PSYCHOLOGY

The Science of Mind and Behaviour

KT-216-935

PSYCHOLOGY
The Science of Mind and Behaviour

Richard Gross

THIRD EDITION

Hodder & Stoughton

A MEMBER OF THE HODDER HEADLINE GROUP

British Library Cataloguing in Publication Data
A catalogue record for this title is available from the British Library

ISBN 0 340 64762 0

First published 1996
Impression number   10 9 8 7 6 5 4 3
Year   1999 1998 1997

Copyright © 1996 Richard Gross

All rights reserved. No part of this publication may be reproduced or transmitted in any form or by any means, electronic or mechanical, including photocopy, recording, or any information storage and retrieval system, without permission in writing from the publisher or under licence from the Copyright Licensing Agency Limited. Further details of such licences (for reprographic reproduction) may be obtained from the Copyright Licensing Agency Limited, of 90 Tottenham Court Road, London W1P 9HE.
Typeset by GreenGate Publishing Services, Tonbridge, Kent
Printed in Great Britain for Hodder & Stoughton Educational, a division of Hodder Headline Plc, 338 Euston Road, London NW1 3BH by Bath Press, Bath

CONTENTS

PREFACE TO THE THIRD EDITION

Much has changed in psychology since 1992 when the second edition of this book was published, making it necessary to update material in all chapters. However, much remains from the second edition, so that anyone familiar with the second edition shouldn't have too much trouble matching the two.

Having said that, there are a number of important changes (apart from the updating) that should be mentioned which have been made largely in response to the comments of readers and which are, of course, intended to make the book a 'better' one; although different people will define this in different ways, the criteria that I use here are 'accessible' and 'user/reader-friendly'.

- Every chapter begins with an *Introduction and Overview*, in which the chapter content is put into a wider context, sometimes historical, sometimes in the form of links with other chapters; major issues and questions that will be discussed in the chapter are identified, along with the key theories and/or content areas.
- Every chapter ends with a detailed *Summary* and *Glossary* of major terms/concepts. The Summary is sufficiently detailed to be used as a major revision aid, although it cannot replace the chapter (otherwise I would simply have written the Summary. The Glossary is much more 'free-standing' (a mini-dictionary), although sometimes a term's definition relates to how it is used in that particular chapter, so that it may have a different meaning in a different context.
- At the end of each chapter there are also recommendations for further reading, mainly books, but occasionally journal articles.
- The text within each chapter is considerably more broken up, both by the use of shorter sections and by the inclusion of Boxes, which are of three main kinds: *Key Study* (which summarize the main aspects of the method and outcome of influential studies, both famous 'classics' and some not so

well-known studies); *Critical/Topical Discussion* (which take a look at how the topic being discussed relates to some general theme, such as cross-cultural psychology, or focus on a particular aspect of the topic which may be politically sensitive or relevant to current social debates, such as sex differences); *Case Study* (which describe in-depth studies of individuals or pairs of twins).

- The inclusion of *Critical/Topical Discussion* boxes reflects a much greater emphasis on recurring themes that seem to have gained widespread attention within psychology as a whole during the last few years, namely *cross-cultural psychology* (often just called 'cultural psychology') and *sociobiology* and the closely related, but even more recent *evolutionary psychology*.
- Some of the longer chapters from the second edition have been split to produce separate chapters. *Motivation* (Chapter 5) and *Emotion and Stress* (Chapter 6) were previously combined, as were *Attitudes and Attitude Change* (Chapter 18) and *Prejudice and Discrimination* (Chapter 19). Also, the philosophical issues of reductionism and free will versus determinism have been taken out of Chapter 2 and combined with Ethics to form a new Chapter 32.
- There is no longer a separate chapter on Comparative Psychology, but much of that material has been retained, although it is distributed throughout a number of chapters, often combined with discussion of sociobiology.

Basic issues in teaching psychology and writing textbooks remain the same: (i) how to achieve an integrated, coherent coverage of a vast subject while having to divide it up into sections, and (ii) how to achieve a balance between breadth and depth, trying to provide an overview of the essential features of a topic while covering it in sufficient detail to prevent the reader from having to do enormous amounts of extra reading. As if this wasn't a tall enough order, the style must also be readable!

While I am confident that the changes are for the better, I hope (and believe) that all the positive features of the second edition have been retained. Overall, I think the page design is far more attractive and much easier to read. I have also tried to correct factual errors and errors of interpretation: once again, thanks to all those who have pointed these out to me.

While the first edition of this book was intended very much for 'A' level and other pre-degree students, it, and the second edition, seemed to meet the needs of a much wider audience; this third edition is now written with that much broader readership in mind. No single book, of course, can meet all the needs of every student/reader, but I believe that this one will meet most of the needs of most of its readers. If that sounds immodest, please let me know what you think after you have used it for a while.

Dedication

To Jan, Tanya and Jo. Thanks for getting us all through the last crazy year or so. Love, peace and tranquility.

The Nature and Scope of Psychology

1 WHAT IS THIS THING CALLED PSYCHOLOGY?

INTRODUCTION AND OVERVIEW

When a psychologist meets someone for the first time at, say, a party and replies to the standard 'opening line', 'What do you do for a living?', the reaction of the newly made acquaintance is likely to fall into one of the following categories:

- 'Oh, I'd better be careful what I say from now on' (partly defensive, partly amused);
- 'I bet you meet some right weirdos in your work' (partly intrigued, partly sympathetic);
- 'What exactly *is* psychology?' (partly inquisitive, partly puzzled).

What these reactions betray (especially the first two) is an inaccurate and incomplete understanding of the subject. The first seems to imply that psychologists are mindreaders and have access to other people's thoughts (they do not), while the second seems to imply that psychologists work only or largely with people who could variously be described as 'mentally ill', 'emotionally disturbed' or 'mad'(they do not – although many do). The third reaction perhaps implies that the borderline between psychology and other subject disciplines is not clearly drawn (it is not) and what this chapter attempts to do is provide a general answer to the question by doing three things:

1 looking at some changing definitions of psychology and some of the major schools of thought within psychology as a whole;
2 outlining the major subdivisions of the subject matter of psychology and seeing what different psychologists actually do;
3 looking at the relationship between psychology and common sense.

DO PSYCHOLOGISTS AGREE AMONG THEMSELVES WHAT PSYCHOLOGY IS?

The word psychology is derived from two Greek words, *psyche* (mind, soul or spirit) and *logos* (discourse or study) which, put together, produce 'study of the mind'.

The appearance of psychology as a subject discipline in its own right is generally dated to 1879, when Wilhelm Wundt opened the first psychology laboratory at the University of Leipzig in Germany. Wundt and his co-workers were attempting to investigate 'the mind' through *introspection*, that is, observing and analysing the structure of their own conscious mental processes (thoughts, images, feelings) as they occurred. Their aim was to analyse conscious thought into its basic elements, perception into its constituent sensations, etc., much as chemists analyse compounds into elements (hence *structuralism*). They recorded and measured the results of their introspections under controlled conditions, i.e. under the same physical surroundings, using the same 'stimulus' (e.g. a clicking metronome), giving the same verbal instructions to each person who participated ('subject' being the term used until recently, but 'participant' will be used throughout this book) and so on. It was this emphasis on measurement and control that marked the separation of the 'new psychology' from its parent discipline of philosophy.

For many hundreds of years, philosophers had been reflecting on and speculating about 'the mind'. Now, for the first time, scientists (Wundt was actually a physiologist by training) were applying some of the basic methods of scientific investigation to the study of mental processes:

> Psychology is the Science of Mental Life, both of its phenomena and of their conditions ... The Phenomena are such things as we call feelings, desires, cognition, reasoning, decisions and the like. (James, 1890)

However, by the second decade of the 20th century, the validity and usefulness of this method were being seriously questioned, in particular by an American psychologist, John B. Watson. Watson believed that introspection produced results which could never be proved or disproved; for example, if my introspection produces different results from yours, how can we ever decide whose is correct? Of course, we cannot, because there is no objective way of doing so: we cannot 'get behind' the introspective report to check its accuracy. Introspection is subjective and only the individual can observe their own mental processes – it cannot be done by another person. Consequently, Watson proposed that psychologists should confine themselves to what is measurable and observable by more than one person, namely behaviour:

> For the behaviourist, psychology is that division of Natural Science which takes human behaviour – the doings and sayings, both learned and unlearned – as its subject matter. (John B. Watson, 1919)

So a new brand of psychology emerged, known as *behaviourism*. It largely replaced Wundt's introspectionism, advocating that human beings should be regarded as complex animals and studied using the same scientific methods as chemistry and physics. This was the only way, Watson believed, that psychology could make any claims to being a science itself: to emulate the natural sciences, psychology must adopt their objective methods. The study of inaccessible, private, mental processes was to have no place in a truly scientific psychology.

Behaviourism (in one form or another) was to remain the dominant force within psychology for the next 40 years or so, especially in the USA and, to a lesser extent, in Britain. The emphasis on the role of learning (in the form of *conditioning*) was to make that topic one of the central areas of research in psychology as a whole. Behaviourist theories of learning are often referred to as *stimulus–response* (S–R) theories, because of their attempt to analyse all behaviour into stimulus–response units, no matter how complex the behaviour. (Strictly, only *classical conditioning* fits the S–R model. The other major form of conditioning, *operant conditioning*, is significantly different but is often included under the S–R rubric; see Chapter 7.) The ideas of Wundt, Watson and James are discussed in much more detail in Chapter 2.

A reaction against both Wundt's structuralism and Watson's behaviourism came in the form of the *Gestalt* school of psychology, which emerged in the 1920s and 1930s in Austria and Germany. The Gestalt psychologists were mainly interested in perception and believed that perceptions could not be broken down in the way that Wundt tried to do with thought and behaviourists advocated for behaviour; one of their central beliefs was that 'the whole is greater than the sum of its parts'.

Starting in 1900, in Austria, Sigmund Freud was beginning to publish his theory of personality in which the unconscious mind was to play such a crucial role. Freud's psychoanalytic theory also represented a challenge, and a major alternative, to behaviourism.

During the 1950s and 1960s, many psychologists began to look to the work of computer scientists in trying to understand the more complex behaviour which, they felt, learning theory (conditioning) had either neglected altogether or greatly oversimplified.

The behaviour in question was what Wundt and the early scientific psychologists had called 'mind' or mental processes, but which were now referred to as cognition or cognitive processes (see James's 1890 definition above). This involves all the ways in which we come to know the world around us, how we attain, retain and regain information, through the processes of attention, perception, memory, problem solving, language and thinking in general.

The cognitive psychologist sees the person as an information processor and cognitive psychology has

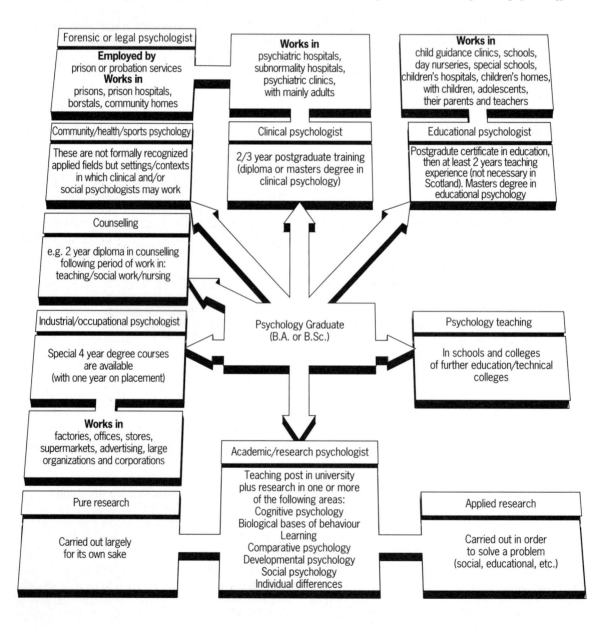

FIGURE 1.1 *The major areas of academic and applied psychology open to psychology graduates*

been heavily influenced by computer science, with human cognitive processes being compared with the operation of computer programs (the computer analogy). Cognitive psychology, along with artificial intelligence, linguistics, philosophy, anthropology and neuroscience (see Fig. 1.2), now forms part of cognitive science, which emerged in the late 1970s,

As we noted earlier, what makes mental (or cognitive) processes different from behaviour is that they are essentially 'private'; that is, you cannot directly and literally observe another person's thoughts or feelings but you can infer what they are likely to be thinking or feeling based on what they are doing; for example, you can infer from a person's furrowed brow or head-scratching that they are trying to puzzle out a problem or make up their mind about something. You can also ask them what they are doing, but ultimately you cannot prove or disprove their account of what is going on inside their head, because nobody else can get inside their head to find out.

Thus we have come full circle back to the behaviourists' original criticisms of introspection. However, mental processes are now accepted as being valid subject matter for psychology, provided we can objectify or externalize them (make them 'public'), as in memory tests or problem-solving tasks. Consequently, what a person says and does are perfectly acceptable sources of data (information) about their cognitive processes, although the processes themselves remain inaccessible to the observer, who can study them only indirectly:

> Psychology is usually defined as the scientific study of behaviour. Its subject matter includes behavioural processes that are observable, such as gestures, speech and physiological changes, and processes that can only be inferred, such as thoughts and dreams. (Clark and Miller, 1970)

More recently (and more concisely):

> *Psychology* is formally defined as the scientific study of the behaviour of individuals and their mental processes ... (Zimbardo, 1992)

HOW CAN WE DIVIDE UP THE WORK THAT PSYCHOLOGISTS DO?

As we have seen, behaviourist and cognitive psychology have been very influential in determining the general direction that psychology has taken in the last 80 years or so and this is reflected in the definitions of their subject which psychologists have given. However, much more goes on under the general heading of 'psychology' than we have outlined so far: there are other theoretical approaches or orientations, other aspects of human (and animal) activity that constitute the special focus of study and finally different kinds of work that different psychologists do.

A distinction which may prove helpful is that between the *academic* and the *applied* branches of the subject (Fig. 1.1). Academic psychologists carry out research (scientific investigation) in a particular area (e.g. perception) and are attached to a university or research establishment where they will also teach first degree students (undergraduates) and supervise the research of postgraduates.

Research is of two major kinds: pure, i.e. done for its own sake and intended, primarily, to increase our knowledge and understanding; and applied, i.e. aimed at solving a particular problem, usually a social problem such as alcoholism or juvenile delinquency. Applied psychology is usually funded by a government institution, like the Home Office or the Department of Education and Industry, or by some commercial or industrial institution.

However, neither of these distinctions is hard and fast: many psychologists work in both academic and applied/practical settings, clinical psychologists especially are engaged in research as an integral part of the evaluation of their work (see below) and pure research may be used for practical ends just as applied research is part of the general 'store of knowledge' which comprises psychology. It may be more useful to distinguish between the psychologist as *investigator* (scientist) and as *practitioner.*

The range of topics that may be investigated is as wide as psychology itself, but a way of classifying them has been suggested by Legge (1975), namely, those which focus on the *processes* or mechanisms underlying various aspects of behaviour and those which focus more directly on the *person.*

● The process approach

This category itself divides into four main areas – the biological bases of behaviour, learning, cognitive processes and comparative – and is often referred to as *experimental psychology.* (This is something of a misnomer, as the experimental method is used in almost all areas of psychology, including the person-oriented approach; it was originally used to distinguish scientific psychology from the philosophy from which it emerged. Sometimes the term 'general' is used instead of 'experimental'.)

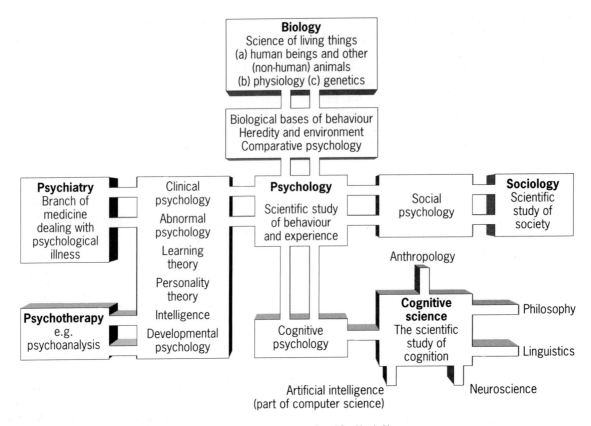

FIGURE 1.2 *The relationship between psychology and other scientific disciplines*

The biological bases of behaviour (Chapters 3–6)

Biopsychologists are interested in the physical basis of behaviour, how the functions of the nervous system (in particular the brain) and the endocrine (hormonal) system are related to and influence behaviour and mental processes. For example, are there parts of the brain specifically concerned with particular behaviours and abilities (*localization of brain function*)? What role do hormones play in the experience of emotion and how are these linked to brain processes? What is the relationship between brain activity and different states of consciousness (including sleep)? What changes occur in the brain when we say that learning has taken place or that a memory has been established? These are just some of the questions that biopsychologists try to answer.

The philosophical issue of *reductionism* often arises in relation to biopsychology; although it is not confined to this area of psychology, controversy has become focused on the 'mind–body' issue (or the relationship between mind and brain) (see Chapter 32). Briefly, some brain or neuroscientists, philosophers

and others believe that the 'mind' can be 'reduced' to or explained totally in terms of brain processes; the implication is that once we know enough about how the brain works, psychology will no longer have a role to play.

A fundamentally important biological process with important implications for psychology is *genetic transmission* (the science of genetics existing in its own right). *The heredity and environment* (or *nature–nurture*) issue, which runs right through psychology, draws on what geneticists have discovered about what kinds of characteristics can be passed from parents to offspring, how this takes place and how genetic factors interact with environmental ones (see Chapters 10, 23, 26, 28 and 30).

Other topics which fall within this area are motivation and stress. (Sensory processes are also biological processes but because of their close connection with perception are dealt with in Chapter 8.)

Learning (Chapter 7)

The learning process permeates most other subdivisions of psychology. This is partly a reflection of the impact of behaviourism on psychology as a whole (at least up to the 1950s), since learning plays such a central part in behaviourist theory where it is studied in the form of conditioning. However, there is much more to learning than conditioning. For example, social learning theorists, while sharing many of the basic principles of conditioning theory, believe that conditioning alone cannot account for much human behaviour. They have focused on *observational learning (modelling)* as an important additional learning process, especially in children (see also Chapters 23 and 27).

A great deal of human learning is closely related to cognitive processes, such as language and perception; for example, Gestalt psychology's insight learning and the learning by rats of 'mental maps' are examples of *cognitive learning*. Conditioning, observational learning and cognitive learning will all feature prominently in the discussion of development (especially Chapters 23 and 27) and the applications of theories of learning are important in the treatment of behaviour disorders (see Chapter 31).

(We should perhaps make a distinction between 'theories of learning', which include all three types mentioned above, and 'learning theory', which usually refers to the behaviourist theories of conditioning, especially those of Pavlov, Watson and Skinner.)

Cognitive processes (Chapters 9–14)

As we noted earlier, cognition means knowing, so cognitive (or mental) processes refer to all those ways in which knowledge of the world is attained, retained and used, including attention, memory, perception, language, thinking, problem solving, reasoning and concept formation ('higher order' mental activities). Although these are often studied for their own sake, they may have very important practical implications too, for example, understanding the memory processes involved in eyewitness testimony. Much of social psychology (listed here as belonging in the person category) is cognitive in flavour, that is, concerned with the mental processes involved in interpersonal perception (e.g. stereotyping) and attitude change (e.g. cognitive dissonance) and is known as *social cognition*. Also, Piaget's theory of development (again, belonging to the person category) is concerned with *cognitive development*.

Because of the major influence of computer science on cognitive psychology and the fact that cognitive psychology now forms part of cognitive science, the relationship between human problem-solving and artificial intelligence is discussed in this section of the book (Chapter 14). According to

cognitive science, both computers and human problem solvers are *information-processing machines*.

Comparative psychology (Chapters 16, 17, 22 and 23)

This is often used synonymously with animal psychology, but the word 'comparative' implies the original purpose of studying animals, namely to increase our understanding of human behaviour. The study of animal behaviour was inspired by Darwin whose 1859 theory of evolution made it seem quite reasonable to believe that, by studying the more simple species from which we have evolved, we should learn more about ourselves.

However, there is a great temptation to extrapolate directly from non-human species to ourselves (see Chapter 2). Moreover, much study of animal behaviour takes place for its own sake and is perhaps more appropriately called 'animal' psychology. At the same time, animals continue to be used as experimental subjects in many areas of psychology, when for ethical and practical reasons humans cannot be used (see Chapter 32).

Ironically, the study of animals was first taken up by psychologists (as opposed to biologists, which Darwin was) and much of their research took place in the laboratory (including Watson's work and that of the behaviourists who followed him). More recently (especially since the 1950s), zoologists have been advocating the 'naturalist' approach to the study of animal behaviour, observing animals in their natural habitats; this *ethological* approach is associated particularly with Niko Tinbergen and Konrad Lorenz. A development of ethology since the late 1970s is *sociobiology*, which attempts to explain all social behaviour (animal and human) in terms of evolutionary forces.

Although there is no separate chapter devoted to comparative psychology, both ethology and sociobiology are discussed in several parts of the book, especially in relation to social and developmental psychology. For example, Lorenz is discussed in the context of aggression (Chapter 17) and Bowlby's theory of attachment in human infants (Chapter 22) was greatly influenced by Lorenz's study of imprinting in goslings.

● The person approach

Social psychology (Chapters 15–20)

Some psychologists would claim that 'all psychology is social psychology' because all behaviour takes place within a social context and, even when we are alone, our behaviour continues to be influenced by others (for example, their potential response to what we are doing). Our *self-concept* is in large measure a reflection of how others have treated us and responded to us in the past (this is actually discussed in Chapter 21) but other people may have a more immediate and direct influence upon us when we are actually in their presence (social facilitation, leadership, conformity and obedience).

Social psychology is also concerned with *interpersonal perception* (forming impressions of others and judging the causes of their behaviour), interpersonal attraction and intimate relationships, attitudes and attitude change, prejudice and discrimination and pro- and anti-social behaviour (especially aggression). Social psychologists tend to draw on the work of general psychology in order to see how this can help them understand the behaviour that goes on between people, including relationships between social groups.

Developmental psychology (Chapters 21–27)

Developmental psychology studies the biological, intellectual, social and emotional changes that occur in the individual over time. One very significant change that has occurred within developmental psychology during the past 25 years or so is the recognition that development is not confined to childhood and adolescence, but is a lifelong process (referred to as the *lifespan approach*). While the ageing process has been studied for many years, the emphasis has tended to be on physical aspects and the associated mental illness (especially senile dementia); it has not had the 'flavour' of a stage of development, unlike pregnancy, infancy, toddlerhood and so on. Also, 'growing old' has traditionally had very negative connotations, compared with 'growing up', which is normally taken to be something desirable and almost an end in itself. It is now generally accepted, however, that adulthood is a developmental stage, quite distinct from adolescence and old age. The first major theorist to acknowledge the lifelong nature of development ('cradle-to-grave') was Erik Erikson, who described the 'Eight Ages of Man', each of which presents the individual with a new developmental task to be worked on.

Developmental psychology is not an isolated or independent field and advances in it depend on progress within psychology as a whole, such as behavioural genetics, (neuro)physiological psychology, learning, perception and motivation and this is reflected in the wide-ranging methods and techniques of study that are used. But developmental psychology also contributes to other areas of psychology; for example, although Piaget's theory of cognitive development was meant to map the changes that take place up to about 15 years of age, he is considered to have made a massive contribution to psychology as a whole.

Individual differences (Chapters 28–31)

As the name suggests, this is concerned with the ways in which people can differ from one another, in particular personality and intelligence. *Personality* can be thought of as those relatively stable and enduring aspects of individuals which distinguish them from others, making them unique, but which at the same time allow people to be compared with each other. Within that general definition, there are several different theoretical approaches, including the *type and trait* approach (Eysenck and Cattell), the *psychodynamic* (Freud, Jung, Adler), the *humanistic* (Maslow, Rogers), the *social learning* approach (Mischell) and the *cognitive* (Kelly). The first of these, the type and trait approach, is closely related to *psychometrics* ('mental measurement'), since this approach makes great use of standardized tests of personality on which to compare large numbers of individuals.

Underlying the psychometric approach is the assumption that every individual can be compared in terms of a specified number of personality traits or dimensions; this represents the *nomothetic* approach (the study of personality 'in general'); by contrast, the humanistic and Kelly's cognitive theories adopt an *idiographic* approach, stressing the uniqueness of individual personality (see Chapters 2 and 29).

The study of *intelligence* is very much concerned with differences between individuals and groups (e.g. racial and age groups) and a great deal of time and money has been invested since 1905 (when Binet and Simon devised the first intelligence test) in constructing new tests and refining old ones. One of the most hotly debated issues in psychology is how to account for differences in measured intelligence between different racial groups in terms of genetic or environmental factors. The status of the tests used is problematic, as is the attempt to define the term 'intelligence' itself.

Another major source of individual differences is mental and behaviour disorders, the subject matter of *abnormal psychology*. This studies the underlying causes of psychological abnormality, including criminality, sexual perversions, drug abuse and alcoholism; it is closely linked with one of the major applied areas of psychology, namely, clinical psychology (see below). There is inevitable overlap between abnormal psychology and the study of (normal) personality: we have to know what the range of individual differences is before we can begin to classify people (or their behaviour) as abnormal or deviant. Psychologists who study abnormality and clinical psychologists are also concerned with the effectiveness of different forms of treatment and therapies.

Three other major sources of individual differences are age, gender and culture; all three are discussed throughout the book, especially in relation to developmental and social psychology and individual differences.

● Comparing the process and person approaches

Is there a real difference between the process and the person approaches after all? I have tried to show how different research areas overlap with others and how, in practice, it is very difficult to separate them, even if it can be done theoretically. However, there are relative differences between them which are important.

The process approach is much more confined to the laboratory, makes far greater use of non-human animals as subjects and makes the general and basic assumption that psychological processes (particularly learning) are essentially the same in all species: any differences that are found between species are only *quantitative* (differences of degree). In contrast, the person approach makes much greater use of field studies (e.g. observing behaviour in its natural environment) and of non-experimental methods (e.g. correlational studies). Mainly human participants are studied and it is assumed that there are *qualitative* differences (differences in kind) between humans and non-human animals.

Our discussion of the person/process approaches has been concerned with the academic branch of psychology. Fortunately, the situation is a little more straightforward as far as applied psychology is concerned, partly because of the special training required (over and above the minimum requirement that all psychologists must possess a psychology degree) and partly because of the place and type of work involved. The three major areas of applied psychology are educational, clinical and industrial (or occupational). (As

these are all concerned with people, they may be considered the applied aspects of the person approach.)

Educational psychology

The educational psychologist has had at least two years teaching experience and has gained a postgraduate qualification in educational or child psychology. The main areas of responsibility include:

● administering psychological tests, particularly intelligence or IQ tests, as part of the assessment of learning difficulties;
● the planning and supervision of remedial teaching;
● research into teaching methods, the curriculum (subjects taught), interviewing and counselling methods and techniques;
● the planning of educational programmes designed to meet the needs of mentally and physically impaired (including the visually impaired and autistic) and other groups of children and adolescents who are not attending ordinary schools (i.e. special education).

Educational psychologists are usually employed by the Local Education Authority (LEA) and work in one or more of the following: child guidance clinics (usually staffed by a psychiatrist, one or more educational psychologists, several psychiatric social workers, one or more child psychotherapists and, sometimes, a speech therapist); the Schools Psychological Service; hospitals, day nurseries, nursery schools, special schools (day and residential) and residential children's homes. The age of clients is up to 18 years, but most will fall into the 5–16 age group.

Working very closely with parents and teachers, educational psychologists advise both groups on how to deal with children and adolescents who have mental and/or physical impairments, behaviour problems or learning difficulties. They are also involved in teacher training.

Clinical psychology

Clinical psychologists are by far the most numerous single group of psychologists: more than one-third of all psychologists classify themselves as clinical and a further 10 percent or so call themselves 'counselling psychologists' (they tend to work with younger clients in colleges and universities rather than in hospitals).

The clinical psychologist has trained for two or three years as a postgraduate and is qualified to:

- assess individuals with learning disabilities, administer psychological tests to brain-damaged patients, devise rehabilitation programmes for long-term psychiatric patients and assess the elderly for their fitness to live independently in their own homes;
- plan and carry out programmes of therapy, usually behaviour therapy/modification (both derived from learning theory principles), but occasionally they may choose psychotherapy (group or individual) in preference to, or in addition to, behavioural techniques (see Chapter 31).

Psychotherapy is usually carried out by psychiatrists (who are doctors who specialize in psychological medicine) or psychotherapists (who are often social workers who undergo a special training, which includes their own psychotherapy) and is based on the psychoanalytic (psychodynamic) theories of personality associated with Freud (see Chapters 29, 30 and 31).

Patients may be of any age but are usually adults, of whom many will be elderly; the clinical psychologist works in psychiatric and subnormality hospitals, psychiatric wards in general hospitals and psychiatric clinics. As we saw earlier, many are engaged in research into abnormal psychology, including the effectiveness of different treatment methods.

Working with the families of patients, clinical psychologists are increasingly involved in community care as psychiatric care in general moves out of the large psychiatric hospitals. They are also engaged in teaching other groups of professionals, such as nurses, psychiatrists and social workers.

A special subgroup of clinical psychologists are the forensic or legal psychologists, who are employed by the prison or probation service. The forensic psychologist may be called as an expert witness in court trials to testify regarding: (i) the credibility of witnesses and defendants; (ii) the fitness of individuals to stand trial; (iii) any other matter seen as requiring the expert opinion of a psychologist (e.g. handwriting). They may work in community homes (once called approved schools), detention centres, youth custody centres and prisons or prison hospitals (for the criminally insane) such as Broadmoor and Rampton.

Industrial or occupational psychology

The responsibilities of the industrial or occupational psychologist include:

- the selection and training of individuals for jobs and vocational guidance, which often involves giving aptitude tests and tests of interest and is

sometimes the responsibility of individuals trained in personnel management, which has a large psychology component;
- industrial rehabilitation, i.e. helping people who, for reasons of illness, accident or redundancy, need to choose and retrain for a new career;
- designing training schemes, as part of 'fitting the person to the job'; this is particularly important at a time when new technology is replacing old methods and sometimes taking over totally the jobs done by particular workers. Teaching machines and simulators (e.g. of an aeroplane cockpit) often feature prominently in such training schemes;
- 'fitting the job to the person' (human engineering or *ergonomics*), whereby applications from experimental psychology are made to the design of equipment and machinery, in order to make the best use of human resources and to minimize accidents and fatigue. Examples of how engineering psychologists have been consulted include telephone dialling codes (memory and attention) and the design of decimal coinage (tactile and visual discrimination); these illustrate very well the interplay between applied and pure research where the former very often depends on the latter and any complete separation between them is not possible;
- advising on working conditions so as to maximize productivity as another facet of ergonomics (the study of efficiency of people in their working environments). Occupational groups involved include computer/VDU operators, those working on production lines and air traffic controllers;
- helping the flow of communication between departments or sections in government institutions or 'industrial relations' in commerce and industry (often called *organizational psychology*). Here the emphasis is on the social, rather than the physical or practical aspects of the working environment.
- helping to sell products and services through advertising and promotions. Many psychologists are employed in the advertising industry, where they draw on what experimental psychologists say about human motivation, attitudes, cognition and so on.

Chartered psychologists

Since 1987, the British Psychological Society (BPS) (the only scientific and professional body for British psychologists incorporated by Royal Charter) has been authorized under its Charter to keep a Register of Chartered Psychologists. Entry to the Register is restricted to members of the Society who have applied for registration and who have the necessary postgraduate qualifications or experience to have reached a standard sufficient for professional practice in psychology without supervision (Gale, 1990).

MAJOR THEORETICAL APPROACHES OR ORIENTATIONS

We have referred several times already to behaviourist, psychoanalytic or cognitive theories or perspectives. It should be apparent by now that we cannot talk about psychologists as if they all shared some basic theory about 'what makes people tick', nor indeed do they agree about what sort of terminology or methodology to use when carrying out their research or formulating their theories.

Different psychologists make different assumptions about what particular aspects of a person are worthy of study, sometimes to the exclusion of others, and this helps to determine an underlying model or image of what human beings are like. In turn, this model or image determines a view of psychological normality, the nature of development, preferred methods of study, the major cause(s) of abnormality and the preferred methods and goals of treatment. These issues and the position of five major theoretical approaches (psychoanalytic, behaviourist, humanistic-existential, neurobiological and cognitive) regarding them are summarized in Table 1.1.

These (together with different versions of each) are the major theoretical approaches that will make their appearance throughout the book (particularly in relation to development and psychological abnormality). It should be evident from even a cursory glance at the table how different and distinctive is the language used by each approach: let us now take a closer look at some of the language used in psychology as a whole.

THE LANGUAGE OF PSYCHOLOGY

As in all sciences, there is a special set of technical terms (jargon) to get used to and this is generally accepted as an unavoidable feature of studying the subject. But over and above these technical words, which scientists speak to fellow scientists, psychologists use, in a technical way, words that are familiar to us from everyday speech and it is here that 'doing psychology' can become a little confusing.

Some examples of this are 'behaviour' and 'personality'. For parents to tell their child to 'behave yourself' is meaningless to a psychologist's ears because behaving is something we are all doing all the time (even when asleep) and to say that someone 'has no personality' is equally meaningless because, as personality refers to what makes a person unique and different from others, you cannot help but have one!

Other terms which denote large portions of the research of experimental psychology, such as memory, learning and intelligence, are called *hypothetical constructs*, that is, they do not refer to anything that can be directly observed but which can only be inferred from observable behaviour. Equally important, they seem to be necessary in order to account for the behaviour that is observed; but there is a danger of thinking of them as 'things' or 'entities', rather than as a way of trying to make sense of behaviour.

Another way in which psychologists try to make sense of something is by comparing it with something else (often something complex is compared with something more simple), that is, they use an *analogy*. Since the 1950s and the development of computer science, the computer analogy has become very popular as a way of trying to understand how the mind works; as we have seen, the language of computer science has permeated the cognitive view of human beings as information processors.

A *model* is a kind of metaphor: it is not meant to be taken too literally but is more of a suggestion as to how we might think of people's behaviour, again in order to understand it better. A model entails a single, fundamental idea or image and is not as complex as a theory (although sometimes the terms are used interchangeably). In Chapter 2, a *theory* is defined as a complex set of inter-related statements which attempt to explain certain observed phenomena. Although, strictly speaking, the role of theory is to explain, in practice, when we refer to a particular theory (e.g. that of Freud or Piaget), we often include description as well. Thomas (1985) defines a theory as 'an explanation of how the facts fit together' and he likens a theory to a lens through which to view the subject matter, filtering out certain facts and giving a particular pattern to those it lets in. A *hypothesis* is defined in Chapter 2 as a testable statement about the relationship between two or more variables; the term is sometimes used to mean something very similar to 'theory' but these two meanings should be kept separate.

	Psychoanalytic or psycho-dynamic (e.g. Freud)	Behaviourist or stimulus–response (e.g. Skinner)	Humanistic-existential (e.g. Rogers)	Neuro-biological or biogenic	Cognitive
Nature of human beings	Individual is in conflict due to opposing demands made by different parts of the personality – id, ego, superego. Behaviour is largely determined by unconscious forces.	Human behaviour is shaped by environmental forces (reinforcement) and is a collection of learned responses to stimuli. The key learning process is conditioning (classical and operant).	The individual is unique, free, rational and self-determining. Free-will and self-actualization make human beings distinct from animals. Present experience is as important as past experience.	Behaviour is determined by genetic, physiological and neurobiological factors and processes. The influence of the central nervous system (especially the brain) is crucial.	The human mind is compared to a computer. People are information processors, selecting information, coding it, storing it and retrieving it when needed. Memory, perception and language are central.
Nature of psychological normality	Adequate balance between id, ego, superego. But conflict is always present to some degree.	Possession of an adequately large repertoire of adaptive responses.	Ability to accept oneself, to realize one's potential, to achieve intimacy with others, to find meaning in life.	Properly functioning nervous system.	Proper functioning of cognitive processes and the ability to use them to monitor and control behaviour.
Nature of psychological development	Psychosexual stages: Oral (0–1); Anal (1–3); Phallic (3–5/6); Latency (5/6–puberty) Genital (puberty–maturity). Sequence determined by maturation. The individual is shaped by early childhood experiences.	None as such. No stages of development. Different behaviour is selectively reinforced at different ages, but the differences between a child and an adult are merely quantitative.	Development of self-concept, in particular self-regard (self-esteem). Satisfaction of low level needs as prerequisite for higher level (growth) needs (in Maslow's hierarchy of needs.)	Stages of behavioural/ psychological development based on changes in brain growth which are genetically determined (i.e. maturation).	Stages of Cognitive development (e.g. Piaget): Sensorimotor (0–2); Preoperational (2–7); Concrete operational (7–11); Formal operational (11–15). Information processing approach–development of memory, perception, language, attention, etc.

TABLE 1.1 *Five major approaches in psychology*

	Psychoanalytic or psycho-dynamic (e.g. Freud)	Behaviourist or stimulus–response (e.g. Skinner)	Humanistic-existential (e.g. Rogers)	Neuro-biological or biogenic	Cognitive
Preferred method(s) of study	**Case-study** (Clinical method)	**Experiment** (Animals and humans, but mainly non-human animals)	**Case study** Q–sort (Rogers)	**Experiment** (mainly non-human animals)	**Experiment** (mainly humans) Artificial intelligence/ computer simulation
Major cause(s) of abnormal behaviour	Emotional disturbance or neurosis caused by unresolved conflicts stemming from childhood. Abnormal behaviour is symptomatic of such conflicts. Main feature is anxiety.	The learning of maladaptive responses or the failure to learn adaptive ones in the first place No distinction between symptoms and the behaviour disorder.	Inability to accept and express one's true nature, to take responsibility for one's own actions and to make authentic choices. Anxiety stems from denying part of the self.	Genetic disorders, organic (bodily) disorders (e.g. brain disease or injury), chemical imbalance, food allergies. Mental illness gives rise to behavioural and cognitive symptoms (e.g. thought disorder in schizophrenia).	Unrealistic or irrational ideas and beliefs about self and others. Inability to monitor or control behaviour through appropriate cognitive processes.
Preferred method(s) of treatment	Insight-orientated psychotherapy (e.g. psychoanalysis). The unconscious is revealed through dream interpretation, free-association, transference.	Behaviour therapy or modification. E.g. systematic desensitization aversion therapy, flooding, behaviour shaping, token economy.	Client-centred therapy; insights come from the client, as present experiences are explored with the therapist.	Physical (somatic) treatments. E.g. chemotherapy (drugs), electro-convulsive therapy (ECT), psychosurgery.	E.g. cognitive–behaviour therapy, rational–emotive therapy, Zen meditation and behavioural self–control.
Goal(s) of treatment	To uncover and work through unconscious conflicts to make them conscious. To achieve reasonable balance between id, ego, superego.	To eliminate maladaptive responses and to acquire adaptive ones.	To rediscover the whole self, which can then proceed towards self–actualization.	To alleviate symptoms and/ or actually reverse the underlying cause(s) of the illness.	To correct unrealistic/ irrational ideas and beliefs so that thinking becomes an effective means of controlling behaviour.

TABLE 1.1 *(continued)*

PSYCHOLOGY AND COMMON SENSE

A common reaction among psychology students, when discussing the findings of some piece of research, is to say 'But we knew that already' implying that 'It's only common sense'. Alternatively, they might say 'But that's not what we normally understand by such-and-such', implying that the research is in some way wrong. So it seems that psychology is often in a contradictory position – either it merely confirms common sense or it contradicts it, in which case psychology seems to be the less credible of the two.

Whereas we would seldom think of ourselves as physicists or doctors, engineers or novelists unless we had received a special education or had special talent, we all consider that we know something about people and why they behave as they do: there is a sense in which we are all psychologists! This is a theme explored at length by Joynson in *Psychology and Common Sense* (1974). He begins by stating that human beings are not like the objects of natural science – we understand ourselves and can already predict and control our behaviour to a remarkable extent. This creates for the psychologist a paradoxical task: what kind of understanding can you seek of a creature which already understands itself?

For Joynson, the fundamental question is 'If the psychologist did not exist, would it be necessary to invent him?'. For Skinner (1971), 'it is a science or nothing' and Broadbent (1961) also rejects the validity of our everyday understanding of ourselves and others (Joynson calls it 'the behaviourists' prejudice'). Yet it seems inevitable that we try to make sense of our own and other people's behaviour (by virtue of our cognitive abilities and the nature of social interaction) and to this extent we are all psychologists. (This is discussed further in relation to interpersonal perception; see Chapter 15.) Heather (1976) points to ordinary language as embodying our 'natural' understanding of human behaviour; in his view, as long as human beings have lived they have been psychologists and language gives us an 'elaborate and highly refined conceptual tool, developed over thousands of years of talking to each other'.

So how can we resolve the dilemma? Legge (1975) and others resolve it by distinguishing between *formal* and *informal* psychology (or professional versus amateur, scientific versus non-scientific). Our common sense, intuitive or 'natural' understanding is unsystematic and does not constitute a body of knowledge; this makes it very difficult to 'check' an individual's 'theory' about human nature, as does the fact that each individual has to learn from their own experience. So part of the aim of formal psychology is to provide such a systematic body of knowledge, which represents the unobservable bases of our 'gut reactions'.

Yet it could be argued that informal psychology *does* provide a 'body of knowledge' in the form of proverbs or sayings or folk wisdom, handed down from generation to generation – for example, 'Birds of a feather flock together', 'Too many cooks spoil the broth' and 'Don't cross your bridges before you come to them'. Perhaps these contain at least a grain of truth: the problem is that for each of them we can find yet another proverb which states the opposite ('Opposites attract', 'Many hands make light work' and 'Time and tide wait for no man' or 'Nothing ventured, nothing gained'). Common sense does not help us to reconcile these contradictory statements but formal psychology can! Indeed, there does seem to be some evidence to support both proverbs in the first pair (see Chapter 16 on interpersonal attraction). Formal psychology tries to identify the conditions under which each statement holds true; they only appear contradictory if we assume that only one or the other can be true! In this way, we can see scientific psychology as throwing light on our everyday, informal understanding, not necessarily as negating or invalidating it.

Legge believes that most psychological research should indeed be aimed at demonstrations of 'what we know already' but that it should aim to go one step further; only the methods of science, he believes, can provide us with the public, communicable body of knowledge that we are seeking. According to Allport (1947), the aim of science is 'Understanding, prediction and control above the levels achieved by unaided common sense' and this is meant to apply to psychology as much as it does to the natural sciences. Just what science involves, and how appropriately we can study people scientifically, is the subject of the next chapter.

CHAPTER SUMMARY

● 'Psychology' literally means 'study of the mind'. Psychology as a separate discipline is usually dated from 1879 when Wundt opened the first psychology laboratory, devoted to the analysis of conscious thought into its basic elements (structuralism) through introspection.

- What made this 'new psychology' different from philosophy was the emphasis on measurement and control, i.e. the application of some of the basic methods of scientific method to the study of mental processes.

- Watson began to challenge Wundt's approach on the grounds that introspection is subjective and there is no way of independently checking the accuracy of introspective reports. For psychology to become a natural science, it must confine itself to what is observable and measurable by more than one person, namely behaviour (behaviourism).

- According to behaviourism, human beings are complex animals who should be studied using the same scientific methods as used in physics and chemistry.

- Behaviourism remained dominant in psychology, especially in America, until the 1950s. Its emphasis on conditioning made learning a central topic in psychology as a whole. Behaviourist theories of learning are often called stimulus–response (S–R) theories (although, strictly, this only applies to classical, as opposed to operant conditioning).

- The Gestalt psychologists rejected both structuralism and behaviourism, claiming that perception in particular, and behaviour in general, cannot be broken down into its elements without destroying the whole.

- Freud began to publish his psychoanalytic theory of personality in 1900; the unconscious mind was the central concept.

- During the 1950s and 1960s psychologists began to 'rediscover' the mind, influenced by the work of computer scientists; they referred to the mind as cognitive processes/cognition, such as attention, perception, memory, problem solving, language and thinking in general. By analogy with the computer, people were seen as information processors. Cognitive psychology forms part of cognitive science.

- Cognitive processes are essentially 'private' and inaccessible to an observer and can only be inferred from behaviour; but if they can be objectified or externalized, as in memory tests, then they are perfectly acceptable subject matter for scientific psychology.

- A distinction is made between academic and applied branches of psychology. Academic psychologists carry out research, which may be pure

or applied; the latter is usually funded by some government department or by commerce or industry. However, these distinctions are not hard and fast. More useful may be the distinction between the psychologist as investigator/scientist and practitioner.

- Areas of research can be divided into those which focus on psychological and biological processes (process approach) and those which focus on the person (person approach). The former is sometimes referred to as 'experimental psychology' but the experimental method is used in all areas of psychology.

- The process approach includes the biological bases of behaviour, learning, cognitive processes and comparative psychology.

- Biopsychologists are interested in how the nervous system, especially the brain, and the endocrine system are related to and influence behaviour and mental processes. This includes the study of localization of brain function, states of consciousness (such as sleep) and the physical changes in the brain associated with learning and memory, motivation and stress.

- Biopsychology often raises the issue of reductionism, especially in relation to the mind–body issue.

- The biological process of genetic transmission is crucial to the heredity and environment/nature-nurture issue.

- Learning is a crucial topic in most areas of psychology, whether in the form of conditioning (reflecting the influence of behaviourism), observational learning, insight learning or other forms of cognitive learning. Conditioning is usually referred to as 'learning theory', while 'theories of learning' refers to the whole range.

- Cognitive processes ('higher order' mental activities) are mainly studied for their own sake but may also have important practical implications, as in eyewitness testimony. Much of social psychology is concerned with the role of cognitive processes in social behaviour (social cognition) and a major theory of development is Piaget's theory of cognitive development.

- Comparative psychology is often used synonymously with animal psychology, inspired by Darwin's theory of evolution. The original aim of learning about ourselves by comparison with non-human species has largely been replaced by studying non-humans for its own sake.

- The early psychological study of animals in the laboratory (by behaviourist psychologists) was followed by the ethological approach of

Tinbergen and Lorenz. Sociobiology represents a later development of ethology and is discussed in relation to several aspects of social and developmental psychology.

- Social psychology is concerned with all the ways in which other people influence us, both in shaping our self-concept and more immediately through social facilitation, leadership, conformity and obedience. It also includes interpersonal perception and attraction, intimate relationships, attitudes and attitude change, prejudice and discrimination, and pro- and antisocial behaviour.

- Developmental psychology is concerned with all aspects of change that occur in the individual over time. Traditionally, this focused on childhood and adolescence, with old age being studied in terms of its negative aspects, but in the last 25 years or so a lifespan approach has become popular, inspired by Erikson's 'Eight Ages of Man'.

- Developmental psychology both draws on other areas of psychology and contributes to psychology as a whole, as in the influence of Piaget's theory of cognitive development.

- Personality represents one source of individual differences, but there are many different theoretical approaches. The type and trait approach of Eysenck and Cattell is closely linked to psychometrics, which involves the use of standardized tests to measure and compare the personality of individuals; this represents a nomothetic approach. Humanistic theories (Maslow, Rogers) and Kelly's cognitive theory adopt an idiographic approach.

- Intelligence, as measured by standardized tests, is another important source of individual and group differences; accounting for differences between racial groups in terms of genetic or environmental factors is one of the most controversial issues in the whole of psychology.

- Mental and behaviour disorders are another form of individual differences, the subject matter of abnormal psychology; this is closely linked to the work of clinical psychologists. Both groups of psychologists are concerned with the effectiveness of different forms of treatment and therapy.

- Age, gender and culture are sources of individual differences which relate to many areas of psychology.

- Although there is considerable overlap between the process and person approaches, there are important differences between them, although these are relative differences.

- The process approach is much more laboratory based, makes far greater use of non-human animal subjects and assumes that the differences between human and non-human species are only quantitative. The person approach makes far greater use of field/naturalistic studies and other non-experimental methods, largely involving human participants and assumes qualitative differences between humans and non-human animals.

- Applied areas of psychology require the psychologist to undergo special training over and above the basic psychology degree.

- Educational psychologists are experienced teachers with a postgraduate qualification in educational or child psychology. They usually work for the Local Education Authority in child guidance clinics, the Schools Psychological Service, special schools and other institutions, mainly with 5–16-year-olds. They administer psychological tests, plan and supervise remedial teaching and special education and carry out research into teaching methods and the curriculum. They work closely with teachers and parents.

- Clinical psychologists represent the largest single group of psychologists (more than a third), with counselling psychologists making up another 10 percent. Clinical psychologists assess learning disability and brain damage, devise rehabilitation programmes for long-term psychiatric patients and assess the elderly for their fitness to live independently.

- They also plan and carry out behaviour therapy/modification (based on conditioning theory), although psychotherapy may sometimes be used, either additionally or instead of behavioural techniques.

- Psychotherapy, which is derived from Freud's psychoanalytic theory, is usually carried out by medically qualified psychiatrists or trained psychotherapists.

- Clinical psychologists work mainly with adults, many of whom will be elderly, in psychiatric and subnormality hospitals and other facilities for psychiatric patients. They are increasingly involved in community care and also engaged in teaching others working in the caring professions.

- Forensic/legal psychologists are clinical psychologists employed by the prison or probation service; they may be called as expert witnesses in criminal cases.

- Industrial /occupational psychologists are involved in job selection and training and vocational guidance, industrial rehabilitation, designing training schemes as part of 'fitting the person to the job', human engineering /ergonomics ('fitting the job to the person'), industrial relations, advertising and promotions.

- Since 1987, the British Psychological Society (BPS) has kept a Register of chartered psychologists, restricted to members with the necessary postgraduate qualifications/experience to practise in psychology without supervision.

- Different theoretical approaches/orientations in psychology make different assumptions about what aspects of the person are worthy of study, helping to determine an underlying model/image of what human beings are like. This is related to definitions of normality and abnormality, preferred methods and goals of treatment, the nature of development and preferred methods of study.

- Psychologists use their own jargon, as do other scientists, but this sometimes involves using familiar words, such as 'behaviour' and 'personality', in unfamiliar, technical ways. 'Personality' is also a hypothetical construct, as are memory, intelligence and learning.

- Psychologists use analogies to help them understand behaviour, as in the computer analogy used by cognitive psychologists, according to which both computers and people are seen as information processors.

- A model is a kind of metaphor, not as complex as a theory, although both are meant to explain or make sense of behaviour. Theories are usually tested in the form of hypotheses derived from the theory.

- There is a sense in which we are all psychologists: we understand ourselves and can predict and control our behaviour, making us very different from the objects of natural science. This creates a dilemma for the psychologist: is he or she necessary? One answer is to distinguish between informal/commonsense psychology (the layperson's understanding of behaviour) and formal/scientific psychology; the latter aims to go beyond commonsense understanding and to provide a public, communicable body of knowledge, in which common sense is enlightened rather than invalidated.

GLOSSARY

Behaviourism Watson's approach, in rejection of Wundt's introspectionism, according to which only behaviour which can be observed and measured by

more than one person can be the subject matter of a truly scientific psychology.

Chartered psychologist Someone who belongs to the British Psychological Society Register, indicating a level of competence and experience that does not require supervision.

Cognition All the ways in which we come to know the world around us; how we attain, retain and regain information, through attention, perception, memory, problem solving, language and other cognitive processes.

Comparative psychology The scientific study of animal (i.e. non-human) behaviour.

Computer analogy Comparison between the mind and the digital computer, both of which are seen as information-processing machines.

Ergonomics Part of industrial/occupational psychology, concerned with 'fitting the job to the person'. More generally, study of the efficiency of people in their working environment or 'human engineering'.

Ethology A branch of zoology which stresses the study of animal behaviour in its natural habitat.

Gestalt psychology School of thought which grew up in Austria and Germany in the 1920s and 1930s in opposition to both structuralism and behaviourism; any attempt to analyse perceptual experience/behaviour into its constituent parts is invalid, since the whole is greater than the sum of its parts.

Hypothetical construct An abstract concept referring to something that cannot be directly or literally observed but which can only be inferred from behaviour, such as learning, intelligence and personality.

Learning theory The theories of classical and operant conditioning (Pavlov, Watson, Skinner), as distinct from 'theories of learning', which include observational learning, insight learning and other forms of cognitive learning.

Lifespan approach The view that psychological development continues throughout an individual's lifetime ('cradle-to-grave'), not just in childhood and adolescence.

Model a kind of metaphor, consisting of a single, fundamental idea or image; a way of thinking about behaviour intended to make it more easily understood.

Psychiatrist A medically trained person who specializes in psychological medicine.

Sociobiology An extension of ethology, which attempts to explain all social behaviour (human and non-human) in terms of evolutionary forces.

Structuralism Wundt's early approach to psychology in which he attempted to analyse conscious thought into its basic elements through introspection (hence 'introspectionism').

Theory a complex set of inter-related statements which attempt to explain certain observed phenomena; usually tested in the form of a hypothesis derived from the theory.

FURTHER READING

Fancher, R. E. (1979) *Pioneers of Psychology*. New York: Norton. 'Studies of the great figures who paved the way for the contemporary science of behaviour': the subtitle to this highly readable and informative account of, amongst others, Wundt and James, Freud, Pavlov and Watson, Piaget and Skinner.

Miller, G.A. (1962) *Psychology: The Science of Mental Life*. Harmondsworth: Penguin. One of the 'classic', largely historical, introductions to psychology.

2

THE SCIENTIFIC NATURE OF PSYCHOLOGY

INTRODUCTION AND OVERVIEW

Having defined psychology as the scientific study of behaviour and cognitive processes (or mind or experience) in the previous chapter, we now need to explore that definition further by considering the nature of science and, more importantly, the nature of psychology as a scientific discipline. To do this, we shall try to identify some of the general characteristics of science, including the nature of scientific method (often taken, incorrectly, to be the same thing), then we shall describe some of psychology's early history as a scientific discipline and finally we shall ask what is perhaps the crucial question, namely, how appropriate is it to use scientific method to study human behaviour and cognitive processes?

Science is a theme that, perhaps inevitably, runs all the way through the remaining 30 chapters of this book, sometimes explicitly, sometimes implicitly. For example, in Chapter 15 (Interpersonal Perception), it is argued that everyone may be thought of as a psychologist in the sense that we all develop 'theories' about what other people are like (theory building being an important feature of science); we use these theories to help us explain/understand, predict and, sometimes, to control others' behaviour (the three main aims of science). Another aspect of interpersonal perception is the attribution process, in which we account for behaviour (both our own and other people's) in terms of its causes, another fundamental feature of 'classical' science (namely, *determinism*); indeed, Heider (1958), the founder of attribution theory, referred to the layperson as a 'naive scientist'.

The nomothetic–idiographic debate is one that has taken place within psychology for much of its history, especially in relation to theories of personality (see Chapter 29). It concerns the most appropriate way of thinking about and studying people, either (a) trying to identify characteristics shared by everyone (nomothetic), or (b) studying people as unique individuals (idiographic). This, in turn, is related to a

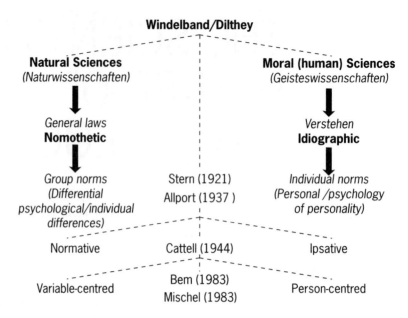

FIGURE 2.1 *Nomothetic–idiographic distinction and its relationship to other corresponding distinctions*

distinction (first made in the 1800s) between the Naturwissenschaften (the natural/physical sciences) and the *Geisteswissenschaften* (humanities or social sciences); ironically, those modern-day psychologists who support a nomothetic approach may still be trying to model psychology on a view of physics (in particular, and natural science in general) which physicists themselves see as outdated, but which may have been valid when Watson delivered his 'behaviourist manifesto' in 1913.

In addition to determinism, 'classical' science is usually portrayed as being unbiased, objective and value free; this view of science is called *positivism*. Even if natural science can be accurately described in this way (which Popper, for example, believes it cannot), psychology seems to face special problems as a positivist science. The fact that psychologists are studying other human beings seems to challenge any simple interpretation of the findings of psychological research: it is a social process of interaction as much as a scientific procedure, which raises both methodological and ethical issues (see Chapter 32), and the values and biases (usually unconscious) of the investigator always play some part in the research process.

Two further features of science are *reductionism* (discussed in Chapter 32) and *empiricism*, the philosophical theory according to which the only source of true knowledge about the world is what comes to us through our senses; this belief proved to be a central influence on the development of physics and chemistry and, in turn, on psychology as a separate scientific discipline.

SOME PHILOSOPHICAL INFLUENCES ON PSYCHOLOGY'S DEVELOPMENT AS A SEPARATE DISCIPLINE

Descartes, the 17th century French philosopher, has had an enormous impact on the development of psychology as a science (as well as on the development of science in general). His distinction between matter and mind is called *philosophical dualism* and is usually contrasted with the view that only matter exists (*materialism*): the universe consists of two fundamentally different 'realities', namely physical matter, which is extended in time and space, and non-material, non-extended mind This is discussed in Chapter 32 in relation to the mind—brain relationship.

Dualism allowed scientists to treat matter as inert and completely distinct from themselves; this meant that the world could be described objectively, without reference to the human observer. Objectivity became the ideal of science and it was extended to the study of human behaviour and social institutions by Comte in the mid-1800s, when it became known as *positivism.*

Descartes also promoted *mechanism*, the view that the material world comprises objects which are assembled like a huge machine and operated by mechanical laws. He extended this view to living organisms, including, eventually, the human body. Because the mind is non-material, Descartes believed that it cannot be studied in the same way as the physical world; rather, it can only be investigated through introspection, i.e. observing one's own thoughts and feelings. He also argued that complex wholes may be understood in terms of their constituent parts and so was one of the first advocates of *reductionism.*

● Science and empiricism

Empiricism refers to the ideas of 17th and 18th century British empiricist philosophers, in particular Locke, Hume and Berkeley, who believed that the only source of true knowledge about the world is sensory experience, i.e. what comes to us through our senses or what can be inferred about the relationships between such sensory facts. They were usually seen as opposed to the *rationalist or nativist* philosophers who believed that knowledge of the world is largely innate or inborn. The word 'empirical'

('through the senses') is often used to mean 'scientific', implying that what scientists do – and what distinguishes them from non-scientists – is carry out experiments and observations as ways of collecting data or 'facts' about the world. Empiricism proved to be one of the central influences on the development of physics and chemistry.

● Empiricism and psychology

University courses in scientific psychology were taught for the first time in the 1870s; before this time, there were no laboratories explicitly devoted to psychological research and the early scientific psychologists had trained mainly as physiologists, doctors, philosophers or some combination of these. According to Fancher (1979), the two professors who set up the first two laboratories deserve much of the credit for the development of academic psychology, namely Wilhelm Wundt (1832–1920) in Germany and William James (1842–1910) in the USA.

The contribution of Wilhelm Wundt

Wundt, a physiologist by training (having first obtained a medical degree), is generally regarded as the 'founder' of the new science of experimental psychology; as he wrote in the preface to his *Principles of Physiological Psychology* (1874), ' ... The work I here present to the public is an attempt to mark out a new domain of science' (quoted in Fancher, 1979). Having worked as assistant to Hermann Helmholtz, the great physiologist who had much to contribute to the psychology of perception (see Chapter 9), Wundt was eventually appointed professor of 'scientific philosophy' at Leipzig in 1875, showing the lack of distinct boundaries between the various disciplines which combined to bring about the development of psychology (Fancher, 1979).

In 1879, he converted his 'laboratory' at Leipzig University (in fact, a small, single room used as a demonstration laboratory) into a 'private institute' of experimental psychology. For the first time, a place had been set aside for the explicit purpose of studying psychology and conducting psychological research. Hence, 1879 is generally accepted as the 'birthdate' of psychology as a discipline in its own right. At first, the institute was small, but it soon began to attract people from all over the world, who returned to their own countries to establish laboratories modelled on Wundt's.

In his *Principles of Physiological Psychology*, he argued that conscious mental states could be scientifically studied through the systematic manipulation of antecedent variables and analysed by carefully controlled techniques of introspection. Introspection was a rigorous and highly disciplined technique for the separation of conscious experience into its most basic elements; participants were always advanced psychology students who had been carefully trained to introspect properly and those who found it too difficult were discouraged from pursuing careers in psychology. The aim of introspection was to analyse conscious experience into elementary sensations and feelings. *Sensations* referred to the raw sensory content of consciousness, devoid of all 'meaning' or interpretation; all conscious thoughts, ideas, perceptions, etc. were assumed to be combinations of sensations which could be defined on just four dimensions: *mode* (visual, auditory, etc.), *quality* (e.g. the colours and shapes of the visual sensations), *intensity* and *duration*. Thus, the introspective analysis of the experience of looking at a moving picture would not contain references to the objects in the picture, but the minute description of patches of light, of differing colours, intensities and durations.

Feelings could also be introspectively analysed in terms of three dimensions: based on the classic experiment in which Wundt himself listened to a metronome beating at varying rates, he identified *pleasantness–unpleasantness*, *tension–relaxation* and *activity–passivity* (inducing a mild excitement or having a slight calming effect).

The attempt to analyse or break down experience into its constituent parts is a form of reductionism. Through introspection, Wundt was trying to cut through the learned categories and concepts that define our everyday experience of the world and thereby expose the 'building blocks' from which even the earliest childhood experiences are constructed, just as chemical compounds are constructed from hydrogen, oxygen and the other chemical elements. Because of the central role of introspection in studying consciousness, Wundt's early brand of psychology came to be called *introspective psychology* and his attempt to analyse conscious thought into its elementary sensations and feelings is known as *structuralism*.

The contribution of William James

James, like Wundt, trained originally in medicine, but he received no further formal academic training after his medical degree. Having first been appointed to teach anatomy and physiology at Harvard University in 1872, by 1875 he was calling his course 'The Relations between Physiology and Psychology'

and it was in connection with this course that he developed his small demonstration laboratory in 1875. In 1878 he dropped anatomy and physiology from his curriculum and for several years he taught 'pure psychology'; although he did relatively little research himself, he used his laboratory to enrich his classroom presentations.

His view of psychology is summarized in his classic and extremely popular *The Principles of Psychology* (1890), which includes chapters on brain function, habit, the stream of consciousness (see Chapter 4), the self (see Chapter 21), attention (see Chapter 11), memory (see Chapter 12), perception (see Chapters 9 and 10), instinct (see Chapter 17), free will (see Chapter 32) and emotion (see Chapter 6). It is ironic that, in view of the impact that James had on the development of psychology, especially through his *Principles* (which has given us the immortal definition: 'Psychology is the Science of Mental Life ... ') and how famous it made him as a psychologist, he was very critical both of the book and of what psychology could offer as a science. After its publication, he became increasingly interested in philosophy and thought of himself less and less as a psychologist, although he was (in 1894) the first American to call favourable attention to the recent work of the then still rather obscure neurologist from Vienna, Sigmund Freud (Fancher, 1979).

According to Fancher, James did not put forward a theory so much as a point of view (as much philosophical as psychological) which directly inspired *functionalism*, a movement especially popular with American psychologists , according to which it is the purpose and utility of behaviour that are important, rather than merely its description. (Functionalism is often contrasted with Wundt's structuralism.) Functionalism, in turn, helped to stimulate interest in individual differences, since they determine how well or poorly individuals will adapt to their environments (see Chapters 28–31). According to Fancher, these attitudes made Americans especially receptive to Darwin's ideas about individual variation, evolution by natural selection and the 'survival of the fittest' when they first appeared in 1859.

● John Watson's behaviourist revolution: a new subject matter for psychology

In 1909, John B. Watson took over the psychology department at Johns Hopkins University and immediately began trying to cut psychology's ties to philosophy and to strengthen those with biology. At first, Watson lived in a kind of 'uneasy alliance' with traditional introspective psychology, which was, for most people, 'real' psychology, i.e. the study of human consciousness. He continued to teach courses based on the work of Wundt and James, while conducting his own research on animals and becoming increasingly critical of the use of introspection. In particular, he argued that introspective reports were unreliable and difficult to verify: it is impossible to check the accuracy of such reports because they are based on purely private experience, to which the investigator has no possible means of access. Surely this is no way for a scientific psychology to proceed! (Fancher, 1979).

The only solution, as Watson saw it, was for psychology to redefine itself and in 1913 he published an article called 'Psychology as the Behaviourist Views It', which is often referred to as the 'Behaviourist Manifesto', a charter for a truly scientific psychology. Although Wundt had been influenced by empiricism through its impact on science as a whole, it was behaviourism which was to represent a rigorous empiricist approach within psychology for the first time. According to Watson:

> Psychology as the behaviourist views it is a purely objective natural science. Its theoretical goal is the prediction and control of behaviour. Introspection forms no essential part of its methods, nor is the scientific value of its data dependent upon the readiness with which they lend themselves to interpretation in terms of consciousness. The behaviourist ... recognizes no dividing line between man and brute. The behaviour of a man, with all its refinement and complexity, forms only a part of the behaviourist's total scheme of investigation.

Three features of this 'Behaviourist Manifesto' deserve special mention:

1 Psychology must be purely objective, excluding all subjective data or interpretations in terms of conscious experience; he was redefining psychology as the 'science of behaviour ', instead of the traditional 'science of mental life'.
2 The goals of psychology should be to predict and control behaviour (as opposed to describing and explaining conscious mental states); this was maintained by the other major behaviourist psychologist, B.F. Skinner (see Chapter 7).
3 There is no fundamental (qualitative) distinction between human and non-human animal behaviour. If, as Darwin had shown, humans evolved from more simple species, then it follows that human behaviour is simply a more complex form

of the behaviour of other species (i.e. the difference is merely one of degree – quantitative; see below). Consequently, rats, cats, dogs and pigeons became the major source of psychological data; since 'psychological' now meant 'behaviour' rather than 'consciousness', animals that were convenient to study and whose environments could easily be controlled could replace people as experimental subjects.

In 1915, Watson was elected president of the American Psychological Association and his presidential address dealt with his recent 'discovery' of Pavlov's work on conditioned reflexes in dogs (see Chapter 7). He proposed that the conditioned reflex could become the foundation of a full-scale human psychology.

Locke had described the mind at birth as a *tabula rasa* ('blank slate'), on which experience makes its imprint. Despite rejecting the mind as a valid subject for a scientific psychology, the extreme environmentalism of Locke's empiricism lent itself very well to the behaviourist emphasis on learning (through the process of Pavlovian or classical conditioning): what the environment shapes simply moves from 'the mind' to observable behaviour.

According to Miller (1962), empiricism provided for psychology both a methodology, which stresses the central role of observation and measurement, and a theory, which comprises:

● the *tabula rasa* view of the mind;
● analysis into elements, such as overt behaviour into stimulus–response units (a form of reductionism);
● *associationism* which explains how simple elements can be combined to form more complex elements.

This distinction corresponds to that between two kinds of behaviourism – *philosophical* behaviourism which, in its most extreme form, involves the rejection of mind (see Chapter 32) and *methodological* behaviourism, which refers to the general belief in the importance of using empirical methods, particularly controlled laboratory experiments, statistics and so on.

Behaviourism also embodied positivism, in particular the emphasis on the need for scientific rigour and objectivity: human beings were now being conceptualized and studied as 'natural phenomena', with their subjective experience, consciousness and other characteristics, which had for so long been taken as distinctive human qualities, being removed from the 'universe': there was no place for these things in the behaviourist world.

In the rest of this chapter we shall consider some of the problems that arise when this 'natural science' approach to the study of people is adopted.

WHAT DO WE MEAN BY 'SCIENCE'?

As summarized in Figure 2.2, a science must involve:

- a definable *subject matter* (which, as we have seen, changed from conscious human thought to human and non-human animal behaviour within

psychology's first 35 years or so as a separate discipline);

- *theory construction*, which is an attempt to explain observed phenomena (for example, Watson's attempt to account for most human and animal behaviour in terms of classical conditioning, and, later, Skinner's attempt to do the same with operant conditioning);

- *hypothesis testing*, which involves making specific predictions about behaviour under certain specified conditions (for example, predicting that by combining the sight of a rat with the sound of a hammer crashing down on a steel bar just behind his head, a small child will come to fear the rat; see Chapter 7 and the case of little Albert);

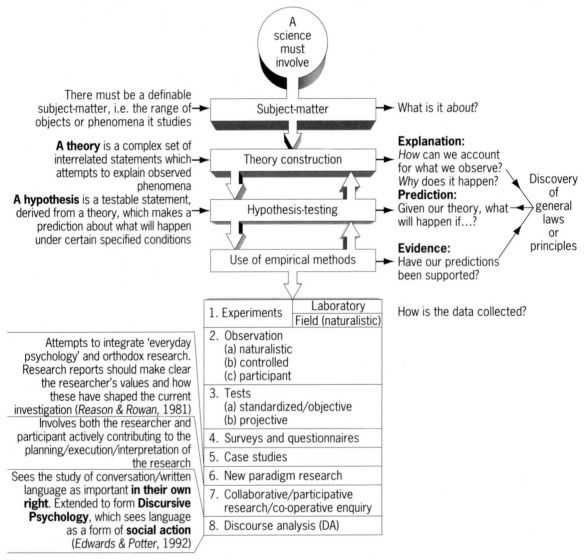

FIGURE 2.2 *A summary of the major features of science*

Common beliefs	Alternative views
1 Scientific discovery begins with simple, unbiased, unprejudiced observation (i.e. the scientist simply 'samples' the world without any preconceptions, expectations, predetermined theories, etc.).	**1** There is no such thing as 'unbiased' or 'unprejudiced' observation. Our observation is always selective, interpretative, prestructured and directed (i.e. we must have at least some idea of what we are looking for, otherwise we cannot know when we have found it).
2 From the resulting sensory evidence ('data'/ 'sense-data'), generalized statements of fact will take shape (i.e. we gradually build up a picture of what the world is like based on a number of separate 'samples').	**2** 'Data' do not constitute 'facts': 'evidence' usually implies measurement, numbers, recordings, etc. which need to be interpreted in the light of a theory. Facts do not exist objectively and cannot be discovered through 'pure observation'. According to Deese (1972) : 'Fact' = Data + Theory.
3 The essential feature of scientific activity is the use of empirical methods, through which the sensory evidence is gathered ('empirical' = 'through the senses' = 'scientific') (i.e. what distinguishes science from non-science is performing experiments, etc.)	**3** Despite the central role of data collection, data alone do not make a science: theory is just as crucial, because without it, data have no meaning (see point 2).
4 The truth about the world (the objective nature of things, what the world 'is really like') can be established through properly controlled experiments (and other ways of collecting 'facts'), i.e. science can tell us about reality as it is independently of the scientist or the activity of observing it.	**4** Scientific theory and research reflect the biases, prejudices, values and assumptions of the individual scientist, as well as of the scientific community to which they belong: science is not value free (see section on p.28 'The importance of theory").
5 Science involves the steady accumulation of knowledge, so that each generation of scientists adds to the discoveries of previous generations.	**5** Science involves an endless succession of long, peaceful periods (normal science) and scientific revolutions (Kuhn, 1962; see Table 2.3).
6 Science involves a cold, detached, impersonal attitude, an automaton-like precision.	**6** Science has a warm, human, exciting, argumentative, creative 'face' (Collins, 1994)

Table 2.1 *Some common beliefs about 'science' and 'scientific method' (based on Medawar, 1963; Popper, 1972)*

- the use of *empirical methods* to collect data relevant to the hypothesis being tested (evidence).

As we saw earlier, explanation and prediction are two widely accepted goals of science, control being a third; to these we could add a fourth, namely the discovery of general laws or principles, which 'feed back' into theory construction and prediction.

● What is meant by 'scientific method'?

This account of what constitutes a science would probably be accepted by most psychologists and philosophers of science. However, this does not in itself tell us how the scientific process takes place, the sequence of 'events' involved (such as where the theory comes from in the first place and how it is related to observation of the subject matter) or the precise relationship between theory construction, hypothesis testing and data collection: these, collectively, are usually referred to as (the) *scientific method*. Table 2.1 summarizes some common beliefs about both science and scientific method together with some alternative views.

As a result of the first two beliefs in particular, Popper has revised the stages of the scientific process as proposed by the inductive method; see Table 2.2 (overleaf).

● Can psychology be called a science if psychologists cannot agree what it is?

As we saw above (and in Chapter 1), definitions of psychology have changed during the 120 or so years of its life; these changing definitions largely reflect

Inductive method (classical view)	Popper's version
1 Observation and method	**1** Problem (usually a refutation of an existing theory or prediction).
2 Inductive generalization	**2** Proposed solution or new theory.
3 Hypothesis	**3** Deduction of testable statements from the new theory (i.e. hypothesis). *
4 Attempted verification of hypothesis	**4** Tests or attempts to refute by methods including observation and experiment.
5 Proof or disproof	**5** Establishing a preference between competing theories.
6 Knowledge	

* This relates to the *hypothetico-deductive method,* which is usually contrasted with/opposed to the inductive method. In practice, the two approaches should be seen as complementary, both playing a part in the scientific process.

TABLE 2.2 *Comparison of the classical, inductive view of science and Popper's revised version*

the influence and contributions of the major theoretical approaches or orientations, such as behaviourism, psychoanalysis, the humanistic-existential, cognitive and neurobiological/biogenic. As shown in Table 1.1. (pp. 12–13), each approach rests upon a different image of what human beings are like, which in turn determines what it is important to study, as well as the methods that can and should be used to study it. In the light of this, different approaches can be seen as not only different facets of the same discipline, but as self-contained disciplines (Kuhn, 1962; Kline, 1988). According to Kuhn (1962), a philosopher of science, this means that psychology has no paradigm (it is preparadigmatic) and therefore it is still in a state of prescience (see Table 2.3).

Valentine (1982) claims that behaviourism comes as close to being a paradigm as anything could, because it provides:

● a clear definition of the subject matter, namely behaviour (as opposed to mental or cognitive processes or private experience);
● fundamental assumptions, in the form of the central role played by learning (in particular, conditioning) and the analysis of behaviour into stimulus–response units, allowing prediction and control;
● a methodology, with the controlled experiment at its core.

But this claim seems to overlook the distinction, which we noted earlier, between two kinds of behaviourism, philosophical and methodological. Most present-day psychologists are not behaviourists in the philosophical sense and methodological behaviourism is about the importance of using empirical methods of research, not a theory about the subject matter of psychology.

● Is a theoretical approach the same as a paradigm?

As Table 2.3 shows, Kuhn himself, as well as psychologists such as Joynson and Boden, maintain that psychology is still in a stage of prescience, i.e. it has not yet evolved a paradigm; this contrasts sharply with the view of Palermo and LeFrancois, who believe that psychology has already had several revolutions, with its current state of normal science involving the cognitive paradigm. A third view, which represents a blend of the first two, is that psychology currently, and simultaneously, has a number of paradigms (sometimes, but not always, with the implication that this makes it prescientific).

For example, Smith and Cowie (1991) identify psychoanalysis, behaviourism, sociobiology, the information-processing approach and the cognitive-developmental approaches as paradigms, with the last being the most important as far as child development is concerned, while Davison and Neale (1994) identify 'four major paradigms of contemporary abnormal psychology', namely, the biological, psychoanalytic, learning (behaviourist) and cognitive.

Lambie (1991) believes that it is a mistake to equate 'paradigm' with 'approach' As we noted in

A field of study can only legitimately be considered a science if a majority of its workers subscribe to a common global perspective or paradigm. Although theory is a crucial feature of a paradigm, there is much more to a paradigm than a particular theory. For example, Glassman (1995) describes it as a superordinate framework or worldview which shapes both theories and evidence. Kuhn identifies three historical stages in the development of a science:

Kuhn's three stages	Where does psychology fit in?
1 *Pre-science* No paradigm has evolved and there are several schools of thought.	Psychology comprises a number of schools of thought, all of which define the subject matter differently. In particular, each school presents a different image of what human beings are like, which in turn determines *what* should be studied and *how* to study it. As well as Kuhn (1962) himself, Joynson (1980) and Boden (1980) argue that psychology is preparadigmatic. … Now in psychology most of the work is of the detailed kind, as if there were an accepted paradigm. Yet … this is by no means the case. In fact, there are various models of psychology, all of which involve different paradigms … (Kline, 1988)
2 *Normal science* A paradigm has emerged and it dictates the kind of research that is carried out; the results are interpreted so as to be consistent with it. The details of the theory are filled in and workers explore how far it can go; disagreements may arise but these can be resolved within the limits allowed by the paradigm.	Behaviourism comes as close to a paradigm as anything could (Valentine, 1982) (see below)
3 *Revolution* A point is reached in almost all established sciences where the conflicting evidence becomes so overwhelming that the old paradigm has to be abandoned and is replaced by a new one (*paradigm shift*). For example, Copernican physics was replaced by Newtonian, which in turn was displaced by Einstein's theory of relativity. When this paradigm shift occurs, there is a return to *normal science*.	Palermo (1971), for example, argues that psychology has already undergone several paradigm shifts. The first paradigm was *structuralism*, represented by Wundt's introspectionism, with its emphasis on identifying the elements of the conscious thoughts and feelings of normal human adults. This was replaced by Watson's *behaviourism,* with its emphasis on the objective observation of the overt behaviour of adults, children and animals. More recently, *cognitive psychology* has put 'mind' back on the psychological map, based on the concept of information processing and the computer analogy. LeFrancois (1983) is another who takes this position. Glassman (1995) disagrees, claiming that there has never been a complete reorganization of the discipline as has happened in physics.

TABLE 2.3 *Kuhn's (1962, 1970) account of the nature and development of science*

Table 2.3, while theory is an essential part of a paradigm, there is much more involved than just theory; for example, different theories can coexist within the same overall approach, such as classical and operant conditioning within 'learning theory' (the behaviourist approach) and Freud's and Erikson's theories both representing the psychoanalytic/psychodynamic approach. One of the 'ingredients' that makes a paradigm different from an approach is its *social psychological* dimension, i.e. paradigms refer to assumptions and beliefs held in common by most, if not all, the members of a given scientific community.

● The importance of theory

Valentine (1992) believes that theories are both logically and psychologically necessary but they also serve a crucial practical function, namely guiding research by helping us to select from an infinite number of possible experiments (Allport, 1955); this is called the *heuristic* function of theories. According to Popper (1959), 'Theories are nets cast to catch what we call "the world", to rationalize it, to explain and to master it'.

Given the critical role of theory in general as a part of science, how can we set about deciding the value of any particular theory? We shall now consider a number of criteria for evaluating a theory, which are listed in Table 2.4.

(a) Falsifiability or refutability
(b) Truth value
(c) Reflexivity
(d) Predicting future events
(e) Internal consistency
(f) Economy
(g) Fertility
(h) Practical usefulness
(i) Changing our image of ourselves as human beings
(j) Presenting an objective, unbiased, value-free account of human behaviour and experience

---

TABLE 2.4 *Checklist of criteria for evaluating a theory*

Falsifiability or refutability – is it possible to find evidence which would show the theory to be false?

According to Popper (1959), it is too easy to obtain evidence to support a theory: showing a theory to be true (the *principle of verification*) is invalid as a way of distinguishing between science and non-science. It must be possible to produce evidence which shows the theory to be false (the *principle of falsification*

or *refutability*). One appeal of Freud's theory, for example, is that – according to its critics, such as Popper and Eysenck (1985) – it can explain anything! To take an example, part of the anal (retentive) personality (caused by strict potty-training) is parsimony (miserliness, thriftiness, meanness). But the opposite behaviour, namely reckless gambling or financial speculating, can also be related to strict potty-training through the unconscious mechanism of reaction formation. In either case, Freud would say that the behaviour supports his psychosexual theory. How could it be falsified? (see Chapters 21 and 29).

Kline (1988) points out an important distinction made by philosophers of science between bold conjectures (new and surprising hypotheses, especially counterintuitive or contrary to common sense predictions; see, for example, Festinger's theory of cognitive dissonance in Chapter 18) and cautious conjectures (hypotheses that follow easily from the theory and which are highly likely to be supported). While support for bold conjectures is generally considered to be good support for the theory, cautious conjectures are only interesting if they turn out to be incorrect. Kline believes that psychologists rarely go in for bold conjectures; instead they use cautious conjectures and regard the theory as confirmed if they are supported; this is particularly true, he says, of users of cognitive models (see Chapters 9–14).

Truth value – does the theory accurately reflect the nature of the phenomena it is trying to explain?

For example, are people actually like Freud's theory says they are? If we answer 'yes', this implies that there is only one version of the truth, so if Freud is right, Skinner, especially when his ideas directly conflict with Freud's, must be wrong. This is an extreme form of *rationalism*, according to which it is possible to choose between different theories on logical and experimental grounds. To some degree, all the criteria listed in Table 2.4 can be thought of as the logical grounds for choosing between different theories, but these criteria tell us that there is no absolute way of doing it, which rationalism seems to require; for example, psychologists and philosophers of science are likely to disagree as to which criteria are the most important.

Also, as we saw in Table 2.1, our observations are always guided by our theories and data are always interpreted in the light of some theoretical concept or other, so we could never carry out the 'ultimate' experiment to choose between different theories.

However, every so often in the following chapters we shall refer to attempts by psychologists to test opposing hypotheses against one another (see the discussion of cognitive dissonance in Chapter 18); the conclusion that is often drawn is that hypothesis A applies under conditions X, while hypothesis B applies under conditions Y. This represents a form of *relativism*, according to which all theories are (equally) credible, all contribute to our understanding of human behaviour and there is no need to choose between them; this is sometimes called an *eclectic* approach.

Reflexivity – can the theory account for its own existence?

Formulating theories is part of human behaviour. Since scientific activity is part of the totality of human behaviour, psychologists are in the unique position of having to account not only for the behaviour of those they are studying, but also for their own behaviour as scientists. In fact, the psychologist as scientist is engaging in behaviour which is very similar to that of those they are studying: as Heather (1976) puts it, the psychologist makes observations about observers, experiments with experimenters and theorizes about theorizers.

Heather believes that the acid test of any psychological theory is its ability to explain its own creation and he maintains that no behaviourist theory (such as Skinner's) is capable of passing the test. According to Freud, all acts of creativity (including constructing a theory) represent a sublimation of unconscious processes and, to this extent, his theory *can* account for itself. But probably the best example of a reflexive theory is Kelly's *personal construct theory*, which is built around the model of 'man the scientist' (see Chapter 29).

Predicting future events – can the theory accurately predict what will happen and explain what has already taken place?

Hypothesis testing is primarily concerned with the accuracy and reliability of predictions, often drawn from a theory, and this is a major way of evaluating the truth value of the theory.

While theories are, by their nature, generalizations, in a psychological context we often want to know how a certain theory will apply to a particular individual. This relates to the idiographic–nomothetic debate, in which the study of people as unique individuals and the study of people in general have, traditionally, been seen as opposed and irreconcilable. However, it makes as much sense to generalize and make predictions about the same individual (individual norms) as it does about groups of people (group norms) (see Chapter 29).

Instead of seeing the two approaches as opposed, they are increasingly being seen as complementary. For example, even though Freud used the case study, which is the idiographic method par excellence, this did not prevent him from formulating a theory of personality meant to apply to people in general, and even Skinner's operant conditioning, which some would argue represents the best (and the worst) of the nomothetic approach, is based on repeated, highly controlled experiments with individual rats (see Gross, 1995).

Internal consistency – do the different parts of the theory fit together to form a coherent structure?

There shouldn't be any contradictions between one part of the theory and another and the terms and concepts used should be logically related. However much Freud's psychoanalytic theory, for example, has been criticized in terms of falsifiability, truth value and its (in)ability to predict future outcomes, the various parts of the theory (such as the structure of personality, levels of consciousness, unconscious motivation and psychosexual development) are generally seen as highly inter-related, consistent and logically connected.

Economy – how many 'unproven' assumptions does the theory make?

In general, the fewer assumptions the better and in addition, the mechanisms it proposes to explain the phenomena in question should be as simple as possible. These requirements are sometimes summed up in the *law of parsimony* or 'Occam's razor', according to which, if we are presented with two theories which are equally 'good' in all other respects, the one which is more simple, more economical, is 'better'.

Fertility – has the theory generated much research, debate and general interest?

According to Thomas (1985), this can take the form of:

● direct replication studies;
● testing certain assumptions or principles not previously tested;
● verification studies (to test whether some theoretical assumption is borne out in real life);

- 'population applicability' (e.g. cross-cultural research);
- 'extended theorizing' (developing and modifying the original theory), as in the neo-Freudian theories of Jung, Adler and Erikson (see Chapter 29) and neo-behaviourist theories, such as Bandura's social learning theory (see Chapters 7, 23 and 27).

Practical usefulness – does the theory offer practical guidance in solving everyday problems (such as childrearing, crime and mental disorder)?

This relates to the aims of psychology as a scientific discipline. Is it appropriate that, in keeping with (other) natural sciences, psychology should aim to explain/understand, predict and control human behaviour and experience?

The title of George Miller's (1969) presidential address to the American Psychological Association was 'Psychology as a Means of Promoting Human Welfare'; in it, he made the distinction between psychology as a natural science and as a means of changing our image of ourselves. As a natural science, psychology aims, theoretically, to provide the 'true' view of human beings' psychological nature and, practically, to apply the theoretical principles which have been discovered in the form of behavioural technologies, i.e. ways of manipulating our circumstances and behaviour to make them fit our desires and goals. In this context, psychologists become the 'experts', the professionals, who present their findings to the rest (the public at large) and apply these findings in the form of behavioural control (such as behaviour therapy and modification; see Chapter 31).

Miller is unhappy with the idea of psychologists as experts; he believes that of the three aims of psychology as a science, understanding and prediction are more appropriate than control, with understanding being the primary goal. In fact, he sees self-understanding as much more important and appropriate than the expert's understanding of others. While psychotherapy in general is seen as providing the person with insight or self-understanding (in contrast with behaviour therapy/modification which is seen as trying to change behaviour), some forms of psychotherapy adopt a much more person-centred approach than others, in particular, Rogers' client-centred therapy (see Chapter 31). Discussion of the aims of psychology (and the aims of therapies based on psychological principles) raises very important ethical issues (see Chapter 32).

In its other role, which is often implicit and unconscious, psychology seems to have the effect of changing our beliefs about what we are like as human beings; rather than discovering means to ends, it may influence the very nature of those ends themselves. This suggests a further criterion.

Changing our image of ourselves as human beings – has the theory had an impact upon what we think we are like and, indirectly, upon the way we behave?

Miller cites Freud's theory in this context: Freud can be seen as having changed the nature of the problems human beings face and it is in this way, rather than through providing practical solutions to those problems we already have, that psychology in general, and theories in particular, might exert their most powerful and significant influence. ' ... the impact of Freud's thought has been due far less to the instrumentalities he provided than the changed conception of ourselves that he implied ... ' (Miller, 1969).

Presenting an objective, unbiased, value-free account of human behaviour and experience–is the theory free of the (unconscious) cultural biases, prejudices, assumptions, experiences and values of the psychologist?

As we have seen, the view that science should be objective, unbiased and value free is called positivism. According to feminist psychologists, there is a major source of bias within both the research and theorizing which make up 'mainstream' academic psychology (as well as the psychology profession itself), namely, *androcentrism* (or the 'masculinist bias'), whereby women's behaviour and experience are compared with those of men, who are implicitly taken (by men) as the standard or norm against which women are judged (see Chapters 23 and 27, for example). Since most psychologists are white, middle-class Americans or Europeans, there is also a very strong tendency to equate 'human' with ' member of Western culture' and to judge members of non-Western cultures against the norms of behaviour and experience which apply to the former; this is called *ethnocentrism* (or the 'Eurocentric bias') (see Chapters 9 and 28, for example). To the extent that such biases actually do influence psychologists' research and theories, psychology cannot be regarded as an objective science. (This is discussed further below.)

HOW APPROPRIATE IS IT TO STUDY BEHAVIOUR USING THE METHODS OF SCIENCE?

We saw when discussing reflexivity that 'doing science' is part of human behaviour; this means that when psychologists study what people do, they are engaging in some of the very behaviours that they are trying to understand (such as thinking, perceiving, problem-solving and explaining). This is sometimes referred to as psychologists being part of their subject matter, which makes it even more difficult to be objective than for other scientists. What objective means here is, 'stepping back from something in order to appreciate what it is really like, its true nature'. But can any scientist be completely objective according to this definition?

One way of trying to answer this question is to consider the social nature of scientific activity. If we conclude that it is as social as any other form of human behaviour, does this necessarily mean that 'the truth' only exists by agreement; that is, science does not, after all, tell us about what things are really like, but only what scientists happen to believe is the truth at any particular time? According to Richardson (1991):

> Whatever the *logical* aspects of scientific method may be (deriving hypotheses from theories, the importance of refutability, etc.), it is a very *social* business. Yet this exposure of scientific activities to national and international comment and criticism is what distinguishes it from the 'folklore' of informal theories ...

Research must be qualified and quantified to enable others to replicate it and in this way, the procedures, instruments and measures become standardized so that scientists anywhere in the world can check the truth of reported observations and findings. This implies the need for universally agreed conventions for reporting these observations and findings (Richardson, 1991).

A more extreme view of the social nature of science is taken by Collins (1994), who argues that the results of scientific experiments are more ambiguous than they are usually taken to be, while theory is more flexible than most people imagine: ' ... This means that science can progress only within communities that can reach consensus about what counts as plausible. Plausibility is a matter of social context so science is "a social construct"'.

● The social nature of science

Kuhn's concept of a paradigm stresses the role of agreement or consensus among fellow scientists working within a particular discipline. Accordingly, the 'truth' has more to do with the popularity and widespread acceptance of a particular framework within the scientific community than with its 'truth value'. The fact that revolutions do occur (i.e. paradigm shifts) demonstrates that 'the truth' can and does change; for example, the change from Newtonian physics to Einsteinian physics reflected the changing popularity of these two accounts. Kuhn (1970) quotes Max Planck, who helped to shape the 'Einsteinian revolution':

> ... a new scientific theory does not triumph by convincing its opponents and making them see the light, but rather because its opponents eventually die, and a new generation grows up that is familiar with it.

But surely the popularity or acceptability of a theory is at least partly determined by how well it is seen to explain and predict the phenomena in question, so that the social and the 'purely' scientific or rational criteria are both relevant (one does not exclude the other). In the absence of any 'ultimate' way of choosing between theories (see above), the need for scientists to have agreed criteria and procedures by which they can test and check each others' research findings assumes even greater significance

As the quotes from Richardson and Collins above make clear, science does not take place in a social vacuum but is a human activity which is part of an international community. Agreed conventions and criteria regarding what counts as 'good science' ('scientific method') help to make scientific knowledge so much more objective and reliable than 'common sense' or informal knowledge, although it is always a matter of degree – as we have seen, there can be no absolute truths even in science.

However, even if there are widely accepted ways of 'doing science', what does this mean for psychology? Is it appropriate to study human behaviour and experience as part of the natural world or is a different kind of approach needed altogether? After all, as we saw earlier, it is not just psychologists who observe, experiment and theorize. One way of trying to understand what this means is to consider the psychology experiment as a social situation.

● The psychology experiment as a social situation

To regard empirical research in general, and the experiment as particular, as objective involves the assumption that the researcher does not influence the behaviour of the person whose behaviour is being investigated, i.e. they only influence the behaviour of the participant (the outcome of the experiment) to the extent that they decide what hypothesis to test, how the variables are to be operationalized, what design to use and so on. But an equally important assumption concerns the people whose behaviour is being studied, namely, that the only factors that matter (which influence their performance) are the variables that are manipulated by the experimenter and which are objectively defined.

Can either of these two assumptions be justified, i.e. is there really nothing else 'going on' in an experiment apart from what can be objectively defined? Is there really nothing that 'passes between' those involved, no unconscious or inadvertent contribution that either the experimenter or participant makes to the outcome?

Experimenters are people too: the problem of experimenter bias

According to Rosenthal (1966), what the experimenter is *like* is correlated with what the experimenter *does*, as well as influencing the participant's perception of, and response to, the experimenter. For example, Rosenthal (1967, cited in Valentine, 1992) described the pattern of behaviour that female experimenters show towards male participants as 'interested modesty'. By contrast, male experimenters' behaviour towards female participants is simply 'interested', taking significantly longer to prepare stimulus materials for female than for male participants. This is a demonstration of *experimenter bias*. Further examples are given in Box 2.1.

Participants are psychologists too: the concept of demand characteristics

What contribution is made to the experiment by the participant, over and above their performance on the experimental task? Instead of seeing the person being studied ('subject') as a passive responder, to whom things are done, Orne (1962) prefers to stress

---

BOX 2.1	Key study: Rosenthal's demonstrations of experimenter bias

Experimenter bias has been demonstrated in a wide range of experiments, including reaction time, psychophysics, animal learning, verbal conditioning, personality assessment, person perception, learning and ability, as well as in everyday life situations (Rosenthal and Rubin, cited in Valentine, 1992).

What they consistently show is that, if one group of experimenters has one hypothesis about what it expects to find and another group has the opposite hypothesis, both groups will obtain results that support their respective hypotheses. These results are not due to the mishandling of data by biased experimenters, but somehow the bias of the experimenter creates a changed environment in which participants actually behave differently.

In two separate studies (Rosenthal and Fode, 1960; Rosenthal and Lawson, 1961, cited in Weisstein, 1993), experimenters who were told that rats learning mazes had been specially bred for brightness ('maze-bright') obtained better learning from their rats than did experimenters who believed that their rats were 'maze-dull'.

In fact, both groups of rats were drawn from the same population and were randomly allocated to the 'bright' or 'dull' condition. The crucial point is that the 'bright' rats did actually learn faster. Somehow, the experimenters' expectations concretely changed the situation, although how this happened is far less clear.

In the case of people, expectations are likely to be conveyed through a variety of non-verbal behaviours. Probably the most famous demonstration is the 'Pygmalion' experiment by Rosenthal and Jacobson, written up in book form as *Pygmalion in the Classroom* (1968). In a natural classroom situation, children whose teachers were told that they would show academic 'promise' during the next academic year showed significantly greater gains in IQ than children for whom such predictions were not made (although this group also made substantial improvements). The children were, in fact, randomly allocated to the 'academic promise' and the control (no such prediction) conditions, but the teachers' expectations actually produced the predicted improvements in the first group, i.e. there was a *self-fulfilling prophecy*.

How do you think the teachers' expectations might have been conveyed to the children and how could these, in turn, have influenced the childrens' IQ test performance?

what the person does, which implies a far more active role. Participants' performance in an experiment could almost be thought of as a form of problem-solving behaviour since, at some level, they see their task as working out the true purpose of the experiment and responding in a way which will support the hypothesis being tested.

In this context, the totality of cues which convey an experimental hypothesis to the participant represent important influences on their behaviour and the sum total of those cues are called the *demand characteristics of the experimental situation* (Orne, 1962). These cues include:

> ... the rumours or campus scuttlebut [gossip] about the research, the information conveyed during the original situation, the person of the experimenter, and the setting of the laboratory, as well as all explicit and implicit communications during the experiment proper.

In addition, the experimental procedure itself may provide cues; for example, if a task is presented twice, with some intervening task (i.e. a repeated measures design), even the dullest college student will realize that some change in performance is expected on the second task compared with the first.

This tendency to identify the demand characteristics is related to the tendency to play the role of 'a good experimental subject', wanting to please and co-operate with the experimenter and not to 'upset the experiment'. For example, Orne points out that, if people are asked to do five push-ups as a favour, they will ask 'Why?' but if the request comes from an experimenter, they will ask 'Where?'. Similarly, he reports an experiment in which people were asked to add sheets of random numbers, then tear the sheets up into at least 32 pieces. Five-and-a-half-hours later, they were still at it and the experimenter had to stop them!

This demonstrates very clearly the strong tendency to want to please the experimenter and it is mainly in this sense that Orne sees the experiment as a social situation, in which the people involved play different but complementary roles: in order for the interaction to proceed fairly smoothly, each must have some idea of what the other expects of them. These expectations are part of the culturally shared understandings of what science in general, and psychology in particular, involves and without them, the experiment couldn't 'happen' (Moghaddam *et al.*, 1993). So not only is the experiment a social situation, but science itself is a *culture-related phenomenon*. This represents another respect in which science cannot claim complete objectivity.

Can anything be done to prevent these sources of bias?

The two most common ways of trying to solve the problem of bias are the *single-blind technique*, aimed at the participant, and the *double-blind technique*, aimed at the experimenter. However, if the single-blind is a (partial) solution, it also creates problems: concealing information from participants about the conditions they are being tested under means that they are being deceived as to the true nature of the experiment and this represents a very serious ethical problem (see Chapter 32). In the double-blind technique, the experimenter who assesses the participant's performance is not the one who originally allocated participants to experimental conditions so neither participant nor experimenter knows under which condition particular participants have been tested.

Using one or both methods does not change the nature of the experimental situation from a social to a non-social one: indeed, by removing some of the potential sources of bias, the experimental situation may appear even more difficult to fathom and so the search for demand characteristics may become all the more necessary!

● The problem of representativeness: how typical of people in general are the participants studied by psychologists?

When discussing the idiographic–nomothetic approaches earlier, we noted that both can be seen as involving generalization from some smaller sample to a larger population. In the case of the nomothetic approach, which is the one adopted by traditional, mainstream, experimental, academic psychology, the generalization is from rather restricted samples of participants to 'people in general'.

But is this valid? Are these samples sufficiently representative of people in general to enable us to base whole theories of human behaviour upon them? Indeed, is it possible, or meaningful, to try to construct theories about 'human beings' or 'people in general' in the first place?

Figure 2.3 captures a fairly typical scene as far as the participant characteristics are concerned: they are

FIGURE 2.3 *Photographs of one of Asch's famous conformity experiments (see Chapter 20). What are the most apparent characteristics of the experimental participants (and how are those similar to/ different from those of Asch)?*

white, male, American, largely middle-class students (characteristics which they have in common with the experimenter!) and therefore, both younger and more intelligent (or, at least, more academically able) than the majority.

Despite the fact that these experiments were carried out in the early 1950s, very little has changed as far as participant samples are concerned: the typical participant in American psychology, at least, is a psychology undergraduate who is obliged to take part in a certain number of empirical investigations as a course requirement (Krupat and Garonzik, 1994) (see Chapter 32). Psychology , as a discipline, has been dominated by psychologists from America, Britain and other Western cultures and the vast majority of participants have been members of those same cultures. Yet the findings from this research, and the theories based upon it, have been applied to people in general, as if culture makes no difference.

An implicit, assumed equation is made between 'human being' and 'person from Western culture'; this is commonly referred to as the Anglocentric or Eurocentric bias, a form of ethnocentrism, which is defined as the tendency to use our own ethnic/cultural group's norms and values to define what is 'natural' and 'correct' for everyone (Triandis, 1990), to define 'reality'. And when members of other cultural groups *have* been studied, they have usually been compared with Western samples, using the behaviour and experience of the latter as the standard. However, *cross-cultural psychology* (or, more commonly 'cultural psychology') does not make this equation between 'human being' and ' member of Western culture' because cultural background is treated as the crucial *independent*

variable; in this way, cultural psychology acts as a 'corrective' to much traditional, mainstream psychology.

In a similar way, the behaviour and experience of men has, according to feminist psychologists, been taken as the standard against which women have been judged; this is called the androcentric or masculinist bias. In addition, they believe that mainstream psychology is *sexist* (regarding women as inferior to men and discriminating against them because they are women) and *heterosexist* (regarding gay men and lesbian women as abnormal and discriminating against them because they are gays or lesbians). Feminist psychologists believe that the major deficiency of mainstream psychology has been to deny the part played by values, resulting in the masculinist bias: so long as the bias remains implicit and unrecognized, the picture that emerges of 'female psychology' has an objective, scientifically valid appearance, i.e. it seems to be telling us 'what women are like'.

Similarly, while the Eurocentric bias goes unrecognized, the findings of research using Western samples appears to tell us, accurately, what 'people in general' are like. Once we realize that scientists, like all human beings, have prejudices, values and so on, their research and theories begin to look much less objective, reliable and valid than they did before.

● The problem of artificiality: how typical of real-life situations are the situations in which psychologists study people?

A major criticism of traditional empirical methods – especially the laboratory experiment – has focused on the artificiality of the laboratory situation and the often unusual and even bizarre tasks that people are asked to perform there, in the name of science. How can we be sure that the way people behave in the laboratory, a situation that is so far removed from what people usually encounter in everyday life, is an accurate indication of how they are likely to behave outside, in everyday settings? According to Heather (1976), we can't!

When we ask if the results of a particular study can be generalized, we usually need to know about both the nature of the sample involved (see above) and the nature of the setting in which those results were obtained (including the experimental task the participants were asked to perform). If the setting (and the task) is seen as similar or relevant enough to everyday situations to allow us to generalize the results, we say that the study has high *external* or *ecological validity.*

Traditionally, participants have been called 'subjects', implying that they are regarded as something less than a person, a dehumanized and depersonalized 'object'; this is consistent with the *mechanistic view* of the person. According to Heather (1976), it is a small step from reducing the person to a mere thing or object ('subject' in the context of the experimental setting) to seeing people as machines or machinelike ('mechanism' = 'machine-ism'). This way of thinking about people is reflected in the popular definition of psychology as the study of 'what makes people tick', which derives from the 19th century view of the universe central to the physical sciences.

● The problem of internal vs external validity: how do we balance the need for experimental control with the wish to study behaviour in realistic settings?

Modelling itself on the natural sciences, which adopt a positivist and mechanistic approach to the investigation of the natural world, psychology attempts to overcome the problem of the complexity of human behaviour by using experimental control.

The purpose of control is to enable the experimenter to isolate the key variable which has been selected (the *independent variable* or IV), in order to observe its effect on some other variable (the *dependent variable* or DV). Assuming that other variables (*extraneous variables*) likely to affect the DV have been properly controlled, the experimenter

can conclude that the IV, and only the IV, is influencing the DV. But how do we know when all the relevant extraneous variables have been controlled? It is fairly easy to control the more obvious *situational variables* (such as room temperature, noise levels and instructions) and *participant variables* (such as gender, age and nationality), but for every variable that is controlled there is probably at least one which isn't.

This is especially true in the case of participant variables: it is the variability or heterogeneity of human beings that makes them so much more difficult to study scientifically than, say, chemicals: chemists don't usually have to worry about how two samples of a particular chemical might be different from each other, but psychologists definitely do have to allow for individual differences between participants.

Furthermore, which variables are controlled and which are not depend on the judgement and intuition of the experimenter – what they believe is important (and possible) to control (Deese, 1972). This implies that control and objectivity are matters of degree, whether it is in physics or psychology: as Popper (1972) points out, it is unrealistic – because impossible – to regard any observation as totally objective, value free or uninfluenced by the experimenter's interests, preferences or expectations (see Table 2.1).

Along with the impossibility of complete control, there is a problem involved in assuming that the IV (or 'stimulus' or 'input') is identical for every participant, i.e. that it can be defined in some objective way, independently of the participant, and that it has a standard effect on everybody. The attempt to define IVs and DVs in this way can be seen as a form of reductionism, which is discussed in Chapter 32.

Complete control would mean that the IV alone was responsible for the DV, including experimenter bias and the effects of demand characteristics; as we saw earlier, this is most unlikely. But even if complete control were possible (i.e. even if we could guarantee the *internal validity* of the experiment), a fundamental difficulty would remain. The greater the degree of control over the experimental situation, the more different it becomes from real-life situations, i.e. the more artificial it gets and the lower its *external validity.* This represents a dilemma for the psychologist as scientist: in order to discover the relationships between variables (necessary for understanding human behaviour in natural, real-life situations), the psychologist must 'bring' the behaviour into a specially created environment (the laboratory), where the relevant variables can be controlled in a way that is impossible in those natural settings. But in doing so, the psychologist has constructed an artificial environment and the resulting behaviour is similarly artificial, i.e. it is no longer the behaviour that the psychologist was trying to understand!

One partial solution is to carry out an experiment in a real-life situation; the control is 'taken' into the real world, rather than the participants being brought into the specially created world of the laboratory. These *naturalistic* or *field experiments* are used mainly in social psychology (see Chapters 15–20).

● The problem of studying animal behaviour: how much can we learn about human behaviour from the study of non-human subjects?

Animal experiments have been used extensively in academic psychology and have often produced much controversy, both scientific/methodological and ethical. It is often very difficult to separate these two sources of controversy, but the ethical issues will be dealt with in detail in Chapter 32. Here, the focus is on the scientific/methodological issues, in particular, the question of generalizing from the results of animal experiments to human behaviour.

In the past, experiments which would not have been allowed if they involved human participants have been carried out using animals (although they wouldn't be allowed today!). Examples include sensory deprivation experiments with chimpanzees and kittens (e.g. Riesen, 1947; Blakemore and Cooper, 1970; see Chapter 10), total social isolation using rhesus monkeys (e.g. Harlow and Zimmerman, 1959; see Chapter 22), inducing extreme stress in monkeys and dogs (e.g. Brady, 1958; Seligman, 1974; see Chapters 6 and 7) and implanting electrodes into rat brains, after which they are 'sacrificed' (i.e. killed) (e.g. Olds and Milner, 1954; see Chapter 5).

Much less controversial from an ethical point of view are the experiments by Skinner, using rats and pigeons, in the highly controlled environment of a Skinner Box (see Chapter 7) and it is this high level of control over crucial variables (both situational and those relating to the animals themselves), which represents the single most important reason for using animal subjects. What other reasons are there for using animals?

There is an underlying evolutionary continuity between humans and other species, which gives rise to the assumption that differences in behaviour between humans and other species are merely quantitative (as opposed to qualitative), i.e. other species may display more simple behaviour and have more primitive nervous systems than humans, but they are essentially of the same kind as those of humans.

As we saw when discussing Watson's behaviourist manifesto earlier, the study of animal behaviour was inspired by Darwin's (1859) theory of evolution, which made it seem quite reasonable to believe that, by studying the more simple species from which we have evolved, we should learn more about ourselves.

Animals are (mostly) smaller and, therefore, easier to study in the laboratory. They also have much shorter lifespans and gestation periods, making it much easier to study their development; many generations can be studied in a relatively short time.

Animal studies can both provide useful hypotheses for subsequent testing with humans and be used to test cause-and-effect relationships where the existing human evidence is only correlational. This is partly to do with the point above and partly to do with the greater degree of control that is possible in animal experiments, in both cases raising fundamental ethical questions.

● The problems of mechanism and determinism: how valid is it to explain human behaviour in terms of cause and effect?

As we saw earlier, 'mechanism' comes from 'machine'. According to Heather (1976), to say that psychology is mechanistic implies a view of people as inert and passive, propelled into motion only by the action of some internal or external force acting upon them. Their behaviour can be completely explained, at least in principle, in terms of 'causes' over which they have no control (i.e. the theory of determinism).

It is generally agreed that a 'cause' cannot be directly observed; strictly speaking, all that can be observed are two events occurring close together in space and/or time (the principle of *contiguity*), one of which we call the 'cause' and the other the 'effect'. But which is which? We normally think of the cause as preceding the effect; in addition, the cause is a *necessary condition* (i.e. the effect won't occur unless the cause occurs) and a *sufficient condition* (i.e. the effect will occur every time the cause occurs). But is this a useful way of thinking about most complex human behaviour? The IV can be thought of as roughly equivalent to a cause and the DV to an effect. However, 'IV' and 'DV' are much more general terms than 'cause' and 'effect'; psychologists are much more likely to talk about 'variable Y systematically changes as a function of changes in variable X' or 'changes in variable X produce changes in variable Y ', than 'variable X causes variable Y'.

The very terms 'cause' and 'effect' imply that, somehow, they exist objectively. However, as we saw earlier, they cannot be observed directly, but must be inferred from what is observed and it is theories which tell us what is supposed to influence what, i.e. what the psychologist identifies as cause and effect will depend on what they believe and expect to find (Deese, 1972). This relates to Deese's more general point that data (i.e. the 'raw material' obtained from observations) must be interpreted according to a theory, otherwise they have no meaning. Different theories, therefore, will identify different causes for essentially the same behaviour, i.e. they will explain the behaviour differently. Yet despite such differences, as in Freud's and Skinner's theories, for example, they can still agree about the extent to which human behaviour is *determined.* Indeed, Freud and Skinner shared one fundamental belief, namely, that free will is an illusion. (This is discussed in Chapter 32 in relation to ethical and philosophical issues.)

CHAPTER SUMMARY

- Science is a theme that pervades psychology. The study of interpersonal perception portrays everyone as a 'naive scientist', formulating theories for explaining, predicting and controlling behaviour, as well as attributing causes to behaviour.
- The nomothetic–idiographic debate corresponds to the distinction between the Naturwissenschaften (natural sciences) and Geisteswissenschaften (humanities/social sciences) respectively.
- Descartes divided the universe into physical matter and non-physical mind, i.e. philosophical dualism; this allowed scientists to describe the physical world objectively, without reference to the human observer.
- Descartes also introduced mechanism into science and extended this view of matter to living

organisms, including the human body. He was an early advocate of reductionism.
- As applied to the study of human behaviour/social institutions, objectivity came to be called positivism (Comte).
- Empiricism is another fundamental feature of science. Empiricist philosophers argued that the only source of true knowledge about the world is sensory experience.
- The early scientific psychologists had trained mainly as physiologists, doctors or philosophers and the two key pioneers were Wundt in Germany and James in the USA.
- Wundt set up his 'private institute' of experimental psychology in 1879, the year that is generally accepted as the birthdate of psychology as a separate discipline.
- At first, the subject matter of scientific psychology was what it had always been, i.e. consciousness. Wundt argued that conscious mental states could be analysed into their basic elements (structuralism) through carefully controlled introspection (hence, 'introspective psychology' or introspectionism).
- Wundt believed that conscious experience could be analysed into elementary sensations, which are the raw sensory content of consciousness, and feelings, which could be analysed in terms of pleasantness–unpleasantness, tension–relaxation and activity–passivity. This represents a form of reductionism.
- James did relatively little research but used his laboratory to enrich his teaching; he popularized psychology through his famous book *The Principles of Psychology*, in which he wrote about many topics that are now part of 'mainstream' academic psychology. He also helped to introduce Freud's theories into the USA.
- James helped to inspire functionalism, particularly popular with American psychologists, which, in turn, helped to stimulate the study of individual differences.
- Watson rejected introspectionism on the grounds that it is based on purely private experience, accessible only to the person who is introspecting. To be an objective, natural science, psychology must replace consciousness with public, observable behaviour as its subject matter.
- The focus on objective behaviour represented one feature of Watson's 'behaviourist manifesto', the others being the prediction and control of behaviour and the study of non-human animals whose behaviour differs from that of humans

only quantitatively. Almost all animal and human behaviour is learned through the process of classical conditioning.

- Watson's behaviourism embodied the extreme environmentalism of Locke's empiricism; this provided for psychology both a methodology and a theory, comprising the tabula rasa view of the mind, analysis into elements and associationism. This corresponds to a distinction between methodological and philosophical behaviourism respectively.
- A science must involve a subject matter, theory construction, hypothesis testing and the collection of data through the use of empirical methods. The relationship between these, and the order in which they take place, refers to (the) scientific method.
- Theory is just as crucial as data, because data on their own have no meaning; they do not constitute objective 'facts' about the world but have to be interpreted in the light of a particular theory . Similarly, theory determines the kind of observations the scientist makes in the first place.
- The classic picture of how science proceeds is induction, which sees simple, unbiased observations leading to generalized statements of fact. An alternative view is the hypothetico-deductive method, according to which testable hypotheses are deduced from a theory.
- Different theoretical approaches/orientations in psychology may be regarded as self-contained disciplines, which implies that psychology lacks a paradigm (Kuhn), i.e. it is still in the prescience stage.
- Some psychologists believe that psychology has already had three paradigms (structuralism, behaviourism, cognitive psychology) and so has undergone revolution. Others maintain that a number of paradigms currently coexist in the form of major theoretical approaches. However, it is probably mistaken to equate a paradigm with a theoretical approach, one important difference being that a paradigm implies consensus within a scientific community.
- A number of criteria are used to evaluate theories in psychology, including: falsifiability/refutability, truth value, reflexivity, predicting future events, internal consistency, economy, fertility, practical usefulness, changing our image of ourselves and presenting an objective, value-free account of behaviour.
- According to the principle of falsification/refutability, a scientific theory must be capable of being shown to be false; finding evidence to support the theory (principle of verification) is too easy. Freud's theory is often criticized for being irrefutable.
- Truth value refers to whether or not a theory accurately reflects the nature of what it is trying to explain. This relates to the issue of whether only one theory can be true and how to choose between competing theories; according to relativism, all theories are credible and there is no need to choose between them.
- Reflexivity refers to a theory's ability to account for its own existence, which Kelly's personal construct theory is able to do very well.
- Theories are generalizations but we often want to know how they apply to a particular individual; this relates to the idiographic–nomothetic debate. However, generalizations can take the form of individual norms as well as group norms.
- A theory should be internally consistent and economical, making as few assumptions as possible.
- The fertility of a theory can be measured in terms of direct replication studies, verification studies, population applicability and extended theorizing.
- The practical usefulness criterion relates to the aims of psychology as a scientific discipline. In terms of Miller's distinction, psychology as a natural science stresses prediction and control, in the form of behaviour therapy and modification, while understanding/self-understanding are more appropriate goals, as in psychotherapy. Psychology's other role is to change our image of ourselves as human beings.
- According to positivism, science should be objective, unbiased and value free. However, there are a number of biases in 'mainstream' Western academic psychology, including androcentrism, sexism, heterosexism and ethnocentrism.
- Because of the impossibility of seeing the world 'as it really is', scientists' attempts to replicate/repeat each others' findings assume great importance. This illustrates the social nature of science. Kuhn's concept of a paradigm implies that 'truth' is more to do with the popularity of a theory and its acceptance by the scientific community than its actual truth value but these two criteria are not mutually exclusive.
- One way in which psychology is different from other sciences is that the psychology experiment is a social situation, in which both experimenter and participant influence the outcome over and above the objectively defined features.
- Experimenter bias seems to create a change in the environment in which the participants actually

behave differently, whether they are people or rats. A very famous demonstration of this is Rosenthal and Jacobson's *Pygmalion in the Classroom.*

- The participant actively tries to work out the true purpose of the experiment, a form of problem-solving behaviour. The totality of cues which convey an experimental hypothesis are called the demand characteristics of the experimental situation (Orne).

- The expectations which the experimenter and participant have of each other are part of the culturally shared understandings of what science in general, and psychology in particular, involves.

- The single-blind and double-blind techniques are the two most commonly used ways of trying to reduce the effects of experimenter bias and demand characteristics.

- Participants in psychology experiments are very unrepresentative of people in general. Generalizing from the study of people from Western culture is a form of ethnocentrism, called the Anglocentric/Eurocentric bias.

- A major problem with laboratory experiments is their artificiality; this is related to the external/ecological validity of experimental studies. Psychologists face the dilemma of trying to balance the need for experimental control with the wish to study behaviour in naturalistic/realistic settings.

- Experiments involve the manipulation of the independent variable to see its effect on the dependent variable, with other relevant (extraneous) variables (both situational and participant) being controlled.

- Experimental design refers to ways of trying to control participant variables (individual differences).

- Not only is complete control impossible, but it cannot be assumed that the independent variable is identical for every participant or that it can be defined independently of the participant.

- The use of animals in psychological research raises both scientific/methodological and ethical questions.

- Watson's 'Behaviourist Manifesto' claimed that there are only quantitative differences between humans and other species, reflecting the evolutionary continuity of Darwin's theory of evolution.

- Much greater experimental control is possible when using animal subjects and this allows the testing of cause-and-effect relationships.

- It seems difficult to explain human behaviour in terms of any simple cause-and-effect analysis, especially as what is a cause and what is an effect depend on the particular theory under consideration.

- Although different theories identify different causes, they may still agree that behaviour is determined; for example, Freud and Skinner both argue that free will is an illusion.

GLOSSARY

Androcentrism A form of bias within psychology, in which women's behaviour/experience is compared with men's, who are implicitly taken as the standard/norm against which women are judged. Also called the masculinist bias.

Demand characteristics Orne's term for the sum of all the cues which convey an experimental hypothesis to the participant, including rumours about the research, information conveyed by the laboratory setting, explicit and implicit communication during the experiment, the experimental procedure and the experimenter as a person.

Double-blind technique An attempt to remove/reduce experimenter bias by concealing from the experimenter who assesses the participant's performance knowledge of the experimental conditions under which particular participants have been tested.

Empiricism Theory of 17th/18th century British philosophers, such as Locke, according to which the only source of true knowledge is sensory experience ('empirical' = 'through the senses'; empirical methods = scientific methods). Contrasted with rationalism/nativism.

Ethnocentrism A form of bias within psychology, in which 'human' is equated with 'member of Western culture', so that the latter represents a standard/norm for judging the behaviour/experience of those from non-Western cultures. Also called the Eurocentric/Anglocentric bias.

External validity The extent to which an experimental (laboratory) situation resembles everyday/naturalistic situations; the greater the external validity, the more the findings can be generalized from the former to the latter. Also called ecological validity/mundane realism.

Experimenter bias The unconscious tendency of experimenters to behave in ways that make it more likely that the hypothesis they are testing will be supported. This may happen through a variety of nonverbal signals to the participant which convey how they are meant to perform.

Functionalism The view that it is the purpose/utility of behaviour that is important, rather than simply describing it. Associated with James and Dewey and often contrasted with Wundt's structuralism.

Internal validity The extent to which an experimental finding/effect can be attributed to the independent variable and no other (extraneous) variables. The greater the experimental control, the greater the internal validity.

Mechanism Originally, the view that the material world consists of objects assembled like a huge machine and operated by mechanical laws. Extended by Descartes to living organisms, including the human body.

Methodological behaviourism The general belief in the importance of using empirical methods, especially controlled experiments, statistics, etc.

Paradigm Kuhn's term for a global perspective or framework which dictates theory construction and empirical research, shared by members of a scientific community; required for a state of normal science.

Philosophical behaviourism The rejection of the mind, either because it does not exist or because it is impossible to study scientifically. Associated mainly with Watson and Skinner.

Positivism The view that science should be objective, unbiased and value free. First applied to the study of human social behaviour by the 19th century philosopher/sociologist Comte.

Principle of falsification Being able to obtain evidence that would show a theory to be false. Popper's criterion for distinguishing between science and non-science. Also called refutability.

Principle of verification Being able to obtain evidence in support of a theory.

Structuralism Wundt's attempt to analyse conscious thought into elementary sensations and feelings, through introspection (hence, 'introspectionism'/ 'introspective psychology').

Single-blind technique Any attempt to conceal from participants information regarding the experimental condition under which they are being tested.

FURTHER READING

Coolican, H. (1994) *Research Methods and Statistics in Psychology*, 2nd edn. London: Hodder and Stoughton. A very thorough but very readable and widely used text covering all major aspects of methodology and statistics; especially relevant here is Chapter 11 on 'New Paradigm Research'.

Deese, J. (1972) *Psychology as Art and Science*. New York: Harcourt Brace Jovanovich. A short, very readable account of scientific method in general and in psychology in particular.

The Biological Basis of Behaviour and Experience

3 THE NERVOUS SYSTEM

INTRODUCTION AND OVERVIEW

Biopsychology is the study of the biological bases, or the physiological correlates, of behaviour and is a branch of neuroscience (or neurobiology), the study of the nervous system (or the 'brain sciences'). While biopsychology often goes under other names (such as psychobiology, behavioural neuroscience, biological psychology and physiological psychology), Pinel (1993) prefers 'biopsychology' because it denotes a biological approach to the study of psychology, where psychology 'commands centre stage': biopsychologists are, above all, psychologists who (like other neuroscientists) bring to their research a knowledge of the biology of their subject matter.

> ... biopsychology's unique contribution to neuroscientific research is a knowledge of behaviour and of the methods of behavioural research ... the ultimate purpose of the nervous system is to produce and control behaviour. (Pinel, 1993).

In other words, biopsychologists are not interested in biology for its own sake, but for what it can tell them about behaviour and mental processes. In general terms :

- The kind of behaviour of which an animal is capable depends very much on the kind of body it possesses; humans can flap their arms as much as they like but they will never fly (unaided) because arms are simply not suited to flight, they are not designed for it, while wings are. However, we are very skilled at manipulating objects (particularly small ones) because that is how our hands and fingers have developed during the course of evolution.
- The possession of a specialized body is of very little use unless the nervous system is able to control it. Of course, evolution of the one usually mirrors evolution of the other: the kind of behaviour of which a species is capable is determined by the kind of nervous system it possesses.
- The kind of nervous system also determines the extent and the nature of the learning of which a species is capable. As you move along the phylogenetic–evolutionary scale, from simple, one-celled amoebae,

through insects, birds and mammals, to primates including *Homo sapiens*, the nervous system becomes gradually more complex and behaviour becomes increasingly the product of learning and environmental influence, as distinct from instinct and other innate, genetically determined factors.

We shall start this chapter by considering the major subdivisions of the nervous system as a whole, then we shall look at some of its basic characteristics, both structural and functional. Moving on to the central nervous system (CNS), we shall concentrate on the brain: we shall discuss major methods of studying the brain, including recent imaging techniques, its major structures and functions, including the localization of brain function. Finally, we shall discuss the autonomic nervous system (ANS) and the endocrine system and see how they interact with each other and with the CNS.

BIOPSYCHOLOGY AND OTHER DISCIPLINES

As we noted above, biopsychology is a branch of neuroscience. According to Pinel (1993), biopsychology, which itself is composed of a number of subdivisions, draws together knowledge from the other neuroscientific disciplines, in particular:

- *neuroanatomy*, the study of the structure of the nervous system;
- *developmental neurobiology*, the study of how the nervous system changes as the organism matures and ages;
- *neurochemistry*, the study of the chemical bases of neural activity, especially those that underlie the transmission of signals through and between neurons (nerve cells);
- *neuroendocrinology*, the study of the interactions between the nervous system and the endocrine glands and the hormones they release;
- *neuropathology*, the study of nervous system disorders; related to this is *neuropsychology*, the study of the behavioural deficits produced in people by brain damage, in particular the outer layer of the cerebral hemispheres (the *neocortex*);
- *neuropharmacology*, the study of the effects of drugs on the nervous system, especially those influencing neural transmission; related to this is *psychopharmacology*, which is concerned with the effects of drugs on behaviour and how these effects are mediated by changes in neural activity.

The recent expansion of this largely applied area of research has led many to suggest that it constitutes a separate discipline;

- *neurophysiology*, the study of the responses of the nervous system, particularly those involved in transmission of electrical signals through and between neurons. This is related to (a) *physiological psychology*, which involves manipulation of the nervous system through surgical, electrical and chemical means under strictly controlled experimental conditions (invasive methods, using mainly non-human animal subjects), and (b) *psychophysiology* which uses non-invasive methods, mainly with human participants, to study the physiology of psychological processes such as attention, emotion, information processing and, increasingly, major mental disorders (especially schizophrenia; see Chapter 30).

All of these disciplines will be 'represented' in various parts of this chapter.

AN OVERVIEW OF THE HUMAN NERVOUS SYSTEM (NS) – STRUCTURE AND FUNCTION

As you can see from Figure 3.1, the NS involves a number of subdivisions. Before looking at these in detail, we need to look at some of the general characteristics of the NS.

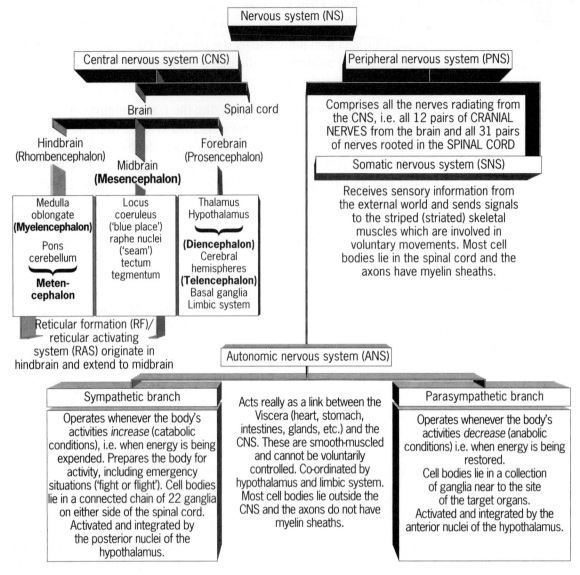

FIGURE 3.1 *Major subdivisions of the human nervous system (including the main subdivisions of the brain)*

The NS as a whole comprises between 10 and 12 billion (i.e. 10–12 thousand million) nerve cells or *neurons*; these are the basic structural units or building blocks of the NS. Other kinds of cell in the NS include *glial* ('glue') cells, which are mostly smaller than neurons and ten times more numerous; there are different kinds of glial cells, the most important being *astrocytes* and *oligodendrocytes*. It used to be thought that they merely 'fill in the space' between neurons, but they are increasingly being seen as capable of passing signals to each other, receiving signals from neurons and perhaps even passing signals to neurons. They also play a vital role in brain development; not only do they supply nutrients and structural support to the neurons and provide a barrier to certain substances from the bloodstream, but oligodendrocytes provide the insulating *myelin sheath* around the axon of the neuron (see below) (Young, 1994).

● Neurons

About 80 percent of all neurons are found in the brain, in particular in the cerebral cortex, the topmost outer layer. Information is passed from neuron to neuron in the form of *electrochemical impulses*; these constitute the 'language' of the NS.

Neurons are of three main kinds:

1 *sensory* (or *afferent*), which carry information from the sense organs to the central nervous system (CNS);
2 *motor* (or *efferent*) which carry information from the CNS to the muscles and glands;
3 *interneurons* (or *connector* neurons), which connect neurons to other neurons and integrate the activities of sensory and motor neurons. Interneurons are the most numerous and constitute about 97 percent of the total number of neurons in the CNS, which is the only part of the NS in which they are found.

Although no two neurons are identical, most share the same basic structure and they work in essentially the same way. Figure 3.2 shows a typical motor neuron. The *cell body* (or *soma*) houses the nucleus (which contains the genetic code), the cytoplasm (which feeds the nucleus) and the other structures common to all living cells. The *dendrites* branch out from the cell body; it is through the dendrites that the neuron makes electrochemical contact with other neurons, by receiving incoming signals from neighbouring neurons. The *axon* is a thin cylinder of protoplasm, which projects away from the cell body and carries the signals received by the dendrites to other neurons. The *myelin sheath* is a white, fatty substance which insulates the axon and speeds up the rate of conduction of signals down the axon and towards the *terminal buttons* (or boutons or synaptic knobs). The myelin sheath is not continuous but is interrupted by the *nodes of Ranvier*.

Neurons vary considerably in length; for example, a neuron in the spinal cord may have an axon 2–3 feet long, running from the tip of the spine down to the big toe, while in the brain, neurons are only a few one-thousandths of an inch long. Axons of motor neurons which terminate in muscles end in a series of branches, tipped by motor endplates, each of which is attached to a single muscle fibre. Impulses at the motor endplate cause the muscle to contract (e.g. the arm is raised).

A *nerve* is a bundle of elongated axons belonging to hundreds or thousands of neurons. Nerves spread out to every part of the body and connect with sense receptors, skin, muscles and internal organs. Twelve pairs of cranial nerves leave the brain through holes in the skull and 31 pairs of spinal nerves leave the spinal cord through the vertebrae; together, they constitute the nerves of the *peripheral nervous system* (PNS) (see Fig. 3.1). Nerves are usually large enough to be seen with the naked eye, while neurons can only be seen with the help of a powerful microscope.

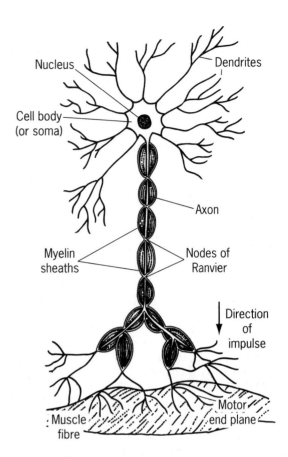

FIGURE 3.2 *A typical motor neuron*

● Communication between neurons

As Figure 3.3 shows, the terminal buttons house a number of tiny sacs or *synaptic vesicles*, which contain between 10 and 100,000 molecules of a chemical messenger, called a *neurotransmitter*. When an electrochemical impulse has passed down the axon it arrives at a terminal button and stimulates the vesicles to discharge their contents into the minute gap between the end of the terminal button (the *presynaptic membrane*) and the dendrite of the receiving neuron (the *postsynaptic membrane*) called the *synaptic cleft* (or gap).

The neurotransmitter molecules cross the synaptic gap and combine with special receptor sites in the postsynaptic membrane of the dendrite of the receiving neuron. The term 'synapse', therefore, refers to the junction between neurons (there is no actual physical contact between them) at which signals are passed from a sending to a receiving neuron through the release of neurotransmitters. However, some neurons use a form of direct electrical influence (these

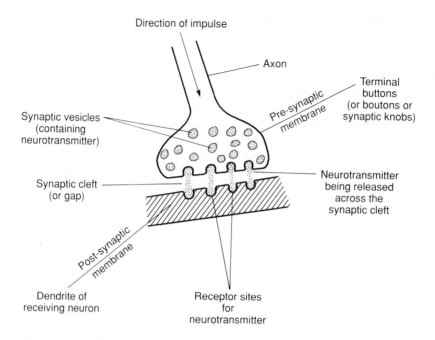

Direction of impulse

Axon

Terminal buttons (or boutons or synaptic knobs)

Pre-synaptic membrane

Synaptic vesicles (containing neurotransmitter)

Synaptic cleft (or gap)

Neurotransmitter being released across the synaptic cleft

Post-synaptic membrane

Dendrite of receiving neuron

Receptor sites for neurotransmitter

FIGURE 3.3 *The synapse*

'electrotonic' synapses are not well understood) and synapses are sometimes found between dendrite and dendrite, axon and cell body and between axon and axon. However, the most common arrangement is for neurons to interconnect at synapses where a form of chemical communication is used (Iversen, 1979).

The electrochemical signal which passes down the axon is called an *action potential*. Before the action potential occurs, an inactive neuron contains positively charged potassium (K+) ions (electrically charged potassium atoms) and large, negatively charged protein molecules. Outside the neuron, in the surrounding fluid, there are concentrations of positively charged sodium ions (Na+) and negatively charged chloride ions (Cl–). The large, negatively charged, protein ions are trapped inside the neuron, while the positively charged sodium ions are kept out by the action of the *sodium–potassium pumps* in the cell membrane, which allow potassium (and chloride) ions to move in and out fairly freely.

The overall effect of this uneven distribution of ions is that the inside of the cell is electrically negative relative to the outside (by about 70 millivolts). The neuron is said to be impermeable to the positively charged sodium ions; this situation describes its resting state or *resting potential*. When an action potential occurs, the inside of the neuron

momentarily changes from negative to positive (+ 40 millivolts), the sodium channels are opened (for 1 millisecond) and sodium ions flood into the neuron (it is now permeable to sodium ions); this sets off a chain reaction, whereby the sodium channels open at adjacent membrane sites all the way down the axon. But almost as soon as the sodium channels are opened, they close again and potassium channels are opened instead, allowing potassium ions out through the membrane and restoring the negative resting potential.

Because the myelin sheath is not continuous but segmented (so that at the nodes of Ranvier the axon is actually exposed), the action potential jumps from one node to another down the axon; this is called *saltatory conduction* and is actually faster than if the sheaths were continuous (see Fig. 3.2).

● Response threshold

The stimulus to the neuron must be intense enough to produce an action potential, that is, it must exceed the *threshold of response*, but once this has been passed, it travels at the same speed to the end of the axon. So an impulse is either present or absent (the *all-or-none rule*). Action potentials are all of the same strength (*amplitude*), so the intensity of the stimulus is measured by:

1 the frequency of firing, whereby the stronger the stimulus, the more often the neuron will fire (a very strong stimulus producing a volley of impulses);
2 the number of neurons stimulated, whereby the stronger the stimulus, the greater the number of neurons stimulated.

However strong the stimulus, there is always a very short interval after each firing (1–2 milliseconds) during which no further impulse can pass; this is the *absolute refractory period*. This is followed by a *relative refractory period*; the stronger the stimulus, the shorter the interval between the absolute refractory period and the next impulse.

● Different types of synapses and neurotransmitters

Some synapses are *excitatory* (they 'instruct' the receiving neuron to 'fire', i.e. to conduct an action potential) while others are *inhibitory* (they 'instruct' the receiving neuron not to 'fire'). Because each neuron may have between 1000 and 10,000 synapses, some of which will be excitatory and some inhibitory, the 'decision' to fire or not will depend on the combined effect of all its receiving synapses; if enough excitatory synapses are active, their combined effect may add up to exceed the threshold for firing of the receiving neuron (this is called *summation*).

Inhibitory synapses are important because they help control the spread of excitation through the highly interconnected NS and so keep activity channelled in appropriate networks or 'circuits'; epileptic seizures or fits, for example, may be caused by excitation of many different brain circuits at the same time and, if it were not for inhibition, we might all be having seizures much of the time.

What makes a synapse either excitatory or inhibitory is the particular neurotransmitter(s) contained within the vesicles of the synaptic button. As we have seen, neurotransmitter molecules cross the synaptic cleft and then attach themselves to specific receptor sites in the postsynaptic membrane; these sites actually consist of large protein molecules. A region on the surface of the receptor site is precisely tailored to match the shape of the transmitter molecule (in a lock-and-key fashion). The effect of the transmitter is brought to an end either by *deactivation* (where it is destroyed by special enzymes) or by *reuptake* (where it is pumped back into the presynaptic axon, either for destruction or recycling).

According to Iversen (1979) and others there are at least 30 different neurotransmitters in the brain, each with its specific excitatory or inhibitory effect on certain neurons; the various chemicals are localized in specific groups of neurons and pathways and are not randomly distributed throughout the brain. Some of the major transmitters and their effects are shown in Table 3.1. As a general rule, a single neuron will store and release the same neurotransmitter in all its axon terminals, so that we can label a neuron by the transmitter it uses and identify in the brain *cholinergic, noradrenergic, dopaminergic* and *serotonergic* neurons, which use ACh, noradrenaline, dopamine and serotonin respectively as their neurotransmitters. However, there is some evidence that more than one kind of transmitter may be released from the same synaptic button depending on the pattern of action potentials reaching it (Lloyd *et al.*, 1984).

While neurotransmitters have a fairly direct influence on receiving neurons, *neuromodulators* 'tune' or 'prime' neurons so that they will respond in a particular way to later stimulation by a neurotransmitter. Included among the neuromodulators are certain *neuropeptides* (which are included in Table 3.1), notably the *enkephalins* ('in the head') and the *endorphins* ('morphine-within'), which are also known as *opioids* because functionally they resemble the opium drugs morphine, heroin and opium itself (see Table 3.2).

Morphine is commonly used for the relief of severe, intractable pain and the discovery of 'opiate receptors' in the neurons strongly suggested that the brain creates its own powerful painkiller; enkephalins and endorphins seemed to fit the bill and they may work by interfering with the release of transmitters from the presynaptic membrane of neurons which transmit information about pain. It is thought that they are released during acupuncture and hypnosis, producing a reduction in perceived pain, although pain information probably still reaches the brain (as it is not the pain receptors which are directly influenced; see Chapter 4). It is also believed that *placebos* ('dummy drugs') work by influencing the release of endorphins in response to the belief that an active drug was given (Hamilton and Timmons, 1995).

Other neuropeptides are founds as *hormones,* including: (i) vasopressin, which is thought to play a role in memory; (ii) corticosteroids ('stress hormones') and adrenocorticotrophic hormone (ACTH), which are involved in stress reactions and emotional arousal (see Chapter 6); and (iii) androgens (male

Neurotransmitter	Effect on receiving Neuron	Related behaviour
1 Acetylcholine (ACh)	Generally *excitatory* but can be *inhibitory* depending on the type of receptor molecule involved	Voluntary movement of muscles, behavioural inhibition, drinking, memory. In Alzheimer's disease, there is a reduction of ACh – due to degeneration of ACh-producing neurons
2 Noradrenaline (norepinephrine) (monoamine transmitter)	*Inhibitory* (in CNS) and *excitatory* (in ANS)	Wakefulness and arousal – behavioural and emotional, eating. Some forms of recurrent *depression* associated with low levels and *mania* with high levels
3 Dopamine (monoamine transmitter)	*Inhibitory* and *excitatory* Monoamine Transmitters	Voluntary movement, emotional arousal. Parkinson's disease caused by atrophy of dopamine-releasing neurons (which link the midbrain to the corpus striatum). Schizophrenia may be caused by over-activity of dopamine in the hypothalamus, limbic system and medial forebrain bundle which mediate emotion and thought. Abnormally high concentrations of dopamine and dopamine receptors in brains of deceased schizophrenics (see Chapter 30)
4 Serotonin	*Inhibitory* and *excitatory*	Sleep, temperature regulation
5 GABA (gamma aminobutyric acid)	*Inhibitory*. It is the most common inhibitor in the CNS (up to one-third of all the brain's synaptic buttons) and is found in all parts of the CNS	Motor behaviour. The inherited disease *Huntington's chorea* may result from degeneration of GABA cells in the corpus striatum which is involved in motor control
6 Glycine	*Inhibitory*. Found in the spinal cord	Spinal reflexes and other motor behaviour
7 Glutamate	*Excitatory*	Unknown
8 Aspartate	*Excitatory*	Unknown
9 Peptides (Neuromodulators, e.g. enkephalins and endorphins)	*Inhibitory* and *excitatory*	Sensory transmission, especially pain

TABLE 3.1 *Major neurotransmitters and their effects*

sex hormones), which regulate sex drive in both sexes (see the later section on the endocrine system).

Other neuromodulators are the *prostaglandins*, which cause long-term shifts in neuronal sensitivity (Lloyd *et al.*, 1984); it is believed that a deficiency in prostaglandins may cause schizophrenia.

● Drugs, mood and behaviour

The effect of drugs on behaviour is mediated by their effect on neurotransmitters. Psychologists are partic-ularly interested in *psychoactive* drugs, i.e.

mood-altering or consciousness-changing drugs ('active' in the 'psyche') which directly alter the level of activity in one or more brain systems (either increasing or decreasing it). Many commonly used drugs interact with receptor molecules in very much the same way as neurotransmitters do; the shape of the drug molecules are sufficiently like that of the neurotransmitters to work as if they were keys to the lock of the receptor molecules (see above). Table 3.2 summarizes the effects on mood and behaviour of some major drugs, together with effects on neuro-transmitters.

Drug	Neurotransmitters affected	Effects on physiology, mood and behaviour
1 Curare (used by South American Indians to poison their arrows)	Acetylcholine (ACh) prevented from acting because the curare molecules cover up the post-synaptic receptor sites of the muscle neurons	Fatal muscular paralysis. The brain is not affected–but all other muscles, including respiratory muscles, are paralysed
2 Botulinum toxin (present in improperly prepared food)	Acetylcholine (ACh)	Paralysis which is often fatal (=botulism)
3 Nerve gases and insecticides	Acetylcholine (ACh)	Fatal muscular paralysis
4 *Stimulants* caffeine nicotine cocaine	Caffeine is found in tea and coffee and many carbonated drinks, particularly colas	*Nicotine* may have a relaxing or stimulating effect, depending on circumstances. It is addictive. Effects of cocaine similar to those of amphetamines but former is addictive
Amphetamines ('speed or uppers') e.g. Benzedrine Dexedrine Methedrine Drinamyl ('Purple Hearts') Hallucinogenic amphetamines Methylenedioxy– amphetamine (MDA)/ MDMA/MDEA (Ecstasy 'E')	Dopamine and noradrenaline– their re-uptake is blocked, making them effective for longer	Amphetamines seem to act more as psycho-motor *stimulants* than anti-depressants (which is often how they are prescribed). Increase alertness, counteract fatigue and lethargy and produce feelings of confidence and decisiveness. Suppress appetite (through stimulation of Reticular Activating System which controls overall level of arousal and 'mimicking' the sympathetic branch of the ANS. But high doses can induce symptoms identical with paranoid schizophrenia
5 *Antidepressants* **A**. Tricyclics/ (imipramine)/ (Tofranil)/ /amitriptyline (Tryptizol) **B**. Monoamine oxidase (MAO) Inhibitors (phenelzine) (Nardil) tranylcypromine (Parnate) **C**. Prozac	(Work by blocking the breakdown of noradrenaline and serotonin) These inhibit the enzyme Monoamine oxidase (MAO) which breaks down the monoamine transmitters subsequent to their release This is a selective serotonin re-uptake inhibitor	Feeling of euphoria. They block rapid eye movement (REM) sleep (see Chapter 4)

TABLE 3.2 *The effect of major psychoactive drugs on neurotransmitters, physiology, mood and behaviour*

Drug	Neurotransmitters affected	Effects on physiology, mood and behaviour
6 *Major tranquillizers* phenothiazines ('anti-schizophrenic drugs')/ (chlorpromazine)/ (Largactil or Thorazine) trifluoperazine (Stelazine)	Dopamine. They bind to dopamine receptor sites (they are dopamine-antagonists) and so prevent dopamine from reaching those receptor sites	Reduce schizophrenic–and other psychotic–symptoms. The reticular activating system is *not* affected, nor the electroencephalogram (EEG). But electrical activity in hypothalamus and limbic system is suppressed
7 *Anti–anxiety drugs* benzodiazepines (minor tranquillizers or anxiolytic sedatives) diazepam (Valium) chlordiazepoxide (Librium) meprobamate (Miltown)	Inosine (which might be a neuro-modulator) binds with the same receptor site as these drugs. It could be the body's own anxiety reliever. GABA	A calming effect, reducing anxiety and tension without depressing the level of alertness. Valium prescribed to patients with Huntington's Chorea may help by stimulating GABA receptors
8 *L-dopa*	Dopamine. The body converts the drug into dopamine	Prescribed for patients with Parkinson's disease. Can sometimes produce symptoms of schizophrenia
9 *Sedatives (or Depressants)* barbiturates '(Downers'/ Barbs') e.g. Luminal (phenobarbitone) Amytal (amylobarbitone), Nembutal, Seconal, Pentothal alcohol	In large quantities these are sleep inducers *(hypnotics)* and may act in a similar way to certain anaesthetics. In smaller doses, they act more like (minor) tranquillizers Combined with alcohol, they can be fatal	In small amounts, barbiturates and alcohol can act as stimulants by reducing anxiety and reducing inhibitions. Larger amounts may cause people to become belligerent and abusive, disorientated and confused and they may experience hallucinations. Larger quantities induce sedation, stupor (sleep), anaesthesia, loss of consciousness and death (Ornstein, 1977) Addicts who are withdrawn from alcohol often suffer 'delirium tremens' (the DTs) which can be fatal
Opiates (narcotics) (codeine, morphine, heroin)	Opium comes from the juice of certain types of poppy; its active ingredients are *codeine* and *morphine.* Morphine is stronger than codeine and *heroin* (derived from morphine) is the strongest narcotic of all. Neural tissue is eventually destroyed after prolonged use of heroin and the *endorphins* are under-produced	At first heroin produces intense pleasure but repeated use produces *tolerance* – i.e. ever-increasing amounts must be taken to achieve the same effect. Tolerance soon gives way to physical and psychological *dependence. Physical dependence* means that the body cannot do without a drug because it has adjusted to /become reliant on the presence of that drug. When someone who is physically dependent stops taking the drug, they suffer withdrawal (abstinence syndrome). If a drug is so pleasurable that users feel compelled to keep taking it – even though the body is not physiologically dependent , they are *psychologically dependent.* Physical dependence + tolerance = *drug addiction*

TABLE 3.2 *(continued)*

Drug	Neurotransmitters affected	Effects on physiology, mood and behaviour
10 *Hallucinogenic drugs* LSD (lysergic acid diethylamide/ 'Acid') psilocybin ('magic mushroom') Mescaline Phencyclidine (PCP or 'Angel Dust')	Structurally similar to serotonin Structurally similar to noradrenaline and dopamine They seem to work by blocking the effects of serotonin, which usually inhibits thought processes and emotions May attach themselves to serotonin receptor sites, preventing the sites from receiving it. The result is that consciousness becomes flooded with remote associations and feelings	LSD produces illusions ; hallucinations, (loss of contact with 'reality'), distortions of time perception. Overdoses can cause psychotic reactions and could kill LSD, psilocybin and mescaline are also referred to as 'psychedelics'. All hallucinogenic drugs are also called psychotomimetic', which means 'imitation of psychosis', because some produce effects very similar to schizophrenia
11 Cannabis sativa ('pot'/'dope') Herbal cannabis ('grass'/'marihuana') Cannabis resin ('Weed'/'the herb') Cannabis oil ('hash'/'hashish')	Precise biochemical mechanisms are not known. It may influence serotonin. Acetylcholine-utilising neurons in limbic system may be disrupted	Small amounts produce a mild, pleasurable 'high' (relaxation, loss of social inhibition, intoxication)(i.e. has a sedative effect). Large amounts can cause hallucinations, such as the perceived slowing down of time and heightened sensitivity to colours, sounds, etc. (i.e. acts like a hallucinogen).

TABLE 3.2 *(continued)*

There are several different ways in which psychoactive drugs have been classified. For example, Hamilton and Timmons (1995) identify three broad groups :

1 *stimulants* produce exaggerations of the conditions normally associated with alert wakefulness; in high doses, they cause overt seizure activity;
2 *depressants* produce exaggerations of the conditions normally associated with relaxation and sleep (which is why they are often referred to as *sedatives*); in high doses , they cause unconsciousness;
3 *hallucinogens* produce distortion of normal perception and thought processes; in high doses, they can cause episodes of psychotic behaviour (see Chapter 30).

The drugs used to treat mental disorders – antidepressants, anti-anxiety drugs and major tranquillizers – are discussed in detail in Chapter 31. (The effect of drugs on mood and behaviour, etc. is an important demonstration of how physical events can affect mental events, one aspect of the 'mind–body' issue; see Chapter 32.)

THE CENTRAL NERVOUS SYSTEM (CNS)

● How do we know what we know? Methods of studying the brain

As with drugs, there are different ways of classifying the various methods that are used to study the brain. Perhaps the simplest classification is in terms of:

- *clinical/anatomical methods,* which involve the study of the effects on behaviour of accidental injury to the brain or brain disease in human beings, or patients who have undergone brain surgery for the treatment of disorders such as epilepsy (in particular, 'split-brain' patients);
- *invasive methods*, in which there is deliberate intervention in the form of surgically removing areas of brain tissue (*ablation*) or causing damage or injury (*lesions*) to particular brain sites or stimulation of the brain, either electrically or chemically. Also included is the recording of the electrical activity of very small areas of the brain, or even single neurons, through the insertion of very fine electrodes (*microelectrode recording*); although no damage is intended, it may nonetheless happen and so this is counted as invasive. These methods involve animal subjects and are extremely controversial from an ethical point of view (see Chapter 32);
- *non-invasive methods*, in which either the brain's electrical activity is recorded by attaching electrodes to the scalp or computerized scanning or imaging techniques are used to study the living human brain. In either case, the brain is not interfered with in any way and there is no risk of damage or injury.

Clinical/anatomical methods

One of the earliest methods used to study the CNS was the study of patients who had suffered brain damage, as the result of an accident or a stroke or tumour. A famous and early example is Paul Broca's discovery of a specialized area of the brain for speech. In 1869, Broca, a French physician, reviewed evidence from a number of cases of brain damage and concluded that injury to a certain part of the left cerebral hemisphere caused the patient's speech to become slow and laboured but that the ability to understand speech was almost completely unaffected. What is now called *Broca's area* seems to control the ability to produce speech and damage to it causes *motor* (or *expressive*) *aphasia*. In 1874, Carl Wernicke reported that injury to a different part of the left hemisphere caused *receptive aphasia*, that is, the inability to understand speech (one's own or someone else's).

These clinical studies of the brain have normally been conducted in parallel with anatomical studies, usually during the course of postmortem examinations; studying structure and function in a complementary way is essential for an adequate

understanding of such a complex organ as the brain. Split-brain patients have undergone surgery for epilepsy when all other treatments have failed. The surgery (*commissurotomy*) involves cutting the tissue which connects the two halves of the brain (the corpus callosum) and Roger Sperry and his colleagues in the 1960s and 1970s made full use of the unique opportunity to study these 'split brains'. Their work will be discussed in detail later in the chapter.

Invasive methods

As we noted above, parts of the brain may be surgically removed (either through cutting or burning out with electrodes – a method called *ablation*) or an area of the brain may be damaged (rather than removed) (the *lesion method*). An early user of the first method was Karl Lashley, working with rats in the 1920s, and it has been used extensively to study the role of the brain in eating (see Chapter 5).

Psychologists are usually interested in destroying areas or structures located deep within the brain; to do this, a *stereotaxic apparatus* is used, which allows the researcher to operate on brain structures that are hidden from view (see Fig. 3.4). While the subjects are exclusively non-human animals, stereotaxic surgery is also used with humans, including psychiatric patients; psychosurgery is discussed in Chapter 31.

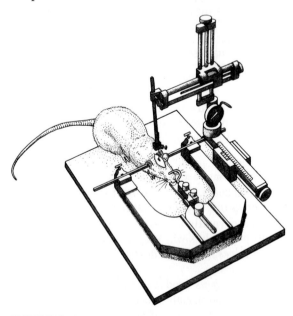

FIGURE 3.4 *A stereotaxic apparatus, used to insert an electrode into a specific portion of an animal's brain (From N. Carlson, 1992. Foundations of physiological psychology 2nd ed. Boston,Allyn and Bacon)*

Instead of surgically removing or damaging the brain, it can be stimulated, either chemically (using micropipettes to drop drugs known to either increase or decrease the activity of particular neurotransmitters onto specific areas of the brain) or, more commonly, electrically, using microelectrodes, whereby precise locations can be stimulated. Again, it is usually non-human animals that are involved (see Chapter 5), but sometimes patients already undergoing surgery for a brain tumour or some other abnormality (such as epilepsy) are studied: the neurosurgeon takes advantage of the fact that the patient is conscious, alert and able to report memories, sensations and so on produced by the stimulation. Penfield pioneered this kind of research in the 1950s.

Microelectrodes are also used to record the electrical activity in individual neurons when the subject (usually a cat or monkey) is presented with various kinds of stimuli. This method was used by Hubel and Wiesel in the 1960s to study visual feature detectors (see Chapters 8 and 9).

Non-invasive methods

The electrical activity of the brain can also be recorded from the outside by fitting electrodes to the scalp; the activity can be traced on paper and typical brainwave patterns associated with various states of arousal have been found. This is the electroencephalogram (EEG), which records action potentials for large groups of neurons and has been used extensively in the study of states of consciousness, including sleep. Related to this is the electromyogram (EMG), which records the electrical activity of muscles, and the electrooculogram (EOG), which records eye movements, both of which are, like the EEG, used in sleep research (see Chapter 4).

A brief change in the EEG may be produced by the presentation of a single stimulus but the effect may well be lost (or obscured) in the overall pattern of waves. However, if the stimulus is presented repeatedly and the results averaged by a computer, other waves cancel out and the evoked response can be detected. This technique is known as the *average*

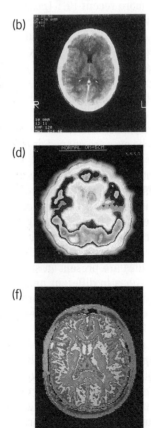

FIGURE 3.5 *Non-invasive techniques (a), (c) and (e) used to study detailed sections of the living human brain (b), (d) and (f)*

evoked potential (AEP) and has shown, for example, that an identical visual stimulus yields different AEPs according to the meaning the participant attaches to it.

A relatively recent method of studying the CNS involves *radioactive labelling*, which takes advantage of the brain's flexible use of bloodborne oxygen. A radioactive isotope is added to the blood, causing low levels of radioactivity, which increase as greater blood flow occurs in more active areas of the brain. A scanner next to the head feeds radiation readings to a computer, which produces a coloured map of the most and least active brain regions; different regions change colour as the person attempts a variety of tasks or is presented with a variety of stimuli.

Another use of computers is the CAT scan (*computerized axial tomography*). A moving X-ray beam takes pictures from different positions around the head and these are converted by the computer into 'brain slices' – apparent cross-sections of the brain. CAT scanning is used primarily for the detection and diagnosis of brain injury and disease but is not as efficient as the more recent PET (*positron emission tomography*), which uses the same computer-calculation approach as CAT but uses radiation for the information from which the brain slices are computed. A radioactive tracer is added to a substance used by the body (e.g. oxygen or glucose). As the marked substance is metabolized, PET shows the pattern of its use; for example, more or less use of glucose could indicate a tumour and changes are revealed when the eyes are opened or closed.

Magnetic resonance imaging (MRI) is like a CAT scan but does not use radiation; instead, it passes an extremely strong magnetic field through the head and measures its effects on the rotation of atomic nuclei of some element in the body; again, a computerized cross-sectional image is produced (Fig. 3.5). So far only hydrogen nuclei have been used; because hydrogen molecules are present in substantially different concentrations in different neural structures, the MRI can use the information to prepare pictures of brain slices which are much clearer (higher resolution) than CAT pictures.

Most recent are *single-photon emission computerized tomography* (SPECT), which, like PET, tracks blood flow through the brain, and *superconducting quantum imaging/interference device* (SQUID), which detects tiny changes in magnetic fields.

These new imaging technologies mean that neuroscientists no longer have to rely on laboratory animals or brain-damaged patients requiring surgery to view what is happening inside the brain as it happens. We can now peer into healthy living brain and observe the moment-to-moment changes that occur in relation to mental activity: although this does not mean that we can now literally look inside someone's mind, it adds to the age-long philosophical debate about the relationship between mind and brain (see Chapter 32).

● What can these methods tell us?

As we noted earlier, psychologists are not interested in the brain for its own sake (as fascinating as this may be) but for what it can tell us about the control of psychological functions and abilities, both subjective and behavioural. It is tempting to infer that if damage to (or loss of) a particular brain area is associated with the loss of (or reduction in) a particular ability, that part of the brain normally controls that ability; unfortunately, there are other possibilities. For example, the damaged area might itself be controlled by a different (undamaged) area or the damage may have disrupted the normal functioning of nearby, or related, intact areas. We shall return to some of these issues later when we discuss split-brain patients.

● How does the brain develop?

One of the most remarkable things about the human brain is not its size or even the number of neurons of which it is composed, but rather the staggering complexity of the interconnections between the neurons. Given that there are somewhere between 8 and 10 billion neurons in the brain, each of which may have between 1000 and 10,000 synaptic connections with other neurons, it has been estimated that there are more possible ways in which the neurons of a single human brain can be interconnected than there are atoms in the known universe!

It is the development of synaptic connections which accounts for much of the increase in brain weight after birth. At birth, the baby has almost its full complement of neurons and the brain is closer to its adult size than any other organ: it represents 10 percent of the baby's total body weight compared with 2 percent of the adult's. At six months, the brain is already half its eventual adult weight; at 12 months, 60 percent; at five years, 90 percent and at ten years 95 percent. The increase in weight is almost 200 percent in the first three years and the brain reaches its maximum weight by about 20 years. While the major development before birth is the growth of neurons, brain growth after birth is the result of four major changes:

1 We have already mentioned the growth of synaptic connections between neighbouring neurons. The continued growth or survival of any given neuron in fact depends on the establishment of synaptic connections with other neurons and the death of individual neurons is extremely common during brain development; indeed, the period of peak development in any one brain area is marked by the greatest rate of cell death in that area that will occur during the lifetime of the organism, a much higher rate than is associated with ageing, for example (see Chapter 24).

2 The neurons do actually increase in size (but not in number).

3 Glial cells develop (see above).

4 The oligodendrocytes produce the myelin sheaths which grow around the axons to insulate the neuron and speed up the conduction of action potentials.

If the absolute size of brains determined level of intelligence, then humans would certainly be surpassed by many species and even if we take brain size: body size ratio, we would still find that house mice, porpoises, tree shrews and squirrel monkeys come higher in the intelligence league than ourselves. Clearly, it is the *kind* of brain which is important and what seems to be unique about the human brain is the proportion of it which is not devoted to particular physical and psychological functions and which is, therefore, 'free' to facilitate our intelligence, our general ability to think, reason, use language and learn.

THE MAJOR STRUCTURES AND FUNCTIONS OF THE BRAIN

During the first five weeks of foetal life, the neural tube changes its shape to produce five bulbous enlargements which are generally accepted as the basic divisions of the brain; these are the *myelencephalon* (the medulla oblongata), the *metencephalon* (the pons and cerebellum), the mesencephalon (the midbrain), the *diencephalon* (thalamus and hypothalamus) and the *telencephalon* (the cerebral hemispheres or cerebrum). The myelencephalon and metencephalon together make up the hindbrain and the diencephalon and telencephalon make up a major portion of the forebrain ('encephalon' means 'within the head') (see Fig. 3. 1).

● The forebrain

The cerebral hemispheres (or cerebrum)

The cerebral hemispheres are the two largest structures at the top of the brain which enfold (and, therefore, conceal from view) most other brain structures. If you were to remove an intact brain, its appearance would be dominated by the massive hemispheres, with just the cerebellum showing at the back (as in Fig. 3.6).

The top layer of the cerebrum (about 1 cm at its deepest) is the *cerebral cortex* (usually just called 'cortex', which means 'bark'); it is highly convoluted

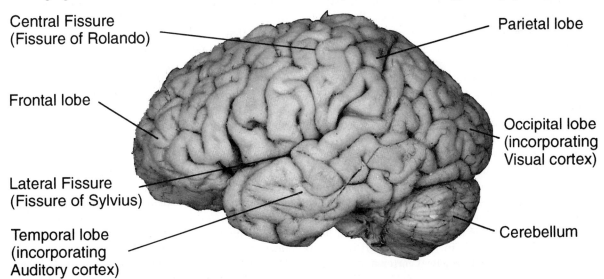

Central Fissure (Fissure of Rolando)

Parietal lobe

Frontal lobe

Occipital lobe (incorporating Visual cortex)

Lateral Fissure (Fissure of Sylvius)

Temporal lobe (incorporating Auditory cortex)

Cerebellum

FIGURE 3.6 *Lateral (side-on) view of the human brain (left cerebral hemisphere)*

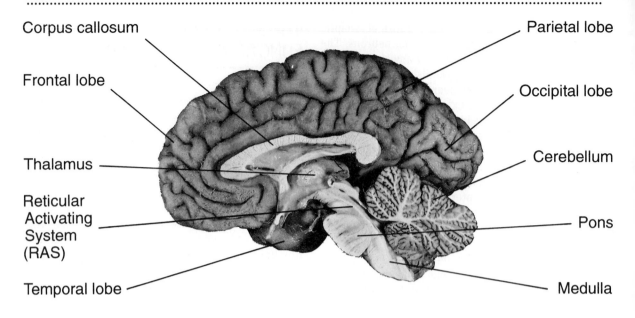

Corpus callosum

Frontal lobe

Thalamus

Reticular
Activating
System
(RAS)

Temporal lobe

Parietal lobe

Occipital lobe

Cerebellum

Pons

Medulla

FIGURE 3.7 *Front-to-back cross-section of the right cerebral hemisphere*

(wrinkled; see Fig. 3.6), which is necessary in order to pack its 2½ square foot surface area into the relatively small space inside the skull. The cortex is pinkish-grey in colour (hence 'grey matter'), but below it the cerebrum consists of much thicker white matter, composed of myelinated axons (the cortex consists of cell bodies).

There is a large crevice running along the cerebrum from front to back (the *longitudinal fissure* or *sulcus*), which divides the two hemispheres, although they are connected further down by a dense mass of commissurial ('joining') fibres called the *corpus callosum* (or 'hard body').

There are two other natural dividing lines in each hemisphere: the *lateral fissure* (or fissure of Sylvius) and the *central fissure* (or fissure of Rolando). The lateral fissure separates the *temporal lobe* from the *frontal lobe* (anteriorly) and from the *parietal lobe* (posteriorly), while the central fissure separates the frontal and parietal lobes. The *occipital lobe* is situated behind the parietal lobe and is at the back of the head. (Remember, this division of the cortex into four lobes – named after the bones beneath which they lie – is a feature of both hemispheres, which are mirror-images of each other.)

The *visual cortex* is found in the occipital lobe , the *auditory cortex* in the temporal lobe, the *somatosensory* (or *body-sense*) cortex in the parietal lobe and the *motor cortex* in the frontal lobe (see Chapter 8). The somatosensory cortex and motor cortex are perhaps the most well-defined areas and both

show *contralateral control*, that is, areas in the right hemisphere receive information from and are concerned with the activities of the left side of the body and vice versa. The crossing over takes place in the medulla (part of the brainstem) and is called *corticospinal decussation*. These areas represent the body in an upside-down fashion, so information from the feet, for example, is received by neurons at the top of the area.

Furthermore, the amount of cortex taken up with the motor activities of, or sensory information from, different parts of the body is associated not with the size of that body part but with the degree of precise motor control or the sensitivity of that part of the body. So fingers, for example, have much more cortex devoted to them than the trunk in the motor cortex and the lips have a very large representation in the somatosensory cortex (see Fig. 3.8). Broca's area is found in the frontal lobe and Wernicke's area borders the temporal and parietal lobes but in the left hemisphere only. (We shall say more about this under localization of brain function below.)

About three-quarters of the cortex does not have an obvious sensory or motor function and is known as the *association cortex*; this is where the 'higher mental functions' (cognition) – thinking, reasoning, learning, etc. – probably 'occur' but, except for certain aspects of memory and perception, these aspects of human intelligence have resisted attempts to localize them. However, there is no doubt that the cortex is not necessary for biological survival (this is

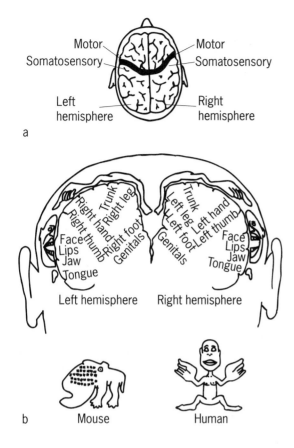

FIGURE 3.8 *Animunculi and homunculi showing how much cortical tissue is devoted to each body area. The mouse explores with its nose and each whisker has its own cortical area. We can use our hands for sensing, although we normally rely more on vision. The large face of the homunculus reflects the large cortical areas necessary for the control of speech*

controlled by various subcortical structures), as some species do not have one to begin with (e.g. birds) and in those that do, surgical removal does not prevent the animal from displaying a wide range of behaviour, although it becomes much more automatic and stereotyped. The human brain has a greater proportion of association cortex than any other species.

According to Suomi (1982), the cortex is of special interest to the developmental psychobiologist because:

- it is the last part of the brain to stop growing and differentiating;
- it undergoes greater structural change and transformation after birth than any other part of the brain;

- a greater number of neural interconnections are made after birth than during the prenatal period.

The sequence of cortical development seems to be: (i) the motor area; (ii) the somatosensory area; (iii) the visual area; and (iv) the auditory area. It is interesting to try to relate this sequence to the nature–nurture debate on perception (see Chapter 10) and Piaget's theory of cognitive development, in which sensorimotor activity plays such a vital part (see Chapter 25).

The thalamus ('deep chamber')

There are actually two thalami, situated deep in the forebrain (between the brainstem and the cerebral hemispheres). Each is an egg-shaped mass of grey matter and represents a crucial link between the cerebrum and the sense organs. All sensory signals pass through the thalamus, which serves as a relay station or major integrator of information flowing in from the sense organs to the cortex; each contains nuclei which are specialized to handle particular types of signal:

- the *ventrobasal complex,* which takes information fed in from the body via the spinal cord;
- the *lateral geniculate* ('bent') *body* (LGB), which processes visual information (see Chapter 8);
- the *medial geniculate body* (MGB), which processes auditory information (see Chapter 8).

The thalamus also receives information from the cortex, mainly dealing with complex limb movements, and these are directed to the cerebellum. Another part of the thalamus plays a part in sleep and waking.

The hypothalamus ('under the thalamus')

For its size (about equal to the tip of your index finger), the hypothalamus is a remarkable and extremely important part of the brain. It plays a major part in homoeostasis (control of the body's internal environment) and motivation, including eating and drinking, sexual behaviour and emotional arousal. Seven areas can be identified, each with its own special function:

1 posterior, sex drive;
2 anterior, water balance;
3 supraoptic, also water balance;
4 presupraoptic, heat control;
5 ventromedial, hunger;
6 dorsomedial, aggression;
7 dorsal, pleasure.

(The role of the hypothalamus, particularly in relation to hunger and thirst, is discussed in detail in Chapter 5.)

The hypothalamus works basically in two ways:

1 by sending electrochemical signals to the entire ANS (see Fig. 3.1), so that it represents a major link between the CNS and the ANS;
2 by influencing the *pituitary gland,* to which it is connected by a network of blood vessels and neurons.

The pituitary gland is situated in the brain, just below and to one side of the hypothalamus, but it is not part of the CNS; it is in fact part of the *endocrine (hormonal) system*, which we shall discuss later in the chapter (see also Chapter 6).

Basal ganglia ('nerve knots')

These are embedded in the mass of white matter of each cerebral hemisphere and are themselves small areas of grey matter, in fact comprising a number of smaller structures:

● the *corpus striatum* ('striped body'), composed of the lentiform nucleus and caudate nucleus;

● the *amygdala* ('almond');
● the *substantia nigra* (which is also part of the *tegmentum,* usually classified as part of the midbrain).

These structures are closely linked to the thalamus and they seem to play a part in muscle tone and posture by integrating and co-ordinating the main voluntary muscle movements, which are the concern of the great descending motor pathway (the *pyramidal system*). Information from the cortex is relayed to the brainstem and cerebellum.

The limbic system ('bordering')

This is not a separate structure but comprises a number of highly inter-related structures which, when seen from the side, seem to nest inside each other, encircling the brainstem in a 'wishbone' (see Fig. 3.9). The major structures are: (i) thalami bodies; (ii) hypothalamus; (iii) mamillary bodies; (iv) septum pellucidum; (v) cingulate gyrus; (vi) hippocampus; (vii) amygdala; (viii) fornix; and (ix) olfactory bulbs.

The human limbic system is very similar to that of primitive mammals and so is often called 'the old

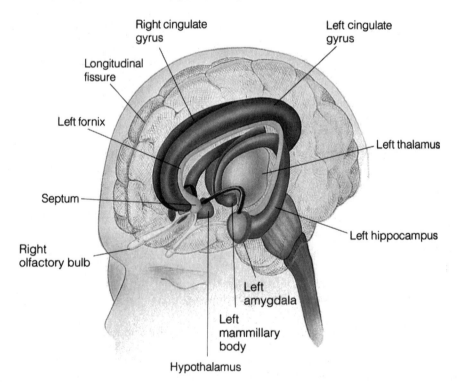

FIGURE 3.9 *The major structures of the limbic system: the thalami bodies, the hypothalamus, the mammillary bodies, the hippocampus, the amygdala, the septum, the fornix and the cingulate gyrus. Also illustrated are the olfactory bulbs, which are connected to several limbic structures. (From J.Pine, 1993) Biopychology. Boston, Allyn and Bacon*

mammalian brain'. It is also sometimes called the 'nose brain' because much of its development seems to have been related to the olfactory sense (and, of course, the olfactory bulb is one of its components). It is closely involved with behaviours which satisfy certain motivational and emotional needs, including feeding, fighting, escape and mating.

The *hippocampus* is involved in memory; someone whose hippocampus is damaged is very easily distracted and they will be unable to carry out an intended sequence of actions (e.g. making a cup of tea) because they have forgotten what they had planned to do (see Chapter 12).

The limbic system as a whole serves as a meeting place between the cortex (or 'neocortex', in evolutionary terms the most recent part of the brain to have developed) and older parts of the brain, such as the hypothalamus. From the cortex it receives interpreted information about the world and from the hypothalamus information about the body's internal state; these are integrated and the 'conclusions' are fed back to the cortex and to the older, subcortical areas.

● The midbrain

This is really an extension of the brainstem and connects the forebrain to the spinal cord. The main structure is the *reticular activating system* (RAS) (reticulum = network) or *reticular formation* (RF), which ascends from the spinal cord to the forebrain carrying mainly sensory information (the ARAS) and descends from the forebrain to the spinal cord carrying mainly motor information. Since it begins in the spinal cord and passes through the brainstem, it is often classified as part of the hindbrain in addition to the midbrain.

The ARAS is vitally important in maintaining our general level of arousal or alertness (it is often called the 'consciousness switch') and plays an important part (but by no means the only one) in the sleep–wake cycle (see Chapter 4). It also plays a part in selective attention and, although it responds unselectively to all kinds of stimulation, it helps to screen extraneous sensory information by, for example, controlling *habituation* to constant sources of stimulation and making us alert and responsive mainly to changes in stimulation (see Chapter 11). Sleeping parents who keep 'one ear open' for the baby who might start to cry are relying on their ARAS to let only very important sensory signals through, so it acts as a kind of sentry for the cortex. Damage can induce a coma-like state of sleep.

The midbrain also contains important centres for visual and auditory reflexes, including the *orienting reflex,* a general response to a novel stimulus. Birds which sight, track and capture prey in flight have very prominent and bulging areas in their midbrain and bats have a very prominent auditory area in the midbrain.

● The hindbrain

Cerebellum ('little brain')

Like the cerebrum, the cerebellum consists of two halves or hemispheres and is even more convoluted than the cortex. It synthesizes all sensory information from vision, the inner ear (which controls balance), the muscles and the joints and can calculate the movements required in a particular sequence of behaviour. So the cerebellum plays a vital role in the co-ordination of voluntary (skeletal) muscle activity, balance and fine movements (such as reaching for things). Motor commands which originate in higher brain centres are processed here before transmission to the muscles.

Damage to the cerebellum can cause hand tremors, drunken movements and loss of balance. The inability to reach for objects normally (*ataxia*) and hand tremors are quite common amongst the elderly.

The cerebellum also controls the intricate movements involved in the swimming of a fish, the flying of a bird, playing a musical instrument or driving a car. Once learned, complex movements like those involved in signing our name, picking up a glass, walking and even talking seem to be 'programmed' into the cerebellum, so that we can do them 'automatically' without having to think consciously about what we are doing; the cerebellum acts like an 'automatic pilot' inside the brain.

The cerebellum accounts for about 11 percent of the entire brain weight and only the cerebrum is larger. Its grey matter in fact consists of three layers of cells, the middle layer of which – the *Purkinje cells* – can link each synapse with up to 100,000 other neurons, more than any other kind of brain cell.

The pons ('bridge')

This is a bulge of white matter which connects the two halves of the cerebellum. It is an important connection between the midbrain and the medulla and is vital in integrating the movements of the two sides of the body. Four of the 12 cranial nerves (which originate in the brain) have their nuclei ('relay stations') here, including the large trigeminal nerve. It is the middle portion of the brainstem.

The medulla oblongata ('rather long marrow')

This is a fibrous section of the lower brainstem (about 2 cm long) and is really a thick extension of the spinal cord. In evolutionary terms, it is the oldest part of the brain and it is the site of the crossing over of the major nerve tracts coming up from the spinal cord and coming down from the brain. It contains vital reflex centres, which control breathing, cardiac function, swallowing, vomiting, coughing, chewing, salivation and facial movements.

The midbrain, pons and medulla together make up the *brainstem*.

THE SPINAL CORD

About the thickness of a little finger, the spinal cord passes from the brainstem down the whole length of the back and is encased in the vertebrae of the spine. The spinal cord is the main communication 'cable' between the brain (CNS) and the peripheral nervous system (PNS), providing the pathway between body and brain.

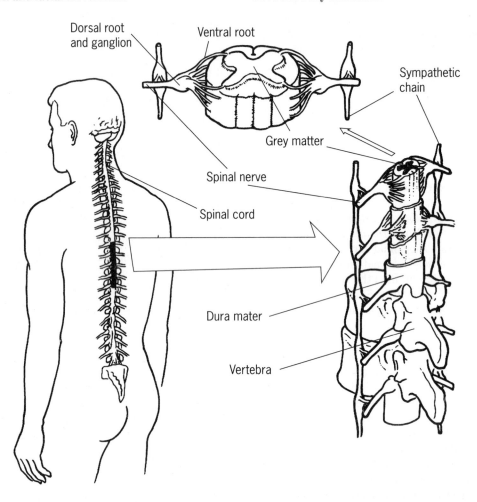

FIGURE 3.10 *The spinal cord and spinal nerves. (From Rosenzweig and Leiman, 1989). The left diagram shows a general view of the spinal column with a pair of nerves emerging from each level. The right diagram shows how the spinal cord is surrounded by bony vertebra and enclosed in a membrane, the dura mater. Each vertebra has an opening on each side through which the spinal nerves pass. The top diagram shows the location of the spinal cord grey matter and the white matter that surrounds it. In the grey matter are interneurons and the motor neurons that send axons to the muscles. The white matter consists of myelinated axons that run up and down the spinal column.*

Messages enter and leave the spinal cord by means of 31 pairs of spinal nerves; each pair innervates a different and fairly specific part of the body and are 'mixed nerves', i.e. they contain both motor (carrying information from the NS to the muscles) and sensory (carrying information from the sensory receptors to the NS) neurons for most of their length. However, at the junction with the cord itself, the nerves divide into two roots – the *dorsal* root (towards the back of the body), which contains sensory neurons, and the *ventral* root (towards the front of the body), which contains motor neurons (Fig. 3.10).

The spinal cord constitutes a simplified model (compared with the brain) of a neurological system which receives sensory information, processes it and then delivers impulses to the muscles for the initiation and co-ordination of motor activity. The basic functional unit of the NS is the spinal reflex arc; for instance, the knee-jerk reflex involves just two kinds of neurons: a sensory neuron conveys information about stimulation of the patella tendon to the spinal cord and this information crosses a single synapse within the grey 'butterfly' (which runs inside the centre of the cord). This causes a motor neuron to stimulate the appropriate muscle groups in the leg, which causes the leg to shoot up in the air.

However, most spinal reflexes are more complex than this. For example, withdrawing your hand from a hot plate will involve an interneuron (as well as a sensory and motor neuron) and two synapses. Commonly, the experience of pain follows 1–2 seconds after you have withdrawn your hand – this is how long it takes for sensory information to reach the cortex.

THE LOCALIZATION AND LATERALIZATION OF BRAIN FUNCTION

So far we have said that the cerebral hemispheres are mirror-images of each other and both divide into four lobes and that Broca's area and Wernicke's area (which deal with speech production and comprehension, respectively) appear only in the left hemisphere.

This (and other evidence) has led to the view that the hemispheres are functionally different (*functional lateralization*) and much of the discussion has focused on language. From studies of stroke victims in particular, it is generally agreed that for the majority of right-handed people, their left hemisphere is dominant for speech (and language ability in general). Someone who is paralysed down their right side must have suffered damage to the left hemisphere and, if they have also suffered *aphasia*, then we can infer that language is normally controlled by the left hemisphere.

One of the difficulties associated with generalizations in psychology (even with something as 'biological' as cerebral function) is the existence of individual differences. Some people seem to have much more lateralized brains than others; others have language more or less equally represented on both sides (*bilateral representation*) (Beaumont, 1988). As far as the left hemisphere being dominant for language, this seems to be true for 95 percent of right-handed patients, while only 5 percent had their right hemisphere dominant. But with left-handers, things are much less clearcut: 75 percent had their left hemisphere dominant, none had the right dominant but 25 percent showed bilateral representation (based on a review by Satz (1979) of all studies between 1935 and 1975; cited in Beaumont, 1988).

Over and above this left–right-handed difference, women show less lateralization than men; for example, damage to one side will, on average, affect a woman's brain less than a man's. Similarly, damage to the right hemisphere will interfere with a man's spatial abilities more than a woman's. So, the left–right specialization is most prevalent in right-handed men (and not 'all people'!(Ornstein, 1986)) (see Chapter 23).

In the majority of right-handed people, is the dominance of the left hemisphere a built-in characteristic or is it modifiable? According to Zaidel (1978), the two hemispheres are fairly equal up until about age five. In general, a child's brain is much more plastic (flexible) than an adult's (Rose, 1976); for example, in children up to three years, brain trauma produces similar effects regardless of which site is damaged. Provided the lesion is not too severe or if it occurs on one side only, considerable recovery is possible – the corresponding area on the other side takes over the function of the damaged area and this seems to be especially true of speech.

This seems to support the conclusions of Lashley who (in the 1920s) studied the effects of brain destruction on rats' learning ability. His (1929) *law of mass action* states that the learning of difficult problems depends upon the amount of damage to the cortex and not on the position or site of the damage, i.e. the greater the cortical damage, the greater the learning difficulty, but Lashley could not find specific neural circuits related to the learning of, or memory for, particular types of problem. The *law of equipotentiality* states that corresponding parts of the brain are capable of taking over the function normally performed by the damaged area.

Similarly, the *principle of multiple control* maintains that any particular part of the brain is likely to be involved in the performance of many different types of behaviour. For example, rats with lesions in their lateral hypothalamus show deficits in certain learning situations, as well as impaired feeding (see Chapter 5). Conversely, the same behaviour (e.g. aggression or emotion) normally involves a number of brain sites and the logical conclusion of this seems to be that the brain functions as a complete unit, an integrated whole. (We shall return to this issue below.)

● Split-brain patients. One brain or two? One mind or two?

Remember that split-brain patients have undergone surgery (normally in the treatment of epilepsy) to cut their corpus callosum, which normally joins the two hemispheres and allows an exchange of information from one to the other. While the surgery may relieve the suffering, it has a major side-effect in that the two hemispheres become functionally separate, i.e. they act as two separate, independent brains. Sperry (based on a number of studies in the 1960s and 1970s, for which he was awarded the Nobel Prize for Medicine in 1981) and Ornstein (1975) believe that split-brain studies reveal the 'true' nature of the two hemispheres and that each embodies a different kind of consciousness (see Chapter 4). A typical split-brain experiment is described in Box 3.1.

These examples show that the right hemisphere is not completely without language ability – otherwise participants could not successfully point or select – but it clearly lacks the left hemisphere's ability to name and articulate what has been experienced. In the second example, both hemispheres are handicapped if information is not conveyed from one to the other – the whole word ('heart') is not perceived by either!

A similar but perhaps more dramatic example involved sets of photographs of different faces – a beautiful young female model, a podgy-cheeked boy, an old man and so on. Each photo was cut down the middle and the halves of two different faces were pasted together. They were then presented in such a way that the left side of the photo would only be

---

BOX 3.1	Key study: when the left brain literally doesn't know what the left hand is doing (Sperry, 1968)

Participants sit in front of a screen with their hands free to handle objects that are behind the screen but which are obscured from sight by the screen. While fixating on a spot in the middle of the screen, a word (e.g. 'key') is flashed onto the left side of the screen for one-tenth of a second to ensure that the word is only 'seen' by the right hemisphere (see Fig. 3.11).

If asked to pick out the key from a pile of objects with the left hand (still controlled by the right hemisphere), this can be done quite easily. However, the participant is unable to say what word appeared on the screen (because the left hemisphere did not receive the information from the right as it would in a normal person); the participant literally does not know why they chose that object.

Again, a word (e.g. 'heart') is flashed on a screen, with 'he' to the left and 'art' to the right of the fixation point. If asked to name the word, participants will say 'art' (because this is the portion of the word projected

to the left hemisphere) but when asked to point with the left hand to one of two cards on which 'he' and 'art' are written, the left hand will point to 'he' (because this was the portion projected to the right hemisphere).

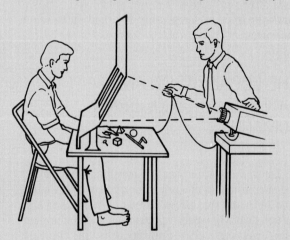

FIGURE 3.11 *Apparatus for studying lateralization of visual, tactual, lingual and associated functions in the surgically separated hemispheres. (From Sperry, 1968)*

visible to the right hemisphere and vice-versa. So, for example, with a picture of an old man to the right and a young boy to the left, participants were asked to describe what they had seen (the left hemisphere responding): they said 'an old man'. But if asked to point with their left hand to the complete photo of the person they had seen (the right hemisphere responding) they would point to the young boy. It seems that two completely separate visual worlds can exist within the same head!

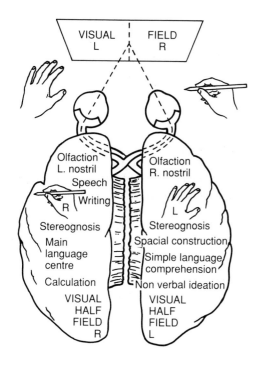

FIGURE 3.12 *Schematic outline of the functional lateralization evident in behavioural tests of patients with forebrain commissurotomy. (From Sperry, 1968)*

These and many more, equally dramatic experiments led Sperry, Ornstein and others to conclude that each of the separated hemispheres has its own private sensations, perceptions, thoughts, feelings and memories – in short, that they constitute two separate minds, two separate spheres of consciousness (Sperry, 1964; see Fig. 3.12). Levy-Agresti and Sperry (1968) concluded that the:

> ... mute, minor hemisphere is specialized for Gestalt perception, being primarily a synthesist in dealing with information input. The speaking, major hemisphere, in contrast, seems to operate in a more logical, analytic, computer-like fashion ...

Ornstein (1986) summarizes the differences like this:

● The left is specialized for *analytic and logical thinking* (i.e. breaking things down into their component parts), especially in verbal and mathematical functions, processes information sequentially (one item at a time) and its mode of operation is primarily linear (straight line).
● The right is specialized for *synthetic thinking* (bringing different things together to form a whole), particularly in the area of spatial tasks, artistic activities, crafts, body image and face recognition, processes information more diffusely (several items at once) and its mode of operation is much less linear (more holistic).

Cohen (1975) argues that long-standing presurgical pathology might have caused an abnormal reorganization of the brains of these split-brain patients, so that generalizing to normal people might not be valid. She cites a study by Kinsbourne in which the left hemisphere of aphasic patients was anaesthetized but they continued to speak fluently but unintelligibly, suggesting that the abnormal speech is produced by the non-specialist right hemisphere. This seems to contradict the conclusions of split-brain studies that the right hemisphere has some understanding of language but is mute!

A number of attempts have been made to move beyond the simplistic left hemisphere/right hemisphere, verbal/non-verbal distinction, both in normal participants and in split-brain patients. In a review of recent research, Annett (1991) says that ' ... it is evident that each hemisphere has some role in the functions assigned to the other'. For example, the right hemisphere has a considerable understanding of language and it has been suggested that it might be responsible for semantic errors made by deep dyslexics. Similarly, the left hemisphere is almost certainly responsible for the production of imagery, 'which is likely to be required in much spatial thinking'.

But are there any distinctive left hemisphere skills? Annett believes the best candidate is sensitivity to differences in rapidly changing acoustic cues, crucial to speech recognition. Another possibility is the production of movement sequence over time, involved in both speech and skilled hand movement.

She cites an interesting study by Poizner *et al.* (1987) of six cases of deaf users of American Sign Language (ASL), all right handers, who had used ASL since early childhood: three suffered a left hemisphere stroke, three a right hemisphere stroke. The former suffered loss of ASL, often remarkably similar to the kinds of disorder seen in normal speakers who suffer strokes at similar locations; the three right hemisphere stroke patients showed no significant loss of ASL. This suggests that left hemisphere specialization for language can occur for a language that is not based on speech (Annett, 1991).

While arguing that right hemisphere processing of language is extremely rare and is found in normal people only as a result of early left hemisphere damage, Gazzaniga (1985) also claims that it is not at all clear that the traditional interpretation of split-brain studies is correct. He argues that the brain is organized in a *modular* fashion, i.e. organized into relatively independent functioning units, which work in parallel. (This is consistent with current connectionist models in artificial intelligence; see Chapter 14.) Many of the modules operate at a non-conscious level, in parallel to our conscious thought; the left hemisphere tries to assign interpretations to the processing of these modules. So brains are organized such that many mental systems coexist in a 'confederation' (similar to Fodor's (1983) idea of mental modules).

According to Sternberg (1990), although Gazzaniga's view is not the common one among neuropsychologists, not all neuropsychologists accept the degree of separation between the hemispheres suggested by Sperry and his co-workers. An alternative view is one of *integration*, i.e. the two hemispheres should be seen as playing different parts in an integrated performance (Broadbent, 1985, cited in Sternberg, 1990). Cohen (1975) agrees that, when normal participants are studied, the two sides of the brain do not function in isolation but form a highly integrated system. Most everyday tasks involve a mixture of 'left' and 'right' skills: in listening to speech, for instance, we analyse both the words and the intonation pattern, while an integrated perception of linguistic and musical elements occurs in the appreciation of opera and analysis of visual shapes and linguistic knowledge are both required in reading; these may be accompanied by imagery and subvocal speech. Far from doing their own thing, the two hemispheres work very much together (Cohen, 1975).

THE AUTONOMIC NERVOUS SYSTEM (ANS)

As Figure 3.1 shows, the ANS is the part of the PNS, which controls the internal organs and glands of the body over which we have little (or no) voluntary

control. It comprises two branches, the *sympathetic*, which takes over whenever the body needs to use its energy, as in an emergency situation (the 'fight or flight' syndrome), and the *parasympathetic*, which is dominant when the body is at 'rest' and energy is being built up.

Essentially, therefore, the two branches work in opposite ways but they are both equally necessary for the maintenance of the delicately balanced internal state of homoeostasis (see Chapter 5). Sometimes a sequence of sympathetic and parasympathetic activity is required: in sexual arousal in men, erection is primarily parasympathetic while ejaculation is primarily sympathetic.

The ANS produces its effects in two ways:

1 by direct neural stimulation of body organs; and
2 by stimulating the release of hormones from the endocrine glands.

In both cases, the hypothalamus is the orchestrator. Table 3.3 summarizes the major sympathetic and parasympathetic effects on the organs and glands and the ANS will be discussed further in Chapter 6 in relation to emotion and stress.

THE ENDOCRINE SYSTEM

As we have said, many of the bodily reactions which result from the ANS are produced by its effect on the endocrine glands, which secrete hormones (chemical messengers which, unlike neurotransmitters, are released directly into the bloodstream and are carried throughout the body).

The effect of hormones is much slower than that of neurotransmitters: an electrochemical impulse can convey a message in a matter of milliseconds, while several seconds may be required for the stimulation, release and arrival of a needed hormone at its destination. Consequently, where an immediate behavioural reaction is required (e.g. a reflex action), the NS plays a major role: hormones are better suited to communicating steady, relatively unchanging messages over prolonged periods of time (e.g. the body changes associated with puberty).

Endocrine glands are ductless and are contrasted with *exocrine* glands (such as salivary, sweat and tear glands) which do have ducts and secrete fluids directly onto the body surface or into body cavities; their influence is, consequently, much less widespread than that of endocrine glands.

Organ or function affected	Sympathetic reaction	Parasympathetic reaction
1 Heart rate	Increase	Decrease
2 Blood pressure	Increase	Decrease
3 Secretion of saliva	Suppressed (mouth feels dry)	Stimulated
4 Pupils	Dilate (to aid vision)	Contract
5 Limbs (and trunk)	Dilation of blood vessels of the voluntary muscles (to help us run faster, for example)	Contraction of these blood vessels
6 Peristalsis (contraction of stomach and intestines)	Slows down (you don't feel hungry in an emergency)	Speeds up
7 Galvanic skin response (GSR) (measure of the electrical resistance of the skin)	Decreases (due to increased sweating associated with increased anxiety)	Increases
8 Bladder muscles	Relaxed (there may be temporary loss of bladder control)	Contracted
9 Adrenal glands	Stimulated to secrete more adrenaline and noradrenaline	Reduced secretion
10 Breathing rate	Increased (through dilation of bronchi)	Decreased
11 Liver	Glucose (stored as glycogen) is released into the blood to increase energy	Sugar is stored
12 Emotion	Experience of strong emotion	Less extreme emotions

TABLE 3.3 *Major sympathetic and parasympathetic reactions*

The major endocrine gland is the *pituitary gland* which, as we have seen, is physically (but not functionally) part of the brain (situated just below the hypothalamus). It is often called the 'master gland' because it produces the largest number of different hormones and also because it controls the secretion of several other endocrine glands. The pituitary comprises two independently functioning parts, the posterior and the anterior. The former transmits hormones which are thought to be manufactured in the hypothalamus, while the latter is stimulated by the hypothalamus to produce its own hormones. The major hormones of the posterior and anterior lobes of the pituitary are shown, with their effects, in Table 3.4.

Other important endocrine glands are the *adrenals* (situated just above the kidneys), each of which comprises the adrenal medulla (inner core) and the adrenal cortex (outer layer). As Table 3.4 shows, the medulla secretes adrenaline and noradrenaline which are the transmitter substances for the sympathetic branch of the ANS; consequently, the 'fight or flight' syndrome is often kept going by a 'closed circuit', whereby the sympathetic NS stimulates the adrenals to produce adrenaline and noradrenaline (initiated by the hypothalamus, which stimulates the pituitary gland to secrete ACTH which, in turn, stimulates the adrenals) which then stimulate the sympathetic nerves, and so on. This closed circuit explains why your heart continues to pound for several seconds after a dangerous or stressful situation has passed (see Chapter 6).

	Hormone	Endocrine gland or organ stimulated	Effects
Anterior pituitary	Growth hormone (somatotropin)	Body tissues	Increases growth of bones and muscles, particularly in childhood and adolescence. Too little produces *pituitary dwarfism* and too much *gigantism*
	Gonadotrophic hormones **1** Luteinizing hormone (LH)	Gonads (Testes–male, Ovaries–Female)	Development of sex (germ) cells — Ova (Female) / Sperm (Male) Production of sex hormones — Oestrogen and Progesterone (Female) / Testosterone (Male)
	2 Follicle-stimulating hormone (FSH)	Ovaries	Production of follicles in ovary during ovulation
	Thyrotrophic hormone (TTH)	Thyroid gland	Secretion of thyroxin which controls metabolic rate–too little causes lethargy and depression, too much causes hyperactivity and anxiety
	Lactogenic hormone (Prolactin)	Breasts	Milk production during pregnancy
	Adrenocorticotrophic hormone (ACTH)	Adrenal glands 1 Adrenal medulla 2 Adrenal cortex	Secretion of adrenaline and noradrenaline. Secretion of adrenocorticoid hormones (or corticosteroids), e.g. cortisol and hydrocortisone (important in coping with stress) (see Chapter 6)
Posterior pituitary	Oxytocin	Uterus (Womb)	Causes contractions during labour and milk release during breast feeding
	Vasopressin (Also a neurotransmitter)	Blood vessels	Causes contraction of the muscle in the walls of the blood vessels and so raises blood pressure
	Antidiuretic hormone (ADH)	Kidneys	Regulates the amount of water passed in the urine

Other endocrine glands include:
(A) *Thymus* – situated in the chest; functions unknown, but thought to involve production of antibodies (see Chapter 6)
(B) *Pancreas* – secretes insulin (Anti-diabetic hormone), given in the treatment of diabetes. Controls the body's ability to absorb glucose and fats.
(C) *Pineal body/gland* – situated near corpus callosum, functions unknown but may play a role in sleep-walking cycle (see Chapter 4)

TABLE 3.4 *Major pituitary hormones and their effects*

CHAPTER SUMMARY

- Biopsychology is the branch of neuroscience that studies the biological bases of behaviour; biopsychologists are first and foremost psychologists and are only interested in biology for what it can tell them about behaviour and mental processes, not for its own sake.
- It is important for psychologists to know about biology because an animal's behaviour depends on the kind of body and nervous system it possesses. Its nervous system determines the extent and nature of the learning it is capable of: the more complex the species, the more of its behaviour is the product of learning and environmental influence.
- Biopsychology draws together knowledge from other neuroscientific disciplines, in particular neuroanatomy, developmental neurobiology, neurochemistry, neuroendocrinology, neuropathology (related to which is neuropsychology), neuropharmacology (related to which is psychopharmacology) and neurophysiology (related to which is physiological psychology and psychophysiology).
- Physiological psychology uses invasive methods to manipulate the nervous system of non-human animals, while psychophysiology uses non-invasive methods to study human psychological processes and mental disorders.
- The nervous system (NS) comprises 10–12 billion neurons, 80 percent of which are found in the brain, mainly in the cerebral cortex. There are ten times as many glial cells, one type of which (oligodendrocytes) provide the myelin sheath around the axon of the neuron, which provides insulation and speeds up the rate of conduction of electrochemical impulses.
- Neurons are either sensory/afferent, motor/efferent or interneurons/connector. They vary enormously in length but they share a basic structure: the cell body/soma, which contains the nucleus and the cytoplasm, dendrites (which receive incoming signals from other neurons) and the axon which carries signals to other neurons; at the end of the axon is the terminal button.
- A nerve is a bundle of elongated axons. Twelve pairs of cranial nerves leave the brain through holes in the skull; 31 pairs of spinal nerves leave the spinal cord through the vertebrae; together they constitute the nerves of the peripheral nervous system (PNS).
- The terminal buttons house synaptic vesicles containing molecules of neurotransmitter; these are released into the synaptic cleft/gap when an electrochemical impulse stimulates the vesicles in the presynaptic membrane and combine with special receptor sites in the postsynaptic membrane.
- Before the electrochemical signal/action potential occurs, the inside of the cell is electrically negative relative to the outside (the resting potential). When an action potential occurs, the inside momentarily changes from negative to positive: the cell becomes permeable to sodium ions which flood in, opening up the sodium channels along the length of the axon. The resting potential is almost immediately restored. The action potential jumps from one node of Ranvier to the next (saltatory conduction).
- Once the threshold of response has been exceeded, action potentials travel at the same speed and are all of the same strength; they are either present or absent (all-or-none rule). The intensity of a stimulus is measured by the frequency of firing and the number of neurons that are stimulated.
- Regardless of the strength of the stimulus, there is an absolute refractory period, followed by a relative refractory period.
- Synapses are either excitatory or inhibitory, depending on the particular neurotransmitter contained within the synaptic button; whether or not a particular neuron will fire depends on the combined effect of all its receiving synapses (summation). Inhibitory synapses are needed to keep activity channelled in appropriate circuits.
- Once the transmitter molecules have crossed into the postsynaptic membrane, their effect is ended either by deactivation or reuptake. Large numbers of neurotransmitters each have their own excitatory or inhibitory effect on certain neurons and are localized in specific groups of neurons and pathways. Normally, a single neuron can be labelled by the transmitter it uses: cholinergic, noradrenergic, dopaminergic and serotonergic neurons use acetylcholine (ACh), noradrenaline, dopamine and serotonin respectively.
- Neuromodulators have a more indirect effect on receiving neurons than neurotransmitters by 'priming' them for later stimulation by a neurotransmitter. Neuromodulators include neuropeptides, in particular the enkephalins and the endorphins/opioids, which seem to be the brain's own painkillers; they are possibly released during acupuncture and hypnosis and may help to explain the placebo effect. Other neuropeptides include

- vasopressin, corticosteroids, adrenocorticotrophic hormone (ACTH) and androgens, all hormones.
- Drugs influence behaviour through their effect on neurotransmitters. The molecules of many commonly used psychoactive drugs are of a very similar shape to those of neurotransmitters and operate in a similar way. Psychoactive drugs can be classified in different ways, such as stimulants, depressants/sedatives and hallucinogens.
- Clinical/anatomical methods of studying the brain involve patients who have suffered accidental brain damage or disease or split-brain patients. Two early examples are Broca's discovery that injury to a specific area in the left hemisphere (Broca's area) causes motor/expressive aphasia and Wernicke's finding that injury to a different part of the left hemisphere (Wernicke's area) causes receptive aphasia. These clinical studies are usually conducted in parallel with anatomical studies, usually during post mortems.
- Invasive methods involve ablation or causing lesions to particular brain sites, stimulating the brain, either electrically (using microelectrodes) or chemically (dropping drugs onto specific brain areas) and microelectrode recording. They are used mainly with non-human animals and involve a stereotaxic apparatus which allows the researcher to operate on areas deep within the brain, but patients undergoing brain surgery are also studied.
- Non-invasive methods include the electroencephalogram (EEG), electromyogram (EMG) and electrooculogram (EOG) and the average evoked potential (AEP). Radioactive labelling involves measuring levels of radioactivity which increase with increased blood flow to more active brain areas; a computer produces a coloured map of the brain, showing the more and less active areas.
- Computers are also used in a number of scanning/imaging devices, such as computerized axial tomography (CAT), positron emission tomography (PET), magnetic resonance imaging (MRI), single-photon emission computerized tomography (SPECT) and superconducting quantum imaging/interference device (SQUID). These techniques provide access to processes associated with mental activity, inside the healthy living brain as they happen.
- Interpreting the results of studies which use these various methods is more complicated than it might at first appear; this is partly to do with the fact that the brain is such a complex, interconnected system.

- It is the amazingly complex interconnections between neurons that make the brain such a remarkable organ and it is the development of synaptic connections which accounts for much of the increase in brain weight after birth. But increase in the size of the neurons, development of glial cells and myelin sheaths also contribute to postnatal brain growth.
- Another unique feature of the human brain is the proportion of it (especially the cortex) which is not devoted to particular physical and psychological functions; neither its absolute size nor the brain size: body size ratio is remarkable.
- The brain develops from the neural tube into the myelencephalon and metencephalon (which together compose the hindbrain), the mesencephalon (midbrain), the diencephalon and telencephalon (which together compose much of the forebrain).
- The cerebral hemispheres/cerebrum enfold and conceal most other brain structures. The top layer is the highly convoluted cortex. The cerebrum is naturally divided by the longitudinal fissure/sulcus (from front to back); each hemisphere is naturally divided by the lateral fissure/fissure of Sylvius and the central fissure/fissure of Rolando.
- These fissures separate the four lobes of each hemisphere: the occipital lobe (which houses the visual cortex), the temporal lobe (auditory cortex), the parietal lobe (somatosensory/body-sense cortex) and the frontal lobe (motor cortex).
- The somatosensory and motor areas are probably the most well defined and both show contralateral control; the crossing over (corticospinal decussation) takes place in the medulla. Highly sensitive parts of the body (e.g. the lips) and those over which we have precise motor control (e.g. the fingers) have much more cortex devoted to them than other parts.
- The association cortex is where higher mental processes 'occur', but as yet most have not been localized. The cortex is not needed for biological survival, which is controlled by various subcortical structures. The sequence of development seems to be: motor, somatosensory, visual and auditory areas.
- The thalamus is a crucial link between the cerebrum and the sense organs. It acts as a relay station for all incoming sensory information and contains specialized nuclei: ventrobasal complex (bodily information via the spinal cord), the lateral geniculate body (LGB) (visual information) and the medial geniculate body (MGB) (auditory information).

- The hypothalamus plays a major role in homoeostasis, motivation, sexual behaviour and emotional arousal. It comprises seven areas: posterior (sex drive), anterior and supraoptic (water balance), presupraoptic (heat control), ventromedial (hunger), dorsomedial (aggression) and dorsal (pleasure). It works either by sending electrochemical signals to the whole ANS or by influencing the pituitary gland, which is located close to the hypothalamus but is part of the endocrine/hormonal system.

- The basal ganglia comprise a number of smaller structures, namely, the corpus striatum, the amygdala and the substantia nigra (part of the tegmentum in the midbrain). These are closely linked to the thalamus and are involved in posture and muscle tone.

- The limbic system ('old mammalian brain'/'nose brain') comprises a number of highly inter-related structures arranged in a 'wishbone', namely, the thalamus, hypothalamus, mamillary bodies, septum pellucidum, cingulate gyrus, hippocampus, amygdala, fornix and the olfactory bulbs. It is involved in motivation and emotion and also integrates information from the cortex (about the outside world) and hypothalamus (about the body's internal state).

- The midbrain is an extension of the brainstem and connects the forebrain to the spinal cord. The reticular activating system (RAS) or reticular formation (RF) begins in the spinal cord and passes through the brainstem; the ascending RAS (ARAS) plays a vital role in maintaining arousal/alertness, is involved in selective attention and the sleep–wake cycle and controls habituation. The midbrain also controls the orienting reflex.

- The cerebellum consists of two hemispheres, each comprising three layers of cells, including Purkinje cells, which can connect with a greater number of neurons than any other kind of brain cell. It plays a vital role in the co-ordination of voluntary muscle activity, balance and fine movements; damage can cause hand tremors, loss of balance and co-ordination. Complex movements involved in skills are performed by the cerebellum acting like an 'automatic pilot'.

- The midbrain, pons and medulla oblongata together make up the brainstem. The pons connects the two halves of the cerebellum and is crucial for integrating the movements of the two sides of the body. The medulla, the oldest part of the brain, is an extension of the spinal cord and contains vital reflex centres for breathing, cardiac function, swallowing, vomiting, coughing and so on.

- The spinal cord is encased in the vertebrae and is the main communication cable between the CNS and the PNS. Messages enter and leave via 31 pairs of spinal nerves, each containing both motor and sensory neurons for most of their length; but at the junction with the cord itself, the nerve divides into the dorsal root (sensory neurons) and the ventral root (motor neurons).

- The spinal reflex arc, such as the knee-jerk reflex, is the basic functional unit of the NS but most spinal reflexes are more complex than this, involving a motor, sensory and interneuron and two synapses.

- There is considerable evidence, such as from the study of stroke victims, that the two cerebral hemispheres are functionally different (functional lateralization). In the case of language, the left hemisphere is dominant in most right-handed people. However, some people seem to have much more lateralized brains than others and others display bilateral representation. Left-handed people are less likely than right-handed, and women are less likely than men, to show lateralization.

- Lateralization does not usually develop until about age five. Children show considerable recovery from brain injury if it is not too extensive or if it occurs on one side only; this plasticity is especially evident in the case of speech. This supports Lashley's laws of mass action and equipotentiality. It is also consistent with the principle of multiple control.

- Split-brain patients have undergone commissurotomy, in which the corpus callosum has been cut, making the two hemispheres functionally separate. In a typical split-brain experiment, participants sit in front of a screen with their hands free to handle objects that are behind the screen but obscured from sight; while fixating on a spot in the centre of the screen, words are briefly flashed on the screen so that they are only 'seen' by the right hemisphere. They are then asked to select an object with the left hand and to say what word appeared on the screen.

- The findings from split-brain studies have led to the view that each hemisphere constitutes a separate mind or sphere of consciousness; the left is specialized for analytic and logical thinking, processes information sequentially and in a linear way, while the right is specialized for synthetic thinking and processes information more diffusely and more holistically.

- The abnormality of the brains of split-brain patients prior to surgery makes generalizing these results more difficult and each hemisphere plays some role in the functions normally attributed to the other. For example, while the right hemisphere lacks the left hemisphere's ability to name and articulate what has been experienced, it has considerable language understanding.

- An alternative to the 'two minds' interpretation is that the brain is organized in the form of modules which work in parallel and often non-consciously; the left hemisphere tries to make interpretations of what these modules are doing. Another alternative is the view that the two hemispheres form part of a highly integrated system, with most tasks involving both 'left' and 'right' skills.
- The autonomic nervous system (ANS) comprises the sympathetic branch (controlling the 'fight or flight' syndrome) and the parasympathetic branch; these work in essentially opposite ways but both are equally necessary for homoeostasis. The ANS works either by direct neural stimulation of body organs or by stimulating the release of hormones; in both cases, the process is orchestrated by the hypothalamus.
- Hormones are released directly into the bloodstream and so their effect is much slower than that of neurotransmitters; this makes hormones better suited to communicating steady, relatively constant messages over extended periods of time, as in the body changes in puberty.
- The pituitary gland produces the largest number of different hormones and controls the secretion of several other endocrine glands. The posterior pituitary transmits hormones thought to be made in the hypothalamus (oxytocin, vasopressin and antidiuretic hormone), while the anterior pituitary is stimulated by the hypothalamus to produce its own hormones (growth hormone/somatotropin, gonadotrophic hormones, thyrotrophic hormone, lactogenic hormone/prolactin and adrenocorticotrophic hormone.
- The adrenal medulla secretes adrenaline and noradrenaline which are the transmitters for the sympathetic branch of the ANS; the adrenal cortex secretes adrenocorticoid hormones/corticosteroids, such as cortisol and hydrocortisone, which are important in coping with stress.

GLOSSARY

Ablation Surgical removal (either through cutting or burning) of parts of the brain.
Absolute refractory period The 1–2 millisecond interval following the firing of a neuron before another impulse can pass (regardless of the strength of the triggering stimulus). The stronger the stimulus, the shorter the interval before the next impulse (*the relative refractory period*).

Action potential The electrochemical signal/impulse which passes down the axon when the inside of the cell momentarily changes from being negatively to being positively charged.

All-or-none rule The presence or absence of an action potential, regardless of the intensity of the triggering stimulus.

Autonomic nervous system (ANS) Branch of the PNS which links the viscera (smooth-muscled organs) and the CNS. The sympathetic branch operates under catabolic conditions (when energy is being used, e.g. 'fight or flight'), while the parasympathetic branch operates under anabolic conditions (when energy is being restored).

Biopsychology The study of the biological bases/physiological correlates of behaviour; a branch of neuroscience ('brain sciences').

Central nervous system (CNS) The brain and spinal cord.

Contralateral control Each hemisphere's control of the activity of/receipt of information from the opposite side of the body. The crossing over (corticospinal decussation) takes place in the medulla.

Functional lateralization The control of particular psychological functions and abilities by one or other hemisphere.

Law of equipotentiality Lashley's claim that corresponding parts of the brain are capable of taking over the function normally performed by a damaged area.

Law of mass action Lashley's claim that the effects of brain damage (for example, on learning) depend on how much is damaged.

Lesion method deliberate damage made to parts of the brain.

Localization of brain function The control of particular psychological functions and abilities by particular regions of the cortex.

Motor aphasia Loss of ability to produce speech due to damage to Broca's area. Also called expressive aphasia.

Neuromodulators Chemicals which 'prime' neurons for responding to later stimulation by a neurotransmitter. They include neuropeptides, notably enkephalins and endorphins (opioids).

Neuropsychology The study of the behavioural deficits produced in people by brain damage, especially in the neocortex.

Neurotransmitter A chemical messenger, stored in synaptic vesicles in the presynaptic membrane; molecules are released across the synaptic cleft whenever an action potential occurs. Examples are serotonin, dopamine, adrenaline and ACh.

Peripheral nervous system (PNS) All the 12 pairs of cranial nerves and 31 pairs of spinal nerves radiating from the CNS to the entire body. It subdivides into the somatic nervous system (SNS) and the autonomic nervous system (ANS).

Physiological psychology Manipulation of the nervous system through surgical, electrical or chemical means (invasive methods) under strictly controlled conditions; used mainly with non-human animals.

Principle of multiple control The claim that any particular part of the brain is likely to be involved in the performance of many different types of behaviour.

Psychopharmacology The study of the effects of drugs on behaviour (especially psychoactive drugs, such as stimulants, depressants and hallucinogens) and how these are mediated by changes in neural activity.

Psychophysiology The use of non-invasive methods to study the physiology of psychological processes, such as attention, emotion, information processing and mental disorders.

Receptive aphasia Loss of ability to understand language due to damage to Wernicke's area.

Somatic nervous system (SNS) Branch of the PNS which receives sensory information from the external world and sends signals to the striped skeletal muscles involved in voluntary movements.

Split-brain patients People, usually epileptics, who have undergone a commissurotomy in which the corpus callosum is cut, so that the two hemispheres are no longer connected.

Summation The combined effect of all the excitatory and inhibitory synapses converging on a particular neuron and exceeding the threshold of firing.

Threshold of response The minimum intensity of a stimulus needed to produce an action potential.

FURTHER READING

Pinel, J.P.J. (1993) *Biopsychology,* 2nd edn. Boston: Allyn and Bacon. An excellent, detailed, but very readable text, with excellent illustrations.

4 STATES OF CONSCIOUSNESS

INTRODUCTION AND OVERVIEW

For the first 30 or so years of its life as a separate discipline, pioneered by figures such as William James and Wilhelm Wundt, psychology took consciousness (i.e. conscious human experience) as its subject matter and introspection (observation of one's own mind) was the primary method used to investigate it (see Chapters 1 and 2). This interest in consciousness is not surprising given psychology's philosophical roots (see Chapter 2) (and James was primarily a philosopher). Then John Watson declared his Behaviourist Manifesto in 1913, according to which psychology must discard all reference to consciousness; any term denoting mental processes was to be banned on the grounds of being unscientific because inaccessible to an observer.

With the 'cognitive revolution' (usually dated at 1956; see Chapter 14), the 'mind' has once again become respectable, legitimate subject matter. Chapters 8–14 illustrate one of the ways in which the mind is studied (i.e. cognitive processes, with information processing as the central approach) and in this chapter we shall examine an alternative, although overlapping way of conceptualizing and studying the mind.

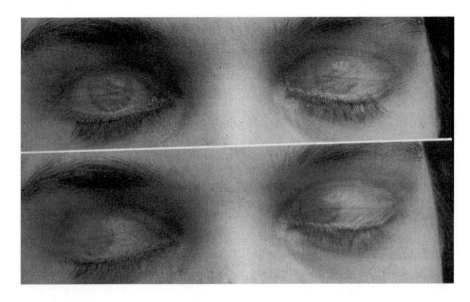

We shall look at some of the different ways in which 'consciousness' has been used by psychologists and the relationship between consciousness and arousal, alertness and attention. A considerable amount of research into sleep as a state of consciousness has taken place since the 1950s, using objective measures of physiological activity in relation to subjective experiences, in particular dreaming. According to Hobson (1995), the rhythm of rest and activity ('... the primordia of sleeping and waking ...') represents one of the most universal and basic features of life; so the study of sleep is of interest to biologists as well as to biopsychologists. We shall discuss theories of the function of sleep and the nature of dreaming. We shall also discuss meditation and hypnosis.

MEANINGS OF 'CONSCIOUSNESS'

Consciousness is usually discussed in relation to humans and nothing more will be said in this chapter about the consciousness of other species, but because of the diverse ways in which psychologists have studied the topic (including animal experiments), some of what we say will have direct bearing on animal consciousness. We should also note that a distinction is usually made between *consciousness*, which is shared by human and non-human animals, and *self-consciousness*, which is unique to human beings (and possibly the higher primates; see Chapters 21 and 26).

We use the term 'consciousness' in a variety of ways in everyday language, for example:

- When we are awake we are conscious but when we are asleep, in a coma or we have been 'knocked out' by a punch to the head, we are unconscious (the term 'unconscious' is often reserved for the last two examples but, as we shall see, when we fall asleep, we do 'lose consciousness').
- When we do something consciously we do it deliberately or knowingly, but to do something automatically or without having to think about it (e.g. an experienced driver or typist) is to do it unconsciously.
- Advertising campaigns (e.g. anti-drug) are aimed at increasing public consciousness or awareness of the subject of the campaign.

Similarly, psychologists and other scientists interested in trying to understand consciousness define it in different ways. Freud, for example, saw consciousness as a whole comprising three levels:

1 the *conscious*, which refers to what we are fully aware of at any one time;
2 the *preconscious*, which refers to what we could become aware of quite easily if we switched our attention to it;
3 the *unconscious*, which refers to what we have pushed out of our conscious minds, through repression, making it extremely inaccessible, although it continues to exert an influence on our thoughts, feelings and behaviour (see Chapter 29).

Although most psychologists would agree that thoughts, feelings, memories, etc. differ in their degree of accessibility (that is, they could all be placed on a continuum of consciousness, with 'completely conscious' at one end and 'completely unconscious' at the other), most would not accept Freud's formulation of the unconscious (based on repression). Indeed, other psychodynamic theorists, in particular Jung, disagreed fundamentally with Freud's view of the unconscious. Although he admitted the existence of repression, Jung distinguished between the personal and the collective unconscious, the former being based on the individual's personal experiences, the latter being inherited and common to all human beings (see Chapter 29).

Rubin and McNeil (1983) define consciousness as 'our subjective awareness of our actions and of the world around us'. Ruch (1984) gives it a much more cognitive emphasis by defining it as:

> ... a process of experiencing the external and internal environment in ways that separate immediate stimuli from immediate responses, that is, stimuli are processed and 'understood' in some sense as against leading directly to mechanical responses.

Both definitions share a view of consciousness as pointing inwards, towards our thoughts, feelings, actions, etc. and outwards, towards external, environmental events (including other people); this mirrors the 'mental' orientation of Wundt and James and the other early psychologists and cognitive psychologists since the mid-1950s and Watson's (and Skinner's) behaviourist orientation respectively.

CONSCIOUSNESS, AROUSAL AND ALERTNESS

Objective physiological measures, such as electroencephalograms (EEGs), electromyograms (EMGs), electrooculograms (EOGs) (see below), breathing and heart rates and other correlates of consciousness, are often described as measures of level of *arousal* or *alertness*. Both subjectively and in terms of overt behaviour, there is an obvious difference between being sleepy and being wide awake in terms of degree of arousal or alertness; less obvious are the smaller changes which occur during normal wakefulness and which are of two kinds – tonic and phasic – mediated by different brain systems (Lloyd *et al.*, 1984).

● Tonic alertness

Changes in tonic alertness reflect intrinsic (and usually quite slow) changes of the basic level of arousal throughout a 24-hour period (or even across a lifetime) and so are closely related to various biological rhythms, in particular the *circadian rhythm* (see below). It was originally thought that the reticular formation (RF) or reticular activating system (RAS) was solely responsible for arousing and maintaining consciousness (in Chapter 3 the RAS was described as a 'consciousness switch'). For instance, if the brainstem is severed below the RAS, the animal will be paralysed but will remain fully alert when awake and will show normal sleep–wake EEG patterns, but if it is sectioned above the RAS, it will fall into a state of continuous slow-wave sleep.

Moruzzi and Magoun (1949) found that electrical stimulation of the RAS of sleeping cats woke them up, in anaesthetized cats it produced long-lasting signs of arousal in their EEGs, and in cats that were not anaesthetized, the effect of RAS stimulation was to produce behavioural signs of arousal, alertness and attention. According to Moruzzi and Magoun, sleep occurs when the activity of the RAS falls below a certain critical level; in sleep, sensory input to the RAS is reduced and the electrical activity sweeping from the

RAS up through the cortex drops below the level required to keep us awake (Diagram Group, 1982).

However, it is now known that other brain structures (both in the thalamus and hypothalamus) are involved in the sleep–wake cycle and the co-ordination of all these systems is necessary for the initiation and maintenance of conscious awareness. Both during wakefulness and sleep, there are periodic, fairly predictable changes in the degree of alertness; the daytime changes are governed by a *diurnal rhythm* and the sleep (night-time) changes by an *ultradian rhythm*.

● Phasic alertness

Changes in phasic alertness involve short-term, temporary variations in arousal, over a period of seconds, initiated by novel and important environmental events. An important component of these changes is the *orienting response* to arousing stimuli (which involves a decrease in heart rate and breathing rate, pupil dilation, tensing of the muscles and characteristic changes in the EEG, which becomes desynchronized). If the stimuli are continuously presented, the orienting response is replaced by *habituation,* whereby the person or animal stops responding to them (see Chapter 3). Habituation is, in fact, a form of *adaptation*; it is more important from a survival point of view to respond to novel stimuli rather than constant ones and since most stimuli are relatively constant, we need to be able to attend selectively to those which are different and/or unexpected. It is the changing aspects of the environment which demand, and usually receive, our attention and the nervous systems of animals and humans have evolved so as to make them especially responsive to change.

CONSCIOUSNESS AND ATTENTION

Another way in which experimental psychologists have studied consciousness is through the concept of attention. Although consciousness is difficult to describe because it is fundamental to everything we do (Rubin and McNeil, 1983), one way of trying to 'pin it down' is to study what we are paying attention to, that is, what is in the forefront of our consciousness and, according to Allport (1980a), 'attention is the experimental psychologist's code name for consciousness'.

● Focal attention

Focal attention (or focal awareness) is what we are currently paying deliberate attention to and what is in the centre of our awareness (this corresponds to Freud's 'conscious'); all those other aspects of our environment, or our own thoughts and feelings which are on the fringes of our awareness but which could easily become the object of our focal attention, are within our *peripheral attention* or awareness (which corresponds to Freud's 'preconscious'); see Chapter 11.

We do seem capable of doing many things quite unconsciously (i.e. automatically, without having to think about what we are doing) and this perhaps is best illustrated by our perceptual abilities. It is difficult to imagine what it would be like if we were aware of how we perceive. For example, to select consciously one version of the ambiguous lady cartoon (see Fig. 9.13), we must either know that there is a young and an old lady 'in' the picture or we must have already perceived both versions (in which case, how did the original perception come about?). You may have had difficulty yourself perceiving the old lady if your immediate perception was of the young lady, even though you consciously 'searched' for and tried to see the alternative version. (This underlines the very important difference between conception and perception.)

Using a rather different (but popular) example, something which we normally do quite automatically (such as walking down stairs) might well be disrupted if we try to bring it into focal awareness. Again, this makes sense in terms of freeing us to attend to those environmental events which are unfamiliar or threatening in some way; if we had to think about our bodily movements when walking, this would add to the long list of sources of stimulation competing for our attention! (see Chapter 11). Perhaps only when first negotiating stairs as a toddler did we ever have to attend focally to ascending and descending them; but even with skills which do require focal attention when they are first acquired (e.g. driving, playing the piano), once they have been mastered, they become automatic and, as Lloyd *et al.* (1984) put it, unconscious processes seem to be 'precipitates' of earlier conscious processes.

Nisbett and Wilson (1977) go so far as to claim that all psychological activities (including social behaviour) are governed by processes of which we are unaware. If people are asked about what they think governed their behaviour after participating in a social psychology experiment, the answers they give do not usually correspond very well with the explanations which psychologists offer for the same behaviour (and which they believe are the real reasons). Nisbett and Wilson argue that our belief that we can account for our own behaviour ('commonsense' or intuitive explanations) is illusory because what really guides our behaviour is not available to consciousness (compare this with Freud's distinction between 'our' reasons and 'the reasons'; see Chapter 29): we do not have direct or 'privileged' access to our cognitive processes themselves , only to the products or outputs of those processes. However, as we saw in Chapter 1, many psychologists take the view that people are psychologists and that commonsense explanations may be as valid as theoretical, scientific ones (Joynson, 1974; Heather, 1976), which seems to be in direct conflict with Nisbett and Wilson.

THE FUNCTIONS OF CONSCIOUSNESS

Like perception, many cases of problem solving seem to involve processes which are 'out of consciousness'; for example, answers often seem to 'pop into our head' and we do not know how we reached them. If what is important is the solution (as opposed to the process involved in reaching it), then consciousness may be seen as incidental to information processing (consistent with Nisbett and Wilson's view). However, while perception and other basic cognitive and behavioural processes may not require consciousness, they are usually at least accompanied by consciousness and if (as far as we know) most other species lack it (or at least our kind of consciousness), then we can infer that it evolved in human beings for some purpose.

The complexity of our nervous system which makes our consciousness possible provided our ancestors with the flexibility of behaviour which helped them survive. However, it is less obvious whether consciousness was itself adaptive or simply a side-effect or byproduct of a complex nervous system. Some psychologists and biologists believe that consciousness is a powerful agent for controlling behaviour which has evolved in its own right; accordingly, non-conscious problem-solving systems are seen as the servants of consciousness; they are guided and integrated by consciousness but carry out automated routines (Ruch, 1984). According to Hilgard's (1977) 'neo-dissociation' theory of hypnosis (see below), the consciousness which solves a problem may be different from that which reports the solution; neither is 'higher' or 'lower' than the other, they are simply different. This is consistent with the work on split-brain patients (discussed in Chapter 3).

Humphrey (1986, 1993) argues that if consciousness (what he calls the 'inner eye') is the answer to anything at all, it must be to a biological challenge which human beings have had to meet, namely the human need to understand, respond to and manipulate the behaviour of other human beings: ' ... The first use of human consciousness was – and is – to enable each human being to understand what it *feels* like to be human and so to make sense of himself and other people *from the inside*' (Humphrey, 1993). This inner eye allowed our ancestors to raise social life to a new level, so that consciousness is essential for human social activity; we are natural psychologists in a way that species lacking consciousness cannot be (see Gross, 1995).

● Two kinds of consciousness

As we saw in Chapter 3, the two cerebral hemispheres are specialized (although they share the potential for many functions and both participate in most psychological activities), so that each is dominant with respect to particular functions.

Ornstein (1986) believes that these two modes of operation represent two distinct modes of consciousness; in daily life we normally just alternate between them and, although they might complement each other, they do not readily substitute for one another (as when you try to describe a spiral staircase or how you tie a shoelace).

Galin and Ornstein (1972; cited in Ornstein, 1986) recorded changes in participants' EEGs when presented with either verbal or spatial tasks: on verbal tasks, alpha rhythms (associated with a waking adult with the eyes closed) in the right hemisphere increased relative to the left, while on spatial tasks, the reverse was true. The appearance of alpha rhythms indicates a 'turning off' of information processing in the area of the brain involved so, on verbal tasks, information processing is being turned off in the right hemisphere, which is the side of the brain not being used (as if to reduce the interference between the two conflicting modes of operation of the two hemispheres).

Similarly, people with damage to the left hemisphere have greater problems with consciously executed writing, while those with right hemisphere damage have greater problems with more automatic writing, such as signing their name. This suggests that the left hemisphere may be more involved in highly conscious processes which require intentional behaviour and the focusing of attention, while the right may be more involved with automatic or unconscious actions and more sensitive to material outside the conscious focus of attention.

CONSCIOUSNESS AND THE ELECTROENCEPHALOGRAM (EEG)

As we saw in Chapter 3, a major method (since the 1930s) of studying the working of the brain is to monitor its electrical activity; exactly the same information can be used to throw light on consciousness, because particular patterns of electrical activity are correlated with other indices of arousal and alertness.

Electroencephalography (literally, 'electric-in-head writing') detects the output of minute electrical 'ripples', caused by changes in the electrical charges in different parts of the brain (usually the synchronized activity of large groups of neurons). Although there are characteristic patterns which are common to all individuals of a particular age or developmental stage, an individual's brain activity is as unique and distinctive as their fingerprints.

The electroencephalogram (EEG) has wires, an amplifier, electromagnetic pens and paper revolving on a drum. One end of each wire is attached to the scalp (with the help of special jelly) and the other to the amplifier, which can register impulses of 100 microvolts (1/10,000 of a volt) or less and magnifies them 1 million times; the impulses are traced on paper by pens and appear as rows of oscillating waves (see Fig. 4.1). The waves vary in frequency and amplitude:

● *Frequency* is measured as the number of oscillations per second – the more oscillations, the higher the frequency. One complete oscillation is a cycle and the frequency is expressed as cycles per second (cps) or hertz (Hz).
● *Amplitude* is measured as half the height from the peak to the trough of a single oscillation. Frequency is the more important of the two measures.

The four major types of wave (measured in frequency) are described in Box 4.1.

Computerized electroencephalography has recently been used to detect evoked potentials, minute voltage changes induced in the brain by fairly

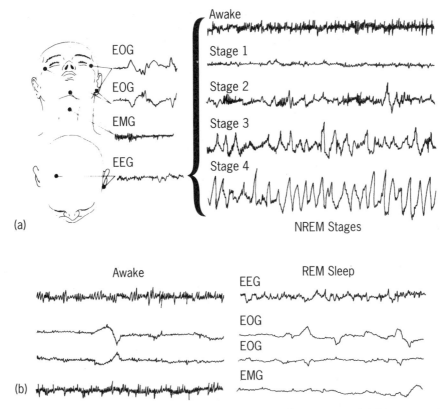

FIGURE 4.1 *Comparison of physiological measures for different types of sleep. (a) The non-rapid eye movement (NREM) stages are represented in typical order of appearance; in reality each one gradually blends into the next. (b) Rapid eye movement (REM) sleep is in some ways similar to waking but in others quite different; the EEG is more similar to waking than to that of any NREM stage and REMs are present, but the body muscles are deeply inhibited*

BOX 4.1	The four major types of brain wave (measured in frequency)

- *Delta* (1–2 Hz) These are found mainly in infants, sleeping adults or adults with brain tumours.
- *Theta* (3–7 Hz) These are found mainly in children aged 2–5 years and in psychopaths; they may be evoked by frustration.
- *Alpha* (8–12 Hz) These are found mainly in adults who are awake, relaxed and whose eyes are closed. They are most reliably recorded from the back of the scalp.
- *Beta* (13 Hz and over) These are found mainly in adults who are awake and alert, whose eyes are open and who may be concentrating on some task or other. They are most reliably recorded from the front and middle of the scalp and are related to activity in the sensory and motor cortex.

specific visual and auditory stimuli; often the average of a number of responses to similar kinds of stimuli is used (the *average evoked potential* (AEP)) in order to amplify the signal-to-noise ratio. AEPs are used to study newborns, some children with learning problems, patients in a coma, stroke victims, tumour patients and patients with multiple sclerosis, but for certain brain conditions, brain scanning has largely replaced the EEG in the past few years (Diagram Group, 1982); see Chapter 3.

SLEEP

● Sleep and the circadian rhythm

Blakemore (1988) asks what would happen if we removed all the external cues to the nature of time (or *zeitgebers*) both natural and manufactured (clocks, mealtimes, day and night). Could our bodies still have their own rhythmic existence?

In 1972, Michel Siffre, a young French cave explorer, spent seven months underground with no cues as to the time of day. He had adequate food, water, books and exercise equipment and his only contact with the outside world was via a telephone which was permanently staffed. He was linked up to a computer and video camera by which scientists on the surface could monitor his physiological functions and state of mind. He organized his life into a fairly normal pattern of alternating periods of activity and sleep and his 'day' was broken up by a normal meal pattern. The remarkable finding was that he chose to live a 25-hour day (not 24). For every real day that passed, he rose an hour later – the clock in his brain was running a little slow:

> For all the advances of modern society, we cannot afford to ignore the rhythms of the animal brain within us, any more than we can neglect our need to breathe or eat. Without the biological clocks in our brains, our lives would be chaotic, our actions disorganized. The brain has internalized the rhythms of Nature, but can tick on for months without sight of the sun ... (Blakemore, 1988)

Most animals display a *circadian rhythm* ('circadian' from the Latin *circa dies* = 'about one day'), a periodicity or rhythmical alternation of various physiological and behavioural functions, synchronized to the 24-hour cycle of light and dark. So, during a 24-hour period, there is a cycle of several physiological functions (e.g. heart rate, metabolic rate, breathing rate, body temperature) which all tend to reach maximum values during the late afternoon and early evening and minimum values in the early hours of the morning. (The disruption of circadian rhythms is discussed in Chapter 6 as a source of stress.)

Rats, like humans, have an inherent rhythm of about 25 hours which dictates their cycle of sleep and waking if they are put in the dark. This internal clock is as reliable and regular as most manufactured ones – the rhythm deviates by no more than a few minutes over several months. So how is the internal (biological) clock reset each day to the cycle of the real world and where is the clock to be found?

It is thought to be a tiny cluster of neurons, the *suprachiasmatic nucleus* (SCN), situated in the medial hypothalamus. For example, damage to the SCN in rats produces complete disappearance of the circadian rhythm – the sleep–wake cycle, eating and drinking, hormone secretion, etc. become completely random during the course of the 24-hour period.

Although most of what is known about the SCN is based on experiments with non-human animals using ablation (see Chapter 3) and although we cannot make direct electrophysiological recordings from the human brain, anatomical studies show that humans have an SCN (Empson, 1993).

The SCN is situated directly above the optic chiasma (the junction of the two optic nerves en route to the brain; see Chapter 8). A tuft of thin nerve fibres branches off from the main nerve and penetrates the hypothalamus above, forming synaptic connections with cells in the SCN. This anatomically insignificant pathway is the link between the outside world and the brain's own clock (Blakemore, 1988). So the retina projects directly onto the SCN, which ensures that the sleep–wake cycle is tuned to the rhythm of night and day – if this connection with the retina is severed, the cycle goes 'haywire'.

So, in human adults at least, it appears that the circadian rhythm does not depend primarily on external cues (although, presumably, it can be adjusted if necessary, using these external cues). But how do we know that the rhythm hasn't been learnt as a result of years of environmental experience?

● The physiology of sleep

When darkness falls, the eyes indirectly inform the *pineal gland* (the 'third eye'), a tiny structure at the top of the brainstem which keeps track of the body's natural cycles and registers external factors such as light and darkness. The pineal gland secretes *melatonin* in response to darkness, making us drowsy; Downing (1988) calls melatonin 'nature's sleeping draught'. Melatonin is a hormone that affects brain cells which produce *serotonin*, a sleep-related transmitter substance. In turn, serotonin is concentrated in the *raphe nuclei* (situated near the pons), which secrete a substance that acts on the RAS to induce light sleep. Jouvet (1967) found that lesions of the raphe nucleus in cats produce severe insomnia and naturally occurring lesions in humans seem to have a very similar effect.

Another important sleep centre is the *locus coeruleus* (LC), a tiny structure (on each side of the brainstem) whose cells are rich in noradrenaline, which it is thought might be involved in inducing active (or rapid eye movement, REM) sleep (see below). The LC may well serve many of the functions previously attributed to the RAS; although it has only two inputs (one excitatory, one inhibitory), its outputs spread to all parts of the brain. Studies with rats suggest that its function might be to increase the animal's sensitivity to environmental stimuli, i.e. to regulate its level of vigilance, rather than arousal as such (Empson, 1993).

Finally, there is evidence that a substance called *factor S* accumulates gradually in the brains of animals while they are awake and that, if this is removed from the fluid surrounding the brain and transferred into another animal, sleep will be induced. It is likely that factor S contributes to our feelings of sleepiness (Diagram Group, 1982).

● Varieties of sleep and the ultradian rhythm

In the typical sleep laboratory, a volunteer settles down for the night with not only EEG wires attached but also wires from an electrooculogram (EOG) (*oculo* meaning 'eye') and from an electromyogram (EMG) (*myo* meaning 'muscle'; see Fig. 4.1).

A typical night's sleep comprises a number of *ultradian cycles* (approximately 90 minutes duration) and each cycle consists of a number of stages which are described in Table 4.1.

The cycle then goes into reverse, so the sleeper re-enters stage 3 and then stage 2, but instead of re-entering stage 1, a different kind of sleep (*active sleep*) appears. Pulse and respiration rates increase,

as does blood pressure, and all three processes become less regular. EEGs begin to resemble those of the waking state (showing that the brain is active, supported by increases in oxygen consumption, blood flow and neural firing in many brain structures) and yet it is even more difficult to wake someone from this kind of sleep than the deep stage 4 sleep and for this reason it is referred to as *paradoxical sleep* (Aserinsky and Kleitman, 1953).

Another characteristic of active sleep are the rapid eye movements (the eyeballs moving back and forth, up and down, together) under the closed lids (hence *rapid eye movement* (REM) sleep). Finally, while the brain may be very active, the body is not; REM sleep is characterized by muscular paralysis (especially the muscles of the arms and legs) so that all the tossing and turning and other typical movements associated with sleep in fact only occur during stages 1–4 which, collectively, are called *non-rapid eye movement* (NREM) *sleep*. (The distinction between REM and NREM sleep was originally made by Dement and Kleitman, 1957.)

Another feature of REM sleep is the appearance of *pontine-geniculo-occipital* (PGO) *spikes/waves*, which are generated in the pons and travel through the lateral geniculate nucleus (LGN), the part of the thalamus that processes visual information which is

---

After we shut our eyes and prepare for sleep, alpha waves (8–12 Hz) begin to punctuate the high frequency beta waves (13 Hz and over) of active wakefulness. The transitional stage from being awake to entering stage 1 sleep is called the *hypnagogic period* and is sometimes included in stage 1.

Stage 1: When we first fall asleep, the EEG is irregular and lacks the pattern of alpha waves which characterizes the relaxed waking state. There is at first a reduction in frequency of the alpha waves, which are then replaced by a low voltage, slow theta wave (3–7 Hz), accompanied by slow rolling eye movements. The heart rate begins to slow down, the muscles relax and it is easy to be woken up.

Stage 2: This is a deeper state of sleep than stage 1 but it is still fairly easy to wake someone. The EEGs show bursts of activity called *sleep spindles* (1–2 second waxing and waning bursts of 12–14 Hz waves). There are also occasional sharp rises and falls in amplitude of the whole EEG (*K complexes*), which last up to about two seconds.

Stage 3: Sleep is becoming deeper, the spindles disappear and are replaced by long slow delta waves (1–2 Hz) for up to 50 percent of the record. The sleeper is now quite unresponsive to external stimuli and so is difficult to wake; heart rate, blood pressure and body temperature all continue to drop.

Stage 4: The sleeper now enters *delta sleep* (deep or 'quiet sleep') (50 percent and more of the record consists of delta waves) and will spend up to 30 minutes in stage 4; about an hour has elapsed since stage 1 began. It is difficult to wake the sleeper – as in stage 3 – but something highly personally relevant (e.g. a baby crying) can rouse even a deep sleeper

Stages 2–4 collectively are called *slow-wave sleep* (SWS); as we pass from Stage 1 to 4, the frequency of the waves decreases and the amplitude/voltage increases. Also, muscle tone steadily declines.

TABLE 4.1 *A typical night's sleep: The 4 stages of non-rapid eye movement (NREM) sleep*

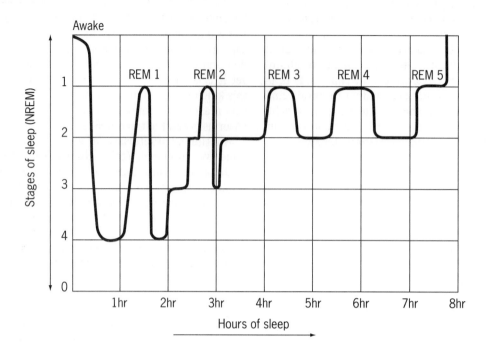

FIGURE 4.2 *A typical night's sleep (note the disappearance of stages 3 and 4 and the relative increase in the length of REM periods)*

then sent to the visual cortex (see Chapter 8). They were discovered in the 1960s by Jouvet working with cats: they typically occur in bursts, starting just before the other signs of REM sleep and continuing throughout the REM period and they often seem to precede individual eye movements. According to the *activation–synthesis model* of dreaming (see below), PGO activity is the prime source of dreaming experience (Empson, 1993).

After 15 minutes or so in REM sleep, we re-enter NREM sleep (stages 2–4) and so another ultradian cycle begins. However, with each 90 minute cycle (of which there are 4–5 on average per night), the duration of the REM sleep increases and that of NREM sleep decreases; the first cycle normally provides the deepest sleep and the shortest REM period and, as the night goes on, we spend relatively more time in REM and less in NREM sleep. In later cycles, it is quite common to go from REM to stage 2 and then straight back into REM sleep (bypassing stages 3 and 4) and natural waking usually occurs during a period of REM sleep (see Fig. 4.2).

This sleep pattern is not only typical but seems to be universal. However much people's lifestyles may vary during the day, sleep proceeds in the same regular pattern, obeying the same rules. There are no apparent differences between men and women, introverts and extroverts, the more and less intelligent, although there are important developmental changes; the most striking thing about sleep patterns within a broad age group, however, is how remarkably uniform they are (Empson, 1993). Also:

> ... While most all-night recording experiments are over brief periods (of up to a week), some very extended studies have been done and there is no evidence that the patterns of sleep we observe over short periods (after the first night) are in any way peculiar to the unfamiliarity of the laboratory environment. (Empson, 1993)

● Sleep and dreaming

About 80 percent of the time, sleeping volunteers, if woken during REM sleep, will report that they have been dreaming, while being woken from NREM sleep only produces a 15 percent 'dreaming rate'.

REMs seem to be a very reliable indicator that someone is dreaming (especially in combination with the fairly high frequency and low amplitude brain waves). To some extent, the nature of the REMs reflects the content of the dream (for instance, dreaming about a tennis match and a back-and-forth movement of the eyes – as would happen in waking life), but it is now generally agreed that there is no one-to-one correspondence between dream action and eye movement, although cues about the general nature of the dream can often be gleaned from the REM record. For example, if the eye movements are small and sparse, we are probably having a peaceful, fairly passive dream, whereas larger and more continuous REMs suggest a more active and emotional dream (Faraday, 1972). (Faraday notes that research has shown that movements of the inner ear also occur during sleep and may be correlated with the auditory content of dreams.)

Not only is there a difference in the number of times that dreams are reported when participants are woken from REM and NREM ('orthodox') sleep, but the kind of mental activity associated with each is very different. Participants woken from NREM sleep tend to report dreams which are shorter, less vivid and less visual than REM dreams and, in fact, they often describe themselves as having been 'thinking' rather than dreaming; NREM sleep is also associated with sleepwalking (somnambulism), sleeptalking and some types of nightmare.

REM sleep has been called 'dream sleep' or the 'D-state' and some have gone as far as to call it the 'third state of existence', because it is in many ways as different from NREM sleep (the 'S-state') as it is from waking. This leads us to ask why we need to dream.

But is it possible that the difference between dreams in REM and NREM sleep is actually an artefact of the ability to *recall* dreams following the 'rude awakening'? Beaumont (1988) argues that being awoken from NREM sleep may lead to the dream being forgotten before the participant is sufficiently awake to report it (since this is a deeper kind of sleep in which the brain is much less active), while being woken from REM sleep may allow the ongoing dream to be remembered and then reported (here the brain is much more active). Clearly, if this is so, then we have stumbled upon a major confounding variable which challenges the very basis of much of the sleep/dream research. There is evidence that an appreciable amount of mental activity does occur during NREM sleep and there are no completely consistent differences between dream reports obtained when participants are woken from either kind of sleep.

However, evidence from studies of sleep deprivation does seem to support the view of REM sleep as a dream-state sleep quite independently of the sleeper's report of having dreamed (or not).

● The effects of sleep deprivation – the REM rebound

As far as rats are concerned, long-term sleep deprivation is definitely not good for their health: it causes impaired thermoregulation, metabolic dysfunction and eventually death (Hobson, 1995). For example, Rechtschaffen *et al.* (1989a, b) selectively deprived rats of either REM or both REM and NREM sleep; after a week of total deprivation, they showed progressive weight loss even in the face of increased food intake. This became more pronounced after two weeks and after four weeks, they died. During this time, body weight plummeted while food consumption soared and body temperature became progressively more unstable.

However, in the case of human beings, studies have been remarkably consistent in failing to show any marked changes in heart and breathing rates, blood pressure, skin conduction, body temperature, EMG or EEG, even when deprivation continues for up to 200 hours (Pinel, 1993). Webb and Bonnet (1979) (cited in Lahey, 1983) limited participants to two hours sleep on one particular night; they suffered no ill effects the following day but that night they fell asleep more quickly and slept longer than usual. Longer periods of sleep deprivation may result in some unpleasant psychological effects but people are remarkably able to do without sleep. Webb and Bonnet gradually reduced the length of sleep in a group of volunteers from eight to four hours per night over a two-month period with no detectable effect.

However, when sleep is *abruptly* reduced (as, say, in the case of hospital doctors, who may be on duty for 72 hours at a stretch), the effects are rather more serious. Irritability, intellectual inefficiency and an intense fatigue and need for sleep ensue, which are more or less the same effects as are produced by depriving participants of approximately two hours of REM sleep (but otherwise allowing them to sleep normally); the following night, there is an increase in REM sleep (so as to compensate for the previous night's loss), which is called the *REM rebound*. When volunteers are able to get by on greatly (but *gradually*) reduced amounts of sleep, it is apparently because they pack their two hours of REM tightly into the sleeping time they do have (thus reducing the amount of NREM sleep in between their dreams); when sleep is abruptly reduced, there is no time to adopt this additional dreaming-sleep pattern.

There has been a good deal of support for the REM rebound phenomenon. For example, Dement (1960) woke participants from their REM sleep on five successive nights (while a control group were only woken during NREM sleep periods). When they were allowed to sleep uninterruptedly, they did 60 percent more dreaming until they had made up their lost REM time. For as many as five nights following their REM deprivation, they spent more time in REM sleep than usual and on some nights they doubled their REM time. These results were consistent with the idea that REM sleep and the dreaming associated with it are especially important, perhaps representing the most important function of sleeping (Empson, 1993).

In cats too, it seems that NREM alone is inadequate. Jouvet (1967) placed cats on a small island surrounded by water and allowed them either to remain awake or to go into NREM sleep. However, whenever they entered REM sleep, they tended to slip into the water and woke up; prolonged deprivation of REM sleep produced abnormal behaviour, including hypersexuality, and, eventually death.

Dement also reported that his participants tended to become paranoid while deprived of REM sleep, ascribing sinister motives to the researcher, developing all kinds of unreasonable suspicions and even hallucinating, as well as becoming nervous, irritable and unable to concentrate. However, he later maintained that these symptoms were not reliably caused by lack of REM sleep and that they were more likely to have been caused by the researcher's expectations, communicated (ironically) through concern for their welfare; Dement had told his participants what he thought the probable results would be and that a psychiatrist would be on duty all the time. After the third day, little sleep at all was achieved (since they had more frequent REM periods and so were woken more frequently) and the symptoms were the combined effects of total sleep deprivation and suggestion. (This is a good example of demand characteristics; see Chapter 2.) Dement replicated his earlier study in 1965 and found no evidence of psychiatric symptoms with REM sleep deprivation.

According to Pinel (1993), the most convincing evidence that REM sleep deprivation is not severely debilitating comes from study of the effects of *tricyclic antidepressants* (see Chapter 31); these selectively block REM sleep but patients who regularly take large doses, and so get little REM sleep for months at a time, experience no serious side-effects that can be attributed to their REM loss.

● Theories of sleep. What is it for?

Our planet is a dangerous place; there is ruthless competition for limited resources and only the fittest survive. And yet all the most advanced animals, normally alert, shrewd, watchful, drop their defences to sleep. Even human beings, the most spectacularly successful species, spend one-third of their lives more or less paralysed and senseless.

If sleep is so risky, it must bestow a huge benefit on animals that indulge in it, or it would have been eliminated by the powerful forces of natural selection. Animals that did not need sleep would surely have evolved and prevailed over their sleepy competitors ... sleep must surely be valuable ... (Blakemore, 1988)

According to Empson (1993), even though physiologists have made great strides in understanding sleep mechanisms, this hasn't greatly helped in understanding what sleep is *for*; only a larger understanding of the role of sleep in human functioning (including its psychology) can answer that question.

While sleep has the features of a *primary drive* (such as hunger and sex), what makes it unique as a primary biological drive is that the need for sleep is reflected in decreased levels of arousal and its satisfaction is associated with further decreases. Sleep, therefore, represents a serious exception to the view that organisms seek a single optimal level of (non-specific) arousal (Lloyd *et al.*, 1984) (see Chapter 5).

The restoration theory

The restoration theory (Oswald, 1966) maintains that both REM and NREM sleep serve a restorative, replenishing function. NREM restores bodily processes which have deteriorated during the day, while REM sleep is a time for replenishing and renewing brain processes through the stimulation of protein synthesis.

The theory also accounts for the large proportion of babies' sleeping time spent in REM sleep; only gradually do we acquire sleep–wake patterns which we associate with the circadian rhythm. During much of their first year, babies are sleeping for about 18 hours per 24, by about 12 months they have two periods of sleep every 24 hours (one day time and one night-time) and not until about five years has an 'adult' pattern become established (probably as a result of both environmental and maturational factors). Within these changing patterns, the relative proportions of REM and NREM sleep change quite dramatically: whereas the newborn spends half of its

18 hours in REM sleep, adults usually spend only one-quarter of their eight hours in REM sleep. The developing brain needs a great deal of protein synthesis for cell manufacture and growth and REM sleep helps to achieve this (see below).

What evidence is there to support Oswald? In patients who survive drug overdoses and withdrawal and other brain 'insults', such as intensive electroconvulsive therapy (see Chapter 31), there are prolonged increases in REM sleep, which are consistent with the estimated time for the half-life of proteins in the brain, i.e. in a six-week period, about half the brain's total protein is replaced and this is the approximate length of the increased REM period (somewhere between six and eight weeks).

Nocturnal secretion of growth hormone (which produces bodily protein synthesis) depends on uninterrupted stage 4 sleep and in adults, a chronic lack of normal stage 4 is found in fibrositis sufferers, whose EEG during sleep is characterized by 'alpha–delta' patterns, a mixture of sleeping and waking EEG; this is typically experienced as fitful, 'unrestorative sleep'. The disturbance of stage 4 in healthy volunteers produces the symptoms of fibrositis.

According to Empson (1993), all this evidence is consistent with a general anabolic function for sleep: REM sleep subserving brain growth, repair and memory functions and slow-wave (stage 4) sleep promoting bodily growth and repair. However, cell repair goes on 24 hours a day (even though it reaches a peak at night), but a more serious objection to the theory is that, far from being a restful state, REM sleep is an active state (at least as far as the brain is concerned) and probably burns up a substantial amount of energy. Indeed, blood flow to the brain increases during REM sleep and this would actually *prevent* high levels of protein synthesis. In view of this kind of evidence, Oswald (1974) maintains that both types of sleep are involved in the process of restoring bodily tissue.

Evolutionary theory

Different species characteristically sleep for different periods. Those at risk from predators, which cannot find a safe place to sleep or which spend large parts of each day searching for and consuming food and water (such as herd animals), sleep very little (e.g. zebras sleep for only 2–3 hours per day) while predators that sleep in safe places and can satisfy their food and water needs fairly quickly sleep for much of the day (e.g. lions often sleep more or less continuously for 2–3 days after gorging themselves on a kill).

The evolutionary theory of sleep (Meddis, 1975, 1977) maintains that sleep is an advantage because it keeps the animal immobilized for long periods and being immobile, it will be less conspicuous to would-be predators and, therefore, safer. The safer the animal from predators, the longer it is likely to sleep. But, as we noted above, a preyed-upon species may sleep for short periods because of the constant need to stay on guard against predators. This means that whatever sleep pattern a species has, it can be explained in 'evolutionary' terms. Long sleep could serve the function of staying out of the way of predators as well as its opposite (i.e. not needing to stay alert because the animal has no natural predator), while short sleep can also serve the function of protection against possible predators. This is an example of *non-falsifiability* (see Chapter 2).

Meddis also argues that the long sleep periods of babies have evolved to prevent exhaustion in their mothers and, in this sense, sleep is still functional – at least for mothers of babies and small children! As to the need for immobilization, this no longer seems viable as an explanation of sleep in humans and so may be regarded as a remnant of our evolutionary past. A variant of the evolutionary theory is *hibernation theory*, which maintains that elaborate mechanisms of sleep have evolved solely to keep us quiet in the dark; animals hibernate to conserve energy and to stay out of possible danger during the winter months.

Any evolutionary theory (like Meddis's) must be able to explain the variety of lifestyles across modern species, involving very great differences in total sleep time. Why has this particular instinct become a universal, while others are as diverse as the habitats of the creatures exhibiting them? Why does almost every known animal show the same patterning of sleep (although there is a great variation in total quantity)? Despite enormous differences in lifestyle, all mammals seem to have to find time for a minimum amount of sleep. If there was no other evidence for the absolute necessity of sleep, the finding that the porpoise has evolved a system of sleeping with the two sides of its brain alternately would be eloquent enough on its own (Empson, 1993).

Empson (1993) characterizes Meddis's theory as a 'waste of time' theory; he claims that it is contradicted by the fact that it is universal among animals, as well as by the finding that sleep deprivation can be fatal (Kleitman, 1927; Rechtschaffen *et al.*, 1989a, b).

A weaker version of the 'waste of time' theory was proposed by Horne (1988), who distinguishes between *core sleep* (which is necessary) and *optional sleep* (which isn't). Evidence from sleep deprivation experiments (both partial and total) shows that accumulated sleep 'debts' are made up to some extent on recovery nights, but never entirely. For example, REM rebound accounts for approximately 50 percent of the REM sleep lost during selective awakenings; so only the first three hours of sleep are truly necessary (core sleep) and the rest is optional (having no physiological function). In animals which sleep longer than three hours, it seems to reduce energy expenditure and keep them immobile.

Empson (1993) criticizes the distinction for being not very useful – most of us eat more than we absolutely need to in order to keep body and soul together, both in variety and quantity, but no biologist would say that, because a proportion of feeding was optional that feeding was only partly functional:

> ... sleep appears to be ubiquitous and necessary; it is a complex function of the brain involving far-reaching changes in body physiology as well as brain physiology. It is difficult to believe that it does not have an important function and the restorative theories provide a coherent account of what this might be. (Empson, 1993)

Hobson's levels

Although not a discrete theory, Hobson (1995) proposes that the function of sleep can be analysed at different levels:

1 At the *behavioural* level, sleep suppresses activity at a time (night-time/darkness) when the chances of finding food or a mate are relatively low; also, such activities have a high energy cost in warm-blooded animals when the temperature is low. This makes sleep behaviourally very efficient. In addition, the enforced nature of sleep and its relation to resting activity serves to unite animals in a family or pair-bonded situation which may encourage sexual behaviour and promote care and development of the young. Hobson finds it incredible that ethologists have failed to recognize and systematically study sleep as a form of behaviour.

2 At the *developmental* level, a function of REM sleep for developing organisms (as we noted when discussing restoration theory earlier) could be the guaranteed activation of neural circuits underlying crucial, survival behaviours. From an evolutionary point of view, there would be great advantages gained from ensuring the organized activation of the complex systems of the brain before the organism has developed the ability to test them in the real world. In both the developing and the adult

animal, REM sleep could constitute a form of behavioural rehearsal.

3 At the *metabolic* level, the recurring cycles of NREM/REM sleep are accompanied by major changes in all the body's physiological systems. NREM involves decreased blood pressure, heart and breathing rates, as well as the release of growth and sex hormones from the pituitary (consistent with the restoration theory), while REM involves increased blood pressure, heart and breathing rates, as well as penile erection and clitoral engorgement.

DREAMING

While a great deal has been discovered about the physiology of sleep and psychologists have developed reliable techniques for establishing when people are likely to be dreaming, there has been no equivalent progress in understanding the nature of dreams. A starting point must be to establish clearly how dreaming differs from waking consciousness.(Empson, 1993).

● So how do dreams differ from waking consciousness?

Empson (1993) identifies four such differences:

1 Dreams happen to us as opposed to being a product of our conscious control: ' ... When dreaming we are the spectators of an unfolding drama, and only rarely does one have the impression of being in control ... ' 'Lucid dreaming', in which the dreamer 'knows' they are dreaming and decides how the dream plot should develop, is very rare.

2 The logic of waking consciousness is suspended (as indeed Freud believed; see Chapter 29).

3 Dreams reported in the laboratory tend to be mundane and lack the bizarre quality of 'normal' dreams; this is probably because only the strangest experiences are remembered when we wake normally after a night's sleep. Also, Faraday (1972) points out that the last dreams of the night tend to be more vivid than earlier ones.

4 Dreams are certainly odd. Empson refers to what has been called the singlemindedness of dreams: the imagery of the dream totally dominates the dreamer's consciousness while, when awake, we normally reflect on the stream of consciousness as it goes on and can be aware of one thing but simultaneously imagine something else.

Hobson (1995) describes dreams as typically including hallucinations (predominantly visual, although auditory, tactile and movement sensations are also prominent, with taste and smell under-represented and pain extremely rare), delusions (believing that the events are real), cognitive abnormalities (such as the occurrence of events that would be physically impossible in the real world), emotional intensification and amnesia (we forget over 95 percent of our dreams), which have led to a comparison between dreams and abnormal states of mind, as in schizophrenia and organic mental disorders, in particular delirium (see Chapter 30).

● Theories of dreaming: why do we dream?

Reorganization of mental structures

According to Ornstein (1986), REM sleep and dreaming may be involved in the reorganization of our *schemas* (mental structures) so as to accommodate new information. People placed in a 'disturbing and perplexing' atmosphere for four hours just prior to sleep (asked to perform difficult tasks with no explanation) spend longer in REM sleep than normal; REM time also increases after people have had to learn complex tasks.

This may explain why REM sleep decreases with age; as we have seen, newborns spend 50 percent of their (approximately) 18 hours of sleep in REM (active) sleep compared with 25 percent spent by adults in their (approximately) eight hours. Oswald suggested that babies' brains need to process and assimilate the flood of new stimuli pouring in from the outside world and that this is (partly) achieved through REM sleep.

Activation–synthesis model (Hobson and McCarley, 1977; McCarley, 1983)

The cortex is highly active during REM sleep, although it receives little external stimulation. Although the motor cortex is highly active (generating activity which would normally produce bodily movement), these commands don't reach the muscles of the limbs but are 'switched off' at a relay station at the top of the spinal column, so we are effectively paralysed (*output blockade*). (This explains the loss of tone in the neck muscles under the chin, one defining feature of REM sleep.)

Not only is the cortex isolated (unable to control muscles) but there is also inhibition of incoming signals produced by the sensory systems (so perceptions of the 'real' world are selectively attenuated) (*input blockade*). Hindbrain and midbrain structures, normally associated with relaying sensory information to the cortex, spontaneously generate signals (*PGO waves*; see above) responsible for cortical activation and are also indistinguishable from signals which would normally have been relayed from the eyes/ears. This activity is under the control of a periodic triggering mechanism in the pontine brainstem (top of the spinal column, at the base of the brain). Giant cell activity precedes REMs in animals and there is no evidence that cortical activity can influence these cells (Empson, 1993).

So the brain is very active during REM (*activation*) and dreams are a conscious interpretation (*synthesis*) of all this activity. The cognitive system, which organizes sensory information into the simplest meaningful interpretation when we are awake, processes all the internally generated signals as if they came from the outside world. In combination with oculomotor activity, PGO waves are sent to the visual and association cortex and the thalamus; what we call a dream is the simplest way of interpreting these internally produced signals by combining them into some meaningful whole. It is the unusual intensity and rapidity of brain stimulation (often involving simultaneous activation of areas not usually activated together when we are awake) which account for the highly changeable and sometimes bizarre content of dreams. According to Hobson (1995), ' ... the now autoactivated and autostimulated brain processes these signals and interprets them in terms of information stored in memory'.

Many dream experiences do seem to reflect the brain's and body's state (and so can be thought of as interpretations of these physical states), e.g. being chased, locked up or frozen with fear may well reflect the blocked motor commands to the muscles, floating, flying and falling experiences may reflect vestibular activation and the sexual content of dreams may reflect vaginal engorgement and penile erection (Ornstein, 1986).

Evaluation of the activation–synthesis model

- A similar neural theory (Rose, 1976) explains dreaming in terms of the relatively random inputs which trigger memory sequences at a time when 'waking' control mechanisms (which normally keep a fairly close watch over these sequences) are either reduced or absent.
- Perhaps there is a sense in which we dream instead of acting (maybe suggesting the need for

rest/restoration for the body). Cats with brain-stem injury act out their dreams by, for example, chasing the mouse of their dreams while ignoring the real mouse in their cage, i.e. they are not paralysed in the normal way during REM sleep.

- Dreams are often incoherent and bizarre; abrupt shifts in imagery may simply be the brain 'making the best of a bad job in producing partially coherent dream imagery from the relatively noisy signals sent up ... from the brain stem' (Ornstein, 1986).

- Does the truth of the activation–synthesis model exclude other theories of dreams? Not necessarily: it may account for 'where dreams come from' but not 'what dreams are for'. Psychological theories focus on the synthesis component (much more than on the activation component) and try to explain its significance for the dreamer. Freud's is probably the best known (and most controversial); dreams are wish fulfilments and, like Jung, he saw *symbolism* as being of central importance; both saw dreams as putting the dreamer in touch with parts of the self usually inaccessible during waking life (see Chapter 29). Hall (1966) saw dreams as 'a personal document, a letter to oneself' and, like Jung, advocated the study of dream series rather than single isolated, dreams.

- The activation–synthesis model has been elaborated by Crick and Mitchison (1983); according to them, we dream in order to forget! The cortex (unlike other parts of the brain) is composed of richly interconnected *neuronal networks* in which each neuron has the capacity to excite its neighbours. Memories are encoded in these networks, with neurons and their many synapses representing different features of memory; these networks are like spider's webs – when one point is excited, a pulse travels throughout the network.

The problem with such a network system is that it malfunctions when there is overload of incoming information (e.g. fantasies, obsessions, hallucinations). To deal with such overload, the brain needs a mechanism to 'debug' or tune the network; this would work best when the system is isolated from external inputs and would have to be able to randomly activate the network in order to eliminate spurious (or 'parasitic') connections (Atkinson *et al.*, 1990). Learning requires constant modification of the brain circuits. Whatever rule is used by the brain to guide the strengthening/weakening of

synaptic connections, it surely makes mistakes, in the form of '... odd backwaters of neural circuitry ... little unwanted pieces of modified circuitry that would disturb the progress of normal learning, if left unpruned ... ' (Blakemore, 1988).

The random pontine brainstem activity which stimulates the cortex during REM sleep has the function of erasing memories which have become 'parasitic' – interpretations which, whatever their origin, have no place in our latest view of the world and are redundant but persistent:

> ... Dreams are, quite literally, a kind of shock therapy, in which the cortex is bombarded by barrages of impulses from the brainstem below, while a different mode of synaptic modification ensures that the unwanted elements of each circuit are unlearned. The perceptual content of dreams would, then, correspond to the internally generated patterns of activity set up in the cerebral cortex as a result of the barrage from below. The fact that the narrative of a dream, though sometimes bizarre, is at least coherent (the dream tells some sort of story) must surely reflect interpretative processes, at higher levels of the brain, probably in the frontal lobes, trying to impose order or plausibility on the chaos of activity in the sensory area of the cortex ... (Blakemore, 1988)

REM sleep is, then, the mechanism for 'cleaning up' the network; we awake with a cleaned-up network and the brain is ready for new input. Trying to remember our dreams, according to Crick and Mitchison, may not be a good idea as they are the very patterns of thought the system is trying to tune out. For others, especially psychoanalysts and other psychodynamic psychologists, it is essential that we do remember our dreams so that we can try to understand their meaning.

● What would happen to an animal that couldn't dream?

According to Crick and Mitchison, its cortex would fill up rapidly with the unwanted junk of unrepresentative experience. In order to survive without dreams, an animal would need a much larger cortex. Two higher mammals which seem to have no REM sleep are the spiny anteater (an Australian marsupial) and the dolphin; both have an abnormally large cortex for their size and evolutionary development. Their oversized brains are needed to accommodate all their useless memories since they have little or no ability to unlearn them (Blakemore, 1988).

HYPNOSIS

Rubin and McNeil (1983) define hypnosis as ' ... an altered state of consciousness, in which the hypnotized subject can be influenced to behave and to experience things differently than she would in the ordinary waking state'. Elsewhere, they define it as '... a state of increased suggestibility (or willingness to comply with another person's directions) that is brought about through the use of certain procedures by another person, the hypnotist'. These two definitions relate to the views of 'state' theorists and 'non-state' theorists respectively, between whom there is a continuing debate.

● Hypnosis as an altered state of consciousness

According to Hilgard (1975), hypnosis is:

> ... the state of consciousness caused in a subject by a systematic procedure for altering consciousness, usually carried out by one person (the hypnotist) to alter the consciousness of another (the subject).

A typical hypnotic procedure is described in Box 4.2.

FIGURE 4.3 *Scene from a hypnotic procedure*

The most influential state theory is Hilgard's *neo-dissociation theory* (1974, 1977), according to which there exist multiple systems of control that are not all conscious at the same time. Normally, these cognitive control systems are under the influence of an 'executive ego' that controls and monitors the other systems. But in hypnosis, the hypnotist takes much of that away such that, in response to suggestion, motor movements are experienced as involuntary, memory and perception are distorted and so on. To demonstrate this principle, Hilgard refers to the *hidden*

BOX 4.2   The hypnotic procedure

The typical procedure begins with a 10–15 minute induction ritual of verbal suggestions designed to induce a passive, sleeplike (but waking) state. For the next 45 minutes or so, the participant is asked to perform a number of tasks, which may be based on the Stanford Hypnotic Susceptibility Scales (Weitzenhoffer and Hilgard, 1959). These scales mainly involve:

(i) *ideomotor* ('thought–movement') tasks, such as 'posture sway' (falling without forcing), 'arm immobilization' (the arm rises less than one inch in ten seconds) and 'verbal inhibition' (not being able to give his/her name within ten seconds).

They also include:

(ii) *sensory hallucinations* (e.g. imagining a fly is in the room and behaving in some appropriate way);

(iii) *temporary amnesia* (only being able to recall three or fewer items from a longer series);

(iv) *age regression* (e.g. the participant is taken back in time and asked to describe events and people in his/her childhood); and

(v) *posthypnotic suggestion* (e.g. after being 'awakened', the participant opens the window when the hypnotist gets out his/her handkerchief, a signal given to the participant while in the hypnotic state).

The more items the participant 'passes', the higher the *susceptibility score*; using these scales, men and women have been found to be equally hypnotizable while people with vivid imaginations and those who feel comfortable taking orders from others tend to be hypnotized more easily. Susceptibility seems to reach a peak up to the age of ten and declines steadily after that. About 5 percent of the population can be induced to a deep hypnotic trance and about 10 percent do not respond at all, with the majority falling somewhere in between these two extremes.

observer phenomenon. This was first demonstrated in relation to the experience of pain and the claimed ability of hypnosis to bring about pain relief (*hypnotic analgesia*) represents some of the strongest evidence in support of the state theory.

Hypnosis and pain

Hilgard claims that hypnosis has been successfully used with dental patients, burn victims, women in childbirth and terminal cancer patients to reduce their pain. One experimental technique for studying pain is the *cold pressor response*, where participants immerse their arm in freezing water and are asked to report how painful it is over a 30-second period. 'Hypnotized' participants are told that the experience will not be painful and usually report very little or no pain (a 'slight tingle', for example). However, physiological measures of pain (such as heart rate and blood pressure) are usually extremely high and when the 'hidden observer' is contacted (by placing a hand on the person's shoulder), it often reports a higher level of pain, only slightly less than the same person reports when not hypnotized (Hilgard, 1978). This occurs because pain *is* experienced during hypnotic analgesia, but the 'part' experiencing pain is dissociated from awareness by an 'amnesic barrier'.

● The non-state view: trance or role playing?

Non-state theorists would argue that the reports of the 'hidden observer' simply reflect what participants think they are expected to say as conveyed by the experimental instructions (Spanos, 1989; Wagstaff, 1981).

Using a wide variety of measures (such as EEG, blood pressure and chemistry, breathing rate, skin temperature and resistance), it is clear that the hypnotic state is not a state of sleep and most researchers (both state and non-state) seem to agree that there is no unique correlate of the hypnotic state. Physiological changes do occur following hypnotic induction, but they seem to be explicable in other ways, such as changes normally associated with changes in attention or a state of relaxation. Does this mean that hypnosis is simply a state of relaxation? While at first they might appear to be different, since participants can appear 'hypnotized' when engaged in strenuous physical activity (such as pedalling an exercise bike), it has been argued that one can still be relaxed (cognitively) even when engaged in physical activity (Edmonston, 1991, cited in Wagstaff, 1995). Perhaps the main problem with the idea that hypnosis is just relaxation is that it does not adequately explain various hypnotic phenomena, such as hallucinations and amnesia (Fellows, 1990, cited in Wagstaff, 1995).

Some of the evidence seems quite convincing; for example, touching the skin with a pencil may cause blisters if the participant has been told it is red hot. Telling participants that they have just eaten a large, fatty meal causes the body to secrete lipase (a fat-digesting enzyme); when they think the meal was rich in protein, pepsin and trypsin are secreted (protein-digesting enzymes). Hypnosis can also affect breathing rate, heart rate and various kinds of glandular activity (Diagram Group, 1982).

Although they differ in what they emphasize, non-state theorists argue that hypnotic phenomena can be readily explained in terms of more everyday psychological concepts and processes, drawn mainly from social and cognitive psychology, such as attitudes, expectancies, beliefs, compliance, imagination, attention, concentration, distraction and relaxation (Wagstaff, 1995). To many non-state theorists, the hypnotic situation is best seen as a social interaction in which both hypnotist and participant enact roles: the participant's role is to present themselves as 'hypnotized' based on previous expectations and cues available in the immediate situation. This does not mean that hypnotic behaviours are necessarily faked or sham (although some may be); the participants may become very involved in the role and may use a variety of strategies to successfully produce the desired effects.

Wagstaff (1991, cited in Wagstaff, 1995) has proposed that hypnotic responding may involve three stages:

1 the participant figures out what is expected on the basis of previous experience and the hypnotist's instructions;
2 the participant uses imaginative or other strategies to try to bring about the suggested effects;
3 if the strategies fail or are judged to be inappropriate, the participant either gives up or reverts to compliance or faking.

● How do we choose between the state and non-state theories?

The problem of compliance or faking is recognized by both state and non-state theorists, largely as a result of the pioneering work of Orne (1959, 1966), who stressed the extent to which any experimental situation is primarily a social situation (see Chapter 2). For many non-state theorists, compliance is an integral component of much hypnotic responding (Spanos, 1991; Wagstaff, 1991), which has led to their use of 'hypnosis' and 'hypnotic' in a purely operational way, i.e. a 'hypnotic' group is one that has been given a hypnotic induction procedure and 'hypnotized'/'hypnotically susceptible' participants are those who tend to respond positively to suggestions in what is defined as a hypnotic context. From this non-state perspective, then, 'hypnosis' exists but (only) as a label for a context rather than as an altered state of consciousness.

There are enormous methodological problems involved in trying to choose between the state and non-state viewpoints. The basic approach has been to compare participants who have been given a hypnotic induction procedure with various control groups designed to test alternative non-state explanations. A key design is Orne's (1979) 'real-simulator', in which 'hypnotized' participants are compared with those instructed to fake excellent hypnotic participants, but without any explicit instructions as to how this is to be achieved. Another popular control group is Barber's (1969) 'task-motivated' group, in which participants are told to try hard to imagine and experience hypnotic suggestions, but without a formal induction procedure. The logic behind these approaches is that if no differences emerge between the hypnotic and control groups, then it is unnecessary to propose a special hypnotic process or state to explain the responses of the hypnotic group; on the other hand, if differences are found, then it is reasonable to assume that hypnotic induction may add a special element (Wagstaff, 1995).

When 'real-simulator' or 'task-motivated' designs are used, some of the early claims for hypnosis are usually not supported; for example, there is no conclusive evidence that hypnotic participants are superior on a range of tasks including appearing blind, colourblind, deaf, acting like a child and recalling childhood events, lifting weights, learning and remembering . Even when tasks involve dangerous or antisocial activities (e.g. picking up a poisonous snake, putting one's hand into a glass of concentrated acid and throwing the acid at the experimenter, peddling heroin, mutilating the Bible and making slanderous statements), simulators are just as likely, occasionally even more so, to perform them as 'reals' (Wagstaff, 1981, 1989). This demonstrates the lack of 'transcendent properties' of hypnosis.

One of the most controversial issues is that of 'trance logic' (Orne, 1959, 1979), which refers to the observation that 'hypnotized' individuals , unlike simulators, seem not to need logical consistency and can tolerate contradictory responses. For example, when 'reals' are shown an empty chair and it is suggested to them that there is a person sitting on it, they tend to report that the image is transparent, i.e. they can see the chair through the person; but simulators tend to report an opaque or solid image, i.e. they cannot see the back of the chair. In terms of neo-dissociation theory, this could reflect the possibility that, during hypnosis, different 'parts' of consciousness are being accessed alternately or simultaneously. However, not all 'reals' display trance logic and later research has produced mixed results.

● Conclusions

According to Wagstaff (1995), research and debate in hypnosis flourishes, but we seem to be no further forward in deciding whether there is an altered state of consciousness that we can call 'hypnosis'. Traditionally, the topic was something of an embarrassment to psychologists, better left to psychiatrists or parapsychologists, but the high standard of research in this area should place it firmly within mainstream psychology.

MEDITATION

Meditation has been defined as a clearing or emptying of the mind through a narrowly focused thought process; the special word or phrase (the *mantra*) used in Transcendental Meditation is an example of this.

According to Burns and Dobson (1984), the different forms and varieties of mediation are all ways of achieving an inner quiet and a heightened awareness and can be thought of as the art of being in the 'here and now'.

Meditation, originally practised in India and other Eastern countries, became popular in the West in the late 1960s, as part of the 'flower power' phenomenon which was, among other things, a rejection by the youth of traditional materialistic values which were seen as severely limiting people's individual freedom. Since then, meditation has been studied by psychologists as a state of consciousness (and a technique for bringing that about) using fairly traditional, scientific techniques.

There are many reported cases of yogis who manage to control their autonomic functions quite voluntarily through meditation, enabling them to endure all kinds of injury and deprivation without suffering any apparent physical harm. A famous example is Ramanand Yogi, a 46-year-old Hindu who, in 1970, through the practice of yoga ('union'), managed to survive for over five hours in a sealed metal box. He was filmed and various physiological measurements were taken while he was inside: he used just over one-half of the calculated minimum amount of oxygen needed to keep him alive (and during one hour, he was averaging just one-quarter).

The secret of yogis' science-defying feats seems to be the trancelike state which is induced by meditation techniques, whereby the body's metabolism is slowed down considerably; others believe that meditation (like hypnosis) is simply an elaborate way of inducing quite normal relaxation responses and that there is nothing unique or magical about meditation.

Over and above any religious beliefs surrounding it, meditation requires:

● a quiet environment where the meditator will not be interrupted;
● a mental device on which to concentrate (such as the mantra, which is repeated continuously);
● a passive attitude as opposed to an active, striving one;
● a comfortable position.

Regular use of this simplified form of meditation encourages a relaxation response, which triggers the parasympathetic branch of the ANS. Ornstein (1986) has suggested that meditation is primarily a right hemisphere 'intuitive' activity and practising meditation for long periods may induce a relative shift in hemisphere dominance. Some research has shown that meditators do better than non-meditators on certain right hemisphere tasks, such as remembering musical tones, but they do worse on verbal problem-solving tasks. However, we cannot be sure that these differences arose because of meditation as the evidence is correlational: there may be other important differences between meditators and non-meditators apart from meditation.

What yogis seem to be able to do through meditation can apparently be achieved in a much more scientifically orientated way through biofeedback (see Chapters 6 and 7).

CHAPTER SUMMARY

● Psychology began life as a separate scientific discipline by focusing on consciousness, studied through introspection. Behaviourism then declared consciousness to be unsuitable subject matter for a scientific psychology. However, since the cognitive revolution, cognitive processes and consciousness, in various guises, have once more become important and popular topics.

● The term 'consciousness' is used in a variety of ways in everyday language and psychologists also define it differently. Freud distinguished three levels of consciousness: conscious, preconscious and unconscious. Most psychologists do not accept Freud's view of the unconscious as based on repression, but they would accept that there is a continuum of consciousness. Jung distinguished between the personal and collective unconscious.

● Consciousness can be seen as pointing inwards towards our thoughts and feelings and outwards towards external events.

● Arousal/alertness can be defined objectively in terms of various physiological measures, such as EEGs, EOGs, EMGs, breathing and heart rates; these are correlates of consciousness.

● Changes in tonic alertness are closely linked to various biological rhythms, especially the circadian rhythm. The RF/RAS plays an important role in arousing/maintaining consciousness; sectioning an animal's brainstem above the RAS will cause continuous slow-wave sleep and electrically stimulating the RAS of sleeping cats wakes them up. If sensory input to the RAS falls below a certain level, we will fall asleep.

● Other brain structures in the thalamus and hypothalamus are also involved in the sleep–wake cycle. Alertness changes in fairly predictable ways both during wakefulness (controlled by a diurnal rhythm) and sleep (ultradian rhythm).

● Changes in phasic alertness involve changes in the orienting response to arousing stimuli; this is complemented by habituation, which is a form of adaptation. From a survival point of view, it is changing aspects of the environment that need to be attended to and both human and non-human nervous systems have evolved such that they are especially responsive to change.

● Consciousness can be experimentally pinned down by studying attention, which can be focal or peripheral. Perception seems to take place largely unconsciously (i.e. outside of focal attention) and many behaviours are carried out quite automatically, allowing us to consciously attend to the unfamiliar or threatening aspects of our environment.

- Nisbett and Wilson claim that all psychological activities are governed by processes that are not available to consciousness; we only have access to the products of those processes and this suggests that consciousness may be incidental to problem-solving. However, these unconscious processes are usually accompanied by consciousness, implying that it must have evolved for some purpose; they may be the servants of consciousness.

- According to Humphrey, the 'inner eye' of consciousness evolved to allow our ancestors to relate to others based on understanding others' experience of being human; consciousness makes human beings natural psychologists.

- The specialized functions of the two cerebral hemispheres represent distinct modes of consciousness: the left hemisphere is more involved in highly conscious processes that require focal attention, while the right hemisphere is more involved with automatic/unconscious behaviour.

- The electroencephalogram (EEG) detects the minute output of large groups of neurons and magnifies them 1 million times; the impulses are traced on paper and appear as rows of oscillating waves, which vary in frequency (measured in hertz (Hz)) and amplitude. The four major types of brain wave are delta (1–2 Hz), theta (3–7 Hz), alpha (8–12 Hz) and beta (13 Hz and over). Computerized electroencephalography measures average evoked potentials (AEPs).

- When Michel Siffre spent seven months underground with no external cues as to the time of day/night, the clock in his brain ran according to a 25-hour cycle. Most animals display a circadian rhythm which is synchronized to the 24-hour cycle of light and dark, involving a rhythmical alternation of various physiological and behavioural functions.

- The internal/biological clock is thought to be the suprachiasmatic nucleus (SCN), part of the hypothalamus. If rats' SCN is damaged, the circadian rhythm disappears. It is situated directly above the optic chiasma and there are synaptic connections between the optic nerve and the SCN; the retina projects directly onto the SCN, ensuring that the sleep–wake cycle is tuned to the rhythm of night and day.

- When darkness falls, the pineal gland begins to secrete melatonin, making us drowsy. It affects brain cells that produce serotonin concentrated in the raphe nuclei; they secrete a substance that acts on the RAS to induce light sleep. The locus coeruleus (LC) is rich in noradrenaline which induces REM sleep; it may also play a role in regulating overall level of vigilance. Factor S accumulates in the brain while we are awake and seems to contribute to feelings of sleepiness.

- Sleep is measured in the laboratory using an electrooculogram (EOG) and electromyogram (EMG) as well as an EEG. A typical night's sleep comprises 4–5 ultradian cycles, each consisting of several stages. The transition from being awake to stage 1 is the hypnagogic period, followed by stages 1–4. Stages 2–4 are collectively called slow-wave sleep (SWS) or 'deep' sleep; stages 1–4 are collectively called non-rapid eye movement (NREM) sleep.

- After completion of the first cycle, it goes into reverse, but instead of re-entering stage 1, active sleep appears. Physiological processes increase and EEGs begin to resemble those of the waking state, yet it is more difficult to wake someone than from stage 4 sleep (making it 'paradoxical'), the body is largely paralysed and rapid eye movements can be seen (rapid eye movement (REM) sleep). REM sleep also involves pontine-geniculo-occipital (PGO) waves.

- With each ultradian cycle, the duration of REM increases and that of NREM decreases, so that relatively more time is spent in REM as the night proceeds; this pattern seems to be universal.

- REMs are a very reliable indicator of dreaming and the nature of the REMs to some extent reflects the dream content. Although dreaming does take place during NREM sleep, it is very different from REM dreams; however, this may be due to a difference in the ability to recall dreams when woken from REM and NREM sleep, rather than a difference in the actual dream content.

- Total sleep deprivation in rats causes progressive weight loss and eventual death, but in human beings the effects are much less clear-cut; although sleep-deprived people may experience some unpleasant psychological effects, when this is done gradually, there are relatively few harmful consequences. However, when sleep is abruptly reduced, people are likely to suffer irritability, intellectual inefficiency and an intense need for sleep.

- When sleep is gradually reduced, REM sleep is concentrated into the sleep time available; this is impossible with abrupt and total sleep deprivation.

- Depriving people of REM sleep produces the REM rebound, suggesting that dreaming associated with REM sleep is perhaps the most important function of sleep.

- When Jouvet deprived cats of REM sleep, their behaviour became abnormal and they eventually died. Although Dement originally claimed that people deprived of REM sleep become psychologically disturbed, these results were later explained in terms of the combined effects of total sleep deprivation and suggestion. Tricyclic antidepressants selectively block REM sleep without producing any serious side-effects.

- Psychologists are still very unclear about the functions of sleep. It is unique as a primary biological drive in that the need for sleep is reflected in decreased levels of arousal.

- According to Oswald's restoration theory, REM and NREM sleep help replenish bodily and brain processes respectively This is consistent with the proportion of babies' sleeping time spent in REM sleep and changes in the proportions of REM to NREM sleep as they develop.

- Patients who have suffered brain 'insults' spend longer in REM sleep during a 6–8-week recovery period, which is the time needed for about half the brain's total protein to be replaced. Stage 4 sleep, which is disrupted in fibrositis sufferers, is crucial for bodily protein synthesis; healthy volunteers who are deprived of stage 4 sleep develop symptoms of fibrositis.

- However, cell repair goes on 24 hours a day and the brain is highly active during REM sleep, using up considerable energy and preventing high levels of protein synthesis. Oswald now maintains that both REM and NREM sleep are involved in restoration of bodily tissue.

- According to Meddis's evolutionary theory of sleep, sleep keeps the animal immobilized and so safer from predators, so longer sleep is associated with greater safety. But danger from predators is also associated with shorter sleep, because of the need to stay alert, and longer sleep is also characteristic of certain predators such as lions. Hibernation theory is a variant of evolutionary theory.

- The need for immobilization no longer seems relevant for human beings, but sleep is a universal instinct: despite enormous variations in lifestyles and total sleep time across species, all mammals sleep. This, together with the fatal effects of sleep deprivation, suggest that sleep is more than a 'waste of time'.

- The distinction between core sleep and optional sleep is supported by the finding that accumulated sleep 'debts', following periods of deprivation, are only partly made up on recovery nights; however, this does not imply that sleep is only partly functional.

- Sleep prevents animals from wasting valuable energy in pursuit of food or a mate and so is behaviourally very efficient; it also keeps animals together, encouraging sexual behaviour and care of the young. REM helps to keep active the complex brain systems which underlie survival behaviours and so represents a form of behavioural rehearsal.

- Dreams differ from waking consciousness in several important ways. They happen to us, the logic of waking consciousness is suspended, they are often bizarre and are 'singleminded'; they include hallucinations, delusions, various cognitive abnormalities and are emotionally intense, but we forget about 95 percent of our dreams. Many of these characteristics occur in mental disorders, such as schizophrenia and delirium.

- REM sleep and dreaming may be involved in the reorganization of our schemas so that we can process new information; this is consistent with the high proportion of babies' total sleep time spent in REM sleep and decreases in REM sleep as we get older.

- Although the brain is highly active during REM sleep, we are effectively paralysed (output blockade) and there is also an inhibition of incoming sensory signals (input blockade). PGO waves are spontaneously generated in the pontine brainstem and are indistinguishable from signals normally received from the eyes and ears. This activation of the brain is consciously interpreted (synthesis) in the form of a dream; according to the activation–synthesis model, dreams are the simplest way of interpreting these internally produced signals.

- Cats with brainstem injury act out their dreams, suggesting that we might dream instead of acting. The bizarre nature of dreams may reflect the 'noisy' signals sent up from the brainstem, together with the intense, rapid and simultaneous stimulation of brain areas not usually activated together in waking life.

- Psychological theories of dreams, such as those of Freud, Jung and Hall, focus on the synthesis component, stressing their significance for the dreamer.

- According to Crick and Mitchison, memories are encoded in the cortex's richly interconnected neuronal networks; when there is overload of incoming information, fantasies, hallucinations and other malfunctions occur. The network needs to be 'debugged' and this happens during REM sleep when the random pontine brainstem activity erases 'parasitic' memories; dreams are a way of 'cleaning up' the network and preparing it for new input and so we need to forget our dreams.

- Neither the spiny anteater nor the dolphin has REM sleep and both have an abnormally large cortex for their size; their oversized brains are needed to store all their unlearned, useless memories.

- There is an ongoing debate between state and non-state theorists as to the nature of hypnosis. Hilgard believes that hypnosis is an altered state of consciousness induced in a participant by a hypnotist using an induction ritual of verbal suggestions. Hypnotic susceptibility is measured by how many behavioural items the participant displays from a standardized scale, such as the Stanford Hypnotic Susceptibility Scales, including sensory hallucinations, temporary amnesia, age regression, and posthypnotic suggestion.

- Men and women are equally susceptible and about 85 percent of the population are neither highly susceptible nor highly resistant; susceptibility reaches a peak at the age of ten, then steadily declines.

- Neo-dissociation theory is the most influential state theory. The hypnotist removes much of the normal 'executive ego' control over our multiple cognitive systems which become dissociated from each other; this is shown by the 'hidden observer phenomenon', first demonstrated in relation to hypnotic analgesia. In the cold pressor response, hypnotized participants report little pain, but physiological measures of pain are high and the hidden observer reports pain levels almost as high as the unhypnotized participant.

- Both state and non-state theorists agree that hypnosis is not a sleep state, nor does it have any unique physiological characteristics; the physiological changes that do occur can be explained in terms of changes in attention or a state of relaxation. However, hypnosis seems to involve more than just relaxation, which cannot adequately explain certain hypnotic phenomena, both psychological and physical.

- Non-state theorists explain hypnotic phenomena in terms of everyday psychological processes such as expectancies, compliance and imagination. The hypnotic situation is essentially a social interaction involving the enactment of roles. Participants may become very involved and use various strategies for producing the desired effects; if these fail, they may revert to compliance or faking. Partly because of this, many non-state theorists define 'hypnosis' and 'hypnotic' operationally.

- The methodological problems involved in trying to choose between the state and non-state viewpoints are enormous. Two popular designs that use controls who have not undergone an hypnotic induction procedure are Orne's 'real-simulator' and Barber's 'task-motivated' group; if there are no differences between hypnotic and control groups, then a special hypnotic state is not needed to explain the responses of the former.

- These designs tend to demonstrate lack of 'transcendent properties'. One of the most controversial issues is Orne's 'trance logic', which has produced mixed results.

- Meditation can take different forms, but they share the goal of achieving an inner calm and a heightened awareness. Originating in Eastern culture, meditation is now studied by scientific psychologists as a state of consciousness and a means of bringing that about.

- There are many reported cases of yogis voluntarily controlling their autonomic functions through meditation, enabling them to endure considerable injury but without any apparent harm . This is explained by some in terms of the induced trance-like state, by others in terms of normal relaxation responses, which trigger the parasympathetic branch of the ANS.

- Meditation might be a primarily right hemisphere activity; practising meditation for long periods may induce a relative shift in hemisphere dominance.

GLOSSARY

Circadian rhythm The rhythmical cycle of various physiological and behavioural functions (heart and breathing rate, body temperature, sleep–wake cycle) synchronized to the 24-hour cycle of light and dark. (*circa dies* = 'about one day').

Electrooculogram (EOG) A visual record of eye movements during sleep, especially rapid eye movements (*oculo* = 'eye').

Electroencephalogram (EEG) A visual record of the electrical activity of the brain recorded via electrodes attached to the scalp. The recording apparatus is called an electroencephalograph.

Electromyogram (EMG) A visual record of muscle movements in the face and neck during sleep; (*myo* = 'muscle').

Focal attention What we are currently paying deliberate attention to, what is in the centre of our awareness; contrasted with peripheral attention.

Hidden observer phenomenon In hypnosis, part of the hypnotized participant's mind which appears to become dissociated from the hypnotized part; for example, while the latter reports no pain (in the cold pressor test), the former reports pain. Central feature of Hilgard's neo-dissociation theory.

Hypnagogic period The transitional stage in between being awake and entering stage 1 sleep, characterized by vivid but largely disconnected images and sensations.

Input blockade The inhibition of incoming signals from the sensory systems to the cortex during REM sleep; attenuation of perception of the external world.

Non-rapid eye movement (NREM) sleep Stages 1–4; stages 2–4 are called slow-wave sleep (SWS).

Output blockade The 'switching off' of signals in the motor cortex, preventing them from reaching the muscles; accounts for the paralysis in REM sleep.

Phasic alertness Short-term, temporary variations in arousal, over a period of seconds, triggered by novel and important environmental events. Relates to the orienting response to novel stimuli and habituation to constant, continuously present stimuli.

Rapid eye movement (REM) sleep Active sleep in which the EEG is much like the waking state, physiological processes increase but waking the dreamer is very difficult ('paradoxical' sleep) and the muscles of the limbs are paralysed. Associated with dreaming.

'Real-simulator' Experimental design for studying hypnosis, in which 'hypnotized' participants are compared with control participants instructed to fake excellent hypnotized participants, but without any explicit instructions as to how to achieve this.

REM rebound The tendency for people deprived of REM sleep to spend more time in REM sleep when allowed to sleep normally.

Sleep spindles 1–2 second bursts of 12–14 Hz waves which are characteristic of stage 2 sleep; this is also marked by K complexes, occasional sharp rises and falls in the amplitude of the whole EEG.

'Task-motivated' Experimental design for studying hypnosis, in which 'hypnotized' participants are compared with control participants told to try to imagine and experience hypnotic suggestions but without a formal induction procedure.

Tonic alertness Intrinsic and usually quite slow changes in the basic level of arousal throughout a 24-hour period; related to biological rhythms, especially the circadian rhythm.

Trance logic The observation that 'hypnotized' participants, unlike simulators, appear not to need logical consistency and can tolerate illogical or contradictory responses.

Ultradian rhythm Rhythmical cycle of various physiological and behavioural functions that takes place during the night, controlling the stages of sleep (NREM = stages 1–4 + REM sleep) which alternate in 90-minute cycles. The daytime equivalent is the diurnal rhythm; both last less than 24 hours.

FURTHER READING

Empson J. (1993) *Sleep and Dreaming,* 2nd edn. Hemel Hempstead: Harvester Wheatsheaf. A very thorough discussion of all the major aspects of the topic, including sleep disorders and sleep in animals.

Wagstaff, G. F. (1995) Hypnosis. In Colman A.M. (ed.) *Controversies in Psychology.* Harlow, Essex: Longman. A brief but excellent overview by the UK's leading hypnosis researcher.

5 MOTIVATION

INTRODUCTION AND OVERVIEW

Trying to define motivation is a little like trying to define psychology itself. Taking the layperson's view of psychology as the study of 'what makes people tick' as a starting point, this can be seen as a way of equating psychology with the study of motivation, since motivation, in a general sense, refers to why people act and think as they do, as does the popular definition.

Asking why people do what they do, and the related question of how, is usually interpreted as a question about causes and much of psychology is an attempt to identify the causes of behaviour, both normal and abnormal. Each of the major theoretical approaches, namely the psychoanalytic, behaviourist, humanistic-existential, neurobiological/biogenic and cognitive, tries to account for the causes of human behaviour; the underlying image of human beings implicit in each theory is, in essence, a theory of the causes of behaviour (See Table, 1.1, p. 12).

Motivated behaviour is goal-directed, purposeful behaviour and it is difficult to think of any behaviour (animal or human) which is not motivated in this sense. However, exactly how the underlying motives are conceptualized and how they are investigated depends very much on the persuasion of the psychologist:

- a *psychoanalytic* psychologist will try to discover unconscious motives and wishes (Freud's personality theory is discussed in Chapter 29);
- a *behaviourist* will search for reinforcement schedules. In Chapter 7, we shall discuss laboratory studies of learning and in particular, of conditioning, which dominated academic psychology in America and Britain up to the early 1950s (see Chapters 1 and 2). For Skinner, not only is 'motivation' too mentalistic a term to be acceptable but it is unnecessary, since behaviour can be explained completely in terms of reinforcement schedules, leaving nothing 'behind'. However, not all learning theorists agree with Skinner, including Hull, whose *drive reduction theory* differs from Skinner's ideas in several important ways;

- a *humanistic* psychologist, such as Maslow, will relate behaviour to self-actualization;
- a *neurobiological* psychologist will look for processes taking place in the nervous system, endocrine system and other bodily systems and processes;
- a cognitive psychologist will try to relate behaviour to the person's thinking.

In this chapter, we shall have something to say about all of these theoretical approaches, but much of the detailed discussion of their claims will be found throughout the rest of the book. We shall begin by looking at some specific definitions of motivation and a brief history of the concept, which has its roots in philosophy. We shall then introduce Maslow's *hierarchy of needs*, which is useful as a framework for discussing other theories since it takes such a comprehensive view of motivation as a whole.

We shall then take a detailed look at *drive theories* of motivation (including that of Hull), which had such a major influence in the early days of psychology as a science. In the form of *homeostatic* drive theories, they continue to be discussed and investigated, especially in relation to two biologically crucial drives, namely hunger and thirst. However, as we shall see, even in the case of 'basic' motives like these, cognitive and other individual variables, plus social and cultural and other environmental variables, play a crucial role in influencing our behaviour and those of other animals.

The rest of the chapter will concentrate on *non-homeostatic* needs and drives, including electrical self-stimulation of the brain (ESB), competence motives and cognitive motives. Finally, we shall take a brief look at *social motives*. In all cases, we shall find considerable overlap between the content of this chapter and that of other chapters in the book.

WHAT IS MOTIVATION AND ARE THERE DIFFERENT KINDS OF MOTIVE?

According to Rubin and McNeil (1983), motives are a special kind of cause which ' ... energize, direct and sustain a person's behaviour (including hunger, thirst, sex and curiosity)'. Similarly, 'Motivation refers, in a general sense, to processes involved in the initiation, direction, and energization of individual behaviour ...

(Geen, 1995). The word 'motive' comes from the Latin for 'move' (*movere*) and this is captured in Miller's (1962) definition:

> The study of motivation is the study of all those pushes and prods – biological, social and psychological – that defeat our laziness and move us, either eagerly or reluctantly, to action.

As we noted in the opening section, different schools of thought within psychology look for the causes of behaviour in very different 'places', i.e. they take very different views as to what kind of causes explain human and animal behaviour. These differences indicate that motives may differ with regard to a number of features or dimensions, including: (i) internal or external; (ii) innate or learned; (iii) mechanistic or cognitive; and (iv) conscious or unconscious. A number of attempts have been made to classify different kinds of motives and these loosely correspond to the major psychological theories outlined above.

Murray (1938) identified 20 different human motives (which he called *needs*), including dominance, achievement and autonomy. Rubin and McNeil (1983) classify motives into two major categories: survival or physiological motives and competence or cognitive motives, with social motives representing a third category. Clearly, humans share survival motives with all other animals and, as we shall see below, we also share certain competence motives. But other motives are peculiarly and uniquely human, notably self-actualization, which lies at the peak of a 'hierarchy of needs' in Maslow's (1954) humanistic theory.

● Maslow's hierarchy of needs: a framework for looking at motivation

Although this is commonly discussed in relation to theories of personality (see Chapter 29), it is just as relevant to any discussion of motivation, since it is concerned with needs. (The book in which he first proposed his hierarchy was called *Motivation and Personality*.) According to Maslow, we are subject to two quite different sets of motivational states or forces : (i) those that ensure survival by satisfying basic physical and psychological needs (physiological, safety, love and belongingness, and esteem); and (ii) those that promote the person's self-actualization, i.e. realizing one's full potential, 'becoming everything that one is capable of becoming' (Maslow, 1970), especially in the intellectual and creative domains:

> We share the need for food with all living things, the need for love with (perhaps) the higher apes, [and] the need for Self-Actualization with [no other species].

While behaviours that relate to survival or deficiency needs (*deficiency* or *D-motives*) are engaged in because they satisfy those needs (a means to an end), those that relate to self-actualization are engaged in for their own sake, because they are intrinsically satisfying (*growth, being* or *B-motives*). The latter include the fulfilment of ambitions, the acquisition of admired skills, the steady increase of understanding about people, the universe or oneself, the development of

creativeness in whatever field or, most important, simply the ambition to be a good human being. It is simply inaccurate to speak in such instances of tension reduction, thereby implying the overcoming of an annoying state, for these states are not annoying (Maslow, 1968).

Another term for tension reduction is *drive reduction;* we shall examine the concept of drive and drive reduction theories a little later in the chapter. The point to remember for the moment is that to reduce the full range of human motives to drives that must be satisfied or removed is simply mistaken.

The hierarchical nature of Maslow's theory (see Fig. 5.1) is intended to highlight the following points:

● Needs lower down in the hierarchy must be satisfied before we can attend to needs higher up; for instance, if you are reading this while your stomach is trying to tell you that it is lunchtime, you probably won't absorb much about Maslow (pun intended!) and the same will apply if you are tired or in pain. Yet you can probably think of exceptions, such as the starving artist who finds inspiration despite hunger or the mountain climber who risks their life for the sake of adventure (what Maslow would call a 'peak' experience – another pun intended!).

● Higher level needs are a later evolutionary development, that is, in the development of the human species (*phylogenesis*), self-actualization is a fairly recent need. This applies equally to the development of individuals (*ontogenesis*): clearly, babies are much more concerned with their bellies than with their brains. However, it is never a case of one need excluding all other needs, but rather one being predominant at any one time and this applies at any stage of development.

● The higher up the hierarchy we go, the more the need becomes linked to life experience and the less 'biological' it becomes. Individuals will achieve self-actualization in different ways, through different activities and by different routes, and this is related to experience, not biology:

> A musician must make music, an artist must paint, a poet must write, if he is to be ultimately at peace with himself. What a man can be, he *must* be. (Maslow, 1968)

This captures nicely the *idiographic* nature of Maslow's theory, i.e. the view that every individual is unique (see Chapter 29).

● The higher up the hierarchy we go, the more difficult it becomes to achieve the need. Many human

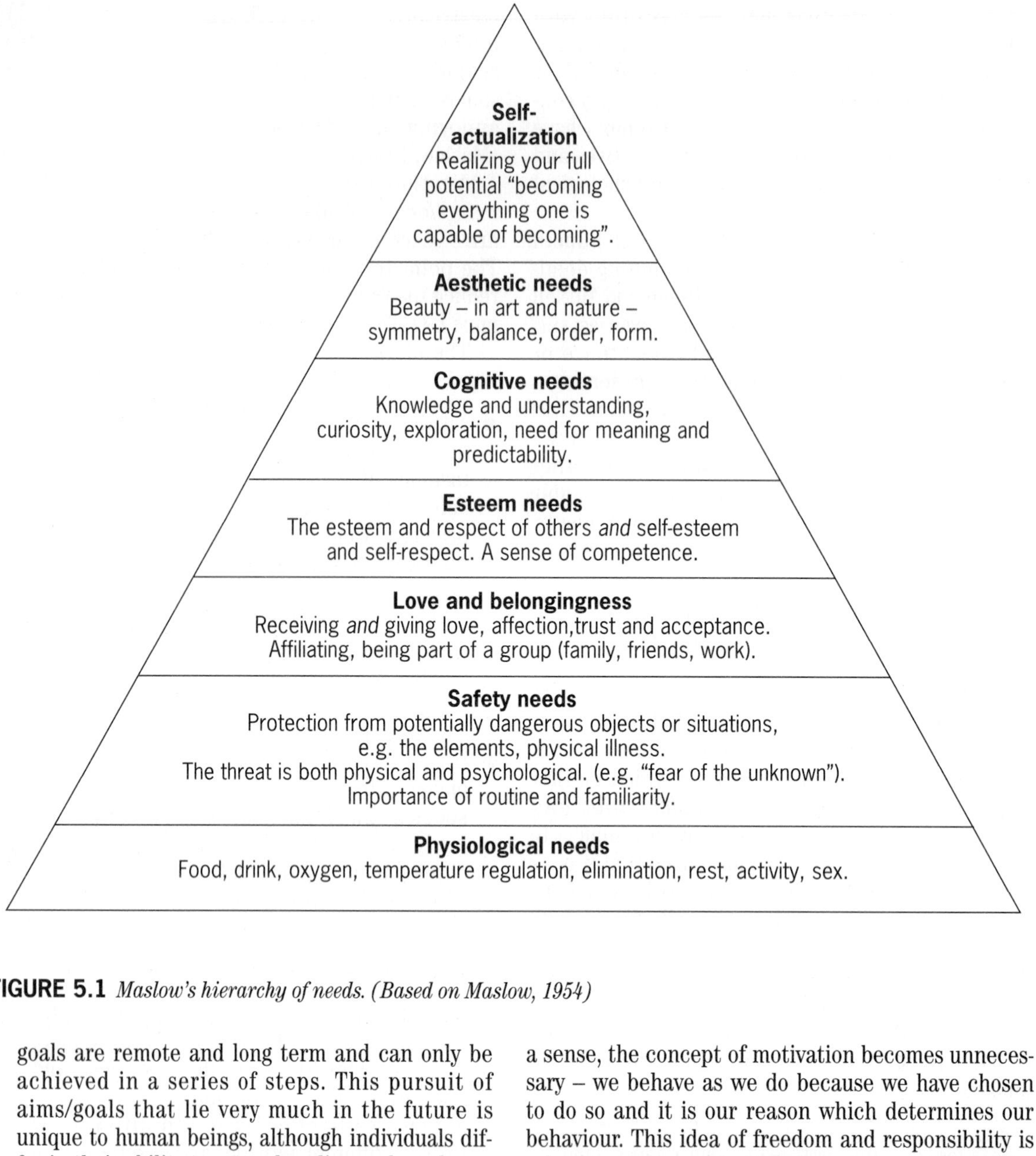

FIGURE 5.1 *Maslow's hierarchy of needs. (Based on Maslow, 1954)*

goals are remote and long term and can only be achieved in a series of steps. This pursuit of aims/goals that lie very much in the future is unique to human beings, although individuals differ in their ability to set and realize such goals.

THE EARLY STUDY OF THE PSYCHOLOGY OF MOTIVATION

As with many other aspects of psychology, the study of motivation has its roots in philosophy (see Chapter 2). *Rationalists* saw human beings as free to choose between different courses of action and so, in a sense, the concept of motivation becomes unnecessary – we behave as we do because we have chosen to do so and it is our reason which determines our behaviour. This idea of freedom and responsibility is a basic premise of both *humanistic* and *cognitive* approaches (see Chapter 32).

The 17th-century British philosopher Hobbes proposed the theory of *hedonism*, which maintains that all behaviour is determined by the seeking of pleasure and the avoidance of pain; these are the 'real' motives (whatever we believe our motives to be) and this basic idea is an important one in Freud's *psychoanalytic theory*, captured in the concept of the *pleasure principle*. Similarly, the basic principles of positive and negative reinforcement can be seen as corresponding to the seeking of pleasure and avoidance of pain respectively and these are central to Skinner's *operant conditioning*.

Freud's theory is often referred to as an *instinct theory* and the concept played a major role in early psychological approaches to motivation. Largely inspired by Darwin's (1859) theory of evolution, which argued that humans and animals differ only quantitatively and not qualitatively, a number of psychologists (including James and McDougall) identified human instincts that were meant to explain human behaviour. McDougall (1908), for example, originally proposed 12 and by 1924 over 800 separate instincts had been identified. But to explain behaviour by labelling it is to explain nothing (e.g. 'We behave aggressively because of our aggressive instinct' is a circular statement) and this, combined with the sheer proliferation of instincts, seriously undermined the whole approach. (However, the concept of instinct – with certain important modifications – remains a central feature of the *ethological* approach to behaviour, in particular, non-human animal behaviour.)

During the 1920s the concept of instinct was largely replaced by the concept of *drive,* a term first used by Woodworth (1918), who compared human behaviour with the operation of a machine: the mechanism of a machine is relatively passive and drive is the power applied to make it 'go'. The concept of drive has taken two major forms: *homeostatic drive theory* (Cannon, 1929), which is a physiological theory, and *drive reduction theory* (Hull, 1943), which is primarily a theory of learning.

HOMEOSTATIC DRIVE THEORY

The term *homeostasis* (from the Greek *homos*, meaning 'same', and *stasis,* meaning 'stoppage') was coined by Cannon in 1929 to refer to the process by which an organism maintains a fairly constant internal (bodily) environment; that is, how body temperature, blood sugar level, salt concentration in the blood, etc. are kept in a state of relative balance or equilibrium. The basic idea is that when a state of imbalance arises (e.g. through a substantial rise in body temperature) something must happen to correct the imbalance and restore equilibrium (e.g. sweating). In this case, the animal does not have to 'do' anything because sweating is completely automatic and purely physiological. However, if the imbalance is caused by the body's need for food or drink (tissue need), the hungry or thirsty animal has

to behave in a way which will procure food or water and it is here that the concept of a homeostatic drive becomes important. Tissue need leads to internal imbalance, which leads to homeostatic drive, which leads to appropriate behaviour, which leads to restoration of internal balance, which leads to drive reduction.

As Green (1980) points out, the internal environment requires a regular supply of raw materials from the external world but while oxygen intake, for example, is involuntary and continuous, eating and drinking are voluntary and discontinuous (or spaced) and while we talk about a hunger and thirst drive, we do not talk about an 'oxygen drive'. Because of the voluntary nature of eating and drinking, hunger and thirst have been the homeostatic drives most researched by biopsychologists.

● Hunger and eating

Does hunger cause eating?

If there is a commonsense theory of eating, it is that we eat because – and when – we are hungry. What could be simpler? If asked why we get hungry, most people would probably say that 'our bodies get hungry', that is, certain events take place in our bodies when we haven't eaten for a certain period of time and these act as the 'signal' to eat; we experience that signal as hunger.

This fits very neatly with the outline of the hunger drive given above. If we place the experience of hunger in between 'internal imbalance' and 'homeostatic drive', we get a nice blend of the commonsense and drive reduction theories, with hunger towards the end of a chain of causation that results in eating.

However, is hunger either a necessary or sufficient condition for eating to occur, i.e. can eating occur in the absence of hunger and is it possible that we might not eat despite being hungry? We have all been tempted by the look or the smell of food when not feeling hungry and we are not usually still hungry by the time the dessert trolley comes along, i.e. we often eat simply because we like it. This suggests that hunger is *not necessary* for eating. Conversely, people who go on diets or hunger strike are not eating (or eating less than they might otherwise do) despite hunger, suggesting that hunger is *not sufficient.*

So there seems to be no biological inevitability about the hunger–eating relationship. However, as Blundell and Hill (1995) point out, under many circumstances there is a close relationship between the pattern of food intake and the rhythmic fluctuation of hunger. For example, many experimental studies confirm the strong link between the intensity of experienced hunger sensations and the amount of food eaten. This fairly consistent finding has been interpreted as showing that there is a causal connection between hunger and the size of a following meal. However, in reality, certain physiological mechanisms are probably producing both the sensations of hunger and the eating behaviour.

Blundell and Hill propose an *appetite control system* in which hunger, eating and physiological mechanisms are coupled together, but the coupling isn't perfect and there will be circumstances where

uncoupling can occur, as in the hunger strike example or in cases of eating disorders (such as obesity and anorexia nervosa; see below). So what might some of these physiological mechanisms be? Assuming that, normally, these are 'coupled' (or correlated) with hunger, what happens when the 'body gets hungry'?

What starts a meal?

As Carlson (1992) points out, the physiological signals that cause eating to begin need not be the ones that cause it to end. There is considerable delay between the act of eating (the correctional mechanism) and a

---

BOX 5.1

Box 5.1 Key study: Cannon and Washburn's (1912) 'Swallow a balloon if you're hungry'.

Cannon originally believed that the hunger drive is caused by stomach contractions ('hunger pangs') and that food reduces the drive by stopping the contractions.

Washburn swallowed an empty balloon tied to the end of a thin tube. Then Cannon pumped some air into the balloon and connected the end of the tube to a water-filled glass U-tube so that Washburn's stomach contractions would cause an increase in the level of water at the other end of the U-tube (see Fig. 5.2). He reported a 'pang' of hunger each time a large stomach contraction was recorded.

These results were soon confirmed by a case study (cited in Carlson, 1992) of a patient with a tube implanted through his stomach wall, just above the navel. He had accidentally swallowed some acid which caused the walls of his oesophagus (the muscular tube that carries food from the throat to the stomach) to fuse shut. The tube was a means of feeding himself and provided a window through which his stomach activities could be observed. When there was food in his stomach, small, rhythmic contractions (subsequently named peristaltic contractions/peristalsis) mixed the food and moved it along the digestive tract; when it was empty, the contractions were large and associated with the patient's reports of hunger.

However, patients who have had their stomachs removed (because of disease) and the oesophagus 'hooked up' directly to the duodenum or small intestine (the upper portion of the intestine through which most of the glucose and amino acids are absorbed into the bloodstream; see below) continue to report feeling hungry and satiated. Even though their stomachs are bypassed, they maintain normal body weights by eating more frequent, smaller meals (Pinel, 1993). Similarly,

cutting the neural connections between the gastrointestinal tract (comprising mainly the stomach and intestines) and the brain (i.e. cutting the vagus nerve) has little effect on food intake in experimental animals or human patients.

These findings suggest that Cannon exaggerated the importance of stomach contractions in causing hunger, but this does not mean that the stomach and the gastrointestinal tract play no part in hunger and satiety. If the vagus nerve is cut, signals arising from the gut can still be communicated to the brain via the circulatory system. Also, the presence of food in the stomach (*stomach loading*) is important in the regulation of feeding: if the exit from the stomach to the duodenum is blocked off, rats still eat normal-sized meals. It seems that information about the stretching of the stomach wall caused by the presence of food is passed to the brain (via the vagus nerve), allowing the brain's feeding centres to control meal size.

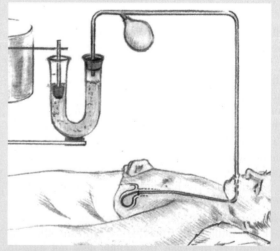

FIGURE 5.2 *The system developed by Cannon and Washburn in 1912 for measuring stomach contractions. (From J.Pinel 1993) Biopsychology. B,A & B*

change in the state of the body, so that while we may start eating because the level of nutrients has fallen below a certain point, we certainly don't stop because that level has been restored to normal. In fact, we usually stop eating long before this, since digestion takes several hours to complete. Therefore, the signals for hunger and for *satiety* (the state of no longer being hungry) are sure to be different.

Probably the earliest formal theory of hunger was proposed by Cannon, which was based on a very famous experiment described in Box 5.1.

The information that is passed from the gut or gastrointestinal tract (GIT) to the brain via the circulatory system concerns the components of the food that has been absorbed. What are the nutrients whose depletion acts as a signal to start eating?

Some of the components of food which might be contenders for this crucially important role are fats (lipids), carbohydrates (including glucose), vitamins/mineral salts and proteins/amino acids. Fats and carbohydrates are burnt up in cellular reactions and provide the energy to fuel metabolic processes. (*Metabolism* refers to all the chemical processes occurring in the body's cells and which are essential for the body's normal functioning; *metabolic rate* refers to the amount of energy the body uses.) When we engage in vigorous physical activity, the muscles are fuelled by fats and carbohydrates, which are stored as energy reserves. The cells that store our fat reserves are called adipocytes, which clump together as *adipose tissue* (or simply 'fat'), and the form in which carbohydrates are stored as energy is *glycogen* (a complex carbohydrate). Two major accounts of why we start eating are the glucostatic and lipostatic theories.

Glucostatic theory

According to the glucostatic theory, which was first proposed in the late 1940s/early 1950s, the primary stimulus for hunger is a decrease in the level of blood glucose below a certain set-point (with a corresponding primary stimulus for satiety being an increase above this set-point). It made sense to see eating as mainly concerned with maintaining a blood glucose set-point because glucose is the body's (especially the brain's) primary fuel. This is an example of a homeostatic system.

The *glucostat* was assumed to be a neuron (probably in the hypothalamus) that detects the level of blood glucose in much the same way as a thermostat measures temperature, i.e. although no one had actually identified the glucostat, it was assumed that there must exist some mechanism that responds to

changes in levels of blood glucose in a functionally equivalent way to a thermostat's response to changes in temperature.

According to Pinel (1993), Mayer's (1955) version of the glucostatic theory was particularly influential because it dealt with a serious problem associated with earlier versions: he proposed that it was glucose *utilization* (the rate at which it is used), rather than absolute blood glucose level, that was regulated by feeding. Under normal circumstances, this distinction is not very important since they are usually highly correlated; by stressing the utilization of glucose, Mayer's version could account for those few occasions where high levels are associated with *hyperphagia* (overeating). For example, people with diabetes mellitus overeat despite high blood glucose levels because their pancreas fails to produce sufficient quantities of insulin (needed for glucose to enter most body cells and to be utilized by them). Utilization of glucose is monitored by glucoreceptors that compare glucose levels entering the brain or leaving it; this information is used to stimulate or inhibit feeding in order to maintain glucose utilization around a prescribed set-point.

Mayer's hypothesis was supported by experiments which appeared to identify the location of the glucoreceptors in the brain. Mayer and Marshall (1956, cited in Pinel, 1993) injected mice with gold thioglucose, reasoning that the glucose would bind to the glucoreceptors (wherever they might be) and that the tissue in the area would be destroyed by the gold (which is a neurotoxin).The mice began to eat huge quantities of food and subsequent examination showed that damage had occurred to tissue in the ventromedial hypothalamus (VMH); they concluded that the VMH is a *satiety centre*. (We shall see below that other, quite separate research, reached the same conclusions.)

However, although a fall in blood glucose may be the most important physiological signal for hunger, it's not the only one. If animals eat a meal that is low in carbohydrate but high in fats or proteins, they still manage to eat a relatively constant amount of calories, even though their blood glucose is reduced slightly. If eating were controlled exclusively by blood glucose, we would expect them to overeat and get fat (Carlson, 1992).

Lipostatic theory

The 1950s and 1960s saw the appearance of a second explanation of a homeostatic mechanism that triggers eating, namely the lipostatic theory. As Green (1994) points out, this focuses on the end product of glucose metabolism, namely the storage of fats (lipids) in adipocytes. As we saw above, clumps of adipocytes form the fatty (adipose) tissues of the body. It was originally observed that body fat is normally maintained at a relatively constant level. For example, Kennedy (1953, cited in Pinel, 1993) argued that everyone has a set-point for body fat and deviations from this lead to compensatory adjustments in the level of food intake.

Similarly, fluctuations in the amount of stored fats largely determine variations in body weight and according to Nisbett's (1972, cited in Green, 1994) version of the lipostatic theory, everyone has a *body weight set-point* around which our weight fluctuates within quite narrow limits; this is determined by the level of fats in the adipocytes. The most frequently cited evidence in support of the lipostatic theory is the failure of short-term dieting programmes to produce long-term weight loss: as soon as dieting stops, the person regains the weight that has been lost.

Other evidence comes from animal experiments which involve making lesions in the hypothalamus. When the lateral hypothalamus (LH) is damaged, rats will stop eating, even when food is readily available, to the point of death from starvation. This failure to feed is called *aphagia* and was originally taken to indicate that the LH normally functions to stimulate eating (and so represents another partial answer to the question 'why do we start eating?'). Keesey and Powley (1975, cited in Green, 1994) deprived rats of food so that their body weight was substantially lowered; when lesions were then made in their LH, they started eating *more* food (not less). In normal rats, the lesion lowers the body weight set-point and the resulting failure to eat occurs because the animal is trying to adjust to this lower target weight. However, if the weight is reduced *before* the lesion is made to below the lesion-produced target, the rat now increases feeding (following the lesion) in order to reach the new (higher) set-point. What this means, of course, is that damage to the LH doesn't affect feeding directly but (as Nisbett suggests) indirectly, by altering the body weight set-point; feeding is aimed at attaining this new target.

Set-point or settling point: thermostat or leaky barrel?

According to Pinel (1993), the glucostatic and lipostatic theories are complementary, rather than mutually exclusive. This is partly because the former was meant to account for the initiation of eating (as well as its termination), i.e. relatively short-term

processes, while the latter was meant to explain long-term feeding habits and the regulation of body weight. Complementary or not, both theories rest on the assumption that, within the nervous system there is a certain kind of eating circuit that involves mechanisms that are sensitive to deviations from one or more hypothetical set-points. This assumption is itself based on another, namely that *homeostasis* implies the existence of set-point mechanisms.

Many current biopsychological theories of eating reject these assumptions in favour of the view that body weight tends to drift around a natural *settling point*, i.e. the level at which the various factors that influence it achieve balance or equilibrium. Pinel (1993) believes that earlier theorists were seduced by the analogy with the thermostat, which is a compelling set-point model. His analogy for a settling point theory is the *leaky barrel model*, according to which the level of fat in the body, like the water level in a leaky barrel, is regulated around a natural settling point rather than a predetermined set-point.

What other factors influence what and how much we eat?

One of the attractions of a settling point theory compared with a set-point theory is that it is more compatible with research findings that point to factors other than internal energy deficits as causes of eating. As we noted earlier, hunger is neither a necessary nor a sufficient condition for eating to take place; even if it were possible to explain *hunger* purely in terms of lowered levels of glucose and fat, for example, we would still need to identify other influences on *eating*.

According to Pinel (1993):

> The modern era of feeding research has been characterized by an increasing awareness of the major role played by learning in determining when we eat, what we eat, how much we eat, and even how the food that we eat is digested and metabolized. The concept of the feeding system has changed from that of an immutable system that maintains glucose and fat levels at pre-determined set points, to that of a flexible system that operates within certain general guidelines but is 'fine-tuned' by experience ... '

Both humans and other animals are drawn to eat (rather than driven to eat) by food's *incentive properties*, i.e. the anticipated pleasure-producing effects of food (its *palatability*). This doesn't deny the importance of internal regulatory factors; in fact, this view suggests how internal regulatory factors exert their effects. According to incentive theories, both internal and external factors influence eating in the same way, that is, by changing the incentive value of available foods. It seems that signals from the taste receptors produce an immediate decline in the incentive value of similar tasting food and signals associated with increased energy supply from a meal produce a general decrease in the incentive properties of all foods.

Support for this view comes from the discovery, by Rolls and Rolls (1982), of LH neurons that respond to the incentive properties of food, rather than food itself. When monkeys were repeatedly allowed to eat one palatable food, the response of LH neurons to it declined (a form of habituation?), although not to other palatable foods. Neurons that responded to the sight of food would come to respond to a neutral stimulus that reliably predicted the presentation of food. This seems to explain very neatly the common experience of our 'mouths watering' at the mere mention of our favourite dish or a picture of it, all examples of classically conditioned responses (see Chapter 7). Similarly smell, and the dinner bell are food-predicting cues which elicit digestive and metabolic events, such as salivation, insulin secretion and gastric secretions (*cephalic phase responses*). Pavlov (1927) was the first to demonstrate that a cephalic phase response can be conditioned: the sight or smell of milk produced abundant salivation in puppies raised on a milk diet, but not in those raised on a solid diet. He is better known for his demonstrations that salivation can be conditioned to the sound of a metronome or the sight of a light bulb being switched on, following his observation that experimental dogs would start to salivate when they heard the footsteps of the person who usually fed them. Feeling hungry at those times of the day when we usually eat (whether or not we are experiencing an energy deficit) is another example of a conditioned response.

If learning is involved in the way humans and other animals respond to foods that are already palatable, might learning be involved in what is found palatable in the first place? Knowing what to eat is partly determined by innate preferences for tastes that are associated in nature with vital nutrients. For example, sweetness detectors on the tongue are probably there because they helped our ancestors to identify food that is safe to eat; even when we are not particularly hungry, we tend to find a sweet taste pleasant and eating something sweet tends to increase our appetite (Carlson, 1992).

However, both humans and other animals also have the ability to learn the relationship between taste and the post-ingestion consequences of eating certain food, as in *taste aversion studies* (e.g. Garcia *et al.*, 1966), in which rats learn to avoid novel tastes that are followed by illness (see Chapter 7). Rats are also able to learn to prefer tastes that are followed by the infusion of nutrients and flavours that they smell on the breath of other rats.

Rats and human beings have in common a metabolism that requires them to eat a variety of different foods, i.e. no single food provides all essential nutrients. Humans generally find a meal that consists of moderate amounts of several different foods more interesting than a huge plate of only one food, however palatable that food might be. If we have access to only one particular food, we soon become tired of it and this is called *sensory-specific satiety*; this clearly encourages the consumption of a varied diet.

It seems that cultural evolution helps the selection of balanced diets. For example, Mexicans increased the calcium in their diet by mixing small amounts of mineral lime into their tortillas. In the industrialized societies of Europe and North America, by contrast, we seem to prefer diets which are fundamentally detrimental to our health, although in recent years there has been a strong campaign in favour of healthy eating. The tendency has been for manufacturers to sell foods that are highly palatable and energy dense, often with little nutritional value, which encourage us to overeat and, as a result, to increase fat deposits and body weight.

Blundell and Hill (1995) note that this does not generate a biological drive to undereat (as a compensation) and this may help to explain the increasing prevalence of obesity in many affluent cultures in the late 20th century. Yet it is understandable, in evolutionary terms, that there should be a strong defence against undernutrition but only a weak one against the effects of overnutrition:

> ... For human beings it can be supposed that during most of the tens of thousands of years of human evolution the biggest problem facing human-kind was the scarcity of food ... Hence, powerful mechanisms will have developed to signal this deficit and to generate an appropriate motivational response. However, the existence of an abundance of food, highly palatable and easily available, is a very recent development in evolutionary terms. Accordingly, it is unlikely that evolutionary pressure has ever led to the development of mechanisms to prevent overconsumption ...

Pinel (1993) notes that the number of different substances consumed each day by most people in industrialized societies is immense and such variety makes it very difficult for our bodies to use their natural ability to learn which foods are beneficial and which are not.

What stops a meal?

In discussing how eating gets started, we inevitably touched on some of the factors that determine when we stop. Just as we start eating for a whole range of reasons, of which hunger is just one, so 'meal size' is influenced by several factors.

According to Blundell and Hill (1995), *satiety* (feeling 'full up' or satisfied) is, by definition, not an instantaneous event but something that occurs over a considerable period of time. It is, therefore, useful to distinguish different phases of satiety associated with different mechanisms which, together, comprise the *satiety cascade*. This involves four mediating processes (sensory, cognitive, post-ingestive and post-absorptive) which maintain inhibition over hunger and eating during both the early and late phases of satiety.

1 *Sensory effects* are generated by the smell, taste, temperature and texture of food and inhibit eating in the very short term.
2 *Cognitive effects* refer to beliefs we hold about the properties of food and may inhibit hunger in the short term.
3 *Post-ingestive effects* include gastric distension, the rate of gastric emptying, the release of hormones (such as CCK; see below) and the stimulation of certain receptors along the gastrointestinal tract.
4 *Post-absorptive effects* refer to mechanisms arising from the action of glucose, fats, amino acids (and other *metabolites*) after absorption across the intestine into the bloodstream. Post-ingestive and post-absorptive effects are the most important as far as the suppression and subsequent control of hunger are concerned.

The concept of a cascade implies that foods of varying nutritional composition will have different effects on satiety by having differing effects on the mediating processes. There is currently considerable research interest in whether protein, fat and carbohydrate differ in their satiating efficiency and their capacity to reduce hunger. One clear finding is that carbohydrates are efficient appetite suppressants and although there have been only a few studies of the effects of fats, it is known that the fat content of food influences its texture and palatability but that it has a disproportionately weak effect on satiety (Blundell and Hill, 1995).

Although the stomach may not be very important in causing hunger (see Box 5.1), it does seem to be important in satiety; for example, we noted that stomach loading and stretching of the stomach wall play a part in reducing hunger. The gastric branch of the vagus nerve carries emergency signals from the stretch receptors in the stomach wall, preventing us from overeating and damaging the stomach. Signals from special receptors that can detect the presence of nutrients are transmitted to the brain by means of a chemical released into the blood by cells in the stomach wall (Carlson, 1992).

After food reaches the stomach, the protein is broken down into its constituent amino acids. As digestion proceeds, food gradually passes into the duodenum (small intestine), which controls the rate of stomach emptying by secreting a peptide hormone (short chains of amino acids) called *cholecystokinin* (CCK). CCK is secreted in response to the presence of fats, detected by receptors in the walls of the duodenum, and many studies have found that injecting CCK into hungry rats causes them to eat smaller meals. Wolkowitz *et al.* (1990, cited in Carlson, 1992) gave people injections of a drug that blocks CCK receptors in the peripheral nervous system (but not in the brain); they reported feeling more hungry and less full after a meal than controls given a placebo.

Hypothalamic regulation of eating: how does the brain control eating?

According to Pinel (1993), it has been known since the early 1800s that tumours of the hypothalamus can cause *hyperphagia* (excessive overeating) and *obesity* in humans. But not until the advent of *stereotaxic surgery* in the late 1930s (see Chapter 3) were experimenters able to assess the effects of damage to particular areas of the hypothalamus on the eating behaviour of experimental animals.

Hetherington and Ranson (1942) found that large, bilateral lesions in the lower, central portion of the hypothalamus (the ventromedial nucleus or VMN) cause hyperphagia, that is, the rat will carry on eating until it becomes grotesquely fat, doubling or even trebling its normal body weight (see Fig. 5.3). Although the VMN was only one of several structures damaged by such lesions, it was generally assumed that the ventromedial hypothalamus

FIGURE 5.3 *Hyperphagic rat. (Adapted from H. Gleitman 1981* Psychology. *New York, Norton)*

(VMH) was the crucial structure. The resulting hyperphagia was taken to indicate that the normal function of the VMH is to inhibit feeding when the animal is 'full' and hence the VMH became known as the *satiety centre;* it has been found in rats, cats, dogs, chickens and monkeys (Teitelbaum, 1967).

As we have seen, the traditional interpretation of the VMH hyperphagia syndrome was that lesioned animals become obese because they overeat. However, recent evidence suggests that the converse is true, i.e. the tendency to become obese causes them to overeat. How? Lesions increase the body's tendency to produce fat (*lipogenesis*) and decrease the tendency to release fats into the bloodstream (*lipolysis*) (possibly as a result of increases in insulin release that occur following lesions). Because the calories eaten are converted to fat at such a high rate, the animal must keep eating to ensure that it has enough calories in its blood to meet its immediate energy requirements.

The VMH syndrome is much more complex than the simple loss of inhibitory control of eating. Paradoxically, VMH rats are not 'hell-bent' on eating –

they won't eat anything and everything. An interesting finding is that the taste of food seems to be especially important in hyperphagic rats; whereas most animals will eat even bad-tasting food ('you'll eat anything if you're hungry enough'), hyperphagic rats are very fussy and will refuse their regular food if quinine is added to it, even if this means that they become underweight (Teitelbaum, 1955). Similar results have been found with obese humans. Why? Some possible answers are given in Box 5. 2.

Not only is the VMH syndrome behaviourally complex, but it is also complex anatomically. VMH lesions do not just involve damage to the VMN, but also to axons that connect the *paraventricular nucleus* (PVN) (situated in the medial hypothalamus) with certain parts of the brainstem. It has been found that microinjections of CCK into the PVN inhibit food intake, whereas microinjections of a supposed hunger peptide, *substance Y,* stimulates eating (Pinel, 1993). It has also been found that two neurotransmitters in the medial hypothalamus play an important role in eating behaviour; noradrenaline stimulates carbohydrate intake, while serotonin inhibits it. Most recent research interest has focused on the role of the PVN.

If the VMH has traditionally been regarded as a 'brake' on eating, the lateral hypothalamus (LH) has been seen as the 'accelerator'. Bilateral lesions to the LH cause aphagia, a refusal to eat, even to the point of death from starvation (Anand and Brobeck, 1951; Teitelbaum and Stellar, 1954). Even rats made hyperphagic by VMH lesions will become aphagic by the addition of LH lesions. These findings suggest very strongly that the LH is a *feeding centre.*

However, the role of the LH is not well understood, partly because the effects are more diffuse than was originally thought. For example, the LH syndrome includes not just aphagia but also *adipsia* (the complete cessation of drinking), both of which are, in turn, part of a more general lack of responsiveness to sensory input. The LH itself is a relatively large, complex and ill-defined area with many nuclei and several major nerve tracts running through it and while electrical stimulation of the LH produces eating, it also triggers drinking, gnawing, temperature changes and sexual activity. Conversely, eating can also be elicited by stimulation of other areas of the hypothalamus, the amygdala, hippocampus, thalamus and frontal cortex. For all these reasons, Pinel (1993) believes that to call the LH a 'hunger centre' is a misnomer.

BOX 5.2   Eating disorders

One possible explanation for the 'finicky' eating of VMH rats is that the lesion reduces their sensitivity to internal cues of satiation (e.g. blood glucose level and body fat content) and instead they become more responsive to external cues (e.g. taste). Schachter (1971) reports that overweight people also seem to pay little attention to internal cues (e.g. hunger pangs) and base their eating habits more on external cues (e.g. the availability and taste of food). However, although there is some evidence that hypothalamic tumours are associated with obesity in obese humans, there is no evidence that the hypothalamus does not function properly in overweight people generally, although it is still possible that it works differently in 'fat' and 'thin' eaters.

Schachter *et al.* (1968) found that while normal-weight people responded to the internal cue of stomach distension ('feeling bloated') by refusing any more food, obese people tended to go on eating. Similarly, when a group of normal and a group of obese people were deprived of one meal and then half of each group was given a roast-beef sandwich and the other half left hungry, only the normal-weight people who had eaten the sandwich ate fewer crackers when allowed to eat their fill – the fact that some of the obese people had eaten a sandwich made no difference to the number of crackers they ate.

Schachter (1971) suggests that it is the availability of food to which the obese people were responding. However, he also found that they are less prepared than normal-weight people to make an effort to find food (e.g. go into the next room to get sandwiches) or to prepare the food in some way (e.g. shell peanuts); so the former tend to keep on eating as long as food is in sight or is ready to eat, regardless of whether their physiological needs have been met, while the latter are more willing to search for food but only if they are genuinely hungry.

Overweight people also tend to report that they feel hungry at prescribed eating times even if they have eaten a short while before; normal-weight individuals tend to eat only when they feel hungry and this is relatively independent of clock time. However, we cannot simply infer that this increased sensitivity to external cues is what causes some people to become obese – it could just as well be an effect of obesity. So what other likely causes are there? Differences in *basal metabolic rate* (how fast we burn up our body's energy stores) largely determine our body weight and these differences seem to be hereditary (Carlson, 1992).

In a review of the literature, Rodin *et al.* (1989, cited in Carlson, 1992) found no evidence to support the role of psychological variables that are often suggested as causes of obesity, such as lack of impulse control, poor ability to delay gratification and maladaptive eating styles (primarily eating too fast). Also, unhappiness and depression seem to be the effects of obesity, rather than causes.

The role of complex psychological variables has been studied much more extensively in relation to *anorexia nervosa* and *bulimia nervosa*. Both of these, but not obesity, are included in the category of 'eating disorders' in DSM-IV (1994), the formal classification of mental and behavioural disorders published by the American Psychiatric Association. In the World Health Organization's classification system (ICD-10, 1992), anorexia and bulimia are categorized under 'behavioural syndromes associated with physiological disturbances and physical factors', while obesity is included in an appendix called 'Other conditions from ICD-10 often associated with mental and behavioural disorders' (see Chapter 30).

Anorexia nervosa (literally, 'nervous lack of appetite') is characterized by deliberate weight loss, induced and sustained by the patient. It occurs most commonly in adolescent girls and young women, but adolescent boys and young men may also be affected, as may children approaching puberty and older women up to the menopause. It is associated with a self-perception of being too fat, an intrusive dread of fatness and flabbiness of the body shape (Fig. 5.4) and the patient imposes a low weight threshold on themselves. There is

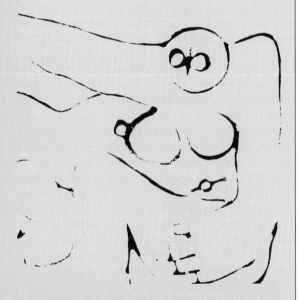

FIGURE 5.4 *A patient's painting of how she sees herself at 'normal' weight – obese, ugly and resentful*

usually undernutrition (of varying degrees) which is produced by restricted dietary choice, excessive exercise, induced vomiting and purging (use of laxatives) and the use of appetite suppressants and diuretics. Also common are endocrine disorders, involving the hypothalamic-pituitary-gonadal system (see Chapter 3), which in women takes the form of *amenorrhoea* (cessation of menstruation) and in men loss of sexual interest and potency (World Health Organization, 1994).

Like the anorexic, the person with *bulimia nervosa* (from *bous* meaning 'ox' and *limos* meaning 'hunger') sees themselves as being too fat, with an intrusive dread of fatness. What makes this different from anorexia are the recurrent episodes of overeating (at least twice a week over a period of three months) in which large amounts of food are consumed in short periods of time ('binges'), which are then followed by one or more of the following: self-induced vomiting,

self-induced purging, alternating periods of starvation, the use of appetite suppressants or diuretics (and, in the case of diabetics, a neglect of their insulin treatment). Again, unlike the anorexic, there is a persistent preoccupation with eating and a strong desire or compulsion to eat (craving).There is often, but not always, a history of anorexia (World Health Organization, 1994).

While the physiological abnormalities and medical complications of anorexia are the result of emaciation, those seen in bulimia result from specific behaviours. For example, vomiting often leads to erosion of dental enamel and can lead to damage of the oesophageal sphincter; bulimic episodes often cause swelling of the parotid glands (the largest of the salivary glands) and laxative abuse can cause profound constipation on laxative withdrawal. Most of these problems are reversed once the person has regained normal eating habits (Cooper, 1995).

● Thirst and drinking

What starts us drinking?

Like the study of eating, the study of drinking has until recently been based on the belief that drinking is motivated by a deficit in the body's water resources, i.e. by deviation from set-points, as part of a homeostatic drive mechanism. However, most drinking (like most eating) occurs in the absence of deficits, which suggests the role of the *positive incentive properties* of potential drinks, i.e. the motivation to drink comes from anticipating their pleasurable effects. We tend to prefer drinks that have a pleasant taste (such as fruit juice) or pleasant pharmacological effects (such as alcohol, coffee and tea).

According to the *positive incentive theory* of drinking, water deprivation increases the positive incentive value of almost all salt-free drinks; after 24 hours without a drink people report that even plain water has a pleasant taste (Rolls *et al.*, 1980, cited in Pinel, 1993). If you add a little saccharine to the water of non-deprived rats, their water intake rockets. Like people, rats with unlimited access to water or other palatable fluids drink far more than they actually need. Conversely, a small amount of quinine is sufficient to substantially decrease rats' water intake.

As with food, sensory-specific satiety has a major effect on drinking. As fond as rats are of saccharine, if saccharine solution is constantly available ('on tap'), they will come to prefer it less than when it is only available periodically. Similarly, animals drink

more when they have access to a variety of drinks, which can produce *polydipsia* (grossly excessive drinking).

A dry mouth and throat are obvious cues to thirst and the *dry mouth theory* of thirst is the counterpart of the stomach contractions theory of hunger (see Box 5.1). Although a dry mouth is one consequence of water deficiency, the evidence suggests that it is not the primary factor in thirst. For example, producing a chronic dry mouth by removal of the salivary glands does not substantially increase water intake, unless rats are fed dry food or kept in a very hot environment. Conversely, blocking the sensation of a dry mouth (e.g. with local anaesthetic) fails to decrease water intake. The most convincing evidence against the dry mouth theory comes from sham drinking, in which water flows down the oesophagus and then out through a fistula before it can be absorbed; despite the lack of a dry mouth, animals sham-drink continuously (Pinel, 1993).

Are there different types of thirst?

For our bodies to function properly, the volume of the body's two fluid compartments must be regulated; these are the *intracellular* (namely, the fluid portion of the cell cytoplasm) and the *extracellular* (comprising the *interstitial fluid*, which refers to the blood plasma, and the cerebrospinal fluid). Of the two types of extracellular compartments, it is the interstitial (or intravascular) volume that is important for understanding thirst. ('Interstitial' refers to the 'seawater' that bathes the body's cells.)

Most of the time, we take in more water and sodium than we need and the kidneys excrete the excess. But if the levels fall too low, correctional mechanisms are activated. Loss of water from either the intracellular or interstitial fluid compartments elicits drinking and this is mediated by two different physiological systems, one that is sensitive to reductions in intracellular fluid volume (or *cellular dehydration*) and one that is sensitive to reductions in blood volume (*hypovolaemia*). Corresponding to these two systems are two types of thirst, namely *osmometric* and *volumetric* respectively.

Osmometric thirst occurs when, for example, we eat very salty food, such as salted peanuts or crisps. Salt doesn't easily pass into cells, so it accumulates in the interstitial fluid, making it *hypertonic* (i.e. a more concentrated solution); water is then drawn from the cells into the interstitial fluid (making it *hypotonic*). Salt consumption has little effect on blood volume and osmometric thirst is usually induced in experimental animals by injecting hypertonic solutions of salt or other solutes that don't pass readily through cell membranes. A number of sources of evidence point to the presence of *osmoreceptors* in the LH and the lateral preoptic area of the hypothalamus (LPH).

If we cut ourselves very badly or suffer an internal haemorrhage or have very heavy menstrual periods, both water and salt are lost from the interstitial fluid, causing hypovolaemia (a drop in blood volume) which in turn causes volumetric thirst, but without causing cellular dehydration. Hypovolaemia is detected by *baroreceptors* (blood pressure receptors) located in the walls of the heart and by *blood flow receptors* in the kidneys. Decreased firing of the baroreceptors triggers the release of *antidiuretic hormone* (ADH) (*vasopressin*) from the posterior pituitary ('on instruction' from the hypothalamus); this in turn stimulates the kidneys to reduce the excretion of water (i.e. more concentrated urine). (It is thought that ADH is actually manufactured in the hypothalamus itself; see Chapter 3.)

What makes us stop drinking?

According to set-point theories, drinking brings about a return to internal water resource set-points; when this has been achieved, drinking stops. However, like hunger, thirst and drinking seem to stop long before enough time has elapsed for the body to have absorbed the water from the stomach and for the water–salt balance in the blood to have been restored.

Even if absorption took place quickly enough to explain cases of water-deprived drinking, we have seen that much spontaneous drinking is not triggered by water deprivation in the first place and even when it is, the amount we drink is not rigorously regulated. For example, in sham-drinking experiments, animals in their first post-deprivation bout of drinking will sham drink an amount that is proportional to the length of the preceding period of deprivation (despite the fact that the water leaves the gastrointestinal tract through a fistula before it can be absorbed). This could be due to previous learning or it could reflect the incentive value of the water, such that the longer the period of deprivation, the greater the incentive value.

Stomach distension probably contributes to satiety; cold water is more thirst-quenching because it moves out of the stomach much more slowly and so provides a clearer stomach-distension signal to the brain. The *mouth-metering mechanism* also plays a part; this gauges the amount of water being ingested and compares the amount needed to restore the water balance.

However, in rats, injections of water directly into the stomach or bloodstream reduces deprivation-induced drinking by only 30 percent of the amount injected, and even total replenishment of an animal's water resources has only a modest (about 30 percent) inhibitory effect on deprivation-induced drinking. As Pinel (1993) observes, these findings pose difficulties for any set-point theory.

DRIVE-REDUCTION THEORY

As indicated earlier, Hull's motivational theory must be considered in the context of his theory of learning. Drive reduction was intended to explain the fundamental principle of *reinforcement*, both positive (the reduction of a drive by the presentation of a stimulus) and negative (the reduction of a drive by the removal or avoidance of a stimulus).

As we have seen in discussing homeostasis, a physiological or tissue need gives rise to a corresponding drive and behaviour which removes the need and consequently reduces the drive. The needs and drives in which Hull was interested were the primary (physiological), homeostatic needs and drives of hunger, thirst, air, avoiding injury, maintaining an optimum temperature, defecation and urination, rest, sleep, activity and propagation (reproduction) and Hull believed that all behaviour (human and animal) originates in the satisfaction of these drives. The essence of drive-reduction theory is represented in Figure 5.5.

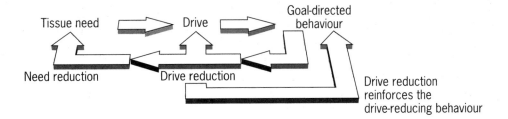

FIGURE 5.5 *Summary of drive-reduction theory*

While the terms *need* and *drive* are often used interchangeably, there is a fundamental difference between them; needs are physiological and can be defined objectively (e.g. in terms of hours without food or blood sugar level) and drives are psychological (behavioural) and constitute *hypothetical constructs*, i.e. abstract concepts that refer to processes and events thought to be taking place inside the person or animal but which cannot be directly observed or measured. However, drives are operationalized as hours of deprivation in Hull's equations (see below). (It is worth noting that the concept of motivation itself is a hypothetical construct.)

Hull proposed a number of equations which were meant to be testable in laboratory experiments. Perhaps the most important of these was:

$$sEr = D \times V \times K \times sHr$$

where *sEr* stands for the intensity or likelihood of any learned behaviour which can be calculated if four other factors are known, namely *D* (the drive or motivation, measured by some indicator of physical need, such as hours of deprivation), *V* (the intensity of the signal for the behaviour), *K* (the degree of incentive, measured by the size of the reward or some other measure of its desirability) and *sHr* (habit strength, measured as the amount of practice given, usually in terms of the number of reinforcements; Walker, 1984).

Criticisms of homeostatic drive reduction theory

Hull's basic premise that animals (and, by implication, people) always learn through primary drive reduction and never learn if drive reduction does not occur can be criticized from several directions.

Even in the case of primary drives, their relationship to needs is very unclear, as we saw when discussing the eating behaviour of obese people. At its simplest, needs can arise without specific drives, as in learning what and how much to eat (see above); for example, we need vitamin C but we wouldn't normally talk of a 'vitamin C drive' (in the way that we talk about a general hunger drive). Conversely, drives can occur in the absence of any obvious physiological need and one important example of a non-homeostatic drive in animals is electrical (self-)stimulation of the brain (ESB) (see Box 5.3). Brain stimulation is such a powerful reinforcer that a male rat with an electrode in its LH will self-stimulate in preference to eating if hungry, drinking when thirsty or having access to a sexually receptive female. This effect has been found in rats, cats, monkeys and pigeons (and humans, occasionally). According to Beaumont (1988), Carlson (1992) and others, the main reward site for ESB is the median forebrain bundle (MFB), a fibre tract which runs from the brainstem up to the forebrain through the LH and the effect seems to depend on the presence of the synaptic transmitters dopamine and noradrenaline. There are also brain sites which, when stimulated, motivate the animal to terminate stimulation.

These reward centres are generally thought of as the neural substrate of 'pleasure', so that any behaviour defined as pleasurable involves their activation; ESB is seen as a 'short-cut' to pleasure, eliminating the need for natural drives and reinforcers. However, there are some very important differences between the effects of ESB and (other) primary reinforcers (see Gross, 1994).

Tolman's *cognitive behaviourism* challenged Skinner's *S–R psychology* because it showed that learning could take place in the absence of reinforcement (*latent learning*). As Hull was defining reinforcement in terms of drive reduction and claiming that learning could not occur without drive reduction, it follows that Tolman was also showing that learning could take place in the absence of drive-reduction (see Chapter 7).

BOX 5.3   Key study: what a rat wouldn't do for a shock

Olds and Milner (1954) found that rats stimulated by an electrode implanted near the septum (part of the limbic system) would make between 3000 and 7500 lever-pressing responses (the response producing shock) in a 12-hour period. Olds (1956) reported that one rat stimulated itself more than 2000 times per hour for 24 consecutive hours and in 1958 reported that rats which normally press a lever 25 times per hour for a food reward will press 100 times per minute for a reward of ESB (see Fig. 5.6).

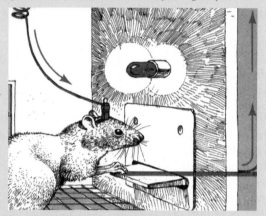

FIGURE 5.6 *Olds (1956) implanted electrodes in the hyporthalamus of rats. The rats could trigger an electrical stimulus by depressing a lever. Clearly, the region where the electrode was implanted constitutes some kind of pleasure centre Adapted from J.Olds ©1956 Pleasure Centres in the brain.* *Scientific American, Inc. All rights reserved*

Hull's theory was also inadequate in that it emphasized primary (homeostatic) drives to the exclusion of secondary (non-homeostatic) drives: primary drives are based on primary (innate) needs while much human (and, to a lesser extent, non-human animal) behaviour can only be understood in terms of secondary (acquired) drives. A number of researchers, notably Miller (1948), Mowrer (1950) and Dollard and Miller (1950), modified Hull's theory to include acquired drives (in particular, anxiety) which led in the 1950s to a great deal of research on avoidance learning (see Chapter 7).

The attachment of babies to their mothers has been explained in terms of a secondary drive (acquired through classical conditioning by associating her with the reduction of the primary hunger drive; see Chapter 22). Phobias can be understood in terms of avoidance learning (whereby avoiding the feared object or situation reduces the fear and so, through negative reinforcement, makes avoidance more likely; see Chapters 7, 30 and 31).

For Mowrer (1950), the secondary drive of anxiety is one of the main instigators of behaviour; striving for social approval, success, power and money can all be seen as being motivated by the wish to avoid the unpleasant consequences which, early in life, became associated with loss of parental love, failure or weakness.

In Maslow's terms, drive-reduction theory deals only with survival needs and ignores completely the self-actualization (or 'growth') needs which make human motivation distinctively different from that of non-human animals. We have seen that, even in the case of primary, homeostatic drives such as hunger and thirst, the relationship between underlying tissue need and drive is far from simple and this is true of non-human animals as well as of humans. Just as ESB cannot be accommodated by drive reduction when considering only animal motivation, so non-human animals seem to have other non-homeostatic drives which they share, to some degree, with humans. The rest of this chapter will be devoted to these important, and pervasive, non-homeostatic needs and drives.

NON-HOMEOSTATIC NEEDS AND DRIVES

● Competence motives: motives without specific primary needs

According to White (1959), the 'master reinforcer' which keeps most of us motivated over long periods of time is the need to confirm our sense of personal competence, defined as our capacity to deal effectively with the environment. It is intrinsically rewarding and satisfying to feel that we are capable human beings, to be able to understand, predict and control our world (which, as you may have spotted, also happen to be the major aims of science; see Chapter 2).

Unlike hunger, which comes and goes, competence seems to be a continuous, ongoing motive. We cannot satisfy it and then do without it until it next appears, because it is not rooted in any specific physiological need and for this reason it is not very helpful to think of the competence motive as a drive which pushes us into seeking its reduction. Another important difference between competence motives

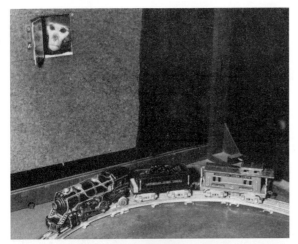

FIGURE 5.7 *Research by Butler and Harlow has shown that animals are motivated to explore and manipulate their environments, quite unrelated to biological drives such as hunger and thirst. Monkeys will learn and work in order to open a door which allows them to view an electric train. They will also work diligently to open locks which lead to no tangible reward.*

and homeostatic drives is that the former often involve the search for stimulation rather than an attempt to reduce it, as in the latter.

One way of seeking stimulation is through curiosity and exploration, which have been demonstrated in a number of species. If rats are allowed to become thoroughly familiar with a maze and then the maze is changed in some way, they will spend more time exploring the altered maze, even in the absence of any obvious extrinsic reward, such as food: they are displaying a *curiosity drive* (Butler, 1954). Butler (1954), Harlow (1953) and Harlow *et al.* (1950, 1956) gave monkeys mechanical puzzles to solve, e.g. undoing a chain, lifting a hook and opening a clasp. The monkeys did these puzzles over and over again, for hours at a time, with no other reward: they were displaying their *manipulative drive* (Harlow *et al.*, 1950) (see Fig. 5.7).

Play and motivation

Much of the behaviour normally described as play can be thought of in terms of the drives for curiosity, exploration and manipulation; indeed, play and exploration are often equated. The purpose of play from the child's point of view is simple enjoyment; it does not consciously engage in play to find out how things work, to try out adult roles or to exercise its imagination but because it is fun and intrinsically satisfying. Any learning which does result is quite incidental, although for the young child there is no real distinction between 'work' and 'play' in an adult sense.

Piaget (1951) distinguishes between play, which is performed for its own sake (and which allows the child to practise its skills and abilities in a relaxed and carefree way) and 'intellectual activity' or learning, in which there is an external aim or purpose; this distinction is meant to apply to the three major types of play he identifies (mastery, symbolic or make-believe and play with rules) but is more blurred in the first. (Piaget's theory is discussed in more detail in Chapter 25.)

It is not just humans who play; the young of many species engage in activities which seem to have little to do with homeostatic or survival needs; however, the higher up the evolutionary scale the species is, the more apparent and purposeful the play becomes and the more the nature of play changes as the young animal develops. As Fontana (1981(a)) points out, even in monkeys, play is mainly confined to physical movement of some kind, such as chasing and romping, and it usually involves other young monkeys; but in humans, play goes through a series of stages (Piaget, 1951) and there is a great variety of types of play, including manipulation of physical objects, physical play with other people, symbolic or imaginative play and so on.

Motivation and adaptation

Piaget saw play as essentially an adaptive activity and, throughout development, play helps to consolidate recently acquired abilities as well as aiding the development of additional cognitive and social skills. In the same way, the competence motives of curiosity, exploration and manipulation undoubtedly have adaptive significance for an individual and, ultimately, for the species. Although the internal conditions which give rise to competence motives are not apparent (in contrast with physiological drives) and although they do not have any obvious, immediate consequences for the

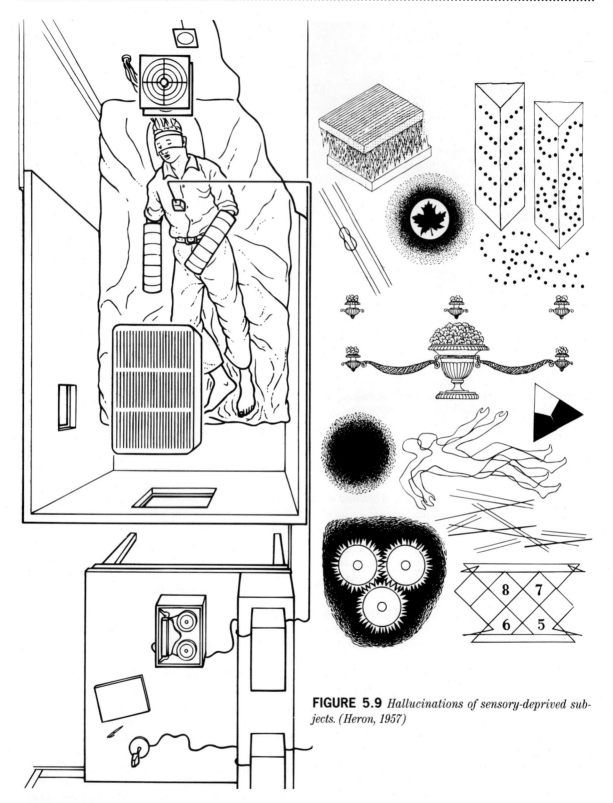

FIGURE 5.9 *Hallucinations of sensory-deprived subjects. (Heron, 1957)*

FIGURE 5.8 *Sensory deprivation cubicle. (Heron, 1957)*

fulfilment of biological needs, investigating and exploring the environment equips an animal with 'knowledge' which can be used in times of stress or danger (Bolles, 1967).

According to *optimal level* (or *arousal*) theories (e.g. Berlyne, 1969), these kinds of behaviours are based on an inbuilt tendency to seek a certain 'optimum' level of stimulation or activity (not unlike a homeostatic model of drive reduction). Exploring the unfamiliar increases arousal, but if the unfamiliar is too different from what we are used to, arousal will be too high (we feel anxious and tense) while if it is not different enough, arousal is too low (we soon become bored).

A number of *sensory deprivation* experiments, involving mature animals, both human and non-human, lend support to optimum level theories. Butler (1954) kept monkeys in small, barren cages where pressing a button brought a reward of opening a small observation window, through which they could see, for example, an electric train (see Fig 5.7). In the classic experiments on sensory deprivation carried out by Hebb and his colleagues at McGill University in the 1950s (Bexton *et al.*, 1954; Heron, 1957), participants almost completely cut off from their normal sensory stimulation (by wearing blindfolds, earmuffs, cardboard tubes on their arms and legs, etc.) soon began to experience extreme psychological discomfort, reported hallucinations and could not tolerate their confinement for usually more than three days (see Figs 5.8 and 5.9).

Cohen and Taylor (1972) studied the psychological effects of long-term imprisonment and found that sensory deprivation and monotony are experiences which are shared by prisoners, explorers, space travellers and round-the-world sailors. Conversely, excessive stimulation ('sensory overload') is also debilitating and may be responsible for some kinds of psychological disorders in our highly urbanized society.

The need for control

Another major kind of competence motive is the need to be in control of our own destiny and not at the mercy of external forces (Rubin and McNeil, 1983). The need for control is closely linked with the need to be free from the controls and restrictions of others, to dictate our own actions and not be dictated to. According to Brehm (1966), when our freedom is threatened, we tend to react by reasserting our freedom, which he called *psychological reactance*.

When people initially expect to have control over the outcomes of their actions, the first experience of not being in control is likely to produce reactance but further bad experiences are likely to result in *learned helplessness* (Seligman, 1975). (This is discussed in relation to stress in Chapter 6.)

There are important individual differences in how control is perceived. Rotter (1966) proposed the *locus of control* concept to refer to our beliefs about what controls events in our everyday lives and how we are reinforced for our actions. Locus of control was first assessed by the Locus of Control Scale, a self-administered questionnaire comprising 23 pairs of opposed statements; the scale contrasts *internals*, who believe they are responsible for what happens to them, with *externals*, who believe that luck, fate and other people and events control most aspects of their lives (see Chapters 6 and 29).

● Cognitive motives: consistency and achievement

Perhaps one of the most researched cognitive motives is the need for *cognitive consistency*, which is discussed in Chapter 18 in relation to attitudes and attitude change. Another which has generated an enormous amount of research and theorizing is *achievement motivation* or *need for achievement* (nAch), which was one of the 20 human motives identified by Murray in 1938; he drew a sharp distinction between 'psychogenic' or psychological needs, which are learned, and 'viscerogenic' or physiological needs, which are innate.

Based on his acceptance of Freud's belief that people express their true motives more clearly in free association than in direct self-reports (or questionnaire-type personality tests), Murray (together with Morgan, 1935) devised the *Thematic Apperception Test* (TAT), which consists of a series of 20 pictures, presented one at a time, ten in each of two sessions separated by at least one day. Slightly different versions are used for men and women, boys and girls. The participant is told the TAT is a test of imagination and asked to make up a story that describes:

● what is happening and who the people are;
● what has led up to the situation;
● what is being thought and what is wanted and by whom;
● what will happen, what will be done.

The pictures are sufficiently ambiguous with regard to the events depicted and the emotions of the characters (Fig. 5.10) to allow a wide range of

FIGURE 5.10 *Sample TAT picture*

interpretations and how a person interprets them reveals their unconscious motives; hence the TAT is a major *projective* test used in motivation and personality research (see Chapter 29). A person who scores high on nAch is concerned with standards of excellence, high levels of performance, recognition of others and the pursuit of long-term goals (i.e. they are ambitious).

McClelland (McClelland *et al.*, 1953, 1958) is the major figure associated with nAch research and has found that high scorers tend to perform better on a number of tasks, including anagram puzzles, are generally more persistent and prefer an 'expert' to a 'friendly' work partner. They also tend to attribute their performance to internal factors (ability, effort, etc.), while low scorers are more likely to attribute theirs to external factors (ease of the task, luck, etc.).

It has been found consistently that nAch scores do not predict the actual behaviour of females as well as that of males. Why should this be? According to Maccoby (1963), females traditionally have not been encouraged to be successful in those areas in which men are expected to excel (and which are reflected in nAch scores), but Horner (1970, 1972), using a story completion task, found that female students showed significantly greater fear of success than male students. This fear of success is likely to

influence behaviour in competitive situations and situations in which success is seen by women as coming into conflict with their relationships with men and their success as women.

Hoffman (1977) followed up Horner's participants and found that the high fear of success scorers married and had children sooner than low scorers; having a baby reaffirms their sense of femininity, removes them from the competitive arena and re-establishes their dependency on their husbands. Significantly, many became pregnant when faced with the possibility of success in an area where they might have been in competition with their husbands.

● Social motives

According to Geen (1995), social motivation refers to the activation of processes involved in the initiation, direction and energization of individual behaviour ' ... by situations in which other people are in close contact with the individual ...'. It is usually assumed that these situations do not provide specific cues for individual behaviour (i.e. they are 'weak'), unlike 'strong' situations , such as those in which there is direct social influence (as in obedience experiments; see Chapter 20). So what kinds of social situation are included as involving social motives?

Geen gives three main examples, *social facilitation* (the enhancing effect on behaviour of the mere presence of others) (see Chapter 20), *social presentation* (behaving in ways that attempt to present a desired or idealized self-image to others) (see Chapter 15) and *social loafing* (the tendency for individual effort to diminish in group task situations, partly as a result of *diffusion of responsibility*) (see Chapter 20).

Each of these phenomena may be thought of as a manifestation of the more general influence of *social anxiety*, i.e. a state created when a person who wishes to make a certain impression on others doubts that this impression can actually be made. But why should the fear of making a bad impression be such a powerful motive for individual behaviour? One answer can be found at quite a low level of Maslow's hierarchy, namely love and belongingness, which includes the need for affiliation, the company of other people, especially family, friends and work colleagues, the need to be accepted by, and included within, society. Certain kinds of conformity can be understood in terms of this basic need (a survival need in Maslow's terms) (see Chapter 20). But does this need itself stem from some other, even more fundamental need?

According to Greenberg *et al.* (1986, cited in Geen 1995), one reason people need to be included within the collective may be that human culture, which society represents, provides a buffer against facing one's own vulnerability and mortality. Society provides a 'cultural drama' that gives meaning to life and without which the individual would experience a dread of being alive. We are, therefore, motivated to play an approved role in that drama: by meeting cultural standards, the individual achieves the approval and acceptance of others and avoids rejection and isolation. This can be seen in relation to safety needs, the second level of Maslow's hierarchy, and includes 'fear of the unknown', the ultimate example of which is the fear of death. This is a topic discussed in Chapter 24 in relation to old age. The general need for others (affiliation) and the influences on our relationships with particular others are discussed in Chapter 16 on interpersonal attraction.

CHAPTER SUMMARY

- The study of motivation is the study of the causes of behaviour and all the major theoretical approaches within psychology as a whole are concerned with identifying these causes.
- While there is general agreement that motivated behaviour is purposeful, goal-directed behaviour, different approaches see the underlying causes in very different ways. These differences relate to internal/ external, innate/ learned, mechanistic/ cognitive and conscious/ unconscious dimensions.
- 'Motive' comes from the Latin for 'move' and denotes that which energizes and gives direction to people's behaviour.
- Motives have been classified in various ways, but the most comprehensive classification is Maslow's hierarchy of needs, which distinguishes survival, deficiency or D-motives and self-actualization, growth, being or B-motives. While the former are a means to an end, the latter are an end in themselves.
- Lower level needs must be satisfied before higher level needs can be attended to; the latter are less 'biological' than the former and are more closely linked to life experience. Higher level needs are also a later evolutionary development, both phylogenetically and ontogenetically. Self-actualization is a uniquely human motive.

- Humanistic and cognitive psychology have their roots in rationalist philosophy, while hedonism can be seen as a central theme in both Freud's psychoanalytic theory and Skinner's operant conditioning.
- Influenced by Darwin's theory of evolution, many early psychologists (e.g. James, McDougall and Freud) tried to explain human behaviour in terms of large numbers of instincts. This approach was replaced by Woodworth's concept of drive.
- Two major forms of drive theory are Cannon's homeostatic drive theory and Hull's drive reduction theory.
- Homeostatic drive refers to what motivates an animal to engage in behaviour that will remove a tissue need, which produced the drive in the first place. Hunger and thirst are the homeostatic drives that have been most researched by biopsychologists.
- Common sense tells us that we eat because we are hungry, but hunger is neither a necessary nor a sufficient condition for eating to occur. However, although there may be no biological inevitability about the hunger–eating relationship, they are often closely related, probably both being produced by certain physiological mechanisms.
- The physiological signals that cause eating to begin and that cause it to end are almost certain to be different; since digestion takes several hours to complete, the signals for hunger and for satiety could not be the same.
- The earliest formal theory of hunger was Cannon's theory of stomach contractions, based on a famous experiment in which Washburn swallowed a balloon . However, later findings showed that patients whose stomachs have been removed still report feeling hungry and satiated, suggesting that Cannon attached too much importance to stomach contractions.
- However, stomach loading is important in regulating feeding and information about the stretching of the stomach wall is passed to the brain via the vagus nerve. Information from the gastrointestinal tract about the components of the absorbed food is also passed via the circulatory system.
- Fats and carbohydrates (including glucose) provide the energy to fuel metabolic processes. Body fat is stored as adipose tissue (clumps of adipocytes) and carbohydrates are stored as glycogen.
- According to the glucostatic theory, the primary stimulus for hunger is a decrease in the level of blood glucose (the body's – especially the brain's

– primary fuel) below a certain set-point. The glucostat (probably a neuron in the hypothalamus) detects the level of blood glucose in the way a thermostat measures temperature.

- Mayer argued that it is glucose utilization that is regulated by feeding and this hypothesis was supported by experiments that seemed to identify the location of glucoreceptors in the brain, namely the VMH.

- Although falls in blood glucose levels may be the most important signal for hunger, it is not the only one. The other major set-point theory is the lipostatic theory, which focuses on the storage of lipids (fats) in the adipose tissue.

- Our level of body fat normally remains fairly constant and everyone has a body weight set-point around which their weight fluctuates within quite narrow limits (determined by the level of adipose tissue). Also, short-term dieting fails to produce long-term weight loss. These observations support the lipostatic theory.

- Damage to the LH does not affect feeding directly but indirectly by altering the body weight set-point; this also supports the lipostatic theory.

- The glucostatic theory was meant to account for the relatively short-term processes of eating initiation (and termination), while the lipostatic theory was meant to explain long-term feeding habits and regulation of body weight. They share the belief in pre determined set-points. Pinel prefers the view that body weight drifts around a natural settling point.

- Eating, in both humans and other animals, is partly determined by food's incentive properties (its palatability).

- Food-predicting cues elicit cephalic phase responses (e.g. salivation) through classical conditioning; these were first demonstrated by Pavlov.

- Although we have an innate preference for sweet tastes and eating something sweet tends to increase our appetite, humans and other animals are also capable of learning the relationship between taste and the post-ingestion consequences of eating certain food, as in taste aversion studies.

- Sensory-specific satiety encourages the consumption of a varied diet, very necessary for rats and people. Rats and people are also capable of learning which diets best meet their biological needs, although people in industrialized societies seem to prefer diets that are fundamentally harmful to health, with obesity becoming increasingly common during the late 20th century.

- According to the satiety cascade, there are different phases of satiety, involving sensory, cognitive, post-ingestive and post-absorptive effects, which inhibit hunger and eating during both early and late phases. This implies that foods of differing nutritional composition will have different effects on satiety; research suggests that carbohydrates are much more efficient appetite suppressants than fats.

- The duodenum (small intestine) controls the rate of stomach emptying by secreting CCK in response to fats; this seems to act as a hunger reducer.

- Lesions in the VMN of the hypothalamus of rats cause hyperphagia and the VMH became known as the 'satiety centre'. But instead of overeating causing obesity, it seems that lesions increase lipogenesis, such that the animal must keep eating to ensure it has enough calories in its blood for its immediate energy needs; i.e. obesity causes overeating.

- The VMH syndrome involves an increased fussiness about the taste of food, one example of the increased sensitivity to external cues of satiation. This also seems to be true of obese humans, who seem to respond to the availability of food and are less prepared than normal-weight people to find food or prepare it in some way. These differences could be caused by obesity, which is at least partly hereditary.

- Anorexia nervosa and bulimia nervosa are both classified as mental/behavioural disorders and both involve a self-perception of being too fat and an intrusive dread of fatness. But while the former suffers from undernutrition due to self-imposed dieting and other means, the latter is preoccupied with eating and typically alternates between eating binges and self-induced vomiting, etc.

- Lesions to the LH cause aphagia, which suggests that it is a feeding centre. However, the effects of LH lesions are much more diffuse than originally thought, including adipsia which, like aphagia, is part of a more general lack of responsiveness to sensory input.

- Drinking has traditionally been seen as motivated by deviation from set-points induced by water deprivation. But most drinking reflects the influence of the positive incentive properties of potential drinks and both rats and humans drink far more than they actually need if palatable drinks are readily available. Sensory-specific satiety also has a major effect on drinking.

- Although there is some support for the dry mouth theory, this is not the primary factor in thirst; the most convincing evidence against the theory comes from sham-drinking experiments.
- Osmometric thirst relates to cellular dehydration/reductions in intracellular fluid volume, while volumetric thirst relates to hypovolaemia/reductions in blood volume.
- Osmometric thirst is detected by osmoreceptors found in the LH and the LPH.
- Volumetric thirst is detected by baroreceptors found in the walls of the heart and by blood flow receptors in the kidneys. Decreased firing of the baroreceptors triggers ADH from the posterior pituitary, which stimulates the kidneys to reduce the excretion of water.
- It is difficult for set-point theories to explain why drinking stops, whether this is water-deprived drinking or not. Both stomach distension and the mouth-metering mechanism play a part in satiety.
- Hull's drive reduction theory was intended to explain the principle of reinforcement. He believed that all human and non-human animal behaviour is based on the satisfaction of primary/homeostatic drives, which stem from primary needs (tissue needs).
- Needs can arise without specific drives and drives can occur in the absence of any obvious tissue need, as in ESB. Brain stimulation is a very powerful reinforcer and can over-ride the primary drives of hunger, thirst and sex.
- The main site for ESB is the MFB, which is generally thought of as the neural substrate of 'pleasure', regardless of the particular activity that produces the pleasure.
- Latent learning shows that learning can take place in the absence of reinforcement and much behaviour can only be understood in terms of secondary (non-homeostatic) drives, such as anxiety and its avoidance.
- While drive reduction theory ignores self-actualization needs, which are unique to human beings, it also fails to recognize that animals share with human beings certain non-homeostatic needs and drives, such as curiosity, exploration, manipulation and play, which are all related to the search for stimulation. They are also linked to the need for competence, which is important for adaptation to our environment.
- According to optimal level theories, there is a built-in tendency to seek an 'optimum' level of stimulation, which helps to explain why both sensory deprivation and sensory overload can be stressful and disturbing.
- One major type of competence motive is the need for control. A first response to loss of control is often psychological reactance, which may be followed by learned helplessness if loss of control is repeatedly experienced.
- People with high internal locus of control believe they are responsible for what happens to them, while those with high external locus of control see external events as controlling their lives.
- Cognitive consistency and need for achievement (nAch) are two very important cognitive motives. Related to the latter are fear of failure and fear of success.
- Many kinds of social behaviour can be seen as a manifestation of social anxiety, which in turn may stem from the more fundamental need for safety and protection from our fear of death.

GLOSSARY

Adipocytes The cells that store the body's reserves of fat.

Adipose tissue Fat; clumps of adipocytes.

Adipsia The complete cessation of drinking.

Anorexia nervosa Eating disorder involving deliberate, self-induced weight loss, related to self-perception of being too fat and dread of fatness ('nervous lack of appetite').

Aphagia The failure to feed, even when food is freely available.

Baroreceptors Specialized blood pressure receptors, in the wall of the heart, that respond to hypovolaemia.

Bulimia nervosa Eating disorder involving episodes of gross overeating ('binges') alternating with self-induced vomiting, etc. Craving for food is coupled with self-perception of being too fat and dread of fatness (*bous* ='ox', *limos* = 'hunger').

Calories The energy content of food.

Cephalic phase responses Food-predicting cues (e.g. dinner bell) which elicit digestive and metabolic events (e.g. salivation).

Cholecystokinin (CCK) A hormone secreted by the duodenum in response to the presence of fats; acts as a satiety signal to the brain by controlling the rate of stomach emptying.

Duodenum The upper part of the intestine; small intestine.

Glucoreceptors specialized cells that monitor levels of glucose in the body.

Glucostat A (hypothetical) neuron (probably in the hypothalamus) that detects blood glucose levels, by analogy with a thermostat.

Glucostatic theory The view that hunger is caused by a decrease in blood glucose below a certain set-point.

Glycogen A complex carbohydrate; the form in which carbohydrates are stored as energy.

Hedonism 17th century philosophy of Hobbes, according to which all behaviour is determined by the seeking of pleasure and the avoidance of pain.

Homeostasis From the Greek *homos* meaning 'same' and *stasis* meaning 'stoppage'; maintenance of a constant internal (bodily) environment.

Homeostatic drive The motivation (e.g. as in hunger drive) to behave in ways (eating) that will satisfy some tissue need (drop in blood glucose) that creates a state of internal imbalance.

Hyperphagia Excessive overeating.

Hypovolaemia Reduction in blood volume.

Incentive property The anticipated pleasure-producing effects of food and drink – their palatability.

Lateral hypothalamus (LH) Area of the hypothalamus whose function is to stimulate eating; lesions cause aphagia.

Lipolysis The release of fats into the bloodstream.

Lipostatic theory The view that hunger is caused by a decrease in body fat from a certain set-point.

Locus of control Beliefs about what controls the events in our everyday lives and the source of the reinforcements for our actions.

Metabolic rate The amount of energy the body uses.

Metabolism All the chemical processes occurring in the body's cells that are essential for normal functioning.

Motive From the Latin *movere* meaning 'move', a special kind of cause which energizes and gives direction to behaviour.

Oesophagus The muscular tube that carries food from the throat to the stomach.

Osmometric thirst Thirst triggered by reduction in volume of intracellular fluid (cellular dehydration).

Osmoreceptors Specialized neurons in the lateral hypothalamus and lateral preoptic hypothalamus that respond to changes in cellular dehydration.

Peristalsis Small rhythmic contractions of the stomach which mix the food and move it along the digestive tract.

Polydipsia Grossly excessive drinking.

Psychological reactance Reasserting our freedom in response to (perceived) attempts to threaten it.

Rationalism The philosophical doctrine that sees human beings as free to choose between different courses of action.

Self-actualization Realizing one's full potential, especially in the intellectual and creative domains. At the top of Maslow's hierarchy of needs.

Sensory-specific satiety The reduction of a food or drink's incentive properties if only that food or drink is accessible.

Sham drinking Experimental procedure in which water flows down the oesophagus, then out through a fistula before it can be absorbed via the stomach.

Stomach loading The presence of food in the stomach.

Vagus nerve The nerve that passes information between the stomach and the brain.

Ventromedial hypothalamus (VMH) Lower, central area of the hypothalamus that acts as a 'satiety centre'; lesions produce hyperphagia.

Volumetric thirst Thirst triggered by reduction in blood volume (hypovolaemia).

FURTHER READING

Carlson, N.R. (1992) *Foundations of Physiological Psychology*, 2nd edn. Boston: Allyn and Bacon. A very thorough, well-illustrated textbook that covers all aspects of physiological psychology.

Pinel, J.P.L. (1993) *Biopsychology*, 2nd edn. Boston: Allyn and Bacon. Like Carlson, a comprehensive text but it has the advantage of being illustrated in colour, helping to make it even more user-friendly.

6 EMOTION AND STRESS

INTRODUCTION AND OVERVIEW

Mr Spock in *Star Trek* is often pointing out to Captain Kirk how much energy human beings waste through reacting emotionally to things when a more logical and rational approach would be more productive. But would we be human at all if we did not react in this way? This is not to advocate 'being emotional' in the sense of losing control of our feelings or being unable to consider things in a calm and detached way; however, it is the richness of our emotions and our capacity to have feelings as well as to think and reason which makes us unique as a species. Emotions set the tone of our experience and give life its vitality; they are internal factors which can energize, direct and sustain behaviour (Rubin and McNeil, 1983).

At the same time, we often respond emotionally to events and situations that we believe make demands on us that we cannot meet, either because we don't have the abilities or resources needed or because they force us to make very difficult choices and decisions. These negative kinds of events and situations are described as *stressful* and our emotional responses to them are often referred to as the experience of stress.

In this chapter, we shall begin by looking at how psychologists have attempted to define and classify emotions, before discussing the major theories of emotion. As we shall see, the more recent theories have emphasized the role of cognitive factors and are collectively referred to as *cognitive appraisal theories*. They stem from Schachter's (1964) *cognitive labelling theory* which encouraged a generation of (mostly) social psychologists to perform experiments which assumed that different emotions are associated with the same state of physiological arousal. That arousal was defined largely in terms of autonomic nervous system (ANS) activity. Since the mid-1980s, the idea that different emotions are associated with different patterns of physiological activity has become much more popular and there is also more interest in the part played by the central nervous system (CNS). We shall then consider some of the links between emotion and stress before asking three critical questions: (i) what causes it ? (ii) what effects does it have? and (iii) how do we cope with it? The answers to all three (inter-related) questions have very important practical implications for people's physical and mental health (see Chapter 31).

EMOTION

● What is it and how can we classify different emotions?

Wundt (1896), one of the founders of scientific psychology (see Chapters 1 and 2), believed that emotional experience can be described in terms of combinations of three dimensions – pleasantness/unpleasantness, calm/excitement and relaxation/tension (based on introspection). Schlosberg (1941) also identified pleasantness/unpleasantness, together with acceptance/rejection and sleep/tension (based on photographs of posed facial expressions). Osgood (1966) too saw pleasantness as one dimension plus activation and control, which correspond to the evaluative, activity and potency factors of the semantic differential; see Chapter 18 (based on live emotional display).

Ekman *et al.* (1972) and Ekman and Friesen (1975) identified six primary emotions (surprise, fear, disgust, anger, happiness and sadness) which they believe are universal, i.e. they are expressed facially in the same way and are recognized as such by members of a diversity of cultures, suggesting very strongly that they are innate (based on photos of posed facial expressions; see Fig. 6.1).

More recently, Plutchik (1980) has proposed an *emotion wheel* (see Fig. 6.2), in which eight basic/primary emotions (composed of four pairs of opposites) are shown inside the circle, with a further eight complex emotions on the outside. The primary emotions correspond to Ekman and Friesen's six, except that 'joy' and 'sorrow' are used for 'happiness' and 'sadness', respectively, plus acceptance and expectancy. Plutchik believes that the primary emotions are both biologically and subjectively distinct.

Happiness   Disgust   Surprise   Sadness   Anger   Fear

FIGURE 6.1 *Six universal facial expressions*

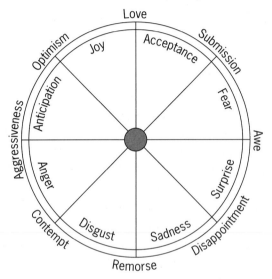

FIGURE 6.2 *The emotion wheel. Plutchik's model arranges eight basic emotions within a circle of opposites. Pairs of these adjacent primary emotions combine to form more complex emotions noted on the outside of the circle. Secondary emotions emerge from basic emotions more remotely associated on the wheel. (From Zimbardo, 1992)*

● What is meant by 'basic' or 'primary' emotions?

For Ekman (1994), 'basic' is meant to emphasize the role that evolution has played in shaping both the unique and the common features that emotions display, as well as their current *function*. Emotions evolved for their adaptive value in dealing with fundamental life tasks, i.e. they helped species to survive, and three major characteristics of emotions follow from this adaptive function:

1   there will be certain common elements in the contexts in which emotions are found to occur, despite individual and cultural differences in social learning;

2   they are likely to be observable in other primates (while it is possible that there are certain emotions that are unique to humans, there is no convincing evidence that this is so);

3   they can be aroused so quickly that they start to happen before we are even aware of them: ' ... Quick onset is central to the adaptive value of emotions, mobilizing us quickly to respond to important events'.

So emotions can occur with very rapid onset, through automatic appraisal (see below), with little awareness and with involuntary changes in expression and physiology; indeed, we often experience emotions as happening to us rather than chosen by us.

As we shall see below, there is recent evidence for distinctive patterns of ANS activity for various emotions and Ekman believes that these patterns are likely to have evolved because they support patterns of motor behaviour that were adaptive for each of these emotions, preparing the organism for quite different actions. For example, fighting might well have been the adaptive action in anger (which is consistent with the finding that blood flow increases to the hands in anger). There may also be unique patterns of CNS activity for each emotion which is not found in other mental activity.

Averill (1994) also recognizes the influence that an evolutionary approach has had in the study of emotions, defining basic emotions as those ' ... that fulfil vital biological functions ... ', i.e. vital to the survival of the species. Like Ekman, he believes that basic emotions should be universal, be seen (at least in rudimentary form) in non-human primates and be heritable. However, what is considered basic also varies between cultures and within the same culture over time; for example, in the Middle Ages, hope was classified as a basic emotion, while today it is regarded as secondary (if it is considered at all) by most emotion theorists (Averill, 1994). But most basic of all, he says, are emotions that are psychologically basic: when people are asked to recount emotional episodes that evoked their 'true feelings', they typically describe incidents that reinforce or transform or enhance their sense of self (Morgan and Averill, 1992).

For each distinct emotion that we may identify, there are three components:

1 the subjective experience of happiness, sadness, anger, etc;
2 the physiological changes which occur, involving the autonomic nervous system (ANS) and the endocrine system, over which we have little, if any, conscious control, although we may become aware of some of their effects (such as 'butterflies in the stomach', gooseflesh, sweating, etc.; see Chapter 3);
3 the behaviour associated with a particular emotion, such as smiling, crying, frowning, running away, being frozen to the spot, etc.

(2) and (3) are sometimes categorized together as 'bodily reactions', with the former being called *visceral* and the latter *skeletal*. This distinction relates to the ANS and central nervous systems (CNS) respectively. However, while running away is largely under voluntary (CNS) control, crying or sweating definitely are not, yet in all three cases we infer another person's emotional state from this observable behaviour.

How these three components are related, the relative emphasis given to each of them and how they are related to our cognitive appraisal or interpretation of the emotion-producing stimulus or situation are what distinguish competing theories of emotion.

● Theories of emotion

Darwin's 'The Expression of Emotions in Man and Animals'

The publication of this book represents the first formal attempt, by any scientist, to study emotion. Based largely on anecdotal evidence, Darwin (1872) argued that particular emotional responses (such as facial expressions) tend to accompany the same emotional states in humans of all races and cultures, even those who are born blind. (This claim has, of course, been supported by the research of Ekman and Friesen; see above.) Like other human behaviours, the expression of human emotion is the product of evolution and so he attempted to understand them by comparing them with similar behaviours in other species.

Based on such comparisons, he proposed a theory of the evolution of emotional expression comprising three main ideas:

1 expressions of emotion evolve from behaviours that signal what an animal is likely to do next;
2 if such behaviours benefit the animal that displays them, they will evolve in ways that make them more effective as a form of communication and their original function may be lost;
3 opposing messages are often signalled by opposing movements or postures (the *principle of antithesis*).

Taking threat displays as an example:

Figure 6.3 The two woodcuts from Darwin's 1872 book The Expression of Emotions in Man and Animals, which he used to illustrate the principle of antithesis. The aggressive posture features ears forward, back up, hair up and tail up; the submissive posture features ears back, back down, hair down and tail down (From J.Pinel 1993) Biopsychology. Boston, Allyn and Bacon

1 Originally, facing one's enemies, rising up and exposing one's weapons were just the early components of animal combat.

2 Once the enemies began to recognize these behaviours as signals of imminent aggression, those aggressors that could communicate their aggressive intent most effectively and scare off their victims without actually fighting had a distinct advantage. As a result, elaborate threat displays evolved and actual combat declined.

3 To be most effective, signals of aggression/submission must be clearly distinguishable, so that they tended to evolve in opposite directions; for example, gulls signal aggression by pointing their beaks towards one another and submission by pointing them away from one another. Similarly, primates signal aggression by staring at one another and submission by averting their gaze (Pinel, 1993). Another example is shown in Figure 6.3.

The James–Lange theory

If there is a commonsense theory of emotion, it is that something happens which produces in us a subjective emotional experience and, as a result of this, certain bodily and/or behavioural changes occur. James (originally in 1878 and then in 1890) and Lange (at first quite independently of James) turned this commonsense view on its head, arguing that our emotional experience is the *result,* not the cause, of perceived bodily changes. To give an example used by James, the commonsense view says that we meet a bear, are frightened and run; the James–Lange theory maintains that we are frightened *because* we run! Again, 'We feel sorry because we cry, angry because we strike, afraid because we tremble ...':

... the bodily changes follow directly the perception of the exciting fact, and ... our feeling of the same changes as they occur is the emotion. (James, 1890)

The crucial factor in the James–Lange theory is *feedback* from the bodily changes (see Fig. 6.4). We label our subjective state by inferring how we feel based on perception of our own bodily changes ('I'm trembling so I must be afraid') which is rather similar to Bem's self-perception theory (see Chapter 18). Is this theory valid?

You may be able to think of situations in which you have reacted in a fairly automatic way (e.g. you've slipped coming down the stairs) and only after you have grabbed the banisters do you become aware of feeling frightened (and a little shaken) – it is almost as if the sudden change in your behaviour has caused the fear, quite apart from why you grabbed the bannisters.

The theory implies that by controlling (deliberately altering) our behaviour, we can control our emotional experiences. Try smiling – do you feel any happier? A crucial test (which James admitted would be very difficult to perform) would be to examine the emotional experience of someone who is completely anaesthetized but not intellectually or motor impaired.

In the examples that James himself gives of inferring emotion from bodily changes (e.g. running away from the bear), he is clearly attaching much more importance to skeletal as opposed to visceral changes; in this respect, the James–Lange theory probably differs from other theories, which usually talk about physiological changes meaning visceral changes. To this extent, there are two important studies which lend support to the James–Lange theory, both of which are described in Box 6.1.

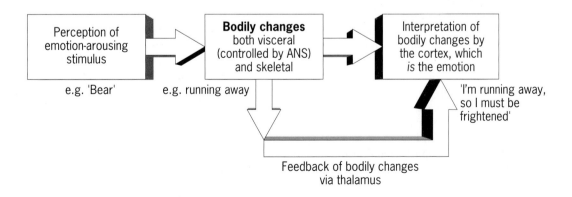

FIGURE 6.4 *The James–Lange theory of emotion*

BOX 6.1 Key study: listen to your heart and smile if you want to be happy

Valins (1966) provided male participants with feedback of their supposed heart rate while watching slides of semi-nude Playboy females. The heart rate was prerecorded and programmed to increase in apparent response to presentation of half the slides, so that participants believed they were reacting to these pictures. These slides were rated as more attractive than those supposedly associated with unchanged heart rate.

Laird (1974) falsely informed 32 students that they were to participate in an experiment to measure activity in the facial muscles. Bogus electrodes were attached to their faces (as if to measure physiological responses) and the participants were instructed to raise their eyebrows, contract the muscles in their forehead and make other facial expressions without realizing the emotional significance of what they were doing. Cartoon slides were then projected onto a screen and, regardless of their content, participants rated those they saw while 'smiling' as funnier. Also, when rating their own emotion, participants described themselves as happier when they were smiling, angrier when frowning and so on.

What the Valins and Laird studies suggest is that overt behaviour may cause subjective feelings without there being any obvious physiological arousal taking place, i.e. visceral changes may not be necessary . But neither Valins (using the *false feedback* paradigm) nor Laird (testing the *facial feedback* hypothesis) attempted to measure any accompanying visceral changes. What if smiling triggers certain physiological changes? Might these be the real cause of our feeling happy, rather than the change in our facial muscles? And if so, isn't this quite damaging to the James–Lange theory, since it places so much stress on behavioural (i.e. skeletal) changes (such as running away out of fear)?

Levenson *et al.* (1990, cited in Carlson, 1992) asked participants to move particular facial muscles (to simulate the emotional expression of fear, anger, surprise, disgust, sadness and happiness) and also monitored several physiological responses controlled by the ANS while this was going on. They found that the simulated expressions did alter ANS activity; for example, anger increased heart rate and skin temperature, fear increased heart rate but decreased skin temperature, while happiness decreased heart rate without affecting skin temperature.

We should also note that in the James–Lange theory, these bodily changes occur spontaneously, not consciously and deliberately, so perhaps for this reason we cannot draw too many conclusions from experiments like those of Valins and Laird. However, both studies strongly suggest that physiological arousal is not sufficient to account for emotional experience and the fact that participants in the Valins study were prepared to infer emotion on the basis of information about their reactions to stimuli suggests it may not even be necessary and that cognitive factors may be sufficient (Parkinson, 1987). (We shall return to this issue below.)

The Cannon–Bard theory

According to Cannon, there are four major faults with the James–Lange theory:

1 It assumes that for each subjectively distinct emotion there is a corresponding set of physiological changes enabling us to label the emotion we are experiencing.
2 Even if 1 were true, physiological arousal would still not be sufficient.
3 Physiological arousal may not even be necessary.
4 The speed with which we often experience emotions seems to exceed the speed of response of the viscera, so how could the physiological changes be the source of sudden emotion?

Cannon (1929) argued that: '... the same visceral changes occur in very different emotional states and in non-emotional states'. In other words, while the James–Lange theory was built on the assumption that different emotional stimuli induce different patterns of ANS activity and that perception of these different patterns results in different emotional experiences, the Cannon–Bard theory claims that the ANS responds in the same way to all emotional stimuli (namely, the sympathetic branch prepares the organism for flight or fight, through increased heart rate and blood pressure, pupil dilation, increased blood flow to the muscles, increased respiration and increased release of adrenaline and noradrenaline from the adrenal medulla; see Chapter 3). This means that there must be more to our emotional experience than simply physiological arousal, otherwise we wouldn't be able to tell one emotional state from another.

What is the evidence for the specificity of the body's response to emotional stimuli?

According to LeDoux (1994), this represents ' ... one of the most pesky problems in emotion research ... '. He points out that the emphasis of research has been on ANS activity and this emphasis is partly due to Cannon's criticism of the James–Lange theory. One early study is that of Ax which is described in Box 6.2.

While Ax's methods would be ethically unacceptable today, his findings have been confirmed by others (e.g. Frankenhaeuser, 1975). Schachter (1957) confirmed Ax's original findings that fear is influenced largely by adrenaline but also found that anger produces a mixed adrenaline–noradrenaline response and pain produces a noradrenaline-like pattern. Schachter and Singer (1962) concluded that:

> Whether or not there are physiological distinctions among the various emotional states must be considered an open question. Any differences which do exist are at best rather subtle and the variety of emotion, mood and feeling states do not appear to be matched by an equal variety of visceral patterns.

This conclusion is consistent with Schachter's *cognitive labelling theory* (1964), which sees physiological arousal as necessary for emotional experience but the nature of the arousal as irrelevant (see below) .

Less extreme and controversial methods than that used by Ax include the *directed facial action method* (in which participants are instructed to make the facial expressions characteristic of various emotions while ANS activity is recorded) and the *relived emotion method* (in which participants are asked to think about previous emotional experiences while these measures are being made). One of the leading researchers in the field is Levenson, who has carried out a series of experiments using both kinds of method.

Levenson maintains that it is a 'myth' that every emotion is autonomically different; it seems far more likely that reliable differences will only be found between emotions for which there are different associated typical behaviours and even among this smaller set, it is quite unlikely that each of them will be unique, i.e. not sharing any features in common. Autonomic uniqueness is doubtful because quite different behaviours can make quite similar demands on certain ANS functions. For example, both anger and fear involve an increase in the availability of oxygenated blood (e.g. increased heart rate) but at the same time the muscles involved in fighting and fleeing are rather different, so we would expect anger and fear to be different with regard to patterns of vasodilation and constriction that regulate blood flow to different muscle groups.

Concentrating on anger, disgust, fear, sadness (negative emotions), plus happiness (positive emotion) and surprise, Levenson and his colleagues have identified a small number of fairly reliable differences in patterns of ANS activity both between the

---

BOX 6.2 — Key study: Ax's 'fear and anger' experiment

In a famous (but ethically highly dubious experiment), Ax (1953) measured various aspects of electrodermal (skin conductance), electromyographic (muscle action potential), cardiovascular and respiratory activity in participants who were deliberately frightened and made angry. Volunteers were told that they were participating in a study of hypertension (high blood pressure). They were asked to lie quietly on a couch while physiological measures were being taken. While electrodes were being attached, it was casually mentioned that the regular technician (who usually operated the technical equipment in an adjacent room) was sick and a man who had recently been fired for incompetence and arrogance was filling in for him.

A few minutes later (following the recording of baseline measures), either the 'anger condition' occurred (followed by the 'fear condition') or vice-versa . In the 'fear condition', a continuous mild shock was administered to one finger (with no warning or explanation) with the intensity gradually increased until the participant complained. Then sparks were made to jump. In the 'anger condition', the technician (who was, of course, an actor) entered the test room and spent five minutes checking the wiring. During this time, he jostled the participant, criticized the attending nurse and blamed the participant for causing a fault in the equipment. Of 14 different measures that were taken, Ax found that seven were significantly different in the two conditions. For example, fear was associated with increased heart rate, skin conduction level, muscle action potential frequency and breathing rate (corresponding to the effects of adrenaline) while anger was accompanied by increased diastolic blood pressure, frequency of spontaneous skin conduction responses and action potential size (indicating the greater influence of noradrenaline).

negative emotions and between the negative emotions as a group and happiness. For example, anger, fear and sadness all produce larger increases in heart rate than disgust, while anger produces a larger increase in finger temperature than fear (Levenson *et al.*, 1990).

These differences have been found consistently across populations differing in occupation, age (from young people to 71–90-year-olds), culture (Americans and Minangkabau males living in Western Sumatra, Indonesia) and gender, as well as across the directed facial action and relived emotion methods. As far as positive emotions are concerned, Levenson believes that they might not be associated with any particular pattern of behaviour or, if they are, it would be characterized by low activity, making little metabolic demand on the ANS:

Instead of having distinctive autonomic signatures ... positive emotions might be associated with a state of physiological quiescence ... their primary function might be to 'undo' the autonomic activation produced by negative emotions ... to restore the organism to its pre-arousal state in a more efficient and rapid manner than would be the case if the negative emotions were allowed to run their natural course. (Levenson, 1994).

What this implies is that, at least in our present state of knowledge, we cannot draw general conclusions about the specificity of the body's response to emotional stimuli – it depends partly on which emotion (positive or negative, and which positive or negative emotion) we are talking about.

Pinel (1993) advocates a position falling between the extreme views represented by the Cannon–Bard and James–Lange theories: on the one hand, the Cannon–Bard view that the ANS responds in the same way to all emotional stimuli is clearly incorrect – several differences have been well documented. On the other hand, there is insufficient evidence to make a strong case for the James–Lange view that each emotion is characterized by a different pattern of ANS activity.

Also, to be fair to James (as we noted earlier), he was probably more concerned with expressive behaviour (running away, trembling, etc.) than he was with visceral responses (which the research we have just reviewed focused on) and it could be argued that Cannon's first criticism is, therefore, not strictly relevant. (Indeed, since we are almost completely unaware of these visceral changes, it would have been very difficult for James to have claimed that it is 'visceral feedback' which constitutes the emotion.)

Even if there were identifiable patterns of physiological response associated with different subjective emotions, Cannon argued that such physiological changes themselves do not necessarily produce emotional states, i.e. physiological arousal is not sufficient. This was demonstrated by Marañon (1924); see Box 6.3. However, the study by Hohmann (1966) (see Box 6.4) suggests that, although physiological changes are not sufficient for the experience of 'full-blooded' emotions, they may be necessary.

BOX 6.3 | **Key study: as if emotion were just a matter of adrenaline**

Marañon (1924) injected 210 people with adrenaline: 71 percent said they only experienced physical symptoms, with no emotional overtones at all, and most of the rest reported 'as if' emotions. The few who experienced genuine emotion had to imagine (or remember) a highly emotional event.

BOX 6.4 | **Key study: real emotions need an intact ANS**

Hohmann (1966) studied 25 adult males with spinal cord injuries who suffered corresponding damage to their ANS and who reported significant changes in the nature and intensity of certain emotional experiences, particularly, anger, fear and sexual feelings. Generally, the higher the lesion was in the spinal cord, the greater the disruption of visceral responses and the greater the disturbance of normal emotional experiences; like Marañon's participants, they too reported 'as if' emotions, a 'mental kind of anger', for example.

According to Schachter (1964), what Marañon's and Hohmann's participants reported is precisely what would be expected from his cognitive labelling theory, which sees emotional experience as a joint function of cognitive and physiological factors (see below).

Cannon (1927) removed the sympathetic nervous system of cats and Sherrington (1900) severed the spinal cord and vagus nerves of dogs; in both cases, feedback from the viscera to the brain was prevented but the animals showed apparently normal emotional reactions. Cannon took these findings to mean that physiological changes may not even be necessary.

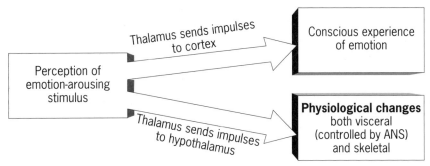

FIGURE 6.5 *The Cannon–Bard theory of emotion*

However, as Lloyd *et al.* (1984) point out, we do not know about the animals' emotional experience. Yet Dana's (1921) study of a patient with a spinal cord lesion lends support to Cannon – despite having no sympathetic functioning and extremely limited muscular movement, the patient showed a range of emotions, including grief, joy, displeasure and affection. But we cannot generalize from a single case, although the Valins and Laird studies both support Dana.

Cannon also argued that, as we often feel emotions quite rapidly and as the viscera are quite slow to react, how could the physiological changes be the source of such sudden emotion (as required by the James–Lange theory)? However, although the viscera are not sensitive to certain kinds of stimulation (such as burning and cutting), they provide much better feedback than Cannon suspected. Many visceral changes can occur sufficiently quickly that they could be the causes of feelings of emotion (Carlson, 1992).

So what is different about Cannon's theory (known as the Cannon–Bard theory)? As Figure 6.5 shows, the subjective emotion is quite independent of the physiological changes involved: the emotion-producing stimulus is processed by the thalamus, which sends impulses to the cortex, where the emotion is consciously experienced, and to the hypothalamus, which sets in motion certain autonomic physiological changes.

Schachter's cognitive labelling theory

According to Schachter (1964), Cannon was wrong in thinking that bodily changes and the experience of emotion are independent and the James–Lange theory was mistaken in claiming that physiological changes cause the feeling of emotion. However, he shares the James–Lange belief that physiological changes precede the experience of emotion because the latter depends both on physiological changes and

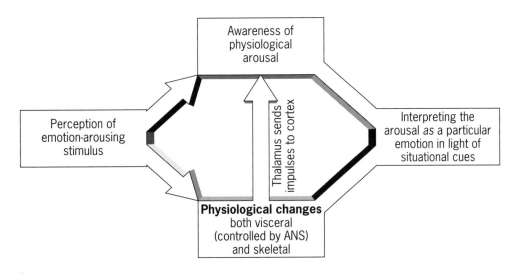

FIGURE 6.6 *Schachter's cognitive labelling theory (or two-factor theory)*

| BOX
6.5 | Key study: Schachter and Singer's (1962) adrenaline experiment |

Participants were given what they were told was a vitamin injection in order to see its effect on vision; in fact, it was adrenaline and they were tested under one of four conditions:

Group A participants were told the real side-effects of the injection (namely palpitations, tightness in the throat, tremor, sweating, etc.).

Group B participants were given false information about the effects of the injection (e.g. itching and headache).

Group C participants were given no information about the effects of the injection (e.g. true or false).

Group D (control group) participants were given a saline injection (and otherwise treated like group C). While waiting for a 'vision test', each participant (one at a time) sat in a waiting room with another 'participant' (in fact, a confederate of the experimenters). For half the participants in each condition, the confederate acted in a happy, frivolous way (making paper aeroplanes, laughing out loud and playing with a hula hoop) (euphoria) while for the other half, he acted very angrily (eventually tearing up the questionnaire which he and the participant were both asked to complete) (anger). (In fact, the group B condition was only run with a euphoric stooge.)

Participants' emotional experiences were assessed by: (i) observers' ratings of the degree to which they joined in with the confederate's behaviour; and (ii) by self-report scales. As predicted, groups A and D were much less likely to join in with the confederate and to report feeling euphoric or angry, while group B and C participants assumed the confederate's behaviour and emotion.

1 If an individual experiences a state of physiological arousal for which they have no immediate explanation, they will 'label' this state and describe it in terms of the cognitions available. So precisely the same state of arousal could receive different labels (e.g. 'euphoria'/'anger' – groups B and C). (Physiological arousal and cognitive labelling are necessary.)

2 If an individual experiences a state of physiological arousal for which they have a completely appropriate explanation (e.g. 'I've just been given an injection of adrenaline') they will 'label' this state accordingly (group A).

3 Given the same circumstances, an individual will react emotionally or describe their feelings as emotions only to the extent that they experience a state of physiological arousal (all 3 groups). (Physiological arousal is necessary.)

Schachter and Wheeler (1962) confirmed these results by injecting participants either with adrenaline or chlorpromazine (which inhibits arousal); controls were injected with a placebo. While watching a slapstick comedy, the adrenaline participants laughed more and the chlorpromazine participants less than the controls.

Another supporting study is that by Dutton and Aron (1974) (Box 6.6). This study confirms Schachter's theory that the autonomic arousal which accompanies all emotions is similar and that it is our interpretation of that arousal that is important, even though this sometimes results in our misidentifying our emotions. Dutton and Aron's suspension bridge participants seemed to be mislabelling their fear as sexual attraction to the interviewer. (What do you think would have been the outcome if the interviewer had been male?)

Evaluation of the cognitive labelling theory

According to Parkinson (1987), the predominant influence in the study of emotion since Schachter has been a cognitive one. The focus of Schachter's model is an atypical state of affairs where the participant is unsure about the cause of arousal (groups B and C). But Schachter (1964) admitted that we usually are aware of a precipitating situation prior to the onset of arousal (which usually takes 1–2 seconds to reach consciousness) and so it is normally perfectly obvious to the person what aspects of the situation have initiated the emotion. However, even here the meaning of the emotion-inducing circumstances requires some cognitive analysis before the emotion can be labelled. Schachter claims that although the *quantitative* aspect of emotion can arise without

on the interpretation of those changes; we have to decide which particular emotion we are feeling, and the label we attach to our arousal depends on what we attribute that arousal to (see Fig. 6.6). Schachter is saying that physiological arousal is necessary for the experience of emotion but the nature of arousal is immaterial – it is how we interpret that arousal that matters and so the theory is also known as the *two factor theory of emotion*.

The classic experiment which demonstrates this cognitive theory of emotion is that of Schachter and Singer (1962) described in Box 6.5. They were testing three inter-related hypotheses regarding the interaction between physiological and cognitive factors in the experience of emotion:

BOX
6.6 Box 6.6 Key study: Falling in love on a suspension bridge (Dutton and Aron, 1974)

The participants were unsuspecting males, aged 18–35, who were visiting the Capilano Canyon in British Columbia, Canada. An attractive female experimenter approached the men and asked them questions as part of a survey she was supposedly conducting on the effects of scenery on creativity. One of the things they were asked to do was to invent a short story about an ambiguous picture of a woman (in fact a picture from the Thematic Apperception Test or TAT), which was later scored for the amount of sexual content, taken to reflect their sexual attraction towards the interviewer.

Some men were interviewed on an extremely unstable suspension bridge, five feet wide, 450 feet long, composed of wooden boards attached to wire cables running from one side of the canyon to the other. This bridge, 230 feet above the canyon, tends to sway, tilt and wobble, giving the impression that one is about to fall over the side, with only very low handrails of wire cable for support (*high arousal condition*). Other men were interviewed on a solid wooden bridge upstream, a mere ten feet above a shallow rivulet, with high handrails and without any swaying or tilting (*low arousal condition*).

As predicted, the stories of the former group contained significantly more sexual imagery. The interviewer also invited the men to call her if they wanted more information about the research. Again in line with predictions, four times as many men from the high arousal condition called her as from the low arousal condition.

To show that arousal was the independent variable, Dutton and Aron also arranged for another group of men to be interviewed ten minutes or more after crossing the suspension bridge, by which time the symptoms of their physical arousal should have been declining. These non-aroused men did not show the signs of sexual arousal shown by the men in the high arousal condition.

FIGURE 6.7 *The Capilano River bridge*

cognitive mediation ('Am I in a state of emotional arousal?') (e.g. Valins), the *qualitative* aspect requires prior cognition ('What emotion is it I am experiencing?') (e.g. Laird). Mandler (1984) has called Schachter's theory the 'jukebox' theory – arousal is like the coin which gets the machine going and cognition is the button we push to select the emotional tune. According to Parkinson (1987), the view that affect (emotion) is post-cognitive is now probably the most popular attitude among emotion theorists. But even accepting the important role of cognitive factors, is our emotional experience really as labile or malleable as Schachter claims, that is, are environmental cues really as easily accepted as the basis for inferences about our own feelings (Fiske and Taylor, 1991)? Using the original Schachter and Singer paradigm, several studies (Plutchik and Ax, 1967; Marshall and Zimbardo, 1979; Maslach, 1979) have concluded that when we look for an explanation of a state of arousal, we don't merely use others' behaviour as a guide to what we are feeling, but we call on many other sources of information as well, particularly our own past history, i.e. we search for previous occasions on which we felt this arousal state to explain why it is occurring now. While other people's behaviour might suggest – or even dictate (through conformity) – how we should behave in that situation, it does not tell us how we are feeling; at the very least, others' behaviour must in some way be appropriate (Weiner, 1992).

These later studies also found that people who don't have a ready-made explanation for their adrenaline-produced arousal are more likely to attach a negative emotional label to it (such as unease or nervousness similar to 'free-floating anxiety'). This suggests that emotional liability is not as great as Schachter maintains, i.e. unexplained arousal is not a neutral state to which one emotional label can be applied as easily as any other, but has a negative, unpleasant quality about it.

According to Schachter, while group A participants could attribute their arousal to the injection (i.e. they had a ready-made explanation and so didn't need an emotional explanation), for those in groups B and C, no such ready-made explanation was available and so the confederate's behaviour was used as a cue for explaining their own state of arousal (as either euphoria or anger). Taking one of James's original examples, fear is a label we give to our state of arousal when we attribute the arousal to a 'frightening' stimulus (the bear). While for the James–Lange theory the original cause of the bodily reactions is irrelevant (because our emotional experience is based on feedback from those bodily reactions), for Schachter it is what we attribute our arousal to, what is responsible for it, that determines the label we give to it. In the adrenaline experiment, the initially unexplained arousal is attributed to the (rather extreme) behaviour of the confederate and so is labelled euphoria or anger accordingly.

In the same way, the men in Dutton and Aron's experiment who were tested on the swaying suspension bridge, unaware of the 'real' cause of their arousal, attributed it to the female interviewer: we know that arousal was the independent variable and it is highly likely that had it not been for the intervention of the attractive interviewer, they would have labelled their arousal 'fear', because it would have been attributed to a frightening stimulus (the bridge).

What all these examples show is that the cognitive labelling theory is essentially based on *attributional principles* and this represents a major form of influence that the theory has had on cognitive theories of emotion in general. For example, Peterson and Seligman (1980) and Abramson and Martin (1981) grafted attribution principles onto Seligman's (1975) theory of learned helplessness (discussed later in relation to stress) in order to try to explain clinical depression. Clearly, the experience of the inability to control the outcome of one particular situation (helplessness) does not

inevitably lead to clinical depression in most people. So what other factors are involved? Abramson and Martin (1981) believe that depression only occurs when people make certain attributions about their helplessness, specifically when they believe it is caused by internal factors (as opposed to environmental), which are perceived as stable (as opposed to variable) and that are believed to reflect a global deficiency (as opposed to one related to a particular kind of bad experience). So people become depressed when they conclude that helplessness is likely to pervade all aspects of their future lives.

According to Weiner (1986, 1992), certain kinds of attribution produce specific emotions. For example, success produces a very general positive feeling (such as happiness), while failure produces a very general negative feeling (such as sadness), but if the outcome (either success or failure) is either very different from what is expected or has very important consequences, we try to figure out the reasons (or causes) for the outcome. These reasons will take the form of internal or external attributions which in turn can be broken down into controllable or uncontrollable; it is the combination of internal/external and controllable/uncontrollable that will determine specific emotional responses. Some examples are given in Figure 6.8. (Weiner's attributional theory of emotion is important for understanding *helping behaviour*; see Chapter 17.)

The misattribution effect and the misattribution paradigm

What the adrenaline and the Dutton and Aron experiments show is that people can make mistakes in how they attribute their arousal, i.e. it is possible to feel euphoric or angry (when one's arousal is in fact due to adrenaline) or sexually aroused (when one's arousal is really (due to) fear). This mislabelling of our feelings and drawing mistaken conclusions about the causes of those feelings is called the *misattribution effect* (Ross and Nisbett, 1991).

As part of their suspension bridge experiment, and in a later experiment, Dutton and Aron (1974, 1989) invited male students to participate in a learning experiment. After meeting an attractive female partner, half the students were frightened with the news that they would be suffering some 'quite painful' electric shocks. Before the experiment was due to begin, they were given a short questionnaire 'to get some information on your present feelings and reactions, since these often influence people on the learning task'. Asked how much they would like to date and kiss their partner,

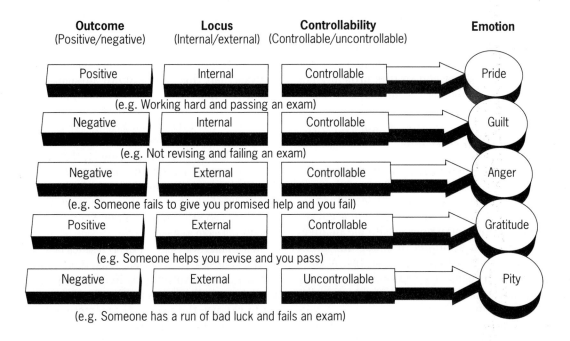

Outcome (Positive/negative)	Locus (Internal/external)	Controllability (Controllable/uncontrollable)	Emotion
Positive	Internal	Controllable	Pride
(e.g. Working hard and passing an exam)			
Negative	Internal	Controllable	Guilt
(e.g. Not revising and failing an exam)			
Negative	External	Controllable	Anger
(e.g. Someone fails to give you promised help and you fail)			
Positive	External	Controllable	Gratitude
(e.g. Someone helps you revise and you pass)			
Negative	External	Uncontrollable	Pity
(e.g. Someone has a run of bad luck and fails an exam)			

FIGURE 6.8 *Examples of how particular kinds of attribution can produce particular emotions. (Based on Weiner, 1986, 1992)*

the aroused (frightened) men expressed more intense attraction than the non-frightened men.

As, by definition, the female partner was sexually attractive, it was far easier for the men to transfer their arousal to her and so mislabel it as sexual arousal as opposed to fear. In this way she represented a salient or credible source of arousal (Olson and Ross, 1988). To take another example, if, using the false feedback paradigm (Valins, 1966; see above), female participants are shown slides of attractive male nudes, it may be easy to alter their preferences among the pictures based on false heart rate feedback, whereas it would be very difficult to achieve if the male nudes were replaced by slides of naked hippos! (This is a deliberately modified version of an example given by Taylor *et al.*, 1994.)

The misattribution effect is most likely to occur when the actual source of the arousal is unclear or ambiguous (Olson and Ross, 1988). For example, while we are unlikely to mistake what we are feeling in the presence of a coiled snake, we might well

do so when bumping into a fellow student in the lunch queue (Taylor *et al.*, 1994). It is also most likely to happen when we don't care very much about how we respond to some thing or situation; when it really matters, people seem to monitor their own attitudes and emotions more carefully and so are less influenced by external cues.

Both these points are very important for evaluating a major practical application of Schachter's theory and subsequent studies using the *misattribution paradigm* (Valins, 1966). Schachter's theory implies that emotional reactions induced by a threatening experience can be reattributed to a neutral or less threatening source, e.g. if you blame some external stimulus rather than your own inadequacies, you may calm down sufficiently to break the vicious circle (see Chapters 30 and 31). According to Taylor *et al.* (1994), when misattribution or reattribution studies were first done, they gave some promise of providing a new therapeutic tool for dealing with disruptive anxieties, fears, depressions, low self-esteem and other seemingly neurotic emotions. A variety of studies have tried to apply reattribution therapies to public speaking anxiety, test anxiety, depression and other unwanted emotions. The general technique has been to try to get the person to reattribute anxieties to less threatening sources. However, the effects have been short-lived, unreliable, limited to weak anxieties or very slight and so it is probably not powerful enough for therapeutic purposes.

Cognitive appraisal or affective primacy – which comes first, thought or feeling?

Perhaps the best known *cognitive appraisal theory* is that of Lazarus (1982) which is a development of Schachter's cognitive labelling theory. According to Lazarus, some degree of cognitive processing is an essential prerequisite for an affective reaction to a stimulus to occur and is an integral feature of all emotional states. A good demonstration of cognitive appraisal is the study by Speisman *et al.* (1964) (see Box 6.7), which is discussed in the context of stress.

For Lazarus, '... emotion results from evaluative perception of a relationship (actual, imagined or anticipated) between a person (or animal) and the environment'. We appraise the implications of the stimulus event for our well-being, i.e. how will the stimulus (which will usually be another person) affect my personal goals? The relationship with the stimulus involves either harm (i.e. thwarting of or threat to goal attainment) or benefit and the particular harms or benefits provide the details of the *relational meaning* (i.e. the significance of our relationship with the stimulus).

He proposes that cognitive appraisal invariably precedes any affective reaction, although it does not have to involve any conscious processing. Zajonc (1984) argues that there is generally little direct evidence of either the existence or nature of such preconscious cognitive processing (although the study of *subliminal perception* (see Chapter 9) suggests otherwise). Zajonc (1980) argues that cognition and affect operate as independent systems and an emotional response may precede cognitive processes under certain circumstances; we often make affective judgements about people even though we have processed very little information about them. For example, we may meet someone very briefly and form a positive or negative impression, despite not being able to remember any detailed information about them later, e.g. hair or eye colour (Eysenck and Keane, 1990).

Zajonc seems to overestimate the amount of cognitive processing which Lazarus and other cognitive appraisal theorists (such as Clore, Ellsworth, Frijda and Scherer) are claiming. For example, Lazarus simply argues that some minimal cognitive analysis at some level always precedes emotional experience, i.e. there needs to be some type of 'meaning analysis', but this can be quite automatic and so 'cognitive appraisal' is quite consistent with the sense of 'immediacy' which so much emotional experience has (and which Frijda (1994) sees as a characteristic of emotion).

But is Lazarus claiming, in effect, that an experience cannot be called an 'emotion' *unless* some cognitive appraisal is involved, i.e. is it part of the definition of an emotion? If so, it could be argued that this is an arbitrary definition and that he wants to have his cake and eat it!

In a similar way, Clore (1994) defines emotions as mental states, so that, by definition, there is substantial cognitive involvement. Neither physiological arousal nor feeling states provide the best way of trying to capture the nature of an emotion; to be an emotion, feelings must signify the results of an appraisal of some kind. Emotions aren't simply particular kinds of feelings, but particular kinds of feelings for particular reasons, i.e. they have emotional causes. This is why feelings that are generated artificially by electrical stimulation or hormone injection or some other non-cognitive means aren't emotions. (see Marañon's study in Box 6.3). For Clore, emotion terms seem to refer to something beyond feelings, to psychological states of which feelings are perhaps a necessary but not a sufficient condition.

Many of the examples which Zajonc gives of emotion without cognition (i.e. affective primacy or 'preferences need no inferences') do not seem to be examples of emotional states at all. For example, when someone leaps out in front of you and shouts 'Boo!', your physiological and bodily response (including your facial expression) would be more accurately described as constituting a *startle reflex* than as the emotion of fear. Startle, although it includes some emotion-like reactions, isn't generally seen as an emotion and while such reactions might lower our threshold for fear, they do not by themselves constitute fear.

Lazarus would have no problem with these examples: he would agree with Zajonc that no cognitive appraisal is required. Nothing in appraisal theory says that an object must be recognized before a sense of pleasure or aversion can be felt and

BOX
6.7
Key study: Subincision in the Arunta

A famous study by Speisman *et al.* (1964) involved showing participants a film on anthropology (*Subincision in the Arunta*) in which the penises of aboriginal boys are seen being cut with a jagged flint knife as part of a puberty rite. This normally causes high levels of stress. However, the sound track was manipulated, so that: (i) the pain, jaggedness of the knife, etc. were emphasized (*trauma*); (ii) the boys' anticipation of entering manhood was stressed (*denial*); (iii) the emotional elements were ignored and the traditions of the tribe were stressed (*intellectualization*); or (iv) there was no commentary at all (*silent control*).

As predicted, arousal (measured by GSR and heartrate) was highest in (i), next highest in (iv) and lowest in (ii) and (iii). What we tell ourselves about external situations influences the level of arousal we experience.

However, we should also ask if the converse is true – does the level of arousal influence how we appraise the situation? Those studies that have failed to replicate Schachter and Singer's findings all suggest that emotion is rather less malleable than Schachter believed: (i) if the dosage is high enough, adrenaline seems to produce an unpleasant mood – even in the group B condition and in the presence of the euphoric 'stooge'; (ii) group B and group C were both more likely to interpret the unexplained arousal negatively, regardless of the mood of the stooge (see above).

according to Ellsworth (1994), Zajonc has identified one of the basic and most important steps in the process, usually (though not necessarily) a very early step. Further appraisals (such as the perception of an obstacle, a sense of being in control or not, attribution of agency, i.e. was the event caused by oneself or someone else ?) result in emotions that are more differentiated than the simple sense of liking or disliking, approach or avoidance.

However, if Zajonc is equating 'emotions' with 'reflexes', then their respective views are poles apart. Yet it would probably be a misrepresentation to say that Lazarus believes that emotion always involves cognitive appraisal while Zajonc claims that it never does. According to Scherer (1994), the classic debate between the two, which had a major impact on the psychology of emotion during the 1980s, was mostly concerned with the level of processing involved, not whether any processing took

place, and this in turn revolved around the definition of 'cognition'.

So what do we mean by 'cognition'?
If 'cognition' means or includes basic sensory processing, then most, if not all, emotions will have some cognitive component. However, LeDoux (1994) and Panksepp (1994), both biologists, suggest that the brain circuitry underlying emotion and cognition are different. Cognition is seen as depending on the neocortex and hippocampus and if 'cognition' is restricted to those processes involving these brain areas, then emotion can occur without cognition, since animals with extensive lesions in these structures still display emotional responses. But doesn't this beg as many questions as it tries to answer, such as whether we can compare human and non-human emotions, even when the animals have intact brains, especially in the light of the definitions of emotion that we discussed above?

According to Davidson and Ekman (1994), the older Lazarus/Zajonc debate has advanced considerably. Most theorists now acknowledge that emotion can be elicited in the absence of conscious cognitive mediation; if a broad view of cognition is taken, most would also agree that some cognitive processing is required for most emotion. The challenge is to specify more precisely the types of cognitive processing that may be critical to the emotion generation process and to identify the neural circuitries that underlie emotion and cognition respectively. We also need to study the interactions between emotion and cognition.

STRESS: WHEN EMOTIONS BECOME HARMFUL

● How are stress and emotion related?

Cox (1978) argues that the experience of stress is usually described in ways associated with emotions – anger, anxiety, depression, fear, grief, guilt, jealousy and shame. Lazarus (1976) refers to these as the 'stress emotions'.

● Pain as an emotional and stressful experience

Although pain is not usually considered to be an emotion:

- it is often associated with emotions, such as anxiety and depression, two of the 'stress emotions';
- it shares with emotion the three main components of subjective experience, physiological/bodily changes and expressive behaviour, together with cognitive appraisal;
- methods used to help people cope with pain are often those used to help people cope with stress.

According to the International Association for the Study of Pain (IASP), pain is '... an unpleasant sensory and emotional experience associated with actual or potential tissue damage, or described in terms of such damage'. This definition indicates that pain is a subjective, personal experience that encompasses both sensory (e.g. pulling, burning, aching) and emotional (e.g. anxiety, depression) qualities. Not only may anxiety be part of the experience of pain, but it is generally accepted that anxiety leads to an increase in the perception of pain. It is also well known that depression often accompanies chronic pain and is positively associated with the pain intensity ratings of chronic pain patients (Bradley, 1995).

The IASP definition recognizes that an individual needn't suffer actual tissue damage at a specific body site in order to perceive pain at that site, as in the 'phantom limb' phenomenon, where someone who has lost an arm or leg continues to feel the presence of the amputated limb: about 50 percent of amputees experience chronic severe pain in their phantom limbs.

Pain is basically a physiological phenomenon, whose biological function is to provoke special reactive patterns aimed at the removal/avoidance of the noxious stimulus and this is true for animals in general. But the physiology of pain and understanding its biological function do not explain the *pain experience*, which includes not only the pain sensation but certain autonomic responses and 'associated feeling states' (Zborowski, 1952). For example, they wouldn't explain the acceptance of intense pain in torture (part of the initiation rites of many traditional, non-industrialized societies), nor the strong emotional reactions of certain individuals to the slight sting of a hypodermic needle.

In human society, pain acquires specific social and cultural significance and members of different cultures may assume differing attitudes towards different types of pain. According to Zborowski (1952), two of these attitudes may be described as *pain expectancy* and *pain acceptance*. Pain expectancy refers to the anticipation of pain as being unavoidable in a given situation (such as childbirth, sport or battle), while pain acceptance is the willingness to experience pain, which is manifested mostly as the inevitable component of culturally accepted experiences, (such as initiation rites and medical treatment). So labour pain is expected as part of childbirth but in most Western cultures it is not *accepted* (and various steps are taken to keep it to a minimum), while in others (such as Poland) it is both expected *and* accepted (and little or nothing is done to relieve it).

Trusting the doctor's ability to ease your suffering (whether this takes the form of a cure or merely the relief of pain and suffering) represents part of the cognitive appraisal aspect of pain; specifically, the belief that the illness/symptoms are controllable. If we attribute our symptoms to something that is controllable, this should make us feel more optimistic; that is, the meaning of our illness may be a crucial factor in how we react to it, which in turn may affect the illness itself.

According to Brody (1995), the patient's health is most likely to change in a positive direction when the meaning of the illness has been changed for the patient in a positive way. For example, when Mr Smith goes to the doctor with an experience that means to him 'I might have cancer' and he leaves with an experience that means ' I have a bad case of bronchitis and it should be better in a few days if I take these antibiotics', there is the greatest likelihood that he will feel better and breathe more easily even *before* the antibiotics begin to take effect. Although 'meaning' is hard to define, one component is giving the patient an explanation (i.e. attribution) for their illness that is both understandable and as reassuring as is truthfully possible. (People often claim that uncertainty is much more stressful than any diagnosis and this may be because uncertainty allows you to 'think the worst'. Similarly, when relatives go missing, having apparently 'disappeared into thin air', or are presumed dead but without a body being found, distress is maintained at a very high level because there is no available explanation.)

A number of methods and techniques used in the treatment of stress are also used for treating (mainly chronic) pain. (This is not surprising, since pain is often a symptom of many stress-induced – or psychophysiological – disorders, such as migraine headaches, and, as we saw above, anxiety can increase the perception of pain caused by medical illness). Bradley (1995) groups these behavioural treatments into three major kinds: contingency management, biofeedback and self-management/cognitive behaviour treatment.

FIGURE 6.9 *Biofeedback*

Contingency management is a form of operant conditioning (see Chapter 7) , whose goal is to achieve sufficient control over the patient's environment that reinforcement is withdrawn from 'pain' behaviours and made contingent on 'well' behaviours. Relatives are trained to reward the display of healthy behaviour at home and to ignore the display of pain behaviour.

Biofeedback involves giving the patient information (via monitors or buzzers) about certain autonomic functions (such as blood pressure, heart rate, muscle tension) so that they are able to bring these functions under voluntary control. Bradley (1995) cites a study in which college students suffering from muscle contraction headaches were given seven 50-minute sessions, twice weekly, using feedback about muscle tension (electromyograph (EMG) biofeedback). They were also urged to practise their newly learned skills at home when free of headaches and at the first signs of a headache. Compared with a waiting-list control condition (no treatment until the study was over) and a placebo condition (which engaged in 'pseudomeditation'), the EMG biofeedback produced significant reductions in EMG and headache activity (see Fig. 6.9).

Duchene (1990) also found convincing evidence for the effectiveness of EMG biofeedback in reducing the acute (as opposed to chronic) pain associated with childbirth among 40 first-time mothers. They were randomly assigned to the experimental or control group, the former attending six weekly training sessions and being loaned biofeedback machines for practice at home. The feedback was provided through both sound and a visual monitor, based on the tension of the abdominal muscles, which the women focused on relaxing when they felt a pain or contraction. All the women were monitored for pain perception, starting at admission and then at various points during labour, again at delivery and once more 24 hours after delivery (to recall the overall pain intensity). While 14 of the 20 control group women requested and had epidurals for pain relief, only eight of the experimental group did so (a significant difference) and the latter's labours were also significantly shorter.

Self-management/cognitive behaviour treatment is based on the premise that patients' expectations influence their emotional and behavioural reactions to life events, so that it is critical that doctors help patients to believe that they can acquire the necessary skills for controlling pain and other forms of disability. Self-management interventions usually involve multiple treatments, such as learning coping skills, progressive muscle relaxation training, practice in communicating effectively with family members and health care providers and providing positive reinforcement for displaying coping behaviour. Patients are encouraged to take responsibility for managing their pain and to attribute their success to their own efforts. (Cognitive behaviour treatment is discussed below in relation to stress.)

● What is stress?

According to Goetsch and Fuller (1995), definitions of stress fall into three categories:

1 stress as a stimulus;
2 stress as a response;
3 stress as interaction between an organism and its environment.

This classification corresponds very closely to three models of stress identified by Cox (1978).

The *engineering model* sees external stresses giving rise to a stress reaction, or strain, in the individual, so the stress is located in the stimulus characteristics of the environment; stress is what *happens* to a person (not what happens within a person).

The concept is derived from Hooke's law of elasticity in physics, which deals with how loads (stress) produce deformation in metals. Up to a point, stress is inevitable and can be tolerated; indeed, moderate levels may even be beneficial (what Selye (1956) called *eustress*). Indeed, complete absence of stress (as measured, say, by anxiety or physiological arousal) could be positively detrimental (for instance, being so relaxed that you fail to notice the car speeding towards you as you are crossing the road). Stress helps to keep us alert, providing us with some of the energy required to maintain an interest in our environment, to explore it and adapt to it; in these respects, stress is similar to motivation and emotion (or is a component of both). However, when stress becomes intolerable (when we are stretched beyond our limits of elasticity), it becomes positively harmful.

The *physiological model* is primarily concerned with what happens *within* the person, that is, with the 'response' aspects of the engineering model, in particular the physiological (and, to a lesser extent, the psychological) changes which occur as a result of stress.

The impetus for this view of stress was Selye's (1956) definition that 'Stress is the non-specific response of the body to any demand made upon it'. Selye's original observations were made when he was a medical student and noticed a general malaise or syndrome associated with 'being ill', regardless of the particular illness. The syndrome was characterized by: (i) a loss of appetite; (ii) an associated loss of weight and strength; (iii) loss of ambition; and (iv) a typical facial expression associated with illness. Further examination of extreme cases revealed major physiological changes, including enlargement of the adrenal cortex, shrinkage of the thymus, spleen and lymphatics (all involved in the body's immune system) and, eventually, deep bleeding ulcers of the stomach and upper gut (confirmed by Cox, 1978). These changes, representing the non-specific response to illness, were supposed to reflect a distinct phenomenon which Selye called the *General Adaptation Syndrome* (GAS) – we shall discuss this further below.

The *transactional model* represents a kind of blend of the first two models and sees stress as arising from an interaction between people and their environment, in particular, when there is an imbalance between the person's perception of the demand being made of them by the situation and their ability to meet the demand, and when failure to cope is important. Because it is the person's perception of this mismatch between demand and ability which causes stress, the model allows for important individual differences in what produces stress and how much stress is experienced; people may also differ in terms of characteristic physiological responses to stress (over and above the GAS). For instance, some will typically have migraine headaches, others break out in a rash, others have stomach pains and so on. There are also wide differences in how people attempt to cope with stress, psychologically and behaviourally, and we shall discuss some of these below.

The engineering model may be seen as primarily concerned with the question 'What causes stress?' (i.e. stress as a stimulus) and the physiological model with the question, 'How do we react (physiologically) to stress?' or 'What are the effects of stress?' (i.e. stress as a response). The transactional model is concerned with both these questions plus the question, 'How do we cope with stress?' (i.e. stress as an interaction between an organism and its environment). We shall now look at these three major issues.

What causes stress?

If, according to the transactional model, the causes of stress depend on how individuals perceive and appraise the demands being made of them, then it follows that these causes don't exist objectively and cannot be defined separately from the individuals involved. This is a view adopted by Lazarus (1966) who points out that individuals differ in terms of what is seen as a *stressor* in the first place. So when asking 'What causes stress?', we need to be aware that we are trying to identify *potential* stressors, the kinds of event or experience that most people are most likely to find exceed their capacity and ability to handle the demands that are involved, with a wide range of individual perceptions of the 'same' event.

Frustration and conflict

Anything which prevents us from achieving our goals is a potential source of stress. Indeed, frustration is usually defined as some kind of negative emotional state which occurs when we are prevented from reaching a goal (Coon, 1983) and so is a common source of stress. But what causes frustration?

Our own inadequacies can prevent us from achieving our goals and ambitions (e.g. we want to be a basketball player but are very short or we want to be a doctor but cannot stand the sight of blood). Or we can be thwarted by a whole range of external/environmental factors over which we have little or no control, such as the train being cancelled, the telephone being out of order or the weather changing for the worse! We shall say more about these everyday hassles below.

Conflicts develop when a person experiences two or more competing or contradictory motives or goals:

- *Approach–approach* conflicts involve having to choose between two equally attractive alternatives, e.g. two equally delicious-sounding dishes on the same menu or two equally interesting courses at college or university (see cognitive dissonance theory in Chapter 18 for a discussion of how such conflict is resolved once the decision has been made).
- *Avoidance–avoidance* conflicts involve having to choose between two equally unattractive alternatives, e.g. going to the dentist or putting up with awful toothache, deciding whether to do your psychology or your sociology essay first. It is a case of having to choose 'between the devil and the deep blue sea'.
- *Approach–avoidance* conflicts involve the same person or situation having both desirable and undesirable qualities, e.g. you are really interested in psychology but you are not so sure about the statistics or you want to go to university but you would like to be working and earning some money.

Disruption of circadian rhythms

As we saw in Chapter 4, the word 'circadian' comes from the Latin *circa dies* and means 'about one day'. It describes a particular periodicity or rhythm of a number of physiological and behavioural functions which can be seen in almost all living creatures.

During a 24-hour period, there is a cycle of many physiological functions (e.g. heart rate, metabolic rate, breathing rate, body temperature) which all tend to reach maximum values during the late afternoon and early evening and minimum values in the early hours of the morning. It might seem fairly obvious that such a rhythm would occur as it is likely that physiological functions would increase during the day when we are active and become depressed at night when we are asleep and inactive. However, many studies have shown that these rhythms persist if we suddenly reverse our activity pattern and sleep during the day and are active during the night. This represents one kind of evidence that these rhythms are internally controlled (i.e. they are *endogenous*).

However, our circadian rhythms are kept on their once-every-24-hours schedule by regular daily cues in the environment. These environmental (*exogenous*) cues are called *zeitgebers* (from the German meaning 'time givers') and the most important for the regulation of mammalian circadian rhythms is the daily cycle of light and dark. So if we persist with our reversal of sleep and activity, after a period of acclimatization, the body's circadian rhythms will have reversed and become synchronized to the new set of exogenous cues.

Individuals differ considerably in how quickly they can reverse their rhythms; it can take 5–7 days for some and up to 14 days for others and some may never achieve a complete reversal. Also, not all physiological functions reverse at the same time – body temperature usually reverses inside a week for most people, while the rhythms of adrenocortical hormone take much longer. During the changeover period all the body's functions are in a state of *internal desynchronization* (Aschoff 1979), which is very stressful and accounts for much of the exhaustion, malaise and lassitude associated with changing work shifts. In shift work, the zeitgebers stay the same, but workers are forced to adjust their natural sleep–wake cycles in order to meet the demands of changing work schedules (Pinel, 1993).

So what happens to job performance (and, therefore, job efficiency) when body temperature and other physiological functions alter rhythm as a result of change in work shift? Hawkins and Armstrong-Esther (1978) studied 11 nurses during the first seven nights of a period of night duty and found that performance was significantly impaired on the first night but improved progressively on successive nights; body temperature had not fully adjusted to night-working after seven nights. There were significant differences between individual nurses, with some appearing relatively undisturbed by working nights and others never really adjusting at all. (The effects of lack of sleep were discussed in Chapter 4.)

Shift workers often report experiencing insomnia, digestive problems, irritability, fatigue, even depression. Workers who rotate shifts each week also have more accidents on the job and lower productivity. Blakemore (1988) refers to a study of workers at the Great Salt Lake Mineral and Chemical Corporation in Utah, who worked a three-weekly schedule: the first week a day shift, second week a night shift, third week an evening shift and so on. Although this is one of the most common shift schedules used in industry, it seems almost deliberately designed to present the worst possible challenge to the rhythms of the body. Blakemore says it is like travelling constantly from West to East and never quite overcoming the resulting jet lag (more of that below). Laboratory animals subjected to this kind of rotating schedule of light and dark suffer from increased heart disease and a shorter lifespan.

The Utah workers were forced to rotate their biological clock backwards by eight hours per week. Czeisler recommended that: (i) the shifts rotate forwards in time (taking advantage of the body's natural preference for a 25-hour cycle); and (ii) each shift should last for three weeks (as most people take more than a week to adjust to a new time zone). The results of these changes were quite dramatic, rapid and remarkable – workers liked the new schedules, enjoyed better health and made better use of their leisure time; productivity rose by 22 percent.

Consistent with these findings, Pinel (1993) reports that companies have had great success in terms of productivity and job satisfaction by scheduling *phase delays*, i.e. whenever possible, shift workers are transferred from their current schedule to one that begins later in the day. It is much more difficult to go to sleep four hours earlier and get up four hours earlier (a *phase advance*) than to go to sleep four hours later and get up four hours later (a *phase delay*).

Another occupational group who are very much affected by disruption to their circadian rhythms are airline pilots who experience jet lag because they cross time zones during the course of the flight. If you have ever travelled across a time zone, you will know what it is like to have your biological rhythms 'out of sync' with your surroundings. If you arrive in Washington DC at, say, 7 p.m. (after an eight-hour flight from London) you may be ready to start your evening's entertainment but as far as your body is concerned, it is sleeping time (back in London it is 1 a.m., the middle of the night).

Knowledge of the characteristics of the biological clock help us to understand an apparently curious feature of jet lag, namely that most people suffer much less when travelling in an East–West direction than a West–East direction. When going West ('chasing the sun'), the day is temporarily lengthened: because the natural or free-running circadian rhythm cycle of the biological clock is 25 hours (see Chapter 4), an increase in day length is much easier to deal with than a decrease. Indeed, the ideal way to travel would be always going East–West, in short hops of one time zone each day, making each day of the journey precisely equal to the body's natural 25-hour rhythm. (This corresponds to a phase-delay change in work shift, while travelling West–East corresponds to a phase advance.)

Melatonin (a hormone produced by the pineal gland) plays a crucial role in the experience of jet lag: its secretion reaches a peak during the night (helping to make us sleepy in the first place; see Chapter 4) and, after a long flight, the cyclical release of melatonin stays locked into the day/night pattern of the home country for some days. This could account for the fatigue felt during the day and the insomnia at night. If jet-lagged volunteers are given melatonin during the evening, far fewer report feeling jet-lagged than controls who receive only a placebo (Blakemore, 1988). Alternatively, exposure to intense light early in the morning promotes phase advances (Czeisler *et al.*, 1989, cited in Pinel, 1993).

Life changes

Holmes and Rahe (1967) examined 5000 patient records and made a list of 43 life events, of varying seriousness, which seemed to cluster in the months preceding the onset of their illness. Out of this grew the *Social Readjustment Rating Scale* (SRRS), a self-administered pencil-and-paper measure on which participants check all those things which have happened to them in some specified time period (usually 6–12 months) (see Table 6.1).

The assumption underlying the scale is that stress is created by events which require change (whether they are desirable or undesirable). Life changes are a mixed blessing – while we may welcome the variety and novelty they provide they also prevent us from achieving certain (other) goals and may force us into setting ourselves new goals and objectives which we have not anticipated. The SRRS was intended to predict the onset of illness; how well has it fared?

A number of studies have shown that people who experience many significant life changes (i.e. a score of 300 life change units (LCUs) or over) are more susceptible to physical and mental illness than those with lower scores, e.g. correlations are usually small but significant and the range of associated symptoms is wide, including sudden cardiac death, heart attacks (non-fatal), TB, diabetes, leukaemia, accidents and even athletics injuries.

How can we be sure that life changes actually cause illness?

The studies which claim to show that life change is responsible for illness are *correlational*; it is possible, therefore, that, instead of life events causing illness, some life events are themselves early manifestations of an illness which is already developing, e.g. being fired from work, sexual difficulties, trouble with in-laws, change in sleeping habits (Brown, 1986).

Many of these studies are also *retrospective,* i.e. people are asked to recall both the illnesses and the stressful life events that occurred during the specified period, which is likely to produce unreliable data (see Chapter 12). For example, someone who is under stress (whatever the cause) may focus on minor physiological sensations and report these as 'symptoms of illness' (Davison and Neale, 1994).

Is change necessarily stressful?

The SRRS, as we have seen, assumes a particular view of stress, i.e. any change is, by definition, stressful, regardless of whether it is usually seen as positive (e.g. marriage) or negative (e.g. death of spouse). According to Davison and Neale (1994), the available evidence seems to indicate that the undesirable aspects of events are at least as important as the fact that they change people's lives. A quick glance at Table 6.1 suggests that life changes have a largely negative feel about them, perhaps especially those in the top ten which, of course, receive the highest LCU scores. This implies that there might be a confusion, within the scale, between 'change' and 'negativity'.

Is all change equally stressful?

Life changes may only be stressful if they are unexpected and, in this sense, uncontrollable, i.e. it may not be change as such that is stressful, but change that is not within our power to prevent or reverse. Studies have shown that when people are asked to classify the undesirable life events on the SRRS as either 'controllable' or 'uncontrollable', only the latter are significantly correlated with subsequent onset of illness.

According to Parkes (1993), the psychosocial transitions that are most dangerous to health are those that:

- demand a major change in our *assumptive world* ('everything that we assume to be true on the basis of our previous experience ...');
- have lasting consequences; and
- take place over a relatively short period of time (i.e. are sudden) and allow little time for preparation. The sudden death of a relative from a heart attack, in an accident or as a result of crime, are examples of the most stressful kind of life changes. (Psychosocial transitions or critical life events will be discussed again in Chapter 24 on adulthood and old age.)

As Brown (1986) suggests, perhaps it is perceived uncontrollability which makes life change stressful and, hence, dangerous to health. Using Rotter's (1966) *Locus of Control Scale* (see Chapter 5) and devising a new scale (the *Life Events Scale*), Johnson and Sarason (1978) found that life events stress was more closely related to psychiatric symptoms (in particular, depression and anxiety) among people rated as high on external locus of control than among those rated as high on internal locus of control, i.e. people who believe that they don't have control over what happens to them are more vulnerable to the harmful effects of change than those who believe they do.

Related to locus of control is Seligman's (1975) concept of *learned helplessness* (see Chapter 7). When dogs, mice, cats and people discover that their behaviour and the delivery of electric shock are independent (i.e. nothing the animal/person does will make any difference, the shock will be given anyway), this learned helplessness is generalized to other situations in which shock *is* contingent on the animal's/person's behaviour.

Seligman believes that human depression can be explained in terms of learned helplessness – the original state of anxiety is replaced by depression when the individual realizes that trauma cannot be controlled and is said to be in a state of inaction (inhibition of coping behaviour) which places them in a highly vulnerable biological position. Learned helplessness is also thought to be involved in drug abuse. We saw above, when discussing theories of emotion, how Peterson and Seligman (1980) have combined the theory of learned helplessness and attribution theory to explain depression.

In Brady's (1958) executive monkey experiment, pairs of monkeys were yoked by an apparatus which gave electric shocks: whenever one received a shock, so did the other (and this happened at 20-second intervals for six hours at a time over a period of several weeks). One of the pair (the 'executive') could prevent shock by pressing a lever; the other also had a lever but pressing it had no effect. The executive developed severe ulcers and eventually died; the other member of the pair showed no apparent ill effects. This seems to contradict the belief that control over the situation usually reduces stress.

Two important points need to be made: (i) Brady's monkeys were not randomly assigned to the executive and non-executive conditions but had been selected on the basis of how quickly they learned to avoid shock (Seligman *et al.*, 1971); and (ii) in a partial replication of Brady's experiment, Weiss (1972), using rats, preceded the shock by a warning signal for the executives who had much less stomach ulceration than their partners. By contrast, Brady's

Rank	Life event	Mean value
1	Death of spouse	100
2	Divorce	73
3	Marital separation	65
4	Jail term	63
5	Death of close family member	63
6	Personal injury or illness	53
7	Marriage	50
8	Fired at work	47
9	Marital reconciliation	45
10	Retirement	45
11	Change in health of family member	44
12	Pregnancy	40
13	Sex difficulties	39
14	Gain of new family member	39
15	Business readjustment	39
16	Change in financial state	38
17	Death of close friend	37
18	Change to different line of work	36
19	Change in number of arguments with spouse	35
20	Mortgage over $10,000	31
21	Foreclosure of mortgage or loan	30
22	Change in responsibilities at work	29
23	Son or daughter leaving home	29
24	Trouble with in-laws	29
25	Outstanding personal achievement	28
26	Wife begins or stops work	26
27	Begin or end school	26
28	Change in living conditions	25
29	Revision of personal habits	24
30	Trouble with boss	23
31	Change in work hours or conditions	20
32	Change in residence	20
33	Change in schools	20
34	Change in recreation	19
35	Change in church activities	19
36	Change in social activities	18
37	Mortgage or loan less than $10,000	17
38	Change in sleeping habits	16
39	Change in number of family get-togethers	15
40	Change in eating habits	15
41	Vacation	13
42	Christmas	12
43	Minor violations of the law	11

TABLE 6.1 *Social Readjustment Rating Scale. The amount of life stress a person has experienced in a given period of time, say one year, is measured by the total number of life change units (LCUs). These units result from the addition of the values (shown in the right column) associated with events that the person has experienced during the target time period. The mean values (item weightings) were obtained empirically by telling 100 judges that 'marriage' had been assigned an arbitrary value of 500 and asking them to assign a number to each of the other events in terms of 'the intensity and length of time necessary to accommodate ... regardless of the desirability of the event relative to marriage'. The average of the numbers assigned each event was divided by 10 and the resulting values became the weighting of each life event. (From Holmes and Rahé, 1967)*

executives had to be constantly vigilant; without a warning signal, they could never be sure whether they would be successful in avoiding the next shock – very stressful! Human executives (many of whom are Type A personalities; see below) are also particularly prone to stress-related diseases and air traffic controllers (who have to be constantly vigilant) have the highest incidence of stomach ulcers in the USA.

The hassles and uplifts of everyday life

The SRRS is useful but, by definition, most of the 43 changes are not everyday occurrences. Kanner *et al.* (1981) designed a *hassles scale* (comprising 117 items, including 'concerns about weight', 'misplacing or losing things', 'rising price of common goods') and an *uplifts scale* (135 items including 'relating well with spouse/lover', 'feeling healthy', 'meeting your responsibilities').

In a study of 100 men and women aged 45–64 over a 12-month period, Kanner *et al.* confirmed the prediction that hassles were positively related to undesirable psychological symptoms and that uplifts were negatively related. They also found that hassles were a more powerful predictor of symptoms than life events (as measured by SRRS) ('divorce', for example, may exert stress by any number of component hassles, such as cooking for oneself, handling money matters and having to tell people about it).

Brown (1986) believes that we need to be able to use the hassles scale to predict *somatic* symptoms, because psychological symptoms occur very close in time to the hassles themselves. Research along these lines has been carried out using the *Assessment of Daily Experience* (Stone and Neale, 1982). This was designed to allow individuals to record and rate their daily experiences in *prospective* studies, i.e. to predict illness on the basis of experiences rather than looking back at illness that has already occurred. The unit of analysis is one day (rather than, say, a six-month period), which makes the events to be rated much more commonplace or mundane ('everyday') than those found in the SSRS, while not excluding major life events. One such study is described in Box 6.8.

Occupation-linked stressors and surviving disasters

We have already referred to several occupational groups when discussing the causes of stress: airline pilots in relation to jet lag, air traffic controllers in relation to the need to be constantly vigilant and

---

BOX 6.8 Key study: looking forward from stress to illness

Stone *et al.* (1987) began a study of the relationship between life experience and health, in which 79 participants provided at least 12 weeks of continuous daily data about symptoms and health-related behaviours (including any treatment sought or given). Respiratory illness was chosen as the critical variable, partly because respiratory infection maximizes the opportunity to detect the delayed effects of events on the onset of symptoms. For example, with rhinovirus infection (a major cause of the common cold) there is a 2–5 day lag between exposure to the virus and the onset of peak symptoms: it would be possible for stress to increase the risk of illness but with symptoms not apparent for 2–5 days. By contrast, a headache is much more likely to appear on the same day as the stressors that have induced it, making a causal link more difficult to interpret.

Stone *et al.* predicted that in the period prior to the onset of respiratory illness there would be an increase in the daily frequency of undesirable events and a corresponding decrease in the frequency of desirable events (relative to 'control days'). The predictions were confirmed: there were significant decreases in desirable events 3–4 days prior to illness onset and significant increases in undesirable events 4–5 days before. The two days immediately prior to illness had average rates of both kinds of event; this effectively rules out the possibility that the results are caused by some bias, such as feeling poorly before the symptoms really show and judging events more negatively as a result (Davison and Neale, 1994).

---

shift workers in relation to disruption of their circadian rhythms. Whether industrial workers or nurses, shift workers as a group face the same stressful conditions when having to adjust their bodily rhythms to their shift. However, nurses, along with other health care professionals (whether on night duty or not) have to contend with other sources of stress, many of which seem to be an inherent feature of their occupation. Some of these are discussed in Box 6.9.

Being the survivor of an accident, particularly a major disaster in which large numbers of other people lost their lives, can become a source of long-term stress. The emotional and behavioural response to such experiences is known as *post-traumatic stress disorder*, which was first formally recognized as a form of mental disorder in *DSM-III* (1980), the

American Psychiatric Association's classification and diagnostic system. The aftermath of the Vietnam war helped to get this new diagnosis generally accepted. Unlike other psychological disorders, apart from describing a cluster of symptoms, it also includes its presumed cause(s), namely, a traumatic event which the person has directly experienced or witnessed that involved actual or threatened death, serious injury or a threat to physical integrity (Davison and Neale, 1994) (see Chapter 30).

● What are the effects of stress?

We have already seen that this is the key question that the physiological model is concerned with and this section will be mainly concerned with the body's response to stress, including the possible mechanisms by which stress can bring about illness.

According to Selye (1956) the General Adaptation Syndrome (GAS) represents the body's defence against stress. Selye argues that the initial symptoms of almost any disease or trauma are virtually identical, that is, the body responds in the same way to any stressor, whether it is external and environmental or whether it arises from within the body itself. His work on stress began quite accidentally during his study of sex hormones, when he observed that injecting extracts of ovary tissue into rats produced the three responses that we noted above in human patients, namely, enlargement of the adrenal glands, shrinkage of the thymus gland and bleeding ulcers. When he used extracts of other organs, as well as substances not derived from bodily tissue, the same responses were produced. He eventually found that this same 'triad' of 'non-specific' responses could be produced by such different stimuli as insulin, cold or heat, X-rays and exercise. Selye (1956) defined stress as:

> ... the individual's psychophysiological response, mediated largely by the autonomic nervous system and the endocrine system, to any demands made on the individual.

Whatever the particular stressor or noxious stimulus, the body responds in the same way; this response is called the GAS, which comprises three stages: the alarm reaction, resistance and exhaustion.

Alarm reaction
This involves physiological changes generally associated with emotion: the sympathetic branch of the ANS is activated and in turn stimulates the adrenal medulla to secrete increased levels of adrenaline and noradrenaline (the 'stress hormones'). These are associated with sympathetic changes such as increased blood sugar level, increased heart-rate and blood pressure, increased blood flow to the muscles, pupil dilation and decreased GSR (the *fight or flight syndrome*; see Chapter 3).

The amount of adrenaline and noradrenaline (*catecholamines*) in the urine reflects the degree of sympathetic-adrenomedullary activity taking place and is correlated with how much stress people report experiencing. The action of the catecholamines is to mimic sympathetic arousal (hence they are called sympathomimetics) and, in fact, noradrenaline is the transmitter at the synapses of the sympathetic branch of the ANS. Consequently, noradrenaline from the adrenals prolongs the action of noradrenaline released at synapses in the ANS. This means that, even if the stressor is short-lived and even after it has been removed, sympathetic arousal will continue. (This is a 'closed-loop' process, making a stress reaction self-perpetuating.)

Resistance
If the stressor is not removed, the body begins to recover from the initial alarm reaction and to cope with the situation. There is a decrease in sympathetic activity, a lower rate of adrenaline and noradrenaline output, but an increase in output from the other part of the adrenal gland, the adrenal cortex.

The adrenal cortex is controlled by the amount of *adrenocorticotrophic hormone* (ACTH) in the blood. ACTH is released from the anterior pituitary (the 'master' endocrine gland) upon instructions from the hypothalamus. The adrenal cortex is essential for the maintenance of life and its removal results in death. The effect of ACTH is to stimulate the adrenal cortex to release *corticosteroids* (or adrenocorticoid hormones), one group of which are the glucocorticoid hormones (chiefly, corticosterone, cortisone and hydrocortisone); these control and conserve the amount of glucose in the blood (*glucogenesis*), which helps to resist stress of all kinds. To the extent that the glucocorticoids convert protein into glucose, make fats available for energy, increase blood flow and generally stimulate behavioural responsiveness, the anterior pituitary-adrenal cortex system is contributing to the fight or flight syndrome.

Exhaustion
Once ACTH and corticosteroids are circulating in the bloodstream, they tend to inhibit the further release of ACTH from the pituitary (through a negative feedback system). If the source of stress is removed during the resistance stage, blood sugar levels will gradually return to normal. However, when the stress situation continues, higher brain centres will

BOX 6.9 Caring for others is bad for your health

According to Seymour (1995), employers are increasingly coming to realize that a stressed workforce is an expensive workforce. A Department of Health/Confederation of British Industry (CBI) report (1991) found that the cost of sickness absences for stress and mental disorders in the UK runs to £5 billion per year.

According to the Health Education Authority (1988), the four most stressful occupations are nursing, social work, teaching and working in the police force. In the case of nursing, some sources of stress seem to be intrinsic to the job, such as having to deal constantly with the pain, anxiety and death of patients, having to support both patients and their families; this is made more demanding because of the very inadequate training or support that nurses receive to handle these traumatic emotional events (Gaze, 1988).

If this wasn't stressful enough, nurses working in particular specialized areas or hospital departments are faced with additional demands. For example, nurses working in intensive care units have to maintain high levels of concentration for long periods of time, are often emotionally drained by continuous close contact with a distressed and frightened family and the process of dying may not follow a natural course – it can be sud-den, but technology (ventilators, etc.) and drugs may prolong it (Fromant, 1988).

Medical staff working in accident and emergency departments are in the front line when it comes to coping with major disasters, such as the Zeebrugge ferry disaster and the Hungerford massacre in 1987 and the Hillsborough football disaster in 1989. However well prepared the staff may be from a practical point of view, it seems impossible to be prepared for the emotional demands made by large-scale death and serious injury. As David Smith, Charge Nurse at the Royal Hallamshire Hospital A and E Department in Sheffield, which dealt with the Hillsborough casualties , put it '... On the day, you deal with what happens. But it's the fall-out afterwards that's the problem' (quoted in Owen, 1990).

Increasing workload seems to be a feature of life in late 20th century Britain and there is a growing trend for professionals to seek legal remedies for workplace pressures. For example, in 1994, senior social worker John Walker successfully sued Northumberland County Council for causing his second nervous breakdown as a result of an excessive caseload and lack of support and in April 1995, junior doctor Chris Johnstone settled out of court with his previous employer, Camden and Islington Health Authority, over a claim about a workload which, he claimed, led him into a suicidal depression.

over-ride the negative feedback system and maintain the pituitary-adrenal excitation. The body's resources are now becoming depleted, the adrenals can no longer function properly, blood glucose levels drop and, in extreme cases, hypoglycaemia could result in death. It is at this stage that psychophysiological disorders develop, including high blood pressure (hypertension), heart disease (coronary artery disease (CAD), coronary heart disease (CHD), asthma and peptic (stomach) ulcers. Selye called these the *diseases of adaptation.*

All these physiological responses to stress are based, originally, on the work of Cannon (1928, 1929) whose theory of emotion we discussed above. His early research basically lay dormant for many years until Selye's (1956) research popularized the notion of stress and brought it to the attention of scientists in many different disciplines (Gatchel, 1995) (see Fig. 6.10).

How does stress make us ill?

One very general way of trying to understand why stress is bad for us is to look at it from an evolutionary perspective. The sympathetic branch of the ANS responds as a unit, so when it is stimulated, there is generalized, undifferentiated arousal. This was probably of crucial importance in our evolutionary past, when our ancestors were frequently confronted by life-threatening dangers: this is precisely what the fight or flight syndrome is for. However, while an increase in heart rate may be necessary to supply more blood to the muscles when facing a hungry-looking bear, it may be quite irrelevant to most of the stressors that we face in modern life, whether these are everyday hassles or major life changes. While most stressors don't present us with physical danger, our nervous and endocrine systems have evolved in such a way that we typically react to stressors as if they did; what may have been adaptive responses for our ancestors have become maladaptive today.

If our bodies react to stressful situations and events so as to prepare us for action, but 'action' (i.e. fight or flight) is not usually what is required, what happens to all that internal activity? In the case of heart rate and blood pressure (BP), chronic stress (stress that continues for long periods of time) will involve repeated episodes of increases in heart rate and BP which, in turn, produce increases in plaque formation within the cardiovascular system.

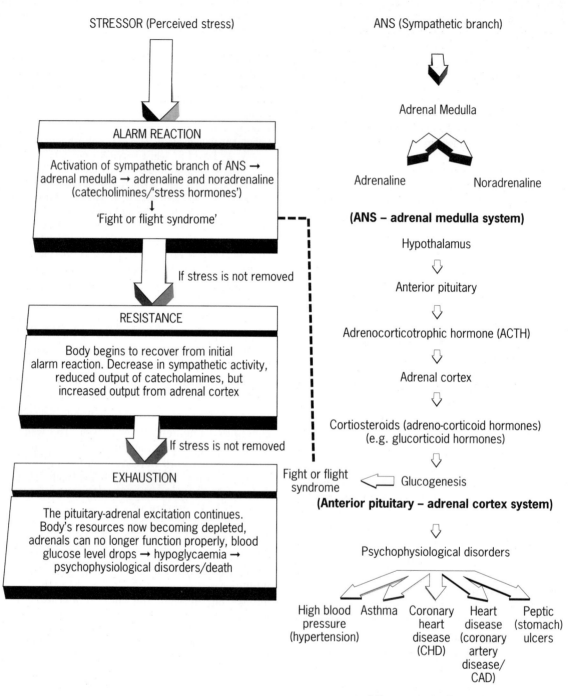

FIGURE 6.10 *Summary diagram of the three stages of the General Adaptation Syndrome (GAS) (Selye) and their relationship to the physiological changes associated with (i) the ANS – adrenal medulla and (ii) anterior pituitary – adrenal cortex systems (Cannon)*

Again, stress produces an increase in blood cholesterol levels, through the action of adrenaline and noradrenaline on the release of free fatty acids. This produces a clumping together of cholesterol particles, leading to clots in the blood and in the artery walls and occlusion of the arteries. In turn, raised heart rate is related to a more rapid build-up of cholesterol on artery walls. High BP results in small lesions on the artery walls and cholesterol tends to get trapped in these lesions (Holmes, 1994).

Stress and the immune system

An important way in which stress may result in disease is through its influence on the body's immune system, a collection of billions of cells which travel through the bloodstream and move in and out of tissues and organs, defending the body against invasion by foreign agents (e.g. bacteria, viruses, cancerous cells); the study of the effect of psychological factors on the immune system is called *psychoimmunology*. People often catch a cold soon after a period of stress (e.g. final exams) because stress seems to reduce the immune system's ability to fight off cold viruses. Goetsch and Fuller (1995) refer to studies that show decreases in the activity of *lymphocytes*, 'natural killer cells' (a particular type of white blood cell which normally fights off viruses and cancer cells), among medical students during their final exams.

A study by Greer *et al.* (1979) in England of women who had been diagnosed as having breast cancer (and actually had a mastectomy) found that those who reacted either by denying what had happened or by showing a 'fighting spirit' were significantly more likely to be free of cancer five years later than women who stoically accepted it or felt helpless. The implication here is that the first two reactions help to muster the immune system's fight against the spread of cancer.

A powerful stressor is the death of a close relative (it comes at the top of the SRRS) and there is considerable evidence linking this (and other kinds of loss and separation) and the immune system. For example:

- a group of men whose wives had died of breast cancer were found to have decreased immune function;
- marital discord has been associated with an increase in illness and death and with changes in immune function;
- people who are divorced are significantly more likely to die of pneumonia than married people;
- women who are separated from their husbands have 30 percent more illnesses and doctor's appointments than married women.

Although some of these findings may be partially attributable to differences in lifestyle (such as smoking and alcohol consumption), there is mounting evidence of the direct effects of stress on the immune system (Goetsch and Fuller, 1995).

The study by Stone *et al.* (1987) described in Box 6.8 also supports this view. In that study, it was also found that changes in mood (that are influenced by daily events) are linked to changes in the level of antibodies contained within immunoglobulin A (IgA), a substance found in tears, saliva, bronchial and other bodily secretions. These antibodies are thought to be the body's first line of defence against invading viruses and bacteria; the higher the level of positive mood, the higher the level of antibodies.

Cohen *et al.* (1991, cited in Davison and Neale, 1994), at the Common Cold Unit in England, gave volunteers nasal drops containing mild cold virus, along with a battery of measures of recent stressors. Increases in exposure to stressors was clearly linked to the rate of infection.

Finally, there is thought to be a link between stress, the body's natural painkillers and the immune system. In 1975, it was discovered that the body makes its own natural painkillers, morphine-like substances called endorphins and enkephalins. (These are discussed in Chapter 3 as *neuromodulators*.) Endorphins are found in the pituitary gland and, although their exact role in stress reactions is still unclear, several studies have suggested that they may help to mediate the body's response to stressful stimuli. If the endogenous production of painkillers helps the body cope with stress, would blocking the effects of endorphins increase its susceptibility to stress? Some support for this hypothesis is provided by a study cited by Goetsch and Fuller (1995) in which a group of normal volunteers were given naloxone, a drug which blocks the effects of endorphins, producing increased anxiety, irritability and depression and difficulty in concentrating and general functioning.

However, animal studies have shown that endorphins also inhibit the immune system and may promote the growth of tumours. Chronic use of painkillers in humans (which may be comparable to the increase in levels of endorphins in response to a stressor) is associated with increased incidence of infection and several immunological abnormalities (including a decrease in T lymphocytes, which defend the body primarily against fungi and viral infections, and phagocytes, cells which absorb dead or foreign material).

Modifiers or mediators of stress: Individual differences in the effects of stress

There is considerable evidence that individuals differ in their response to stressful situations, such that some are more susceptible or vulnerable than others; according to the transactional model of stress, this is exactly what we would expect to find and is what the model is trying to explain. If stressors cannot be defined objectively (i.e. independently of the person experiencing the stress) and if some people are more vulnerable to the harmful effects of stress (given that a situation or event has been perceived as making excessive demands), we need explanations at the *level of the person* (as distinct from the level of physiology) to account for these differences. According to Cox (1978), in concentrating his attention on the body's physiological response to stressor events, Selye ignored the role of psychological processes; according to the transactional model, much of the physiological response is not directly determined by the actual presence of the stressor agent but by its psychological impact on the person.

Some of the major individual differences that we shall discuss here are personality, gender and ethnic background.

Personality

The Type A personality (sometimes referred to as a *behaviour pattern* rather than a personality type) (Friedman and Rosenman, 1974) is, typically, a middle-class American male who has a chronic sense of time urgency, an excessive competitive drive and is very aggressive and hostile towards others. He is always setting himself deadlines, has 'hurry sickness', cannot bear waiting his turn, has to do several things at once, is insecure about his status and needs the admiration of peers to bolster his self-esteem. The Type B person is less driven and relatively free of such pressures.

How does this relate to stress?

The Type A personality is seen as being at risk, specifically, for high blood pressure and coronary heart disease (CHD). A longitudinal study, the Western Collaborative Group Study (WCGS) (Rosenman et al., 1975) was begun in 1960 and involved over 3000 men, aged 39–59, all well at the start of the study, which continued for 8 ½ years. Type A men were almost 2½ times as likely to develop

coronary heart disease as their Type B counterparts; when adjustments were made for traditional risk factors (e.g. age, smoking, blood cholesterol, blood pressure, heart disease in the family, diabetes, low levels of education, lack of exercise), Type A men were still twice as likely to suffer heart attacks, etc. Type As with CHD were more than five times as likely to have a second myocardial infarction (heart attack) as Type Bs with CHD. These findings have been replicated in Sweden, Belgium, Honolulu, England, New Zealand and Canada.

As Davison and Neale (1994) point out, these results don't mean that Type As are highly likely to develop CHD; it is a *relative* risk, whereby of the 7 percent of participants who had developed CHD at the end of the 8½ year study, two-thirds were Type A and one-third were Type B. Although by the late 1970s many researchers were concluding that it is one of the significant risk factors, the vast majority of Type As *don't* develop CHD and many Type Bs *do*.

However, there are also several more recent studies which have failed to support the concept of a distinct Type A personality. In a review of the research, Evans (1990) concludes that, as a global measure, Type A has yet to show itself as an indisputable risk factor for coronary heart disease.

One methodological problem involves the use of two different means of assessing personality type, namely the *structured interview* (Rosenman et al., 1964) and the *Jenkins Activity Survey* (Jenkins et al., 1974) which is a self-report inventory. According to Davison and Neale (1994), these two measures are not highly correlated, which could account for some of the inconsistencies in the research literature. More specifically, while the Jenkins Activity Survey is better at detecting a person's job involvement, competitive striving and fast pace of living, the structured interview is better at detecting hostility.

Type A or hostility?

Recent research is increasingly pointing towards hostility as the best single predictor of CHD; in fact, hostility is a better predictor than the Type A pattern as a whole. But does hostility cause CHD or are they merely correlated? Holmes (1994) concludes that, overall, the relationship between personality factors and cardiovascular disorders is probably due to *both* the influence of personality (Type A and hostility) on arousal, which in turn leads to cardiovascular problems, *and* to genetic factors that lead to hostility and arousal, which then leads to coronary artery disease.

Other personality variables

Although Type A behaviour has been the most extensively investigated personality factor in current health psychology, other research investigating personality in relation to disease-proneness and health behaviours includes Temoshok's (1987) study of Type C personality in relation to cancer (cited in Weinman, 1995). The *Type C personality* has difficulty expressing emotion and tends to suppress or inhibit emotions, particularly negative ones such as anger. While there is no clear-cut evidence that these personality characteristics can actually cause cancer, it does seem likely that they influence the progression of cancer and, hence, the survival time of cancer patients (Weinman, 1995).

In contrast to the adverse effects of Type A and Type C, other personality variables can be protective in various ways. For example, *hardiness* (Kobasa, 1979) describes individuals with a high sense of personal control over events in their lives and a strong sense of commitment or involvement, together with a tendency to see environmental demands or changes as challenges (rather than as stressors). This is similar to the individual with high internal locus of control (see above and Chapter 5).

Cultural/ethnic background

According to Thoreson and Powell (1992, cited in Davison and Neale, 1994), the Type A construct is still a very useful and important one, provided more careful attention is paid to (among other things) cultural aspects. For example, competitiveness and striving for achievement are common goals in capitalist societies, but probably not in more traditional, communal ones.

In a similar way, the SRRS has been criticized for not taking account of cultural and ethnic differences in the kinds of potential stressors that people are exposed to. For many years it has been noted that both the physical and mental health of African Americans is worse than that of whites, especially the spread of AIDS and hypertension. While this is partly to do with the direct negative effects of poverty, such as poor diet, low levels of education and poor medical care, there are many psychological stressors involved as well, many of which are related, more or less directly, to racism.

Anderson (1991) describes *acculturative stress,* which refers to the emotional challenges posed by discrepancies between the values, beliefs, norms and behaviours of African Americans and those of the majority white community, in which they often live as outcasts and strangers. Anderson further distinguishes three categories of stressors:

- Level 1 stressors (*chronic*), such as racism, overcrowding, poor living conditions and noise;
- Level 2 stressors (*major life events*), such as those included in the SRRS;
- Level 3 stressors (*daily events, hassles*).

While acculturative stress can be present at all three levels, it most often occurs at level 3. On a day-to-day basis, the African American faces pressures to become assimilated into the mainstream white society while at the same time facing obstacles to assimilation, and any successful assimilation may compromise their sense of African-American identity.

Gender

At every age from birth to 85 and over, more men die than women. But despite this lower mortality, women have higher rates of *morbidity* (i.e. generalized poor health and specific diseases). For example, women have higher rates of diabetes, amnesia, gastrointestinal problems and rheumatoid arthritis, visit their doctors more often, use more prescribed drugs and account for two-thirds of all surgical procedures in the USA (Davison and Neale, 1994). Why this gender difference?

Women might have some biological mechanism which protects them from life-threatening diseases. For example, oestrogen may protect against CHD; hormone replacement therapy lowers the rate of mortality from CHD, perhaps by maintaining raised levels of high-density lipoprotein (HDL), the 'good cholesterol'. Frankenhaeuser (1983) found that, compared with male students, female students failed to show a significant increase in adrenaline output in response to a stressful situation (doing an IQ test). She links females' relative unresponsiveness to their higher life expectancy, i.e. they suffer less stress-related damage during their lifetime. Additional findings (Frankenhaeuser *et al.*, 1983) that female engineering students and bus drivers show male patterns of adrenaline response to stressors suggest that socialization into gender roles may be the crucial variable, rather than any biological sex difference (see Chapter 23).

Another possible explanation could lie in the finding that women are less likely than men to be Type A personalities and are also less hostile than men. It has been suggested (by Eisler and Blalock, 1991, cited in Davison and Neale, 1994) that the Type A pattern is part and parcel of a rigid commitment to the traditional male gender role, which emphasizes achievement, mastery, competitiveness, not asking for help or emotional support, excessive need for control, the tendency to become angry and express it when frustrated. They link these attributes to men's greater vulnerability to coronary problems and other stress-related health risks.

In the early 20th century, most deaths were due to epidemics and infection, but now the main cause of death are diseases that are affected by lifestyle. Also, during the last 30 years or so, while the death rate from CHD among men has declined, for women it has stayed fairly constant, i.e. the gap in mortality rates between men and women is closing. Why? One possibility is that lifestyle differences between them are also decreasing, with women smoking and drinking much more than they used to (Davison and Neale, 1994).

● How do we cope with stress?

As we saw when defining stress, what is stressful for one person may not be for another (i.e. we cannot define stress-as-stimulus objectively). Although the basic physiological (bodily) responses to a stressor may be common to everyone, we have seen how factors such as personality, cultural/ethnic background and gender can all mediate the effects of a perceived source of stress (stress-as-response). In addition, even among those who appraise a situation as stressful, the effects of the stress may vary depending on how the individual copes with the situation (Lazarus, 1966) – the appraisal of an event as harmful or threatening in some way is really only the beginning of the stress process, not the end.

This initial or primary appraisal is then followed by secondary appraisals, in which we consider the different means of coping at our disposal; essentially, we search for coping responses that will reduce or remove the threat. What choices are open to us? Clearly, we evaluate the choices in terms of our perception of the threat, weigh up the costs and benefits of the various options and then select the one that seems most appropriate.

> ... Thus, the relationship between a stressful event and coping represents a dynamic interplay or process. Coping behaviour can be seen as a series of transactions between an individual who has a certain set of resources, values, and commitments with a particular environment with its own demands and constraints. (Gatchel, 1995)

Cohen and Lazarus (1979) have classified all the coping strategies that a person might use into five general categories:

1 *Direct action response*, in which the individual tries to directly change or manipulate their relationship to the stressful situation, such as escaping from it or removing it.

2 *Information seeking*, in which the individual tries to understand the situation better and to predict future events that are related to the stressor.

3 *Inhibition of action*, which involves doing nothing. This may be the best course of action if the situation is seen as short term.

4 *Intrapsychic or palliative coping*, where the individual reappraises the situation (for example, through the use of psychological defence mechanisms) or changes their 'internal environment' (through drugs, alcohol, relaxation or meditation).

5 *Turning to others* for help and emotional support.

These five categories of coping overlap with the distinction between *problem-focused* and *emotion-focused* coping (Lazarus and Folkman, 1984). Problem-focused coping involves taking direct action in order to solve the problem or seeking information that is relevant to a solution. This clearly subsumes (1) , (2) and perhaps certain examples of (5). Emotion-focused coping involves trying to reduce the negative emotions that are part of the experience of stress, with (4) being the best example of this alternative. Lazarus and Folkman argue that effective coping depends on the situation and sometimes using both kinds might offer the 'best solution'.

In the transactional model (Cox, 1978), the 'stress response' refers to both psychological and physiological means of coping, corresponding respectively to the individual's and the body's attempt to meet the demands being made upon it. In turn, the psychological response has two components, cognitive defence and behavioural response, and the consequences of both (perceived and actual) are continuously being appraised in relation to the stressful situation.

However, sometimes the term 'coping response' or mechanism is used in contrast to 'defence mechanism' (e.g. Grasha, 1983; Savickas, 1995). The *ego defence mechanisms* (discussed in detail in Chapter 29) are mainly associated with the anxiety produced by conflict, as described in Freud's psychoanalytic theory. By their nature, defence mechanisms involve some degree of distortion of reality and self-deception and, while desirable in the short term, as long-term solutions to stress they are unhealthy and undesirable. They reduce tension, anger and depression and other negative emotions but do nothing to help remove or change the stressor itself or the fit between the person and their environment. *Coping*

Copying mechanism	Description	Corresponding defence mechanism
1 Objectivity	Separating one thought from another or our feelings from our thoughts, which allows us to obtain a better understanding of how we think and feel and an objective evaluation of our actions	Isolation
2 Logical analysis	Carefully and systematically analysing our problems in order to find explanations and make plans to solve them, based on the realities of the situation	Rationalization
3 Concentration	The ability to set aside disturbing thoughts and feelings in order to concentrate on the task in hand	Denial
4 Empathy	The ability to sense how others are feeling in emotionally arousing situations so that our interactions take account of their feelings	Projection
5 Playfulness	The ability to use past feelings, ideas and behaviour appropriately to enrich the solution of problems and to otherwise add some enjoyment to life	Regression
6 Tolerance of ambiguity	The ability to function in situations where we or others cannot make clear choices because the situation is so complicated	–
7 Suppression	The ability consciously to forget about or hold back thoughts and feelings until an appropriate time and place to express them arises	Repression
8 Substitution of thoughts and emotions	The ability consciously to substitute other thoughts and feelings for how we really think or feel in order to meet the demands of the situation	Reaction formation

Sublimation can be thought of as a coping mechanism and a defence mechanism, because it involves channelling anxiety in socially desirable ways and so is positive and constructive

TABLE 6.2 *Some major coping mechanisms and their corresponding defence mechanism (based on Grasha, 1983)*

mechanisms, by contrast, are conscious ways of trying to adapt to stress and anxiety in a positive and constructive way, by using thoughts and behaviours oriented towards searching for information, problem-solving, seeking help from others, recognizing our true feelings and establishing goals and objectives:

'... In effect, coping improves fit [between the individual and the environment], whereas defence maintains misfit while reducing perceived stress' (Savickas, 1995).

Table 6.2 shows eight major coping mechanisms, together with the equivalent defence mechanisms.

● Stress management

Much of what we have said about coping with stress refers to what people do in a largely spontaneous way, i.e. without seeking help from professionals. In this informal sense we all 'manage our stress' more or less effectively. But in a more formal sense, stress management refers to a range of psychological techniques that are used in a quite deliberate way, in a professional setting, to help people reduce their stress. These techniques may be used singly or in combination.

In the case of *biofeedback* (which we discussed above in relation to pain control), the focus is on treating the symptoms of stress rather than the stressor itself. The same is true for a number of procedures used to bring about a state of relaxation, in particular *progressive muscle relaxation* (also an important component of *systematic desensitization*, used mainly for the treatment of phobias; see Chapter 31), *meditation* and *hypnosis* (both of which were discussed in Chapter 4).

Cognitive restructuring is a general term that refers to a number of specific methods aimed at trying to change the way individuals think about their life situation and self, in order to change their emotional responses and behaviour. This approach to stress management is based largely on the work of Beck (the treatment of *automatic thoughts*) and Ellis (*rational emotive therapy*), two major forms of cognitive behaviour therapy (again, see Chapter 31). This approach includes the provision of information to reduce uncertainty and to enhance people's sense of control. In a general sense, cognitive approaches can be seen as focusing on the appraisal processes studied by Lazarus (e.g. Lazarus, 1966; Lazarus and Folkman, 1984).

CHAPTER SUMMARY

- Early psychologists identified various dimensions of emotional experience, including pleasantness/unpleasantness.
- Ekman and Friesen identified six primary emotions which are universal and, probably, innate. Plutchik's emotion wheel also incorporates primary emotions but distinguishes these from complex emotions.
- Ekman and Averill adopt an evolutionary approach to understanding primary or basic emotions, which includes their current function. Also,

basic emotions should be present, in some form, in non-human primates.
- But what are considered 'basic' emotions differ between cultures and over time within the same culture and they may not be biologically but psychologically or culturally basic (Averill).
- For each distinct emotion there is the subjective experience, physiological changes, associated behaviour and cognitive appraisal of the emotion-producing stimulus/situation.
- Darwin's theory of emotion sees emotional behaviours (such as threat displays) as having evolved because they benefited those animals that used them effectively, i.e. they removed the need for actual combat.
- The James–Lange theory turns the commonsense theory of emotion on its head by claiming that our emotional experience is the result of perceived bodily changes, in particular, skeletal changes.
- The studies by Valins (using the false feedback paradigm) and Laird (testing the facial feedback hypothesis) support the James–Lange theory, although they fail to take into account any visceral changes that may be taking place. They both suggest that physiological arousal is not sufficient to account for emotional experience.
- Cannon criticized the James–Lange theory for assuming that different emotional states are associated with different patterns of ANS activity. The Cannon–Bard theory claims that the ANS responds in the same way to all emotional stimuli.
- Recent research into the specificity of bodily responses to emotional stimuli uses the directed facial action method and the relived emotion method. Levenson reports differences between anger, disgust, fear and sadness (negative emotions), but it is difficult to draw any general conclusions about specificity. However, both the James–Lange and Cannon–Bard theories take too extreme a view about the issue.
- The Marañon and Hohmann studies support Cannon's claim that physiological arousal is not sufficient for emotional experience, although they indicate that it is necessary. However, Cannon's own study of cats, plus those of Sherrington and Dana, suggest that it might not even be necessary.
- According to Schachter's cognitive labelling theory, the experience of emotion depends both on physiological changes and the interpretation of those changes, so Cannon was mistaken in claiming that emotional experience and bodily changes are independent.

- The Schachter and Singer 'adrenaline experiment' demonstrates that while physiological arousal is necessary, the nature of the arousal is irrelevant; what's crucial is the cognitive label we give that arousal.

- The Dutton and Aron 'suspension bridge' experiment, as well as supporting Schachter's theory, also demonstrates that our labelling of our arousal may be mistaken, i.e. it might involve a mislabelling or misattribution (the misattribution effect). This is most likely to occur when the actual source of the arousal is unclear/ambiguous or when we don't particularly care about how we respond.

- Failure to replicate the adrenaline experiment suggests that (a) emotional experience is much less malleable than Schachter claims, (b) unexplained arousal is likely to be interpreted negatively.

- Cognitive labelling theory is essentially based on attributional principles. Several attributional theories of emotion have grown out of it, such as Abramson and Martin's theory of depression and Weiner's theory.

- Also influenced by Schachter's theory is Lazarus's (and other versions of) cognitive appraisal theory, which clams that some minimal cognitive analysis always precedes emotional experience, although this can be unconscious and automatic. Zajonc's affective primacy theory claims that emotional responses can occur without any cognition being involved.

- The basic disagreement between Lazarus and Zajonc seems to be about the level of processing involved, rather than whether or not any cognitive processing takes place. This, in turn, centres around the definition of 'cognition'.

- There are a number of similarities and links between emotion and stress and these can be illustrated by taking the example of pain. It is often associated with emotions such as anxiety and depression, it shares with emotion the three main components of subjective experience, physiological changes and expressive behaviour, together with cognitive appraisal, and methods used to treat pain are often those used to treat stress. Pain is often related to psychophysiological (i.e. stress-related) disorders.

- Although pain is essentially a biological phenomenon, it also has social, cultural and psychological significance, the latter including our explanations/attributions of pain, such as whether or not it is controllable.

- Contingency management, biofeedback and self-management/cognitive behaviour treatment are behavioural treatments used to treat pain and stress.

- Stress is usually defined as a stimulus, a response or as an interaction between an organism and its environment.

- The engineering model is mainly concerned with the causes of stress, the physiological model focuses on the effects of stress (particularly the physiological effects), while the transactional model addresses the additional issue of how we cope with stress.

- According to Lazarus, stress cannot be defined objectively, i.e what counts as a stressor depends on the individual's perception of an excessive demand being made on his/her capacities.

- Frustrations and conflicts can cause stress. Three main kinds of conflict are approach–approach, avoidance–avoidance and approach–avoidance.

- Disruption of circadian rhythms (the' biological clock'), which involves the internal desynchronization of all the body's functions, can be very stressful. It occurs when shift workers change their shift pattern and when we cross time zones (as in jet lag).

- The negative effects are increased when the biological clock is brought forward (a phase advance), as when shifts start earlier or when time zones are crossed in a West–East direction.

- The Social Readjustment Rating Scale (Holmes and Rahe) is a major way of measuring stress, which it does in terms of life change units. It was intended to predict the onset of illness, so that the greater the amount of life change, the greater the likelihood of future illness.

- Studies which claim to have found support for this prediction are correlational and retrospective and the SRRS assumes that all change is inherently stressful. We need to distinguish between change that is predictable/controllable and that which is not. People rated high on external locus of control (Rotter) are more vulnerable to the harmful effects of change and learned helplessness (Seligman) is seen as a major feature of clinical depression.

- The hassles scale (Kanner *et al.*) is designed to measure everyday stressors, which seem to be a better predictor of ill health than the life events of the SRRS.

- The Assessment of Daily Experience (Stone and Neale) is another alternative to the SRRS and has been used in prospective studies to predict the onset of respiratory illness.

- Many occupations, including the health care professions, seem to be inherently stressful, as in the case of nurses having to deal continuously with illness, death, distress and suffering.
- Surviving disasters of various kinds, such as the Hillsborough football disaster or the Vietnam war, can result in post-traumatic stress disorder.
- The General Adaptation Syndrome (GAS) (Selye) refers to the body's response to any stressor. It comprises the alarm reaction, resistance and exhaustion. Two main bodily systems are involved: the sympathetic branch of the ANS which stimulates the adrenal medulla to produce adrenaline and noradrenaline (the catecholamines), and the anterior pituitary- adrenal cortex system, which involves the release of corticosteroids.
- While most stressors do not present us with physical danger, our nervous and endocrine systems have evolved in such a way that we typically react to stressors as if they did. These once-adaptive responses are maladaptive today.
- There are a number of ways in which stress can result in physical illness, including its influence on the immune system. Studies have found stressful situations to be associated with decreased lymphocyte activity, decreased levels of antibodies found within immunoglobulin and increased incidence of infection and immunological abnormalities due to increased output of endorphins/enkephalins (the body's natural painkillers).
- Personality, gender and ethnic background all act as modifiers/mediators of the response to stress. Perhaps the most researched is the Type A personality (Rosenman *et al.*), who is especially vulnerable to high BP and CHD. Recent research suggests that hostility is the best single predictor of CHD.
- Type C personality (Temoshok) has difficulty expressing emotion and is thought to be more cancer-prone than other personality types.
- The greater incidence of high BP among African Americans has been attributed to the direct and indirect effects of racism, one facet of which is acculturative stress (Anderson).
- Women seem to be relatively unresponsive to stress-producing situations, which may help explain their longer average life expectancy. Women are also less likely than men to be Type A personalities, although the gap in death rates from CHD between men and women is closing.
- Secondary appraisal involves a search for coping responses that will reduce/remove the stressor (Lazarus). Five categories of coping response are direct action response, information seeking, inhibition of action, intrapsychic/palliative coping and turning to others (Cohen and Lazarus). This overlaps with problem-focused and emotion-focused coping (Lazarus and Folkman).
- 'Coping mechanism' is sometimes contrasted with 'defence mechanism', referring to conscious/constructive and unconscious/distorting solutions respectively.
- Stress management refers to a range of psychological techniques used deliberately to help reduce stress, including biofeedback, progressive muscle relaxation, meditation, hypnosis and cognitive restructuring (based on Beck's and Ellis's forms of cognitive behaviour therapy).

GLOSSARY

Adrenocorticotrophic hormone (ACTH) Hormone released from the anterior pituitary which stimulates the adrenal cortex to release corticosteroids, which help the body to cope with stress.

Biofeedback A psychological method for treating pain, hypertension, migraine headaches (and other stress-related symptoms), in which patients are given information (via monitors) about certain autonomic (involuntary) functions (e.g. heart rate) so that these can be brought under voluntary control.

Circadian rhythms Any biological rhythm with a period of about 24 hours (such as the sleep–wake cycle). (*circa dies* = 'about one day')

Cognitive appraisal Process in which we assess the (likely) effect of a stimulus/event on our well-being and then respond emotionally to it . The appraisal is an integral part of the emotional state. Also very important in relation to stress – both the perceived cause and coping responses.

Cognitive behaviour treatment/therapy A form of psychotherapy in which individuals are encouraged to change the way they think about their life situation/themselves (*cognitive restructuring*), in order to alter their emotional responses and behaviour. Used mainly for treating stress, depression and anxiety.

Directed facial action method Technique for studying the physiological changes accompanying emotional states, in which participants are asked to make facial expressions characteristic of various emotions.

Facial feedback hypothesis The claim that emotional states are determined by feedback from the facial muscles, e.g. deliberately smiling will induce a feeling of happiness (e.g. Laird).

False feedback paradigm Method of studying emotional experience which involves providing participants with false information about their physiological responses to emotional stimuli. The feedback is used to infer their preferences for certain stimuli over others (e.g. Valins).

General Adaptation Syndrome (GAS) Selye's term for the body's general response to any stressor, comprising the alarm reaction, resistance stage and exhaustion stage.

Learned helplessness In depressed people, the belief that nothing they do will affect the outcome of events (based on past negative experiences). Based originally on Seligman's experiments with dogs.

Locus of control Rotter's term for an individual's relatively stable view of events as being largely beyond their control (high external) or as controllable (high internal).

Misattribution effect The process by which we mislabel our feelings and draw mistaken conclusions about their causes (e.g. Dutton and Aron).

Misattribution paradigm Method of studying emotion in which environmental cues are deliberately manipulated in order to produce the misattribution effect (e.g. Schachter and Singer).

Psychophysiological disorders Bodily/physical illnesses that are caused/aggravated by stress, such as migraine headaches, stomach ulcers, hypertension (high blood pressure). Previously called 'psychosomatic'.

Social Readjustment Rating Scale (SRRS) Self-administered pencil-and-paper scale for measuring stress in life change units – the higher the score, the greater the stress.

Specificity (of physiological response) The view that for each subjectively distinct emotion there is a corresponding set of physiological changes.

Stress Negative emotional states/physiological responses produced by a stressor.

Stress management General term for a range of psychological techniques for helping people to reduce stress, including biofeedback, progressive muscle relaxation, meditation, hypnosis and cognitive restructuring.

Stressor The cause or source of stress: stress-as-stimulus.

Transactional model (of stress) A view of stress as arising from an interaction between individuals and their environment, specifically, where there is a perceived mismatch between demands made and capacity to respond.

Two-factor theory of emotion Another term for Schachter's cognitive labelling theory.

Type A personality Typically, a middle-class American male with a chronic sense of time urgency, an excessive competitive drive and hostility towards others, who is prone to hypertension and coronary heart disease (Friedman and Rosenman).

Zeitgebers (*'time givers'*) Environmental (exogenous) cues relating to the maintenance of circadian rhythms (such as the light–dark cycle).

FURTHER READING

Ekman, P and Davidson, R.J. (eds) (1994) *The Nature of Emotion: Fundamental Questions*. New York: Oxford University Press. A collection of original chapters by leading researchers in the field, covering all aspects of emotion.

Cox, T. (1978) *Stress.* London: Macmillan Education Ltd. An excellent source for theories of stress and research into the effects of stress on health, plus its management/alleviation. Also useful for emotion and the links between emotion and stress.

Lazarus, R.S. (1991) *Emotion and Adaptation*. Oxford: Oxford University Press. An excellent review of the topic, including his own ideas, by one of the key figures in modern emotion research.

7 LEARNING

INTRODUCTION AND OVERVIEW

When discussing the history of psychology as a scientific discipline and identifying the major theoretical approaches within psychology as a whole, we saw in earlier chapters how the *behaviourist* approach has exerted a major influence in psychology. In view of the central role of learning in philosophical behaviourism, it is not surprising that the topic of learning should itself be one of the most researched and discussed in the whole of psychology.

However, the concept of learning illustrates very well the discrepancy between the everyday, commonsense use of a term and its technical, scientific use (see Chapter 1). When the layperson talks about learning , the emphasis is usually on *what* has been learned, for example, learning to drive or to use a computer, learning French or learning about the causes of the Vietnam war. But when psychologists use the term, their focus is on the *process* of learning itself, almost irrespective of the end product; they ask 'How does it work?' rather than 'What does it lead to?'.

Another important difference is that when we focus on the end product we tend to judge the learning to be deliberate; when you learn to drive, for example, you pay to acquire certain specific skills which will get you your driving licence. But, for the psychologist, learning can take place without there being a 'teacher' as such: we can learn by merely observing others, who may not even know they are being watched, let alone be trying to teach us anything. We can also learn without other people being involved at all; for example, if two 'events' occur often enough in the environment (e.g. lightning followed by thunder) then we can learn that they are related without anyone trying to teach us.

So the concept of learning is a very broad one as far as psychologists are concerned, covering both 'formal' (i.e. deliberate) and 'informal' (i.e. unintentional) varieties. In either case, what happens when learning takes place (i.e. the process) is the same, but psychologists differ widely as to what exactly the process involves and different theories of learning embody different views about just what is involved. John B.Watson, the founder of behaviourism, based his explanation of human learning on Ivan Pavlov's *classical conditioning of dogs,* where the learner is passively responding to environmental events. A much more active view of learning was proposed by Edward Thorndike, whose work was built upon by arguably the most famous and influential behaviourist of all, Burrhus F. Skinner, who saw *operant conditioning* as the crucial form of both human and animal learning.

Other behaviourists were very critical of this emphasis on conditioning and Edward Tolman was one of the first psychologists to acknowledge the part played by *cognitive factors*. Tolman's *cognitive behaviourism* represented a radical departure from the theories of Watson and Skinner and helped to loosen the behaviourist stranglehold on psychology in general and the study of learning in particular. *Social learning* theorists are behaviourists who, like Tolman, see cognitive factors as a crucial part of the learning process, such as Bandura's theory of *observational learning*. Insight learning and learning sets are other examples of how thinking forms part of the learning process.

In discussing all these theories in this chapter, we shall see how they have influenced so many other areas of research, reflecting the importance of the topic of learning within psychology as a whole.

HOW CAN LEARNING BE DEFINED?

As we saw in Chapter 1, learning is a *hypothetical construct*, that is, it cannot be directly observed but can only be inferred from observable behaviour. So, for example, if a person's performance on a task at Time 1 differs from performance on the task at Time 2, we might infer that learning has taken place. But if that change is observed on just that one occasion , we may be much more hesitant about making such an inference. Learning, therefore, normally implies a fairly permanent change in a person's behavioural performance. Again, temporary fluctuations in behaviour can occur as a result of fatigue, drugs, temperature changes and so on and this is another reason for taking permanence as a minimum requirement for saying that learning has taken place.

However, permanent changes in behaviour can also result from things that have nothing to do with learning, for example, the effects of brain damage on behaviour or the changes associated with puberty and other maturational processes. So if some change in behaviour is to be counted as learning, the change must be linked in some way to past experience of some kind (regardless of whether there was any attempt to bring about that change).

For these reasons, psychologists usually define learning as (a) '... a relatively permanent change in behaviour due to past experience' (Coon, 1983) or (b) '... the process by which relatively permanent changes occur in behavioural potential as a result of experience' (Anderson, 1995).

● Learning versus performance.

Anderson's definition has one major advantage over Coon's, namely, it implies a distinction between *learning* (behavioural potential) and *performance* (actual behaviour). Think of all the things you know and can do but which you are not displaying at this present moment – if you can swim you are almost certainly not doing so as you read this chapter, but you could readily do so if faced with a pool full of water! So what you could do (potential behaviour based on learning) and what you are actually doing (current performance) are two different things but ultimately, of course, the only proof of learning is a particular kind of performance (such as exams).

We can relate the learning–performance distinction to what we said earlier about what counts as learning. Performance, but not learning, can fluctuate due to fatigue, drugs, emotional factors, etc. and so is much more variable than learning, which is more permanent. (Exams come to mind again – many students have left an exam knowing what they could not demonstrate during the exam itself.)

Learning and other abilities

A rather different kind of definition is offered by Howe (1980), for whom learning is ' ... a biological device that functions to protect the human individual and to extend his capacities'. In this context, learning is neither independent of nor entirely separate from several other abilities, in particular memory and perception. Indeed, learning and memory may be regarded as two sides of the same coin (see Chapter 12).

According to Howe, learning is also cumulative, i.e. what we learn at any time is influenced by our previous learning, so that developmental and learning processes are closely interlinked. Also, most instances of learning take the form of adaptive changes whereby we increase our effectiveness in dealing with the environment; this has undoubted survival value. Anderson (1995) defines learning as ' ... the mechanism by which organisms can adapt to a changing and non-predictable environment'.

Some basic questions about learning

While it is generally agreed by psychologists that learning is: (i) relatively permanent and (ii) due to past experience, there is much less agreement about exactly what changes when learning takes place and what kinds of past experience are involved. Put another way, how do the changes occur and what mechanisms are involved?

A dimension along which psychologists differ regarding the above is the extent to which they focus on the overt, behavioural changes as opposed to the covert, cognitive changes. As we have seen in Chapters 1 and 2, behaviourists such as Watson and Skinner emphasize the former to the exclusion of the latter, while cognitive psychologists are more interested in the latter as they are reflected in the former.

We will now take a detailed look at different theories of learning.

BEHAVIOURIST APPROACHES – LEARNING THEORY (CLASSICAL AND OPERANT CONDITIONING)

Figure 7.1 shows the major figures in the behaviourist tradition and how they relate to each other. Historically (or chronologically) Skinner does not belong at the top but at the bottom – he was born several years after the others but he appears at the top because of the distinction he made (in 1938) between *respondents* (or respondent behaviour),

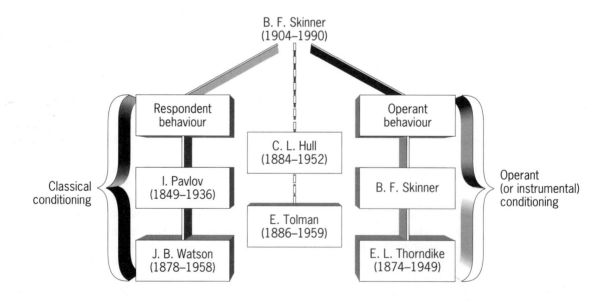

FIGURE 7.1 *Major figures in the behaviourist (learning theory) tradition*

which are triggered automatically by particular environmental stimuli, and *operants* (or operant behaviour) which are not tied to stimuli in that way and which are essentially voluntary.

Related to this distinction is the one between classical (Pavlovian) conditioning and operant (instrumental or Skinnerian) conditioning. Although both represent the behaviourist stimulus–response (S–R) approach to learning, there are some important differences between them, hence Skinner's distinction. Neither Hull nor Tolman fits easily into either of the two major types of conditioning, which is why they are placed between the others (Hull's theory was discussed in Chapter 5).

● Classical conditioning (or why do dogs drool over bells?)

Ivan Pavlov (Fig. 7.2) was a physiologist interested in the process of digestion in dogs, for which research he was awarded the Nobel Prize in 1904 (the year Skinner was born). He developed a surgical technique whereby a dog's salivary secretions could be collected in a tube attached to the outside of its cheek so the drops of saliva could be easily measured (Fig. 7.3). In the course of his physiological investigations, Pavlov noticed that the dogs would often start salivating *before* any food was given to them, for

FIGURE 7.2 *Ivan Pavlov (1849–1936)*

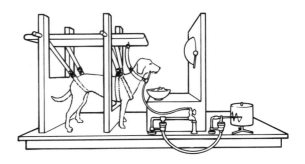

FIGURE 7.3 *The apparatus used by Pavlov in his experiments on conditioned reflexes*

example, when they looked at the food or saw the feeding bucket or even when they heard the footsteps of the approaching laboratory assistant who was coming to feed them.

These observations led to the study of what is now called classical (or Pavlovian) conditioning, whereby a stimulus (a bell) which would not normally produce a particular response (salivation) eventually comes to do so by being paired with another stimulus (food) which *does* normally produce the response. The basic procedure is summarized in Figure 7.4.

Before conditioning, the taste of food will naturally and automatically make the dog salivate but the sound of a bell will not so the food is referred to as an *unconditioned stimulus* (UCS) and the salivation is an *unconditioned response* (UCR) – an automatic, reflex, biologically built-in response. The dog does not have to learn to salivate in response to food: it does so naturally. During conditioning the bell is paired with the food. Because the bell does not naturally produce salivation it is referred to as a *conditioned stimulus* (CS), i.e. its coming to produce salivation is conditional upon it being paired with the UCS. (It is also neutral with regard to salivation prior to conditioning.) If the bell and food are paired often enough, the dog starts to salivate as soon as it hears the bell and before the food is presented. When this occurs we say that conditioning has taken place and the salivation is now referred to as a *conditioned response* (CR) because it is produced by a conditioned stimulus (CS) – the bell.

This basic procedure can be used with a variety of conditioned stimuli, e.g. buzzers, metronomes, lights, geometric figures and so on. The exact relationship between the CS and the UCS can also be varied to give different kinds of conditioning. For example, in the example shown in Figure 7.4, the CS is presented about half a second before the UCS and is called

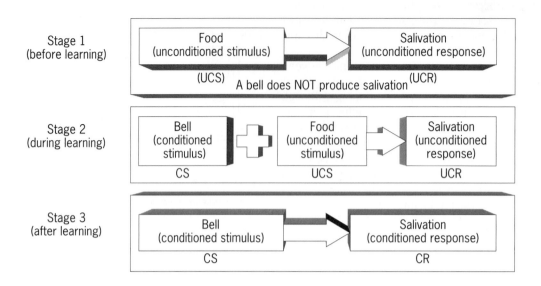

FIGURE 7.4 *The basic procedure involved in classical conditioning*

delayed or *forward* conditioning. This and three other alternatives are shown in Table 7.1.

Higher order conditioning

Pavlov demonstrated that a strong CS could be used in place of food to produce salivation in response to a new stimulus which had never been paired with food. For example, if the CS is a buzzer, it can be paired with, say, a black square in such a way that after ten pairings (using delayed conditioning) the dog will salivate a small but significant amount at the sight of the black square before the buzzer is sounded.

Remember that the black square had never been associated with food directly but only indirectly, through association with the buzzer which had been associated with food; it is as if the CS were functioning as a UCS. The buzzer and food situation is referred to as *first order* conditioning and the black square and buzzer situation as *second order* conditioning. Pavlov found that, with dogs at least, learning could not go beyond third or fourth order

1 **Delayed or forward**	The CS is presented before the UCS and remains 'on' while the UCS is presented and until the UCS appears. Conditioning has occurred when the CR appears before the UCS is presented. A half second interval produces the strongest learning – as the interval increases, so the poorer the learning becomes. This is the kind of conditioning typically used in the laboratory, especially with animals.
2 **Backward**	The CS is presented after the UCS; generally this produces very little, if any, learning in laboratory animals. However, much advertising uses backward conditioning (e.g. the idyllic tropical scene is set and then the coconut bar is introduced).
3 **Simultaneous**	The CS and UCS are presented together; conditioning has occurred when the CS on its own produces the CR. This kind of conditioning occurs often in real-life situations (e.g. the sound of the dentist's drill accompanies the contact of the drill with your tooth).
4 **Trace**	The CS is presented and removed before the UCS is presented, so that only a 'memory trace' of the CS remains to be conditioned. The CR is usually weaker than in delayed or simultaneous conditioning.

TABLE 7.1 *Four types of classical conditioning based on different CS–UCS relationships*

conditioning. Even so, conditioning is beginning to look a rather more complex process than it did when we first described it.

Generalization and discrimination

Other phenomena involved in classical conditioning (as well as in operant) which make it a more complex and versatile process are generalization and discrimination.

In *generalization* the CR transfers spontaneously to stimuli that are similar to, but different from, the original CS. For example, if a dog is trained using a bell of a particular pitch and it is then presented with a bell a little higher or lower in pitch, it will still salivate, although only one bell (the original CS) was actually paired with food. However, if the dog is continually presented with bells that are increasingly different from the original, the CR will gradually weaken and eventually stop altogether; the dog is showing *discrimination* (see Fig. 7.5).

In addition to spontaneous discrimination, as in the above example, Pavlov trained dogs to discriminate in the original conditioning procedure. For example, if a high-pitched bell is paired with food but a low-pitched bell is not, the dog will start salivating in response to the former but not to the latter (discrimination training).

An interesting phenomenon related to discrimination is what Pavlov called *experimental neurosis.* He trained dogs to salivate to a circle but not to an ellipse and then gradually changed the shape of the ellipse until it became almost circular. As this happened the dogs started behaving in 'neurotic' ways – whining, trembling, urinating and defecating, refusing to eat and so on. It was as if they did not know how to respond – was the stimulus a circle (in which case, through generalization, they 'ought' to salivate) or was it an ellipse (in which case, through discrimination, they 'should not' salivate)?

Extinction and spontaneous recovery

After dogs had been conditioned to salivate to a bell, if the bell was repeatedly presented without food, the CR of salivation became gradually weaker and eventually stopped altogether; this is called *extinction.* When this happens, it might seem as if the association between the bell and the food has faded so that the dog has 'unlearnt' the original connection. But this is not the case: when dogs were removed from the experimental situation, following extinction, and then put back a couple of hours or so later and Pavlov re-presented the bell, the dogs started salivating again. Although there had been no further pairing of the bell and food, the CR of salivation reappeared in response to the bell, a phenomenon called *spontaneous recovery*. It shows that extinction does not involve an 'erasing' of the original learning but rather a learning to inhibit or suppress the CR when the CS is continually presented without a UCS.

Does classical conditioning apply to human behaviour?

There have been many laboratory demonstrations involving human participants and the basic procedure is useful as a way of thinking about how certain fairly automatic responses may be acquired in real life. Also, as we shall see in Chapter 31, the impact of conditioning principles (both classical and operant) within clinical psychology has been considerable, i.e.

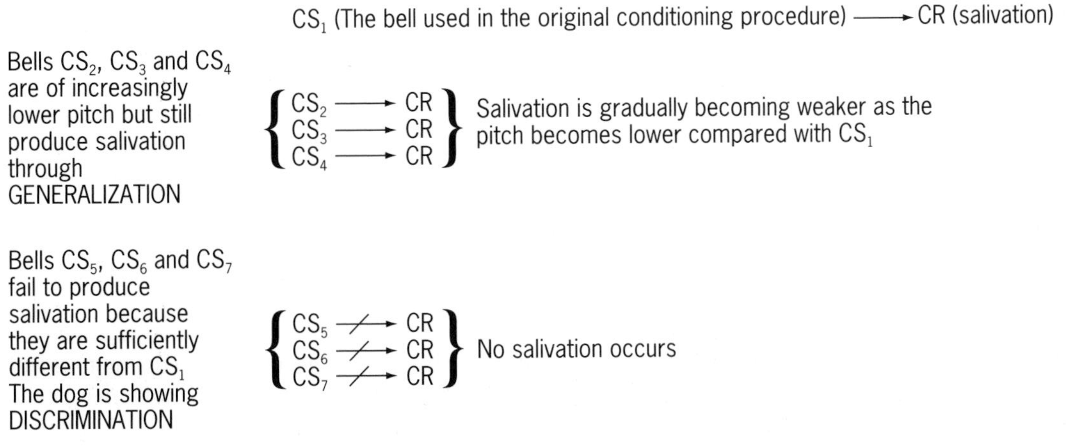

CS_1 (The bell used in the original conditioning procedure) $\longrightarrow$ CR (salivation)

Bells CS_2, CS_3 and CS_4 are of increasingly lower pitch but still produce salivation through GENERALIZATION

$$\left\{ \begin{array}{l} CS_2 \longrightarrow CR \\ CS_3 \longrightarrow CR \\ CS_4 \longrightarrow CR \end{array} \right\}$$ Salivation is gradually becoming weaker as the pitch becomes lower compared with CS_1

Bells CS_5, CS_6 and CS_7 fail to produce salivation because they are sufficiently different from CS_1 The dog is showing DISCRIMINATION

$$\left\{ \begin{array}{l} CS_5 \nrightarrow CR \\ CS_6 \nrightarrow CR \\ CS_7 \nrightarrow CR \end{array} \right\}$$ No salivation occurs

FIGURE 7.5 *An example of discrimination occurring spontaneously as a result of generalization stopping*

BOX 7.1	Key study: the case of little Albert (Watson and Rayner, 1920)

Albert B's mother was a wet-nurse in a children's hospital. Albert was described as 'healthy from birth' and 'on the whole stolid and unemotional'. When he was about nine months old his reactions to various stimuli were tested – a white rat, a rabbit, a dog, a monkey, masks with and without hair, cotton wool, burning newspapers and a hammer striking a four-foot steel bar (just behind his head). Only the last of these elicited a fear response and so constituted the UCS (with fear the UCR); the other stimuli were neutral because they did not produce fear.

When Albert was just over 11 months old, the rat and the UCS were presented together; this occurred seven times altogether over the next seven weeks, by which time the rat (CS) on its own came to produce the fear response (now a CR).

The CR transferred spontaneously to the rabbit, the dog, a sealskin fur coat, cotton wool, Watson's hair and a Santa Claus mask, but it did not generalize to Albert's building blocks or to the hair of two observers (i.e. Albert showed discrimination).

Five days after conditioning, the CR produced by the rat persisted; ten days after conditioning it was 'much less marked' but one month after conditioning it was still evident.

Whether Watson and Rayner had intended to remove the CR is not known – Albert's mother removed him from the hospital.

BOX 7.2	Key study: the case of Little Peter (Jones, 1924)

Little Peter was a two-year-old living in a charitable institution. Jones was mainly interested in those children who cried and trembled when an animal (e.g. a frog, rat or rabbit) was shown to them and Peter, who in other respects was regarded as well adjusted, had an extreme fear of rats, rabbits, fur coats, feathers, cotton wool, frogs and fish (it was not known how these fears had arisen).

Jones, supervised by Watson, put a rabbit in a wire cage in front of Peter while he ate his lunch and, 40 sessions later, Peter ate his lunch with one hand and stroked the rabbit (now on his lap) with the other. In a series of 17 steps the rabbit (in the cage) had been brought a little closer each day, was then let free in the room and eventually sat on Peter's lunch tray.

This is an early example of a method of removing fears (or phobias) called *systematic desensitization;* it is used a great deal today (see Chapter 31).

they can be used deliberately to change people's behaviour in a certain direction (see also Table 1.1, p.12).

The first attempt to apply Pavlov's findings to humans was made by Watson. Working with Rayner (1920), Watson succeeded in inducing fear in a young child through classical conditioning (Box 7.1) in what is considered to be one of the most ethically dubious psychology experiments ever conducted.

Watson and Rayner might have attempted to remove little Albert's fear using the method of direct unconditioning employed by Jones (1924) to treat Little Peter (Box 7.2).

If a fear of rats can be deliberately induced (as in Little Albert's case) or removed (as in Little Peter's), does classical conditioning also help to explain how fears are acquired, spontaneously, in everyday life? We can see how, for example, a fear of the dentist could be learnt in this way, e.g.:

- drill hitting a nerve (UCS)→pain/fear (UCR);
- sound of drill (CS)+ drill hitting nerve (UCS)→pain/fear (UCR);
- sound of the drill (CS)→fear (CR).

You could become conditioned to more than one CS in the same 'sitting' – it all depends on what you notice at the time. For example, if you are looking at the dentist peering into your mouth, you may become afraid of faces seen upside down or if the dentist is wearing a mask you may acquire a fear of masks too. Also, through generalization, you can come to fear all drill-like noises or white coats worn by medical personnel or lab technicians, and so on. Generalization may be useful up to a point but discrimination may be just as important ; for example, carpenters need to use electric drills and it is necessary for them to do so without trembling with fear.

As we shall see in Chapter 30, human fears may often be perpetuated through avoiding the object of our fears, i.e. we do not give the fear a chance to undergo extinction. (This occurs in conjunction with operant conditioning whereby the avoidance behaviour becomes strengthened through negative reinforcement, which will be discussed later in this chapter.)

● Operant conditioning (or why do rats press levers?)

When Skinner (Fig. 7.6) drew the distinction between respondent and operant behaviour, he was not rejecting the discoveries of Pavlov and Watson but arguing that most animal and human behaviour is not elicited by specific stimuli in the way they described. Instead, he was interested in how animals operate on their environment and how this operant behaviour is instrumental in bringing about certain consequences which then determine the probability of that behaviour being repeated.

Skinner saw the learner as much more active than did Pavlov or Watson, for whom behaviour was automatically brought about by stimuli – unconditioned stimuli before learning and conditioned stimuli after learning. In classical conditioning, there is a certain necessity and inevitability about the response – the animal has no choice but to respond in a particular way. But in operant conditioning things are much less certain: behaviour is emitted by the organism (not elicited by the stimulus), so is essentially voluntary (as opposed to reflex or involuntary) and the likelihood of a particular behaviour being emitted is a function of the past consequences of such behaviour.

FIGURE 7.6 *B.F. Skinner (1904–1990) (Bettman Archive Inc.)*

Just as Watson's ideas were based on the earlier work of Pavlov, so Skinner's study of operant conditioning grew out of the earlier work of another American, Edward Thorndike.

Thorndike and the law of effect

Thorndike built puzzle-boxes for use with cats; their task was to operate a latch which would automatically cause the door to spring open. Each time they managed to escape there was a piece of fish waiting for them, which was visible from inside the puzzle-box (Fig. 7.7). (The cats were deprived of food for a considerable time before the experiments began and so were highly motivated.) Each time, after eating the fish, the cats were put straight back in and the whole process was repeated.

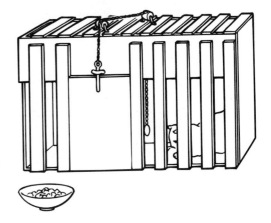

FIGURE 7.7 *Thorndike's puzzle-box*

At first the cats struggled to get out, behaving in a purely random fashion, and it was only by chance that the first escape was made. But each time they were returned to the puzzle-box it took them less time to operate the latch and make their escape. For instance, with one of the boxes, the average time for the first escape was five minutes but after 10–20 trials this was reduced to about five seconds. How did Thorndike account for this?

The learning, he said, was essentially random or trial and error; there was no sudden flash of insight into how the releasing mechanism worked but rather a gradual reduction in the number of errors made and hence escape time. As to exactly what was being learned in this trial-and-error way, Thorndike proposed a 'connection between the situation and a certain impulse to act' or between the stimulus (the manipulative components of the box) and the response (the behaviour which allowed the cat to escape). Further, the stimulus–response connection is 'stamped in when pleasure results from the act, and stamped out when it doesn't' – this is Thorndike's famous *law of effect* (1898).

The law of effect is crucially important as a way of distinguishing classical and operant conditioning (as Skinner was to do 40 years later):

1 It points out that what happens *as a result* of behaviour will influence that behaviour in the future, whereas in classical conditioning it is, in a sense, what happens *before* behaviour (pairing of

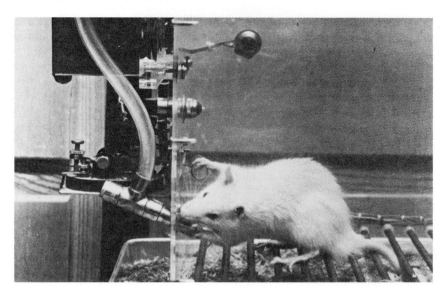

FIGURE 7.8 *A rat in a Skinner box*

the CS and UCS) that is crucial and which determines the behaviour.

2 It points out that the animal is not indifferent to the nature of those consequences – responses that bring about 'satisfaction' or pleasure are likely to be repeated and those which bring about 'discomfort' are likely not to be. (In classical conditioning the UCS works essentially in the same way whether it is food (something pleasant) or electric shock (something unpleasant or aversive), since the response is produced *by* it and not vice versa.)

Skinner's 'analysis of behaviour'

Skinner used a form of puzzle-box known as a *Skinner box*, which was designed for a rat or pigeon to do things in rather than escape from. This box has a lever (in the case of rats), under which is a food tray and the experimenter decides exactly what the relationship shall be between pressing the lever and the delivery of a food pellet. In this sense, the experimenter has total control of the animal's environment but it is the rat that has to do the work (Fig. 7.8).

Another modification of Thorndike's work was Skinner's use of the term *strengthen* in place of 'stamping in' and *weaken* in place of 'stamping out' in Thorndike's law of effect. For Skinner, Thorndike's terms were too mentalistic while his own were more objective and descriptive. The analysis of behaviour, according to Skinner, requires an accurate but neutral representation of the relationship (or contingencies) between:

1 antecedents (the stimulus conditions, e.g. the

lever, the click of the food dispenser, a light that may go on when the lever is pressed);

2 behaviours (or operants, e.g. pressing the lever);

3 consequences (what happens as a result of the operant behaviour).

This is the ABC of operant conditioning. We shall look at (1) and (3) in more detail.

'Behaviour is shaped and maintained by its consequences'

This quote from Skinner represents his version of the law of effect; the consequences of operants can be *positive reinforcement; negative reinforcement* or *punishment* and their effects on behaviour are summarized in Figure 7.9.

You will see that positive and negative reinforcement have the same effect on behaviour, namely strengthening it (making it more probable), but each works in a different way, from the opposite direction. Positive reinforcement involves presenting something the animal likes (e.g. food) while negative reinforcement involves the removal or avoidance of some 'aversive' (literally 'painful') state of affairs (e.g. electric shock). Punishment has the opposite effect on behaviour, i.e. weakening it (making it less probable) – through the presentation of an aversive stimulus.

Let us take the example of a rat pressing a lever in a Skinner box (Fig. 7.10).

The difference between negative reinforcement and punishment should now be clear: in the former, an aversive stimulus comes to an end or is avoided altogether, while in the latter the aversive stimulus begins.

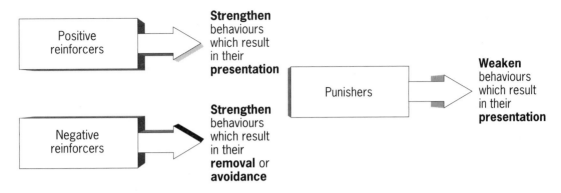

FIGURE 7.9 *The consequences of behaviour and their effects*

What is the difference between a reinforcer and reinforcement?

You may have spotted that in Figure 7.9 the term reinforc*er* (and punish*er*) is used ,while in Figure 7.10 I have referred to reinforc*ement* (and punish*ment*); the difference is between a thing and a process. Food itself is a reinforcer, electric shock a punisher; the process whereby food is presented as a result of lever-pressing is (positive) reinforcement and when electric shock is presented instead it is called punishment.

But we should note here just how Skinner defines these terms or, more accurately, how he decides that something is or is not a reinforcer or a punisher. It is, in fact, a decision that must be made retrospectively, that is, after food or shock, etc. has been made contingent on, say, lever-pressing on a number of occasions. So, if the behaviour is strengthened when followed by food, we can call the food a reinforcer and if the shock weakens it we can call the shock a punisher; therefore, reinforcers and punishers cannot be defined independently of the effects they have on behaviour.

This kind of definition could be accused of circularity ('a reinforcer is whatever strengthens behaviour' and 'whatever strengthens behaviour is a reinforcer') and it seems to make the task of predicting behaviour rather tricky because Skinner is saying that we have to 'wait and observe' just what the effects on behaviour are. A partial solution (of an empirical if not a logical kind) is to ensure that rats and pigeons are highly motivated to learn the relationship between pressing levers or pecking discs and receiving food by starving them for several hours before the experiments begin!

A partial justification for 'waiting and seeing' is that, according to Skinner, this is a more rather than a less scientific way of going about things, since the intended effect may not always coincide with the actual effect. Take an example from parent–child interaction: if children who feel deprived of their parents' attention find that the parents respond when they are naughty, they are more likely to go on being naughty, even if the parents' response is to shout or smack. Being shouted at or smacked is at least a form of attention and is preferable to being ignored. So, whereas the parents' intention is to stop

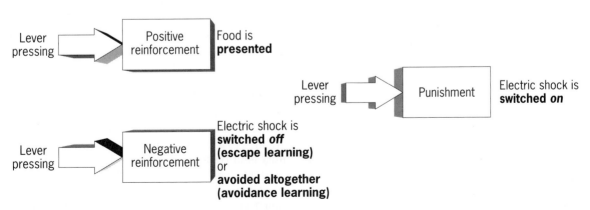

FIGURE 7.10 *Three possible consequences of lever pressing in a Skinner box*

the child being naughty, the actual effect may be the opposite, i.e. an intended punishment may turn out to be a positive reinforcement!

Similarly, a positive reinforcement can only loosely be called a reward as 'reward' implies that the rewarder expects to strengthen behaviour, whereas 'positive reinforcement' refers to what has been shown to strengthen the behaviour of the rewarded person or animal.

Primary and secondary reinforcers

As well as the distinction between positive and negative reinforcement, an important distinction also exists between two types of reinforcer: primary and secondary. *Primary* reinforcers (e.g. food, water, sex) are naturally reinforcing in themselves, whereas *secondary* reinforcers acquire their reinforcing properties through association with primary reinforcers; that is, we have to *learn* (through classical conditioning) to find them reinforcing.

Examples of human secondary (or conditioned) reinforcers are money, trading stamps, cheques and tokens (see Chapter 31 for a discussion of token economy programmes used with psychiatric patients and other groups).

In a Skinner box situation, if a click accompanies the presentation of each pellet of food, the rat will eventually come to find the click on its own reinforcing; this is demonstrated by using the click as a reinforcer for getting the rat to learn some new response. A famous demonstration of the power of secondary reinforcers is the study by Wolfe (1936). He used the Chimp-O-Mat machine, which chimpanzees learned to operate to obtain poker chips, as a secondary reinforcement for solving problems.

Secondary reinforcers are often important because they 'bridge the gap' between the response and the primary reinforcer which may not be immediately forthcoming.

Schedules of reinforcement

Another important aspect of Skinner's work (Ferster and Skinner, 1957) is concerned with the effects on behaviour of how frequently and how regularly (or predictably) reinforcements are presented. He identified five major schedules, each of which is associated with a characteristic pattern of responding and, as Walker (1984) observes, this part of Skinner's research is largely counterintuitive, which makes it all the more interesting.

To summarize first, rats and pigeons (and probably most mammals and birds) typically 'work harder'

(e.g. press the lever at a faster rate) for scant reward: when reinforcements are (i) relatively few and far between and (ii) relatively irregular or unpredictable, not only will they go on working but will do so long after the reinforcement has been withdrawn altogether! So each schedule can be analysed in terms of *pattern and rate of response* and *resistance to extinction*. This is summarized in Table 7.2.

A convenient way of displaying visually the rate of response is to plot responses cumulatively, as steps along a vertical axis, against the time when they are made along the horizontal axis. Skinner called this a 'cumulative record' and an example is shown in Figure 7.11.

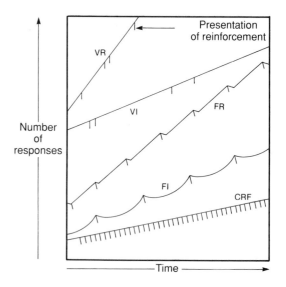

FIGURE 7.11 *Typical cumulative records for a response (such as level pressing) reinforced using five schedules of reinforcement*

A continuous schedule is usually only used when some new response is being learned; once it is being emitted regularly and reliably it can be maintained by using one of the four partial or intermittent schedules. But, of course, this change must be gradual: if the animal is used to being reinforced every time it makes a certain response and it is then switched to a Variable Ratio (VR) 50 (i.e. on average, every 50th response is reinforced), it will soon stop responding. Skinner (1938) originally used an interval schedule because a reinforcer is guaranteed, sooner or later, so long as one response is made in the interval.

Reinforcement schedule	Example	Pattern and rate of responding	Resistance to extinction	Example of human behaviour
1 Continuous reinforcement (CRF)	Every single response is reinforced	Response rate is low but steady	Very low – the quickest way to bring about extinction	1 Receiving a high grade for every assignment 2 Receiving a tip for every customer served
2 Fixed interval (FI)	A reinforcement is given every 30 seconds (FI 30) – provided the response occurs at least once during that time	Response rate speeds up as the next reinforcement becomes available; a pause after each reinforcement. Overall response rate fairly low	Fairly low – extinction occurs quite quickly	1 Being paid regularly – every week or month. 2 Giving yourself a 15-minute break for every hour's studying done
3 Variable interval (VI)	A reinforcement is given on average every 30 seconds – but the interval varies from trial to trial. So the interval on any one occasion is unpredictable	Response rate is very stable over long periods of time. Still some tendency to increase response rate as time elapses since the last reinforcement	Very high – extinction occurs very slowly and gradually	Many self employed people receive payment irregularly – depends when the customer pays for the product or service
4 Fixed ratio (FR)	A reinforcement is given for a fixed number of response – however long this may take. E.g. one reinforcement every 10 responses (FR 10)	There is a pronounced pause after each reinforcement and then a very high rate of responding leading up to the next reinforcement	As Fixed interval	1 Piece work – the more work done, the more money earned. 2 Commission – extra money for so many goods made or sales completed
5 Variable ratio (VR)	A reinforcement is given on average every 10 responses (VR 10) but the number varies from trial to trial. So the number of responses required on any one occasion is unpredictable	Very high response rate – and very steady	Very high – the most resistant of all the schedules	Gambling

Table 7.2 *Common reinforcement schedules and associated patterns of response and resistance to extinction*

Shaping – the reinforcement of successive approximations

Reinforcement can also be used to build up relatively complex behaviour – behaviour which the animal does not normally display or which is not part of its natural repertoire – by reinforcing closer and closer approximations to the desired behaviour.

First, the behaviour must be broken down into a number of small steps, each of which is reinforced in sequence, so that gradually what the animal can do is much more like what the experimenter is trying to teach it. This is what animal trainers have been doing for hundreds of years and is the method of reinforcement Skinner used to teach pigeons to play ping-pong or turn a full (anticlockwise) circle. Most skills in humans are learned in this step-by-step manner, whether this happens deliberately and consciously (as in driving) or spontaneously and unconsciously (as in acquiring speech).

Shaping also provides an important foundation for *behaviour modification,* used to teach mentally handicapped people to use the toilet, feed and dress themselves and other social skills. It has been used also to develop speech in autistic children (see Chapter 31).

Negative reinforcement – escape and avoidance learning

Figure 7.10 shows that two forms of negative reinforcement are escape and avoidance learning; these are the two major ways in which negative reinforcement has been studied in the laboratory. Escape learning is relatively simple; for example, rats can learn to press a lever to turn off electric shock. Avoidance learning is more complex and more relevant to certain aspects of human behaviour.

Most laboratory studies have used a shuttle box, a box divided into two compartments, sometimes with a barrier or door between the two compartments; electric shock can be delivered through the floor of either compartment independently of the other. Neither side is permanently safe but only one is electrified at a time; the problem for the animal is to find which is the safe side on any one occasion. A warning signal is given whenever the electrified side is to be changed, so the animal can always avoid being shocked if it switches sides when it hears (or sees) the warning signal. But why should it? According to the two factor theory (Mowrer, 1960) or the two process theory (Gray, 1975) the animal first learns to be afraid (through classical conditioning the light or buzzer warning signal elicits an anticipatory emotional response of fear or anxiety) and then learns a response to reduce the fear (jumping the barrier is negatively reinforced through avoiding the shock before it is switched on).

Miller (1948) attempted to separate out the classical from the operant factors. At first he trained rats to run out of a white room, through a small door, into a black room by giving them shocks in the white room. After pretraining, the door was closed and could only be opened by the rat turning a wheel. Even though no further shocks were given, the residual 'aversiveness' of the white room (acquired through classical conditioning) was sufficient to motivate the rats to learn quickly to turn the wheel so that they could run through into the 'safe' room, thus relieving their anxiety (negative reinforcement).

An interesting and important difference can now be seen between positive and negative reinforcement in relation to extinction. If we try to teach a rat a new response in order to get it into a black box which used to contain food, it will soon stop responding; but if a rat successfully escapes from a white room which used to be dangerous, it may go on escaping indefinitely. In the former case it soon 'discovers' that the food is no longer available but in the latter it does not stay around long enough to 'discover' that the shock is no longer happening.

Therefore, responses which are motivated by conditioned fear or anxiety should persist longer (take longer to extinguish) than those motivated by positive incentives. Avoidance learning prevents the learner from testing reality and this has been found in dogs and humans (Solomon and Wynne, 1953; Turner and Solomon, 1962). In humans, phobias may be seen as persisting in this way and one therapeutic attempt to bring about extinction through forced reality testing is called *flooding* or *implosion therapy* (see Chapter 31).

Punishment

Skinner has always maintained that positive reinforcement (and, to a lesser extent, negative reinforcement) is a much more potent influence on behaviour than punishment, both with animals and humans, largely because punishment can only make certain responses less likely – you cannot teach anything new by punishment alone. Other psychologists either disagree with Skinner or emphasize different reasons for the ineffectiveness of punishment.

Campbell and Church (1969) argue that punishments are, if anything, a stronger influence on behaviour than the incentive effects of reinforcements (at least as far as laboratory animals are concerned). The problem, however, is the unpleasant side-effects of stress, anxiety, withdrawal, aggression and so on (see Chapter 27 for discussion of this in relation to children).

Estes (1970) trained two groups of rats to press a lever for food, after which they were given extinction trials. For Group A, the first few extinction trials involved strong electric shock every time they pressed; from then on, the food was simply withheld. For Group B, food was withheld on all the extinction trials (and no shocks). In the first stage of extinction, Group A rats did make fewer responses but they later resumed their previous rate of responding and, by the end of the experiment, had made as many responses as Group B. Estes concluded that punishment merely suppressed the lever pressing in the short term, but did not weaken it. Other experiments have shown that the strength and duration of the suppression effect depend on the intensity of the punishment and the degree of deprivation. However, the response is still suppressed rather than unlearned.

Howe (1980) points out that when alternative ways of obtaining reinforcers are available, punishment has a more powerful suppressive effect on the punished behaviour. For example, Azrin and Holtz (1966) combined punishment and reinforcement so that response A was punished while response B, incompatible with A, was positively reinforced. This is something that Skinner advocates with human beings.

The antecedents of behaviour – stimulus control

A crucial difference between classical and operant conditioning is to do with the role of the stimulus in relation to the response. Whereas in classical conditioning the stimulus elicits or triggers the response in an automatic way, in operant conditioning the stimulus indicates the likely consequence of emitting a particular response, i.e. the operant behaviour is more likely to occur in the presence of some stimuli than others. If the rat has been reinforced for pressing the lever, it is more likely to go on emitting that response as the lever becomes associated both with reinforcement and the action of pressing (probably through classical conditioning). Technically, lever pressing has now come under the control of the lever stimulus – but there is still no inevitability about pressing it, only an increased probability. (This is why the term S–R psychology is sometimes used only to refer to classical conditioning.)

Similarly, drivers' behaviour is brought under the stimulus control of traffic signals, road signs, other vehicles, pedestrians and so on. Much of our everyday behaviour can be seen in this way; sitting on chairs, answering the telephone, turning on the television, etc. are all operants which are more likely to occur in the presence of those stimuli because of the past consequences of doing so.

A special case of stimulus control is a discriminative stimulus. In the Skinner box, for example, if a rat is reinforced for lever pressing only when a light is on, the light soon becomes a discriminative stimulus, i.e. the rat only presses when the light is on. If you learn to ask your teachers questions only when they are sitting at their desk (and not when standing by the board) because this has been the occasion for discussion in previous lessons, then your question-asking behaviour is under the stimulus control of your teachers' behaviour.

● Does conditioning work in the same way for all species?

According to Walker (1984), the fact that many experiments involving a variety of species can all be described as classical conditioning (since in all cases a response comes to be elicited by a new stimulus) does not in itself mean that there is only one mechanism involved or only one explanation which applies, equally, to all species and all cases. Although conditionability seems to be an almost universal property of nervous systems (including those of sea snails, flatworms and fruit flies), many psychologists have argued that there can be no general laws of learning (Seligman, 1970). But what might such laws be?

One example is the law of contiguity: events (or stimuli) which occur close together in time and space are likely to become associated with each other. Most of the examples of conditioning we have considered so far would appear to 'obey' the law of contiguity. But can we find exceptions and, if so, how can we explain them? For one possible answer, see Box 7.3.

Findings from taste aversion experiments show that the use of slow-acting rat poisons are really a waste of time and effort because the interval between food consumption and illness can be several hours without abolishing the aversion (i.e. the association between the poison and the illness is still learnt). However, as Mackintosh (1984) has pointed out, the time interval does have some effect – everything else being equal, 30 minutes will show a more marked aversion than 300 minutes (although there

BOX 7.3 Key study: learning to feel as sick as a rat

A famous and important exception to the law of contiguity are *taste aversion* studies (Garcia and Koelling, 1966; Garcia et al, 1966). In the Garcia et al study, rats were given a novel-tasting solution, e.g. saccharine-flavoured water (the CS), prior to a drug, e.g. apomorphine (the UCS), which has a delayed action, inducing severe intestinal illness (the UCR). In two separate experiments the precise time-lapse between tasting the solution and the onset of the drug-induced nausea was either (a) 5, 6, 7, 8, 9, 10, 11, 12, 15, 16, 17, 18, 19, 20, 21 and 22 minutes, or (b) 30, 45, 75, 120 and 180 minutes. In (a), the rats received just four treatments (one every third day) and in (b) five were given (one every third day) and in all cases a conditioned aversive response to the solution was acquired (i.e. intestinal illness became a CR – a response to the solution alone). In some replications, just a single treatment has been needed. Illness seems to be naturally attributed to tastes.

will be some learning in the latter). While rats can also be conditioned to novel smells, auditory, visual and tactile stimuli are not so readily associated with internal illness.

As for pigeons, it is impossible to deter them from water and, for other species, taste aversions are very difficult to establish, even if the animal is made very ill. In almost all species aversions are learned more easily to new flavours than to familiar ones (saccharine solution is a novel taste for the rat).

Thus there seem to be definite biological limitations on the ability of animals to develop a conditioned aversion. Similarly, the average rat will learn very quickly to avoid shock in a shuttle box and will also learn very quickly to press a lever for food. However, rats do not learn very readily to press a lever to avoid shock. Again, pigeons can be trained quickly to fly from one perch to another in order to avoid shock but it is almost impossible to train them to peck a disc to avoid shock.

Findings like these have led Bolles (1980) and others to conclude that we cannot regard the basic principles of learning as applying equally to all species in all situations; we must take into account the evolutionary history of the species as well as the individual organism's learning history.

An important idea in this context is Seligman's concept of *preparedness* (1970). Animals are biologi-

cally prepared to learn actions that are closely related to the survival of their species (e.g. learned water or food aversions) and these prepared behaviours are learned with very little training. By the same token, there are also contraprepared behaviours, which are contrary to an animal's natural tendencies and so are learned with great difficulty, if at all. Seligman believes that most of the behaviour studied in the laboratory falls somewhere in between these two extremes.

Oakley (1983) believes that preparedness in conditioning is an inherited characteristic. If, in the history of a species, individuals have often been exposed to certain biologically significant kinds of association, then the ability to learn rapidly about such associations becomes genetically transmitted. These genetic constraints apply to both classical and operant conditioning.

What about preparedness in humans? Much of the relevant data relates to how easily certain conditioned fear responses can be induced in the laboratory or how common certain phobias are compared with others (the 'naturally occurring ones'). For instance, Ohman *et al.*, 1975a,b) paired slides of snakes and spiders with a strong electric shock and quickly established conditioned emotional responses to these slides but not to slides of flowers, houses or berries.

Seligman (1972) observed that human phobias tend to fall into certain narrow categories, most of them being of animals or dangerous places. Most common of all were the fear of snakes, spiders, the dark, high places and closed-in places and often there is no previous evidence for the fear actually having been conditioned (this is discussed further in Chapters 30 and 31). Another interesting finding is that classically conditioned responses extinguish faster in humans than animals. According to Weiskrantz (1982), this is because the CRs are modulated by more complex human memories.

These findings in turn raise further questions, including what exactly is learned during conditioning and what is the role of cognitive factors in conditioning? We shall consider these two questions together.

● Is conditioning more complex than it seems? What is the role of cognition?

According to Mackintosh (1978), conditioning is not reducible to the strengthening of S–R associations by the automatic action of a process called reinforcement. It is more appropriate to think of it as a matter of detecting and learning about *relations between events,* whereby animals typically discover what signals or causes events that are important to them, such as food, water, danger or safety. Mackintosh goes on to say that instead of treating salivation or lever pressing as what is learned, we could regard it simply as a convenient index of what the subject has learned, namely that certain relationships exist in its environment.

Indeed, Pavlov himself described the CS as a 'signal' for the UCS, the relationship between CS and the UCS as one of 'stimulus substitution' and the CR as an 'anticipatory' response (or 'psychic secretions'), suggesting that his dogs were *expecting* the food to follow the bell, etc.

To support this interpretation, Rescorla (1968) presented two groups of animals with the same number of CS–UCS pairings, but the second group also received additional presentations of the UCS on its own without the CS. The first group showed much stronger conditioning than the second, indicating that the most important factor (in classical conditioning anyway) is how predictably the UCS follows the CS, not how often the CS and UCS are paired.

Many investigators regard conditioning as involving the formation of a central representation of causal relations (or, at least, predictive ones) between events: stimulus event A predicts stimulus event B (the CS predicts the UCS). But the learning may also take the form: stimulus event A predicts that stimulus event B will not occur. This is called *conditioned suppression* or *inhibition.*

Pavlov (1927) first trained a dog with three separate stimuli: a flashing light, the tone of C sharp and a rotating disc; all of these were signals for food. Then an *inhibitory combination* was formed by sounding a metronome along with the rotating disc; this combination was never followed by food and the dog learned not to salivate. Then the metronome was sounded along with the tone and flashing light, which produced a virtual elimination of salivation. Pavlov concluded that the metronome had become a *conditioned inhibitor.*

Another demonstration of the complexity of conditioning is the phenomenon of *blocking* (Kamin, 1969). If, for example, an animal is shown a light, quickly followed by an electric shock, the light soon comes to elicit fear as a CR. If a noise is then added (noise + light + shock), then the noise should also soon become a CS, because it too is being paired with shock.

However, this is not what happens; if the noise is later presented alone, it fails to produce a CR. Why? It seems that the noise has somehow been 'blocked' from becoming a CS because of the previous conditioning to the light. In cognitive terms, since the light already predicts shock, the noise is irrelevant, it provides no additional information – the animal already 'knows' that shock will follow the light.

Turning now to operant conditioning, the complexity of learning is well illustrated by *learned helplessness* (Seligman, 1974, 1975). Dogs were strapped into a harness and given a series of shocks from which they could not escape. They were later required to learn avoidance behaviour in a shuttle box – they had to jump a barrier within 10 seconds of a warning signal or suffer 50 seconds of painful shock. Whereas control dogs, which had not been subjected to the inescapable shocks, learned the avoidance response very quickly, about two-thirds of the experimental dogs seemed unable to do so. They seemed passively resigned to suffering the shock and even if they did successfully avoid the shock on one trial, they were unlikely to do so on the next. Some dogs had to be pushed over the barrier 200 times or more before this learned helplessness wore off.

According to Seligman, the dogs learned that no behaviour on their part had any effect on the occurrence (or non-occurrence) of a particular event (i.e. the shock). This has been demonstrated using human participants by Miller and Norman (1979) and Maier and Seligman (1976) have tried to explain depression in humans in terms of learned helplessness (see Chapters 5, 6 and 30).

Skinner's claim that reinforcements and punishments automatically strengthen and weaken behaviour has been challenged by many, including Bandura (1977) who maintains that: (i) they provide the learner with information about the likely consequences of certain behaviour under certain conditions, that is 'what leads to what' and whether we are 'right' or 'wrong' (*feedback*), and (ii) they motivate us by causing us to anticipate future outcomes – our present behaviours are largely governed by the outcomes we expect them to have.

While Bandura is addressing his comments primarily to human behaviour, one of the earliest challenges to Skinner's view came from a fellow student of learning in rats, Edward Tolman.

● Tolman's cognitive behaviourism – latent learning and cognitive maps

Tolman, although working within the behaviourist tradition in the 1920s, 1930s and 1940s, would today be regarded as a cognitive psychologist, because he explained the learning of rats in terms of inferred

BOX
7.4 Key study: Learning your way around – who needs reinforcement!

Tolman and Honzik (1930) showed that learning can take place in the absence of reinforcement (contrary to Skinner's position) in the following way.

Group 1 rats were reinforced every time they found their way through a maze to the food box; Group 2 were never reinforced; and Group 3 received no reinforcement for the first ten days of the experiment but did so from day 11. Group 1, as you might expect, learned to run the maze quickly and made fewer and fewer mistakes. Again, not surprisingly, Group 2 never decreased the time it took them to find the food and they wandered the same maze aimlessly much of the time. Group 3, however, having apparently made no progress during the first ten days (of no reinforcement) showed a sudden decrease in the time it took to reach the goal box on day 11 when they received their first reinforcement and caught up almost immediately with Group 1 (see Figures 7.12 and 7.13).

Clearly the Group 3 rats had been learning their way through the maze during the first ten days but that learning was *latent* (or 'behaviourally silent'), that is, it did not show up in their actual behaviour (performance). With the incentive of the reinforcement on day 11, that previously 'hidden' learning was demonstrated, allowing Group 3 rats to catch up very quickly with the Group 1 rats, which had been reinforced from the beginning. So Tolman and Honzik had produced evidence for the view that reinforcement may be important in relation to *performance* of learned behaviour but that it is not necessary for the learning itself.

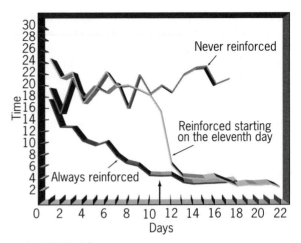

FIGURE 7.12 *The results of Tolman and Honzik's study of latent learning in rats*

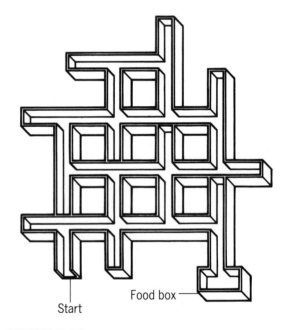

FIGURE 7.13 *The maze used in Tolman and Honzik's study of latent learning in rats*

cognitive processes, in particular *cognitive* or *mental maps*. He also distinguished between learning and performance (or 'knowing' and 'doing'). See Box 7.4.

Having established the role of reinforcement, Tolman wanted to know exactly what it is that is learned (and which does not require reinforcement). Tolman's theory (1948) of *place learning* (or *sign learning*) maintains that rats learn something about 'what leads to what' in the maze, that is, they learn *expectations* as to which part of the maze will be followed by which other part of the maze. Tolman called these expectations *cognitive maps* and they represent a primitive kind of perceptual map of the maze, an understanding of the spatial relationships that constitute the maze (much like the mental map you have of familiar streets, those that lead to your home

or to college). What is the evidence for this?

Like all cognitive processes, a cognitive map cannot be directly observed but only inferred from actual behaviour. However, it is difficult to know how else to explain the findings that rats will take shortcuts to the food box if the old path is blocked or how, if the maze were rotated, they could find the usual food location from several different starting points (Tolman et al, 1946).

These findings suggest that it is not the individual movements of walking or swimming, etc. that constitute the learning of the maze but rather something to do with the geographical characteristics of the maze. In a direct test between these two opposed interpretations, Restle (1957) flooded a maze immediately after a group of rats had learnt to run it and they were able to swim to the goal-box with no more errors than when they had walked. This clearly supports Tolman's theory of sign learning.

● Applications of conditioning

The three major ways in which conditioning principles have been put to practical use with people are:

1 *behaviour therapy* and *behaviour modification*, which constitute major forms of treatment of behaviour disorders and which are discussed in detail in Chapter 31;
2 *biofeedback*;
3 *programmed learning* or *instruction*.

Biofeedback techniques grew out of experiments with rats (Miller and Dicara, 1967; Dicara and Miller, 1968), in which, it was claimed, involuntary, autonomic, responses were brought under control using operant conditioning. Briefly, paralysed rats were positively reinforced by hypothalamic electrical stimulation whenever their breathing rate – and other

autonomic functions – changed in the desired direction. This was quite a startling finding, because until then it had been believed that autonomic behaviour could only be conditioned through classical methods and that operant methods could only be applied to voluntary behaviour.

However, these results have always been considered to be highly controversial and have never been replicated (Walker, 1984); even Miller himself (1978) has spoken out against accepting the results from any experiments using curarized (paralysed) animals (on scientific rather than ethical grounds, it should be noted).

Nevertheless, research into biofeedback has continued, but with mixed fortunes. As used with people, the basic procedure involves providing individuals with information, i.e. feedback, about specific aspects of their biological functioning (e.g. heart rate, breathing rate, blood pressure, EEG and GSR – see Chapter 4). On the strength of this information, they are trained to control these biological functions (of which we are normally unaware) at will.

In a typical training session, the individual (who will often be a patient receiving biofeedback as a treatment condition in an experimental study) is connected to various recording machines and when, say, blood pressure falls within a certain predetermined

---

Skinner believed that much conventional teaching and learning is slow and inefficient. Programmed instruction can remove these obstacles to learning on the basis of six principles:

1 The material to be learned is broken down into a number of elements – separate items of information (or *frames).*

2 The material is presented in a predetermined sequence, such that each step or increment is so small that the probability of making errors is almost zero; this *continuous reinforcement* schedule ensures a high level of motivation.

3 For every correct response, an immediate reinforcement is provided in the form of the learner being told that the response is correct *(immediate feedback);* an incorrect response takes the learner back to that item (usually after a brief account of why the answer is incorrect). In either case, learners are checking their own progress.

4 At each step, the learner must emit (or voluntarily produce) a correct answer in order to receive a reinforcement; in this way, reinforcement is contingent upon appropriate behaviour and learners are actively participating in their learning.

5 The reinforcement of correct responses to a number of small steps (successive approximations) making up the material to be learned represents a form of *shaping.*

6 Learners work at their own pace, which allows for any individual differences in speed of learning.

TABLE 7.3 *Skinner's principles of programmed instruction*

range, a signal is given (such as waves on a monitor screen, a buzzer or a light), which , of course, is the feedback.

Biofeedback has been applied to an enormous range of clinical problems, including many psychophysiological disorders, and we saw in Chapter 6 some examples of its use in coping with pain . One of the controversial aspects of biofeedback is the possibility of alternative explanations for its successes ; for example, when blood pressure and heart rate are shown to be controllable, this might be due to subtle muscular movements or changes in breathing, i.e. changes in the autonomic functions may be a consequence of control over voluntary functions. Also, many researchers believe that simple training in voluntary muscle relaxation is often at least as effective – and sometimes more so – as biofeedback for the treatment of stress-related disorders (see Chapter 6).

Programmed learning or *instruction* is a method of instruction that systematically applies the principles of operant conditioning to the learning situation. The first 'teaching machine' was devised by Pressey, an educational psychologist, in 1926. It consisted of a series of multiple choice questions used for testing what students had already been taught. Skinner (1954, 1958) advocated the extension of this technique for initial learning.

Not only did Skinner believe that all learning (human and animal) takes place according to the principles of (operant) conditioning but also that the usual classroom situation is not an ideal place for learning to happen. The teacher typically has little control over crucial variables such as students paying attention, their motivation and the reinforcements they receive and often it is the aversive consequences of the classroom which dominate (such as trying to avoid failure or the teacher's disapproval).The principles on which programmed learning is based are summarized in Table 7.3.

The kind of programmed learning which Skinner devised and advocated is *linear*, i.e. it comprises a predetermined sequence of steps which is the same for all students and each step must be correctly answered before moving on to the next. By contrast, *branching* programmes usually comprise larger frames (chunks of information and explanations rather than very short, simple questions and bits of information) and they allow alternative routes through the material, depending on the accuracy of the learner's answers. This allows more able students to skip familiar material and move on to more advanced material. Branching also enables a learner who makes an error to find out why the answer is wrong by directing them to branch off from the main stem of the programme and work through some special review material.

Both linear and branching programmes can take the form of books (programmed texts), teaching machines (in which, for example, a frame is exposed in the left-hand window and the student writes the answer in the right-hand window or pulling a lever moves the answer under a perspex cover, revealing the correct answer and the next frame) or computer assisted instruction (CAI). CAI usually involves an elaborate, complex, branching programme; the learner either operates a teletype keyboard or uses a special probe to indicate the answer on a monitor.

SOCIAL LEARNING THEORY AND OBSERVATIONAL LEARNING

A major alternative to conditioning (as an attempt to explain learning) comes from social learning theory (SLT) . This originated in the USA in the 1940s and 1950s as an attempt to reinterpret certain aspects of Freud's psychoanalytic theory in terms of conditioning theory (or orthodox learning theory) (Dollard and Miller, 1950). This was carried on in the 1960s and 1970s, notably by Albert Bandura (Fig. 7.14), who tried to make Freud's concept of identification more objective and scientifically viable by studying it in the laboratory in the form of *imitation* (see Chapter 23).

FIGURE 7.14 *Albert Bandura (born 1925)*

● What are some of the important similarities and differences between SLT and orthodox learning theory?

Along with other behaviourist psychologists, SL theorists regard all behaviour as being learned through the same mechanisms, according to the same principles of learning. However, where they differ significantly from Pavlov, Watson, Skinner and so on is in their interest specifically in human learning, especially the acquisition of social and moral behaviour (we shall be discussing both theories in relation to moral development in Chapter 27).

Although SL theorists agree that we should observe what is observable, they also believe that there are important *cognitive* or *mediating variables* which intervene between stimulus and response and without which we cannot adequately explain behaviour. These cognitive variables cannot be directly observed but can only be inferred from observing actual behaviour. We shall say more about this later on.

SL theorists do not deny the importance of classical and operant conditioning but they do think that these learning processes cannot adequately account for the appearance of *novel* behaviour, that is, behaviour which the individual has not displayed before. Classical conditioning can explain how a response shifts from one stimulus to another (stimulus substitution) while operant conditioning can explain how spontaneously produced responses, through selective reinforcement and shaping, become more likely to be repeated. But if these were the only two kinds of learning, the child's behavioural repertoire would be very limited indeed.

Consequently SL theorists have emphasized a kind of learning that is distinct from conditioning, namely *observational learning*, that is, learning through watching the behaviour of another person. There are several important points to note about the concept of observational learning:

- The person whose behaviour is observed is called the *model;* hence 'modelling' is normally used synonymously with 'observational learning'.
- The learning takes place spontaneously, with no deliberate effort on the learner's part or any intention to teach on the model's part.
- Both fairly specific behaviours (e.g. nailbiting) and more general, emotional states (e.g. fear of the dentist) can be modelled (the latter through facial expressions, body posture, etc.).

Observational learning, as such, takes place without any reinforcement (Bandura, 1965); mere exposure to the model is sufficient for learning to occur. However, whether the learning actually reveals itself in the behaviour (i.e. is imitated) depends, among other things, on the consequences of the behaviour, both for the model and the learner (Bandura et al, 1963). So, whereas for Skinner the role of reinforcement is central to the learning process itself, for the SL theorists it is important only in so far as it determines the likelihood of learned responses actually being demonstrated. This, of course, is the crucial distinction between learning and performance which we came across when discussing Tolman's cognitive behaviourism.

Much of the SLT research has centred on the characteristics of models that make them more or less likely to be imitated and the conditions under which the learning will be performed.

● Reinforcement as information about the future

We noted earlier that Bandura takes a very different view from Skinner of how reinforcement works and this relates directly to the learning–performance distinction which Bandura makes but which Skinner does not. According to Skinner, reinforcement works automatically; the strengthening of a response simply 'happens' and the learner, human or animal, is not required to assess or evaluate the effects of their behaviour. Bandura (1977), on the other hand, maintains that 'Reinforcement serves principally as an informative and motivational operation rather than as a mechanical response strengthener'.

By 'informative' he means that the consequences of our behaviour (reinforcement or punishment) tell us under what circumstances it would seem wise to try a particular behaviour in the future, that is, they improve our prediction of whether a given action will lead to pleasant or unpleasant outcomes in the future. While Skinner believes that a consequence exerts its influence in reverse (i.e. strengthening the behaviour that preceded the reinforcement or punishment), Bandura argues that the consequence exerts its influence forwards, into the future, by giving the learner information about what effects can be expected if he or she behaves that way again in similar circumstances. For these reasons, we can learn from observing others (as well as from our own behaviour), because watching others can provide the same information as to what kind of behaviour leads to which consequence.

By 'motivational', Bandura means that we are more likely to try to learn the modelled behaviour if we value the consequences related to that behaviour. But as Bandura also makes the distinction between learning and performance, the motivational effect of reinforcement (as we noted above) may be greater in relation to the demonstration of learning rather than the learning itself.

● The role of cognitive factors in observational learning

The learning process is much more complex for Bandura than it is for Skinner. In Bandura's (1974) view, '... contrary to mechanistic metaphors, outcomes change behaviour in humans through the intervening influence of thought'. He believes that there are five major functions involved in observational learning:

1 *Paying attention*. The learner must attend to the pertinent clues in the stimulus situation and ignore those aspects of the model and the environment that are incidental and do not affect the performance the learner seeks to learn. Especially with complex behaviour, failure to reproduce the behaviour properly later on is often due to misdirected attention at the time of modelling.

2 Recording a *visual image* or *semantic code* for the modelled behaviour in memory. Without an adequate coding system, the learner fails to store what has been seen or heard (see Chapter 12). There are obvious developmental trends in the ability to learn from models; whereas an infant's use of modelling is confined mainly to immediate imitation, the older child can defer (postpone) imitation because of its superior use of symbols. The codes must, of course, be suitable for transforming into overt actions (see Chapter 25).

3 *Memory permanence*. This refers to devices such as rehearsal and use of multiple codes to help retain the stored information over long periods.

4 *Reproducing the observed motor activities* accurately. This usually requires a number of trials to get the muscular feel of the behaviour (through feedback). Again, there are developmental trends involved here, whereby the older child enjoys greater muscular strength and control.

5 *Motivation*. Behaviourists have traditionally equated this with the role of the consequences of behaviour but we have already discussed the differences between Bandura's and Skinner's interpretation of the nature of reinforcement and how it works.

Some evidence for the role of cognitive factors is provided by a study by Bandura et al (1963) in which children were asked to reproduce the actions of a model seen on a film. Group 1 simply watched the film, Group 2 were asked to describe the model's actions as they saw them on the film and Group 3 were asked to count while watching the film (an interfering task). It was found that Group 2 children were able to reproduce the behaviour of the model most accurately and thoroughly through the aid of verbalization. As expected, Group 3 children did worst of all, with Group 1 children somewhere in between.

We shall have more to say about the role of cognitive factors in modelling in Chapter 27 on moral development.

INSIGHT LEARNING

Insight learning represents a view of learning as 'purely cognitive' and stems from a theoretical approach in psychology which is diametrically opposed to the S–R approach, namely, the *Gestalt* school. The Gestalt psychologists are best known for their work on perception (see Chapter 9) and their view of learning is directly linked to their view of perception; indeed, insight learning can be defined as a perceptual restructuring of the elements that constitute a problem situation, whereby a previously missing 'ingredient' is supplied and all the parts are seen in relation to each other, forming a meaningful whole (see Chapter 14 for a discussion of Gestalt studies of problem solving).

For example, imagine a chimpanzee in its cage reaching for a banana which lies outside the cage; its arm is not long enough to get the banana but also outside the cage is a stick which the chimp can reach and which is long enough to reach the banana. After reaching with its arm unsuccessfully, it suddenly reaches for the stick and uses it to rake in the banana.

Köhler (1925), one of the leading Gestalt psychologists, used this and similar problems to demonstrate insight learning, which he saw as opposed to the trial-and error-learning involved in S–R approaches. In the latter, stimulus and response become associated when, by chance, the animal produces the correct response (or 'solves the problem') and is reinforced for doing so. However, the correct response does not appear suddenly, it merely takes less and less time on each subsequent trial and there is no 'understanding' involved (e.g. Thorndike's cats in puzzle-boxes).

By contrast, in insight learning a sudden solution is the rule (usually preceded by long pauses, during which there is inspection of the whole visual field) and, once the solution has appeared, it can be repeated immediately the next time the problem is confronted. What is learned is not a specific set of conditioned associations but a cognitive relationship between a means and an end and this makes transfer to other, similar problem situations easier.

For example, Sultan (Köhler's most intelligent chimp) was able to pull into the cage the longer of two sticks by using the shorter one and then, with the longer one, was able to pull in a piece of fruit. Again, he was able to join two sticks together in order to make a stick long enough to rake in some fruit. In a different kind of problem, he learned to stack boxes, one on top of the other, to reach bananas suspended from the ceiling (Fig. 7.15).

However, a couple of qualifications need to be made. Firstly, animals do not usually demonstrate insight learning very easily unless all the elements that constitute the problem are in their field of vision at the same time. For example, the chimp has to be able to see the fruit and sticks (or boxes) together before it can grasp their relationship and solve the problem. People, by contrast, could immediately think of a stick and go looking for one; language is an important tool for thinking in this kind of problem-solving situation. Secondly, Köhler has been criticized for his belief that insight involves a sudden restructuring of the situation independent of the animal's past experience. There is evidence that insightful solutions can be facilitated by 'hints' or cues, especially if the elements of the problem situation are already familiar to the learner. This is captured especially well in another solution that Sultan found to the banana problem; he succeeded in breaking off a branch from a sawn-off castor oil bush, located inside the cage, which he used to rake in a banana lying outside the cage. Although Köhler described this as happening in 'one single quick chain of action' and despite its appearance as a 'flash of insight', it did not come 'out of the blue', out of nowhere. Sultan was very familiar with bananas and with castor oil bushes, as well as with sticks.

● Insight learning and the act of creation

According to Arthur Koestler (1970), all acts of 'creation', whether in painting, humour, poetry or science, share one basic characteristic, namely the juxtaposition of two concepts or ideas or images which were previously separate. When two things, previously unrelated, are seen as belonging together in some way, a joke or a scientific discovery is made. He cites the story of Archimedes, who was asked to judge whether a beautiful crown, allegedly made of pure gold, had in fact been adulterated with silver. Short of melting it down, he was stumped – he knew the specific weight of gold (its weight per volume unit) but how was he to measure the volume of such a complicated and ornate object as the crown?

One day, while getting into his bath, Archimedes noticed the familiar sight of the water level rising and in a flash ('Eureka!') he realized that the volume of water displaced was equal to the volume of his immersed body and that here was a way that the volume of the crown could also be measured. So, two already familiar pieces of knowledge, the specific weight of gold and water displacement equalling object immersion, were, for the first time, related to each other and in that moment a discovery was made. Only someone with Archimedes' knowledge could

FIGURE 7.15 *Köhler's experiments with chimpanzees*

have made such a discovery; in Koestler's terms, he was *ripe* for making the discovery. In the case of chimpanzees, their ripeness includes their manual dexterity, their advanced sensory motor co-ordination (biological) and their familiarity with sticks, bananas, etc. (experiential or environmental); the former are reminiscent of Seligman's concept of preparedness (see above).

● Do we have to choose between trial and error and insight?

Koestler believes that the debate between the S–R and cognitive theorists derives to a large extent from a refusal to take seriously the notion of ripeness. Rats and cats have generally been presented with tasks for which they are biologically ill-fitted and so the resulting learning was bound to appear gradual, piecemeal and at first quite random. Köhler and the Gestalt school, by contrast, set chimps problems for which they were (almost) ripe and so gave the impression that all learning is based on insight. So, is there a middle ground?

Gagné (1970) has attempted to answer the question regarding the relationship between simple and complex forms of learning. Is there a continuity between them and, if so, what form does this take? His solution is to regard eight major varieties of learning as hierarchically related, each building on earlier, more simple abilities which therefore represent prerequisites for later, more complex abilities. These are summarized in Table 7.4.

According to Harlow (1949), S–R learning and insight learning are related; essentially, they are two different phases of the same, continuous process, with S–R learning predominant in the early stages and insight developing out of prior S–R connections. Harlow suggests that the concept of a *learning set* (or 'learning to learn') represents an intervening process between S–R and insight learning; the greater the number of sets, the better equipped the learner is to adapt to a changing environment and a very large number of different sets 'may supply the raw material for human thinking'.

To study learning sets, Harlow gave monkeys a variety of discrimination tasks. In the simplest, the

1 **Signal learning**	The establishment of a simple connection in which a stimulus takes on the properties of a signal (*classical conditioning*)
2 **Stimulus–response learning**	The establishment of a connection between a stimulus and a response where the response in a voluntary movement and the connection is instrumental in satisfying a need or motive (*operant conditioning*)
1 and 2 are prerequisites for: 3 **Chaining**	The connecting of a sequence of two or more previously learned stimulus–response connections
4 **Verbal association**	The learning of chains that are specifically verbal, important for the acquisition and use of language. Enables a number of learned connections involving words to be emitted in a single sequence
3 and 4 are prerequisites for: 5 **Discrimination learning**	Making different responses to similar stimuli. Involves more than simply making isolated stimulus–response connections because it is necessary to deal with the problem of interference between similar items
5 is a prerequisite for: 6 **Concept learning**	Learning to make a common response to stimuli that form a class or category but which differ in their physical characteristics. Requires representing information in memory, classifying events and discriminating between them on basis of abstracted properties
6 is a prerequisite for: 7 **Rule learning**	A rule is a chain of two or more concepts (e.g. 'if A then B')
7 is a prerequisite for: 8 **Problem-solving**	Involves recombining old rules into new ones, making it possible to answer questions and solve problems, especially important for real-life human problem-solving situations

Table 7.4 *Gagné's hierarchy of learning*

monkey had to choose between two objects, one of which was designated the 'correct one'. In a more complex task, the monkey had to find the 'odd one out' of three objects. In both types of task, the pair of objects or set of three was changed each time a correct discrimination was made. So, for example, the monkey might be shown a small red square and a large blue circle and would be given six trials in which to choose the 'correct' one (for which a food reward was given). When this had been achieved, a different pair of objects (e.g. a green triangle and a black circle) was presented and once again the monkey had six trials in which to make the correct discrimination.

In one study, involving 344 of these two-object tasks, the results were dramatic. Learning the first few discriminations was difficult but it gradually became easier as the number of different tasks increased, until after 300 the solution was immediate (solved on the first trial). Remember that the same pair of objects was never used more than once. According to Harlow, a learning set involves learning a general skill applicable to a whole new class of problems or again, it consists of learning a simple rule or code, based on a conceptual (not a perceptual) relationship. To this extent, Harlow demonstrated that insightful learning itself is (at least partially) learned and grows out of more random, trial-and-error learning.

● Learning set and transfer of learning

Learning set represents a special case of a more general phenomenon known as *transfer of learning* (or training). Essentially, transfer refers to the influence of earlier learning on later learning which we saw, when defining learning at the beginning of the chapter, to be an inherent feature of the learning process in general (Howe, 1980).

Howe maintains that some kinds of transfer take the form of simple stimulus generalization (equivalent to Gagné's signal learning) while in more complex learning situations transfer may depend on the acquisition of rules or principles that apply to a variety of different circumstances (Gagné's concept, rule learning and problem-solving). Learning sets can be viewed as intermediate between simple generalization and the more complex transfer phenomena involved in hierarchically organized skills.

It used to be thought that certain disciplines (such as Latin or maths) were so general in their transferability that they could 'train the mind' to cope with almost any demand that might subsequently be made of it. However, it is now recognized (especially for motor skills) that the effect of training is much more limited and is restrained by the degree of similarity of the components of different tasks; and yet the notion of similarity itself is a complex one.

For instance, in a mirror-drawing task, practice under one condition (e.g. drawing the outline of a star without the mirror) interferes with performance under the other conditions (drawing using only the mirror-image of the star), producing *negative transfer*. Yet tracing patterns of very different appearance might seem to constitute dissimilar tasks but in fact there is considerable *positive transfer* from practising one pattern using only the mirror-image to being able to trace another under the same conditions. Positive transfer also occurs when people practise with their non-preferred hand. The normal laboratory procedure for studying transfer is as follows:

- experimental group – learns A, learns B, tested on B;
- control group – learns B, tested on B

If learning A *enhances* the learning of B, then we say that positive transfer occurs; if A *interferes* with B then we speak of negative transfer, and if A makes *no difference* either way then there is no transfer.

Transfer is commonly analysed in S–R terms: (i) where the S–R relationships are the same (e.g. A and B require the same response), then we expect to find positive transfer; (ii) where the S–R relationships are different (A requires one response and B a different, incompatible response) ,then we expect negative transfer.

Again, when an old response is required by a new stimulus there is positive transfer; when a new response is required by an old stimulus there is negative transfer. Learning sets, of course, are one form of positive transfer and positive transfer in general illustrates the cumulative nature of learning, whereby new learning builds on prior learning. Not only is learning cumulative but, as we said early in the chapter, it is closely intertwined with other processes, particularly perception and memory which are covered in the next section of the book (See Chapters 9 and 11).

CHAPTER SUMMARY

- Learning is one of the central areas of research in psychology and has played a major part in the development of psychology as a scientific discipline.

- Psychologists are interested in learning as a process, which may or may not involve one person trying to teach something to another.

- Theories of learning differ as to the nature of the process involved, especially the role played by cognitive factors, but all would agree that learning involves a relatively permanent change in behaviour due to past experience.

- An important distinction is that between learning and performance, referring to potential and actual behaviour respectively.

- Learning is cumulative and adaptive, closely related to other abilities, particularly memory.

- Skinner distinguished between respondent and operant behaviour, which correspond to classical (or Pavlovian) and operant (or instrumental) conditioning respectively.

- In classical conditioning, the pairing of a conditioned and an unconditioned stimulus results in the former eliciting a response that formerly was only produced by the latter.

- Delayed or forward, backward, simultaneous and trace conditioning differ according to the relationships between the conditioned and the unconditioned stimuli.

- Generalization, discrimination, extinction and spontaneous recovery represent conditioning phenomena which make it more complex and versatile. Spontaneous recovery demonstrates that extinction involves a learning to inhibit or suppress the conditioned response.

- Watson applied classical conditioning to human behaviour for the first time by inducing fear of a rat in Little Albert .

- Jones removed animal phobias from Little Peter using an early form of systematic desensitization. This is one kind of behaviour therapy which, along with behaviour modification, forms an important part of clinical psychology.

- Compared with classical, operant conditioning sees learning as much more active. Skinner was interested in how animals operate on their environment and how their activity is instrumental in producing certain consequences.

- Skinner's work was based on Thorndike's law of effect. He designed a form of puzzle-box (a Skinner box), and called the consequences of behaviour positive reinforcement, negative reinforcement and punishment.

- Reinforcement (both positive and negative) strengthens behaviour, while punishment weakens it.

- Primary reinforcers are naturally reinforcing, while secondary (or conditioned) reinforcers come to be reinforcing through association with primary reinforcers, as in the token economy.

- Different schedules of reinforcement can be analysed in terms of pattern/rate of response and resistance to extinction. Variable schedules involve high, steady rates of response and high resistance to extinction compared with fixed and continuous schedules.

- Shaping involves the reinforcement of successive approximations to the desired behaviour.

- Two forms of negative reinforcement are escape and avoidance learning, which have been explained by the two factor theory, according to which both classical and operant conditioning are involved. The persistence of human phobias can be understood in terms of avoidance learning.

- Punishment seems to involve a suppression of behaviour and is most effective when combined with the reinforcement of an incompatible response.

- In operant conditioning, the stimulus makes certain behaviour more likely to occur, but this is not inevitable as it is in classical conditioning. This is called stimulus control.

- Taste aversion experiments contribute to the view that the basic principles of conditioning do not apply equally to all species in all situations.

- Preparedness helps to explain experimental findings which show that different species acquire certain conditioned responses more or less easily and why certain human phobias are more common than others.

- Rather than a simple strengthening of S–R associations, conditioning can be thought of as the learning about relations between events or the formation of central representations of causal relations between events.

- Seligman's concept of learned helplessness illustrates the complexity of (operant) conditioning and has been used to explain human depression.

- Tolman's theory of latent learning is meant to show that learning can take place in the absence of reinforcement; what rats learn when they run a maze is a cognitive map of the maze, not the individual movements of walking or running that take them to the food box.

- Biofeedback is commonly used to treat psychophysiological disorders and uses operant methods to change autonomic responses.
- Programmed learning is a method of instruction that systematically applies operant conditioning principles to educational situations. A basic distinction is between linear and branching programmes.
- Social learning theorists are primarily concerned with explaining human learning and stress the role of cognitive variables. The key learning process involved is observational learning and, like Tolman, they distinguish between learning and performance.
- Bandura stresses the informational and motivational aspects of reinforcement, as well as fundamental cognitive processes such as attention and memory.
- Insight learning involves the perceptual restructuring of the elements that constitute some problem situation and was proposed by Gestalt psychologists such as Köhler. According to Koestler, insight is central to all acts of creation, but the person (or animal) must be ripe for making the discovery.
- Insight and trial-and-error aren't necessarily opposed forms of learning. Gagné's hierarchy of learning and Harlow's concept of learning set show that they are related, not exclusive. Learning set represents a special case of the more general transfer of learning.

GLOSSARY

Biofeedback Based on operant conditioning, a technique for treating psychophysiological disorders in which autonomic functions are brought under voluntary control.

Classical conditioning A form of learning in which a conditioned and an unconditioned stimulus become associated, such that the former comes to elicit a response previously elicited only by the latter. Also known as Pavlovian or respondent conditioning.

Cognitive (or mental) map Tolman's term for a rat's primitive understanding of the spatial relationships of a maze.

Conditioned response (CR) The name for the unconditioned response when triggered by the conditioned stimulus alone.

Conditioned stimulus (CS) A stimulus which, through being paired with an unconditioned stimulus, comes to elicit the unconditioned response without the unconditioned stimulus.

Discrimination Process by which the conditioned response is produced by certain stimuli but not others.

Extinction The gradual weakening and eventual cessation of the conditioned response when the conditioned stimulus is repeatedly presented without the unconditioned stimulus.

Generalization Process by which the conditioned response spontaneously transfers to stimuli that are similar to, but different from, the original conditioned stimulus.

Higher order conditioning The pairing of a stimulus with the conditioned stimulus, such that the former triggers the conditioned response without ever having been paired with the unconditioned stimulus.

Insight learning A cognitive theory, based on Gestalt principles, which sees learning as a perceptual restructuring of the elements making up a problem situation.

Latent learning Tolman's hypothesis that learning can take place without reinforcement, although it may not show up in the animals' behaviour without reinforcement.

Law of effect The relationship between stimulus and response is 'stamped in' by a pleasurable outcome and 'stamped out' by an unpleasant outcome (Thorndike, 1898)

Learned helplessness Seligman's term for the failure to acquire avoidance responses, due to previous experience of being prevented from escaping from an aversive situation.

Learning A relatively permanent change in behaviour (-al potential) as a result of past experience.

Learning set Harlow's term for 'learning to learn'; the learner acquires the 'rules' for solving a particular type of problem based on limited examples.

Negative reinforcement Removal or prevention of an aversive stimulus, contingent on some response and which strengthens it (i.e. makes it more likely to be repeated).

Operant behaviour Voluntary behaviour emitted in the presence of certain environmental stimuli.

Operant conditioning A form of learning in which voluntary behaviour becomes more or less likely to be repeated depending on its consequences. Also known as Skinnerian or instrumental.

Positive reinforcement Presentation of a pleasurable stimulus, contingent on some response and which strengthens it (i.e. makes it more likely to be repeated).

Preparedness Seligman's view that different species are biologically equipped to acquire certain conditioned responses more easily if they have high survival value.

Primary reinforcer A stimulus that is naturally reinforcing, such as food and water.

Programmed learning/instruction A method of instruction that systematically applies the principles of operant conditioning, as in teaching machines and computer-assisted instruction.

Punishment Presentation of an aversive stimulus, contingent on some response and which weakens it (i.e. makes it less likely to be repeated).

Respondent behaviour Involuntary behaviour, automatically triggered (elicited) by particular environmental events or stimuli.

Schedules of reinforcement Rules for the presentation of reinforcers in relation to an operant response. Reinforcement can be continuous or partial/intermittent.

Secondary reinforcer A stimulus that becomes reinforcing through association with a primary reinforcer, such as money and tokens. Also known as conditioned reinforcers.

Shaping Reinforcement of successive approximations to some desired behaviour.

Skinner box A form of puzzle-box used for investigating operant conditioning, with a lever or illuminated disk and a dispenser for food reinforcements.

Social learning theory An alternative to conditioning theory which stresses the role of cognitive factors in human behaviour, especially observational learning/modelling.

Spontaneous recovery The reappearance of the conditioned response, following extinction and after a rest period, without any additional conditioning taking place.

Stimulus control In operant conditioning, learning to emit a particular response in the presence of certain stimuli but not others. Past reinforcements make this more probable, but never inevitable.

Stimulus–response (S–R) approach The behaviourist theories of Watson and Skinner, according to which most behaviour can be analysed into stimulus–response connections, acquired through conditioning.

Taste aversion studies Experiments in which animals develop, through conditioning, an aversion for tastes whose past consumption has been followed by illness.

Transfer of learning The influence of earlier on later learning; positive transfer enhances later learning, while negative transfer impedes it.

Trial-and-error learning Random learning involving a gradual reduction in number of errors and time to complete a task.

Unconditioned response (UCR) An automatic, reflex, involuntary, biologically built-in response.

Unconditioned stimulus (UCS) A stimulus that triggers an unconditioned response.

FURTHER READING

Walker, S. (1984) *Learning Theory & Behaviour Modification.* London: Methuen A clear introduction to the basic concepts and issues, including the clinical applications of classical and operant conditioning.

Anderson, J.R. (1995) *Learning & Memory: An Integrated Approach.* New York: John Wiley & Sons. As the title suggests, an attempt to look at learning and memory as two sides of the same coin, so just as useful for Chapter 12 of this book as for the present one.

Sensory and Cognitive Processes

8 SENSORY PROCESSES

INTRODUCTION AND OVERVIEW

When we move our eyes or our heads, the objects we see around us remain stable. Similarly, when we follow an object that is itself moving, we attribute the movement to the object and not to ourselves. When we approach people in the street we do not experience them as gradually growing 'before our very eyes' and objects seen from various angles are still recognized as 'the same' object as they are when seen from head-on.

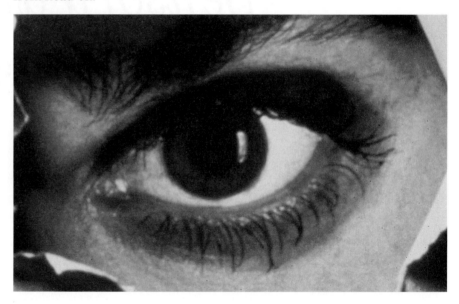

It is estimated that 80% of external information we receive reaches us through our eyes

These examples of how we experience the world may seem mundane and 'obvious' until we realize what is actually taking place physically. If we compare what we experience (namely, a world of objects that remain stable and constant) with what our sense organs receive in the form of physical stimulation (an almost continuous state of flux), it is almost as if there are two entirely different worlds involved: the one we are consciously aware of is a world of 'things' and people (perception) and the one we are not aware of is a world of sense data (sensation).

How are sensation and perception related? Essentially, perception cannot occur in the absence of sensation (i.e. the physical stimulation of the sense organs), but the sense data constitute only the 'raw material' from which our conscious awareness of objects is constructed. So, to the extent that we perceive the world as it really is, we do this indirectly, through analysing, interpreting and trying to make sense of sensations. It feels like we are in direct and immediate contact with the world as we do not have to work out consciously what objects are (not usually, at least). However, our awareness of things is the end product of a long and complex process, which begins with physical energy stimulating the sense organs (light in the case of vision, sound waves in the case of hearing and so on) and ends with the brain interpreting the information that it has received from the sense organs. (We shall look later at how the visual system processes visual information.) So whereas the visual system as a whole is involved in (visual) perception, in sensation only the sense organs (the eyes) are directly stimulated; but, of course, the sense organs are part of the perceptual system as a whole.

In this chapter, we shall focus on the physical processes that are crucial to perception, i.e. sensation, and in the next chapter the emphasis will be on the psychological processes, i.e. perception. But, hopefully, it is clear from the preceding paragraph that both are usually involved and we are not usually aware of any such distinction. Psychologists have concentrated most of their efforts on vision and to a lesser extent audition and this will be reflected in this chapter.

THE SENSES: PROVIDING THE RAW MATERIAL OF PERCEPTION

According to Ornstein (1975) we do not perceive objective reality but, rather, our construction of reality – our sense organs gather information which the brain modifies and sorts and this 'heavily filtered input' is compared with memories, expectancies and so on until, finally, our consciousness is constructed as a 'best guess' about reality.

In a similar vein, James (1902) maintained that '... the mind, in short, works on the data it receives much as the sculptor works on his block of stone'. However, different artists use different materials and, similarly, different sensory systems provide different kinds of sense data for the perceiver-sculptor to 'model'. Each of our various sensory systems is only designed to respond to a particular kind of stimulation but a related and equally important point (often overlooked) is that they also function as data reduction systems (Ornstein, 1975).

To the extent that something cannot be sensed (i.e. our senses are not responsive or sensitive to it) it does not exist for us; while we normally regard our senses as the 'windows' to the world, a major job they perform is to discard 'irrelevant' information and to register only what is likely to be of practical value (clearly, something which has occurred as a result of evolutionary forces). We would be overwhelmed if we responded to the world as it is; different forms of energy are so diverse that they are still being discovered and all species have developed particular sensitivity to certain of these which have aided their survival. A good example is the frog, whose visual system contains specialized kinds of detectors, one of which responds only to small, dark objects coming into the field of vision and which move quite close to the eye. Clearly, the frog has evolved its own specialized 'bug-perceiving' subsystem.

Bruce and Green (1990) define perception as the ability to detect structures and events in the surroundings. This requires that an animal be sensitive to at least one form of energy which can provide

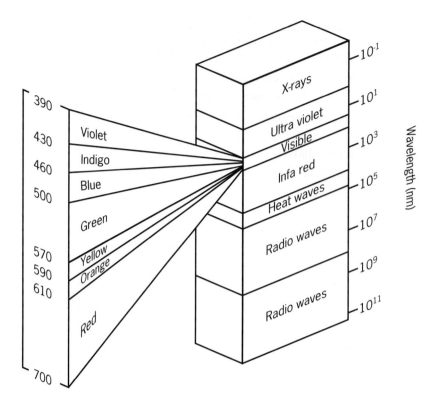

FIGURE 8.1 *The spectrum of electromagnetic radiation. Wavelengths are given in nanometres (1 nm = 10⁻⁹ m). The visible part of the spectrum is shown on the left, with the colours of different wavelengths of light. (Redrawn from Bruce and Green, 1990)*

information about the environment, e.g. chemical substances diffusing through the air or water, mechanical energy (pressure on the body surface, forces on limbs and muscles or waves of sound pressure in the air or water), electric or magnetic fields:

> Sensitivity to diffusing chemicals and to mechanical energy gives an animal considerable perceptual abilities but leaves it unable to obtain information rapidly about either its inanimate world or about silent animals at a distance from itself ... The form of energy that can provide these kinds of information is light, and consequently most animals have some ability to perceive their surroundings through vision ... (Bruce and Green, 1990)

Light is one form of electromagnetic radiation, which includes radio waves, microwaves, infrared and ultraviolet light, as well as the visible spectrum . Although the entire spectrum ranges from less than 1 billionth of a metre to more than 100 metres, the human eye, by design, responds only to the tiny portion between 380 and 780 billionths of a metre *(nanometres)* which we call light. (Although pressure on the eyeball produces sensations of light, it is external

sources of light which normally produce the sensation; Figure 8.1.)

HOW CAN SENSORY SYSTEMS BE CLASSIFIED ?

The senses have been classified in several ways. For example, Sherrington (1906) identified three kinds of receptors:

1 *exteroceptors* (which tell us about the external environment);
2 *interoceptors* (which tell us about the internal environment);
3 *proprioceptors* (which deal with the position of our body in space and its movement through space).

Exteroception includes the five 'traditional' senses of sight (vision), hearing (audition), smell (olfaction), taste (gustation) and touch (cutaneous or skin senses). Interoception includes the internal receptors

Sense modality	Sense organ (accessory structure)	Sense receptor (transducer)	Brain area (cortex unless otherwise indicated)
Vision (sight)	Eye (in particular, the lens)	Rods and cones (in the retina)	Occipital lobe-striate cortex, extrastriate, (prestriate) cortex (via optic nerve)
Audition (hearing)	Outer ear (pinna) Middle ear (eardrum and ossicles) Inner ear (cochlea)	Specialized hair cells in the organ of Corti situated in the cochlea	Temporal lobe (via auditory nerve)
Gustation (taste)	Tongue (in particular the taste buds and papillae, the ridges around the side of the tongue)	Special receptors in the taste buds which connect with sensory neurons (nerve cells)	Temporal lobe (via gustatory nerve)
Olfaction (smell)	Nose (in particular the olfactory mucosa of the nasal cavity)	Transducers in the olfactory mucosa	Temporal lobe and limbic system (via olfactory bulb and olfactory tracts)
Skin or cutaneous senses (touch)	Skin	There are about 5 million sensors of at least 7 types, e.g.: 1 Meissner's corpuscles (touch) 2 Pacinian corpuscles (stretching and vibration) 3 Krause end bulbs (cold)	Parietal lobe (somatosensory cortex) and cerebellum
Proprioception (kinaesthetic and vestibular senses)	Inner ear (semicircular canals) (in particular the vestibular sacs)	Vestibular sensors or otoliths ('earstones'), tiny crystals attached to hair cells in vestibular sacs which are sensitive to gravity	Cerebellum (via vestibular nerve)

TABLE 8.1 *Sense organs, sense receptors and brain areas for the six major sensory systems/modalities*

for oxygen, carbon dioxide, blood glucose and so on. Proprioception is usually subdivided into: (i) the kinaesthetic sense which monitors movements of the limbs, joints and muscles; and (ii) the vestibular sense, which responds to gravity and the movements of the head.

Gibson (1966) rejected proprioception as a distinct sensory system (and saw taste and smell as representing the same system) and Legge (1975) includes proprioception under the general heading of interoception.

CHARACTERISTICS OF SENSORY SYSTEMS

However we classify them, sensory systems (or *modalities*) have certain characteristics in common:

- As we have already seen, they each respond to particular forms of energy or information.
- They each have a *sense organ* (or accessory structure), which is the first 'point of entry' for

the information that will be processed by the system (the sense organ, as it were, 'catches' the information).

● They each have *sense receptors* (or transducers), specialized cells which are sensitive to particular kinds of energy and which then convert it into electrical nerve impulses, the only form in which this physical energy can be dealt with by the brain (see Chapter 3).

● They each involve a specialized part of the brain which interprets the messages received from the sense receptors and (usually) results in conscious awareness of an object, a person, a word, a taste, etc. (i.e. we perceive).

● A certain minimum stimulation of the sense receptors is necessary before any sensory experience will occur; this is known as the *absolute threshold*. In practice, instead of finding a single intensity value below which people never detect the stimulus and above which they always detect it, a range of values is found and the absolute threshold is taken to be the value at which the stimulus is detected 50% of the time.

● Sensory thresholds: a link between sensation and perception

Not only does the absolute threshold vary from individual to individual but it varies for the same individual at different times, depending on physical state, motivation, physical conditions of presentation and so on.

The *difference threshold* is the minimum amount of stimulation necessary to discriminate between two stimuli and is also known as the *just noticeable difference (jnd)*. Weber's law states that the jnd is a constant value but this, of course, will differ from one sense modality to another; for example, $\frac{1}{133}$ is the value needed to tell apart the pitch of two different tones and $\frac{1}{5}$ for discriminating between saline solutions.

Fechner (1860) reformulated Weber's law and the Weber-Fechner law (as it has come to be known) states that large increases in the intensity of a stimulus produce smaller, proportional increases in the perceived intensity. Fechner's was one of the first attempts to express mathematically a psychological phenomenon and was an important contribution to *psychophysics*, which studies the relationship between physical stimuli and the subjective experience of them and which is of enormous historical importance in the development of psychology as a science.

The Weber-Fechner law holds only approximately through the middle ranges of stimulus intensities and an alternative approach is *signal detection theory*, which rejects the notion of thresholds altogether. Each sensory channel always carries noise (any activity which interferes with the detection of a signal); the stronger the stimulus, the higher the signal-to-noise ratio and the easier it is to detect the stimulus. The detection of a stimulus, therefore, then becomes a statistical matter, i.e. a question of probabilities.

THE VISUAL SYSTEM

The fundamental job of a single-chambered eye (such as the human eye) is to map the spatial pattern in the *optic array* (a term introduced by Gibson (1966) to refer to the pattern of light reaching a point in space from all directions) onto the retina by forming an image: all light rays striking the eye from one point in space are brought to a focus at one point on the retina (Bruce and Green, 1990). Visual acuity is a way of describing the efficiency with which the eye does this ('... the ability to see the details of objects ...' (Pinel, 1993)) and acuity is limited by several processes, in particular:

● the efficiency with which the optical apparatus of the eye maps the spatial pattern of the optic array onto the retina;

● the efficiency with which the receptor cells convert that pattern into a pattern of electrical activity;

● the extent to which information available in the pattern of receptor cells activity is detected by the neural apparatus of the retina and the brain.

We shall look at each of these aspects of acuity in turn.

● The sense organ: the eye

Ornstein (1975) describes the eye as 'the most important avenue of personal consciousness' and it is estimated that 80% of the information we receive about the external world reaches us through vision (Dodwell, 1995). As we noted earlier, research interest has focused largely on vision, both as a sensory system and a perceptual system. The sense organ of vision is the eye and its major structures are shown in Figure 8.2.

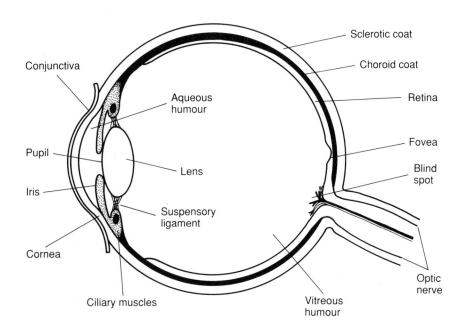

FIGURE 8.2 *The major structures of the human eye*

The conjunctiva is a transparent, delicate membrane, covering the inside of the eyelids and the front of the eye. It contains nerves and many tiny blood vessels which dilate (expand) if the eye is irritated or injured (the eye becomes bloodshot). The cornea is a transparent membrane which protects the lens and through which light enters the eye.

The pupil (the hole in the iris) regulates the amount of light entering the eye via the *iris* (the coloured part of the eye), which has tiny sets of muscles that dilate and contract the pupil. (Pupil size is also regulated by the ciliary muscles.) In bright light, the pupil contracts to shut out some of the light rays; when light is dim or we are looking at distant objects, the pupils dilate to let more light in; here it is sensitivity rather than acuity which is crucial. Ultimately, pupil size is controlled by the autonomic nervous system (ANS) and so is outside conscious control; the parasympathetic branch of the ANS controls change in pupil size as a function of change in illumination, while the sympathetic branch dilates the pupils under conditions of strong emotional arousal (e.g. an 'emergency' situation when we need to see 'better'; see Chapters 5 and 6).

The lens, situated just behind the iris, is enclosed in a capsule held firmly in place by the suspensory ligaments. It focuses light on the retina as an inverted (upside-down) image and its shape is regulated by the ciliary muscles. As with certain reptiles, birds and other mammals, the lens of the human eye thickens and increases its curvature (and the ciliary muscles contract) when focusing on nearby objects; when viewing more distant objects, it becomes flatter (and the ciliary muscles are fully relaxed). This process is called *accommodation* and increases the power of the lens (a measure of its performance) – the ability to accommodate over a wide range is clearly useful to primates, which typically examine the detail of objects at close range.

Between the cornea and the lens is the anterior chamber filled with aqueous humour, a clear, watery fluid, and behind the lens is the posterior chamber (larger than the anterior) filled with vitreous humour, a jellylike substance. Both fluids give the eyeball its shape and help to keep it firm.

The sclerotic coat is the thickest layer of the eyeball and forms the outer, white part of the eye. It consists of a strong, fibrous membrane, except in the front where it bulges to form the cornea. The choroid coat is a dark layer containing black-coloured matter which darkens the chamber of the eye and prevents reflection of light inside the eye; in front, it becomes the iris which is seen through the transparent cornea.

Primates' eyes make the largest, most rapid and most precisely controlled eye movements of all animals except the chameleon. The human eye is held in position by a dynamic balance between three pairs of antagonistic muscles and instability in this balance produces a continuous, small-amplitude tremor, which means that the retinal image is in constant motion.

Sampling the optic array is achieved by three kinds of movement:

1 Sudden, intermittent jumps of eye position (*saccades*) occur while trying to fixate an object when looking directly at it (foveal vision). Even when we think we are looking steadily at something or when we read or look at a picture, our eyes make several saccades each second to scan it.
2 Once an object has been fixated, smooth and continuous pursuit movements keep it in foveal vision as the object or the observer moves.
3 If the distance of the object from the observer changes, convergence movements, also smooth and continuous, keep it fixated by the foveas of both eyes.

According to Bruce and Green (1990), the human eye at any instant samples a relatively large portion of the optic array (the peripheral visual field) with low acuity and a much smaller portion (the central or foveal visual field) with high acuity. Beaumont (1988) believes that constant alteration of the retinal image serves three useful purposes:

1 It gives more time to the pigments to replace themselves after bleaching (see below).
2 Any nervous tissue becomes less responsive with repeated stimulation and so also needs a chance to recover.
3 It helps reduce the probability that parts of the retina will become obscured by blood vessels by giving an opportunity for slightly different parts of the stimulus to be viewed by different sets of receptors.

● Is the eye a camera?

In a camera, light striking each light-sensitive grain in the film comes from a narrow segment of the optic array and this is also true of the retinal image (Bruce and Green, 1990). Both also have a lens which projects the image onto the film or the retina. So the camera is a useful analogy for understanding the optics of the eye. However, Bruce and Green point out a number of important differences:

● Judged by the same standards as a camera, even the most sophisticated eye forms an image of an extremely poor quality. Optical aberrations produce blur, aberrations of the lens and cornea cause distortions in the image and the curvature

FIGURE 8.3 *The eye as a camera?*

of the retina means that images of straight lines are curved and metrical relations in the image do not correspond to those in the world.

● As we have seen, the image is constantly moving; a camera which moved in this way would produce blurred pictures.
● The retinal image has a yellowish cast, particularly in the macular region, and contains shadows of the blood vessels which lie in front of the receptor cells in the retina. Could the retinal image be 'cleaned up' to the point where it resembles a photograph?
● The question implies that the role of the eye is to take a snapshot of the world at each fixation and send a stream of pictures to the brain to be examined there. But while the purpose of a camera is to produce a picture to be viewed by people, the purpose of the eye and brain is to extract the information from the changing optic array needed to guide a person's actions or to specify objects or events of importance. The extraction of information about pattern begins in the retina itself – the optic nerve does not transmit a stream of pictures to the brain (as a TV camera does to a TV set) but instead transmits information about the pattern of light reaching the eyes. The brain then has to interpret that information.

The retina is the innermost layer of the eyeball, formed by the expansion of the optic nerve which enters at the back and a little to the nasal side of the eye. It is a delicate membrane, comprising three main layers:

1 rods and cones, photosensitive cells which convert light energy into electrical nerve impulses (and which form the rear layer of the retina);

2 bipolar cells, connected to the rods, cones and ganglion cells;

3 ganglion cells, whose fibres (axons) form the beginning of the optic nerve leading to the brain.

● The receptors: rods and cones

Most of the eye's structures are, in fact, accessory structures and Gregory (1966) has estimated that only about 10% of the light entering the eye actually reaches the transducers (rods and cones), the rest being absorbed by the accessory structures.

The rods are 1000 times more sensitive than cones and are far more numerous – in each retina there are 120 million rods and 7 million cones. Their distribution around the retina also differs: cones are much more numerous towards the centre of the retina, in particular in the fovea (a pitlike depression which is in fact part of a cone-rich area called the macula lutea) where there is a concentration of about 50,000 cones, while the rods are distributed fairly evenly around the periphery (but are not found in the fovea).

The rods are specialized for vision in dim light (including night-time vision) and contain a photosensitive chemical (rhodopsin) which changes structure in response to low levels of illumination; they help us see black, white and intermediate greys (achromatic colour) and this is referred to as *scotopic vision*. The cones are specialized for bright light vision (including daylight) and contain iodopsin; they help us see chromatic colour (red, green, blue, etc.) and provide *photopic vision* (from 'photon', the smallest particle of light which travels in a straight line). (Colour perception and defects in perceiving colour are discussed below.)

Human vision, like that of most species, must be adapted to operate in a range of light intensities and this is reflected in the structure of the retina. Rods have a deeper stack of pigment-filled layers of folded membrane in the outer segment than cones; this means that a photon passing through a rod is less likely to come out the other end, making rods far more sensitive than cones (i.e. they are more likely to respond to low levels of illumination). According to Bruce and Green (1990), this difference explains the correlation between the rod:cone ratio in an animal's retina and its ecology: diurnal animals (those which are active by day and sleep at night) have a higher proportion of cones than nocturnals, though pure-cone retinas are rare (mostly confined to lizards and

snakes), as are pure-rod retinas (confined to deep-sea fish and bats, which never leave their dark habitats).

A further adaptation of the retina in animals active in dim light is in the form of a silvery tapetum lucidium behind the retina, which reflects light back through it, so giving the rods a second 'bite' at the stream of photons (although at the cost of increasing blur through imperfect reflections). This explains the glow of a cat's eyes when caught in a car's headlights (Bruce and Green, 1990).

When focusing on objects in bright light, the most sharply-defined image is obtained by looking directly at them, thereby projecting the light onto the fovea (which, remember, is packed with cones). In night light, however, the sharpest image is actually produced by looking slightly to one side of the object (e.g. a star in the sky), thereby stimulating the rods which are found in the periphery of the retina.

The dense packing of cones helps explain acuity – the more densely packed the receptors, the finer the details of a pattern of light intensity which can be transformed into differences in electrical activity. The difference between a human's acuity and, for example, a falcon's is the result of a difference in receptor packing, with receptors being three times more densely packed in the falcon.

The chemical difference between the rods and cones also explains the phenomenon of *dark adaptation*. If you go into a dark cinema from bright sunlight, you will experience near blindness for a few seconds because the rods need a little time to take over from the cones, which were responding outside (i.e. the rhodopsin in the rods is being regenerated or resynthesized, having been 'bleached' by the bright sunlight). It takes 30 minutes for the rods to reach their maximum level of responding.

The 127 million rods and cones are 'reduced' to 1 million ganglion cells which make up the optic nerve; this means that information reaching the brain has already been 'refined' to some extent compared with the relatively 'raw' information received from other sensory nerves. However, the degree of reduction or *summation* differs considerably for different areas of the retina: in the periphery, up to 1200 rods may combine to form a single ganglion cell and thus connect to a single axon in the optic nerve, providing only very general visual information; while at the fovea, perhaps only 10–12 cones are summed for each ganglion cell and this provides much more detailed information. Two other kinds of cell, horizontal and amacrine, interconnect with groups of the other cells and connect them together, which increases further the degree of information processing which takes place in the retina itself. Horizontal cells connect receptors and bipolar cells, while amacrine cells connect bipolar and ganglion cells.

The first step in analysing the transformation of pattern occurring in the retina is to establish the relationship between input and output (i.e. the pattern of light falling on the retina and the rate at which ganglion cells fire impulses). Each ganglion cell has a *receptive field*, a region of the retina, usually roughly circular, in which stimulation affects the ganglion cell's firing rate. There are (at least) three kinds of ganglion cell, each with a different kind of receptive field:

1 on-centre cells are more neurally active when light falls in the centre of the receptive field but less active when it falls on the edge;
2 off-centre cells work in the opposite way;
3 transient cells have larger receptive fields and seem to respond to movements, especially sudden ones.

The combined activity of on-centre and off-centre cells provides a clear definition of contours ('edges') where there is a sudden change in brightness. These contours are essential in defining the shape of objects to be perceived (Beaumont, 1988). (Further analysis of contours takes place in the striate cortex by simple, complex and hypercomplex cells – see below.) As Beaumont (1988) points out, the retina appears to be built back-to-front: the receptors don't point to the source of the light but towards the supporting cells at the back of the eye. Before it arrives at the receptors,

light must pass through the layers of retinal cells and blood vessels inside the eye. In view of all this, it is surprising that such high-quality vision can still be achieved (Fig. 8.4). (You may sometimes become aware of this in the form of a treelike after-image after a lightning flash, which are the shadows of the blood vessels thrown upon the retina, or when you look up at the sky, especially a cloudless blue sky, and you see small transparent bubbles floating in front of you, which are red blood cells.)

● Visual pathways: from eye to brain

As we have seen, the 127 million receptors in each eye are combined to form the 1 million optic nerve fibres, which means that there is a massive integration and channelling of information.

As you can see from Figure 8.5, the pathways from the half of each retina closest to the nose cross at the optic chiasma (or chasm) and travel to the opposite hemisphere (crossed pathways), while the pathways from the half of each retina furthest from the nose (uncrossed pathways) travel to the hemisphere on the same side as the eye. This means that if somebody fixates on a point straight ahead of them, so that the eyes converge, the image of an object to the right of fixation falls on the left half of each retina and information about it passes along the crossed pathway from the right eye to the left hemisphere and along the uncrossed pathway from the left eye to the left hemisphere – no information is passed directly to the right hemisphere.

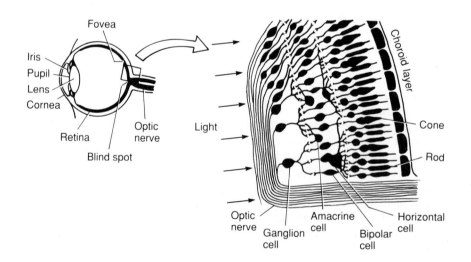

FIGURE 8.4 *A diagrammatic section through the eye and a section through the retina at the edge of the blind spot. (From Atkinson et al., 1983)*

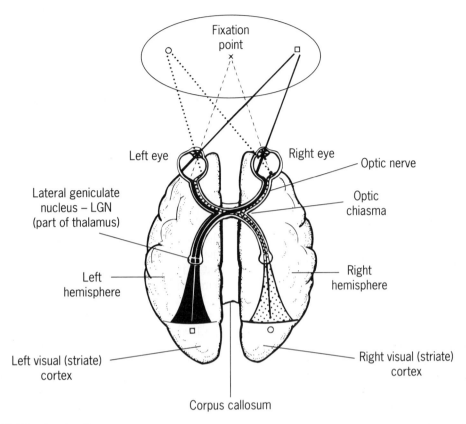

FIGURE 8.5 *The visual system*

All these relationships are reversed for an object to the left of the fixation point, so that information is passed directly only to the right hemisphere. Therefore it follows that any damage to the visual area of just one hemisphere will produce blind areas in both eyes; however, the crossed pathway ensures that complete blindness in either eye will not occur.

Before reaching the cortex, the optic nerve travels through the lateral geniculate nucleus (LGN) which is part of the thalamus; optic nerve fibres terminate at synapses with LGN cells arranged in layers (laminae). Each lamina contains a retino-opic map of half the visual field.

LGN cells have concentric receptive fields similar to those of retinal ganglion cells and each is thought to be driven by one or more of the same receptive field type. Axons of LGN cells form the optic radiations and project to the occipital lobe. In monkeys, all LGN cells project to area 17, which is the visual or striate cortex (called the geniculostriate path).

In humans, the geniculostriate path must be intact for conscious experience of vision to be possible – people with damage to their visual cortex will report complete blindness in part or all of the visual field. Even so, they will show some ability to locate or even identify objects which they cannot consciously see (what Weiskrantz (1986) calls *blindsight*). The most thoroughly investigated patient is D.B., who had an operation meant to reduce the number of severe migraines he suffered. He was left with an area of subjective blindness but was able to detect whether or not a visual stimulus had been presented to the blind area and could also identify its location, although he seemed to possess only a rudimentary ability to discriminate shapes. This suggests that, while most visual functions rely on the 'primary' geniculostriate path, the 'secondary' retinotectal path (some ganglion cells are projected to the paired superior colliculi structures in the midbrain) carries enough information to guide some actions in an unconscious way. However, in the intact brain, those two paths do not function independently: the cortico-tectal path provides the superior colliculi with input from the cortex.

The first recordings from single cells in the striate cortex of cats and monkeys were made by Hubel and

called the 'functional architecture' of the visual cortex).

The six main layers of the striate cortex can be recognized under the microscope. The cortical area devoted to the central part of the visual field is proportionately larger than that devoted to the periphery. Hubel and Wiesel (1977) suggest that the cortex is divided into roughly square blocks of tissue (about 1 mm square), extending from the surface down to the white matter, which they call hypercolumns.

● Are there other regions of the cortex where visual information is processed?

Single-cell recordings have revealed many regions of the extrastriate (or prestriate) cortex, anterior to the striate, which can be considered 'visual areas'. But it has proved more difficult to map these, compared with the striate cortex.

Maunsell and Newsome (1987) reviewed studies involving macaque monkeys and concluded that there are 19 visual areas, covering large areas of the occipital, temporal and parietal lobes (Fig. 8.6). The deep folding of the cortex means that some areas, lying within folds (sulci), are not visible from the exterior; for this reason, two important areas not shown in Figure 8.6 are V3 (lying in the lunate sulcus between V2 and V4) and the middle temporal area (MT) in the superior temporal sulcus (anterior to V4).

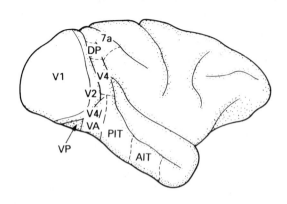

FIGURE 8.6 *Side view of the right cerebral hemisphere of a macaque monkey. Area VI is the striate cortex. (From Maunsell and Newsome, 1987)*

Wiesel (1959, 1962, 1968). They found cells with concentric fields in a layer of the cortex where input fibres from the LGN terminate (simple fields), but in other layers cells had quite different receptive fields (complex fields). They identified three kinds of cortical cells:

1 *Simple cells* respond only to particular features of a stimulus (e.g. straight lines, edges and slits) in particular orientations and in particular locations in the animal's visual field. For example, a bar presented vertically may cause a cell to 'fire' but if the bar is moved to one side or out of vertical, the cell will not respond.

2 *Complex cells* also respond to lines of particular orientation – but location is no longer important, e.g. a vertical line detector will respond wherever it is in the visual field. It seems that complex cells receive inputs from larger numbers of simple cells sharing the same orientation sensitivity.

3 *Hypercomplex cells* are 'fed' by large numbers of complex cells and are similar to complex cells except that they take length into account too (i.e. they are most responsive to a bar or edge not extending beyond their receptive field).

However, some researchers have come to doubt the existence of a third distinct class of cell (Bruce and Green, 1990). Despite this, the visual cortex is by no means a homogeneous mass of tissue with cells of different kinds randomly scattered; instead, it shows astonishingly precise and regular arrangement of different cell types (what Hubel and Wiesel (1962)

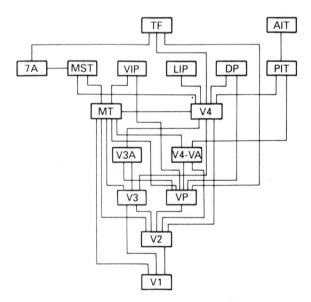

FIGURE 8.7 *The hierarchical organization of extrastriate visual areas in the macaque money as proposed by Maunsell and Newsome. (From Maunsell and Newsome, 1987)*

Each area sends output to several others and most, if not all, connections are matched by reciprocal connections running in the opposite direction. Van Essen (1985) lists 92 pathways linking the visual areas. Most can be classified as either ascending (leading away from V1) or descending (leading towards V1); when classified in this way, a consistently hierarchical pattern emerges, with areas placed at different levels (Fig. 8.7).

Does each area have its own specified function? Zeki (1978) proposed a 'parcelling model', whereby the simple representation of the visual field in V1 and V2 is parcelled out to be analysed by a number of areas working in parallel, one analysing patterns of motion, another colour, etc. However, Maunsell and Newsome (1987) and Van Essen (1985) believe that there might be two main pathways operating in parallel, one concerned with the analysis of motion and spatial layout, the other with colour, form and object recognition. Some of the evidence regarding processing of colour is discussed in the next section.

● Colour vision and colour blindness

Light can be described physically by its energy spectrum (intensities at different wavelength) or phenomenologically by three dimensions: (i) brightness (perceived intensity); (ii) hue (perceived colour); and (iii) saturation (the purity of hue, i.e. how much colour or how much white). Although both hue and saturation are aspects of 'colour', it is hue which is intended when discussing theories of colour vision and colour vision defects.

As we have already seen, the cones are the photoreceptors responsible for chromatic vision. We have also seen that the rods and cones contain photosensitive pigments (which change their chemical constitution on exposure to light – as does photographic film), rhodopsin ('visual purple') in the case of rods and iodopsin in the case of cones. Rushton and Campbell (1954; cited by Rushton, 1987) were the first to measure the visual pigments in the living human eye, applying the familiar observation that a cat's eye will reflect back light shone in its eye. Using a photomultiplier tube, they measured the very faint light reflected from the human eye (we have a very black surface behind the retina – the choroid coat -instead of the cat's shining tapetum lucidium) and identified rhodopsin, plus red and green pigments. However, insufficient blue light is reflected to measure the blue cone pigment (Rushton, 1987).

Later, Marks *et al.* (1964; cited by Rushton, 1987), in the USA, used fresh retinas from monkeys and human eyes removed during surgery to measure visual pigments in single cones. They found the blue-, green and red-sensitive cones, thus supporting the Young-Helmholtz trichromatic theory; Rushton and Campbell's findings were also confirmed using living colour-blind participants who possessed only one of the two pigments measured by them.

● The trichromatic theory

The trichromatic theory (Young, 1801) claims that colour is mediated by three different kinds of cone, each responding to light from a different part of the visible spectrum – blue-sensitive, green-sensitive and red-sensitive cones are maximally responsive to short, medium and long wavelengths, respectively. While the sum of the three wavelengths (B + G + R) determines brightness, their ratio or pattern (B:G:R) determines colour. This is essentially what is believed today (Rushton, 1987).

This explains the painter's experience that mixing a few paints will produce a whole range of colours. It also implies that every colour (including white) should excite B, G and R cones in a characteristic set of ratios, such that a mixture of red and green and blue lights, adjusted to produce this same set of ratios, should appear white or whatever the initial colour was. This was systematically tested by Maxwell (1854), who found that every colour can be matched by a suitable mixture of blue, green and red 'primaries' (the trichromacy of colour). This was later confirmed by Helmholtz (Rushton, 1987). Hence, this is often called the Young-Helmholtz trichromatic theory.

● The opponent colour theory

The major alternative to the trichromatic theory is the opponent colour (tetrachromatic) theory (Hering, 1878), which claims that colour analysis depends on the action of two types of detector, each having two modes of response – one signals either red or green, the other signals yellow or blue. (Brightness depends on a system that signals white or black – therefore, one can see colour that looks greenish and bluish and dark but not one that looks both reddish and greenish or both light and dark, etc.; Troscianko, 1987.)

What evidence is there to support the opponent colour (or opponent process) theory?

- If you stare at a coloured surface (e.g. red) and then look at a plain surface, you will perceive an after-image which is coloured in the 'opposite direction' (i.e. green). This is called a complementary (or negative) after-image.
- People with defective colour vision (usually called 'colour-blind') usually fail to distinguish between red and green; this is the most common form of defect, caused by a recessive sex-linked gene which affects more males (about 8%) than females (about 0.4%). Sufferers have dichromatic vision (whereas those with normal vision have trichromatic) such that they possess only red- or green-sensitive cone pigments, but they can match every colour of the rainbow exactly with a suitable mix of only two coloured lights (e.g. red and blue) – most people need the green primary as well if every colour is to be matched.

Next most common is true colour-blindness, whereby there is an absence of any cones at all (these people have monochromatic vision) and least common of all is yellow-blue blindness. These findings are clearly consistent with the opponent colour theory.

- While the retina encodes in terms of three constituent components (a blue, green, red 'component' system) output through the ganglion cells and onto the LGN becomes recoded in terms of opponent processes (DeValois *et al.*, 1966). There seem to be four kinds of LGN cells: those which increase activity to red light but decrease with green (R+ G–), those which increase activity to green light but decrease with red (G+ R–), and similarly for blue and yellow (B+ Y–) and yellow and blue (Y+ B–). Still other LGN cells simply respond to black and white (Beaumont, 1988).

Evidence such as this has led to the generally held view that a complete theory of colour vision must draw on elements from both theories; indeed, Helmholtz himself showed that the two theories are not incompatible, as a simple transformation could change the three receptor outputs to two different signals plus one additive signal (Troscianko, 1987).

BOX 8.1 Land's (1964, 1977) 'Mondrian' experiment and retinex theory of colour constancy

Land used a large, complex display ('colour Mondrian') – a patchwork of different coloured matt papers, randomly arranged so that each colour was surrounded by several others. The display was illuminated by mixed light from projectors with red, green and blue filters. Each projector also had an independent brightness control.

Observers selected one of the papers (e.g. white) and Land measured the amounts of red, green and blue light coming from the white paper. They then selected a second paper (e.g. red) and once again the amounts of red, green and blue light were measured.

Land then changed the illumination so that the red light from the red paper was exactly equal to the red light from the white paper (this required only a small change, since roughly the same amounts of red light are reflected from a red and white paper). A substantial change was required to adjust the other projectors so that exactly the same amounts of green and blue came from the red paper as had previously come from the white paper (much less green and blue are reflected from a red paper). When all three projectors were turned on together, each observer reported 'red' despite the fact that the physical properties of the light from that paper were the same as the light from the white paper (using previous illumination).

In this way, Land went from paper to paper and showed that nearly the full range of colour sensations could be produced from a single mixture of red, green and blue light (thus supporting the trichromatic theory).

If perceived colour were determined solely by the spectral composition of the reflected light, the initially red paper would be seen as white. But observers displayed *colour constancy* and this led Land to propose his retinex theory (1977), whereby the information from each of the sets of receptor mechanisms produces a separate lightness image, a comparison of these images is carried out and it is this comparison which determines the colour which is perceived. Again, the three lightnesses provide the co-ordinates of a 3-D space and, whereas a colour space based on the *absolute absorptions* in the three classes of receptor will predict only whether two physical stimuli will match, a space based on the three lightnesses will predict how colours actually look, because between them they give the reflectance of the object in different parts of the spectrum (i.e. a measure of the *relative absorptions*).

'Retinex' ('retina' and 'cortex') implies that the formation of lightnesses could occur in the retina or cortex; the retinal-cortical structure acts as a whole.

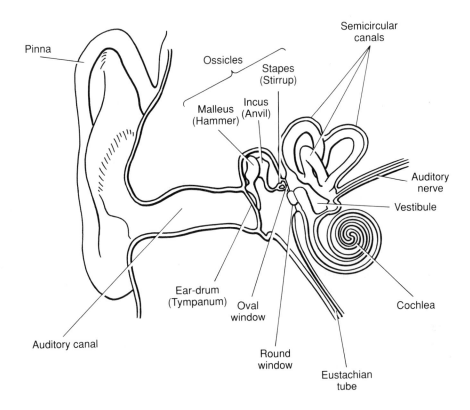

FIGURE 8.8 *The major structures of the human ear*

Retinex theory and colour constancy

Any chromatic light hitting the retina is composed of different amounts of the three primary colours (e.g. turquoise might be 70% blue, 30% green) so blue-sensitive cones would 'fire' quite quickly and green-sensitive ones quite slowly (and red-sensitive would not fire at all). However, perceived colour is not solely determined by the wavelength composition of the light reflected from the object (the *spectral reflectance* of the object) but by several other factors including:

- the relative proportions of different wavelengths in the light falling on the object (the spectral composition of the illumination);
- prior stimulation of the retina (as shown by complementary or negative after-images);
- the nature of the surroundings, such as the simultaneous contrast created by adjacent areas of different colour or brightness (e.g. a grey square will look brighter set against a black background than against a white background);
- our familiarity and knowledge of an object's colour, which is part of the psychological phenomenon of colour constancy (see Chapter 9).

According to McConn (1987), our visual system is built to tell us about the permanent colours of objects as opposed to the spectral composition of the light falling on a local area of the retina. A powerful demonstration of colour constancy is provided by Land (1964, 1977), the inventor of the Polaroid camera. His 'Mondrian' experiment and retinex theory are described in Box 8.1.

THE AUDITORY SYSTEM

The sense organ: the ear

When we hear sounds we are detecting changes in air pressure as they occur at the ear. These changes have a cyclical pattern and move in a wavelike fashion. So sounds (i.e. pure tones, a sound which corresponds to a sine wave) can be thought of as having a *frequency* (the number of cycles per second, measured in hertz) and *intensity* (the height or amplitude of the wave). Real sounds, of course, are complex and comprise many components with different frequencies and intensities (but these can be thought of as composed of a collection of pure tones; Beaumont, 1988).

Sound waves arrive at the pinna (Fig. 8.8), where they are 'trapped' and passed into the auditory canal (the two structures comprise the outer or external ear). From here, the sound waves travel to the eardrum (tympanum or tympanic membrane) which is deflected so that it moves with the same frequency as the sound waves. Linked to the eardrum is the first of three small bones, the malleus ('hammer'), which transmits the eardrum's movements to the incus ('anvil') which in turn passes vibrations onto the stapes ('stirrup'). This mechanical arrangement not only transmits but amplifies the wave. The three bones are collectively known as the ossicles and they, together with the eardrum, comprise the middle ear. From here sound passes into the inner ear via the stapes which rests against the oval window which is the 'gateway' to the inner ear and the receptors.

● The receptors

The auditory receptors are contained in the cochlea, a fluid-filled structure, consisting of a coiled tube of bone resembling a snail's shell. It is divided into sections of fluid by various membranes, including the basilar membrane. Pressure at the oval window causes pressure changes in the cochlear fluid which in turn causes the basilar membrane to vibrate. This has the effect of bending the hair cells of the organ of Corti (attached to the basilar membrane). These hair cells are the auditory receptors and synapse with neurons with long axons, which form part of the auditory (cochlear) nerve. The hair cells are forced against the fairly rigid tectoral membrane and this contact produces nerve impulses in the hair cells, which pass to ganglion cells and then to the cortex via the auditory nerve.

When pressure waves are transmitted to the basilar membrane, one part vibrates much more strongly than the rest, depending on the frequency of the original sound wave – high frequency sounds vibrate the end near to the middle ear, while low frequency sounds vibrate the other end (von Bekesy, 1960). However, the precise mechanism by which hair cells produce neural potentials is still poorly understood (Beaumont, 1988).

The inner ear also contains sensory receptors for balance and positional sense – the vestibular and kinaesthetic senses – in particular, the vestibular sacs contained within the semicircular canals.

● The auditory pathways

The auditory nerve (the 8th cranial nerve) comprises about 31,000 neurons (compared with approximately 1 million in the optic nerve) and travels through the medial geniculate body (MGB), part of the thalamus, en route to the upper part of the temporal lobe. Unlike vision, cortical cells are not arranged topographically (in terms of the spatial location of the stimulus), so that different groups of cells seem to deal with different frequencies.

Impulses from the auditory nerve at one side of the head pass up to the MGB and the cortex on both sides of the brain (in vision, remember, the visual field at one side only projects to the opposite hemisphere). But it is still true that the pathway from one ear to the opposite hemisphere is larger and more important than that passing to the same-side hemisphere. Damage to the auditory nerve on one side of the head will cause deafness in the ear on that side. However, deafness rarely results from brain damage, due to the projection from each ear to both sides of the brain (bilateral projection). Brain damage is usually on one side only, thus altering hearing thresholds (acuity) but not producing complete deafness (Beaumont, 1988).

● Auditory sensory processing and hearing defects

The major psychological (phenomenological) aspects of sound are:

● pitch;
● loudness;
● timbre;
● location (or localization).

Pitch is the equivalent of hue in relation to light. It corresponds to the frequency of the sound wave which, as we have seen, is encoded by the vibration of different regions of the basilar membrane. Throughout the auditory system there are neurons which respond most actively to stimulation of a given frequency; this information can, therefore, be passed fairly directly to the cortex. But most cells do not respond to a highly specific frequency and some respond over quite a broad range. There is also a curious absence of cells responsive to lower frequencies (although there is good discrimination of pitch at this level; Beaumont, 1988).

Young adults can hear frequencies between 20 and 20,000 hertz. Dogs, bats and porpoises can detect much higher frequencies. The jnd is less than 1 Hz at 100 Hz and 100 Hz at 10,000 Hz.

Loudness or intensity involves more complex coding. It is not coded independently of frequency, so the response of a given cell in the auditory pathway will differ for two tones, even if they are of the same loudness. There seem to be insufficient neurons to separately encode all the levels of loudness we can detect at each frequency, so the coding of loudness must involve the joint activity of several cells (Beaumont, 1988).

Loudness is measured in decibels (dB): a change of 10 dB corresponds to a change in sound power of ten times; 20 dB = 100 times; 30 dB = 1000 times and so on.

Timbre is the quality of sound (for example, the sound of different musical instruments producing the same note). We do not usually hear pure tones but tones composed of a *fundamental* plus a range of harmonies and overtones. In everyday life, complex sounds comprise a bundle of different frequencies. Some cells in the auditory cortex might only respond to complex sounds.

Location of sound is identifying where the sound is coming from and, as with visual depth perception (see Chapter 9), there is more than one cue involved: two major cues are *phase differences* and *intensity differences*. Both of these are related to the fact that our ears occupy different positions on our heads, so that sound has to travel less distance to reach one ear than the other, thereby involving an *interaural time difference*.

In phase differences, pressure waves originating from the sound source are likely to arrive at the two ears at a different phase in their cycles – at a given moment the wave arriving at, say, the left ear may be going up while that at the right may be going down. As there are cells which respond at particular phases in the cycle, these phase differences can be detected by cells higher up in the auditory system. Unless the stimulus is directly in front or behind, some pattern of phase differences will be generated by any complex sound. This cue is used for low frequency sounds.

Intensity differences refer to the fact that intensity will be greater at the nearer ear. The head produces a 'sound shadow', which decreases the intensity of the sound reaching the further ear and, as the head blocks high frequencies more than low frequencies, this cue is used for high frequency sounds. If you wear stereo headphones and increase the relative loudness in one ear, the sound will appear to shift towards that side of space. The same effect can be produced to some extent by altering the balance control on a stereo system (Beaumont, 1988).

The fact that we tend to confuse sounds coming from in front with those coming from behind is consistent with this two-cue 'theory' – phase and intensity differences are virtually non-existent for sound sources directly in front of or behind the observer.

Finally, the two main kinds of hearing deficits are: (i) *conduction loss,* in which thresholds are raised roughly equally at all frequencies due to poor conduction in the middle ear, and (ii) *sensorineural loss,* in which threshold increase is unequal, with large increases occurring at higher frequencies. This usually results from inner ear damage, often involving some destruction of the hair cells (which do not regrow). This is quite common in elderly people, rock musicians, airport runway crews and pneumatic drill operators (Atkinson *et al.*, 1990).

CHAPTER SUMMARY

- An important distinction is made between the physical process of sensation and the psychological process of perception. Sensation is necessary for perception, since sense data represent the 'raw material' from which conscious awareness of the world is constructed.
- Each sensory system is sensitive to a particular form of physical energy , but each also acts as a data reduction system.
- Being able to detect information rapidly about the inanimate world or other, silent animals is very important for survival, which is why most species have evolved visual abilities.
- Light is one form of electromagnetic radiation. The human eye responds to only a tiny fraction of the visible electromagnetic spectrum (380-780 nanometres).
- The senses have been classified in several ways. Exteroceptors include the five traditional senses of sight, hearing, smell, taste and touch, interoceptors include the internal receptors for oxygen, etc. and proprioceptors are usually subdivided into the kinaesthetic sense and the vestibular sense.
- Every sense modality comprises a sense organ/accessory structure, sense receptors/transducers, a specialized brain area that processes the sensory messages and an absolute threshold.
- The Weber-Fechner law is an attempt to predict difference threshold/jnd and is an important part of psychophysics, which studies the relationship between physical stimuli and subjective experience.

- Signal detection theory rejects the notion of thresholds and instead uses the concept of signal-to-noise ratio.
- The fundamental job of the human eye is to focus an image of the optic array onto the retina with maximum acuity. About 80% of our information about the world comes through vision.
- The pupil regulates the amount of light entering the eye by contracting or dilating. Pupil size is controlled by the ciliary muscles and by the ANS.
- The lens focuses light on the retina as an inverted image and its shape is regulated through accommodation.
- The retinal image is continuously moving and other kinds of movement include saccades, pursuit movements and convergence.
- Although the camera is a useful analogy for understanding the optics of the eye, the differences are greater than the similarities, especially the fact that what is sent to the brain is not a picture but information about the pattern of light reaching the eyes, which must then be interpreted.
- The retina contains 120 million rods and 7 million cones, the photosensitive cells which convert light energy into electrical nerve impulses. It also comprises bipolar and ganglion cells.
- The rods help us see achromatic colour (scotopic vision) and the cones help us see chromatic colour (photopic vision).
- When focusing on objects in bright light, the sharpest image is obtained by projecting the image onto the fovea, which is densely packed with cones.
- The rods and cones are 'reduced' to 1 million ganglion cells (summation) but this varies according to which part of the retina is involved.
- There are (at least) three kinds of ganglion cell, each with a different kind of receptive field.
- The retina appears to be built back-to-front, with light having to pass through layers of retinal cells and blood vessels before reaching the rods and cones.
- The pathways from the half of each retina closest to the nose cross at the optic chiasma/chasm, through the lateral geniculate nucleus, then onto the visual/striate cortex in the occipital lobe. This is called the geniculostriate path.
- Cases of blindsight suggest that the retinotectal path carries enough information to allow some 'unconscious' vision. Normally, these two paths work together.
- Hubel and Wiesel identified simple, complex and hypercomplex cells in the striate cortex of cats and monkeys, which respond to particular stimulus features. These are arranged in a remarkably precise and regular way called hypercolumns.
- Research with monkeys has shown that large areas of the occipital, temporal and parietal lobes are involved in vision.
- The Young-Helmholtz trichromatic theory of colour vision stresses the ratio or pattern of the three wavelengths of light, while the opponent colour/tetrachromatic theory is based on the two modes of response of two types of detector.
- Some of the evidence supporting the opponent colour theory comes from the study of people with defective colour vision ('colour-blind'). Both theories are seen as valid and complementary.
- According to retinex theory, perceived colour is not solely determined by the wavelength of the light reflected from the object, but also by a number of other factors, including colour constancy.
- The outer/external ear (pinna and auditory canal), middle ear (tympanum and ossicles) and the cochlea are all part of the sense organ of the auditory system.
- The cochlea contains specialized hair cells in the organ of Corti, attached to the basilar membrane. These are the auditory sense receptors .
- The auditory nerve travels through the medial geniculate body en route to the temporal lobe.
- Two major cues to the location of sound are phase differences and intensity differences ; these relate to low and high frequency sounds respectively. They both involve inter-aural time differences.
- The two main forms of hearing deficits are conduction loss and sensory-neural loss.

GLOSSARY

Absolute threshold In psychophysics, the minimum stimulation of a sense receptor necessary for any sensory experience to occur.

Accessory structure First point of entry for incoming sensory information. Also known as *sense organ.*

Accommodation Changes in the shape of the lens depending on the distance of the object being observed.

Blindsight Demonstration of certain visual abilities in patients with damage to their visual cortex ,who otherwise report complete blindness in part or all of their visual field. Mediated by the intact retinotectal path.

Cochlea Fluid-filled coiled tube of bone, divided

into sections of fluid by various membranes, including the basilar membrane. Contains the hair cells of the organ of Corti, the auditory receptors.

Cones Photosensitive cells in the retina, sensitive to bright light (chromatic colour).

Convergence Smooth and continuous changes in the position of the eyeballs, relative to each other, caused by changes in the distance of objects from the observer.

Dark adaptation Process by which the eyes adjust from bright light to low levels of illumination. Takes about 30 minutes for rhodopsin in the rods to be fully regenerated.

Difference threshold In psychophysics, the minimum amount of stimulation necessary to discriminate between two stimuli. Also known as *just noticeable difference* or *jnd*.

Electromagnetic radiation Forms of energy including radio waves, microwaves, ultraviolet, X-rays. The human eye responds only to a tiny fraction of the entire spectrum (the visible spectrum), i.e. 380-780 nanometres.

Exteroceptors Sense receptors which tell us about the external world. Includes the five traditional senses (sight, hearing, smell, taste, touch).

Fovea Pitlike depression, near the centre of the retina, packed with cones. Produces the sharpest image in bright light.

Geniculostriate path The main optic pathway between the lateral geniculate nucleus and the visual/striate cortex.

Interaural time difference The difference in the time it takes for sound to reach the two ears, due to their different position on the head. A major cue for the location of sound.

Interoceptors Sense receptors which tell us about the internal environment, including receptors for oxygen, carbon dioxide and blood glucose.

Lateral geniculate nucleus (LGN) Part of the thalamus, through which the optic nerve travels en route to the visual cortex.

Medial geniculate body (MGB) Part of the thalamus, through which the auditory nerve travels en route to the temporal cortex .

Opponent colour theory Theory of colour vision based on the action of two types of cell that respond to light of a specific range of wavelengths and are actively inhibited from responding to other wavelengths.

Optic array The pattern of light converging on a point in space from all directions.

Optic chiasma (or chasm) Point at which the optic

nerves from the half of each retina closest to the nose cross and travel to the opposite hemisphere.

Ossicles Three bones (malleus, incus, stapes) which, with the tympanum or eardrum, comprise the middle ear.

Proprioceptors Sense receptors including the kinaesthetic sense (which monitors movements of limbs, joints and muscles) and the vestibular sense (which responds to gravity and head movements).

Psychophysics Scientific study of the relationship between physical stimuli and psychological responses to them. Very important in the history of psychology as a science.

Pupil Hole in the iris which regulates the amount of light entering the eye. Pupil size is controlled by the iris, the ciliary muscles and the ANS.

Receptive field A roughly circular region of the retina whose stimulation affects the firing rate of ganglion cells or cells in the visual cortex to which it is related.

Retina Innermost layer of the eyeball, a delicate membrane comprising three main layers of cells (rods and cones, bipolar cells and ganglion cells, whose axons constitute the optic nerve).

Retinex theory Theory of colour vision, according to which perceived colour is determined not simply by the wavelengths of light reflected from an object, but also by several other factors, including colour constancy.

Retinotectal path A 'secondary' optic pathway in which ganglion cells are projected to the superior colliculus in the midbrain.

Rods Photosensitive cells in the retina, sensitive to dim light (achromatic colour).

Sensation The physical stimulation of the sense organs, necessary for the psychological process of perception

Signal detection theory Mathematical account of sensory experience which rejects the concept of a 'threshold' and measures the strength of a stimulus in terms of *signal-to-noise ratio*.

Summation The reduction of rods and cones to a smaller number of ganglion cells (127 m to 1 m).

Transducer Specialized cells that respond to specific kinds of energy, which is then converted to nerve impulses. Also known as *sense receptor.*

Trichromatic theory Theory of colour vision based on the ratio of three primary colour receptors (blue-, green- and red-sensitive). Also known as the *Young-Helmholtz theory.*

Visual acuity The ability to see the details of an object.

FURTHER READING

Gregory, R.L. & Colman, A.M. (eds) (1995) *Sensation and Perception.* London: Longman. Four of the five chapters in this book are relevant here : 'Fundamental Processes in Vision' (Dodwell); 'Hearing' (Moore); 'The Skin, Body and Chemical Senses' (Schiffman); 'Psychophysics' (Laming).

9 PERCEPTION 1: PROCESSES AND THEORIES

INTRODUCTION AND OVERVIEW

Chapter 8 began with the claim that sensation and perception, although related, are distinct. Perception requires stimulation of the sense organs (and, more importantly, the sense receptors) but there is more to perception than just this physical stimulation, which merely provides the 'raw material' for perception. But what is the 'extra' ingredient that turns a merely physical process (sensation) into a psychological one (perception)? Is this a valid way of thinking about the relationship between two such interdependent processes? What assumptions are we making when drawing such a distinction?

These questions touch on some of the fundamental similarities and differences between major psychological theories of perception. Two major issues which different theories attempt to resolve are:

1 Is our awareness of the world of objects, people, etc. essentially
   determined by the information presented to the sensory receptors, so
   that we perceive what things are like in a fairly direct way based on
   sensory information ('bottom-up processing') or is perception the end
   result of a process which begins with sensory stimulation but which
   also involves making inferences about what things are like, so that we
   perceive them indirectly, drawing on our knowledge and expectations
   of the world ('top-down' processing)?

2 Is the way we perceive largely the result of learning and experience
   (empiricism) or is it essentially an innate ability, requiring little if any
   learning (nativism)? (This is, of course, an example of the nature-
   nurture issue which is dealt with in Chapter 10.)

Fortunately, it is relatively easy to classify the major theories of
perception in terms of these two issues, since researchers who believe
that perception is an indirect process, based on top-down processing,
also tend to be empiricist (Bruner, 1957; Neisser, 1967; Gregory, 1972,
1980), while the major theorist who believes in direct perception
(bottom-up processing) is Gibson (1966, 1979) who, while influenced by
the Gestalt psychologists, is probably best thought of as an empiricist.
Bruce and Green (1990) also refer to the indirect/top-down theories as
'traditional' and Gibson's direct theory as 'ecological' (indeed, this was
Gibson's own term, implying basically that visual information from the
whole physical environment is available for analysis by retinal receptor
cells). The Gestalt psychologists represent the major nativist approach
(see Table 9.1).

In this chapter, we shall concentrate on one of each kind of theory,
namely Gregory's, Gibson's and the Gestalt theory (the 'three Gs'),
together with the computational theory of Marr. Most of the 'basic'
perceptual phenomena, such as perceptual constancy, illusions,
perceptual set, perceptual defence, depth perception and perception of
movement, will be discussed in relation to one of the major theories. At
the end of the chapter, we shall discuss theories of *pattern recognition*,
which may be seen as the central problem of perception.

	Direct (bottom-up) (ecological)	Indirect (top-down) (traditional)
Empiricist	Gibson	Gregory, Bruner, Neisser, Marr
Nativist	Gestalt	

TABLE 9.1 *A classification of theories of perception*

DEFINITIONS OF PERCEPTION

Definitions of perception are usually drawn from theories like Gregory's and these definitions make clear that there is a difference between sensation and perception. According to Gregory himself (1966):

> Perception is not determined simply by stimulus patterns; rather it is a dynamic searching for the best interpretation of the available data ... perception involves going beyond the immediately given evidence of the senses.

According to Coon (1983), perception is '... the process of assembling sensations into a useable mental representation of the world' and again, 'Perception creates faces, melodies, works of art, illusions, etc. out of the raw material of sensation'.

These definitions also make it clear that perception does involve sensory stimulation which, in turn, makes it necessary to distinguish between perception proper and experiences which are indistinguishable from these but which do not involve sensory stimulation, namely hallucinations (see Chapter 30), e.g. 'seeing pink elephants' in the absence of any.

Coon's reference to illusions suggests another distinction, namely that between accurate (true or veridical) perception, whereby our interpretation matches the objective nature of the object or stimulus, and mistaken or false perception, where we in some way misinterpret what is presented to the senses. Illusions, of course, are examples of mistaken perception (while hallucinations are generated by the brain and involve no external stimulus). Illusions have been used a great deal by Gregory (and other empiricists) to demonstrate how accurate or veridical perception works (see below).

● But why should it be necessary to 'explain' perception at all?

Usually, perception seems so immediate and instantaneous that it is difficult to understand that there is anything to be explained. But there is and psychologists see this explanation of how we are able to perceive the world around us through our senses '... as a *problem* ...'(Greene, 1990).

One special problem, according to Greene (1990), is to explain the process by which *physical* energy received by the sense organs forms the basis of *perceptual* experience (the sensation/perception distinction again). If you think of some of the ways in which the eye is *not* a camera and how the retinal image is distorted (relative to the object which projects it; see Chapter 8), then you will have some idea of the 'problem of perception'. Further, the retinal image is inverted (and yet we see the world the right way up) and it is two-dimensional (the retina is curved and flat) yet we see a three-dimensional world, which suggests that our perception of objects, etc. cannot be adequately accounted for by the facts of sensory stimulation alone. As Dodwell (1995) says, '... To perceive seems effortless. To understand perception is nevertheless a great challenge'.

Perceptual constancy, visual illusions and *perceptual set* all demonstrate the interpretative, indirect, 'top-down' nature of perception, which is the view taken by Gregory.

GREGORY'S THEORY OF PERCEPTION

● Perceptual constancy

Just as it is necessary to select from all the available sensory stimulation which surrounds us (in order to prevent 'sensory overload'), so it is often necessary to supplement it, because the total information that we might need could be missing (not directly available to the senses). This is what Gregory means by 'going beyond the immediately given evidence of the senses' (i.e. inferences). Gregory was very much influenced by Helmholtz, the famous 19th century German physiologist, who first proposed that perceptions are 'unconscious inferences' and used visual illusions to demonstrate his ideas (see below).

We often view objects from angles such that their 'true' shape and size are not reflected in the retinal image they project; for example, rectangular doors often project trapezoid-shaped images, round cups often project elliptical-shaped images and people of normal size often project very small images, and yet we usually perceive them as rectangular, round and normal-sized, respectively. These are examples of *shape* and *size constancy*, the ability to perceive objects as we know them to be despite changes in the sensory stimulation which they produce. (Whether this ability is learned or inborn is discussed in Chapter 10.)

An impressive demonstration of the mechanisms which produce constancy is provided by *after-images*. If you stare at a bright light for a few seconds, the after-image this causes has a fixed size, shape and position on the retina. But if you quickly look at a nearby object and then at one further away, the after-image seems to shrink and swell, seeming largest when we are looking at the most distant object. Why should this happen? A real object casts a smaller image the further away it is and to maintain perceptual constancy, the image is 'scaled up' by the brain *(constancy scaling);* the same scaling effect is applied to after-images, producing changes in their apparent size. Another easy but quite convincing demonstration is to draw your outline in the mirror in a steamy bathroom, closing one eye as you do so – the image, which appeared life-size as you drew it (guided by constancy), seems half the normal size as you stand back from it.

But do size and shape constancy always work? Clearly, there are times when they do not: your knowledge that those things moving about down there are cars and people does not persuade you when you look down from a very tall building – they do *look* more like ants than people! Perception can be more powerful than conception. But this is an exception to the rule.

As we move our heads around, we produce a constantly changing pattern of retinal images and yet we do not perceive the world spinning around; kinaesthetic feedback from the muscles and the organs of balance in the ear is integrated with the changing retinal stimulation by the brain so as to inhibit perception of movement – this is called *location constancy.* To keep the world from swinging crazily every time we move our eyes, the brain subtracts the eye-movement commands from the resulting changes on the retina and this helps to keep people and objects 'in their place'.

In *colour constancy,* familiar objects retain their colour (strictly, they retain their hue) under a variety of lighting conditions (including night light), provided there is sufficient contrast and shadow. Again, this is not a foolproof process and we do sometimes make mistakes but clearly there is not a one-to-one correspondence between wavelength of light and colour perception (see Chapter 8).

Related to colour constancy is *brightness constancy;* for example, we perceive coal as black even in bright sunlight and paper as white even in deep shadow, although the coal may actually be reflecting more light than the paper (as measured by a photometer or light meter).

So visual information from the retinal image is often sketchy and incomplete and the visual system has to 'go beyond' the retinal image in order to test hypotheses which fill in the 'gaps' (Greene, 1990). In order to make sense of the various sensory inputs to the retina, the visual system must draw on all kinds of evidence, including distance cues, information from other senses and expectations based on past experience. For all these reasons, perception is an indirect process involving a construction based on physical sources of energy.

● Visual illusions

These represent yet another example of how we go beyond the information given, whereby what we perceive may not be physically present in the stimulus (and hence not present in the retinal image). Gregory (1983) has identified four types of illusion, which are summarized in Table 9.2.

Gregory explains illusions in terms of a *perceptual hypothesis* which is not confirmed by the 'data'; that is, our attempt to interpret the stimulus figure turns out to be misplaced or inappropriate, resulting in the experience of an illusion. It is our attempt to construe the stimulus in keeping with how we normally construe the world which misleads us, in particular reading depth and distance cues into 2-D drawings.

When perceptual cues conflict, the visual system has to 'bet' as to what the correct interpretation is. For instance, in the Ponzo illusion, it can either accept the equal lengths of the two central lines as drawn on the page (a flat, 2-D surface), which would involve the assumption that they are equidistant from the observer, or it can 'read' the whole figure as representing a railway track converging into the distance, so that the two horizontal lines represent sleepers, the top one of which would be further away from the observer (nearer the horizon) but appears longer since it 'must' be longer in order to produce the same length image on the retina.

Clearly, the second interpretation is inappropriate, since the figure is in fact drawn on a flat piece of paper (i.e. there are no actual distance differences) and the result is the illusion experience. But this case of mistaken perception illustrates (as do all illusions) how the perceptual system normally operates, namely by formulating a perceptual hypothesis, a 'best guess' which is then tested against sensory inputs. As Gregory (1972) puts it, '... perception is an active process of using information to suggest and test hypotheses'. What we perceive are not the data but the interpretation of them: '... a perceived object is a hypothesis, suggested and tested by sensory data ...' (Gregory, 1966).

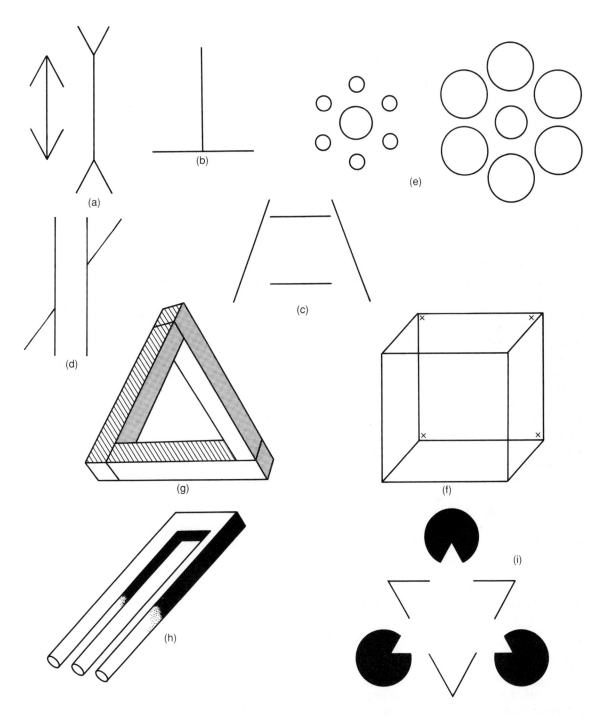

FIGURE 9.1 *Common illusions. (a) Müller-Lyer illusion (1889). The arrow with the outgoing fins is seen as longer, but they are the same length; (b) Horizontal vertical illusion (Fick, 1851). The vertical line is seen as longer, but they are the same length; (c) Ponzo illusion (1928). The top line of the two central lines is seen as longer but they are the same length; (d) Poggendorff illusion (Zöllner, 1860). A diagonal line appears bent but it is not; (e) the Titchener circles (Wundt, 1898). The central circle in the left-hand group is seen as larger than that in the right-hand group but they are the same size; (f) Necker cube. The crosses can be seen as being drawn either on the back side of the cube or on the top side (looking down);(g) the Penrose impossible triangle; (h) another impossible object; (i) the Kanizsa triangle.*

Type of illusion	Examples	Description
Distortions	Müller-Lyer, horizontal-vertical, Ponzo, Poggendorff, Titchener, circle (Fig. 9.1.(a–e))	We genuinely misperceive, i.e. we make a perceptual mistake
Ambiguous figures	Rubin vase (Fig. 9.9), Necker cube (Fig. 9.1.(f))	The same input results in different perceptions through a switch of attention
Paradoxical figures	Penrose impossible objects (Fig. 9.1 (g) and (h))	In the case of the 'impossible triangle', we make the false assumption that the three corners are all the same distance from us. A 3-D 'version' of the triangle can be made, in which the corners aren't actually touching but appear to do so when viewed from a particular angle
Fictions	Kanizsa triangle (Fig. 9.1.(i))	We 'see' what is literally not there, not 'given' in the stimulus. Gregory calls this a 'surprising absence of signals'

TABLE 9.2. *Classification of visual illusions (based on Gregory, 1983)*

In the case of ambiguous figures, we make two alternative hypotheses about what sort of object could be responsible for that sort of pattern on our retina – clearly, the sensory information is not adequate in accounting for the perceptual experience since the figure can be seen in more than one way (i.e. there cannot be a one-to-one correspondence between sensation and perception). With the Necker cube, for example, a spontaneous 'flipping' occurs but the sensory stimulation has not changed in any way. The same applies to reversible figures like the Rubin vase and Leeper's ambiguous lady (see Figs. 9.12 and 9.14).

However, Gregory stresses that the hypothesis is not a separate process from the perception itself: '... the experience that one has in perception *is* a hypothesis. I wouldn't separate the hypothesis from the perception ... perceptions are predictive hypotheses. They're suggested by available data ...' (Gregory, 1983).

● The perceptual hypothesis explanation of the Müller-Lyer illusion

According to Gregory, the arrow with the ingoing fins provides linear perspective cues which suggest it could be the outside corner of a building; the ingoing fins, accordingly, are seen as walls receding away from us so that the shaft is closer to us. For the arrow with the outgoing fins, the situation is reversed; perspective cues suggest it could be the inside corner of a room so that the outgoing fins are seen as walls approaching us, in which case the shaft is in some sense further away from us (Fig.

9.2). However, the retinal images produced by the shafts are equal and, according to size constancy, if equal-sized images are produced by two lines, one of which is further away from us than the other, then the line which is further away must actually be longer!

All this interpretation is, of course, taking place quite unconsciously and so quickly that we perceive the illusion immediately. The role of learning in perception of the illusion also tends to support Gregory's interpretation as evidenced by the study of cataract patients and crosscultural studies (see Chapter 10).

However, if (as in Fig. 9.3) the perspective cues are removed but the illusion remains then this strongly suggests that Gregory's *misapplied size constancy theory* is itself misapplied. Also, Robinson

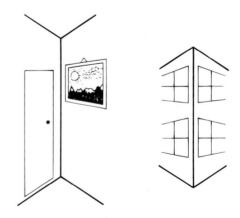

FIGURE 9.2 *A representation of Gregory's explanation of the Müller-Lyer illusion in terms of depth cues and size constancy*

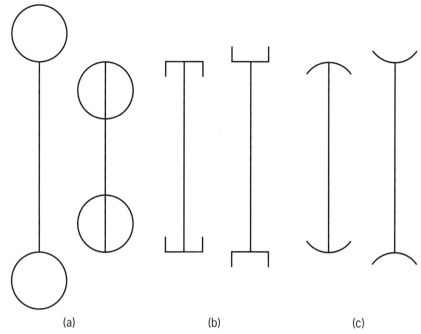

(a)   (b)   (c)

FIGURE 9.3 *The Müller-Lyer illusion with the depth cues removed. (a) Delboeuf (1892); (b) Delboeuf (1892), Brentano (1892); (c) Delboeuf (1892)*

FIGURE 9.4 *Judd's (1899) Müller-Lyer figure used by Morgan (1968)*

(1972) suggests that it is more likely that the apparent distance of the shaft is caused *by* the apparent size of the shafts than vice-versa (as claimed by Gregory).

Robinson (1972) also cites a study by Morgan (1968) using a Müller-Lyer figure (Judd, 1899) with a dot placed halfway along the shaft (Fig. 9.4). The dot clearly seems to be nearer the left-hand end and it the only way Gregory could explain this is to suppose that the arrowheads make the shaft appear to slope away from the observer, thus offering a rather odd perspective interpretation of the figure. Gregory (1971) in fact claims to have demonstrated such a slope using an apparatus designed to measure apparent depth. Using both eyes, the observer, in the dark, sees a small light which can be adjusted in distance. Using only one eye, the observer sees a luminous display of the Müller-Lyer (or some other) illusion and by means of a sheet of neutral tinted perspex at 450° to the line of sight, the light can be superimposed onto the luminous display. So the light can be put at different points on the display, thus mapping the apparent distance of various parts of the figure. Gregory has shown that the outgoing fins do appear to be closer to the observer than the shaft (i.e. they represent inside corners), while the ingoing fins appear to be further away (i.e. outside corners), thus supporting his applied constancy scaling explanation.

However, Eysenck and Keane (1990) believe that Gregory was mistaken when he claimed that everyone perceives the luminous figure as 3-D and when the illusion is perceived, it may be due simply to the fact that the apparently longer shaft is part of a longer (overall) object (Eysenck, 1984). Clearly, not all illusions can be explained in terms of the same (unconscious) processes (e.g. size constancy). According to Robinson (1972), it is very unlikely that the large number and the variety of illusions can be explained by a single principle.

● Other kinds of illusions

So far, we have been talking about illusions in a very restricted and special sense, namely as visual stimuli which have been deliberately created to be illusions. However, we are surrounded by illusions which we do not normally think of in this way, partly, perhaps, because they are so commonplace:

- All drawings, paintings, etc. are 2-D, but because of perspective cues used by the artist, we infer depth and distance (the third dimension); we add something which is not physically present in the stimulus. This also applies to the images projected onto our television and cinema screens, which also employ another kind of illusion – that of movement. Perhaps the ultimate illusion is the computer-generated virtual reality.

- *Illusions of movement.* Just as it is possible for changes in patterns of stimulation on the retina not to be accompanied by perception of movement, so it is possible to perceive movement *without* a successive pattern of retinal stimulation (i.e. apparent movement or motion).

If you look at a spot of light in an otherwise completely dark room, the light will appear to move (even though it is stationary); this is called the *autokinetic effect.* However, if other lights are introduced, the effect disappears (because a frame of reference has been introduced).

Moving pictures are based upon *stroboscopic motion,* where a succession of stationary images is projected onto a screen sufficiently quickly to produce an illusory impression of continuous movement. A simpler form of this is the *phi phenomenon,* much researched in the laboratory, whereby a number of separate lights turned on and off in quick succession will create the impression of a single light moving from one position to another.

Finally, when the only information we have about movement is visual (that is, there are no proprioceptive cues), we tend to assume that larger objects remain stationary while smaller ones move. A famous demonstration of this was carried out by Duncker (1939) who shone a light onto a screen and then moved the screen to one side; most participants reported that they saw the light move (in the opposite direction to the actual movement of the screen). This is an example of *induced movement.* Other examples include the moon seen through a thin cover of moving clouds (where it is the moon – the smaller object – which is seen to move) and the common experience of sitting in a train alongside another train and not being sure which one has started to pull out of the station.

● Veridical perception of movement

What these movement illusions show is that the brain normally uses more than just retinal images when perceiving real movement. The assumption that larger objects are less likely to be moving than smaller ones is one extra 'rule' that is used, so that judgements about relative size are important extra bits of information. However, as we have seen, this can mislead us as much as it can inform us.

Clearly, there must be changes in the retinal image; indeed, it seems that the receptors only respond to *changes* in the environment. As we saw in Chapter 8, the eyes are constantly making minute, oscillatory movements which keep the receptors stimulated. A device for stabilizing the retinal image (Cornsweet, 1970) shows that these movements are necessary for seeing things *at all.* A tiny slide projector, mounted on a contact lens, is attached to the cornea and a slide projected onto a screen; since the lens and the projector move with the eye, the retinal image is stabilized (i.e. eye movements and the movement of the image on the screen 'cancel each other out' and so the retinal image stays in the same place). After initially seeing the picture with normal acuity, within a few seconds it begins to fade and after a minute disappears altogether.

If you turn your head slowly around with your eyes open, you will create a succession of different retinal images but you will *not* perceive movement. Clearly, therefore, changes in the retinal image cannot be a sufficient basis for the perception of movement. Conversely, when an unchanging object moves across your visual field and you follow it with your eyes, the retinal image remains the same but you *do* perceive movement.

Another important cue to movement is *configuration change.* Objects moving in the environment usually do so against a background of stationary (or differently moving) objects and the nose and other anatomical borders to the visual field also provide stationary reference points against which to judge movement (which causes a configuration change or change in the overall pattern and interrelationship between objects). However, although in practice this is often an important source of information, it may not be a necessary one. Gregory (1973) points out that if a lighted cigarette is moved about in a dark room it will be perceived as moving, even though there are no background cues or frames of reference.

It seems that the brain is capable of distinguishing between eye movements which signal movement of objects (real movement) and eye movements (and movements of the head) which do not (as when you scan a stationary scene and things stay in their proper place). Probably the superior colliculus plays an important role in making this distinction (see Chapter 8). Gregory (1973) describes two systems:

1 the image-retina system, which responds to changes in the visual field which produce changes in the retinal image;

2 the eye-head system, which responds to movements of the head and eyes.

He argues that the perception of movement is the product of an interplay between the two systems.

● Perceptual set

Many very important and famous studies of perception relate, directly or indirectly, to the concept of perceptual set, one which lies at the heart of the view that perception is an active process involving selection, inference and interpretation. Allport (1955) defined perceptual set as '... a perceptual bias or predisposition or readiness to perceive particular features of a stimulus', i.e. the tendency to perceive or notice some aspects of the available sense data and ignore others.

According to Vernon (1955), set works in two ways: firstly as a *selector*, whereby the perceiver has certain expectations which help focus attention on particular aspects of the incoming sensory stimulation; and secondly, as an *interpreter*, whereby the perceiver knows how to deal with the selected data, how to classify, understand and name it and what inferences to draw from it.

What determines set?

There are several factors which can influence or induce set, most of which are to do with the perceiver *(perceiver* or *organismic variables)* and some of which are to do with the nature of the stimulus or the conditions under which it is being perceived *(stimulus* or *situational variables)*. Both kinds of variable influence perception only indirectly, through directly influencing set which, as such, is a perceiver variable or characteristic (Fig. 9.5).

Context, instructions and other situational variables

The way that instructions create set is, essentially, through inducing expectations on the part of the perceiver. There are many examples of selective perception outside the laboratory where set is a key variable: a great deal of occupational and professional training can be seen as equipping the trainee with a system of sets which will enhance performance in various ways, such as the police being trained to notice and remember car registration numbers or the physical characteristics of (potential) law-breakers.

Often, there is an interaction between expectation and context, as in the letter/number series below:

E D C ฿A   16 15 14 ฿ 12

The physical stimulus is the same in each case but is perceived differently because of the context in which it appears; we expect it to be a letter B when in a sequence of other letters and the number 13 when in a sequence of other numbers (Minturn and Bruner, 1951). We may fail to notice printing errors or writing errors for the same reason; for example, 'The cat sat on the map and licked its whiskers'. If

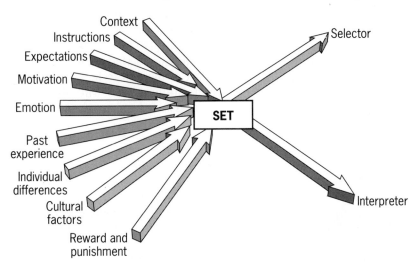

FIGURE 9.5 *The indirect influence of perceiver and stimulus variables on perception through their direct influence on set*

BOX
9.1

Key study: a card trick with a difference

Bruner and Postman (1949) presented participants with unusual playing cards, i.e. with the colour and suit combinations reversed (e.g. black hearts and red spades). The cards were presented tachistoscopically and, not surprisingly perhaps, at very short exposures people tended to report that the cards were normal (basing their reports on one feature and assuming that the other matched it). But at longer exposures, they sometimes reported 'brown or purple hearts' or 'cards in black with red edges', which suggested a genuine perceptual distortion ('compromise perceptions', an almost literal blending of stimulus information and stored information).

you can't spot the deliberate mistake, look at Figure 9.6. What do you read in the triangles? What words are actually written in the triangles? What you perceive and what is physically present should, in each case, be different.

These last three examples demonstrate the interaction between expectation and past experience; a classic experimental demonstration of this is the study by Bruner and Postman (1949), described in Box 9.1.

Allport (1955) distinguished six types of motivational-emotional influence on perception:

1 bodily needs (normally studied as the effects of physiological deprivation);
2 reward and punishment;
3 emotional connotation;
4 individual values;
5 personality;
6 the value of objects.

Two principles of perception related to the concept of set are *perceptual accentuation/sensitization*,

whereby things that are relevant or salient for us are perceived as larger, brighter, more attractive, more valuable, etc. and *perceptual defence*, whereby things that are threatening or anxiety-provoking in some way are more difficult to perceive at a conscious level (McGinnies, 1949).

● Effects of emotional connotation: perceptual defence

McGinnies (1949) coined the term 'perceptual defence' to refer to the findings from laboratory experiments that subliminally-perceived words (below the threshold of consciousness) which evoke unpleasant emotions take longer to perceive at a conscious level than neutral words. Perceptual defence is, in turn, linked to the more general – and less defence-orientated – concept of *subliminal* perception, i.e. '... perception occurring even though the stimulus input is presented so briefly or at such low intensity as to be below the threshold of conscious awareness' (Eysenck and Keane, 1990).

A number of studies have shown that recognition can occur before perception enters conscious awareness ('autonomic discrimination without awareness' – the 'subception effect'). Somehow, enough information about the stimulus is transmitted to the autonomic nervous system to determine different levels of GSR but not enough reaches the brain centres responsible for correct verbal identification. Another way this phenomenon has been studied is through what cognitive neuropsychologists call 'blindsight' (Weiskrantz, 1986; see Chapter 8), which seems to provide very strong evidence that extensive perceptual processing can occur despite an absence of conscious awareness.

Dixon (1971) reviewed a number of studies which showed that verbal stimuli which are too quick or too dim to be consciously perceived will nonetheless affect the observer's associative processes. It has been found that: (i) associations

FIGURE 9.6 *What is actually written in the triangles?*

BOX
9.2 Key study: emotionality and
perceptual defence

McGinnies (1949) presented participants, via a
tachistoscope, with 11 emotionally neutral words
(such as 'apple', 'broom' and 'glass') and seven emo-
tionally-arousing, taboo words (such as 'whore',
'penis', 'rape', 'bitch'). Each word was presented for
increasingly long durations until it was named and
there was a significantly higher recognition threshold for the taboo words (i.e. it took longer for
participants to name them). The taboo words also
produced a greater GSR and more of them were distorted when being named.

following the subliminal perception of a word were
linked to its meaning (Marcel and Patterson, 1978);
(ii) self-ratings of anxiety increased following the
subliminal presentations of unpleasant words, such
as 'cancer' (Tyler *et al*, 1978); (iii) GSRs increase to
the subliminal presentation of emotive picture stimuli, such as a breast (O'Grady, 1977).

The earliest and most famous study of perceptual
defence is described in Box 9.2.

A number of studies have challenged McGinnies's
conclusion regarding perceptual defence. For example, Howes and Solomon (1950) argued that the
higher threshold for taboo words was due to the
greater reluctance of participants to say them out
loud without more confidence in their guesses.

Perhaps the most serious question that has been
asked is whether perceptual defence is a truly perceptual phenomenon or whether the increased
recognition threshold for taboo words is due to some
kind of response bias (Eysenck, 1984). Hardy and
Legge (1968) asked participants to detect the presence of a faint auditory stimulus while watching a
screen on which emotive or neutral words were presented subliminally. Though nearly all failed to
notice that any words had been presented, the auditory threshold was higher when emotive words were
being presented. This effect was due to reduction in
sensitivity to stimulation as opposed to a shift in
response bias – the experimental design effectively
precluded any report suppression. Hardy and Legge
concluded that perceptual defence is a genuine perceptual phenomenon.

However, there remains a paradox. According to
Howie (1952), when we talk about perceptual
defence we are speaking of 'perceptual processing as
somehow being both a process of knowing and a

process of avoiding knowing', i.e. how is it that the
perceiver can selectively defend themselves against
an emotional stimulus *unless* they have already perceived and identified it (Eysenck, 1984)?

The concept of subliminal perception in general,
and perceptual defence in particular, becomes more
acceptable if perception is thought of not as a unitary process but one involving multiple processing
stages and mechanisms, with consciousness perhaps
representing just the final level of processing
(Erdelyi, 1974; Dixon, 1981), i.e. consciousness may
not be essential to cognition (Eysenck, 1984). As
Baddeley (1990) says, '... there is by now relatively
substantial evidence to suggest that a subject's
behaviour may be influenced by information that he
is not able to report consciously ...'.

● Evaluation of Gregory's 'perceptual hypothesis' theory

Gordon (1989) describes Gregory's theory as representing '... the most explicit and fullest treatment of
the central idea of empiricism ...'. But he also argues
that there is a serious problem regarding the relationship between knowledge and hypotheses – for
example, illusions persist despite full knowledge of
why they occur. For example, although we *know* that
the shafts of the arrows in the Müller-Lyer illusion
are the same length, we can't help but see the arrow
with the outgoing fins as longer. Why doesn't this
knowledge enable us to modify our hypotheses in an
adaptive way? And just what are these hypotheses?
How do we modify them? And what's the difference
between different kinds of learning which do occur,
some very rapid (for example, having the old lady
pointed out to us in the ambiguous lady – Fig. 9.13),
some very slow (for example, adapting to wearing
distorting goggles – see Chapter 10)? Gordon (1989)
believes that the computational approach to vision
(such as Marr's, which we shall discuss later in the
chapter) shows that it is possible to give much more
detailed accounts of what the central constructive
processes ('top-down' processing) might be than anything Gregory offers.

Gordon also points out that if perception is essentially constructive, how does it ever get started? How
is it that there seems to be such communality among
the perceptions of different people if we have all had
to construct our own idiosyncratic worlds?
Brunswick's answer would be in terms of *probabilistic functionalism* (1952, 1956), according to which
the selection of appropriate cues is vital to survival,
i.e. the world is common to all perceivers and this

may account for regularities in the perceptions of all creatures sharing a particular ecological niche.

Are our retinal images really as impoverished as Gregory claims, i.e. are they as ambiguous and lacking detailed information ? If they are, how does he account for the fact that perception is typically accurate, that our hypotheses are usually correct? Illusions are not 'paradigm' (typical) cases of perceptual experience. Eysenck and Keane (1990) suggest that Gregory is perhaps more successful in explaining visual illusions than perception as a whole, since illusions are artificial, simplified, unrealistic stimuli compared with naturally-occurring objects and scenes.

Support for the constructivist theory comes from studies of the importance of context on perception (see above) which usually involve very brief presentations of stimuli, thus maximizing the impact of knowledge, expectations, etc. ('top-down' processes) and reducing the impact of 'bottom-up' processes. But since such conditions occur relatively infrequently in everyday life, constructivist theories such as Gregory's may be more relevant to explaining perception in artificial laboratory situations than perception as it takes place under natural conditions.

GIBSON'S THEORY OF DIRECT PERCEPTION

In the real world, retinal images only rarely contain projections of single, isolated objects. Usually they are much richer than this and typically include other objects, background, even the distant horizon. In addition, movement is a vital part of perceiving, something that is often overlooked in laboratory research.

In summing up Gregory's contribution, Gordon (1989) states that '... empiricists may have underestimated the richness of sensory evidence when perceivers operate in the real world ...'. Again:

> ... it is possible that we perceive constructively only at certain times and in certain situations. Whenever we move under our own power on the surface of the natural world and in good light, the necessary perceptions of size, texture, distance, continuity, motion, and so on, may all occur directly and reflexively ... (Gordon, 1989)

Let us consider some of the basic ideas of Gibson's theory of direct perception and ecological optics (a 'bottom-up' approach).

FIGURE 9.7 *Optic flow as a pilot approaches the landing strip. (From Gibson, 1950)*

While for most empiricists the starting point in trying to explain perception is the retinal image, for Gibson this involves the mistake of describing the input for a perceiver in the same terms as that for a single photoreceptor, namely a stream of photons. The correct starting point for Gibson is a pattern of light extended over time and space, which can be thought of as an optical array containing all the visual information from the environment striking the eye. It provides unambiguous, invariant information about the layout of objects in space and this information takes three main forms: *optic flow patterns, texture gradient* and *affordances.*

Perception essentially involves 'picking up' the rich information provided by the optic array in a direct way which involves little or no (unconscious) information processing or computations or internal representation.

In the Second World War, Gibson was given the task of preparing training films which would describe the problems pilots experience when taking off and landing. He needed to know exactly what information pilots have available to them. His answer was optic flow patterns (OFPs) which can be illustrated by considering a pilot approaching the landing strip (Fig. 9.7) – the point towards which the pilot moves appears motionless, with the rest of the visual environment apparently moving away from that point, i.e. all around that point there is an apparent radial expansion of textures flowing around one's head. This lack of apparent movement of the point towards which we move is an invariant, unchanging feature of the optic array. Such OFPs can provide pilots with unambiguous information about their direction,

	MONOCULAR	BINOCULAR	
PICTORIAL (secondary) These refer to features of the visual field itself (and so are static).Most monocular cues are pictorial	Relative size		In an array of different-sized objects, smaller ones are usually seen as more distant (especially if they are known to have a constant size).
	Relative brightness		Brighter objects normally appear to be nearer.
	Superimposition (or overlap)		An object which blocks the view of another is seen as being nearer.
	Linear perspective		Parallel lines (e.g. railway tracks) appear to converge as they recede into the distance.
	Aerial perspective		Objects at a great distance appear to have a different colour (e.g. the hazy, bluish, tint of distant mountains).
	Height in the horizontal plane		When looking across a flat expanse (e.g. the sea), objects that are more distant seem higher (i.e. closer to the horizon) than nearer objects, which seem lower (closer to the ground).
	Light and shadow		3-D objects produce variations in light and shade (e.g. we normally assume that light comes from above).
	Texture gradient		Sand, for instance, looks more textured close up than when it stretches away from us, when it looks more smooth,uniform and fine-grained.
	Motion parallax. This is the major *dynamic* depth cue (either monocular or binocular).		Refers to the speed of apparent movement of objects nearer or further away from us. Generally, objects further away seem to move more slowly than nearer objects (e.g. telegraph poles seen from a train window flash by when close to the track).
NON-PICTORIAL (primary) These refer to the activity of the eyes, either one (monocular) or both (binocular).	Accommodation	Retinal disparity Convergence	
	(These are described in Chapter 8)		

TABLE 9.3 *A classification of depth cues*

speed and altitude. Gibson was so impressed by the wealth of sensory information available to pilots in OFPs that he subsequently devoted himself to analysing the kinds of information available in sensory data under other conditions (Eysenck and Keane, 1990).

Gibson called one such set of conditions *texture gradients* (or gradient of texture density). Textures expand as you approach them and contract as they pass beyond your head and this happens whenever you move towards something, so that over and above the behaviour of each texture element, there is a 'higher-order' pattern or structure, available as a source of information about the environment; i.e. the flow of the texture is *invariant*. This is an example of an important cue to depth, which is perceived directly (i.e. without the need for any inferences). Other examples of directly perceived, invariant higher-order features of the optic array relevant to depth perception include *linear perspective* and *motion parallax* .These are examples of pictorial depth cues; examples of other pictorial as well as non-pictorial cues are given in Table 9.3.

So for Gibson, the third dimension (depth) is available to the senses as directly as the other two dimensions, automatically processed by the sense receptors and automatically producing the perceptual experience of depth.

The third major feature of the optic array, *affordances,* is closely related to Gibson's concept of 'ecological optics'. To understand an animal's perceptual system, we need to consider the environment in which the system has evolved, particularly the patterns of light (optical array) which reach the eye from the environment (ecological optics). When an object moves further away from the eye its image gets smaller (relative size). Most objects are bounded by texture surfaces and the grain of texture (or texture gradient) gets finer as the objects recede. Objects obscure a part of the textured ground against which they are seen (superimposition) and the further away an object is, the closer it will be to the horizon (height in the horizontal plane). The crucial point here is that objects are not judged in complete isolation – the optical array commonly contains far more information than that associated with a single stimulus object, something overlooked by the use of classical optics and laboratory experiments (Gordon, 1989) (see Table 9.3).

● Evaluation of Gibson's theory

According to Marr (1982), Gibson asked the critically important question: 'How does one obtain constant perception in everyday life on the basis of continually changing sensations?'. This is exactly the right question, showing that Gibson correctly regarded the problem of perception as that of recovering from sensory information 'valid properties of the external world'. But he failed to realize two equally critical things, namely that:

> First, the detection of physical invariants, like image surfaces, is exactly and precisely an information-processing problem, in modern terminology. And second, he vastly underrated the sheer difficulty of such detection. (Marr, 1982)

Workers in artificial intelligence (of whom Marr is one) have set themselves explicit goals, including devising a system which will simulate the process of seeing: trying to create some model which will actually extract variants has proved very difficult. But Gordon (1989) wonders whether, equally, Marr has underemphasized the importance of motor activity.

An interesting study by Lee and Lishman (1975) tends to support Gibson's belief in the importance of movement in perception and the artificiality of separating sensory and motor aspects of behaviour. This is described in Box 9.3.

The concept of affordances is, arguably, the most controversial aspect of Gibson's theory. These are directly perceivable, potential uses of objects (e.g. a ladder 'affords' climbing, a chair 'affords' sitting) and which ones are detected will depend on the perceiver's species and current psychological state. The concept of affordances is part of Gibson's (1979)

BOX 9.3   Key study: if the room sways, there may be an experiment going on

Lee and Lishman (1975) used a specially built swaying room (suspended above the floor) designed to bring texture flow under experimental control. As the room sways (so changing the texture flow), adults typically make slight unconscious adjustments and children tend to fall over. Normally, the brain is very skilled at establishing correlations between changes in the optic flow, signals to the muscles and staying upright.

Arguably, the single most important reason for having a visual system is to be able to anticipate when contact with an approaching object is going to be made. Lee and Lishman (1975), for example, believe that estimating 'time to contact' is crucial for actions such as avoidance of objects and grasping them and thus represents extremely important ecological information. (This can be expressed as a formula :

$$\text{Time to contact} = \frac{\text{Size of retinal image}}{\text{Rate of expansion of retinal image}}$$

and is a property shared by all objects, hence it is another invariant and a demonstration of the unambiguity of the retinal image.)

Measures of optical flow have also provided some understanding of how skilled long-jumpers control their approaches to the take-off position (Gordon, 1989).

attempt to show that all the information needed to make sense of the visual environment is directly available in the visual input, i.e. a pure bottom-up approach.

According to Bruce and Green (1990), the concept is at its most powerful/useful in the context of simple visually-guided behaviour, such as that of insects. It makes sense here to speak of an animal detecting the information available in the light needed to organize its activities and the idea of the animal needing to have a conceptual representation of its environment seems redundant.

But what about people? Gibson's concept may apply to the detection of distance and other variables involved in the guidance of locomotion, but humans don't just perceive and act in a physical environment but also in a cultural environment. Is Gibson seriously claiming that no *knowledge* of writing or the postal system is needed in order to detect that a pen affords writing or that a letterbox affords posting a letter, that these are directly perceived invariants?

● Seeing and seeing as

Fodor and Pylyshyn (1981) make the distinction between 'seeing' and 'seeing as'. 'What you see when you see a thing depends upon what the thing you see is. But what you see the thing as depends upon what you know about what you are seeing ...' (Fodor and Pylyshyn, 1981).

This view of perception as 'seeing as' is the fundamental principle of the *transactionalists* (e.g. Ames: see Ittelson, 1952). They argue that because the sensory input is always ambiguous, the interpretation

selected is the most likely one in the light of what has been perceived in the past. A very famous demonstration is the Ames distorted room (Fig. 9.8), which is constructed in such a way that when viewed with one eye through a special peephole, a person at one end may look like a dwarf and a person at the other end like a giant and if they cross the room they appear to change size. The perceiver is put into a situation of having to choose between two different beliefs about the world built up through past experience: (i) rooms are rectangular and consist of right angles, etc. (and as seen through the peephole, the Ames room looks perfectly normal and regular); and (ii) people are usually of 'average' height. Most observers choose the former and so judge the people to be of an odd size – but the case of a wife who saw her husband in the Ames room and judged the room to be odd shows that particularly salient past experience can override more generalized beliefs about the world.

Fodor and Pylyshyn (1981) believe that Gibson's ecological approach has little useful to say about seeing as but provides useful insights into seeing. Bruce and Green (1990) agree, saying '... Most human activity takes place within a culturally defined environment and ... people see objects and events as what they are in terms of a culturally given conceptual representation of the world'.

The Ames room is, of course, another kind of visual illusion and it is the near impossibility of Gibson's theory to account for mistaken (non-veridical) perception which is perhaps its greatest single weakness. He argues that most laboratory demonstrations of 'mistakes' occur in circumstances very different from those prevailing in the natural environment (e.g. 2-D

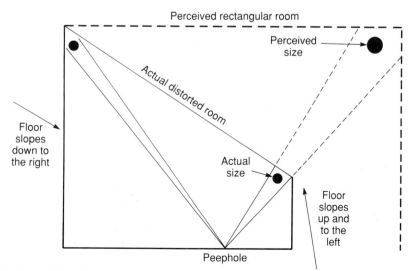

FIGURE 9.8 *The Ames distorted room*

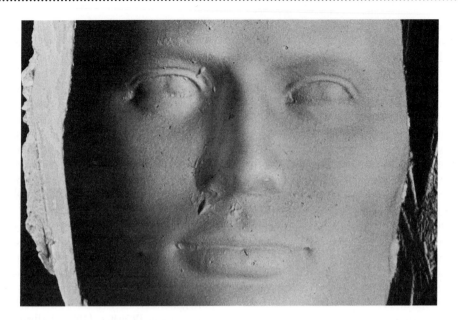

FIGURE 9.9 *Picture of the inside of a hollow mask – it is impossible not to see it as a normal face. (From Gregory, 1970)*

illusions, presented briefly as opposed to 3-D objects perceived over relatively long periods).

But his claim that illusions are merely trick figures dreamt up by psychologists to baffle ordinary people does not apply to all cases; at least some produce effects similar to those found in normal perception and one particularly striking example is the *'hollow face' illusion* (Fig. 9.9) – there is sufficient information here to see the mask as hollow but we stubbornly fail to do so. If we move our head from side to side, the face appears to follow us, in blatant disregard of the actual motion perspective present (Bruce and Green, 1990). Gregory's (1971) explanation is simply that the improbability of it being a hollow face and not a normal face is so great that the truth is totally rejected:

> The hollow face is not an example of an illusion which involves static observers or monocular viewing and is a difficult one for the ardent Gibsonian to discuss as a laboratory trick. We must invoke a memory of some sort here to explain why we see what we are used to seeing despite useful information to the contrary. (Bruce and Green, 1990)

For Gibson, there is no distinction between sensation and perception; indeed, his 1966 book is entitled *The Senses Considered as Perceptual Systems*. If all perception were veridical, his case might be stronger. Eysenck (1984) claims that, in a sense, Gibson's theory is too good because he is arguing that stimulation of the sense receptors provides so much valuable information that space perception is essentially perfect (which, clearly, it is not).

● Similarities and differences between Gibson and Gregory – and a compromise

Both theories would agree that:

- visual perception is mediated by light reflected from surfaces and objects;
- some kind of physiological system is needed to perceive;
- perception is an active process ('A perceiving organism is more like a map-reader than a camera' (Gibson, 1966));
- perceptual experience can be influenced by learning.

However, the nature of the learning involved is quite different for the two theorists, which relates to some of the other fundamental differences between them.

While for Gregory, as we have seen, meaningless sensory cues must be supplemented by memory, habit, inference, expectation, etc. in order to construct a meaningful world, for Gibson the environment (initially the optic array) supplies us with a much richer and more usable source of information, indeed, all the information that we need for living in the world. Perceptual learning consists not in 'gluing' together sensory 'atoms', but in coming to differentiate and discriminate between the features of the environment as presented in the optic array.

Dodwell (1995) suggests that two different kinds of learning are involved, constructive or synthetic in Gregory's case, analytic in Gibson's, and there is no good reason to restrict the number of different types of perceptual learning that are theoretically possible. To the extent that Gibson acknowledges the role of learning (albeit a different kind of learning from Gregory), he may be considered an empiricist, together with his emphasis on what is provided by the physical world. But in certain other respects, Gibson may also be considered a nativist. He was very much influenced by the Gestalt psychologists (see below) and, like them, he stressed the organized quality of perception. In his 'global psychophysics' (1950), he argued that visual stimulation arising from the world has a coherence and 'wholeness' which is not based on the observer's knowledge or activity, a view very similar to the concept of a 'Gestalt'. However, for Gibson, this organized quality is inherent in the optic array, i.e. it is part of the physical structure of the light impinging on the observer's eye, whereas for the Gestaltists, it was a function of how the *brain* is organized.

So is there a middle ground between Gibson and Gregory, a theoretical synthesis? According to Eysenck and Keane (1990, 1995), the relative importance of bottom-up and top-down processes is affected by a variety of factors: bottom-up may be crucial when viewing conditions are good but top-down may become increasingly important if the stimulus is presented very briefly and/or the stimulus is ambiguous, etc. Gibson seems to have concentrated on optimal viewing conditions, while Gregory and other constructivists have tended to use suboptimal viewing conditions.

Clearly, in most circumstances, both bottom-up and top-down processes are needed: the most clearly worked out model of such interdependence is Neisser's (1976) analysis-by-synthesis model (Fig. 9.10). He assumes a *perceptual cycle* involving

schemata, perceptual exploration and *stimulus environment.* Schemata contain collections of knowledge based on past experience (see Chapter 12) which serve the function of directing perceptual exploration towards relevant environmental stimulation. Such exploration often involves moving around the environment and leads the perceiver to sample actively the available stimulus information. If the sampled information fails to match that in the relevant schema, then the hypothesis is modified accordingly. An initial analysis of the sensory cues/features (bottom-up) might suggest the hypothesis that an object is, say, a chair. This will set in motion a search for the expected features (e.g. four legs and a back), based on our schema of a chair *(synthesis* – a top-down process). But if the environmental features start to disconfirm the original hypothesis (e.g. there are only three legs and no back), then a new hypothesis must be proposed and tested (this is a stool) and the appropriate stool-schema activated.

So perception never occurs in a vacuum, since our sampling of sensory features of the environment is always guided by our knowledge and past experience. In this way, perception is also seen as an interactive process, involving both bottom-up feature analysis and top-down expectations.

GESTALT PSYCHOLOGY – PERCEPTION IS ORGANIZED

If the key process in Gregory's theory is inference and in Gibson's direct perception of invariants, then the key concept in the Gestalt approach is that of *organization.* Ehrenfels (1890) claimed that many

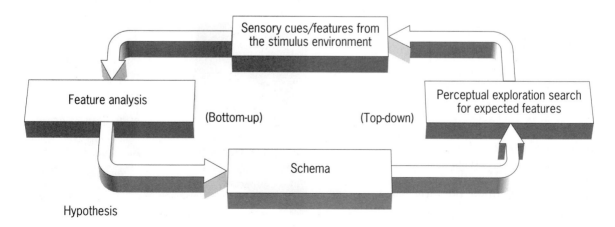

FIGURE 9.10 *Neisser's (1976) analysis-by-synthesis model of perception*

groups of stimuli acquire a pattern quality which is over and above the sum of their parts; for example, a square is more than a simple assembly of lines – it has 'squareness'. This 'emergent property' he called *Gestalt qualität* (form quality). Based on this claim, the Gestalt psychologists considered *perceptual grouping* into whole structures to be the fundamental phenomenon involved in perception (Roth, 1995).

Wertheimer (1880–1943) began work in 1910 on the phi phenomenon, which demonstrates that the perception of (apparent) movement occurs as a result of the temporal and spatial relationships between the (component) stimuli: the whole is greater than the sum of its parts. Wertheimer worked at Frankfurt University with the assistance of two young psychologists, Köhler (1887–1967) and Koffka (1886–1941), and these are the three central figures in Gestalt psychology.

According to Gordon (1989), the discoveries of Gestalt theory '... are now part of our permanent knowledge of perception ...' and that includes the distinction between figure and ground demonstrated by the famous Rubin vase (Rubin, 1915; Fig. 9.12). A major philosophical influence on Gestalt psychology was *phenomenology*, the belief that a perceptual theory should be trying to explain everyday experience. For example, Koffka asked 'Why do things look as they do?' (which Gordon claims is '... the most famous question in the history of perception'). A perceptual theory must explain the stability and coherence of our world of everyday experience – we perceive objects, not sensations, and the proper approach to this world is that of the phenomenologist: 'There seems to be a single starting point for psychology, exactly as for all the other sciences: the world as we find it, naïvely and uncritically' (Köhler, 1947).

● The principles of perceptual organization

If it is true that we perceive objects not as combinations of isolated sensations (colours, shapes, sizes, etc.) but as *Gestalten* (variously translated as 'organized wholes', 'configurations' or 'patterns'), how is this achieved? We apply certain principles which can all be summarized under the *law of Prägnanz*, according to which 'Psychological organization will always be as "good" as the prevailing conditions allow. In this definition, the term "good" is undefined' (Koffka, 1935).

Attneave (1954) defined 'good' as possessing a high degree of internal redundancy, i.e. the structure

FIGURE 9.11 *A collection of light and dark patches – or a close-up of a photograph of an eye?*

of any unseen part is highly predictable from the visible parts, and Hochberg's 'minimum principle' (1978) maintains that if there is more than one way of organizing a given visual stimulus, the one most likely to be perceived is the one requiring the least amount of information to describe it.

In practice, the 'best' way of perceiving is to see things as symmetrical, uniform and stable and this is achieved through proximity, closure, continuity and symmetry, similarity, figure-ground and the part-whole relationship. These are all manifestations of the more general, inclusive law of Prägnanz (Fig. 9.13) and are described in Table 9.4.

FIGURE 9.12 *The Rubin vase*

Proximity

Elements which appear close together – in space or time – tend to be perceived together, so that Figure 9.13(a) is normally seen as three pairs of parallel lines and 9.13(b) as a group of three dots, followed by a pair, followed by a single dot. An auditory example would be the perception of a series of musical notes as a melody because they occur soon after one another in time.

Closure

Closed figures are more easily perceived than open or incomplete ones, so that we tend to close incomplete figures, as in Figure 9.12(c), (d) and (e), in order to give their familiar meaning.

Continuity and symmetry

Similar parts of a figure which appear in straight or curved lines tend to stand out; when they make recognizable shapes (such as circles and squares) they become conspicuous. So, for example, the crosses in Figure 9.13(f) are seen as composing a square, those in 9.13(g) a circle and those in 9.13(h) a straight line. Again, music is perceived as continuous rather than a series of distinct, separate sounds and the same applies to speech.

Similarity

Like elements tend to be perceived together, as belonging to the same pattern. In Figure 9.13(i), for example, we tend to see alternating rows of dots and crosses (rather than columns of dots and crosses intermingled); if we turn it on its side (9.13(j)), we now see columns of dots alternating with columns of crosses. When we hear all the separate voices in a choir as one entity, the principle of similarity is operating.

Figure-ground

Some part of a stimulus always stands out as being in the foreground (the figure) and everything else as background (ground); the figure is what we attend to at any particular time and the ground represents the context in which the figure is presented and from which it derives its meaning.

According to Rubin (1915), the figure has 'thinglike' qualities, while the ground is relatively uniform; the figure also seems to be nearer and the ground extends unbroken behind it.

Figure 9.13 (the famous Rubin vase) illustrates the figure-ground principle and is also reversible, i.e. it can be seen in two ways – when we attend to the vase, the profiles constitute ground and when we switch attention to the profiles, they become the figure.

A famous example of a reversible figure-ground phenomenon is Leeper's ambiguous lady (Fig. 9.14). Can you see an attractive young lady and an old hag? Objectively, they are both present in the picture but it is impossible to see them both simultaneously. A map is another example – we normally see the land as figure and the sea as ground, since we are more familiar with the shape of Africa, for example, than the shape of the Atlantic.

An auditory example is following one conversation out of several going on in a 'cocktail party' situation (usually the one we are involved in) but a reversal can occur if, for example, our name is mentioned by someone on the other side of the room. Try repeating 'over-run' out loud and you will find the two words alternating as figure and ground.

Part-whole relationship

Figure 9.13(f), (g) and (h) illustrate the principle that 'the whole is greater than the sum of its parts': each pattern is composed of 12 crosses but the gestalts are different despite the similarity of the parts (and are determined largely through proximity and continuity/symmetry).

Another example is the case of water (H_2O), which is composed of a mixture of hydrogen (H) and oxygen (O) but the properties of water are very different from those of hydrogen or oxygen taken separately. Again, the notes in a musical scale played up the scale produce a very different sound compared with the same notes played down the scale and the same melody can be recognized when hummed, whistled or played with different instruments and in different keys.

TABLE 9.4 *The Gestalt principles of organization*

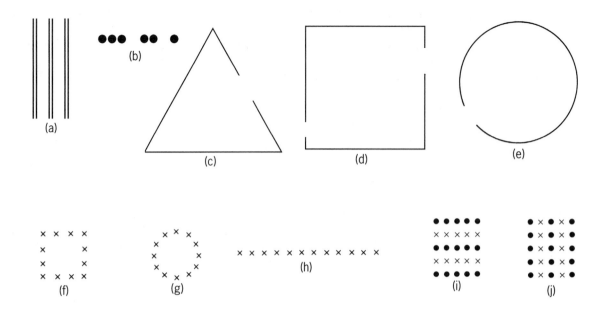

FIGURE 9.13 *The Gestalt principles of organization. (a) Proximity; (b) proximity; (c) closure; (d) closure; (e) closure; (f) continuity and symmetry; (g) continuity and symmetry; (h) continuity and symmetry; (i) similarity; (j) similarity.*

● Assessment of Gestalt principles

According to Gordon (1989), most contemporary psychologists would agree that the Gestaltists were correct about many things: geometric illusions continue to fascinate both theorists and experimenters, we do seem to respond to relationships between stimuli rather than to absolute values, wholes are more than the sum of their parts and stimuli are organized into patterns. 'The spontaneous groupings in perception are fascinating and reliable phenomena and are still being researched 80 years after Wertheimer's demonstration ...' (Gordon, 1989). Similarly, Roth (1986) believes that the most comprehensive account of perceptual grouping is still that provided by the Gestalt psychologists in the 1920s.

However, many writers agree that the laws (especially Prägnanz) are (as originally expressed) at best only descriptive and at worst extremely vague, imprecise and difficult to measure. For example, Greene (1990) asks what exactly makes a circle or square a 'good' figure? Yet there has been a recent revival of interest in Gestalt principles and many experiments (as opposed to verbal reports or 'demonstrations') have been carried out. According to the principles, some figures should look 'better' than others: will people recognize good figures when they see them (Greene, 1990)?

FIGURE 9.14 *Leeper's ambiguous lady*

● Experimental tests of Gestalt laws

Pomerantz (1981) reviewed a number of experiments which provide objective measures of perceptual grouping. If a set of elements lend themselves to perceptual grouping, then people should have difficulty responding to one element of the set while ignoring others. Conversely, if a set of elements don't lend themselves to grouping, it should be easy to do this. One relevant study is the experiment by Pomerantz and Garner (1973), which is described in Box 9.4.

Navon (1977) tested the hypothesis that the overall Gestalt should be perceived before the individual (component) parts. He distinguished between *local* (more specific and so 'part-like') and *global* (more 'whole-like') features. Participants looked briefly at a large (global) letter composed of many small (local) letters while deciding as quickly as possible whether an H or an S had been presented auditorily. When the global letter was the same as the auditory letter, auditory discrimination was faster but when they were different, there was an interference effect and it was much slower. More surprisingly, performance on the auditory task was totally unaffected by the nature of the local letters – most participants failed to notice that large letters were constructed from smaller ones. This suggests that global features are perceived more readily than local, as predicted by Gestalt principles. Why?

Perhaps when there is only enough time for a partial perceptual analysis, it is usually more valuable to obtain information about the general structure of a perceptual scene than about a few isolated details. The experiment shows that the whole can be perceived before its parts, but it is not clear how much

---

BOX 9.4 Key study: trying to ignore what comes naturally

One objective measure of grouping is how quickly participants can sort or classify one element presented with others which they must try to ignore. For example, Pomerantz and Garner (1973) used a pile of cards, each with a pair of brackets printed on it. Participants had to sort the cards into two piles (A and B) according to whether the left-hand bracket on each card looked like '(or)'. Participants were told to ignore the right-hand bracket completely. In one condition, the pair of elements were predicted to be groupable, in the other condition, non-groupable. (There was an experimental and a control pack in each condition; see Fig. 9.15.) They predicted that reaction times for the groupable cards would be longer than for the non-groupable cards.

The results confirmed the hypotheses, showing that there are objective correlates for the perceptual phenomenon of grouping. Elements seen as grouped are also processed differently – less efficiently (more slowly) because participants were trying to select out one element from a group. Under conditions where the experimental task was to attend to all elements of a group, groupable elements are processed more efficiently.

What is it about the groupable elements which makes them groupable? Presumably, similarity and proximity are involved. Pomerantz and Schwaitzberg (1975) systematically manipulated proximity by using cards with brackets drawn further and further apart. Given a suitable separation between the paired elements, grouping effects disappeared (i.e. there was no longer a difference between sorting times for control and experimental packs of 'groupable' stimuli).

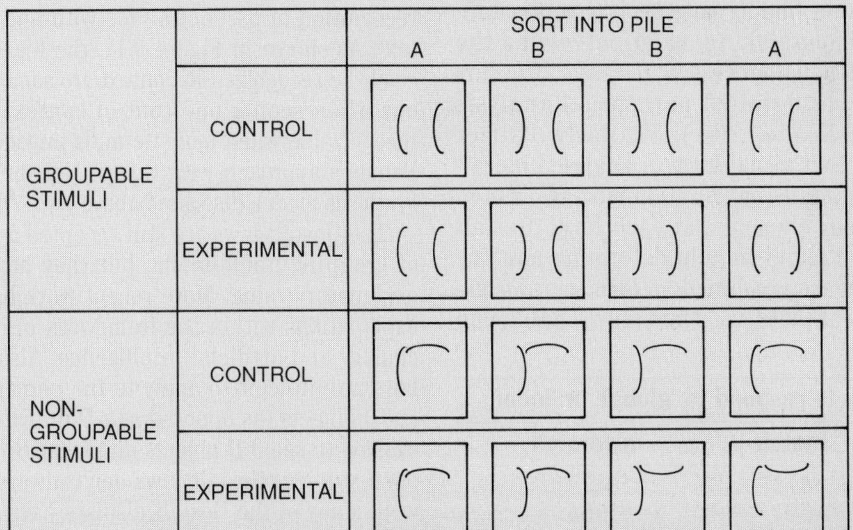

FIGURE 9.15 *Experimental test of grouping used by Pomerantz and Garner*

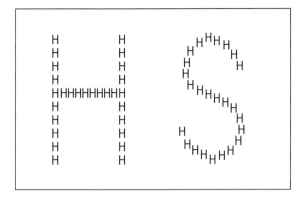

FIGURE 9.16 *Example of (a) matching and (b) non-matching local and global letters, as used by Navon (1977)*

control people have over their perceptual processes. For example, if someone *wanted* to perceive the local features while ignoring the global, could they (Eysenck and Keane, 1990)? Navon (1977) tried to answer this in a further experiment, using the same kinds of stimuli. This time participants had to decide as quickly as possible whether the global letter was an H or an S or, alternatively, whether the local letters were Hs or Ss. On half the trials, the local and global elements matched (Fig. 9.16(a)), while on the other trials they didn't (Fig. 9.16(b)). Decision speed with global letters was unaffected by the nature of the local letters, but decision speed with local letters was greatly slowed when there was a mismatch (see Table 9.5).

What this latter finding suggests is that it is difficult or even impossible to avoid perceiving the whole and that global processing necessarily occurs before any more detailed perceptual analysis (Eysenck and Keane, 1990). Similarly, Palmer (1977) argues that visual form is analysed hierarchically, from overall configuration moving down to basic features or elements, at each level. Gestalt principles were found to help determine how the low-level units are combined to form more organized gestalten at that level. Marr (1976) also found

the Gestalt principles useful in achieving accurate *segmentation,* that is, how visual information is used to decide which regions of a visual scene belong together and form coherent structures. He devised a computer program aimed at achieving segmentation (of a teddy bear, for example) using the Gestalt principles and got very encouraging results, obtaining appropriate segmentation of the teddy's outline, eyes and nose. However, some scenes are ambiguous and require using knowledge about objects in order to achieve segmentation (e.g. two leaves overlapping substantially in a bowl of flowers; Marr, 1982).

● Conclusions

The Gestalt notion that pattern recognition often depends on the overall shape of a visual stimulus, rather than on its individual features, has received some support. However, there are clearly cases in which it does not apply. Factors such as the sizes of the local and global features, the viewing conditions and the nature of the observer's task are all likely to play a part in determining the role played by individual features in pattern recognition (Eysenck and Keane, 1990). In everyday life, it is obviously easier sometimes to process 'forests' and sometimes easier to process 'trees' (Roth, 1986).

Some theorists (e.g. Palmer, 1975) have suggested that under most circumstances, the interpretation of parts and wholes takes place in a top-down and bottom-up direction simultaneously, such as in the recognition of parts of a face with and without context. As shown in Figure 9.17, the features that can easily be recognized in context are somewhat ambiguous when seen alone (out of context) – although recognizable when more detail is provided. (Compare Palmer's approach with that of Neisser's analysis-by-synthesis model, discussed above.)

The Gestalt laws are still accepted as descriptions of grouping phenomena, but they have very little explanatory value. More recent work has looked for explanations within the framework of cognitive psychology and artificial intelligence. Also, the Gestalt laws are difficult to apply to the perception of solid (3-D) objects (as opposed as 2-D drawings). Our eyes evolved to see 3-D objects and when 3-D arrays have been studied, Gestalt laws don't always stand up so well. Many of the Gestalt displays have very low ecological validity, i.e. the '... naturalness of stimuli, how representative they are of the objects and events which organisms must deal with in order to survive' (Gordon, 1989). Part of this low ecological validity is

Time in msecs to respond to 'global' or 'local'		
condition	match	mismatch
Global	471	477
Local	581	664

TABLE 9.5 *Decision time for global and local letters under match or mismatch conditions. (Based on Navon, 1977)*

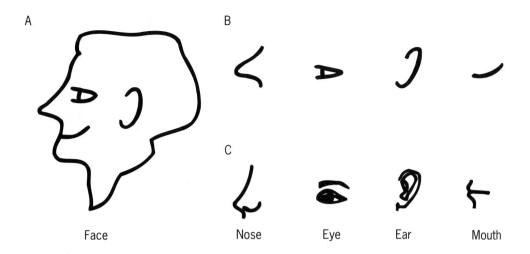

FIGURE 9.17 *The features that can easily be recognised in context (A) are rather ambiguous when seen alone – out of context (B), although recognizable when more detail is provided (C). (Based on Palmer, 1975).*

the Gestalt emphasis on *single* objects – in the real world we're faced with 'whole' scenes in which the 'parts' are single objects (Humphreys and Riddoch, 1987).

MARR'S COMPUTATIONAL THEORY OF VISION

To the extent that Gibson believes that all the information we need for veridical perception is contained in the optical array, there is no 'problem' of perception that needs resolving. For Gregory, there is a problem: how do we account for our (usually) accurate perception given the highly ambiguous and often incomplete nature of the retinal image? But he was not concerned with spelling out the precise mechanisms by which useful information about a scene is extracted from an image of that scene. Marr (1982), however, regarded this as crucial and his whole theory is an attempt to propose a solution to the 'vision problem'

A way of putting the 'problem' in perspective is to consider what would be necessary if we were to attempt to design a computer to perform certain tasks which people can do relatively easily. It turns out that what comes 'naturally' to us is in fact so complex and so poorly understood that attempts to give a machine this ability prove astonishingly unsuccessful (see Chapter 14).

Frisby (1986) asks us to imagine that we are trying to design a robot capable of assembling some blocks (as part of an industrial assembly process). How would we go about designing a visual system that could match the visual capabilities of a person for seeing what needs to be done to construct a tower? First, the robot needs an optical device of some kind (e.g. a TV camera) that could capture one or more images of the scene. Secondly, the images would have to be analysed and interpreted in some way to provide useful information about the scene (e.g. information about the distance of the blocks from the robot, their shape, etc.). While all this information is so readily provided by our own visual system, it is natural to think it must be easy to enable a robot to extract such information from its input images (Frisby, 1986). But it is not!

So the vision problem can be defined as finding out how to extract useful information about a scene from images of that scene; 'useful information' is that which will guide the thoughts or actions of the total system of which the visual system is a part. For this reason, vision is sometimes described as the business of making explicit information about a scene which is only implicit in the original image – the *computational approach* aims to specify the computations which are necessary to extract useful information from images.

Marr (a mathematician by training) began by studying the computations performed by the cerebellum but soon became dissatisfied with speculating about neural structures as such and decided what was missing was an analysis of the *functions* they perform. Even if you knew the functions of every cell or connection in the brain, this still would not be enough – he said it would be like trying to understand flight simply by examining a bird's feathers (Gardner, 1985). In other words, in order to understand how something works, we need to know what it is *for*.

● Marr's metatheory of vision

Asking what the visual system is for relates to the first of three levels at which, according to Marr, any process must be understood, namely:

1   the *computational theory level:* a theoretical analysis of the tasks performed by perception (visual, in this case) and the methods needed to perform them;
2   *the algorithmic level:* identifying the actual operations by which perceptual tasks are achieved – processes and representations in a biological visual system, algorithms in a computer;
3   *the hardware level:* the mechanisms underlying the operations of the system – neuronal or nervous system structures in a biological visual system, electronic components in a computer.

Most of Marr's work relates to the first and second levels; as we have seen, he began at the third level and decided that the vision problem needs to be approached from the opposite direction, i.e. we need to know the function of the system as a whole before we try to understand its physical implementation. Vision must start with an image on the retina but what we experience is the external world. Light stops at the retina and from then on all there is are nervous impulses – there are no pictures in our head (but that's what we experience). It follows that this neural activity is representing the world symbolically and these symbolic representations of various aspects of the world, initially obtained from the retinal image, are combined into the description we call seeing (Marr, 1982).

● Working out the computational theory

Marr believed that the theory should see the main job of vision as deriving a representation of shape. Vision can do much more than this, of course, but he believed that information about brightness, colour, etc. is of secondary importance. So how is the visual system able to derive reliable information regarding the shapes of objects in the real world from information contained in the retinal image?

His answer was that vision is organized as an information-processing system comprising a series of successive stages which represent independent visual *modules.* The four basic stages of visual representation are summarized in Box 9.5 and in Figure 9.18. Each stage or module takes as its input the information it receives from the previous stage and makes it into a more complex description or representation of the input. By taking the image as the starting point (i.e. the result of light rays from objects or scenes in the real world being focused onto a light-sensitive surface, either a screen or the retina), Marr's approach is strictly bottom-up (Roth, 1995).However, there are also top-down aspects to the theory, as we shall see below when discussing 3-D object recognition.

● 3-D model representation and object recognition

Having referred to the 3-D model representation as involving top-down processes (drawing on stored knowledge about what objects look like), Marr, in fact, argued that in many cases, 3-D structures can be derived from the 2½-D sketch using only general principles of the kind used in the earlier stages. This view rests on the simple observation that stick-figure representations (especially of animals and plants) are easy to recognize (Garnham, 1991). The brain automatically transposes the contours derived from the 2½-D sketch onto axes of symmetry which resemble stick figures composed of pipe cleaners (Gardner, 1985). The 3-D model will comprise a unique description of any object one can distinguish – the same object should always produce the same unique description no matter what the angle of viewing.

But how are these stick figures related to the people, animals and plants, etc. we usually see?

Marr argued that people's bodies, etc. can be represented as jointed cylinders or, more realistically, as generalized cylinders which change their size along their length (Fig. 9.19). He then showed that the cylinders which compose an object can be computed from the 2½-D sketch: the lines running down the centre of these cylinders (important in the recognition process) make up the stick figures. Once a generalized cylinder representation of objects in a scene has been computed, it can be compared with stored representations of objects in a catalogue of 3-D models, where objects are represented in 'standard' orientations (Garnham, 1991).

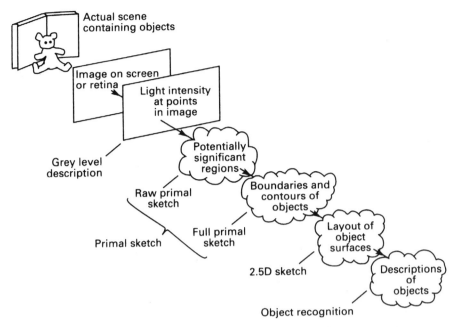

FIGURE 9.18 *The four basic stages or modules in Marr's model of the processing of a visual image. (From I.Roth and V. Bruce (1995)* Perception and Representation: Current issues *2nd ed. Buckingham: Open University Press)*

BOX 9.5 | The four stages (modules) of Marr's computational theory of vision

complex scenes, the images of different objects may occlude each other. Overall, it provides a more useful, less cluttered description of the image – hence 'sketch'.

The image (or grey-level description)

Its function is to represent the intensity of light at each point in the retinal image, so as to discover regions in the image and their boundaries. Regions and boundaries are parts of images, not parts of things in the world, so this represents the starting point of the process of seeing.

Primal sketch

Such useful attributes of a 3-D scene as surface markings, object boundaries and shadows can be recovered from the image by locating and describing the places where the intensity of the image changes relatively abruptly from place to place. There are really two modules involved at this stage. The function of the raw primal sketch is to describe potentially significant regions, i.e. those which may correspond, in the real world, to the edges of objects, the boundaries between overlapping objects and the texture of objects. The full primal sketch provides information about how these regions 'go together' to form structures, i.e it provides a functional explanation for the Gestalt grouping principles. Grouping is necessary since, for example, in

2½-D sketch

Its function is to make explicit the orientation and depth of visible surfaces, as if a 'picture' of the world is beginning to emerge. It is no longer an image because it contains information about things in the world which provide the image. However, it describes only the visible parts of the scene and so is not fully three-dimensional; object recognition requires that the input representation of the object is mapped against a representation stored in memory, so that non-visible parts are taken into account. (This is essentially what perceptual constancy involves.) Also, the sketch changes with the observer's viewpoint (i.e. it is viewpoint dependent) and so descriptions at this stage are not invariant.

3-D model representation

Its function is to make shapes and their spatial organization explicit as belonging to particular 3-D objects, independently of any particular position or orientation on the retina (i.e. viewpoint independent). The observer now has a model of the external world. Knowledge about the nature and construction of the object is now utilized (top-down processing). It can be thought of as object recognition.

Cylinder

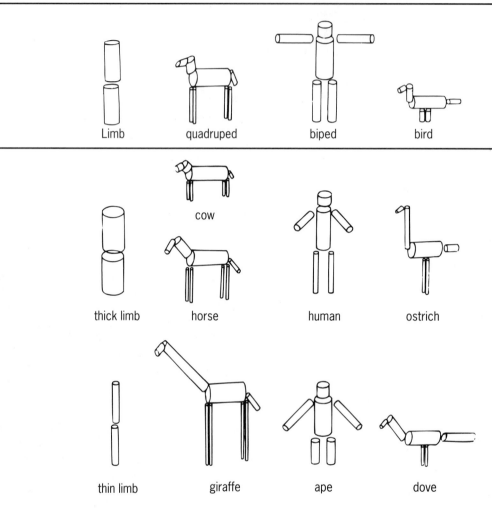

FIGURE 9.19 *Cylinders of various sizes can be combined to represent the shapes of various (parts of) objects. (From Marr and Nishihara, 1978)*

● Evaluation of Marr's theory

According to Harris and Humphreys (1995), Marr was the first to popularize the computational approach and his framework remains the widest-ranging computational account of visual object recognition, and Gordon (1989) says that Marr's work is regarded by many as the most important development in perception theory in recent years.

For Roth (1995), the first question that we should ask is : does Marr's model work, i.e. does it generate a symbolic representation which corresponds to the significant components of the input? The algorithms were implemented by Marr and Hildreth (1980) and, broadly speaking, they achieved what was claimed by the model. However, as Roth points out, the fact that the program works does not mean that biological vision systems work in the same way. The main evidence supporting the relevance of Marr's model to biological vision comes from the classic neurophysiological studies of Hubel and Wiesel of the response to light of single cells in the retina and visual cortex of cats and monkeys; these are discussed in the section on pattern recognition at the end of this chapter.

Marr and Hildreth are not the only ones to have devised an algorithm for generating the raw primal sketch and it has been claimed that some of these produce a better fit with data from human perceptual experiments. Despite this, the general claim that the early stage of vision consists of a representation of simple components, such as edge segments, is generally accepted (Roth, 1995).

However, the account of the 3-D model is clearly much weaker than the earlier stages. This is not surprising since the problems are much more formidable. As we have seen, the early stages make only very general assumptions about the structure of the external world and don't require knowledge of specific objects. Although a bottom-up approach is not an inevitable consequence of the computational approach, it has dominated recent research, at least partly because it is easier to derive computational theories from the early stages of perception, where the relationships between the stimulus and the world are much easier to specify (Harris and Humphreys, 1995).

Similarly, Gardner (1985) argues that most of Marr's theory focuses on the steps prior to recognition of real objects in the real world ('... the most central part of perception ...'): '... the procedures he outlined for object recognition may prove applicable chiefly to the perception of figures of a certain sort for example, the mammalian body, which lends itself to decomposition in terms of generalized cylindrical forms' (Gardner, 1985). According to Harris and Humphreys (1995), researchers are beginning again to consider whether top-down, domain-specific knowledge (see Chapter 14) might be used. This trend has been encouraged partly by *connectionist models* of visual perception (see Chapter 14) and partly by Biederman's (1987) *recognition-by-components theory* (see below), according to which stored knowledge about objects may be contacted directly from 2-D information in the image, without the elaboration of 2½-D and 3-D descriptions.

Nevertheless, Marr's general approach, and in particular the argument for computational theories, '... is likely to remain as one of the most important contributions of research in artificial intelligence to psychological theory. Such theories are able to guide empirical and theoretical research, even if the detailed models specified at any one time later turn out to be wrong' (Harris and Humphreys, 1995).

PATTERN RECOGNITION – WHAT MAKES A 'T' A 'T'?

In a sense, pattern (or object) recognition is the central problem of perception and is almost synonymous with perception itself: how are we able to recognize, identify and categorize objects? What are the processes by which sensory information is converted into a psychologically meaningful perception? Eysenck (1984) defines pattern recognition as 'assigning meaning to visual input by identifying the objects in the visual field' and believes that the ease with which we normally succeed in identifying objects in fact conceals the 'amazing flexibility of the human perceptual system as it copes with a multitude of different stimuli', a remarkable achievement.

A common way of illustrating the problem is to think of all the different ways in which a particular stimulus might be presented; for instance, letters of the alphabet, as in Figure 9.20. What do all these marks on the page have in common? To say that obviously they are all letter Ts is too easy and, in a sense, begs the question. How are we able to recognize them as Ts, what makes them identifiable in this way, what makes a T a T? These are what theories of pattern recognition (PR) attempt to answer. There are three major kinds of theory:

1 template-matching;
2 prototype;
3 feature detection.

FIGURE 9.20 *What makes a 'T' a 'T'?*

● Template matching hypothesis

As with all theories of PR, the template matching hypothesis (TMH) sees PR as the comparison of information which has just stimulated the sense organs (retained in sensory memory) with the relatively permanent information acquired during our lifetime, i.e. a match is made between the incoming sensory information and something in our long-term stores. But what exactly is this something?

According to the TMH, the memory system stores a large number of constructs or internal representations *(templates)* and we compare incoming stimulus information with these miniature copies of previously presented patterns or objects. But if there is an unlimited number of ways of presenting the letter T, for example, it follows that there would have to be an unlimited number of separate templates, each corresponding to a specific visual input. To be able to store that many templates, our cerebrum would be so bulky that we would need a wheelbarrow to cart it around. Clearly, this is neurologically impossible but even if it were possible, it would require an enormously time-consuming search (Solso, 1995).

But if we have to compare an incoming stimulus with a miniature copy of it, how do we ever recognize even slightly unfamiliar patterns – we would need to have come across the 'new' pattern before in order to have a template for it. This, of course, is nonsense! The fact that we normally recognize so many patterns so quickly and can recognize unfamiliar shapes and forms suggests that TMH is not a valid explanation of most human PR. However, it is used by computers when 'reading', i.e. matching specific letter configurations against specific configurations in its memory (like a key in a lock). This is one reason

why they are so bad at recognizing any slight deviation from the highly specific configurations in their memories (see Chapter 14).

It is also the basis of price-coding in supermarkets. Each packet has a special bar code which identifies the item for which the computer supplies the price; this is then entered on the cash-register tape (see Fig. 9.21).

A recent alternative to TMH is Biederman's recognition-by-components theory (or geon theory). According to Biederman (e.g. 1987), human information processing uses a limited number of simple geometric 'primitives' that may be applied to complex shapes ('geon'stands for 'geometrical ions'). All complex forms are composed of geons; for instance, a cup consists of a cylinder (for the container portion) and an ellipse (for the handle) (see Fig. 9.22).The recognition of an object consists of recognition-by-components, in which 24 distinct, simple forms can be combined to produce more complex ones (in much the same way as an unlimited number of words are produced by combining a small number of letters). (Also compare Biederman's geons with Marr and Nishihara's generalized cylinders.)

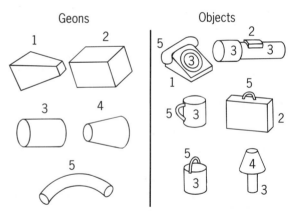

FIGURE 9.22 *(From I Biederman (1990) Higher–level vision. In EN Oskerson, SM Kosslyn and JM Hollerbach (eds).* An invitation to cognitive science. *MA; MIT Press)*

One test of geon theory is the use of *degraded forms,* as shown in Figure 9.23. The identification of any given visual object is determined by whichever stored object representation provides the best fit with the component- or geon-based information obtained from the visual object. But how do we segment an object in order to establish the number of parts or components making it up? Biederman agreed with Marr and Nishihara that the *concave* parts of contour are particularly important in segmentation (Solso, 1995).

FIGURE 9.21 *The bar codes on the goods we buy identify them. When the bar code is read by a computerised cash register, the computer supplies the price, which is then entered on the cash register tape. The code is read by template matching on the basis of the positions, widths and spacing of the lines.*

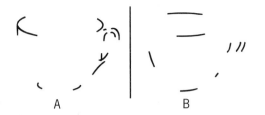

FIGURE 9.23 *65 percent of the contour has been removed from a drawing of a cup; (A) preserves part of the contour providing information about concavities but (B) does not. (From I Biederman, 'Human Image Understanding; Recent Research and a Theory' in* Computer Vision, *Graphics and Image Processing 32, 29–72 © 1985 Academic Press)*

● Prototype theories

Instead of proposing that what we store is a template for each individual pattern, we could suggest a smaller number of *prototypes*, 'abstract forms representing the basic elements of a set of stimuli' (Eysenck, 1984). Whereas template theories treat each stimulus as a separate entity, prototype theories maintain that similarities between related stimuli play an important part in PR, whereby each stimulus is a member of a category of stimuli and shares certain basic properties with other members of the category.

While the idea of a prototype is intuitively appealing, the precise nature of prototypes and the matching process is not very explicit and prototype theories fail to explain how PR is affected by the context as well as by the stimulus itself (Eysenck, 1984). Just what those properties are which are shared by a category of stimuli is what we want to know but what prototype theories fail to tell us; for example, to define the prototype for the letter T as an 'idealized' letter T, the 'best' representation of the pattern, just begs the question. This is where *feature detection* comes into its own.

● Feature detection theories

By far the most researched and influential theories of PR maintain that each stimulus pattern can be thought of as a configuration of elementary features. Letters of the alphabet, for example, are composed of combinations of about 12 basic features (including straight vertical lines, horizontals and closed curves). For example, an A may be analysed into two diagonals (/\ ), one horizontal (–), a pointed head (ʌ) and an open bottom(⌒). The evidence for this is of two main kinds: behavioural and neurological.

Behavioural studies

A common experimental technique is a visual scanning task in which participants search lists of letters as rapidly as possible in order to find a specified target letter which occurs in unpredictable positions in the lists. Clearly, finding the target letter involves recognizing a particular pattern and rejecting others and if recognition entails the detection of elementary features, then the task should be more difficult the more features the target and non-target letters have in common. For example, it should be easier to find Z in a list comprising C,G and O than when the non-target letters are M,X and E. This has been confirmed by Neisser (1964) and Rabbitt (1967).

A more direct approach is to observe eye movements and fixation. Such studies assume that if you gaze for a relatively long time at a certain feature in a pattern, you are extracting more information from it than a feature which is only scanned briefly. Yarbus (1967) claimed that the perception of features within complex patterns depends not only on the nature of the physical stimuli but also relates to higher-order cognitive processes, such as attention and purpose (see Fig. 9.24).

Neurological studies

There is considerable evidence that the visual systems of a wide variety of vertebrates contain both peripheral (retinal) and central (cortical) cells that respond only to particular features of visual stimuli (Hubel and Wiesel, 1959, 1962, 1963, 1968; Barlow *et al*, 1972). As we saw in Chapter 8, Hubel and Wiesel, for example, using cats and monkeys, identified three kinds of cortical cells – simple, complex and hypercomplex. But do these different kinds of cell constitute the feature detectors postulated by feature detection theories?

Marr (1982) tried to construct a computerized feature detection system and found that the activity in any one cell is too variable and ambiguous to be thought of as feature detection as such; however, it might provide the first step in the analysis of features present in the visual input. Perhaps these neurological detectors are a necessary precondition for any higher-level (cognitive) pattern analysis taking place. However, there are also some more basic criticisms. Eysenck (1984), for example, argues that feature theories typically assume a *serial* form of processing, with feature extraction being followed by feature combination and, finally, by PR. Hubel and Wiesel (1962) saw the sequence of simple, complex and hypercomplex cells representing a serial flow of information, whereby only particular information is

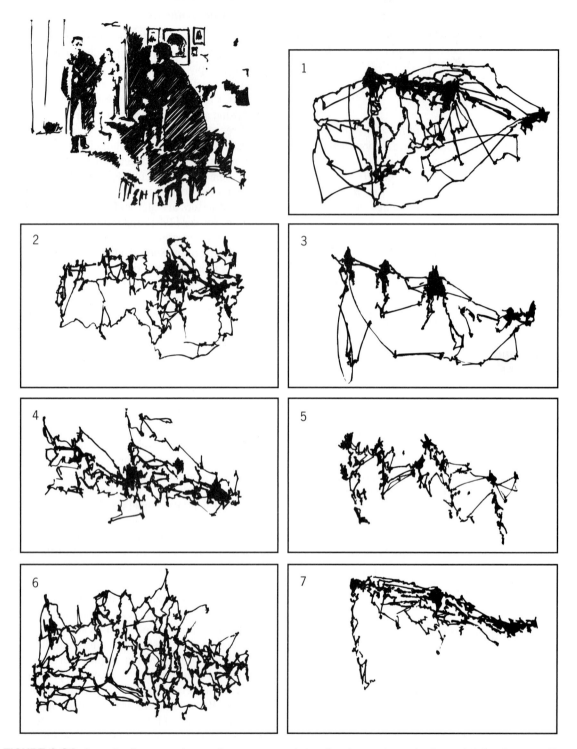

FIGURE 9.24 *Records of eye movements of someone examining the picture shown in the top left-hand square. Trace 1 was made when the participant examined the picture at will. In Trace 2, the participant was asked to estimate the economic status of the people shown , in Trace 3 , to judge their ages, in Trace 4, to query what they had been up to prior to the arrival of the visitor, in Trace 5, to remember their clothing, in Trace 6, to remember their positions (and objects) and in Trace 7, to estimate how long the visitor had not seen the family. (Redrawn from Yarbus, 1967)*

processed at any one time before being passed on to the next level upwards and so on. (This is very similar to the stages of Marr's computational theory.)

Yet it is widely accepted that a great deal of *parallel* (non-serial) processing takes place in the visual cortex and that the relationship between the three kinds of cell is more complex than originally thought. An interesting and famous example of non-serial processing is Selfridge's (1959) computer program for the recognition of Morse code and a small set of handwritten letters, which he called *Pandemonium* (the capital of Hell in Milton's *Paradise Lost)*. The components are four kinds of demons:

1 *Image demons,* who simply copy the pattern, much as the retina records visual patterns.
2 *Feature demons,* who analyse the information from the image demons in terms of combinations of features.
3 *Cognitive demons,* who are specialized for particular letters and will 'scream' according to how much the input from the feature demons matches their special letter.
4 *A decision demon,* who chooses the 'loudest scream' and hence, the name of the letter.

Finally, several writers have pointed out that feature detection theories do not take sufficient account of the context and certain perceiver variables, such as expectations (e.g. Palmer, 1975; Norman, 1976; Eysenck, 1984) and we have seen some examples of their influence throughout this chapter. Clearly, the same features can produce different patterns (especially if they are ambiguous) and different features can produce the same pattern depending on context, which can tell us what patterns are likely to be present and hence what to expect. Indeed, we may fail to notice the absence of something or a distorted form of a stimulus (e.g. typing or printing errors) because of its high predictability. This influence of context and expectation on the analysis of sensory features illustrates top-down or *conceptually-driven processing;* most feature detection theories to date seem to be bottom-up or *data driven.*

One effect of context on PR may be to allow a partial and selective analysis of the stimuli to be recognized, i.e. PR involves selectively attending to some aspects of the presented stimuli but not others. PR and selective attention, therefore, can be seen as closely related (Solso, 1979). We will discuss attention in Chapter 11.

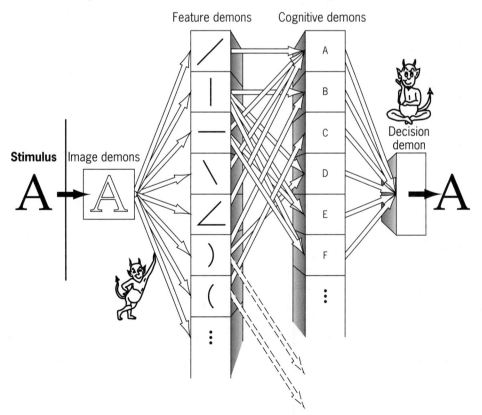

FIGURE 9.25 *A representation of Selfridge's Pandemonium model of pattern recognition. (Based on Ruch, 1984)*

CHAPTER SUMMARY

- One important issue that distinguishes different theories of perception is whether it is a top-down or a bottom-up process. Another is the nature-nurture issue.

- Most definitions of perception reflect top-down theories, which distinguish between sensation and perception and which regard perception as a problem that needs to be explained.

- According to Gregory, we often need to draw inferences from the available sensory information, as in shape, size, location, colour and brightness constancy. The constancies demonstrate that perception is a process of construction based on physical sources of energy.

- Visual illusions also illustrate how we go beyond the information given. Four major categories of illusion are distortions, ambiguous figures, paradoxical figures and fictions.

- Gregory explains illusions, such as the Ponzo and Müller-Lyer, as the result of a misplaced perceptual hypothesis, in which a flat, 2-D drawing is interpreted as if it had depth.

- Illusions of movement include the autokinetic effect, stroboscopic motion, the phi phenomenon and induced movement.

- A number of factors contribute to the perception of real movement in addition to the retinal image. These include judgements about relative size and configuration change. The perception of movement is the product of an interaction between the image-retina system and the eye-head system.

- Perceptual set acts as a selector and as an interpreter; it is determined by a number of factors, both perceiver/organismic and stimulus/situational. Instructions, expectations, past experience and context often interact to induce set.

- Related to set are perceptual accentuation/sensitization and perceptual defence. The latter is related to the more general concept of subliminal perception. Despite a controversial history, it seems that perceptual defence is a genuine perceptual phenomenon.

- Gregory's theory has been challenged because of the emphasis given to illusions, which are not typical of perceptual experience in general. In everyday life, bottom-up processes may play a greater role than he claims.

- Gibson's theory of direct perception is bottom-up and starts with the optical array; this provides unambiguous, invariant information about the layout of objects in space in the form of optic flow patterns, texture gradient and affordances.

- Depth is automatically and directly available to the senses, based on pictorial cues (relative size, relative brightness, superimposition, linear perspective, aerial perspective, height in the horizontal plane, light and shadow, texture gradient and motion parallax), and non-pictorial cues (accommodation, retinal disparity and convergence).

- Gibson seems to have underplayed the importance of culturally determined knowledge in perception; he implies that there is no difference between seeing and seeing as, the latter pertaining to cultural learning and experience.

- For the transactionalists , 'seeing as' is the fundamental principle of perception, and the Ames distorted room is a classic demonstration of how basic beliefs about the world are built up through past experience.

- Gibson's theory has great difficulty accounting for illusions, where perception is mistaken.

- Both Gregory and Gibson believe that perceptual experience is influenced by learning. For Gregory, it is constructive/synthetic, for Gibson it is analytic. This makes them both empiricists.

- Neisser's analysis-by-synthesis model represents an important integration of Gregory's top-down and Gibson's bottom-up approaches.

- The key concept in Gestalt psychology is perceptual organization and a major feature of this approach are the principles of perceptual grouping. These can be summarized under the law of Prägnanz and include proximity, closure, continuity and symmetry, similarity, figure-ground and the part-whole relationship.

- One criticism of the concept of a Gestalt is the difficulty of defining a 'good figure'. However, several experiments have provided objective measures of perceptual grouping.

- Although the Gestalt laws are accepted as descriptions of grouping phenomena, they have little explanatory value and Gestalt demonstrations have low ecological validity.

- Marr's computational theory is an attempt to solve the vision problem, i.e. finding out how to extract useful information about the shape of objects from images of them. To understand how vision works, we must first know what its function is .

- This information is extracted in four stages or modules, namely the image (or grey-level description), primal sketch (which comprises a raw and a full primal sketch), 2½-D sketch and 3-D model representation, which can be thought of as object recognition.

- Often, 3-D structures are derived using stick-figure representations which, in turn, are made up of the lines running down the centre of generalized cylinders. This can explain the perception of people, animals, etc.
- Pattern recognition is the central problem of perception and is almost synonymous with it.
- The template matching hypothesis has to assume a separate template for each individual object or pattern, which is neurologically impossible.
- Biederman's recognition-by-components theory (or geon theory) is an alternative to TMH.
- Prototype theories propose a smaller number of abstract representations or idealized forms of categories of objects.
- Feature detection theories see patterns as configurations of elementary features. These have been tested behaviourally through visual scanning tasks, observation of eye movements and fixation and neurologically through study of individual cells in the retina and visual cortex.
- Most theories of PR assume serial processing and ignore the fact that much parallel processing takes place in the visual cortex. One exception is Selfridge's *Pandemonium.*
- The influence of context and expectations on PR illustrates conceptually-driven processing, while most feature detection theories are data driven.

GLOSSARY

Affordances Gibson's term for the directly perceivable, potential uses of objects (e.g. a ladder 'affords' climbing).

Analysis-by-synthesis Neisser's model in which bottom-up processes (analysis) interact with top-down processes (synthesis) in a perceptual cycle.

Autokinetic effect Visual illusion, in which a stationary spot of light in an otherwise completely dark room appears to move.

Bottom-up processing In perception, awareness of objects that is determined solely by the incoming sensory information. Also known as *data-driven* processing.

Computational approach The approach to vision which aims to make explicit the stages involved in extracting useful 3-D information from 2-D images.

In Marr's theory, image/grey-level description, primal sketch, 2½-D sketch, 3-D model representation (object recognition).

Ecological optics Gibson's view that to understand an animal's perceptual system, we need to consider the environment in which the system evolved.

Feature detection theories Explanations of pattern recognition, according to which each stimulus pattern is a configuration of elementary features.

Gestalt German word for 'organized whole', 'configuration' or 'pattern'.

Induced movement Visual illusion in which movement is attributed to the wrong object, as in the moon behind clouds.

Law of Prägnanz The 'umbrella' principle of perceptual grouping in Gestalt theory, incorporating proximity, closure, continuity and symmetry, similarity, figure-ground and part-whole relationship.

Misapplied size constancy theory Gregory's explanation of visual illusions (e.g. Ponzo and Müller-Lyer) in terms of inappropriate assumptions about the 3-D nature of 2-D drawings.

Optic flow patterns The apparent radial expansion of textures flowing around our head as we approach a point, which appears motionless (as in a pilot bringing a plane down towards a landing strip).

Optical array In Gibson's theory, the pattern of light containing all the visual information from the environment reaching the eye. Provides unambiguous, invariant information about the layout of objects in space.

Parallel processing In pattern recognition, the simultaneous detection, combination and identification of features/ patterns (e.g. Pandemonium).

Pattern recognition Process of recognizing, identifying and categorizing objects. Almost synonymous with 'perception'.

Perceptual accentuation Tendency to perceive things that are important for us as larger, brighter, more attractive, etc. Also called perceptual sensitization.

Perceptual constancy Perceiving things as they 'are' (as we know them to be), despite changes in angle of viewing, distance, lighting conditions, etc. Major types are shape, size, location, colour, brightness.

Perceptual defence Process by which things that are threatening or anxiety-provoking are more difficult to perceive at a conscious level.

Perceptual set A bias, predisposition or tendency to notice certain aspects of the available sense data and to ignore others. Acts as selector and interpreter.

Phi phenomenon Visual illusion, in which a number

of separate lights turned on and off in quick succession will appear as a single light moving from one position to another.

Prototypes In pattern recognition, an abstract form representing an 'idealized' object category; incoming stimuli are recognized as an example of a particular category .

Recognition-by-components theory Biederman's view that all complex forms are composed of simple geometrical forms ('geons'); pattern recognition consists of recognizing these components. Also called geon theory.

Segmentation Marr's term for the use of visual information to decide which regions of a visual scene belong together and form coherent structures ('wholes').

Serial processing In feature detection theories, a sequence of processes, from feature extraction to feature combination to pattern recognition.

Stroboscopic motion Visual illusion, in which a succession of stationary images projected onto a screen sufficiently fast will give impression of continuous movement.

Subliminal perception Perception that occurs below the threshold of conscious awareness (due to very brief or low-intensity presentations of a stimulus).

Template matching hypothesis Theory of pattern recognition, according to which incoming sensory information is matched against an internal representation/miniature copy of objects.

Texture gradients The apparent expansion of textures as you approach and contraction as they pass beyond your head. Also called gradient of texture density.

Top-down processing In perception, awareness of objects which is the end result of a process that begins with sensory stimulation but involves inferences based on knowledge/expectations, etc.Also known as conceptually-driven processing.

Transactionalists Psychologists (e.g. Ames) who believe that we use past experience to help us interpret inherently ambiguous sensory input. Perception is 'seeing as'.

Visual illusions Perceptual experiences in which the perceived stimulus differs in some way from the objective stimulus. Include distortions, ambiguous figures, paradoxical figures, fictions and illusions of movement.

FURTHER READING

Roth, I. & Bruce, V. (eds) (1995) *Perception and Representation:* Current Issues , 2nd edn. Buckingham: Open University Press. Thorough, up-to-date, discussion with stress on Marr's computational approach and the perception/recognition of faces.

Solso, R.S. (1995) *Cognitive Psychology*, 4th edn. Boston: Allyn and Bacon, Chapters 3 and 4.

10 PERCEPTION 2: THE DEVELOPMENT OF PERCEPTUAL ABILITIES

INTRODUCTION AND OVERVIEW

The subject of this chapter illustrates one of those themes and debates that runs through psychology as a whole, namely the nature–nurture or heredity–environment issue. As with other aspects of behaviour where this debate goes on (such as psychological sex differences – Chapter 23, language development – Chapter 26, intelligence – Chapter 28 and schizophrenia – Chapter 30), the questions that are asked are deceptively simple and often conceal crucial assumptions and value judgements.

In the case of perception, there are additional reasons for not expecting any simple answers. As we saw in Chapter 9, perception is a complex set of interconnected and overlapping abilities (e.g. perception

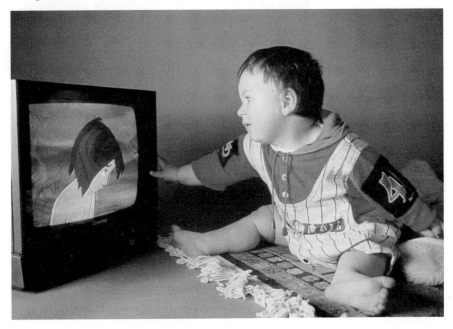

of depth, shape and movement) and several sense modalities are involved. To ask whether perception is learnt or innate is to oversimplify the issue. Philosophers, who considered this question long before psychologists began to study it scientifically, tended to oversimplify their questions and, consequently, produced oversimplified answers, which were of two distinct types:

- According to *nativists,* we are born with certain capacities to perceive the world in particular ways; these capacities are often immature or incomplete at birth but develop gradually thereafter. Psychologists of a nativist persuasion believe that this development after birth proceeds through the genetically-determined process of maturation, with learning playing only a minor role or none at all. This type of philosophy is best illustrated by the Gestalt school of psychology.
- *Empiricists* maintain that all our knowledge and abilities are acquired through experience, that is, are learned (the word 'empirical' means 'through the senses'). As we saw (Chapter 9), transactionalists are one school of psychology embodying the empiricist philosophy.

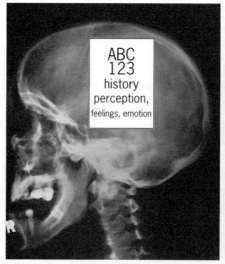

Nativist

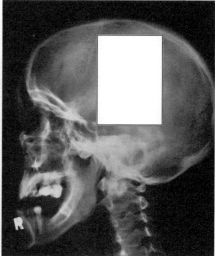

Empiricist

Most present-day psychologists would consider themselves neither nativists nor empiricists but rather *interactionists,* believing that we may be born with capacities to perceive the world in certain ways but that stimulation and environmental influences in general are crucial in determining how – and even whether – these capacities actually develop. Different perceptual abilities may be more or less affected by genetic or environmental factors, but it is certain that any perceptual ability is the product of an interaction between both sets of factors; both are always involved, although it is not always obvious exactly what part they play. (There is a sense in which empiricists are also interactionists. According to Segall (1994), to an empiricist, every perception is the result of an interaction between a stimulus and a perceiver shaped by prior experience (as in Gregory's theory of perceptual hypotheses; see Chapter 9). But this is a different kind of interaction from the one described above, which represents a 'blend' of innate/biological and learned/experiential influences. It is in this latter sense that 'interactionist' will be used in this chapter.)

This chapter will attempt to answer the nature-nurture question by considering five major types of evidence: the study of newborn babies, animal experiments, studies of human cataract patients, studies of perceptual adaptation/readjustment and cross-cultural studies.

OVERVIEW OF THE KINDS OF EVIDENCE RELEVANT TO THE NATURE–NURTURE DEBATE

Investigating the perceptual abilities of *newborn babies* (or neonates) represents the most direct way of investigating the nature–nurture issue. In general, the earlier a particular ability appears, the more likely it is to be under the influence of genetic factors. However, the fact that it develops some time after birth does not necessarily mean it has been learnt, as it could take time to mature. There are other special difficulties involved in studying speechless participants, as we shall see below.

Animal experiments often involve depriving animals in some way of normal sensory and perceptual stimulation and recording the long-term effects of this deprivation on their sensory and perceptual abilities. Some studies reverse this and actually provide the animals with 'extra' experience and stimulation. Still others study the animal's brain to see how it controls perceptual abilities. From a research point of view, the main advantage of studying animals is that we can manipulate their environments in ways which are not permissible with humans. Deprivation studies can tell us how much and what kinds of early experience are necessary for normal perceptual development in those species being studied, but we must be very cautious about generalizing these findings to humans and we

must be aware of the ethical objections to such research (see Chapter 32).

Studies of *human cataract patients* represent the human counterpart to animal deprivation studies. These patients have been deprived of normal visual experience through a physical defect, rather than through experimental manipulation or interference, and constitute a kind of 'natural experiment'. Their vision is restored through surgical removal of the cataract and the abilities that are evident immediately after removal of the bandages are normally taken to be innate and unlearned. However, there are special problems involved here too: generalizing from 'unusual' adults can be hazardous and it is not always obvious whether abilities that do not appear have to be learned or are 'present' but not being used.

In studies of *perceptual adaptation* or *readjustment,* human volunteers wear special goggles which distort the visual world in various ways. If they can adapt to such a distorted-looking world, then human 'perceptual habits' cannot be as fixed or rigid as they would be if they were under genetic control – perhaps the way we perceive is itself originally learned. However, we need to ask what kind of adaptation is taking place: is it actually perceptual or is it merely motor, that is, learning to move about successfully in a very different-looking environment? If the latter is the case, then we cannot conclude necessarily that our perceptual 'habits' are habits at all (i.e. learned in the first place) but only that we are good at changing our body movements to 'match' what we see.

Cross-cultural studies attempt to test whether or not the way that people in Western culture perceive things is universal, that is, perceived in the same way by people who live in cultures very different from our own. The most common method of testing is to present members of different cultural groups with the same stimulus material, usually visual illusions. A major advantage of cross-cultural studies is that they act as a buffer against generalizing from a comparatively small sample of the earth's population (Price-Williams, 1966), i.e. unless we study a particular process in different cultures, we cannot be sure what kinds of factors influence that process. So, if we find consistent differences between different cultural groups, unless we have good, independent reasons for believing that these differences are biologically caused then we are forced to attribute them to environmental factors, be they social customs, ecological, linguistic or some combination of these. Such studies, therefore, enable us to discover the extent to which perceiving is structured by the nervous system (and so common to all human beings) and to what extent by experience. However, as we shall see, psychologists cannot agree as to the key features of such cultural experience.

● Overview of the evidence: what general conclusions can we draw ?

Although most psychologists regard perceptual abilities as the product of an interaction between genetic factors (nature) and environmental factors (nurture), some attempts have been made to test directly the merits of the nativist and empiricist positions and we shall discuss some of these when we look at the work of Bower, with infants. By the same token, most of the evidence which supports the nativist theory derives from infant studies; as we noted above, the earlier a particular ability appears, the less opportunity there has been for learning to have occurred and so the more likely it is that the ability is under genetic control.

Although the bulk of the evidence supports the interactionist position, there are grounds for concluding that relatively simple perceptual abilities are more under genetic control and less susceptible to environmental influence, while the situation is reversed in the case of more complex abilities. The most clear-cut demonstration of this comes from human cataract patients and so we shall start with these.

STUDIES OF HUMAN CATARACT PATIENTS

These represent the 'natural' counterpart in humans of the animal experiments described below. They are based on case studies of patients who have undergone an operation for the removal of cataracts to 'restore' their sight (a cataract is a film over the lens of the eye and can either be present at birth or develop any time afterwards). Most of the evidence comes from the work of von Senden, a German doctor who, in 1932, reported on 65 cases of people who had undergone cataract-removal surgery; the earliest case was reported in 1700, the latest in 1928.

Von Senden's original data was taken up again by Hebb in 1949, who analysed the findings in terms of *figural unity*, the ability to detect the presence of a figure or stimulus, and *figural identity*, being able to name or in some other way identify the object, to 'say' what it is. Hebb concluded that while the first seemed to be innate, the second seemed to require learning.

Initially, cataract patients are typically bewildered by an array of visual stimuli (rather like the 'booming, buzzing confusion' which William James believed was the perceptual experience of newborn babies). However, they can distinguish figure from ground (i.e. some object from its background), fixate objects, scan them and follow moving objects with their eyes. But they cannot identify by sight alone those objects which are already familiar through touch (and this includes faces), distinguish between various geometrical shapes without counting the corners or tracing the outline with their fingers or say which of two sticks is longer without feeling them, although they can tell there is a difference. They also fail to show perceptual constancy. For example, even after visual identification has occurred (i.e. things are recognized through sight alone), there may be little generalization to situations other than the one in which the object was originally recognized, e.g. a lump of sugar held in someone's hand may not be identified correctly when suspended from a piece of string. (Interestingly, as we shall see later in the chapter, Bower believes that size and shape constancy are probably innate; Hebb's findings suggest this is not so.)

So the more simple ability of figural unity seems to be available very soon after cataract removal and does not seem to depend on prior visual experience, while the more complex figural identity seems to

BOX 10.1 The case of S.B. (Gregory and Wallace, 1963)

S.B. was 52 when he received his sight after a corneal graft operation. His judgement of size and distance were good, provided that he was familiar with the objects in question. He could recognize objects visually if he was already familiar with them through touch while blind so, unlike most of the 65 cases analysed by Hebb, he displayed good *crossmodal transfer*, i.e. recognition through one sense modality (touch) being substituted by another (vision). However, he seemed to have great difficulty in identifying objects visually if he was not already familiar with them in this way: a year after his operation he still could not draw the front of a bus although the rest of the drawing was very well executed (Fig. 10.1). S.B. was never able to use his newfound ability to see to his fullest extent; for instance, he did not bother to turn on the light at night but would sit in the dark all evening.

As the months passed, it became clear that S.B. was in some ways like a newborn baby when it came to recognizing objects and events by sight alone. For instance, he found it impossible to judge distances by sight alone; he knew what windows were, from touching them both from inside a room and from outside (while standing on the ground) but, of course, he had never been able to look out from a top-floor window and he thought 'he would be able to touch the ground below the window with his feet if he lowered himself by his hands' (Gregory and Wallace, 1963). The window in question was the one in his hospital room – 40 feet above the ground!

He never learnt to interpret facial expressions such as smiles and frowns, although he could infer a person's mood from the sound of their voice.

require a long period of training. Hebb believes that this is how these two aspects of perception normally develop. Further evidence comes from the case of S.B. (Box 10.1).

Although these 65 cases seem to underline the importance of experience as far as all but the most simple perceptual abilities are concerned, there are certain problems involved in interpreting the results:

- Adult patients are not the same as babies; while the sensory systems of babies are all relatively undeveloped, adults have other well-developed sensory modalities which tend to compensate for the lack of vision (touch and hearing in particular). These other channels may actually hinder visual learning because the patient, in order to use vision, may have to actually 'unlearn' previous experience. As people tend to find it easier to use the channel they already know best or use most often, S.B.'s ability to recognize familiar objects through vision alone but continued preference for touch over vision may reflect this tendency to stick with what is familiar, rather than experiment with the unknown. This may be a safer conclusion to draw than Hebb's, which is that figural identity is (normally) largely learned.

- It seems that, traditionally, cataract patients have not been very adequately prepared for their 'new world of vision'; their resulting confusion and general emotional distress following the operation may result in a rather inaccurate picture of what they can and cannot actually see. Referring to S.B. again, when blind he would cross the street on his

FIGURE 10.1 *This was drawn after S.B. had had some experience of sighted travel. Basically it shows the parts he knew by touch but clearly he had also, by this time, noticed the bright advertisement for Typhoo Tea on the side of the bus*

own, but once he could see the traffic it frightened him so much that he refused to cross on his own. In fact, he died three years after his operation, at least partially from depression. (Depression was also common amongst von Senden's cases.)

- We do not know what physical deterioration of the visual system may have occurred during the years of blindness and so cannot be sure that the absence of figural identity is due to lack of visual stimulation and learning (which Hebb believes are responsible) rather than to some physical damage.

- The reliability of the case histories themselves is open to doubt; presumably the standards for reporting in 1700 were not as strict as they are today, so that there is great variability in the ages of the patients when they underwent surgery and when their cataracts first appeared and hence in the amount of visual experiences prior to the defect.

ANIMAL EXPERIMENTS

In an early experiment, Riesen (1947) deprived one group of chimps of light by raising them in darkness, except for several 45-second periods of exposure to light while they were being fed. This continued until they were 16 months old, when they were compared with a group of normally-reared chimps. The deprived group showed markedly inferior perceptual abilities when tested at 16 months. While they did show pupil constriction to light and were startled by sudden, intense illumination, they did not blink in response to threatening movements made towards their faces or show any interest in their toys unless they accidentally touched them with some part of their bodies.

As Weiskrantz (1956) pointed out, the visual deficiencies in the deprived group were probably due to failure of the retinas to develop properly; when the retina is not stimulated by light, fewer of the retinal cells develop and the visual cortex too may begin to degenerate. So, Riesen's experiment may show only that a certain amount of light is physically necessary to maintain the visual system and allow it to mature normally.

In an effort to overcome these objections to his original study, Riesen later (1965) reared three chimps from birth to seven months of age, under three different conditions:

1 Debi spent the whole time in darkness;
2 Kova spent 1½ hours per day exposed to diffuse or unpatterned light by wearing translucent goggles; the rest of the time was spent in darkness;
3 Lad was raised in normal lighting conditions.

As expected, only Debi suffered retinal damage. Lad was no different, perceptually, from any other normally-reared chimp. It was Kova who was of special interest because, while she did not suffer any retinal damage, she was only exposed to unpatterned light, so that she did not see 'objects' as such but only patches of light, different colours and brightnesses – not distinguishable shapes or patterns. She was noticeably retarded as far as her perceptual development was concerned.

Riesen also fitted translucent goggles to monkeys, chimps and kittens for the first three months of their lives. Some simple perceptual abilities remained intact, such as differentiating colours, size and brightness, but more complex abilities did not, e.g. following a moving object, differentiating between geometrical shapes, perceiving depth and distinguishing a moving object from a stationary one. Riesen's studies as a whole suggest that :

● light is necessary for normal physical development of the visual system (at least in chimps, some monkeys and kittens); and
● patterned light is also necessary for the normal development of some of the complex visual abilities (in those species).

Therefore, environmental stimulation of certain kinds seems to be essential for normal perceptual development. If perception were wholly innate, environmental factors (over and above those which can actually harm the developing organism or actively prevent maturation from taking place) should not have any effect; Riesen has shown, however, that they do. Other animal experiments have also shown the impact of early experience on perceptual abilities.

Hubel and Wiesel (1962) used cats reared in full or partial blindfolds (translucent goggles); the receptive fields of the latter failed to develop normally (see Chapter 8). In a later study, Hubel (1979) found evidence that the brain itself can be affected by visual deprivation. He surgically closed either the left or right eyelid of several monkeys when they were two weeks old. This reduced the amount of light striking the retina; the eyelid remained closed until 18 months of age. He then opened the eye and injected a radioactive substance, which would be transported to the visual cortex, into the non-deprived eye. Pictures were taken of slices of cortex with radiation-sensitive film, allowing a study of the ocular dominance columns, which are groups of cells in the cortex that respond to input from either the right or the left eye (see Chapter 8). The columns of the open eye were greatly expanded while those of the closed eye had shrunk dramatically.

Held and Hein (1963) were concerned with the effects of deprivation on the ability of kittens to guide their movements through vision. Given that a kitten's perceptual abilities are not entirely innate, to what extent is the acquisition of these abilities dependent on exposure to visual stimulation *and* motor activity? They used an apparatus called the kitten carousel (Fig. 10.2). For the first eight weeks after birth, kittens were kept in darkness and then spent about three hours each day in the carousel (the rest of the time being spent in the dark). The 'active' kitten could move itself around (its legs were free) and its movements were transmitted to the 'passive' kitten via a series of pulleys, i.e. every time the active kitten moved the passive kitten moved the same distance, at the same speed, etc. The significant thing to note is that both kittens had exactly the same visual experience (both type and amount) but one could move itself about while the other was dependent on the first one's movements.

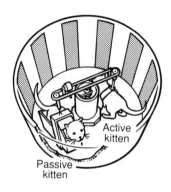

FIGURE 10.2 *The kitten carousel. (From Held, 1965)*

After several weeks of this arrangement, they were tested for 'paw-eye co-ordination'. The active kittens were markedly superior; for example, after 30 hours exposure they all showed visually-guided paw placement (if gently lowered towards the floor, they extended their paws, which is a typical response for normally-reared kittens). None of the passive kittens could do this after 30 hours, nor did they blink in response to an approaching object. They also failed to show the normal reluctance to step onto the deep side of the *visual cliff apparatus* (see below and Fig. 10.11). But does this mean that they could not actually perceive depth? In fact, the passive kittens soon learned the normal avoidance responses when allowed to run around in a lighted environment. This suggests that, rather than having failed to learn depth perception as such, they simply had not learned the correct motor responses associated with depth perception. So we must distinguish between perception on the one hand and *sensory-motor co-ordination* on the other (see perceptual readjustment studies, below).

● A brief evaluation of animal experiments

A general problem with animal studies (as with studies of human infants) is that we can only infer their perceptual experiences through observing their behaviour or their physiological responses – they

---

BOX 10.2 | **Key study: the effects of being raised in a vertical or horizontal world**

Blakemore and Cooper (1970) looked at quite specific environmental effects. They raised kittens from birth in darkness, except for a five-hour period each day when they were placed in a large drum or round chamber which had either vertical or horizontal stripes on the walls. A collar prevented the kittens from seeing their own bodies, so that the stripes were the only visual stimuli they encountered.

At five months old, the kittens were tested for line recognition by being presented with a moving pointer held either vertically or horizontally. Those reared in the 'vertical world' would only reach out to touch a vertical pointer, while those raised in the 'horizontal world' reached only for a horizontal pointer. Depending on the kind of visual experience they had had for the first five months, the kittens acted as if they were blind in the presence of the other kind of visual stimulus.

This 'behavioural blindness' mirrored 'physiological blindness'. By placing microelectrodes into individual cells in the visual cortex, Blakemore and Cooper found that those kittens raised in a vertically-striped environment did not possess cells that fired in response to bars of light moved horizontally and the reverse was true for the kittens raised in the horizontally-striped environment. The only receptive fields to have developed were those which reflected the early visual experience of the kittens.

However, this does not show conclusively that responding to lines at different angles develops solely through environmental influence. It is possible that receptive fields for all angles are present at birth and that where a kitten sees only vertical lines, those fields which would otherwise have responded to horizontal lines are 'taken over' by vertical fields. Nevertheless, these findings seem to suggest very strongly that the type of environment is important in the development of at least certain kinds of perceptual ability in some species: in kittens, perception does seem to be at least partly learned.

cannot tell us more directly what they can or cannot see. We cannot be certain that animals deprived in particular ways do not perceive particular stimuli, only that *they do not behave as if they do*. It is possible that certain perceptual abilities have developed, but if they have not become linked to the animal's behaviour, we may have no way of knowing.

PERCEPTUAL ADAPTATION/READJUSTMENT STUDIES

The basic hypothesis being tested here is that human beings are capable of perceiving the world in a different way from normal and adjusting to this altered perception, thus demonstrating that perception is largely learned. The greater the degree of adaptation to a new perceptual world, the more significant the role of learning is taken to be. Compared with other species that have been tested, such as salamanders (Sperry, 1943) and chickens (Hess, 1956), human beings come out on top as far as this adaptability is concerned. It follows that the less adaptation a particular species shows, the greater the control by genetic factors in the perceptual abilities of that species.

One of the earliest recorded human studies was that of Stratton (1896; Box 10.3).

Gilling and Brightwell (1982) report a recent replication of Stratton's inverted goggles experiment (Box 10.4).

Snyder and Pronko (1952) made goggles which inverted and reversed the visual world. Their volunteers wore them continually for 30 days and were able to adapt to the changes. Two years after the experiment, these participants coped just as well when refitted with the goggles as first-time participants at the end of the thirty-day period, showing that motor adaptations are extremely resistant to forgetting.

Kohler (1962) used an optical device which inverted the image without reversing left and right (more like Stratton's than Snyder and Pronko's). His volunteers were disoriented and even nauseous at first, but after several days they adjusted and lived reasonably normally. Kohler concluded that upright vision could be achieved if the person moved about and touched objects in the environment and the more familiar the object was, the more easily this could be achieved. The fact that some had an

---

BOX 10.3   Key study: turning the world upside down

Stratton (1896) fitted himself with a telescope on one eye which 'turned the world upside down'. (The other eye was kept covered – if both eyes had worn telescopes it would have proved too much of a strain, especially to the eye movement muscles.) He wore the telescope for a total of 87 hours over an eight-day period; he wore blindfolds at night and at other times when not wearing the inverting lens. As far as possible, he went about his normal routine. For the first three days he was aware that part of his environment – the part not in his immediate field of vision but on the periphery – was in a different orientation. But by the fourth day he was beginning to imagine unseen parts as also being inverted and by the fifth day he had to make a conscious effort to remember that he actually had the telescope on. He was able to walk round the house without bumping into furniture and when he moved, his surroundings looked 'normal'; however, when he concentrated hard and remained still, things still appeared upside down. By the eighth day, everything seemed 'harmonious'; he began to 'feel' inverted but this was quite normal and natural to him.

When Stratton removed the telescope, he immediately recognized the visual orientation as the one that existed prior to the start of the experiment. He found it surprisingly bewildering, although definitely not upside-down. This absence of an inverted after-image or after-effect is quite a crucial finding: it means that Stratton had not actually learnt to see the world in an upside-down fashion, otherwise removal of the telescope would have caused the now normal (right way up) world to look upside-down again! Instead, it suggests that the adaptation took the form of learning the appropriate motor responses in an upside-down-looking world. (Compare this with the question of depth perception in Held and Hein's kittens.) Having said this, Stratton did experience an after-effect which caused things before him to 'swing and sweep' as he moved his eyes, showing that location constancy had been disrupted.

In another experiment, Stratton made goggles which visually displaced his body so that he always appeared horizontally in front of himself – wherever he walked he 'followed' his own body image, which was suspended at right angles to his actual body. When he lay down, his body would appear above him, vertically, again at right angles (Fig.10.3). After three days, he was able to go out for a walk on his own – and lived to tell the tale!

inverted after-effect when they removed the apparatus also suggests that the adaptation may actually be visual in nature and not simply sensorimotor. However, the after-effect lasted only for the first few minutes, which suggests that any purely perceptual learning that did occur was not very substantial.

The importance of moving about in the physical environment when adapting to a perceptually distorted world was confirmed by Held. Based on his work with the kitten carousel, he got one human participant to push another around on a trolley inside a large drum, while both wore goggles that shifted everything to one side. They both had identical visual experiences (as did the active and passive kitten) but the one who did the pushing made a faster and more efficient adjustment (as did the active kitten).

● What conclusions can we draw from adaptation studies ?

- It seems that when volunteers adapt to a distorted perceptual world, they are not, for the most part, actually learning to see 'normally' but are developing the appropriate motor behaviour which helps them to get around and function efficiently in their environment. What is learnt is not a new way of perceiving the world but a new set of body movements.
- The visual system, at least in adults, is extremely flexible and can adjust to distorted conditions. This strongly suggests that learning plays an important role in perceptual development, since a totally or largely innate system would not allow such adaptation to occur.
- Because the volunteers are adults, who have already undergone a great deal of learning and in whom maturation has already taken place, it is difficult to generalize from these studies to how babies develop under normal circumstances. Just because an adult is able to learn to perceive the world in a different way, we cannot automatically assume that babies originally have to learn to perceive the world as they do.

CROSS-CULTURAL STUDIES

As we noted earlier, these have mainly involved testing members of different cultural groups using the same test materials, usually visual illusions; two of the most commonly used have been the Müller-Lyer and the horizontal-vertical (see Chapter 9).

The pioneering study was carried out by Rivers *et al.* in 1901. They went to the Murray Islands, a group of islands situated in the Torres Straits (between New Guinea and Australia). Compared with English adults and children, the Murray Islanders were less prone to the Müller-Lyer. This was attributed to the fact that the natives limited their attention strictly to the task they were asked to perform (i.e. judge the length of the arrow shafts), while Europeans tended to regard the figure as a whole (including the arrowheads). By contrast, the horizontal-vertical illusion was more marked among the Murray Island men; this, together

FIGURE 10.3 *One of Stratton's experiments in which goggles displaced the wearer's body image at right angles*

BOX
10.4

The case of Susannah Fienues (Gilling and Brightwell, 1982)

Susannah Fienues, a young art student, wore inverted goggles (fitted with a prism as opposed to a lens) for a period of seven days. After first putting them on she reported:

The cars are going upside down. They're going the wrong way. It's all going completely the wrong way to what you'd expect. It's really strange.

After one hour, she reported:

... In fact, looking at people in cars was quite normal, I didn't think they were upside down, and I just got adjusted to it, I think. But the difficult thing is just walking and being very disorientated, because how you feel is completely different to what you're doing... As for things being upside down, it just doesn't feel like that at all because I know very well that I'm sitting here and so I think my brain still knows that, so it's all right.

Like Stratton, she at first had great difficulty in pouring milk from a jug into a glass. By the fourth day, she could walk without difficulty, even with poise, from the bedroom to the sitting room. And she could now pour the milk! She felt 'Just fine...I don't notice that things are upside down at all'. She could write her name normally but only if she closed her eyes and didn't see her hand as she wrote it. With her eyes open, she could write it so that it appeared normal to her but inverted to anyone else!

By seven days her early problems seemed to have vanished – she could ride her bike, walk, run, climb stairs, turn corners, make coffee and put records on. 'The only thing that's still quite difficult is eating and using a knife and fork.' Again:

... It's become more and more difficult to imagine myself standing upright or sitting down normally. I almost want to sit upside down because I can't quite imagine myself sitting normally.

This account supports the view of vision as an active process, enabling us to deal with the world. When Susannah removed the goggles, she was annoyed that nothing seemed any different! She reverted to normal vision within a few minutes, very relieved that the experiment was over. Like Stratton, she learnt to match her vision with signals reported by the rest of her body:

... She was not just seeing, but sampling the world as a whole with her senses, and organizing them so that they told stories which could be sensibly related to each other. She saw with her whole body, the whole apparatus of her senses, as it were, and not just with her eyes ...

with the pronounced character of the illusion in children, led Rivers to conclude that it was due to some physiological condition or, at least, to some simple and primitive psychological condition (Price-Williams, 1966).

Probably the largest study was that of Segall *et al* (1963), which is described in Box 10.5.

Another illusion that has been used in cross-cultural research, but less often than the other two, is the *rotating trapezoid*. This is attached to a motor and revolves in a circle. It has horizontal and vertical bars fixed to it to give the impression of a window (see Fig. 10.4.) Most Western observers report seeing a rectangle that oscillates to and fro, backwards and forwards, rather than a trapezoid revolving through 360° (which is what it actually is and does). This seems to be based on the assumption that it is a window (or window-type object). (This effect is reduced when it is viewed binocularly, i.e. with both eyes, rather than monocularly, i.e. with one eye closed; it is also reduced when the horizontal bars are removed.)

On the assumption that it is normally interpreted as a window by people who are used to seeing windows and who bring with them expectations of rectangularity, we might expect that people from cultures where windows (as we know them) are not an everyday sight might see the rotating trapezoid for what it is. One such cultural group are the Zulus, who not only do not have Western-style windows but tend to live in a rather circular environment. Allport and Pettigrew (1957) compared urban and rural Zulus with each other and with Europeans.

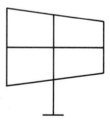

FIGURE 10.4 *The rotating trapezoid (as used by Allport and Pettigrew, 1957)*

Under optimal conditions (using one eye and further away) there were no differences between the three groups. But under less than optimal conditions (using both eyes and from a shorter distance) the rural Zulus – who live in the traditional circular culture – were less likely to perceive an oscillating rectangle than the other two groups and were more likely to perceive a rotating trapezoid.

BOX 10.5 Key study: cultural differences in the perception of geometric illusions

Segall *et al.* (1963) spent six years studying African children and adults and inhabitants of the Philippines, comparing them with each other as well as with South Africans of European descent and Americans from Illinois (in the American Mid-West). On the Müller-Lyer illusion, the Africans and Filipinos were much less susceptible than the other two groups, but there were some interesting results for the horizontal-vertical illusion.

Two of the African tribes studied, the Batoro and the Bayankole, were at the top end of the illusion scale, that is, they were most likely to see it. Both tribes live in high, open country where you can see for miles without 'interference'; hence, vertical objects, such as trees or mountains, become important focal points and are used to estimate distances.

A third tribe, the Bete, who live in a jungle environment, were at the bottom end of the scale – they were least likely of all the groups to see the illusion. Europeans and Americans tended to come somewhere in between the three African tribes.

The implication is that ecology, i.e. the physical environment which a cultural group occupies, is closely tied to the susceptibility of that group to visual illusions; as we shall see below, some psychologists believe that ecology actually determines susceptibility.

Stewart (1973) found that rural Tongan children were less likely to see the Ames distorted room than children living in the city of Lusaka (Zambia) and European children. She found the same differences for other illusions (including the Müller-Lyer) and, interestingly, the greater the exposure to a 'rectangular' environment, the greater the susceptibility to the Müller-Lyer illusion. How can we account for the differences?

One of the first attempts to explain the results of cross-cultural studies was Segall *et al.*'s (1966) carpentered world hypothesis. Referring to members of Western culture, they say:

> We live in a culture in which straight lines abound and in which perhaps ninety per cent of the acute and obtuse angles formed on our retina by the straight lines of our visual field are realistically interpretable as right angles extended in space.

What they are saying, in effect, is that we tend to interpret illusion figures, which are usually 2-D draw-

ings, in terms of our past experiences, so that in Western culture (which is a 'carpentered world') we add a third dimension (depth) which is not actually present in the drawing. This misleads us as to the true nature of the stimulus, resulting in what we call an illusion. This explanation is very similar to Gregory's (see Chapter 9). We are more or less likely to experience the illusion depending on what our cultural experience tells us the drawing could represent.

● An evaluation of the carpentered world hypothesis

Is there any evidence which does not support it? Mundy-Castle and Nelson (1962) studied the Knysma forest dwellers, a group of isolated, white, illiterate South Africans. Despite the rectangularity of their environment, they were unable to give appropriate 3-D responses to 2-D symbols on a standard test and on the Müller-Lyer figure their responses were not significantly different from non-Europeans, although they differed significantly from literate, white adults.

Jahoda (1966) compared the Lobi and Dagomba tribes of Ghana, who live in open parkland in round huts, with the Ashanti, who live in dense forest in roughly rectangular huts. The prediction that the Lobi and Dagomba would be significantly more susceptible to the horizontal-vertical while the Ashanti would be significantly more susceptible to the Müller-Lyer was not supported.

Finally, Gregor and McPherson (1965) found no significant differences between two groups of Australian aborigines on the two illusions, despite one group living in a relatively urbanized, carpentered environment and the other living primitively out of doors. However, both groups were significantly less prone to the Müller-Lyer than Europeans and more prone to the horizontal-vertical.

● The perception of pictures: is it a cultural phenomenon?

Based on the studies of Mundy-Castle and Nelson, Jahoda and Gregor and McPherson, it has been suggested that Segall *et al* exaggerated the influence of ecology on cultural differences in perception. Jahoda, for example, has stressed the importance of considering the possible effects of exposure to Western education and other cultural variables (which were largely overlooked in the Segall *et a.l* study). He believes that many of the findings may reflect the inability of some cultural groups to interpret 2-D drawings or other representations of the 3-D world, something which we take so much for granted because we encounter them from birth onwards. But it may be very difficult for people who are not familiar with them through a lifetime of exposure to interpret them in this way: the tendency to see pictures as depicting objects in the real world may itself be culturally determined.

It seems there are two separate processes involved when we 'read' pictures. Firstly, we must learn to make perceptual inferences about the real world (what is the picture of?) and secondly, we must learn the conventions which the picture-maker is using in order to assess the real world (for instance, all the depth cues, such as linear perspective, relative size and superimposition; see Chapter 9).

Cross-cultural research, mainly in Africa, shows that the interpretation of pictures is far from automatic; rather than an inborn ability, it is a skill of considerable complexity. Three very famous studies seem to lend support to this view – the first indirectly (see Box 10.6) , the second two directly.

Deregowski (1972) refers to a description given by a Mrs Fraser (who taught health care to Africans in the 1920s) of an African woman slowly discovering that a picture she was looking at portrayed a human head in profile:

> She discovered in turn the nose, the mouth, the eye, but where was the other eye? I tried by turning my profile to explain why she could see only one eye, but she hopped round to my other side to point out that I possessed a second eye which the other lacked.

The woman was treating the picture as an object rather than as a 2-D representation of an object – she had not learnt to 'infer' the depth in the picture, i.e. the parts that were not immediately visible (which clearly she could do when looking at a real face). Her 'object' turned out to have only two dimensions and this is what she found bewildering.

Hudson (1960) used a series of pictures depicting hunting scenes (two of which are shown in Fig. 10.5). They have been used in many parts of Africa with participants drawn from a variety of tribal and linguistic groups. They were shown one picture at a time and asked to name all the objects in the picture in order to determine whether or not the elements were correctly recognized. Then they were asked about the relationship between the objects – 'What is the man doing?', 'What is closer to the man?' and so on. If participants take note of the depth cues and make the 'correct' interpretations, they are classified as having 3-D depth perception; if not, they are judged to

---

BOX 10.6   Key study: Size constancy is a relative thing; or, confusing your buffalo with your insects.

Turnbull (1961) studied the Bambuti pygmies, who live in the dense rainforests of the Congo, a closed-in world without open spaces. Turnbull brought a pygmy out to a vast plain where a herd of buffalo was grazing in the distance. The pygmy said he had never seen one of those insects before; when told they were buffalo, he was offended and Turnbull was accused of insulting his intelligence. Turnbull drove the jeep towards the buffalo; the pygmy's eyes widened in amazement as he saw the insects 'grow' into buffalo before him. He concluded that witchcraft was being used to deceive him.

This is a good illustration of lack of *size constancy*, an important cue we use to 'read' pictures. The sight of the buffalo from such a distance was so far removed from the pygmy's experience that he could only believe that they were small animals (insects) rather than much larger ones (buffalo) which only looked smaller (by virtue of the small retinal image produced by large objects viewed from a distance). He could not apply size constancy for such great distances (but presumably he could for shorter ones) and if he could be deceived in this way when looking at real, live buffalo, how much more insulted would he have felt if he had been shown a photograph of the same scene? Directly relevant to this question is the study by Deregowski (1972).

---

have 2-D perception. According to Deregowski (1972), '... The results from African tribal subjects were unequivocal: both children and adults found it difficult to perceive depth in the pictorial material. The difficulty varied in extent but appeared to persist through most educational and social levels.'

However, it may not be a simple matter of cultural differences in the ability to identify 2-D pictorial representations of the 3-D world but also the conditions under which people from different cultural groups are asked to recognize things depicted in pictures. There seem to be three important questions we should ask about such studies (Gross, 1994):

1 Do these studies make it difficult for people from non-Western cultures to give 'correct' responses?

2 Could it be that the drawings used in some of these studies emphasize certain depth cues while ignoring others, thus putting non-Western perceivers at a double disadvantage?

FIGURE 10.5 *Pictorial depth perception is tested by showing participants a picture such as the left-hand illustration. A correct interpretation is that the hunter is trying to spear the antelope which is nearer to him than the elephant. An incorrect interpretation is that the elephant is nearer and is about to be speared. The picture contains two depth cues: overlapping objects and known size of objects. The right-hand illustration depicts the man, elephant and antelope in true size ratios when all are the same distance from the observer. (From Hudson, 1960)*

3 Is it also possible that what is taken as a difference in perception is really a matter of stylistic preference?

To answer (1), Deregowski *et al.* (1972) studied the Me'en tribe of Ethiopia, who live in a remote area still largely unaffected by Western culture. When members of the tribe were shown drawings of animals, they responsed by feeling, smelling, tasting or rustling the paper, showing no interest in the visual content of the picture itself. However, when the unfamiliar paper was replaced by pictures painted on (familiar) cloth, they responded to the drawing of the animal. These animals were 30 cm high (compared with only 5 cm on the paper) and, without exception, despite almost certainly not having seen a picture before, seven out of ten correctly identified the first cloth picture as a buck and ten out of ten identified the second as a leopard. As Serpell (1976) says:

> Given a sufficiently salient stimulus, with distracting cues removed such as the novelty of paper or the distinct white band of the border, immediate recognition may be possible simply by stimulus generalization, one of the most basic characteristics of learning.

At the same time, several participants misidentified the buck and leopard as other four-legged animals and, in some cases, recognition seems to have been built up gradually, by helping them to trace the outline of the animal with a finger.

Under optimal conditions, pictures do seem to be recognizable without any prior learning; unlike words, most pictures are not entirely arbitrary representations of the real world – their arbitrariness '... lies in what features they choose to stress and what features to leave out and it is these conventions governing this choice which the experienced picture perceiver must learn' (Serpell, 1976).

In answer to (2), one of the things the experienced picture perceiver has learned is the Western artist's use of relative size to represent distance. So, in Hudson's pictures a major cue to the relationship between the man, elephant and antelope is their relative size against the background knowledge of their normal sizes. Hudson also uses the cues of overlap (or superimposition) and linear perspective (see Chapter 9), e.g. in one drawing the elephant and a tree were shown near the apex of a pair of converging straight lines representing a road. Since the laws of perspective were a late discovery in European art (Gombrich, 1960) and the assumption of parallel edges to a road is promoted by a 'carpentered' environment, it is not too surprising that African children seldom understand this cue. Hudson (1960) found overlap (if noticed) to be the most effective of his three cues.

But there is also a contradiction between these depth cues and others in the real world, namely

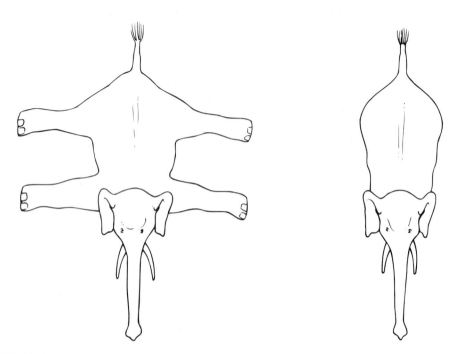

FIGURE 10.6 *The split-elephant drawing (left) was generally preferred by African children and adults to the top-view perspective drawing (right). One person, however, did not like the split drawing because he thought the elephant was jumping around in a dangerous manner. (From Deregowski, 1972)*

binocular disparity and motion parallax, both of which are missing from Hudson's pictures (and, indeed, from all pictures). Also missing is gradient of density (or texture gradient). Serpell (1976) refers to an unpublished report by Kingsley *et al.* in which an artist redrew one of Hudson's pictures adding pebbles to the road and grass in open terrain, each surface showing a gradient of density, while everything else remained unchanged. Twelve-year-old Zambian children gave 64% 3-D answers under these conditions compared with 54% on Hudson's original. When colour and haze around distant hills, etc. were added, the figure rose to 76%.

According to Berry *et al.* (1992), texture gradient is a powerful depth cue in photographs but is hardly ever used in stimulus material in cross-cultural studies. To the first-time observer, these pictures, therefore, may display unusual qualities. Another depth cue missing from Hudson's pictures is height in the horizontal plane (or elevation). McGurk and Jahoda (1975, cited in Berry *et al.*, 1992) used a test in which elevation was the crucial cue. Using non-verbal responses, participants are asked to place models of people on a response board in similar positions to those occupied by the figures in the stimulus pictures. Using this method, even four-year-olds from Ghana, Hong Kong and Zimbabwe showed evidence of depth perception. All this points to the original Hudson pictures making the perception of depth difficult for non-Western people.

In answer to (3), much of the research seems to imply a belief that the Western style of pictorial art represents the real world in an objectively correct fashion; by implication, the person who does not understand it is 'deficient' in some way. But since 'artistic excellence' is not identical with 'photographic accuracy' (Gombrich 1960), Serpell (1976) asks if it may be possible that members of different cultures 'reject' Western art forms on aesthetic grounds and that all the research has mistakenly described a stylistic preference as a difference in perception.

Hudson (1962) and Deregowski (1969b, 1970) found that Africans with limited Western education slightly preferred unfolded, 'split', 'developed' or 'chain-type' drawings (Fig. 10.6 (left)) to 'orthogonal' or perspective drawings (as in Fig. 10.6 (right)). Why? Often it is because the latter fails to show some of the important features (recall the African woman shown the photograph by Mrs Fraser).

The importance of artistic convention increases the more symbolic and abstract the art is – the convention is part of the fund of common experience shared by the artist and the audience. Duncan *et al.*

(1973) point out that the small lines used by cartoonists to imply motion are the least understood of all the pictorial conventions which have been shown to rural African schoolchildren. And where the artist had drawn a boy's head in three different positions above the same trunk to indicate the head was turning around, half the children thought he was deformed.

Likewise, Western observers require guidance from an anthropologist to understand the art forms of American Indians (Boas, 1927) (see Fig. 10.7).

FIGURE 10.7 *Stylized bear rendered by the Tsimshian Indians on the Pacific coast of British Columbia is an example of split drawing developed to a high artistic level. According to anthropologist Franz Boas, the drawings are ornamental and not intended to convey what an object looks like. The elements represent specific characteristics of the object. (From Deregowski, 1972)*

STUDIES OF HUMAN INFANTS

As we noted before, studies on human infants represent the most direct way of trying to settle the nature-nurture issue. However, the fact that the baby cannot tell us what it sees and hears presents problems of its own, the most important being that the investigator has to *infer* what the baby perceives; we can never be sure that the inference is correct.

Again, if newborns do not show a particular ability this does not necessarily mean that such abilities have to be learnt – they may develop some time after birth through the action of genetic 'time switches' involved in the process of maturation. The general rule is that the earlier an ability appears, the more likely it is to be genetically controlled and not the result of learning.

Clearly, perception is not a single ability but a series of abilities. Vision (which has been the most widely studied sense modality in babies, as it has in general; see Chapters 8 and 9) involves perception of colour, shape, size, depth, movement, etc. Some of these may be largely innate, while others may be largely due to the effects of experience. We must be specific about which aspect of perception we are talking about when trying to establish to what extent, and in what ways, genetic and environmental factors have their influence.

● Asking the right questions

In 1890, William James wrote 'The baby, assailed by eyes, ears, nose, skin and entrails at once, feels it all as one great booming, buzzing confusion'.

Until quite recently, many people (including psychologists) agreed with James that the baby's perception of the world is hazy, poorly defined, unstructured, even chaotic. Many have gone so far as to believe that babies are born blind. But studies of newborns in the last 20 years or so have taught us that to ask 'Can the baby see or not, or hear or not?' is the wrong kind of question. Instead, we should ask 'What and how well can the baby see and hear?'.

● Methods used to study infant perception

Psychologists make inferences about infants' perception in two ways: firstly, by looking at what the baby *possesses* by way of sensory equipment (its structural and physical attributes) and secondly, by observing what the baby *does* (including physiological changes in the presence of various stimuli). In both cases we ask 'What is the baby likely to be seeing or hearing?' and 'How soon can particular abilities be expected, or seem to, develop?'.

A general and widely used method is to present two stimuli simultaneously. If the infant spends more time looking at one than the other, then it is inferred that (i) it can actually tell the difference (discriminate) between them; and (ii) that it prefers the one it looks at longer. This is called the *spontaneous visual preference technique* (or preferential looking). The same basic technique has been used to study other modalities, including taste and smell.

For example, Steiner (1977, 1979) studied newborns' differential responses to tastes and smells by their facial expressions. The psychophysical evidence is compelling that four basic qualities together make up taste experience, namely sweet, salt, sour and bitter. Steiner systematically gave the newborns sweet, sour and bitter substances and photographed their 'gustofacial' responses. Sweet produced expressions of 'satisfaction', often accompanied by a slight smile and sucking movements. Sour produced lip pursing, often accompanied by or followed by nose wrinkling and eye blinking. Bitter produced expressions of dislike and disgust and rejection, often followed by spitting or even prevomiting movements.

Cernoch and Porter (1985) compared breastfed babies with bottlefed babies, 12–18 days old, for olfactory recognition of their mother, father and a stranger. They were photographed while exposed to pairs of gauze pads worn under the arm by each of the adults the previous night. Only breastfeeding babies showed a clear preference for their own mother's scent, no baby recognized its father's scent and nor did the bottlefed recognize their mother's. (Mothers can recognize their baby's scents after 1–2 days.)

Another method involves reflecting light on the cornea to monitor the baby's vision and then filming the reflection of the cornea. This gives the researcher a more precise reading of what the baby is looking at than is possible from simply noting the orientation of the head or the general direction of the gaze (as in the first method).

Another approach is to measure the baby's *sucking rate,* via a dummy or pacifier, as a response to different stimuli. A baseline rate is recorded before the stimulus is presented (i.e. the baby's normal or spontaneous sucking rate). When the stimulus is presented, the baby at first tends to suck noticeably slower or faster but after a while *habituation* sets in (that is, the baby stops responding to it as a novel stimulus) and a return to the baseline rate occurs. The stimulus is then changed in some way and if there is another increase or decrease in sucking rate, it is inferred that the baby can tell the difference – it is responding to the change as a novel stimulus.

Habituation is used as a method in its own right and has been used to study perception in every modality. It presumably reflects two components: (i) the baby's developing mental representation of a stimulus and (ii) the continuing comparison of whatever stimulus is present with that representation. If an external stimulus and a mental representation match, the baby 'knows' the stimulus, so there is little reason for it to continue looking. But mismatches maintain the baby's attention, so that a novel (and discriminable) test stimulus presented after habituation to a familiar one typically re-excites attention. This method has been used especially to study the perception of form, orientation, location, movement and colour (Bornstein, 1988).

Conditioned head rotation involves the baby sitting on its (usually) mother's lap. On one side is a loudspeaker and when a tone or speech syllable is played through the speaker and the baby responds by orienting towards it, it receives a positive reinforcement in the form of a colourful mechanical toy which appears just above the speaker. This method can help measure the development of several abilities basic to sound perception, such as detection of sounds of different frequencies, localization of sound in space and response to complex sounds which specify speech (Bornstein, 1988).

A sixth method is to attach a dummy or nipple to audiovisual equipment so that when the baby sucks, a tape-recording is switched on or an image projected onto a screen can be brought into sharper focus the harder the baby sucks.

Two important physiological measures are the baby's heart rate and breathing rate – a decrease in these is usually taken to indicate that something has caught the baby's attention.

According to Bornstein (1988), conditioned head rotation and habituation are less ambiguous than some of the other methods, such as preferential looking, because they '... draw even more actively on definitive behavioural acts ...' and for this reason are currently among the most widely used methods. They can all be considered as measures of the baby's behaviour, from which we then infer what the baby is likely to be perceiving. A more direct approach is to study the baby's visual apparatus.

● What visual equipment do babies possess?

We know that the nervous system as a whole is still immature (as we might expect). The optic nerve is thinner and shorter than an adult's and is only partially myelinated (insulated by a myelin sheath), so that visual information is transmitted inefficiently to an equally undeveloped cortex for interpretation. However, myelination is complete by about four months after birth. (Without myelination of the optic nerve, we could probably only see diffuse flashes of light.)

The human eye at birth is about half the size and weight of an adult's; the eyeball is shorter and this reduces the distance between the retina and the lens, making vision less efficient. However, the newborn's eyeball is anatomically identical to the adult's – all the parts are there but their relationship to each other is different and they do not all develop at the same rate.

Perceiving colour

According to Bornstein (1988), studying colour presents formidable technical problems, one of them being the fact that colour (hue) and brightness covary; clearly each must be controlled in order to study the other. Adults, at least, can be asked to match brightness.

Bornstein (1976) used a habituation technique with three-month-olds and found they could discriminate blue-green from white and yellow from green (these tests are normally failed by red-green 'colour-blind' people). These findings have been confirmed in a number of studies. Bornstein sums up their findings by saying that '... infants one month and certainly two months of age and older are known to possess largely normal colour vision, based on their discrimination of colour stimuli in the absence of brightness cues' (Bornstein, 1988).

The retina and the rods and cones are all fairly well developed at birth, so the basis for colour vision is present in the newborn. (These two kinds of retinal cells become differentiated by the seventh month of pregnancy at the latest.)

Perceiving brightness

The fovea (which is packed with cones and thus provides the clearest image of an object when viewed in daylight or other bright light) is fairly well developed at birth; by four months after conception it has become structurally differentiated.

We know that babies react to bright light while still in the womb – if a bright light is shone on a pregnant woman's belly, the baby may move towards it. (Perhaps some of the baby's movements in the womb, known as 'quickening', which usually begin around the fourth month, stem from this attraction to light.) Also, the pupillary reflex (a response to bright light whereby the pupil contracts, thus reducing the amount of light that enters the eye) is present even in premature babies. Similarly, the blink reflex to bright light is present at birth. According to Bornstein (1988), a baby's sensitivity to brightness is reasonably similar to an adult's.

Perception of movement

The ability to follow a moving stimulus depends upon a reflex called the *optokinetic reflex* (or *optic nystagmus*), which consists of a series of back-and-forth eye movements called visual saccades (you can spot them if you watch the eyes of somebody who is reading; see Chapter 8). This reflex is present soon after birth; for instance, within 48 hours of birth, babies can track a slowly moving object. It is only about half as efficient as an adult's at this time, but it improves rapidly during the next three months.

If a series of fine, vertical stripes is passed across the baby's field of vision, they will produce visual saccades; if the stripes are made finer and finer (so that eventually they appear grey) the saccades stop. Babies are more successful at tracking horizontal than vertical movement but even then it will be jerky – they refixate often, gazing at the moving object and then shifting their gaze to a different spot. One possible reason for this jerkiness is that *convergence* is absent at birth, although it usually appears two days after birth and is fully developed by 2–3 months. Convergence is essential for fixation and depth perception (see Chapter 9).

Also essential for efficient vision is *accommodation*. At birth, the eye operates rather like a fixed-focus camera, that is, the baby only sees clear-cut images of objects that are about 20 cm from its face and anything nearer or further will tend to look blurred. There is no real accommodation at all at first, which is due to the immaturity and weakness of the ciliary muscles which focus the lens by changing its shape. Conveniently, however, 20 cm is approximately the distance between the baby's face and the face of the person feeding it, which gives the baby plenty of opportunity to examine the adult face and become familiar with it. By two months, the baby is beginning to accommodate to the distance of objects and by four months the ability to accommodate has reached adult standards. This improvement, like many of the others we have noted above, seems to be very largely due to maturation.

Visual acuity

Related to the ability to see clear, well-defined images is the efficiency of the baby's vision. The newborn's visual acuity is about 30 times poorer than in the adult but despite this imperfect vision, the baby likes to see an image in as clear a way as possible. Kalnins and Bruner (1973) found that babies 1–3 months old will learn to operate the focus on a projector in order to make the picture clearer; the focus was connected directly to a nipple and was arranged so that appropriate sucking rates would bring the blurred picture into focus. The babies also looked less at an out-of-focus image than at a clear-cut image.

Visual acuity improves rapidly during the first 4–6 months and between six and 12 months will come within adult ranges. It may not reach 20:20 until ten or 11 years of age and there are important individual differences as to the eventual attainment of 20:20 vision.

A method of investigating acuity is through *visually-evoked potentials* (VEPs). Electrodes are attached to the scalp, above the visual cortex, and a visual stimulus is presented. If the electrical activity changes, then the baby is judged to be perceiving the stimulus. There is evidence that VEPs exist in newborns, showing that some degree of acuity is present then (see Chapter 3).

● What babies do

Perceiving pattern or form

Fantz (1961) presented 30 babies, aged 1–15 weeks, with a variety of stimuli and used the time spent looking at each of these as an index of the baby's visual preferences. They were shown, at weekly intervals, pairs of stimuli comprising: bullseyes, horizontal stripes, checkerboards, two sizes of plain square, a cross, a circle and two triangles (of the same area; Fig. 10.8). There was a distinct preference, at all ages, for the bullseye over the stripes and for the checkerboard over the plain square. The bullseye was most looked at of all the stimuli and next most popular was the checkerboard.

So there seems to be a very early, if not inborn, preference for more complex over less complex stimuli, that is, stimuli which contain more information and in which there is more 'going on'. However, this preference for complexity also seems to be a function of age. Fantz's babies, tested weekly, were presented with progressively narrower stripes and as they got older they could distinguish targets with narrower and narrower stripes.

Other researchers have also found this preference for complexity as a function of age. In another experiment, Fantz (1961) showed that babies 2–4 months old prefer patterns to colour or brightness. Six discs

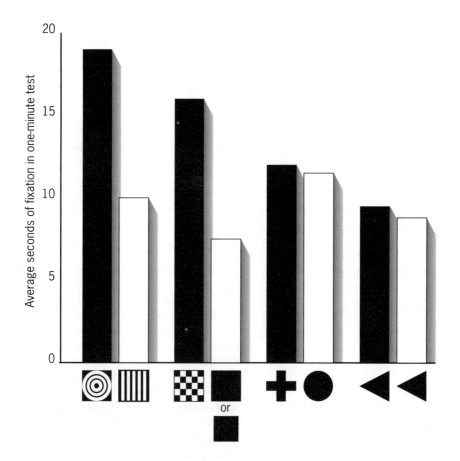

FIGURE 10.8 *The bars indicate looking time for each of the stimulus patterns presented in pairs. (From Fantz, 1961)*

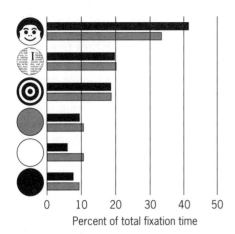

Percent of total fixation time

FIGURE 10.9 *The upper bar of each pair indicates looking time for 2–3-month-olds, the lower bar for babies of four months old. (From Fantz, 1961)*

BOX 10.7

Key study: does shape perception change in the first few months?

Slater and Morison (1987) wanted to know if infants who are made familiar with a number of different instances (*exemplars*) of the same shape (triangle, square, cross, circle) would extract the overall shape and learn to disregard the changes to the parts of the stimulus. If so, they should show a novelty preference when a different exemplar of the same shape is paired on postfamiliarization trials with an exemplar of a different shape (i.e. they should respond to the latter as a novel stimulus, but show no response to the former).

During the familiarization phase, each newborn and 3–5-month-old saw six exemplars of one stimulus shape, followed by two postfamiliarization trials (paired presentation of a different exemplar of the familiar shape and a novel shape). The newborns did not show a preference for the novel shape but the 3–5-month-olds did (the difference was statistically significant):

> ... During the first two months infants can discriminate between shapes, but they probably do so on the basis of differences in lower-order variables, such as orientation, contrast ... and so on. Shortly after this something like true form perception begins and infants respond to higher-order variables ... such as configurational invariance and form categories. (Slater, 1989)

---

were shown: one was plain red, one plain white and one plain yellow, the others were a face, printed matter and a bullseye. At all ages there was a preference for the face over either the printed matter or the bullseye and all three were preferred to the plain discs (Fig. 10.9).

The preference for increasing complexity seems to indicate that the capacity for differentiation steadily improves, possibly because the ability to scan becomes more efficient and thorough. Studies of eye movements give precise indications of what babies are looking at. At first, when a baby finds a stimulus interesting, it continues to scan it but it tends to limit itself to the focus of interest; for example, Salapatek (1975) found that very young infants confine their scanning to one corner of a triangle which seems to indicate a preference for areas of greatest contrast. (Another example is the eyes and hairline of the face.) Only later does the baby begin to explore all around the stimulus and inside it (e.g. all corners of the triangle or the nose and mouth of a face), i.e. the baby now attends to the whole pattern and not just to specific parts.

An experiment suggesting a change in how form is perceived in early infancy was conducted by Slater and Morison (1987; cited by Slater, 1989) and is described in Box 10.7.

The perception of 'facedness'

It is generally agreed that the human face is probably the most interesting and attractive stimulus experienced by the baby – it is three-dimensional, contains high-contrast information (particularly the eyes, mouth and hairline), is constantly moving (eyes, mouth, head), is a source of auditory stimulation (voice) and regulates its behaviour according to the baby's own activities. So it neatly combines all the stimulus dimensions which babies seem to (innately) prefer (complexity, pattern, movement, etc.). However, does the baby gradually come to prefer faces because they contain all these preferred elements or is there an inborn predisposition to respond to the face *as a face,* an innate perceptual knowledge of the face?

Fantz takes the latter view. In a famous study (1961), he presented four-day-olds to six-month-olds with all possible pairs of three stimuli, which were black against a pink background and the approximate shape and size of an adult's head (Fig. 10.10). At all age levels, infants looked more at the schematic representation (a) than they did at the scrambled face (b), while the control stimulus (c)

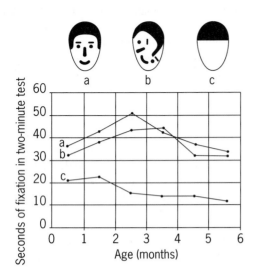

FIGURE 10.10 *Looking time for each of three facelike stimuli. (From Fantz, 1961)*

was largely ignored. Even though the difference in the time spent looking at (a) and (b) was slight, Fantz concluded that 'There is an unlearned, primitive meaning in the form perception of infants', such that there is an innate preference for facedness.

However, Hershenson *et al.* (1965) pointed out that (a) and (b) are both more complex than (c) and that may account for their preference over (c), as opposed to their resemblance to human faces. So they presented newborns with all possible pairs of three equally complex stimuli:

1 a real female face;
2 a distorted picture, which retained the outline of head and hair but altered the position of the other features;
3 a scrambled face, as in Fantz's experiment (stimulus (b)).

They found no preference for any of these three and concluded that a preference for real faces is not inborn and usually does not appear until about four months of age.

More recently, Kleiner (1987) compared newborns' and two-month-olds' preferences between two-dimensional facelike patterns and abstract patterns and found a clear age difference. Newborns preferred the abstract patterns, while two-month-olds preferred the facelike patterns, the former containing greater contrast. Similar results have been found for six-week-olds and three-month-olds.

Melhuish (1982) showed pictures of the mother's face and female strangers' faces to one-month-olds, one at a time for 30 seconds at a time. Although there was no preference for the mother's face, the infants did look longest at the faces with the highest contrast. Although infants as young as five weeks may be able to discriminate between the photographed face of their mother and a female stranger, it seems that this is based on the outer boundary of the face (hair-face outline), with internal features becoming important only from 45 months.

But what happens if the facelike stimuli are equated for contrast or in other ways contrast is made irrelevant to the responses and discriminations required? As Slater (1989) points out, people are so important to the infant that it would not be surprising to find that neonates learn quickly to discriminate between them and there is a great deal of evidence that this is so. As we saw earlier, 2-3-week-old breastfed babies recognize their mother's breast odour and very quickly show a preference for the mother's voice compared with that of a female stranger (Lipsitt, 1977).

Bushnell and Sai (1987, cited in Slater, 1989) showed newborns their mother's (live) face and the face of a female stranger (matched for overall brightness of face and hair colour). There was a clear preference for the mother's face, indicating a quickly learned visual preference (the babies' mean age was two days, five hours).

But is there any evidence of a *specific* response to the human face (as opposed to a more general learning ability)? Slater (1989) cites a study in which newborns less than an hour old turned their heads and eyes significantly more to track a 2-D schematic facelike stimulus than to track a 'scrambled face', which in turn was preferred to a blank face with no internal detail (thus supporting Fantz's early findings). Other studies have shown that babies as young as 2-3 months old show a preference for slides of female faces judged by adults as attractive compared with less attractive faces. Could there be an unlearned aesthetic appreciation of faces (Slater, 1989)?

Instead of taking the view that there is a genetically-determined preference for the human face as such, Rheingold (1961) believes that infants develop a selective responsiveness to it (and things that resemble it) as it embodies all the stimulus dimensions that babies seem, innately, to prefer, conveniently 'packaged' in a very attractive and stimulating form. For this reason, she calls the human face a supernormal stimulus. However:

... a growing body of converging evidence – early learning of and preference for the mother's face, visual following of facelike stimuli, imitation of facial gestures, aesthetic perception of faces – gives strong support to the claim that the human face has special, species-specific visual significance for the infant from birth onwards. (Slater, 1989)

Perceiving depth

This has been one of the most researched aspects of infant perception and has perhaps become the focus for the heredity-environment issue. If babies can perceive depth at birth or very soon afterwards, this suggests that the ability is genetically determined; the earlier it develops, the more likely it is that learning does not play a very important role.

It has been investigated in rather different ways but probably the most famous study, and one of the earliest, was carried out by Gibson and Walk (1960) using the *visual cliff apparatus*. As you can see from Figure 10.11, this consists of a central platform, on one side of which is a sheet of plate glass and immediately below this a black and white checkerboard design (the 'shallow side'). On the other side is another sheet of plate glass, this time with the checkerboard design placed on the floor, a distance of about four feet, giving the appearance of a drop or 'cliff' (the' deep side'). The baby is placed on the central platform and its mother calls to it and beckons it, first from one side, then from the other.

Gibson and Walk used babies aged 6–14 months; most would not crawl onto the 'deep side' and this was interpreted as indicating depth perception (that is, they perceived the visual cliff or apparent drop and therefore did not venture onto it). The few who did (either by backing onto it or resting one foot on it for support) did so 'accidentally' – their poor motor control was responsible rather than their inability to perceive depth.

But can we be sure that a baby old enough to crawl has not *learnt* to perceive depth? Gibson and Walk took their findings as strong support for the view that depth perception is (probably) inborn, but since they only used babies who could already crawl, we cannot be certain how early this ability normally appears. They also tested other species on the visual cliff and found supporting evidence. Chicks less than one day old never hopped down onto the deep side; goat kids and lambs, tested as soon as they could stand, also avoided it; rats, if they could feel the glass with their very sensitive whiskers, stepped down on either side; and four-week-old kittens avoided the deep side unless they were reared in the dark (in which case they tended to fall down on either side). If forcibly placed on the deep side, these young animals would 'freeze'. An interesting alternative to crawling as a measure of depth perception in infants was conducted by Campos *et a.l* (1970) (see Box 10.8).

Another way of investigating depth perception is to observe how babies react when an object approaches their faces from a distance. Bower *et a.l* (1970) found that babies just 20 days old show an *integrated avoidance response*, i.e. they throw back

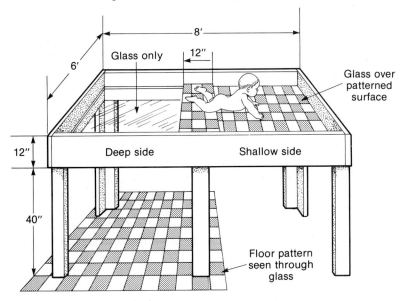

FIGURE 10.11 *The visual cliff. (From Dworetzky, 1981)*

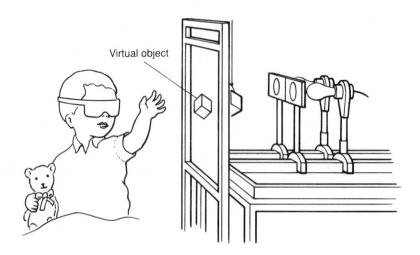

Virtual object

FIGURE 10.12 *A baby wearing polarizing goggles attempts to grasp a virtual intangible object in front of the screen (Bower, 1979). (From Barnes-Gutteridge, 1974)*

BOX 10.8	Key study: using heart rate as an indirect measure of depth perception

Campos *et al.* (1970) studied two-, three-and-a-half- and five-month-olds and they used heart rate as the index of depth perception. Even the youngest showed a drop in heart rate, showing interest, when placed on the deep side; they were also less likely to cry and were more attentive to what was underneath them and they clearly were not frightened by what they saw. There were no such changes when they were placed on the shallow side. Therefore it seems that even two-month-olds can perceive depth and that avoidance behaviour is probably learnt (perhaps after the baby has had a few experiences of falling).

their head, shield their face with their hands and even cry, indicating some very early depth perception. If a large box is moved towards the baby's face, from the visual information that the box is getting larger it seems to understand that it is getting closer and would be harmful and, accordingly, puts its arm in front of its face to protect itself. (This occurs even with one eye closed but not when equivalent pictures were seen on a screen, showing that motion parallax is the critical cue for distance.)

To underline the importance (and inseparability) of heredity and environment, Bornstein (1988) concludes his review of studies of depth perception by saying: '... No matter how early in life depth perception can be demonstrated, the ability still rests on some experience; no matter how late its emergence, it can never be proved that only experience has mattered'.

Perceiving 3-D objects

The Bower *et al.* study of the integrated avoidance response, as well as demonstrating depth perception, also suggests that the baby sees the box as a solid, 3-D object and Bower (1979) investigated this hypothesis by presenting 'solid' objects which were not solid at all but illusions of 3-D objects created by using special polarizing filters and goggles. Babies aged 16–24 weeks old are sat in front of a screen. A plastic, translucent object is suspended between lights and the screen so it casts a double shadow on the back; when the screen is viewed from the front, using polarizing goggles, these double shadows merge to form the image of a single 3-D object (Fig. 10.12).

None of the babies showed any surprise when they grasped the real, solid objects but when they reached for the apparent objects and discovered there was nothing solid to get hold of, they all expressed surprise and some even showed distress. Clearly, they expected to be able to touch what they could 'see'. Bower believes that this ability is innate.

Perceptual organization: the visual constancies and Gestalt principles

Perceptual constancy represents a major form of organization which seems to be a necessary prerequisite for many other types of organization (see Chapter 9). Empiricists would argue that constancy is learned and that babies and young children are likely to be 'tricked' by the appearance of things – if something looks smaller, for example (it projects a smaller retinal image), then it *is* smaller. Nativists, on the other hand, would claim that, like all perceptual abilities, constancy is innate so that the baby can judge the size of an object regardless of the retinal image produced by the object.

Bower (1966) tested these two opposing hypotheses experimentally. Initially, he trained two-month-olds to turn their heads at the sight of a 30 cm cube at a distance of 1 metre (when they turned their heads in the desired direction, an adult popped up in front of the baby and cried 'peek-a-boo', a very powerful positive reinforcer for babies). When they were looking at the cube consistently, it was replaced by: (i) a 30 cm cube at a distance of 3 metres (this would produce a retinal image one-third the size of the original); (ii) a 90 cm cube at a distance of 1 metre (this would produce a retinal image three times the size of the original); or (iii) a 90 cm cube at a distance of 3 metres (this would produce exactly the same sized image as the original; Fig. 10.13).

How often the baby turned its head towards each of these three cubes could be used as a measure of how similar to the original the baby considered it to be; i.e. if the baby generalized its head-turning response mainly to (i), this would be evidence for size constancy. This is what the nativists predict: the baby will respond to the actual size of the cube, regardless of distance. If the head-turning response generalized mainly to (iii), this would be evidence for lack of size constancy: as predicted by the empiricists, the baby at first would 'compare' retinal images and base its perception of similarity on these, regardless of distance.

What Bower found was that, compared with 98 head-turns produced by the original cube, (i) produced 58, (ii) produced 54 and (iii) produced 22.

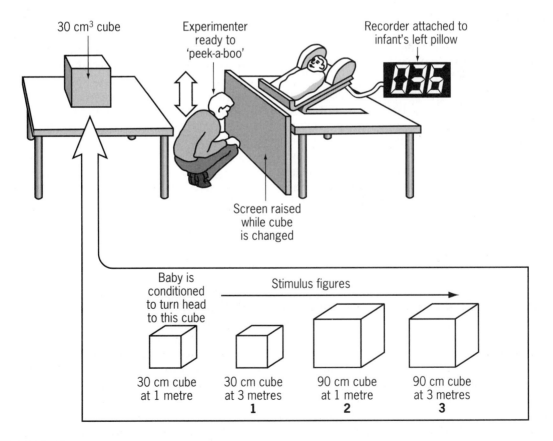

FIGURE 10.13 *Bower's 'peek-a-boo' experiment*

This seems to represent clear support for the nativists: babies responded most to the cube of the same size, regardless of distance, next came the cube the same distance away as the original but of a different size and last of all came the cube of a different size and distance, but giving the same retinal image as the original. It is the difference between (i) and (iii) which constitutes the critical findings.

More recent studies, using recovery from habituation as an index of size constancy, have confirmed that the ability to perceive the true size of an object is present by 18 weeks (Slater, 1989). Using a similar procedure to the one described above for size constancy, Bower (1966) studied *shape constancy*. If a two-month-old was trained to turn its head to look at a rectangle, it would continue to do so when the same rectangle was turned slightly (to produce a trapezoid retinal image).

Slater (1989) refers to studies which suggest that newborns are able to extract the constant real shape of an object that is rotated in the third dimension, i.e. they can recognize an object form independently of (transformations in) its orientation in space (shape constancy). Bornstein (1988), after reviewing recent studies of both shape and size constancy, concludes that '...babies still only in the first year of life can perceive form qua form'. Other perceptual constancies include feature, identity and existence.

Feature constancy is the ability to recognize the invariant features of a stimulus despite some detectable but irrelevant transformations – and this ability is present at birth. If newborns have been habituated to a moving stimulus, they will show a novelty preference when shown the same stimulus paired with a novel shape, both of which are stationary (i.e. they respond to the new shape, showing that they perceive the familiar stationary stimulus as the same stimulus as when it was moving).

Feature constancy is a necessary prerequisite for *identity constancy*, the ability to recognize a particular object as being exactly the same object despite some transformation. But how could we distinguish empirically between identity constancy and (mere) feature constancy?

A study which perhaps comes closest to demonstrating identity constancy is one by Bower (1971) in which babies were seated in front of mirrors which could produce several images of the mother. Babies below 20 weeks old smiled, cooed and waved their arms to each of the 'multiple mothers', whereas older babies became quite upset at seeing more than one mother. This suggests that it is only the older babies

who are aware that they have only one mother and can therefore be said to have identity constancy.

Existence constancy refers to the belief that objects continue to exist even when they are no longer available to the senses, what Piaget called *object permanence* (see Chapter 25). Together, existence and identity constancy comprise the *object concept*, which may appear around the middle of the first year rather than earlier. They are both more sophisticated than shape and size and feature constancies – the object concept may arise out of these 'basic' constancies.

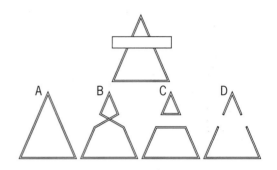

FIGURE 10.14 *The stimulus figures used in Bower's study of closure. (After Bower, 1977)*

Bower was also interested in how the infant's perception is organized in terms of certain Gestalt principles (see Chapter 9). He wanted to find out if closure is an inborn characteristic (as the Gestalt psychologists claim) by training two-month-olds to respond to a black wire triangle with a black iron bar across it and then presenting them with four triangle stimuli (Fig. 10.14). The fact that they generalized their response to a complete triangle suggests that they 'understood' that underneath the black iron bar lay a complete, unbroken triangle and given that they were unlikely to have encountered many triangular stimuli in their lifetime, Bower's findings support the view that closure is an inborn feature of infant perceptual ability.

● Conclusions

As we have said, studies of human infants represent the most direct way of testing the nature–nurture controversy with regards to perception, but the evidence they provide must be considered in the light of the evidence from the four other major kinds of research and vice-versa.

Because each perceptual ability must be considered separately (e.g. colour, depth and constancy) there is no simple overall answer to the question of whether nature or nurture, heredity or environment, is more important in influencing the course of perceptual development, except one which makes clear the virtual impossibility of trying to disentangle their effects:

> ... At present we are only part-way towards a description of the changes in visual competence in early infancy, and the causes of the changes are also poorly understood. Newborns are competent learners and some developments may be a consequence of perceptual experience; others may result from endogenous maturational processes, perhaps linked to the increasing involvement of the visual cortex. (Slater, 1989)

Similarly:

> ... Some perceptual capacities are given congenitally – even, apparently, in the basic functioning of the sensory systems – whereas other perceptual capacities develop during infancy and maturity. Perceptual development after birth (or whenever the onset of experience takes place) is doubtlessly some complex transaction of these two principal forces [genetic/maturation and experience/environmental influence]... basic mechanisms in many cases can impose perceptual structure early in life, but... perceptual development is determined and guided by a transaction of these structural endowments in combination with experience. Thus, neither nativism nor empiricism holds sway over perceptual development; rather, innate mechanisms and experience together co-determine how children come to perceive the world veridically. (Bornstein, 1988)

CHAPTER SUMMARY

- The nature–nurture or heredity–environment controversy is debated in many areas of psychology and usually involves an oversimplification of the issues involved.
- Two extreme philosophical theories are nativism and empiricism, with most psychologists taking an intermediate interactionist position.
- The five main types of evidence that are relevant to the influence of nature–nurture in perception are the perceptual abilities of newborn babies (or neonates), animal experiments, studies of human cataract patients, studies of perceptual adaptation/readjustment and cross-cultural studies.
- Studying neonates represents the most direct source of evidence but we still have to disentangle the effects of maturation and learning. Also, we can only infer what their perceptual experience is.

- Animal experiments usually involve deprivation of normal sensory experience, which raises serious ethical questions. There is also the problem of generalizing the results of such studies to humans.
- Studies of human cataract patients represent the human counterpart to animal experiments, but there are problems in the interpretation of the research findings, such as poor psychological preparation for seeing, possible physical deterioration of the visual system and dubious reliability of the case histories.
- Studies of perceptual adaptation/readjustment demonstrate the flexibility of human perception, but caution is needed in deciding what kind of adaptation is involved – perceptual or motor.
- Cross-cultural studies help to identify the influences on perceptual development, in particular the role of learning and experience. Psychologists disagree as to the key features of cultural learning.
- While the evidence overall supports the interactionist position, more simple perceptual abilities seem to be controlled by genetic factors and more complex abilities by environmental influences.
- When analysing data from cataract patients, Hebb distinguished between figural unity (e.g. figure-ground), which he believed is largely innate, and figural identity (e.g. perceptual constancy), which is largely learnt .
- Experiments such as those of Riesen and Hubel and Wiesel, using blindfolds and translucent goggles, suggest that light is necessary for normal physical development of the visual system and that patterned light is necessary for the normal development of the more complex abilities in chimps, cats and some monkeys.
- Specific environmental influences can have specific effects, as shown by Blakemore and Cooper's experiment in which kittens were raised in either a horizontal or vertical 'world'.
- Held and Hein's kitten carousel experiment demonstrates the importance of motor activity in the development of perceptual abilities, as well as the need to distinguish between perception and sensorimotor co-ordination.
- In general, the greater the degree of adaptation to a new perceptual world (created through wearing inverting goggles, for example), the greater the role of learning is taken to be.
- Studies like those of Stratton, Susannah Fienues, Snyder and Pronko and Kohler illustrate the

enormous adaptability of the human visual system. The common lack of after-effects following the removal of the distorting goggles suggests that the adaptation involves learning appropriate motor behaviour.

- Cross-cultural studies involve giving members of different cultural groups the same test materials, usually visual illusions, including the Müller-Lyer, horizontal-vertical and the rotating trapezoid.

- Based on their large-scale study in Africa, the Philippines and the USA, Segall *et al.* proposed the carpentered world hypothesis to explain why different cultural groups are more/less susceptible to different illusions. This stresses the role of the physical environment on perception.

- Evidence that contradicts the carpentered world hypothesis has led to the proposal that exposure to Western education and other cultural variables may be more important, such as 2-D drawings and photographs.

- Many studies (such as those by Deregowski) show that interpretation of pictures is not an inborn ability, but a very complex skill. In addition, studies using pictures (such as Hudson's) make it more difficult for people from non-Western cultures to give correct answers, as well as highlighting certain depth cues while ignoring others.

- Cross-cultural research may also have mistakenly described a preference for different artistic styles as a difference in perception.

- Psychologists infer what babies can perceive by studying what they possess (their sensory equipment) and their behaviour. Several methods are used, mainly concerned with the latter, including the spontaneous visual preference technique, reflecting light on the cornea, measuring sucking rate, habituation, and conditioned head rotation.

- While the newborn's nervous system as a whole is immature and visual information is transmitted inefficiently, the eyeball is anatomically identical to the adult's and the retina and fovea are fairly well developed . Several basic reflexes are present, including the pupillary, blink and optokinetic, but convergence and accommodation are both absent at first.

- Babies show a very early, if not inborn, preference for complex stimuli, but this is a function of age. This is probably related to improvement in the ability to scan the whole pattern, rather than just areas of greatest contrast.

- One aspect of form perception that has been extensively investigated is 'facedness'. Fantz was the first to claim that babies have an inborn preference for faces as such, but this is often difficult to separate from the preference for complexity. However, evidence that babies quickly learn to prefer their mother's face (and voice) is contributing to the view that the human face has species-specific significance from birth onwards.

- Depth perception has been studied using the visual cliff apparatus and has been the focus for the nature-nurture debate. Heart rate measures support Gibson and Walk's original claim (based on crawling) that depth perception is probably innate.

- Bower believes that babies have an inborn understanding of the solidity of 3-D objects, as well as size and shape constancy and the Gestalt principle of closure.

- A distinction is made between feature constancy (present at birth), identity constancy (which develops by about five months) and existence constancy (which, together with identity constancy, comprises the object concept, which appears at about six months).

- The generally accepted conclusion is that some perceptual abilities are present at birth, while others develop later; perceptual development after birth involves a complex interaction between genetic/maturational and environmental/experiential influences.

GLOSSARY

Carpentered world hypothesis Segall *et al.*'s explanation of cross-cultural differences in response to visual illusions. Members of Western cultures learn to interpret 2-D illusions as having depth as a result of being surrounded by the straight lines of buildings/other manufactured objects.

Crossmodal transfer The ability to recognize through one sense modality (e.g. vision) objects that were previously only recognized through another (e.g. touch).

Empiricism The philosophical theory according to which perceptual (and other) abilities are acquired through experience (i.e. learned).

Existence constancy Belief that objects continue to exist even when they are no longer available to the senses. (Corresponds to Piaget's concept of object permanence.)

Feature constancy Ability to recognize the constant

features of a stimulus despite some detectable but irrelevant transformation.

Figural identity The ability to name or in some other way identify an object.

Figural unity The ability to detect the presence of a figure or stimulus.

Identity constancy Ability to recognize a particular object as being exactly the same object despite some transformation.

Integrated avoidance response Baby's response to an object approaching its face: throwing back its head, shielding face with hands, even crying. An early indicator of depth perception.

Interactionism The view that both innate/genetically determined and environmental influences contribute to the development of perceptual (and other) abilities.

Kitten carousel Apparatus devised by Held and Hein for studying the role of movement in visual perception. Comprises a large drum, inside which an 'active' kitten is free to walk which, via a system of pulleys, automatically moves the 'passive' kitten (carried in a basket).

Nativism The philosophical theory according to which perceptual (and other) abilities are innate or develop through the genetically-determined process of maturation.

Object concept Term used to refer collectively to identity and existence constancy.

Perceptual adaptation/readjustment The learning of new bodily movements in order to successfully get around in a visual world that has been changed through wearing distorting goggles.

Rotating trapezoid illusion A large trapezoid, with horizontal and vertical bars to give the impression of a window, attached to a motor which turns it in a circle. Most Western observers report a rectangle that oscillates backwards and forwards.

Spontaneous visual preference technique Method used to study infant perception, in which two stimuli are presented simultaneously. If the baby spends longer looking at one, it is inferred that it can discriminate between them and that it prefers the one it looks at longer. Also called preferential looking.

Supernormal stimulus An object or pattern that brings together, in exaggerated form, several stimulus characteristics. For Rheingold, the human face possesses all the stimulus dimensions that babies innately prefer (movement, complexity, etc.).

Visual cliff Apparatus devised by Gibson and Walk for studying depth perception. Consists of a central platform, with an apparent drop on one side ('cliff' or deep side) and a 'shallow' side on the other.

FURTHER READING

Slater, A. & Bremner, G. (eds) (1989) *Infant Development.* London: Lawrence Erlbaum Associates.A detailed, quite advanced textbook on most aspects of infant development. Especially relevant here are Chapter 2 (Slater: 'Visual Memory and Perception in Early Infancy), Chapter 4 (Bower: 'The Perceptual World of the New-Born Child').

Bornstein, M.H. & Lamb, M.E. (eds) (1988) *Perceptual, Cognitive and Linguistic Development: Part II of Developmental Psychology : An Advanced Textbook*, 2nd edn. London: Lawrence Erlbaum Associates. As the title says, this is also an advanced textbook but the chapter by Bornstein (Chapter 4 : 'Perceptual Development Across the Life-Cycle') is very readable and very useful for discussion of the nature-nurture issue.

Berry, J.B., Poortinga, Y.H., Segall, M.H. & Dasen, P.R. (eds) (1992) *Cross-cultural Psychology: Research and Applications.* New York: Cambridge University Press. Widely regarded as the 'classic' in this area of psychology. Chapter 6 is particularly useful here.

11 ATTENTION

INTRODUCTION AND OVERVIEW

When discussing the topic of perception in Chapter 9, several references were made to the concept of *selection*. For example, one of the major ways in which perceptual set functions is to bias what aspect of a stimulus/stimulus situation we notice. This, in turn, presupposes that we are not capable of noticing everything that is physically available to the senses at any particular moment: in other words, when we describe perception as being a selective process, we are in fact talking about selective attention, a major concern of the present chapter. According to Greene and Hicks (1984):

> The topics of perception and attention merge into each other since both are concerned with the question of what we become aware of in our environment. We can only perceive things we are attending to; we can only attend to things we perceive ...

Much of what arrives at the senses is never perceived, that is, we are not aware of it at any one time. Given the amount of stimulation that surrounds us and the limited capacity of the brain to process and interpret sensory information, it seems inevitable (and highly desirable) that we should only be able to attend to certain things and not others. Think of how chaotic things would be if, for example, we were constantly aware of the clothes on our body or the sound of our own breathing, or the sight of our arms and legs as we walk – quite apart from all the stimulation provided by other people and the physical world around us.

Traditionally, the topics of perception and attention have been studied in different ways, the former assuming that participants are attending to particular stimuli presented to them, the latter focusing on just what it is that is 'perceived' and what isn't at any one time. But in Chapter 9 we saw that perception is not always conscious – if *subliminal perception* is a genuine perceptual process then we cannot, after all, see awareness as a factor common to the two topics of perception and attention, as Greene and Hicks (1984) suggest.

As we saw in Chapter 1, the dominant paradigm within cognitive psychology as a whole is the *information-processing approach,* at the heart of which lies the belief that the human mind can be compared with a digital computer (the computer analogy). Some writers consider

that the computer analogy is most evident in explanations of attention and memory (see Chapter 12) ; for example, the concepts of a buffer store and a limited capacity processor are drawn from information technology and are crucial to the study of attention.

Another key feature of theories of attention is how they relate to the distinction between serial and parallel processing. Briefly, serial processing involves a step-by-step process, in which each operation is carried out in turn, while in parallel processing, two or more operations are performed at the same time. All the early theories, starting with Broadbent's (1958) filter model and other 'bottleneck' theories of selective attention (Treisman, Deutsch and Deutsch), as well as early attempts to explain divided attention (e.g. Kahneman's central capacity theory) assumed serial processing. Later theories (e.g. Allport's multichannel theory) assume parallel processing and hierarchical theories (e.g. Baddeley's theory of 'working memory') see both types of processing as being involved.

Assumptions about serial or parallel processing reflect changes in the underlying computer analogy which in turn reflect developments in computer technology. For much of the 1950s and 1960s, computers were

only capable of serial processing and it was these general properties that were used to understand the mind. By the 1970s, many different programming languages had been developed, which resulted in the use of particular languages and more specific aspects of computer software for modelling human thought. During the 1980s and 1990s, machines capable of massive parallel processing started to be built and theorists have returned to the view that cognitive theories should be based more closely on the parallel processing capabilities of the brain (Eysenck and Keane, 1995; Jarvis, 1994).We shall have much more to say about the computer analogy, and the serial/parallel processing distinction, in Chapter 14.

● What do we mean by attention?

Like so many terms in psychology, attention has been used in several different ways. A very famous definition is that of William James (1890), according to whom:

> It is the taking possession by the mind, in clear and vivid form, of one out of what seem several simultaneously possible objects or trains of thought. Focalization, concentration of consciousness are of its essence. It implies withdrawal from some things in order to deal effectively with others.

This definition seems to suffer from the same problem that we noted above when discussing the relationship between attention and perception, namely that we cannot necessarily equate attention with consciousness (see below). However, James' definition does serve to underline the selective nature of attention, which is echoed in Solso's (1995) very recent definition , namely 'the concentration of mental effort on sensory or mental events'. But again, this is only one of two major ways in which attention has been defined and investigated: a crucial distinction is made between:

1. attention as the mechanisms by which certain information is registered and other information is rejected (whether or not the latter enters conscious awareness) – *selective or focused attention;*
2. attention as some upper limit to the amount of processing that can be performed on incoming information at any one time – *capacity or divided attention.*

The term has also been used to refer to arousal level, vigilance and the ability to stay alert and concentrate. These were discussed in Chapters 4 and 5.

● How has attention been studied?

Eysenck (1984) identifies two basic experimental techniques used to study attention:

1. People are presented with two or more simultaneous 'messages' and are instructed to process and respond to only one of these. The most popular way of doing this is to use *shadowing,* whereby one message is fed into the left ear and a different message into the right ear (through headphones) and people have to repeat one of these messages aloud as they hear it.

   The shadowing technique is really a particular form of *dichotic listening* (Broadbent, 1954) which refers to the simultaneous reception of two different stimulus inputs, one to each ear. Shadowing was first used by Cherry (1953) who wanted to study the cocktail party situation, in which the individual manages to select one or two voices to listen to from the hubbub of numerous conversations taking place at the same time and in the same room. The participant is instructed to select, which can tell us something about the selection process and what happens to unattended stimuli (i.e. it is used to study selective attention). Most studies have studied auditory attention.

2. In the *dual-task* technique, people are asked to attend and respond to both (or all) the messages. Whereas shadowing focuses attention on a particular message, the dual-task method deliberately divides people's attention and this provides useful information about a person's processing limitations and also about attention mechanisms and their capacity. Variables which seem to affect performance on such dual tasks are: (i) task similarity; (ii) task difficulty; and (iii) practice (e.g. the effects of automaticity).

THEORIES OF SELECTIVE ATTENTION: WHAT DO WE NOTICE WHEN WE'RE NOT PAYING ATTENTION?

A number of theories, based largely on the shadowing technique, have tried to account for selective attention by proposing that somewhere in the processing of information there is a bottleneck or filter (partly due to neurological limitations), at which point the attended message is passed on for further processing and the non-attended message is either filtered out altogether (and so has no effect on behaviour) or is processed only to a limited degree. These *single channel models* (Broadbent, 1958; Deutsch and Deutsch, 1963; Treisman, 1964; Norman, 1969, 1976) differ essentially over the position of the filter and hence how much (and what kind of) processing of the non-attended message takes place.

● Broadbent's filter model (1958)

The 'modern era of attention' began with the publication of Broadbent's (1958) *Perception and Communication,* which also had a great impact on the development of cognitive psychology as a whole. In it, he argued that the world is composed of many more sensations than can be handled by the perceptual and cognitive capabilities of the human observer. In order to cope with the flood of available information, humans selectively attend to only some of the cues and tune out much of the rest. Attention is, therefore, the result of a limited-capacity information-processing system, what Solso (1995) calls a 'pipeline' theory.

According to Broadbent, the bottleneck occurs very early in processing and is based on the major physical properties of the incoming stimuli. For example, much early research suggested that very

---

<table>
<tr><td>**BOX 11.1**</td><td>Key study: why use one ear when two will do?</td></tr>
</table>

Gray and Wedderburn (1960) presented, to alternate ears, the syllables composing a word plus random digits, so that when a syllable was 'heard' by one ear, the other ear would 'hear' digits. For example, in one experiment, participants heard:

Left ear: OB 2 TIVE
Right ear: 6 JEC 9

FIGURE 11.1 *'Intelligent' use of both ears*

(In other experiments, phrases were used in place of words, such as 'Dear Aunt Jane', 'Mice eat cheese', and 'What the hell'.)

According to Broadbent, when participants were asked to repeat what they had heard in one ear (or channel) they should have reported 'ob-two-tive' or 'six-jec-nine'; this is nonsense, of course, but the filter model maintains that it is the physical nature of the auditory signal (i.e. which ear receives which input) and not meaning which determines what is attended to and, hence, what is recalled. What they actually reported was 'objective' or the complete phrase (e.g. 'Dear Aunt Jane') , i.e. they acted 'intelligently'.

---

little, if any, of the non-attended message could be recalled, except: (i) the speaker's gender; and (ii) whether it consisted of words or pure tones (Cherry, 1953; Treisman, 1964). Participants were unable to identify its content, the language in which it was spoken, whether it changed from English to German or whether it was English played backwards. Even a word repeated 35 times was not recalled (Moray, 1959). The filter is also 'tuned' to other physical characteristics, such as volume, brightness, intensity and novelty.

However, Broadbent's model could not account for a feature of the cocktail party situation, whereby we can be engaged in one conversation but can switch our attention if we hear our name mentioned in another. Moray (1959) found that this happened about a third of the time in a shadowing task. Gray and Wedderburn's findings also seem to pose serious problems for Broadbent (see Box 11.1).

Broadbent had himself demonstrated that we can switch channels in an early (1954) study. Using a *split-span procedure*, participants heard six digits, three to each ear in simultaneous pairs, at half-second intervals (261–795). They were asked to recall the digits in either of two ways: (i) pair-by-pair (i.e. 27/69/15) or (ii) ear-by-ear (261–795). The ear-by-ear method of recall was much easier and produced more accurate recall. This led Broadbent to suggest that ears act like separate channels which can only be attended to one at a time. The pair-by-pair method of recall is more difficult because it requires a continuous switching from one channel to the other – this takes time and so is less efficient. By contrast, the ear-by-ear method requires only one switch of attention from one channel to the other. (Note that the participants in Gray and Wedderburn's study were able to switch attention rapidly from channel to channel, more easily than Broadbent's model seems to suggest.)

However (and this is the crucial point) as participants successfully reported *some* of the items presented to the other ear, these must be held in a temporary buffer store. Broadbent's model is shown in Figure 11.2. For this kind of reason, Solso (1995) believes that it is mistaken to portray Broadbent's model as a crude either/or theory, in which information is processed in either one channel or another. Indeed, Broadbent was quite explicit in rejecting such an extreme view, although he stressed the limitations of the information processed by the unattended ear, both the quantity and detail.

Experience with grammatical and semantic aspects of language override the instructions to attend only to one ear, which might help to explain the

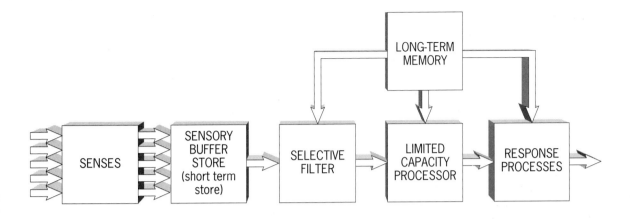

FIGURE 11.2 *Broadbent's filter model*

'chicken and egg' situation whereby switching channels seems to be facilitated by meaning but we need to switch channels in order to detect the meaning! However it occurs, the fact that selection can be based on meaning is inconsistent with Broadbent's theory.

Are there methodological problems with shadowing experiments?

- Because participants are usually not asked about the non-shadowed message until the end of the experiment, it is possible that they have forgotten what they have actually noticed during the shadowing task (which would also contradict Broadbent's model). Norman (1969) stopped people without warning in the middle of a shadowing task and they were able to recall the last few words of the non-shadowed message if questioning occurred within 30 seconds of being interrupted (see Chapter 12).
- In the initial shadowing studies, the assumption was made that if participants were not consciously aware of the meaning of the non-attended message, it was because there was no processing of meaning taking place. But what about the possibility of unconscious processing (Eysenck and Keane, 1990, 1995)?

   A number of studies have shown that when certain words in the shadowed message are followed by electric shock and then later appear in the non-attended message, there is an associated change in GSR. For example, Von Wright *et al.* (1975) asked participants to attend to long lists of words and sometimes an electric shock was received when the Finnish word for 'suitable' was presented. Then they shadowed one auditory word list while a second list was simultaneously presented to the other ear. When the previously shocked word (or a word with a very similar sound or meaning) was presented in the non-shadowed list, there was a noticeable GSR change (although these changes were detected only on a fraction of the trials).

- The participants in the early shadowing experiments had had little or no previous experience of shadowing messages, so almost all their available processing resources had to be allocated to the shadowing task. Underwood (1974) asked inexperienced participants to detect digits presented to either the shadowed or non-shadowed ear ; they succeeded 8% of the time on the latter compared with 67% by an experienced researcher in the field (Moray).

● Treisman's attenuator model (1964)

This model retains much of the 'architecture' of Broadbent's, but sees the bottleneck as being much more flexible. Treisman's *stimulus-analysis system* proceeds through a hierarchy (Fig. 11.3). First, initial screening evaluates the signal on the basis of gross physical characteristics (much like Broadbent's) but instead of 'irrelevant' messages being excluded, the *attenuator* ('perceptual filter') 'turns their volume down' so that they are still 'available for higher level processing'. 'The channel filter attenuates irrelevant messages rather than blocks them completely' (Treisman, 1964). Secondly, further analysis is based on individual words, grammatical structure and word meaning.

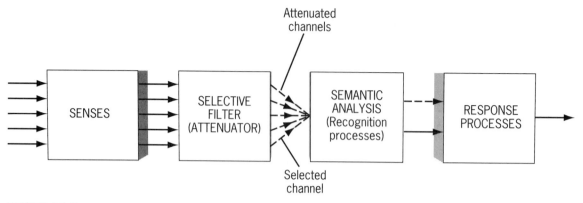

FIGURE 11.3 *Treisman's attenuator model*

Clearly, Treisman's model can account for the cocktail party situation much more easily than Broadbent's: it seems to provide a logical explanation of how we can 'hear' something while not attending to it and how we attend to the meaning rather than the physical characteristics of the message alone. But how are the executive decisions made. Does a simple attenuator have the capacity to analyse the intricate features of a message and check them with some master control to see whether they should or should not pass through and can it do so as quickly as is necessary (Solso, 1979)? And although Treisman's model can account for the extensive processing of non-shadowed messages in a way that is impossible for Broadbent, so can the pertinence model.

● The pertinence model (Deutsch and Deutsch, 1963; Norman, 1969, 1976)

This model, originally proposed by Deutsch and Deutsch in 1963 and revised by Norman in 1969 and 1976, puts the bottleneck much nearer the *response* end of the processing system by proposing that all signals are fully analysed from the start and then passed on to an attenuator, which passes on the message for further processing in a toned-down form (Fig. 11.4). Compared with Treisman's model, the decision as to the *pertinence* or relevance of a message occurs much earlier and it is this that determines the response.

If every signal is analysed initially, this would seem to make the model very uneconomical (Solso, 1979) because a great number of irrelevant stimuli need to be checked with long-term memory store before further processing can occur; it also makes it rather rigid and inflexible (Eysenck, 1984). But is there any evidence that *all* incoming information is

analysed initially? Some important evidence is reported in Box 11.2.

● An evaluation of single channel models

Wilding (1982) believes that more is known about non-attended messages than either Broadbent's or Treisman's models can accommodate, but not as much as proposed by the pertinence model. Many researchers have begun to question whether any filter theory which assumes a single, general purpose, limited-capacity central processor can, in principle, account for the complexities of selective attention (Norman and Bobrow, 1975; Neisser, 1976; Allport, 1980b) and much of the relevant evidence comes from dual-task studies, which are more directly concerned with processing *capacity*. So we shall now turn our attention (pun intended!) to studies of divided attention.

STUDIES OF DIVIDED ATTENTION: CAN WE DO TWO THINGS AT THE SAME TIME?

Many of the earlier shadowing experiments overlooked a number of critical variables which can influence performance on these tasks, including practice, degree of similarity between competing tasks, the difficulty of tasks and so on. According to Hampson (1989), there are more similarities between selective/focused and divided attention than might be thought: factors which make the one easier also tend to make the other easier, since '... anything which minimizes interference between processes, or keeps them "further apart" will allow

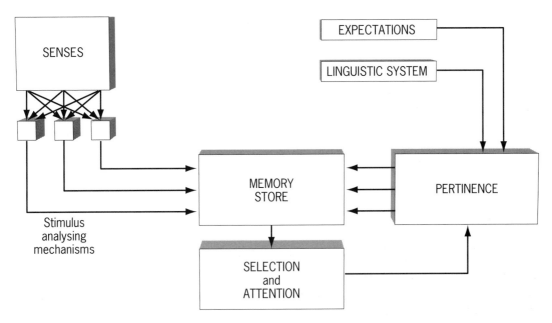

FIGURE 11.4 *Norman's late selection model*

BOX 11.2	Key study: can we choose between the pertinence and attenuator models?

Treisman and Geffen (1967) used a shadowing task in which participants had to repeat the shadowed message aloud but also had to indicate (by tapping) when they heard a certain 'target' word, which could occur in either ear. The pertinence model would predict that the target item should be detected and produce a response in whichever ear it appeared, while the filter model would predict that it would not be detected if it appeared in the non-shadowed ear. What were the results?

Participants detected 87% of the target words in the shadowed ear but only 8% in the non-attended ear, which seems to represent unequivocal support for Broadbent. However, Deutsch and Norman (1967) rejected the experiment as a valid test of the pertinence model on the grounds that participants had to shadow *and* tap in one message but only tap in the other and this made the shadowed target words more

important than the non-shadowed ones. However, when Treisman and Riley (1969) removed this bias by telling participants to stop shadowing and to tap as soon as they detected a target in either message, there was still a greater detection of shadowed target words than non-shadowed (although it was a less dramatic difference than in the 1967 experiment). Other studies have also failed to support the pertinence model, e.g. Kahneman (1973), Neisser (1976).

Johnston and Heinz (1978) have proposed a more flexible model, whereby selection is possible at several different stages of processing and in a 1979 experiment found that the amount of processing of a non-shadowed message varies as a function of task-demand in a way which is more consistent with Treisman's model than those of Deutsch and Deutsch or Norman. Johnston and Wilson (1980) found that non-target words were processed semantically when participants did not know at which ear target words would arrive (*divided attention condition*), but they were not semantically processed when they did know (*focused attention condition*). This suggests that the amount of processing received by non-target stimuli is often only as much as is required to perform the experimental task.

them to be dealt with more readily either selectively or together'.

A clear example of interference in a dual-task situation is an experiment conducted by Shaffer (1975). (Notice that shadowing, used to study selec-

tive attention, is often used in dual-task experiments.) A skilled typist performed an audio-typing task which involved listening to the material to be typed presented via headphones to *one* ear. This was combined with each of two concurrent tasks: (i) a

BOX 11.3

Divided attention and the role of task similarity, practice and task difficulty (based on Eysenck and Keane,1995)

● **Task similarity**

Allport et al. (1972) found that when participants try to shadow passages of prose while learning auditorily presented words, subsequent recognition-memory performance for the words was no better than chance. But when shadowing was combined with visually presented words to learn, memory was significantly better and it was better still (90% correct) when pictures were the to-be-remembered material.

What different kinds of similarity are relevant in dual-task performance? Wickens (1984) reviewed the evidence and concluded that two tasks interfere to the extent that they involve the same stimulus modality (visual/auditory), make use of the same stages of processing (input/internal processing/output) and rely on related memory codes (verbal/visual). While response similarity also seems to be important, *similarity of stimulus* modality has probably been the most thoroughly explored..

In addition to their experiments already described, Allport *et al.* (1972) report findings which demonstrate both a quite astonishing capacity that some people show for handling two inputs simultaneously and also the importance of similarity of modality in influencing that capacity. They studied skilled pianists who had to shadow continuous speech while simultaneously sight-reading music which they had not seen before; they in fact performed as well on the sight-reading as they did when there was no concurrent, shadowing task.

● **Practice**

Why might practice make it easier to perform two tasks simultaneously? Firstly, participants may develop new strategies for performing each of the tasks so as to minimize interference. Secondly, the demands a task makes on attention or other central resources may be reduced as a function of practice. Thirdly, while a task may initially require the use of several specific processing resources, practice may produce a more economical mode of functioning using fewer such resources. (This is discussed further in relation to automatic processing; see below.)

● **Task difficulty**

As with similarity, there is a question as to how difficulty should be defined. But we cannot simply assume that the demands of the two tasks performed together equal the sum of the demands of the same tasks when performed separately because, when they are performed together, fresh demands of co-ordination and avoidance of interference are introduced.

---

shadowing task in which the shadowed message was presented to the ear not receiving the input to be typed and (ii) a task of reading aloud visually presented material. In both cases, performing the audio-typing task and a concurrent task led to considerably poorer performance on one or both tasks, compared with performance when the tasks were carried out separately. Clearly there was *interference* between the tasks because of their similarity – the audio-typing task involves the auditory input modality (speech via headphones) as did the shadowing task; although here the output modalities were different (typing = motor; shadowing = articulatory), the interference caused by the similarity of the input was sufficient to cause decrement in actual performance. The reading aloud task involved visual input (and so was different from the audio-typing auditory input) but this time the output modality was the same for both (i.e. articulatory). The interference here stemmed from what the person actually had to do.

Some of the research into divided attention using dual-task techniques in relation to the three variables of task similarity, practice and task difficulty is summarized in Box 11.3.

● Automatic versus controlled processing

In cases of people who demonstrate quite remarkable capacity to do two things at the same time (such as Allport *et al*'s pianists), the tasks used are very different from each other (e.g. sight-reading and shadowing prose). This contrasts with the shadowing experiments investigating selective attention, where very similar 'messages' are used (e.g. digits presented to both ears). Another important difference is to do with the participants – they are often highly skilled and thoroughly practised in one of the tasks – in Shiffrin and Schneider's (1977) terms, these participants are displaying *automatic processing (or automaticity.)*

According to Eysenck and Keane (1995), there is fairly general agreement about what this means:

● automatic processes are fast;
● they do not reduce the capacity for performing

other tasks (i.e. they make no demands on the person's attention);

• they are not available to consciousness;
• they are unavoidable (such that they always occur when the appropriate stimulus is presented, even if it is outside the field of attention). Automatic processing is contrasted with controlled processing (which corresponds to focused attention, sometimes called 'focal' attention or awareness; see Chapter 4).

Learning to drive a car clearly results in automaticity. At first, focused attention is required for each component part of the skill so that any slight distraction (such as being asked a question by a passenger in the car) can disrupt performance (with potentially dangerous consequences!). However, an experienced driver can quite happily engage in conversation, listen to the radio or even read a map while driving. This applies to other psychomotor skills (such as playing a musical instrument), as well as using language and social interaction skills. Skilled performance may free consciousness for the more demanding and changing 'onslaught of activities' that require focused attention; the importance of studies of automaticity is that they may tell us something about the complex activity that seems to occur outside conscious experience (Solso, 1995) (see Fig 11.5).

But is it always so easy to demonstrate automaticity empirically? For example, the claim that it makes *no* demands on the person's attention is rarely the case. Again, regarding its 'unavoidability', the *Stroop effect* is usually seen as involving unavoidable and automatic processing. Here, colour words are presented (e.g. 'blue') in a conflicting coloured ink (e.g. 'blue' written in red ink) and the experimental task is to name the colour (i.e. red). The colour *words* usually interfere with the task, probably because reading is such a well-learned, unavoidable, automatic activity. However, Kahneman and Henik (1979) found that the effect was much greater when the distracting information was in the same *location* as the colour which was to be identified, rather than at an adjacent location within the central fixation area – this suggests that the Stroop effect may not be automatic and unavoidable after all.

Shiffrin and Schneider (1977) found that attention can be divided among several information sources with reasonable success when automatic processes are used. This is quite different from focused attention, where some sources of information must be attended to and others ignored – controlled processes largely prevent unwanted processing from occurring, whereas automatic processes disrupt performance because of automatic responses to to-be-ignored stimuli. According to Eysenck (1982, quoted in Eysenck and Keane, 1990), 'Automatic processes function rapidly and in parallel but suffer from inflexibility; controlled processes are flexible and versatile but operate relatively slowly and in a serial fashion'. While Shiffrin and Schneider's distinction was based on their use of visual tasks, Eysenck and Keane point out that very similar results have been obtained for auditory tasks.

● Automaticity and practice

A central feature of Shiffrin and Schneider's (1977) theory of automatic processing is the claim that some processes become automatic as a result of practice. But Eysenck and Keane (1990) point out that this tells us very little about what is actually happening – is it just a speeding up of the processes involved or is there a change in the nature of the processes themselves?

Norman and Shallice (1980) and Shallice (1982) argue that, instead of automatic versus attentional or controlled processing, it is preferable to identify three levels of functioning:

1 *fully automatic processing* controlled by schemata (i.e. organized plans) which occur with very little conscious awareness of the process involved;
2 *partially automatic* processing, which involves contention scheduling (a way of resolving conflicts

FIGURE 11.5 *At first, learning to drive a car, like other psychomotor skills, requires focused attention. The experienced driver however displays automaticity*

between competing schemata) and which generally involves more conscious awareness than fully automatic processing but which occurs without deliberate direction or conscious control;

3 *deliberate control* by a supervisory attentional system, which is involved in decision making and troubleshooting and allows flexible responding in novel situations.

Eysenck and Keane (1990) believe this approach is superior to that of Shiffrin and Schneider, which assumes a single control system. The three levels approach provides a more natural explanation for the fact that some processes are fully automatic while others are only partially so. But what exactly happens as automaticity develops through prolonged practice?

According to Logan (1988), Shiffrin and Schneider fail to spell out in any detail *why* practice has the effect it does; like Eysenck and Keane, he argues that their model is largely descriptive and explains very little. As summarized by Eysenck and Keane, Logan makes the following assumptions:

● Separate memory traces are stored away every time a stimulus is encountered and processed.

● Practice with the same stimulus produces storage of more and more information about the stimulus and what to do with it.

● This increase in the knowledge base leads to rapid retrieval of relevant information as soon as the appropriate stimulus is presented.

● 'Automaticity is memory retrieval: performance is automatic when it is based on a single-step, direct-access retrieval of past solutions from memory' (Logan, 1988).

In the absence of practice, the task of responding appropriately to a stimulus requires thought and the application of rules; after prolonged practice, the appropriate response is stored in memory and can be accessed very rapidly.

CONCLUSIONS: ATTENTION AS CENTRAL CAPACITY, MODULES OR SOME COMBINATION OF THE TWO?

What seems to emerge from the research and theory discussed above is that some tasks require a greater degree of attention than others. This is why more than one thing can be done at the same time – no one of them requires the full capacity of the atten-

tion system (e.g. audio-typing and shadowing prose). But however skilled one is at a particular activity and, therefore, however much attention can be devoted to some other concurrent task or tasks, surely there is some overall limit to how many things we can do simultaneously.

This implies that there is some sort of limited-capacity central processor which co-ordinates and allocates a central (finite) pool of attentional resources to different tasks (like the Treasury allocating resources to different government departments). Indeed, *resource allocation* is a term used to describe how attention becomes divided between tasks (as well as how money is divided between government departments). This view of attention as a flexible process which can be spread across tasks as required seems to fit the facts of everyday observation very well – it seems intuitively right. (You might be having a cup of coffee at this moment as you read, something which you are so skilled at that you hardly need to give it any of your attention – drinking coffee that is!).

A way of saying that a particular task does not require our conscious (focused) attention is to say that it requires little mental effort; tasks which require a lot of mental effort make heavy demands on the central, limited-capacity processor. This concept of mental effort forms an important part of Kahneman's (1973) theory of attention, which assumes that there is an overall limit to a person's capacity to perform mental work (see Fig. 11.6).

When we are aroused and alert (see Chapters 4 and 5), we have more attentional resources available than when we are tired and lethargic. If we are both motivated and skilled, we will have attentional capacity 'left over'. It follows that we can attend to more than one thing at a time as long as the total mental effort required does not exceed the total capacity available (we can't 'overspend'). Kahneman believes that allocation of attentional resources depends on a central allocation policy adopted by the central processor, which constantly evaluates the level of demand. If level of demand becomes excessive, the central allocation policy must decide which tasks should receive more attention.

The research on attentional capacity strongly suggests that attention is a far more flexible system than is suggested by models of selective attention (particularly Broadbent's filter model). In keeping with this view, Kahneman's model sees attention as a central dynamic process rather than the result of an automatic filtering of perceptual input. Neisser (1976) suggests that attention should be thought of not as a

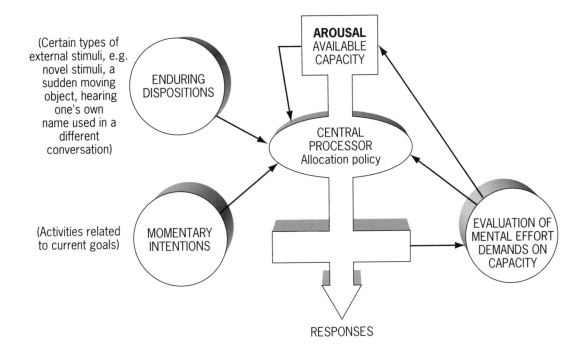

FIGURE 11.6 *Kahneman's model of attention*

mechanism or process but as a skill. Rather than see-ing a one-way flow of information from input through to responses, Kahneman sees attention as involving a constant perceptual evaluation of the demands required to produce appropriate responses.

Yet Kahneman is not without his critics. One diffi-culty is to do with how much of the monitoring of task demand and allocation of attention is an unconscious process, i.e. how are decisions made to channel our attention to a difficult task, say? Spelke *et al.* (1976) argue that people's ability to develop skills in special-ized situations is so great that it may never be possible to define the general limits of cognitive capacity and so the concept of attention-as-capacity is largely redundant.

Allport (1980b, 1989) rejects the concept of a gen-eral purpose, limited-capacity processor altogether. The concept of attention, he says, is often used syn-onymously with 'consciousness' with no proper specification of how it is supposed to operate and it has done little, if anything, to increase our under-standing of the problems it is meant to explain. Instead, he proposes a number of different specific processing mechanisms or *modules;* when two simul-taneous (dual) tasks are highly similar, they compete for the same modules and this leads to mutual inter-ference, but dissimilar tasks involve different

modules and so no interference occurs.

Some of the most convincing evidence for the modular theory comes from cognitive neuropsychol-ogy, in particular the study of language in brain-damaged patients. However, if there are sev-eral independent processors or modules that operate in parallel, we would need to explain how they are co-ordinated so as to produce coherent behaviour.

Theories that attempt to do this are called *synthe-sis theories,* representing a compromise position based on a hierarchical structure. For example, Baddeley (Baddeley and Hitch, 1974; Baddeley, 1986) has proposed two specific systems (an articulatory loop and a visuospatial scratch pad) in addition to a central capacity processor (which is modality-free). This could explain why overt repetition of an over-learned sequence of digits (which uses an articulatory loop) does not interfere with verbal rea-soning (which uses the central processor).The central processor (attention) is at the top of the hierarchy and is involved in the co-ordination and control of behaviour. Below are specific processing mechanisms which operate relatively separately from each other (i.e. in a modular fashion). Processes at the bottom tend to be more automatic than those at the top. Without some kind of overall control, there would probably be chaos.

The Baddeley 'solution' relates, in fact, to his model of *working memory,* an attempt to explain what short-term memory is for and how it operates. It is interesting to note that we began this chapter by relating attention to perception; we end it by suggesting an important link between attention and memory, the topic of the next chapter.

CHAPTER SUMMARY

- The topics of attention and perception are closely related, since both involve selection from all the available sensory stimulation. However, they have traditionally been studied in different ways.

- The dominant paradigm in cognitive psychology is the information-processing approach, central to which is the computer analogy.

- Changes in the computer analogy since the 1950s reflect developments in computer technology, in particular, the ability of computers to carry out serial or parallel processing.

- There are many definitions of attention, but a crucial distinction is made between selective or focused and divided attention or capacity.

- A major method used for studying selective attention is shadowing, a particular form of dichotic listening, while divided attention is studied primarily using the dual-task technique.

- Theories of selective attention tend to centre around the idea of a bottleneck or filter and are referred to as single channel models. Broadbent's filter model, Treisman's attenuator model and the pertinence model of Deutsch and Deutsch, and Norman differ essentially as to the position of the filter.

- According to Broadbent, the bottleneck occurs very early in processing and is based on the physical properties of the incoming stimuli. This, however, fails to account for the cocktail party situation, as well as the findings of several shadowing experiments in which participants' reports include meaningful information from the non-shadowed message.

- Broadbent's model recognizes that a certain amount of information from the non-shadowed message is held in a temporary buffer store, but its amount and detail are very limited and do not include meaning.

- There are a number of methodological problems with shadowing experiments, such as the possibility of forgetting information from the non-shadowed message, of unconscious processing and participants' lack of experience of shadowing messages.

- Treisman's model sees the bottleneck as much more flexible than Broadbent's, 'turning down' non-shadowed messages rather than rejecting them.

- The pertinence model can also account for the extensive processing of non-shadowed messages, by claiming that *all* incoming information is fully analysed from the start. This represents a very inflexible system and there is very little supporting evidence. The bottleneck is seen as much nearer to the response end of the processing system.

- Many early shadowing experiments failed to take account of certain critical variables for task performance, in particular practice, degree of similarity between competing tasks and difficulty of tasks. These can influence both selective and divided attention but they have been investigated mainly in relation to the latter.

- When people demonstrate remarkable divided attention, the tasks involved are very different from each other and they are often highly skilled and practised in one of the tasks, i.e. they display automatic processing or automaticity.

- Shiffrin and Schneider contrast automatic processing with controlled processing, which corresponds to focused attention. The former is rapid, parallel and inflexible, while the latter is slow, serial and flexible.

- Norman and Shallice prefer to identify three levels of functioning: fully automatic and partially automatic processing and deliberate control.

- There seems to be some upper limit to how many things we can do simultaneously, which implies some limited-capacity central processor. According to Kahneman, the central processor adopts a central allocation policy, which determines how much attention is given to different tasks, depending on the amount of mental effort involved.

- Allport rejects the central processor concept and, instead, proposes a number of different specific processing modules, which are independent and operate in parallel.

- A compromise between central processor theories and modular theories are synthesis theories, which propose a central processor plus specific systems, arranged hierarchically. One example is Baddeley's theory of working memory.

GLOSSARY

Automatic processing The high degree of skill and practice displayed by experienced drivers, typists etc., such that little, if any, conscious or controlled processing is required. Also known as automaticity.

Bottleneck In theories of selective attention, the point at which the attended message is passed on for further processing and the non-attended message is either filtered out or processed only to a limited extent. Also known as the filter.

Cocktail party situation Cherry's term for our ability to concentrate on one or two voices when several conversations are taking place at the same time. Sometimes called the cocktail party problem.

Computer analogy The comparison made between the human mind and a digital computer.

Controlled processing Consciously attending to the performance of some skill-related behaviour, as when the skill is first being acquired. Corresponds to focal attention or awareness.

Divided attention The upper limit to how much processing can be performed on incoming information at any one time. Also known as capacity.

Dual-task technique Method for studying divided attention, in which participants are asked to attend to two or more concurrent messages/tasks.

Information-processing approach The dominant paradigm within cognitive psychology, which sees the human mind as comparable to a digital computer.

Mental effort In Kahneman's theory, the demands made on the central, limited-capacity processor.

Modular theories (of attention) The view that attention comprises a number of independent, specific processing mechanisms working in parallel (e.g. Allport).

Parallel processing A process in which two or more operations are carried out at the same time.

Resource allocation How attention becomes divided between tasks.

Selective attention The mechanisms by which certain information is registered and other information is rejected. Also known as focused attention.

Serial processing A step-by-step process, in which each of a series of operations is carried out separately.

Shadowing A form of dichotic listening, in which two different messages are fed to the two ears, via headphones; one message must be repeated aloud as it is heard. Used mainly for studying selective attention.

Stroop effect The interference produced when colour words (e.g. 'blue') are presented in a conflicting coloured ink (e.g. 'blue' written in red ink) and the task is to name the colour (i.e. red). An example of automatic processing.

Synthesis theories (of attention) Compromise between central processor theories and modular theories, which propose a hierarchical structure, as in Baddeley's theory of working memory.

FURTHER READING

Eysenck, M.W. & Keane, M.T. (1995) *Cognitive Psychology – A Student's Handbook*, 3rd edn. London: Lawrence Erlbaum Associates. A detailed, comprehensive, but relatively non-threatening textbook. The chapter on attention discusses all the issues in this chapter in depth, together with topics such as action slips/absentmindedness not dealt with here.

Solso, R.L. (1995) *Cognitive Psychology*, 4th edn. Boston: Allyn & Bacon. Another comprehensive but fairly user-friendly textbook. The attention chapter includes sections on the neuropsychology of attention and relates attention to consciousness.

12 MEMORY

INTRODUCTION AND OVERVIEW

As we saw in Chapter 7, learning is defined in terms of relatively permanent changes in behaviour due to past experience and memory is a crucial part of the learning process – without memory, we could not benefit from past experience. Unless, in some way, our prior learning can be 'recorded', it cannot be used at a later date. However, trying to define learning and memory independently of each other is very difficult, as they represent two sides of the same coin: (i) learning depends on memory for its 'permanency' and, conversely, (ii) memory would have no 'content' without learning.

Therefore, we could define memory as the *retention of learning* or *experience,* showing how interdependent the two processes are. As Blakemore (1988) says, 'In the broadest sense, learning is the acquisition of knowledge and memory is the storage of an internal representation of that knowledge ...'. And again:

... without the capacity to remember and to learn, it is difficult to imagine what life would be like, whether it could be called living at all. Without memory, we would be servants of the moment, with nothing but our innate reflexes to help us deal with the world. There could be no language, no art, no science, no culture. Civilization itself is the distillation of human memory. (Blakemore, 1988)

There is another interesting parallel between the twin topics of learning and memory, namely that both featured prominently in the early days of psychology as a science (see Chapters 1,2 and 7). William James (1890), one of the pioneers of psychology, was arguably the first to make a formal distinction between *primary* and *secondary memory,* which correspond to short-term and long-term memory respectively; this distinction lies at the heart of the very influential *multistore model* of Atkinson and Shiffrin (1968). Hermann Ebbinghaus (1885) is usually regarded as the pioneer of the experimental study of memory, using himself to study such basic phenomena as learning curves and forgetting curves and inventing nonsense syllables for the purpose.

For much of the first half of the 20th century, memory was not a respectable topic for experimental psychologists, reflecting the dominance of behaviourism which rejected mental processes as being worthy of scientific effort. However, some behaviourists, particularly in the USA, studied 'verbal behaviour' using paired-associate learning, in which pairs of unrelated words are presented, the first member of the pair representing the 'stimulus' and the second the 'response'. This *associationist* approach kept the study of 'memory' firmly within the behaviourist framework and was most clearly seen in *interference theory* (e.g. McGeoch, Underwood), which continues to be discussed as a major theory of forgetting.

Since the 'cognitive revolution' in the 1950s, memory has become an integral topic within the information-processing approach, central to which is the computer analogy (see Chapters 11 and 14). The respectability that memory has regained since the decline of behaviourism can be seen most clearly perhaps in the study of mental imagery.

In this chapter, we shall discuss all the major theories of remembering and forgetting (more than just two sides of the same coin) and this will include major modifications of the basic distinction between short- and long-term memory. As we shall see, challenges to this distinction have led to considerable interest in the study of *everyday memory,* i.e. memory phenomena that are relevant to our everyday lives, such as *autobiographical memory* and so-called *flashbulb memories.* While memory is still largely studied in the laboratory, psychologists are increasingly recognizing the need to understand its real-world significance.

THE MEANINGS OF 'MEMORY'

As we saw in Chapter 1, memory (like learning) is a hypothetical construct and, as such, is an abstract concept which refers to three distinguishable but interrelated processes:

1 registration (or reception);
2 storage;
3 retrieval (see Fig. 12.1).

Registration can be thought of as a necessary condition for storage to take place but, as we shall see below, it is not a sufficient condition, i.e. not everything which registers on the sense receptors is stored. Similarly, *storage* can be seen as a necessary, but not a sufficient, condition for *retrieval*, i.e. you can only recover information which has been stored (you cannot remember something you do not know) but the fact that you know it is no guarantee that you will remember it on any particular occasion. This is the crucial distinction between *availability* (whether or not the information has been stored) and *accessibility* (whether or not it can be retrieved), which is especially relevant to theories of forgetting.

STORAGE

In practice, storage is studied through testing people's ability to retrieve; this is equivalent to the distinction we made in Chapter 7 between learning and performance: learning corresponds to the storage aspect of memory, while performance corresponds to the retrieval aspect of memory.

However, there are several kinds of retrieval; so, as tested by recall, for example, storage may seem not to have occurred (no learning) but as tested by recognition, storage (and hence learning) might be demonstrated. For these reasons, it is useful to distinguish between memory as storage and memory as retrieval, with 'remembering' often used to denote the latter.

As we noted at the beginning of the chapter, it was James who originally made the distinction between primary and secondary memory, although Ebbinghaus (1885) would have accepted the distinction. Hebb (1949), Broadbent (1958), Waugh and Norman (1965) and many others have also made the distinction , but perhaps the most well-known version is Atkinson and Shiffrin's *multistore model* (1968, 1971), in which they are called *short-term* and

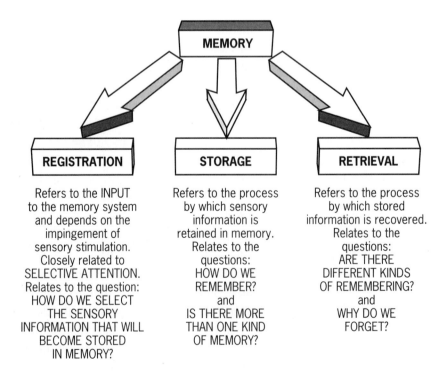

FIGURE 12.1 *The three processes of memory*

long-term memory respectively. Strictly speaking, short-term memory (STM) and long-term memory (LTM) refer to experimental procedures for investigating primary and secondary memory respectively, which are assumed to underlie them; however, we shall use STM and LTM to refer to both (Fig. 12.2).

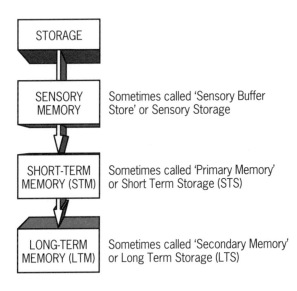

FIGURE 12.2 *The three forms of storage*

● Sensory memory

Although most research and theorizing have concentrated on STM and LTM, logically the place to start is with sensory memory (sometimes called 'sensory buffer store' or 'sensory storage'). Sensory memory gives us an accurate account of the environment as experienced by the sensory system, i.e. we retain a kind of 'literal copy' of the stimulus for a brief period of time following exposure; any information which is not attended to or processed further is forgotten. So, clearly, sensory memory is closely related to registration and it is probably more accurate and helpful to think of it as part of the process of perception and a necessary requirement for storage proper (i.e. STM).

Sensory memory seems to be *modality specific,* that is, the storage (such as it is) occurs within the sensory system that received the information and not at some central location. Additional information entering the same sensory channel immediately disrupts the storage. For example, if, shortly after a visual array is presented, a second visual stimulus is presented, the memory of the initial array may be lost. However, if the second stimulus is a sound or smell it will not interfere with memory of the visual

stimulus. *Iconic memory* is a brief visual memory system (an icon is an image) which allows visual images to be stored for about half a second) and its auditory equivalent is *echoic memory* which stores sounds for up to two seconds). If we had no iconic memory , we would perceive a film as a series of still images interspersed with blank intervals rather than as a continuously moving scene and without echoic memory, instead of hearing speech as such we would hear a series of unrelated sounds (Baddeley, 1995) (see Chapters 8 and 9).

Sperling (1960, 1963) studied the iconic store and showed that more information is available immediately after visual stimulation than can be recalled even a few seconds later. He showed participants an array comprising three rows of four letters in a 4 × 3 matrix for 50 milliseconds (¹⁄₂₀ of a second). When asked to recall as many as possible from the whole matrix (*whole reports* or *span of apprehension*) they recalled, on average, 4.32 letters (out of 12), although they commonly reported having seen more than they could actually remember. In another condition (*partial reports*), participants were required to recall the top, middle or bottom row, depending on whether they heard a high-, medium- or low-pitched tone. Although they could not know in advance which tone would be heard, they succeeded in recalling an average of 3.04 of the letters from each row, which meant that between nine and ten words were available immediately after presentation. Clearly, the information must have been lost rapidly in the first condition: in the time it took to try to recall the whole array approximately five words were lost and this was supported by the finding that the advantage of partial reports was lost if the auditory signal was delayed for a second or so.

Similar effects have been reported for the echoic store by several researchers, including Broadbent (1958) and Treisman (1964). It seems that iconic memory involves storage of stimuli which have been discriminated in terms of physical features only (e.g. size, shape, colour, location) as distinct from their meaning and Morton (1970) reported that the echoic store (what he called the *precategorical acoustic store*) works in the same way.

This reference to Broadbent and Treisman highlights the considerable overlap between the areas of attention and memory. For example, Broadbent's filter model (see Chapter 11) was in many ways the main precursor of the multistore approach to memory and there is a definite resemblance between sensory memory (or storage) and Broadbent's sensory 'buffer' store (Eysenck and Keane, 1990; see Fig. 11.2).

● Short-term memory (STM)

According to Lloyd *et al.* (1984) probably less than one-hundredth of all the sensory information that impinges every second on the human senses reaches consciousness and of this, only 1/20 achieves anything approaching stable storage.

Clearly, if memory ability were limited to sensory memory, our capacity for retaining information about the world would be extremely limited as well as very precarious. However, according to models of memory such as Atkinson and Shiffrin's multistore model (1968, 1971), some information from sensory memory is successfully passed on to STM, which allows us to store information long enough to be able to use it and, for this reason, it is often referred to as 'working memory'. (However, 'working memory' has different connotations as used by Baddeley and Hitch (1974) and Hitch (1980); see below.)

We can analyse STM (and LTM) in terms of three dimensions:

1 capacity (how much information can be stored);
2 duration (how long the information can be held in storage);
3 coding (in what ways sensory input is transformed or processed so that it can be stored, i.e. how it is represented by the memory system).

Capacity

Ebbinghaus (1885) and Wundt (in the 1860s) were two of the first psychologists to maintain that STM is limited to six or seven bits of information, but the most famous account is given by Miller in his article 'The magical number seven, plus or minus two' (1956). In this article Miller showed how *chunking* can be used to expand the limited capacity of STM by using already established memory stores to categorize or encode new information.

If we think of STM's capacity as seven 'slots' (plus or minus two), each slot being able to accommodate one bit or unit of information, then seven individual letters would each fill a slot and there would be no 'room' left for any additional letters. However, if the letters are chunked into a word, then the word would constitute a unit of information and there would still be six free slots. In the example below, the 25 bits of information can be chunked into (or reduced to) six words, which could quite easily be reduced further to one 'bit' (or chunk) based on prior familiarity with the words:

S A V A O

R E E E G

U R S Y A

O O D N S

F C N E R

To be able to chunk, you have to know the 'rule' or the 'code', which in this case is: starting with F (bottom left-hand corner) read upwards until you get to S and then drop down to C and read upwards until you get to A, then go to N and read upwards and so on. This should give you 'four score and seven years ago'.

Whenever we reduce a larger to a smaller amount of information we are chunking and this not only increases the capacity of STM but also makes it more likely that the information will be stored for longer. It also represents a form of encoding information by imposing a meaning on otherwise meaningless letters or numbers, etc.: (i) arranging letters into words, words into phrases, phrases into sentences; (ii) converting 1066 (four bits of information) into a date (one chunk), so a string of 28 numbers could be reduced to seven dates; (iii) using a rule to organize information, e.g. the series 149162536496481100121 (21 bits) is generated by the rule by which $1^2 = 1$, $2^2 = 4$, $3^2 = 9$ and so on. The rule represents a single chunk and that is all that has to be remembered.

These examples demonstrate how chunking allows us to bypass the seven-bit 'bottleneck'; although the amount of information contained in any one chunk may be unlimited (e.g. the rule in (iii) above can generate an infinitely long set of digits), the number of chunks which can be held in STM is still limited to seven plus or minus two.

Duration

It seems that, unaided, we can hold information in STM for between 15 and 30 seconds (according to Atkinson and Shiffrin, 1971), but this can be extended through *rehearsal* or repetition. Rehearsal seems to require some kind of speech (either overtly or mentally) whereby we 'say' the information to keep it 'circulating' within STM (e.g. repeating a telephone number out loud until we dial it), but it is easily disrupted by either external distractions (e.g. someone asking you for change while you are repeating the number) or internal ones (e.g. thinking about your own telephone number).

Coding

As we have just noted, it seems that in rehearsal information is maintained in the memory system acoustically (the *sounds* of the items are repeated and stored); although it can be visual, this is likely to be slower than acoustic rehearsal. Coding in STM therefore seems to be primarily acoustic, i.e. information from sensory memory (including visual) is converted into sound and is stored in this form.

● Long-term memory (LTM)

Capacity

It is generally accepted that LTM has *unlimited capacity*. It can be seen as the storehouse of all things in memory which are not currently being used but which are potentially retrievable. It enables us to deal with the past and to use that information to deal with the present; in a sense, LTM allows us to live in the past and present simultaneously.

According to Bower (1975), some of the kinds of information contained in LTM include:

1 a spatial model of the world around us;
2 knowledge of the physical world, physical laws and properties of objects;
3 beliefs about people, ourselves, social norms, values and goals;
4 motor skills, problem-solving skills and plans for achieving various things;
5 perceptual skills in understanding language, interpreting music, etc. Many of these are included in what Tulving (1972) calls *semantic memory* (see below).

Duration

Information can be held for between a few minutes and several years (which may in fact span the individual's entire lifetime).

Coding

There are at least two forms of coding in LTM: a *semantic code*, which deals with material in terms of verbal meaning, and an *imagery* or *visual code*, which takes a pictorial form. The former seems to be more common, especially when we have to deal with abstract material for which it is difficult to conjure up appropriate images. However, it has also been suggested that an acoustic code is used in LTM (see Table 12.1).

RETRIEVAL

'Remembering' can take many different forms (Fig. 12.3). However, they are all ways of recovering or locating information which has been stored; they also represent different ways of measuring memory in the laboratory.

● *Recognition* is a sensitive form of remembering, whereby something or somebody strikes us as familiar without our necessarily being able to name or otherwise identify it. Or we may recognize certain objects or faces as having been 'present' in a test situation when the 'target' items are present with other 'distractor' items (which were not originally present). This is the kind of remembering involved in multiple choice tests – the answers from which you have to choose one can be regarded as retrieval cues.

	Capacity	Duration	Coding
STM	7 bits of information. Can be increased by chunking	15–30 seconds (unaided) Can be increased by rehearsal	Acoustic
LTM	Unlimited	From a few seconds to several years (perhaps permanently)	(i) Semantic (ii) Visual (iii) Acoustic

TABLE 12.1 *Summary of major differences between STM and LTM*

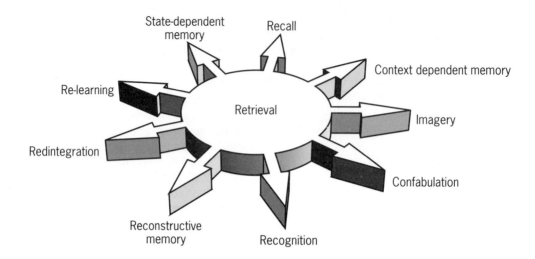

FIGURE 12.3 *Different forms of remembering or retrieval*

- *Recall* is a more stringent form of remembering and usually involves the active searching of our memory stores. When we recall, we reproduce something learned some time earlier and often the retrieval cues are missing or very sparse. This is the kind of remembering involved in timed essays.

- *Relearning* is the most sensitive measure of all – even though something may seem to be totally 'forgotten', it may be easier to learn second time around than it was originally. In experiments it is usually expressed as a:

Savings score =

$$\frac{\text{Original trials} - \text{Relearning trials}}{\text{Original trials}} \times \frac{100}{1}$$

- *Reconstructive memory* is the kind of remembering involved when information is passed from one person to another, often by word of mouth, as in the spreading of rumours or gossip. It is not simple reproduction of the past but interpretation of the past in the light of our beliefs, schemas, expectations and so on and so often involves a distortion of objective truth. This was first investigated by Bartlett (1932) and underlies much of the research on eyewitness testimony that we shall discuss later in the chapter.

- *Confabulation* refers to a kind of memory error often made under conditions of high motivation or arousal – if we are unable to recall a certain item, we may manufacture something that seems appropriate. Our recollection of some past event often reflects the combined recollection of several events of that kind , plus the 'filling in' of the missing details. Patients with Korsakov's syndrome are very prone to confabulation.

- *Redintegration* is the recollection of past experiences on the basis of a few cues, which might be souvenirs, particular smells, melodies – almost anything, in fact, which serve as reminders. Only a portion of the information is immediately available and a search of memory gradually leads to the redintegration of knowledge into some kind of coherent whole. The search is rather like a detective's investigation, but every so often some item will 'pop up', quite unrelated to what is currently being consciously thought about. This kind of remembering is involved in the recollection of childhood involved in psychoanalysis (see Chapters 30 and 31).

- *Cue-dependent memory* refers to the similarity or difference between the state (e.g. alcohol or no alcohol) and the context (e.g. the room) in which the original learning took place and in which the learning is remembered. Generally, if two different states or contexts are involved, retrieval is poor. We shall return to this in relation to theories of forgetting.

- *Imagery* is the basis of many kinds of *mnemonic*

Device	Example
Method of loci ('method of places' or the 'house technique;)	You have to imagine a short walk through a series of locations, perhaps a journey through a familiar street, past well-known buildings or through the rooms in your house or college. Take each of the (unrelated) words to be remembered in turn (e.g. the items on a shopping list) and associate it with each of your locations. The more bizarre the association, the greater the probability of recalling the words.
Associations	You find a relationship between the unrelated words by weaving them into a sensible story.
Rhyme and rhythm	E.g. 'Thirty days hath September' etc.
Numeric pegword system (pigeonhole technique)	Numbers are associated with a rhyming object and you picture the items to be remembered in relation to the relevant pegword. E.g.: One-bun Egg Two-shoe Sausage Three-tree Potatoes The items to be remembered are hooked onto the pegword by constructing an image which includes the first item with the bun, the second item with the shoes, etc. (egg on a bun, sausage in a shoe, potatoes growing on a tree).

TABLE 12.2 *Some of the most commonly used mnemonic devices*

devices (memory aids) and there is much evidence that we can remember verbal material better if we can 'hook it' onto some visual image – this relates both to initial learning (how the material is encoded) and retrieval (see Table 12.2). Imagery is discussed further later in the chapter.

THE MULTISTORE MODEL (ATKINSON AND SHIFFRIN, 1968, 1971)

So far, we have been discussing STM and LTM differences without looking specifically at Atkinson and Shiffrin's model (Fig. 12.4). This is sometimes called the *dual memory theory* (Atkinson *et al.*, 1990) because of the emphasis on STM and LTM in which stored information has been coded, in contrast with sensory memory which holds information from the environment in roughly its original or 'sensory' form.

Sensory memory, STM and LTM are referred to by the model as permanent structural components of the memory system and represent intrinsic features of the information-processing system of humans. In addition to these structural components, the memory system comprises relatively transient processes called *control processes*, of which rehearsal is one. Rehearsal serves two main functions: (i) to act as a buffer between sensory memory and LTM by maintaining incoming information within STM; and (ii) to transfer information to LTM.

Finally, how does information transfer from sensory memory to STM? According to Atkinson and Shiffrin, it is scanned and matched with information in LTM and if a match occurs (i.e. *pattern recognition;* see Chapter 9), the information from sensory memory might then be fed into STM along with a verbal label from LTM.

The three main kinds of evidence for the multistore model that we shall discuss are:

1 two-component tasks;
2 studies of coding;
3 the study of brain-damaged patients.

● Two-component tasks

The most economical way of accounting for performance on certain memory tasks in the laboratory is in terms of a distinction between STM and LTM. For example, if participants are presented with 20 words, one after the other, and then asked to recall them immediately afterwards in any order (*free recall*) typical results would be as shown in Figure 12.5.

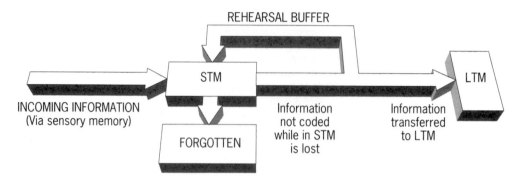

FIGURE 12.4 The multistore model of memory. (Based on Atkinson and Shiffrin, 1971)

The probability of recalling any word depends on its position in the list (its serial position) and hence the graph shown in Figure 12.5 is called a *serial position curve*. Participants typically recall those items from the end of the list first and get more of these correct than earlier items (the *recency effect*). According to Murdock (1962), this is true no matter how long the list. Items from the beginning of the list are recalled quite well relative to those in the middle of the list (the *primacy effect*) but not as well as those at the end. Poorest recall is for items in the middle portion of the curve.

The implication is that the recency effect reflects words being retrieved from STM, whereas the primacy effect reflects retrieval from LTM. The last items are only remembered if recalled first and tested immediately, as demonstrated by Glanzer and

Cunitz (1966); when recall is delayed by, for example, counting backwards in threes (thus preventing rehearsal), the recency effect disappears while recall of earlier items is largely unaffected. They presented two groups of participants with the same list of words: one group recalled the material immediately after presentation while the other group recalled after 30 seconds. The first group showed a recency effect (indicating STM retrieval) and the second group showed a primacy effect (indicating LTM retrieval; Fig. 12.6).

A second kind of task involves what has become known as the *Brown-Peterson technique* (Brown, 1958; Peterson and Peterson, 1959) and is concerned specifically with the effects of the length of the recall interval on recall (Fig. 12.7).This is described in Box 12.1.

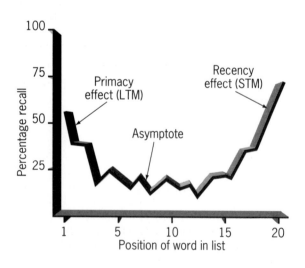

FIGURE 12.5 *A typical serial position curve. (Based on Glanzer and Cunitz, 1966)*

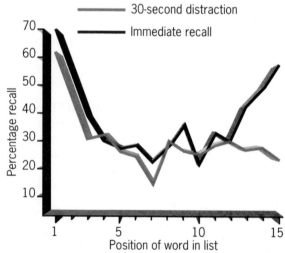

FIGURE 12.6 *The effect of distraction prior to recall on the serial position curve. (Based on Glanzer and Cunitz, 1966)*

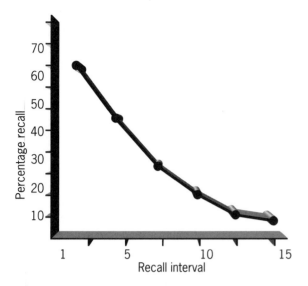

FIGURE 12.7 *The effects of an interfering task on recall. (Based on Peterson and Peterson, 1959)*

The rapid loss of information from memory when rehearsal is prevented is usually taken as evidence for the existence of a STM with rapid decay of the memory trace or displacement; the kind of forgetting involved in LTM is thought to be different and this difference in forgetting represents further support for the multistore model (see below). However, not everyone accepts this interpretation of the findings.

BOX 12.1	Key study: demonstration of the Brown-Peterson technique

Peterson and Peterson (1959) used trigrams, which are nonsense syllables comprising three consonants (e.g. CPQ). Only one trigram was to be remembered on each trial, something that would be well within the participants' capabilities if allowed normal rehearsal (i.e. repeating it over and over to themselves). But this was prevented by getting them to count backwards in threes, aloud, for 3, 6, 9, 12, 15 or 18 seconds or not at all, after which a tone was sounded as a signal for them to stop counting and try to recall the trigram (Glanzer and Cunitz had done this for a period of 30 seconds in their second experiment). Even with very small amounts of information, nearly 70% is forgotten after only a 9-second delay and 90% after 18 seconds. (The remaining 10% is thought to be retained over a longer period and is processed by LTM.)

For example, Gruneberg (1970) argues that they could be a feature of any memory system and do not necessarily imply a distinction between two separate stores.

Is rehearsal all of a kind?

The concept of rehearsal itself, so important in Atkinson and Shiffrin's model, has also been criticized as both unnecessary and too general. Craik and Watkins (1973), for example, asked participants to remember only certain words (those beginning with a particular letter) from lists presented either

FIGURE 12.8 *Elaborative rehearsal is much more like the rehearsal involved in a play than is maintenance rehearsal.*

rapidly or slowly; the position of critical words relative to non-critical ones determined the amount of time a particular word spent in STM and the number of potential rehearsals given to it. Retention over long periods was found to be unrelated to either duration in STM or the number of explicit or implicit rehearsals. An earlier study by Glanzer and Meinzer (1967) found that participants required to repeat items aloud recalled fewer of them than those allowed an equal period of silent rehearsal. Perhaps in silent rehearsal the material is not being merely repeated but recoded into a different form which enhances recall.

As a result of these and other findings, Craik and Watkins (1973) distinguished between *maintenance* (or rote) *rehearsal* and *elaborative rehearsal*. Maintenance rehearsal involves repeating the items in the form in which they were presented and is sufficient to retain them in the short term. Elaborative rehearsal involves elaboration of the items, for example semantic recoding (giving them a meaning) or associative linking of words with pre-existing knowledge, and is necessary for long-term retention. It seems that maintenance rehearsal is not necessary for storage, as illustrated by Jenkins' (1974) study in which participants showed they could remember material even though they were not expecting to be tested and so were unlikely to have rehearsed the material (this is *incidental learning*).

It seems, therefore, that it is the *kind* of rehearsal or processing that is crucial rather than the amount and this idea has been investigated in particular by Craik and Lockhart (1972), in the form of the *levels of processing* approach (which will be discussed in detail later in the chapter).

● Studies of coding

If we take again the familiar example of trying to remember a telephone number, we keep it in STM by auditory rehearsal (using an acoustic code), that is, we say it over and over regardless of whether we have looked it up in the directory or the operator has given it to us. Experimental findings tend to support this view of STM.

Conrad (1963, 1964) presented participants with sequences of six consonants and found that the errors they made in trying to remember them were similar in *sound* to the correct item (e.g. b/d, p/v, m/n) despite the fact that they had been presented visually. In fact, they made the same kind of acoustic errors as they did when trying to detect similar spoken consonants against a noisy background. Similarly, Baddeley (1966) found that immediate recall of the order of short lists of unrelated words was seriously impeded if the words were acoustically similar (e.g. caught/short/taut/nought) but not if they were semantically similar (e.g. huge/great/big /wide). After a delay, however, exactly the opposite effect occurred.

It seems that the phonemic or grammatical features of prose sentences are forgotten almost immediately, while the semantic features are well remembered even after a long delay, i.e. when we recall a conversation, speech or lecture, it is the *meaning* that we remember (we often report the 'gist' of the conversation or whatever) rather than the particular words or phrases used. Therefore, there is considerable support for the view that STM uses an acoustic code and LTM a semantic code. However, not everyone accepts this view.

When discussing chunking in relation to STM capacity, we used the term 'meaning' to describe what is involved in reducing large amounts of information to smaller and more manageable amounts so as to increase the capacity of STM. According to Miller (1956), chunking represents a *linguistic recoding* which seems to be the 'very lifeblood of the thought process'. He says that it is not surprising that such compression of information can occur when you consider how lexical information is normally processed: our capacity to read and understand is largely based on the chunking of letters into words, words into phrases and phrases into sentences. Therefore, the capability of STM to handle a vast amount of information is facilitated by our ability to chunk information; however, this cannot occur until certain information in LTM is activated and a match made between the incoming items and their representation in LTM.

This is illustrated by an experiment by Miller and Selfridge (1950) in which participants were presented with a number of 'sentences' (of varying lengths) which represented different approximations to true English sentences; the task was to recall the words in their correct order. Immediate recall was greater the closer the sentence approximated normal English, suggesting that knowledge of semantic and grammatical structure (presumably stored in LTM) is used to facilitate immediate memory.

More recently, Bower and Springston (1970) used a letter sequence which participants had to recall. In one condition, letters were read so that they did not form a well-known group and so could not be matched with information stored in LTM (fb, iph, dtw, aib, m), while in another they did (fbi, phd, twa, ibm). The latter were more readily recalled; they were clustered along the lines of acronyms familiar to most college students and, in effect, the pause after 'fbi', etc. allowed participants to 'look it up' in their mental lexicon and so encode the letter in a chunk.

So, clearly, an acoustic code is not the only one used in STM. Equally, you only have to think of all the voices and melodies we can remember over long periods of time and which are, presumably, acoustically coded and of all the faces, scenes, skills and so on which are difficult to process verbally to realize

BOX 12.2	The case of H.M. (based on Blakemore, 1988)

H.M. had been suffering epileptic fits of devastating frequency since the age of 16. At 27 he underwent surgery, using a technique never used before, which miraculously cured his epilepsy – but at a terrible cost. The hippocampus was removed on both sides of his brain (see Chapter 3). He was left with severe anterograde amnesia – he had near normal memory for anything which he had learned prior to the surgery but he had severe memory deficits for events which occurred after the surgery. For example, within the first few hours after the operation, he was unable to recognize the medical staff and could not find his bedroom.

His STM was generally normal; for instance, he could retain verbal information for about 15 seconds without rehearsal and for much longer with rehearsal. However, he could not transfer information into LTM or, if he could, he could not retrieve it. He seemed entirely incapable of remembering any new fact or event. He had almost no knowledge of current affairs because he forgot all the news almost as soon as he had read about it; he had no idea what time of day it was unless he had just looked at the clock; he could not remember that his father had died or that his family had moved house and he would reread the same magazine without realizing he had already read it.

Although he could recognize friends, state their names and relate stories about them, he could do so only if he knew them before the surgery. People he met after the operation remained, in effect, total strangers to him and he had to 'get to know them' afresh each time they came into his house. Brenda Milner has known him for 25 years yet she is a stranger to him each time they meet.

He was able to learn and remember perceptual and motor skills, although he had to be reminded each day just what skills he knew how to do. However, '... new events, faces, phone numbers, places, now settle in his mind for just a few seconds or minutes before they slip, like water through a sieve, and are lost from his consciousness' (Blakemore, 1988).

● The study of brain-damaged patients

If STM and LTM really are distinct, then there should be certain kinds of brain damage which impair one without affecting the other. One such form of brain damage is *anterograde amnesia* and a famous case is that of H.M. (Milner *et al.*, 1978; Box 12.2).

An equally dramatic, but in many ways more tragic case than that of H.M is that of Clive Wearing (Box 12.3).

What conclusions can we draw from the study of amnesic patients?

The kind of amnesic syndrome displayed by H.M. and Clive Wearing has been interpreted by Atkinson and Shiffrin as 'perhaps the single most convincing demonstration of a dichotomy in the memory system', i.e. a distinction between STM and LTM. According to Parkin (1987), the *amnesic syndrome* is not some general deterioration of memory function but a selective impairment in which some functions, such as learning novel information, are severely impaired while others, including memory span and language, remain normal. There is ample evidence that they both retained normally functioning STMs, which is consistent with evidence from experimental studies using free recall with amnesic patients and normal (control) participants.

As we saw in the section on two-component tasks, serial position curves show a separation of STM (recency effect) and LTM (primacy effect); if amnesics really do have an intact STM, they should show similar recall to normal participants for items later in the list (i.e. similar recency effect, based on STM) but poorer recall for items earlier in the list (i.e. different primacy effect, based on LTM). This is exactly what is found (e.g. Baddeley and Warrington, 1970). These results have led most psychologists to accept that in the amnesic syndrome, STM function is preserved but LTM function is impaired.

However, there are two ways of interpreting this difference in STM and LTM functioning: it may mean that the problem for amnesics is one of transfer from STM to LTM, which would be perfectly consistent with the multistore model, or, alternatively, it could be due to difficulties in retrieval (Warrington and Weiskrantz, 1968, 1978), i.e. the information is successfully transferred and stored in LTM but it cannot easily be recovered when required. This interpretation is more consistent with Craik and Lockhart's depth of processing approach (1972) – the amnesic may not be able to process most kinds of new information deeply enough

that a single, semantic code is not the only one used by LTM. According to Wickelgren (1973), it could be that the mode of coding reflects the processing which has occurred in a given context, rather than being a property of the memory store itself (see the later section on Levels of Processing).

BOX
12.3

The case of Clive Wearing (based on Blakemore, 1988; Baddeley, 1990)

Clive Wearing used to be the chorus master of the London Sinfonietta and a world expert on Renaissance music, as well as a BBC radio producer. In March 1985 he suffered a rare brain infection caused by the cold sore virus (*Herpes simplex*). The virus attacked his hippocampus and destroyed it, along with other parts of his cortex. Like H.M., he lives in a snapshot of time, constantly believing that he has just awoken from years of unconsciousness. For example, when his wife, Deborah, enters his hospital room for the third time in a single morning, he embraces her as if they had been parted for years, saying, 'I'm conscious for the first time' and 'It's the first time I've seen anybody at all'.

Deborah describes her husband like this: 'Clive's world now consists of a moment, with no past to anchor it and no future to look ahead to. It's a blinkered moment.'

At first his confusion was total and very frightening to him. Once he held a chocolate in the palm of one hand, covered it with the other for a few seconds till its image disappeared from his memory. When he uncovered it, he thought he had performed a magic trick, conjuring it up from nowhere. He repeated it again and again, with total astonishment and growing fear each time.

Like H.M., he can still speak and walk, as well as read music, play the organ and conduct. In fact, his musical ability is remarkably well preserved. Also like H.M, he can learn new skills (e.g. mirror-reading). Over the course of a few days of testing, the speed of reading such words doubles and it can be done just as well three months later. Yet for Clive it is new every time. But unlike H.M., his capacity for remembering his earlier life was extremely patchy. He could still remember general features, including where he had been to school, what Cambridge college he attended, highlights such as singing for the Pope on his visit to London and some particular dramatic musical events he had organized. But in all cases his capacity to recall detail was extremely poor.

He showed considerable impairment in other areas too. He had written a book on an early composer (Lassus) and could still recall just a few relevant features about his life but with no richness or detail. When shown pictures of Cambridge (where he'd spent four years as an undergraduate and had often visited subsequently) he only recognized King's College Chapel – the best known and most distinctive Cambridge building – but not his own college. He couldn't remember who wrote *Romeo and Juliet* and when shown photos of the Queen and the Duke of Edinburgh he thought they were singers he had known from a Catholic church.

Such amnesic patients' lives are effectively ruined because of a lack of *conscious* recollection; according to Deborah, 'without consciousness he's in many senses dead'. If he goes out alone he gets lost and cannot find his way back – he cannot tell anyone who finds him where he's come from or where he's going. In his own words, his life is 'Hell on earth – it's like being dead – all the bloody time'.

for retrieval from LTM but can do so to allow STM retrieval.

Another major implication of these clinical findings is that the idea of a 'unitary' LTM is a gross oversimplification, i.e. there must be different kinds of LTM (see next section).

The other major kind of amnesia is *retrograde amnesia* where the patient fails to remember what happens before the surgery or accident which causes it. It can be caused by head injuries, electroconvulsive therapy (ECT), carbon monoxide poisoning and extreme stress. As in anterograde amnesia, there is typically little or no disruption of STM and the period of memory loss may be minutes, days or even years. When retrograde amnesia is caused by brain damage it is usually accompanied by anterograde amnesia. Similarly, patients who are suffering from Korsakov's syndrome (caused by severe, chronic alcoholism involving damage to the hippocampus) usually experience both kinds of amnesia. Both H.M. and Clive Wearing suffered only anterograde amnesia.

What seems to be involved in retrograde amnesia is a disruption of the *consolidation process* whereby, once new information has entered LTM, a consolidation time is needed for it to become firmly established physically in the brain.

ALTERNATIVES TO THE MULTISTORE MODEL

In this section we shall discuss three major attempts to modify and revise Atkinson and Shiffrin's multistore model, namely:

1 episodic and procedural memory;
2 levels of processing;
3 working memory.

None of these represents an outright rejection of that model; rather, they all share the view that it is an oversimplified account of the highly complex human memory.

● Episodic and procedural memory

As we saw when discussing H.M. and Clive Wearing, whatever their brain damage prevented them from doing, they were still able to use many basic skills (e.g. talking and walking, playing the organ, reading) and were even capable of acquiring certain new skills (and retaining these) – but they did not know that they knew them! So, clearly, certain parts of their LTM (or certain *kinds* of LTM) were still intact and this makes it necessary to distinguish between different kinds of LTM remembering not allowed for by the multistore model, which sees LTM as unitary.

Tulving (1972) distinguished between episodic and semantic LTM. *Episodic memory* (EM) is an 'autobiographical' memory responsible for storing a record of our past experiences – the events, people, objects and so on which we have personally encountered. This usually includes details about the particular time and place in which objects and events were experienced (i.e. they have a spatio-temporal context). So they relate to questions such as 'Where did you go on your holiday last year?' and 'What did you have for breakfast this morning?'. They have a subjective (self-focused) reality but most could, in theory anyway, be verified by others.

Semantic memory (SM) is our store of general, factual knowledge about the world, including concepts, rules and language, '... a mental thesaurus, organized knowledge a person possesses about words and other verbal symbols, their meanings and referents ...' (Tulving, 1972).

The essential feature of SM is that it can be used without reference to where and when that knowledge was originally acquired. For example, we don't remember 'learning to speak' (at least, not our native language) – we just 'know English'. However, SM can also store information about ourselves; for example, when we are asked how many brothers and sisters we have or how much we like psychology, we do not have to remember specific past experiences in order to answer. Similarly, much of our SM (e.g. our 'general' knowledge about computers) is built up from past experiences with particular computers (which are part of EM), through abstraction and generalization. What this suggests is that, instead of regarding EM and SM as two quite distinct systems within the

brain (which is what Tulving originally intended), it might be more valid to see SM as made up from multiple EMs (Baddeley, 1995).

When Tulving first drew the distinction, he maintained that episodic memory is synonymous with *autobiographical memory* (AM). He claimed that recalling a list of words as part of an experimental task taps EM, since the process of learning the words constitutes a specific experience or episode. In the same way, forgetting of words in a free-recall task can be thought of as a failure in our EM since, clearly, we already know the words as part of our SM but we have failed to remember that they appeared in that particular list just presented to us. However, Cohen (1993) argues that learning word lists is not what most people understand by AM. Instead, she claims that AM is a special kind of EM concerned with specific life events that have a self-reference, i.e. they have personal significance. Accordingly, she distinguishes between *autobiographical* EM and *experimental* EM; taking part in an experiment in which we are required to learn lists of words is an example of the latter.

Flashbulb memories refer to a special kind of EM, namely the kind of vivid and detailed recollections people often have of some major public event (national or international), such as the dismantling of the Berlin Wall or the resignation of Margaret Thatcher. People can usually recall exactly where they were, what they were doing and with whom when the news broke. According to Brown and Kulik (1982), there is a neural mechanism that is triggered by events that are emotionally arousing, unexpected or extremely important, with the result that the whole scene becomes 'printed' on the memory. However, Neisser (1982) argued that the durability of flashbulb memories stems from their frequent rehearsal and reconsideration after the event and the detail of people's memories and their vividness aren't necessarily signs of their accuracy – we can be very confident about something and still be mistaken!

Tulving (1985) among others (such as Anderson, 1985) distinguished a third kind of LTM, namely *procedural* memory (PM).This refers to information from LTM which cannot be inspected consciously. For example, riding a bike is a complex skill which is even more difficult to describe. (This corresponds to Bruner's 'enactive' mode of representation, a kind of 'muscle memory'; see Chapter 25.) Similarly, native speakers of a language cannot usually describe the complex grammatical rules by which they speak correctly (perhaps because they were not learnt

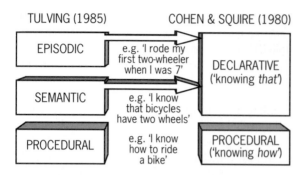

FIGURE 12.9 *Distinctions between different kinds of LTM*

consciously in the first place; see Chapter 26). By contrast, EM and SM are both capable of being inspected consciously and the content of both can be described to another person.

Overlapping with Tulving's distinction is Cohen and Squire's (1980) distinction between declarative and procedural memory, which in turn corresponds to Ryle's (1949) distinction between *knowing that* and *knowing how*, respectively (see Fig. 12.9). Anderson (1983) argues that when we initially learn something, it is learned and encoded declaratively, but with practice it becomes compiled into a procedural form of knowledge. (This can be seen as corresponding to the distinction between controlled versus automatic processing or focused versus divided attention, discussed in Chapter 11.)

How does all this help us understand the kind of LTM deficiencies experienced by patients like H.M. and Clive Wearing? Certainly, most aspects of their PM seemed to be intact (and they could both acquire new skills) but both their EM and SM were partially impaired. For instance, H.M. was given extensive training (by Gabrieli *et al.*, 1983) in the task of learning the meaning of unfamiliar words which had come into popular use since his operation. He made very little progress, despite extensive practice every day for ten days. According to Eysenck and Keane (1990), most other amnesics similarly fail to update their SM to take account of changes in the world since onset. For example, Baddeley (1984) reports that many do not know the name of the current Prime Minister or President and have very poor recognition for faces of people who have become famous only quite recently.

When new learning does occur in amnesic patients, which may include psychomotor skills, problem solving or cued verbal learning, they typically deny having encountered the task before despite simultaneously showing quite clear evidence of learning. All these examples of learning share one crucial characteristic – they allow the patient to demonstrate learning without the need for conscious awareness of the learning process. Declarative learning/memory involves conscious recollection of the past and its adequate functioning seems to be disrupted by damage to a number of cortical and subcortical areas (including the temporal lobes, hippocampus and mamillary bodies); this is seriously impaired in amnesic patients. On the other hand, procedural learning/memory involves more automatic processes and so does not require conscious recollection and does not appear to be impaired by brain damage to these areas (Baddeley, 1995).

● Levels of processing (LOP)

According to Craik and Lockhart (1972), it is not rehearsal as such which is important but what is done with or to the material during rehearsal. It is the attentional and perceptual processes occurring at the time of learning which determine what information is stored in LTM. The distinction between maintenance and elaborative rehearsal that we noted above is a direct result of the LOP approach (since the latter involves a greater depth of processing) (Baddeley, 1990).

As we have seen, the multistore model distinguishes between *structural* components (sensory memory, STM and LTM) and *control* processes (e.g. rehearsal, attention and coding), with the latter being tied to the former; emphasis is put on the sequence of stages that information goes through as it passes from one structural component to another when being processed. The LOP approach, on the other hand, begins with hypothesized processes and then formulates a memory system (the structural components) in terms of these operations. This can be seen as the multistore model in reverse.

Craik and Lockhart (1972) (and Neisser, 1976) see memory, essentially, as the *byproduct* of the processing of information; the durability of memory (or trace persistence) is a direct function of the depth of processing. Incoming stimuli are subjected to a series of analyses, starting with a shallow, sensory analysis, passing through an intermediate, phonetic level and finishing with a deeper, semantic analysis (Table 12.3). Which level is used depends on both the nature of the stimulus and the time available for processing. The general rule is that the deeper the level of processing used, the less likely the material is to be forgotten.

Level	Description
1. **Structured or shallow level**	Is the word written in capital letters or not? (What does it look like?)
2. **Phonetic or phonemic level**	Does the word rhyme with some other word? (What does it sound like?)
3. **Semantic level**	Does the word mean the same as some other word? (What does it mean?)

TABLE 12.3 *The three levels or depths of processing. (Based on Craik and Lockhart, 1972)*

It is important to note that, despite these important differences, Craik and Lockhart still assumed a separate STM but instead of seeing its main role as the transfer of information to LTM, they emphasized its processing function. However, it is doubtful whether they actually needed to do this. For example, as we saw earlier, STM is traditionally associated with phonological (acoustic) processing and LTM with semantic. But rather than regarding these forms of coding as characteristics of the two stores, Craik and Lockhart regarded the coding itself as primary and saw depth of processing as influencing how permanently information is remembered (Baddeley, 1990). One demonstration of this is an experiment by Craik and Tulving (1975) which is described in Box 12.4.

Whilst finding support for the LOP approach, Craik and Tulving (1975) also argued that depth of processing is not the only factor influencing LTM. They found support for the view that *elaboration* of processing is also important, i.e. the amount of processing of a particular kind. In one experiment they manipulated elaboration by varying the complexity of a sentence frame from simple ('She cooked the _____ ') to complex ('The great bird swooped down and carried off the struggling _____ '). Participants were given an unexpected cued recall test, whereby they were given the sentence frame and asked to recall the word which had been presented with it. For those words compatible with the sentence frame, cued recall was twice as high for words accompanying complex compared with simple sentences. Since the same deep or semantic level of processing was involved in both conditions, there must be some additional factor involved, i.e. elaboration.

However, Craik and Tulving seemed to be assuming that there is a direct relationship between the

---

BOX 12.4 Key study: depth of processing and the retention of words in episodic memory

Craik and Tulving (1975) presented participants with words via a tachistoscope and asked them one of four questions about each word: (i) is the word in capital letters? (e.g. TABLE/table); (ii) does the word rhyme with *wait*? (e.g. hate/chicken); (iii) is the word a type of food? (e.g. cheese/steel); (iv) would the word fit the sentence 'He kicked the — into the tree'? (e.g. ball/rain).

Of these, (i) corresponds to structural processing, (ii) to phonetic processing and (iii) and (iv) to semantic processing. Participants had to answer 'yes' or 'no' to each question and were subsequently given an unexpected test of recognition, which involved presentation of the words they had seen intermixed with the same number of words they had not seen; they had to say which they had seen before.

There was a significantly better recognition with deeper levels of processing. Also, recognition was superior if the answer was 'yes' than if it was 'no'.

---

sheer number of elaborations and the probability of recall. But what about the *kind* of elaboration involved?

Bransford *et al.* (1979) found clear evidence for the importance of the nature of the elaboration (e.g. 'A mosquito is like a doctor because they both draw blood') rather than the number of elaborations (e.g. 'A mosquito is like a racoon because they both have heads, legs and jaws'). Despite the former involving fewer elaborations (it is minimally elaborated), such similes were better remembered than the latter which is multiply elaborated. Why?

According to Eysenck (1979) and others, it is encodings which are distinctive or unique in some way which are more likely to be remembered. This represents an alternative way of conceptualizing the basic concept of depth – it may be the non-distinctiveness of shallow encodings (as opposed to their shallowness as such) which leads to their poor retention (Eysenck, 1984, 1986).

Eysenck (1984, 1986) believes that it is often difficult to choose between LOP, elaboration and distinctiveness because they co-vary (i.e. occur together). We know that retention cannot be predicted solely on the basis of LOP because more elaborate or distinctive semantic encodings are usually better remembered than non-elaborate or non-distinctive ones. A study by Eysenck and Eysenck (1980) shows that a shallow LOP can cause remembering that is almost as good as a deep LOP, as long as it is also distinctive. It is possible that all three make separate contributions to LTM but distinctiveness, which relates to the nature of processing and takes account of relationships between encodings, is likely to prove more important than elaboration, which is only a measure of the amount of processing (Eysenck, 1984, 1986).

Evaluation of the LOP approach

● According to Eysenck (1984, 1986), LOP was probably the most influential theoretical approach in memory during the 1970s, but it rapidly went out of favour after that. He says that most psychologists believe it contains a grain of truth but is a substantial oversimplification. We should note, though, that Craik and Lockhart themselves claim that their approach does not constitute a *theory* of memory but offers a new way of interpreting existing data and provides a conceptual framework for memory research.

● Eysenck (1984, 1986) believes that Craik and Lockhart were absolutely right to argue that perception, attention and memory are inter-dependent; once it is recognized that memory traces are formed as a result of perceptual and attentional processes, it becomes necessary for memory research to focus on these processes. At this general level, LOP has made a major contribution. Prior to 1972, remarkably few experiments compared the effects on memory of different kinds of processing – it had been implicitly assumed that any particular stimulus will typically be processed in a very similar way by all participants on all occasions. According to Parkin (1987), LOP has made a significant contribution to our understanding of memory; in attempting to explain a wide range of memory phenomena, it is now accepted that changes in the *processing strategy* may provide the basis for an explanation.

● Probably the most serious problem with LOP is the difficulty of measuring or defining depth independently of the actual retention score, i.e. if 'depth' is defined as 'how many words are remembered' and if 'how many words are remembered' is taken as a measure of 'depth', we are faced with a circular definition. One attempt to provide an independent measure of depth is in terms of the kind of orienting task used and a famous example of this approach is the experiment by Hyde and Jenkins (1973) (see Box 12.5). According to Baddeley (1990),' ... there is no generally accepted way of independently assessing depth of processing. This places major limits on the power of the levels of processing approach'.

● Eysenck (1984, 1986) argues that the original theory focused too narrowly on the processing activities occurring at the point of acquisition (operationally defined as the kind of orienting task involved) and virtually ignored all the other determinants of LTM. More specifically, learning and memory are affected by at least four types of factors: (i) the nature of the task; (ii) the kind of stimulus material used; (iii) individual characteristics of the participants (e.g. idiosyncratic knowledge); and (iv) the nature of the retention test used to measure memory. In many LOP experiments, several orienting tasks are used but only one kind of stimulus material (usually words), one fairly homogeneous set of participants and one kind of retention test (e.g. Hyde and Jenkins (1973) used only free recall).

BOX 12.5 Key study: trying to define depth of processing in terms of orienting task

Hyde and Jenkins (1973) used five orienting tasks, meant to vary in the amount of processing of meaning involved. These were: (i) rating words for pleasantness; (ii) estimating the frequency with which the words are used in English; (iii) detecting the number of 'e's and 'g's in the words; (iv) deciding the part of speech appropriate to each word (noun/verb/adjective/'some other'); and (v) deciding whether or not the word fitted various sentence frames ('it is the ___/'it is____'). Hyde and Jenkins defined (i) and (ii) as involving semantic (deep) processing and (iii)–(v) as involving non-semantic (shallow) processing. The prediction, of course, was that (i) and (ii) would produce significantly higher retention and this was indeed found. However, the assumption that (i) and (ii) involved thinking of the word's meaning while (iv) did not has been challenged. If it is only an assumption, we are again faced with the lack of an adequate, independent measure of 'depth'.

However, there are often large interactions between the four factors and an important demonstration of this is a study by Morris *et al.* (1977). They predicted that stored information (whether deep or shallow) will be remembered only to the extent that it is relevant to the memory test used; so deep or semantic information would be of little use if the memory test involved learning a list of words and later selecting words that rhymed with the stored words, while shallow rhyme information would be very relevant. They called this *transfer-appropriate processing*. Their results supported their prediction and represent an experimental disproof of LOP, specifically the idea that deep processing is intrinsically more memorable than shallow processing; they also demonstrate that how memory is tested must be taken into account when we are trying to predict the consequences of some processing activity.

According to Parkin (1993), different orienting tasks vary in the extent to which they require participants to treat the stimulus as a word (e.g. 'Is "tiger" a mammal?' compared with 'Does "tiger" have two syllables?'), yet retention tests always require participants to remember words. Since semantic tasks, by definition, always require attention to be paid to stimuli as words, the superior retention they produce could reflect the bias of the retention test towards the type of information being encoded – the orienting task and the retention test are both concerned with the same type of information, which is not the case when other kinds of task are used.

● Working memory

Just as Tulving's and Cohen and Squire's distinctions challenge the earlier concept of a unitary LTM, so the concept of *working memory* (WM) (Baddeley and Hitch, 1974) challenges the earlier concept of a unitary STM. They adopted a functional approach, i.e. they wanted to answer the question: what is memory for? They did not reject the multistore model's view of STM as rehearsing incoming information for transfer to LTM, but claimed that it is more complex and versatile than this.

According to Cohen (1990):

'The concept of the short-term store as a working memory store emphasizes that it is an active store used to hold information which is being manipulated. Working memory is the focus of consciousness – it holds the information you are consciously thinking about now ...'

The original model has been itself modified and elaborated (Baddeley, 1981, 1986) and in its current form consists of a central executive, at the top of a hierarchy, controlling or directing the activities of three other components, the articulatory loop, visuospatial

scratch pad and primary acoustic store (see Fig. 12.10). (The original model did not include the primary acoustic store – this was added by Salame and Baddeley, 1982.)

The *central executive* is the most important component because it is used when dealing with any task which makes cognitive demands. It is so called because it allocates attention to incoming information (see Chapter 11) and directs the operation of the other components ('slave systems'; Baddeley, 1990). It is a very flexible system that can process information in any sensory modality (it is modality-free) and in a variety of different ways. It can also store information for brief periods of time. According to Baddeley (1981), '... the Central Executive is becoming increasingly like a pure attentional system'.

The *articulatory* (or *phonological*) *loop* can be regarded as a verbal rehearsal loop that we use when we, for example, try to remember a telephone number for a few seconds by muttering it to ourselves. It is also used to hold the words we are preparing to speak aloud. So it uses an *articulatory/phonological* code, which represents information as it would be spoken (the 'inner voice'). The *visuospatial scratch pad* (or *sketch pad*) can also rehearse information but deals with visual and/or spatial information, for example, driving along a familiar road approaching a bend and thinking of the spatial layout of the road around the bend (Eysenck, 1986). So it uses a visual code, which represents information in the form of visual features, such as size, shape and colour ('the inner eye'). Baddeley (1986) describes it as '... a system especially well adapted to the storage of spatial information, much as a pad of paper might be used by someone trying, for example, to work out a geometric puzzle'.

The *primary acoustic store* receives auditory input directly; visual input can only enter it indirectly after being converted to a phonological form (i.e. processed by the articulatory loop). It uses an acoustic/phonemic code, which represents information in the form of auditory features such as pitch and loudness (the 'inner ear').

Some feel for how WM works can be gained from trying to work out how many windows there are in your present home. Most people attempt this by forming a visual image of their home and then counting the windows, either by imagining looking from outside or walking through the rooms. The visuospatial sketch pad is the system used for setting up and manipulating the image, the articulatory loop is involved in the process of subvocal counting, while the whole operation is organized and run by the central executive (Baddeley, 1995).

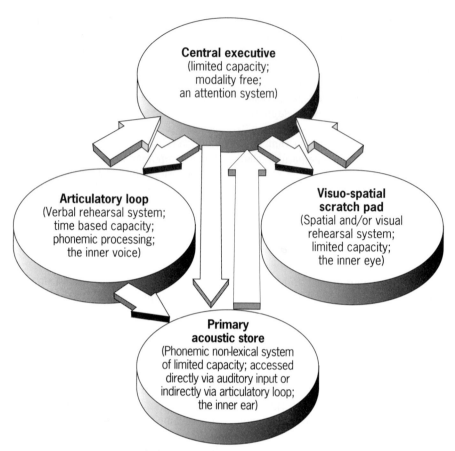

FIGURE 12.10 *The working memory model. (From Cohen et al., 1986)*

WM has been studied mainly by the use of the con-current or interference (or dual-) tasks method (very similar in design to dual-task studies of divided attention; see Chapter 11). Assuming that each com-ponent of WM has a limited capacity, if two tasks make use of the same component(s), then perfor-mance of one or both tasks should be worse when performed together than when performed separately. If they require different components, it should be possible to perform them as well together as sepa-rately. An example involves the use of *articulatory suppression:* the participant rapidly repeats out loud something meaningless (such as 'hi-ya' or 'the') and this uses up the resources of the articulatory loop so that it cannot be used for anything else. If this pro-duces poorer performance on another concurrent task, then we can infer that this second task also uses the articulatory loop (Eysenck, 1986).

Evaluation of working memory

● Eysenck (1986) believes that it is almost univer-sally agreed that it is much more realistic to

assume that WM comprises several relatively inde-pendent processing mechanisms than to see STM as a single, unitary store. It is also useful to treat attentional processes and STM as parts of the same system, mainly because they are probably used together much of the time in everyday life.
● The notion that any one component of WM may be involved in the performance of a great number of apparently very different tasks is a valuable insight. For example, the articulatory loop seems to play a part in memory span tasks, mental arithmetic, ver-bal reasoning and reading (Eysenck, 1986).
● Baddeley (1990) believes that the articulatory loop is far from being just '... a way of linking together a number of laboratory phenomena ...' and one reason is that it, or some similar system, plays an important role in learning to read. He says that if you select a group of children with specific problems in learning to read (despite nor-mal intelligence and supportive family background), one of the most striking features they have in common is an impaired memory span. But they also tend to do rather poorly on

tasks which do not directly test memory, such as phonological manipulation and awareness (e.g. judging whether words rhyme or taking a word and deleting the first phonemes before repeating it, for example, 'spin' becomes 'pin'). So what is it that is causing the difficulty in learning to read? While in the normal development of reading these factors undoubtedly interact, in a minority of children some form of phonological deficit (detectable before the child has even begun to learn to read) seems to prevent that learning. It seems likely that this deficit is related to the development of the phonological loop system, although at present we know too little about it to draw any firm conclusions (Baddeley, 1990).

- It is generally agreed that we know least about the most generally important component, namely the central executive – and this perhaps is the model's greatest limitation. It can apparently carry out an enormous variety of processing activities in different conditions which poses obvious problems in terms of describing its precise function – it even suggests that the notion of a single CE may be as inappropriate as that of a unitary STM (Eysenck, 1986). However:

... we should not abandon the notion of some general Central Executive. If the human mind really consisted of nothing but numerous specific processing mechanisms operating in isolation from each other, it seems likely that total chaos would result. At the very least, some central system seems to be needed in order to co-ordinate the activities of the specific mechanisms, and the Central Executive seems well suited to that role. (Eysenck, 1986)

MEMORY AND THE REPRESENTATION OF KNOWLEDGE

According to Eysenck and Keane (1990), what psychologists have generally called knowledge is information that is represented mentally in a particular format and is structured or organized in some way. This leads to two interrelated questions about the nature of knowledge:

1 What format do mental representations take?
2 How are these mental representations organized?

Despite its obvious importance, this area was neglected until quite recently when attempts to provide a knowledge base for computer systems stimulated an interest in how '... this enormously important but complex facility operates in people' (Baddeley, 1990). In this section, we shall begin by taking a fairly general look at the role of organization in memory (including imagery), then we shall discuss some specific models of how knowledge is represented in semantic memory.

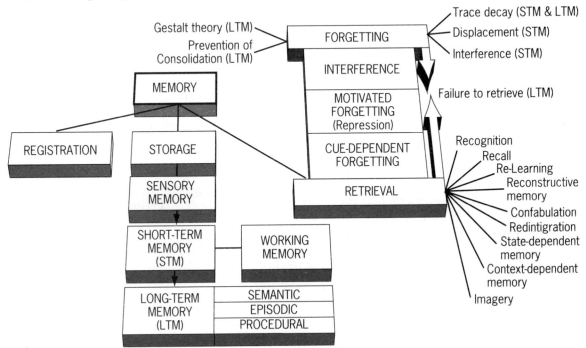

FIGURE 12.11 *A summary of the three components of memory and theories of forgetting*

● The organized nature of memory

When discussing the limited capacity of STM, we noted that chunking is a way of increasing this limited capacity by imposing a meaning on unrelated items of information. We do this by integrating and relating the incoming material to knowledge that we already possess in LTM, i.e. we *organize* it, giving it a structure that otherwise it does not have. As Baddeley (1995) says, 'The secret of a good memory, as of a good library, is that of organization; good learning typically goes with the systematic encoding of incoming material, integrating and relating it to what is already known'.

Organization can either be imposed by the experimenter (EO) or spontaneously by the participant, which Tulving (1980) called 'subjective organization' (SO). He was attempting to account for the findings, from many studies, that in free recall of randomly selected words, participants consistently tend to recall groups of words in the same order, despite changes in the order of presentation on each trial. The earlier interpretation was that the organization simply reflected pre-existing associations (based on a passive, associationistic view), but Tulving saw participants as actively imposing their own organization on the lists.

Mandler (1967) found that instructions to organize will facilitate learning, even though the participant is not trying to remember the material. He used a pack of 52 cards with a word printed on each; the task was to place the cards into seven columns. Half were told to try to remember the words, but not the other half. After five sorting trials, recall was tested; those instructed to just organize the cards recalled as many words as participants instructed to remember them, which suggests that organization was equivalent to learning.

BOX 12.6   Key study: helpful hierarchies

Bower *et al.* (1969) gave participants the task of learning a list of 112 words arranged into conceptual hierarchies (see Fig. 12.12). For the experimental group, the words were organized in hierarchical form (28 on each of four trials) while the control group was shown 28 words on each of four trials but they were selected randomly. The former recalled a mean of 73 words correctly while the latter recalled only 21 on average. Clearly, organization can facilitate retention.

A classic study of organization is that of Bower *et al.* (1969), which is described in Box 12.6.

● Imagery as a form of organization

According to Paivio (1969), probably the most powerful predictor of the ease with which words will be learned is their 'concreteness', that is, how easily the word evokes a mental image. Richardson (1972) has also stressed the importance of imagery as an aid to memory and regards it as a process of organization, for to produce an image of a single stimulus will not improve recall. In a 1974 experiment, Richardson tested free recall of a series of 'concrete' and 'abstract' words and by varying the interval between presenting the stimulus and recalling it, he concluded that the 'effect of imageability lies in secondary memory'; in other words, 'concrete' words were recalled significantly more efficiently from LTM (compared with 'abstract' words) whereas there was no difference with recall from STM.

Bower (1972) showed that asking participants to form a mental image of pairs of unrelated nouns (e.g.

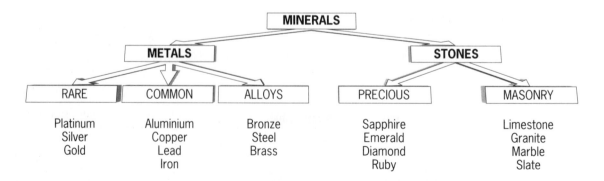

FIGURE 12.12 *An example of a conceptual hierarchy used in Bower et al.'s (1969) experiment*

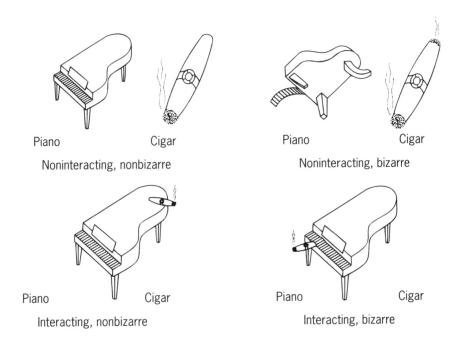

FIGURE 12.13 *Examples of pictures used to associate piano and cigar in the Wollen et al. (1972) study of image bizarreness. From Wollen, K.A., Weber, A. & Lowry, D.H.* Cognitive Psychology, *Volume 3. Copyright © 1972 Academic Press*

'dog' and 'bicycle') where the two words were interacting in some way resulted in significantly better recall than when they were instructed merely to memorize the words (75% correct recall versus 45% correct). Bower considers that the more unusual the details of the image, the better. Paivio (1971) believes that a general theme or principle, rather than specific content, is more easily retrieved by converting information into visual images. Whenever abstract material can be converted into concrete ideas, recall is enhanced. Exclusive reliance on the verbal system for encoding and retrieving information is a mistake.

BOX 12.7 The mind of a mnemonist (Luria, 1968)

S. was a reporter for a Moscow newspaper in the early 1920s. His astounding ability to produce reports, rich in the minutest factual detail without ever taking notes, so amazed the editor that he sent him for psychological evaluation. Luria, who for years had been studying human memory and amnesia caused by various forms of disease, had never encountered anyone like S. There seemed to be no limit either to the capacity of his memory or its durability. He could recall, without error, a list of words that increased up to 30, 50 and eventually 70 and he could remember nonsense material after days, months and even years. He could commit to memory, in a few minutes, long lists of numbers and recall them perfectly, hours, days or weeks later. Luria tested him 30 years after they first met and S. could still remember perfectly the numbers of tables he had previously learned!

He seemed to have spontaneously developed mnemonic tricks. For example, he would associate, in his mind's eye, lists of objects he wished to remember with familiar features of a street or some other familiar place. He mentally placed each object at some point on the scene; all he had to do to remember the list was to recall the mental image of the scene and locate each object on display. He would imagine himself walking along a Moscow street looking in each hiding place for the object he had put there. 'Sometimes I put a word in a dark place and have trouble seeing it as I go by,' he wrote (this is the *method of loci*). His recall was accompanied by extreme *synaesthesia*, i.e. sensory information from one modality evokes a sensation in another, for example, colours are associated with tastes. He once said to Luria, 'What a crumbly yellow voice you have'. These synaesthetic components seemed to provide a background for each item to be recalled.

Apart from objects interacting or not interacting, images can differ in terms of their bizarreness. So, for example, an image of a dog riding a bicycle does not just involve the two things interacting, but is also rather bizarre. Wollen *et al.* (1972) studied the relative contribution of these two dimensions by giving pictures to participants to help them learn paired associates, such as 'piano-cigar'. Figure 12.13 shows all four combinations of these two dimensions. They found a large effect of interaction but not of bizarreness, which suggests that interaction promotes elaborative encoding that aids later recall. However, the Wollen *et al.* study used an unrelated design and when related designs are used, bizarre images stand out from the rest as the most distinctive, producing the best recall (Anderson, 1995). (See the discussion of the LOP approach above.)

Paivio (1986) has proposed the *dual coding hypothesis* to account for the effects of imagery on verbal learning. Mental activity involves interaction between two interconnected but functionally independent subsystems: (a) a non-verbal imagery system, which processes information about objects and events; and (b) a verbal system which is specialized for handling speech and writing. Within the latter, each known word is assumed to be represented by a *logogen;* images are represented in an equivalent way called *imagens*. The two systems are connected via *referential* links which allow a word to be associated with its relevant image and vice-versa. This can help explain the better learning of concrete words – they activate both verbal and non-verbal codes, while abstract words activate only a verbal code. Similarly, pictures are easier to memorize than words representing those pictures, because a picture is more likely to activate a verbal code as well as an imaginal one, while words are less likely to evoke a picture (especially if they are abstract) (Parkin, 1993).

A dramatic illustration of the role of imagery is the man with the exceptional memory documented by Luria in The *Mind of a Mnemonist* (1968; see Box 12.7). Luria's S. can be seen as illustrating *eidetic imagery* (from the Greek *eidos* meaning 'that which is seen').

Table 12.2 gives some examples of mnemonic devices (memory aids), many of which make use of imagery. What they all have in common is either the reduction or elaboration of the way we encode information: we either strip away irrelevant information in order to have as little as possible to remember or we elaborate the information to be stored (either verbally or through imagery). An example of (verbal) reduction is the acronym ROYGBIV, an aid to remembering the colours of the spectrum (Red/Orange/Yellow/Green/Blue/Indigo/Violet); of course you must be able to remember the code and also decode it. Alternatively, an elaboration of this acronym is 'Richard of York Gave Battle in Vain', which is decoded in the same way.

● Knowledge and semantic memory

Perhaps the best known model of SM, and the one which has generated most research and debate, is the *hierarchical network model* (Collins and Quillian, 1969, 1972). This is concerned with our memory for words and their meanings and the information involved is organized hierarchically, as shown

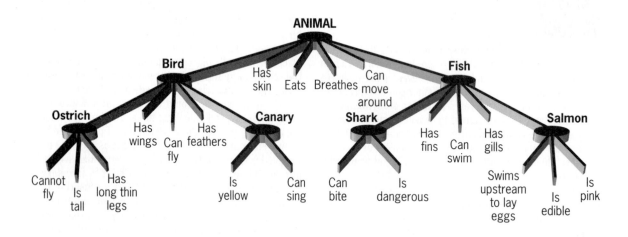

FIGURE 12.14 *Part of the semantic memory network for a three-level hierarchy. (From Collins and Quillian, 1969)*

in Figure 12.14. SM is portrayed as a network of concepts which are connected with other concepts by pointers; each word or concept is represented by a particular node in the network. The meaning of a particular word is given by the configuration of pointers that connect that word with other words.

Some pointers indicate the properties of a word, e.g. a canary 'can sing' and 'is yellow'; other pointers indicate the category the word belongs to – at a lower, more specific level, the category of *bird* and at a higher, more general level, the category *animal*. Since all birds (or almost all) have certain properties in common (e.g. have wings, can fly and have feathers) these are stored together with the concept *bird;* it would be unnecessary (redundant) for them to be stored with each kind of bird. Similarly, the properties shared by canaries, birds and animals need only be stored at the highest level, that of animal – this is the most economical way of storing a great deal of information. Since, by implication, whatever is stored at a higher level (e.g. animal) applies to lower level words (e.g. canary), a hierarchical organization involves little redundancy, i.e. a relatively large amount of information can be stored in a relatively small space.

How does the model explain the way we go about comprehending and verifying simple sentences? If we were asked whether the statement 'A canary can sing' is true, we would only need to find the word 'canary' and retrieve the properties stored with that word. However, to verify 'A canary can fly' we would first have to find 'canary' and then move up one level to 'bird' before retrieving the property 'can fly'. Assuming that it takes time to move from one level to another, it should take longer to verify 'A canary can fly' than to verify 'A canary can sing' and it would take even longer to verify 'A canary has skin'. The model assumes that the various properties stored with each word are scanned simultaneously.

Collins and Quillian presented participants with various sentences, including the examples given above, which they had to judge as true or false by pressing an appropriate button as quickly as possible; reaction time was used as a measure of difficulty. The main finding was that the time taken to decide that a statement is true increased as a function of the number of levels that had to be worked through to verify it. Thus, more time was needed to verify 'A canary is an animal' than 'A canary is a bird', which is what the model, of course, predicts.

However, it has been pointed out that it takes longer to verify 'A canary is an animal' because there are more animals than birds. So the findings of Collins and Quillian could be accounted for in terms of the relationship between category size and reaction time. Again, some members of a category are judged as more typical than other members, e.g. 'canary' and 'ostrich' both belong to the category *bird* but a 'canary' is judged to be a more typical bird than an 'ostrich'. So when determining whether instances belong to a category, participants respond faster to typical instances ('A canary is a bird') than to atypical ones ('An ostrich is a bird'). That should not happen according to the hierarchical model – presumably the same distance has to be travelled in both cases (Baddeley, 1990).

Conrad (1972) found evidence that response time may reflect the relative frequency with which certain attributes are commonly associated with a particular concept. Controlling for frequency, she reran Collins and Quillian's experiment and found no evidence for longer response times to categories meant to be stored at higher levels. These results strongly suggest that 'semantic relatedness' (what attributes are commonly associated with particular concepts) could fairly easily account for the original findings. The Collins and Quillian model assumes that all attributes are equally important or salient in determining the members of a concept – it seems likely that they are not. Similarly, Rips *et al.* (1973) found that it took longer to verify 'A bear is a mammal' than 'A bear is an animal' which is the opposite of what the hierarchical model predicts, since 'animal' is higher up in the hierarchy than 'mammal'.

The findings could be explained in terms of how easy (or difficult) it is to imagine concepts at different levels: the higher up the hierarchy you go, the more abstract the category becomes and the more difficult it becomes to form a mental image of it, e.g. it is easier to picture a canary than 'an animal'. This could explain the findings at least as well as the distance as such that must be crossed (see the discussion of imagery above).

In the light of these criticisms, Collins and Loftus (1975) proposed a revised network model. The major changes include:

- The network is no longer hierarchically organized, making it more flexible.
- The new concept of *semantic distance* denotes that highly related concepts are located close together and distance reflects how easily 'excitation' can flow from one node to the next.
- A range of different types of link is introduced, such as class membership associations (or *is a* links – 'A dog is a mammal', including some negative instances, such as 'A dolphin is not a fish'), *has*

links ('An animal has skin'), *can* links ('A bird can fly'), *cannot* links ('An ostrich cannot fly'), etc.

It no longer sees the memory network in terms of logical, hierarchical relationships, i.e. human memory may simply not be as logical and systematic as originally proposed, and it allows for an individual's personal experience and the structure of the environment to act as at least partial influences on the relationship between concepts. It also introduced the concept of *spreading activation*, whereby when two concepts are stimulated an activation from each spreads throughout the network until they are linked. This takes time, because semantically related concepts are closer together than semantically unrelated concepts.

Nevertheless, Johnson-Laird *et al.* (1984) believe that there are many examples where the interpretation offered by the network will tend, in actual discourse, to be overridden by the constraints of real-world knowledge; for example, 'The ham sandwich was eaten by the soup'. This would appear to be nonsensical until you put it into the context of a restaurant, where waiters/waitresses sometimes label customers in terms of their order. Johnson-Laird *et al.*, call this failure to 'escape from the maze of symbols into the world' the *symbolic fallacy:* you have to know the relationship between symbols and what they refer to. (We shall return to this issue in Chapter 14 in the form of the controversy over whether computers can think.)

● Schema theory and everyday memory

According to Baddeley (1990), it became increasingly obvious during the 1970s that SM must contain structures considerably larger than the simple concepts involved in network models such as that of Collins and Loftus. This 'larger unit' of SM is the *schema*, a concept first used by Bartlett in 1932 and which we shall discuss in depth in the section on reconstructive memory. Just as importantly, any theoretical approach to everyday memory must try to explain why it works in such a 'hit-and-miss' way, i.e. our memories are often vague, incomplete and distorted.

What governs the complex pattern of remembering and forgetting? According to Cohen (1993), *schema theory* represents the most influential approach to this fundamental problem. At its core is the belief that what we remember is influenced by what we already know and that our use of past experience to deal with new experience is a fundamental feature of the way the human mind works. Our knowledge is stored in memory as a set of schemas, simplified, generalized mental representations of everything we understand by a given type of object or event based on our past experience. They operate in a 'top-down' way to help us interpret the 'bottom-up' flood of information reaching our senses from the world.

The term 'schema' was borrowed from the neurologist Henry Head, who used it to represent a person's concept of the location of limbs and body (rather like having a homunculus – little man – inside one's head, keeping track of the position of one's limbs; Baddeley, 1990). Two major modern schema theories are those of Rumelhart (1975) and Schank (1975) and Schank and Abelson (1977). There is a good deal of overlap between them and the broad characteristics which they share are summarized by Rumelhart and Norman (1983/85) as follows:

● *Schemas have variables or slots.* Schemas are packets of information which comprise a fixed, compulsory value plus a variable or optional value. For example, a schema for buying something in a shop would have relatively fixed slots for the exchange of money and goods, while the variable values would be the amount of money and the nature of the goods. In particular cases, a slot may be left unspecified and can often be filled with a 'default' value (a best guess given the available information).

● *Schemas can be related together to form systems.* They are not mutually exclusive packets of information but can be overlapping. For example, a schema for a picnic may be part of a larger system of schemas including 'meals', 'outings' and 'parties'.

● *Schemas represent knowledge at all levels of abstraction.* Schemas can relate to abstract ideologies, abstract concepts (e.g. justice), or concrete objects (e.g. the appearance of a face).

● *Schemas represent knowledge rather than definitions.* Schemas embody knowledge and experience of the world rather than abstract rules.

● *Schemas are active recognition devices.* This is very similar to Bartlett's 'effort after meaning', whereby we try to make sense of ambiguous and unfamiliar information in terms of our existing knowledge and understanding (see below).

According to Schank (1975) and Schank and Abelson (1977), we develop schemas or scripts which represent commonly experienced social events, such as catching a bus and going to a restaurant. These allow us to fill in much of the detail not specified in any text that we might read. For example:

Name:	Restaurant	**Roles:**	Customer
Props:	Tables		Waiter
	Menu		Cook
	Food		Cashier
	Bill		Owner
	Money		
	Tip		
Entry conditions:	Customer is hungry	**Results:**	Customer has less money
	Customer has money		Owner has more money
			Customer is not hungry

Scene I:	Entering	**Scene 3:**	Eating
	Customer enters restaurant		Cook gives food to customer
	Customer looks for table		Customer eats food
	Customer decides where to sit		
	Customer goes to table		
	Customer sits down		
Scene 2:	Ordering	**Scene 4:**	Exiting
	Customer picks up menu		Waitress writes bill
	Customer looks at menu		Waitress goes over to customer
	Customer decides on food		Waitress gives bill to customer
	Customer signals waitress		Customer gives tip to waitress
	Waitress comes to table		Customer goes to cashier
	Customer orders food		Customer gives money to cashier
	Waitress goes to cook		Customer leaves restaurant
	Waitress gives food order to cook		
	Cook prepares food		

TABLE 12.5 *A simplified version of Schank and Abelson's (1977) schematic representation of activities involved in going to a restaurant (from Bower et al., 1979)*

We had a tandoori chicken at the Taj Mahal last night. The service was slow and we almost missed the start of the play ...

can only be interpreted by bringing in a great deal of additional information (Baddeley, 1990). We need to have schemas that predict what would happen next and fill in those aspects of the event which are left implicit in the text. Scripts are essential ways of summarizing common cultural assumptions which not only help us to understand text and discourse but also predict future events and behave appropriately in given social situations. Scripts contain the sequences of actions one goes through when carrying out stereotypical events (e.g. 'catching a bus' or 'eating out') and would also include the sorts of objects and actors we are likely to encounter.

Schank and Abelson (1977) built their scripts into a computer program (SAM) which they claim is capable of answering questions about restaurants and understanding stories about restaurants (see Chapter 14). Table 12.5 shows their script for eating at a restaurant.

Bower *et al.* (1979) asked people to list about 20 actions or events, in order, which commonly occur while eating at a restaurant and found considerable

agreement. For example, at least 73% mentioned sitting down, looking at the menu, ordering, eating, paying the bill and leaving. Also, at least 48% included entering, giving the reservation name, ordering drinks, discussing the menu, talking, eating salad or soup and ordering dessert, eating dessert and leaving a tip. So there were at least 15 events which formed part of many people's knowledge of what is involved in going to a restaurant. These findings broadly agreed with Schank and Abelson's restaurant script. Interestingly, when such events were incorporated into stories, people tended to falsely recall aspects of the passage which were not explicitly included but which were consistent with the script. The order of events was also changed to fit what would 'normally' happen. (This is exactly what Bartlett would have predicted would happen.)

● An evaluation of schema theory

Cohen (1993) points out a number of criticisms, including:

● the whole idea of a schema is too vague to be useful;
● there is an overemphasis on the inaccuracies of memory, overlooking the fact that complex events

are sometimes remembered very precisely and accurately (especially the unexpected, unusual aspects);

● how are schemas acquired in the first place? There seems to be a kind of 'Catch-22' involved here, since without schemas we are unable to interpret new experiences, and new experiences are needed to build up schemas

These and similar criticisms led Schank (1982) to propose his *dynamic memory theory*, an attempt, as the name implies, to take account of the more dynamic aspects of memory. It represents a more elaborate version of the original, as well as a more flexible, less rigid model. It is meant to clarify the relationship between general knowledge schemas

and memory for specific episodes, based on a more hierarchical arrangement of memory representations. *Memory organization packets* (MOPs) are at the bottom of the hierarchy, storing specific details about particular events; at higher levels, the representations become more and more general and schema-like. MOPs are not usually stored for very long and become absorbed into the event schemas which store those features that are common to repeated experience. However, details of unusual or atypical events are retained (Cohen, 1993).

RECONSTRUCTIVE MEMORY AND EYEWITNESS TESTIMONY

As we saw in the previous section, Bartlett's concept of a schema is central to theories which attempt to explain the structure and organization of knowledge in LTM. Because of the large amount of work on the organizational aspects of memory and because of the growing recognition of the need to study meaningful material (as opposed to lists of unrelated words, etc.), there has been a 'rediscovery' of the work of Bartlett (*Remembering*, 1932).

One of two major methods used by Bartlett was *serial reproduction*, in which one person reproduces the original story, a second person has to reproduce the first reproduction, a third has to reproduce the second reproduction and so on until six or seven reproductions have been made. The method is meant to duplicate, to some extent, the process by which rumours or gossip are spread or legends passed from generation to generation. One of the best-known pieces of material Bartlett used was 'The War of the Ghosts' which is difficult for people from Western culture because of its style and some of its unfamiliar content and underlying beliefs and conventions. It is reproduced, in full, in Box 12.8. Ian Hunter (1964) used 'The War of the Ghosts' (and a serial reproduction method) and found similar characteristic changes to those reported by Bartlett, including:

● The story becomes noticeably shorter, e.g. Bartlett found that after six or seven reproductions, it shrank from 330 to 180 words.

● Despite becoming shorter, and details being omitted, the story becomes more coherent; no matter how distorted it might become, it remains a story because the participants are interpreting the story as a whole, both listening to it and retelling it.

● It also becomes more conventional, that is, it retains only those details which can be easily

---

BOX 12.8   The War of the Ghosts

The title of this story is 'The War of the Ghosts'. One night two young men from Egulac went down to the river to hunt seals and while they were there it became foggy and calm. Then they heard war-cries and they thought: 'Maybe this is a war party'. They escaped to the shore and hid behind a log. Now canoes came up and they heard the noise of paddles and saw one canoe coming up to them. There were five men in the canoe and they said: 'What do you think? We wish to take you along. We are going up the river to make war on the people'. One of the young men said 'I have no arrows'. 'Arrows are in the canoe', they said. 'I will not go along. I might be killed. My relatives do not know where I have gone. But you', he said, turning to the other, 'may go with them.' So one of the young men went but the other returned home. And the warriors went on up the river to a town on the other side of Kalama. The people came down to the water and they began to fight and many were killed. But presently the young man heard one of the warriors say: 'Quick, let us go home; that Indian has been hit'. Now he thought: 'Oh, they are ghosts'. He did not feel sick but they said he had been shot. So the canoes went back to Egulac and the young man went ashore to his house and made a fire. And he told everybody and said: 'Behold I accompanied the ghosts and we went to fight. Many of our fellows were killed and many of those who attacked us were killed. They said I was hit and I did not feel sick.' He told it all and then he became quiet. When the sun rose he fell down. Something black came out of his mouth. His face became contorted. The people jumped up and cried. He was dead.

BOX 12.9 Crosscultural perspective: remembering as a cultural activity

An important implication of Bartlett's work is that memory is a social phenomenon that cannot be studied as a 'pure' process. Because he emphasized the influence of previous knowledge and background experience, remembering is integrally related to the social and cultural contexts in which it is practised. When members of Western and non-Western cultures are compared on tasks devised in psychology laboratories, such as free recalling lists of unrelated words, the former do better; this seems to reflect the meaninglessness of such tasks for the latter.

According to Mistry and Rogoff (1994), culture and memory are enmeshed skills and 'remembering' is an activity with goals whose function is determined by the social and cultural context in which it takes place. This helps to explain the phenomenal memory for lines of descent and history of Itamul elders in New Guinea, needed to resolve disputes over claims to property by conflicting clans. Bartlett himself described the prodigious ability of Swazi herdsmen to recall individual characteristics of their cattle. But since Swazi culture revolves around the possession and care of cattle, this ability is not so surprising. What these examples show is that remembering is a means of achieving a culturally important goal, rather than the goal itself (Mistry and Rogoff, 1994).

BOX 12.10 Key study: a definite case of misleading the witness

Loftus and Zanni (1975) showed 100 students a film of a multiple car accident and they were then asked to complete a 22-item questionnaire, six of which were 'critical' questions. For half the students, the critical questions began 'Did you see *a* (broken headlight)?' and for the other half, they began 'Did you see *the* (broken headlight)?', the only difference being in the form of the article.

Of course, usually when we use the definite article we are assuming the existence of the denoted object, but when we use the indefinite article no such assumption is being made: the influence of the form of question was reflected in the results. When asked about something which had not in fact appeared in the film, 15% in the *the* group said 'Yes' compared with only 7% of the *a* group, who were also more likely to say 'Don't know', both when the object had been present and when it had not.

In another experiment (Loftus and Palmer, 1974), Loftus explored the influence of changing a single word in certain critical questions on judgement of speed. For some participants, the critical question was 'About how fast were the cars going when they *hit*?'; for others, 'hit' was replaced by 'smashed', 'collided' 'bumped' or 'contacted'. These different words have very different connotations regarding speed and force of impact and, again, these were borne out in the judgements of speed: 'smashed' produced an average speed estimate of 40.8 mph, 'collided' 39.3 mph, 'bumped' 38.1 mph, 'hit' 34.0 mph and 'contacted' 31.8 mph. A different group of participants was asked to estimate the speed of cars for just 'hit' or 'smashed' with a control group not asked about speed at all.

assimilated to the shared past experience and cultural background of the participants.

● It becomes more clichéd, i.e. any peculiar or individual interpretations tend to be dropped.

Bartlett concluded that *interpretation* plays a large and largely unrecognized role in the remembering of stories and past events. We reconstruct the past by trying to fit it into our existing schemata and the more difficult this is to do, the more likely it is that elements are forgotten or distorted so that it fits. Bartlett refers to *efforts after meaning*, i.e. trying to make the past more logical, more coherent and generally more 'sensible', which involves making inferences or deductions about what could or should have happened. Rather than human memory being computer-like, with the output matching the input, Bartlett and Hunter believe that we process information in an active attempt to understand it. Memory is an 'imaginative reconstruction' of experience (Bartlett, 1932).

● Eyewitness testimony

This view of memory as reconstructive in nature is also taken by Elizabeth Loftus, who has investigated it mainly in relation to *eyewitness testimony* (EWT). Loftus argues that the evidence given by witnesses in court cases is highly unreliable; her research strongly suggests that it is the form of questions that witnesses are asked which mainly influences how they 'remember' what they 'witnessed'. 'Leading questions' are of special interest, because they can introduce new information which can alter the witness's memory of an event – by their form or content they suggest to a witness the answer that should be given, as in the classic 'Have you stopped beating your wife?'. Lawyers, of course, are skilled at deliberately asking such questions and undoubtedly, police also use such questioning when interrogating suspects and witnesses to a crime.

Loftus studied the influence of questioning in the laboratory using students as eyewitnesses and films of automobile accidents as the events they had to remember and report. Two well-known studies are described in Box 12.10.

Loftus and Palmer (1974) wanted to find out if participants were truly misremembering, i.e. does memory itself undergo change as a result of misleading questions or is the existing memorial representation of the accident merely being supplemented by the misleading questions? Theoretically, this is a very important issue – the idea of *memory as reconstruction* is that memory itself is transformed at the time of retrieval; that is, what was encoded originally changes when it is recalled.

Loftus tested this by retesting the 'smashed', 'hit' and control groups a week later, asking them a new series of questions (without seeing the film again). This time the critical question asked whether the witness had seen any broken glass (although there was none in the film). If 'smashed' really influenced participants such that they remembered the accident as more serious than it was, then they might also 'remember' details that were not shown but which are consistent with an accident occurring at high speed, such as broken glass. The results showed that

32% of the 'smashed' group reported seeing the non-existent glass, compared with 14% of the 'hit' group and 12% of the controls. This suggests that the answer to the question about the glass was determined by the earlier question about speed, which had changed what was originally encoded when seeing the film.

However, some researchers have challenged this conclusion. For example, Bekerian and Bowers (1983) showed that the old trace had survived and could be accessed by using an appropriate method of retrieval: if the questions followed the order of the events in strict sequence, rather than being asked in the relatively unstructured way as Loftus and Burns had done, participants were not influenced by the bias introduced by the subsequent questions. '... In short, the Loftus effect is not due to destruction of the memory trace but is due to interfering with its retrieval' (Baddeley, 1995). And besides, are eyewitnesses really as unreliable as Loftus believes? There are several kinds of evidence which suggest they are not.

● Stephenson (1988) points out that the bulk of the work on EWT has been carried out in laboratories and has concentrated on eyewitness identification of people seen under fairly non-threatening conditions or even people seen on films. In sharp contrast were the participants of a study by Yuille and Cutshall (1986), described in Box 12.11.

BOX 12.11 A case study of eyewitness memory of a crime (Yuille and Cutshall, 1986; cited in Stephenson, 1988)

The incident involved a gun shooting which occurred on a spring afternoon outside a gun shop in full view of several witnesses (in Vancouver, Canada). A thief had entered the gun shop, tied up the proprietor and stolen some money and a number of guns. The store owner freed himself, picked up a revolver and went outside to take the thief's licence number. The thief, however, had not yet entered his car and in a face-to-face encounter on the street, separated by six feet, the thief fired two shots at the store owner. After a slight pause the store owner discharged all six shots from his revolver. The thief was killed whereas the store owner recovered from serious injury. Witnesses viewed the incident from various vantage points along the street, from adjacent buildings or from passing automobiles and they witnessed various aspects of the incident, either prior to and including the actual shooting or after the shots were fired (Yuille and Cutshall, 1986).

Twenty-one of the witnesses were interviewed by the police shortly after the event and 13 of them agreed to take part in a research interview 4–5 months later. In both sets of interviews (police and research), verbatim accounts of the incident were obtained and follow-up questions were asked in order to clarify points of detail. Also, the researchers asked two misleading questions based on Loftus's '*a* broken headlight'/'*the* broken headlight' technique. The sheer volume of accurate detail produced in both sets of interviews is truly impressive. The researchers obtained much more detail than did the police, because they were concerned with memory for details which had no forensic value. Witnesses who were central to the event gave more details than did peripheral witnesses, but there was no overall difference in accuracy between the two groups.

Regarding the errors in recall, there were few, if any, inventions and many of those that were made could plausibly be attributed to perceptual distortion stemming from the disadvantageous viewpoint of one or two peripheral witnesses. Significantly, the wording of the misleading questions had no effect and those who were most deeply distressed by the incident (e.g. suffered nightmares) were the most accurate of the witnesses.

- Some laboratory research also suggests that participants will not inevitably be misled by leading questions. Loftus herself (1979), for example, found that if the misleading information is 'blatantly incorrect', it will have no effect. Participants saw colour slides of a man stealing a red purse from a woman's bag; 98% correctly remembered the colour of the purse and when they read a narrative description of the event containing a 'brown purse', all but two continued to remember it as red. Thus, memory for obviously important information which is accurately perceived at the time is not easily distorted (Cohen, 1986).

- In the previous example, the purse's colour is the focus of the whole incident, not a peripheral detail. Cohen (1986) believes that people are more likely to be misled if: (i) the false information concerns insignificant details which are peripheral to the main event; (ii) the false information is given after a delay, when the memory of the actual event has had time to fade (but note the accuracy of the recall after 4–5 months in the Yuille and Cutshall study above); (iii) participants are not aware that they may be deliberately misinformed and so have no reason to distrust the information.

● Conclusions

Loftus *et al.* (1970) believe that people often do little better than guess when trying to identify an alleged criminal in an identity parade. It is evidence such as this which led to the publication of the Devlin Report (1976) which recommends that the trial judge be required to instruct the jury that it is not safe to convict on a single EWT alone, except in exceptional

circumstances (e.g. the witness is a close friend or relative) or when there is substantial corroborative evidence. The safeguards recommended are much stronger than those of the US Supreme Court but are similar to those of American legal experts (Brown, 1986). (For further discussion of EWT, see Gross, 1994.)

THEORIES OF FORGETTING

To understand why we forget, we must consider the distinction made earlier between *availability* and *accessibility;* the former refers to whether or not material has been stored in the first place, while the latter refers to being able to retrieve what has been stored (the question of retrievability). In terms of the multistore model, since information must be transferred from STM to LTM for permanent storage, availability has to do mainly with STM and the transfer of information from STM into LTM, while accessibility has to do mainly with LTM.

This suggests that one way of looking at forgetting is to ask what prevents information staying in STM long enough to be transferred to LTM (some answers are *trace decay, displacement* and *interference)* and another is to ask what prevents us from locating the information that is in LTM (some answers being *interference, motivated forgetting* and *cue-dependent* forgetting, which are all to do with failure to retrieve). *Trace decay* and *prevention of consolidation* have also been proposed as explanations of LT forgetting (in terms of availability), while Gestalt theory is concerned with what happens to long-term memories once transfer from STM has occurred (see Fig. 12.15).

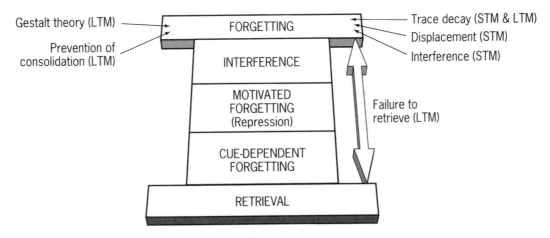

FIGURE 12.15 *Different theories of forgetting, including retrieval failure*

● Trace decay

Essentially this is an attempt to explain why forgetting increases with time. James (1890) claimed that the limiting factor in STM is simply the passage of time: a stimulus decays from STM as its neural after-effects decay. More recent supporters include Brown (1958), Peterson and Peterson (1959) and Wingfield and Byrnes (1972).

The underlying assumption is that learning leaves a 'trace' in the brain, that is, there is some sort of physical change after learning that was not there before and forgetting is due to a spontaneous fading or weakening of the neural memory trace over time. Hebb (1949) argued that the physiological basis of memory is dualistic, that is, there are two phases involved in the formation of memory: (i) a group of nerve cells excite each other, resulting in a very brief memory trace; and (ii) with repeated neural activity, a structural neural change occurs. The first phase corresponds roughly to STM and forgetting is due to neural decay; the second phase corresponds roughly to LTM and forgetting must be due to the intervention of some other information. So, for Hebb, trace decay applies only to STM.

This belief represents a major argument in support of the multistore model. However, the idea of trace decay has been extended to LT forgetting, in the form of *decay through disuse;* that is, if certain knowledge or skills are not used or practised for long periods, the memory trace corresponding to them will fade

and hence they will be forgotten. Yet a good deal of remembering goes on when we think decay might have eradicated it, especially in the case of motor skills (e.g. driving, typing, playing the piano) with no intervening practice. The ability of a delirious person to remember a foreign language not spoken since childhood also testifies against any simple decay through disuse explanation. But how satisfactory is trace decay as an account of ST forgetting?

Waugh and Norman (1965) used a *serial probe technique* in which sequences of 16 digits are presented at the rate of 1–4 per second and one of the 16 is then selected (the probe) and the task is to name the digit which *follows* the probe. Simple trace decay would predict much better retention of the rapidly presented digits since there is less time between presentation and test. However, they found no such relationship.

In a famous early study, Jenkins and Dallenhach (1924) found that when participants were allowed to sleep during the interval between learning and recall of nonsense syllables, they remembered many more of them than those who stayed awake for an equivalent period. Two groups learnt a ten-item list of nonsense syllables either late at night or early in the morning. The 'night' group were woken after one, two, four or eight hours and tested for recall (as well as being tested immediately after learning). The 'day' group reported back to the lab at the same intervals but continued their daily activities. As shown in Figure 12.16, in both groups recall declined with time but it declined to a greater extent in the day group. If decay is a natural result of the passage of time alone, then we should have expected equal forgetting in both groups. The results suggest that it is what happens in between learning and recall that determines forgetting in STM, not time as such (and this would seem to apply to LT forgetting too).

Although some data exist suggesting that neurological breakdown occurs with age and disease (such as Alzheimer's disease), there is no evidence that the major cause of forgetting from LTM is neurological decay (Solso, 1995). The major alternative to trace decay is *interference* (see below).

● Displacement

In a limited capacity ST store, new items tend to displace old ones; this, of course, rests on the assumption of a limited number of 'slots' into which new material can be inserted ('the magic number seven, plus or minus two'), so that when a new piece of information is to be introduced, one of the existing

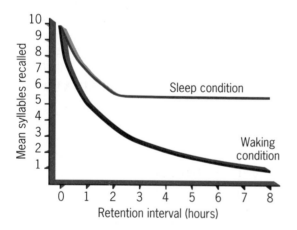

FIGURE 12.16 *Average recall of nonsense syllables by participants allowed to sleep between learning and recall (sleep condition) and those who stayed awake for the equivalent period (waking condition). Adapted from Jenkins and Dallenbach (1924)*

seven slots would need to release its existing material to make way for it. (In terms of memory traces, new material will have high trace strength and older items low trace strength.) Glanzer *et al.* (1967) tested the trace decay, displacement and interference theories and found displacement to be a major factor, but they also found a small effect of time delay, suggesting a possible decay component.

Shallice (1967) found that although rapidly presented digits did show less marked forgetting (suggesting trace decay), elapsed time was less important than the number of subsequent items in determining the probability of recall (which suggests displacement). However, despite this apparent evidence, it is far from clear that displacement refers to a process distinct from either decay on the one hand or interference on the other (or some mixing of the two).

● Interference

According to this theory, forgetting increases with time solely because of increasing interference between competing memories. As our store of information grows, it becomes increasingly difficult to identify or locate a particular item and this constitutes a *failure to retrieve* from LTM. Near the beginning of the storage process, interference from extraneous material can prevent new information from passing from STM into LTM.

As we noted at the beginning of the chapter, interference is conceptualized in stimulus-response (S-R) terms and is commonly studied experimentally using paired associate learning. According to the associationist framework within which it has been studied, associative bonds are formed between specific stimuli and specific responses and these associative connections are held in memory provided other competing information does not interfere with them.

Interference lends itself to closer experimental control than most other theories of forgetting. The

usual procedure for studying interference in the laboratory is shown in Figure 12.17. Normally, the first member of each pair in list A is the same as in list B but the second member of each pair is different in the two lists. In *retroactive inhibition* (RI), the learning of a second, later, list (B) interferes with the recall of the original list A (so the interference works backwards) while in *proactive inhibition* (PI), list A interferes with the recall of later learned list B (and so works forwards).

McGeoch (1942) argued strongly for the importance of RI, which he defined as 'a decrement in retention resulting from activity, usually a learning activity, interpolated between an original learning and a later measurement of retention'. He concluded that the greater the similarity between the two lists, the greater the interference; for example, a list of numbers learned before or after a list of adjectives is likely to interfere very little. However, if the same stimulus is associated with a different response, interference will be very marked (compare this with negative transfer of learning which we discussed in Chapter 7). Why?

Some explanations focused on *response competition,* with associations between similar responses being difficult to discriminate (e.g. McGeoch, 1936), while others argued that *unlearning* (a process similar to the extinction involved in conditioning, whereby the responses on the first list are not 'reinforced' during the learning of the second list) took place, with the interpolated task actually weakening the association between the original stimulus and response (e.g. Melton and Irwin, 1940). Whatever the correct explanation, not all forgetting could be attributed to RI; in fact, some researchers, notably Underwood (1957), claimed that PI is the more important of the two, with the amount of forgetting in any one set of material an increasing function of the amount of similar material that has been learned in the past. Underwood also found that PI increases with time (one of the factors

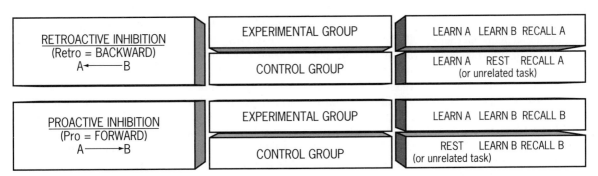

FIGURE 12.17 *The usual procedure for studying interference in the laboratory*

that make it more important) while RI decreases. How did he account for this difference?

While RI is affected by both response competition and unlearning, the responses on the first list undergo *spontaneous recovery* and so RI decreases over time. By contrast, PI involves only the former – the first list is increasingly able to exert response competition on the second and so PI increases over time. Anderson (1995) agrees that PI might be a more powerful influence than RI, based on a discussion of studies of sleep. The famous Jenkins and Dallenbach experiment (1924; see above) is consistent with other studies which show that less is forgotten during sleep which, as we saw earlier, is certainly consistent with interference theory. However, sleep studies test only the hypothesis that forgetting is due to RI; but what about the influence of material learned prior to retention (i.e. PI)?

Evaluation of interference theory

Although experimental demonstrations of interference are quite plentiful, real-life situations in which we must learn incompatible responses to the same stimulus are quite rare. Most of the experimental support has used nonsense syllables but interference is much less easy to demonstrate when meaningful material is used. How can we reconcile these apparently contradictory findings? One solution is to refer once more to Tulving's distinction between episodic and semantic memory.

When someone has to learn the response *bell* to the stimulus *woj*, the word *bell* is not actually 'learned' in the lab but is already part of the person's SM; what is learned is 'bell-as-a-response-to-woj', an event which is dependent on the specific laboratory situation (and which is stored in EM). If studies of interference are largely studying EM, then the 'laws' of interference are also largely based on EM as opposed to SM and it is likely that, whereas EM is susceptible to interference, SM is much more resistant, since it is more stable and structured. No amount of new information is going to cause me to forget the things I know and that are stored in my SM (Solso, 1995).

In a similar way, Baddeley (1990) points out that it has been very difficult to demonstrate significant PI outside the laboratory, one reason being that when learning of potentially interfering material is spaced out over time interference is greatly reduced but in the laboratory it is rather artificially compressed in time, thus increasing the probability of interference. So the major problem is generalizing the results to real-life situations, i.e. experimental studies of interference have low *ecological validity*.

● The Gestalt theory of forgetting

Not surprisingly, the Gestalt account of forgetting is closely related to the Gestalt theory of perception (see Chapter 9). It is the only theory of forgetting which proposes that memories undergo *qualitative changes* over time: complex memories change so as to become more internally consistent in the direction of 'good form'. For example, irregular shapes will increasingly be remembered as more regular and symmetrical. Although there is no convincing evidence of such changes in shape memory, some supporting evidence comes from reconstructive distortions of memory for stories towards greater simplicity and consistency; however, the latter changes are not spontaneous, as the Gestalt theory would require (see reconstructive memory above).

● Prevention of consolidation

Once new information has entered LTM, a consolidation time is needed for it to become firmly recorded (this is the *consolidation process*): time-dependent changes occur in the nervous system, as a result of learning. We saw earlier that patients who have been the victims of concussion or brain injury or who have undergone brain surgery or electroconvulsive therapy (ECT) commonly suffer retrograde amnesia, that is, loss of memory for events which have occurred prior to the event.

There is evidence to show that retention of a learned response increases with increase in the interval between training and ECT; an hour's delay permits almost perfect retention. Also, certain drugs (strychnine, nicotine, caffeine and amphetamine) given immediately after a learning trial seem to speed up the consolidation process (see Chapter 3).

● Cue-dependent forgetting

Tulving (1974) used the term *cue-dependent forgetting* to refer jointly to: (i) state-dependent; and (ii) context-dependent forgetting. According to Tulving, accessibility (i.e. retrievability) is governed by *retrieval cues* or routes which can either be encoded with the to-be-remembered material (at the time of learning) or can be provided later as prods or pointers which govern where in the memory the search will take place. Psychological or physiological *states* represent *internal cues* while environmental or contextual variables represent *external cues*. Forgetting or, more accurately, the failure to retrieve something from memory is a failure of the retrieval cues to match the encoded nature of items in memory (Solso, 1995).

Examples of *state-dependent* forgetting would be learning something while drunk, while smoking marijuana or under the influence of some other drug and trying to remember it while sober, not smoking marijuana or not under the influence of any drug. Regarding *context-dependent* forgetting, Abernethy (1940) asked one group of participants to learn and recall in the same room, while a second group learned and recalled in different rooms; the recall of the first group was much better. Godden and Baddeley (1975) had divers learn word lists either on land or 15 feet under water; recall later was either in the same context or a different one and in the latter conditions there was a 30% decrement in recall. They repeated the study in 1980 using recognition as the measure of remembering and found no effect; they concluded, therefore, that context-dependent forgetting applies to recall only. Baddeley (1995) points out that effects as large as those found in the 1975 study occur only with a very dramatic change of environment. Less marked changes can produce detectable effects, but on the whole, studies that have compared examination performance in the original lecture room with performance in an unfamiliar examination hall (a very common example of context-dependent

BOX 12.12	Key study: demonstrating the availability/accessibility difference

A contextual cue used by Tulving and Pearlstone (1966) took the form of the category name of words that participants had to learn. They were read lists of varying numbers of words (12, 24 or 48) containing categories of one, two or four exemplars per list along with the category name; they were asked only to memorize the exemplars (e.g. category name = animal, exemplar = dog).

Half the participants free-recalled by writing the words on a blank piece of paper but the other half were provided with the category names as cues and they recalled more words; this advantage was most apparent with the 48-word lists (see Fig. 12.18). However, when the first group were later given the category names, their recall improved, which illustrates very well the distinction between availability and accessibility; the category name cues helped make accessible what was in fact available, so they knew more than they could retrieve under the cueless conditions.

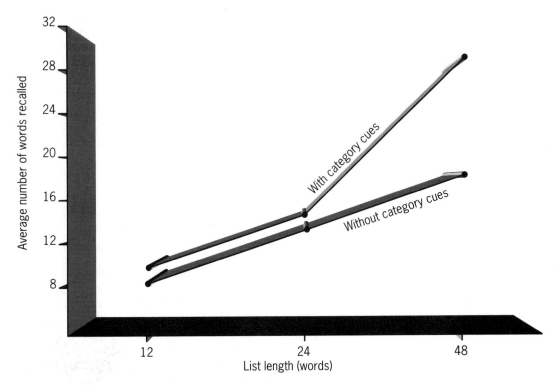

FIGURE 12.18 *Average number of words recalled with and without category cues. Adapted from Tulving and Pearlstone (1966). From Solso, R.L. (1995) Cognitive Psychology (4th edn.). Boston: Allyn & Bacon*

forgetting) do not suggest any significant differences.

This probably reflects the fact that when we are learning, the surroundings are not a particularly salient feature of the situation. However, the *internal environment* can have subtle but powerful effects; for example, mood can have a contextual effect on memory such that someone in a sad mood is typically much more likely to recollect earlier unhappy events from their life than someone in a happy mood or vice-versa (Bower, 1981, cited in Baddeley, 1995).

A different kind of contextual variable is that used by Tulving and Pearlstone (1966) (see Box 12.12).

But how closely related to the recall cue must the encoding cues be in order to operate as effective retrieval cues? According to Tulving's (1983) *encoding specificity principle* (ESP), cues only help retrieval if they have been encoded at the time of learning: in the Tulving and Pearlstone experiment, the category names were presented along with the exemplars and so, presumably, were encoded at the time of learning. The ESP, according to Tulving, explains why recall is sometimes superior to recognition (even though recognition is generally considered to be easier than recall).

However, not everyone accepts the ESP. For example, Jones (1979) distinguishes between two kinds of cues: (i) those which may not have been encoded in the original learning and so do not form part of the information to be recalled (based on extrinsic knowledge); and (ii) those that have been encoded during learning and which do (based on intrinsic knowledge). They both aid recall but probably work in different ways. The problem is being able to define a cue encoded at learning independently of its ability to stimulate recall of information. An effective recall cue is inferred to have been encoded while an ineffective one is inferred not to have been and this is rather circular.

● Motivated forgetting (repression)

As we shall see in Chapter 29, Freud believed that forgetting is motivated; that is, we forget for a reason (or reasons). In the case of repression, painful, disturbing or threatening thoughts or ideas are actively pushed out of our conscious minds and are made unconscious in order to protect ourselves against them. Unconscious or repressed memories are exceedingly difficult to retrieve (are inaccessible) but remain available ('in storage') and continue to exert a great influence over us even though we have no awareness of them.

| BOX 12.13 | Key study: testing Freud's repression hypothesis |

Levinger and Clark (1961) looked at the retention of associations to negatively-charged words (such as 'quarrel', 'angry', 'fear') compared with those for neutral words (such as 'window', 'cow', 'tree'). When asked to give immediate free associations to the words, the emotional words tended to produce a longer response latency (i.e. it took the participants longer to respond); they also produced higher GSRs, a measure of emotional arousal.

As soon as the word association test had been completed, the participants were given the cue words again and asked to try to recall the associations they had previously given. They were particularly poor at remembering the associations to the emotionally-charged words, exactly what Freud's repression hypothesis predicted. The study stood for some years as perhaps the best demonstration that some kind of repressive process might operate in human memory (Parkin, 1993).

However, an alternative interpretation was proposed by Eysenck and Wilson (1973). This was based on research carried out in the 1960s which showed that on immediate test, highly arousing words tend to be poorly retained whereas after a delay, the effect reverses. If the items are being repressed, then they should continue to be repressed, whereas if arousal is the crucial variable, then the effect should reverse. This was confirmed in a study by Parkin *et al.* (1982), who replicated the Levinger and Clark study but added a delayed recall, in which the participants were asked to recall their associations seven days after the original test, thus supporting the arousal-based interpretation of Levinger and Clark's findings, i.e. higher levels of arousal inhibit immediate recall but facilitate longer term recall.

Although similar results have been found more recently, other studies have found a general inhibition of emotional responses at all retention levels. According to Parkin (1993), the question of emotional inhibition remains open.

Repression and the 'return of the repressed' have been apparently demonstrated in several studies but the interpretation of the evidence is controversial. According to Anderson (1995), there is little doubt that traumatic experiences can produce memory disturbances, although by their very nature they defy controlled experimental analysis. However, there is plentiful clinical evidence that is at least consistent with Freud's repression hypothesis; also, according to Freud, repression does not require extreme emotional

BOX 12.14 Critical discussion: recovered memories – remembering what never happened?

Since the early 1990s, in North America, there has been considerable publicity given to court cases where parents are being sued for damages by their teenage or adult children, who accuse them of child sexual abuse (CSA) which has been remembered during the course of psychotherapy. The assumption made is that these recovered memories had been repressed since the alleged CSA happened and that the safety and support provided by the therapist allows them to become conscious many years later.

However, accused parents, as well as retractors (people who had recovered memories of CSA, accused their parents, then later denied the accusations) have also sued therapists and hospitals for planting false memories into their children's minds. In May 1994, Gary Ramona was awarded $500,000 after the jury decided that therapists had planted false memories of CSA in the mind of his daughter, Holly. The False Memory Syndrome Foundation was set up in the US in 1992 and in 1993, the British False Memory Society was founded, with 550 families currently on its books (Patel, 1994).

One difficulty with accepting recovered memories as literal recollections of past events is that they might have (supposedly) happened at a very early age, when experience is not verbalized as it is later on. According to the 1995 BPS report on recovered memories, CSA which is alleged to have occurred before four years of age and which doesn't continue beyond that age might not be retrievable in adulthood in a narrative form, i.e. describable in words. Very early memories are implicit rather than explicit and are reflected in behaviour, outside conscious awareness. This means that we don't need the concept of repression in order to explain the 'forgetting' of childhood experiences, but it also implies that some recovered memories could be false (or at the very least inaccurate).

According to a survey of 810 chartered psychologists, about 90% believe that recovered memories are sometimes or usually 'essentially correct', a negligible number believe that they are always correct, about 66% believe that false memories are possible and over 14% believe that one of their own clients has experienced false memories (BPS, 1995).

Related to the concept of repression is perceptual defence, which was discussed in Chapter 9.

As far as clinical evidence is concerned, it is widely accepted that repression plays a crucial role in different types of *psychogenic amnesia* such as fugue and multiple personality disorder (see Chapter 30), i.e. a loss of memory that is associated with a traumatic experience (as opposed to brain injury or surgery). A relatively common form of psychogenic amnesia is *event-specific* amnesia, i.e. loss of memory for a fairly specific period of time, such as violent criminals who claim they cannot remember carrying out their crime. Even when both malingering and the effects of intoxication at the time the crime was committed have been ruled out, there are still a substantial number of criminals who seem to have repressed memory of their crime (Parkin, 1993).

Parkin (1993) also cites recent evidence that repressive mechanisms may play a beneficial role in enabling people with *posttraumatic stress disorder* to adjust (see Chapter 6). For example, survivors of the Holocaust judged to be better adjusted were significantly less able to recall their dreams when woken from REM sleep (see Chapter 4) than less well-adjusted survivors (Kaminer and Lavie, 1991). However, when the term 'repression' is used, it does not necessarily imply a strictly Freudian interpretation; rather, '… we are simply acknowledging that memory has the ability to render part of its contents inaccessible as a means of coping with distressing experiences. The mechanism by which memory achieves this, however, is an elusive one' (Parkin, 1993). This is also the view taken by the recent British Psychological Survey on 'Recovered Memories' (BPS, 1995) (see Box 12.14).

CHAPTER SUMMARY

- Memory can be defined as the retention of learning or experience; these are two interdependent processes.
- Some of the pioneers of experimental psychology studied memory, notably Ebbinghaus, who used nonsense syllables to establish learning and forgetting curves.
- Up until the 1950s, memory was either avoided altogether or was studied as a form of 'verbal behaviour', using paired-associate learning, firmly within the behaviourist framework.
- Since the 'cognitive revolution', memory has been studied largely from an information-processing

experiences but is much more 'commonplace'. A famous experimental test of repression is the study by Levinger and Clark (1961) described in Box 12.13.

approach and there has been a recent move towards the study of everyday memory.

- 'Memory' can refer to registration, storage or retrieval. Storage corresponds to availability, retrieval to accessibility.

- Many psychologists have distinguished between short-term storage (primary memory or STM) and long-term storage (secondary memory or LTM).

- Sensory memory is necessary for STM. It is modality specific and works in a similar way to the sensory buffer store in Broadbent's filter model of attention.

- STM and LTM can be analysed in terms of capacity, duration and coding.

- The limited capacity of STM can be increased by chunking, which draws on LT storage to encode new information in a meaningful way. Rehearsal is a way of holding information in STM for longer intervals and the primary code used by STM is acoustic.

- LTM has an unlimited capacity and contains all our basic knowledge of the world. It holds information indefinitely and it uses a semantic code and an imagery/visual code.

- Retrieval takes many forms, including recognition, recall, relearning, reconstructive memory, confabulation, redintegration, state- and context-dependent memory and imagery.

- The most influential model of memory that distinguishes between STM and LTM is the multistore model of Atkinson and Shiffrin. STM and LTM are structural components, with rehearsal a major control process.

- Two-component tasks, such as those producing a serial position curve and the Brown-Peterson technique, support the STM-LTM distinction, as do studies of the kind of coding errors made in tasks involving STM and LTM.

- Studies of brain-damaged, amnesic patients, such as H.M. and Clive Wearing, also appear to support the STM-LTM distinction. While STM continues to function fairly normally, LTM functioning is impaired, but opinions differ as to whether this reflects difficulty in transfer from STM to LTM or is to do with LTM retrieval difficulties.

- The distinction between maintenance and elaborative rehearsal represents an important challenge to the multistore model.

- LTM is not unitary, but comprises episodic and procedural as well as semantic memory. Autobiographical memory and flashbulb memories are two kinds of episodic memory.

- Declarative memory/learning corresponds to episodic and semantic memory, all involving conscious or explicit knowledge. Procedural memory involves more automatic processes.

- The levels of processing (LOP) approach sees memory as a byproduct of how information is processed or coded. Semantic processing will produce longer storage than structural or phonetic processing.

- Opinions differ as to the relative importance of the elaboration and the distinctiveness of processing.

- A major problem with LOP is trying to measure depth independently of the actual retention score. One proposed solution is in terms of orienting tasks. Another is to concentrate on what it is relevant to remember given how memory will be tested (transfer-appropriate processing).

- Working memory (WM) adopts a functional approach to understanding STM and sees it as comprising a central executive, articulatory loop ('inner voice'), visuospatial scratch pad ('inner eye') and primary acoustic store ('inner ear'). The central executive is an attentional system and WM is studied using concurrent/interference tasks (as is divided attention).

- Both chunking and imagery are forms of organizing information; this makes the information easier both to store and to retrieve. An important issue is the importance of interacting images relative to their bizarreness.

- Imagery plays an important part in mnemonic devices, such as the method of loci.

- An influential model of SM is the hierarchical network model, which sees the memory network in terms of logical, hierarchical relationships between words and concepts. This has been modified to include semantic distance and spreading activation, making it more flexible and realistic.

- Schema theory sees schemas as the 'unit' of SM, rather than simple concepts. Our knowledge is stored in memory as simplified mental representations of objects and events, which we use to interpret new experiences. One influential form of schema theory is the notion of scripts; these represent commonly experienced social events such as going to a restaurant.

- Bartlett introduced 'schema' into psychology to help explain the interpretation and reconstruction involved when we try to remember meaningful material, such as stories. This implies that memory is not a 'pure' process that can be studied outside the social and cultural context in which it takes place.

- Seeing memory as reconstructive has influenced

much of the research into eyewitness testimony (EWT). An important theoretical issue is whether 'leading questions' actually change earlier memories or simply interfere with their retrieval.

● Some naturalistic research suggests that EWT may be more reliable than it appears to be based on laboratory experiments.

● Forgetting can be understood as a failure in the transfer of information from STM to LTM (trace decay, displacement, interference) or the loss of information once transfer has occurred (decay through disuse, prevention of consolidation) or failure to retrieve form LTM (interference, motivated forgetting, cue-dependent forgetting) or changes in LT memories (Gestalt theory).

● As far as decay theory is concerned, it seems that the passage of time in itself is not important, but rather what happens in between learning and recall. This is the focus of interference theory.

● An important distinction is between retroactive inhibition (RI) and proactive inhibition (PI). There is evidence that PI is more important, partly because it increases with time.

● A major limitation of interference theory is the low ecological validity of the experiments used to test it, especially the use of nonsense syllables.

● Cue-dependent forgetting refers jointly to state- and context-dependent forgetting. Psychological or physiological states represent internal cues and environmental or contextual variables represent external cues or routes to retrieving stored information.

● Motivated forgetting/repression is based on Freud's psychoanalytic theory and has stimulated much research and debate. Experimental evidence is not very supportive, but clinical evidence involving psychogenic amnesia, posttraumatic stress disorder, etc. is much more so.

● There is currently great controversy over recovered memories of child sexual abuse and false memory syndrome.

GLOSSARY

Accessibility The retrievability of information that has been stored in memory.

Anterograde amnesia Memory loss for events occurring after brain injury or whatever the cause may be.

Availability In the context of memory, whether or not information has been stored.

Brown-Peterson technique Method for studying the effects of length of recall interval on recall of lists of words, etc.

Chunking A way of increasing the capacity of STM by reducing large amounts of unrelated information to a smaller amount of meaningful information. A form of organization, drawing on knowledge from LTM.

Confabulation A kind of memory error in which we manufacture details of some event in order to fill in the gaps.

Consolidation process Time needed for information in LTM to become firmly recorded physically in the brain.

Cue-dependent forgetting Forgetting that occurs due to a mismatch between the state or context in which the original learning and subsequent recall take place.

Declarative memory Term used to refer to SM and EM, which can be inspected consciously and described ('knowing that'). A form of explicit memory.

Displacement A theory of forgetting from STM in which new information replaces information which previously occupied one of the small number of slots.

Elaborative rehearsal The elaboration of items by giving them a meaning which they didn't originally have.

Encoding specificity principle The belief that cues only help retrieval if they are encoded at the time of learning.

Episodic memory (EM) A form of LTM responsible for storing the events, people, etc. that we have experienced personally (they have a *spatiotemporal context*). Sometimes used synonymously with 'autobiographical' memory.

Flashbulb memories A special kind of EM relating to vivid and detailed recollections of what we were doing /where we were when news broke of some major national/international event.

Interference A theory of forgetting which stresses the competition between memories. In LTM, there is a failure to retrieve, in STM, extraneous material prevents new information passing into LTM.

Levels of processing Alternative to the multistore model, which sees memory as the result of how deeply information is processed.

Long-term memory (LTM) Unlimited capacity storage system, which can retain information from a few minutes to a lifetime. Uses both semantic and imagery/visual codes.

Maintenance rehearsal The repetition of items acoustically, either aloud or silently.

Mnemonic devices Memory aids, often using

imagery, which either reduce or elaborate the encoding of information.

Multistore model Model of memory in which STM and LTM represent structural components of the memory system, with control processes (especially rehearsal) directing the flow of information between them.

Paired-associate learning Procedure for studying memory using pairs of unrelated words/nonsense syllables, in which the first member of the pair represents the 'stimulus' and the second member the 'response'.

Proactive inhibition Interference caused by the learning of earlier material with the recall of later material (so it works forwards).

Procedural memory A form of LTM relating to our ability to perform complex skills which cannot be inspected consciously or described ('knowing how'). A form of implicit memory.

Psychogenic amnesia Memory loss caused by psychological stress or trauma.

Recall A stringent form of retrieval, in which we actively search our memory stores (as in timed essays).

Recognition A sensitive form of retrieval, in which a target item is matched with something stored in memory (as in multiple choice tests).

Reconstructive memory The kind of remembering involved in storytelling and eyewitness testimony, in which we draw on existing schemas to make inferences about events in order to make them more meaningful and coherent.

Recovered memories Memories, often of child sexual abuse, which surface during psychotherapy after many years of repression.

Retroactive inhibition Interference caused by the learning of later material with the recall of earlier material (so it works backwards).

Retrograde amnesia Memory loss for events occurring before the brain injury or whatever the cause may be.

Schema A simplified, generalized, mental representation of everything we understand by a given type of object or event, based on past experience. (Plural = 'schemas' or 'schemata'.)

Script One kind of schema which represents commonly experienced social events (such as eating in a restaurant).

Semantic memory (SM) A form of LTM which stores our general factual knowledge about the world, including concepts, rules and language.

Sensory memory A basic form of storage, which provides very brief, literal copies of sensory experience needed for STM. Modality specific. Also called *sensory buffer store.*

Serial position curve Graph showing the probability of recalling a particular word depending on its position in the list. Typically, it shows a strong recency effect and a weaker primacy effect.

Short-term memory (STM) Limited capacity, limited duration storage system, confined largely to an acoustic store. Capacity can be increased by chunking and duration by rehearsal.

Trace decay A theory of forgetting which sees the increase of forgetting over time as caused by the fading of the neural memory trace. Applies to both STM and LTM.

Transfer-appropriate processing How well information will be remembered, depending on the extent to which it is relevant to the test of memory that is used.

Working memory A functional model of STM, in which a central executive, at the top of a hierarchy, controls the activities of an articulatory loop, visuospatial scratch pad and primary acoustic store. The central executive is an attentional system.

FURTHER READING

Baddeley, A. (1990) *Human Memory: Theory and Practice*. London: Lawrence Erlbaum Associates. An extremely broad, detailed but readable textbook by one of the leading figures in the field.

Parkin, A.J. (1993) *Memory: Phenomena, Experiment and Theory*. Oxford: Blackwell. A much briefer text than Baddeley's, with chapters on developmental aspects of memory.

13 LANGUAGE AND THOUGHT

INTRODUCTION AND OVERVIEW

The relationship between language and thought is one of the most fascinating and complex issues within psychology and it has been debated by philosophers for over 2000 years. Our thinking often goes on through the medium of imagery and our thoughts and feelings are often expressed (unconsciously) through gestures and facial expressions and in other non-verbal ways. Artists 'think' non-linguistically. We have all had the experience of knowing what we want to say but being unable to find the right words and students often do poorly in essays because they cannot put into words what they 'know'.

From all of these examples, it would appear that thinking is possible without language. But psychologists differ greatly as to how they see the exact relationship between the two; their views fall into three main categories:

- *Thought is dependent on, or caused by, language.* This is the view taken by Whorf, Sapir, Bruner, Watson and Bernstein, as well as *social constructionists*, an extremely diverse group of theorists.

Sapir and Whorf, the first a linguist and anthropologist, the second a linguist, were both interested in comparing languages, which they saw as a major feature of a culture. Individuals, of course, are born into a particular culture and a particular language community, so there was an expectation that language would be the greatest influence. Language, because it is shared by all members of a culture (or 'subculture'), is more obviously 'public' than the much more private, individual 'thought'.

Watson, the founder of behaviourism, stressed the role of environmental influences on the individual almost to the exclusion of any 'internal' psychological factors so, once again, language is the greater influence because it is 'public' and can be studied objectively (at least in its spoken form) while thought is too inaccessible to others to be even worthy of scientific investigation.

According to Bruner, language is essential if thought or knowledge are not to be limited to what can be learned through actions (the enactive mode of representation) or images (the iconic mode), i.e. language is crucial for the development of the symbolic mode (see Chapter 25). In a rather similar way, Bernstein, a sociologist, sees language codes as a major influence on intelligence, especially in the context of education and social class. Partly influenced by certain approaches within sociology, social constructionists (such as Gergen) see language as providing a basis for all our thought, a system of categories for dividing up experience and giving it meaning.

- *Language is dependent on, and reflects, thought.* Probably the most extreme version of this view is Piaget's, according to which language reflects the individual's level of cognitive development.

(Piaget's ideas will be discussed in detail, with Bruner's, in Chapter 25.)

- *Thought and language are originally quite separate activities* which come together and interact at a certain point of development (about two years old). This is associated mainly with Vygotsky, whose developmental theory as a whole is discussed in Chapter 25.

DOES LANGUAGE DETERMINE THOUGHT?

● The linguistic relativity hypothesis

The philosopher Ludwig Wittgenstein claimed that 'The limits of my language mean the limits of my world', by which he meant that we can only think about and understand the world through language, so that if our language does not possess certain ideas or concepts, then they cannot exist for us. Many psychologists argue that language may determine how we think about objects or events, while others contend that language actually determines the ideas, thoughts and perceptions themselves, i.e. what we think.

Among those who adopt this latter view are Benjamin Lee Whorf, an amateur linguist, and Edward Sapir, a linguist and anthropologist (and Whorf's tutor). They reached very similar conclusions quite independently of each other, but their theory has become known as the *Sapir–Whorf linguistic relativity hypothesis* (often referred to as the 'Whorfian hypothesis'). According to Whorf (1956).

> We dissect nature along lines laid down by our native languages. The categories and types that we isolate from the world of phenomena we do not find there because they stare every observer in the face; on the contrary, the world is presented in a kaleidoscopic flux of impressions that has to be organized by our minds – and this means largely by the linguistic systems in our minds. We cut nature up, organize it into concepts and ascribe significance as we do, largely because we are parties to an agreement to organize it this way – an agreement that holds throughout our speech community and is codified in the pattern of our language ...

What Whorf is saying is that language determines our concepts and we can think only through the use of concepts (this is *linguistic determinism*). It follows that acquiring a language involves acquiring a world view (that is, how we cut nature up – it does not come 'ready sliced') and that people with different languages have different world views, that is, they cut nature up differently (this is, strictly speaking, what the linguistic relativity hypothesis maintains). We shall be discussing below differences in the way the spectrum is cut up linguistically; the analogy of thin, medium and thick-sliced is not as outrageous as it might first sound!

What kind of evidence did Sapir and Whorf base their hypothesis on?

Whorf compared Standard Average European (SAE) languages, such as English, French and Italian (Indo-European), with Native American languages, particularly Hopi. Vocabulary determines the categories we use to perceive and understand the world. For instance, whereas in English we have a single word for snow, the Inuit Eskimos have approximately 20 (including one for fluffy snow, one for drifting snow, another for packed snow, and so on). The Hopi Indians (whose language Whorf studied for several years) have only one word for 'insect', 'aeroplane' and 'pilot' and the Zuni Indians do not distinguish, verbally, between yellow and orange.

FIGURE 13.1 *According to Whorf, the fact that Inuit Eskimos have 20 different words for snow means that they literally perceive more varieties of snow than native English speakers who have only one or two words*

But it is not only the vocabulary of a language that determines how and what we think and perceive but also the grammar. In the Hopi language, no distinction is made between past, present and future; it is a 'timeless language' (compared with English), although it does recognize duration, i.e. how long an event lasts. In European languages, 'time' is treated as an objective entity, as if it were a ruler with equal spaces or intervals marked off, and there is a clear demarcation between past, present and future (corresponding to three separate sections of the ruler). We say 'ten days' in much the same way as we say 'ten men', although we cannot experience ten days simultaneously. By contrast, the Hopi Indians do not talk about an objective period of time but only as it appears subjectively to the observer. For example, they say 'I stayed until the sixth day' or 'I left on the sixth day' (instead of 'I stayed for six days').

Again, the Hopi Indians get by without tenses for their verbs and have no words or grammatical forms which refer directly to 'time'. Instead, they use different verb endings according to how certain the speaker is about an event (whether they have actually seen it or have just heard about it) or different voice inflections which express whether the speaker is reporting an event, expecting an event or making a generalization about events.

In English, we think of nouns as denoting objects and events and verbs as denoting actions. But in the Hopi language, 'lightning', 'wave', 'flame', 'meteor', 'puff of smoke' and 'pulsation' are all verbs, as events of necessarily brief duration must be verbs; so, for example, 'it lightninged', 'it smoked' and 'it flamed'.

All these differences, according to Sapir and Whorf, determine differences in how native speakers think about, perceive and remember the world: the world *is* different according to what language we speak (or perhaps, more accurately, the language we 'think in').

Some questions (and question marks) about the Whorfian hypothesis

- According to Pullum (1989, cited in Newstead, 1995), the Inuit Eskimos have relatively few words for snow, much of Whorf's evidence was anecdotal (Berry *et al.*, 1992) and generally he exaggerated the differences between Hopi and SAE (Jackendoff, 1993).
- But even if the differences in vocabulary and grammar were well established, would this justify the conclusions that he and Sapir drew? Does the finding that Inuit Eskimos have 20 words for snow necessarily mean that native speakers of Inuit actually perceive more varieties of snow than speakers of English? Did Whorf show that the Hopi Indians cannot discriminate between past, present and future in essentially the same way as SAE speakers?

  Judith Greene (1975) asks us to imagine a Hopi linguist doing a Whorfian analysis of English: would they think that we have 'primitive' beliefs that ships are really female or that mountains have feet or that 'driving a car', 'driving off in golf' and 'driving a hard bargain' all involve the same activity? Of course not; we do distinguish between the grammar of a language and our perceptual experience. The fact that we can translate from Hopi into English and vice-versa implies that there is a universally-shared knowledge of the world, which is independent of the particular language in which it is expressed.
- A crucial question that Whorf seems to have overlooked is *why* do Eskimos have so many names for

snow and SAE languages so few? One answer is that the more significant an experience or some feature of our environment is for us, the greater the number of ways of expressing it in the language, i.e. instead of our language determining our perceptions, our perceptions (reflecting what is important for us) might be influencing our language.

> ... The development of specific language codes ... is dependent on cultural needs; the learning of these codes by members of a language group also involves the learning of significant values of the culture, some of which must be related to survival ... (Solso, 1995)

- It is extremely difficult to put the Whorfian hypothesis to direct experimental test. Miller and McNeill

---

BOX 13.1 Key study: How Navaho children shape up on cognitive development

Carroll and Casagrande (1958) compared Navaho children (both those who spoke only Navaho, *Navaho-Navaho,* and those who spoke English and Navaho, *English-Navaho)* and American children (of European descent, who spoke only English) on the development of form or shape recognition.

The Navaho language stresses the importance of form. For example, verbs of handling involve different words according to the type of object being handled, so that long and flexible objects (such as string) have one word form, while long, rigid objects (like sticks) have another and flat and flexible objects (like cloth) have yet another word form. It is also known (from other research) that American children of European descent develop object recognition in this order: size, colour and form or shape.

If the Navaho language has influenced cognitive development (as Sapir and Whorf predict it would) then the developmental sequence of the Navaho-Navaho children should differ from that of the English children – they should be superior. And this indeed was what Carrol and Casagrande found: the Navaho-Navaho children were best at form recognition and showed it earliest, next came the English children and last of all the English-Navaho children.

These results appear to lend support to the Sapir–Whorf view but why did the English children come second and not third? According to the researchers, they were atypical, having had a great deal of experience of shape classification at nursery school. If the English-Navaho children are taken as the relevant control group, the study can be taken as supporting the Whorfian hypothesis, but if the English children are the relevant control group, then it cannot.

(1969) distinguish between three rather different versions, all consistent with Whorf's general theoretical position but varying in the strength of the claims they make. For the sake of simplicity, we shall distinguish between: (i) the *strong version,* which claims that language determines thought; and (ii) the *weak version* (which combines the 'weak' and 'weakest' according to Miller and McNeill), which claims only that language affects perception and memory. Most of the criticisms that we have considered so far relate to the strong version, but almost all the research relates to the weak version. Box 13.1 summarizes one of the few studies that is relevant to the strong version.

Testing the weak version of the linguistic relativity hypothesis

According to Whorf, if a language does not make certain discriminations in its verbal labels, then native speakers of that language will be unable to make the corresponding perceptual discriminations. Taking a previous example, since the Zuni language does not distinguish between yellow and orange, Zuni speakers should not be able to perceive the difference between these two colours – they would be 'blind' for these two colours. Does this reflect the way things really are?

Lenneberg and Roberts (1956) found that the number of errors made by bilingual Zuni-English speakers in distinguishing orange and yellow fell midway between that of monolingual Zuni and monolingual English speakers. This suggests that the two languages do not determine two different sets of perceptions which in some way conflict, but rather two sets of labels for essentially the same colour perceptions.

Other studies (see below) show that speakers can learn new labels for colours, indicating that there are no differences in what is actually perceived by native speakers of different languages. Instead, language serves to draw attention to differences in the environment and acts as a label to help store these differences

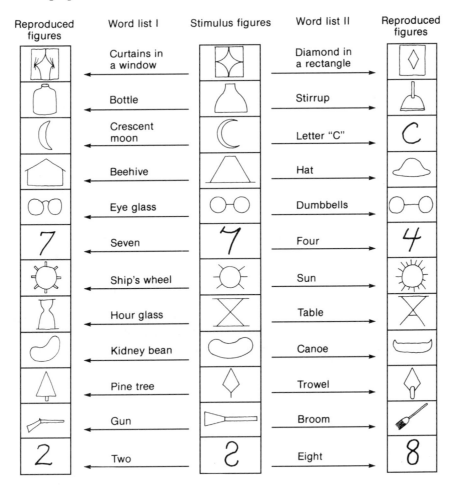

FIGURE 13.2 *Stimulus figures, word lists and reproduced figures. (From the experiment by Carmichael et al., 1932)*

in memory; sometimes the label we apply to what we see may distort our recall of what was seen, since the label determines how we code our experiences into memory storage. This was well illustrated in a famous experiment by Carmichael *et al.* (1932). Two separate groups of participants were given identical stimulus figures but two different sets of labels. After a period of time, both groups were asked to reproduce the figures. The drawings of both groups were distorted in comparison with the original stimulus according to which label had been presented (Fig. 13.2)

So there seems to be very little direct evidence to support the original ('strong') form of the linguistic relativity hypothesis, but rather more support for the weaker version. According to Brown (1956), language merely predisposes people to think or perceive in certain ways or about certain things – it does not determine these thoughts and perceptions. But can we go one step further and ask if there is there any evidence that would actually *contradict* the Whorfian hypothesis?

The perception of colour: searching for universal linguistic structures

Some of the most influential studies of colour coding have identified *universal linguistic* structures, i.e. universal characteristics of human thought processes that produce universal linguistic structures. (This is very much in line with Piaget's position and relates to the second of the three major views on the relationship between language and thought.)

Despite a diversity of terms denoting colour, all languages apparently select colour terms from the 11 basic (or *focal*) colour categories of black, white, red, green, yellow, blue, brown, purple, pink, orange and grey. In English, all 11 are used but the Ibibio of Nigeria use only four, and the Jalé of New Guinea only two. However, this does not indicate an arbitrary division of the colour spectrum: if a language has fewer than 11 terms, those it lacks come from categories lower down in the list. For example, Jalé names only the first two categories (black and white) and Ibibio the first four (black, white, red and green) and so on down the list. According to Berlin, and Kay (1969) the

focal colours become encoded in the history of a language in a (largely) fixed order, as shown in Fig. 13.3; they see these various stages as representing steps in the evolution of languages.

Of course, the smaller the number of terms, the wider the range of colours they apply to. So, for example, green in Ibibio encompasses the English green, yellow and blue. Therefore, according to Whorf, speakers of Ibibio should be unable to perceive the same colour differences that English speakers can. Do the findings bear him out? The influential study by Berlin and Kay is described in Box 13.2

Heider (1972) studied 23 native speakers of diverse languages drawn from seven of the major language families of the world. They were asked to write down the name they would give for each colour chip (as used by Berlin and Kay, 1969). Focal colours were given shorter names and were named faster than non-focal colours and it was the same colours that were the most codable in different languages. Heider also gave a colour memory test, very similar to that used by Brown and Lenneberg (1954), to a sample of Dani speakers (a Stone Age agricultural people of Indonesian New Guinea) and to a sample of Americans. The Dani language has only two basic colour terms – 'mola' for bright, warm hues and 'mili' for dark, cold hues. After the random presentation of both focal and non-focal colours and following a 30-second delay, participants had to select from an array of many colours those they had previously been shown. Despite the substantial linguistic differences between the Dani and English speakers, both samples recognized the focal colours better than the non-focal. It seems that focal colours have a higher codability than non-focal even for those focal colours for which there is no basic term in the person's language.

In a second study with the Dani, eight focal and eight non-focal colours were paired with a separate response word. Despite the fact that all the words were unfamiliar, the Dani participants needed significantly fewer trials to learn the new focal terms than the non-focal. Heider (1972) concluded that:

> ... far from being a domain well suited to the study of the effects of language on thought, the colour-space

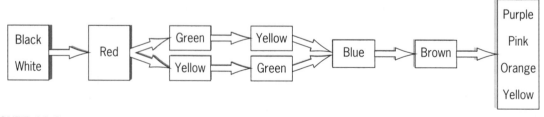

FIGURE 13.3 *The sequence in which terms for focal colours emerge in the history of languages. (Berlin & Kay, 1969)*

BOX 13.2

Key study. Basic colour terms: their universality and evolution

Two anthropologists, Berlin and Kay, used a chart with an array of 329 small coloured chips comprising virtually all the hues that the human eye can discriminate. The hues were at all levels of brightness and all at maximum saturation (see Chapter 8). They asked native speakers of 20 languages (other than English) to (a) trace the boundaries of each of their native language's basic colour terms, and (b) to point to the chip which was the best example of each basic colour term.

A basic or focal colour was defined by a list of linguistic criteria, including (i) a term should consist of only a single unit of meaning (e.g. 'red' as opposed to 'dark red'), and (ii) it should name only colours and not objects (e.g. 'purple' as opposed to 'wine').

As expected from anthropological research, there was considerable variation in the placement of boundaries. However, the choice of best examples was surprisingly similar. Figure 13.4 shows that the most typical or focal chips for basic colours are neatly clustered. The largest clusters were for black and white and red, for which all the 20 languages have colour terms, then 19 for green, 18 yellow, 16 blue, 15 brown and purple, 14 grey and 11 pink and orange. Large parts of the diagram remain outside the areas covered by the basic colour terms. Berlin and Kay concluded that 'colour categorization is not random and the foci of basic colour terms are similar in all languages'.

Their results led them to reinterpret the findings of an earlier study by Brown and Lenneberg (1954), who had claimed that the *codability* of a colour (measured partly as the speed with which it was named) is correlated with accuracy of memory (how accurately a colour could be remembered in a recognition task). Berlin and Kay proposed instead that there may be areas of the colour space that are perceptually more salient to all peoples and these areas become both more codable and can be better remembered as a direct result of their salience.

would seem a prime example of the influence of underlying perceptual-cognitive factors on the formation and reference of linguistic categories.

More specifically, what Heider (sometimes referred to as Rosch – her married name) means is that the results should be explained in terms of *physiological factors* underlying colour vision rather than linguistic factors. Is there any evidence that focal colours are learnt (i.e. discriminated) *before* any verbal colour labels are learnt, which would represent a very serious contradiction of Whorf?

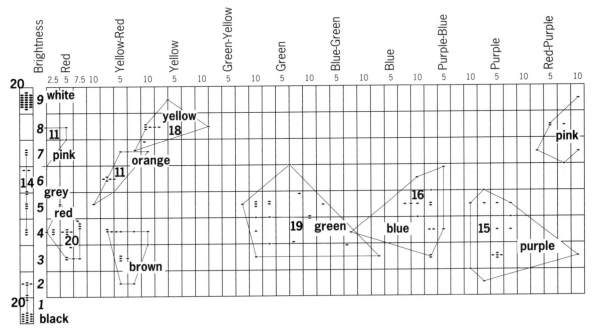

FIGURE 13.4 *Clusters of dots representing foci (averaged over participants) in each of 20 languages. The number in each cluster indicates the number of languages that had a basic term for the colour concerned. (Numbers in the margins refer to parameters of the Munsell colour system.) (Berlin & Kay, 1969)*

According to Bornstein (1988), '... pre-verbal infants categorize the visible spectrum into relatively discrete hues of blue, green, yellow and red: which are similar to those of adults ...' Many psychologists now believe that Whorf overestimated the significance of language differences. The studies of colour coding contribute to the conclusion, widely accepted, that:

> ... language as an instrument for thinking has many cross culturally invariant properties. As humans we may not all be sharing the same thoughts, but our respective languages do not seem to predestine us to different kinds of thinking. (Berry *et al.*, 1992)

● Peripheralism

Another theory which maintains that language determines thought is that of Watson (1912; see Chapter 1). Watson claimed that all thought processes are really no more than the sensations produced by tiny movements of the speech apparatus which are too small to produce audible sounds. In fact, he was trying to deny thought altogether and so 'reduce' it to silent speech. His theory is known as *peripheralism,* that is, thinking does not occur centrally in the brain but peripherally in the voicebox.

In 1912 his theory was very speculative because there were no instruments precise enough to detect such movements. However, movements of the larynx have since been detected. Yet this does not tell us that these movements are thoughts or even that they are necessary for thinking to occur, only that they accompany thinking. An experiment by Smith *et al.* (1947) leaves little doubt that, in fact, these movements are not necessary. Smith injected himself with a drug (curare) which causes total paralysis of the skeletal muscles and thus causes complete respiratory paralysis, so that he had to be kept breathing artificially. He was later able to report the thoughts and perceptions he had during his paralysis.

Furth (1966) demonstrated experimentally that people who are born deaf and mute, and who do not learn any sign language, are of average ability in thinking and intelligence as adults. Watson would have predicted that such individuals would be incapable of thinking. (It is evidence such as Furth's which lends support to Piaget's view that it is the development of cognitive structures which is of primary importance, with language merely reflecting those structures.)

An important study which suggests that language plays a rather more central role in cognitive development is the Luria and Yudovich study of the Russian twins described in Box 13.3.

BOX 13.3 | **Key study: the case of the Russian twins (Luria and Yudovich, 1956)**

Luria and Yudovich (1956) studied a pair of five-year-old identical twin boys in Russia, whose home environment was unstimulating and who played almost exclusively together. They had only a very primitive level of speech development, received very little encouragement to speak from adults and made little progress towards a symbolic use of words.

Luria described their speech as *synpraxic,* a primitive form of speech in which the child cannot detach the word from the object or action which it denotes. Their communication with each other consisted of words and actions inextricably mixed. Words on their own had no permanent meanings and could only be understood in a concrete situation; also, their meanings changed according to the situation in which they were used and the tone of voice in which they were spoken. For example, one of their names (Lioshia) could mean:

'I (Lioshia) am playing nicely' or
'Let him (Lioshia) go for a walk' or
'Look (Lioshia) what l have done'

They hardly ever used speech to describe objects or events or to help them plan their actions, they could not understand other people's speech and their own represented a private system of communication, a kind of signalling (rather than symbolic) system. However, they were normal in most other ways and did not appear to be mentally retarded, although they never played with other children and when they played with each other the content was always very primitive and monotonous; for example, there was never any attempt to build or construct things.

The twins were separated and placed in different nursery schools. One was given special remedial training for his language deficiency and the other was not. Although the twin given special treatment did make more rapid progress and, ten months later, was still in advance of his brother, equally significant is the fact that both made progress and the synpraxic speech died away. So we must be cautious in drawing any firm conclusions about the effects of the special training that only one twin received.

However, Luria and Yudovich conclude by saying:

> The whole structure of the mental life of both twins was simultaneously and sharply changed. Once they acquired an objective language system, the children were able to formulate the aims of their activity verbally and after only three months we observed the beginnings of meaningful play.

● Restricted and elaborated codes

As a sociologist, Bernstein was interested in the role of language as a social (rather than an individual) phenomenon, especially as it relates to cultural deprivation. Essentially, Bernstein (1961) claims that working- and middle-class children speak two different kinds of language (codes) – a *restricted code* and an *elaborated code*, respectively. Since the relationship between potential and developed intelligence is mediated through language, the lack of an elaborated code prevents working-class children from developing their full intellectual potential. These language codes, according to Bernstein, underlie the whole pattern of relationships (to objects and people) experienced by middle-class and working-class families, as well as the patterns of learning which their children bring with them to school.

Bernstein studied the effect of social class differences in language on the child's intellectual ability by comparing the performance of boys from lower working-class homes with boys from famous public schools on tests of verbal and non-verbal intelligence (see Chapter 28). Working-class boys who scored high on the non-verbal test scored lower on the verbal test (sometimes there was a difference of up to 26 points) but scores for the public school boys did not show this pattern. These differences in verbal and non-verbal IQ for the working-class boys were attributed to their poor linguistic background, i.e. their restricted code

(or 'public language'). Some of the main characteristics of these two codes are shown in Table 13.1.

Stones (1971) gives examples of imaginary conversations on a bus between a mother and child:

Mother: Hold on tight.

Child: Why?

Mother: 'Hold on tight.

Child: Why?

Mother: You'll fall.

Child: Why?

Mother: I told you to hold on tight, didn't I?

This would be a fairly typical restricted code-type of conversation: the words are being used more as signals than symbols, with very little attempt to explain or reason on the mother's part. Now contrast this with an elaborated code mother and her child:

Mother: Hold on tight, darling.

Child: Why?

Mother: If you don't you'll be thrown forward and you'll fall.

Child: Why?

Mother: Because if the bus suddenly stops, you'll jerk forward onto the seat in front.

Child: Why?

Restricted code	Elaborated code
1 Grammatically crude, repetitive, rigid, limited use of adjectives and adverbs, uses more pronouns than nouns. Sentences often short, grammatically simple and incomplete.	I Grammatically more complex, flexible. Uses a range of subordinate clauses, conjunctions, prepositions, adjectives, adverbs. More nouns than pronouns. Sentences longer and more complex.
2 Context-bound, i.e. the meaning not made explicit but assumes listener's familiarity with the situation being described, e.g. 'He gave me it'; listener cannot be expected to know who 'he' or what 'it' refers to.	2 Context-independent, i.e. the meaning is made explicit, e.g. 'John gave me this book'.
3 'I' rarely used and much of the meaning conveyed non-verbally.	3 'I' often used, making clear the speaker's intentions, as well as emphasizing the precise description of experiences and feelings.
4 Frequent use of uninformative but emotionally reinforcing phrases such as 'you know', 'don't I'.	4 Relatively little use of these reinforcing phrases.
5 Tends to stress the present, the here-and-now.	5 Tends to stress past and future, rather than the present.
6 Doesn't allow expression of abstract or hypothetical thought.	6 Allows expression of abstract or hypothetical thought.

TABLE 13.1 *Characteristics of the restricted and elaborated codes (Bernstein, 1961)*

Mother: Now, darling, hold on tightly and don't make such a fuss.

Bernstein's theory has important implications for education:

- Although lower working-class pupils can achieve a good deal of mechanical learning, they are much more handicapped in attempting academic work. The restricted code acts as a filter to restrict what gets through from the teacher who, by definition, is an elaborated code user; the middle-class child has access to both codes.
- Schooling is conducted almost entirely in an elaborated, formal code. Hence the middle-class children merely have to develop their language skills, while working-class children have to change theirs, i.e. school is continuous with the home for middle-class but not for working-class children. The older the child gets, the more difficult it becomes to overcome this disadvantage because the educational system becomes more and more abstract.
- The middle-class child is used to attending to long speech sequences (middle-class parents place more emphasis on verbal explanations as part of their disciplinary techniques), while the working class child (often used to communicating in a noisy, even chaotic environment) may find concentrating very difficult and may even have learnt how *not* to attend.
- Middle-class parents encourage their children to ask questions and if they cannot answer them themselves will consult a book or refer the child to one. The world is presented as rational and knowable – it can be mastered and understood. Working-class parents, on the other hand, are generally less responsive to their child's questions and may be unable or unwilling to 'point the child in the right direction'. The working-class child might then come to regard the world as largely unknowable or only knowable by others. Clearly, asking and answering questions, using books and other reference materials and generally being inquisitive and wanting to find out about the world are all fundamental parts of formal schooling.

An evaluation of Bernstein's theory

Some support for Bernstein comes from a study by Hess and Shipman (1965). They studied 163 American mothers and their four-year-olds and found social class-related differences in communication which seemed to influence the child's intellectual development. In particular, they drew attention to 'a lack of meaning in the mother-child communication system' for low-status families, that is, language was used much less to convey meaning (to describe, explain, express and so on) and much more to give orders and commands to the child. Hess and Shipman claim that 'The meaning of deprivation is a deprivation of meaning'.

If true, these implications of having only a restricted code are of quite crucial importance. They amount to the impossibility of upward social mobility (moving 'up' from working-class status to middle-class status). How could a working-class child (limited to a restricted code) ever grow up to become a teacher, who is a middle-class elaborated code user? But we know this does happen. Clearly, any theory formulated in terms of two basic types tends to oversimplify things as they really are, so that a more helpful way of thinking about language codes may be to see restricted and elaborated codes as two ends of a continuum.

Perhaps the most serious criticism of Bernstein's theory is to do with the very terms 'restricted' and 'elaborated'. They imply a value-judgement of middle-class speech as being in some way 'superior', that is, it resembles 'standard' (or 'the Queen's') English much more than working class speech does. But this is very difficult to defend on objective grounds.

In a similar fashion, the English spoken by black children and adults, according to Bernstein, is a restricted code and this makes their thinking less logical than that of white, middle-class children and adults.

Labov and black English

Bereiter and Englemann (1966) point out that certain inner-city, black dialects of American English are often called 'substandard' rather than 'non-standard' and are often attacked as illogical. One reason given for this attack is that speakers of these dialects often omit the present tense *copula* (the verb 'to be'), producing such sentences as 'He a fool' instead of the standard 'He is a fool'. But which version is more logical?

Labov (1970) showed that speakers of both dialects are, in fact, expressing the same ideas and understand each other equally well. Also, many prestigious world languages, such as Russian and Arabic, like black English, also omit the present tense of the verb 'to be', yet they are never called illogical. This suggests that black English dialects are frowned upon as a matter of convention or prejudice and not because they are poorer vehicles for expressing meaning and thinking logically.

Again, the structure of black English (phonology, grammar, etc.) differs in important ways from standard English and as intelligence tests are administered in standard English, black children are clearly under a linguistic handicap (this also applies to the white, working-class child). It has been argued that black English speakers are not making grammatical 'errors' but are correctly using a separate dialect of English; black English is different from standard English but is just as logical. Bernstein based his view of black English on a limited sample; but in addition, many children from low-income black families simply would not or could not speak freely and comfortably in their full language when around whites.

Similarly, Labov has pointed out that the social situation is a powerful determinant of verbal behaviour. He describes the dramatic changes that can take place when the testing conditions are changed. A young black boy, Leon, was shown a toy and asked, by a friendly white interviewer, to tell him everything he could about it. The boy said very little and remained silent for much of the time. In a second situation, Leon was interviewed by a black interviewer. This time, he answered the questions with single words or indistinct sounds. However, when sitting on the floor sharing a bag of crisps with his best friend and with the same black interviewer introducing topics in the local dialect, Leon emerged as a lively conversationalist. If the first two situations had been relied upon, Leon would have been labelled 'non-verbal' or 'linguistically retarded'.

The picture that is emerging is that black children are actually *bilingual*. At home, in the playground, in their neighbourhoods, they speak an accepted vernacular but in the classroom, they are forced to use another form of the English language with which they are unfamiliar. The school 'register' may be used when the children talk to people who seem to be in authority and only when using the register are their sentences short and their grammar simple and intonation strange. Once out of school, their natural register is easy, fluent, creative and even gifted. It is unquestionably non-standard English (not substandard); in fact, it is another language, with its own grammar. Labov's findings certainly do not support the view that such children lack the language needed for abstract thinking.

● Social constructionism

According to Burr (1995), 'social constructionism' (e.g. Gergen, 1973) can be thought of as a theoretical orientation which lies behind a number of recent alternative approaches to the study of human beings as social animals, including 'critical psychology', 'discourse analysis' and 'poststructuralism'.

One general characteristic of this approach is the belief that language is a pre-condition for thought. Our ways of understanding the world derive not from objective reality but from other people – past and present. We are born into a world where the conceptual frameworks and categories used by the people in our culture already exist. Indeed, these frameworks and categories are an essential part of our culture since they provide meaning, a way of structuring our experience of both ourselves and the world of other people. These ideas have much in common with the strong version of the Whorfian hypothesis. (The social constructionist view of language has much to contribute to the understanding of prejudice and discrimination (see Chapter 19), gender (see Chapter 23) and personality (see Chapter 29)).

ARE LANGUAGE AND THOUGHT SEPARATE AND INDEPENDENT?

According to Vygotsky, thought and language start out as separate and independent activities. In very young children (as in animals) thought precedes language (it is pre-verbal, as in sensorimotor intelligence) and language is devoid of thought (for example, when the baby cries or makes other sounds with its vocal apparatus, it is usually expressing feelings or trying to attract attention or fulfilling some other social aim).

Then, at about two years, there is a crucial moment when pre-linguistic thought (actions, perceptions, images, etc.) and pre-intellectual language

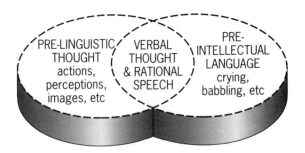

FIGURE 13.5 *Summary of Vygotsky's theory of language and thought*

(crying, babbling, etc.) 'meet and join to' initiate a new kind of behaviour ... thought becomes verbal and speech rational' (Vygotsky, 1962).

Vygotsky's theory can be represented as two overlapping circles, one representing pre-linguistic thought, the other pre-intellectual language; where they overlap represents verbal thought and rational speech (Fig. 13.5).

Between the ages of two and seven, language performs two functions: (i) an *internal* one of monitoring and directing internal thought; and (ii) an *external* one, namely communicating the results of the child's thinking to others. But the child cannot yet distinguish them, which results in *egocentric speech* – the child talks out loud about its plans and actions and is neither thinking privately nor communicating publicly to others but is caught somewhere in between, i.e. the child cannot distinguish between speech for itself (what Piaget called *autistic speech*) and speech for others (which Piaget called *socialized speech*).

Then, at about seven years (when concrete operational thought usually begins) the child starts to restrict its overt language to the purposes of communication, while the thought function of language is now internalized as internal speech or verbal thought. Piaget originally claimed that egocentric speech is just a kind of running commentary on the child's behaviour and that when it declines at around seven, it 'disappears' to be replaced by socialized speech (communicative speech). Vygotsky, on the other hand, noted that egocentric speech becomes more and more unlike social speech just as it begins to disappear. His experiments showed that when six- or seven-year-olds are trying to solve a difficult problem or are thwarted in their attempts to do something (for example, their pencil breaks in the middle of drawing a picture), so that they have to revise their plans, they often revert to overt verbalization. (Adults, too, often 'think out loud' in similar situations, for example 'Now where did I put it?' or 'Now what am I going to do?, especially if they believe there is no one around who can hear them.)

These findings convinced Vygotsky that the function of egocentric speech is similar to that of inner speech: it does not merely accompany the child's activity but serves 'mental orientation, conscious understanding; it helps in overcoming difficulties, it is speech for oneself, intimately and usefully connected with the child's thinking. In the end it becomes inner speech'.

The positions of Piaget and Vygotsky are summarized in Figure 13.6.

By 1962, Piaget had come to share Vygotsky's view regarding the function and fate of egocentric speech. Both inner speech and egocentric speech differ from speech for others in that they do not have to satisfy the grammatical conventions: they are both elliptical (abbreviated) and incomplete, concerned more with the essential meaning rather than how it is expressed. Inner speech, Vygotsky says, is a dynamic, shifting, unstable thing, fluttering between word and thought'.

Overt speech can sometimes resemble inner speech in its abbreviated nature, long after egocentric speech has been replaced. For instance, people who know each other very well, like married couples, may often talk in a kind of shorthand which would not be used with anybody else: 'Tea?' asked with a rising inflection, and perhaps at a certain hour of the day, will be interpreted correctly as 'Would you like a cup of tea, dear?' (this is reminiscent of the child's one-word sentences or holophrases which adults have to interpret according to the context; see Chapter 26). Friends or colleagues often share a vocabulary which would be meaningless to an outsider; the more familiar we are with others, the more shared experiences we have in common and the less explicit our speech has to be. In Bernstein's terms, we slip into a restricted code when we are talking to familiar people, in familiar surroundings, whom we assume see things as we do.

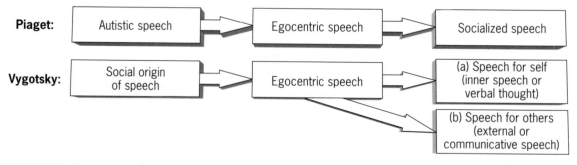

FIGURE 13.6 *Piaget's and Vygotsky's views on egocentric speech*

CONCLUSION

According to Eysenck and Keane (1990), '...It seems intuitively plausible to assume that language is the servant of thought rather than its master'. They maintain that renewed interest in the relationship between language and thought was stimulated by Fodor's (1983) *Modularity of Mind,* in which he argued that different cognitive abilities function independently of each other (these are separate modules of the mind or cognitive processors), including one dedicated to language processing. It follows that the process of language comprehension is not influenced by non-linguistic information, including thought.

While Fodor's position is probably too extreme, there is reason to believe that many aspects of language processing are relatively separate from non-linguistic processes. Cognitive neuropsychological evidence indicates that there are processing components devoted to specific aspects of language processing at both the comprehension and the production levels (see Chapters 3, 4 and 26).

CHAPTER SUMMARY

- There are many examples which suggest that thinking can take place without language, but there is a great variety of views concerning the exact relationship between them.
- Whorf, Sapir, Bruner, Watson, Bernstein and social constructionists share the view that thought is dependent on, or caused by, language.
- According to Bruner, language is essential for the symbolic mode of representation, otherwise thought and knowledge will be limited to actions and images.
- Piaget sees language as dependent on, and reflecting, the individual's level of cognitive development.
- According to Vygotsky, thought and language are originally quite separate activities which come together at about two years of age.
- The Sapir-Whorf linguistic relativity hypothesis (or 'Whorfian hypothesis') claims that language determines our concepts. Acquiring a language means acquiring a particular world view.
- Standard Average European (SAE) languages and native American languages, such as Hopi, differ in both vocabulary and grammar in ways that cause differences in how native speakers think about, perceive and remember the world.
- Whorf has been criticized for exaggerating these differences and for equating the presence or absence of certain words or grammatical features with the ability or inability to perceive certain aspects of the world.
- Whorf also failed to ask why these linguistic differences might have evolved. Having many words for snow might have survival value for the Inuit Eskimos.
- An important distinction has been made between the strong and the weak versions of the Whorfian hypothesis. The study by Carrol and Casagrande involving Navaho children lends some support to the strong version, but most research has focused on the weak version.
- Studies which show that speakers can learn new labels for colours suggest that language serves to draw attention to colour differences and other features of the environment, providing labels to help store these differences in memory. Verbal labels determine how we code our experiences into memory storage.
- Studies of colour coding have identified universal linguistic structures, which reflect universal characteristics of human thought. All languages appear to select colour terms from 11 basic or focal colour categories and those which use fewer do so in a predictable order. This represents steps in the evolution of languages.
- According to Berlin and Kay, focal colours are more salient to all peoples and this explains both why they are more codable *and* more easily remembered
- Despite considerable differences between Dani and English speakers, both samples recognized focal colours better than non-focal colours. Dani speakers also learn new names for focal colours faster than for non-focal colours.
- Heider believes that focal colours reflect the role of physiological factors rather than linguistic ones and there is evidence that babies learn to discriminate colours long before any verbal labels are learnt.
- Watson's peripheralism claims that all thought processes are simply the sensations produced by tiny movements of the speech apparatus; this represents his behaviourist rejection of the mind.
- The study of twins by Luria and Yudovich suggests that language plays a central role in cognitive development, contrary to the views of Piaget.

- Bernstein's distinction between restricted and elaborated codes can help explain the failure of working class children to achieve their intellectual potential. For them, home and school are not continuous as they are for middle class children.
- Bernstein's distinction involves a value judgement, with the elaborated code being seen as superior. This also applies in the case of the English spoken by black children and adults.
- Labov and others argue that black English is different (non-standard) rather than inferior (substandard) and that in familiar, non-threatening situations, black dialects are as fluent and grammatically complex as standard English. Black children are actually bilingual.
- Social constructionists regard language as a precondition for thought. Language gives us a set of meanings and a framework for structuring our experience, which are essential parts of our culture.
- According to Vygotsky, thought and language are initially separate and independent. At about two, thought becomes verbal and speech becomes rational. Egocentric speech results from the child's failure to distinguish between the internal and external functions of speech.
- For Vygotsky, the function of egocentric speech is similar to that of inner speech and, at about seven, it becomes inner speech. They both differ from speech for others in not following grammatical conventions.
- Fodor's *Modularity of Mind* argued that language and thought represent quite separate, independent modules or cognitive processors.

the cause of our concepts, the only means of knowing the world; if our language has no term for something, then it cannot exist for us.

Linguistic relativity hypothesis The theory of Sapir and Whorf that our language provides us with a particular understanding/perception of the world. Really a form of linguistic determinism. Often called the Whorfan hypothesis.

Peripheralism The view that thought processes can be reduced to the sensations produced by tiny movements of the speech apparatus too small to produce audible sounds. Proposed by Watson, founder of behaviourism.

Restricted code According to Bernstein, a form of language that is grammatically simple and rigid, context-bound, preventing the expression of abstract/hypothetical thought. The only form of language available to working-class people. Also called 'public language'.

Social constructionism Theoretical orientation underlying many recent alternative approaches to the study of human beings (such as 'critical psychology'). One central assumption is that our understanding of the world does not reflect objective reality but is based on the categories/frameworks provided by our language.

Synpraxic speech A primitive form of speech in which the child cannot detach a word from the object or action to which it refers.

Universal linguistic structures Uses of language that are common to all peoples across all cultures, which reflect universal characteristics of human thought, such as the hierarchy of colour words.

GLOSSARY

Egocentric speech According to Vygotsky, the result of a young child's failure to distinguish between the internal and external functions of speech. 'Talking out loud' serves similar functions to that of inner speech, which it becomes at about seven; for Piaget, it simply 'disappears'.

Elaborated code According to Bernstein, a form of language that is grammatically complex and flexible, context-independent, allowing the expression of abstract/hypothetical thought. The language of middle-class people and the educational system.

Linguistic determinism The theory that language is

FURTHER READING

Whorf, B.J. (1956) *Language, Thought and Reality: Selected Writings of Benjamin Lee Whorf*, (ed. J.B. Carroll). Cambridge, MA: MIT Press. A good example of the need to read the original research to fully appreciate the issues.

Rosch, E. (1977) Human categorization, in *Studies in Cross-Cultural Psychology, Volume 1*, (ed. N. Warren). New York: Academic Press. A detailed but readable account of the colour perception research, within the broader context of 'By what principles do humans divide up the world in the way they do?', by one of the leading researchers in the field.

14 THINKING, PROBLEM-SOLVING AND ARTIFICIAL INTELLIGENCE

INTRODUCTION AND OVERVIEW

In Chapters 9–13, we discussed some basic cognitive processes, in particular perception, attention and memory, and we have also looked at the ways in which all of these might be influenced by language, the latter being what many philosophers and psychologists have argued is unique to human beings (see Chapter 26). These basic cognitive processes are all aspects of 'thought', although there is more to thinking than just those particular examples. Another way in which psychologists have chosen to look at both human and animal thought is to study problem-solving, a problem being defined as arising whenever a path to a desired goal is blocked, literally in the case of rats running mazes (Greene, 1987). There is another sense, though, in which '... all thinking involves *problem solving,* no matter how simple, immediate and effortless it may appear ...' (Boden, 1987a).

A good example of this would be perception. You will remember from Chapter 9 that the immediacy and accuracy of perception suggests that there is nothing that needs explaining, that there is no 'vision problem'. But we saw that most psychologists agree in rejecting that view, although they disagree as to how to 'solve the problem'. The scientist who has addressed himself most directly to this issue is Marr, who attempted to provide an answer to the question of how useful information about a scene (some part of the external world) can be extracted from images of that scene, i.e. what *computations* must be performed.

Much of the work of computer simulation and artificial intelligence (AI) has been centred around problem-solving, i.e. attempts to produce computer programs which will solve 'human problems' so that we might understand better how *we* solve them. This work is based on the argument that both computers and human problem solvers are

information-processing machines (Greene, 1987), whether the problem is of the perception type (i.e. a fundamental cognitive process which pervades everything we do and which, of course, we share with animals) or of the puzzle type (i.e. tasks specially constructed in order to make their solution difficult, from chess through to Rubik's cube).

Although research into human problem solving was taking place during the 1920s and 1930s, significantly, it was taking place in Germany and elsewhere in Europe, where the impact of American behaviourism was minimal. It was not until the mid-1950s that behaviourism's domination, including its rejection of the mind as suitable subject matter for a scientific psychology, was overturned by the rise of cognitive psychology (the 'cognitive revolution'); this was largely inspired by computer scientists, including those working in artificial intelligence.

PROBLEM-SOLVING RESEARCH

Some of the earliest research was carried out and inspired by the Gestalt psychologists who, based on their theory of perceptual organization (see Chapter 9), saw the essence of problem-solving (PS) as the *perceptual restructuring* of the problem, resulting in insight. Some of the classic experiments were those performed by Köhler (1925) with chimps (see Chapter 7).

Maier (1931) devised the 'two string and pendulum' problem, in which a room has two strings hanging from the ceiling, plus several other objects (for example, poles, pliers and extension cords). The problem was to tie the two strings together, although they were too far away to be able to reach one while holding the other. Several different solutions were produced but the most 'insightful' and infrequently produced is the 'pendulum' solution: take the pliers and tie them to one of the strings and swing them; holding on to the other string, the 'pendulum' can be caught on its upswing. Maier demonstrated a striking example of 'problem restructuring' by first allowing participants to reach a point where they became stuck and then (apparently accidentally) brushing past the string to set it swinging. Soon after this happened, they tended to produce the pendulum solution, even though most claimed not to have noticed the 'subtle hint' about how to solve the problem.

Duncker (1926, 1945) performed experiments on *functional fixedness* (or 'fixity'). Participants were given a candle, box of tacks and several other objects and their task was to attach the candle to a wall over a table so that it did not drip onto the table underneath. Most tried to tack the candle directly to the wall or glue it by melting it. Few thought of using the inside of the tack-box as a candle-holder and tacking that to the wall – participants were 'fixated' on the box's normal function and they needed to reconceptualize it (to use *lateral thinking*; de Bono, 1967). Their past experience was leading them away from the solution – they needed to look at a familiar object in an unfamiliar way.

	Jar A	Jar B	Jar C
Initial State	8	0	0
Intermediate States	3 —(5)→ 5		0
	3	2 —(3)→	3
	6	2 ←(3)	0
	6	0 —(2)→	2
	1 —(5)→ 5		2
	1	4 —(1)→	3
Goal State	4 ←(1)	4	0

FIGURE 14.2 *The shortest series of moves to the solution of the water-jug problem. The arrows indicate the direction of pouring and the circled numbers indicate how much has been poured.*

In evaluating the Gestalt approach, Eysenck and Keane (1990) claim that the concepts of 'insight' and 'restructuring' are attractive because they are easily understood, especially when accompanied by perceptual demonstrations, and '... convey something of the mysterious dynamism of human creativity'. But as theoretical constructs, they are radically underspecified – it is very unclear under what conditions they will occur and exactly what insight involves (see Chapter 7). However, in many ways, the spirit of Gestalt research, with its emphasis on the goal-directed and non-associationist nature of thinking, provides a basis for the *information-processing approach*. It also left a large body of experimental problems and evidence which any later theory had to be able to reinterpret; '... the legacy of the school was, therefore, substantial' (Eysenck and Keane, 1990).

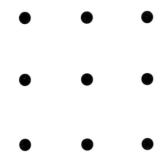

FIGURE 14.1 *Scheerer's nine-dot problem*

Similar is Scheerer's (1963) *nine-dot problem* (Fig. 14.1). The problem is to draw four continuous straight lines, connecting all the dots, without lifting the pencil from the paper. Most people fail because they assume that the lines must stay within the square formed by the dots – they 'fixate' on the shape of the dots. (The solution can be found over the page – Fig. 14.3.)

Finally, Luchins (1942) and Luchins and Luchins (1959) devised the *water-jug problems*. In one version, there are three jugs, A, B and C, which can hold eight, five and three litres, respectively. A is full, B and C are empty. The participant has to find a way of getting four litres into A and four litres into B (without any measures on the jugs). Figure 14.2 shows the shortest series of moves to solution (based on Eysenck and Keane, 1990). Luchins also used the jug problems to demonstrate *problem-solving set* (a form of functional fixedness).

● Classifying problems – adversary and non-adversary

Before discussing how artificial intelligence (AI) has helped us understand human PS, it seems useful to categorize different kinds of problem and look at a wider range of problems than those devised by the Gestalt school.

Garnham (1988) distinguishes between two broad classes of problem: *adversary* and *non-adversary*. Adversary problems involve two or more people who pit their wits against each other; the prototype example is chess. Garnham says that game-playing is a special kind of PS in which the problem is to find a

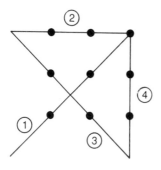

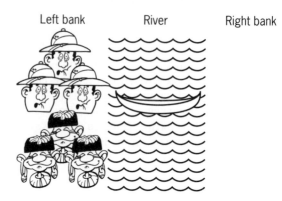

Left bank   River   Right bank

FIGURE 14.3 *The solution to the nine-dot problem. The 'trick' is to draw the lines outside the square of dots*

FIGURE 14.5 *The missionaries and cannibals problem*

winning strategy or the best current move. The focus of AI research here has been on two-player games in which each player always has complete information about the state of play and in which there is no element of chance. Apart from chess, games used include noughts and crosses (tic-tac-toe) and draughts (checkers). (Compare these with backgammon, which does involve an element of chance, and card games which do not involve complete information because you're not supposed to see your opponent's hand.)

Most problems fall into the non-adversary category, in which another person is only involved as the problem setter – so the Gestalt problems fall into this category. Some of the most commonly used include:

- The eight-puzzle (Fig. 14.4). A 3×3 matrix containing the numbers 1-8, with one vacant square, must be moved until the numbers are in order.
- The missionaries and cannibals (or 'hobbits and orcs') problem (Fig. 14.5). The three missionaries and three cannibals must be transported across the river in a single boat which can only hold two

people but needs at least one to get it across the river. The cannibals must never outnumber the missionaries on either bank (or they'll be eaten).

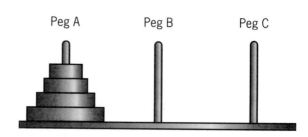

Peg A   Peg B   Peg C

FIGURE 14.6 *The Tower of Hanoi problem*

- The Tower of Hanoi problem (Fig. 14.6). There are three vertical pegs with four (or more) discs of increasing size stacked on one peg. The problem is to transfer the discs to the second peg, moving only one at a time and never placing a larger disc on top of a smaller one.

$$\frac{DONALD}{ROBERT} + GERALD$$

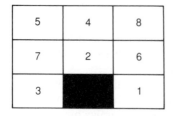

5	4	8
7	2	6
3	■	1

FIGURE 14.4 *The eight-puzzle*

- Cryptarithmetic (Bartlett, 1958). Given that D = 5 and each letter stands for a digit (0-9), find the digits which make the sum correct.

EARLY AI RESEARCH INTO PROBLEM-SOLVING

● The 1956 cognitive revolution

It is almost unanimously agreed among psychologists that cognitive psychology (the 'cognitive revolution') began in 1956. A number of events occurred in that year which converged to form a radical shift in the direction that psychology as a discipline was to take :

● At a meeting at the Massachusetts Institute of Technology (MIT), Chomsky introduced his ideas on his theory of language (see Chapter 26), Miller presented a paper on the 'magical number seven' in short-term memory (see Chapter 12) and Newell and Simon presented a paper on the Logical Theory Machine (or Logic Theorist) with a further paper by Newell, Shaw and Simon (1958), which was then extended into the General Problem Solver (GPS) (Newell and Simon, 1972).

● The first systematic attempt to investigate concept formation from a cognitive psychological perspective was reported (Bruner *et al.*, 1956).
● At Dartmouth College, New Hampshire (the 'Dartmouth Conference'), ten academics met to discuss the possibilities of producing computer programs that could 'behave' or 'think' intelligently. These academics included McCarthy (generally attributed with having coined the term 'artificial intelligence'), Minsky, Simon, Newell, Chomsky and Miller.

A new way of thinking about and investigating cognitive processes had emerged, namely the *information-processing approach,* at the centre of which lay the *computer analogy,* i.e. the view that human cognition can be understood by comparing it with the functioning of digital computers. In Kuhn's (1970) terms, the information-processing approach marked a paradigm shift, replacing behaviourism as the dominant paradigm (see Chapter 2).

● The General Problem Solver, algorithms and heuristics

The GPS was a computer program designed to simulate the entire range of human PS and represented the first computational model of psychological phenomena. The GPS was originally based upon records of what people are thinking as they perform some experimental task – usually this meant asking people to report verbally how they were going about the problem they were trying to solve (a kind of running commentary on their own PS performance) called *protocol analysis.* The kind of operations which human participants indicated they were using were then built into the computer program and, subsequently, the validity of the GPS was tested against further protocol analysis. This new research methodology, however, soon ran into serious difficulties. Garnham (1988) identifies two major problems:

1 it is difficult to measure the goodness of fit between protocol and the so-called 'traces' of a computer program;
2 it is unclear how people's commentary on what they are doing relates to the mental operations actually contributing to the solution of the problem. Even more serious is the fact that in some cases, such as object recognition and language understanding, none of the mental operations which underlie our abilities is available to consciousness at all, making protocol analysis inappropriate.

The Logic Theorist (the forerunner of the GPS) was designed to prove theorems in propositional calculus (as formalized by Whitehead and Russell in *Principia Mathematica)* and in their attempt to simulate this particular ability, Newell *et al.* developed the idea of *heuristics* which are procedures that can be used to prove theorems or solve problems, but which cannot be guaranteed to find a solution, even if there is one. Heuristics are contrasted with *algorithms,* which are procedures that do offer such a guarantee. For many problems, such as finding proofs in propositional calculus or winning in chess, algorithmic procedures can take unrealistic amounts of time; when people solve such problems, they must be using heuristic methods (Garnham, 1988). Heuristics, therefore, are rules of thumb, '... guidelines for selecting actions that are most likely to lead a solver towards a goal, but may not always do so' (Greene, 1987).

The Logic Theorist used a number of heuristics which, even for simple proofs, speeded it up compared with an algorithmic procedure. Even though there were many theorems it could not prove (mainly due to limitations of memory and the amount of time it was allowed to run), the Logic Theorist was important because the idea of heuristics dominated research on theorem proving and PS up to the mid-1960s. It was incorporated into the GPS which, as we have seen, was a more direct simulation of human thinking than the Logic Theorist.

● Solving non-adversary problems

Means-end analysis

Simon (1979) describes one general heuristic strategy as incorporating progress tests which indicate whether the solver is 'getting warmer', i.e. getting nearer to the goal. This was formulated in the GPS and later programs as *means-end analysis* (MEA). In essence, it involves selecting operations which will reduce the distance between the current situation and the current goal. For example, in a geometry theorem-solving program, at each point the program selects a method, carries out certain deductions, then tests to see if these have succeeded in narrowing the distance from the current goal. Depending on the outcome, the program either moves on to the next step, tries a different method or gives up altogether. The major aim of any heuristic is to reduce a problem to manageable proportions by increasing the selectivity of the program in choosing which operations to perform: '... The means-end heuristic provides a method for evaluating the relevance of actions according to whether they are useful in achieving a current goal' (Greene, 1987).

However, it is often not possible to achieve the main goal all in one step, so another important characteristic of MEA is to break down the main goal into subgoals (or a problem into subproblems), each of which has to be solved before the final (main) goal can be reached. (Many real-life situations are of this kind, especially if they involve large amounts of time, e.g. 'getting to a foreign country' or 'getting to university'.) So the basic procedure would be as shown in Figure 14.7.

PS programs using MEA have had some success in simulating the verbal protocols of human solvers when the problem has a fairly clear goal or subgoal structure, for example, the Tower of Hanoi. This particular application of MEA illustrates a major approach to describing the search for problem solution called *problem-reduction representation*: each operator (possible moves) divides one goal into a set of subgoals, each of which is easier to achieve. For example, in the Tower of Hanoi, the overall goal is to move four discs from A to B, moving one disc at a time and never placing a larger disc on top of a smaller one. This overall goal can be subdivided into three subgoals:

1 transfer the three smaller discs from A to C;
2 transfer the largest disc from A to B;
3 transfer the three smaller discs from C to B.

(1) and (3) can be reduced further. (2) can be achieved directly, assuming that (1) has been achieved. Complete reduction analyses the problem into moves of single discs whose preconditions are met; they correspond to the rules (*control strategies*) about only moving one disc at a time and only smaller discs being placed on a larger one (not vice-versa).

Garnham (1991) calls problem reduction a 'divide and conquer' approach and he considers it to be a powerful tool. But is it always this clear just what the subgoals are?

The missionaries and cannibals problem is a good example of how the final goal may be obvious enough while the subgoals may be far less obvious. Indeed, many puzzles are selected for experiments precisely

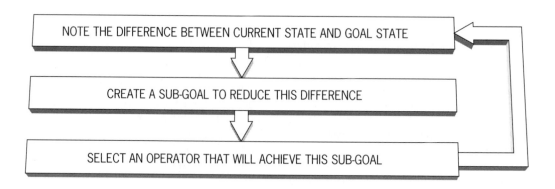

FIGURE 14.7 *Outline of major steps involved in subgoal MEA*

because the basis for selecting the shortest set of moves to reach the final goal is obscure. So how do you measure progress towards the final goal in such problems? It certainly cannot be measured simply by the total number of people transported from the left to the right, because if there are too many cannibals the missionaries will get eaten! While it is possible for a computer to work out a sequence of all possible moves and then to plot the quickest path of moves towards a solution, people cannot hold this type of structure in their limited capacity working memories. The water-jug problem poses the same difficulties for human solvers. (If a computer program did systematically check every possible move until the goal were reached, it would be using a 'check-every-move' algorithm.)

A further problem with MEA as a heuristic for PS is that it is sometimes necessary to move further away from a goal in order to achieve a solution. One reason that the missionaries and cannibals problem is so difficult is that at one point it becomes necessary to take a missionary and a cannibal back to the left bank from where they started, thus apparently increasing the distance from the final goal of getting them all over to the right bank (Greene, 1987).

Newell (1973) developed a computer program which simulates the reactive kind of PS, where people react to situations as they arise (as opposed to trying to carry out a preplanned sequence of actions based on a MEA of the whole problem). It is a more 'bottom-up' approach than MEA and its basic form is that of a 'production', which is a rule comprising a condition plus an action: if such-and-such a situation, then do such-and-such; they are known as *production systems* (Greene, 1987).

State-space theory

The search strategy that would be appropriate in cases such as the missionaries and cannibals problem would be *state-space representations,* which are tailored to the use of operators which change one state of the world into another. The basic component is a state of the world or, strictly, a state of that part of the world relevant to the problem. For example, in the missionaries and cannibals problem, a typical state of the world might be as shown in Figure 14.8. Operators can change one state into another. So, using the operator which takes one missionary and one cannibal from the left to the right bank in the boat, State (1) can be changed into State (2); from each state it is usually possible to reach several others, using different operators. A map of all states that can be reached

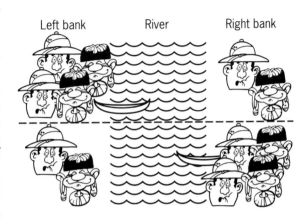

FIGURE 14.8 *Two possible states in the missionaries and cannibals problem*

from the initial state by applying one or more operators is called the *state-space* (or problem-space), which can be represented by tree diagrams (state-action trees) with the initial state at the top and paths to other states branching beneath it. For many problems, such trees can be extended indefinitely:

A solution to the problem is, therefore, a sequence of action that gets from the starting state along the branches of the tree to the goal state (Garnham, 1991).

● How does this apply to real-life, everyday problems?

Garnham (1988) believes that in everyday problems, and those requiring a high degree of creative thinking, it is usual for one or more of: (i) the initial state; (ii) the goal state; or (iii) the operators to be ill-defined (i.e. not made explicit) and this makes AI programs designed to solve such problems difficult to write. But in the missionaries and cannibals problem (and the Tower of Hanoi) , all three are clearly specified (they are well-defined problems) and AI programs are relatively successful in solving them. Is state-space theory a useful way of thinking about how people solve puzzles?

It has proved quite successful for a narrow range of puzzle-like, well-defined problems, but most puzzles people have to solve are not like this. Two major differences between puzzle problems and real-life problems (according to Greene, 1987) are:

1 Puzzle-problems are unfamiliar problems about which the solver has little knowledge, whereas many everyday problems require considerable amounts of knowledge. The knowledge which is

relevant in puzzle-problems is called *general-purpose* or *domain-independent* heuristic knowledge. For example, MEA can be applied in a wide range of different situations (domains). They are generally applicable but not always very efficient, which is why in AI they are often called universal, weak methods. By contrast, everyday problems (which, as we have said, are often ill defined), require substantial *domain-specific* knowledge – this also applies to skill in adversary problems, such as chess (see below).

2 The knowledge required to solve puzzles is present in the statement of the problem, whereas much of the difficulty with everyday problems is finding the relevant information needed to solve them.

Clearly, people do not construct in their minds potentially infinite state-action trees (although if they did they would be able to read solutions directly from the trees), but their subjective reports do indeed suggest that they think of puzzles in terms of states and actions. So when people are deciding what action to perform, do they 'look ahead' in their mind's eye and see which sequence of actions gets them nearest to the goal state? To do this they would need to construct part of a state-action tree in their mind but it looks as though people do not do so – at least not in experimental studies where people try to solve unfamiliar puzzles; instead, they consider only the immediate possibilities and choose from these. However, a possible exception to this general rule is the expert, for example, the chess master (Garnham, 1991) (see below).

● Solving adversary problems: the case of chess

According to Garnham (1988), two-person games are best described using state-space theory, with states corresponding to board positions and operations to moves by either player. The search tree has the initial board position at the top and different levels of the tree correspond to moves by each player.

Good chess players think through the consequences of a move before making it, which is equivalent to a pattern through a state-action tree. The number of possible sequences of moves is frighteningly large (in computational terms, a *combinatoric explosion* of possibilities – there are an estimated 10^{20} possible games of chess, compared with a mere 10^{12} microseconds per century; Garnham, 1988), so players only think through a very small proportion; only rarely

can they think through to a win, lose or stalemate situation. It follows that they must have some means of evaluating the intermediate positions they think through to in order to decide which they prefer – these are called 'quiet positions', because there is no imminent danger of losing a piece (except in exchange for the opponent's piece). Clearly, a major consideration in evaluating such a position is the number of pieces left to each player.

Since what is good for one player is bad for the other, players must assume that their opponents will always choose the move which is worst for them. This assumption is the basis of the *minimax procedure* used in computer chess programs: players should *min*imize the *max*imum loss their opponents can inflict on them. It can in principle be used to choose among all possible moves or among a smaller set initially selected by some other method. Programs used to be like human players – they selected a small number of moves to follow up, then used minimax to analyse these in detail. Programs run on small computers still operate in this way. However, top programmers have access to the most powerful machines available and they often revert to a more algorithmic method, for example, examining every possible position that can be reached in the next five moves by each player (which involves comparing hundreds of thousands of positions). While modern computers can perform many millions of operations per second (through 'brute force' methods), this provides few insights for cognitive scientists, since it bears no relationship to the way that people solve difficult problems (Garnham, 1991). Even the best human players have an extremely limited *lookahead* compared with such powerful computers (a few hundred board positions).

But how good are those chess-playing programs which do not use brute force methods and which, like human players, set bounds to their lookahead? According to Boden (1987b), some of them play very respectable chess: the Greenblatt chess Program, for instance, wins over 80% of its games against non-tournament players as well as a fair proportion of tournament matches. However, there is no prospect of a chess master being beaten by a program in the near future. Even with heuristics, there are far too many alternatives to be considered for the program to be likely to pick the right one: as it cuts down the range of alternatives, it is as likely as not to lose the best move:

... Master chess players develop global perceptual schemata in terms of which they can *see* threats and oppositions on the board much as a lesser mortal can *see* complex emotional response in a cartoon face ... (Boden, 1987b)

A move towards more ecologically valid research is to study how experts solve problems compared with novices (as opposed to powerful computers).

● Expert versus novices: the importance of knowledge and experience

According to Greene (1987), what is missing from AI accounts of human PS so far are the different experiences people bring to different tasks. MEA, for instance, is meant to be typical of all PS by all problem solvers. It was originally presented as a general characteristic of human thinking which can, in principle, be applied to any problem and the selection of actions to attain the desired goal is considered to be a universal feature of human behaviour. Implicit in this view is the belief that it is only limitations in working memory (WM) capacity that prevent humans from applying MEA in all cases.

BOX 14.1 Key study: do grand masters simply have better memories?

De Groot (1965, 1966) compared the performance of five grand masters and five expert players on choosing a move from a particular board position. He asked participants to think aloud and then determined the number and type of different moves they had considered. Grand masters did not consider more alternative moves or search any deeper than experts and yet they took slightly less time to make a move. Independent raters judged the final moves of the masters to be superior to those of the experts.

His initial explanation for these differences was in terms of knowledge of different board positions stored in LTM. It is well known that good players study previous games and can recall their own game in detail; this use of prior knowledge excludes any need to consider irrelevant moves and a host of alternatives. He gave his participants a five-second presentation of board positions from actual games and asked them to reconstruct them from memory – the masters were correct 91% of the time compared with 41% accuracy for the experts; clearly, the masters could recognize and encode the various configurations of pieces using prior knowledge. When pieces were randomly arranged on the board (i.e. not in a familiar pattern), both groups did equally badly, i.e. neither group had the knowledge available to encode the configuration because they were (equally) unfamiliar.

However, the ability to implement a particular PS strategy depends on knowledge. Thinking mechanisms may be universal but solvers are categorized as experts or novices in relation to different problem situations: expertise is more far-reaching than simple knowledge of the rules which apply to a particular problem (otherwise we would all be chess masters!). Chess experts are in fact no better at recalling random arrays of pieces, which suggests there is nothing special about their WM. The gain from expertise is that it places less strain on WM: since PS strategies are already available, 'the more you know, the less you have to think' (Greene, 1987). (Compare this with controlled vs automatic processing in relation to attention; see Chapter 11.)

> Like problem solving in other ... domains ... chess playing needs more than quick thinking and a retentive memory: it requires an appreciation of the overall structure of the problem, so that intelligent action can be economically planned ... (Boden, 1987b)

Chase and Simon (1973) (amongst others) replicated de Groot's findings (see Box 14.1). Experts spent less time, made fewer errors, needed fewer glances, took in more information per glance than novices when asked to memorize or reproduce briefly presented, meaningful board patterns. But there were no differences when the patterns were random. Better players also recall clusters often based on attack or defence configurations, implying some sort of abstract knowledge representation:

> ... It appeared, thus, that intelligent systems rely to a great extent on stored problem patterns when they face a familiar task. Instead of creating solutions from scratch for every problem situation, they make use of previously stored information in such a way that it facilitates their coping with the current problem. (Sternberg, 1990)

The usefulness of prior knowledge is at least as important in more natural domains, for instance, language processing. Sternberg says that a complete understanding of even a very simple sentence pair requires a memory structure that includes beliefs and expectations about people's normal behaviour in the world; '... knowledge, thus, is a necessary ingredient of any intelligent system' (Sternberg, 1990).

● Expert systems (or intelligent knowledge-based systems)

Expert systems (ESs) are important because they promise to be the first major application of AI research (Garnham, 1991). It is assumed that most kinds of human expertise are in short supply and ESs are aimed at making it more widely available. According to Garnham (1988), 'ES' and 'intelligent knowledge-based system' are amongst the most common terms in AI, especially with respect to its applications. 'Knowledge engineering' is the new term for writing ESs.

Basically, an ES is a program that embodies (some of) the knowledge of a human expert in a domain in which expertise comes with experience (Garnham, 1988). In fields such as medicine, it is difficult to formulate the knowledge an expert has, since if that knowledge could be explicitly formulated, human experts would be easier to train.

What kind of problems do ESs solve?

Amongst the most successful ESs to date are DEN-DRAL, which helps organic chemists to establish the structure of complex molecules, and XCON, which decides how the various parts of expensive bespoke computer systems should be put together. More controversial are MYCIN and CADUCEUS, both involved in medical diagnosis and discussed further below.

As they are intended to do (some of) the work of human experts, the first condition a problem must satisfy, if it is to be tackled by an ES, is that there should be recognized experts at solving it and their performance should be demonstrably better than that of non-experts (e.g. a medical consultant compared with both the layperson and non-specialist GPs). The case of medical diagnosis illustrates certain other features a problem should have:

- There is no simple set of rules a medical expert can follow in diagnosing illness; if there were, diagnosis could be performed by non-intelligent programs (and there would probably be no experts). Instead, consultants draw on wide experience of the connection between manifestations of illnesses and underlying causes.
- A single manifestation (symptom, sign, test result) may indicate a number of different diseases, but it is unlikely to be associated with any one of them in every case. Further, some of the data that diagnosis is based on may be misleading or incorrect, i.e. reasoning about diagnosis is, in some sense, probabilistic.
- Diagnosis does not depend on general knowledge but requires a large but manageable amount of domain-specific knowledge.

What should ESs do?

Apart from the primary goal of solving domain-specific problems (e.g. medical diagnosis), they should be able to explain how they reached a particular conclusion because they usually interact with people in solving problems and those users often need to know how a decision has been reached.

Where does the ES knowledge come from?

As we have seen, it comes from human experts and the process of encoding it into the system is called *transfer of expertise*. If what differentiates experts from novices is the mastery of a body of knowledge, it might seem to be a relatively straightforward matter to transfer that knowledge by asking them. However, experts cannot always formulate explicitly the knowledge they use, nor can they say how they combine different items of information to make a judgement about a particular case. Lengthy interviews may need to be conducted in which experts are asked to give their opinions on sample cases and these data may have to be supplemented by survey data; for example, patterns of medical symptoms and test results are correlated with eventual diagnosis. This makes the writing of ESs difficult and time consuming.

● Two examples of ESs – MYCIN and CADUCEUS

MYCIN diagnoses bacterial infections requiring antibiotics and is intended for situations where drugs must be prescribed before the micro-organism responsible for the infection has been properly identified (a laboratory culture may take up to two days to grow). A chronically sick patient needs earlier treatment, so drugs have to be prescribed on the basis of symptoms and the results of quick tests. MYCIN interacts with a medical expert, requesting information and suggesting treatments. It asks only specific questions related to the hypothesis it is currently considering.

CADUCEUS embodies the knowledge of a single expert (Jack D. Myers MD), a specialist in internal medicine at the University of Pittsburgh. It knows about many more illnesses than MYCIN, tries to mimic the way Myers reasons, not just reach the same conclusions, and stores its knowledge about illness in a semantic network (see Chapter 12) as distinct from a set of 'if-then' production rules (which is true of most). It essentially considers related hypotheses in parallel and also incorporates a preference that medical experts have for formulating at least a partial diagnosis fairly quickly and then using that to give focus to further investigation (Garnham, 1988).

While ESs have now been used in medicine for over 20 years, they are only just beginning to make their appearance in nursing. Two examples are CANDI (Computer-Aided Nursing Diagnosis and Intervention), developed by Chang *et al.* (1988) in the USA based on the diagnosis of patient problems as part of the nursing process, and the Glasgow University Expert Systems in Nursing Group (GUESS-ING), which has designed experiments to find the cognitive skills of clinically excellent nurses in the area of pressure sore risk and preventative care planning. These were then formalized into a computer program which can be used as both a decision support and a tutoring tool (Jones *et al.*, 1989; both are cited by Eaton, 1991).

● Evaluation of ESs

According to Boden (1987a), ESs are much less flexible than their human counterparts and most in actual use are considerably less complex than either MYCIN or DENDRAL, which were the prototypes and both of which took many work-years to build:

> ... In almost every case, their 'explanations' are merely recapitulations of the previous firing of if-then rules... for they still have no higher-level representations of the knowledge domain, their own problem-solving activity, or the knowledge of their human user. (Boden, 1987a)

Some researchers are trying to provide ESs with causal reasoning, so that they can not only arrive at a conclusion but also explain the reason to the user. Boden claims that ESs cannot integrate knowledge from distinct domains, using concepts and patterns of inference from one domain to reason (by analogy) in another. Genuine expertise, she argues, requires both high-level knowledge and analogical thinking.

Inevitably, perhaps, ESs raise ethical issues. Those used in the medical domain are especially prone to criticism by virtue of the nature of the domain – patient diagnosis and treatment – and ultimately it is the recipient of the health care who is most affected. But the professionals who come into direct contact with them might see them as both allies and enemies (to anthropomorphize a little) or

predominantly as one or the other depending on their status in the hierarchy, how much of an expert one is thought to be:

> It is commonly asserted that knowledge is power. If expert knowledge becomes more accessible, will the balance of power change? There are social consequences to the use and development of these new systems. There is animosity by some as they feel expert systems usurp the human expert. (Eaton, 1991)

WHAT COMPUTERS CAN AND CANNOT DO – THE SCOPE OF AI

So far we have talked about computers as problem solvers and have looked at some of the important differences between them and human problem solvers. Also, apart from our discussion of ESs, we have discussed problems of the puzzle variety, i.e. the non-everyday type of problem, such as the Tower of Hanoi and missionaries and cannibals. But what about the kind of problem we referred to in the Introduction, such as vision and language understanding, which humans are 'designed' for? Can computers be programmed to mimic these basic human abilities and, if so, what can we learn about the way we use them?

To try to answer these questions, we need to take a closer look at what computers are, what AI is and some attempts to program computers to do what humans are particularly good at doing – seeing and understanding language.

● What is AI?

According to Garnham (1988), AI is '... the science of thinking machines ...' and, again:

> ... an approach to understanding behaviour based on the assumption that intelligence can best be analyzed by trying to reproduce it. In practice, reproduction means simulation by computer. AI is, therefore, part of computer science ...

Newell and Simon originally distinguished the broad field of AI from a particular part of it, namely the *computer simulation* of human behaviour. While the former was the attempt to make machines behave intelligently – by whatever means – computer simulation was a particular method for producing intelligent machines, namely, making them reproduce human behaviour, and the goal of computer simulation was to provide a model of human cognitive functioning.

According to Garnham (1988), most contemporary AI research is influenced more or less by consideration of how people behave – very few researchers simply try to build clever machines disregarding the principles underlying its behaviour and many still have the explicit goal of writing a program which works in the way people do (such as Marr in relation to vision; see Chapter 9). However, the term computer simulation is rarely used these days (Garnham, 1988).

So cognitive psychologists and workers in AI share an interest in the scientific understanding of cognitive abilities and they should work together to increase that understanding. The majority of AI workers probably do wish to further our knowledge of the mechanisms underlying behaviour and to make general statements about knowledge representation, vision, thinking, language and so on.

These kinds of abilities are all part of 'intelligence' in the broadest sense of that term and psychology has always had intelligence (in various senses) as one of its central concerns (see Chapters 25 and 28). Just as workers in AI need to have an idea of what intelligence or thinking is before they can make a machine which is intelligent or can think, so AI research can provide insights into human cognitive processes – the relationship between psychology and AI is a reciprocal one. As we saw in Chapter 1, since the late 1970s cognitive psychology and AI have both become component disciplines in the new discipline of cognitive science, along with neuroscience, linguistics, philosophy and anthropology. By the late 1970s, cognitive psychologists had more in common with AI researchers than with other psychologists and AI researchers had more in common with cognitive psychologists than with other computer scientists (Garnham, 1998).

Boden (1987b) defines AI as '...the science of making machines do the sorts of things that are done by human minds ...': the 'machines' in question are, typically, digital computers. However, she is at pains to make clear that AI is *not* the study of computers but the study of intelligence in thought and action. Computers are its tools because its theories are expressed as computer programs which are tested by being run on a machine.

● What is a computer?

The initial concept of the 'computer' and the first attempts to build the modern digital computer were made by the Cambridge mathematician, Charles Babbage (1792–1871). The mathematical theory of computability was first developed in the 1930s. It specified what computers can and cannot do and how much time and memory they need for the computations they can perform. A number of mathematicians were independently searching for the smallest set of basic operations needed to perform any possible computation.

One very influential approach was that of Turing (1936) who described an abstract computing device (a Turing machine) which performs its calculations with the help of a tape divided into squares, each with a symbol printed on it. Its basic operations comprise reading and writing symbols on the tape and shifting the tape to the left or right. It uses a finite vocabulary of symbols but the tape is indefinitely long. It only has a finite number of internal states – when it reads the symbol on a square, its state may change, depending on what state it is currently in and on what the symbol is; additional bits of machinery (e.g. more tape) do not increase the range of computations but only increase speed. A universal Turing machine can mimic the operation of any other Turing machine. To do this it must be given a description of how that machine works, which can be written onto its tape in standard Turing machine format.

Every general-purpose digital computer is an approximation to the universal Turing machine (since no real machine has an indefinitely large memory); when it runs a program, it behaves as if it were a machine for performing just the task the program performs:

> This special property of digital computers, that they can mimic any discrete machine, is described by saying that they are *universal* machines. The existence of machines with this property has the important consequence that, considerations of speed apart, it is unnecessary to design various new machines to do various computing processes. They can all be done with one digital computer, suitably programmed for each case... as a consequence of this all digital computers are in a sense equivalent. (Turing, 1950)

The basic active components of *digital* computers are normally in one or two stable states (on/off) making them essentially *binary* in nature, i.e. they use only two symbols (e.g. 0/1) as in binary arithmetic. They can symbolize an indefinitely large number of things (as can the 26 letters of the Roman alphabet) because they can be grouped together in indefinitely many ways. As described by

Turing, they are machines which change accordingly to the problem to be solved (based upon the particular instructions contained within the program). 'Digital' refers to the finger and the fingers can be used as a kind of abacus, a simple form of computing machine. Computers are, in essence, autonomous abaci – working without continuous human intervention (Gregory, 1981).

The other main kind of computer is *analogue*, which are, generally, continuous mechanisms which represent more or less abstract quantities by physical parameters (e.g. lengths, angles and voltages).

● What can computers do and how do they do it?

Strictly, of course, computers are metallic objects (*hardware*) and when we ask what they can do (and, later, when we ask whether they are intelligent), it is not the physical machine as such that we are interested in but the procedures which they perform, the calculations and other operations they carry out as required by the program (the *software*), i.e. the computer-as-an-information-processing device. Although originally designed as calculating machines (after all, 'compute' means to 'calculate'), a computer is not a mere 'number cruncher' or supercalculating arithmetic machine; computers do not crunch numbers, they manipulate symbols (Boden, 1987a).

Computers can only 'think' in abstract symbols. In itself, a symbol is meaningless; there need be no intrinsic similarity between a symbol and what it symbolizes. The meaning is assigned by a human user, who interprets it in a particular way. For this reason, symbolic representation is said to be *propositional*, i.e. it represents what is the case in formal language rather than being a physical analogue of something in the world. (An example of an analogue process would be a mental image, which bears a much closer relationship to what it is an image of than any symbol, such as a word.) Boden (1987a) points out that some programming languages are more readily amenable than others to symbolizing certain things – ALGOL, for example, is similar to algebraic notation and so, not surprisingly, it is much easier to write sensible mathematical programs with it than some 'non-algebraic' programming language. However, just as numbers can be expressed in words (e.g. 'ten'), so matters usually expressed in words can be expressed in numbers (e.g. '30120' could be a symbol for a cat, as

opposed to 'cat', and so would have no numerical meaning).

Computers, therefore, can crunch numbers if specifically programmed to do so but this is not their essential computational function; although originally developed with mathematical problems in mind, digital computers are, in fact, general-purpose symbol manipulating machines. It is up to the programmer to decide what interpretations can sensibly (that is, consistently) be made of the symbols of machine and programming languages which, in themselves, are meaningless (Boden, 1987a).

● Strong and weak AI and the computational theory of mind

One of the definitions given earlier of AI was Garnham's (1988) appealingly simple, 'the science of thinking machines'. It is now time to look at that definition a little more closely and to ask whether 'thinking' is to be taken literally or metaphorically. Putting this another way, do computers actually think/behave intelligently (i.e. are they reproducing or duplicating the human equivalent) or are they merely simulating (mimicking) thought/intelligence? This distinction corresponds to the one made by Searle (1980) between strong and weak AI, respectively:

> According to weak AI, the main value of the computer in the study of the mind is that it gives us a very powerful tool, e.g. it enables us to formulate and test hypotheses in a more rigorous and precise fashion than before. But according to strong AI the computer is not merely a tool; rather, the appropriately programmed computer really is a mind in the sense that computers given the right program can be literally said to understand and have other cognitive states. Further, because the programmed computer has cognitive states, the programs are not mere tools that enable us to test psychological explanation but the programs are themselves explanations ... (Searle, 1980)

Searle is a philosopher who is very critical of strong AI, a view advocated by computer scientists such as Minsky, who defines AI as '... the science of making machines do things that would require intelligence if done by men'. The implication of such a definition is that machines must be intelligent if they can do what humans can do, although this rather begs the question as to what it means to display intelligence. Underlying strong AI is the *computational theory of mind* (CTM), one supporter of whom is Boden (1987a):

... Intelligence may be defined as the ability creatively to manipulate symbols, or process information, given the requirements of the task in hand. If the task is mathematical, then numerical information may need to be processed. But if the task is nonnumerical (or 'semantic') in nature ... then the information that is coded and processed must be semantic information, irrespective of the superficial form of the symbols used in the information code ...

As we noted earlier, symbolic representation is propositional, i.e. since a symbol has no inherent similarity to what it symbolizes, it represents something in a purely formal way. Computer programs comprise formal systems, 'a set of basic elements or pieces and a set of rules for forming and transforming the elements or pieces' (Flanagan, 1984). In computer languages, symbols stand for whatever objects, relations or processes we wish but the computer manipulates the symbols, not their meaning. Programs consist of pure *syntax* (rules for manipulating symbols) and are devoid of *semantic content* (reference to anything in the world). For the computer, there is nothing 'outside' it to which these symbols refer, which is why they have no 'content', only 'form'. It is the human programmer who then attaches the meaning to these symbols.

But, according to CTM, all intelligent systems are defined as symbol manipulators which, of course, include human minds. So if symbols are meaningless to a computer, it follows that they are meaningless also to a human mind. But in that case, what is the 'meaning' which, according to Boden, the human programmer attaches to the meaningless symbols? And how do we account for *intentionality*, which Searle (amongst others) believes is an essential characteristic of genuine mentality or consciousness, (i.e. mental states are about things in the world, they have an external reference to something outside themselves and this is (part of) what we mean by saying that the world is meaningful to us and that we understand it)?

Searle's attack on strong AI and CTM takes the form of a *Gedanken* experiment ('thought experiment') called the Chinese room, which is described in Box 14.2.

● The Chinese room and the Turing test

Searle believes that he has demonstrated quite conclusively that there is more to intelligence and understanding than mere manipulation of symbols. In particular, he is trying to refute the major methodological presupposition of strong AI, namely the

---

BOX 14.2   The Chinese room (Searle, 1980)

Suppose that I am locked in a room and am given a large batch of Chinese writing. Suppose that I know no Chinese, either written or spoken, and that I am not even confident that I could recognize Chinese writing as Chinese writing distinct from, say, Japanese writing or meaningless squiggles. After this first batch of Chinese writing, I am given a second batch together with a set of rules for correlating the second batch with the first batch. The rules are in English and I understand them as well as any other English native speaker. They enable me to correlate one set of formal symbols with another set of formal symbols and all that 'formal' means here is that I can identify the symbols entirely by their shapes. I am then given a third batch of Chinese symbols together with some instructions, again in English, which enable me to correlate elements of this third batch with the first two batches and these rules instruct me how to give back certain Chinese symbols with certain sorts of shapes in response to certain sorts of shapes provided by the third batch. Unknown to me, the people giving me all these symbols call the first batch a 'script', the second batch a 'story', the third batch 'questions', the symbols I give back in response to the third batch, 'answers to the questions' and the set of English rules 'the program'. I am also given stories in English which I understand, questions in English about these stories and I give back answers in English.

After a while I get so good at following the instructions for manipulating the Chinese symbols and the programmers get so good at writing the program that, from the point of view of somebody outside the room, my answers are indistinguishable from those of native Chinese speakers, just as my answers to the English questions are indistinguishable from those of other native English speakers. However, although from the external point of view my answers to the Chinese and the English questions are equally good, in the English case this is because I am a native speaker of English while in the Chinese case this is because I am manipulating uninterpreted formal symbols and in this respect I am simply behaving like a computer, i.e. performing computational operations on formally specified elements. For the purposes of the Chinese, I am simply a realization of the computer program.

Turing test (or Imitation Game) proposed by Turing (1950) as an objective way of trying to answer the question 'Can machines think?' (see Box 14.3). According to Garnham (1988), there are no accounts of machines playing the Imitation Game but there are anecdotes about computers being mistaken for people and ELIZA (a program that simulates the speech of a non-directive, client-centred therapist; see Chapter 31) figures in most of them. These stores are rather embarrassing for supporters of CTM, because ELIZA is not a very intelligent program (Boden, 1987a).

However, supporters of strong AI claim that it is only a matter of time before computers will pass the Turing test and once they do so, terms such as thought, understanding, awareness, happiness, pain, etc. could be applied equally to computers and human participants. Clearly the Turing test represents an operational, behaviouristic definition of 'thinking' because it is defined as an appropriate kind of 'output' or performance, regardless of what may be going on 'inside'. Yet this is precisely the definition which the Chinese room is aiming to show is invalid.

But isn't the Chinese room a highly restricted and artificial environment? Gregory (1987) argues that, like us, AI programs must have knowledge of the world in order to deal with the world. Imagine rearing a baby in the Chinese room; how could it learn the meaning of the Chinese (or any other) symbols in such a restricted environment? Years of active exploration in infancy are essential for us to learn to read meanings in the neural signals from our senses; extended to perception as a whole, the Chinese room environment would prevent correlations between symbols and events developing as it has no view of the outside world, provides no opportunity for exploration as a way of building up a store of knowledge and relating these to Chinese (or other) symbols:

> The Chinese room parable does not show that computer-based robots cannot be as intelligent as we are – because *we* wouldn't be intelligent from this school either. (Gregory, 1987)

According to Boden (1993), a computer program is a program for a computer: when a program is run on suitable hardware, the machine does something as a result. There's no magic about it; input peripherals (teletypes, cameras, sound analysers) feed into the internal computations, which lead eventually to changes in output peripherals (VDU screen, speech synthesizers). In between, the program makes several things happen; many symbols are manipulated inside the system itself. The machine is engineered in such a way that a given instruction produces a specific operation and in this sense, a programmed instruction is not merely a formal rule; rather, its

BOX 14.3 The Imitation Game or Turing test (Turing, 1950)

This is played with three people, a man (A), a woman (B) and an interrogator (C), who may be of either sex. The interrogator stays in a room apart from the other two. The object of the game for the interrogator is to determine which of the other two is the man and which is the woman. He knows them by the labels X and Y and at the end of the game he says either 'X is A and Y is B' or 'X is B and Y is A'.

The interrogator is allowed to put questions to A and B thus: Will X please tell me the length of his or her hair? Now suppose X is actually A, then A must answer. It is A's object in the game to try to cause C to make the wrong identification. His answer might therefore be: My hair is shingled and the longest strands are about nine inches long.

In order that tones of voice may not help the interrogator, the answers should be written or, better still, typewritten. The ideal arrangement is to have a teleprinter communicating between the two rooms.

We now ask the question: What will happen when a machine takes the part of A in this game? Will the interrogator decide wrongly as often when the game is played like this as he does when the game is played with a man and a woman? These questions replace our original 'Can machines think?'

I believe that in about 50 years time it will be possible to program computers, with a storage capacity of about 10^9, to make them play the imitation game so well that, on average, the interrogator will not have more than a 70% chance of making the right identification after five minutes of questioning. When this occurs, there is no contradiction in the idea of thinking machines.

essential function is to make something happen (the 'executive' function of programs). According to Newell and Simon, meaning and understanding are based in what a creature can do in the world.

Boden (1993) contends that a functioning program is comparable to Searle-in-the-Chinese-room's understanding of *English* (not Chinese). A word in a language one understands is a mini-program, which causes certain processes to be run in one's mind; clearly, this does not happen with the Chinese words because Searle-in-the-room does not understand Chinese, but Searle fails to draw the parallel between his understanding of the English rules and computer programs because he assumes that programs are 'all syntax and no semantics'.

● Do we need brains to be brainy?

Supporters of strong AI, by analogy with the computer, analyse human intelligence in terms of the possession and operation of appropriate programs (a form of *machinomorphism*). Thus, our bodies – including our brain – are seen as in no way necessary to our intelligence: in Boden's terms (quoted in Rose, 1992), 'You don't need brains to be brainy'. This is a form of *functionalism* which represents a solution to the mind-body (mind-brain) problem – it is the program (software) that matters (the computational theory of mind) with the brain (hardware) being incidental. This can be seen as a new form of *dualism* (Putnam, 1975; see Chapter 32) which Russell (1984) sees as posing a real dilemma for CTM. On the one hand, CTM is claiming that the 'mind' does not depend on any particular physical realization but, on the other hand, computer simulation is meant to be a realistic model of how the brain carries out information processing.

Flanagan (1984) believes that, while Searle may not have proved the impossibility of strong AI, he is certainly correct that merely running a computer program is not sufficient for our kind of mentality. So what else is needed? He finds it implausible that our evolutionary history, genes, biochemistry, anatomy and neurophysiology have nothing essential to do with our defining features (even though it remains logically possible). Searle (1987) believes that mental states and processes are real biological phenomena in the world, as real as digestion, photosynthesis, lactation, etc., in that they are 'caused by processes going on in the brain' which are entirely internal to the brain. Again, the intrinsically mental features of the universe are just higher level physical features of brains.

Penrose (1987) agrees that there is more to understanding than just carrying out some appropriate program (software) and that the actual physical construction of the brain (hardware) is also important. He argues that a computer designed to follow the logical operations of every detail of the workings of the human brain would itself not achieve 'understanding' even though the person whose brain is being considered would claim to understand.

Searle's view has been referred to as *carbon/protoplasm chauvinism* (Torrance, 1986), i.e. his only basis for denying that robots think is that they are not made of flesh and blood. His views about the causal properties of the brain have been attacked by many as obscure. Is he proposing that intentionality is a substance secreted by the brain (Gardner, 1985)? Gardner argues that if Searle is claiming that, by definition, *only* the human brain or brain-like mechanisms can display intentionality/understanding, then there is no point to the controversy and the Chinese room loses its force. A major problem is that we simply do not know what makes the brain conscious and so we cannot design a conscious machine, one that would exactly duplicate its physical nature. Still, the brain is a physical entity and it is conscious, so it must have some design features (presumably physical) which make it conscious (McGinn, 1987). This does not mean that a machine could not be conscious; only that it would have to be the same kind of machine the brain is, whatever kind that is. In support of Searle, Teichman (1988) states that while we know that the computer hardware does not produce (initiate) the program, it is highly probable that the brain does help to produce mental states.

Gregory (1987) believes that intelligence isn't necessarily embodied in living organisms or protoplasm but may occur in a computer system based on silicon (or any other material). The emphasis here is on the process as opposed to the substance – though there must be physical mechanisms to carry out the processes, strong AI claims that any physical system capable of carrying out the necessary processes can be described as intelligent, even if it is 'made of old beer cans', in Searle's words.

● An evaluation of AI: drawing some preliminary conclusions

So far in this chapter, we have been discussing what Rose (1992) calls the *holistic* approach to AI, what Le Voi (1993) calls the *rule-based* approach, which has been the most popular and influential approach for most of AI's 40-year history. As we have seen, this attempts to create behaviour by a computer which mimics/simulates the behaviour of a natural intelligence, i.e. human beings, by programming the computer with a large collection of rules (production rules). The sequential activation of these rules produces behaviour more or less like the intended target (such as expert medical diagnosis by an ES).

To achieve better and more accurate models of human performance in areas such as memory, language and PS, rule-based systems could grow more extensive sets of production rules and larger memories, apparently endlessly; in principle, it seemed that all human behaviour could potentially be simulated by a sufficiently complex system (Le Voi, 1993).

However, despite the obvious power of this approach, some psychologists began to question the appropriateness of this way of modelling human cognition (irrespective of whether it could successfully create an artificial intelligence). For example, Le Voi discusses Anderson's (1983) ACT* (Adaptive Control of Thought), which is an attempt to construct a comprehensive model of cognition using a relatively small set of components (declarative /procedural /working memory; see Chapter 12). The WM component, unlike the real, psychological WM, does not have a limited capacity, which it would need to have in order to simulate human memory; as it stands, it cannot provide any insights into why humans have a limited capacity WM in the first place.

A second example from ACT* is *generalization*, widely accepted as being a fundamental aspect of human cognition (as illustrated in schemas, for example; see Chapter 12). This is programmed into ACT* (in the form of creating more general rules from specific ones), but while this may successfully produce humanlike behaviour, it gives no insight into how or why we do it in a seemingly effortless way

The traditional, rule-based approach is linked to the CTM, i.e. it is a mind-modelling approach, according to which we don't need brains to be brainy: what is important about cognition can be described at an abstract level, independent of the machinery (brain or computer) which underlies it. If cognitive processes are understood as the processing of information, then since it can be encoded in many different physical forms (e.g. printed in books, recorded on tape), it does not matter whether it is stored and manipulated by the electrical and chemical activity of the brain or by the on/off states of transistors in a computer; in other words, computers that bear no physical resemblance to brains can be programmed to simulate cognitive abilities (Garnham, 1991).

● Why does the brain matter?

In addition to the objections we discussed earlier regarding the relevance of having a brain, many psychologists and neurobiologists, as well as workers in AI, began to express serious doubts about the rule-based approach and CTM in terms of how the brain works compared with the operation of most digital, von Neumann computers.

These earlier generations of computers were essentially serial processors, i.e. they could perform – although admittedly incredibly fast – only one operation at a time in sequence (i.e. in a linear fash-

ion). This puts limits on their speed of operation, since information can be passed no faster than the speed of light (the 'von Neumann bottleneck'; Rose, 1992). AI researchers became convinced that real brains do not work like this at all, but instead carry out many operations in parallel and in a distributed manner, i.e. many parts of a network of cells are involved in any single function and no single cell is uniquely involved in any. If computers could be designed to be more like brains, the speed limitation could be overcome. These considerations caused an explosion of interest in new computer designs based on *parallel distributed processing* (PDP) principles, promising new generations of machines

CONNECTIONISM OR PARALLEL DISTRIBUTED PROCESSING – THE NEW AI

However valid the criticisms of strong AI made by Searle and others may have been when they were made, changes in AI itself have rendered those criticisms less valid and less necessary. The major development which, according to Gordon (1989), could 'revive the status of the computer as a model [of the mind]' is the parallel distributed processing (PDP) approach. Similarly, Gardner (1987) refers to the PDP approach as representing an alternative 'model view' of cognition, a response to the increasingly obvious limitation of the serial digital von Neumann computer. The pioneers of this new approach were Rumelhart *et al.* (1986).

The central principle of this new brain-modelling approach is *connectionism*, which is based on the idea that the brain is composed of networks of neurons with multiple connections between them. If the aim of AI is to construct models which offer insights into human cognition, then it was necessary to look much more closely at the microstructure of the brain itself to see if insights into the power of this natural information-processing engine might help develop a more realistic modelling system. Most PDP researchers were interested in how individual components (neurons) might operate collectively to produce the brain's information-processing capacity.

● PDP models and 'neural networks'

Because of the obvious influence of the brain's structure (networks of interconnected neurons), PDP or connectionist models are often called 'neural networks' and Rumelhart *et al.* (1986) describe their work as engaging in *'neurally inspired* modelling of cognitive processes'. However, in reality, the vast majority of these models have little more than an entirely superficial relationship to neural anatomy; they are mathematically based computational models based on networks of parallel processing computational units; characteristics of the units are usually derived from known properties of mathematical concepts (not of neurons) (Le Voi, 1993). Although PDP modelling has brought about new developments in computer architecture (hardware), they are still made of silicon chips (not protoplasm).

Ironically, the origins of these modern developments are some of the earliest computers which attempted to develop abstract models of brain cells and to discover how large networks of cells would work together. During the 1930s and 1940s, Lashley tried to discover the brain sites where learning and memory occurred but his 'search for the engram' (1950) failed (see Chapter 3). Hebb (1949) proposed that groups of interconnected neurons continue to show increased activity after termination of the stimulus and that clusters of neurons showing reverberating activity act as functional units. He further claimed

that modifications to such an interacting cluster or network could be the basis of short and long-term learning; he called them *cell assemblies.* Both Rosenblatt's *perceptron* (1959) and Selfridge's (1959)/Selfridge and Neisser's (1960) *Pandemonium* (see Chapter 9) tried to model learning phenomena in terms of self-modifying connection strengths between neuronlike elements.

Unlike these earlier models, the 'memory' does not reside in any one single cell or pair of connected cells within the network, but is a property of the network as a whole; this is related to the *existence of hidden layers,* arrays of units between input units and output units (Fig. 14.9). This is consistent with a fundamental fact about the brain's 'wiring': the vast majority of neurons are not in direct communication with the outside world (either by sensory input or motor output) but connect internally, receiving messages from and replying to other neurons, i.e. there is a vast amount of internal processing of any messages arriving in the brain and also a great deal of private traffic between these neurons (interneurons) before any external responses are made. The hidden layers in PDP models are meant to serve almost as such interneurons and massively increase the power of the networks to 'learn', generalize and predict (Rose, 1992).

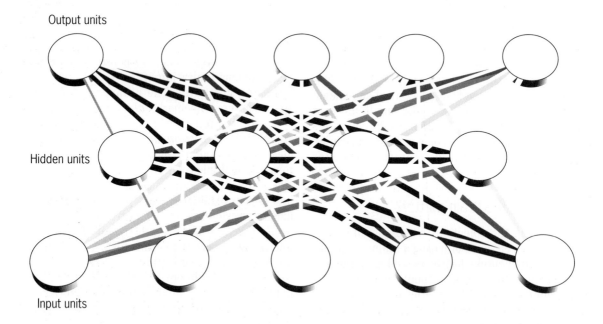

FIGURE 14.9 *Schematic diagram of a connectionist machine. The circles represent the processing units and the lines represent the connections along which activation passes from one unit to another. Activation in one unit may either increase or decrease the activation in another unit to which it is connected, depending on whether the connection is positive (facilitatory) or negative (inhibitory). (Based on Garnham, 1991)*

● What can PDP models do?

When PDP models were developed, they were found to have some remarkable properties, many of which are known to be characteristics of human behaviour; for example, they seem to be inherently capable of generalizing from many specific cases without needing arbitrary specific add-ons to the model so that it could 'do' generalization, i.e. this was one of the 'natural' behaviours of PDP models.

This is linked to their ability to learn and remember. A characteristic feature of human memory is that if it is presented with a partial cue, it will recall other information to complete or supplement the cue (for example, recognizing someone from just seeing the back of their head): the memory system has been cued with part of the content of the memory trace in order to produce recall (*content addressability*). Various previous computer models found it difficult (though not impossible) to model content addressability because the computer naturally addresses memory by location, not content: information is looked up in a computer by knowing *where* it is stored. Because content addressability is such a central feature of human memory, any cognitive model of memory must adequately reproduce it and PDP models are particularly well suited to learn how to group or categorize objects based on *exemplars* (Le Voi, 1993).

The most important method of learning is called *backwards error propagation using the Generalized Delta Rule (GDR)* (back propagation/error propagation for short). The network can be set a problem in the form of an input pattern; a successful solution comprises a matching or otherwise acceptable output pattern. Only parts of the output pattern will match at first – the discrepancy between input and output is fed back ('propagated back') into the hidden layer, such that connections to outputs which are (nearly) correct are strengthened (according to some predetermined rule) while others may be left unchanged or even weakened. There is no supervisory control of the network, no central executive guiding the overall flow of information (Gordon, 1989). Since all knowledge resides in the connections themselves, advocates of PDP models have offered a reconceptualization of major cognitive processes. Memory, for example, is viewed as a set of relationships existing between various aspects of facts or events as they are encoded in groupings or patterns of units, instead of a set of facts or events stored in the brain. What is actually stored, according to this view, are the connections and strengths among units which allow the patterns to be recreated subsequently. Learning involves finding the right connection strengths so that proper patterns of activation are produced under the appropriate conditions (Gardner, 1987).

● Some advantages of PDP models

Connectionists argue that, although rules are not explicitly encoded into their machines, those machines can learn to behave as if they were following rules. One example is Rumelhart and McClelland's English past-tense learning machine, meant to mimic some aspects of how a child learns past-tense endings. Verbs are divided into a number of subclasses and associated with each subclass is the change required to produce the past tense from the present. Regular verbs, which followed the *-ed* rule, formed the largest group; other subgroups comprised irregular verbs that are similar to one another (e.g. blow/grow/know/throw). Any new verb was assimilated to one of those categories, sometimes producing errors (e.g. 'grind' > 'grind' as opposed to 'ground').

To the casual observer, Rumelhart and McClelland's machine behaved very impressively, but a sophisticated analysis by Pinker and Prince showed that it did not know the detailed rules of the English past-tense system. Instead of following the complex rules of language, these machines may be following simpler rules which reflect statistical regularities, i.e. probabilities of one thing going with another (cited by Garnham, 1991). (This is similar to the controversy over the learning of language by chimps; see Chapter 26.) Connectionism is basically an associationist approach (see Chapter 2) which partly explains why it cannot cope adequately with the complex rule-governed, information-processing character of much cognition, especially language and reasoning.

FIGURE 14.10 *Figures from a digital watch face*

Even connectionists concede that PDP models deal more effectively with perception and other 'lower level' (subsymbolic) processes than with 'symbol-laden' activities like language. Nevertheless, PDP models are very attractive to psychologists who want to know why human information processing has the characteristics it has.

Le Voi (1993) identifies three major advantages of representing information/knowledge in a distributed (as opposed to a local) way: economy, redundancy and robustness to damage.

1 *Economy* is neatly illustrated by digital clocks and watches. Each number in these displays is represented by activity across seven segments or units which compose it (see Fig. 14.10), i.e. the representation of each number is distributed over all seven units and no single unit selectively represents any specific number. So, only seven units are needed for ten numbers. Similarly, it is suggested that representation of memories in the brain is distributed over a collection of individual units (neurons) and their connections (synapses) (neural networks).

2 *Redundancy* refers to the fact that the original representation encoded more information than was needed to maintain the representation, which leads directly on to

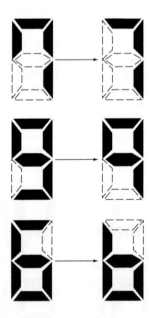

FIGURE 14.11 *Even if one of the cells or segments fails, the others can still represent the number well enough for it to be recognized. This illustrates redundancy and robustness to damage in a distributed system.*

3 *Robustness to damage,* which is a direct result of large numbers of units being involved in the original representation. The adult human brain loses hundreds of thousands of neurons every day, but this does not affect our cognitive processes; the brain is robust to the loss of parts of its information-processing potential and even when the rate of loss increases (as with ageing), loss of performance is still slow ('graceful degradation') rather than sudden and catastrophic. In most conventional computers, when even a single crucial instruction or component is faulty, the whole system breaks down; not so with PDP systems (see Fig. 14.11).

● Some problems with PDP models

Le Voi (1993) cites a model comprising a three-layer network with hidden units for reading English words, devised by Seidenberg and McClelland (1989). Despite their success in simulating experimental results of human reading, some aspects of the model's performance are decidedly non-human. Some of the errors the model makes are made quite commonly by children learning to read (e.g. 'dose' being pronounced like 'rose' and 'womb' like 'comb'); however, others (e.g. 'romp'/'ramp', 'bronze'/'branz', 'zip'/'vip' and 'taps'/'tats') are almost never made by people. More serious perhaps is that the GDR seems incompatible with the idea of one-trial learning, but neither example represents a fundamental, inherent limitation to PDP models.

The key question is whether there are any aspects of human cognition to which this approach cannot be applied (or for which PDP models are an inappropriate level of analysis). Ironically, in view of the earlier criticisms of the rule-based approach which the PDP approach was trying to correct, it is the rule-governed nature of language that might be one such example (e.g. Fodor and Pylyshyn, 1988); although Fodor and Pylyshyn acknowledge that the brain is almost certainly a massively parallel distributed processing machine, they argue that PDP models are merely accounts of low-level implementation of a rule-based cognitive system.

CONCLUSIONS: CAN COMPUTERS EVER BE LIKE BRAINS?

According to Penrose (1990), connectionism, if it is to work, depends on a relatively fixed, stable relationship of units within a 'neural network', modified only in response to specific inputs and then responding in a deterministic way to this modified response. However, there is a built-in indeterminacy in the way that individual neurons and their synaptic connections operate, i.e. their responses are inherently unpredictable; yet, despite this unpredictability at the level of the individual units/components, the system as a whole is predictable. Consciousness, intelligence and memory are properties of the brain as a system, not properties of the individual units, and they could not be predicted from analysing the units (they are called *emergent properties*). For these reasons, Penrose argues that connectionism is reductionist (see Chapter 32).

According to Rose (1992), the very concept of AI implies that intelligence is simply a property of the machine itself. However, agreeing with Penrose but taking his criticisms further, Rose argues that the neuronal system of brains, unlike a computer, is radically indeterminate:

> ... brains and the organisms they inhabit, above all human brains and human beings, are not closed systems, like the molecules of a gas inside a sealed jar. Instead they are open systems, formed by their own past history and continually in interaction with the natural and social worlds outside, both changing them and being changed in their turn ...

This openness creates a further level of indeterminacy to the functioning of both brain and behaviour. Unlike computers, brains are not error-free machines and their mode of operation is not simply reducible to a small number of hidden layers. Compared with digital computers, brains perform linear computations relatively slowly, yet they can make judgements with such apparent ease that computer modellers, both the rule-based and connectionist kinds, remain baffled (Rose, 1992). At least for the foreseeable future, it seems that brains will continue to outperform computers when doing the kinds of things that they were naturally designed to do.

CHAPTER SUMMARY

- There is a sense in which all thinking is problem-solving (PS), as in the case of perception which may appear straightforward but turns out to be extremely complex (the 'vision problem').
- Much of what goes on in computer simulation and artificial intelligence has focused on PS and is based on the belief that both computers and human problem solvers are information-processing machines, whether the 'problem' is a basic, pervasive, cognitive process or a deliberately constructed puzzle.
- Early research into PS was conducted by Gestalt psychologists, who saw PS as essentially the perceptual restructuring of the problem resulting in insight. Problems included Maier's two strings and pendulum, Scheerer's nine-dot problem, Luchins' water-jug problems and Duncker's tasks involving a candle, box of tacks, etc. designed to demonstrate functional fixedness.
- While the Gestalt approach leaves a lot to be desired scientifically, it left a legacy for later theories to build on, including the information-processing approach.
- In adversary problems, such as chess, noughts and crosses and draughts, each player who is trying to find a winning strategy has complete information about the state of play; there is no element of chance. Most problems are non-adversary (including the Gestalt problems), including the eight puzzle, the missionaries and cannibals, the Tower of Hanoi, and cryptarithmetic.
- The 'cognitive revolution' is usually traced to 1956, when a number of events took place, including a meeting at MIT, at which Newell and Simon introduced their Logic Theorist (later to be called the General Problem Solver (GPS)), and the famous Dartmouth Conference. What emerged was the information-processing approach, central to which was the computer analogy.
- The GPS was a computer program designed to simulate the entire range of human PS. It was originally based on protocol analysis, but it is unclear how people's reports relate to the cognitive processes actually contributing to the problem solution even if we have conscious access to those processes.
- The Logic Theorist involved heuristics, general rules of thumb for PS which cannot guarantee a solution, unlike algorithms, which are also very time consuming. Heuristics were incorporated into the GPS and dominated PS research for several years.
- Means-end analysis (MEA) is a general heuristic strategy which involves selecting operations that will reduce the distance between the current situation and the current goal; the aim is to make a problem more manageable by becoming more selective as to what actions are worth performing.
- The main goal/problem often needs to be broken down into subgoals/subproblems, as in the Tower

of Hanoi, where there is a clear goal/subgoal structure; this is done by problem reduction representation, using operators. However, in the missionaries and cannibals and water-jug problems, while the final goal may be obvious enough, the subgoals are not.

- Where it may not be possible to carry out a pre-planned sequence of actions, a more reactive, 'bottom-up' production systems approach may be used.

- With problems such as the missionaries and cannibals, state-space representations would be the most appropriate search strategy, in which operators change one state into another. The problem solution is a sequence of action that goes from the starting point along the branches of the tree diagram/state-action tree to the goal state.

- The missionaries and cannibals and Tower of Hanoi are well-defined problems, making it relatively easy for AI programs to solve them; they involve general-purpose/domain-independent knowledge.

- Everyday problems are often ill-defined and require domain-specific knowledge, but it is also often unclear what information is needed to solve them.

- Two-person games, such as chess, are best described using state-space theory. Good players think through the consequences of a move before making it, which is equivalent to a pattern through a state-action tree. But this can only involve a very small proportion of the vast number of possible moves.

- A general heuristic used in computer chess programs is the minimax procedure, but more powerful machines use more algorithmic, 'brute force' methods; even the best human players have an extremely limited lookahead by comparison.

- Chess programs which play more like human players are still not as good as chess masters who develop global perceptual schemata which allow them to see possible threats.

- MEA was originally presented as a general feature of human thinking which can be applied to any type of PS, limited only by WM. But experts do not have superior WM than novices, nor have chess grand masters stored more board positions in LTM than chess experts. Experts rely on stored problem patterns to help them solve current problems, so that they don't have to create solutions from scratch.

- Expert systems (ESs) represent a major application of AI. They are computer programs that embody the knowledge of a human expert, so that they can do some of the work that human experts do, such as medical diagnosis (e.g. MYCIN and CADUCEUS) and nursing (e.g. CANDI and GUESSING). Expertise involves a great deal of domain-specific knowledge.

- ESs are written using transfer of expertise/knowledge engineering; since it is often difficult for experts to formulate explicitly the knowledge they use, the writing of ESs is difficult and time consuming.

- ESs are much less flexible than human experts and are generally unable to explain their solutions, except to repeat their 'if-then' rules. They also raise ethical issues, especially in the context of medical diagnosis.

- Originally, computer simulation was seen as a method for producing intelligent machines (AI); the goal of computer simulation was to provide a model of human cognition. But most contemporary AI is guided by beliefs about human behaviour, directly or indirectly, so cognitive psychologists and AI researchers share a reciprocal interest in the scientific understanding of cognitive abilities and both form part of cognitive science.

- Computers are the tools used by AI to express and test its theories, which take the form of computer programs. An influential theory of what a computer is is Turing's abstract computing device/Turing machine; every general-purpose digital computer is an approximation to a universal Turing machine, since the same computer, if suitably programmed, can mimic any computing process.

- Digital computers (as opposed to analogue) are binary in nature, allowing them to symbolize an indefinitely large number of things. Strictly, computers are physical machines (hardware), but it is usually what they can do, i.e. the computer-as-information-processing-device, that psychologists are interested in.

- Although originally designed as powerful calculators, computers are general-purpose, symbol-manipulating machines; in themselves, symbols are meaningless (symbolic representation is propositional) and meaning is assigned by the human programmer.

- An important and controversial philosophical distinction is that between weak AI and strong AI. According to the former, computers merely simulate/mimic thought or intelligence, while according to the latter, they are actually (literally) reproducing/duplicating them (i.e. they are thinking/being intelligent).

- Underlying strong AI is the computational theory of mind (CTM), according to which intelligence is the ability to manipulate symbols or process information relative to the task in hand; this is as true of a human mind as it is of a computer. But this view of symbols as meaningless in themselves conflicts with intentionality.

- Searle tries to refute CTM with his famous Chinese room thought experiment; he believes that it shows that there is more to intelligence than mere symbol manipulation, because the man in the Chinese room successfully manipulates Chinese symbols without understanding Chinese. Supporters of CTM would argue that the man in the room successfully passes the Turing test/Imitation Game, which is all that is required for a machine to be described as intelligent. Supporters of strong AI claim that it is only a matter of time before actual computers will pass the Turing test.

- The Chinese room thought experiment has been criticized on several counts, including the fact that it describes a highly restricted and artificial environment. Also, Boden claims that a functioning program is comparable to the man-in-the-Chinese-room's understanding of English and not Chinese, as claimed by Searle.

- According to CTM, the mind does not need any particular physical realization, since it is the possession and operation of appropriate programs that define intelligence, i.e. 'you don't need a brain to be brainy'. But many biologists, psychologists and others believe that there must be certain design feature of the brain (as yet unknown) that have evolved to make it conscious; Searle's belief that robots cannot think because they aren't made of flesh and blood has been branded carbon/protoplasm chauvinism.

- The appropriateness of the rule-based approach as a way of modelling human cognition has been seriously challenged in recent years; this is partly due to CTM's claim that the possession of a brain/the structure and mode of operation of the human brain are irrelevant. While digital computers process information in a serial fashion, brains operate in a parallel and also in a distributed manner. These considerations led to the development of parallel distributed processing (PDP).

- The central principle of this new brain-modelling approach is connectionism, i.e. how individual units/neurons might operate collectively to produce the brain's information-processing capacity. Despite the obvious influence of what is known about the brain's neural networks, PDP models are mostly quite unlike neural anatomy (they are based on mathematical concepts) and new PDP machines are still made of silicon chips.

- Some of the very earliest computers tried to develop abstract models of brain cells and the operation of networks of cells, such as Lashley's 'engram', Hebb's cell assemblies and Rosenblatt's perceptron. Unlike these earlier models, PDP networks have hidden layers of units in between input and output units; this is consistent with the vast internal connection/processing that takes place in the brain.

- PDP models seem naturally capable of generalizing, remembering (as demonstrated by content addressability) and learning, which takes place mainly through back/error propagation; there is no central executive guiding the overall flow of information, so the network seems to be using feedback to gradually move towards a matching output 'all by itself'.

- According to PDP models, memory does not comprise facts or events stored in the brain; what is actually stored are the connections and strengths among units. Learning involves finding the right connection strengths so that proper patterns of activation are produced.

- Although rules are not explicitly built into their machines, connectionists argue that they learn to behave as if they were following rules. This can be seen in a machine designed to learn English past-tenses, but critics have argued that its performance merely reflects statistical regularities, rather than linguistic rules. Connectionists themselves admit that PDP models deal more effectively with processes that do not involve symbols.

- Three major advantages of distributed representations of knowledge are economy, redundancy and robustness to damage, all of which are displayed by the brain.

- Connectionism assumes that units within a network respond in a deterministic way to changes that occur in response to specific inputs. But the responses of individual neurons are highly unpredictable and yet the brain as a total system is predictable; its properties (such as consciousness) could not be predicted from analysis of the units.

- Brains and human beings are open systems, constantly interacting with the natural and social world; this creates a further level of indeterminacy of both brain and behaviour. Brains may not be error-free machines, but they can perform certain tasks that are currently beyond the capability of any computer.

GLOSSARY

Adversary problems Games, such as chess, involving two or more players, where the aim is to find a winning strategy and where all players have complete information about the state of play.

Artificial intelligence (AI) An approach to understanding behaviour based on the assumption that intelligence can best be analysed by trying to reproduce/duplicate it (strong AI) or mimic/simulate it (weak AI) by means of computer programs. AI forms part of cognitive science, along with cognitive psychology, neuroscience, linguistics and philosophy.

Computational theory of mind (CTM) Definition of intelligence as the manipulation of symbols, either in human beings or computers, regardless of any particular physical realization (such as a brain).

Connectionism The central principle involved in parallel distributed processing (PDP), based on the idea that the brain is composed of networks of neurons with multiple connections between them.

Expert system (ES) A computer program that embodies (part of)the knowledge of a human expert in a domain where expertise comes with experience (e.g. medical diagnosis). Written according to transfer of expertise/knowledge engineering.

Functional fixedness The tendency to focus on the normal function of an object, based on past experience, when, in the context of problem solving, it needs to be seen in an unfamiliar way. Also called *fixity.*

General Problem Solver (GPS) Newell and Simon's computer program, an extension of the Logic Theorist, designed to simulate the entire range of human problem-solving. The first computational model of psychological processes.

Heuristics A rule of thumb for problem-solving, which narrows down the options for possible solutions but without guaranteeing a solution. Contrasted with algorithms which are much more time consuming but do guarantee a solution.

Means-end analysis (MEA) A general heuristic

strategy used in the GPS which reduces the distance between the current situation and the current goal. Often involves breaking down the main goal/problem into subgoals/problems.

Minimax procedure A strategy used in computer chess programs, whereby players minimize the maximum loss that an opponent can inflict on oneself.

Non-adversary problems Puzzles, such as the missionaries and cannibals/Tower of Hanoi problems, that are created deliberately for use in the study of problem solving.

Protocol analysis Records of what people are thinking as they perform an experimental task, usually by asking them to report verbally on how they are going about solving a problem.

State-space representation A search strategy appropriate for solving problems such as missionaries and cannibals, whereby one state is changed (by operators) into another state. Problem solution involves a sequence of action from the starting state, along the branches of the state-action tree/tree diagram, to the goal state.

Turing test The major methodological criterion of strong AI, according to which a human interrogator communicates, via a teletype, with two others, one of which is a person, the other a computer. If the interrogator only has a 70% chance of correctly identifying which is which, the computer has passed the test and has demonstrated that it can 'think'. Also called the Imitation Game.

FURTHER READING

Le Voi, M. (1993) Parallel distributed processing and its application in models of memory, in G. Cohen, G. Kiss and M. Le Voi (eds) *Memory: Current Issues,* 2nd edn. Buckingham: Open University Press. A very thorough but readable account of PDP, an extremely complex and technical topic for the non-computer scientist.

Broadbent, D. (ed.) (1993) *The Simulation of Human Intelligence.* Oxford: Blackwell.
A collection of original chapters by several key figures, including Penrose, Newell, Boden and Broadbent, one of the 'founders' of cognitive psychology.

Social Behaviour

15 INTERPERSONAL PERCEPTION

INTRODUCTION AND OVERVIEW

We could quite appropriately begin a textbook of psychology with a chapter on interpersonal perception, as this is concerned with how we all attempt to explain and predict the behaviour of other people. To this extent, we all do in our everyday lives what the professional psychologist does as a scientist (see Chapters 1 and 2), since it is impossible to interact with people and not try to make sense of their actions and to anticipate how they are likely to behave in the future. So in this chapter, we shall be examining the key processes involved in our day-to-day attempts to understand and predict the behaviour of others. Probably in no other area of psychology does the unique nature of the discipline as a whole become so apparent, namely, the fact that psychologists are studying 'themselves': they are part of the subject matter and in order to study human behaviour, they must utilize the very same processes they are attempting to explain!

We shall begin by trying to answer two important questions:

1 What is the relationship between general perception and interpersonal perception?
2 What is the difference between the professional psychologist and the amateur (lay person)?

Then we shall look at the concept of *social cognition,* which will serve as a framework for the rest of the chapter. In general terms, this is the study of how people understand their social worlds, i.e. the cognition of people, their behaviour and the settings in which that behaviour occurs (Schneider, 1995). While person perception has deep roots in social psychology, it flourished during the 1950s, 1960s, and 1970s, with research and theorizing about (a) forming impressions of other people: this was investigated mainly from the perspective of the perceiver (central vs. peripheral traits, the primacy-recency effect, implicit personality theories and stereotyping), but we shall also look at it from the point of view of the actor (the person being perceived), i.e. we shall discuss some of the ways in which we all try to influence the impression that others form of us, through impression management (or self-presentation); (b) attribution theories: these try to account for how we all explain behaviour – our own as well as other people's – in terms of its causes; we shall discuss some of the ways in which attribution principles have been applied to other aspects of social behaviour.

However, since the 1980s, these traditional areas of person perception have more or less been replaced by 'social cognition', which differs from the earlier research not so much in terms of the phenomena under investigation but in terms of the overall approach. While impression formation and attribution theories were very 'cognitive' in that they were concerned with the content of our thoughts about others (as has always been true of social psychology in general), 'content' was the operative word; social cognition, by contrast, was very much a reflection of the information-processing approach that was having such an impact in cognitive psychology in particular and in psychology as a whole. One important feature of this approach is that it focuses on the often unconscious, automatic processes that underlie the impressions and causal attributions that we make and that we are conscious of (i.e. the 'content' of person perception) (see Chapters 4 and 11).

HOW ARE PERCEPTION OF OBJECTS AND PERCEPTION OF PEOPLE RELATED?

Figure 15.1 shows that interpersonal perception is the perception of others (sometimes called 'person perception'); the other component of social perception is the perception of self (see Chapter 21). As we shall see, the way we perceive others involves:

1 *selection* (e.g. focusing on people's physical appearance or on just one particular aspect of their behaviour;

2 *organization* (e.g. trying to form a complete, coherent impression of a person);

3 *inference* (e.g. attributing characteristics to someone for which there is no direct or immediate evidence, as in stereotyping).

While these principles are common to both types of perception, there are also fundamental differences between perceiving inanimate objects and perceiving other people:

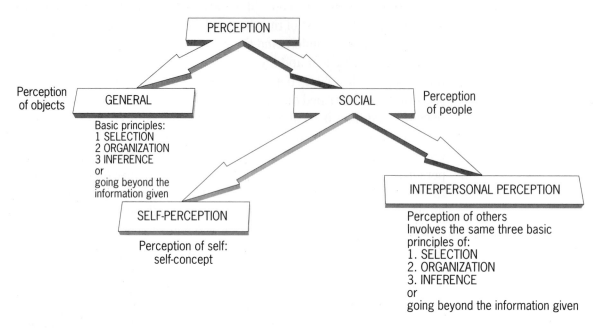

FIGURE 15.1 *Relationship between general and social perception*

- People *behave* (but objects do not); it is often behaviour which provides the data for making inferences about what people are like.
- People *interact* with other people (but we do not interact with objects or they with each other); one person's behaviour can influence another's, so that each one's behaviour towards the other is at least partly a product of the other's behaviour towards them.
- People *perceive* and *experience* (but objects cannot); one person's perception can influence the other's (probably through their behaviour, especially their non-verbal behaviour), so that each person's perception of the other is at least partly a product of the other's perception of them.

Some psychologists (particularly the phenomenological psychologists) regard experience as the major source of 'data' (as opposed to behaviour) in social interaction, e.g. Laing (1967) argued that the task of *social phenomenology* is to relate 'my experience of your behaviour to your experience of my behaviour' so that it studies the relationship between experience and experience.

In Laing's book '*Knots*' (1972), he dramatically (and often humourously) demonstrates (in the form of short prose poems and diagrammatic poems) the kinds of tangles that human relationships can get into. Here are two of the shorter and more straightforward examples:

(a) Jack frightens Jill he will leave her because he is frightened she will leave him.

(b) *Jack:* 'You are a pain in the neck.
To stop *you* giving me a pain in the neck
I protect my neck by tightening my neck muscles,
Which gives me the pain in the neck you are.'
Jill: 'My head aches through trying to stop you giving me a headache.'

For Laing, 'knots' like these illustrate how 'my experience of another is a function of the other's experience of me' – and vice-versa.

ARE WE ALL PSYCHOLOGISTS?

As we noted at the outset, everyone, as part of their everyday living in a social world, tries to 'figure people out', explain, predict and, very often, control others' behaviour; these also happen to be the three traditionally accepted aims of science, including psychology (see Chapter 2). Judy Gahagan (1984) defines interpersonal perception as 'the study of how the layperson uses theory and data in understanding people'. She breaks this definition down further into three main components:

1 The study of how people perceive others as *physical objects* and form impressions of their physical

appearance, actions and the social categories to which they can be assigned. Often the first thing we notice about other people is some aspect of their appearance (e.g. clothes, hair) and to this extent we are treating them as no more than 'things'. This is usually the first step involved in stereotyping, since it is usually on the basis of their physical appearance that we assign people to groups.

2 The study of how people perceive others as *psychological entities* – we form impressions of what kind of person they are or we infer what their feelings, motives, personality traits, etc. might be (having already identified them, for example, as belonging to a particular group – gender, racial, occupational, and so on).

3 The study of the layperson as a *psychologist.* According to Nisbett and Ross (1980), 'We are all psychologists. In attempting to understand other people and ourselves, we are informal scientists who construct our own intuitive theories of human behaviour. In doing so, we face the same basic tasks as the formal scientist ... . 'Intuitive theories' is another way of referring to the 'implicit personality theories' which we shall be discussing later in the chapter.

We shall return to this theme at various points in the chapter but for now, let us focus on some of the important differences between the psychologist and the lay person. According to Gahagan (1984, 1991):

● The layperson uses his/her theories for pragmatic (or practical) and immediate purposes, as opposed to gaining knowledge for its own sake.

● The layperson is rarely a disinterested observer of another's behaviour – we usually have a vested interest in what is going on and are usually emotionally involved to some extent. The professional, as a scientist, has to be 'detached' and objective (although complete detachment is impossible; see Chapter 2).

● The layperson may be completely unaware of the reasoning they have followed when making inferences about others and this reasoning may change from one situation to another. So the layperson's theories are not spelled out or articulated (hence 'implicit' personality theories) and may not be consistent. But psychologists must try to be consistent and make their reasoning explicit so that other psychologists can examine it.

THE PERSON AS THINKER: THE ROLES OF COGNITION IN SOCIAL PSYCHOLOGY

We have already noted that social psychology has always been strongly cognitive, i.e. people are *thinking organisms* (as opposed to emotional organisms or mindless automatons) who 'reside' between stimulus and response (a S–O–R model as opposed to a S–R model; see Chapters 1 and 7).We have also noted that *social cognition* represents a fairly recent way of looking at the thinking involved in our social interactions.

According to Fiske and Taylor (1991), there are four general views of the thinker within social psychology or four guises that the cognitive tradition has assumed :

1 *Consistency seekers.* This refers to the principle of *cognitive consistency,* around which a number of theories of attitude change were built in the 1950s, the most influential being Festinger's cognitive dissonance theory (see Chapter 18). All the theories claimed that cognitive inconsistency produces a strong motivation to reduce the inconsistency.

2 *Naive scientist.* This refers to the first of the social cognition guises, with attribution theories being central to the view that, by trying to infer unobservable causes from observable behaviour, we all operate as amateur scientists (see above). This view was first proposed by the 'father of attribution theory', Fritz Heider, in 1958 but most attribution theories were formulated between the mid-1960s and early 1970s. As we shall see below, these theories were *normative,* i.e. they attempted to account for how people ought to attribute causes to behaviour under 'ideal' conditions; they also took the 'naive scientist' model too far by seeing ordinary people as completely logical and systematic in their thinking.

3 *Cognitive miser.* Partly as a reaction against normative attribution theories, Nisbett and Ross (1980), Taylor (1981) and others introduced the term 'cognitive miser' to convey the idea that people are limited in their capacity to process information, so they take shortcuts whenever they can, adopting strategies that simplify complex problems. While this leads them to draw biased and hence inaccurate conclusions (relative to what the normative theories predict), seeing people as

fallible thinkers represents a much more descriptively accurate account of how people actually think about behaviour. This is reflected in studies of error and bias in the attribution process (see below) but also, more generally, in what are called *heuristics* (Tversky and Kahneman, 1974) or 'rules of thumb'. Some examples are given in Table 15.1.

4 *Motivated tactician*. This refers to a development of the cognitive miser view, 'putting back' the motivational and emotional variables that were removed from the original cognitive consistency model. The motivated tactician is a '... fully engaged thinker who has multiple cognitive strategies available and chooses among them based on goals, motives, and needs ...' (Fiske and Taylor, 1991). This corresponds to what Leyens and Codol (1988) call the 'cognitive-affective human being'.

● Evaluation of social cognition: what has happened to the 'social'?

Critics of social cognition (such as Moscovici, 1982; Zajonc, 1989) have argued that it may have been 'too successful', i.e. it may have taken social psychology too far towards cognitive psychology, such that there may not be any 'social' in social cognition. Many of the cognitive processes and structures that have been proposed seem to be unaffected by social context, i.e. they seem to be taking place within an apparently isolated person who is thinking about social objects. But this is not what is meant by 'social cognition'; instead, we should be focusing on the link between people and the social object. This is truly social because it is concerned with how cognition is socially constructed, shared and maintained by different members of a given social group or even a whole society. To study 'social' cognition by studying what is going on inside the head of individuals is *reductionist* (see chapter 32).

Stereotypes illustrate the shared nature of cognition, but perhaps the best example of how cultural knowledge may be constructed and transmitted is Moscovici's (1961, 1981) theory of social representations. *Social representations* refer to

> ... a set of concepts, statements and explanations originating in daily life in the course of inter-individual communications. They are the equivalent, in our society, of the myths and belief systems in traditional societies; they might even be said to be the contemporary version of common sense. (Moscovici, 1981)

Moscovici (1961) showed that people have simplified (and often mistaken) ideas about Freud's psychoanalytic theory but they know the name 'Freud', just as they might know Einstein's name and have some equally simple and inaccurate ideas about what he said about relativity. This illustrates the *personification* of new and complex ideas, i.e. linking them with a person. Complex ideas are also often converted into the form of visual images, as in a cartoon where the darker side of a person's nature is portrayed as a devil (in one balloon) and his/her conscience as an angel (in another); this kind of *figuration* is sometimes used to convey Freud's concepts of the id and

---

Availability: judging the frequency or probability of an event according to the number of instances of it that can readily be brought to mind (remembered) and so which are cognitively available. For instance, being able to think of several friends who are studying psychology in other colleges or universities leads you to believe that psychology is nationally one of the most popular subjects (which it actually is!).

Representativeness: deciding whether a particular person or event is an example of a particular schema (e.g. if X has particular characteristics – has long hair, is wearing a skirt, has a high-pitched voice and is called Jo – then there is a very good chance that X is female, but not necessarily!). In the example, there is a match between this person in front of you and your stereotyped belief (or prototype) of a (typical) female.

Simulation: judging what is likely to be/have been the outcome of some event or incident according to how easily different outcomes can be brought to mind. For example, it can help explain why we are often much more angry and upset by 'near misses' than when we 'missed it by a mile' – we can imagine *'if only* I had...' or *'if only* that man in front of me ...' much more easily in the former than in the latter.

Anchoring: when you have no information about a specific event, you may draw on information about a similar event as a reference point or 'anchor'. For example, if asked to estimate how many hours per week a fellow psychology student studies, in the absence of any specific knowledge, you may base your answer on how many (or few!) hours you yourself put in.

TABLE 15.1 *Some examples of heuristics used in uncertain or ambiguous situations*

FIGURE 15.2 *A representation of Freud's concept of the id, ego, and superego, using figuration*

superego respectively (with the person himself being the ego, see Fig 15.2) Both personification and figuration relate to the need to *objectify*, i.e. to make the abstract concrete (Moscovici and Hewstone, 1983) (see Chapter 12). We also need to anchor new and unfamiliar ideas into some pre-existing system (see Table 15.1).

Together, objectifying and anchoring help us to master the social world and to facilitate our communication with others and these are precisely the two main functions of social representations. In a way, the study of social representations is the study of the transformation from knowledge to common sense (Moscovici and Hewstone, 1983) or 'popular consciousness' and the theory of social representations 'explains how the strange and the unfamiliar become, in time, the familiar' (Farr and Moscovici, 1984, in Leyens and Codol, 1988). It is the study of how social representations evolve and are communicated between groups and individuals that makes this true social cognition.

FORMING GLOBAL IMPRESSIONS OF PEOPLE – FITTING THE PIECES TOGETHER

The two major explanations of how global perception takes place are:

1 central versus peripheral traits;
2 the primacy–recency effect.

● Central versus peripheral traits

The basic idea here is that certain information which we have about a person (i.e. certain traits we believe they possess) is more important in determining our overall impression of that person than any other information. The classic study is that of Asch (1946), which is described in Box 15.1.

Based on Asch's study, Kelley (1950) set out to check Asch's findings and see whether the description of the target person as 'warm' or 'cold' would influence participants' behaviour towards a real (as opposed to hypothetical) person. This is described in Box 15.2.

For Asch, a set of traits produces an integrated impression or configuration (a *Gestalt*) in which the

---

BOX 15.1   Key study: building our impressions around something warm or cold

Asch (1946) presented participants with a list of adjectives describing a fictitious person. One group had the following list: intelligent, skillful, industrious, *warm*, determined, practical and cautious. A second group had the same list, except that the word 'cold' replaced the word 'warm'. These lists were called the stimulus lists.

Both groups were then presented with a second list (the response list) of 18 trait words (different from the stimulus list) and were asked to underline those adjectives which described the target person. The two groups chose significantly and consistently different words from the second list. For example, the 'warm' group saw the character as generous, humourous, sociable and popular, while the 'cold' group saw him as having the opposite traits. There were also certain qualities attributed to him equally by both groups, e.g. reliable, good-looking, persistent, serious, restrained, strong and honest.

The words 'warm' and 'cold' seemed to have a major effect on the overall impression of the target person for the two groups. When Asch used 'polite' and 'blunt' (instead of 'warm' and 'cold') participants underlined almost identical words in the response list. Asch concluded from this that 'warm-cold' represented a *central* trait or dimension, while 'polite-blunt' represented a *peripheral* trait or dimension. And the central traits which seem to influence our global perception in this way are implicitly evaluative, i.e. they are to do with whether the person is liked or disliked, popular or unpopular, friendly or unfriendly, kind or cruel, etc.

BOX
15.2
Key study: the 'warm-cold' variable in a naturalistic setting (Kelley, 1950)

Students at the Massachusetts Institute of Technology were told that their regular teacher would not be coming and they would be having Mr X instead; Kelley also told them that they would be asked to assess him at the end of the session. Mr. X was a male member of staff not known to the students. Before he arrived, they were given some biographical notes about the substitute teacher; for half the students these included the description 'rather warm' and for the other half 'rather cold' – otherwise the biographies were identical.

There then followed a 20-minute discussion between the teacher and the students, during which Kelley recorded how often each student attempted to interact with the teacher. After he left the room, students assessed him on 15 rating scales (e.g. 'knows his stuff-doesn't know his stuff', 'good-natured-irritable'). Those who had read the 'warm' description consistently responded more favourably to him than those who had read the 'cold' description. The two groups also responded differently when asked to write a free description. Fifty six per cent of the 'warm' group participated in the discussion, compared with 32% of the 'cold' group. So not only had Kelley confirmed Asch's findings regarding the central nature of the 'warm-cold' dimension, but he had also demonstrated a relationship between how students perceived the target person and their attempts to interact with a real person (as opposed to Asch's fictitious person).

meaning of one trait has been influenced by the others (with some traits – central traits – exerting a major organizing influence compared with peripheral traits, which have little or no influence) and which can generate inferences about additional traits not given in the set. By contrast, Bruner and Tagiuri (1954) argued that both general impressions and inferences about additional traits are due to people's *implicit personality theories* (see below); this does not contradict Asch, since he was not opposed to the view that inference is involved, just as Bruner and Tagiuri were not opposed to Gestalt ideas.

Wishner (1960) found that the impact of the traits 'warm' and 'cold' on inferences about other traits depends on their prior associations with those traits. So 'warm' and 'cold' affect inferences of traits like 'generous' and 'popular' because these traits are all associated in people's implicit personality theories,

while 'warm' and 'cold' do not affect inferences of other traits, such as 'reliable' and 'honest'. This suggests that central traits do not need to be incorporated into different Gestalten in order to have the effects on trait inferences which Asch found. Indeed, Asch found only negligible differences in the traits inferred when 'warm' and 'cold' were presented alone and those inferred when they were presented in a list of traits (as in the experiment described in Box 15.1).

However, although the trait associations in people's implicit personality theories may account for differing impressions of a warm and cold person, the meaning of various traits may nevertheless be altered by the context in which they appear, as Asch originally suggested. For example, Zebrowitz (1990) cites studies in which, if someone is described as 'proud', this trait is rated as closer in meaning to 'confident' when it appears in the context of positive traits, but as closer to 'conceited' when it appears in the context of negative traits.

Wishner also showed that whether a trait is central or not is a relative matter, i.e. it depends on what else is known about the person. So, for example, in Asch's study, 'warm–cold' was central in relation to generous/humourous/sociable/popular, but peripheral (or at least neutral) in relation to reliable/good-looking/persistent/serious/restrained/strong/ honest. So, rather than saying a trait is central or not, we should say that whether a trait is central in a particular study will depend on the pattern of correlations with other traits in the study.

● The primacy–recency effect

The other major explanation of global perception concentrates on the *order* in which we learn things about a person: the *primacy effect* refers to the greater impact of what we learn first about someone ('first impressions count') and the *recency effect* refers to the greater impact of what we learn later on. A famous study of primacy–recency is that of Luchins (1957) (see Box 15.3).

Initial support for a primacy effect came in an earlier study, again by Asch (1946). He used two lists of six adjectives describing a hypothetical person (intelligent, industrious, impulsive, critical, stubborn and envious), one in the above order and the other in the reverse order. Participants given the first list (where the first words denoted desirable qualities) formed a favourable overall impression, while those given the second list (where the first words denoted undesirable qualities) formed an unfavourable overall impression.

BOX
15.3

Key study: forming an impression of Jim (Luchins, 1957)

Participants were matched on measures of personality and then allocated to one of four groups: group 1 heard a straightforward description of an extrovert character called Jim; group 2 heard a straightforward introvert description. (These were control groups used to establish that participants could accurately identify extroverts and introverts – there was a 75% success rate.) Group 3 heard the first half of the extrovert description followed by the second half of the introvert description; and group 4 heard the reverse of group 3 (so for groups 3 and 4 the descriptions were contradictory). The extrovert and introvert descriptions are shown below.

All the participants were then asked to rate Jim in terms of introversion-extroversion. Group 1 judged him to be the most extroverted and group 2 the most introverted (as you would expect) and, although the judgements of groups 3 and 4 were less extreme, group 3 rated Jim as being more extrovert than group 4. Remember, they all received the same information about Jim, only the order was different. Luchins concluded that the earlier elements of the description had a greater impact than the later elements, so he had found evidence for the primacy effect.

Extrovert description

Jim left the house to get some stationery. He walked out into the sunfilled street with two of his friends, basking in the sun as he walked. Jim entered the stationery store which was full of people. Jim talked with an acquaintance while he waited for the clerk to catch his eye. On his way out, he stopped to chat with a school friend who was just coming into the store. Leaving the store, he walked toward school. On his way out he met the girl to whom he had been introduced the night before. They talked for a short while and then Jim left for school.

Introvert description

After school Jim left the classroom alone. Leaving the school, he started on his long walk home. The street was brilliantly filled with sunshine. Jim walked down the street on the shady side. Coming down the street toward him, he saw the pretty girl whom he had met on the previous evening. Jim crossed the street and entered a candy store. The store was crowded with students and he noticed a few familiar faces. Jim waited quietly until the counterman caught his eye and then gave his order. Taking his drink, he sat down at a side table. When he had finished his drink he went home.

Both the Luchins and Asch studies involved hypothetical people. In Jones *et al*'s study (1968), an actual person was used (a stooge of the experimenters). Participants watched a student trying to solve a series of difficult multiple-choice problems and were then asked to assess his intelligence. It was arranged so that the student always solved 15 out of 30 correctly but one group saw him get most of the right answers at the beginning of the series, while another group saw him get most of the right answers at the end. Which group do you think assessed him as more intelligent?

The common sense prediction would be that when the student improved as the series went on (i.e. got most right towards the end) he would be judged as more intelligent than when he seemed to be getting worse as the series went on (got most right towards the beginning) – in the first case he would seem to be learning as he went along, in the second case his early successes could be attributed to guesswork or 'beginner's luck'. Jones *et al* made the common sense prediction that there would be a recency effect. However, the opposite was found – the student under the first condition was judged as being more intelligent – there was a primacy effect. Significantly, when asked to recall how many problems the student had solved correctly, those who had seen the 15 bunched at the beginning said 20.6 (on average) while those who had seen them bunched at the end said 12.5 (on average), so these memory distortions (over- and underestimations) also reflected the impact of the primacy effect.

● How can we account for the primacy effect ?

Luchins says that when later information is discrepant with earlier information, people tend to regard the first information as revealing the 'real' person and to explain away or dismiss the later information as not representative or typical, i.e. it is discounted because it contradicts what came first. Anderson (1974) maintains that people pay more attention to information presented when they are first trying to form an impression about someone and, having formed some initial impression, they pay less attention to any subsequent information.

Asch's explanation is that the first bit of information affects the *meaning* of later information, so that the latter is made consistent with the former and so, effectively, does not contradict it. For example, if you initially find out that someone is courageous and frank, when you later learn that he is also undecided, you may take that to mean 'open-minded' rather than 'wishy-washy' (Zebrowitz, 1990). But does the primacy effect always prove more powerful than the recency effect? The answer seems to be that it does, but only under certain conditions.

Luchins reasoned that if the primacy effect is due to decreased attention being paid to later information, then it should be possible to destroy the effect by warning against making snap judgements. He found this to be true and it was particularly effective if it was given between the presentation of the two inconsistent pieces of information about the same individual. In a similar vein, Hendrick and Constanini (1970) found that primacy seems to prevail unless participants are specifically instructed to attend closely to all the information.

Evidence exists that a negative first impression is more resistant to change than a positive one. Why should this be? One explanation may be that negative information carries more weight because it is likely to reflect socially undesirable traits or behaviour and, therefore, the observer can be more confident in attributing the trait or behaviour to the person's 'real' nature. (This is relevant to Jones and Davis's attribution theory; see below.) Another explanation may be that it is more adaptive for us to be aware of negative traits than positive ones, since the former are potentially harmful or dangerous to us.

Finally, Luchins found that, although the primacy effect may be important in relation to strangers, as far as friends and other people whom we know well are concerned, the recency effect seems to be stronger. For example, we may discover something about a friend's childhood or something that happened to them before we knew them, which might change our whole perception of them. This raises the fundamental question 'How well do we (or can we) know anybody?'.

INFERRING WHAT PEOPLE ARE LIKE – IMPLICIT PERSONALITY THEORIES AND STEREOTYPING

● The halo effect

Asch's original finding that the inclusion of the word 'warm' produces a more positive impression compared with the same list including the word 'cold' demonstrates what is called the *halo effect*. If we are told that a person has a particularly favourable characteristic (e.g. 'warm', which suggests the person is likeable), then we tend to attribute them with other favourable characteristics (a *positive* halo). The reverse is true if we are told the person is 'cold' (and therefore unlikeable) – we attribute them with a *negative* halo. The halo effect seems to illustrate very well two basic principles of perception (see Fig. 15.1):

1 We like to see people in as consistent (or organized) a way as possible. It is simpler to regard someone as having either all good or all bad qualities than a mixture of good and bad. Two quite extreme examples of this are when lovers regard each other as perfect and faultless ('love is blind') and the 'mirror image phenomenon', where enemies see each other as all bad (see Chapter 19 on prejudice).
2 The halo effect is a very general form of implicit personality theory; these enable us to infer what people are like when we have only very limited information about them.

● Implicit personality theories

As we saw earlier, we all have 'implicit' theories about what makes people 'tick' and one kind of implicit theory is to do with how personality is structured and what traits tend to go together or cluster. Zebrowitz (1990) refers to these as 'person type' implicit personality theories.

Our *names* are a part of the central core of our self-image (see Chapter 21) and names can sometimes form the basis for others' expectations. Harari and McDavid (1973) pointed out that first names, like surnames, are often associated with particular characteristics, partly determined by the media (e.g. the hero and heroine are often called Stephen and Elizabeth and the villains and fall guys Elmer and Bertha). They asked experienced teachers to evaluate a set of short essays written by 11-year-olds who were identified by first name only. Some essays were randomly associated with four names stereotyped by other teachers as attractive and favourable (David, Michael, Karen and Lisa) and four stereotyped as unattractive and unfavourable (Elmer, Hubert, Bertha and Adelle). Although the same essays were associated with different names for different teachers, those written by 'attractive' names were graded a full letter grade higher than those by 'unattractive'

... the general inclination to place a person in categories according to some easily and quickly identifiable characteristic such as age, sex, ethnic membership, nationality or occupation, and then to attribute to him qualities believed to be typical to members of that category. (Tagiuri, 1969)

... a shared conception of the character of a group...(Brown ,1986)

... the process of ascribing characteristics to people on the basis of their group memberships ...(Oakes et al., 1994)

... widely shared assumptions about the personalities, attitudes and behaviour of people based on group membership, for example ethnicity, nationality, sex, race and class ... (Hogg and Vaughan, 1995)

TABLE 15.2 *Some definitions of 'stereotype' and stereotyping*

names and, significantly, the effect was stronger with boys' names than with girls'.

Another kind of implicit personality theory involves inferring what somebody is like psychologically from certain aspects of their *physical appearance*. Allport (1954) pointed to popular stereotypes of this kind, such as the totally unfounded beliefs that fat people are jolly, high foreheads are a sign of superior intelligence, eyes too close together is a sign of untrustworthiness and redheads have fiery tempers.

A number of studies have demonstrated the 'attractiveness' stereotype, i.e. the inference that physically attractive people also have more attractive personalities (e.g. Dion *et al.*'s (1972) 'What is beautiful is good'). This and other studies are discussed further in Chapter 16.

Clearly, our readiness to attribute characteristics to photos of people on the basis of their physical appearance is related to our stereotypes of males and females in general. The above findings suggest that we have a generalized notion of what defines attractiveness in men and women and we then apply this to particular cases. So a tall woman would be perceived differently from a short woman and a tall man – in all three cases, their psychological characteristics are equally 'hidden' but we are usually prepared to describe them very differently based on what we believe makes a man or woman attractive. This represents a kind of interaction between implicit personality theories that see certain personality traits (or certain physical characteristics and

personality traits) as belonging together, on the one hand, and group stereotypes on the other.

● Stereotypes and stereotyping

In discussing implicit personality theories above, we often referred to 'stereotypes'. Stereotypes can be thought of as a special kind of implicit personality theory that relates to an entire group. The term was introduced into social science by Lippman (1922), who defined stereotypes as 'pictures in our heads'. Table 15.2 gives some other definitions.

The process of stereotyping involves the following reasoning: (i) we assign someone to a particular group (e.g. on the basis of their physical appearance); (ii) we bring into play the belief that all members of the group share certain characteristics (the stereotype); and (iii) we infer that this particular individual must possess these characteristics.

The basic method of studying ethnic stereotypes is that used by Katz and Braly (1933) in one of the best known and earliest studies of its kind. One hundred undergraduates at Princeton University, USA, were presented with a list of ethnic groups (Americans, Jews, Negroes, Turks, Germans, Chinese, Irish, English, Italians and Japanese) and 84 words describing personality. They were asked to list, for each ethnic group, the five or six traits which were 'typical' of that group. The aim was to find out whether traditional social stereotypes (as typically portrayed in papers and magazines) were actually held by Princeton students. In fact, they showed considerable agreement, especially about derogatory traits. One of the rather disturbing aspects of the findings was that most of the students had had no personal contact with any members of most of the ethnic groups they had to rate. Presumably, they had absorbed the images of those groups prevalent in the media.

In 1951, Gilbert studied another sample of Princeton students and this time found less uniformity of agreement (especially about unfavourable traits) than in the 1933 study. Many expressed great irritation at being asked to make generalizations at all.

In 1967, Karlins *et al.* repeated the study (but reported their findings in 1969). Again many students objected to doing the task but there was greater agreement on the traits they did assign compared with the 1951 study. There seemed to be a re-emergence of social stereotyping but in the direction of a more favourable stereotypical image. A summary of the main findings from these three studies is given in Table 15.3.

Group	1933	1951	1967
Americans	industrious intelligent materialistic ambitious progressive	materialistic intelligent industrious pleasure-loving individualistic	materialistic ambitious pleasure-loving industrious conventional
Japanese	intelligent industrious progressive shrewd sly	imitative sly extremely nationalistic treacherous	industrious ambitious efficient intelligent progressive
Jews	shrewd mercenary industrious grasping intelligent	shrewd intelligent industrious mercenary ambitious	ambitious materialistic intelligent industrious shrewd
Negroes	superstitious lazy happy-go-lucky ignorant musical	superstitious musical lazy ignorant pleasure-loving	musical happy-go-lucky lazy pleasure-loving ostentatious

TABLE 15.3 *The five traits most frequently assigned to four ethnic groups by three generations of Princeton students (as reported by Katz and Braly, 1933; Gilbert, 1951; Karlins et al., 1969) (from Brown, 1986)*

● The traditional view of stereotypes: are they inherently bad?

For most of the time that psychologists have been studying stereotypes and stereotyping, they have condemned them for being both false and illogical, and dangerous, and people who use them have been seen as prejudiced and even pathological (see Chapter 19).

Lippman (1922), for example, described stereotypes as selective, self-fulfilling and ethnocentric, constituting a '... very partial and inadequate way of representing the world'. The research started by Katz and Braly (1933) was intended to trace the link between stereotypes and prejudice: stereotypes are public fictions arising from prejudicial influences 'with scarcely any factual basis'. So should they be dismissed as completely unacceptable ?

According to Allport (1954), most stereotypes do contain a 'kernel of truth'. Lippman had recognized the categorization processes involved in stereotyping as an important aspect of general cognitive functioning and Allport built on these ideas, arguing that 'The human mind must think with the aid of categories ...'. However, he also believed that prejudiced people tend to make extremely simple dichotomous (either/or) judgements compared with tolerant, non-prejudiced people.

Asch (1952) also rejected the view of stereotyping as 'faulty processing'. In a great many situations the behaviour of individuals (for example, members of audiences, committees, families, football teams, armies) *is* determined by their group membership, so that representing people in terms of these group memberships (i.e. stereotyping) could be seen as an important way of representing social reality. In keeping with his belief in Gestalt principles, Asch argued that groups have distinct psychological properties which cannot be reduced to the characteristics of the individual members

Sherif (1967) also argued that stereotypes are not in themselves deficient but serve to reflect the reality of intergroup relations. Instead of asking if they are objectively true or accurate, stereotypes need to be understood in this intergroup context and, to this extent, they are highly flexible since changes in the relationship with other groups will result in changes to the stereotyped images of those groups.

● The changing face of stereotypes: are they 'normal' after all?

All the researchers whose views of stereotyping have been discussed so far are American. According to Taylor and Perkins (1994), there are compelling reasons why American psychologists should condemn stereotyping and wish to rid society of this evil. One of these is the political ideology, according to which everyone who lives in America is first and foremost 'American' regardless of the country they might have come from or their ethnic/cultural origins. This is the 'melting pot' idea, whereby differences are 'boiled away', leaving just one culture.

By contrast, European social psychologists, notably Tajfel, had been brought up in contexts where it was normal to categorize people into groups, where they expected society to be culturally diverse and where people were proud of their cultural identity. From this personal experience, Tajfel and others mounted a challenge to the American view of stereotyping. Tajfel (1969), for example, reconceptualized stereotyping as the product of quite normal cognitive processes common to all (non-prejudiced) individuals; specifically, it is a special case of categorization, which involves an exaggeration of similarities within groups and of differences between groups (the *accentuation principle*). According to Oakes *et al.* (1994), Tajfel's contribution is widely seen as having been revolutionary; one effect of his ideas was to move researchers away from studying the content of stereotypes and towards the study of the *process* of stereotyping in its own right.

● Stereotyping as a normal cognitive process

According to Brislin (1993):

> ... Stereotypes should not be viewed as a sign of abnormality. Rather, they reflect people's need to organize, remember, and retrieve information that might be useful to them as they attempt to achieve their goals and to meet life's demands ...

Stereotypes are 'categories about people' (Allport, 1954; Brislin, 1981) and categories in general, and stereotypes in particular, are shortcuts to thinking. From a purely cognitive point of view, there is nothing unique about stereotypes – they are universal and inevitable, '... an intrinsic, essential and primitive aspect of cognition ...' (Brown, 1986).

Yet definitions claim that they are exceptionless generalizations, i.e. every skinhead is aggressive, every American is materialistic, etc. without exception. Can

---

BOX 15.4	Key study: what does the 'typical' mean in 'stereotypical'?

McCauley and Stitt (1978) chose Germans as the target group plus three 'typical' traits (efficient/extremely nationalistic/scientifically-minded), and two 'atypical' traits (pleasure-loving/superstitious). Junior college students were told they would be asked a series of questions which they would not be able to answer exactly (e.g. 'What percentage of American cars are Chevrolets?'). Intermixed with these were critical questions about Germans – 'What percentage of Germans are efficient/extremely nationalistic/ scientifically-minded/pleasure-loving/superstitious?' and, corresponding to these, 'What percentage of people in the world generally are efficient/ extremely nationalistic/scientifically-minded/pleasure-loving/superstitious? 'The results are shown below.

What do these results mean? None of these values is even close to 100%, so clearly 'typical' does *not* mean 'true of all' (an exceptionless generalization) and 'scientifically-minded' is not even attributed to a majority of Germans. What 'typical' seems to mean is 'true of a higher percentage of the group in question than of people in general' (Brown, 1986), i.e. *characteristic*. This is what the diagnostic ratio is intended to show; it is calculated simply by dividing the percentage for Germans by the percentage for people in the world – anything over 1.00 represents a trait which belongs to the stereotype, anything below 1.00 represents a trait which does not. Stereotypes, then, seem to be schemas about what particular groups are like relative to 'people in general': they are not exceptionless generalizations.

Trait	% People in the world	% Germans	Diagnostic ratio
Efficient	49.8	63.4	1.27
Extremely nationalistic	35.4	56.3	1.59
Scientifically- minded	32.6	43.1	1.32
Pleasure-loving	82.2	72.8	0.89
Superstitious	42.1	30.4	0.72

this possibly be the case? Clearly, the degree of generalization involved is too great to make a stereotype factually true; no group is completely homogeneous and individual differences are the norm, and yet the Katz and Braly instruction to list the traits typical of each ethnic/national group was thought to have been understood by the Princeton students as an instruction to list the traits *true of all members* of each group (Brown, 1986). However, the early studies never actually found out exactly what was understand by 'typical'. But we noted that in the 1951 study (and again in 1967), some students were objecting to doing what was being asked of them. In fact, fairly substantial numbers actually refused to do it, sensing that characterizing ethnic groups at all would be interpreted as an ignorant or even morally wrong.

Brown (1986) cites a very interesting study by McCauley and Stitt (1978), which attempted to find out just what people do mean when they say a trait is typical of a group (see Box 15.4).

● Recent stereotyping research

The view of stereotyping as a normal cognitive process has led to exciting new developments in stereotype research, both in the USA and elsewhere (Taylor and Perkins, 1994). For example, instead of seeing comments such as 'They're all the same' as simply bigoted and discriminatory, recent research has shown that such statements may stem from a very natural cognitive process, called the *outgroup homogeneity effect* (Quattrone, 1986): people tend to perceive members of an outgroup as highly similar to each other (stereo-

FIGURE 15.3 *When white participants saw a picture similar to this for a brief period of time, about half of them 'remembered' seeing the black man holding a razor. This is taken to reflect the way that stereotypes can influence the encoding and retrieval of information.(Based on Buckhout, 1974)*

type), whereas they tend to see all kinds of individual differences among members of their own group (the *ingroup differentiation hypothesis;* Linville *et al*, 1989). (These could be seen as an extension of Tajfel's accentuation principle; they are all consequences of the act of categorization.)

This differential perception of ingroup and outgroup members is not necessarily indicative of outgroup prejudice, but is the natural outcome of social interaction patterns. We tend to interact with members of our own groups and this encourages a simplified social representation of other groups; in this context, it is both necessary and useful to see all outgroup members as similar. (This is one reason why Allport's 'contact hypothesis' encourages equal status contact in the pursuit of common goals; see Chapter 19.) Ironically, study of the processes involved in stereotyping has suggested that it is the content that needs to be - and can - be modified: the process may be 'hard-wired' as an element of human cognition so that there is nothing we can do about it (Taylor and Perkins, 1994).

The *illusory correlation* (Chapman, 1967; Hamilton and Gifford, 1976) refers to the process in which, when two variables that are unusual or distinct in some way happen to become linked on one occasion, people tend to believe that they are always linked in that way. For example, if a member of a minority ethnic group is involved in a serious crime, majority group members are likely to associate the two, such that 'muggers are likely to be...' becomes part of the negative stereotype of that group. In turn, negative stereotypes can influence other important cognitive processes, such as attention, perception and memory (see Chapters 9, 11 and 12) and these can influence behaviour. So it is not stereotypes themselves which are dangerous or objectionable, but how they affect the way that stereotyped individuals are treated.

● Stereotyping and (other) cognitive processes

Buckhout (1974) gave participants a series of drawings in which some stereotypical pattern was violated. One drawing (see Fig. 15.3) showed a casually dressed white man threatening a well-dressed black man on a subway train, with the white man holding a razor; it was assumed that most whites would have a stereotype of blacks in which the tendency towards violent crime was a component (the illusory correlation). After seeing the picture briefly, approximately half the (white) participants 'remembered' seeing a black man holding a razor; this is consistent with what we know about the role of expectations in perception and how perception influences memory, Research findings like this clearly have very important implications for the reliability of eyewitness testimony (see Chapter 12).

Similarly, Rothbart *et a.l* (1979) found that people often recall better those facts that support their stereotypes (a case of *selective remembering)* and Howard and Rothbart (1980) found that people have better recall of facts which are critical of the minority than facts which are favourable (a case of *negative memory bias).*

Duncan (1976) showed participants a video of a discussion between two males and told them it was a 'live' interaction over closed circuit television; they had to classify various pieces of behaviour. At one point, the discussion became heated and one actor gave the other a shove – the screen then went blank. Duncan wanted to see how participants classified the shove; they could choose from 'playing around', 'dramatizing', 'aggressive behaviour' and 'violent behaviour'. They saw a version of the same film which differed only in the race of the two actors – two whites, two blacks, a white who shoved a black or a black who shoved a white. Many more participants classified the black man's shove as violent behaviour, especially if he shoved a white man!

Our expectations of people's personalities or capabilities may influence the way we actually treat them, which in turn may influence their behaviour in such a way that our expectation is confirmed. This is known as the *self-fulfilling prophecy* and is an illustration of how stereotypes can (unwittingly) influence our behaviour, and not just our perception and memory.

INFLUENCING HOW OTHERS SEE US: IMPRESSION MANAGEMENT

When defining interpersonal perception, we said that it involves the use of 'theory and data' in the understanding of people. So far, we have dealt with part of the theory side (implicit personality theories and stereotypes), but now we shall turn to the data side.

Our impressions of others are, to some degree, 'at the mercy' of what they ' present' in the form of physical appearance and behaviour (verbal and non-verbal), both deliberately and unintentionally. It is difficult to think of a social situation in which we

are not trying (consciously or otherwise) to manipulate how others perceive us. This fundamental aspect of social interaction is referred to as *impression management* or *self-presentation,* which Turner (1991) defines as '...the process of presenting a public image of the self to others...'. Sometimes we may be trying to influence particular people on a particular occasion (e.g. a job interview) or we may be trying to maintain an image of ourselves which we believe is shared with other people in general (e.g. that we are caring or competent or attractive). Yet whatever the situation, it does seem that impression management is going on all the time.

It is widely agreed that we are usually trying to influence other people in a positive way, i.e. we want them to have a favourable impression of us (Schlenker, 1980; Turner, 1991). Clearly, this is very relevant to interpersonal attraction: instead of simply sitting back and letting others be impressed (or not), we can take an active role in making ourselves likeable to others (Duck, 1988) (see Chapter 16). According to Turner, a number of studies suggest that concerns with self-presentation may underlie a whole range of phenomena, including bystander intervention, aggression, deindividuation (see Chapter 17), conformity (see Chapter 20) and cognitive dissonance (see Chapter 18).

Because behaviour is the vehicle for conveying impressions, a number of writers have likened the process of impression management to that of acting. To create a successful impression requires the right setting, props (e.g. the way you are dressed), skills and a shared understanding of what counts as 'backstage'. The person who takes *self-disclosure* too far (see below), for instance, may be regarded as bringing onto stage what should be kept 'backstage' and so creates an unfavourable impression. Goffman, a Canadian sociologist, is one of the best-known exponents of this 'dramaturgical' analysis of social interaction, in books such as *Stigma* (1963) and *The Presentation of Self in Everyday* Life (1971).

Impression management requires us to 'take the role of the other' (see Cooley and Mead's theories of self, Chapter 21), i.e. we must be able, psychologically, to step into someone else's shoes to see how the impression looks from their viewpoint and to adjust our behaviour accordingly. How do we do it? How do we try to impress another person favourably? Fiske and Taylor (1991), in a review of the literature, identify five major components which are summarized in Table 15.4.

- In *behaviour matching,* we try to match the target person's behaviour; an example would be that if they are self-disclosing, we will be too, to a comparable degree.

- When we conform to *situational norms,* we use our knowledge of what is appropriate behaviour in a particular situation to adopt that behaviour ourselves. For every social setting, there is a pattern of social interaction which conveys the best identity for that setting – the 'situated identity'. High self-monitors (see below), in this respect, are more likely to be successful in making a favourable impression.

- Appreciating or flattering others (*ingratiation*) can sometimes produce a favourable response from the target person, especially if the appreciation is sincere. But flattery, if seen for what it is, can backfire on the flatterer who will be seen as deliberately trying to achieve their own ends.

- If we show *consistency* among our beliefs, or between our beliefs and behaviour, we are more likely to impress other people favourably, since inconsistency is generally taken as a sign of weakness.

- Our *verbal* and *non-verbal behaviour* should match, which they usually do if we are sincere. However, if we are flattering, for instance, or in some other way being dishonest, the non-verbal channel will often 'leak', giving away our true feelings. When people perceive an inconsistency between what we are saying and what we are conveying with our body, the non-verbal channel is usually taken as conveying the 'true' message (Argyle et al., 1972; Mehrabian, 1972).

TABLE 15.4 *Major components involved in impression management (based on Fiske and Taylor, 1991)*

Do we always try to convey positive impressions?

- We may feel constrained by the impressions which others already have of us and we act in order to 'muddy the waters'. For instance, if you are continually being told how good a son or daughter you are, the responsibility this places on you might encourage you to behave in the opposite fashion, so that you 'free yourself' from the expectation that you will go on behaving dutifully and respectfully, etc.

- You might protect yourself from anticipated failure either by engaging in behaviours that will produce insurmountable obstacles to success, so that when the inevitable failure happens you have a ready-made excuse (*behavioural self-handicapping*), or by blaming, in advance, things about yourself which could explain the failure (apart from your lack of competence). For example, teachers at exam time get quite used to students telling them how badly they are going to do because of lack of sleep, not having been well, having been unable to revise, always getting anxious about exams and so on (*self-reported handicaps*).

One way of thinking about *self-handicapping* is to see it as an attempt to influence the kind of attribution that other people make about our behaviour, i.e. we want them to see our failures as caused by factors that are 'beyond our control' and that don't, therefore, threaten the positive impression they have of us

(and that we have of ourselves). Making excuses for, as well as confessing, our socially undesirable behaviour after it has occurred can also be explained in attributional terms (Weiner, 1992).

Self-monitoring

While people in general are concerned with the impressions they make on others, people differ in the extent to which they can and do exercise intentional control over their self-presentation; *high self-monitors* are particularly talented in this way compared with *low self-monitors* (Snyder, 1995). Self-monitoring refers to the extent to which people normally attend to external, social situations as guides for their behaviour, as opposed to their own internal states.

High self-monitors are concerned with behaving in a socially appropriate manner and so are more likely to monitor the situation (rather than themselves), looking for subtle cues as to 'how to behave'. They are more skilled in using facial expressions and their voice to convey particular emotions, are more likely to initiate conversations and can interpret non-verbal communication more accurately compared with low self-monitors (Ickes and Barnes, 1977; Snyder, 1979). While their perceptiveness and social sensitivity enable them to interact effectively in diverse settings, carried to an extreme, they can be accused of being self-interested opportunists who change themselves and their opinions to suit the situation (Snyder, 1987). All of this means, of course, that their behaviour shows greater *cross-situational*

High scorers will tend to agree with the following:

● I would probably make a good actor.
● I'm not always the person I appear to be.
● In different situations and with different people, I often act like very different persons.

Low scorers will tend to agree with the following:

● I have trouble changing my behaviour to suit different people and different situations.
● I can only argue for ideas which I already believe.
● I would not change my opinions (or the way I do things) in order to please someone else or win their favour.

TABLE 15.5 *Some sample items from the Self-Monitoring Scale (Snyder, 1987, in Snyder, 1995)*

inconsistency – that is, they behave differently in different situations.

By contrast, low self-monitors remain 'themselves' regardless of the situation and rarely bend or adapt to the norms of the social setting: what they are monitoring is their behaviour in relation to their own enduring needs and values. They may think of themselves as principled people who 'stick up' for what they believe, etc. but, carried to extremes, they can be seen as insensitive, inflexible and uncompromising (Snyder, 1987). They show greater *cross-situational consistency* because their behaviour is governed much more by personal characteristics, which are more enduring than the norms associated with different situations.

Snyder (1987) has developed a pencil and paper test (the Self-Monitoring Scale) which consists of a number of statements with which the respondent has to agree or disagree. Some examples are given in Table 15.5.

● Self-disclosure

How accurately others perceive us is determined partly by how much we reveal to them about ourselves and this special kind of communication is called *self-disclosure;* it can be thought of as a social skill which represents an important element in the overall process of self-presentation. Wiemann and Giles (1988) define it as '...the voluntary making available of information about one's self that would not ordinarily be accessible to the other at that moment ...'.

According to Jourard (1971), we disclose ourselves in many ways – through what we say and do (as well as what we omit to say and do) and this includes facial expressions, gestures and other forms of non-verbal communication (NVC). This means that we have greater control over some aspects of self-disclosure than others since, generally, we have greater control over verbal than non-verbal behaviour. However, Jourard believes that the decision to self-disclose (or to become 'transparent') is one taken freely and the aim in disclosing ourselves is to 'be known, to be perceived by the other as the one I know myself to be'. Jourard believes that we can learn a great deal about ourselves through mutual self-disclosure and our intimacy with others can be enhanced. It is a way of both achieving and maintaining healthy personality but only if the self-disclosure meets the criterion of *authenticity* (or honesty).

What factors influence how much we disclose to others? Five major factors have emerged from the research:

1 reciprocity;
2 norms;
3 trust;
4 quality of the relationship;
5 gender.

● *Reciprocity.* The more personal the information we disclose to someone, the more personal the information they are likely to disclose to us. This relates to the norm of reciprocity (Gouldner, 1960), according to which our social behaviours 'demand' an equivalent response from our partner. In this way, one disclosure begets another of approximately equal valence (positive or negative information) and depth of intimacy (Weimann and Giles, 1988) and, step-by-step, relationships become more intimate (Altman and Taylor, 1973 – see 'Quality of Relationships' below). Sometimes, we might feel the other person is 'overdoing it' and giving too much away (or doing so too quickly), but we are still likely to reveal more about ourselves than we otherwise would.
● *Norms.* The situation we are in often determines how much (or what kind of) disclosure is appropriate; for instance, it is acceptable for someone we meet at a party to tell us about their job but not to reveal details about medical problems or political beliefs.
● *Trust.* Generally, the more we trust someone, the more prepared we are to self-disclose to them.
● *Quality of relationships.* Altman and Taylor's (1973) *social penetration theory* maintains that the more intimate we are with somebody, the greater the range of topics we disclose to them and the more deeply we discuss any particular

topic. Equally, a high degree of mutual self-disclosure can enhance the intimacy of the relationship and is an excellent predictor of whether couples stay together over a four-year period.

● *Gender.* Women generally disclose more than men and Jourard (1971) argues that men's limited self-disclosure prevents healthy self-expression and adds stress to their lives.

As with impression management as a whole, self-disclosure is very relevant to the understanding of interpersonal attraction and relationships and we shall discuss it further in Chapter 16.

JUDGING THE CAUSES OF BEHAVIOUR – THE ATTRIBUTION PROCESS

Most of our impressions of others are based on what they actually do – their overt behaviour – and the setting in which it occurs and how we judge the *causes* of their behaviour will have a major influence on the impression we form about them. Was their behaviour something to do with them, as a person, for instance, their motives, intentions or personality (an *internal* cause) or was it something to do with the situation, including some other person or some physical feature of the environment (an *external* cause)? Unless we can make this sort of judgement, we cannot really use the person's behaviour as a basis for forming an impression of them and although we might mistakenly attribute the cause to the person instead of the situation, attribution still has to be made.

● Attribution and the naive scientist

The process by which we make this judgement about causes is called the *attribution process* and was first investigated by Heider (1958). In a famous study, Heider and Simmel (1944) demonstrated the strength of the human tendency to explain people's behaviour in terms of their intentions by showing that we sometimes attribute intentions to inanimate objects! (See Box 15.5.)

At the beginning of the chapter, we noted that there is a sense in which we are all psychologists and perhaps this is seen most clearly in the case of *attribution theory*, which promises to '...uncover the way in which we, as ordinary men and women, act as

---

BOX 15.5   Key study: even geometrical figures have intentions

Heider and Simmel (1944) showed animated cartoons of three geometrical figures (a large triangle, a smaller triangle and a disc) moving around, in and out of a large square. Participants tended to see them as having human characteristics and, in particular, as having intentions towards each other. A common perception was to see the two triangles as two men in rivalry for a girl (the disc), with the larger triangle being seen as aggressive and a bully, the smaller triangle being seen as defiant and heroic and the disc as timid. (Compare the notion of intentionality in adults with what Piaget calls *animism* in the child; see Chapter 25.)

---

scientists in tracking down the causes of behaviour; it promises to treat ordinary people, in fact, as if they were psychologists ... ' (Antaki, 1984). However, '... Although it sounds as if it is one theory, it is ... actually more like a set of mini-theories ...' (Antaki, 1984). We shall now discuss three of these 'mini-theories', namely the *correspondent inference theory* (Jones and Davis, 1965), the *co-variation model* (Kelley, 1967, 1972), and Weiner's (1986) *attributional theory of motivation and emotion.*

● Correspondent inference theory (Jones and Davis, 1965)

Very much influenced by Heider, Jones and Davis (1965) believe that the goal of the attribution process is to be able to make *correspondent inferences,* that is, to infer that both the behaviour and the intention that produced it correspond to some underlying, stable feature of the person (i.e. a *disposition*). An inference is 'correspondent' when the disposition attributed to an actor 'corresponds' to the behaviour from which the disposition is inferred. For instance, if someone gives up his seat on the bus to allow a pregnant woman to sit down and we infer that he is 'kind and unselfish', this is a correspondent inference because both the behaviour and the disposition can be labelled in a similar way ('kind and unselfish'). But if we attribute the behaviour to compliance with someone else's demands ('he' is a husband whose wife has *told* him to give up his seat), then we would not be making a correspondent inference.

According to Jones and Davis, a precondition for a correspondent inference is the attribution of *intentionality* and they specify two criteria or conditions for this: we have to be confident that the actor (a) is capable of having produced the observed effects, and (b) knew the effects the behaviour would produce. Having made these preliminary decisions, how do we then proceed to infer that the intended behaviour is related to some underlying disposition?

One answer suggested by Jones and Davis is the *analysis of uncommon effects:* when more than one course of action is open to a person, a way of understanding why they chose one course rather than another is to compare the consequences of the action that is taken with the consequences of those which are not, i.e. what is distinctive (or uncommon) about the effects of the choice that is made? For instance, if you have a strong preference for one particular university, even though there are several that are all similar with regard to type of course, number of students, reputation and so on, the fact that all the others require you to be in residence during your first year suggests that you have a strong preference for being independent and looking after yourself. Generally, the fewer the differences between the chosen and the unchosen alternatives, the more confidently we can infer dispositions and the more negative elements that are involved in the chosen alternative, the more confident still we can be of the importance of the distinctive consequence. (If living out of residence means a lot of extra travelling or is more expensive, then the desire to be self-sufficient assumes even greater significance.)

However, the analysis of uncommon effects can lead to ambiguous conclusions and other cues must also be utilized, in particular, choice, social desirability, social role and prior expectations.

- *Choice* is self-explanatory: is the actor's behaviour influenced by situational factors or a result of free will?
- *Social desirability* relates to the norms associated with different situations. Much of the time, the need to explain other people's behaviour does not actually arise – to the extent that we 'conform', there is 'nothing to explain'. We base our impressions of others more on behaviour which is in some way unusual, novel, bizarre or antisocial than on behaviour that is expected or conventional. The former seems to provide more information about what the person is like, largely because when we behave unconventionally we are more likely to be ostracized, shunned or disapproved of.

For example, since at a funeral we are expected to dress soberly, look sad and talk respectfully of the person who has died, when we see people behaving in this way we can easily attribute their behaviour to the situation ('that's how one acts at funerals'). If somebody arrives in brightly-coloured clothes, making jokes and saying what a lout the deceased was, they are 'breaking the rules', their behaviour needs explaining and is likely to be attributed to characteristics of the person who is acting in this socially undesirable way. This was demonstrated in an experiment by Jones *et al.* (1961) described in Box 15.6.

BOX 15.6 Key study: if you want to be an astronaut, be a loner

Jones *et al.* (1961) played a tape-recording of a job interview where the applicant was, supposedly, applying to be an astronaut or a submariner. Prior to hearing the tape, participants were informed of the ideal qualities for the job: astronauts should be inner-directed and able to exist without social interaction, while submariners should be other-directed and gregarious – the participants believed that the candidates also understand these ideal qualities.

The tape presented the candidate as either displaying these qualities or behaving in the opposite way and participants had to give their impressions of the candidate. When the candidate behaved in the opposite way, they more confidently rated the candidate as actually being like that, compared with those who heard a 'conforming' candidate.

- *Roles* refer to another kind of conformity. When people in well-defined roles behave as they are expected to, this tells us relatively little about their underlying dispositions (they are 'just doing their job'). But when they display out-of-role behaviour, we can use their actions to infer 'what they are really like'.
- *Prior expectations* are based on past experiences with the same actor. The better we know someone, the better placed we are to decide whether their behaviour on a particular occasion is 'typical' and, if it is 'atypical', we are more likely to dismiss it or play down its significance or explain it in terms of situational factors.

● Co-variation Model (Kelley, 1967, 1972)

Also based on Heider's early work, Kelley concentrated on how we make judgements about internal and external causes. His co-variation model (1967) aims to explain cases where we have knowledge of how the person being studied usually behaves in a variety of situations and how others usually behave in those situations. *The principle of co-variation* states that 'an effect is attributed to one of its possible causes with which, over time, it co-varies', i.e. if two events repeatedly occur together, we are more likely to infer that they are causally related than if they very rarely occur together. If the behaviour to be explained is thought of as an effect, the cause can be one of three kinds and the extent to which the behaviour co-varies with each of these three kinds of possible cause is what we base our attribution upon. To illustrate the three kinds of causal information, let us take the hypothetical example of a student, called Sally, who is late for her psychology class:

1 *Consensus* refers to the extent to which other people behave in the same way, i.e. are other students late for psychology class? If all (or most) other students are late, then consensus is high (she's in good company) , but if Sally is the only one, consensus is low.

2 *Distinctiveness* refers to the extent to which Sally behaves in a similar way towards other, similar, 'stimuli' or 'entities', i.e. is Sally late for other subjects? If she is, then distinctiveness is low (there's nothing special or distinctive about psychology), but if she is only late for psychology, then distinctiveness is high.

3 *Consistency* refers to how stable Sally's behaviour is over time, i.e. is Sally regularly late for psychology? If she is, consistency is high; if she is not (this is a 'one-off'), then consistency is low.

Kelley believes that a combination of low consensus (Sally is the only one late), low distinctiveness (she is late for all her subjects) and high consistency (she is regularly late) will lead us to make a *person (internal or dispositional) attribution;* that is, the cause of Sally's behaviour is something to do with Sally, e.g. she is a poor timekeeper. However, any other combination would normally result in an *external* or *situational attribution*, e.g. if Sally is generally punctual (low consistency) or if most students are late for psychology (high consensus), then the cause of Sally's lateness might be 'circumstances' in the first case or the subject and/or the teacher in the second (Table 15.6).

Evaluation of Kelley's model

A number of empirical studies have found support for Kelley. McArthur (1972) presented participants with one-sentence descriptions of various behaviours relating to emotions, accomplishments, opinions and actions, for example, 'Sue is afraid of the dog', 'George translates the sentence incorrectly'. Each sentence was accompanied by high or low consensus information, high or low distinctiveness information and high or low consistency information. The task was to attribute each behaviour to characteristics of the actor, the stimulus (target), circumstances or some combination of these. There was strong support for Kelley.

However, not all three types of causal information are used to the same extent in laboratory studies. For example, Major (1980) found that participants show a marked preference for consistency over the other two, with consensus being the least preferred. Similarly, Nisbett and Borgida (1975) found surprisingly weak effects of consensus information when they asked university students to explain the behaviour of a participant in a psychology experiment. This participant, like most others, had agreed to tolerate a high level of electric shock. However, those who were told that 16/34 participants had tolerated the highest possible shock level were no more likely to make situational attributions than those who had been given no consensus information at all. Why? Nisbett and Borgida argued that people's judgements are less responsive to the dull and abstract base rates that constitute consensus information than to the more vivid information regarding the behaviour

Consensus	Distinctiveness	Consistency	Causal Attribution
Low	Low	High	Person (actor) (Internal)
Low	High	Low	Circumstances (External)
High	High	High	Stimulus (target) (External)

TABLE 15.6 *Causal attributions based on three different combinations of causal information (based on Kelley, 1967)*

of one, concrete target person. However, consensus information can have more of an impact if it is made more salient (e.g. it is contrary to what we might expect most people to do) (Wells and Harvey, 1977).

Finally, and perhaps most seriously, Kelley seems to have overestimated people's ability to assess co-variation. He originally compared the social perceiver to a naive scientist (as did Heider), trying to draw inferences in much the same way as the formal scientist draws conclusions from data. More significantly, it is a *normative* model which states how, ideally, people should come to draw inferences about the behaviour of others. However, the actual procedures that people use are not as logical, rational and systematic as the model suggests.

Causal schemata

More recently, Kelley (1972) has offered an alternative model which is meant to cover those situations (perhaps the majority) in which we do not have information about consensus, distinctiveness and consistency. Indeed, often the only information we have is a single occurrence of the behaviour of a particular individual. In such cases, we must rely on what Kelley calls *causal schemata,* which are general ideas about 'how certain kinds of causes interact to produce a specific kind of effect' (Kelley, 1972). Fiske and Taylor (1991) argue that causal schemata provide the social perceiver with a 'causal shorthand' for accomplishing complex inferences quickly and easily. They are based on our experience of cause–effect relationships and what we have been taught by others about such relationships and they come into play when causal information is otherwise ambiguous and incomplete. The two major kinds of causal schemata are:

1 multiple necessary causes;
2 multiple sufficient causes.

● Experience tells us that, for example, to win a marathon you must not only be fit and highly motivated but you must have trained hard for several months beforehand, you must wear the right kind of running shoes and so on. Even if all these causes are present, success cannot be guaranteed, but the absence of any one of them is likely to produce failure so, in this sense, success is more informative than failure. This is an example of *multiple necessary causes.*
● In the case of *multiple sufficient causes,* any one of several causes is sufficient to produce a particular outcome. For example, a film star or sporting personality might promote a particular brand of coffee or aftershave either because he

or she genuinely believes in the product or because of the fee – either is a sufficient cause. Since it is reasonable to assume that it is the fee which accounts for the appearance in the commercial, we discount the other cause ('belief' in the product) according to the *discounting principle* (Kelley, 1972).

● Attributional theory of emotion and motivation (Weiner, 1986)

As the name suggests, Weiner's theory is really an application of basic attributional principles to human emotion and motivation (see Chapter 5). According to Weiner, the attributions we make about our own and other's successes and failures produce specific kinds of emotional response, but these attributions are more complex than described by Heider, Jones and Davis or Kelley.

For Weiner, there are three dimensions of causality:

1 causes can be internal/external (person/situation) – the *locus* dimension;
2 causes can be stable/transient (permanent/temporary) – the *stability* dimension;
3 causes can be controllable or uncontrollable - the *controllability* dimension.

For example, we may blame failure in an exam on a really difficult paper (external, stable, uncontrollable), which is likely to make us feel angry, or on the really bad headache we woke up with on the morning of the exam (internal, unstable, uncontrollable), which may make us feel both angry and disappointed. However, a third possibility is that we blame our failure on our basic lack of ability (internal, stable, uncontrollable), which is likely to make us feel quite depressed. The important point is that not all internal or external causes are of the same kind: in Weiner's view, causes are *multidimensional.* This, together with the emotional responses associated with different attributions, has very important implications for a number of behaviours, including impression management (see above), self-esteem (particularly in the context of gender differences in achievement motivation; see Chapters 5 and 23) and helping behaviour (see Chapter 17).

● Sources of error and bias in the attribution process

As we have already seen, people are far less logical and systematic (less 'scientific') than required by Kelley's co-variation model; research into sources of error and bias seems to provide a much more accurate account of how people actually make causal attributions. Zebrowitz (1990) defines sources of bias as '... the tendency to favour one cause over another when explaining some effect. Such favouritism may result in causal attributions that deviate from predictions derived from rational attributional principles, like covariation ...'. We shall describe some of the main examples of bias in this final part of the chapter.

The fundamental attribution error (FAE)

Even though almost all behaviour is the product of *both* the person and the situation, our causal explanations tend to emphasize one or the other. According to Jones and Nisbett (1971), it could be part of human nature to act in this way: we all want to see ourselves as competent interpreters of human behaviour and so we naively assume that simple explanations are better than complex ones. To try to analyse the interactions between personal and situational factors would take time and energy and usually (as we have seen) we seldom have all the relevant information anyway. The *fundamental attribution error* refers to the general tendency to overestimate the importance of personal or dispositional factors relative to situational or environmental factors as causes of behaviour (Ross, 1977). This will tend to make the behaviour of others seem more predictable which, in turn, enhances our sense of control over the environment.

Heider (1958) believed that behaviour represents the 'figure' against the 'ground', comprising context, roles, situational pressures and so on, i.e. behaviour is conspicuous and situational factors are (comparatively) less easily perceived (see Chapter 9).

Zebrowitz (1990) argues that:

> ... the fundamental attribution error is best viewed as a bias towards attributing an actor's behaviour to dispositional causes rather than as an attribution error. This bias may be limited to adults in Western societies and it may be most pronounced when they are constrained to attribute behaviour to a single cause ...

Related to the FAE, but not usually cited as an example of an attribution error, is the *just world hypothesis* (Lerner, 1965, 1980), according to which 'I am a just person living in a just world, a world where people get what they deserve', i.e. we believe that when 'bad' things happen to people it is because they are in some way 'bad' people, so that they have at least partly 'brought it on themselves'. This can help explain the phenomenon of 'blaming the victim', as in cases of rape where the woman is often accused of having 'led the man on' or giving

him the sexual 'green light' before changing her mind. Myers (1994) gives the example of a German civilian who, on being shown round the Bergen-Belsen concentration camp after the British liberation, commented 'What terrible criminals these prisoners must have been to receive such treatment'. What this person seems to be expressing was the unacceptability of the conclusion that such horrors as had obviously been perpetrated in that camp could happen to innocent people – if they happened to them, why couldn't they happen to me? Believing in a just world gives us a sense of being in control – so long as we are 'good', only 'good' things will happen to us.

In combination with the FAE, the just world hypothesis can help to explain prejudice (see Chapter 19) and helping behaviour (see Chapter 17).

The actor–observer effect (AOE)

Related to the FAE is the tendency for actors and observers to make different attributions about the same event (Jones and Nisbett, 1972; Nisbett *et al*, 1973). Actors usually see their own behaviour as primarily a response to the situation and so quite variable from situation to situation (the cause is external), while the observer typically attributes the same behaviour to the actor's intentions and dispositions and so quite consistent across situations (the cause is internal). (The observer's attribution to internal causes is, of course, the FAE.) .

Nisbett *et al.* (1973) found that students:

- assumed that actors would behave in the future in ways similar to those they had just witnessed;
- described their best friend's choices of girlfriend and college major in terms referring to dispositional qualities of their best friend (while more often describing their own similar choices in terms of properties of the girlfriend or major);
- attributed more personality traits to other people than to themselves.

Why should this occur? One answer is that what is perceptually salient or vivid for the actor is different from what is perceptually salient or vivid for the observer (this is the figure–ground explanation which we noted when discussing the FAE). An important study by Storms (1973) described in Box 15.7 supports this perceptual salience explanation of the AOE.

Self-serving attributional bias

A number of studies have found that the AOE is most pronounced when judging negative behaviours and

BOX 15.7 Key study: videotape and the attribution process (Storms, 1973)

Two actor participants at a time engaged in a brief, unstructured conversation while two observers looked on. Later, a questionnaire was used to measure the actors' attributions of their own behaviour in the conversation and the observers' attributions of the behaviour of one of the two actors to whom they had been assigned. Visual orientation was manipulated by the use of videotapes of the conversation, so that the *no video* (control) group simply completed the questionnaire, the *same orientation* group simply saw a video of what they saw during the original conversation (before completing the questionnaire) and the *new orientation* group saw a video which reversed the original orientation, with actors seeing themselves and observers seeing the other actor (again, before completing the questionnaire).

As predicted, in the first two groups the usual AOE was found. But, also as expected, the AOE was reversed in the third group, i.e. actors made more dispositional attributions than did observers.

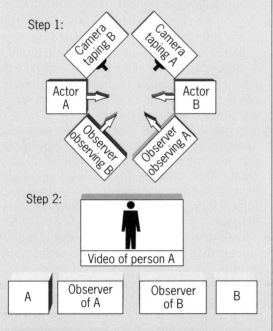

FIGURE 15.4 *Diagram depicting the arrangement in the Storms (1973) experiment*

incompetent in some way, so we are more likely to 'blame' our failures on something external to ourselves; this is the *self-protecting bias* which protects our self-esteem. But we are quite happy to take the credit for our successes; this is the *self-enhancing bias* which enhances our self-esteem. Together, they are referred to as *self-serving attributional bias* (Miller and Ross, 1975). There is some evidence that positively valued outcomes (e.g. altruism) are more often attributed to people, and negatively valued outcomes (e.g. being late) to situational factors, regardless of who committed them. However, when either the self or someone closely associated with the self has committed the action, credit for positive events and denial of responsibility for negative ones are even stronger.

An interesting exception to this general rule is the case of very depressed people. Abramson *et al.* (1978) found that they tend to explain their failures in terms of their own inadequacies and their successes more in terms of external factors, such as luck and chance (see Chapter 6). Depressed people are displaying a different *attributional style* from non-depressed people, but there is also evidence that women are more likely than men to cope with stress by blaming themselves for their plight and to attribute their achievements to external factors (Davison and Neale, 1994). Differences in attributional style can also help to explain why married couples differ in their degree of happiness (see Chapter 16).

The importance of the consequences

The more serious the consequences of the actor's behaviour, the more likely the FAE is to be made: the more serious the outcome, the more likely we are to judge the actor as responsible, regardless of the perceived intentions of the actor. This was demonstrated by Walster (1966), who gave participants an account of a car accident in which a young man's car had been left at the top of a hill and then rolled down backwards. One group was told that very little damage was done to the car and no other vehicle was involved; a second group was told that it collided with another car, causing some damage; while a third group was told that the car crashed into a shop, injuring the shopkeeper and a small child. When they had to assess how responsible the car owner was, the third group found him more 'guilty' or morally culpable than the second group and the second group found him more guilty than the first.

may be absent or even reversed for positive ones. Why? Naturally, no one wants to admit to being

If more serious consequences can result in greater blame and responsibility, can the reverse inference occur, i.e. can belief that an act is intentional affect perception of the seriousness of the consequences? Darley and Huff (1990) found that judgements of the damage caused by an action depended on whether participants believed it was done intentionally, through negligence or accidentally. Although the damage done was described in an identical way, those who read that the act was done intentionally inflated their estimation of the amount of damage done compared with those who believed the damage was caused unintentionally (either through negligence or accident).

Another facet of the consequences of behaviour is how these consequences affect us personally *(personal* or *hedonic relevance):* the more they affect us (the greater the hedonic relevance), the more likely we are to hold the actor responsible. Going one step further than hedonic relevance is *personalism,* which is the perceiver's belief that the actor intended to harm the perceiver; in terms of Jones and Davis's theory, this increases the chances of making a correspondent inference.

CHAPTER SUMMARY

- Interpersonal perception refers to how we all attempt to explain, predict and to some degree control the behaviour of other people; in these ways, we can all be thought of as psychologists.
- Although social psychology in general, and interpersonal perception in particular, has always been concerned with the content of people's thoughts about others, social cognition now emphasizes the information-processing approach.
- Both object and person perception involve selection, organization and inference. But there are also crucial differences between them, due to the fact that only people behave, interact with each other, perceive and experience.
- Social phenomenologists regard experience, rather than behaviour, as the major source of 'data' in social interaction.
- There are important differences between the implicit personality theories of the lay person and the formal scientific theories of psychologists, including the purposes to which their respective theories are put.
- Four views of people as thinking organisms have been identified: consistency seekers, naive scientists, cognitive misers and motivated tacticians.
- As cognitive misers, we use heuristics as shortcuts to thinking, including availability, representativeness, simulation and anchoring.
- Some critics have claimed that social cognition is too much concerned with the thinking that goes on inside the heads of individuals and overlooks the links between people and social objects.
- According to Moscovici, social representations arise from everyday communications between individuals. They refer to 'common sense', simplified, widely shared understanding of complex theories and ideas, such as Freud's psychoanalytic theory, and involve personification and figuration.
- According to Asch, central traits exert a major organizing influence on our overall impression of a person, while peripheral traits have little or no influence. An alternative, but not contradictory explanation is that overall impressions and inferences about additional traits reflect our implicit personality theories.
- According to Wishner, whether a trait is central or not is a relative matter, depending on the pattern of correlations with other traits; this will vary between different studies.
- A second major explanation of global perception is the primacy–recency effect. While most of the evidence supports a primacy effect with regard to strangers, a recency effect may be more powerful with regard to people we know well. A recency effect can also be produced if people are warned not to make snap judgements.
- The halo effect is one kind of implicit personality theory; these enable us to infer what people are like when we have only limited information about them. These theories may be based on people's names and various aspects of their physical appearance, including how physically attractive they are.
- Stereotypes represent a special kind of implicit personality theory which characterize entire groups.
- Traditionally, American researchers studied stereotypes in relation to prejudice and they were seen as false, illogical overgeneralizations. However, even some of the early researchers recognized the reality of group behaviour and the role of stereotypes in reflecting intergroup relations.
- European psychologists saw the categorization of people as normal and expected; gradually the emphasis shifted from studying the content of

stereotypes to stereotyping as a process. From a cognitive point of view, stereotyping is a normal mental shortcut.

- The act of categorizing people produces the accentuation principle, outgroup homogeneity effect and the ingroup differentiation hypothesis. The illusory correlation can help explain the formation of negative stereotypes of minority groups.

- Stereotyping is dangerous because of how it may affect basic cognitive processes, such as attention, perception and memory. Stereotypes may also influence people's behaviour towards members of outgroups, as well as the behaviour of outgroup members themselves through the self-fulfilling prophecy.

- We actively try to influence the impression that others form of us through impression management/self-presentation. This has been compared with acting on stage and involves behaviour matching, appreciating/flattering others, showing consistency among our beliefs and matching our verbal and non-verbal behaviour.

- Usually, we try to influence others positively, but self-handicapping represents an exception to this general rule. This, and other kinds of impression management, can be explained in terms of attribution principles.

- Self-monitoring refers to the degree to which impression management is important for individuals; high self-monitors try to match their behaviour to the situation, while low self-monitors are always trying to 'be themselves'.

- Self-disclosure can be thought of as a social skill which plays an important part in self-presentation. Important factors that influence self-disclosure include reciprocity, norms, trust, quality of relationship and gender.

- Attribution theories are psychologists' attempts to explain the attribution process, which tries to identify the causes of behaviour. An important distinction is between internal/person causes and external/situational causes.

- Correspondent inference theory sees the goal of the attribution process as being able to infer dispositions , which explain both the behaviour and the intention to act that way. Dispositions are inferred from intentionality, analysis of uncommon effects, choice, social desirability, roles and prior expectations.

- According to Kelley's co-variation model, internal or external attributions are based on high or low values of three kinds of causal information: consensus, distinctiveness and consistency.

- Kelley's model is a normative model which overestimates the logical nature of people's thinking. Causal schemata help to explain how attribution takes place in the absence of causal information.

- Weiner's attribution theory identifies three dimensions of causality: locus, stability and controllability.

- Research into sources of error and bias provides a more accurate account of how the attribution process takes place than the normative theories do. Major examples include the fundamental attribution error, the actor–observer effect, self-serving attributional bias and the importance of the consequences (e.g. hedonic relevance, personalism).

GLOSSARY

Accentuation principle A special case of categorization, according to which we exaggerate the similarities within a group and the differences between groups.

Actor-observer effect Tendency for actors to see their behaviour as caused mainly by situational factors and for observers to see actors' behaviour as caused mainly by dispositional factors.

Analysis of uncommon effects In Jones and Davis' theory, comparing the consequences of a chosen action with those of non-chosen actions; what is distinctive/uncommon about the former provides clues as to dispositions.

Anchoring heuristic Relating some event for which you have no information to a similar event which serves as a reference point/anchor.

Attribution process The lay person's attempts to explain behaviour in terms of its causes.

Attribution theory Formal psychological accounts of the attribution process.

Attributional style General tendency to make certain kinds of attributions about one's successes and failures.

Availability heuristic Judging the frequency or probability of an event according to the number of instances of it that can readily be remembered.

Causal schemata 'Causal shorthand' which we use when causal information is ambiguous or incomplete. Main types are multiple necessary and multiple sufficient.

Central traits Personality characteristics (e.g. warm and cold) which have a major influence on our overall impression of a person.

Cognitive miser A view of people as limited in their

capacity to process information, so that they need to take shortcuts to help simplify complex problems.

Consensus The extent to which other people behave in the same way as the actor.

Consistency How regularly the actor behaves in a particular way in the same situation.

Correspondent inference theory Jones and Davis' theory of attribution which sees the goal of attribution to infer dispositions from behaviour.

Distinctiveness The extent to which the actor behaves in similar ways in similar situations or towards similar 'stimuli'.

Fundamental attribution error General tendency to overestimate the importance of personal/dispositional (internal) causes relative to situational (external) causes of behaviour.

Halo effect A kind of implicit personality theory, in which one positive (or negative) trait is used to infer other positive (or negative) traits.

Hedonic relevance Tendency to hold an actor responsible/make a fundamental attribution error if his/her actions affect us personally; this is enhanced if we believe that the action was meant to harm us *(personalism)*.

Illusory correlation Process whereby two variables that are unusual or distinctive in some way, which happen to become linked on a single occasion, come to be seen as always linked (e.g. race and crime).

Implicit personality theory An informal, intuitive belief about how personality is structured, which allows us to infer what people are like when we have very limited information about them; 'person schema'.

Impression management The active attempt to influence the impression that others form of us, usually in a positive direction. Also known as *self-presentation.*

Ingroup differentiation hypothesis Tendency to perceive individual differences between members of one's ingroup.

Just world hypothesis General belief that bad things only happen to bad people; this involves 'blaming the victim'.

Naive scientist A way of thinking about the ordinary person as trying to infer unobservable causes from observable behaviour, much like the formal scientists; first proposed by Heider.

Norm of reciprocity The 'rule' which states that social behaviours should receive an equivalent response from our social partners.

Outgroup homogeneity effect Tendency to perceive members of an outgroup as highly similar to each other ('they all look the same').

Peripheral traits Personality characteristics (e.g. polite and blunt) that have little influence on our overall impression of a person.

Principle of co-variation The basis of Kelley's attribution theory, according to which if two events repeatedly occur together (co-vary), we infer that they are probably causally related.

Representativeness heuristic Deciding whether a particular person or event is an example of a particular schema or general category.

Self-disclosure A component skill involved in impression management, in which we voluntarily make information about ourselves available to others.

Self-handicapping Protecting the self from anticipated failure, either through behavioural self-handicapping or self-reported handicaps. A form of impression management.

Self-monitoring The degree to which people try to adapt their behaviour to match the demands of particular social situations. High self-monitors do this to a considerable degree, low self-monitors hardly at all.

Self-serving attributional bias Tendency to blame our failures on external factors (self-protecting bias) and take the credit for our successes (self-enhancing bias).

Simulation heuristic Judging what is likely to be/have been the outcome of some event or incident according to how easily different outcomes can be imagined.

Social cognition In general, people's thoughts and beliefs about all aspects of their social environment; more specifically, thoughts and beliefs that arise through social interaction and which influence interaction.

Social phenomenology Theory which sees experience as the major source of data in social interaction, as opposed to behaviour.

Social representations 'Common sense', simplified, widely shared understanding of complex ideas and theories (e.g. Freud's psychoanalytic theory) which arise from everyday communication between individuals.

Stereotypes a kind of implicit personality theory which relates to the characteristics of an entire social group.

FURTHER READING

Fiske, S.T. and Taylor, S.E. (1991) *Social Cognition*, 2nd edn. New York: McGraw-Hill. Considered by many the 'classic' in this area of psychology, it is frequently cited by other writers.

Zebrowitz, L.A. (1990) *Social Perception*. Milton Keynes: Open University Press. Much shorter than the Fiske and Taylor but very thorough.

16 INTERPERSONAL ATTRACTION AND INTIMATE RELATIONSHIPS

INTRODUCTION AND OVERVIEW

According to popular belief, it is love that makes the world go round but according to Rubin and McNeil (1983), liking perhaps more than loving is what keeps it spinning. How are liking and loving related and how are they different? Are there different kinds of love and is this important for understanding the way that romantic relationships develop over time and why some will eventually break down? How do we get into relationships in the first place?

When people are asked 'What is it that makes your life meaningful?' or 'What is necessary for your happiness ?', most people say, before anything else, satisfying close relationships with friends, family and romantic partners (Berscheid, 1985, cited in Myers, 1994). As important as family relationships are, we shall focus in this chapter on those intimate relationships over which we have some choice. When we talk of relationships breaking up (or down), we often use phrases that imply a degree of choice (e.g. 'Why don't you get out of that relationship?' or 'I wish I'd never got involved in the first place') and one way of trying to understand the way that relationships end is to see it as the process of relationship formation put into reverse. We don't often talk about ending relationships with relatives, however bad they get, and that is because 'we can't choose our parents ...'.

Traditionally, social psychologists have concentrated on *interpersonal attraction* (really an aspect of interpersonal perception; see Chapter 15) which relates to the question 'How do relationships start?'. But during the last 20 years or so, the emphasis has shifted to two questions which logically follow the first, namely (a) What keeps people in intimate relationships together (their maintenance and progression)? and (b) Why and how do relationships go wrong (relationship breakdown or dissolution)?

THE NEED FOR OTHER PEOPLE: AFFILIATION AS A PRECONDITION FOR ATTRACTION

Before discussing the research and theory relating to interpersonal attraction, we should consider the basic human need for the company of other human beings, i.e. *affiliation* (or affiliative needs). In Chapter 5, we saw that the need to belong and to be accepted by others is one of Maslow's basic survival needs and in Chapter 20 we shall see that this can help explain certain types of influence that others can exert on us, such as pressure to conform. Conformity can also be explained in terms of the need to evaluate our beliefs and opinions by comparing them with other people's beliefs and opinions, especially in ambiguous or unstructured situations, which is the central idea in Festinger's (1954) *social comparison theory*.

According to Duck (1988), we are more 'affiliative' and inclined to seek others' company under certain conditions than others, for example, when we are anxious, when we have just left a close relationship (the 'rebound' situation) and when we have moved to a new neighbourhood. A famous experiment by Schachter (1959) illustrates the way that increased anxiety can increase our affiliative needs – see Box 16.1. A more recent study by Kulik and Mahler (1989) reached the same conclusions but involved patients about to undergo coronary bypass surgery; most preferred to share a room with someone who had already undergone coronary surgery, rather than another patient waiting for the same operation. The main motive for this preference seemed to be the need for information about the stress-inducing situation (see Chapter 5).

LIKING, LOVE AND INTIMACY

In *Liking and Loving* (1973), Rubin defines liking as positive evaluation of another and loving as more than an intense liking, being qualitatively different and comprising three main components:

1 *Attachment:* the need for the physical presence and emotional support of the loved one. (On the Love Scale, an attachment item is 'If I could never be with ____ I would feel miserable'.)

2 *Caring:* a feeling of concern and responsibility for the loved one. ('If ____ were feeling badly my first duty would be to cheer him/her up'.)

3 *Intimacy:* the desire for close and confidential contact and communication, wanting to share certain thoughts and feelings with the loved one more fully than with anyone else. ('I feel that I can confide in ____ about practically everything'.)

Caring corresponds to Fromm's definition of love (1962) as 'the active concern for the life and growth of that which we love'.

The *Love Scale* can also be applied to same-sex friends and Rubin found that females reported loving their friends more than men, but there was no difference in scores on the Liking Scale. Other studies suggest that women's friendships tend to be more intimate than men's, engaging in more spontaneous joint activities and more exchange of confidences. Rubin and McNeil (1983) suggest that loving for men may be channelled into single, sexual relationships while women may be better able to experience attachment, caring and intimacy in a wider range and variety of relationships.

It has been suggested that love is a label that we learn to attach to our own state of physiological arousal (see Chapter 6), but most of the time love does not involve intense physical symptoms; love, therefore, is more usefully thought of as a particular sort of attitude that one person has towards another (Rubin and McNeil, 1983). However, should we distinguish between different types of love ?

Berscheid and Walster (1978) agree that love does not usually involve intense physiological arousal by distinguishing between *companionate love* (sometimes called 'true love' or 'conjugal love'), 'the affection we feel for those with whom our lives are deeply entwined', including very close friends and marriage partners) and *passionate* or *romantic love* (also referred to as obsessive love, infatuation, 'love sick' or 'being in love').They define romantic love as

---

BOX 16.1

Key study: a stress shared is a stress halved or 'anxiety loves anxious company' (Schachter, 1959)

Female psychology students were led to believe that they would be receiving electric shocks. One group was told that the shocks would be painful (high anxiety condition), while another group was told they would not be at all painful (low anxiety condition). They were then told that there would be a delay while the equipment was set up and they were given the option of either waiting alone or with another participant; their choice (waiting alone or with someone else) was the dependent variable, so no actual shock was given. But the experiment is still ethically very dubious. As predicted, the high anxiety group showed a greater preference for company (20 out of 32) than the low anxiety group (ten out of 30).

In a separate, but related experiment, all the participants were told that the shocks would be painful, but for half the choice was between waiting alone and waiting with another participant in the same experiment and for the other half it was between waiting alone and waiting with another student who was waiting to see her teacher. For the first group, there was a strong preference for waiting with another high-anxiety participant, while the second group preferred to wait alone. This suggests strongly that social comparison was the motive for affiliation (rather than distraction) – if we have something to worry about, we prefer to be with other worriers.

'A state of intense absorption in another. Sometimes lovers are those who long for their partners or for complete fulfilment. Sometimes lovers are those who are ecstatic at finally having attained their partner's love and, momentarily, complete fulfilment. A state of intense physiological arousal.' These are qualitatively different but companionate love is only a more extreme form of liking ('the affection we feel for casual acquaintances') and corresponds to Rubin's 'love'.

Rubin (1973)	**Liking**	**Loving**	
Berscheid & Walster (1978)		**Companionate vs.**	**Passionate/Romantic**
Sternberg (1988)		Intimacy + Commitment **Fatuous** Passion + Commitment	Intimacy + Passion **Consummate** Intimacy + Passion + Commitment

TABLE 16.1 *The relationship between liking and different types of love*

Similarly, Sternberg (1988) has proposed a 'triangular' model of love, in which three basic components (intimacy, passion and decision/commitment) can be combined so as to produce *consummate love;* when only two are combined, the resulting love is either romantic, companionate or fatuous (see Fig. 16.1 and Table 16.1). Berscheid and Walster's and Sternberg's models are multidimensional, in contrast with Rubin's, according to which love is a single, underlying dimension on which individuals can be ranked in terms of the strength of feeling for a partner. These distinctions are important for understanding how intimate relationships change over time.

sometimes make specific mention of marriage /married partners.

According to Kerckhoff and Davis (1962),who compared 'short-term couples' (less than 18 months) with 'long-term couples' (18 months or more) over a seven-month period, relationships pass through a series of 'filters'. Initially, similarity of *sociological* (or demographic) variables will determine the likelihood of individuals meeting in the first place. To some extent, our choice of friends and partners is made for us: social circumstances reduce the 'field of availables' (Kerckhoff, 1974), i.e. the range of people that are realistically available for us to meet (as opposed to those who are theoretically available).

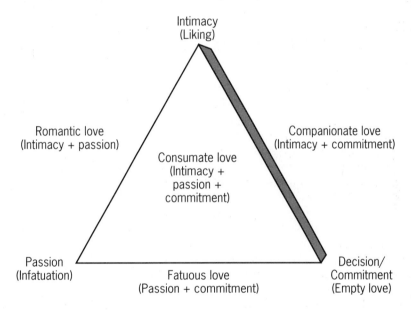

FIGURE 16.1 *Robert Sternberg's (1988) model of different kinds of love as combinations of three basic components of love. (From Myers, D.G. (1994)* Exploring Social Psychology. *New York, McGraw-Hill)*

THE DYNAMIC NATURE OF RELATIONSHIPS: STAGE THEORIES OF HOW RELATIONSHIPS CHANGE

Our own experience tells us that our intimate relationships change and develop over time and this is what we expect will happen; indeed, those which stagnate ('we're not going anywhere'), especially if they are sexual/romantic in nature, may well be doomed to failure (Duck, 1988). A number of theories have been proposed charting the course of relationships, which are usually meant to cover both sexual and non-sexual kinds although they

There is considerable preselection of the types of people we come into contact with, namely those from our own ethnic, racial, religious, social class and educational groups. These are the types of people we tend to find most attractive initially since similarity makes communication easier and we have something immediately in common with them, as a group; so at this point, attraction has little to do with other people's individual characteristics.

The next 'filter' involves the *psychological* characteristics of individuals, specifically agreement on basic values. This was found to be the best predictor of the relationship becoming more stable and permanent. Those who had been together for less than 18 months tended to have a stronger relationship when the partners' values coincided but with couples of longer standing, similarity was not the most important factor. The best predictor of a longer term commitment was found to be complementarity of emotional needs, which constitutes the third filter. Both similarity and *complementarity* will be discussed further below.

According to Murstein's (1976, 1986, 1987) *stimulus-value-role (SVR) theory*, intimate relationships proceed from a *stimulus* stage, in which attraction is based on external attributes (such as physical appearance), through a *value* stage, in which similarity of values and beliefs becomes much more important, and finally to a *role* stage, which involves a commitment based on successful performance of relationship roles, such as husband and wife. Although all three factors have some influence throughout a relationship, each one assumes greatest significance during one particular stage (see Fig. 16.2).

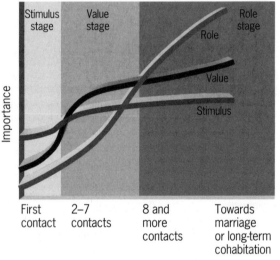

FIGURE 16.2 *States of courtship in SVR theory (Murstein, 1987, based on Brehm, 1992)*

For Levinger (1980), relationships pass through five stages:

1 acquaintance or initial attraction;
2 building up the relationship;
3 consolidation or continuation;
4 deterioration or decline;
5 ending.

At each stage there are positive factors that promote the development of the relationship and corresponding negative factors that prevent its development or cause it to fail. For example, repeated interaction with someone will make initial attraction more likely,

while infrequent contact will make this very unlikely (this relates to proximity which is discussed below). Again, similarity of attitudes and other characteristics helps a relationship to build (stage two), while dissimilarity will make this difficult.

Brehm (1992) points out that many studies have provided only weak evidence for a fixed sequence of stages in intimate relationships: 'stages' are probably best regarded as 'phases' that take place at different times for different couples. However, the claim that relationships do change and develop is not in dispute and it is useful to think of this as involving a beginning, a middle and an end, corresponding to the three questions that were posed at the start of the chapter, namely :

1 How do relationships get started, i.e. what determines *interpersonal attraction?*
2 What keeps people in intimate relationships together, i.e. what contributes to the *maintenance* of relationships?
3 Why do relationships go wrong and how do they end, i.e. what causes the *breakdown* or *dissolution* of relationships?

The rest of the chapter will be an attempt to provide answers to these three questions.We should note here that these broad 'phases' imply considerable overlap, so that specific theory and research discussed in relation to one could easily relate to another and will almost certainly have implications for a later phase.

HOW RELATIONSHIPS GET STARTED: INTERPERSONAL ATTRACTION

A general theoretical framework for explaining initial attraction is that we are attracted to individuals whose presence is *rewarding* for us (e.g. Clore and Byrne, 1974; Lott and Lott, 1974). Rewards can be direct (produced by an individual) or by association (the other person takes on the emotional tone of the surrounding situation): the more rewards someone provides for us, the more we should be attracted to that individual. Rewards will not be the same for everyone, but a number of factors have been found to be influential in initial attraction, including proximity, exposure and familiarity, physical attractiveness, similarity and reciprocal liking. These can be seen as influencing attraction through their reward value.

● Proximity, exposure and familiarity

This really represents a minimum requirement for attraction because it represents a minimum requirement for interaction. Clearly, the further apart two people live, the lower the probability that they will ever meet, let alone become friends or marry each other.

In one well-known study, Festinger *et al.* (1950) studied friendship patterns in a university campus housing complex for married students. People were more friendly with those who lived next door (41 percent), next most friendly with those living two doors away and least friendly with those who lived at the end of the corridor (10 percent). Families separated by four flats hardly ever became friends and in two-storey blocks of flats, the residents tended to interact mainly with others living on the same floor. On any one floor, people who lived near stairways had more friends than those living at the end of the corridor.

What proximity provides is the increased opportunity for interaction which, in turn, increases familiarity and there is considerable evidence that, far from breeding contempt, familiarity breeds fondness ; this is what Zajonc (1968) calls the *mere exposure*

effect. He found that the more times university students saw meaningless Chinese-like characters or (previously) unfamiliar Turkish words, the more likely they were to say it meant something good, and the more often they saw photographs of men's faces, the more they liked them (see Fig. 16.3). According to Argyle (1981), the more two people interact, the more polarized their attitudes towards each other become, usually in the direction of greater liking which, in turn, increases the likelihood of further interaction, but only if the interaction is as equals. A famous demonstration of the impact of familiarity is the study by Newcomb (1961)– see Box 16. 2.

This preference for what is familiar extends to our own facial appearance. Mita *et al.* (1977, cited in Myers, 1994) photographed women students and later showed each student her actual picture together with a mirror-image of it. Most students preferred the latter – this is how we are used to seeing ourselves – while their friends preferred the latter – this is how others are used to seeing us!

So it seems that we like what we know and what we are familiar with, perhaps because it is predictable, and most of the research on familiarity has supported the positive outcome of repeated exposure. On the other hand, repeated exposure to something or somebody may reveal the less acceptable and desirable qualities and even a single

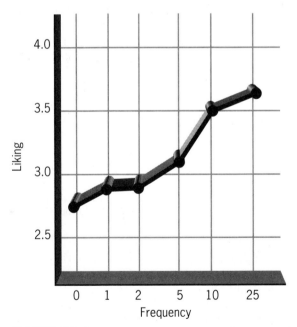

FIGURE 16.3 *The relationship between frequency of exposure and liking. Participants were shown photographs of different faces and the number of times each face was shown was varied. The more they saw a particular face, the more they said they liked the person shown. (Based on Zajonc, 1968)*

BOX 16.2 Key study: does it matter who your room-mate is, since familiarity breeds fondness?

Newcomb (1961) offered male students free board and lodging at a rented boarding house at Michigan University if they participated in a study of the acquaintance process. They were randomly assigned a room and during the first year of the study it seemed that it was similarity of attitudes, beliefs and values which was the strongest determinant of liking. In the second year, using different students, Newcomb assigned each student a room-mate who was either highly similar to himself or as different as possible, on a wide range of attitudes, beliefs and values. Based on the first year's results, it was predicted that similarity would again be the major influence, but it turned out to be familiarity that was the key factor – room-mates became friends far more often than would have been expected on the basis of their characteristics.

encounter with a person can cause dislike if he or she fails to respect the 'rules' governing physical proximity. So can proximity breed contempt?

Not liking others who become 'too familiar'

If we are sitting in an otherwise empty row of seats in a train, for instance, and someone comes and sits right next to us, we may well feel uneasy and suspicious (especially if the stranger is of the opposite

---

BOX 16.3   Key study: beware of space invaders in the library

In the 'Library Study' (Felipe and Sommer, 1966), the unsuspecting participants were female students studying at a large table with six chairs on either side of the table; there were at least two empty chairs on either side of each student and one opposite and there were a number of experimental conditions in which, for example, the experimenter: (i) sat next to her and moved his chair nearer to hers; (ii) sat two seats away from her (leaving one chair between them); (iii) sat three seats away; and (iv) sat immediately opposite her.

The students were more likely to leave, move away, adjust the chair or erect barriers (such as putting a bag on the table between themselves and the 'intruder') when he sat next to them, as in condition (i). Similar results were found for psychiatric patients (Felipe and Sommer, 1966) and for people sitting on park benches (Sommer, 1969). In the last study, the experimenter sat six inches away from someone on an otherwise empty bench and these participants were much more likely to move away – and sooner – than control participants who were not joined by the over-friendly stranger.

---

sex). In a series of studies by Sommer, the experimenter deliberately sat close to unsuspecting people when there was plenty of other available space, in order to see how likely they were to react to this invasion of their *personal space* (see Box 16.3).

The term 'personal space' was first used by the anthropologist Edward T. Hall (1959, 1966) to describe the human behaviour which resembled the 'individual distance' of zoo animals (Hediger, 1951), i.e. the distance which two individuals of the same species try to keep between each other. It has been likened to an invisible bubble that surrounds us. According to Hall, we learn *proxemic rules,* which prescribe: (i) the amount of physical distance that is appropriate in daily relationships; and (ii) the kinds of situations in which closeness or distance is proper. Hall identifies four main regions or zones of personal space, which are summarized in Table 16. 2. Our feelings for others may depend on whether these culturally determined rules are followed and these rules are themselves influenced by the nature of the relationship. For instance, relatives and intimate friends are allowed much closer proximity – and bodily contact – than mere acquaintances or strangers. As far as bodily contact is concerned, there are different rules for different relatives depending on their gender and this applies to friends too; this was demonstrated in a famous study by Jourard (1966); see Figure 16.4.

There are important cultural differences regarding proxemic rules. Each zone of personal space allows the use of different cues of touch, smell, hearing and seeing, which are more important in some cultures than others. Watson and Graves (1966) observed discussion groups of Americans or those from Arab countries; in the latter, there was more direct face-to-face orientation, greater closeness and

I Intimate distance (0–18 inches)	This may involve actual bodily contact and is reserved for our most intimate relationships
2 Casual-personal distance (1½ feet – 4 feet)	This is the distance in which we usually interact with close friends, trusted acquaintances, at parties or with those who share special interests with us
3 Social-consultative distance (4 feet – 12 feet)	This is the distance commonly found between colleagues at work and is used for most business and formal contacts
4 Public distance (12 feet and beyond)	This is used for large, public meetings and lectures and meetings with high-ranking persons

TABLE 16.2 *Hall's four zones of personal space (1959, 1966)*

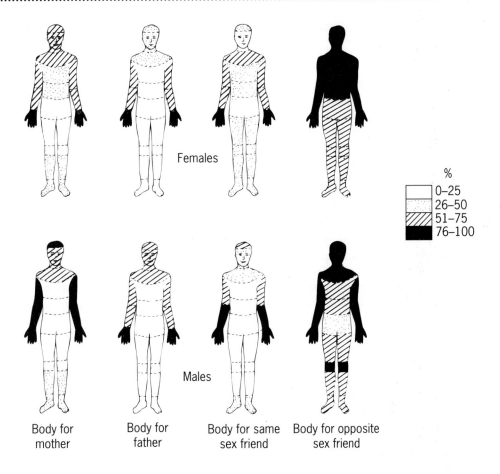

Females

%
0–25
26–50
51–75
76–100

Males

Body for mother Body for father Body for same sex friend Body for opposite sex friend

FIGURE 16.4 *Male and female 'bodies for others', as experienced through the amount of touching received from others (Jourard, 1966)*

touching. South Americans and Arabs have been called 'contact cultures', while the Scots and Swedes have been called 'non-contact cultures'. The caste system in India represents a highly formalized, institutionalized set of proxemic rules.

Proximity is just one of several kinds of social act which make up the degree of intimacy which exists between two people. According to Argyle and Dean (1965), we all have a tendency to approach others and seek their company and at the same time we have an opposing tendency to avoid others and to remain separate and independent. The balance between these two opposing tendencies is 'negotiated', non-verbally, in each social situation in which we find ourselves, so that we try to find a mutually acceptable *level of intimacy,* that is, a level with which we feel comfortable. Clearly, the people in the studies by Sommer *et al.* felt uncomfortable when the experimenter sat himself right next to them – he was making the situation too intimate for them.

Individual differences have also been found to interact with proxemic rules. Hildreth *et al.* (1971, cited in Nicholson, 1977) found that criminals convicted of violent crimes were much more sensitive to physical closeness with others than non-violent criminals. Nicholson (1977) refers to the concept of a *body-buffer zone,* defined as the point at which a person begins to feel uncomfortable when approached by another (a concept similar to Hall's personal space). Violent criminals compared with non-criminals (and schizophrenics compared with other kinds of psychiatric patients) tend to have larger body-buffer zones, that is, they more easily begin to feel uneasy when others walk towards them.

Successful friendships may require an initial establishment of boundary understandings, i.e. in Hall's terms, strangers must be 'invited' into our intimate zone and not 'trespass' from an initial casual personal distance, while in Argyle and Dean's *equilibrium model* of intimacy, strangers who make a situation uncomfortably intimate too soon are unlikely to become friends.

● Similarity: do birds of a feather flock together?

We have already discussed this to some extent in relation to stage theories of relationship development and we have also seen that in the first year of his 1961 study, Newcomb found that similarity of attitudes, values and beliefs was the major determinant of liking among room-mates, at least when they were randomly assigned

Most studies suggest that the critical similarities are those to do with beliefs, attitudes and values. In an early study of Bennington College, an expensive American East Coast women's university college with a liberal tradition amongst the teaching staff and senior students, Newcomb (1943) found that many students coming from conservative backgrounds adopted liberal attitudes in order to gain the liking and acceptance of classmates. Griffitt and Veitch (1974) paid 13 males to spend ten days in a fall-out shelter. Those with similar attitudes and opinions liked each other most by the end of the study, particularly if they agreed on highly salient issues.

Why should similarity be so important? According to Rubin (1973), similarity is rewarding because:

● Agreement may provide a basis for engaging in joint activities.
● A person who agrees with us helps to increase our confidence in our own opinions, which enhances our self-esteem. According to Duck (1992), the validation that friends give us is experienced as evidence of the accuracy of our personal constructs (see Chapter 29).
● Most people are vain enough to believe that anyone who shares their views must be a sensitive and praiseworthy individual.
● People who agree about things that matter to them generally find it easier to communicate.
● We may assume that people with similar attitudes to ourselves will like us and so we like them in turn (this is called *reciprocal liking*; see page 391).

Although similarity of attitudes and values may be most important, these are often not immediately evident when we first meet someone – our attitudes, etc. tend to emerge as our relationships develop and so perhaps it is more appropriate to discuss this aspect of similarity in relation to the maintenance of relationships. One of the most immediately apparent things about a person is their physical attractiveness, which has been studied as an influence on attraction in its own right, as well as one aspect of similarity.

● Physical attractiveness

We noted in Chapter 15 that an important kind of implicit personality theory is the *attractiveness stereotype,* i.e. the belief that attractive-looking people also have more attractive personalities. Dion *et al.* (1972) found that photographs of attractive people, compared with unattractive people, are consistently credited with more desirable qualities – sexually warm and responsive, kind, strong, outgoing, nurturant, sensitive, interesting, poised, sociable, exciting dates, better character, happily married, socially and professionally successful and enjoying more fulfilling lives. (An interesting exception to this general pattern was that there was no difference between attractive and unattractive photographs regarding judgements of expected competence as a parent.)

Given the importance of stereotypes in influencing our first impressions of other people, it would seem that attractive people have a 'head start' in this early phase of relationship development. However, Dermer and Thiel (1975) found that extremely attractive women were judged (by female participants) to be egotistic, vain, materialistic, snobbish and less likely to be successfully married. This suggests that it is not always to our advantage to be seen as highly attractive and one situation where this may apply is where a criminal's good looks played a part in the crime. For example, if a woman is standing trial for fraud, accused of having charmed a man into giving her money for some non-existent cause, she is more likely to be found guilty if she is very attractive. In attribution theory terms, her good looks may make the jury more likely to make a correspondent inference (see Chapter 15) .

Similarly, adults (including parents) may treat children differently according to their physical appeal (quite unconsciously, of course). Adults may also expect that good-looking children will be better behaved than less attractive ones; when the former do behave badly, they may have their behaviour excused by adults making situational, as opposed to dispositional, attributions. Dion (1972) used photographs of seven-year-old children plus accounts of their misbehaviour (either mild or severe) and found that adult participants were more likely to attribute antisocial tendencies (i.e. to make a dispositional attribution) to the unattractive children, if the misbehaviour was serious.

Dion and Dion (1995) observe that stereotyping based on facial attractiveness appears at least as early as six years old; they also suggest that it might be linked to the just world hypothesis, such that there is a positive bias towards 'winners', equivalent to 'blaming the victim' (see Chapter 15).

Who is attractive? The importance of culture and gender

FIGURE 16.5 *The current definition of an 'ideal figure'*

Different cultures have different criteria of what constitutes physical beauty: chipped teeth, body scars, artificially elongated heads and bound feet have all been regarded as beautiful and in Western culture, definitions of beauty change over time, as in the 'ideal' figure for women. (See the section on body image and eating disorders in Chapter 6.) Traditionally, facial beauty has been generally regarded as more important in women than men, while in men it is their stature, particularly height, plus a muscular body and (currently) firm, rounded buttocks which influence how attractive they are judged to be.

What the above examples demonstrate is that it is impossible to define 'attractive' objectively. However, it seems that 'average' (e.g. not too big or too small) may be one way of moving away from a purely subjective definition, as shown in a study by Langlois and Roggman (1990, cited by Myers, 1994). They digitized the faces of up to 32 college students and used a computer to average them. Students judged the composite faces as more appealing than 96 percent of the individual faces

According to Brehm (1992), in the context of personal ads and commercial dating services, the primary 'resource' (or reward) offered by females seeking a male partner is (still) physical attractiveness, which matches what men are actually seeking from a female partner. But this appears to be an almost universal male preference, not one confined to Western culture (Buss, 1989); we shall return to this finding when we discuss complementary needs later in the chapter.

Physical attractiveness and the matching hypothesis

According to Roger Brown (1986), *social exchange theory* (which we shall discuss in the next section) clearly predicts that individuals who are willing to become romantically involved with each other will be fairly closely matched in their ability to reward one another (the *matching hypothesis/phenomenon* or *similarity hypothesis*).

Ideally, we would all have the most beautiful/handsome, charming, generous and in other ways desirable partners because we are all perfectly selfish (according to the theory). But, of course, this is impossible and so we have to find a compromise solution. The best general bargain that can be struck is a *value-match*, i.e. a subjective belief that our partner is the most rewarding we could realistically hope to find.

One of the major ways in which the matching hypothesis has been empirically investigated is the 'computer dance'. Male and female students buy tickets for a 'Welcome Week' computer dance (at a university at the start of an academic year) and complete detailed questionnaires about themselves which the computer, supposedly, uses in order to make ideal matches. The students are rated (without their knowledge) for physical attractiveness and are assigned a partner purely randomly. The first such study was carried out by Walster (Hatfield) *et al.* (1966), involving 752 freshers at the University of Minnesota: physical attractiveness proved to be the single most important factor that determined liking, for both males and females, and the best single predictor of how likely it was that a woman would be asked out again – regardless of the man's.

While this is strong evidence for the impact of physical appeal in initial attraction, this finding is contrary to what the matching hypothesis predicts, i.e. if we settle for a value-match, then only those men who happened to be matched (by chance) with a date whose attractiveness level closely resembled their own would have asked for a second date. In the study, students were already assured of a date before interacting with their partners, with whom they spent a whole 2½ hours before being asked to express their liking for them (during the intermission). According to Berscheid et al. (1971), a more valid test of the matching hypothesis would be where one has to choose a dating partner. So later computer-dance studies have asked participants to specify in advance what kind of partners they would like. Here, people rated as high, low or of average attractiveness tended to ask for dates of a corresponding level of attractiveness, thus supporting the matching hypothesis (Dion and Berscheid, 1970; Berscheid and Walster, 1974).

The implication is, then, that the kind of partner we would be satisfied with is one whom we feel will not reject us, rather than one whom we positively desire. However, Brown (1986) disagrees. He says the matching phenomenon results from a well-learned sense of what is 'fitting' rather than a fear of being rebuffed, i.e. we learn to adjust our expectations of rewards in line with what we believe we have to offer others.

Despite the more recent support for the matching hypothesis, computer dance studies still only test interpersonal attraction based on, at most, a few hours interaction. Berscheid and Walster (1974) claim that 'Couples who have formed viable affectional relationships should appear to outside observers to be of approximately equal levels of physical attractiveness'. They cite a study by Silverman (1971) of 'fait accompli' matching (i.e. matching which has already occurred). Couples were observed in naturalistic dating settings – bars, social events, theatre lobbies. Two males and two females formed the observer team. The observed couples were predominantly 18–22 years old and unmarried. Each observer independently rated the dating partner of the opposite sex on a five-point scale. There was an extremely high degree of similarity between the attractiveness of the couple members. Also, the more similar their attractiveness, the happier they seemed to be with each other (as reflected by the degree of intimacy, e.g. holding hands) – 60 percent of highly similar, 46 percent of moderately similar and 22 percent of least similar couples appeared happy.

However, the observers saw both dating partners together, so a 'halo' emanating from one dating partner might have influenced the observers' rating of the other partner (Berscheid and Walster, 1974), i.e. the expectation of similarity could have biased the observers' ratings towards a more similar rating of the one member based on the rating of the other. Also, it is possible that the degree of matching could have occurred by chance, since 85 percent of the couples were not separated by more than one scale point and no couple by more than 2.5 points: the scale did not permit discriminations to be made between individuals because there were only five points on the scale! A study which gets around the problem of seeing the couple actually together is Murstein's (1972), which is described in Box 16.4.

Price and Vandenberg (1979) went a step or two further by studying married couples aged between 28 and 60. Allowing for age effects on attractiveness (e.g. young people tend to rate older people as less attractive, everything else being equal), they concluded that 'The matching phenomenon [of physical attraction levels between marriage partners] is stable within and across generations'.

BOX 16.4	Key study: testing the matching hypothesis by matching the photographs

Murstein (1972) took photographs, first of 99 engaged or steady couples, then a separate sample of 98. Judges rated the photographs for physical attractiveness on a five-point scale without knowing who the couples were ('who belonged to whom'). The couples had to rate their own and their partner's physical attractiveness. Judges' ratings strongly supported the matching hypothesis – partners received very similar ratings and these were significantly more alike than the same ratings given to 'random couples' (i.e. the actual couples randomly sorted into couples to form a control group). How partners rated themselves (self-concept for attractiveness) was significantly more similar than self-ratings for random couples, thus also supporting the matching hypothesis, but partners' ratings of each other did not prove significant. These results apply (more or less equally) to both samples. Murstein (1972) concluded that 'Individuals with equal market value for physical attractiveness are more likely to associate in an intimate relationship such as premarital engagement than individuals with disparate values'.

● Reciprocal liking: Liking others because they like us

It is certainly very flattering when someone pays us compliments and generally seems to like us; perhaps it also puts us under a certain obligation to reward the other person in turn (see Chapter 15). According to Aronson's *reward-cost principle* (e.g. 1980), we are most attracted to a person who makes entirely positive comments about us over a number of occasions and least attracted to one who makes entirely negative comments about us. This in itself may seem rather obvious. More interesting, however, is Aronson and Linder's *gain-loss theory* (1965), according to which someone who starts off by disliking us and then comes to like us will be liked more than someone who likes us from the start. Equally, someone who begins by liking us and then adopts a negative attitude towards us will be disliked more than someone who dislikes us from the start.

HOW RELATIONSHIPS ARE MAINTAINED: WHAT KEEPS PEOPLE TOGETHER?

If you are asked what all the important relationships in your life have in common, you may say something to the effect that they are all rewarding, i.e. they provide you with security, happiness, contentment, fun and so on and (if you are honest) you will probably also acknowledge that they can be complex, demanding and, at times, even painful. If all relationships involve both positive and negative, desirable and undesirable aspects, what determines our continued involvement with them (if we have that kind of choice) ?

Social exchange theory (Thibaut and Kelley, 1959; Blau, 1964; Homans, 1974; Berscheid and Walster, 1978) provides a general framework for analysing all kinds of relationships, both intimate and non-intimate, and represents an extension of reward theory that we discussed earlier in the chapter. According to Homans (1974), we view our feelings for others in terms of profits, i.e. the amount of reward obtained from the relationship minus the cost – the greater the reward and lower the cost, the greater the profit and the greater the attraction.

According to Blau (1964), our interactions are 'expensive'; they take time, energy and commitment and may involve unpleasant emotions and experiences, so what we get in return must outweigh what we put in. Similarly, Berscheid and Walster (1978) argue that in any social interaction, people exchange rewards (e.g. information, affection, status, money, skills and attention) and the degree of attraction or liking will reflect how each person evaluates the rewards they have received relative to those they have given.

But is it appropriate to think of relationships with other people in these economic, even capitalistic terms? Social exchange theory sees people as fundamentally selfish and human relationships as based primarily on self-interest. Are we really like this? As with many attempts in psychology to explain behaviour, exchange theory offers a metaphor for human relationships and it should not be taken too literally. However, according to Rubin (1973), although we like to believe that the joy of giving is as important as the desire to receive, we must face up to the fact that our attitudes toward other people are determined to a large extent by our assessments of the rewards they hold for us.

At the same time, Rubin believes that social exchange theory is not an adequate, complete account: 'Human beings are sometimes altruistic in the fullest sense of the word. They make sacrifices for the sake of others without any consideration of the rewards they will obtain from them in return'. And altruism is most often and most clearly seen in close interpersonal relationships (see Chapter 17).

Indeed, some psychologists make the distinction between 'true' love and friendship, which are altruistic, and less admirable forms which are based on considerations of exchange (Brown, 1986). Erich Fromm, for instance, in *The Art of Loving* (1962), defines true love as giving, as opposed to the false love of the 'marketing character' which depends upon expecting to have the favours returned. Some empirical support for this distinction comes from a study by Mills and Clark (1980, Cited in Brown, 1986) who identified two kinds of intimate relationship:

1 the *communal* couple, in which each partner gives out of concern for the other;
2 the *exchange* couple, in which each keeps mental records of who is 'ahead' and who is 'behind'.

Social exchange theory is really a special case of a more general account of human relationships, namely *equity theory*. The major extra 'ingredient' which is added to reward, cost and profit is investment: 'A person's investments are not just financial; they are anything at all that is believed to entitle him to his rewards, costs and profits. An investment is any factor to be weighed in determining fair profits or losses' (Brown, 1986). Equity does not mean equality, but a constant ratio of rewards to costs or profit to investment, i.e. equity theory involves a concern with fairness in some way. Brown (1986) believes that equity theory captures a profoundly important generalization about social life, namely that 'Humans in society always acquiesce in some forms of inequality, always find it fair that rewards (or benefits or goods) should be unequally distributed among individuals'.

So it is *changes* in the ratio of what you put in and what you get out of a relationship which are likely to cause changes in how you feel about the relationship, rather than the initial ratio. You may believe it is fair and just that you give more than you get, but if you start giving very much more than you did and receiving proportionately less, then you are likely to become dissatisfied.

Some versions of social exchange theory do in fact take account of factors other than the simple and crude profit motives of social interactors. For example, Thibaut and Kelley (1959) introduced the two important concepts of *comparison level* (CL) and *comparison level for alternatives* (CL alt). CL is basically the average level of rewards and costs that one is used to in relationships; it is the basic level that is expected to be obtained in any future relationship. So, if my obtained reward:cost ratio in a current relationship falls below my CL, I shall be dissatisfied with the relationship, whereas if it is above

my CL, I shall be satisfied. CL alt is basically my expectation about the reward:cost ratio which could be obtained in other alternative relationships. If the ratio in any current relationship exceeds my CL alt, then I am doing better in it than I could do elsewhere, so I should feel satisfied and will probably choose to remain in it. This implies that the endurance of a relationship (as far as one partner is concerned) could be due to the qualities of the (other) partner and the relationship or to the negative and unattractive features of the perceived alternatives or to the perceived costs of leaving (Duck, 1988).

However, this still portrays people as fundamentally selfish and some psychologists (Walster *et al.*, 1978; Duck, 1988) prefer to see relationships as being maintained by an equitable distribution of rewards and costs for both partners – social actors are seen as being concerned with the equity of outcomes both for themselves and their partners. According to Murstein *et al.* (1977), concern with either exchange or equity is negatively correlated with marital adjustment; in both cases, people in close relationships don't think in terms of rewards or costs at all – until they start to feel dissatisfied (Argyle, 1987). Similarly, Murstein and MacDonald (1983) claim that, although the principles of exchange and equity play a significant role in intimate relationships, a great conscious concern with 'getting a fair deal', especially in the short term, makes compatibility very hard to achieve, both in

---

BOX 16.5   Critical discussion: do our genes dictate what we want in a mate?

Buss (e.g. 1988) argues that the chances of reproductive success should be increased for men who mate with younger, healthy adult females, as opposed to older, unhealthy ones. Fertility is a function of the mother's age and health, which also affects pregnancy and her ability to care for her child. Since reproductive success is crucial to the survival of a species, natural selection should favour those mating patterns that promote the survival of offspring. Men often have to rely on a woman's physical appearance in order to estimate her age and health, with younger, healthier women being perceived as more attractive. For women, mate selection depends on their need for a provider to take care of them during pregnancy and nursing; men seen as powerful and controlling resources that contribute to the mother and child's welfare will be seen as especially attractive.

Whatever virtues this sociobiological argument may or may not have, it seems to take male-female relationships out of any cultural or historical context; the very use of the term 'mate selection' seems to capture this. Perhaps women have been forced to obtain desirable resources through men because they have been denied direct access to political and economic power; traditionally, a woman has been regarded as the property of a man, whereby her beauty increases his status and respect in the eyes of others (Sigall and Landy, 1973). What Buss conveniently seems to overlook is that in his (1989) cross-cultural study, 'kind' and 'intelligent' were universally ranked as more important than 'physically attractive' or 'good earning power' by *both* men and women! And how can Buss's argument account for homosexual relationships, which clearly do not contribute to the survival of the species, despite being subject to many of the same sociopsychological influences involved in heterosexual relationships (Brehm, 1992)? Homosexual relationships are discussed separately in Box 16.6.

friendship and, especially, in marriage. (This corresponds to the 'exchange' couple, described by Mills and Clark (1980); see above.)

● Complementarity: do opposites attract?

According to Winch (1958), happy marriages are often based on each partner's ability to fulfil the needs of the other (*complementarity of needs*). For example, a domineering person could more easily satisfy a partner who needs to be dominated than one who is equally domineering and Winch found some empirical support for this view. However, although some complementarity may evolve as a relationship develops, people seem, if anything, slightly more likely to marry those whose needs and personalities are similar (the matching phenomenon) (e.g. Berscheid and Walster, 1978). According to Buss (1985, cited in Myers, 1994), 'The tendency of opposites to marry, or mate ... has never been reliably demonstrated, with the single exception of sex'.

Despite the lack of evidence for complementarity of personality, what about complementarity in resources (Brehm, 1992)? As we noted earlier, men seem to give a universally higher priority to 'good looks' in their female partners than do women in their male partners, while the situation is reversed when it comes to 'good financial prospect' and 'good earning capacity'. Based on a study of 37 cultures (including Nigeria, South Africa, Japan, Estonia, Zambia, Columbia, Poland, Germany, Spain, France, China, Palestinian Arabs, Italy and The Netherlands)

involving over 10,000 people, Buss (1989) concluded that these sex differences '... appear to be deeply rooted in the evolutionary history of our species ...'. This sociobiological explanation of male/female preferences is discussed further in Box 16.5.

● Compatibility

Complementarity, as far as it exists, can be seen as a component of *compatibility*, but as we have seen above, evidence for similarity is far greater and it plays a much larger part in keeping couples together. Hill *et al.* (1976) studied 231 steadily dating couples over a two-year period, at the end of which 103 couples had broken up (45 percent). The surviving couples tended to be more alike in terms of age, intelligence, educational and career plans, as well as physical attractiveness, while those who split up often mentioned differences in interests, background, sexual attitudes and ideas about marriage.

Could the splitting up or staying together have been predicted from the initial questionnaire data? It seems they could to a significant degree: about 80 percent of the couples who described themselves as being 'in love' at the start stayed together, compared with 56 percent who did not. Of couples in which both members initially reported being equally involved in the relationship, only 23 percent broke up, but where one member was much more involved than the other, 54 percent did so. The latter type is a highly unstable couple in which the one who is more involved (putting more in but getting less in return)

BOX 16.6	Topical discussion: how similar are homosexual and heterosexual relationships?

According to Kitzinger and Coyle (1995), since the mid-1970s psychological research on homosexuality has moved away from a 'pathology' model towards one comprising four overlapping themes :

1 Belief in a basic, underlying similarity between homosexual and heterosexual people.
2 Rejection of the concept of homosexuality as a central organizing principle of the personality in favour of recognizing the diversity and variety of homosexuals as individuals.
3 Asserting that homosexuality is as natural, normal and healthy as heterosexuality.
4 Denial of the notion that homosexuals pose any threat to children, the nuclear family or the future of society as we know it.

As far as the first of these is concerned, Bee (1994) concludes that '... gay partnerships are far more like heterosexual relationships than they are different. The urge to form a single, central, committed attachment in early adult life is present in all of us, gay or straight'. However, Kitzinger and Coyle point out some important differences, including the following:

● Although many homosexual partners do live together, cohabitation seems to be far less common for them than for straight couples.
● Compared with straight couples, sexual exclusivity (only having one sexual partner) seems to be rather less common in lesbian and much less common in gay male relationships.
● Most lesbians and gay men actively reject traditional husband-wife or masculine-feminine roles as a model for enduring relationships, preferring equality in status and power (Peplau, 1991).

may feel dependent and exploited, while the one who is less involved (putting less in but getting more in return) may feel restless and guilty (which implies some sense of fairness).

Marital satisfaction is another way of looking at compatibility. In a review of a number of studies that looked at marital satisfaction and communication, Duck (1992) found that happy couples give more positive and consistent non-verbal cues than unhappy couples, express more agreement and approval for the other's ideas and suggestions, talk more about their relationship and are more willing to compromise on difficult decisions. Lauer and Lauer (1985, cited in Baron and Byrne, 1991) asked several hundred couples married for at least 15 years why they thought their marriage had lasted: they stressed friendship (e.g. 'My spouse is my best friend'), commitment ('Marriage is a long-term commitment'), similarity ('We agree on how and how often to show affection') and positive affect ('We laugh together') as the basic elements in an enduring relationship. These findings could be seen as implying a successful transition from passionate to companionate love.

RELATIONSHIP BREAKDOWN AND DISSOLUTION: WHY AND HOW DO RELATIONSHIPS GO WRONG?

Duck (1988, 1992) identifies a number of antecedents of divorce and marital unhappiness, i.e. factors making it more likely that the marriage will end in one or both of these:

● Marriages where the partners are younger than usual tend to be more unstable. (This can be related to Erikson's concept of intimacy whereby teenage marriages, for example, involve individuals who have not yet fully established their sense of identity and so are not ready for a commitment to one particular person; see Chapter 21.) Also, there seems to be a link between the rising divorce rate and the increasing trend towards early parenthood which allows young couples little time to adjust to the new relationships and responsibilities of marriage; then financial and housing problems are added with the arrival of a baby (Kellmer Pringle, 1986).
● Marriages between couples from lower socioeconomic groups and lower educational levels tend to

be more unstable. (These are also the couples which tend to have their children very early in marriage.)
● Marriages between partners from different demographic backgrounds (race, religion, etc.) also tend to be more unstable. (This can be related to Kerckhoff and Davis's filter model; see above.)
● Marriages between people who have experienced parental divorce as children or who have had a greater number of sexual partners than average before marriage tend to be more unstable.

Clearly, these factors on their own cannot adequately explain why marriage break-up occurs, since only a certain proportion of marriages involving young, lower class individuals or those from different cultural backgrounds, etc. actually end in divorce. Conversely, many divorces will involve couples who do not fit any of these descriptions. So what other factors may be involved?

According to Brehm (1992), there are two broad types of cause:

1 *structural* (specifically, gender, duration of the relationship, the presence of children and role strain created by competing demands of work and family);
2 *conflict resolution*.

● Gender differences

Men and women seem to differ in their perception of problems in a relationship. In general, women report more problems and there is some evidence that the degree of female dissatisfaction is a better predictor than male unhappiness of whether the relationship will end. Does this mean that women are more sensitive to relationship problems than men? An alternative explanation is that men and women come into relationships with different expectations and hopes and that those of men are generally fulfiled to a greater extent than those of women.

Consistent with this possibility is evidence of gender differences in the specific type of problems that are reported. For example, although divorcing men and women are equally likely to cite communication problems as a cause of their splitting up, women stress basic unhappiness and incompatibility more than men do. Again, men seem particularly upset by 'sexual withholding' by a female partner, while women are distressed by a male partner's sexual aggression.

● Duration of relationships and the passage of time

The longer partners have known each other before marriage, the more likely they are to be satisfied in the marriage and the less likely they are to divorce. However, couples who have cohabited before marriage report fewer barriers to ending the marriage and the longer a relationship lasts, the more people blame their partners for negative events. Two major views of changes in marital satisfaction over time are the linear and the curvilinear

According to the *linear model* (e.g. Pineo, 1961, cited in Brehm, 1992), there is an inevitable fading of the romantic 'high' of courtship before marriage. Also, people marry because they have achieved a 'good fit' with their partner; any changes that occur in either partner will reduce their compatibility. For example, if one partner becomes more self-confident (ironically, through the support gained from the relationship), there may be increased conflict between two 'equals' competing for superiority. The linear model is represented in Figure 16.6.

The *curvilinear model* (e.g. Burr, 1970, cited in Brehm, 1992) is represented in Figure 16.7. The middle portion of the curve seems to be closely associated with the arrival and departure of children: marital satisfaction declines as children are born and grow up, then increases again as they mature and leave home. While it is generally agreed that there is a decline in satisfaction during the early years, whether there is an actual increase or just a levelling off after that remains a matter of debate. According to Gilford and Bengtson (1979, cited in Brehm, 1992),

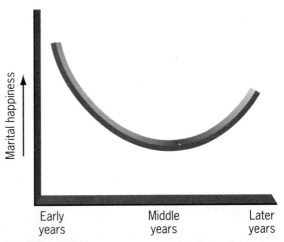

FIGURE 16.7 *A curvilinear life cycle. (Based on Brehm, 1992)*

it is an oversimplification to talk about 'marital satisfaction' ; instead, we should look at two life cycles: (i) the pattern of positive rewards; (ii) the pattern of negative costs. This produces the following:

● early years: very high rewards and very high costs;
● middle years: decline in both;
● later years: continuing decline in costs and increase in rewards.

(Marriage, divorce, and parenthood, including conflicts between work and family responsibilities, will be discussed further in Chapter 24.)

● Conflict resolution

According to Duck (1988), some kind and degree of conflict is probably inevitable in all relationships and the process of resolving conflicts is often a positive one, promoting growth of the relationship.The important question, therefore, is not whether there is conflict but how conflict is handled. However, if conflicts recur, indicating a lack of agreement and an inability to resolve the underlying source of conflict, the partners may come to doubt each other as reasonable persons, leading to a 'digging in of the heels', a disaffection with each other and, ultimately, a 'strong falling out'.

According to Bradbury and Fincham (1990), happy and unhappy couples resolve conflict in typically different ways, which can be understood as different attributional patterns (see Chapter 15): happy couples use a *relationship-enhancing* pattern, while unhappy couples use a *distress-maintaining* pattern (see Figure 16.8).

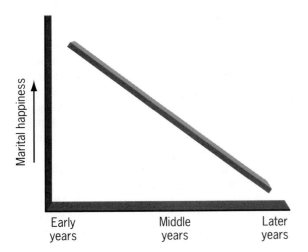

FIGURE 16.6 *A linear life cycle. (Based on Brehm, 1992)*

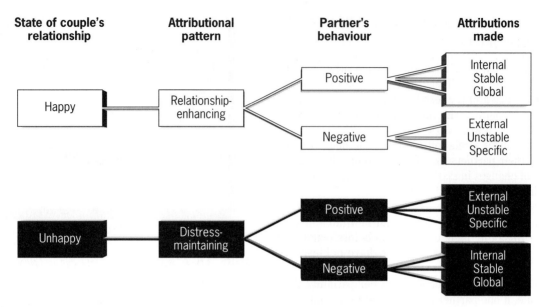

FIGURE 16.8 *Attributions made by happy and unhappy couples according to Bradbury and Fincham (1990).* *(From Brehm S.S. (1992)* Intimate Relationships *(2nd ed.) New York, McGraw-Hill)*

● Rule-breaking and deception

The rules in question are 'relationship rules', the expectations which each partner has of the other. For example, Argyle and Henderson (1984) and Argyle *et al.* (1985) identified a number of rules thought to apply to all or most relationships, such as 'Should respect the other's privacy', 'Should not discuss what is said in confidence', 'Should be emotionally supportive'. There are additional rules for particular types of relationship. Relationships fall into clusters, with similar rules applying within a cluster; for example, one cluster includes spouse, siblings and close friends and another includes doctor, teacher and boss. Deception represents probably the most important rule that should not be broken ; although what counts as deception will depend on the nature of the relationship, if you cannot trust your friend or partner, the relationship is almost certainly doomed.

● The process of relationship dissolution

Relationships are highly complex and this is as true of relationship break-up as it is of their formation and maintenance. It applies to the break-up of friendships and sexual relationships and not just marriages, particularly if the relationship is a long-term one that has embraced many parts of the person's emotional, communicative, leisure and everyday life (Duck, 1988).

The most useful way of looking at the break-up of a relationship is to regard it as a process, not an event, which takes place over a period of time. As Duck (1988) says, '... Breaking up not only is hard to do, but also involves a lot of separate elements that make up the whole rotten experience'.

Lee (1984) proposed five stages of premarital romantic break-ups: (i) *dissatisfaction* (D) is discovered; then (ii) it is *exposed* (E); (iii) there is some *negotiation* (N) about it; (iv) attempts are made to *resolve* (R) the problem; and finally (v) the relationship is *terminated* (T). He surveyed 112 such break-ups – (E) and (N) tend to be experienced as the most intense, dramatic, exhausting and negative aspects of the whole experience. Those who skipped these stages (by just walking out) felt less intimate with their ex-partner, even while the relationship had been going satisfactorily. Where the whole passage from (D) to (T) is particularly prolonged, people reported feeling more attracted to their ex-partner and experienced greatest loneliness and fear during the break-up.

Duck (1982) proposed a model of relationship dissolution, which is summarized in Table 16.3.

Each person needs to emerge from the relationship that has 'died' with an intact reputation for relationship reliability. 'Dressing the grave' involves 'erecting a tablet' which provides a credible, socially acceptable account of the life and death of the relationship. While helping to save face, it also serves to keep alive some memories and to 'justify' the original commitment to the ex-partner:

> ... Such stories are an integral and important part of the psychology of ending relationships ... By helping the person to get over the break-up they are immensely significant in preparing the person for future relationships as well as helping them out of old ones. (Duck, 1988)

Breakdown – Dissatisfaction with relationship

Threshold : *'I can't stand this any more'*

INTRAPSYCHIC PHASE
Personal focus on partner's behaviour
Assess adequacy of partner's role performance
Depict and evaluate negative aspects of being in the relationship
Consider costs of withdrawal
Assess positive aspects of alternative relationships
Face 'express/repress dilemma'

Threshold : *'I'd be justified in withdrawing'*

DYADIC PHASE
Face 'confrontation/avoidance dilemma'
Confront partner
Negotiate in 'Our Relationship Talks'
Attempt repair and reconciliation?
Assess joint costs of withdrawal or reduced intimacy

Threshold : *'I mean it'*

SOCIAL PHASE
Negotiate post dissolution state with partner
Initiate gossip/discussion in social network
Create publicly negotiable face-saving/blame-placing stories and accounts
Consider and face up to implied social network effect, if any
Call in intervention team

Threshold : *'It's now inevitable'*

GRAVE-DRESSING PHASE
'Getting over' activity
Retrospective; reformative postmortem attribution
Public distribution of own version of break-up story

TABLE 16.3 *A sketch of the main phases of dissolving personal relationships. (Based on Duck, 1982, from Duck, 1988)*

CHAPTER SUMMARY

- Intimate relationships with relatives and romantic partners represent crucial factors in determining people's general happiness.
- The study of relationships traditionally concentrated on interpersonal attraction, i.e. how relationships get started; more recently, psychologists have investigated the maintenance and break-up/dissolution of relationships.
- The need for affiliation represents a precondition for attraction and can be related to the need for social comparison. Both are enhanced under conditions of increased anxiety.
- Loving is qualitatively different from liking and involves attachment, caring and intimacy. An important distinction is between passionate/romantic and companionate love. Sternberg's 'triangular' model also distinguishes fatuous and consummate love.
- According to Kerckhoff and Davis's 'filter model', relationships pass through a series of filters, from similarity of sociological variables, through agreement on basic values, to complementarity of emotional needs. This and other 'stage' theories are not strongly supported by empirical evidence, but it is generally agreed that relationships do change and develop.
- A general theoretical framework for explaining initial attraction is that the presence of others must be rewarding; this can help to explain the impact of proximity, exposure and familiarity, physical attractiveness, similarity and reciprocal liking.
- Proximity is a prerequisite for attraction; it provides increased opportunity for interaction, which increases familiarity through the mere exposure effect.
- However, people can become too familiar by invading our personal space and this can make them immediately dislikable. Proxemic rules dictate the appropriate distance to keep between ourselves and another person in different situations.
- There are important cultural and individual differences regarding proxemic rules and proximity is just one of several social acts constituting a mutually acceptable level of intimacy.
- Similarity of attitudes and values is a powerful influence on attraction, but this usually only emerges as the relationship develops. However, physical attractiveness is immediately apparent.

- The impact of physical attractiveness is partly due to the attractiveness stereotype, which can produce different attributions for the socially unacceptable behaviour of attractive and unattractive people.
- There are important cultural differences in what counts as physical beauty and most cultures have different criteria for what is attractive in men and women. There is also a universal tendency for men to regard physical attractiveness as more important than women.
- Physical attractiveness has been studied extensively in relation to the matching hypothesis/phenomenon. Early studies used the 'computer dance' method; when people are asked to specify how attractive they would like their date to be before being assigned a partner, they usually respond in line with their own level of attractiveness.
- Computer dance studies involve the creation of artificial couples, but the matching hypothesis has also received support from studies of real couples, despite certain methodological problems.
- According to the gain-loss theory, reciprocal liking is increased if someone who initially dislikes us then comes to like us.
- Social exchange theory is an extension of reward theory and is a major explanation of all kinds of relationships, both intimate and non-intimate. It sees people as fundamentally selfish, concerned only with getting as much out of a relationship as possible.
- Critics of the theory argue that humans are capable of altruism as well as selfishness, as demonstrated by the distinction between communal and exchange couples.
- Social exchange theory is a special case of equity theory, which refers to a constant ratio of rewards to costs and involves the concept of fairness; changes in the reward-cost ratio are likely to cause dissatisfaction with the relationship.
- Thibaut and Kelley's version of social exchange theory is less crude than other versions; it includes the concepts of comparison level and comparison level for alternatives, which put the present relationship in the context of past and future relationships.
- There is little evidence for the complementarity of psychological needs but there is more support for complementarity in resources, in particular, women's ability to reward men with physical beauty and men's ability to reward women with financial/material security.

- Sociobiologists argue that the universal male preference for physical attractiveness and female preference for financial security are genetically determined, part of the evolutionary history of the human species. But this ignores cultural and historical factors depriving women of power.
- Complementarity and similarity are both determinants of compatibility, which can be studied in terms of marital satisfaction.
- Despite a move away from a pathological model of homosexuality, psychologists make assumptions about the basic similarity between homosexual and heterosexual relationships that may not be valid.
- Marriages are more unstable if the couple are teenagers, from lower socioeconomic groups and different demographic backgrounds, whose parents were divorced, who have been sexually active prior to marriage and who experience early parenthood.
- There are important gender differences regarding the perception of relationship problems, possibly reflecting differences in expectations.
- While it is widely agreed that marital satisfaction decreases quite early on, the linear model sees this as a fairly steady decline over the course of married life, whereas the curvilinear model sees the decrease being followed by an increase, associated with the children leaving home.
- Conflict is an inherent part of all relationships; what is crucial is how constructively it is resolved. Happy couples tend to deal with conflict in a relationship-enhancing way, while unhappy couples use a distress-maintaining pattern of conflict resolution.
- Rule-breaking is a major cause of relationship breakdown, especially deception.
- Relationship breakdown is a process, involving a number of stages or phases. According to Duck's model, relationships that have ended need to be 'buried' in a way that enables ex-partners to move on and develop new relationships.

GLOSSARY

Affiliation The basic human need for the company of other human beings (affiliative needs).

Body-buffer zone Similar to 'personal space', the point at which a person begins to feel uncomfortable when approached by another person.

Companionate love The affection we feel for those, both very close friends and romantic partners, with whom our lives are interlinked. Qualitatively different from passionate love.

Comparison level The average level of rewards and costs one is used to based on past relationships.

Comparison level for alternatives Our expectation about the reward-cost ratio that we could obtain from future relationships.

Complementarity of needs The ability of each partner to fulfil the emotional needs of the other.

Contact cultures Cultures in which there is a high degree of face-to-face orientation, physical closeness and bodily contact, even between strangers (e.g. South Americans and Arabs). Contrasted with non-contact cultures (e.g. Scots and Swedes).

Distress-maintaining pattern Pattern of attribution used by unhappily married couples to resolve conflict.

Equity theory Theory of social relationships, according to which relationships are attractive if they are seen as fair, i.e. they involve a constant ratio of rewards to costs/profit to investment.

Field of availables The range of other people who are realistically available for us to meet (as opposed to those who are only theoretically available). Correspond to our sociological/demographic membership groups.

Gain-loss theory The belief that if someone starts off by disliking us and then switches to liking us, we will like the person more than if they like us from the start; the reverse is true if the person starts off by liking us.

Matching hypothesis Derived from social exchange theory, the prediction that individuals who are willing to become romantically involved will be closely matched in their ability to reward each other. Tested by measuring similarity on characteristics including physical attractiveness, values and attitudes.

Mere exposure effect The process in which the more often we are exposed to a stimulus (person, object, etc.), the more familiar it becomes and the more we like it.

Passionate love A state of intense physiological arousal accompanied by longing for the company of and a wish to become absorbed in the loved one. Contrasted with companionate love. Also called *romantic love*.

Personal space The distance that is maintained between two people, sometimes compared to an invisible bubble that we carry around with us.

Proxemic rules The rules governing personal space: the amount of physical distance that is appropriate in everyday interactions and the kinds of situations in which closeness/distance is appropriate.

Relationship-enhancing pattern Pattern of attribution used by happily married couples to resolve conflict.

Reward theory A theory of relationships, according to which the more rewards someone provides for us, the more we will find him/her attractive.

Reward-cost principle The tendency to be most attracted to someone who makes entirely positive comments about us and least attracted to someone who makes entirely negative comments about us.

Social exchange theory Theory of social relationships (both intimate and non-intimate), according to which we are most attracted to relationships which provide us with maximum profit. A special form of equity theory.

Value-match A subjective belief that our partner is the most rewarding we could realistically hope to find . Relates to the matching hypothesis.

FURTHER READING

Brehm, S. S. (1992) *Intimate Relationships*, 2nd edn. New York: McGraw-Hill. An excellent source of research and theory, written by one of the authorities in the field.

Kitzinger, C. and Coyle, A .(1995) Lesbian and gay couples: speaking of difference. *The Psychologist*, 8 (2), 64–9. An extremely interesting article which compares and contrasts straight and gay relationships and contains much useful material about the more traditional, heterosexual research.

17 PROSOCIAL AND ANTISOCIAL BEHAVIOUR

INTRODUCTION AND OVERVIEW

What do human kidney donors and rabbits banging their feet on the ground have in common? Very little, you may say. However, on closer inspection, they both seem to be doing something that has the effect of benefiting another – person or rabbit. This is self-evident in the case of one person donating a kidney to another; in the case of the rabbit, banging the feet is used as a warning to other rabbits of some threat or danger These are both examples of helping behaviour, a form of prosocial behaviour; they are also often cited as cases of altruism, i.e. helping that is performed in order to benefit others and with no expectation of benefit or gain for the benefactor. However, are people – let alone rabbits – capable of acting in a purely unselfish way?

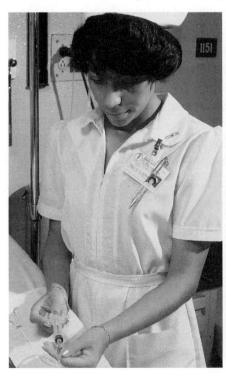

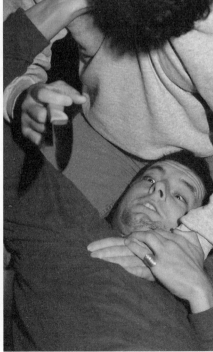

According to *universal egoism* (the view that people are fundamentally selfish), which has been and still is the dominant ethos in social science (including psychology), altruism is an impossibility (Dovidio, 1995). Similarly, sociobiologists consider that acts of apparent altruism turn out to be acts of selfishness in disguise. However, as we saw in Chapter 16, and as we shall see further below, not everyone shares this view; much depends on exactly how these terms are defined.

The question of whether people are by nature selfless or selfish has been debated by philosophers for centuries. William McDougall, in his *An Introduction to Social Psychology* (1908), the first social psychology textbook, proposed that 'sympathetic instincts' are the basis for altruistic activity – and are stronger in women. However, only about 20 studies of helping were published before 1962. The murder of Kitty Genovese in 1964 provided the stimulus for research into helping and altruism, pioneered by Latané and Darley in the late 1960s, which in turn opened the floodgates (Schroeder *et al.*, 1995).

Although only one form of antisocial behaviour (behaviour that has the effect of harming another person), *aggression* has been of interest to psychologists for much of its history. McDougall traced aggressive behaviour to the aggressive instinct (see Chapter 5) and Freud saw the aggressive instinct as a powerful driving force within the personality as a whole (see Chapters 21 and 29). Like Freud, Konrad Lorenz, the famous ethologist, saw aggressive energy as building up over time, reflecting the instinctive nature of aggression. Other explanations of aggression have combined elements of instinct theories with those of learning theory, such as the *frustration-aggression hypothesis,* and Berkowitz's modifications of this, such as the *aggressive–cue theory*. Bandura's study of aggression in relation to *observational learning* stimulated research into the effects of violence in the media in general and, more recently, the specific effects of so-called 'video nasties' in the context of tragedies such as the murder of James Bulger. Perhaps the 'purest' social psychological account of aggression is the theory of *deindividuation.*

BOX 17.1	The case of Kitty Genovese (From *New York Times*, March 27th, 1964)

37 Who Saw Murder Didn't Call the Police

Apathy at Stabbing of Queens Woman Shocks Inspector

By Martin Gansberg

For more than half an hour 38 respectable, law-abiding citizens in Queens watched a killer stalk and stab a woman in three separate attacks in Kew Gardens.

Twice the sound of their voices and the sudden glow of their bedroom lights interrupted him and frightened him off. Each time he returned, sought her out and stabbed her again. Not one person telephoned the police during the assault; one witness called after the woman was dead.

That was two weeks ago today. But Assistant Chief Inspector Frederick M. Lussen, in charge of the borough's detectives and a veteran of 25 years of homicide investigations, is still shocked.

He can give a matter-of-fact recitation of many murders. But the Kew Gardens slaying baffles him – not because it is a murder, but because the 'good people' failed to call the police.

'As we have reconstructed the crime,' he said, 'the assailant had three chances to kill this woman during a 35-minute period. He returned twice to complete the job. If we had been called when he first attacked, the woman might not be dead now.'

'He Stabbed Me!'

She got as far as a street light in front of a bookstore before the man grabbed her. She screamed. Lights went on in the 10-storey apartment house at 82–67 Austin Street, which faces the bookstore. Windows slid open and voices punctured the early-morning stillness.

Miss Genovese screamed: 'Oh, my God, he stabbed me! Please help me! Please help me!'

From one of the upper windows in the apartment house, a man called down: 'Let that girl alone!'

The assailant looked up at him, shrugged and walked down Austin Street toward a white sedan parked a short distance away. Miss Genovese struggled to her feet.

Lights went out. The killer returned to Miss Genovese, now trying to make her way around the side of the building by the parking lot to get to her apartment. The assailant grabbed her again.

'I'm dying!' she shrieked.

'I'm dying!'

A City Bus Passed

Windows were opened again, and lights went on in many apartments. The assailant got into his car and drove away. Miss Genovese staggered to her feet. A city bus, Q-10, the Lefferts Boulevard line to Kennedy International Airport, passed. It was 3.35 a.m.

The assailant returned. By then, Miss Genovese had crawled to the back of the building where the freshly painted brown doors to the apartment house held out hope of safety. The killer tried the first door; she wasn't there. At the second door, 82–62 Austin Street, he saw her slumped on the floor at the foot of the stairs. He stabbed her a third time – fatally.

It was 3.50 by the time the police received their first call, from a man who was a neighbour of Miss Genovese. In two minutes they were at the scene. The neighbour, a 70-year-old woman and another woman were the only persons on the street. Nobody else came forward.

The man explained that he had called the police after much deliberation. He had phoned a friend in Nassau County for advice and then he had crossed the roof of the elderly woman to get her to make the call.

'I didn't want to get involved,' he sheepishly told police.

Suspect is Arrested

Six days later, the police arrested Winston Moseley, a 29-year-old business-machine operator, and charged him with the homicide. Mosely had no previous record. He is married, has two children and owns a home at 133–19 Sutter Avenue, South Ozone Park, Queens. On Wednesday, a court committed him to Kings County Hospital for psychiatric observation.

The police stressed how simple it would have been to have gotten in touch with them. 'A phone call,' said one of the detectives, 'would have done it.'

Today witnesses from the neighbourhood, which is made up of one-family homes in the $35,000 to $60,000 range with the exception of the two apartment houses near the railroad station, find it difficult to explain why they didn't call the police.

Lieut. Bernard Jacobs, who handled the investigation by the detectives, said:

'It is one of the better neighbourhoods. There are few reports of crimes. You only get the usual complaints about boys playing or garbage cans being turned over.'

The police said most persons had told them they had been afraid to call, but had given meaningless answers when asked what they had feared.

'We can understand the reticence of people to become involved in an area of violence,' Lieutenant Jacobs said, 'but where they are in their homes, near phones, why should they be afraid to call the police?'

He said that his men were able to piece together what happened – and capture the suspect – because the residents furnished all the information when detectives rang doorbells during the days following the slaying.

'But why didn't someone call us that night?' he asked unbelievingly.

Witnesses – some of them unable to believe what they had allowed to happen – told a reporter why.

A housewife, knowingly if quite casual, said, 'We thought it was a lovers' quarrel'. A husband and wife both said, 'Frankly, we were afraid'. They seemed aware of the fact that events might have been different. A distraught woman, wiping her hands in her apron, said, 'I didn't want my husband to get involved'.

One couple, now willing to talk about that night, said they heard the first screams. The husband looked thoughtfully at the bookstore where the killer first grabbed Miss Genovese.

'We went to the window to see what was happening,' he said, 'but the light from our bedroom made it difficult to see the street'. The wife, still apprehensive, added: 'I put out the light and we were able to see better'.

Asked why they hadn't called the police, she shrugged and replied, 'I don't know'.

HELPING AND BYSTANDER INTERVENTION: APATHY OR ALTRUISM?

As we noted above, the two pioneers in this area, Latané and Darley, were 'inspired' by a real event involving a murder victim, Kitty Genovese (Box 17.1).

The Kitty murder, together with findings from their laboratory studies, led Latané and Darley to introduce the concept of the *unresponsive bystander* (or *bystander apathy*) to denote people's typically uncaring attitude towards others in need of their help (the title of their 1970 book was *The Unresponsive Bystander: Why Doesn't He Help?*). Before we look at the research in detail, one major conclusion should be mentioned: while the American media thought it remarkable that out of 38 witnesses not a single one did anything to help, Latané and Darley believed that it was precisely *because* there were so many that Kitty Genovese was not helped. So how does the presence of others contribute to the intervention (or lack of it) of a particular individual in an emergency and what other influences are involved?

● Latané and Darley's decision model of bystander intervention

According to Latané and Darley's *decision model*, before someone helps another, that person must:

● notice that something is wrong;
● define it as an emergency;
● decide whether to take personal responsibility;
● decide what kind of help to give;
● implement the decision to intervene.

This represents a logical sequence of steps, such that a negative response at any one step means that the bystander will not intervene and the victim will not receive help (at least not from *that* bystander). This model is summarized in Figure 17.1.

Apart from the Kitty murder, what evidence did Latané and Darley base their model on?

Defining the situation: when is an emergency not an emergency?

In one of the first of the bystander experiments (Latané and Darley, 1968), participants were shown into a room in order to complete some questionnaires. In one condition they were alone, in another condition there were two others present. After a while, steam (resembling smoke) began to pour through a vent in the wall. Latané and Darley wanted to see how quickly they would react. If no one reacted within six minutes, the experiment was terminated, by which time the steam was so thick it was difficult to see the questionnaires. Seventy-five percent of those working alone reported the smoke, half of them within two minutes, while 62 percent of those in the three-person groups carried on working for the full six minutes. In only one three-person group was it reported within the first four minutes.

Latané and Rodin (1969) obtained similar results when participants heard the female experimenter in an adjoining room fall, cry out and moan. They were much faster to react when alone than when others were present. In postexperimental interviews, each participant reported feeling very hesitant about showing anxiety, so they looked to others for signs of anxiety, but since everyone was trying to appear calm, these signs were not found and each person defined the situation as 'safe'. This is called *pluralistic ignorance*. In a variation of Latané and Rodin's experiment, 70 percent of participants on their own responded within 65 seconds; two friends together responded within a similar time; two strangers together were less likely to react at all, but more slowly if they did; and if someone was paired with a

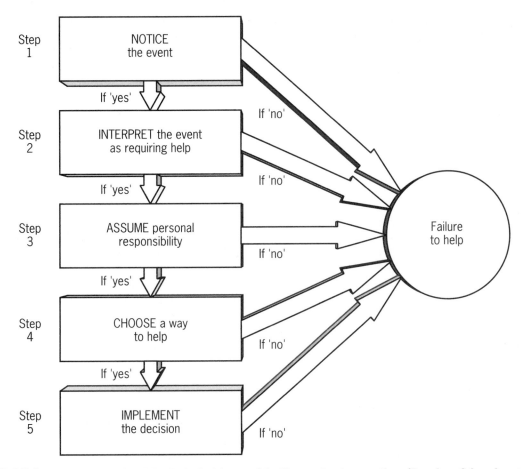

FIGURE 17.1 *Steps in Latané and Darley's decision model of bystander intervention. (Based on Schroeder et al. (1995)* The Psychology of Helping and Altruism. *New York, McGraw-Hill)*

confederate who had been instructed not to intervene at all, that person showed the least and slowest reaction of all.

Can pluralistic ignorance account for the inaction of the witnesses to Kitty Genovese's murder? There seems little doubt that they realized at the time what was going on. Although one woman claimed that she thought it was a 'lover's quarrel', most claimed they were afraid to intervene (they did not deny that help was needed!) and Kitty's second lot of screams (if not the first) must have made the nature of the situation quite unambiguous.

Genuine ambiguity may sometimes account for lack of intervention, as in situations of domestic violence. According to Shotland and Straw (1976), we would be much more likely to help a victim if we believed he/she did not know the attacker than if we believed a relationship existed between the two. Male participants were shown a staged fight between a man and a woman. In one condition the woman

screamed 'I don't even know you', while in another, she screamed 'I don't even know why I married you!' Three times as many men intervened in the first condition than in the second condition.

Accepting responsibility: when does an emergency oblige me to intervene?

A well-known study by Darley and Latané (1968) is described in Box 17.2.

How can we explain such findings? While pluralistic ignorance may make it less likely that we will define a situation as an emergency in the first place ('if the others look calm and aren't rushing around there can't be anything wrong'), this hardly applies in a situation where participants are in cubicles and are in contact with other supposed participants via an intercom system. The best explanation is *diffusion of responsibility*, i.e. the denial of personal responsibility and the belief that someone else will

BOX 17.2

Key study: the stresses of urban living or, let someone else take the strain

Darley and Latané (1968) examined how the presumed presence of others can influence intervention even when information about the seriousness of the emergency cannot possibly be conveyed through their actions or words, but where it is clear that an emergency is happening.

College students were recruited to discuss the problems of living in a high-pressure urban environment. Instead of face-to-face discussion, they communicated via an intercom system ('so as to avoid any embarrassment'). Each participant would talk for two minutes and then each would comment on what the others had said. The 'other' participants were, in fact, tape recordings. Early in the discussion the victim (a confederate) casually mentioned that he had epilepsy and that the anxiety and stress of urban living made him prone to seizures. Later, he became increasingly loud and incoherent, choking, gasping and crying out before lapsing into silence.

Darley and Latané were interested in the percentage of participants who responded within five minutes (by coming out of the small room to look for the victim). Of those who believed they were the only other participant, 85 percent intervened; of those who believed there were two others (three altogether), 62 percent intervened; and of those who believed there were five others (six altogether), only 31 percent intervened. The most responsive group was also the fastest to respond. These findings were confirmed by Latané et al. (1981).

be increased. However, if you believe you are the one who is best equipped to help, the presence of others will have relatively little effect on your behaviour. For example, if a swimmer is in trouble, we will usually let the lifeguard go to the rescue and even if we were the only other person at the pool, we would be extremely unlikely to dive in if we couldn't swim ourselves! But if we are an excellent swimmer and are trained in life-saving skills, we would be much more likely to help even if others were present (Baron and Byrne, 1991).

Piliavin et al. (1981) pointed out what they believe is a confusion between *diffusion*, which occurs when responsibility is accepted by the participant but shared by all the witnesses, and *dissolution*, which occurs when the behaviour of other witnesses cannot be observed and the participant 'rationalizes' that someone else must have already intervened. However, whichever label is applied, all the studies confirm the original finding that the presence of others inhibits an individual from intervening (Pilivian et al., 1981) and yet there are limits to diffusion of responsibility. Piliavin et al. (1969) found that help was offered on crowded subways in New York as frequently as on relatively empty ones (see below). As Brown (1985) suggests, perhaps it is more difficult not to help in a face-to-face situation and in an enclosed space.

According to Schroeder et al. (1995), we should not take the inhibiting effects of other people as indicating bystander apathy, as Latané and Darley did. People may be truly concerned about the victim's welfare but sincerely believe that someone else is more likely – or better qualified in some way – to help. For example, Bickman (1971) replicated the 'seizure' experiment but manipulated the participants' belief about proximity to the victim. Those who believed that the other person was as close to the victim as they were (in the same building) and equally capable of helping showed diffusion of responsibility (i.e. they were less likely to help than those who believed they were alone). However, when they believed that the other person was in another building and so unable to help, they helped as much as those who believed they were alone.

probably do what is necessary: the more bystanders that are present (or believed to be present), the lower the probability that any one of them will accept responsibility. This is more likely to happen when the victim is remote, e.g. can only be 'heard' from some other room in the building (as in the seizure experiment). Kitty Genovese could both be heard and seen (by those who made the effort to look out of their windows) and the second lot of screams must have made it obvious that no one had gone for help after the first lot!

Related to diffusion of responsibility, and something which may interact with it, is the *competence* of the bystander to intervene and offer appropriate help (as perceived by the bystander). In the presence of others, one or more of whom you believe is better equipped to offer help, diffusion of responsibility will

● Evaluation of the decision model

According to Schroeder et al. (1995), the Latané and Darley model provides a valuable framework for understanding bystander intervention. Although originally designed to explain helping in emergency situations, aspects of the model have been successfully applied to many other situations, ranging from preventing someone from drinking and driving, to deciding to donate a kidney to a relative.

However, it does not provide a complete picture. For example, it does not tell us very much about why 'no' decisions are taken at any of the five steps, particularly after the situation has been defined as an emergency and personal responsibility has been accepted, i.e. there is a great deal that takes place between steps 3 and 5. Also, as Dovidio (1995) points out, the model focuses on why people *don't* help others – we also need to ask why they *do*.

A major alternative to the decision model is the *arousal: cost–reward model* (Piliavin *et al.*, 1969, 1981; Dovidio *et al.*, 1991). This is a kind of 'fine-tuning' of some of the processes outlined in the decision model, which identifies a number of critical situational and bystander variables which can help predict how likely intervention is to take place under any particular set of circumstances. The model was first introduced by Piliavin *et al.* (1969)

as a 'heuristic device' in attempting to account for the results of the New York subway experiment (see Gross, 1994) and was subsequently revised and expanded to cover both emergency and non-emergency helping (Piliavin *et al.*, 1981).

The model identifies two conceptually distinct but functionally interdependent influences on helping:

1 *Arousal* in response to the need or distress of others is an emotional response which is the basic motivational construct; when attributed to the distress of the victim, it is experienced as unpleasant and the bystander is motivated to reduce it. But this represents only 'half' the story.
2 *cost–reward* involves cognitive processes by which bystanders assess and weigh up the anticipated costs and rewards associated with both helping and not helping. (This corresponds to the *exchange theory* explanation of intimate relationships that we discussed in Chapter 16; the arousal component is what distinguishes the arousal: cost–reward model from exchange theory.)

Costs of helping/not helping and likely outcome	Examples
1 Costs of helping are *low*	You're not likely to be injured yourself; the victim is only shocked.
Costs of not helping are *high* *Likelihood of intervention is VERY HIGH – and direct.*	You will feel guilty; others will blame you.
2 Costs of helping are *high*	You don't like the sight of blood, you're unsure what to do.
Costs of not helping are *high* *Likelihood of intervention is FAIRLY HIGH – but indirect*	It is an emergency – the victim could die. Call for an ambulance/police or ask another bystander to assist.
OR *redefine the situation* (see text)	Ignore the victim and/or leave the scene.
3 Costs of helping are *high*	'This drunk could turn violent or throw up over me' 'Who would blame me for not helping?'
Costs of not helping are *low* *Likelihood of intervention is VERY LOW*	Bystander may well turn away, walk away , change seats, etc.
4 Costs of helping are *low*	'It wouldn't hurt me to help this blind man cross the street'
Costs of not helping are low	He seems capable of looking after himself and there's very little traffic on the road'
Likelihood of intervention is FAIRLY HIGH	Bystanders will vary, according to individual differences and how they perceive the norms that operate in the particular situation.

TABLE 17.1 *The costs of helping and not helping in emergencies/non-emergencies and the likelihood and type of intervention, as predicted by the arousal: cost–reward model. (Based on Piliavin et al., 1969, 1981)*

According to the model, '... People are aroused by the distress of others and exhibit emotionally empathic reactions to the problems and crises of others ... also ... the severity and clarity of another person's emergency and the relationship to the victim systematically influence arousal ...' (Dovidio *et al.*, 1991). While arousal and helping are often only correlated, the model clearly sees arousal as *causing* the helping; in a major review of the evidence, Dovidio *et al.* (1991) conclude that research demonstrates that emotional reactions to others' distress do indeed play an important causal role in motivating helping. The model proposes that bystanders will choose the response that most rapidly and completely reduces the arousal, incurring as few costs as possible: the emotional component provides the motivation to do *something,* while the cognitive component determines what the most efficient or effective response will be.

● The cost–reward analysis

Most research has probably concentrated on this part of the model and within this component the focus has been on the relative costs of helping and not helping. The *costs of helping* include lost time, effort, possible physical danger, embarrassment, disruption of ongoing activities and psychological aversion (as in the case of a victim who is bleeding, or drunk). *The rewards of helping* include fame, gratitude from the victim and relatives, the intrinsic pleasure and self-satisfaction derived from the act of helping, the avoidance of guilt (for not helping) and even money. The *costs of not helping* include guilt, blame from others and cognitive and/or emotional discomfort associated with knowing that another person is suffering.

We should note that what is high cost for one person may be low cost for another (and vice-versa) and this may differ, for the same person, from one situation to another (and even from one occasion to another, depending on mood, for example).

Table 17.1 shows how the model predicts different outcomes based on all combinations of high and low costs for helping and not helping.

Table 17.1 is based largely on the model as it had been proposed prior to 1981 and reflects considerable empirical support from studies carried out before that date, as reviewed in Piliavin *et al.*'s (1981) *Emergency Intervention.* In that book, and again in Dovidio *et al.* (1991), the model was elaborated by considering the influence of a new range of variables, such as bystander personality and mood,

the clarity of the emergency, characteristics of the victim, the relationship between the victim and potential helpers and attributions made by potential helpers of the victim's deservingness. Many of these variables interact and they contribute to (a) how aroused the bystander is, and (b) the perceived costs and rewards for direct intervention; we shall discuss some of these interactions below when we consider particular variables.

A distinction is made between two kinds of costs associated with not helping, namely *personal costs* (e.g. self-blame, public disapproval) and *empathy costs* (e.g. knowing that the victim continues to suffer).'... In general ... costs for *not* helping affect intervention primarily when the costs for helping are low' (Dovidio *et al.*, 1991). Although indirect helping becomes more likely as the costs for helping increase, as in serious emergencies (Piliavin *et al.*, 1981), overall it is relatively infrequent, perhaps because it is difficult for bystanders to pull themselves away from such involving situations in order to seek other people to assist (Schroeder *et al.*, 1995). The most common (and positively effective) way of resolving the high-cost-for-helping/high-cost-for-not -helping dilemma (see section 2 of Table 17.1) is *cognitive reinterpretation*, which can take one of three forms:

1 redefining the situation as one *not* requiring help (i.e. a non-emergency);
2 diffusing responsibility;
3 denigrating (blaming) the victim. (This can be seen as another application of the 'just world' hypothesis–see Chapter 15.)

These all have the effect of reducing the perceived costs of not helping. (They could also be seen as *rationalizations* which reduce the bystander's cognitive dissonance; see Chapter 18.) Schroeder *et al.* (1995) stress that cognitive reinterpretation does *not* mean that bystanders are uncaring (or 'apathetic'); on the contrary, it is the fact that they do care that creates the dilemma in the first place.

Let us take a look at some specific factors that the model predicts will influence the costs of helping/not helping and, hence, that will affect the likelihood of bystander intervention.

The cost of time

The importance of loss of time as a motive for not helping was shown in a content analysis of answers given in response to five written traffic accident scenarios (Bierhoff *et al.*, 1987). We are often in a hurry

| BOX 17.3 | Key study: if you need help, make sure you don't get in the way of a late Samaritan |

Darley and Batson (1973) carried out a study with students at a theological seminary. They were instructed to present a talk in a nearby building; for half of them, the talk was to be on the Good Samaritan, for the other half, it was to be about jobs most enjoyed by seminary students. Each student was then told: (i) he was ahead of schedule and had plenty of time (to get to the other building); (ii) he was right on schedule, or (iii) he was late. On the way to give their speech, all the students passed a man slumped in a doorway, coughing and groaning (a confederate). Although the topic given for the talk had little effect on helping, time pressures did- the percentages offering help were 63, 45 and 10 for conditions (i), (ii)) and (iii), respectively.

Ironically, on several occasions, the 'late' students who were on their way to talk about the Good Samaritan literally stepped over the victim!

in many real-life situations and waiting can be very frustrating; hence the willingness to sacrifice time for a person in need can be seen as generous (time is money; Bierhoff and Klein, 1988). The most often mentioned motives for helping were enhancement of self-esteem and moral obligation; also quite common were empathy and reciprocity. Another relevant – and revealing – study is that of Darley and Batson (1973), summarized in Box 17.3.

This experiment shows that seemingly trivial variables can exert a profound effect on altruistic responses (Bierhoff and Klein, 1988). By contrast, Bierhoff (1983) asked students to volunteer for a psychology experiment. If they participated without payment, the money would be sent to children in need. They could choose up to 12 half-hour sessions and, on average, students volunteered for 3.71 sessions. What these results indicate is that the general level of helpfulness is higher than some pessimists might have assumed. The willingness to work two hours for people in need is a substantial contribution which should be taken as an indication that people tend to be altruistic in many situations (Bierhoff and Klein, 1988).

Different types of helping

Certain kinds of casual helping (McGuire, 1994, cited in Schroeder et al., 1995) or low-cost altruism

(Brown, 1986) seem to be fairly common, such as giving a stranger directions or telling them the time. Latané and Darley (1970) had psychology students approach a total of 1500 passers-by in New York to ask them such routine, low-cost favours; depending on the nature of the favour, between 34 and 85 percent of New Yorkers proved to be 'low-cost altruists'. However, most people refused to tell the student their name.

Clearly, not all helping is the same; generally, as the type of intervention that is required changes from casual helping through 'substantial personal helping' (e.g. helping someone move house) and 'emotional helping' (e.g. listening to a friend's personal problems) to 'emergency helping' (which is what is involved in most of the studies we have discussed so far), the costs of intervention increase – but so do the costs of not helping.

Helping different kinds of victim

| BOX 17.4 | Key study: good samaritanism – an underground phenomenon? |

Piliavin et al. (1969) had student experimenters pretend to collapse in subway train compartments – they fell to the floor and waited to see if they were helped. Sometimes they would be carrying a cane, sometimes they would wear a jacket which smelled very strongly of alcohol and would be carrying a bottle in a brown paperbag. As predicted, help was offered much less often in the 'drunk' condition than the 'lame' condition (20 percent compared with 90 percent within 70 seconds). In a second study, the person who 'collapsed' bit off a capsule of bloodlike dye and this trickled down his chin; the helping rate dropped from 90 percent to 60 percent. People were much more likely to get someone else to help, especially someone they thought would be more competent in an emergency (Piliavin and Piliavin, 1972).

One of the most famous of all bystander studies is the New York subway field experiment (Piliavin et al., 1969), which is described in Box 17.4.

Similarly, Piliavin et al. (1975) found that when the victim had an ugly facial birthmark, the rate of helping dropped to 61 percent. Other studies have reported that a stranded motorist who is dressed smartly and is well groomed is far more likely to receive help from passing motorists than one who is casually dressed and has long hair.

In general, it seems that the greater the victim's distress, injury or disfigurement, or the more disapproving we are of them (especially if we blame their plight on their undesirable behaviour – as in the case of drunk victims), the more likely we are to perceive them as being different from ourselves which, in turn, makes it less likely that we will offer them help. The psychological costs of helping someone perceived as being different from ourselves seem to be greater than the same help offered to someone perceived as being similar. On this basis, we would expect help to be offered less often to someone of a different racial group from the bystander; however, the evidence is not as clearcut as this. For example, in the New York subway experiment, there was no evidence of same-race helping when the victim was apparently ill, but when he appeared drunk, blacks were much more likely to help a black drunk and whites a white drunk.

This is related to what is called *aversive racism*, a moderate, subtle form of racist bias (e.g. Gaertner and Dovidio, 1986). Many whites who may truly believe that they are not prejudiced still harbour unconscious negative feelings. As a result of possessing both conscious, non-prejudiced convictions and unconscious, prejudiced feelings, aversive racists discriminate in certain situations but not others. Where the social norms for appropriate behaviour are clear and unambiguous (e.g. people who are ill should be helped), aversive racists will not discriminate; if they did behave in a discriminatory way, their self-concept

(as non-racists) would be threatened and this would mean that significant costs were incurred by not helping a victim on the grounds of race/ethnic group. However, when social norms are weak or ambiguous or where they can justify a negative response based on some factor other than race/ethnic group (e.g. drunks can turn nasty, so leave them alone), then discrimination will occur. A study which demonstrates aversive racism is described in Box 17.5.

Personality differences

People who are characteristically more sensitive to the needs of others might experience greater arousal in response to another's plight or experience this arousal more negatively or perceive greater costs for not helping. Helpers are generally more 'other-oriented' (versus 'self-oriented') than non-helpers. One particularly interesting study (Oliner and Oliner, 1988, cited in Dovidio *et al.*, 1991) compared 231 non-Jews who helped save Jews in Nazi Europe with 126 non-savers; the former had stronger beliefs in equality and showed greater empathy.

As Table 17.1 shows, individual differences will have their main impact when both the costs for helping and not helping are low and when the situation is ambiguous and 'psychologically weak' or less 'evocative'. But the more emergency-like the situation (and hence the more compelling and evocative it is), the less relevant person variables will be. Indeed, several studies have failed to find personality differences in helping in emergency situations (Dovidio *et al.*, 1991).

Gender differences

Women may experience greater empathy for others' needs than men and are more attentive to others' needs, which would predict greater helping by women. On the other hand, Eagly and Crowley (1986) reviewed 172 studies and found that men turn out to be significantly more helpful than women. How can we reconcile these two things? One answer is to do with traditional gender roles on the one hand and the kind of helping required in most experimental studies of bystander intervention on the other.

According to Eagly (1987), the female gender role involves *communal helping* – caring for others, providing friends with more personal favours, emotional support, counselling about personal problems, etc. than men. By contrast, the male gender role involves *agentic helping*, namely heroism and chivalry; thus they are more likely to help another when there is an audience present to witness the helping act or other potential witnesses are available. Most studies of

---

BOX 17.5 Key study: diffusion of responsibility as a 'cover' for racism

Gaertner and Dovidio (1977) used the cubicle and intercom procedure, as in the Darley and Latané (1968) experiment; see Box 17.2. White bystanders, who believed they were the only witness to an emergency and when appropriate behaviour was clearly defined, did not discriminate against a black victim; in fact, they were slightly more likely to help a black than a white victim (94 percent compared with 81 percent). But when they believed there were other bystanders, they helped a black victim about half as often as a white victim (38 and 75 percent respectively).

The opportunity to diffuse responsibility offered a non-race-related excuse to treat blacks differently, thereby allowing them to avoid recognizing racial bias as a factor (Schroeder *et al.*, 1995).

bystander intervention (at least those involving emergencies) seem to require agentic helping.

We-ness

This '... connotes a sense of connectedness or the categorization of another person as a member of one's own group ...' (Piliavin *et al.*, 1981). The closer the relationship to the person in need, the greater the initial arousal and costs for not helping, while the costs for helping will be lower.

● Evaluation of the arousal: cost–reward model–are we fundamentally selfish?

Why do we help others? This is the crucial question as far as altruism is concerned, because, as we saw at the beginning of the chapter, altruism is usually defined as helping that is motivated by the wish to benefit another person; so helping may be done for non-altruistic reasons (see Fig. 17.2). The question is: is helping *ever* motivated by a genuine wish to benefit others?

The arousal: cost–reward model (like exchange theory on which it is partly based) assumes an economic view of human behaviour – people are motivated to maximize rewards and minimize costs (Dovidio *et al.*, 1991). Faced with a potential helping situation, we weigh the probable costs and rewards of

alternative courses of action, then arrive at a decision that produces the best outcome – *for ourselves*. This is one form of universal egoism: everything we do, no matter how noble and beneficial to others, is really directed towards the ultimate goal of self-benefit. Those who advocate the *empathy-altruism hypothesis,* while not denying that much of what we do (including much that we do for others) is egoistic, claim that there is much more than just egoism; at least under some circumstances, we are capable of a qualitatively different form of motivation, with the ultimate goal of benefiting someone else. The egoism-altruism debate has been a central focus in research on helping behaviour over the past ten years or so (Dovidio *et al.*, 1995).

Empathic emotions include sympathy, compassion, tenderness and so on and are associated with empathic concern. These empathic emotions can and should be distinguished from the more self-oriented emotions of discomfort, anxiety and upset which are associated with personal distress. (This corresponds to the distinction made above between personal and empathic costs for not helping.) While personal distress produces an egoistic desire to reduce one's own distress, empathic concern produces an altruistic desire to reduce the other's distress. These are qualitatively different. These two views are summarized in Figure 17.2. According to Darley (1991), one of the

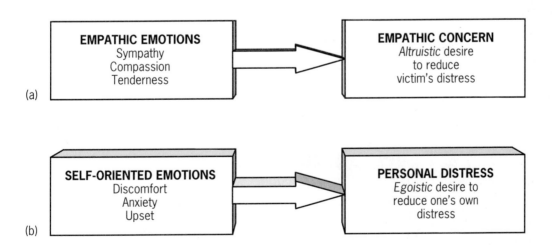

FIGURE 17.2 *Summary of (a) empathy – altruism hypothesis, and (b) universal egoism account of helping behaviour*

two pioneers of bystander intervention research, who is clearly a universal (or at least a Western capitalist) egoist:

> In the United States and perhaps in all advanced capitalistic societies, it is generally accepted that the true and basic motive for human action is self-interest. It is the primary motivation, and is the one from which other motives derive. Thus it is the only 'real' motivation, a fact that some celebrate and some bemoan but most accept ... To suggest that human actions could arise for other purposes is to court accusations of naïveté or insufficiently deep or realistic analysis.

If, according to universal egoists, all human acts of apparent altruism are really driven by self-interest, we might not be surprised to find a similar interpretation of the equivalent behaviours in non-human animals to which we shall now turn.

● Biological altruism – are rabbits that unselfish?

The animal kingdom abounds with examples of altruistic behaviours. For instance, certain small birds, such as robins, thrushes and titmice, warn others of the approaching threat from a hawk; they produce a distinctive thin reedy whistle which, because of its acoustic properties, makes the source very difficult to locate Nevertheless, by giving the

FIGURE 17.3 *Apparent altruism: Selfishness in disguise*

warning signal, an individual is drawing attention to itself in a dangerous situation; a more selfish act would be to keep quiet. Dolphins will often group round an injured individual to push it to the surface where it can breathe, rather than abandon it. In African wild dogs, the most social of all carnivorous mammals, when there are young in the pack most adults go off on a hunting expedition leaving the pups to be cared for by an adult, usually, but not always, the mother. When the hunters return, they regurgitate food for all the animals in the camp, which occasionally also includes sick and crippled individuals (Wilson, 1976).

Chimps display an interesting form of altruism when they temporarily abandon their normally vegetarian diet and indulge in meat eating. Adult chimps (usually the males) sometimes hunt and catch young monkeys and through a system of elaborate begging gestures, other troop members can share the catch. Curiously, they do not share in this way with leaves and fruit.

Perhaps most striking of all is the altruism of the social insects, which display '... altruistic suicide comparable with that sometimes displayed by man ...' (Wilson, 1976). A large percentage of ants, bees and wasps are ready to defend the nest with an insane charge against intruders, which may involve inevitable suicide through their heads being ripped off (as in the social stingless bees of the tropics), viscera torn out (honey bee workers) or their whole body being blasted by 'exploding glands' (an African termite).

And, of course, there is the altruistic rabbit.

● The paradox of altruism – aren't rabbits naturally selfish?

From the point of view of Darwin's theory of natural selection, it is truly remarkable for members of a species to help each other in these ways and quite the opposite of what could be considered 'natural'. According to Darwin (*The Origin of Species*, 1859), individual animals survive if they are able to adapt to their environment by virtue of physical (and behavioural) characteristics they possess and which are produced by random genetic variation or mutation. These better adapted individuals will, on average, have more offspring and, since those offspring will tend to carry the genes for those adaptive characteristics and behaviours, those genes and characteristics become more and more commonplace in the population. In this way, animal populations become differentiated and when different strains become so different that they can no longer interbreed (because their genotypes are too dissimilar), a new species has evolved. This process of natural selection therefore '... operates single-mindedly and relentlessly in favour of traits that improve the chances of survival and the number of offspring of the *individual* animal acting' (Brown, 1986).

But surely this is the complete reverse of what happens when an animal acts altruistically? Any animal which regularly acted in a way which benefited others by risking its own safety and survival would be drastically reducing its own chances of having any offspring at all – these individuals would not last long enough to reproduce successfully! Natural selection predicts that individuals will act to the benefit of themselves alone and not their group or species.

The 'paradox of altruism' refers to this apparent contradiction between Darwin's theory of natural selection and observed facts about altruistic behaviour in a number of species. Is it possible for an animal to behave altruistically *and* in accordance with the laws of natural selection at the same time? It seems so, because altruism turns out to be only apparent, i.e. altruistic behaviour is only selfish behaviour in disguise and, to understand this, we need to shift our attention away from the individual, self-contained, organism to the gene as the fundamental unit of evolution. This is the approach of sociobiology.

● The 'sociobiological solution': the selfish gene instead of the selfish rabbit

Sociobiology represents an extension of Darwin's evolutionary theory and was defined by Wilson (1975), one of its most prominent exponents, as 'the systematic study of the biological basis of all social behaviour'. It attempts to understand all types of social behaviour (including altruism, aggression, dominance and sexual behaviour) in evolutionary terms and this extends to human social behaviour.

Hinde (1982) believes that Wilson's 1975 book *Sociobiology: The New Synthesis* represents a landmark in biology, helping to bring evolutionary theory and behavioural biology together. However, Hinde is also very critical of Wilson's claims that, eventually, sociobiology would engulf ethology and comparative psychology and that behaviour should be reduced to neurophysiology and sensory physiology. As Hinde points out, altruism, for example, can by definition only apply to a dyad or larger group and not to an individual (see Chapter 32). So how does sociobiology resolve the 'paradox of altruism'?

The most general explanation of apparent altruism is Hamilton's theory of *kin selection* (1964). If we think of an individual animal as a set of genes rather than as a separate, 'bounded' organism, then it should be regarded as distributed across kin, i.e. it shares some proportion of its genes with relatives, according to how close the relationship is. It follows that it is possible for an individual to preserve its genes through its own self-sacrifice; if a mother dies in the course of saving her three offspring from a predator, she will have saved 1½ times her own genes (since each offspring inherits one half of its mother's genes). So, in terms of genes, an act of apparent altruism can turn out to be extremely selfish – surrendering your own life as an individual may reap a net profit as far as the survival of your genes in your relatives is concerned (see *The Selfish Gene* by Dawkins, 1976).

This means that individuals are selected to act not to maximize their own fitness (measured in terms of their own survival and reproduction) but to maximize their *inclusive fitness* (measured in terms of their own survival and reproduction *and* that of relatives; Hinde, 1982). So we seem to have resolved the paradox presented by examples of self-sacrifice; when a male lion defends his mate, a honey bee dies when stinging an enemy or a mother bird attracts a predator away from her offspring by feigning a broken wing, we can invoke the principle of inclusive fitness to explain apparently altruistic behaviour which is, fundamentally, selfish. The key is kinship, '... the sharing of common genes by related individuals ...'(Wilson, 1976). While all the examples of self-sacrifice we noted earlier amongst the social insects involve individuals which are either sterile or of very low reproductive potential, '... by their sacrifice they are (in terms of Darwinian fitness) increasing the reproductive chances of their fertile relatives thus ensuring that their (shared) genes are transmitted to future generations ... ' (Wilson, 1976).

However, we are left with another difficulty – what should we make of cases of altruism on the part of animals which are *not* related? Clearly, kin selection cannot accommodate such cases. Trivers (1971) has proposed the principle of *delayed reciprocal altruism*, by which animals will 'return favours' to other animals which have done them a good turn or a good turn is worthwhile because it is likely to be returned. For example, male baboons who do not have a female partner sometimes form a temporary alliance with another solitary male baboon: while the latter attacks a male who is 'courting' a female and so distracts the male's attention, the former mates with the female. Those males who often give this kind of help seem to be more likely to receive help in return, so that reciprocation occurs (Packer, 1977). According to Hinde (1982), other examples are best understood as individuals achieving better results if they make a joint effort (almost a case of 'two heads are better than one'). For instance, it pays two pied wagtails to defend a winter feeding territory, even though they are not related, because in this way then can achieve a higher feeding rate.

● Sociobiology and human nature

According to Wilson (1976), to understand behaviour we need to look at our evolutionary history, both in the recent period as hominids (i.e. the past 10 million years or so) and as part of the animal kingdom as a whole:

> ... the role of sociobiology with reference to human beings ... is to place the social sciences within a biological framework ... constructed from a synthesis of evolutionary studies, genetics, population biology, ecology, animal behaviour, psychology and anthropology ...

In the last chapter of the original *Sociobiology: The New Synthesis* (1975) and later in *On Human Nature* (1978), Wilson argues that all aspects of human culture and behaviour (like the behaviour of all animals) are coded in the genes and have been moulded by natural selection. Wilson acknowledges that about 100,000 years ago, cultural evolution became more important than biological evolution:

> ... As a result it seems clear that human social evolution is more cultural than genetic. Nevertheless, I consider that the underlying emotion of altruism, expressed powerfully in virtually all human societies, is the consequence of genetic endowment ... (Wilson, 1978)

The critical issue for sociobiology, according to Wilson, is the relative contributions to human behaviour of genetic endowment and environmental experience. Our overall social behaviour, he says, most closely resembles that of Old World monkeys and apes (our closest relatives biochemically and anatomically) – this is exactly what you would expect if behaviour is not based on experience alone but is a result of the interplay between experience and the pattern of genetic possibilities. It is the evolution of this pattern which sociobiology seeks to analyse.

He includes within the list of human patterns aggression (including greater aggressiveness of males and their dominance over females), the mother-child bond, language, the incest taboo, the sexual division of labour, altruism, allegiance, conformity, ethics, genocide, indoctrinability, love, spite, territoriality and xenophobia. These behaviours constitute a universal 'human nature' and are thus shared by all human societies; they are the expression of specific genetic structures and are, therefore, the result of evolutionary adaptation through natural selection. But are these claims justified?

- One criticism made of Wilson is that the image of society he depicts is today's European-American capitalist society, but clearly many societies do not fit this mould. Any exceptions to his claimed universal human behaviours he calls 'temporary' aberrations or deviations.
- Is there any direct evidence for the existence of specific genetic structures for the social behaviours listed above? According to Rose *et al.* (1984), up to the present time no one has ever been able to relate any aspect of human social behaviour to any particular gene or set of genes Thus, all statements about the genetic basis of human social traits are necessarily purely speculative. At the most, genes provide human beings with the capacity and inclinations to engage in prosocial actions (for example, through empathy and the communication of emotions), but do not directly cause prosocial behaviour (Schroeder *et al.*, 1995).
- A logical error made by sociobiologists is to treat categories like altruism, dominance, aggression, tribalism and territoriality as if they were natural objects with a concrete reality '... rather than realizing that these are historically and ideologically conditioned constructs ...' (Rose *et al.*, 1984). Mistaking abstract concepts for concrete objects is called *reification* (see Chapter 28 on Intelligence).
- According to Rose *et al.*, (1984), sociobiology is a reductionist, biologically determinist explanation of human existence. (See Chapter 32). Similarly:

> ... Genetics has as little to tell us about human societies as nuclear physics has to tell us about genetics. In the same way that we do not turn to physics to understand genetics, we should not turn to genetics in order to understand human history and culture. (Science as Ideology Group, 1976)

● Biological and psychological altruism

The sociobiological explanation of altruism fails to make the fundamental distinction between biological and psychological altruism (or what Sober, 1988, 1992, cited in Schroeder, 1995, calls *evolutionary* and *vernacular altruism* respectively); the former is displayed by birds, bees, ants, etc., the latter by higher mammals, in particular primates and especially human beings. We would not normally attribute the rabbit which warns its fellow-rabbits of an approaching hunter with altruistic motives or intentions (we would be guilty of anthropomorphism if we did); this is simply part of its biologically determined repertoire of behaviour conditions.

If psychological altruism is primarily a human form of helping, we might also want to ask if humans are also capable of biological altruism. In terms of kin selection, the situation is far more complex among humans than it is with other species. One reason for this, according to Brown (1986), is that the closeness of kinship is construed very differently from one society to another, so there is no simple correspondence between perceived and actual (genetic) kinship. If altruistic behaviour directly reflected actual kinship, rather than learned conceptions of kinship, it would be impossible for adoptive parents to give their adopted children the quality of care they do. As a species, much of our behaviour is altruistic and kin selection can only account for a small portion of our total behaviour-for-others; some principle such as delayed reciprocal altruism is also needed. However, we are still trying to impose a biological explanation on human social behaviour and this may not be the most appropriate way of trying to understand it; as Brown (1986) says, 'Human altruism goes beyond the confines of Darwinism because human evolution is not only biological in nature but also cultural, and, indeed, in recent times primarily cultural'.

Biological or evolutionary altruism may be triggered under very specific conditions, such as a highly arousing emergency situation; people often do display a rapid, almost unthinking, reflexive type of helping in extreme situations such as natural – and other kinds of – disasters. Piliavin *et al.* (1981) found considerable evidence of this impulsive helping in a review of a large number of experiments involving apparently real emergencies; it is generally unaffected by social context (such as diffusion of responsibility) or the potential costs of intervention. They proposed that clear, realistic situations, especially if they involve friends or acquaintances, produce high levels of arousal and focus attention on the victim's plight. As a result, the bystander is most concerned with:

the costs for the victim receiving no help. Personal costs of helping (to the bystander) become peripheral and are not attended to. Therefore, the impulsive helping behaviour that may appear irrational to an uninvolved observer ... may be a quite 'rational' response for a bystander attending primarily to the costs for the victim receiving no help. (Piliavin *et al.*, 1981)

This description comes very close to Sober's definition of evolutionary altruism (Schroeder *et al.*, 1995). Where very close friends or loved ones are the (potential) victims, impulsive helping is even more likely because of increased arousal and sensitivity to the other's distress (Clark *et al.*, 1989).

So both sophisticated reasoning (as in psychological altruism) and more primitive, non-cognitive, biological mechanisms may permit humans to perform a range of altruistic behaviours well beyond those of other species. According to Schroeder *et al.* (1995):

... We may well indeed be a uniquely compassionate and altruistic beast ... altruism may be both a behaviour that has evolved because it is vital to the survival of humanity and a behaviour that is learned and reinforced by most societies because it is vital to the survival of their culture.

AGGRESSION: WHAT IS IT?

We all seem to recognize aggression when we witness it, but defining it often proves much more difficult. When used as a noun, aggression usually conveys some behaviour which is intended to harm another (or at least which has this effect). Yet even this is too broad a definition, since self-defence and unprovoked attack may both involve similar 'amounts' and types of aggression but only the latter would normally be considered 'antisocial' (and the law also recognizes this distinction). When used as an adjective, aggression sometimes conveys an action carried out with energy and persistence (Lloyd *et al.*, 1984), something which may even be regarded as socially desirable.

According to Berkowitz (1993), aggression always refers to some kind of behaviour, either physical or symbolic, that is carried out with the intention of harming someone. He reserves the term *violence* for an extreme form of aggression, a deliberate attempt to do serious physical injury. Similarly, Moyer (1976) argues that aggression may be no more than verbal or symbolic but violence denotes 'a form of human aggression that involves inflicting physical damage on persons or property'.

A number of other important distinctions have been made; e.g. hostile aggression is aimed solely at hurting another (gratuitous or 'aggression for the sake of aggression', which would exclude self-defence) while *instrumental* aggression is a means to an end (and so would include self-defence; Buss, 1961; Feshbach, 1964). Humanistic psychologists (e.g. Maslow, 1968) have distinguished between *natural* or positive aggression, which is aimed largely at self-defence or combating prejudice and other social injustice, and *pathological* aggression or violence, which results when our inner nature has become twisted or frustrated.

● Theories of aggression

The study of aggression represents another example of the nature–nurture issue: the question being asked is whether aggression, as a characteristic of human beings, is biologically determined or the product of learning and environmental influences. Though in most respects very different, Lorenz's ethological theory and Freud's psychoanalytic theory both see aggression as instinctive, with aggressive energy needing to be released regularly if it is not to build up to dangerously high levels. By contrast, the *frustration-aggression hypothesis* sees both instinctive and learned reactions as involved, while the *social learning approach* and *deindividuation* emphasize cognitive aspects of learning from others' behaviour and the influence of others on individual behaviour respectively.

● The ethological approach

Ethologists consider aggression to be instinctive in all species and clearly important in the evolutionary development of the species, allowing individuals to adapt to their environment, survive in it and, hence, successfully reproduce. When space or food are scarce, many species limit their reproduction and survive by marking off living space which they defend against 'trespassers'; this is known as *territoriality.* Aggressiveness is clearly important in competing successfully for limited resources, in defending territory and for basic survival. Are there any human parallels?

According to Ardrey (1966), in *The Territorial Imperative,* people strive to acquire land and possessions, form strong attachments to them and are willing to defend (sometimes violently) what they believe is rightfully theirs. However, to infer from these superficial similarities that a fundamentally similar territorial instinct is at work is greatly to oversimplify human behaviour, which is vastly more complex than any comparable animal behaviour.

Probably the most famous and most comprehensive ethological account of human aggression is that of Konrad Lorenz in *On Aggression* (1966). He believes that it is legitimate to make direct comparisons between different species, although his theory of human aggression is based on the study of non-primates and mainly non-mammals, in particular fish and insects. He defines aggression as 'the fighting instinct in beast and man which is directed *against* members of the same species'. In animals it is basically constructive, but in humans it has become distorted. In what ways?

Probably the major difference between animal and human aggression is to do with *ritualization,* which refers to a way of discharging aggression in a fixed, stereotyped pattern whereby fights between members of the same species result in relatively little physical harm to either victor or vanquished but at the same time allow a victor to emerge. For instance, the fighting that takes place between stags is highly ritualized and the triumphant one is the male who 'makes his point' rather than the one who kills or incapacitates his opponent. In the same way, wolves will end their fight with the loser exposing its jugular vein – but its exposure is sufficient and no blood is spilled. (This is rather like two sword-fighters, one of whom loses his sword and faces his victor, inviting him to 'run me through' but, by this stage, the fight has already been won and lost.)

Sometimes, antagonists may approach each other in a threatening manner but not actually engage in combat – one will show *appeasement rituals* (or gestures) which prevent the other from engaging in actual conflict. For example, in one species of jackdaw, individuals live in close proximity and to prevent mutually destructive conflict, a very effective appeasement gesture has developed; the nape section at the bottom of the head is clearly marked off from the rest of the body by its plumage and colouring and when one bird 'offers' its nape to an aggressor, the latter will never attack, even if on the verge of doing so.

So through these various kinds of ritual, animals avoid destroying each other. But in human beings, according to Lorenz, although aggression remains basically adaptive, it is no longer under the control of rituals. This does not mean that human appeasement responses are not effective (e.g. smiling, cowering, cringing or begging for mercy) and, indeed, Lorenz believes that they are normally very effective. So what is it about human beings that makes us appear so aggressive? According to Lorenz, it is our technology. However naturally aggressive we are as a species compared with other species, our superior brains have enabled us to construct weapons which remove combat from the eye-to-eye situation and so the effectiveness of appeasement rituals is reduced. Indeed, the deadliest weapons (as measured by the number of victims who can be killed or injured at one time) are precisely those which can be used at the greatest distance from the intended victims (e.g. bombs and intercontinental nuclear missiles). According to Lea (1984), 'We have developed a technology which enables our intentions to override our instincts'.

An evaluation of Lorenz's theory of aggression

- In keeping with his belief that humans are naturally highly aggressive, Lorenz maintains that their 'natural condition' is that of 'warrior'. However, he seems to be in a minority of one in this respect. It is generally agreed that early man was not a warrior but a 'hunter-gatherer' (such as the present-day Eskimos, Pygmies of the Ituri forest, Aborigines, Kalahari Bushmen, the Punan of Borneo and so on), who live in small clans which hardly ever come into contact with other groups of people (Siann, 1985).
- Even without the most primitive weapons, other primates, including chimps, can and do kill each other. Goodall (1978) describes warfare between two colonies of chimps which ended in the killing of every male in one of the groups and Lea (1984) points out that infanticide is one of the more common kinds of unrestrained aggression among animals. He cites Hrdy's (1977) study of Hanuman langurs, an Indian monkey species, in which incoming males commonly kill infants despite the attempts of females to resist this male aggression. Infanticide is not confined to primates: male lions that succeed in taking over a 'pride' of females (so displacing other adult males) will often attack and kill any cubs that are present (which then makes the females more available for mating). According to Lea (1984), Lorenz's claim that animal aggression always stops before an animal is killed is basically a myth.
- According to Leakey and Lewin (1977), cultural influences are far more important determinants of human aggression than biological factors. Whatever potential for aggression we may have

inherited as a species, it is culturally over-ridden and repackaged into forms which fit current circumstances. Learning plays no part in Lorenz's theory of aggression which, at least when applied to primates and human beings, makes it inadequate. Cultures differ in the degree and kind of aggression which are permissible and socializing influences can over-ride any innate differences which may exist between males and females (see Mead's study of three New Guinea tribes in Chapter 23).
- Lorenz's view of aggression, in humans and animals, as being spontaneous rather than reactive has been criticized. Like the other three instincts or drives (namely, hunger, sexuality and flight, which collectively he calls the 'big four'), aggressive behaviour does not occur in response to environmental stimuli but spontaneously, when instinctive aggressive energy builds up and demands discharge. (This is called the *hydraulic model* of instinct.) The evidence for this energy model is very sparse indeed. According to Siann (1985) it amounts to the male cichlid fish, which attacks its female mate, and an anecdote about Lorenz's maiden aunt! This view of aggression as being inevitable because aggressive energy builds up, unrelated to external events, has come under fire from many modern biologists and ethologists, who believe that aggression in animals is reactive and modifiable by a variety of internal and external conditions (Hinde, 1974).
- Although it is generally agreed that fighting between animals of the same species is highly ritualized, some critics of Lorenz have pointed out that he did not take account of how the *goals* of behaviour influence the degree of ritual; for example, antelopes are much more likely to use rituals when fighting over territory than when competing for a sexual partner.

● Freud's psychoanalytic approach

Freud's theory will be discussed in detail in Chapter 29, where we shall see that his personality theory is normally regarded as an instinct theory. It was not until late in his life that Freud recognized aggression as an instinct distinct from sexuality (libido) and it was the horrific carnage of the First World War which provided the impetus for the re-working of his theory of aggression. In *Beyond the Pleasure Principle* (1920) and *The Ego and the Id* (1923), he distinguished between the life instinct (or *Eros*), including sexuality, and the death instinct (*Thanatos*).

Thanatos represents an inborn destructiveness and aggression, directed primarily against the self. The aim (as with all instincts in Freud's view) is to reduce tension or excitation to a minimum and, ultimately, to its total elimination. This was the idyllic state we enjoyed in the womb, where our needs were met as they arose, and, for a while, at our mother's breast but after this, the only way of achieving such a Nirvana is through death. However, self-directed aggression conflicts with the life instinct (particularly the self-preservative component), so we eroticize it by combining it with libido (producing sadism, masochism and sadomasochism), direct it towards others or take some of this outwardly directed aggression back into our own personality in the form of the superego (the moral part of personality; see Chapter 27).

Because the impulse to self-destruction is so strong, Freud believed that we must destroy some other thing or person if we are not to destroy ourselves; conflict with the life instinct results in our aggression being displaced onto others. More positively, aggression can be sublimated into sport, physical occupations and domination and mastery of nature and the world in general. Like Freud, Lorenz also argued that we need to acknowledge our aggressiveness and to control it through sport (e.g. the Olympics), expeditions, explorations and so on, especially if international co-operation is involved

(Lorenz called these 'displacement' activities). Another similarity between them is the view of aggression as spontaneous and not reactive, that is, aggressive energy builds up until eventually it has to be discharged in some way.

Some support for Freud (and Lorenz) is provided by studies of people who commit brutal crimes (see Box 17.6).

Ultimately, of course, *Thanatos* always wins its struggle with *Eros* and sometimes it enjoys a premature victory in the form of suicide.

Unlike his ideas on sexuality, Freud's ideas on aggression made little impact either on the public imagination or on other psychologists (including other psychoanalysts) until the publication of *Frustration and Aggression* by Dollard *et al.* (1939) (see below), *Human Aggression* by Storr (1968) and *The Anatomy of Human Destructiveness* by Fromm (1977). Storr, a psychoanalyst, dedicated his book to Lorenz and in the Introduction to the book, he says:

> That man is an aggressive creature will hardly be disputed. With the exception of certain rodents, no other vertebrate habitually destroys members of his own species ... the extremes of 'brutal' behaviour are confined to man; and there is no parallel in nature to our savage treatment of each other ... we are the cruellest and most ruthless species that has ever walked the earth; and that, although we may recoil in horror when we read in newspaper or history book of the

---

BOX 17.6 Key study: the overcontrolled violent criminal

Megargee (1966) reported that brutally aggressive crimes are often committed by overcontrolled individuals; they repress their anger and over a period of time the pressure to be aggressive builds up. Often it is an objectively trivial incident which provokes the destructive outburst, with the aggressor then returning to their previously passive state and once more seeming incapable of violence.

In case after case, the extremely assaultive offender proves to be a rather passive person with no previous history of aggression. In Phoenix, an 11-year-old boy who stabbed his brother 34 times with a steak knife was described by all who knew him as being extremely polite and soft spoken with no history of assaultive behaviour. In New York, an 18-year-old youth who confessed he had assaulted and strangled a seven-year-old girl in a Queens church and later tried to burn her body in the furnace was described in the press as an unemotional

person who planned to be a minister. A 21-year-old man from Colorado who was accused of the rape and murder of two little girls had never been a discipline problem and, in fact, his stepfather reported, 'When he was in school the other kids would run all over him and he'd never fight back. There is just no violence in him'.

In these cases the homicide was not just one more aggressive offence in a person who had always displayed inadequate controls, but rather a completely uncharacteristic act in a person who had always displayed extraordinarily high levels of control:

> ... the extremely assaultive person is often a fairly mild-mannered, long-suffering individual who buries his resentment under rigid but brittle controls. Under certain circumstances he may lash out and release all his aggression in one, often disastrous, act. Afterwards he reverts to his usual overcontrolled defences. Thus he may be more of a menace than the verbally aggressive 'chip-on-the-shoulder' type who releases his aggression in small doses. (Megargee and Mendelsohn, 1966)

atrocities committed by man upon man, we know in our hearts that each one of us harbours within himself those same savage impulses which lead to murder, to torture and to war.

Storr identified four forms of psychopathology (mental disorder) attributable to the inadequate resolution of the aggressive drive, namely depression, schizoid behaviour, paranoia and psychopathy (see Chapter 30).

● The frustration-aggression hypothesis

Intended partly to 'translate' some of Freud's psychoanalytic concepts into learning theory terms, Dollard, Doob, Miller, Mowrer and Sears published *Frustration and Aggression* (1939), in which they proposed their *frustration-aggression hypothesis*. According to this, '... aggression is always a consequence of frustration and, contrariwise, ... the existence of frustration always leads to some form of aggression'.

While agreeing with Freud that aggression is an innate response, Dollard *et al.* argued that it would only be triggered by frustrating situations and events. Some support for this view comes from the displacement of aggression, where a substitute object is found for the expression of aggressive feelings because they cannot be vented openly and directly towards their real object. An example of this displacement of aggression is the scapegoating found in racial discrimination (see Chapter 19).

However, it soon became apparent that the frustration-aggression hypothesis, in its original form, was an overstatement. Miller (1941) revised it by claiming that frustration is an instigator of aggression but situational factors (e.g. learned inhibition, fear of retaliation) may prevent actual aggressive behaviour from occurring; i.e. although frustration may make aggression more likely, it is far from being a sufficient cause of aggression.

Frustration can produce a variety of responses (of which aggression is but one), including regression (see Chapter 29), depression and lethargy (Seligman, 1975; see Chapters 6 and 7). Frustration may also produce different responses in different people in different situations. According to Miell (1990), for example, experiments seem to suggest that frustration is most likely to produce aggression if (a) the person is close to achieving his or her goal, or (b) the frustrating event seems arbitrary. (Berkowitz (1993) says that if a frustration is either arbitrary or illegitimate it is seen as unfair.) This is demonstrated in a study by Kulik and Brown (1979), which is described in Box 17.7.

One of the important cognitive factors identified by Kulik and Brown is the *attribution of intention*, i.e. the person who refused to pledge any money to charity was seen as deliberately frustrating the participants. According to Berkowitz (1993), we are not usually bothered by a failure to reach our goals unless we believe that the frustrater intentionally or improperly tried to interfere with our efforts, i.e. the attribution must involve a cause that is seen as internal, controllable and improper (in violation of generally accepted rules of conduct). This is consistent with Weiner's (1986) attributional theory of emotion and motivation; see Chapter 15.

This attributional perspective is consistent with how we defined aggression earlier, i.e. it is the (perceived) intention to harm another person. If there are mitigating circumstances, the attribution made by the victim may change (the cause is now seen as external and uncontrollable, although still improper); apologizing or confessing can have similar effects (Weiner, 1992) and represent important aspects of impression management (see Chapter 15).

It has been found that a particular type of attributional style is involved in chronic aggression in children. Aggression is quite stable in children over time and those who display chronic aggression have a strong attributional bias towards seeing others as

BOX 17.7	Key study: getting frustrated by other people is all right as long as they have a good reason

Kulik and Brown (1979) found that frustration was more likely to produce aggression if it was not anticipated and if participants believed that the person responsible for frustrating them did so deliberately and without good reason, showing the importance of cognitive factors as cues for aggressive behaviour.

Participants were told they could earn money by telephoning people and persuading them to make a pledge to charity; some expected that about two-thirds of those contacted would agree to make a pledge, while others expected a very low response rate. All the people telephoned were confederates, none of whom agreed to pledge. The first group of participants showed more aggression by slamming down the phone, speaking more aggressively, etc. Also, those given reasonable excuses (such as 'I can't afford it') showed less aggression than those given less reasonable excuses (such as 'Charities are a waste of time and a rip-off').

acting against them with hostile intent, especially in ambiguous situations; such biased attributions often lead to retaliatory aggression (Taylor *et al.*, 1994).

Another modification of the original frustration-aggression hypothesis was proposed by Bandura (1973), who argued that frustration might be a source of arousal, but frustration-induced arousal (like other types of arousal) could have a variety of outcomes, of which aggression is only one. Whether it actually occurs is more the result of learned patterns of behaviour triggered by environmental cues.

● Aggressive-cue theory

In some ways quite similar to Bandura, Berkowitz (1966) argued that frustration produces anger rather than aggression; what is important about frustration is that it is psychologically painful and anything which is psychologically (or physically) painful can lead to aggression. For anger or psychological pain to be converted into actual aggression, certain *cues* are needed; these are environmental stimuli associated either with aggressive behaviour or with the frustrating object or person. Aggressive or violent behaviour

is, at least partly, a reaction to specific features of the surrounding situation which 'pull out' responses that heighten the strength of the behaviour. This happens either when the environmental stimuli have an aggressive meaning for the aggressor (they are associated in the person's mind with aggression) and/or when they somehow remind the aggressor of decidedly unpleasant experiences; this is the *aggressive-cue theory*. The basic experimental procedure used by Berkowitz to test the aggressive-cue theory is summarized in Box 17.8.

Berkowitz and Geen (1966) introduced the confederate to the real participant either as Bob Anderson or Kirk Anderson. As expected, the largest number of shocks were delivered by participants who were angry (had received seven shocks from the confederate), had witnessed the violent film and believed the confederate's name was Kirk – his name was linked to the witnessed aggression through Kirk Douglas. In a parallel experiment, the confederate was introduced either as Bob Kelly, Bob Dunne or Bob Riley; Dunne was the name of the victorious character in *Champion* and Kelly (played by Kirk Douglas) was the loser. As predicted, the confederate received more shocks from participants who had seen the violent film, but most importantly, he was shocked most when he was called Kelly. In both cases (i.e. the confederate called 'Kirk' or 'Kelly' receiving the most shocks), participants encountered someone who reminded them of the victim in the witnessed aggression: he was associated with an instance of successful (i.e. rewarded) aggression, which will make it more likely that anger will be converted into aggression (Berkowitz, 1993).

In an experiment by Berkowitz and Le Page (1967), when it was the participant's turn to evaluate the confederate's solution, he was taken to a 'control room' and was shown the shock apparatus (in fact, a simple telegraph key). For one group of participants, there was a shotgun and a revolver on a table next to the shock key; for a second group, two badminton rackets and some shuttlecocks. For each participant, these objects were pushed aside by the experimenter, who said that 'they must have been left there by another experimenter'. There was a third group for whom there were no 'planted' objects. As predicted, it was found that angry participants delivered more shocks to the confederate if a shotgun and revolver were nearby (objects that are, for most people, associated with violence) than when neutral objects such as badminton rackets were present. This is known as the *weapons effect* (see Fig. 17.4).

BOX 17.8	Berkowitz's paradigm for investigating cue-related aggression

In a series of experiments, Berkowitz used the same basic procedure whereby, when participants arrive, they are told they will be paired with another person (a confederate) in a study concerned with the physiological reactions to stress. To do this, they will be asked to offer a written solution to a problem. Stress will be introduced by their solution being evaluated by their partner, who will deliver between one and ten electric shocks to them (according to their evaluation of the solution). After completing their solutions, half the participants receive a single shock, while the rest receive seven (all fairly mild), the lower number of shocks indicating a very favourable evaluation.

Following this first stage, participants take their turn in evaluating the confederate's solution, either after seeing a violent film (*Champion,* depicting a brutal prize fight and starring Kirk Douglas) or a non-violent film (showing highlights of an exciting track race) or in the presence of objects that are/are not associated with violence. Aggression is measured in terms of the number of shocks the participant delivers.

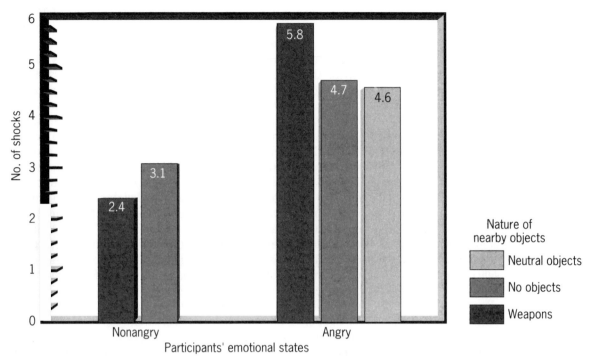

FIGURE 17.4 *Mean number of shocks given as a function of presence of weapons. (Adapted from Berkowitz & LePage (1967). Copyright 1967 by the American Psychological Association. Adapted by permission.)*

These and several other similar studies seem to suggest that people's actions towards others are sometimes influenced in a relatively thoughtless, automatic way by particular details of the immediate situation: the mere physical presence of weapons, even when not themselves used in the performance of aggressive actions, may still increase the occurrence of such behaviour. As Berkowitz (1968) put it, 'Guns not only permit violence, they can stimulate it as well. The finger pulls the trigger, but the trigger may also be pulling the finger'. Apart from some failures to replicate these findings, critics have argued that participants disregarded the explanation of what the weapons, etc. were doing there and realized that the experimenter expected them to be aggressive, i.e. they were responding to the *demand characteristics* of the experimental situation (see Chapter 2). Berkowitz (1993) cites a study by Turner and Simons (1974) in which the more that participants believed the experimenter was interested in their aggressive responses, the less punitive they were towards the confederate, i.e. the increased aggression produced by exposure to weapons came about despite participants' suspicions, not because of their beliefs about what the experimenter expected to happen.

Berkowitz (1995) points to a number of successful replications, including studies carried out in Belgium, Canada, Croatia, Italy and Sweden. In the Swedish study (Frodi, 1975), the weapons effect was shown by high school boys even when they had not been 'angered' (i.e. shocked). According to Baron (1977):

... It is clear that Berkowitz's more general proposal that aggression is 'pulled' or elicited from without by external stimuli rather than merely 'pushed' from within has attained widespread acceptance ... his views in this regard have been highly influential in causing social psychologists to shift their search for the determinants of aggression largely from internal conflict and motives to external environmental factors ...

● The social learning theory approach and the effects of the media

In Chapter 27 we shall look in detail at the work of Bandura and other social learning theorists who believe that *observational learning* (or *modelling*) is a fundamental form of social learning over and above conditioning (see Chapter 7). Bandura's basic experimental procedure involved exposing young children to an aggressive model and then observing the children's behaviour, with the main dependent variable being the number of acts of imitative aggression shown. The model was seen assaulting a large, inflatable rubber doll called a Bobo doll and the children had access to one of these after observing the model; hence, Bandura's experiments are often called the 'Bobo doll experiments'.

According to Baron (1977), the Bobo doll experiments constitute the 'first generation' (or 'phase one') of scientific research into the effects of media violence; almost all involved filmed (symbolic) models. The basic finding was that young children can acquire new aggressive responses not previously in their behavioural repertoire, merely through exposure to a filmed or televised model. If children could learn new ways of harming others through such experience, then the implication was that mass-media portrayals of violence might be contributing, in some degree, to increased levels of violence in society (Baron, 1977). However, Bandura himself (1965) warned against such an interpretation in the light of his finding that learning of aggressive responses does not necessarily mean that they will be displayed in the child's behaviour (see Chapters 7 and 27); nevertheless, the mere possibility of such effects was sufficient to focus considerable public attention on his research.

There were also a number of methodological problems with the Bobo doll research which made it very difficult to generalize from it to 'real world' media influence. This helped to promote 'phase two' of the study of the effects of media violence, with Berkowitz being one of the leading figures (see above). However, before we can study the effects of TV violence, we need to ask:

● How much actual violence is there on TV?
● Do viewers perceive violence in the same way as it is defined by researchers?

Two questions specifically related to the effects of TV violence are:

● How is TV supposed to have its effect on attitudes and behaviour?
● How have these effects been studied?

These questions are discussed in a review of the research literature by Gunter and McAleer (1990).

How much violence is there on TV?

The basic method used by researchers to quantify the amount of violence on television uses simple counting techniques. Violence is defined objectively by researchers who then code samples of TV programmes for any incidents which match their own violence definitions.

Perhaps the largest American study is that by Gerbner et al. (1972) and Gerbner and Gross (1976), who monitored samples of all major network prime-time and weekend daytime programmes since 1967. They defined violence as: 'The overt expression of physical force (with or without a weapon) against self or other, compelling action against one's will on pain of being hurt or killed, or actually hurting or killing'. Violent accidents and natural disasters were included. This analysis of violence provided the framework for British research, beginning with Halloran and Croll (1972) and the BBC's Audience Research Department (1972). Both studies agreed that, although a common feature of programming, violence was not as prevalent on British TV as on American TV.

By far the largest and most recent British study to date is that by Cumberbatch (1987), commissioned by the BBC. It analysed all programmes broadcast on all four channels (with the exception of commercials and Open University) in four separate weeks,

---

BOX 17.9 Key study: how much violence is there on British TV? (Cumberbatch, 1987)

Thirty percent of programmes contained some violence. The overall frequency was 1.14 violent acts per programme, 1.68 acts per hour; each act lasts, on average, for 25 seconds and so violence occupies just over 1 percent of TV time. However, if boxing and wrestling are excluded, the average duration is 13 seconds (0.5 percent); if verbal threats are included, the average frequency rises to 1.96 acts per hour.

Top of the list were spy, fantasy, cartoon, war, detective, crime and thriller programmes and bottom were quiz, game and chat shows, plus (non-contact) sports. However, injuries as such from violent acts were rare – on 26 percent of occasions, violence resulted in death but in 61 percent *no* injuries were shown as the victims simply showed pain or were stunned. Again, the portrayal was quite sanitized, with 83 percent of violence showing no blood at all, while considerable blood and gore featured in only 0.2 percent of cases. Only 13 percent of violence was portrayed as retaliation, while aggressors were 50 percent more likely to be baddies than goodies and violence took place more than twice as often in a criminal context than in upholding the law.

between May and September 1986. This amounted to 1412 hours of TV, 2076 programmes (930 BBC, 1146 ITV and Channel 4). The study used a definition of violence that was very similar to that used by Gerbner and Gross.

The primary unit for counting was the *violent act*, '... a coherent uninterrupted sequence of actions involving the same agents in the same role ...'. So, in a violent scene, if A attacked B, B retaliated and C intervened to help A defeat B, this would count as three violent acts. What did Cumberbatch find? His main findings are summarized in Box 17.9.

While about 75 percent of people believe that there is more violence now on TV than there was about ten years ago, according to Cumberbatch most people are mistaken: violence and concerns about violence have clearly increased in society in the last decade but this has not been reflected by a proportional increase on television, even in the news. He concludes by saying:

> ... While broadcasters may take some comfort from our data on trends in television violence, they must expect to be continually reminded of their responsibilities in this area and be obliged to acknowledge that a significant minority of people will remain concerned about what's on the box. (Cumberbatch, 1987)

How do viewers perceive TV violence?

Much of the concern, of course, centres on children. Cumberbatch found that, while violence was more likely after 9 p.m. and that generally violence in children's TV was rare, the main exception was cartoons. Indeed, until recently, much of the public controversy over the harmful effects of TV on children has focused on very popular cartoons such as 'Tom and Jerry' and 'Popeye'. American cartoons are twice as likely to be violent as British ones but most cartoons are American.

However, do children take cartoons as representing 'reality'? According to Gunter and McAleer (1990), viewers can be highly discriminating when it comes to portrayals of violence. They do not invariably read into TV content the same meanings as do researchers. Merely knowing how often certain predefined incidents occur in programmes does not tell us how significant these features are for viewers. Thus, viewers' perceptions of how violent TV is may not accord with objective counts of programme incidents. However, *realism* does appear to be an important element in viewers' perceptions of violence; real-life incidents in news and documentaries

are generally rated as more violent than violence presented in fictional settings.

Research suggests that children are very similar to adults as far as their judgements of the *amounts* of violent content are concerned. But their *ratings* of violence do differ from those of content analysers, i.e. programmes which are extremely violent according to 'objective' counts of violent acts can be seen by children as 'hardly containing any violence' and this is especially true of cartoons. In reflecting the attitudes and perceptions of the audience, research into the amount of violence on TV, therefore, ought to include at least some subjective input from viewers. This would provide an indication of which types of programmes or portrayals viewers themselves regard as violent and with what degree of seriousness (Gunter and McAleer, 1990).

How does TV violence affect attitudes and behaviour?

Four specific effects of TV violence have been investigated – arousal, disinhibition, imitation and desensitization.

- *Arousal* refers to a non-specific, physiological response, whose 'meaning' will be defined by the viewer in terms of the type of programme being watched (Zillman, 1978; see Chapter 6). Watching TV violence supposedly increases the overall level of emotional arousal and excitement. However, there does not seem to be any strong overall relationship between perceiving a programme as violent and verbal report of emotional arousal, although the more *realistic* the violence is perceived to be, the greater the reported arousal and involvement are likely to be.
- *Disinhibition* refers to the reduction of inhibition about behaving aggressively oneself or coming to believe that aggression is a permitted or legitimate way of solving problems or attaining goals. Berkowitz's aggressive-cue theory, which we discussed earlier, is relevant here.
- *Imitation* is perhaps the most direct link between watching TV and the viewer's own behaviour and is directly related to Bandura's studies of imitative aggression. But social learning theorists acknowledge the role of cognitive factors as mediating between stimulus and response, so what we have said about how TV violence is perceived and interpreted and the importance of realism are clearly crucial intervening variables (both in children and adults).

● *Desensitization* refers to the reduction in emotional response to TV violence (an increased acceptance of violence in real life) as a result of repeated viewing of TV violence. As with drug tolerance, increasingly violent programmes are required to produce an effect (i.e. an emotional response) in order to satisfy the 'need'.

A study by Drabman and Thomas (1974) supports the desensitization hypothesis. Eight-year-olds saw either a violent or a non-violent programme before witnessing a real (staged) fight between two other children in a playroom. The former were less likely to tell an adult what was happening than the latter.

How have the effects of TV violence been studied?

Most of the research which is related to these four proposed effects has consisted of *laboratory experiments*, designed to demonstrate the causal link between watching TV violence and increased viewer aggression. But most studies involve small, unrepresentative samples under highly contrived, unnatural viewing conditions. Their measures of TV viewing and aggression tend to be so far removed from normal, everyday behaviour that whether laboratory findings have any meaning in the outside world is something which can be debated quite strongly (Gunter and McAleer, 1990).

Much more ecologically valid are *field experiments*, in which children or teenagers are assigned to view violent or non-violent programmes for a period of a few days or weeks. Measures of aggressive behaviour, fantasy, attitude, etc. are taken before, during and after the period of controlled viewing. To ensure control over actual viewing, children in group or institutional settings are studied, mostly nursery schools, residential schools or institutions for adolescent boys. Almost without exception, they confirm the results of laboratory studies – in general, children who view violent TV are more aggressive than those who do not. A good example is a study by Parke *et al.* (1977); see Box 17.10.

Field experiments use real TV programmes which are viewed in natural settings and aggression occurs in a situation where naturally occurring consequences are present. However, the situation cannot be as well controlled as in the laboratory – we cannot be so sure that the *only* difference between the two groups is the kind of programme viewed, particularly as it is not always possible to assign participants completely randomly. In the Parke *et al.*, study, for example, it was cottages (i.e. pre-existing groups) which were assigned to violent or non-violent programmes, not individuals. Also, by definition, such participants (juvenile delinquent males) are hardly representative of children or adolescents in general. And when pre-schools are used, home viewing is not controlled during the study.

BOX 17.10   Key study: creating violence – a cottage industry?

Parke *et al.* (1977) studied Belgian and American male juvenile delinquents living in small-group cottages in low security institutions. Their normal rate of aggressive behaviour was assessed (using several measures of physical and verbal aggression) and then the boys in one cottage were exposed to five commercial films involving violence over a period of one week, while boys in another cottage saw five non-violent films during the same period. The former showed significant increases in aggressive behaviour for some of the categories but increases in other measures of aggression were confined to boys who were naturally high in aggression (and who saw the violent film).

BOX 17.11   Key study: introducing television – a natural experiment in Canada (Williams, 1986)

Naturalistic observation of children's behaviour was combined with teacher and peer ratings of their aggression in a community where TV had only recently been introduced for the first time. This community was compared with one in which there was a single TV channel and another which had several. The major finding was that aggressive behaviour in 6–11-year-olds increased over a two-year period following the introduction of TV but no such increase was found in those communities where TV was already available. This was true for verbal and physical aggression, both sexes and for longitudinal (children aged 6–7 prior to TV reception and 8–9 two years later) and cross-sectional (children of the same age at each testing) samples, regardless of the child's initial level of aggression or how much TV they watched.

This represents very strong evidence for the claim that viewing violence leads to an increase in aggressive behaviour (Gunter and McAleer, 1990). The study is discussed further in relation to TV and sex role stereotyping; see Chapter 23.

A common alternative to both laboratory and field experiments is the *correlational survey,* in which participants indicate which programmes they like best and watch most often; the amount of violent content in these choices is then compared with measures of aggression given by peers, teachers, parents, self-reports (or some combination). Gunter and McAleer (1990) claim that the evidence from such studies is very inconclusive, the most consistent finding being that the overall amount of viewing of TV violence is related to self-reports of aggressive behaviour. Of course, it is possible that those who watch more violent television and 'video nasties' differ in other important respects from those who watch less; for instance, something to do with their personality and/or their family environment may account for their attraction to portrayals of violence in the first place, in which case we cannot be sure that it is the observation of violence which causes their greater behavioural aggression.

Probably the most useful kind of study is the *longitudinal panel study* which, like experiments but unlike correlational surveys, can tell us about cause and effect and which normally uses sound sampling methods. The aim is to discover relationships which may exist or develop over time between TV viewing and social attitudes and behaviour and so it is concerned with the cumulative influence of TV – the claim is that the link between the two should increase with age.

For example, in a 20-year follow-up of 400 children, heavy exposure to TV violence at age eight was associated with violent crime and spouse and child abuse at age 30, at all socioeconomic and intelligence levels (Huesmann and Eron, 1984). Sims and Gray (1993, cited in Newson, 1994), in a paper presented to the House of Lords Broadcasting Group, pointed to a vast world literature linking heavy exposure to media violence to subsequent aggressive behaviour. Sims and Gray cite a review by Bailey (1993) of 40 adolescent murderers and 200 young sex offenders in Britain which showed repeated viewing of violent and pornographic videos to be a 'significant causal factor'. This was particularly important in the case of adolescents who abused in a babysitting context, where videos provided 'a potent source of immediate arousal for the subsequent act', including mimicry of the violent images. 'Video nasties' are discussed further in Box 17.12.

However, not all studies have reached these conclusions. For example, in a three-year study of 3200 elementary school children and teenagers by Milavsky *et al.* (1982), measures of verbal and physical aggressive behaviour were obtained by friends (in the case of the children) while the teenagers gave self-reports. The children were interviewed six times, the teenagers five times. They were given checklists of programmes available on the major networks (preclassified for violent content), so information was obtained both about general viewing patterns and

---

BOX 17.12 Critical discussion: what's nasty about 'video nasties'?

Elizabeth Newson, in a discussion paper presented to members of both Houses of Parliament in March, 1994, cites the brutal and sadistic murder of two-year- old James Bulger in 1993 by two ten-year-olds, Robert Thompson and Jon Venables. One of the most disturbing things about the case was that it involved a prolonged act of torture, in which there was '... both the expectation and the attainment of *satisfaction* of some sort through doing deliberate and sustained violence to a very small child (described *by the children* as a 'baby') whose distress was unremitting ...'

A variety of causes have been proposed (including the 'evil freaks' explanation) for this horrific event, which is by no means an isolated case. While there was debate during the 1980s about 'video nasties', more recently concern has increased regarding their more

serious, long-lasting effects. It now seems that professionals in child health and psychology underestimated the degree of brutality and sustained sadism that filmmakers were capable of inventing and willing to portray, as well as children's access to such material. There must be special concern when, in the context of *entertainment/amusement,* either children or adults are repeatedly exposed to images of vicious cruelty. Newson quotes Medved (1992), for whom one of the many evils of video nasties is that they '... advance the ... appalling idea that the most appropriate response to the suffering of others is sadistic laughter ...'

While there has not yet been time to carry out longitudinal studies of the effects of sadistic videos, Sims and Gray (1993; see above) point out that 'Unlike traditional gruesome stories, the viewer is made to identify with the *perpetrator* of the act, and not with the victim' and 'Watching specific acts of violence on the media has resulted in mimicry by children and adolescents of behaviour that they would otherwise, literally, have found unimaginable' (quoted in Newson).

levels of exposure to violent programmes. Only small associations were found and compared with the influence of family background, social environment and school performance, the significance of television viewing as an indicator of aggressiveness was very weak (Gunter and McAleer, 1990). However, an interesting 'natural experiment' in Canada strongly points to television as a distinct and significant influence; see Box 17.11.

Conclusions

In their overall evaluation of the evidence, Gunter and McAleer (1990) state that:

> ... the measurement of television's effects, and of factors that mediate those effects, is highly complex ... we are still a long way from knowing fully the extent and character of television's influence on children's aggressive behaviour.

According to Taylor *et al.* (1994):

> ... media violence is not a sufficient condition to produce aggressive behaviour, nor is it a necessary one. Aggressive behaviour is multiply determined and media violence in and of itself is unlikely to provoke such behaviour ... However ... media violence can be a contributing factor to some aggressive acts in some individuals ...'

Putting the discussion into a wider social and political context, Taylor *et al.,* argue that television and movies contribute only a small amount to crime and violence over and above the contribution of social factors such as unemployment, racial prejudice and the widespread availability of drugs and guns.

TV violence and catharsis

One argument in defence (if not in favour) of watching television violence is that witnessing others being aggressive will help the viewer to 'get it out of their system' (strictly, this is *vicarious catharsis*), thus making the viewer less likely to behave aggressively. The argument is based partly on Freud's and Lorenz's theory of aggression, but the evidence appears to contradict it.

The basic research paradigm used to test this hypothesis is that of Berkowitz (see Box 17.8). The results of several such experiments show that:

- regardless of the level of anger aroused, participants who witness aggression deliver more shocks than those who witness non-violent programmes;
- anger-aroused participants generally respond more punitively than non-aroused participants;

- anger-aroused participants who witness violence respond most punitively of all.

This last finding in particular contradicts the vicarious catharsis hypothesis and instead supports a social learning theory explanation.

However, rather than thinking of catharsis as a process which can occur in anybody, researchers are increasingly suggesting that if such a discharge of hostile feelings can occur at all, it is probably restricted to certain types of personality or those with high levels of certain cognitive skills, such as fantasizing and daydreaming, and those with highly developed imaginations. For some children at least, fictional violence can have positive effects, which throws some doubt on the popular view that violence on television, etc. is harmful to all children, even if they view a great deal. For these children, violence may provide a means through which they can reduce their angry feelings (Gunter and McAleer, 1990).

Similarly, if social learning theorists are correct in what they say about the harmful effects of watching television, it follows that watching television can also be beneficial by promoting prosocial behaviour. According to Gunter and McAleer (1990), studies have shown that portrayals of kindness, generosity, being helpful and socially responsible can exert both short-term and longer term influences on similar behaviours among children.

● Aggression and deindividuation

We have already seen in this chapter how the presence of others can have an inhibiting effect on the helping behaviour of an individual. Can being in the company of other people have a detrimental influence on a person's behaviour, including the tendency to behave more aggressively?

The concept of *deindividuation* has been used to try to explain why it is that people in groups may behave in an uncharacteristically aggressive way (and in other antisocial ways) relative to their individual behaviour. If people believe that they will be identified and consequently punished, they will inhibit their aggressive impulses but in urban settings identification may be difficult and this may reduce people's fear of punishment, with the effect that they are more 'free' to behave in antisocial ways. When an individual's identity is lost in a mass of people and when the markers of personality are reduced, the individual is said to be deindividuated (Gergen and Gergen, 1981).

One of the earliest studies of crowd behaviour was that of Le Bon (1895) and, based on his work, Festinger *et al.* (1952) first introduced the concept of deindividuation, defining it as a state of affairs in a group where members do not pay attention to other individuals as individuals and, correspondingly, the members do not feel they are being singled out by others. Belonging to a group not only provides people with a sense of identity and belongingness (see Maslow's hierarchy of needs – Chapter 5), but allows individuals to merge with the group, to forego their individuality and to become anonymous – in other words, to deindividuate. Is there any evidence to support this view?

Most relevant studies have been laboratory experiments but one interesting field study was conducted by Diener *et al.* (1976), who observed 1300 trick-or-treating children on Halloween night. When they were completely anonymous (for instance, wearing costumes which prevented them from being recognized and going from house to house in large groups), they were most likely to steal money and candy.

Zimbardo (1969) emphasized the absence of self-awareness and self-evaluation; under certain conditions, an individual changes their self-perception and that of others and engages in uninhibited behaviour and this is deindividuation. He also regarded anonymity as a major source of deindividuation and was the first to operationalize anonymity by having participants wear hoods and masks (see Box 17.13).

However, manipulating anonymity has not always proved very easy (Brown, 1985). Some of Zimbardo's (1969) participants were Belgian soldiers who wore hoods, but they did not behave more aggressively; instead, they became self-conscious, suspicious and anxious and the apparently individuated controls retained their 'normal' level of deindividuation related to their status as uniformed soldiers. One of the functions of uniform in the 'real world' is precisely to reduce individuality and hence, at least indirectly, to increase deindividuation. A standard uniform is a clear sign for others, at least, that the wearer belongs to the group or the institution and, to that extent, the uniqueness of the individual is rendered less important or apparent. Dispossessing someone of their 'civilian' clothes is a major technique of depersonalizing the inmate in 'total institutions' such as prisons and psychiatric hospitals (Goffman, 1968, 1971).

As Brown (1985) observes, the victims of aggression are often dehumanized by, amongst other things, shaving their heads and dressing them in ill-fitting clothes so that they appear less human and so can be humiliated and abused more easily (see the prison simulation experiment by Zimbardo *et al.*, Chapter 20). While it may be true that the deindividuation produced by wearing military or police uniform increases the likelihood of brutality, it can just as easily work the other way – the anonymity of massed ranks of police or soldiers may make them appear less human and thus make them a more obvious target for a rioting crowd's violence.

Again, is group behaviour always as unreasonable and uncontrolled as Zimbardo and others have proposed? For example, Brown (1988) refers to the US urban riots of the 1960s, where looting and violence were not completely random but showed signs of selectivity. Similarly, the St Paul's black-police civil disturbances in Bristol in 1984 were violent but at the same time were relatively controlled; violence was aimed at specific targets and avoided others (such as local shops and houses) and was geographically confined to a small area in the heart of the community. Far from losing their identities, the rioters seemed quite unanimous in a new sense of pride in their community produced by their activities (Brown, 1988).

| **BOX 17.13** | **Key study: if you don't want to get shocked, ask to see the other person's face (or, someone else's anonymity can be bad for your health)** |

Zimbardo (1969) had female students deliver electric shocks to another student 'as an aid to learning'. Half wore bulky lab coats and hoods that hid their faces, were spoken to in groups of four and were never referred to by name; the other half wore their normal clothes, were given large name tabs to wear and were introduced to each other by name and could see each other dimly while giving the shock. The student who received the shock was seen through a one-way mirror and pretended to be in extreme discomfort – writhing, twisting, grimacing and finally tearing her hand away from the strap. The hooded, deindividuated participants gave twice as much shock as the individuated group; if they were told that the student receiving the shock was honest, sincere and warm she did not receive any less shock than those who believed she was conceited or critical; by contrast, the individuated participants did adjust the shock they administered according to the victim's character.

Just as television need not produce harmful effects, so deindividuation does not necessarily produce antisocial behaviour; under proper circumstances, deindividuation can be liberating. This was well illustrated by the *black room experiment* (Gergen *et al.*, 1973), which involved participants spending an hour together, either in a completely dark room or in a normally lit room. In the dark room, they at first chatted in a lively manner and explored the physical space and then began to discuss serious matters before conversation faded to be replaced by physical contact; 90 percent of participants deliberately touched other participants, almost 50 percent hugged and 80 percent admitted to being sexually aroused. By comparison, controls talked politely, in the light, for the whole hour. It seems that we can become uninhibited in the dark where the usual norms of intimacy no longer prevail – we feel less accountable for our behaviour in such situations but this state of deindividuation can be to the mutual benefit of all participants (Gergen and Gergen, 1981).

CHAPTER SUMMARY

- According to universal egoism, which has been and still is the dominant ethos of social science, altruism is an impossibility. Whether people are naturally selfless or selfish has been debated for centuries by philosophers and by social psychologists since McDougall's first textbook.

- Helping is one form of prosocial behaviour which has been studied largely as bystander intervention. This area of research was triggered by the murder of Kitty Genovese which, together with early laboratory experiments, led Latané and Darley to introduce the concept of the unresponsive bystander/bystander apathy.

- According to Latané and Darley's decision model, a bystander will pass through a logical series of steps before any help is actually offered; a negative response at any step will mean that no help is offered. The second step involves defining the situation as an emergency, which may not happen due to pluralistic ignorance. Step three involves accepting personal responsibility, but the more potential helpers there are (believed to be) present, the more likely it is that diffusion of responsibility will take place.

- Strictly, the denial of personal responsibility should be called 'dissolution'. How competent we

feel to offer appropriate help will influence diffusion of responsibility. Whatever factors contribute to it, not caring about what happens to the victim is not one of them.

- The decision model provides an incomplete picture, as well as emphasizing why people do not help, rather than why they do. The arousal: cost–reward model represents an extension of the decision model, identifying a number of critical situational and bystander variables which help predict the likelihood of helping under particular circumstances.

- Arousal represents the motivational part of the model, while cost–reward involves the cognitive weighing up of anticipated costs and rewards for both helping and not helping. The model sees people as fundamentally selfish; we try to reduce our arousal and incur as few costs as possible.

- Various combinations of high and low costs for helping and not helping are associated with differing probabilities that help will be offered and whether it will be direct or indirect. Perhaps of most interest is the high-cost-for-helping /high-cost-for-not-helping dilemma. The most common solutions are redefining the situation, diffusing responsibility and blaming the victim, all forms of cognitive reinterpretation.

- The costs of helping and not helping will differ according to a number of variables, including the type of helping required, characteristics of the victim (such as perceived similarity to the bystander), personality and gender of the bystander and the relationship between bystander and victim.

- Helping can only be called altruism if the motive is to benefit the victim (empathic concern). According to the empathy-altruism hypothesis, human beings are capable of altruistic acts, but according to universal egoism, helping is always motivated by personal distress.

- There are many examples in the animal kingdom of altruistic behaviours which endanger the lives of the altruistic individuals and the social insects display 'altruistic suicide' on a very large scale. This seems to contradict a basic principle of Darwin's theory of natural selection, namely that better adapted individual animals will survive and so have more offspring carrying the genes that aided that survival.

- According to sociobiologists, the 'paradox of altruism' can be resolved by seeing altruistic behaviour as selfish behaviour in disguise. Apparently altruistic acts reflect the attempt by an individual animal's 'selfish genes' to secure their own survival, either through saving the lives of close relatives (kin selection) or doing unrelated animals favours that will be returned in the future (delayed reciprocal altruism).

- Sociobiologists extend this argument to human social behaviour, including altruism. This has been criticized as a biologically determinist account of human existence, i.e. it tries to reduce human history and culture to genetics, as well as failing to distinguish between biological/evolutionary and psychological/vernacular altruism, which corresponds to non-human and human behaviour respectively.

- While non-humans are incapable of psychological altruism, humans are capable of biological altruism (impulsive helping), triggered by highly arousing emergency situations, especially where friends or relatives are involved.

- Aggression is a difficult term to define and there is more than one type; it usually implies behaviour that is meant to harm another person.

- According to ethologists, aggression is instinctive in all species, including humans, and has aided their survival, in particular through territoriality.

- Lorenz argues that aggression between members of non-human species is characterized by ritualization and appeasement rituals/gestures, which prevent conflict resulting in serious injury or death. In humans, these have been over-ridden by destructive technology.

- Lorenz's account of human aggression is based on the false view of humans as 'natural warriors'. He also seriously underestimated the extent to which members of other species do kill each other, together with the role of cultural, as opposed to biological, evolution.

- Freud distinguished between the life and death instincts, with aggression being an expression of the latter. Our inborn self-destructive instinct is 'diverted' into outwardly directed aggression. Both Freud and Lorenz believed that aggression builds up spontaneously and needs regular release; some support for this view comes from studies of overcontrolled violent criminals.

- The frustration-aggression hypothesis represented an attempt to integrate some of Freud's ideas with those of learning theory, such as in the displacement of aggression. However, a number of modifications were made to the original theory, concerning the conditions under which frustration is likely to produce aggression; these include the kind of attribution that is made about the aggressor's behaviour.

- A major modification to the original theory is Berkowitz's aggressive-cue theory, according to which environmental stimuli which have an aggressive meaning or are associated with the frustrating object/person are necessary for anger to be converted into aggressive behaviour. One demonstration of this is the weapons effect.

- Bandura's Bobo doll experiments were carried out in the context of his social learning theory which gives central place to observational learning/modelling; they represent the first phase of scientific research into the effects of media violence. Berkowitz's testing of his aggressive-cue theory represents the second phase.

- Before we can study the effects of media violence, we need to ask how much violence is actually presented and whether viewers perceive violence in the same way as it is defined by researchers. Content analysis studies show that there is considerable violence, although this differs between Britain and the US, according to different types of programme, and has actually decreased in recent years in Britain.

- Children are able to distinguish cartoon violence from realistic violence and are generally more aroused by, and disturbed by, the latter.

- Specific effects of TV violence that have been studied are arousal, disinhibition, imitation and desensitization. These have involved a range of research methods, including laboratory and field experiments; the latter are more ecologically valid but are still very limited methodologically. A consistent finding from both types of experiment is that children who watch violent TV are more aggressive than those who do not.

- A common alternative to experiments is the correlational survey but correlational data cannot tell us about cause and effect. This can be remedied by longitudinal panel studies which chart the cumulative influence of TV over several years. If the link between exposure to violence and aggressive behaviour increases with age, this points to the causal effect of the exposure. The natural experiment by Williams in Canada supports the general view that TV violence is a causal factor in its own right.

- Berkowitz's research shows that watching violence only increases the likelihood of further violence, rather than reducing it through vicarious catharsis. However, some children may release angry feelings through watching others' aggression, just as watching TV can promote prosocial behaviour through modelling.

- One of the evils of 'video nasties' is that viewers are made to identify with the aggressor, rather than the victim; they also lead to imitation of otherwise unimaginable acts.
- Deindividuation explains aggression in terms of the reduction of inhibition against antisocial behaviour when individuals are part of a group. In this setting, people change their self-perception and that of others, resulting in a loss of individuality and an increase in anonymity.
- Anonymity has been operationalized by wearing hoods and masks, which make it more likely that individuals will give more punitive electric shocks to an innocent person. However, group/crowd behaviour is not always unreasonable and uncontrolled but can be selective and anonymity can reduce inhibitions to produce positive effects, as in the black room experiment.

GLOSSARY

Agentic help Typically shown by men, involving heroism and chivalry towards strangers, with an 'audience' present.

Aggression A form of antisocial behaviour, either physical or symbolic, carried out with the intention of harming someone. Hostile aggression is gratuitous (done for its own sake); instrumental aggression is a means to an end (e.g. self-defence).

Aggressive-cue theory Berkowitz's view that for anger to be turned into aggression, there need to be environmental stimuli which either have an aggressive meaning or remind the aggressor of the frustrating object/person. One demonstration of this is the weapons effect.

Altruism Helping behaviour that is carried out in order to benefit others, with no expectation of personal gain or benefit.

Appeasement rituals Gestures displayed by one animal which prevent the threatening behaviour of another becoming an actual attack.

Arousal: cost–reward model Piliavin *et al.*'s extension of the decision model. Arousal refers to the emotional response to others' distress which motivates us to do something about it; the most effective response is determined by a cognitive weighing up of the costs and rewards of helping and not helping.

Aversive racism A moderate, subtle form of racial bias, usually unconscious, which manifests itself where the norms for appropriate behaviour are weak/ambiguous or a negative response can be justified on non-racial grounds.

Biological altruism The type of altruism displayed by non-human animals, which does not involve motives/intentions; manifests as impulsive helping in humans. Also called *evolutionary altruism.*

Catharsis Release of aggressive feelings through observing someone else's aggressive behaviour (strictly vicarious catharsis).

Communal helping Typically shown by women, involving caring for others and giving emotional support to friends and family.

Decision model Latané and Darley's account of bystander intervention, according to which help is offered only after a number of logically sequenced steps have been taken, including decisions about the nature of the situation and personal responsibility.

Deindividuation Loss of a sense of individuality (anonymity) and personal responsibility/accountability in a group or crowd situation.

Delayed reciprocal altruism Altruistic acts performed to the benefit of unrelated animals, either to return a previous favour or because it is likely to be returned in the future.

Desensitization Reduction in emotional response to televised violence as a result of repeated exposure.

Diffusion of responsibility The tendency to deny personal responsibility by believing that someone else will probably offer the help that is needed. Usually occurs when other bystanders cannot actually be observed (and 'dissolution' is probably a more accurate term). An example of how the presence of others can inhibit individuals from intervening.

Disinhibition Reduction of inhibition about behaving aggressively, linked to the belief that aggression is a legitimate way of solving problems/attaining goals.

Empathy-altruism hypothesis The view that people are capable of altruism, associated with empathic concern.

Eros The life instincts (including sexuality) in Freud's psychoanalytic theory.

Frustration-aggression hypothesis Dollard *et al.*'s theory of aggression, according to which aggression is always caused by frustration and frustration will always produce some form of aggression.

Helping behaviour A form of prosocial behaviour that has the effect of benefiting another person.

Hydraulic model Lorenz's theory of instincts, according to which instinctive energy (including aggression) spontaneously accumulates over time unless it is discharged.

Inclusive fitness The ability of an individual animal *and* its relatives to survive and produce offspring.

Kin selection Sacrificing our life in order to save that of relatives who share some proportion of our genes; this ensures the survival of our own genes.

Paradox of altruism Apparent contradiction between Darwin's theory of natural selection and observed cases of altruistic behaviour in several species – often involving the death of the altruistic individual.

Pluralistic ignorance The misconception, shared by bystanders, that a situation is 'safe', due to everyone trying to conceal signs of anxiety, such that everyone appears calm. A form of inhibition produced by the presence of others.

Psychological altruism The major type of altruism displayed by human beings, involving motives/intentions. Also called *vernacular altruism*.

Ritualization A way of discharging aggression in a stereotyped pattern, which prevents fights between members of the same species resulting in serious injury.

Sociobiology Extension of Darwin's evolutionary theory; the systematic study of the biological basis of all social behaviour (including altruism and aggression), including human social behaviour.

Thanatos The death instincts (notably aggression) in Freud's psychoanalytic theory.

Universal egoism The view that people are fundamentally selfish, which sees altruism as impossible; associated with personal distress.

Unresponsive bystander Latané and Darley's term for people's typically uncaring attitude towards others who need their help. Also 'bystander apathy'.

Violence An extreme form of aggression involving an attempt to do serious physical injury.

FURTHER READING

Berkowitz, L. (1993) *Aggression: Its Causes, Consequences and Control*. New York: McGraw-Hill. A thorough review of the whole field by one of the leading figures.

Schroeder, D.A., Penner, L.A., Dovidio, J.F. and Piliavin, J.A. (1995) *The Psychology of Helping and Altruism: Problems and Puzzles*. New York: McGraw-Hill. A very thorough, very readable, up-to-date review by some of the leading researchers in the field.

18 ATTITUDES AND ATTITUDE CHANGE

INTRODUCTION AND OVERVIEW

According to Gordon Allport, writing in 1935, 'The concept of attitudes is probably the most distinctive and indispensable concept in contemporary American social psychology ...' More than 50 years later, Hogg and Vaughan (1995) claim that '... Attitudes continue to fascinate research workers and remain a key, if controversial, part of social psychology'. However, the study of attitudes has undergone many important changes during that time, with different questions becoming the focus for theory and research.

According to Stainton Rogers *et al.* (1995), four fundamental questions that psychologists have tried to answer over the last 70 years are:

1 Where do attitudes come from? How are they moulded and formed in the first place?
2 How can attitudes be measured?
3 How and why do attitudes change? What forces are involved and what intrapsychic mechanisms operate when people shift in their opinion about a particular 'attitude object'?
4 How do attitudes relate to behaviour? What is it that links the way people think and feel about an 'attitude object' and what they do about it?

In this chapter, we shall concentrate on the answers that have been offered to questions (3) and (4), although we shall also have something to say about the other two.We shall also discuss these questions in relation to prejudice, considered as an extreme attitude , in the next chapter.

During the 1940s and 1950s, the focus of research was on attitude change, in particular the study of *persuasive communication;* much of the impetus for this came from the use of propaganda during the Second World War, as well as the more general concern over the influence of the mass media, which were becoming an increasingly powerful force, particularly in the United States. The 1950s saw the birth of a number of theories of attitude change, the most influential of these being Festinger's theory of *cognitive dissonance.*

ALL THE TASTE OF GROUND COFFEE
—— IN AN INSTANT ——

From the Kenco Coffee Company

According to Hogg and Vaughan (1995), the 1960s and 1970s was a period of decline and pessimism in attitude research, at least partly due to the apparent failure of research to find any reliable relationship between measured attitudes and behaviour. However, the 1980s saw a revival of interest, stimulated to a large extent by the cognitive approach which was having an impact in social psychology generally. Attitudes, therefore, represent one important aspect of *social cognition*. Attitude change, and the relationship between attitudes and behaviour, are discussed further in the next chapter .

WHAT ARE ATTITUDES?

As with other hypothetical constructs, there is no single definition with which all psychologists would agree and a sample of definitions is given in Table 18.1. According to Rosenberg and Hovland (1960), attitudes are 'predispositions to respond to some class of stimuli with certain classes of response'. These classes of response are:

1 *affective:* what a person feels about the attitude object, how favourably or unfavourably it is evaluated;
2 *cognitive:* what a person believes the attitude object is like, objectively;
3 *behavioural* (sometimes called the 'conative'): how a person actually responds, or intends to respond, to the attitude object based on (1) and (2).

This so-called *three-component* model, which is much more a model of attitude structure than a simple definition (Stahlberg and Frey, 1988), is shown in Figure 18.1. It sees an attitude as an intervening/mediating variable between observable stimuli and responses, illustrating the influence that behaviourism was still having, even in social psychology, at the start of the 1960s. This multi-component model is not without its problems, in particular, the assumption that the three components are highly correlated; the debate about

the attitude-behaviour relationship concerns the correlation between the affective and cognitive components on the one hand and the behavioural component on the other. We shall return to this below.

Most of the definitions in Table 18.1 are unidimensional, because they focus on only one component, namely the affective or evaluative component. This 'narrowing' of the concept of attitude makes it necessary to distinguish it from other, overlapping concepts, in particular beliefs and values.

ATTITUDES, BELIEFS AND VALUES: WHAT IS THE DIFFERENCE?

We often use these terms interchangeably and there is certainly considerable overlap between them; however, they are not identical. An attitude can be thought of as a blend or integration of beliefs and values.

Beliefs represent the knowledge or information we have about the world (although they may be inaccurate or incomplete) and, in themselves, are non-evaluative. According to Fishbein and Ajzen (1975), 'a belief links an object to some attribute' (e.g. 'America' and 'capitalist state'). To convert a belief into an attitude, a 'value' ingredient is needed which, by definition, is to do with an individual's

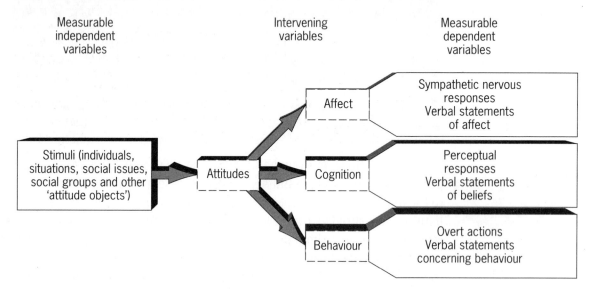

FIGURE 18.1 *Three-component view of attitudes (Rosenberg and Hovland, 1960). From Stahlberg, D. & Frey, D. (1988) Attitudes 1: Structure, Measurement and Functions. In Hewstone, M. et al. (Eds)* Introduction to Social Psychology. *Oxford, Blackwell*

'An attitude is a mental and neural state of readiness, organized through experience, exerting a directive or dynamic influence upon the individual's response to all objects and situations with which it is related.' (Allport, 1935)
'A learned orientation, or disposition, toward an object or situation, which provides a tendency to respond favourably or unfavourably to the object or situation.' (Rokeach, 1968)
'... attitudes have social reference in their origins and development and in their objects, while at the same time they have psychological reference in that they inhere in the individual and are intimately enmeshed in his behaviour and his psychological make-up.' (Warren and Jahoda, 1973)
'the term *attitude* should be used to refer to a general, enduring positive or negative feeling about some person, object, or issue.' (Petty and Cacioppo, 1981)
'an *attitude* is an *evaluative disposition toward some object*. It's an evaluation of something or someone along a continuum of like-to-dislike or favourable-to-unfavourable ...' (Zimbardo and Leippe, 1991)

TABLE 18.1 *Some definitions of attitudes*

sense of what is desirable, good, valuable, worthwhile and so on.

A *value,* according to Rokeach (1968), is '... an enduring belief that a specific mode of conduct or end-state of existence is personally or socially preferable to an opposite or converse mode of conduct or end-state of existence'. While most adults will have many thousands of beliefs, they have only hundreds of attitudes and a few dozen values. Rokeach distinguished between *terminal values* (desirable end-states or goals, for example, wisdom, an exciting life, equality and brotherhood) and *instrumental values* (desirable attributes, for example, competence, helpfulness and intellectualism); the former are desirable in themselves while the latter are desirable as means to the achievement of the former.

Probably the best known classification of values is that of Allport *et al.* (1951). Their scale of values attempts to measure the relative importance for an individual of six value orientations:

1 *theoretical* (problem-solving, knowing how things work);
2 *aesthetic* (the arts, theatre, music, etc.);
3 *political* (political systems and power structures);
4 *economic* (financial issues in general);
5 *social* (general concern for the welfare of other people);
6 *religious* (concern with life after death, moral issues, etc.).

These value orientations may be regarded as corresponding to Rokeach's terminal values. According to Tetlock (1989, cited in Hogg and Vaughan, 1995), terminal values underlie all kinds of political ideology, which can vary as a function of two dimensions : (a) it may assign different priorities to particular values, such as 'individual freedom' or 'national security'; (b) it may be pluralistic, allowing for a variety of values which might sometimes conflict (as in most democracies) or monistic, which only tolerates one predominant value system (as in totalitarian regimes and dictatorships).

According to Fishbein and Ajzen's (1975) *expectancy-value model,* attitudes are a function of beliefs, when beliefs are represented as the sum of the expected values of the characteristics attributed to the attitude object. Each characteristic has an expectancy and a value attached to it; for example, I may have a definite expectancy (high subjective probability) that European integration (the attitude object) will contribute to political stability in Europe (a positively evaluated characteristic). To predict an attitude from such beliefs, expectancy and value terms associated with each characteristic are multiplied together and the products are added:

$$\text{Attitude} = \text{Expectancy} \times \text{Value}$$

According to the theory, we should hold positive (or negative) attitudes towards things that we believe have good (or bad) characteristics. It implicitly assumes that we form attitudes by adding together a number of characteristics of attitude objects, but sometimes we may only take one or a few characteristics into account or we might form attitudes based on affective responses or behaviours, rather than beliefs (Jonas *et al.*, 1995).

● The function of attitudes: what are they for?

According to Hogg and Vaughan (1995):

'... attitudes are basic and pervasive in human life ... Without the concept of attitude, we would have difficulty construing and reacting to events, trying to make decisions, and making sense of our relationships with people in everyday life ...'

Knowledge function	We seek a degree of predictability, consistency and stability in our perception of the world; attitudes give meaning and direction to experience, providing frames of reference for judging events, objects and people.
Adjustive (instrumental or utilitarian) function	We obtain favourable responses from others by displaying socially acceptable attitudes, so they become associated with important rewards (such as being approved of and accepted by others); these attitudes may be publicly expressed but not necessarily believed, as in compliance (see Chapter 20).
Value-expressive function	We achieve self-expression through cherished values. The reward may not be gaining social approval but confirmation of the more positive aspects of one's self-concept, especially a sense of personal integrity.
Ego-defensive function	Attitudes help protect us from admitting personal deficiencies. For example, prejudice helps us to sustain our self-concept by maintaining a sense of superiority over others. Ego defence often means avoiding and denying self-knowledge. This function comes closest to being unconscious in a Freudian sense (see Chapter 29).

TABLE 18.2 *Four major functions of attitudes (Katz, 1960)*

In other words, attitudes provide us with ready-made reactions to and interpretations of events, just as other aspects of our cognitive 'equipment' do, such as schemas (see Chapter 12) and stereotypes (see Chapters 16 and 19). Attitudes save us energy, since we don't have to work out how we feel about objects or events each time we come into contact with them.

However, not all attitudes will serve the same function and a major classification of the functions of attitudes is that of Katz (1960). He was concerned with the motives which attitudes serve and sees some of these motives as conscious and others as unconscious; his approach is probably the closest that modern theories come to a Freudian, psychodynamic view of attitudes. His theory is summarized in Table 18.2. What Katz's functional approach implies is that some attitudes will be more resistant to efforts to change them than others, in particular those that serve an ego-defensive function; this is especially important when trying to account for prejudice and attempts to reduce it (see Chapter 19).

A classification that is similar to Katz's was proposed by Smith *et al.* (1956):

- *object appraisal* refers to the adaptive function of attitudes in meeting day-to-day problems (corresponding to Katz's knowledge function);
- *social adjustment* refers to the usefulness of an attitude in social relationships (corresponding to Katz's adjustive function);
- *externalization* involves responding to an external event in terms of some unresolved internal conflict, thus distorting it (corresponding to Katz's ego-defensive function);

- *quality of expressiveness* which is more concerned with how attitudes reflect an individual's deeper pattern of life, a person's expressive nature or style of operating and so is not really about functions at all (Reich and Adcock, 1976).

ATTITUDES AND BEHAVIOUR: HOW ARE THEY RELATED?

Given that attitudes can only be inferred from what a person says and does, once we have established people's attitudes, are we then in a position to accurately predict how they will behave? As we saw when discussing the three components of attitudes, the behavioural component would seem to be highly correlated with the cognitive and affective components. But is this true in practice? Do people's expressed attitudes (cognitive and affective components) coincide with their overt actions (behavioural component)?

An early, classic study which shows the inconsistency of attitudes and behaviour is that of LaPiere (1934), which is described in Box 18.1.

Wicker (1969) reviewed 42 studies and found that correlations between measured attitudes and behaviour rarely reach 0.30 and average only about 0.15; he concluded that attitudes are typically unrelated or only slightly related to overt behaviours. But is this the only conclusion that can be drawn?

- It is generally agreed that attitudes are only one

BOX 18.1	Key study: doing one thing but feeling another – the 'acceptable' face of prejudice

Beginning in 1930 and for the next two years, LaPiere travelled around the USA with a Chinese couple (a young student and his wife), expecting to encounter anti-Oriental attitudes which would make it difficult for them to find accommodation. But in the course of 10,000 miles of travel they were discriminated against only once and there appeared to be no prejudice. They were given accommodation in 66 hotels, auto camps and 'Tourist Homes' and refused at one. They were also served in 184 restaurants and cafes and treated with '... more than ordinary consideration ...' in 72 of them.

However, when each of the 251 establishments visited was sent a letter six months later asking: 'Will you accept members of the Chinese race as guests in your establishment?', 91 percent of the 128 which responded gave an emphatic 'No', one establishment gave an unqualified 'Yes' and the rest said 'Undecided: depend upon circumstances'.

BOX 18.2	Key study: attitudes can predict behaviour if you ask the right questions

Davidson and Jaccard (1979) tested the correspondence hypothesis by analysing correlations between married women's attitudes towards birth control and their actual use of oral contraceptives during the two years following the study.

When 'attitude towards birth control' was used as the attitude measure, the correlation was 0.08; clearly, the correspondence here was very low. However, when 'attitudes towards oral contraceptives' were measured, the correlation rose to 0.32 and when 'attitudes towards using oral contraceptives' were measured, the correlation rose still further to 0.53. Finally, when 'attitudes towards using oral contraceptives during the next two years' was used, it rose still further, to 0.57. Clearly, in the last three cases, correspondence was much higher.

determinant of behaviour; they represent *predispositions* to behaviour but how we actually act in a particular situation will depend on the immediate consequences of our behaviour, how we think others will evaluate our actions and habitual ways of behaving in those kinds of situations. In addition, there may be situational factors influencing behaviour; for example, in the LaPiere study, the high quality of his Chinese friends' clothes and luggage and their politeness, together with the presence of LaPiere himself, may have made it more difficult to show overt prejudice and, besides, to turn away three guests is clearly against the financial interests of a hotel (at least in the short term). Thus, sometimes we experience a conflict of attitudes and behaviour may represent a compromise between them. (A different kind of conflict situation is where there are pressures on us to conform; see Chapter 20.)

- Again, the same attitude may be expressed, behaviourally, in a variety of ways and in varying degrees; for example, having a positive attitude towards the Labour Party does not necessarily mean that you actually become a member or that you attend public meetings. However, if you don't vote Labour in a general election, people may question your attitude. In other words, an attitude should predict behaviour to some extent, even if

this is extremely limited and specific. Indeed, Ajzen and Fishbein (1977) argue that attitudes *can* predict behaviour, provided the definitions or measurements of both variables are very specific, i.e. there needs to be a high degree of *correspondence* between them. They argue that much of the earlier research suffered from either trying to predict specific behaviours from general attitudes or vice-versa and this accounts for the generally low correlations. The LaPiere study also did this. Box 18.2 describes a study by Davidson and Jaccard (1979) which rectified this shortcoming.

- According to Jonas *et al.* (1995), the earlier failures to demonstrate a consistent relationship between attitudes and behaviour can be understood in terms of the *reliability* and *validity* of the measures used. For example, a single instance of behaviour is an unreliable indicator of an attitude because the performance of the behaviour depends on many factors in addition to the attitude (as we noted earlier). Yet if a number of rather unreliable behavioural indicators of an attitude are combined to form a composite index, the non-attitudinal factors should cancel each other out and it should show a higher correlation with the attitude. This *aggregation principle* (Fishbein and Ajzen, 1974) has been demonstrated in a number of studies.

- Similarly, a single behavioural observation may also be rather invalid, because it embodies specific

FIGURE 18.2 *A demonstration of attitude-behaviour consistency that amazed the world; a pro-democracy Chinese student stands up for his convictions and defies tanks sent in against fellow rebels in Tiananmen Square, Beijing, China. Some 2000 demonstrators died in the subsequent massacre and the student was tried and shot a few days later.*

features that are not included within the attitude being investigated. According to Ajzen and Fishbein (1977), each single measure of behaviour involves (a) a specific action, (b) directed at a target, (c) in a context, (d) at a time or occasion. By contrast, many of the most commonly studied attitudes indicate only the target of an attitude (or the 'attitude object', such as one's attitude towards contraception). What is needed is a representative sample of all the behaviours that are relevant to the attitude in question: the more narrowly defined the attitude, the narrower will be the range of behaviours that are relevant. So, referring back to the Davidson and Jaccard study of contraception, as the attitude was defined more narrowly or specifically, so the correlation with behaviour increased; the range of behaviours that are relevant to 'using oral contraceptives during the next two years' is very small compared with 'birth control'. Ajzen (1988) called this the *principle of compatibility.*

● According to Hogg and Vaughan (1995), what has emerged in the 1980s and 1990s is a view that attitudes and overt behaviour are not related in a simple one-to-one fashion. In order to predict someone's behaviour, it must be possible to account for the interaction between attitudes, beliefs and behavioural intentions, as well as how all of these connect with the later action. As part of this equation, we need to know both how strong and how valuable an individual's beliefs are – some will carry more weight than others in relation to the final act.

One attempt to formalize these links is the *theory of reasoned action* (TRA) (Fishbein and Ajzen, 1974; Ajzen and Fishbein, 1980). Essentially, the theory claims that the proximal (immediate) cause of behaviour is a person's intention to engage in that behaviour. It assumes that (i) human behaviour is rational; (ii) target behaviour is under the actor's conscious control; (iii) the intention is itself a function of both the actor's attitude towards engaging in the behaviour (a personal variable) and their perception of the extent to which significant others think that they should engage in it (*subjective norm*, a social variable). While the TRA has been tested in relation to quite diverse behaviours with quite encouraging results (Jonas *et al.*, 1995), certain crucial criticisms have led to modifications of the original theory.

For example, the TRA is limited to explaining volitional or voluntary behaviour and therefore largely ignores the fact that some behaviours are less under our control than others. Consequently, the *theory of planned behaviour* (TPB) (Ajzen, 1988) was designed to take account of non-voluntary ,as well as voluntary behaviours, by adding to the TRA a new predictor of intention, namely *perceived behavioural control,* our perception of how easy or difficult it is to perform the behaviour reflecting both past experience and current obstacles. Perceived control is, in turn, a function of our belief about how likely it is that we possess the resources and opportunities needed to execute the behaviour. Research has shown that adding this variable can often improve the predictability of intention and behaviour (Jonas *et al.*, 1995). For example, Terry *et al.* (1993, cited in Hogg and Vaughan, 1995) applied features of both the TRA and the TPB to the study of safe sex behaviour as a response to the threat of HIV; target behaviours included monogamous relationships (one partner only), non-penetrative sex and the use of condoms.

Most modern theories agree that attitudes are represented in memory and that the accessibility of an attitude is a factor that can exert a strong influence on behaviour (Fazio, 1986) (see Chapter 12). By definition, strong attitudes are more accessible and exert more influence over behaviour because they can be automatically activated. What makes an attitude more accessible? One factor that seems to be important is direct experience. For example, Fazio and Zanna (1978) found that measures of students' attitudes towards psychology experiments were better predictors of their future participation if they had already taken part in several experiments than if they had only read about them. One explanation for this and similar findings is the *mere exposure effect* (Zajonc, 1968), according to which the more contact we have with something or somebody, the more we like them (see Chapter 17).

THE MEASUREMENT OF ATTITUDES

By definition, an attitude cannot be measured directly because it is a hypothetical construct. Consequently, it is necessary to find adequate indicators of an attitude and most methods of attitude measurement are based on the assumption that they can be measured by people's beliefs or opinions about the attitude object (Stahlberg and Frey, 1988). Most attitude scales rely on verbal reports and usually take the form of standardized statements which clearly refer to the attitude being measured. Such scales make two further assumptions: (i) that the same statement has the same meaning for all respondents; and, more fundamentally, (ii) that subjective attitudes, when expressed verbally, can be quantified, i.e. represented by a numerical score. Some of the major methods of attitude measurement are shown in Table 18.3.

● Some alternative methods of measuring attitudes

A problem with attitude scales (self-report methods) is that participants may be reluctant to reveal their true feelings, which can produce a source of bias called *social desirability,* that is, giving answers which the participant thinks are expected or 'proper' rather than giving honest answers; incorporating a lie scale can help detect this tendency to give socially desirable answers (see Chapter 29). Reassurance that their answers will remain anonymous and stressing the importance of giving honest answers can also help reduce social desirability.

A very different kind of solution is to use cleverly planned inconspicuous observation, a good example of which is Milgram.'s (1965) *lost letter technique.* This was designed to measure people's political attitudes and involves the distribution, throughout a city, of large numbers of letters, stamped but unposted and addressed to different political organizations, such as 'Friends of the Nazi Party' and 'Friends of the Communist Party'. Depending on the rate at which the letters were returned, Milgram was able to assess the popularity of each organization and the corresponding ideological bias of particular parts of the city. While this technique can be criticized on ethical grounds (along with other naturalistic studies in which participants are unaware that they are participating in a study; see Chapter 32), Milgram (1992) stresses that the technique guarantees the anonymity of those who took part.

Another alternative to attitude scales is the *bogus pipeline technique* (Jones and Sigall, 1971), which involves participants being convinced that they cannot hide their true attitudes. They are connected to a machine that resembles a lie detector and told that it can measure both the strength and direction of emotional responses, implying that there is no point in lying. Several studies have shown that participants are indeed convinced and are less likely to conceal

Thurstone's equal appearing intervals scale (1928)

Strictly, this is a technique for constructing an attitude scale. First, about 100 statements are collected, relevant to the attitude object, representing the whole attitude continuum, i.e. they must range from extreme positive to extreme negative. They should be short and unambiguous. Next, about 100 'judges' (representative of the population for whom the scale is intended) are asked to evaluate the statements on an 11-point scale; they are asked to rate each one on an equal interval basis. Any items which produce substantial disagreements are discarded, until 22 remain, two for each of the 11 points on the scale (11 favourable, 11 unfavourable). The average numerical scale position of each statement is calculated. Finally, the 22 statements (in random order) are given to participants who are asked to check every statement with which they agree. The final attitude score is the mean scale value for all endorsed statements.

Though revolutionary in its time, the Thurstone scale is rarely used today, partly because it is so time-consuming to construct, partly because of the assumption that it is an interval (as opposed to ordinal) scale.

LIKERT SCALE

'I believe that under no circumstances can animal experiments be justified'

5	4	3	2	1
Strongly agree	Agree	Undecided	Disagree	Strongly disagree

Likert scale (1932)

This comprises a number of statements, for each of which participants indicate whether they strongly agree/agree/undecided/disagree/strongly disagree. If possible, statements are selected so that for half the statements 'agree' represents a positive attitude and for the other half, it represents a negative attitude. This controls for acquiescent response set, the tendency to agree or disagree with items consistently or to tick the 'undecided' point on the scale. It is one of the most popular standard attitude scales, partly because it proves more statistically reliable than the Thurstone scale, partly because it is easier to construct. It makes no assumptions about equal intervals.

Sociometry (Moreno, 1953)

This represents a method for assessing interpersonal attitudes in 'natural' groups (at school, college, work, etc.), i.e. who likes whom. Each group member is asked to name another who would be their preferred partner for a specific activity or as a friend. The product of these choices is a sociogram which charts the friendship patterns, revealing the popular and unpopular members, the isolates, etc. Each circle represents a group member; the arrows indicate direction of preference. Can you identify the most popular (and the most likely leader)? (See Chapter 20.)

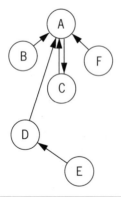

Continued opposite

TABLE 18.3 *Some major methods used in the measurement of attitudes*

socially undesirable attitudes (such as racial prejudice) (Hogg and Vaughan, 1995). The ethical objections are fairly obvious: the technique requires that participants are deceived into revealing aspects of themselves that they otherwise would conceal.

PERSUASIVE COMMUNICATION: HOW EASY IS IT TO CHANGE SOMEONE'S MIND?

According to Laswell (1948), in order to understand and predict the effectiveness of one person's attempt to change the attitude of another, we need to know 'Who says what in which channel to whom and with what effect'. Similarly, Hovland and Janis (1959) say

Guttman scalogram method

This is based on the assumption that a single, unidimensional trait can be measured by a set of statements that are ordered along a continuum of difficulty of acceptance. The statements range from those that are easy for most people to accept to those that most people could not endorse. Such scale items are cumulative, since accepting one item implies acceptance of all those 'below' it. It is constructed so that responses follow a step-like order (Hogg and Vaughan, 1995).

GUTTMAN SCALE
Attitude towards mixed-ethnic housing

How acceptable	Statement
Least	*Generally speaking, people should be able to live where they want.*
	Real estate agencies should not discriminate against minority groups
	The local council should actively support the idea of open housing.
	There should be a local review board that would pass on cases of extreme discrimination of housing.
Most	*There should be laws to enforce mixed-ethnic housing.*

Semantic differential (Osgood et al., 1957)

This assumes a hypothetical semantic space in which the meaning or connotation of any word or concept can be represented somewhere on a seven-point scale. Unlike other scales, this allows different attitudes to be measured on the same scale. The attitude object is denoted by a single word (e.g. 'father') and the scale comprises several bipolar pairs of adjectives (a value of seven usually being given to the positive end and one to the negative end).In the list opposite, 'good-bad' illustrates the evaluative factor, 'strong-weak' the potency factor and 'active-passive' the activity factor.

good _ _ _ _ _ _ _ **bad**

strong _ _ _ _ _ _ _ **weak**

active _ _ _ _ _ _ _ **passive**

TABLE 18.3 *(continued)*

that we need to study: (i) the source of the persuasive communication, that is, the communicator (Laswell's 'who'); (ii) the message itself (Laswell's 'what'); (iii) the recipient of the message or the audience (Laswell's 'whom'); and (iv) the situation or context.

Figure 18.3 shows each of these four factors together with the major aspects of each which have been investigated. Note that it is how the recipient perceives the source which is crucial (although the experimenter usually assumes that the manipulation of source variables will determine how the source is perceived). Also note that the four factors overlap and interact with each other, which often makes it difficult to know where to categorize a particular variable; for example, in Figure 18.2, the trustworthiness of the source includes not being seen as deliberately trying to change the audience's mind; this could just as validly be classified as a message or a recipient factor.

How is attitude change measured? The basic paradigm in attitude-change research involves three steps or stages:

1 measure people's' attitude towards the attitude object (*pre-test*);
2 expose them to a persuasive communication (manipulate a source, message or situational variable or isolate a recipient-variable as the independent variable);
3 measure their attitudes again (*post-test*).

If there is a difference between pre- and post-test measures, then the persuasive communication is judged to have 'worked'.

● How does persuasion work?

According to *theories of systematic processing,* what is important is that the recipient processes the message content in a detailed way. This approach began with Hovland *et al.*'s (1953) proposal that the impact of persuasive messages can be understood in terms of a sequence of processes :

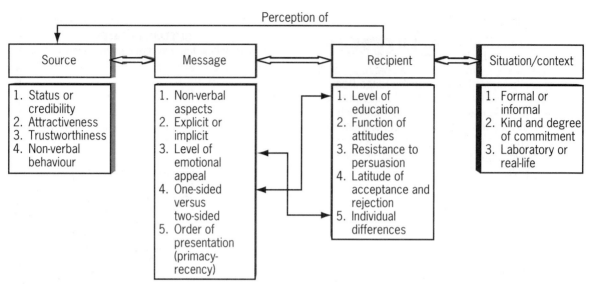

FIGURE 18.3 *The four major factors involved in persuasive communication (arrows between boxes indicate examples of interaction between variables)*

Attention to message → Comprehension of the content → Acceptance of its conclusions

If any of these fails to occur, persuasion is likely not to occur.

McGuire (1969) proposed a longer chain of processes: we should be asking has the recipient: (i) attended to the message; (ii) comprehended it; (iii) yielded to it (i.e. accepted it); (iv) retained it; and (v) acted as a result? As with Hovland *et al.*'s theory, the failure of any one of these steps will cause the sequence to be broken, so that later steps do not occur.

These early theories are related very closely to the early research into persuasive communication that was conducted for the US War Department's Information and Education Department and which has provided a great deal of information regarding *when* attitude change is most likely to occur and *how*, in practical terms, it can be produced. However, it told us less about *why* people change their attitudes in response to persuasive messages. (This early, largely pragmatic approach, is known as the Yale approach and Hovland was one of the leading figures involved).

A more recent approach is the *dual-process approach* or *cognitive perspective* (e.g. Chaiken, 1987), which sees the key questions as: (i) what cognitive processes determine whether someone is actually persuaded? (ii) what do people think about when exposed to persuasive appeals? and (iii) how do their various cognitive processes determine whether and to what extent they experience attitude changes (Baron and Byrne, 1991)? Chaiken's (1987) answer to these questions is in the form of his

heuristic model of persuasion. Heuristics (see Chapter 14) are rules of thumb – mental shortcuts – which we use in processing social or any other kind of information. When a situation is personally involving (for example, it involves attitudes which are salient for the individual concerned), careful, cognitive analysis of the input occurs, whereby the degree of attitude change depends largely on the quality of the arguments put forward.

However, when personal involvement is low, individuals rely on various heuristics to determine whether to change their attitudes. Much of the Yale approach, in fact, deals with the content of these heuristics, e.g. experts are more believable than non-experts and so we are more persuaded by the former, as we are by likeable sources (compared with non-likeable). Other heuristics include: (i) we are more persuaded by a greater than a smaller number of arguments backed up by statistics; and (ii) 'if other people think something is right (or wrong), then I should too'. Heuristics must be available and accessible in order to influence persuasion.

The functions of attitudes also represent an important feature of the cognitive analysis of persuasion (e.g. Katz's four functions; see Table 18.2). Sharitt (1990) argues that there is a relationship between attitude function and persuasion, such that persuasive messages that emphasize the appropriate attitude function of a given product should be more successful in changing attitudes than those which focus on other attitude functions. So, for example, a commercial which emphasizes the utilitarian (or practical) aspects of, say, air conditioners should be

FIGURE 18.4 *A First World War poster campaign, inducing people to invest in the war effort. Most people were sufficiently ego involved that source credibility was irrelevant, nor was suspicion of the source's motives aroused since it was in everybody's best interest to invest in the war effort.*

more successful than one which emphasizes their social identity function (i.e. they allow us to express our identity and project a particular kind of social image) and vice-versa for a commercial for perfume.

● Empirical studies of persuasive communication: source, message, recipient and situational variables

The source

Status or credibility

An important ingredient of status or credibility is whether the source is perceived as being an expert (or at least knowledgeable) in relation to the attitude object; in general, the more expert the source, the more likely we are to be persuaded. A famous demonstration of this is the experiment by Hovland and Weiss (1951) described in Box 18.3; the study also demonstrates the effects of prejudice.

Hovland and Weiss, as well as other studies, found a *sleeper effect,* i.e. when attitudes were retested 3–4 weeks later, the original differences between different sources greatly decreased, so that there was an increasing acceptance of the message from the low-status source and a decreasing acceptance of the high-status source. However, this only occurs if participants are not reminded of the identity and characteristics of the source. So, presumably, the source's identity becomes detached from the actual message with time. According to Hovland, the connection between the arguments and the conclusion of a message is remembered longer than the connection between a 'cue' (such as communicator credibility) and the conclusion. So the sleeper effect represents a delayed form of attitude change.

According to Johnson and Scileppi (1969), credibility is only important in relation to attitude issues with which the participant is only mildly involved; when ego involvement is high, the effect vanishes, perhaps because more attention is paid to the content of the message. Also the more important the attitude issue is to our self-concept, the more suspicious we are of attempts to influence us about it (Reich and Adcock, 1976), which represents an important interaction between source and recipient variables.

In the laboratory, if there is a conflict between a powerful expert figure and the participant's peers, the former is usually more influential but in real-life situations, the reverse seems to be true. Furthermore,

---

BOX 18.3 Key study: you can always trust an expert – as long as they're on your side

Hovland and Weiss (1951) asked American participants to read a statement about the practicality of atomic submarines: those who were told it was written by J. Robert Oppenheimer (one of the scientists who helped develop the atomic bomb) were more convinced of its truth than those who were told its source was *Pravda* (the official newspaper of the then Soviet Union). A similar effect was found when the article concerned antihistamine drugs and the source was either the *New England Journal of Medicine* or a mass-circulation magazine.

Hovland and Weiss collected additional questionnaire data which confirmed that participants saw the medical journal as more credible (in the sense of trustworthy) but there were no differences in how well the articles were remembered (and, therefore, attended to originally).

some peers appear to be more influential than others. In a study by Lazarsfeld *et al.* (1948) of voting behaviour in the USA, it emerged that the majority of voters were not being directly influenced by the media but indirectly through peers (relatives, friends, colleagues, etc.) considered to be 'in the know' regarding political matters. These peers were referred to as *opinion leaders* and Lazarsfeld put forward the *two-step flow hypothesis,* whereby influences stemming from the media first reach opinion leaders who, in turn, pass on what they have read and heard to their everyday associates for whom they are influential.

Attractiveness

A source who is charming, humorous and has a pleasant manner is more persuasive (everything else being equal) than one who does not have these qualities. An unattractive or unlikeable source might produce a 'boomerang effect' whereby the audience responds by adopting attitudes which are contrary to those being advocated. This is one reason that politicians (especially in the USA) devote so much effort to enhancing their personal appeal to voters (Baron and Byrne, 1991) and is part of the process of creating a 'media style'.

Trustworthiness

This relates to the perceived intentions and motives of the source, in particular, are they deliberately trying to influence me and is there an ulterior motive for doing so? Walster and Festinger (1962) found that if participants believe they are 'merely overhearing' a message, they are more likely to be influenced by it than those who hear the same message presented directly to them. An overheard source is less likely to be suspected of ulterior motives and, to this extent, is more trustworthy.

Non-verbal behaviour

This is important largely because of how it contributes to the source being perceived as attractive and trustworthy. One especially relevant dimension of non-verbal behaviour is proximity and personal space (see Chapter 17). For example, there is evidence that most attitude change is produced when the source stands 14–15 feet away and least at a distance of 1–2 feet; participants in the latter condition probably feel that their intimate zone is being encroached and they resent this.

Abelson and Zimbardo (1970) advised campaigning candidates and door-to-door canvassers to keep a distance of 4–5 feet, a respectful distance when talking to strangers, especially when you are on the stranger's 'territory'; this corresponds to Hall's social-consultative distance.

The message

Non-verbal aspects

Following on from what we have said about the source, face-to-face communication may be more effective than attempts by the media to change attitudes because when the source receives feedback from the recipient (in the form of facial expressions, eye contact, body posture and so on) they are in a better position to anticipate objections and to modify the message and present counterarguments. Maslow *et al.* (1971) found that over and above the content of a message, the confidence with which it is presented is a crucial variable. (Confidence could just as easily be discussed as a source-variable as a message-variable.)

Explicit or implicit

The question here is whether the argument should be clearly spelled out (so that no one is left in any doubt as to the conclusions to be drawn) or whether an implicit message is more effective, leaving recipients to work out the conclusions for themselves. McGuire (1968) believes that implicit messages may be more effective if the recipient is capable of, and likely to, draw the conclusions; but for recipients of low intelligence or motivation, explicit messages may be preferred.

Level of emotional appeal

Can people be frightened into changing their minds? One of the most famous attempts to induce attitude change through the manipulation of fear was by Janis and Feshbach (1953) (see Box 18.4).

It would seem from the studies described in Box 18.4 that, in McGuire's terms, you can frighten people into attending to a message, comprehending it, yielding to it and retaining it but not necessarily into acting upon it; indeed, fear may be so great that action is inhibited rather than facilitated. However, this general conclusion needs to be qualified in three main ways:

1 If the audience is told how to avoid undesirable consequences and believes that the preventative action is realistic and will be effective, then even high levels of fear in the message can produce changes in behaviour and the more specific and precise the instructions, the greater the behaviour change (Fig. 18.5). The presence of such instructions is referred to as the *high availability factor.*

2 In situations of minimal or extreme fear, the message may fail to produce any attitude change,

BOX
18.4 Key study: fear of the dentist as a means to healthier teeth

Janis and Feshbach (1953) randomly assigned American high-school students to one of four groups (one control and three experimental). The message was concerned with dental hygiene and degree of fear arousal was manipulated by the number and nature of consequences of improper care of teeth which were referred to (and shown in colour slides); each message also contained factual information about the causes of tooth decay and some advice about caring for teeth.

The high fear condition involved 71 references to unpleasant effects, including toothache, painful treatment and possible secondary diseases, including blindness and cancer; the moderate fear condition involved 49 references, and the low fear condition just 18. (The control group heard a talk about the eye.)

Before the experiment, participants' attitudes to dental health and their dental habits were assessed as part of a general health survey; the same questionnaire was given again immediately following the fear-inducing message and one week later.

As far as how worried participants were about their teeth (an index of attitude change), it seemed that fear had worked, that is, the stronger the appeal to fear, the greater their anxiety. However, as far as actual changes in dental behaviour were concerned, the high fear condition proved to be the least effective; 8 percent of the high fear group had adopted the recommendations (changes in toothbrushing and visiting the dentist in the weeks immediately following the experiment), compared with 22 percent and 37 percent in the moderate and low fear conditions respectively. Similar results were reported by Janis and Terwillinger (1962) when they presented a mild and strong fear message concerning the relationship between smoking and cancer.

Is it fair to force your baby to smoke cigarettes?

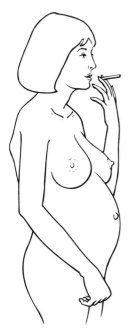

This is what happens if you smoke when you're pregnant.

Every time you inhale you fill your lungs with nicotine and carbon monoxide.

Your blood carries these impurities through the umbilical into your baby's bloodstream.

Smoking can restrict your baby's normal growth inside the womb.
It can make him underdeveloped and underweight at birth.
It can even kill him.
Last year, in Britain alone, over 1,500 babies might not have died if their mothers had given up smoking when they were pregnant.

If you give up smoking when you're pregnant your baby will be as healthy as if you'd never smoked.

The Health Education Council

FIGURE 18.5 *Example of public health campaign poster in which an appeal to fear is combined with the high availability factor*

let alone any change in behaviour. According to McGuire (1968), there is an inverted U-shaped curve in the relationship between fear and attitude change (Fig. 18.6). In segment 1 of the curve, the participant is not particularly interested in (aroused by) the message: it is hardly attended to and may not even register. In segment 2, attention and arousal increase as fear increases, but the fear remains within manageable proportions. In segment 3, attention will decrease again but this time because defences are being used to deal with extreme fear; for example, the message may be denied ('it couldn't happen to me') or repressed (made unconscious and hence forgotten).

3 There are important individual differences regarding normal levels of anxiety (either as a personality trait or in connection with the issue in question, which McGuire calls *initial level of concern*). Clearly, a person who has a high level of initial concern will be more easily pushed into segment 3 than someone with a low level of initial concern; the former may be overwhelmed by a high-fear message (in which case defences are used against it) while the latter may not become interested and aroused enough for the message to have an impact. So different degrees of fear will have different effects upon different individuals depending on their initial level of anxiety (another important interaction). Janis and Feshbach reanalysed their original data and found that high-anxiety participants (who reported frequent

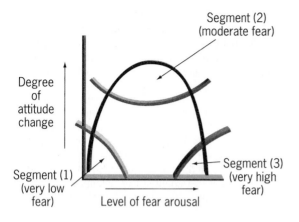

FIGURE 18.6 *Inverted-U curve showing relationship between attitude change and fear arousal. (Based on McGuire, 1968)*

shortage of breath, heart-pounding, etc.) were less influenced by a high-fear message than low-anxiety participants, but were more influenced by a low-fear message.

One-sided versus two-sided arguments

Hovland *et al.* (1949) presented two groups of over 200 soldiers with a series of radio transcripts, arguing that it would take at least two years to end the war with Japan (during the Second World War): one group received a strictly one-sided message and the other a strictly two-sided message. Overall, the two messages produced the same net change in attitudes. However, when education was taken into account, important differences emerged: those who were better educated (had at least completed high school) were more influenced by a two-sided argu-

ment while those who were less well educated were more influenced by a one-sided presentation. Hass and Linder (1972) suggest that this might be related to the recipient's knowledge of counter-arguments; recipients who are aware of arguments opposed to the speaker's point of view are most persuaded by two-sided messages which explicitly refute these arguments.

Order of presentation (primacy-recency)

Having decided to make a two-sided presentation, which side of the argument should come first – the one you want your audience to hold or the counter-position? This, of course, is another instance of the *primacy-recency* issue which we saw when discussing memory (Chapter 12) and interpersonal perception (Chapter 15).

Early research showed a primacy effect but Hovland *et al.* (1957) thought primacy was more powerful only under certain conditions: (i) if both sides are presented by the same person and the recipient is not initially aware that conflicting arguments will be presented; (ii) if recipients make some kind of public commitment at the end of the first message (e.g. they agree to their views being published in a magazine).

Another important factor is the time interval between the two messages. Miller and Campbell (1959) used material from a simulated jury trial and their findings are shown in Figure 18.7. If the second sequence of events is taken as representing the summing up in a trial, where the defence lawyer goes first and is followed by the prosecution lawyer, the implication is that the defence has an advantage. Hass and Linder (1972) advocate that when there are no delays at all, the opposing argument should be

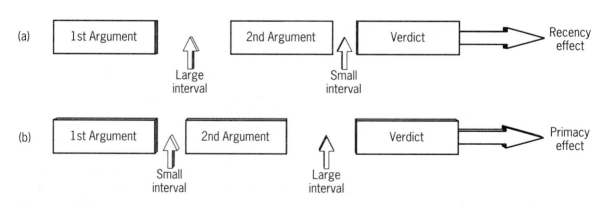

FIGURE 18.7 *The influence of time on primacy-recency in a two-sided argument. (Based on Miller and Campbell, 1959)*

given first and then strongly refuted; in this way attention is drawn to the speaker's viewpoint for most of the presentation. (This, of course, is exactly what the prosecuting lawyer does, except that the opposing argument is presented by another person, i.e. the defence lawyer.)

The recipient

Level of education
We have discussed this already in relation to the Hovland *et al.* study of soldiers (1949) but without saying why the better educated should be more influenced by a two-sided argument. Perhaps they are intellectually better equipped to handle conflicting arguments and are more used to doing so; they might find a two-sided argument more challenging and also may not want to think of themselves as being easily persuaded (as in a one-sided argument).

Resistance to persuasion
In general, it seems that resistance is strongest when counter-arguments are available and weakest when they are not. According to McGuire and Papageorgis (1961), people can be 'inoculated' against attempts to persuade them: by analogy with medical immunization recipients are given a mild 'dose' of an argument against their own opinion, sufficient to activate a defensive counter-argument. Recipients were first exposed to an opposing argument and then were given statements countering these arguments and reinforcing their initial attitudes. A week later, they read a different message which also challenged their initial attitude and they were then less likely to be persuaded by it than others who had not been inoculated (including some who had received support for their opinion but no attack).

Does simply warning someone in advance help them resist a persuasive message? According to Kiesler and Jones (1971) the more committed we are to an issue, the more resistant we are likely to be, regardless of any advance warning. When a warning does have an effect it does so by drawing on that commitment and, perhaps, by prompting us to anticipate counter-arguments and prepare arguments against these (a kind of 'self-inoculation'). Also, the better informed we are about a topic, the more resistant we are likely to be. Forewarning provides us with extra time to muster our defences (especially if we know about the content of the message) and to recall relevant facts and information which may prove useful in arguing against the per-

suasive message. According to Baron and Byrne (1991), '... to be forewarned is to be forearmed, at least in cases in which we care enough about the topic in question to engage in active processing about it'.

When we feel that another person is trying to exert undue pressure on us, we often react by doing the very opposite of what the other wants us to do or adopting the very opposite attitude (*negative attitude change*). This response to perceived threats to our personal freedom is called *reactance* (Brehm, 1966) and represents a strong source of motivation to resist persuasion.

Latitude of acceptance and rejection
The greater the discrepancy between the attitude a person already holds and the one which the communicator wants the person to hold, the less likely it is that any shift in attitude will occur, i.e. if the persuasive message lies outside a person's *latitude of acceptance* (arguments they are prepared to accept), then it will be rejected (and so will fall within the person's *latitude of rejection*).

Sherif and Hovland (1961) found that unacceptable statements tend to be perceived as even more hostile or unfavourable than they really are (*contrast*), while those which are not so extreme may be gradually incorporated into the person's latitude of acceptance (*assimilation*). The more extreme the person's initial position and the greater the ego involvement in it: (i) the smaller the latitude of acceptance; (ii) the greater the latitude of rejection; (iii) the greater the contrast effect; and, consequently, (iv) the less the attitude change. Laboratory experiments normally use issues which are relatively unimportant, together with a high-credibility source; compared with field studies, this has the effect of increasing the latitude of acceptance and hence making attitude change more likely. This throws serious doubt on the ecological validity of laboratory studies of persuasive communication.

Individual differences
Earlier we discussed anxiety in relation to the impact of messages which appeal to fear, but other important and interacting sources of individual differences include gender, self-esteem, persuasibility and intelligence.

Many early studies suggested that women are more easily persuaded but this may simply have been the product of the experimenter's choice of 'male-dominated' issues, such as politics and the economy (Aronson, 1980). Indeed, studies carried out more recently have shown that while women may be more easily persuaded about 'male' issues, men are equally persuasible in relation to 'female' issues, such as home management and family relationships (Sistrunk and McDavid, 1971).

Is there a personality factor which can be called persuasibility? McGuire (1968) thinks there is but that it may not manifest itself equally in relation to both comprehension and yielding and he makes a similar point in relation to intelligence: we would expect a negative correlation between intelligence and persuasibility if the latter is thought of in terms of yielding but because there is a positive correlation between intelligence and comprehension, the overall relationship between intelligence and persuasibility is not a straight line but a curvilinear one (as in the inverted-U curve in Fig. 18.6). Similarly, McGuire believes that there is a curvilinear relationship between self-esteem and persuasibility: people low in self-esteem will be either less attentive or more anxious when processing a message, while those with high self-esteem will be less susceptible to persuasion because they are more self-confident.

Situation or context

Informal situations, such as group discussions, often prove more effective than formal situations, such as speeches and lectures, partly because of differences in the perception of who is trying to influence whom and for what motives. Role-play is another kind of informal situation which has been found effective, both in a therapeutic setting (Kelly, 1955) and experimentally (Janis and Mann, 1965). In the latter, participants who played the role of cancer patients showed significantly greater changes in their attitudes and their smoking behaviour than those who heard information via a tape-recorder or controls, who did neither.

In a group context, participants may be obliged to make some kind of public commitment to a particular attitude which may initially reflect pressures to conform (see Chapter 20) but which may then bring about genuine attitude change through the reduction of cognitive dissonance (see below). Opinions which are expressed privately or anonymously are far less likely to bring about attitude change. Also, as we have already noted, laboratory studies are much more likely to produce attitude change than real-life situations, for a variety of reasons.

THEORIES OF ATTITUDE CHANGE: THE NEED FOR COGNITIVE CONSISTENCY

The most influential theories of attitude change have concentrated on the principle of *cognitive consistency*, whereby human beings are seen as internally active information processors who sort through and modify a large number of cognitive elements in order to achieve some kind of cognitive coherence. It is really a part of human nature, a basic human need, and so such theories may be seen not just as theories of attitude change but also as theories of human motivation (see Chapter 5).

Three of the best known consistency theories are Heider's balance theory (1958), Osgood and Tannenbaum's congruity theory (1955) and Festinger's cognitive dissonance theory (1957), which we shall now examine in detail.

● Cognitive dissonance theory

The central idea is that whenever an individual simultaneously holds two cognitions which are psychologically inconsistent, they experience dissonance, which is a negative drive state – a state of 'psychological discomfort or tension' which motivates the individual to reduce it by achieving consonance. Attitude change is seen as a major way of reducing dissonance. Cognitions are 'the things a person knows about himself, about his behaviour and about his surroundings' (Festinger, 1957) and any two cognitions can be consonant (A implies B), dissonant (A implies not-B) or irrelevant to each other.

A classic example of when dissonance is likely to arise is if we smoke and also believe that smoking causes cancer: assuming that we would rather not have cancer, the cognition 'I smoke' is psychologically inconsistent with the cognition 'smoking causes cancer'. Perhaps the most efficient (and certainly the healthiest!) way to reduce dissonance is to stop smoking, but most of us will work on the other cognition; for example, we might:

- belittle the evidence about smoking and cancer (e.g. 'The human data is only correlational');
- associate with other smokers (e.g. 'If so-and-so smokes, then it can't be very dangerous');
- smoke low-tar cigarettes;
- convince ourselves that smoking is an important and highly pleasurable activity;

● make a virtue out of it by developing a romantic, devil-may-care image and flaunting danger by smoking, etc.

All these possible ways of reducing dissonance demonstrate that dissonance theory regards the human being not as a rational creature but a *rationalizing* one, attempting to appear rational both to others and to oneself. The theory has been tested under three main headings:

1 dissonance following a decision;
2 dissonance resulting from effort;
3 dissonance resulting from counter-attitudinal behaviour.

Dissonance following a decision

If we have to choose between two equally attractive objects or activities, then one way of reducing the resulting dissonance is to emphasize the undesirable features of the one we have rejected; in this way we are trying to add to the number of consonant cognitions and reduce the number of dissonant ones.

This was demonstrated in a study by Brehm (1956) in which female participants had to rate the desirability of several household appliances on an eight-point scale. When they had done this, they had to choose between two of the items (their reward for participating), which for half were ½ to 1½ points apart on the scale (high-dissonance condition), while for the other half they were a full three points apart (low-dissonance condition). When they were asked to re-evaluate the items they had chosen and rejected, they showed increased liking for the chosen item and decreased liking for the rejected one. So far, so good.

The theory also predicts that we will tend to actively avoid information which emphasizes the desirable qualities of the item we have rejected (because that will add to the dissonance) as well as actively seeking information which praises the desirable qualities of the item we have chosen (because that will reduce dissonance by increasing consonance). So if we have had a difficult time deciding which new car to buy, we will avoid advertisements for other cars and go out of our way to find advertisements for our own. Is there evidence to support

---

BOX 18.5 Key study: preferring things that turn out for the worst

In a study by Aronson and Mills (1959), female college students volunteered for a discussion on the psychology of sex, with the understanding that the research was concerned with the dynamics of group discussion. Each student was interviewed individually and asked if she could participate without embarrassment: all but one said yes.

If she had been assigned to the *control condition*, she was simply accepted but for acceptance to the *severe embarrassment condition*, she had to take an 'embarrassment test' (reading out loud to a male experimenter a list of obscene words and some explicit sexual passages from modern novels – remember the year was 1959!) and for acceptance to the *mild embarrassment condition*, she had to read aloud words like 'prostitute' and 'virgin'. They then all heard a tape-recording of an actual discussion (by a group which they believed they would later join) which was about sex in lower animals and extremely dull. They then had to rate the discussion and the group members in terms of how interesting or dull and intelligent or unintelligent they found them.

As predicted, the severe embarrassment group gave the most positive ratings, because they had experienced the greatest dissonance!

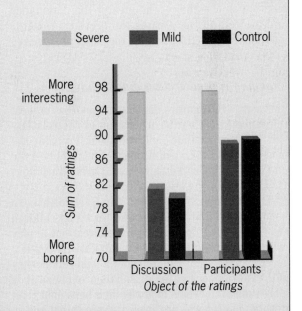

FIGURE 18.8 *Female students' ratings of how interesting a group discussion was in relation to degrees of embarrassment which they suffered in order to get accepted for the discussion. (Based on Aronson & Mills, 1959)*

this prediction? Several studies have suggested that there is a tendency to prefer advertisements showing the car people had recently bought but no corresponding avoidance of advertisements showing other cars.

Dissonance theory predicts that there will be selective exposure to consonant information, i.e. seeking consistent information which is not present at the time. However, there is more to selective perception than selective exposure: other aspects include selective attention (looking at consistent information which is present) and selective interpretation (perceiving ambiguous information as being consistent with our other cognitions). Each of these has been investigated and in a review of the literature, Fiske and Taylor (1991) conclude that the evidence overall is stronger for selective attention and interpretation than for selective exposure.

Dissonance resulting from effort

One of the classic dissonance experiments (Aronson and Mills, 1959) is described in Box 18.5.

The study shows that, when a voluntarily chosen experience turns out badly, the fact that we chose it motivates us to try to think that it actually turned out well: the greater the sacrifice or hardship associated with the choice, the greater the dissonance and, therefore, the greater the pressure towards attitude change (this is called the *suffering leads to liking effect*).

Engaging in counter-attitudinal behaviour

This aspect of cognitive dissonance theory is of most relevance to our earlier discussion of the relationship between attitudes and behaviour. Probably the most famous of all the dissonance experiments is the one carried out by Festinger and Carlsmith (1959) (see Box 18.6).

The findings of Festinger and Carlsmith have been confirmed by several studies in which children are given either a mild or a severe threat not to play with an attractive toy (Aronson and Carlsmith, 1963: Freedman, 1965). If children obey a mild threat, they will experience greater dissonance because it is more difficult for them to justify their behaviour than it is for children who are given a severe threat and so the mild threat condition produces greater reduction in liking of the toy.

But does counter-attitudinal behaviour always and inevitably produce dissonance and attitude change? It seems not – dissonance only occurs when *volitional* (voluntary) behaviour is involved, that is,

---

BOX 18.6 Key study: the 'one dollar/20 dollar' experiment (Festinger and Carlsmith, 1959)

College students were brought, one at a time, into a small room to work for 30 minutes on two extremely dull and repetitive tasks (stacking spools and turning pegs). Later, they were offered either one dollar or 20 dollars to enter a waiting room and to try to convince the next 'participant' (in fact, a female stooge) that the tasks were interesting and enjoyable. Common sense would predict that the 20-dollar group would be more likely to change their attitude in favour of the tasks (they had more reason to do so) and this is also the prediction which would be made by reinforcement or *incentive theory* (Janis *et al.*, 1965) which maintains that the greater the reward or incentive, the greater the attitude change (liking for the tasks).

However, Festinger and Carlsmith found, as predicted by dissonance theory, that it was in fact the one-dollar group which showed the greater attitude change (*this is called the less leads to more effect*). Why? The large, 20-dollar incentive gave those participants ample justification for their counter-attitudinal behaviour and so they experienced very little dissonance; by contrast, the one-dollar group experienced considerable dissonance because they could hardly justify their counter-attitudinal behaviour in terms of the negligible reward, hence, the change of attitude to reduce the dissonance.

---

when we feel we acted of our own free will: if we believe we had no choice, there is no dissonance and hence no attitude change. A study by Freedman (1963) shows that dissonance theory and reinforcement theory are not necessarily opposed to each other – their respective predictions may both be confirmed when applied to the conditions of voluntary or involuntary behaviour.

Another variable which influences dissonance, and which interacts with voluntary or involuntary behaviour, is the degree of *commitment*. Carlsmith *et al.* (1966) used a procedure similar to that of Festinger and Carlsmith's one dollar/20 dollar experiment and also found that the smaller reward produced the greater attitude change. However, this dissonance effect was only found under conditions where participants lied to another person in a highly committing, face-to-face situation (they had to make an identifiable video recording). Where they merely had to write an essay and were assured of complete anonymity, then an incentive effect was found (i.e. the bigger the reward, the greater the attitude change). (In the Festinger and Carlsmith study, this face-to-face variable was not manipulated.)

● Evaluation of dissonance theory

Can the results of dissonance experiments be explained differently?

Not only do dissonance effects occur under certain specified conditions (e.g. volition and commitment), but some critics have argued that even under those conditions it is possible to explain the findings in other ways.

A major critic of dissonance theory has been Bem. He claims that dissonance as such is neither a necessary nor sufficient explanation and he rejects any reference to hypothetical, intervening variables. According to his *self-perception theory* (1965, 1967), any self-report of an attitude is an inference from observation of one's own behaviour and the situation in which it occurs. If the situation contains cues (e.g. offer of a large 20 dollar incentive) which imply that we might have behaved that way regardless of how we personally felt (we lie about the task being interesting even though it was boring), then we do not infer that the behaviour reflected our true attitudes. But in the absence of obvious situational pressures (one dollar condition), we assume that our attitudes are what our behaviour suggests they are. In terms of attribution theory (see Chapter 15), the 20 dollar group can easily make a situational attribution ('I did it for the money'), whereas the one dollar group had to make a dispositional attribution ('I did it because I really enjoyed it').

Eiser and van der Pligt (1988) believe that, conceptually, it is very difficult to distinguish between the two theories. Perhaps, as with dissonance and incentive theories, both processes operate but to different extents under different circumstances. Fazio *et al.* (1977), for example, argue that dissonance may apply when people behave in a way which is contrary to their initial attitude (*counter-attitudinal behaviour*), while self-perception may apply better where their behaviour and initial attitude are broadly consistent (*attitude-congruent behaviour*).

There is no doubt that we do sometimes 'work backwards' from behaviour to 'internal states', e.g. our stomach rumbles or we have 'second helpings' at a meal and then infer how hungry we must have been or we shout at someone and infer that we are angry. These would be good examples of attitude-congruent behaviour but are fairly trivial compared with situations in which we experience some kind of conflict between what we think and what we do. We should also note that conflict is as often between two attitudes or beliefs as it is between attitudes and behaviour – yet Bem's self-perception theory (based as it is on attribution principles) requires some overt behaviour from which we then make an inference about our attitudes. However, such behaviour often simply does not occur.

Another general issue is whether what matters is our own inferences about the way we behave or the inferences we feel others might draw about us (*impression management theory;* see Chapter 15). Tedeschi *et al.* (1971) argue that the effects of many dissonance experiments might not reflect genuine cases of 'private' attitude change but rather an adoption of a public response that protects participants against the possible accusation of insincerity (i.e. the need is to appear consistent rather than a drive to actually be consistent). Impression management theorists (Tedeschi and Rosenfield, 1981; Schlenker, 1982) no longer tend to claim that changes in attitude responses are a mere pretence. Instead, much attitude change is seen as an attempt to avoid social anxiety and embarrassment or to protect positive views of one's own identity. Accordingly, the roots of the 'tension' hypothesized by Festinger may be in people's social concerns with how others might evaluate them and how they should evaluate themselves. So the one dollar group's attitude change is genuine but is motivated by social (rather than cognitive) factors.

Does dissonance really exist?

An objection that can be made to experiments like the one dollar/20 dollar study is that the reasoning involved is circular: (i) the only evidence for the greater dissonance of the one dollar group is the fact that they rated the task as more interesting; and (ii) the fact that they rated the task as more interesting is evidence of the greater dissonance. Is there any independent evidence for the existence of dissonance? What kind of evidence would we accept? What about physiological evidence? Croyle and Cooper (1983) found evidence for more persistent increase in physiological arousal as measured by GSR (galvanic skin response) in participants who wrote a counter-attitudinal essay under high-choice as compared with low-choice instructions or with those who wrote an essay consistent with their own opinion. However, feelings of unpleasant tension may also be produced by factors less directly related to the notion of dissonance, e.g. the belief that a decision will have bad consequences (Cooper and Fazio, 1984). According to such an interpretation, attitude change in such experiments should depend both on the amount of arousal experienced (from whatever sources) *and* on how the participant interprets/explains this arousal.

Support for this notion comes from a study (Zanna and Cooper, 1974) in which participants wrote a counter-attitudinal essay under instructions which implied either high or low freedom of choice. Consistent with previous findings, the prediction that high-choice participants change their opinions more than low-choice was confirmed. The novel feature of the experiment was that participants were also given a placebo pill; they were either told it would make them feel tense or relaxed or told nothing about it at all. The dissonance theory prediction was upheld when participants were given no information and even more strongly when they were told it would relax them. But when told the pill would make them feel tense, no difference between the high and low choice conditions was found. Why?

If participants believe the pill will either relax them or have no effect and they also believe they are acting of their own free will, they change their opinions, presumably because they experience an internal state of dissonance. But if told the pill will make them tense, they will (mis)attribute their tension to the pill and so little attitude change will occur (as is also true of low freedom of choice participants). This attribution explanation is consistent with Bem's self-perception theory and so the Zanna and Cooper experiment offers support for both Festinger and Bem. (Compare this with Schachter and Singer's attribution theory of emotion; see Chapter 6.)

● Conclusions

Despite these and other challenges and reconceptualizations:

> ... cognitive dissonance theory remains one of the most widely accepted explanations of attitude change and many other social behaviours. It has generated over one thousand research studies and will probably continue to be an integral part of social psychological theory for many years ... (Hogg and Vaughan, 1995)

CHAPTER SUMMARY

- Attitudes have always represented one of the most important topics in social psychology. Two central issues that have been investigated are attitude change and the relationship between attitudes and behaviour.

- The concept of an 'attitude' is a hypothetical construct and has been defined in many ways. The three-component model of attitude structure sees attitudes as comprising an affective, cognitive and behavioural component but most definitions are unidimensional, stressing the affective or evaluative component.

- Attitudes have much in common with beliefs and values, but they need to be distinguished.

- Rokeach distinguishes between terminal and instrumental values and a well-known classification of (terminal) values is that of Allport *et al.*, which identifies theoretical, aesthetic, political, economic, social and religious value orientations.

- Terminal values underlie all kinds of political ideology, which may be pluralistic or monistic.

- Attitudes serve the vital cognitive function of providing a ready-made set of responses and interpretations of objects and events . However, different motives underlie different attitudes. Katz identifies the knowledge, adjustive, value-expressive and ego-defensive functions and a similar classification was proposed by Smith *et al.*

- Early research into the relationship between attitudes and behaviour showed that attitudes are very poor predictors of behaviour. However, attitudes represent only one of several determinants of behaviour, including situational factors.

- Attitudes can predict behaviour, provided there is a close correspondence between the way that the two variables are defined and measured (the principle of compatibility). Also, measures of a representative sample of behaviours relevant to the attitude must be made (the aggregation principle).

- The widely accepted view today is that attitudes and overt behaviour are not related in a simple one-to-one way; to predict behaviour, we need to know how a person's attitudes, beliefs and behavioural intentions all interact with each other and how they connect with later action.

- The theory of reasoned action is one attempt to account for these interactions in relation to voluntary behaviour and the theory of planned behaviour attempts to account for non-voluntary behaviours too, by adding the concept of perceived behavioural control.

- Attitudes that are more accessible will tend to have a greater influence on behaviour; accessibility is increased by direct experience.

- Attitudes cannot be measured directly. Most methods of measurement rely on verbal reports which relate to people's opinions about the attitude object; they assume that attitudes can be quantified and that the same statement has the same meaning for all respondents.

- Thurstone's equal appearing interval scale, the Likert scale, the Guttman scalogram method, the semantic differential and sociometry are some of the major methods used in the measurement of attitudes.

- An alternative to these self-report methods, which attempt to get round problems such as acquiescent response set and social desirability, are the lost letter technique and bogus pipeline technique. Whatever their methodological advantages, they pose very serious ethical questions.

- Persuasive communication has traditionally been studied in terms of the influence of four interacting factors: the source of the persuasive message, the message itself, the recipient of the message and the situation/context.

- Theories of systematic processing see the impact of persuasive messages as dependent on a sequence of processes, including attending to the message, comprehending it, accepting its conclusions, retaining it and acting as a result.

- The more recent cognitive perspective focuses on why people change their attitudes (not merely when and how it is likely to happen).The heuristic model of persuasion, for example, explains why we are more likely to be persuaded when the situation is not personally involving or if the arguments are convincing.

- An important aspect of the status or credibility of the source is their perceived expertise. But this becomes less important with time (the sleeper effect). If the source is attractive and trustworthy (not seen as deliberately trying to persuade you) and respects your personal space, you are more likely to be persuaded.

- If the message is presented confidently, it is more likely to be effective and explicit messages may be more effective if the recipients do not draw their own conclusions.

- People can be frightened into attending to, comprehending, accepting and retaining a message, but the high availability factor is necessary for any behaviour change to take place.

- There appears to be an inverted U-shaped curve in the relationship between fear and attitude change. The effects of emotional messages will also depend on individual differences in prior levels of anxiety.

- People with higher levels of education are more likely to be influenced by a two-sided message. When both sides of the argument are presented, there is evidence for a primacy effect, although this will depend on certain conditions.

- Recipients can be helped to resist persuasion by being given a mild 'dose', sufficient to activate a defensive counter-argument. Warning recipients in advance also helps resist a persuasive message, especially if the issue is important enough for them to think about it in advance. Attempts to persuade us may result in negative attitude change and/or reactance.

- The more extreme the message, the more likely it is that it will fall outside the recipient's latitude of acceptance and so be rejected (i.e. it will fall within the latitude of rejection).

- Gender differences in persuasibility reflect the kinds of issues that are studied, not any inherent difference.

- There seems to be a curvilinear relationship between intelligence and persuasibility and between self-esteem and persuasibility.

- Generally, informal situations seem to be more effective than formal ones, especially where some kind of public commitment to a particular attitude is required. Also, laboratory studies are much more likely to produce attitude change than real-life situations.

- The major theories of attitude change share the basic principle of cognitive consistency; the one that has proved most influential is Festinger's theory of cognitive dissonance.

- Dissonance is most likely to occur (i) after making a very difficult choice or decision; (ii) when putting ourselves through hardship or making a sacrifice only to find it was for nothing; or (iii) when engaging in counter-attitudinal behaviour. The latter seems to depend on the behaviour being voluntary or volitional and where there is a high degree of commitment.

- The results of studies such as the 'one dollar/20 dollar' experiment have been interpreted in ways that are contrary to cognitive dissonance theory, such as Bem's self-perception theory. One proposal is that dissonance theory applies under conditions of 'true' counter-attitudinal behaviour, while self-perception theory applies to attitude-congruent behaviour.

- Another alternative theory is impression management theory, which stresses the social rather than the cognitive motivation underlying attitude change.
- A controversial issue is whether it is possible to define/measure dissonance independently of attitude change.

GLOSSARY

Acquiescent response set Tendency to consistently agree or disagree with items on a rating scale or to tick the 'undecided' point on the scale.

Aggregation principle Combining a number of unreliable behavioural indicators of an attitude to form a composite index will cancel out the non-attitudinal factors involved in any single behaviour. This will produce a higher attitude-behaviour correlation.

Attitude A blend or integration of beliefs and values. A predisposition to behave.

Belief The non-evaluative knowledge/ information we have about the world (corresponding to the cognitive component of an attitude).

Bogus pipeline technique An alternative to attitude scales, which involves participants being deceived into believing that a particular machine can measure both the strength and direction of emotional responses.

Cognitive consistency Coherence or balance between our different thoughts, beliefs, etc. Seen as a basic human need.

Cognitive dissonance A state of psychological discomfort produced when our cognitions are inconsistent (including counter-attitudinal behaviour).

Expectancy-value model The view that attitudes are a function of beliefs, which are the sum of the expected values of the attributes of the attitude object.

Guttman scalogram Method of attitude measurement which assumes that a unidimensional trait can be measured by a set of statements ordered along a continuum of difficulty of acceptance.

Heuristic model of persuasion A cognitive theory of why people are persuaded; people use mental shortcuts to avoid analysing the content of a message, especially when the issue is of little importance for them.

High availability factor In a high fear persuasive message, specific instructions about how to avoid the undesirable consequences predicted by the message.

Latitude of acceptance The range of arguments that we are prepared to accept.

Latitude of rejection The range of arguments that goes beyond what we are prepared to accept.

Less leads to more effect When we accept a small inducement to voluntarily engage in some counter-attitudinal behaviour, our attitude undergoes a greater change than if we had accepted a large inducement.

Likert scale Method of attitude measurement comprising a set of statements, for each of which respondents indicate whether they strongly agree/agree/undecided/disagree/ strongly disagree.

Lost letter technique Observational method of studying political attitudes, which involves the distribution of letters addressed to different political organizations to see the return rate for different organizations.

Principle of compatibility Matching the way that 'attitude' and 'relevant behaviour' are measured, so that they are equally specific.

Self-perception theory Bem's view that we infer our attitudes from observing our own behaviour just as we infer others' attitudes from observing their behaviour.

Semantic differential Method of attitude measurement comprising several bipolar pairs of adjectives on a seven-point scale, designed to measure the connotative meaning of any attitude object.

Sleeper effect the tendency, over time, for the source and content of a persuasive message to become detached.

Social desirability Tendency to answer questions on a self-report scale dishonestly, in the direction of 'proper' or expected answers.

Sociometry Method of assessing interpersonal attitudes by asking members of natural groups to make friendship/partner choices; this produces a sociogram.

Suffering leads to liking effect The greater the sacrifice or hardship associated with our choice to do something that turns out badly, the more we come to believe that it actually turned out well.

Theory of planned behaviour (TPB) An extension of the TRA that takes account of non-voluntary behaviour by adding the concept of perceived behavioural control.

Theory of reasoned action (TRA) Theory that sees a person's intention to act as the immediate cause of the behaviour. Deals only with voluntary behaviour.

Three component model A view of the structure of attitudes, comprising an affective component (what we feel about the attitude object), a cognitive component (our beliefs about it) and a behavioural component (our actual or intended behaviour).

Thurstone's equal appearing intervals scale Method of attitude measurement comprising a set of 22 statements (11 favourable, 11 unfavourable). Respondents have to check every one they agree with, each statement being located on an 11-point scale that is assumed to be an interval scale.

Two-step flow hypothesis View that the mass media have a direct effect on only a minority of people (opinion leaders), who then pass on the media messages to their peers.

Value A sense of what is desirable, good, worthwhile, etc. (corresponding to the affective component of an attitude). May be terminal or instrumental.

FURTHER READING

Ajzen, I. (1988) *Attitudes, Personality and Behaviour.* Milton Keynes: Open University Press. Thorough discussion of most of the issues dealt with here by one of the leading researchers in the field. Part of a series of books on social psychology.

Zimbardo, P.G. & Leippe, M.R.(1991) *The Psychology of Attitude Change and Social Influence.* New York: McGraw-Hill. A very readable, but detailed text that, as the title implies, discusses attitude change in the broad context of social influence. Also part of an excellent series on social psychology.

19 PREJUDICE AND DISCRIMINATION

INTRODUCTION AND OVERVIEW

> ... fifty years after the [Nazi] extermination and concentration camps were liberated, genocide continues unabated, neither punished nor prevented. In what used to be ... [Yugoslavia], torture, murder, rape, and starvation are everyday occurrences ... (Hirsch, 1995)

While genocide – the systematic destruction of an entire cultural, ethnic or racial group – is the most extreme form of discrimination, the prejudice that underlies it is essentially the same as that which underlies less extreme behaviours, i.e. prejudice is an *attitude* that can be expressed in many ways or which may not be expressed overtly at all. Like other attitudes, prejudice can be regarded as a disposition to behave in a prejudiced way (i.e. discrimination); this represents another example of the issue regarding the relationship between attitudes and behaviour that we discussed in the last chapter.

Two other questions that we asked about attitudes in Chapter 18 we shall be trying to answer here about prejudice (a) where does it come from, how do people become prejudiced? (b) how is it possible to reduce or even to prevent prejudice? This second question has much greater practical significance than it does in relation to attitudes in general – the quote from Hirsch testifies to that.

We shall begin by trying to define prejudice, before discussing three major theoretical approaches to explaining prejudice:

1 those that locate the cause of prejudice within the psychological make-up of individuals, including the very influential authoritarian personality theory of Adorno *et al*;
2 those that focus on the role of external, environmental factors and which try to account for intergroup conflict, such as Sherif's realistic conflict theory;
3 those which emphasize the impact of group membership, such as Tajfel and Turner's social identity theory.

Both (2) and (3) can be thought of as social psychological approaches, because they stress the interaction between personal (individual) and social variables, in contrast with (1) which focuses on the individual in relative isolation from social influences.

All the theories that seek to explain prejudice and discrimination also have implications for how they can be reduced or prevented; but we shall also discuss attempts and strategies which are not tied directly to any of these theories.

WHAT IS PREJUDICE?

● Prejudice as an attitude

As an extreme attitude, prejudice comprises the components of all attitudes:

- The *cognitive* component is the stereotype (see Chapter 15).
- The *affective* component is a strong feeling of hostility.
- The *behavioural* component can take different forms. Allport (1954) proposed five stages of this component:

  1 *antilocution* – hostile talk, verbal denigration and insult, racial jokes, etc.

  2 *avoidance* – keeping a distance but without inflicting any harm;
  3 *discrimination* – exclusion from housing, civil rights, employment, etc.;
  4 *physical attack* – violence against the person and property;
  5 *extermination* – indiscriminate violence against an entire group (including genocide).

'Discrimination' is often used to denote the behavioural component (in contrast with 'prejudice' which denotes the cognitive and affective components). However, as with all attitudes, the cognitive and affective components may not necessarily be manifested behaviourally (as in the LaPiere study discussed in Chapter 18). But conversely, discrimination does not necessarily imply the presence of cognitive and affective components – people may discriminate if the prevailing social norms dictate that they do so and if their wish to become or remain a member of the discriminating group is stronger than their wish to be fair and egalitarian, etc.(see below).

● Definitions of prejudice

Almost all definitions of prejudice stress the hostile, negative kind (although, strictly, prejudice can also

---

'... an antipathy based on faulty and inflexible generalization directed towards a group as a whole or towards an individual because he is a member of that group. It may be felt or expressed.' (Allport, 1954)

'... Prejudice is an attitude (usually negative) toward the members of some group, based solely on their membership in that group...' (Baron and Byrne, 1991)

'Prejudice is a learned attitude towards a target object that typically involves negative affect, dislike or fear, a set of negative beliefs that support the attitude and a behavioural intention to avoid, or to control or dominate, those in the target group ... Stereotypes are prejudiced beliefs ... when prejudice is acted out, when it becomes overt in various forms of behaviour, then discrimination is in practice ... (Zimbardo and Leippe, 1991)

TABLE 19.1 *Some definitions of prejudice and discrimination*

be positive – just as stereotypes can be positive – or 'neutral') and the research which tries to identify how prejudice arises, and how it might be reduced, also concentrates on hostile prejudice. Three examples are given in Table 19.1.

The definitions in Table 19.1 locate prejudice squarely within the individual – it is an attitude which represents one aspect of social cognition. However, Vivian and Brown (1995) prefer to see prejudice as a special case of *intergroup conflict:* although they are conceptually distinct, they often coexist. Intergroup conflict occurs when '... people think or behave antagonistically towards another group or its members in terms of their group membership and seem motivated by concerns relating to those groups'. They also distinguish intergroup conflict and interpersonal conflict, a distinction that we shall return to when discussing attempts to reduce prejudice.

Defining prejudice in terms of intergroup conflict 'lifts' it to the social plane. Consistent with this is Fernando's (1991) distinction between 'racial prejudice' and 'racism'; the former denotes an attitude possessed by the individual (corresponding to the definitions of Allport and Baron and Byrne), while the latter refers to a political and economic ideology, which is a characteristic of society. Similarly, Littlewood and Lipsedge (1989) argue that '... Racist attitudes may be manifest as a highly articulated set

---

| **BOX 19.1** | Prejudice and discrimination in health care: not all patients are equal |

According to Rose and Platzer (1993), the attitudes of many nurses are grounded in their assumptions about people's heterosexual nature and their lack of knowledge about different lifestyles and how these affect people's health. Ignorance about how lesbians and gay men live can lead nurses to ask inappropriate questions during assessments, leading them to form mistaken judgements.

For example, one lesbian patient who was receiving a cervical smear test was asked if she was sexually active. After saying she was, she was asked what contraceptive she used and replied 'none'. She was then asked if she was trying to become pregnant, which she was not. She had to disclose her lesbianism in order to ensure that health professionals did not make incorrect assumptions about her, which could have led to an incorrect diagnosis. In another example, one patient's

charts were labelled 'high risk'. These labels, which were clearly visible to other patients and members of staff, were there simply because he was gay and so was seen as being at risk of having HIV – the nurses simply assumed that gay men were likely to be HIV positive and that heterosexual men were not. Such assumptions are, of course, linked to stereotypes about what gay men do, rather than to a knowledge of sexual behaviours, which can differ widely regardless of sexual orientation.

One nurse in an accident and emergency department refused to give a male patient an analgesic suppository (a pain-relieving capsule inserted into the anus) 'in case he liked it'. Such examples suggest that homosexuality is seen only in terms of sexual behaviour and not lifestyle, which means that nurses' abilities to see patients as individuals with particular nursing needs are being hampered. There is a false but commonplace belief that lesbians and gay men are less discriminating in their sexual habits than heterosexuals and that they would want to engage in sexual activity in any setting and regardless of personal preferences (Rose and Platzer, 1993).

of beliefs in the individual, but they are also found in less conscious presuppositions, located in society as a whole ...'. The crucial point is that, strictly, it is societies that are racist and individuals who are racially prejudiced and if 'racism' is a feature of society as a whole, then this is also true of the other 'isms', in particular, sexism, heterosexism and ageism.

● There is more to prejudice than racism

Until relatively recently, most of the theory and research into prejudice and discrimination was concerned with racism, '...the quite specific belief that cultural differences between ethnic groups are of biological origin and that groups should be ranked in worth' (Littlewood and Lipsedge, 1989). However, as we noted above, gender (as in sexism), sexual orientation or preference (as in heterosexism) and age (as in ageism) are all the basis for hostility and discrimination. (While we have the ready-made 'racially prejudiced' as an alternative to 'racist', we do not usually talk about 'sexual prejudice, 'sexual orientation prejudice' or 'age prejudice', although these are the grammatical equivalents.) Sexism will be discussed in Chapters 23 and 32, ageism in Chapter 24 and heterosexism in Chapter 30. This chapter will concentrate on racism, but in Box 19.1 there is a discussion of heterosexism in relation to health care, showing that a great deal of prejudice and discrimination of all types is unconscious, reflected in basic, stereotyped assumptions that we make about others which then influence our behaviour towards them, which does not have to be overtly hostile or 'anti'. It is perhaps this pervasive form of heterosexism, etc. that is the most difficult to break down, because we are unaware of it and because it reflects the prejudices that are prevalent in mainstream society.

THEORIES OF THE CAUSES OF PREJUDICE AND DISCRIMINATION

As we noted earlier, attempts to explain prejudice and discrimination fall into three broad categories:

1 those which see prejudice as stemming from *personality* variables and other aspects of the psychological make-up of individuals;
2 those which emphasize the role of external, *environmental* factors;

3 those which focus on the effects of the mere fact of *group membership*.

Each approach may be important to a complete understanding of the causes of intergroup conflict and prejudice and to their reduction (Vivian and Brown, 1995).

● Prejudice stemming from the psychological make-up of individuals

The authoritarian personality

In 1950, Adorno *et al.* proposed the concept of the *authoritarian personality* (in a book of the same name), a type of person who is prejudiced by virtue of specific personality traits which predispose them to be hostile towards ethnic, racial and other minority or outgroups.

They began by studying anti semitism in Nazi Germany in the 1940s and drew on Freud's theories to help understand the relationship between 'collective ideologies' (such as fascism) and individual personality (Brown, 1985). After their emigration to the USA, studies began with over 2000 college students and other native-born, white, non-Jewish, middle-class Americans (including school teachers, nurses, prison inmates and psychiatric patients), which involved interviews concerning their political views and childhood experiences and the use of projective tests (in particular, the thematic apperception test or TAT; see Chapter 5) designed to reveal unconscious attitudes towards minority groups.

A number of scales were developed in the course of their research:

● *Antisemitism (AS) scale.* This defined antisemitism as 'stereotyped negative opinions describing the Jews as threatening, immoral, and categorically different form non-Jews, and of hostile attitudes urging various forms of restriction, exclusion, and suppression as a means of solving the 'Jewish problem'. The 52 items were phrased so as to express a subtle hostility without seeming to offend the democratic values most respondents would feel bound to support, a kind of 'fair-minded and reasonable veneer' (Brown, 1965). Some examples of the items used are given in Table 19.2.
● *Ethnocentrism (E) scale.* The term was first used by Sumner in 1906: 'A view of things in which one's own group is the centre of everything, and all others are scaled and rated with reference to it

Antisemitism (AS) scale	1	The trouble with letting Jews into a nice neighbourhood is that they gradually give it a typically Jewish atmosphere.
	2	I can hardly imagine myself marrying a Jew.
Ethnocentrism (E) scale	1	Negroes have their rights, but it is best to keep them in their own districts and schools and to prevent too much contact with whites.
	2	America may not be perfect, but the American Way has brought us about as close as human beings can get to a perfect society.
Political and economic conservatism (PEC) scale	1	A child should learn early in life the value of a dollar and the importance of ambition, efficiency and determination.
	2	In general, full economic security is harmful; most men wouldn't work if they didn't need the money for eating and living.

Potentiality for fascism (F) scale

1 Conventionalism	Obedience and respect for authority are the most important virtues children should learn.
2 Authoritarian submission	Young people sometimes get rebellious ideas, but as they grow up they ought to get over them and settle down.
3 Authoritarian aggression	Sex crimes, such as rape and attacks on children, deserve more than mere imprisonment; such criminals ought to be publicly whipped or worse.
4 Anti-intraception	When a person has a problem or worry, it is best for him not to think about it, but to keep busy with more cheerful things.
5 Superstition and stereotypy	Some people are born with an urge to jump from high places.
6 Power and toughness	People can be divided into two distinct classes: the weak and the strong.
7 Destructiveness and cynicism	Human nature being what it is, there will always be war and conflict.
8 Projectivity	Nowadays when so many different kinds of people move around and mix together so much, a person has to protect himself especially carefully against catching an infection or disease from them.
9 Sex	Homosexuals are hardly better than criminals and ought to be severely punished.

TABLE 19.2 *Sample items from the various scales used by Adorno et al. (1950)*

... Each group ... boasts itself superior ... and looks with contempt on outsiders. Each group thinks its own folkways the only right one...'. The scale comprised 34 items and some examples are given in Table 19.2.

● *Political and economic conservatism (PEC) scale.* The definitive component of conservatism is attachment to things as they are and a resistance to social change. This is the only scale to include items supporting both sides of the issues. Examples are given in Table 19.2.

● *Potentiality for fascism (F) scale* (sometimes called the implicit antidemocratic trends scale). According to Brown (1965), Adorno *et al.* never referred to the F scale as the authoritarianism scale but since it is supposed to identify the kind of personality the book is talking about, it is rea-

sonable to suppose that the scale could also be correctly called the authoritarianism scale (as it has been in many subsequent research reports). The scale was revised several times during the course of the research, but the items never referred directly to minority groups or politicoeconomic issues. It was intended to measure implicit authoritarian and antidemocratic trends in personality, making someone with such a personality susceptible to explicit fascist propaganda.

The 38 items were subclassified under nine general headings; these and examples of each are shown in Table 19.2.

Table 19.3 shows the correlations between the different scales. The pattern of intercorrelations suggests that (a) scores on the AS, E and F scales all correlate

	AS	E	PEC	F
AS		0.80	0.43	0.53
E			0.57	0.65
PEC				0.57
F (final version)		0.75		

TABLE 19.3 *Correlations between scores on the different scales used by Adorno et al. (1950)*

with each other much more strongly than any of them does with the PEC score; and, following from this, (b) people who are antisemitic are also likely to be hostile towards 'Negroes', 'Japs' and any other minority group or 'foreigner' (all outgroups), i.e. the authoritarian personality is prejudiced in a very generalized way.

What is the authoritarian personality like?

Typically, the authoritarian personality is hostile to people of inferior status, servile to those of higher status, contemptuous of weakness, rigid and inflexible, intolerant of ambiguity and uncertainty, unwilling to introspect feelings and an upholder of conventional values and ways of life (as represented by religion, for example). This belief in convention and intolerance of ambiguity combine to make minorities 'them' and the authoritarian's membership group 'us'; 'they' are by definition 'bad' and 'we' are by definition 'good'.

How does the authoritarian personality come to be prejudiced?

These personality characteristics really only tell half the story as far as the link between personality and prejudice is concerned. Based on the interview and TAT data, Adorno *et al.* claimed that authoritarians have often experienced a harsh, punitive, disciplinarian upbringing, with little affection. While they consciously have a very high opinion of their parents, they often reveal considerable latent (unconscious) hostility towards them, stemming from the extreme frustration they experienced as children. Drawing on Freudian theory, Adorno *et al.* proposed that such unconscious hostility may be displaced onto minority groups (so that they become the objects of the authoritarian's hostility); authoritarians also project onto these groups their own unacceptable, antisocial impulses (especially sexual and aggressive) so that they feel threatened by members of these groups. Authoritarians 'suffer' from 'self-glorification', i.e. they have very little self-insight and their prejudice serves a vital ego-defensive function, which protects them from the unacceptable parts of themselves (see Chapter 18).

Evaluation of the authoritarian personality theory

While there is some evidence that is broadly consistent with the theory, there are a number of serious methodological and other problems which make it untenable; some of these will be discussed in later sections.

● The items on the AS, E and F scales (all Likert-type questions; see Chapter 18) were all worded in such a way that agreement with them always implies antisemitism, ethnocentrism and potential fascism respectively. Adorno *et al.* recognized the possibility that someone with an acquiescent response set (see Chapter 18) might mechanically achieve a high score without necessarily being antisemitic, etc. but they rejected it.

● The interview and TAT data were intended partly to validate the F scale, but the clinical interviews were flawed since the interviewer knew the interviewee's F score; this represents a serious source of *experimenter bias* (see Chapter 2).

● According to Brown (1988), the theory cannot explain the widespread uniformity of prejudice in certain societies or subgroups within societies. If prejudice is to be explained in terms of individual differences, how can it then be manifested in a whole population or at least a vast majority of that population? In pre-war Nazi Germany, for example (and in many other places since), consistent racist attitudes and behaviour were shown by hundreds of thousands of people who must have differed on most other psychological characteristics. Similarly, how can the theory account for the sudden rises and falls of prejudice in particular societies at specific historical periods? Again taking the example of antisemitism in Nazi Germany, this arose during a decade or so which is much too short a time for a whole generation of German families to have adopted new forms of childrearing practices giving rise to authoritarian and prejudiced children (Brown, 1988).

Even more dramatic was the anti-Japanese prejudice among Americans following the attack on Pearl Harbor. Such examples '... strongly suggest that the attitudes held by members of different groups towards each other have more to do with the objective relations between the groups – relations of political conflict or alliance, economic interdependence and so on – than with the familial relation in which they grew up! (Brown, 1988).

The open and closed mind

Another criticism made of the authoritarian personality theory is that it assumed that authoritarianism is a characteristic of the political right and so implied that there is no equivalent authoritarianism on the left. The best known attempt to redress this balance is that of Rokeach (1960), who developed a *dogmatism scale*: 'ideological dogmatism' refers to a relatively rigid outlook on life and intolerance of those with opposing beliefs. High scores on the dogmatism scale reveal: (i) closedness of mind; (ii) lack of flexibility; and (iii) authoritarianism, regardless of particular social and political ideology.

So an individual with left-wing or progressive beliefs can espouse them in just as rigid and dogmatic a way as someone with right-wing or reactionary views – they can be equally extreme (and closed) regardless of their particular content. A measure of general authoritarianism must be free of ideological content, since it can be found in people of every political persuasion, as well as in Freudians, etc.; the best way to think about it is as a mode of thought, rather than as a set of beliefs (Brown, 1965). The dogmatic individual tends to accentuate differences between 'us and them' (e.g. 'The USA and USSR have just about nothing in common'), displays self-aggrandizement (e.g. 'If I had to choose between happiness and greatness, I'd choose greatness'), a paranoid outlook on life ('I often feel people are looking at me critically') and is uncompromising in their beliefs and intolerant of others. These characteristics serve as defences against the dogmatic person's self-inadequacy.

Rokeach (1960) gave the F scale and the dogmatism scale to five English groups of different political persuasions, including a group of 13 communist students. While the communists scored low on the F scale, they had the highest dogmatism scores, which supported Rokeach's claim that the F scale measures only right-wing authoritarianism.

At the same time as he published his dogmatism scale, Rokeach proposed his *belief congruence theory,* according to which the similarity or 'congruence' of individuals' belief systems largely determines their attitudes towards one another: we are generally more attracted to those who share our beliefs, since this validates and legitimizes our own (Byrne, 1971; Festinger, 1954; see Chapter 16). Racial prejudice is seen as the result of perceived differences in belief (belief incongruence) between members of different racial/ethnic groups and this is ultimately more important as a determinant of discrimination than the differences in group membership.

To test the theory, Rokeach devised the *race belief paradigm,* an experimental procedure in which individuals are presented with 'stimulus persons' who vary in terms of their attitudinal and ethnic similarity to the participant. While there is some support for the theory, both from laboratory and field studies (Hogg and Vaughan, 1995), Brown and Turner (1981) warned against applying concepts intended to explain interpersonal behaviour to the realm of intergroup behaviour, since each is controlled by different psychological processes. As a laboratory procedure, the race belief paradigm is an explicitly interpersonal situation (so that individual beliefs are most salient); but when race is made salient, the usual findings can be reversed, i.e. the situation now becomes explicitly intergroup. Rokeach himself recognized the limitations of the belief congruence theory as a complete explanation of prejudice, admitting that it does not apply to situations where racism is institutionalized (as was apartheid in South Africa) or widely socially supported (as in the southern USA). But does this leave very much?

Toughmindedness and tendermindedness

Eysenck (1954) proposed two independent dimensions: *radicalism-conservatism* (the R factor), corresponding to right/left wing political beliefs; and *toughmindedness-tendermindedness* (the T-factor), the terms first used by William James to refer to two poles of human temperament, with toughmindedness corresponding to authoritarianism and dogmatism. A toughminded person will be attracted to extreme political ideologies, be it fascism *or* communism; the authoritarian person is toughminded and conservative, while the humanitarian is tenderminded and radical (Fig. 19.1). While the R-factor represents social attitudes acquired during one's lifetime by social and political experience, the T-factor is a manifestation of certain fundamental personality traits, namely toughmindedness and extroversion and tendermindedness and introversion (see Chapter 29).

Scapegoating: frustration, aggression and prejudice

According to the *frustration-aggression hypothesis* (Dollard *et al.*, 1939), frustration always gives rise to aggression and aggression is always caused by frustration (this was discussed in much more detail in Chapter 17). The source of frustration (i.e. what prevents us from achieving our goals) might often be seen as a fairly powerful threat (e.g. parents or

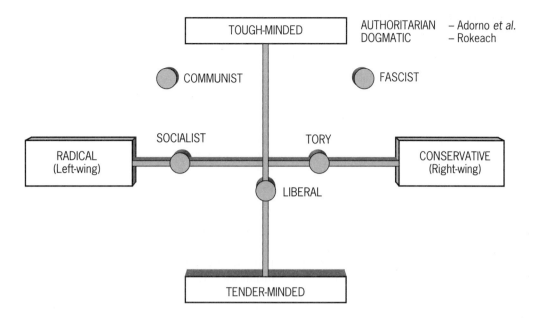

FIGURE 19.1 *Eysenck's two scales (corresponding to the R and T factors), their relationship to Adorno et al. and Rokeach's theories, plus the locations of some 'typical' political attitudes. (Based on Eysenck, 1954)*

employer) or may be difficult to identify at all (e.g. the unemployed may blame 'the government' or 'the recession' or something equally intangible). Drawing on Freudian theory, Dollard *et al.* claim that when we need to vent our frustration but we are unable to do this in a direct way (for whatever reason), we do so indirectly by displacing it onto a substitute target.

The substitute object is, of course, the scapegoat but the choice of scapegoat is not usually random. In England during the 1930s and 1940s, the scapegoat was predominantly the Jews, who were replaced by West Indians during the 1950s and 1960s and during the 1970s, 1980s and 1990s by Asians from Pakistan. In the southern USA, lynchings of blacks from 1880 to 1930 were related to the price of cotton; as the price dropped, so the number of lynchings increased (Hovland and Sears, 1940). While this is consistent with the concept of displaced aggression, the fact that whites chose blacks as scapegoats rather than some other minority group suggests that there are usually socially approved (legitimized) groups which serve as targets for frustration-induced aggression.

Limitations of the 'individual make-up' approach

When discussing Rokeach's race belief paradigm above, we noted the distinction between interpersonal and intergroup behaviour. Several writers (e.g. Billig, 1976; Brown, 1988; Hogg and Abrams, 1988) have argued that any account of prejudice

and discrimination in terms of individuals is reductionist, i.e. the social nature of prejudice and discrimination requires a social explanation (see Chapter 32). Adorno *et al.* imply that racism is the product of the abnormal personality of a small minority of human beings rather than a social and political ideology; this distinction is of great practical as well as theoretical importance, because what is considered to be the cause of prejudice has very real implications for the reduction of prejudice. In fact, Adorno *et al.* recognized that, as important as personality dynamics are, it is society which provides the content of attitudes and prejudice and it is society which defines who are the outgroups. According to Brown (1985), 'cultural or societal norms may be much more important than personality in accounting for ethnocentrism, outgroup rejection, prejudice and discrimination'. This takes us onto the second major approach .

● The role of external/environmental factors

The impact of social norms: prejudice as conformity

Although research on the authoritarian personality has been valuable, individual bigotry can explain only a small proportion of racial discrimination. For example, even though overt discrimination has been, traditionally, greater in the southern USA, white southerners have not scored higher than whites from the north on measures of authoritarianism (Pettigrew, 1959). So, clearly, conformity to social norms can prove more powerful as a determinant of behaviour than personality factors.

Minard (1952) found that black and white coalminers in West Virginia followed a pattern of almost complete integration below ground but almost complete segregation above! This only makes sense when viewed in terms of conformity to the norms which operated in those different situations.

Pettigrew (1971) also found that Americans in the south are no more antisemitic or hostile towards other minority groups than those from the north (as the authoritarian personality explanation would require); i.e. prejudice is not the generalized attitude which Adorno *et al.* claim it is. According to Reich and Adcock (1976), the need to conform and to not be seen as different may cause milder prejudices, but active discrimination against, and ill treatment of, minorities is best seen as reflecting a prejudice which already exists and which is maintained and legitimized by conformity.

Intergroup conflict: relative deprivation theory

The notion of relative deprivation was first used by Stouffer *et al.* (1949) in their classic wartime study of American soldiers; its role in intergroup conflict was developed more formally by Davis (1959). In the context of the frustration–aggression hypothesis, it is when people feel deprived of something they feel

entitled to that they experience frustration: the discrepancy between our actual attainments (such as standard of living) and expectations (the standard of living we feel we deserve) is our *relative deprivation*. When attainments suddenly fall short of rising expectations, relative deprivation is particularly acute, resulting in collective unrest; this is expressed as a J-curve (Davies, 1969, cited in Hogg and Vaughan, 1995; see Fig. 19.2) and a good example of such acute relative deprivation is the 1992 Los Angeles riots. The immediate cause was the acquittal, by an all-white jury, of four LA police officers accused of beating a black motorist, Rodney King. Against a background of rising unemployment and deepening disadvantage, this was seen by blacks as symbolic of their low esteem in the eyes of the white majority (Hogg and Vaughan, 1995). The great sense of injustice at the acquittal seemed to demonstrate in acute form the injustice which is an inherent feature of discrimination – and of relative deprivation.

The LA riots are an example of what Runciman (1966) called *fraternalistic* relative deprivation (based on a comparison either with dissimilar others or with other groups) as opposed to *egoistic*, which is based on comparison with other similar individuals. Vanneman and Pettigrew (1972) found that whites who expressed the most anti black attitudes were those who felt most strongly that whites as a group are badly off relative to blacks; objectively, they were actually better off, showing the subjective nature of relative deprivation. It has been pointed out that the most militant blacks seem to be those with higher socioeconomic and educational status; these individuals probably have higher expectations, both for themselves and for their group, and consequently experience relative deprivation more acutely (Vivian and Brown, 1995).

Intergroup conflict: realistic conflict theory

When members of a group believe that another group can achieve its goals only at their own group's expense (and vice-versa), hostility develops between the groups, along with the discrimination commonly associated with such hostility. Data from many nations and historical periods show that the greater the competition for scarce resources, the greater the hostility between various ethnic groups; for instance, a number of studies have found high levels of racism among lower class whites who felt that blacks were taking away their jobs.

According to Sherif's (1966) *realistic conflict theory*, intergroup conflict arises as a result of a conflict

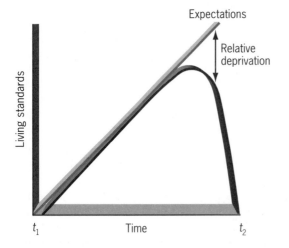

FIGURE 19.2 *The J-curve hypothesis of relative deprivation. (Based on Davies, 1969)*

BOX
19.2 Key study: the Robber's Cave experiment (Sherif *et al.*, 1961)

The setting was Robber's Cave State Park in Oklahoma, where 22 white, middle-class, Protestant, well-adjusted boys, spent two weeks at a summer camp; they were randomly assigned to two groups of 11, each occupying a separate cabin, out of sight of each other. None of the boys knew any of the others prior to their arrival at the camp.

During the first stage of the experiment, each group co-operated on a number of activities (e.g. pitching tents, making meals, a treasure hunt) and soon a distinct set of norms emerged which defined the group's identity; one group called itself the 'Rattlers and the other called itself the Eagles. Towards the end of the first week, they were allowed to become aware of the other's existence and an 'us and them' language quickly developed.

The second stage began with the announcement that there was to be a grand tournament between the two groups, comprising ten sporting events, plus points awarded for the state of their cabins and so on; a splendid trophy, medals and four-bladed knives for each of the group members would be awarded to the winning group.

Before the tournament began, the Rattlers' flag was burned and the camp counsellors (the experimenters) had to break up a fight between the two groups. With some 'help' from the counsellors, the Eagles won and later the Rattlers stole their medals and knives.

There was a strong preference for the ingroup: Rattlers stereotyped all Rattlers as brave, tough and friendly and (almost) all Eagles as sneaky, stinkers and smart alecks; the reverse was true for the Eagles.

with adults from industrial organizations meeting for two-week periods.

Tyerman and Spencer (1983) challenged Sherif *et al.*'s conclusions that competition is a sufficient condition for intergroup conflict by observing English boy scouts at their annual camp. The boys knew each other well before the start of camp and much of what they did there was similar to what the Rattlers and Eagles did at Robbers Cave. They were divided into four 'patrols' who competed in situations familiar to them from previous camps, but the friendship ties which existed prior to arrival at camp were maintained across the patrol groups; competition remained friendly and there was no increase of ingroup solidarity. Tyerman and Spencer believe that the four groups continued to see themselves as part of the whole group (a view deliberately encouraged by the leader) and concluded that Sherif *et al.*'s results reflect the transitory nature of their experimental group. The fact that the English boys knew each other beforehand, had established friendships, were familiar with camp life and had a leader who encouraged co-operation were all important contextual/situational influences on the boys' behaviour. It seems that 'competition' may not, after all, be a sufficient condition for intergroup conflict and hostility.

If we accept this conclusion, the question arises whether it is a necessary condition. In other words, can hostility arise in the absence of conflicting interests? This leads us on to the third major approach.

● The influence of group membership

Minimal groups

According to Tajfel *et al.* (1971), the mere perception of the existence of another group can itself produce discrimination: when people are arbitrarily and randomly divided into two groups, knowledge of the other group's existence is a sufficient condition for the development of pro-ingroup and anti-outgroup attitudes; this is known as the *minimal group*.

Tafjel *et al.* argue that, before any discrimination can occur, people must be categorized as members of an ingroup or an outgroup (making categorization a necessary condition) but, more significantly, the very act of categorization by itself produces conflict and discrimination (making it also a sufficient condition). These conclusions are based on the creation of artificial groups among 14–15-year-old schoolboys from Bristol. The criteria which were used were arbitrary and superficial and differed from experiment to experiment. They included:

of interests: when two groups want to achieve the same goal but cannot both have it, hostility is produced between them. Indeed, he claims that conflict of interest (or competition) is a sufficient condition for the occurrence of hostility or conflict and he bases this claim on one of the most famous field experiments in social psychology, the Robber's Cave experiment described in Box 19.2, which Brown (1986) describes as the most successful field experiment ever conducted on intergroup conflict.

Clearly the competition threatened an unfair distribution of rewards (the trophy, medals and knives) and the losing group inevitably saw the winners as undeserving. Sherif *et al.*'s results have been confirmed

- chronic 'overestimators' or 'underestimators' on a task involving estimating the number of dots appearing on slide projections;
- preference for paintings by Klee or Kandinsky;
- the toss of a coin.

Once these arbitrary groups had been formed, the boys worked alone in cubicles on a task which required them to allocate points, as in a game, which could be exchanged at the end for one-tenth of a penny each. The points could be allocated either to fellow group members or to members of the other group. The only information each boy had about another boy was whether or not he was a member of the same group or the other group, otherwise he was anonymous, unknown, unseen and identified only by a code number. The allocation of points was always to the advantage of ingroup members and to the detriment of outgroup members – even when a co-operative strategy would have maximized the outcome for the ingroup (see Fig. 19.3).

A
MATRIX 1

-19	-16	-13	-10	-7	-4	-1	0	1	2	3	4	5	6
6	5	4	3	2	1	0	-1	-4	-7	-10	-13	-16	-19

MATRIX 2

12	10	8	6	4	2	0	-1	-5	-9	-13	-17	-21	-25
-25	-21	-17	-13	-9	-5	-1	0	2	4	6	8	10	12

B
MATRIX 3

1	2	3	4	5	6	7	8	9	10	11	12	13	14
14	13	12	11	10	9	8	7	6	5	4	3	2	1

MATRIX 4

18	17	16	15	14	13	12	11	10	9	8	7	6	5
5	6	7	8	9	10	11	12	13	14	15	16	17	18

C
MATRIX 5

-14	-12	-10	-8	-6	-4	-2	-1	3	7	11	15	19	23
23	19	15	11	7	3	-1	-2	-4	-6	-8	-10	-12	-14

MATRIX 6

17	14	11	8	5	2	-1	-2	-3	-4	-5	-6	-7	-8
-8	-7	-6	-5	-4	-3	-2	-1	2	5	8	11	14	17

FIGURE 19.3 (A) *Examples of matrices used by Tajfel. The numbers represented points (later translated into awards or penalties in money) to be assigned by a participant to other individuals; by checking a box, the participant assigned the number of points in the top of the box to one person and the number in the bottom of the box to another person; he did not know the identity of these people but only whether each was a member of his own group or the 'other group'. (The groups had been established by the experimenters on grounds that were artificial and insignificant.) Each matrix appeared three times in a test booklet with each row of numbers labelled to indicate whether the partici-pant was choosing between two members of his own group (ingroup) other than himself, two members of the outgroup or one member of the ingroup and one member of the outgroup. Choices were scored to see if participants chose for fairness, maximum gain to their own group or maximum difference in favour of the ingroup. (Based on Tajfel, 1970)*

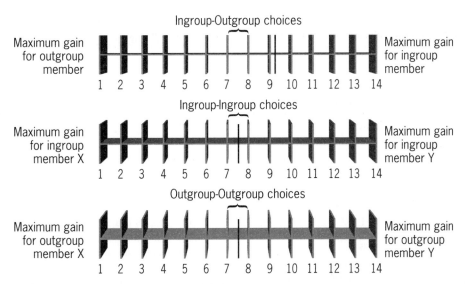

FIGURE 19.3 (B) *Results were scored by ranking the choices from 1 to 14, depending on which box was checked. The end of the matrix at which the ingroup member got the minimum number of points (and the outgroup member the maximum) was designated 1; the other end, giving the ingroup member the maximum, was 14. The mean choices (long vertical lines) are shown here. In the intergroup situation the participants gave significantly more points to members of their own group than to members of the other group. In the intragroup situations, however, the means of the choices fell at Rank 7.5, between the choices of maximum fairness (brackets). (Based on Tajfel, 1970)*

In the Tajfel *et al.* experiments, the actual group assignments were always made randomly whatever the boys believed to be the basis for the categorization. But Billig and Tajfel (1973) and Locksley *et al.* (1980) went even further in the creation of minimal groups by actually *telling* the participants that they were being randomly assigned, tossing the coin in front of them and giving them obviously meaningless names (such as As and Bs or Kappas and Phis). Even under these conditions the groups still showed a strong ingroup preference.

Brown (1988) points out that intergroup discrimination in this minimal group situation has proved to be a remarkably robust phenomenon. In more than two dozen independent studies in several different countries, using a wide range of experimental participants of both sexes (from young children to adults), essentially the same result has been found: the mere act of allocating people into arbitrary social categories is sufficient to elicit biased judgements and discriminatory behaviours.

However, Wetherall (1982) maintains that intergroup conflict is not inevitable. She studied white and Polynesian children in New Zealand and found the latter to be much more generous towards the outgroup, reflecting cultural norms which emphasized co-operation. The minimal group paradigm has also been criticized on several grounds, especially its

artificiality (e.g. Schiffman and Wicklund, 1992; and see Gross, 1994).

Social identity theory (SIT)

How can we account for the minimal group effect? Tajfel (1978) and Tajfel and Turner (1986) offer an explanation in the form of *social identity theory* (SIT). According to SIT, individuals strive to achieve or maintain a positive self-image which has two components – personal identity (derived from personal traits, relationships with other individuals and so on) and social identity (see Chapter 21). In fact, each of us has several social identities, corresponding to the number of different groups with which we identify and, in relation to each one, the more positive the image of the group, the more positive will be our own social identity and hence our self-image. By emphasizing the desirability of the ingroup(s) and focusing on those distinctions which enable our own group to come out on top, we help to create for ourselves a satisfactory social identity and this can be seen as lying at the heart of prejudice.

Members of minimal groups in the laboratory (compared with controls who are not assigned to a group) have been found to show higher self-esteem. For example, Lemyre and Smith (1985) claimed that it was indeed the opportunity to display intergroup discrimination that increased self-esteem: control participants who were categorized but could only distribute rewards between two ingroupers or two outgroupers or could not distribute rewards at all showed lower self-esteem than experimental participants able to make intergroup decisions.

SIT is not limited to minimal group experiments. Part of its attraction is its ability to make sense of a wide range of phenomena in naturalistic contexts, including wage differentials (size of wage relative to comparable groups of workers), ethnolinguistic groups (attempts by various ethnic or national groups to maintain the integrity of their native language) and occupational groups (for example, biases in nursing in favour of registered as opposed to enrolled nurses); (Brown (1988).

Some individuals may be more prone to prejudice because they have an intense need for acceptance by others. For such individuals, personal and social identity may be much more interlinked than for those with a lesser need for social acceptance. The need for a sense of security and superiority can be met by belonging to a favoured ingroup and showing hostility towards outgroups. Prejudice can be seen as an adjustive mechanism which bolsters the self-concept of individuals who have feelings of personal inadequacy. It becomes a 'prop' for these individuals (but with potentially undesirable social implications).

Evaluation of SIT

While there is considerable empirical support for the theory, much of this comes from minimal group experiments; any serious methodological problems with the latter will reduce the validity of the former. Also, and perhaps most seriously, it is argued that the evidence as it stands only shows a positive ingroup bias and not derogatory attitudes or behaviour towards the outgroup, which is what we normally understand by 'prejudice', i.e. although there is abundant evidence of intergroup discrimination, this appears to stem from raising the evaluation of the ingroup rather than denigrating the outgroup (Vivian and Brown , 1995).

A recent development of SIT is *self-categorization theory* (Turner, 1985; Turner *et al.*, 1987), which claims that social identity extends into the private self and that social norms define and shape the activity of the private self and vice-versa (Turner, 1991). This is discussed further in relation to conformity (see Chapter 20).

THE REDUCTION OF PREJUDICE AND DISCRIMINATION

Perhaps an obvious place to start in trying to answer the question 'How can prejudice and discrimination be reduced?' is to see what the theories of their causes have to offer.

- The *authoritarian personality* theory implies that, by changing the personality structure of the prejudiced individual, the need for an ego-defensive 'prop' such as prejudice is removed. By its nature, this is practically very difficult to achieve, even if it is theoretically possible. Equally difficult is the prevention of the kind of childrearing pattern which, according to Adorno *et al.*, determines the authoritarian personality in the first place.

- According to the *frustration–aggression hypothesis* and the theory of *relative deprivation,* preventing frustration, lowering people's expectations, and providing people with less antisocial ways than discrimination of venting their frustrations are all possible solutions, but this may involve putting the historical clock back or changing social conditions in quite fundamental ways.

- *Realistic conflict* theory makes it very clear that removing competition and replacing it with superordinate goals and co-operation will remove or prevent hostility; this will be discussed further below.

- *SIT* and *self-categorization* theory imply that if intergroup stereotypes can become less negative and automatic and if boundaries between groups can be made more blurred or more flexible, then group memberships may become a less central part of the self-concept, making positive evaluation of the ingroup less inevitable. We shall return to this theme below.

● The contact hypothesis

Probably the first formal proposal of a set of social-psychological principles for reducing prejudice was Allport's (1954) *contact hypothesis* (as it has come to be called), which is summarized in a very famous quote:

> Prejudice (unless deeply rooted in the character structure of the individual) may be reduced by equal status contact between majority and minority groups in the pursuit of common goals. The effect is greatly enhanced if this contact is sanctioned by institutional supports (i.e. by law, custom or local atmosphere) ...

Most programmes aimed at promoting harmonious relations between groups that were previously in conflict have operated according to Allport's 'principles', in particular *equal status contact* and the *pursuit of common (superordinate) goals*.

Equal status contact

When people are separated and segregated, the stage is set for *autistic hostility*, i.e. ignorance of others which leads to a failure to understand the reasons for their actions. Lack of contact means there is no 'reality testing' against which to check our own interpretations of others' behaviour and this in turn is likely to reinforce negative stereotypes. By the same token, ignorance of what 'makes them tick' will probably make 'them' seem more dissimilar from ourselves than they really are and there is much independent evidence from the interpersonal attraction research that the greater the (perceived) similarity, the greater the liking (see Chapter 16). It follows that bringing people into contact with each other at least offers the possibility that this negative cycle can be reversed (see Fig. 19.4).

Related to autistic hostility is the *mirror-image phenomenon* (Bronfenbrenner, 1960), whereby enemies come to see themselves as being in the right (with 'God on our side') and the other side as in the wrong and the offender; in the same way, they tend to attribute to each other the same negative characteristics (the 'assumed dissimilarity of beliefs'). By increased contact, there is the opportunity to disconfirm our stereotypes and the outgroup loses its strangeness and becomes more differentiated, i.e. it no longer consists of interchangeable 'units' but is a collection of unique individuals. (This represents a reduction in the illusion of outgroup homogeneity; see Chapter 15.)

However, it is generally agreed that increased contact by itself is not sufficient to reduce prejudice. Despite evidence that we prefer people who are familiar, if this contact is between people who are consistently of the same unequal status, then 'familiarity may breed contempt'. Aronson (1980) points out that many whites (in the USA) have always had a great deal of contact with blacks – as dishwashers, toilet attendants, domestic servants and so on; such contacts may simply reinforce the stereotypes held by whites of blacks as being inferior. Similarly, Amir (1994) argues that we need to ask '... Under what conditions does intergroup contact have an impact, for whom, and regarding what outcomes?'.

One early study of equal status contact was that of Deutsch and Collins (1951), who compared two kinds

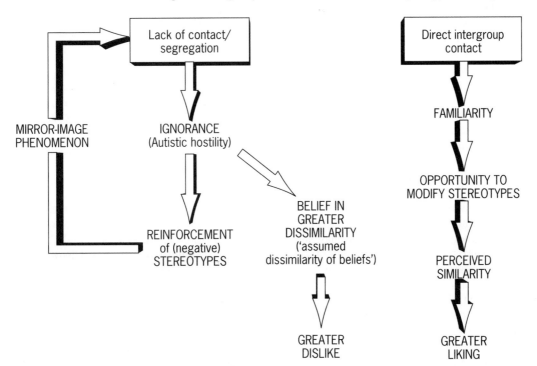

FIGURE 19.4 *Summary of how the negative cycle of lack of contact/segregation between racial/ethnic groups and reinforcement of negative stereotypes can be broken by direct contact (as advocated by Allport's contact hypothesis)*

of housing projects, one of which was thoroughly integrated (blacks and whites were assigned houses regardless of race) and the other segregated. Residents of both were intensively interviewed and it was found that both casual and neighbourly contact were greater in the integrated housing with a corresponding decrease in prejudice among whites towards blacks. So it appeared to be environmental support which was sustaining prejudice in the segregated project.

The Minard study of miners in West Virginia (1952) suggests that the change was confined to situations in which it was socially permissible to be unprejudiced; black and white miners were (equal status) colleagues in the mine, but the norms that operated 'above ground' clearly did not permit equality of status. Consistent with this are studies by Stouffer (1949) and Amir (1969) which found that inter-racial attitudes improved markedly when blacks and whites served together as soldiers in battle and on ships, but relationships were not so good at base camp.

It might be thought that desegregation of American schools would provide a major test of the effectiveness of equal status contact in reducing prejudice and a number of studies have been carried out to this end; however, the results are very discouraging. Stephan (1978) reviewed a number of studies and concluded that desegregation as such seems not to have reduced white prejudice towards blacks and black prejudice towards whites seems to have increased. Several studies have found that, at first, interaction and friendship are totally governed by group attitudes and then slowly start to take account of personal qualities. However, racial attitudes change very little.

If intergroup contact does reduce prejudice, it is not because it encourages interpersonal friendship (as Deutsch and Collins would claim) but because of changes in the nature and structure of intergroup relationships. According to Brown and Turner (1981) and Hewstone and Brown (1986), if the contact between groups is interpersonal (people are seen as individuals and group memberships are largely insignificant), then any change of attitude may not generalize to other members of the respective groups. At the very least, individuals must be seen as typical members of their group if any generalization is to occur. But what if 'typical' means, in practice, 'stereotypical' and the stereotype is negative, e.g. the black reinforces the white's stereotype of blacks? A study by Wilder (1984, cited in Vivian and Brown, 1995) suggests that at the very least the encounter with the 'typical' group member must be a pleasant experience.

BOX 19.3 Key study: the jigsaw classroom technique (Aronson et al., 1978)

Children are assigned to small, inter-racial learning groups, in which each member is given material which represents one piece of the lesson to be learned. Each child must learn its part and then communicate it to the rest of the group and, at the end of the lesson, each child is tested on the whole lesson and is given an individual score. Each child must therefore learn the full lesson but each is dependent on the others in the group for parts of the lesson that can only be learned from them; hence, there is complete mutual interdependence. What are its effects?

The experiment has been replicated in scores of classrooms with thousands of students, and the results are consistent and clear-cut. Aronson (1992) believes that the jigsaw method enhances students' self-esteem, improves academic performance, increases liking for classmates and improves some inter-racial perceptions, compared with children in traditional classrooms. However, although the children of different racial/ethnic groups who had actually worked together came to like each other better as individuals, their reduced prejudice did not generalize to those ethnic groups as a whole. However, most experiments of this type are small-scale and relatively short-term interventions.

According to Aronson (1992), although interdependence – especially through the jigsaw technique – is clearly a promising strategy, it is not a perfect solution. While it does produce beneficial effects with high-school students, it works best with young children, before prejudiced attitudes have an opportunity to become deeply ingrained.

Pursuit of common goals

In a co-operative situation, the attainment of one person's goal enhances the chances of attainment of the goals of other group members and this is the reverse of a competitive situation (Brown, 1986). One of the few attempts to alter the classroom experience in order to realize equal status contact *and* mutual co-operation is the *jigsaw classroom technique* of Aronson *et al.* (1978) described in Box 19.3.

In the Robber's Cave field experiment, Sherif *et al.* (1961) introduced a third stage in which seven equal status contact situations were created (including filling out questionnaires together, seeing movies and having meals together). None of these, nor all of them in combination, did anything to reduce friction. However, it was also arranged that the camp's drinking water supply was cut off and the only way of restoring it was by a co-operative effort by the Rattlers and Eagles. Similarly, in order to afford to hire a movie, the two groups agreed to make an equal contribution and on a trip to Cedar Lake, one of the trucks got stuck and they all had to pull on a rope together to get it started again. Other co-operative tasks involved making meals and pitching tents. In the final few days, the group divisions disappeared and they actually suggested travelling home together in one bus; 65 percent of their friendship choices now were made from the other group and their stereotypes changed too, becoming much more favourable.

However, the imposition of superordinate goals as a recipe for conflict reduction may not always be effective and, indeed, may sometimes even increase antagonism towards the outgroup, if the co-operation fails to achieve its aims. It may also be important for groups engaged in co-operative ventures to have distinctive and complementary roles to play, so that each group's contributions are clearly defined. When this does not happen, liking for the other group may actually decrease, perhaps because group members are concerned with the integrity of the ingroup (Brown, 1988).

But what if attempts are made to 'redraw the boundaries' between in- and outgroups? If, as claimed by minimal group experiments, the mere categorization of oneself as a member of a particular group is sufficient to produce discrimination against other (out-) groups, it follows that recategorization should reduce it, i.e. people formerly viewed as outgroup members come to be viewed as belonging to the ingroup. According to Baron and Byrne (1991), evidence exists to suggest that strategies based on shifting individuals' perceived boundaries between 'us' and 'them' constitute a very promising approach to the problem of intergroup bias.

CONCLUSIONS: WHAT TO DO WITH STEREOTYPES?

If stereotyped beliefs about other groups (whether racial, ethnic, gender, sexual orientation or age) form such a crucial part of our prejudices, then we must try to change people's stereotypes if we are to have any hope of reducing prejudice and discrimination.

There are, however, at least two major barriers in the way to achieving this:

1 '... In many cultures, stereotypes of certain groups are so negative, so pervasive, and have existed for so many generations that they can be considered part of the culture into which children are socialized ...' (Brislin, 1993).
2 Stereotypes (like other schemas; see Chapters 12 and 15) represent a way of simplifying the extraordinarily complex social world we inhabit by placing people into categories. This alone would explain why they are so resistant to change, but they also influence selective attention and selective remembering, processes that are to a large extent outside conscious control. For example, Devine (1989) found that both low- and high-prejudiced people are vulnerable to the automatic activation of the cultural stereotype of African Americans.

BOX 19.4 | Key study: the blue eyes-brown eyes experiment

Aronson and Osherow (1980) reported an experiment with third graders (nine-year-olds) in the USA, conducted by their teacher, Jane Elliott.

She told her class one day that brown-eyed people are more intelligent and 'better' people than those with blue eyes. Brown-eyed students, though in the minority, would be the 'ruling class' over the inferior blue-eyed children and be given extra privileges and the blue-eyed students were to be 'kept in their place' by such restrictions as being last in line, seated at the back of the class and given less break time. They also had to wear special collars as a sign of their low status.

Within a short time, the blue-eyed children began to do more poorly in their schoolwork and became depressed and angry and described themselves more negatively. The brown-eyed group grew mean, oppressing the others and making derogatory statements about them.

The next day, Elliott announced that she had lied and that it was really blue-eyed people who are superior. The pattern of prejudice and discrimination quickly switched from the blue-eyed as victims to the brown-eyed. She then debriefed the children. The purpose of the exercise was to provide the children with an opportunity to experience the evils of prejudice and discrimination in a protected environment.

However, these automatic stereotyped reactions (like one that I am still 'guilty' of, namely inferring that 'doctor' denotes 'he') can be seen simply as habits that can be broken, so that prejudice reduction is a process (rather than an all-or-none event) which involves learning to inhibit these automatic reactions and deciding that prejudice is an inappropriate way of relating to others (Devine and Zuwerink, 1994). Motivating individuals in some way to pay careful attention to others and to focus on their unique attributes rather than their 'group' attributes can be effective.

Relying on stereotypes to form impressions of strangers (*category-driven processing*) represents the least effortful route, while relying on the unique characteristics of the target person (*attribute-driven processing*) represents the most effortful route (Fiske and Neuberg, 1990). While people are very skilled at preserving their stereotypes ('You're OK, it's the others'), the more often they come into contact with members of a particular group who do not fit the stereotype (through attribute-driven processing), the more likely the stereotype (category-driven processing) is to lose its credibility.

Finally, propaganda, education and conscious-ness- raising can all contribute to the reduction and prevention of prejudice. The now quite famous experiment by Jane Elliott (see Box 19.4), which was described in her book *The Eye of the Storm* (and featured in the TV programme '*A Class Divided*'), demonstrates the potential impact of experiencing prejudice and discrimination as a way of understanding its evils. Prejudice is mindless; if we teach people, especially children, to be mindful of others, to think of them as complex, whole individuals, stereotypic reactions could be reduced (Hogg and Vaughan, 1995).

CHAPTER SUMMARY

- As an extreme attitude, prejudice comprises a cognitive component (stereotype), an affective component (hostility) and a behavioural component, which (in the case of racial prejudice) can range from verbal insults to genocide. 'Discrimination' is often used to refer to any kind of prejudiced behaviour.

- Most definitions of prejudice identify it as the characteristic of an individual, but it is often associated with intergroup conflict.

- Racism, sexism, heterosexism and ageism can all be regarded as ideologies, which are a characteristic of society, not individuals.

- A great deal of prejudice and discrimination is unconscious and reflected in stereotyped assumptions that we all make about others; this includes health care professionals and their patients.

- Theories of the causes of prejudice are of three main kinds: those stressing the psychological make-up of individuals, those stressing environmental factors and those which focus on group membership.

- The most famous 'individual' theory is Adorno *et al.*'s authoritarian personality. This was based on a large sample of white, non-Jewish Americans given clinical interviews (including the TAT test) and four Likert-type scales, the antisemitism, ethnocentrism, political and economic conservatism and potentiality for fascism scales. The last of these is taken to be the 'authoritarianism scale'.

- Adorno *et al.* found quite strong correlations between the AS, E and F scales and concluded that the authoritarian personality is prejudiced in a very generalized way. This reflects a personality structure which divides the world rigidly into 'us' and 'them' and a punitive, unloving upbringing, from which considerable repressed hostility towards the parents is displaced and projected onto minority groups.

- Methodological problems with Adorno *et al.*'s data include acquiescent response set and experimenter bias. A major theoretical problem is how a theory of individual differences can account for the uniformity of prejudice as was found in Nazi Germany.

- Rokeach's theory of ideological dogmatism identifies authoritarianism as an extreme way of thinking (the 'closed mind') rather than a particular political persuasion.

- Belief congruence theory claims that similarity of beliefs is more important than ethnic membership in determining racial prejudice; Rokeach tested it using the race belief paradigm.

- Eysenck distinguished radicalism-conservatism and toughmindedness-tendermindedness, the latter corresponding to authoritarianism and dogmatism.

- According to Dollard *et al.*'s frustration-aggression hypothesis, frustration inevitably produces aggression which is often displaced onto minority groups, which act as scapegoats; these are not chosen randomly but are socially approved. This makes any explanation of prejudice/discrimination solely in terms of individuals incomplete and reductionist.

- Discrimination can occur in the absence of prejudice, as when people conform to social norms that demand it.
- According to relative deprivation theory, when attainments fall short of expectations we experience frustration; fraternalistic relative deprivation will produce intergroup hostility, particularly if there is a sudden shortfall of attainments.
- According to Sherif's realistic conflict theory, competition between groups for scarce resources is a sufficient condition for hostility to occur between them. This was demonstrated in the Robber's Cave field experiment.
- Minimal group experiments demonstrate that intergroup conflict can occur without competition and that the mere categorization of oneself as belonging to one group rather than another is sufficient for intergroup discrimination.
- The minimal group effect is explained in terms of Tajfel's social identity theory; this claims that a major component of self-concept is social identity and this reflects the various groups we belong to. We try to increase our self-esteem by accentuating the desirability of the ingroup. Prejudice can be seen as part of the attempt to boost our self-image.
- All the major theories of the causes of prejudice and discrimination have implications for their reduction.
- An important framework for attempts to reduce prejudice is Allport's contact hypothesis, which stresses the need for equal status contact and the pursuit of common goals between members of different ethnic groups.
- When groups are segregated, autistic hostility and the related mirror-image phenomenon can result, with the likely reinforcement of negative stereotypes; unequal status contact can also reinforce stereotypes.
- While interpersonal contact can increase liking for the individuals involved, it rarely generalizes to the ethnic group as a whole. When this does happen, it is because of changes in intergroup relationships.
- The jigsaw classroom technique is a widely used method involving interdependence in the pursuit of common goals; it too seems to work at an interpersonal, rather than intergroup level.
- The pursuit of common goals may only be beneficial if it actually succeeds and if the groups involved have distinctive and complementary roles.
- Stereotypes (category-driven processing) are very resistant to change because they often form part of the culture and because they help us to simplify an extremely complex social world. They can be activated automatically/unconsciously, but like other habits they can be broken if people are encouraged to focus on the unique characteristics of individuals (attribute-driven processing).

GLOSSARY

Ageism Belief in the basic inferiority of the elderly and discriminating against them because they are elderly.

Antisemitism Anti-Jewish prejudice.

Attribute-driven processing Using the unique characteristics of strangers to form an impression of them.

Authoritarian personality According to Adorno *et al.*, someone who is prejudiced against all minority groups, who sees the world as divided into 'us' and 'them' and displaces repressed hostility onto these groups.

Belief congruence theory Rokeach's view that similarity of beliefs is more important than similarity of ethnic group as a determinant of discrimination.

Category-driven processing As in stereotyping, using categories to form impressions of strangers.

Contact hypothesis Allport's proposal that prejudice can be reduced through equal status contact between members of minority and majority groups in the pursuit of common (superordinate) goals.

Dogmatism Rokeach's term for extreme closed-mindedness, regardless of particular political or other content.

Ethnocentrism The belief that one's own ethnic/cultural group is superior to all others and the tendency to judge other groups from the standpoint of one's own.

Heterosexism Belief in the basic abnormality of lesbians and gay men and discriminating against them because they are lesbian or gay.

Intergroup conflict Thinking or acting antagonistically towards another group or its members in terms of their group membership.

Jigsaw classroom technique Method for trying to reduce prejudice by creating small, inter-racial, learning groups, in which each child contributes part of the lesson, making them interdependent on each other for successful learning of the whole lesson.

Minimal group paradigm Tajfel's method for studying the importance of group membership, in which people are arbitrarily assigned to one or other group and then have to allocate points to unknown ingroup or outgroup members.

Prejudice An extreme attitude comprising a negative stereotyped belief, a strong feeling of hostility and a disposition to discriminate against members of the disliked group.

Race belief paradigm Experimental procedure for testing belief congruence theory, in which attitudinal and ethnic similarity of a 'stimulus person' are manipulated .

Racism Belief in the basic inferiority of particular racial/ethnic groups (predominantly whites about blacks) and discriminating against them because they belong to these groups.

Radicalism-conservatism (R-factor) One of Eysenck's two independent dimensions, corresponding to left/right-wing political beliefs respectively.

Realistic conflict theory Sherif's account of intergroup conflict, according to which a conflict of interests (competition) is a sufficient condition for hostility and conflict.

Relative deprivation The discrepancy between actual attainments and expectations; a sudden shortfall in attainments will result in collective unrest. Can be *egoistic* or *fraternalistic*.

Scapegoat A substitute target for frustration-induced aggression.

Self-categorization theory Turner's development of social identity theory, which sees social identity as extending into the private self.

Sexism Belief in the basic inferiority of females and discriminating against them because they are female.

Social identity theory Based on minimal group experiments, Tajfel's view that prejudice and discrimination occur as an attempt to raise self-esteem, since social identity is a major component of self-image.

Toughmindedness-tendermindedness (T factor) One of Eysenck's two independent dimensions, with toughmindedness corresponding to authoritarianism and dogmatism.

FURTHER READING

Allport, G.W. (1954) *The Nature of Prejudice*. Reading, MA: Addison-Wesley.The classic work, which still inspires theory and research in the field.

Paludi, M.A. (1992) *The Psychology of Women*. Debuque, Iowa: W.C.B. Brown & Benchmark. An excellent text for readers interested in sexism, in all its forms, including within psychology itself.

20 SOCIAL INFLUENCE

INTRODUCTION AND OVERVIEW

Most, if not all, human behaviour can only be properly understood if it is thought of as social in nature, that is, as being directly or indirectly bound up with and influenced by the behaviour of others. According to Allport (1968), social psychology as a discipline can be defined as 'an attempt to understand and explain how the thoughts, feelings and behaviours of individuals are influenced by the actual, imagined, or implied presence of others'.

As useful as this definition may be, it raises the question of what 'counts' as social influence, i.e. what is this chapter going to include that has not already been dealt with in the earlier chapters on social psychology? Trying to manipulate other people's impressions of us through impression management (Chapter 15) and deliberate attempts to change people's attitudes through persuasive communication (Chapter 18) represent active forms of influence. By contrast, the way that others can inhibit bystander intervention, through pluralistic ignorance and diffusion of responsibility (Chapter 17), reflects more the influence of the 'mere presence' (actual, imagined, or implied) of other people.

In this chapter, we shall consider a number of additional social influence processes, some of which have been referred to or briefly discussed in previous chapters. Using the criterion of non-deliberate/deliberate (passive/active) attempts to change people's thoughts, feelings and behaviours, we could put social facilitation (and related effects such as social loafing) and conformity (and the related processes of risky shift and group polarization) in one category, with leadership (and power) and obedience in another category. Minority influence, which we shall discuss in relation to conformity, can be seen as a much more active form of influence than most studies of conformity; trying to classify different kinds of social influence will always be rather arbitrary.

So is there anything that these different forms of influence have in common? According to Turner (1991), '... The key idea in understanding what researchers mean by social influence is the concept of a social norm. Influence relates to the processes whereby people agree or disagree about appropriate behaviour, form, maintain or change social norms and the social conditions that give rise to, and the effects of such norms ...' He defines a *social norm* as '... a generally accepted way of thinking, feeling or behaving that is endorsed and expected because it is perceived as the right and proper thing to do. It is a rule, value or standard shared by the members of a social group that prescribes appropriate, expected or desirable attitudes and conduct in matters relevant to the group ...'

Another possible common denominator is compliance, with which we shall begin our discussion of social influence processes.

COMPLIANCE: DOING WHAT OTHERS WANT US TO DO

In cases of active social influence, the influencer is trying to change the thoughts, feelings or behaviours of another person in a particular way, i.e. to get them to *comply* with the attempt to influence. For example, in the context of obedience, people comply with the orders/instructions of someone perceived to be a legitimate authority figure. However, compliance is also used to denote a kind of conformity in which people change their behaviour or expressed attitudes while 'under surveillance' (i.e. in the group situation), only to revert to their 'real' attitudes when away from the group (Kelman, 1958). A major reason given for this kind of conformity is *normative influence* (Deutsch and Gerard, 1955), i.e. fear of rejection by the group. Compliance is contrasted with internalization (Kelman, 1958) or true conformity (Mann, 1969), in which people are converted to the group's attitudes, etc., i.e. they truly believe the attitudes they express in the group and continue to express them when away from the group situation; the motive behind this is *informational influence* (Deutsch and Gerard, 1955).

Compliance also occurs whenever we do what someone else 'asks' us to do, i.e. whenever people make direct requests, such as friends asking us a 'favour' or a salesperson 'inviting' us to try a product or service. Many researchers believe that attempts to gain compliance through direct requests is the most common form of social influence (Hogg and Vaughan, 1995). What kinds of strategy do people adopt to maximize the probability of compliance with a direct request?

Cialdini (1988) has reviewed social influence strategies in situations in which salespeople are trying to sell a product and identifies several ways in which influence might occur:

1 *Norm of reciprocity.* Giving away a free sample or a free estimate for a job may put the customer under a sense of obligation. This is based on the social norm that 'we should treat others the way they treat us'. This can apply to other relationships too, as in the belief that 'one good turn deserves another'.

2 *'Foot in the door' tactic.* Getting someone to agree to a small request makes them more willing to comply with a larger request at some later point than if the larger request had been made initially. This can be explained partly in terms of people's need to appear consistent – both to themselves and others (see Chapter 18). According to Hogg and Vaughan (1995), this represents one of three multiple-request tactics, whereby an initial request functions as a set-up for a second (real) request. The other two are: (a) the 'door in the face' tactic, in which the initial request is large and unreasonable and is followed up with a second, much more reasonable request, which is more difficult to refuse; it is seen as a concession by the requester and makes the other person feel obliged to reciprocate, so both requests need to come from the same person if it is to be effective; and (b) the 'low ball' tactic, in which the requester changes the rules halfway through and manages to get away with it; for example, having induced a customer to commit themselves to a purchase, the salesperson then reveals certain hidden costs that weren't previously mentioned. (The term comes from US baseball; in the UK, we might talk of 'moving the goal posts'.)

3 *Ingratiation*. Agreeing with others and in other ways showing how we are similar to them, showing what attractive and competent people we are, all part of the attempt to get them to like us; this is often the first step in the influence process.

4 *'Social proof'*. Showing that a product or service is good, for example, by impressing the customer with their general popularity or among particular social groups that the customer may wish to emulate.

FIGURE 20.1 *American cigarette advertisement. In England, such direct social influence is banned*

5 *Increasing the desirability of a product* by stressing its scarcity value, the fact that it is about to be taken off the market or its 'forbidden' nature.

According to Smith (1995), some of these (in particular, the norm of reciprocity, 'foot in the door' and stressing the scarcity value of a product) are Machiavellian strategies (named after Machiavelli, the 16th century Italian statesman and writer and generally implying unscrupulous, cunning or devious behaviour) that are likely to be used when a quick sale is all that counts.

SOCIAL FACILITATION: THE INFLUENCE OF THE MERE PRESENCE OF OTHERS

Triplett (1898), carrying out what is widely considered to be the first social psychology experiment (and the first study of social motivation; see Chapter 5), studied the effects of competition on the average time it took children to complete 150 winds of a fishing reel. Each child was tested under two conditions, working alone and working in pairs, each child competing against the other member of the pair; performance was clearly superior in the pairs condition.

However, according to Floyd Allport (1924), Triplett's narrow view of the role of competition could be broadened to include a more general principle, namely, an improvement in performance can be produced by the mere presence of conspecifics (i.e. members of the same species), a form of influence he called *social facilitation*. Allport instructed his participants not to try to compete against one another (and also prevented any collaboration) while engaging on a variety of tasks, which included crossing out all the vowels in a newspaper article, multiplication and finding logical flaws in arguments. He still found they performed better when they could see others working than when they worked alone and he called this form of social facilitation the *co-action effect*. Social facilitation can also be seen when an individual performs a task in front of an audience (other people who are not doing what the person is doing) – this is the *audience effect*. Other studies have shown that social facilitation can occur by simply telling participants that others are performing the same task elsewhere (Dashiell, 1935).

The considerable research interest in social facilitation (much of it involving a range of species and a range of behaviours, from eating to copulation) died down at the end of the 1930s. But it was revived by Zajonc's (1965) *drive theory*, according to which social facilitation depends on the nature of the task, in particular, how simple and well learned it is. According to Zajonc, 'an audience impairs the acquisition of new responses and facilitates the emission of well-learned responses', i.e. things a person already knows how to do (e.g. cancelling numbers and letters and simple multiplication) are done better when others are present, but things which are complex or which participants are required to learn are done less well when others are present. These findings have been confirmed by others. Why should this be?

An instinctive response to the presence of others (in whatever capacity) is an increase in drive level (or level of arousal) and since, up to a certain level, arousal enhances the performance of well-learned behaviour, the presence of others will facilitate performance on simple tasks. However, when the task is complex, the effect of increased arousal is to make it more likely that incorrect or irrelevant responses will be performed and, hence, more errors are made. The arousal produced by the presence of others, together with that produced by the task itself, produce a level beyond the optimum for ideal performance (Zajonc's explanation is based on Hull's learning theory; see Chapter 7).

Zajonc's claim that the presence of others instinctively increases arousal has been challenged by, for example, Cottrell (1972), who proposed the *evaluation apprehension model* as an alternative: we quickly learn that the social rewards and punishments (such as approval and disapproval) are dependent on others' evaluations of us, so the presence of others triggers an acquired arousal drive based on evaluation apprehension (a form of social anxiety). According to Hogg and Vaughan (1995), the evidence, on balance, suggests that the '... mere presence of others appears to be a sufficient cause of, and evaluation apprehension not necessary for, social facilitation effects'. Zajonc (1980) elaborated his earlier model by proposing that socially generated drive may be the product of *uncertainty*. The presence of others implies the possibility of action on their part and that the individual must always be alert to possible changes in the environment caused by the behaviour of others; uncertainty may be caused by the inability to anticipate how they will act (Geen, 1995).

● The 'Ringelmann effect', social inhibition and social loafing

Can the presence of others have an inhibiting effect on performance, as well as a facilitating effect? Several years after Triplett's experiments, Ringelman, a French professor of engineering, reported a series of studies in which the presence of others seemed to produce a loss in motivation. (The studies had actually been conducted prior to Triplett's research, making them the very first experiments in social psychology – Geen, 1995; Smith, 1995). Ringelman found that the more members there were in a tug-of-war team, the less hard each member pulled, i.e. as the size of the group increases, so the amount of force exerted per person decreases. He explained this largely in terms of a loss of physical co-ordination, but he conceded that loss of motivation could also be involved.

Latané et al. (1979) revived the Ringelmann effect under the name of *social loafing*. Early demonstrations involved simple physical acts, such as shouting and hand clapping, individually or in groups, with the general result that the intensity of output per person declined as additional members were added. For example, when participants were asked to cheer and clap as loudly as possible, the amount of noise produced per person (compared with individual performance) dropped by 29 percent in a two-person group, 49 percent in a four-person group and 60 percent in a six-person group. Later studies have shown the effect to be very reliable and general, occurring in both physical and cognitive tasks, in laboratory and naturalistic settings, in both genders and in several cultures.

Social loafing can be defined as the tendency for individuals to work less hard (loaf) on a task when they believe that others are also working on the task and that one's own effort will be pooled with that of the other group members, compared with either working alone or coactively (i.e. others are doing the same task but independently of each other). According to Geen (1995), the data are consistent with one of the major claims of *social impact theory* (Latané and Nida, 1980), namely that when a person is a member of a group subjected to social forces, the impact of those forces on each person in the group is diminished in inverse proportion to (among other things) the number of people in the group – the larger the group, the smaller the impact. Why?

Geen (1995) identifies four main explanations: 'free riding', equalization of perceived output, evaluation apprehension and matching to standard.

● *'Free riding'* (Kerr, 1983) occurs when each member of a group perceives that there is a high probability that some other members of the group will solve the problem at hand and that the benefits from this person's performance will go to all members. Each individual concludes that his or her contribution is dispensable and so puts little effort into the group task and the importance of individual effort decreases as the size of the group increases (rather like diffusion of responsibility in bystander intervention; see Chapter 17). Related to this is the *sucker effect*, according to which, if people expect their fellow group members to become free riders, they may respond by loafing in an effort to bring equality to an inequitable situation ('Why should I make more effort than the others?' or ' I'm no sucker').

- Evaluation apprehension, as we noted above, refers to anxiety about how others will judge us. If, as has been claimed, the tasks commonly used in social loafing studies are boring and meaningless, people will try to avoid doing them: if the efforts of group members are pooled, individuals can remain anonymous ('hide in the crowd', which is very similar to free riding) . However, making each person's contribution identifiable eliminates social loafing (Williams et al., 1981), which suggests that participants become apprehensive about being evaluated by the experimenter. This is especially likely when participants believe that their performance is being compared with that of their co-actors performing the same task so that they are, effectively, in competition. The higher the level of evaluation apprehension, the lower the level of social loafing (Harkins and Jackson, 1985).

  When the tasks used are more realistic and more relevant to everyday life, in more group-oriented (collectivist) cultures such as China and Japan, social loafing effects are not merely eliminated but are actually reversed: the presence of others enhances performance on the same tasks which, in more individualist, Western cultures produce social loafing (Smith and Bond, 1993).

- *Matching to standard* assumes that apprehension over the possibility of being evaluated by the experimenter causes the participant to match a standard for performance set by the experimenter (and that this matching is avoided under conditions that allow social loafing). According to Szymanski and Harkins (1987), the explicit statement of a standard relevant to the activity is sufficient to reduce social loafing.

CONFORMITY

What the definitions in Table 20.1 have in common is the reference to group pressure. They do not specify particular groups with particular beliefs or practices but any group which is important for the individual at the time. The group may be composed of people who are significant others for the individual, for example, family or peers (membership groups), or it may be a reference group, whose values the individual admires or aspires to but which does not involve actual membership.

● Empirical studies of conformity

An early study by Jenness (1932) could be regarded as one of the very first empirical studies of conformity, although it is usually discussed in the context of social facilitation. Jenness asked individual students to estimate the number of beans in a bottle and then had them discuss it to arrive at a group estimate. When they were asked individually to make a second estimate, there was a distinct shift towards the group's estimate. Soon afterwards, Sherif (1935), using a similar procedure, conducted one of the classic conformity experiments, which is described in Box 20.1.

While Sherif believed that he had shown that conformity does indeed take place, others, notably Asch, were very critical of his findings. According to Asch, the fact that the task used by Sherif was ambiguous (i.e. there was no right or wrong answer) made it difficult to draw any definite conclusions about conformity: conformity should be measured in terms of the individual's tendency to agree with other group members who unanimously give the wrong answer on a task where the solution is obvious or unambiguous. If people yield to group pressure when the answer is obvious, this is a much stricter test of conformity than where there is no correct or incorrect answer to begin with.

'... yielding to group pressures'. (Crutchfield, 1962)

'The essence of conformity is yielding to group pressures but it may take different forms and be based on motives other than group pressure' (Mann, 1969)

'... a change in belief or behaviour in response to real or imagined group pressure when there is no direct request to comply with the group nor any reason given to justify the behaviour change ...' (Zimbardo and Leippe, 1991)

Table 20.1 *Some definitions of conformity*

BOX
20.1 Key study: If the light appears
to move, it must be the Sherif

Sherif (1935) used a visual illusion called the *autokinetic effect*, whereby a stationary spot of light seen
in an otherwise dark room appears to move.

He told his participants that he was going to
move the light and that their task was to say how far
they thought the light moved. They were tested individually at first, being asked to estimate the extent
of movement several times. The estimates fluctuated
to begin with but then 'settled down' and became
quite consistent. However, there were wide differences between participants. They then heard the
estimates of other participants – this represented
the group situation (there were usually three per
group). Under these conditions, the estimates of different participants converged, i.e. they became more
alike: a *group norm* developed which represented
the average of the individual estimates.

Just as different individuals produced different
estimates, so did different groups. This happened
both under the conditions already described and
also when participants were tested in small groups
right from the start. According to Sherif, participants, in their groups, used others' estimates as a
frame of reference in what was an ambiguous situation. Note that (i) participants were not in any way
instructed to agree with the others in the group
(unlike the Jenness study), despite initially wide
differences between individuals; (ii) when participants were tested again individually, their estimates
closely resembled the group norm (rather than
their original, individual, estimates).

BOX
20.2 Key study: The Asch
paradigm – conformity as
being in line with the Feds

Asch (1951) gave participants the simple perceptual
task of matching one line (a standard line) with
another (a comparison line), each presented on a
separate card (Fig. 20.2); they had to say which of A,
B or C was the same length as the standard line. A
group of 36 control participants, who were tested
individually, made only three mistakes when tested
20 times each (using different standard and comparison lines), showing that the task was simple – the
answer was obvious and unambiguous!

In the original experiment, students were tested
in groups of 7–9, in which only one person was a
'real' (naive) participant, the others being confederates of Asch who had been instructed beforehand
to give the same wrong answers on certain trials
('critical' trials).

They were seated either in a straight line or
round a table and it was arranged so that the real
participant was always the last to answer (or the last
but one). On the first two trials, the confederates all
gave the right answer, as did the real participant
(these were neutral trials). However, on the third
trial, all the confederates agreed on the 'wrong'
answer. During the next 20 minutes, there were 11
more critical trials (making 12 in all) plus four more
neutral trials (making six in all).

Standard line

Comparison lines

FIGURE 20.2 *Stimulus cards used in Asch's
conformity experiments (1951, 1952, 1956)*

In a series of experiments beginning in 1951, Asch
used a procedure (the *Asch paradigm*) which is
probably the most influential procedure for investigating conformity; it is described in Box 20.2.

The basic conformity rate was about 32 percent,
i.e. on average, participants gave wrong answers on
one-third of the critical trials by agreeing with the
confederate majority. This is a staggeringly high figure considering how unambiguous the task was;
according to van Avermaet (1988), 'The results reveal
the tremendous impact of an "obviously" incorrect
but unanimous majority on the judgements of a lone
subject ...'

However, the overall figure of 32 percent conceals
large individual differences. About 25 percent of participants showed no conformity at all and remained
independent throughout the critical trials; about 47
percent gave between one and seven incorrect

answers and about 28 percent gave eight or more
incorrect answers, making about 75 percent who
conformed at least once. Only about 5 percent conformed on every single critical trial.

When interviewed at length following the experiment, participants gave a number of specific reasons for conforming. Some wanted to act in accordance with the experimenter's wishes and convey a favourable impression of themselves by not 'upsetting the experiment' (which they believed they would have done by disagreeing with the majority); they thought some obscure 'mistake' had been made. A few, who had no reason to believe that there was anything wrong with their eyesight, genuinely doubted the validity of their own judgements by wondering if they were suffering from eye strain or if their chairs had been moved so that they could not see the cards properly Some denied being aware of having given incorrect answers – they had unwittingly used the confederates as 'marker posts' (Smith, 1995). Others said that they wanted to be like everyone else, did not want to 'appear different', 'be made to look a fool', a 'social outcast' or 'inferior'. So, for these participants there was a discrepancy between the answer they gave in the group and what they privately believed: they knew the 'wrong' answer was wrong but went along with it nonetheless. Contrast this with Sherif's participants, for whom there was no conflict between the group's estimate and their own, individual estimates.

So far, we have described the original, basic experiment. Asch (1952, 1955) subsequently varied the basic situation and manipulated different variables in order to identify the crucial influences on conformity.

Does the rate of conformity go on increasing as the size of the majority goes on increasing?

It seems not. Where there is a real participant and just one confederate, the conformity rate is very low indeed (about 3 percent), as you might expect ('it's my word against yours'). Where there are two confederates and one participant, conformity begins to increase (13.6 percent) and with three confederates it reaches 31.8 percent which, as we have seen, was the overall conformity rate. But beyond three, conformity does not continue to rise. So, for example, 15 confederates to one real participant does not produce more conformity than a ratio of three to one. This finding suggests that it is the *unanimity* of the majority which is important (i.e. the confederates all agree with each other) rather than the actual size of the majority (the number of confederates) – it is consensus, not numbers, that matters: '... a unanimous majority of three is, under the given conditions, far more effective than a majority of eight containing one dissenter ...' (Asch, 1951).

However, Gerard *et al.* (1968) and Latané and Wolf (1981) argue that adding more confederates will increase conformity although the rate of increase falls with each extra majority member. Mann (1969) disagrees with Asch and these later studies by arguing that there is a linear relationship between group size and conformity, i.e. as group size increases, so conformity goes on increasing. However, adding more members will only produce more conformity if the majority members are perceived as independent judges and not as sheep following each other or as members of a group who have jointly reached a judgement. According to Hogg and Vaughan (1995), the most robust finding is that conformity reaches its full extent with a 3–5 person majority, with additional members having little effect. Campbell and Fairey (1989, cited in Hogg and Vaughan, 1995) believe that group size may have a different effect depending on the type of judgement being made and how motivated the participant is: where there is no objectively correct answer (such as musical preference) and where participants need to be accepted, group size will have a mainly linear effect, but where there is a correct answer and their main concern is to be correct, a majority of two or three will be as effective as larger majorities.

What is the effect of another member of the group agreeing with the real participant?

In short, it is to reduce conformity from 32 percent to 5.5 percent, whether the member who agrees is another real participant or a confederate. Just as significantly, a dissenter who disagrees both with the real participant *and* the majority has almost as much effect on reducing conformity as one who gives the correct answer (i.e. agrees with the real participant). In both cases, the majority is no longer unanimous. However, this reduction in conformity only seems to apply to unambiguous stimulus situations (like Asch's perceptual task) and not where opinions are being asked for (Allen and Levine, 1968).

What happens when the participant has a 'supporter' at the beginning and then loses that support?

In one situation, the fourth confederate to answer gave the correct answer on the first half of the critical trials but then switched to the incorrect majority answer for the second half. Under these conditions, conformity increased from 5.5 to 32 percent, i.e. the conformity rate is that which would have occurred if there had been no supporter to begin with.

In the original experiment, were participants justified in fearing that they would be ridiculed by the rest of the group if they gave the answer they believed to be correct?

It seems they were. When a group of 16 naive participants and a single confederate were tested, the confederate's wrong answers on the critical trials were greeted with sarcasm, exclamations of disbelief and ridiculing laughter!

Will task difficulty affect conformity?

When Asch made the comparison lines more similar in length, so that the task was more difficult, participants were more likely to yield to the incorrect majority answer and this was especially true when they felt confident that there was a right answer. When tasks are more ambiguous, in the sense that they involve expressing opinions or stating preferences (so there is no objectively correct answer), conformity actually decreases.

Is conformity rate affected by giving answers in private?

Critics of Asch's experiment have pointed out that participants may conform because they are reluctant or too embarrassed to expose their private views in face-to-face situations. If so, the level of conformity should decrease if they are allowed to write their answers down or where there is no face-to-face contact between the group members or where they remain anonymous in some other way. For example, Deutsch and Gerard (1955) used partitions which shielded participants from each other, with responses showing up on a light panel in front of them – the real participant had to press one of three buttons. Under these conditions, conformity was lower than in Asch's face-to-face situation. Indeed, when Asch himself allowed the naïve participant to answer in writing (while the confederates still gave their answers publicly), conformity dropped to 12.5 percent. Crutchfield (1954) also used a non-face-to-face procedure and his research is described in Box 20.3.

● An evaluation of Asch's research

Replications

The Asch studies have stimulated a great deal of research. Larsen (1974) found significantly lower conformity rates than Asch had found among groups of American students and suggested that this was

---

BOX 20.3	Key study: Testing conformity the Crutchfield way – private booths

Crutchfield criticized Asch's experiments for being time-consuming and uneconomical, since only one participant could be tested at a time. He therefore changed the experimental situation so that several (usually five) real participants could be tested at the same time. Altogether, he tested over 600.

Each participant sat in an open cubicle which had a panel with an array of lights and switches; neighbouring panels could not be seen. Questions, pictures and other kinds of stimuli were projected on to the wall and participants were told that the lights on the display panel indicated the answers of other participants. In fact, everyone saw an identical display and so received the same information; each believed that they were the last to respond. The answers were wrong on approximately half the trials. Crutchfield presented a variety of tasks and conformity to the wrong answers differed according to the type of task involved:

● On the Asch-type perceptual judgement, he found 30 percent conformity.

● When asked to compete a series of numbers (as in IQ tests), he also found 30 percent conformity.

● When he presented a star which was obviously smaller in area than a circle (by about one-third, in fact), there was 46 percent agreement that the circle was smaller than the star.

● Some of his participants were army officers attending a three-day assessment programme. Thirty seven per cent of them agreed with the statement 'I doubt whether I would make a good leader' when it was presented in the booth but significantly, none of them agreed with it when tested privately.

● A substantial proportion of college students agreed with statements which, under more 'normal' circumstances, they would not be expected to. For example: (i) 60–70 percent of the population of the USA is aged 65 or over; (ii) American males are, on average, taller than American females, by eight or nine inches; (iii) the life expectancy of American males is only about 25 years; (iv) Americans sleep four to five hours per night, on average, and eat six meals a day; (v) free speech being a privilege rather than a right, it is proper for a society to suspend free speech when it feels itself threatened.

because of a changed climate of opinion in America in the 1970s towards independence and criticism and away from conformity. However, in a later (1979) study, Larsen *et al.* found results very similar to those of Asch. Perhaps the pendulum had begun to swing back again.

Perrin and Spencer (1981) found very low rates of conformity (one out of 396 trials) for a group of British students; but they were engineering, maths and chemistry students and so were perhaps better able to resist conformity pressure because of their special knowledge and experience. Significantly, in the same study, young offenders on probation showed very similar rates of conformity to Asch's; the confederate majority consisted of probation officers and the experimenter was an 'authority figure'. Brown (1985) makes the interesting suggestion that it may not be just students who have changed since the 1950s but the experimenters too; that is, they may not *expect* so much conformity and this may be conveyed, unwittingly, to the participants (see Chapter 2 on *'experimenter effects'*).

In a review of 31 conformity studies using Asch's paradigm, Smith and Bond (1993) conclude that conformity rates tend to be lower among members of individualist cultures in North America and north-west Europe (an average of 25.3 percent) than collectivist cultures in Africa, Asia, Oceania and South America (37.1 percent). This has implications for how we respond to the question 'Is conformity good or bad?' (see below).

How should Asch's findings be interpreted: majority or minority influence?

Despite a minority of participants remaining totally independent and a majority remaining independent most of the time, '... the pervasive inference drawn from these studies has been of the weakness of the individual in face of the group and the strength of spontaneous pressures for conformity inherent in the group context' (Turner, 1991). However, on nearly two-thirds of the critical trials, participants successfully resisted conformity pressures, i.e. conformity was the exception rather than the rule. Either way, the Asch paradigm is usually interpreted as the pitting of a lone individual (the naive participant) who embodies 'the truth' or 'reality' against a mistaken majority sometimes unanimous, sometimes not (the confederates).

BOX 20.4 | **Critical discussion: How do minorities influence majority opinion?**

Moscovici (1976) reanalysed Asch's results and concluded that conformity rates varied widely according to the proportion of trials on which confederates gave incorrect answers. In deciding whether or not to conform, participants were paying attention to the consistency of others' judgements. As a result, he conducted a series of experiments designed to show how minorities can, over time, change the majority's views by giving consistent responses. For example, in a colour-judging task, a confederate minority was instructed to consistently describe a blue-green colour as green: the views of majority participants as to where the boundary might be drawn between the colours considered to be blue or green shifted and the effect persisted when further judgements were asked for after the minority had withdrawn.

Although his results have not always been replicated, studies of minority influence show that it is achieved not so much by a particular style of behaviour in the group, but more by a combination of attributes and behaviour (Smith, 1995). Moscovici (1980) proposes that while majorities impose their views through directly requiring compliance (which often requires 'surveillance'), minorities use more indirect means to achieve a more lasting conversion, perhaps the most important behavioural style being consistency. But why should consistency be so important? According to Hogg and Vaughan (1995), it has five main effects:

1 It disrupts the majority norm, producing uncertainty and doubt.
2 It draws attention to itself as an entity.
3 It conveys the existence of an alternative, coherent point of view.
4 It demonstrates certainty and an unshakeable commitment to this point of view.
5 It shows that the only solution to the current conflict is the minority viewpoint.

Apart from consistency, minorities are more efficient if they are seen to have made significant personal/material sacrifices (*investment*), if they are seen as acting out of principle rather than ulterior motives (*autonomy*) and if they display a balance between being 'dogmatic' (*rigidity*) and 'inconsistent' (*flexibility*) (Hogg and Vaughan, 1995).

Finally, minorities will have more influence if they are seen as being similar to the majority in terms of age, gender and social category (Clark and Maass, 1988) and particularly if they are categorized as ingroup members.

Contrary to this view, Moscovici and Faucheux (1972) advocated that we think of the naive participant as embodying the 'conventional', self-evident opinion of the majority (for example, the earth is round, man evolved from apes), while the confederates represent unorthodox, unconventional, eccentric and even outrageous viewpoints or theories (for example, the conviction that the earth is flat or that man was created in the Garden of Eden).Instead of the confederates being the majority (which they are purely numerically), Moscovici and Faucheux see them as a minority (they represent very unconventional beliefs) who succeed in influencing the majority (the numerically minority naive participant who represents the conventional, majority view) 32 percent of the time. According to this interpretation, those participants who remained independent are the conformists. Looked at in this way, the conformity experiments seem to provide evidence relating to the question 'How do new ideas come to be accepted?' rather than 'What processes operate to maintain the status quo?'

Moscovici (1976) criticized the conventional 'majority' approach to social influence. He argues that there is a *conformity bias,* according to which all social influence serves the need to adapt to the status quo for the sake of uniformity and stability. But normative change is sometimes needed to adapt to changing circumstances and this is very difficult to explain from a conformist bias; what is needed is an understanding of the dynamics of *active minorities.* If minorities did not have influence, how could innovations, whether in science, politics, art or any other arena of human social activity, ever happen? So how do minorities exert their influence over prevailing majority opinion (see Box 20.4)?

● Theories of conformity – why do people conform?

One very influential and widely accepted account of group influence is Deutsch and Gerard's (1955) distinction between informational and normative influence. A major motive underlying *informational influence* is the need to be right, to have an accurate perception of reality. So when we are uncertain, when we face an ambiguous situation, we look to others to help us perceive the stimulus situation accurately (or define the situation; see Chapter 17). This involves a social comparison with other group members in order to reduce the uncertainty. Underlying *normative influence* is the need to be accepted by other people and to make a favourable impression on them. We conform in order to gain social approval and avoid rejection – we agree with others because of their power to reward, punish,

FIGURE 20.3 *A minority of one faces a unanimous majority. (Courtesy William Vandivert and Scientific American, November 1955)*

accept or reject us. How does this basic distinction relate to the major conformity experiments?

● When discussing Sherif's experiment, we noted that the autokinetic effect is an ambiguous situation (there is no actual movement of the light and so there cannot be any right or wrong answers). Under these conditions, participants were only too willing to validate their own estimates by comparing them with those of others; the results were consistent with Sherif's *social reality hypothesis*, which states that '... The less one can rely on one's own direct perception and behavioural contact with the physical world, the more susceptible one should be to influence from others ...' (Turner, 1991). Clearly, informational influence was involved. According to Festinger's (1954) *social comparison theory*, people have a basic need to evaluate their ideas and attitudes and, in turn, to confirm that they are correct; this can provide a reassuring sense of control over one's world and a satisfying sense of competence. In novel or ambiguous situations, social reality is defined by what others think and do and it is significant that Sherif's participants were relatively unaware of being influenced by the other judges : '... They appear to be largely unconsciously adjusting their judgement in the light of others' reports to arrive at a stable, agreed picture of a shared but initially unstructured world' (Turner, 1991).

● In Asch's experiment (and to a large extent in Crutchfield's too), most participants were not uncertain about the correct answer but were faced with a conflict between two sources of information which in unambiguous situations normally coincide, namely their own judgement and that of others. If they chose their own judgement, they risked rejection (ridicule, etc.) by the majority and so normative influence was involved. However, some participants were unaware of any conflict or of having given an incorrect response, which reflects informational influence.

Related to those two kinds of influence are two major kinds of conformity. Sherif's participants used others' judgements to help them attain a more accurate perception of reality, so that when tested again individually, following the group situation, their answers were closer to the group norm than to their own initial (individual) judgement. This illustrates *internalization* (Kelman, 1958), whereby our public and private beliefs or opinions coincide, i.e. we believe what we say and we say what we believe (Mann (1969) preferred to call this *true conformity*). It can be thought of as a conversion to other people's point of view. By contrast, most of Asch's participants

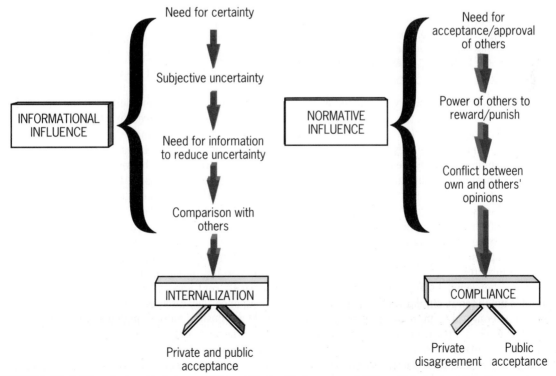

FIGURE 20.4 *The relationship between different kinds of influence and different kinds of conformity*

BOX 20.5 **Key study: Showing the compatibility of informational and normative influence**

Insko *et al.* (1983) had participants, in groups of six, judge whether a colour shown on a slide was more similar to another colour shown to the left or to one shown to the right.

On critical trials, four confederates who answered before the naive participant and another who answered last, gave answers which deviated from those given by most participants in a control condition who were tested alone. There were two independent variables: (i) participants answered either publicly or privately; and (ii) the experimenter could or could not determine which response was more correct (in the 'determined' condition, the experimenter referred to an apparatus through which he could accurately measure which response was more correct; in the 'undetermined' condition, this was said to be impossible).

Two hypotheses were tested: (i) there will be greater conformity in the public than the private condition due to normative influence; and (ii) there will be greater conformity in the determined than the undetermined condition due to informational influence. Both hypotheses were confirmed. Also, the determined condition produced greater conformity in both private and public conditions and all four conditions produced greater conformity than the control condition. Hence, even with 'objective stimuli', informational influence can add to the effect of normative influence (van Avermaet, 1988).

faced a conflict and a compromise was reached in the form of *compliance,* whereby the answer they give publicly (in the group) is not the one which is privately believed – what they say they don't believe and what they believe they don't say (see Fig. 20.4).

While the informational-normative influence distinction has proved very influential, like all distinctions it faces the problem of false dichotomy, i.e. are they really separate, opposite forms of influence or are they complementary? A study by Insko *et al.* (1983) suggests that they can indeed operate together; see Box 20.5.

Remember that when Asch made the three comparison lines much mo re similar and hence the task more difficult, conformity increased; clearly, informational influence is involved here. If we believe there is a correct answer and we are uncertain what that answer is, it seems quite logical to expect that an individual will be more influenced by a unani-

mous majority. This is why having a supporter or the presence of a dissenter has the effect of reducing conformity – by breaking the group consensus the subject is shown both that disagreement is possible and that the group is fallible: '... the more consensual the group and the more isolated the individual (i.e. the less others agree with the deviant), the greater the power of the group to define reality, induce self-doubt in the deviant as to both her competence and social position, and threaten her with ridicule and rejection for being different' (Turner, 1991). In other words, both informational and normative influence can operate in conjunction with each other and should not be seen as opposed processes of influence.

● Conformity and group belongingness

The distinction between informational and normative influence has been called a *dual process dependency model* of social influence (e.g. Turner, 1991). But this has been challenged on the grounds that it underestimates the role of group 'belongingness': an important feature of conformity is that we are influenced by the group because we feel that we belong, psychologically, to it, which is why its norms are relevant standards for our own attitudes and behaviour. The dual process model tends to emphasize the interpersonal aspects of conformity experiments, which could just as easily occur between individuals as between group members.

According to Abrams *et al.* (1990), we only experience uncertainty when disagreement arises with those with whom we expect to agree, in particular, those whom we regard as members of the same category or group as ourselves in respects which are relevant to judgements made in a shared stimulus situation. Social influence results from a process of self-categorization whereby we perceive ourselves as a group member, possessing the same characteristics and reactions as other group members. Turner (1982) calls this mode of influence, when group membership is salient, referent *informational influence.*

According to this view, Sherif's participants were influenced by their assumption that the illusion is objectively real and by their expectation to agree. Indeed, once they discover that the autokinetic effect is only an illusion, mutual influence and convergence cease (Sperling, 1946, cited in Abrams *et al.*, 1990): the need to agree at all is removed. But if we believe that there is a correct answer and we are uncertain what it is, only those whom we categorize as belonging

BOX 20.6 Key study: Knowing what to think by knowing who you are

Abrams *et al.* (1990) used the Sherif paradigm with psychology students but manipulated categorization: confederates were introduced as students at a nearby university, but were either fellow psychology students or students of ancient history. The convergence that Sherif had found in his original experiment only occurred in the former condition, i.e. when others were categorized as being equivalent to self (i.e. a member of the ingroup). So self-categorization may set limits on informational influence.

It should also set limits on normative influence, since individuals will presumably have a stronger desire to receive rewards, approval and acceptance from those categorized in the same way as themselves than from those categorized differently. Using the Asch paradigm but again manipulating categorization, Abrams *et al.* found that conformity exceeded the usual level of 32 percent in the ingroup condition but was greatly below this level in the outgroup condition.

to 'our' group will influence our judgement – not just anyone will do. As Brown (1988) says, '... There is more to conformity, it seems, than simply "defining social reality": it all depends who is doing the defining'. This was demonstrated in a study by Abrams *et al.* (1990), described in Box 20.6. According to this self-categorization approach, people conform because they are group members, which implies that what is important is not the validation of physical reality or the avoidance of social disapproval but the upholding of a group norm; people are the source of information about the appropriate ingroup norm.

● Individual differences in conformity

Another way of trying to understand why people conform is to consider individual differences, i.e. are some people more likely to conform than others and if so, why?

Crutchfield (1955) found that people who tend to conform tend to be intellectually less effective, have less ego strength, less leadership ability, less mature social relationships and feelings of inferiority; they also tend to be authoritarian, self-sufficient, more submissive, narrow-minded and inhibited and have relatively little insight into their own personalities compared with those who tend not to conform. But

does this constitute a conforming personality, i.e. is a person who conforms in one situation also likely to conform in other situations? McGuire (1968) concluded that consistency across situations is not high. The authoritarian personality (Adorno *et al.*, 1950) is perhaps as close to such a personality type as can be found (see Chapter 19).

Men with low self-esteem tend to conform more often than those who are self-assured. This, in turn, relates to gender differences: there is a tendency for men in general to conform less than women, at least partly because men are more likely to see dissent or independence as a way of expressing their competence, while women tend to see co-operation and agreement with others as expressing competence (Zimbardo and Leippe, 1991). However, personality seems to be the crucial variable – Maslach *et al.* (1987) found that men with personal qualities and interests that are stereotypically 'feminine' conform as much as women with these same qualities and interests and conversely, women and men with stereotypically 'masculine' qualities and interests conform less.

People with a high need for social approval, regardless of gender, conform more readily than those with a low need, which suggests that conforming is a way of gaining the approval of others, i.e. if approval or acceptance is the real motive underlying conforming behaviour, then instead of talking about a conforming personality, we should talk about conformity as a means to an end, a means of satisfying certain needs which are more important to some people than to others.

● Is conformity good or bad?

According to Maslach *et al.* (1985), *dissent* is sometimes basically just an expression of disagreement, refusing to go along with the crowd, while at other times it is more creative ('Here's a better idea, folks'). The former may be an attempt to remain independent, almost as a matter of principle (what Willis (1963) might call *anticonformity*), which may betray a basic fear of loss of personal identity, while constructive dissent and independence are positive qualities.

Conformity, in most circumstances, serves a valuable social purpose: conformity to certain rules and norms '... lubricates the machinery of social interaction. It enables us to structure our social behaviour and predict the reactions of others ...' (Zimbardo and Leippe, 1991); and yet the term conformity is often used to convey undesirable behaviour. In laboratory research, it has most often been studied in terms of the '... conspiratorial group ... [being] shown to limit, constrain, and distort the individual's response ...' (Milgram, 1965) and there is the implicit assumption that independence is 'good' and conformity is 'bad'. Asch (1952) in fact made this value judgement quite explicit. However, as Gahagan (1975) points out, conformity can be highly functional, facilitating the satisfaction of social and non-social needs, as well as being necessary, to some extent, for social life to proceed at all. Indeed, in the context of his famous studies of obedience, Milgram showed that the presence of two defiant peers significantly reduced the obedience rate among naive participants and he wrote an article in 1965 called 'Liberating effects of group pressure'. We shall discuss these and his obedience experiments later in the chapter.

● Risky shift, groupthink and group polarization

Based on the traditional interpretation of conformity studies , i.e. that they are concerned with majority influence and with how the status quo is maintained, the commonsense prediction is that groups, relative to individuals, will be more cautious and conservative; convergence towards a group mean in Sherif's experiment is perhaps the clearest demonstration of this prediction. However, Stoner (1961) found the opposite to be true. He presented participants with 12 decision dilemmas faced by hypothetical people and their task was to advise the person about how much risk to take; initially this was done individually, then in groups of about five.

To everyone's amazement, the group decisions were usually riskier than the individuals', i.e. the group advised the hypothetical person to take a greater risk than the average of the individuals' advice and this came to be called the *risky shift phenomenon*. Stoner sparked a wave of research into group decision making, which initially found considerable support for risky shift, involving brief discussions, people of varying ages, occupations and from 12 different countries. However, it was eventually found that risky shift was not, after all, universal; it was possible to present decision dilemmas on which people became more cautious after discussion (Myers, 1994). So is there a general principle that will predict how risky or cautious people's advice will be?

In the context of decision dilemmas, there seems to be a strong tendency for discussion to accentuate individuals' initial leanings, i.e. group discussion tends to enhance the individual's advice, whether this is risky or not. For this reason, risky shift came to be

seen as part of a much wider phenomenon called *group polarization* (Moscovici and Zavalloni, 1969), the tendency for groups to make decisions that are more extreme than the mean of individuals' initial positions, in the direction already favoured by that mean (Myers and Lamm, 1975; Wetherell, 1987). So groups are likely to adopt more extreme views than individual members, but this can be in either a riskier or a more cautious direction. Why does it occur?

According to Brown (1986), the mere exchange of information about who chose what can produce polarization and in discussion, group members may point out relevant information that others have missed and may argue persuasively for its importance. In addition, Turner (1991) argues that polarized decisions are reached because group members wish to define their identity more positively and distinctively, in contrast to members of other groups whom they might expect to adopt more average positions. This is supported by studies in which groups are told of the presumed decisions of other groups relevant to them (Doise, 1969, cited in Smith, 1995).

An example of how group decisions may become very extreme is *groupthink* (Janis, 1971, 1982), defined as a mode of thinking in which the desire to reach unanimous agreement over-rides the motivation to adopt proper, rational, decision-making procedures. Using archive material (people's retrospective accounts and content analysis), Janis analysed how the decisions were taken that led to certain major political/military fiascoes, such as Pearl Harbor (1941), the Bay of Pigs invasion of Cuba (1961) which led to the Cuban Missile Crisis (1962), and the Vietnam War. It has been suggested that groupthink is merely a specific instance of risky shift, in which a group that already tends towards making risky decisions polarizes, through discussion, to an even riskier one (Myers and Lamm, 1975). Janis believes that groupthink stems from an excessively cohesive, closeknit group, the suppression of dissent in the interests of group harmony and a directive leader who signals what decisions he or she favours. It is to leadership that we now turn.

LEADERS AND LEADERSHIP

Early research tried to identify the individual qualities that lead particular individuals to emerge as group leaders; this is often referred to as the *trait approach*. Later research has focused on the effectiveness of those who are appointed to a formal

FIGURE 20.5 *Hitler, Napoleon Bonaparte, Lenin, Ghandi. All great leaders, but are there any qualities they all had in common? Were they all 'born leaders'?*

leadership role, usually within large (usually business) organizations; this is often referred to as the *situational approach,* since it is concerned with the leader's dependence on the group and views leadership as a complex social process.

To an extent, focus on 'the leader' implies a trait approach (i.e. what is it about leaders as individuals, and compared with other individuals, that makes them leaders? Are leaders 'born or made'?), while 'leadership' denotes a process involving a leader, followers, group norms, goals and tasks and complex interactions between them, i.e. a situational approach (i.e. under what circumstances will a leader prove to be effective?).

● The trait approach: what do you need to become a leader?

The search for the qualities which make good leaders was influenced by the 'great man theory' of history, i.e. the view that

'... the fate of societies ... is in the hands of key, powerful, idiosyncratic individuals who by the force of their personalities reach positions of influence from which they can direct and dominate the lives of others. Such men are simply born great and emerge to

take power in any situation regardless of the social or historical context. (Huczynski and Buchanan, 1991)

Stogdill (1974) reviewed a large number of empirical studies and concluded that leaders are slightly more intelligent, self-confident, dominant, sociable and achievement-orientated than followers; they also tend to be older, more experienced and taller (!). But overall, the findings are inconclusive, i.e. leaders are not consistently found to be particular kinds of people who differ in predictable ways from non-leaders. Brown (1985) and Turner (1991) conclude that early research established that there is no consistent set of personality traits which distinguishes leaders from others – the kinds of traits a leader needs will vary from group to group and problem to problem. This is the view taken by another early leadership researcher, Bales (1950), who stressed the *functional demands* of the situation, i.e. the most effective leader in a given context is the person who is best equipped to help the group fulfil its objectives in that context; at another time and place, someone else may well emerge as leader. A good demonstration of this comes from Sherif *et al.*'s (1961) Robber's Cave field experiment (see Chapter 19): when competition with the other group was increased, one of the groups replaced its leader with a physically much stronger boy.

● Leadership styles as an alternative to personality traits

An early and famous study of leadership style is that of Lewin *et al.* (1939), which is described in Box 20.7.

Although the findings of the Lewin *et al,.* study strongly suggest that it is style of leadership (which is not necessarily a fixed characteristic) rather than personality (which is) that is important, Brown (1985) argues that individuals, their groups and leaders can only be understood in the context of the wider society of which they form a part. The 'democratic' style is, implicitly, the favourable and acceptable one of the three studied by Lewin *et al.* because that was the one prevalent in American society during the 1930s.

A number of additional leadership styles have been identified since the Lewin *et al.* study. For example, Bales (1950) distinguished between task specialist and socioemotional specialist, styles which he believed were inversely related, so that no one individual can display both styles simultaneously. In the Ohio State Leadership studies (e.g. Fleischman, 1973; Stogdill, 1974), in which subordinates in mainly military and industrial groups were asked to assess their leaders' behaviour and effectiveness, two

---

BOX 20.7 Key study: It's not what you're like but how you act

Lewin *et al.* (1939) wanted to investigate the effects of three kinds of adult behaviour on a group of ten-year-old boys attending after-school clubs (concerned with model making). The clubs were led by adults who acted in one of three ways: autocratic, democratic or laissez-faire.

The *democratic group* met two days before the other two groups. The leader discussed various possible projects and allowed the boys to choose workmates and generally to make their own decisions. He explained his comments and joined in with the group activities. The boys got on much better with each other and seemed to like each other more than the boys who had an autocratic leader. Although slightly less work was actually done, approaches to the leader were usually task-related. When he left the room, the boys carried on working, showing greater independence, and they co-operated with each other when things went wrong.

Autocratic leaders told the boys what sort of models they would make and with whom they would work. They

sometimes praised or blamed them for their work but did not explain their comments and, although friendly, were aloof and impersonal. The boys became aggressive towards each other when things went wrong and were submissive in their approaches to the leader (which were often attention seeking). If he left the room, the boys stopped working and became either disruptive or apathetic. However, the models they made were comparable, both in quantity and quality, to those of the boys in the democratic group.

Laissez-faire leaders left the boys very much to their own devices, only offered help when asked for it (which was not very often) and gave neither praise nor blame. The boys were aggressive towards each other, although less so than the boys with an autocratic leader. Very little work was done, whether the leader was present or not and they were easily discouraged when things were not going exactly right.

The leader was changed every seven weeks and was instructed to adopt one of the other kinds of leadership style: each group was exposed to only one leadership style (but enacted by three different leaders). This was meant to ensure that the boys' behaviour could be attributed to leadership style and not to the personality of the leader.

---

styles emerged, *initiating structure* and *considera-tion* (for others) (corresponding to Bales' task specialist and socioemotional specialist respectively). Unlike Bales, these two styles were seen as independent dimensions and the most effective leaders are precisely those who score above average on both. Similarly, Sorrentino and Field (1986) carried out detailed observations of 12 problem-solving groups over a five-week period; those members observed to score high on both of Bales' styles were subsequently elected leaders (see Fig. 20.6).

Despite the improvement offered by the study of leadership styles over the trait approach, the focus is still on the leader as an individual. To provide an adequate understanding of leader effectiveness, the study of leadership behaviour needs to be comple-

mented by an analysis of the role of *situational factors;* the need for an interactionist perspective gradually became apparent from observations that effective leadership is not just about the 'right mixture' of leadership styles, because what this right mixture is depends on the nature of the group. The first major theory to recognize that the effectiveness of particular leadership styles depends on situational factors was Fiedler's contingency model.

● Fiedler's contingency model of leadership

Fiedler's (1965) *contingency model* of leadership effectiveness is mainly concerned with the fit or match between a leader's personal qualities or

Lewin et al (1939)	Bales (1950)	Fleischman (1973) Stogdill (1974)	Fiedler (1965)
Autocratic	Task-specialist	Initiating structure	Task orientated (low LPC scorer)
Democratic		|	
Laissez-faire	Socioemotional specialist	Consideration (for others)	Relationship-orientated (High LPC scorer) (see text)

TABLE 20.2 *Relationship between different distinctions made between different kinds of leadership style*

leadership style, on the one hand, and the requirements of the situation on the other.

Fiedler began by measuring the extent to which leaders distinguish between their most and least preferred co-worker (LPC) and developed a scale which gave an LPC score. Leaders are asked to think of all those who have ever worked under them (subordinates) and to select the one who was the most difficult to work with. They then rate this person on 18 bipolar scales (e.g. pleasant-unpleasant, boring-interesting, friendly-unfriendly) which gives an LPC score: leaders with a high LPC score still see their least preferred co-worker in a relatively favourable light and also tend to be more accepting, permissive, considerate and person oriented in relationships with group members (*relationship oriented*). By contrast, a low LPC score implies a very negative attitude towards the least preferred co-worker and low scorers also tend to be directive, controlling and dominant in relationships with group members (*task oriented*).

Fiedler then investigated the fit between these two styles of leadership and the needs of the situation; the basic hypothesis is that the effectiveness of a leader is contingent upon the fit between the leader's style and the degree of 'favourableness', i.e. to what extent the situation allows the leader to exert his or her influence. The degree of favourableness is determined by three situational variables, each of which can have a high or low value:

1 *Quality of leader–member relations* refers to the extent to which the leader has the loyalty and confidence of the members and to the general psychological atmosphere of the group.
2 *Task structure* refers to the complexity of the task and the number of possible solutions: the more unstructured the task, the more the leader must motivate and inspire members to find solutions.
3 *Position-power* refers to the power inherent in the leader's role, for example, the rewards and punishments at their disposal and the organizational support from superiors.

Fiedler's basic hypothesis is that low LPC leaders will be most effective in situations which are either very favourable (high values of the three situational variables) or very unfavourable (low values of each), while high LPC leaders will be most effective where the degree of favourableness is neither very high nor very low (see Fig. 20.7). What is the rationale behind this hypothesis?

When the situation is very favourable, leaders do not have to waste any time worrying about the morale of group members and they have the means

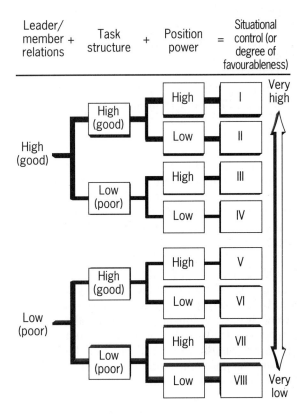

FIGURE 20.6 *Eight segments (or octants) produced by high and low values of leader/member relations, task structure and position power in Fiedler's contingency model. (Adapted from Hogg and Vaughan, 1995, based on Fiedler, 1967,1971,1981)*

and power to be totally task related. Similarly, when the situation is highly unfavourable, leaders have very little to lose by being fairly autocratic: trying to win over the group by a more considerate approach will probably fail anyway, resulting in lost time and reduced effectiveness. At intermediate levels of favourableness, the leader may, by adopting a suitable, relationship-oriented style, be able to improve the relationships with the members enough to compensate for an ill-defined task and lack of authority (Brown, 1988).

An evaluation of Fiedler's contingency model

According to Hogg and Vaughan (1995), there is considerable empirical support for the model, which is considered to be the most useful approach to the analysis of leadership. (see Fig. 20.7). However, a number of criticisms have been made about some of the model's basic assumptions. For example, Fiedler claims that leadership style is a relatively fixed characteristic of the leader (i.e. it is part of the leader's personality), so that leaders will find it difficult to modify their leadership style. But the test-retest reliability of LPC scores is relatively low (Rice, 1978) and, as we saw earlier, Lewin *et al.* (1939) managed to train their confederate leaders to adopt different styles easily. Turner (1991) asks what LPC scores actually mean and what their relationship is to the leader's actual behaviour.

Another criticism involves Fiedler's assumption that the quality of the leader-member relations is the most important of the three situational variables, with the leader's legitimate power being the least important. Not only is this assumption not justified but, as Hogg and Vaughan (1995) observe, couldn't their relative order of importance itself be a function of contextual factors? They also argue that the contingency model ignores the group processes responsible for the rise and fall of leaders and the situational complexity of leadership. However, Smith (1995) believes that Fiedler has steadily improved the model by examining the influence of additional leader qualities, such as intelligence and prior experience.

● Leadership as a process

Whatever the merits of Fiedler's model, it implicitly sees leadership as a one-way influence process, but to understand leadership adequately, it must be seen as a two-way process. Leadership involves leaders and followers in various role relationships and there are several paths to becoming validated as a leader. The question of *validation* is to do with how the leader comes to occupy the role, i.e. how do they achieve legitimacy as a leader? In a formal group structure, the leader is assigned by an external authority and is imposed on the group (an *appointed* leader); in an informal group structure, the leader achieves his/her authority from the group members (who may withdraw their support just as they gave it) and is called an *emergent leader*. Conversely, even in formal structures there are emergent (or 'informal') leaders who exert influence among their peers by virtue of their personal qualities, especially how verbal they are.

Even in the case of appointed leaders, leadership is a complex social process, involving a transaction or exchange between the group members. The leader is dependent on the rest of the group for liking and approval and their attitudes towards the leader will influence the process of leadership. What is easily overlooked is that leaders are actually members of the groups they lead. At one and the same time, they represent and embody the group's norms (they are conformists) and are agents of change, steering it in new directions, i.e. they can change prevailing norms (they are also deviants). But they first have to 'earn' the right to bring about change by building up 'credit' with the rest of the group (what Hollander, 1958 called *idiosyncrasy credit*), through initially conforming closely to established norms, showing the necessary competence to fulfil the group's objectives, being seen as identifying with the group's ideals and aspirations and in other ways. Merei (1949) brought older children, who had previously shown leadership potential, into small groups of younger children in a Hungarian nursery. The most successful leaders were those who initially complied with existing group practices and who only gradually, and later, introduced minor changes; they had built up sufficient idiosyncrasy credit.

Hollander's is a much more dynamic view of leadership than Fiedler's, but both neglect two features of the leader's interactions with others :

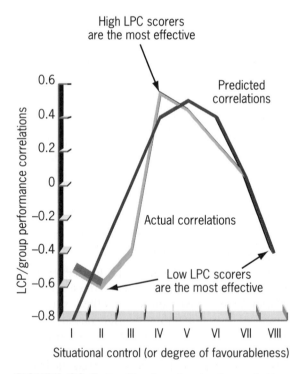

FIGURE 20.7 *Predicted and actual correlations between LPC scores and group performance as a function of situational control (or degree of favourableness). (Based on data from Fiedler 1965.)*

1 The focus of leadership research has been on the links between leaders and their immediate subordinates. But in practice, of course, leaders devote substantial time to their own superiors, relevant colleagues and many others within – and sometimes outside – the organization in which they work. Leaders play a crucial role as 'linking pins' between various groups within a large institution (Likert, 1961). Later theories have developed this idea and reformulated the concept of leadership to emphasize how leader effectiveness can be thought of as successful management of the conflicting needs and demands of the leader's *role set*, i.e. all those who make demands on the occupant of a particular role (e.g. Smith and Peterson, 1988). Taking this broader view of a leader's interactions implies that the leader uses different leadership styles , i.e. forms of influence, with different members of the role set (Smith, 1995).

2 Leaders not only lead their groups but, in varying ways, lead them against other groups. This is illustrated well by the familiar tactic of political leaders who are unpopular at home pursuing an aggressive foreign policy, such as Thatcher in the Falklands War (1982) and Bush in the Gulf War (1991).This *intergroup dimension* of leadership is usually overlooked (Hogg and Vaughan, 1995).

● Can anyone become a leader?

A number of laboratory studies have imposed a particular communication network on a group of participants (e.g. a five-person wheel or 'Y' or chain) in each of which one person is randomly assigned to the central position, so that the other group members can only communicate via that central person and not directly with each other (Fig. 20.8). From studies like these, Brown (1985) concludes that when people are put into positions where the group has to depend on their efforts, they tend to accept the challenge and behave like leaders. Just as crucially, they are recognized as leaders by the rest of the group. Compared with people occupying peripheral positions, they tend to send more messages, to solve problems more quickly, to make fewer errors and to be more satisfied with their own and the group's efforts. Although recognizing that not anyone can fill any role, Brown (1985) concludes that finding oneself in a position of leadership may bring out hidden talents; certainly as far as laboratory studies are concerned, it seems to be primarily the position in the network, and not personality, which accounts for the assumption of the leadership role.

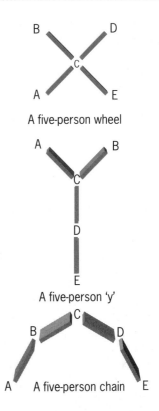

FIGURE 20.8 *Examples of communication networks used in laboratory studies of leadership*

Similarly, Turner (1991) concludes that, given certain minimum 'qualifications', it is probable that anyone can act as an effective leader in the right group at the right time. There is no personality type with a mystical, special 'divine right' to lead (although recent research suggests that being a charismatic figure may be a distinct advantage; see Smith, 1995). Indeed, people whom we think of as outstanding leaders are probably those who are the most flexible and adaptable: surely a basic requirement of leadership is to be able to see what is needed at any given moment and to adapt one's behaviour accordingly. Instead of seeing Lewin *et al.*'s democratic/autocratic styles, or any of the other distinctions we noted earlier, as opposites, the ideal leader may be the person who can be both or either as and when the situation demands.

● Leadership and power

Clearly, leadership and power are closely related concepts, but just as there are different kinds of leader (e.g. appointed and emergent) so there are different kinds of power. A comprehensive classification has

Legitimate power: the formal power invested in a particular role (e.g. President of the USA, Prime Minister, headteacher, bank manager) regardless of the personality of the particular role occupant.

Reward power: control over valued resources ('rewards'), including salary/wages, food, love, respect, co-operation; the individuals will include parents, work colleagues, friends, employers and store-owners.

Coercive power: control over feared consequences ('punishments'), including the withdrawal of rewards, demotion, dismissal, loss of love, etc. Both here and in reward power, power is largely inherent in the role itself, but personality can play some part.

Expert power: possession of special knowledge, skills and expertise (e.g. doctors, teachers, plumbers, car mechanics). Related to informational power, which is to do with access to important sources of information, e.g. computer facilities such as the Internet.

Referent power: personal qualities, such as charm, magnetism, ability to persuade and 'win' people over. The charismatic leader has great referent power, often exceeding their legitimate power. But parents, teachers, etc. may also have referent power in addition to their legitimate, reward, coercive and expert power.

TABLE 20.3 *Five kinds of power (as proposed by French and Raven, 1959)*

been proposed by French and Raven (1959) and is summarized in Table 20.3.

In the context of the trait approach, might we have inadvertently stumbled across a characteristic which is consistently displayed by every leader, namely the lust for power? If we accept Adler's theory of the 'will to power', i.e. the tendency in each of us to overcome our fundamental feeling of inferiority (see Chapter 29), then leaders could be seen as satisfying their will to power in that particular way and this would lend further support to the notion of desire for power as a characteristic of all leaders. However, Gergen and Gergen (1981) warn us against this conclusion: although leadership does imply power, it would be a mistake, they argue, to assume that everyone who possesses power is highly motivated to achieve it. They claim that many political leaders, for example, are recruited and encouraged by others who promote them to powerful positions and their needs for affiliation may be far stronger than their needs for power.

OBEDIENCE

According to Milgram (1992), conformity and obedience have in common the '... abdication of individual judgement in the face of some external social pressure ...' However, the differences are just as important

1 In conformity, there is no explicit requirement to act in a certain way, whereas in obedience we are being ordered or instructed to do something.

2 In conformity, those who influence us are our peers (equals) and the behaviour of individuals becomes more alike (homogenization of behaviour). In obedience, there is a difference in status from the outset, with the authority figure influencing another person; there is no mutual influence.

3 Conformity has to do with the psychological 'need' for acceptance by others and entails going along with one's peers in a group situation; obedience has to do with the social power and status of an authority figure in a hierarchical situation. While we typically deny that we conform (because this seems to detract from our sense of individuality), we usually deny responsibility for our behaviour in the case of obedience ('He made me do it').

Brown (1986) says that conformity behaviour is affected by *example* (from peers or equals) while obedience is affected by *direction* (from somebody in higher authority).

● Empirical studies of obedience

In the conformity experiments of Sherif, Asch and Crutchfield, participants showed conformity by giving a verbal response of some kind or pressing buttons representing answers on various tasks. In the most famous and controversial of all obedience experiments, Milgram's participants were required to 'kill' another human being.

Milgram was attempting to test the 'Germans are different' hypothesis. This hypothesis has been used by historians to explain the systematic destruction of millions of Jews, Poles and others by the Nazis during the 1930s and 1940s. It maintains that: (i) Hitler could not have put his evil plans into operation without the co-operation of thousands of others; and (ii) the Germans have a basic character defect, namely a readiness to obey authority without question

Public Announcement

WE WILL PAY YOU $4.00 FOR ONE HOUR OF YOUR TIME

Persons Needed for a Study of Memory

*We will pay five hundred New Haven men to help us complete a scientific study of memory and learning. The study is being done at Yale University.

*Each person who participates will be paid $4.00 (plus 50c carfare) for approximately 1 hour's time. We need you for only one hour: there are no further obligations. You may choose the time you would like to come (evenings, weekdays, or weekends).

*No special training, education, or experience is needed. We want:

Factory workers	Businessmen	Construction workers
City employees	Clerks	Salespeople
Laborers	Professional people	White-collar workers
Barbers	Telephone workers	Others

All persons must be between the ages of 20 and 50. High school and college students cannot be used.

*If you meet these qualifications, fill out the coupon below and mail it now to Professor Stanley Milgram, Department of Psychology, Yale University, New Haven. You will be notified later of the specific time and place of the study. We reserve the right to decline any application.

*You will be paid $4.00 (plus 50c carfare) as soon as you arrive at the laboratory.

- -

TO:
PROF. STANLEY MILGRAM, DEPARTMENT OF PSYCHOLOGY, YALE UNIVERSITY, NEW HAVEN, CONN. I want to take part in this study of memory and learning. I am between the ages of 20 and 50. I will be paid $4.00 (plus 50c carfare) if I participate.

NAME (Please Print)..................................

ADDRESS ....

TELEPHONE NO. .... Best time to call you ....

AGE........ OCCUPATION................... SEX......
CAN YOU COME:

WEEKDAYS .... EVENINGS ......WEEKENDS.........

FIGURE 20.9 *Announcement placed in a local newspaper to recruit participants. (From Milgram, 1974)*

regardless of the acts demanded by the authority figure, and that it is this readiness to obey which provided Hitler with the co-operation he needed. It is really the second part of the hypothesis which Milgram was trying to test. He had originally planned to take his experiment to Germany, once it was completed at New Haven, Connecticut, but, as we shall see, that proved unnecessary.

The participants in the original (1963) experiment were 20–50-year-old men, from all walks of life. They answered advertisements in local newspapers or that came by post, which asked for volunteers for a study of learning to be conducted at Yale University. It would take about one hour and there would be a payment of $4.50 (see Fig. 20.9). The basic experimental procedure is described in Box 20.8.

Milgram had asked 14 psychology students to predict what would happen for 100 participants in this situation. They thought that a few would break off early on, most would stop somewhere in the middle

and a few would continue right up to 450 volts. He also asked 40 psychiatrists, who predicted that less than 1 percent would administer the highest voltage. These estimates were based on what Milgram called the 'remote' victim experiment, which was the first of a series of 18 different experiments, all variations on the same basic theme. In this particular experiment, Mr Wallace was heard to pound loudly on the wall at 300 volts and, after 315 volts, no further answers were given and no further pounding was heard. The shockingly (pun intended!) high figure for those who actually went on giving shocks up to and including 450 volts was 65 percent, with every teacher giving shocks up to at least 300 volts. Those who continued after 300 volts either refused to carry on somewhere between 315 and 375 or went all the way up to 450 volts.

In the second experiment (voice feedback), teachers heard a tape-recorded series of verbal responses, which they believed were the spontaneous reactions of Mr Wallace to the increasing shock levels:

At 75 volts, he made a little grunt (as he did at 90 and 105 volts).

At 120 volts, he shouted to the experimenter that the shocks were becoming painful.

At 135 volts, he made painful groans.

At 150 volts, he cried out, 'Experimenter, get me out of here! I won't be in the experiment any more! I refuse to go on!' This continued with rising intensity until

At 180 volts, he shouted, 'I can't stand the pain.'

At 270 volts, he let out an agonized scream. [He continued to insist on being released.]

At 300 volts, he shouted desperately that he would no longer provide answers.

At 315 volts, he let out a violent scream, reaffirming vehemently that he was no longer participating.

After 330 volts, ominous silence!

(The teacher was instructed to treat no response as if it were an incorrect response, so the shocks could continue beyond 300 volts.) In addition, the experimenter had a script prepared for whenever the teacher refused to continue or showed any resistance or reluctance to do so:

Prod 1: 'Please continue' or 'Please go on.'
Prod 2: 'The experiment requires that you continue.'
Prod 3: 'It's absolutely essential that you continue.'
Prod 4: 'You have no other choice, you *must* go on.'

BOX 20.8	Key study: Could you kill a man? Probably – if Milgram asked me to

255–300	Intense shock
315–360	Intense to extreme shock
375–420	Danger: severe shock
435–450	XXX

When participants arrived at Yale University Psychology Department, they were met by a young, crew-cut man in a laboratory coat, who introduced himself as Jack Williams, the experimenter. Also present was a Mr Wallace, supposedly another participant, in his late fifties, an accountant, a little overweight and generally a very mild and harmless-looking man (Fig. 20.10). In fact, Mr Wallace was an assistant of Milgram and everything that happened after this was pre-planned, staged and scripted: everything, that is, except the degree to which the real participant obeyed the experimenter's instructions.

The participant and Mr Wallace were told that the experiment was concerned with the effects of punishment on learning and that one of them was to be the teacher and the other the learner. Their roles were determined by each drawing a piece of paper from a hat: both, in fact, had 'teacher' written on them. Mr Wallace drew first and called out 'learner', so, of course, the real participant was always the teacher.

They all went into an adjoining room where the learner (Mr Wallace) was strapped into a chair with his arms attached to electrodes which would deliver a shock from the shock generator situated in an adjacent room. The teacher and experimenter (Mr Williams) then moved next door where the generator was situated; the teacher was, in fact, given a 45-volt shock to convince him that it was real, for he was to operate the generator during the experiment. However, that was the only real shock that either the teacher or the learner was to receive. The generator (which Milgram himself had built and which looked authentic) had a number of switches, each clearly marked with voltage levels and verbal descriptions, starting at 15 volts and going up to 450 in intervals of 15:

15–60	Slight shock
75–120	Moderate shock
135–180	Strong shock
195–240	Very strong shock

The teacher had to read out a series of word pairs (e.g. 'blue–girl', 'nice–day', 'fat–neck') and then the first of one pair (the stimulus word) followed by five words, of which one was the original paired response. The learner had to choose the correct response to the stimulus word by pressing one of four switches, which turned on a light on a panel in the generator room. Each time he made a mistake, the teacher had to deliver a shock and each successive mistake was punished by a shock 15 volts higher than the one before.

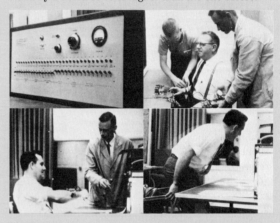

FIGURE 20.10 *1 Shock generator used in the experiments. Fifteen of the 30 switches have already been depressed. 2 Learner is strapped into chair and electrodes are attached to his wrist. Electrode paste is applied by the experimenter. Learner provides answers by depressing switches that light up numbers on an answer box. 3 Subject receives sample shock from the generator. 4 Subject breaks off experiment. On right, event recorder wired into generator automatically records switches used by the subject. (Copyright 1965 by Stanley Milgram from the film Obedience, distributed by the Pennsylvania State University, Audio Visual Services.) (From Milgram, 1974)*

There were also 'special prods' to reassure the subject that he was not doing the learner any permanent harm: 'Although the shocks may be painful there is no permanent tissue damage, so please go on'.

In this second (voice feedback) condition, 62.5 percent of participants went on giving shocks up to 450 volts. Many displayed great anguish, verbally attacked the experimenter, twitched nervously or broke out into nervous laughter. Many were observed

to 'sweat, stutter, tremble, groan, bite their lips and dig their nails into their flesh. Full-blown, uncontrollable seizures were observed for three subjects'. One experiment had to be stopped because the participant had a violently convulsive seizure.

Why was there such a high level of obedience? Milgram tried to answer this crucial question by devising some variations to the basic experiment (using the voice feedback condition as the baseline) in order to identify the critical variables.

1 In post-experimental interviews, many participants said that they had continued giving shocks because the experiment was being carried out at Yale, a very prestigious and highly respected American university. Milgram therefore transferred the experiment to a rundown office building located in downtown Bridgeport, Connecticut (Experiment 10). In this setting, the obedience rate was 47.5 percent (for those continuing up to 450 volts), indicating that the awe-inspiring nature of the original location was not a crucial factor, although it clearly played some part.

2 The proximity of the teacher to the learner proved to be of greater significance than the physical setting. Remember that in the original experiment the teacher and learner were in separate but adjoining rooms, so that the teacher heard the learner (via a tape-recorder) but could not see him. When they were in the same room (about 1½ feet apart), so that the teacher could see as well as hear the learner, the obedience level dropped to 40 percent (Experiment 3). It dropped further still to 30 percent when the teacher was required to force the learner's hand onto the shock plate (Experiment 4). Clearly, it became much more uncomfortable to see the effects of their obedience, so that considerably fewer participants were prepared to go all the way. However, these figures of 40 and 30 percent are still alarmingly high.

3 Another variation involved giving the teacher social support for refusing to obey (Experiment 17). The real participant was teamed with two other 'teachers' (confederates of Milgram). Teacher 1 read out the list of word pairs, Teacher 2 informed the learner if the answer was correct or not and Teacher 3 (the real participant) threw the switch. After 150 volts, Teacher 1 announced that he was not going to continue and moved to another part of the room; the participant had to take over the reading of the word pairs. After 210 volts, Teacher 2 also refused. In all cases, the experimenter continued to order Teacher 3 to proceed as described above. Only 10 percent of real participants continued all the way to 450 volts – they stopped obeying either immediately after one of the confederates did so or very shortly afterwards.

   What this experiment represents is a demonstration of conformity counteracting the effects of obedience; as Milgram (1965) says, '...The effects of peer rebellion are most impressive in undercutting the experimenter's authority ...'. He identifies several specific factors that contribute to the group's effectiveness, including instilling in the participant the idea of defying the experimenter – it may not have occurred to some as a response possibility. Indeed, some made very revealing remarks afterwards, such as 'I didn't realize I could' (i.e. refuse to obey). So the 'demands of the situation' seem to be crucial, that is, how participants interpret and define what is possible or permissible (see Chapter 2). Also, as long as the two confederates are involved there is a 'dispersion (diffusion) of responsibility' for shocking the learner; once they have withdrawn, responsibility becomes focused on the naive participant.

4 When the teacher was paired with another, confederate, teacher and the real participant had only to read out the word-pairs (the confederate threw the switches) there was 92.5 percent obedience. Clearly, it was easier to shift responsibility from themselves to the confederate for what the learner was suffering since 'their hand was not on the button' (Experiment 18).

5 The proximity of the experimenter to the teacher was also found to be crucial. When the experimenter left the room, having given the initial instructions, and issued subsequent instructions by telephone, the obedience level dropped to 20.5 percent (Experiment 7). Participants often pretended to press the shock button or pressed the button for a lower voltage than they were meant to. This suggests that they were trying to compromise between what their conscience was telling them to do and what the experimenter was telling them to do; in his absence, it was easier to disobey him and to obey the dictates of conscience!

● So why do people obey in the Milgram experiment?

In the experimenter's absence, participants are forced to accept responsibility for their own actions, while in his presence, with all the prods and prompts, it was much easier to deny personal responsibility (they were merely 'doing what they were told'). But clearly it was not as cut and dried as this. We saw earlier that many showed obvious signs of distress and conflict. The experimenter was, it seems, being seen as a legitimate authority in that situation, which was totally convincing and very real for the participants (*experimental realism*). The conflict is between two opposing sets of demands – the external authority of the experimenter who says 'Shock' and the internal authority of the conscience which says, 'Don't shock'.

The point at which conscience triumphs is, of course, where the participant (finally) stops obeying the experimenter – at that point the experimenter, in a sense, ceases to be a legitimate authority in the eyes of the participant. Thirty five per cent in the original experiment reached that point somewhere before 450 volts; for many, the crucial 'prod' was when the experimenter said, 'You have no other choice, you *must* go on'. They were able to exercise the choice which, of course, they did have and so at that point they stopped obeying.

The most common mental adjustment in the fully obedient participant is to see himself as an agent of external authority (the 'agentic state'), a typical response being: 'I wouldn't have done it by myself, I was just doing what I was told', as if he had no choice (this is similar to the concept of deindividuation; see Chapter 17). This agentic state (the opposite of autonomy) is what allows humans to function in an organized, hierarchical, social system – for the group to function as a unified whole, individuals must be able to give up responsibility and defer to others of higher status in the social hierarchy. Legitimate authority replaces the individual's own self-regulation (Turner, 1991).

In these studies, the experimenter wore a grey, not a white, laboratory coat, which was meant to be ambiguous (i.e. a white one might have suggested a medical technician) but which indicated his position as an authority figure. Other studies have shown that the fact that someone is wearing a uniform is often reason enough for them to be obeyed. For example, in a study by Bickman (1974), researchers approached people on the streets of New York and ordered them either to pick up a paper bag or give a coin to a stranger. Half of the researchers were dressed in neat street clothes and half in a guard's uniform. Under 40 percent obeyed the civilians but more than 80 percent obeyed the 'guard'.

According to Milgram (1974), 'A substantial proportion of people do what they are told to do, irrespective of the content of the act and without limitations of conscience, so long as they perceive that the command comes from a legitimate authority'.

● An evaluation of Milgram's research

In evaluating Milgram's experiments, ethical issues are usually more prominent than scientific ones. These are discussed in detail in Chapter 32. However, we should note here that Milgram asks whether the ethical criticisms are based as much on the nature of the (unexpected) results as on the procedure itself. Aronson (1988) asks if we would question the ethics if none of the participants had gone beyond the 150 volt level, which is the point at which most people are expected to stop according to Milgram's students and the 40 psychiatrists he consulted. Aronson has manipulated the results experimentally and finds that the higher the percentage going right up to 450 volts, the more harmful the effects of the experiment are judged to be.

The criticism that his sample was unrepresentative of the American population seems to be unjustified. Altogether, 636 participants were tested (in the 18 separate experiments as a whole), representing a cross-section of the population of New Haven, thought to be a fairly typical small American town. However, Milgram admits that those who went on obeying up to 450 volts were more likely to see the learner as responsible for what happened to him and not themselves! They seemed to have a stronger authoritarian character and a less advanced level of moral development. But this was a matter of degree

Study	Country	Participants	% obedient
Milgram (1963)	USA	Male general population	65
		Female general population	65
Rosenhan (in Milgram, 1974)	USA	Students	85
Ancona & Pareyson (1968)	Italy	Students	85
Mantell (1971)	Germany	Male general population	85
Kilham & Mann (1974)	Australia	Male students	40
		Female students	16
Burley & McGuiness (1977)	UK	Male students	50
Shanab & Yahya (1978)	Jordan	Students	62
Miranda et al. (1981)	Spain	Students	Over 90
Schurz (1985)	Austria	General population	80
Meeus & Raaijmakers (1986)	Holland	General population	92

Table 20.4 *Obedience rates based on Milgram's procedure from different countries (adapted from Smith and Bond, 1993)*

only. As Rosenthal and Rosnow (1966) and others have found, people who volunteer for experiments are considerably less authoritarian than those who do not.

While only 40 women were included in Milgram's sample (Experiment 8), they showed a 65 percent obedience rate, just like their male counterparts. These results are included in Table 20.4 which shows the results of cross-cultural replications of Milgram's procedure.

Despite the interesting differences in obedience rates in different countries, we cannot be very confident that they actually tell us very much about cultural differences, since important details of the procedure often differed between studies. For example, in the Australian study, the female participants were asked to give shocks to a female victim, while the victim in Milgram's experiments was always a man (Smith and Bond, 1993).

Finally, it has been claimed that what happened to Milgram's participants cannot be generalized to real-life outside the laboratory. So, in Aronson's terms, do Milgram's experiments have *mundane realism?* Milgram defends himself by maintaining that the essential process involved in complying with the demands of an authority figure is the same, whether the setting is the artificial one of the laboratory or a naturally occurring one outside it. In discussing the relationship between participant and experimenter, Colman (1987) says that although it possesses a special quality of implicit trust and dependency, '... the occasion we term a psychological experiment shares its essential structural properties with other situations composed of subordinate-superordinate roles'.

Milgram (1974) himself acknowledges the enormous differences (some more obvious than others) between his laboratory studies of obedience and Nazi Germany:

> ... yet difference in scale, numbers and political context may turn out to be relatively unimportant as long as certain essential features are retained. The essence of obedience consists in the fact that a person comes to view himself as the instrument for carrying out another person's wishes, and he, therefore, no longer regards himself as responsible for his actions. Once this critical shift of viewpoint has occurred in the person, all the essential features of obedience follow.

A study of great relevance to this issue was conducted by Hofling *et al.* (1966), which aimed to discover whether nurses would comply with an instruction which would involve them having to infringe both hospital regulations and medical ethics (Box 20.9).

There is, of course, an important difference between the situations facing Milgram's participants and Hofling's nurses: the former were being asked to inflict pain upon another human being, while the latter were being asked to do something quite consistent with their role and, presumably, in the patient's best interests. Or was it? The 21 nurses who complied probably did not question that it was, since

---

| **BOX 20.9** | Key study: Obedience in a natural setting (Hofling *et al.*, 1966) |

Identical boxes of capsules were placed in 22 wards of both public and private psychiatric hospitals in the USA. The capsules were in fact placebos (consisting of glucose) but the containers were labelled '5 mg capsules of Astrofen'; the labels also indicated that the normal dose are 5 mg with a maximum daily dose of 10 mg. While the nurse was on duty, a 'doctor' (a confederate 'Dr Smith from the Psychiatric Department') instructed the nurse, by telephone, to give 20 mg of Astrofen to his patient, a Mr Jones, as he was in a desperate hurry and the patient needed the capsules. He said that he would come in to see Mr Jones in 10 minutes time and that he would sign the authorization document for the drug when he got there.

To comply with this request, the nurse would be breaking three basic procedural rules:

1 the dose was above the maximum daily dose of 10 mg;
2 drugs should only be given after written authority has been obtained;
3 the nurse must be absolutely sure that 'Dr Smith' was a genuine doctor.

A real doctor was posted nearby, unseen by the nurse, and observed what the nurse did following the telephone call – did she comply, did she refuse or did she try to contact another doctor? Twenty one out of 22 nurses complied unhesitatingly! Eleven later said that they had not noticed the dosage discrepancy.

In interviews, 22 graduate nurses who had not participated in the actual experiment were presented with the same situation as an issue to discuss; 21 said that they would not have given the drug without written authorization, especially as it exceeded the maximum daily dose.

BOX 20.10 Key study: The prison simulation experiment (Zimbardo et al., 1973)

The participants were recruited through advertisements placed in a city newspaper asking for student volunteers for a two-week study of prison life. They would be paid 15 dollars a day (210 dollars in all, quite a lot of money for a poor student) and over 100 volunteers came forward initially.

They were given clinical interviews and 25 were eventually selected. They were judged to be emotionally stable, physically healthy, 'normal to average' on the basis of extensive personality tests and also law abiding (they had no history of convictions, violence or drug abuse). They were told that their assignment to the role of either prisoner or prison guard would be determined by the toss of a coin. They all stated a preference for being prisoners. So at the start of the study there were no measurable differences between those who were to be assigned to one or other role; they were a relatively homogeneous sample of white, middle-class college students from all over the USA and Canada. They all had an equal chance of being either prisoner or guard.

The 'mock prison' represented an attempt to simulate functionally some of the significant features of the psychological state of imprisonment. The basement of Stanford University in California was converted into a mock prison and the experiment began one Sunday morning when the students who had been allocated the prisoner role were 'arrested' by the Palo Alto police, charged with a felony, told their constitutional rights, searched, handcuffed and taken in the back seat of a squad car to the police station to be booked. After being fingerprinted and having identification forms prepared for his 'jacket' (central information file), the prisoner was taken, blindfold, to 'Stanford County Prison' where he was stripped naked, skin-searched, deloused, issued a uniform, bedding, etc.

Prisoners wore a loose-fitting smock with an identification number front and back, plus a chain bolted around one ankle; they also wore a nylon stocking to cover their hair (instead of being shaved). The guards wore military khaki-style uniforms, silver reflector sunglasses (which made eye contact impossible) and they carried clubs, whistles, handcuffs and keys to the cells and main gate. Although the guards worked eight-hour shifts, the prisoners were imprisoned in their cells around the clock, allowed out only for meals, exercise, toilet privileges, head counts and work.

After an initial rebellion had been crushed, the prisoners reacted passively as the guards stepped up their aggression each day, which made the prisoners even more passive and dependent, and made them feel helpless, that they were no longer in control of their lives. In less than 36 hours, one prisoner had to be released because of uncontrolled crying, fits of rage, disorganized thinking and severe depression. Three more developed similar symptoms and had to be released on successive days. A fifth prisoner developed a rash over his whole body which was triggered when his 'parole' had been rejected. The entire experiment, planned to run for two weeks, was stopped after six days because of the pathological reactions of the prisoners who had originally been selected for their normality.

Social power became the major dimension on which everyone and everything was defined. Every guard at some time or another behaved in an abusive, authoritarian way; many seemed positively to enjoy the newfound power and the almost total control over the prisoners which went with the uniform. For example, Guard A said: 'I was surprised at myself – I made them call each other names and clean the toilets out with their bare hands. I practically considered the prisoners cattle and I kept thinking I have to watch out for them in case they try something'. Guard B (preparing for the visitors' first night): 'I made sure I was one of the guards on the yard, because this was my first chance for the type of manipulative power that I really like – being a very noticed figure with complete control over what is said or not.' Guard C: 'Acting authoritatively can be fun. Power can be a great pleasure.'

the request came from a Dr Smith from the Psychiatry Department.

● The power of social situations

It seems that built into our social roles is a polarity (pair of opposites) which might be expressed as domineering-servile, powerful-powerless, dominant-submissive. Rather than asking what makes some people more obedient than others or how we would have reacted if we had been one of Milgram's participants, we should be asking how we would behave if we were put into a position of authority ourselves. How easily could we assume the role and use the power that goes with it?

An intriguing but also rather frightening experiment by Zimbardo et al. (1973) explored these questions. Their famous Prison Simulation Experiment is described in Box 20.10.

How can we account for the behaviour of the prisoners and prison guards? Zimbardo and Ruch (1977) argue that the abnormal behaviour of both groups is best viewed as a product of transactions with an environment that supports such behaviour. As they were randomly assigned their roles, showed no prior personality pathology and received no training, how was it that they assumed their roles as quickly and completely as they did?

First, presumably, they had learned stereotypes of guard and prisoner roles from the mass media as well as from social models of power and powerlessness (for example, the parent-child, teacher-student, employer-employee relationships). We are able to draw on our experience and knowledge of other role relationship whenever we are faced with new ones, whether we are called upon to be 'in charge' or to be the submissive or powerless one.

Secondly, environmental conditions facilitate role playing. A brutalizing atmosphere, like the 'mock' prison, produces brutality and perhaps this kind of aggression is latent in all of us. Had the roles been reversed, those who suffered as the prisoners may just as easily have inflicted suffering on those who were randomly chosen as guards. (In contrast to the Milgram experiment, there seemed to be no conflict for the guards, quite the reverse, in fact. Clearly the role of teacher and the requirement that he should deliver painful electric shocks were seen as inconsistent with each other. But a guard is someone who is meant to behave in an aggressive and brutal way; hence, no conflict.) Both studies testify to 'the power of social, institutional forces to make good men engage in evil deeds' (Zimbardo, 1973). (The prison simulation experiment has also come under fire on ethical grounds; see Chapter 32.)

● Conclusions

Could it be that underlying the ethical condemnation of studies such as those of Milgram and Zimbardo *et al.* is a rather different response which is more difficult to articulate, namely the shock and horror at what Arendt called 'the banality of evil' (the subtitle of her 1965 book about the Israeli trial of Adolf Eichmann, the Nazi war criminal)? To believe that 'ordinary people' could do what Eichmann did or what Milgram's participants or Zimbardo's prison guards did is far less acceptable than that Eichmann was an inhuman monster or that experimental participants have been put under immorally high levels of stress.

Following the trial (and conviction) of William Calley for the Mi Lai 'sanctioned massacre' in 1968 during the Vietnam war, a national survey was made of the reaction of the American public to the trial: 51 percent said that they would follow orders if commanded to shoot all inhabitants of a Vietnamese village. Kelman and Lawrence (1972), who conducted the survey, concluded that many Americans regard Calley's actions at Mi Lai as 'normal, even desirable, because [they think] he performed them in obedience to legitimate authority'.

According to Kelman and Hamilton (1989, cited in Hirsch, 1995), many of the greatest crimes against humanity are committed in the name of obedience; these include the Nazi extermination of the Jews, the Mi Lai massacre, the massacre of Native Americans and 'ethnic cleansing' in Bosnia. 'Genocide' (the term first used in 1944 by an international lawyer, Raphael Lemkin) tends to occur under conditions created by three social processes:

1 *Authorization.* This relates to what we earlier called the 'agentic state', i.e. obeying orders from legitimate authorities because of where they come from.
2 *Routinization.* The massacre becomes a matter of routine, a mechanical, highly programmed operation.
3 *Dehumanization.* Reducing the victims to something less than human, allowing suspension of the usual moral prohibition on killing.

These ingredients of genocide can be seen as personified in Eichmann who, at his trial, denied ever killing anybody but took great pride in the way he transported millions to their death 'with great zeal and meticulous care' (Arendt, 1965).

The comments of a German judge (1992) when sentencing a former East German border guard for having killed a man trying to escape to the West (three years earlier) echoes the spirit of the Nuremberg Accords, following the Nazi war crime trials: 'Not everything that is legal is right ... At the end of the twentieth century, no one has the right to turn off his conscience when it comes to killing people on the orders of authorities' (quoted in Berkowitz, 1993).

CHAPTER SUMMARY

- ● Social influence is central to social psychology as a whole; it is involved in research areas such as impression management, persuasive communication and bystander intervention.
- ● Social influence can be active or deliberate, as in leadership and obedience, or passive or non-deliberate, as in social facilitation and conformity.

Other forms of influence, such as minority influence, are more difficult to classify in this way.

- A common feature of all social influence is the concept of a social norm. Compliance could also be considered a common denominator which is seen in conformity, obedience and whenever we respond to other people's direct requests. Sales techniques may include the norm of reciprocity, 'foot in the door' tactic, ingratiation, 'social proof' and stressing the scarcity value of a product.

- Early studies of social facilitation stressed the element of competition, but it later emerged that this is not necessary; neither the co-action effect nor the audience effect involves direct competition.

- A major explanation of social facilitation is Zajonc's drive theory, which describes the interaction between the presence of others, level of arousal and familiarity of a task. While Zajonc sees others as triggering an instinctive increase in arousal, Cottrell's evaluation apprehension model sees the arousal as an acquired drive based on the rewards and punishments that others provide.

- The 'Ringelmann effect' describes one way in which the presence of others can inhibit performance ; this was later revived and renamed social loafing and refers to situations where individuals believe that their effort will be pooled with that of other group members.

- Major explanations of social loafing include 'free riding', evaluation apprehension and matching to standard.

- Definitions of conformity commonly refer to group pressure, whether the group is a membership or a reference group.

- One of the earliest major conformity studies is that of Sherif, using the autokinetic effect, in which individual estimates converged to form a group norm. Asch criticized Sherif's use of an ambiguous task and in his own experiments used a comparison of lines task for which there was a correct answer.

- The 'Asch paradigm' produced a basic conformity rate of about 32 percent, although there were important individual differences. Participants gave several different reasons for conforming, which included not wanting to be different from the rest of the group, despite knowing that their answer was wrong.

- In a series of subsequent experiments, Asch tested the influence of specific variables on conformity rate. He found that the unanimity/consensus of the majority is crucial, not its size, although this has been disputed. Having a supporter or the presence of a dissenter both reduce conformity through the majority no longer being unanimous.

- Conformity is increased when the task is made more difficult (more ambiguous) and reduced when participants give their answers in non-face-to-face situations or in written form. However, Crutchfield found that conformity rate will differ according to the type of task, despite testing being conducted in separate cubicles.

- Replications of Asch's experiment have produced higher or lower rates of conformity according to when and where they were conducted; historical and cultural factors seem to play a part.

- Asch's findings are usually interpreted as showing the impact of majority influence. But statistically, conformity is the exception rather than the rule. Moscovici believes that the confederate majority should be thought of as embodying unconventional, minority beliefs and that conformity experiments relate to how new ideas come to be accepted.

- Minorities are needed to produce innovation and change, in politics, science, etc. One way in which they achieve change is through consistency, together with investment, autonomy and rigidity/flexibility balance.

- Two major motives for conformity are the need to be right (informational influence) and the need to be accepted by others (normative influence). Informational influence is related to Sherif's social reality hypothesis and Festinger's social comparison theory and it is demonstrated through internalization/true conformity (as in Sherif's experiment). Normative influence is linked to compliance (as in Asch's experiments).

- Informational and normative influence are not opposed forms of influence, but this dual process dependency model tends to emphasize the interpersonal aspects of conformity experiments. In contrast, referent informational influence stresses the importance of group membership and self-categorization.

- There is evidence of individual differences in the tendency to conform, but there is unlikely to be a 'conforming personality'. However, women in general and men with 'feminine' qualities and interests are more likely to conform than men in general or women with 'masculine' qualities and interests. Conformity is a way of satisfying the need for social approval.

- While independence is often seen as preferable to conformity, conformity also serves an important social function and Milgram has shown how it can have liberating effects in an obedience situation.

- The evidence for the risky shift phenomenon is mixed; it has come to be seen as part of group polarization, in which group decisions tend to become more extreme than the mean of individuals' initial positions. One demonstration of group polarization is groupthink, which stems from excessively cohesive groups with a directive leader.

- The trait approach is the earliest approach to the study of leaders, focusing on leader emergence. The attempt to identify personality traits that distinguish leaders from non-leaders has proved largely unsuccessful.

- An alternative to the trait approach is the study of leadership styles. An early typology was Lewin *et al.*'s democratic/autocratic/laissez-faire styles; others include task specialist/socioemotional specialist and initiating structure/consideration. These still focus on the leader as an individual.

- Fiedler's contingency model takes an interactionist perspective, looking at leadership style (measured as high LPC scorer/relationship oriented or low LPC scorer/task oriented) in relation to situational factors (quality of leader-member relationship, task structure, position-power). It is a model of leader effectiveness rather than leader emergence.

- Despite considerable evidence in support of Fiedler's model, it is based on certain key assumptions which have been challenged. It implicitly sees leadership as involving one-way influence and so ignores the complex transaction between the leader and group members.

- Leaders have complex role sets within the organization, as well as leading their groups against other, external groups. This intergroup dimension is usually overlooked.

- Studies of communication networks suggest that most people are capable of assuming a leadership role if faced with that situation. Perhaps the most effective leaders are those who can adapt their leadership style to suit the functional demands of the situation.

- The concepts of leadership and power are closely related. Five major kinds of power include legitimate, reward, coercive, expert/informational and referent; the charismatic leader has great referent power.

- While both conformity and obedience involve the abdication of personal responsibility, obedience involves orders from someone in higher authority, with the influence being one way only. Milgram's series of 18 obedience experiments involve a basic procedure (remote victim/voice feedback) and variations on this, involving the manipulation of critical variables.

- Increasing the proximity to the victim, reducing the proximity of the experimenter and having the social support of 'rebel' fellow teachers all reduced obedience, while having someone else actually deliver the shock increased it.

- Two related variables that are crucial for understanding obedience are acceptance/denial of responsibility and the 'agentic state'. The wearing of uniform is also important.

- Milgram's experiments have caused great ethical controversy but have also been criticized on scientific grounds. The results have been widely replicated, but identical procedures have not always been used, making it difficult to draw comparisons.

- The mundane realism of the procedure is supported by Hofling *et al.*'s naturalistic experiment involving nurses and Milgram believes that obedience is essentially the same process regardless of the particular context.

- Zimbardo's prison simulation experiment, like Milgram's obedience studies, demonstrates the power of social situations to make people act in uncharacteristic ways: a brutalizing atmosphere, like a prison, can induce brutality in people who are not usually brutal.

- Many of the greatest crimes against humanity are committed in the name of obedience. Genocide tends to occur under conditions of authorization, routinization and dehumanization.

GLOSSARY

Agentic state The state of mind, fundamental to obedience, in which individuals come to see themselves as the instrument of the will of an authority figure.

Asch paradigm Basic experimental procedure for studying conformity, in which a naive participant is put into a group of confederates who, on a certain number of predetermined trials, will give a (unanimous) and obviously wrong answer to a question.

Compliance A type of conformity, in which there is discrepancy between public and private attitudes/opinions. Relates to normative influence. Also used to refer to obedience or responding to another's direct request.

Conformity Yielding to (peer) group pressure.

Contingency model Fiedler's account of leadership

effectiveness, which analyses the fit/match between leadership style (task oriented/relationship oriented, measured as low/high LPC score respectively) and situational factors.

'Door in the face' tactic Getting someone to agree to a second, more reasonable request, after an initial large, unreasonable request has been refused.

Drive theory Zajonc's theory of social facilitation, according to which performance on a task is enhanced (social facilitation) or not depending on the degree of arousal (drive level) that is instinctively induced by the presence of others; drive level is partly determined by the familiarity of the task.

Evaluation apprehension model Cottrell's alternative to drive theory, according to which the arousal induced by others is an acquired drive, based on the rewards and punishments that others provide when evaluating our performance.

'Foot in the door' tactic Getting someone to agree to a small request so that later on they will be more willing to comply with a larger request.

Group polarization Tendency for groups to make decisions that are more extreme than the mean of individual members' initial positions, either more or less risky.

Groupthink A mode of thinking in which the desire to reach unanimous agreement over-rides the wish to adopt proper, rational, decision-making procedures; an example of group polarization.

Idiosyncrasy credit A leader's earned right to change group norms, based on initially conforming with prevailing norms and identifying with group ideals.

Ingratiation Trying to influence someone by getting them to like you (through agreeing with them, showing yourself to be similar, attractive, competent, etc.).

Internalization A type of conformity, in which private attitudes/beliefs coincide with publicly expressed attitudes/beliefs. Relates to informational influence and can be thought of as a conversion to a group norm. Also called *true conformity.*

'Low-ball' tactic Changing the rules halfway through, as in getting someone to commit themselves to something and then pointing out the 'hidden costs'.

Norm of reciprocity Treating others as they treat you or 'one good turn deserves another'.

Referent informational influence A form of social influence in which group membership is crucial: we only experience uncertainty when we disagree with those who belong to 'our' group/category. This is based on self-categorization.

Reference group A group whose values we admire/aspire to, although we don't actually belong (as distinct from a membership group).

Risky shift phenomenon Tendency for group decisions to be riskier than the average of the individual members' decisions. One aspect of group polarization.

Social comparison theory Festinger's view that people have a basic need to evaluate their ideas and attitudes and confirm that they are correct. In novel/ambiguous situations, we turn to others to help define social reality, through what they think and do.

Social facilitation An improvement of performance on a task due to the mere presence of other members of the same species (conspecifics), who either work independently on the same task (co-action effect) or observe (audience effect).

Social impact theory The view that when a person is a member of a group that is subjected to social forces, the impact of those forces on each member is reduced in inverse proportion to the number of group members.

Social loafing Tendency for individuals to work less hard (loaf) on a task when they believe that others are also working on it and that one's own effort will be pooled with that of the other group members, compared with working alone or co-actively.

Social norm A rule, value or standard shared by the members of a social group that defines appropriate, expected or desirable attitudes and behaviour.

FURTHER READING

Milgram, S. (1992) *The Individual In A Social World: Essays and Experiments,* 2nd edn. New York: McGraw-Hill. While not exclusively devoted to social influence, this is a fascinating collection of reprinted journal articles and other papers revealing the creative mind of a very important researcher who died, prematurely, in 1984.

Turner, J.C. (1991) *Social Influence*. Milton Keynes: Open University Press. A short but thorough discussion of all the main aspects of the topic, by one of the leading figures in the field.

Developmental Processes

21 CHILDHOOD AND ADOLESCENCE: THE DEVELOPMENT OF PERSONALITY AND SELF-CONCEPT

INTRODUCTION AND OVERVIEW

All the chapters in this section of the book could be thought of as dealing with various aspects of personality development, if personality is defined as the totality of ways in which individuals function as people. This would include the development of our first relationships with other human beings (and how these affect our later relationships – Chapter 22), how we develop a sense of our own sexual identity (and how that relates to our actual behaviour as males and females – Chapter 23), the development of our knowledge and understanding and ability to use and understand language (Chapters 25 and 26) and, finally, the development of our sense of right and wrong (and how this relates to our actual moral behaviour – Chapter 27).

However, some of the theories to be discussed in these later chapters are concerned with fairly specific aspects of development and for this reason are not usually thought of as theories of *personality* development. Conversely, certain other theories, such as learning theory or social learning theory, although always included in chapters on development, are not strictly *developmental* theories at all, as they are not primarily (or, sometimes, even at all) concerned with explaining psychological change.

Two theories which meet both these 'conditions' (i.e. they are theories of personality and theories of development) are Freud's *psychoanalytic theory* and Erikson's *psychosocial theory*. Freud emphasized development during the first 5–6 years of life, while Erikson saw development as a lifelong process, spanning childhood, adolescence and adulthood (see Chapter 24). Consequently, Freud's is perhaps more accurately described as a theory of *childhood development,* while Erikson is best known for his views on *adolescent development.* Both Freud's and Erikson's views have contributed to what is called the 'classical' theory of adolescence which, together with sociological and anthropological ideas, portrays adolescence as an extremely difficult transition in the life of every person. However, a major alternative to this view is Coleman's *focal theory,* which presents a much more balanced view based on more representative samples of adolescents.

According to Hampson (1995), the human capacity for self-awareness permits us to try to see ourselves as others see us. When personality psychologists study personality via self-reports, such as questionnaires (see Chapter 29), they are assessing people's perceptions of themselves; social psychologists also study people's self-perceptions through their study of the self-concept. This self-perception changes in fairly predictable ways from infancy onwards, with adolescence being a crucial period for its development, according to Erikson. Discussion of the self-concept brings together theory and research from both developmental and social psychology, but even when tracing how self-perception changes in the individual, we shall see that it is inherently social; this is reflected in the early theories of James, Cooley and Mead, as well as the more recent extensions of these, which see the self as constructed in language (e.g. Harré).

FREUD'S PSYCHOANALYTIC THEORY

Freud's theory of personality development is closely related to the other aspects of his theory, in particular his theory of the structure of personality and his motivational theory. His theory as a whole is also closely tied to his work as a psychotherapist and it is quite common to refer to all of these as 'psychoanalysis'; however, it might be helpful to reserve that term to denote Freud's form of psychotherapy and to distinguish it from 'psychoanalytic theory'.

The sheer volume of Freud's work, the fact that his theories were intended to cover all aspects of human behaviour, together with the great influence his work has had within psychology as a whole, make it impossible to do him justice in part of one chapter, so here we shall be concentrating on his stages of *psychosexual development.* Chapters 23 and 27 will discuss other aspects of his developmental theory, while in Chapter 29 we shall look at more

FIGURE 21.1 *Sigmund Freud (1856–1939)*

general aspects of his personality theory. Psychoanalysis will be discussed in Chapter 31.

● Biographical sketch

Sigmund Freud (see Fig. 21.1) was born in 1856 in Moravia, which was then part of the Austrian Empire and is now in the Czech Republic. He spent most of his life in Vienna, from where he fled, in 1937, when the Nazis invaded. Neither Freud himself, being Jewish, nor his theories were very popular with the invaders and he escaped to London, where he died in 1939. He had wanted to be a research scientist but anti-Semitism forced him to choose a medical career instead and he worked in Vienna as a doctor, specializing in neurological disorders (disorders of the nervous system). He constantly revised and modified his theories right up until his death but much of his psychoanalytic theory was produced between 1900 and 1930. Most of what is discussed in this chapter represents the 'final version' of the theory.

● Influences on Freud's thought

Freud originally attempted to explain the workings of the mind in terms of physiology and neurology. Helmholtz, one of the leading physicists of his day (see Chapter 9), had formulated the law of conservation of energy, which states that energy (like mass) can be transformed but not destroyed. In 1874, Brücke, an eminent physiologist, argued that the living organism is a dynamic system to which the laws of physics and chemistry apply. Freud was to put these two principles together and extend them by applying them to the (non-physical) personality. Quite early in his treatment of patients with neurological disorders, Freud realized that symptoms which had no organic or bodily basis could imitate the 'real thing' and that they were as real for the patient as if they had been neurologically caused. So he began to search for psychological explanations of these symptoms and ways of treating them.

In 1885 he spent a year in Paris learning hypnosis from the neurologist Charcot; he then started using hypnosis with his patients in Vienna. However, he found its effects to be only temporary at best and it did not usually get to the root of the problem; nor was everybody capable of being hypnotized. An alternative approach was being developed by Breuer, another Viennese doctor. Breuer was using the *cathartic method,* where patients would talk out their problems; Freud adopted Breuer's method and called it *free association* which became one of the three fundamental tools of psychoanalysis (see Chapter 31).

Freud began his self-analysis during the 1890s and in 1900 published *The Interpretation of Dreams,* in which he outlined his theory of the mind, followed by *The Psychopathology of Everyday Life* (1904), *A Case of Hysteria* and *Three Essays on the Theory of Sexuality* (1905).

Two of Freud's closest colleagues, Carl Jung and Alfred Adler, helped him form the psychoanalytic movement and the first International Psychoanalytic Congress was held at Salzburg in 1908. *The Journal of Psychoanalysis* was first published in 1909 and, in that year, Freud and Jung made a lecture tour of the USA. (Jung's and Adler's theories are described in Chapter 29.)

The structure of personality

Freud believed that the personality or *'psychic apparatus'* consists of three parts (which are not parts of the brain or in any way physical); the *id,* the *ego* and the *superego.*

The id

Although part of the personality, the id responds directly to the instincts, those demands arising from within the body itself, for instance, the biologically based needs for food, warmth, sexual gratification and so on. For Freud, the human organism is a complex energy system and the kind of energy needed to fuel or operate the psychic apparatus is psychic energy, which performs psychological work: the source of psychic energy is the id:

> It contains everything that is inherited, that is present at birth, that is laid down in the constitution – above all, therefore, the instincts ... (Freud, 1964)

The wishes and impulses arising from the body's needs build up a sort of pressure or tension (*excitation*) which demand immediate release or satisfaction. When this happens, we experience pleasure but when it is prevented, we experience pain or frustration. Since the id is in closer touch with the body than with the outside world and since it is not affected by logic or reason and its sole aim is to reduce excitation to a minimum, it is said to be governed by the *pleasure principle* (seeking pleasure and avoiding pain). For this reason, the id can be thought of as the infantile part of the personality, what we are before the social environment has begun to exert any influence over us (including other people), the presocialized part of our make-up.

At birth, we are 'bundles of id' and the id retains its infantile character throughout our lives. Whenever we act on impulse, selfishly, or demand something 'here and now', it is our id that is controlling our behaviour (it is the 'spoiled child' of the personality). In its earliest, most primitive form, the id acts in a reflex way to release tension, for example, blinking or the eye watering to remove dust or dirt, sneezing to remove an irritation from the nostril and automatic opening of the bladder when pressure on it reaches a certain level. However, not all tension can be released in this reflex way, for instance, hunger does not automatically produce food but only irritability and crying, etc. These signals have to be interpreted by another person if the baby is not to starve to death.

Indeed, if the id were capable of satisfying the body's needs in a reflex way, there would be no need for psychological development – so not only is some degree of frustration and discomfort inevitable, they are also necessary for development beyond the reflex level:

> It is the dark, inaccessible part of our personality ... We approach the id with analogies: we call it a chaos, a cauldron full of seething excitations ... It is filled with energy reaching it from the instincts, but it has no organization ... but only a striving to bring about the satisfaction of instinctual needs subject to the observance of the pleasure principle. The logical laws of thought do not apply to the id ... there is no recognition of the passage of time ... (Freud, 1933)

The main development that occurs in the id is the *primary process,* a form of thinking in which an image of the object needed to reduce tension is produced. So, for example, through repeated association of food and hunger-reduction, the hungry baby, if not fed immediately, may conjure up an image of food. However, the id is incapable of distinguishing between the subjective memory-image and the real thing – that is left to the ego.

The ego

The ego is '... that part of the id which has been modified by the direct influence of the external world through the medium of conscious perception' (Freud, 1923). It gradually develops (starting at a few months) as psychic energy is 'borrowed' from the id and directed outwards towards external reality.

The ego can also be described as the 'executive' of the personality, the planning, decision-making, rational and logical part of us, which engages in *secondary process thinking,* which is roughly equivalent to the cognitive processes of perception, attention, memory, reasoning, problem solving and so on. It enables us to distinguish between a wish and reality, inside from outside, subjective from objective and so on, and is governed by the *reality principle.*

While the id demands immediate gratification for some need arising within the body, the ego will postpone its satisfaction until the appropriate time and place ('deferred gratification'). However, this does not imply any kind of moral code – what the ego considers 'right' or 'correct' is what others would find acceptable or what is objectively possible in the situation – it is the consequence of the act rather than the act itself which is the ego's priority. For example, whereas the id would have us scratch wherever and whenever an itch arises, the ego takes reality into account by deciding that scratching in public might offend others and may lead to our being ostracized. So the ego, like the id, is amoral, but the feelings, needs, reactions and so on of other people are taken into account; again, while the id is concerned only with what it wants, the ego is equally concerned with how to get it:

> The ego seeks to bring the influence of the external world to bear upon the id and its tendencies, and endeavours to substitute the reality principle for the pleasure principle which reigns unrestrictedly in the id. For the ego, perception plays the part which in the id falls to instinct. The ego represents what may be called reason and common sense, in contrast to the id, which contains the passions ... (Freud, 1923)

The superego

Not until the superego has developed can we describe the person as a moral being. Morality involves the internalization of a set of moral values which determine that certain behaviour is good or bad, right or wrong, in itself. So the superego represents the moral or judicial branch of the personality and its development is discussed in detail in Chapter 27. It comprises two components:

1 the *conscience,* which threatens the ego with punishment (in the form of guilt) for bad behaviour;
2 the *ego-ideal,* which promises the ego rewards (in the form of pride and high self-esteem) for good behaviour:

> The long period of childhood, during which the growing human lives in dependence on its parents, leaves behind it ... the formation in his ego of a special agency in which the parental influence is prolonged. It has received the name of *superego.* In so far as this superego is differentiated from the ego or is opposed to it, it constitutes a third power which the ego must take into account ... (Freud, 1940)

● Conflict and the ego

As shown in Figure 21.2, the ego can be viewed as 'located' squarely in the middle of the psychic apparatus, the point of convergence of conflicting demands from three sources – external reality, the id and the superego. Where external reality makes demands on the ego (e.g. someone threatening you with a knife), the resulting conflict is called *external* or *reality conflict*. When the ego fears being overwhelmed by the power of the id's demands for instinctual gratification, the result is *neurotic conflict*. Where the ego feels threatened by punishment from the conscience, the result is *moral conflict*.

Freud believes that conflict is inevitable; we live in society which, for its own survival, cannot allow us to give free expression to our id impulses and our ego develops in order to ensure that the individual acknowledges social and material reality. The superego develops in order to assist the ego in keeping the very powerful id in its place but it can only do so by making demands on the ego – there is no direct 'contact' between the id and the superego. Consequently, the ego, part of which constitutes our *conscious self*, is caught in the middle of opposing sets of demands, it is the battleground on which three opposing factions (reality, the id and the superego) fight for supremacy. But the ego is, at the same time, the arbitrator and has to find ways of keeping all the factions 'happy', of satisfying all their demands and not responding to some at the expense of others! How is this achieved? For Freud, all behaviour is a compromise which can

take three major forms – dreams, neurotic symptoms and defence mechanisms (these will be discussed in Chapter 29).

● Freud's instinct theory

Psychoanalytic theory is often described as an instinct theory. From what we have said about the id, it should be evident that Freud believed that personality is based on biological drives, mainly sexual and aggressive in nature, rooted in the body with its unalterable hereditary constitution. However, this needs to be qualified in two main ways.

1 Although Freud saw personality development as largely bound up with development of the sexual instinct (libido) which passes through a maturational, biologically determined sequence of stages, he also stressed the influence of the reactions of significant others (especially parents) on the child's behaviour as it passes through the stages. Freud sees adult personality types arising directly from experiences the child has had at a particular developmental stage (see below).

2 Freud's concept of an instinct was very different from the earlier view of unlearned, largely automatic (preprogrammed) responses to specific stimuli (based on non-human species). He saw instincts as relatively undifferentiated energy, capable of almost infinite variation through experience; indeed, instead of using the German *Instinckt* he used *Trieb* which is most accurately translated as 'drive'.

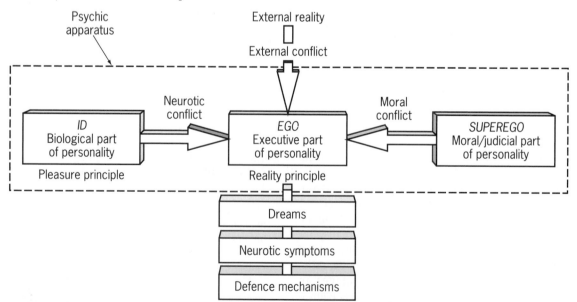

FIGURE 21.2 *The psychic apparatus, showing sources of conflict and ways of resolving it*

In *Beyond the Pleasure Principle* (1920), he distinguished two main groups of instincts, the life instincts (*eros*) which include libido (sexual energy)and the death instincts (*thanatos*), comprising, primarily, aggression. Libido later came to refer to all kinds of psychic (drive) energy, the principal components of which are sexual. However, Freud did not maintain that no other instincts exist or that 'everything is sex' (see Chapter 17).

● Psychosexual development

One of the most radical aspects of Freud's theories is the notion of *infantile sexuality*, the view that babies and young children (and not just adolescents and adults) have sexual experiences and are capable of sexual pleasure. As a way of trying to illustrate how revolutionary this part of the theory was, Table 21.1 compares the Victorian concept of sexuality (the 'official' view) with Freud's in terms of the four major components of an instinct, namely, source, impetus or force, aim and object.

According to Freud, sexuality is not confined to adults but is evident from the moment of birth. In order to understand Freud's theory of infantile sexuality, we must understand his use of the term sexuality: he used it to describe the desire for physical, sensuous pleasure of any kind and, far from being a highly specific drive towards heterosexual gratification (i.e. genital stimulation), sexuality can be satisfied in a variety of ways. The essence of sexual pleasure lies in the rhythmical stroking or stimulation of virtually any part of the body and, accordingly, he describes the baby as 'polymorphously perverse'. Why did he define sexuality in this unusual way?

1 In sexual perversions, adult behaviour may be directed towards persons of the same sex, the individual him/herself, animals, inanimate objects, etc. so sexual desire is not necessarily aimed exclusively at adult members of the opposite sex.

2 Even with adult members of the opposite sex, genital intercourse is not the only form of sexual behaviour enjoyed.

3 Infants often show behaviour similar to adult perverts, e.g. interest in urination and defecation, thumb sucking, exposing their naked body and enjoying seeing others naked.

Components of an instinct	Victorian view of sexuality	Freud's view (infantile sexuality)
Source: Where in the body does it arise?	Arises exclusively in the genital area, so doesn't appear before puberty	Present at birth, passing through a series of predetermined stages of psychosexual development, each focused on a different part of the body (erogenous/erotogenic zone): oral (0–1), anal (1–3), phallic (3–5/6), latency (5/6–puberty), genital (puberty-maturity).
Impetus/ force: How much excitement is produced?	Varies, in adults, from one time to another: gratification reduces it to a minimum, frustration increases it. It is absent in children, so impetus is zero	Can be as strong in a baby (oral stage) as in an adult (genital stage). In itself, one kind of sexuality is no more or less strong than any other. The difference between stages is qualitative (difference in kind) rather than quantitative.
Aim: What is it for? What is its purpose?	Primary aim = procreation (reproduction); secondary aim = release of sexual tension.	Primary aim = release of sexual tension (i.e. pleasure); procreation is almost incidental.
Object: What or whom is needed in order to satisfy it?	Legal spouse.	At first, ourselves, i.e. our own body, as in sucking, later on masturbation (i.e. auto-eroticism). From the genital stage onwards, we need an adult sexual partner of the opposite sex.

Table 21.1 *Comparison between Freud's theory of infantile sexuality and the Victorian view of sexuality*

Freud believed that current (adult) neuroses are the result of inadequate solutions to the problems experienced in childhood at one or more psychosexual stage. Each stage (the sequence being maturationally determined) involves a particular way of achieving gratification and the degree and kind of satisfaction which the child experiences at each stage will depend on how the child is treated by others, in particular its parents. Both excessive gratification and extreme frustration can produce permanent consequences for the individual (*fixation*) and the nature of these consequences is a function of the particular stage at which it occurs and the form it takes. The most satisfactory balance is between gaining enough pleasure to be willing to move on to the next stage but not so much that the individual is content to stay there!

Development for Freud is a complex interaction between a biologically programmed timetable of change and the environmental or social context in which it happens (Stevens, 1995) and if we want to understand the adult, we need to retrace their childhood; hence 'the child is father to the man'.

● Oral stage (0–1 year)

In order to survive, the newborn baby must obtain nourishment through its mouth; but the nerve endings in the lips and mouth are particularly sensitive so that the baby derives pleasure from sucking quite independently of the feeding process (*non-nutritive sucking*). The mouth is also important for finding out about objects.

The oral stage is divided into two: the earlier *receptive* or *incorporative substage* (lasting for the first few months) and the later *biting* or *aggressive substage*. In the former, the baby is passive and almost totally dependent; the major oral activities are sucking, swallowing and mouthing. In the latter, gums are hardening and teeth erupting; biting and chewing become the most important activities. Biting the breast or fingers, etc. can express the baby's *ambivalence*, its experience of both loving and hating the same object (i.e. the mother) at the same time.

● Anal stage (1–3 years)

The most sensitive and pleasurable body zone is now the anal cavity, the sphincter muscles of the lower bowel and the muscles of the urinary system. (Because the urinary functions are involved as well as the anal, it is sometimes called the anal-urethral

stage.) The primary concern is with expelling and retaining faeces and the stage divides into the earlier *expulsion* and the later *retention* substages. In the former, the child experiences its first encounter with external restrictions on its wish to defecate where and when it pleases, in the form of parents trying to potty-train it. This represents a crucial time for the child to learn to earn praise and approval – love from parents is no longer unconditional but now depends on what the child does. In the latter substage, when sensuous pleasure can now be derived from deliberately holding in ('holding onto') its faeces, parents come to be seen for the first time as authority figures:

> The contents of the bowels ... have other important meanings for the infant. They are clearly treated as part of the infant's own body and represent his first 'gift': by producing them he can express his active compliance with his environment and by withholding them, his disobedience. (Freud, 1905)

● Phallic stage (3—5/6 years)

Sensitivity now becomes concentrated in the genitals and masturbation (in both sexes) becomes a new source of pleasure. The child becomes aware of anatomical sex differences, which sets in motion the set of conflicting emotions which Freud called the *Oedipus complex*, based on the mythical king of Thebes (see Box 21.1). The word *'phallic'* comes from the Greek phallus which means penis and Freud chose this word to imply, firstly, that the penis

---

BOX 21.1 **The story of Oedipus**

In the classical Greek tragedy *Oedipus Rex*, by Sophocles, Oedipus, as a baby, was left to die by his father, Laius, who had been warned by an oracle that his son would one day murder him. But Oedipus was rescued and grew up in another city, not knowing he was adopted. As a young man, he learned that he was destined to murder his father and marry his mother, so he left the place he knew as home and on his journey he met Laius, quarrelled with him and slew him. Then, by solving the riddle of the sphinx, he released Thebes (his birthplace) from the creature's power and, as a reward, married Jocasta (his mother). A plague broke out, attributed to Laius's murder, and Oedipus set about finding the murderer! When he discovered the truth, he blinded himself by gouging out his eyes.

and the clitoris are equivalent and secondly, that females do not experience their vaginas as a source of pleasure until puberty. When girls compare their 'phallus' with that of boys, they feel inferior, resentful and jealous or envious.

In the case of boys (who, like girls, take the mother as their first love-object), beginning at about three, their love for their mother becomes increasingly passionate and this brings them into conflict and rivalry with their father. The little boy does not want to share his mother with anyone and so he is jealous of the father who already 'possesses' her and he wants him dead (which, for a three-year-old, means 'out of the way'). However, his father is bigger and more powerful and eventually he comes to fear that he may lose the thing he values most in the world, namely, his penis. Partly because he has been punished for masturbating and may actually have been threatened with all its nasty consequences and partly because he has observed the absence of a penis in girls, the boy comes to fear that his father will cut off his penis *(fear of castration* or *castration anxiety)*.

To resolve the dilemma, the boy represses the desire for his mother (i.e. makes it unconscious) and identifies with his father, i.e. he comes to think, feel and act as if he were his father. This way, at least, he keeps his male organ and can have the mother vicariously, since by becoming like his father, he can indirectly have what his father has.

The equivalent situation for girls is often referred to as the *Electra complex,* a term coined by Jung. But having originally used the term, Freud rejected it because he felt it gave the misleading impression that the experience of boys and girls is very similar and he mostly referred to it as the *female Oedipus complex.* While the boy's Oedipus complex ends with fear of castration, the girl's begins with the belief that she has already been castrated, since little boys have something she does not, namely a penis. The situation is more complex for girls than boys: while boys have to make one 'move', from a romantic attachment to their mother to identification with their father, girls, who take their mother as their first love-object, become romantically attached to their father before finally identifying with their mother.

Why does the girl become attracted to her father? Freud's answer is *penis envy.* Following her discovery of anatomical sex differences and her consequent belief that she has already been castrated (for which she blames her mother), a girl feels inadequate for not having a penis. Eventually realizing that it is unrealistic to hope for one, she substitutes the wish for a penis with the wish for a baby and she turns to

her father as a love-object, hoping that he will provide her with this replacement for her anatomical deficiency. At this point according to Freud, '... the girl has turned into a little woman' (Freud, 1925).

But why does she identify with her mother? Freud admitted that he was much less clear about the girl's motive for identifying with the mother than he was about the boy's motive for identifying with the father: if boys fear castration by their more powerful father, then surely this is sufficient reason to repress desire for the mother and to try to become like the father! It is referred to as *identification with the aggressor* ('If you can't beat them, join them') and the essential motive, therefore, is fear. But what do girls have to fear if they believe they have already been castrated? The girl may fear the loss of her mother's love and to ease the pain that results from this fear (or threats of love withdrawal), she internalizes the images of the mother and this entails being the 'good' child that her mother would wish her to be ('If I'm not what she wants me to be she'll stop loving me'). This process of internalization is known as *anaclitic identification* and, like identification with the aggressor, is defensive, since it keeps the mother 'alive' inside the child.

What Freud was quite sure about was that the girl's identification is much weaker and less complete than the boy's with his father and this has significant implications for their psychological development, particularly in relation to the superego ('the heir to the Oedipus complex'; see Chapter 27).

● Latency period (5/6–puberty)

Freud uses the term 'latency' to indicate that only quantitative changes occur in the libido during these few years prior to puberty – there are no new qualitative changes as in the earlier stages. But this does not mean that the child is asexual: it falls 'victim' to 'infantile amnesia' and represses the sexual preoccupations of the earlier years, allowing social and intellectual development to proceed. There is a 'halt and retrogression in sexual development', which is both culturally determined ('a product of education') and 'organically determined and fixed by heredity' (Freud, 1905). Much of the child's energies are channelled into developing new skills and acquiring new knowledge; play becomes largely confined to other children of the same gender (helping the child to control sexual thoughts).

In relative terms, the balance between the id, ego and superego is greater during latency than at any other time in the child's life; indeed, latency represents the calm before the storm of puberty,

| BOX 21.2 | Freud's theory of Play (based on Millar, 1972) |

Like all behaviour, play is motivated behaviour (i.e. caused by the child's feelings and emotions, both unconscious and conscious). In common with dreams and fantasy, play is determined by wishes. The child can distinguish play from reality, but uses objects and situations from the real world to create a world of its own in which to repeat pleasant experiences at will and to order and alter events in the most pleasing way it can. For instance, children want to be grown up and do what adults do – in play this is possible.

But how does this account for the frequency with which unpleasant experiences are repeated in play? For example, children who hate taking medicine dose their dolls or they graphically re-enact a frightening accident or event. Given that we try to keep excitation to a minimum, so that all increases in excitation are felt as unpleasant and all decreases as pleasurable, repeating distressing or upsetting experiences in play is, in fact, an attempt to feel pleasure, since repetition reduces the excitation associated with them. This impulse to repeat (repetition compulsion) is part of the urge to return to an earlier, more stable, tension-free state (i.e. death) (see Chapter 17).

Through play, the child can master disturbing experiences by actively bringing them about rather than being a passive and helpless victim; this view contributed to the development of play therapy and the use of projective tests of personality (see Chapters 30 and 31).

Given that conflict and frustration are inevitable, then much play can be seen as the special use of *ego defence mechanisms*, such as (a) *projection* – dolls, imaginary companions, evil witches, etc. behave maliciously; (b) *displacement* – immersing doll-baby or toy in water or throwing it about helps relieve a jealous sibling's feelings without harming the new baby brother or sister; (c) *regression* – blowing bubbles may represent a return to oral overindulgence or frustration; (d) *sublimation* – sand and water play are acceptable, while playing with faeces is not.

which marks the beginning of the genital stage. The relative harmony within the child's personality is now disrupted and the id begins to make powerful new demands in the form of heterosexual desires, so that members of the opposite sex are now needed to satisfy the libido (we shall discuss this further below in relation to adolescence).

● An evaluation of the Oedipus complex theory

One criticism of Freud's Oedipal theory ('the central phenomenon of the sexual period of early childhood'; Freud, 1924) is that, even if true for Western cultures, the Oedipus complex may not apply to all cultures and to all historical periods. For instance, Malinowski (1929) studied the Trobriand Islanders in the South Pacific, a culture in which the mother's brother, not the child's father, is the figure of authority, although the father continues to have a normal sexual relationship with the mother. Under these circumstances, sons tend to have a very good relationship with their father, free of the love-hate ambivalence which Freud saw as an inherent feature of the Oedipus complex; however, the relationship with the uncle is not usually so good. This not only suggests that the complex is not universal, but that sexual jealousy and rivalry, as major components in the whole 'family drama', may be much less important than Freud believed.

Fisher and Greenberg (1977), in a major review of empirical studies of Freudian theory, concluded that children do have to cope with erotic feelings towards the opposite-sex parent and feelings of hostility towards the parent of the same sex. They also reported that fear of castration (expressed indirectly as concern about physical injury, fear of death, fear of bodily harm or attack) is relatively common in men and is intensified when they are exposed to erotic heterosexual stimulation. Women do seem to be more motivated by fear of loss of love.

One indirect kind of evidence comes in the form of the powerful appeal of fairy tales. According to Stevens (1995), these often involve themes that are strange, to say the least, unless they are regarded as fantasies relating to psychosexual stages (see Bettelheim's *The Uses of Enchantment: The Meaning and Importance of Fairy Tales*, 1976); for example, characters are often eaten, heads are cut off or a beanstalk soars magically into the sky until it is cut down to destroy a threatening giant. The problem with this kind of 'evidence', however, is that you have to believe in the validity of psychoanalytic ideas before you can use them to interpret the imagery of the fairy tale, i.e. the evidence assumes what it is trying to 'prove' (a circular argument).

Stevens (1995) argues that Freud's theories were a 'distillation' or integration of insights derived from a number of sources: his own self-analysis, observation of everyday life, broad knowledge of philosophy,

| BOX 21.3 | Key study: Analysis of a phobia in a 5-year-old boy – the case of little Hans (Freud, 1909) |

Hans had a phobia of being bitten by a horse and was especially afraid of white horses with black around the mouth and wearing blinkers; he tried to avoid horses at all costs. [Freud's interpretation: fear of being bitten represented Hans's fear of castration.]

Hans was particularly frightened when he once saw a horse collapse in the street. [Freud's interpretation: seeing the horse collapse reminded him, unconsciously, of his death wish against his father, which made him feel guilty and afraid.] Is there any reason to believe that Hans saw the horses as symbolizing his father?

● Hans once said to his father as he got up from the table: 'Daddy, don't trot away from me'.
● On another occasion, Hans said: 'Daddy, you are lovely, you're so white'. This suggests he may have thought his father resembled a white horse (as opposed to a dark one).
● Hans's father had a moustache ('the black on the horse's mouth').
● His father wore glasses, which resembled blinkers as worn by horses.
● Hans had played 'horses' with his father, with Hans usually riding on his father's back.

Hans claimed that his fear stemmed from the time he saw a horse collapse in the street: 'When the horse in the bus fell down it gave me such a fright really; that was when I got the nonsense' (i.e. the phobia). This was confirmed by Hans's mother but his father, and Freud, paid little attention to this plausible explanation of the phobia.

Freud believed Hans was a 'little Oedipus', loving to be in bed with his mother and going to the bathroom with her and regarding his father as a rival and wanting him out of the way. But rather than the father being 'the aggressor', it seemed to be the mother who made explicit threats of castration. For instance, she once said to him, 'If you do that [touch his penis] I shall send for doctor A to cut off your widdler. And then what'll you widdle with?'. She threatened to abandon him; Hans said, 'Mummy's told me she won't come back'. Again:

'It's only in the big bath that I'm afraid of falling in' (Hans).
'But Mummy baths you in it. Are you afraid of Mummy dropping you in the water?' (Father).
'I'm afraid of her letting go and my head going in' (Hans).

---

the arts and science, as well as clinical evidence, i.e. case studies of his patients. With one exception, his patients were adults and a common criticism of his theory of psychosexual development is that any valid theory of child development must be based on studies of children. In the light of this criticism, the case of little Hans assumes even greater significance (Box 21.3).

It seems very difficult for at least two reasons to regard the case of little Hans as evidence for the Oedipus theory:

1 Freud had already made up his mind what was wrong with him and interpreted all the data accordingly; little Hans was seen by Freud as confirming the Oedipal theory which had already been proposed in the *Three Essays on the Theory of Sexuality* (1905) – Freud saw Hans as a 'little Oedipus'.
2 Hans's psychoanalysis was conducted primarily by the father (not Freud), a follower of Freud's ideas. The two men conferred and consulted each other but Freud himself only met Hans on one or two occasions. (By the way, Hans's mother had been a patient of Freud before her marriage.) Freud him-

self was aware of the methodological objections which could be raised: how could the father be objective in his observations and psychoanalyse someone with whom he was so emotionally involved? Also, the child will be susceptible to his father's suggestions. Doesn't this immediately invalidate the case study as an independent confirmation of Freud's Oedipal theory? (This and other issues dealing with the scientific nature of Freud's theory will be dealt with in Chapter 29.)

One of the most serious problems faced by much of Freud's theory in general, and the case of little Hans in particular, is that of alternative explanations. Is Freud's interpretation of Hans's phobia the only reasonable, feasible one? Amongst those who offer alternative interpretations are two very eminent psychoanalysts, Erich Fromm and John Bowlby.

According to Fromm (1970) (Fig. 21.3), Freud wanted to find support for the theory of sexuality based on adults by directly reviewing material drawn from a child. While Freud claims that the dread of castration came from 'very slight allusions', Fromm believes that there were clear, strong threats – made

FIGURE 21.3 *Erich Fromm (1900–1980). (UPI/Bettmann Archive Inc.)*

by the mother. Freud's extreme patriarchal attitude prevented him from conceiving that the woman *could* be the main cause of fear. Indeed, '... clinical observation amply proves that the most intense and pathogenic fears are indeed related to the mother; by comparison, the dread of the father is relatively insignificant' (Fromm, 1970)

It would seem that Hans needed his father to protect him from a menacing mother. Fromm believes that the successful outcome of the therapy was due not so much to the interpretations made of Hans's fear as the protective role of the father and the 'super-father' (Freud). He believes the fear of horses has two origins: (i) fear of the mother (due to her castration threat); and (ii) fear of death (he had witnessed a funeral and then later a fallen horse which he thought dead). To avoid both fears he developed a fear of being bitten which protects him both from horses and from experiencing (consciously) both types of anxiety.

Fromm suggests that rather than being directed towards his father (as the Oedipus theory states), Hans's hostility is aimed at his mother (based on her castration threats, her 'treason' at giving birth to Hanna and his desire to be free from fixation on her). Hans's yearning to take his father's place was not necessarily an expression of hate or desire for the father's death but the universal tendency to want to be grown up and no longer be subjected to adult power. Indeed, there is much evidence of great warmth and friendship in their relationship. Besides, the phobia was no more serious than those which

occur in many children and it would probably have disappeared by itself without any treatment and without the father's support and interest (Fromm, 1970).

Bowlby's (1973) reinterpretation of little Hans is in terms of *attachment theory* (see Chapter 22). He asks whether Hans's anxiety about the availability of attachment figures played a larger part than Freud realized. Agreeing with Fromm, Bowlby argues that most of Hans's anxiety arose from threats by the mother to desert the family. The main evidence for this interpretation includes the father's account that the mother was in the habit of using threats of an alarming kind to discipline Hans, including the threat to abandon him. The symptoms did not come out of the blue; Hans had been upset throughout the preceding week. They began when Hans had woken up one morning in tears. Asked why he was crying he said to his mother, 'When I was asleep, I thought you were gone and I had no Mummy to coax with' ('coax' = cuddle).

When his sister, Hanna was born, Hans was kept away from his mother. The father stated that Hans's 'present anxiety, which prevents him leaving the neighbourhood of the house, is in reality the longing for [his mother] which he felt then'. Freud confirms this by describing Hans's 'enormously intensified affection' for his mother as 'the fundamental phenomenon in his condition'. According to Bowlby (1973), '... distinct from and preceding any fear of horses, Hans was afraid his mother might go away and leave him'.

A fascinating postscript to this case study (Freud, 1922) lends support to various aspects of both Fromm and Bowlby's interpretations. Hans's parents had divorced (but we are not told exactly when) and each had remarried. At age 19, Hans was living on his own, was on good terms with both parents and only regretted that as a result of the family break-up he had been separated from Hanna of whom he was so fond.

● Oedipus complex, seduction theory and child abuse

In 1896 (prior to publication of his theory of infantile sexuality), Freud gave a lecture to the Society for Psychiatry and Neurology in Vienna called 'The Aetiology of Hysteria' in which he described his findings that in 18 cases of previously unexplained hysteria referred to him, each patient had been sexually abused in childhood – either by an adult or by an older sibling. This claim that repressed memories of childhood sexual abuse are the primary causal factor in the development of hysteria and other forms of neurosis is known as the *seduction theory*.

However, he soon began to doubt the validity of the theory and he ultimately (1905) concluded that memories of child sexual abuse are often fantasies derived from repressed remnants of incestuous desires for the opposite-sex parent (the Oedipus complex); i.e. having originally believed that children were the victims of actual abuse, he claimed instead that the 'abuse' was in the mind of the child, it happened in the child's fantasy.

According to Powell and Boer (1994), the recent evidence that child sexual abuse is surprisingly common and that many clients seem to uncover forgotten memories of such abuse during adult psychotherapy has led to a re-examination of Freud's possible motives for abandoning the seduction theory. By far Freud's most ardent critic has been Masson (1984) who, in *The Assault on Truth*, accused Freud of cowardice for having rejected the reality of child sexual abuse, partly to escape the criticism of his medical colleagues who refused to acknowledge that incest could be so common.

In Freud's defence, a number of writers have argued that he never completely discarded the seduction theory (e.g. Jacobs, 1992). But more importantly, and rather more indirectly in support of Freud, Masson's interpretation of events has itself been challenged. A number of writers, quite independently of each other, have shown that Masson failed to appreciate the misleading nature of Freud's claims, both in the seduction theory papers themselves and especially in his retrospective historical accounts (e.g. Cioffi, 1974; Esterson, 1993; Israels and Schatzman, 1993; Powell and Boer, 1994). For example, according to Israels and Schatzman (1993), Masson attributed to Freud a version of the seduction theory that never existed, namely that his patients told him stories of abuse, i.e. they were consciously aware of having been abused. But in Freud's own version, his hysterical patients suffered from unconscious memories of abuse. Powell and Boer (1994) believe that Freud was aware that he often used highly suggestive, even coercive tactics in eliciting memories of abuse from his patients and that the evidence that they were real was weak; recognition of these problems may have played an initial role in his eventual rejection of the seduction theory. (The recent debate about 'recovered memories' and 'false memory syndrome' is discussed in Chapter 12.)

● Psychosexual development and personality types

We noted earlier that both excessive gratification and extreme frustration (especially during the oral stage) could produce long-lasting consequences, notably the kind of personality traits that the adult possesses. The process by which these traits are determined is *fixation*. However, fixation is not an all-or-none thing, it can vary in degree. There are many examples of how commonplace oral fixation is: for example, smoking, nail biting, pen sucking and kissing are all 'oral' activities, while many swear words make reference to anal-urinary activities ('crap', 'shit', 'piss', for example). These examples show that the early stages of development all leave their mark or imprint to varying degrees.

Freud was equally interested in more extreme examples of fixation and identified two major personality types – the *oral* and the *anal*. Some of the major traits associated with these, together with traits and activities resulting from the use of defence mechanisms, are shown in Table 21.2.

Is there any evidence to support Freud?

Kline and Storey (1977) found evidence for two oral characters, one in which dependency, fluency, sociability, liking of novelty and relaxation clustered together (*oral optimistic*) and one in which independence, verbal aggression, envy, coldness and hostility, malice, ambition and impatience clustered together (*oral pessimistic*). Storey (1980) found a relationship between these scores and smoking, food preferences and nail biting. Fisher and Greenberg (1977) concluded that people who are unusually preoccupied with oral themes tend to crave approval and support from significant others. As far as the anal personality is concerned, Kline (1972), Fisher and Greenberg (1977) and Pollak (1979) found evidence for the clustering of three major character traits, namely orderliness, parsimony and obstinacy.

Fisher (1978) found that racial prejudice based on skin colour can be predicted by participants' attitudes to cleanliness and thrift, implying that colour prejudice is at least partly the consequence of an unconscious connection between skin colour and faeces. As Fonagy (1981) points out, such predictions certainly seem highly counterintuitive and difficult to account for except in psychoanalytic terms. However, the fact that there is substantial evidence for the *existence* of oral and anal personality types does not mean that these traits come about in the way Freud believes. So what is the evidence that

Oral (0–1)	Incorporative	Fixation through over-indulgence		1 Cheerful, unrealistically optimistic; 'life is easy.' 2 'I am the centre of the universe'; self centredness. 3 Dependent – can't bear others' disapproval.
			Passive	Through *sublimation*: interest in languages, compulsive talker, ventriloquist, thirst for knowledge'.
		Fixation through frustration	Dependent	1 Greedy, acquisitive. 2 Envious, pessimistic. 3 Addict, parasite 4 Gluttonous. 5 Thumb-sucker. 6 Smoker.
	Aggressive	Fixation through over-indulgence	Active	
		Fixation through frustration	Biting	1 Cynical 2 Verbally, 'biting', sarcastic, scornful, disdainful, contemptuous. 3 Nail-biter.
Anal (1–3)	Expulsive	Orderliness could represent a *reaction formation* against the wish to mess.		
		a) Orderliness		1 Preoccupation with punctuality, routine; everything must be in its proper place. 2 Obsessive-compulsive behaviour (in extreme cases). 'Performing' for others, giving presents, donating to charity etc, could be *sublimations* of wish to 'perform on the potty' for parents. Sculptors, potters, gardeners are all *sublimating* the wish to smear.
	Retentive	b) Parsimony c) Obstinacy	1 Miserly, thrifty. 2 Wilfully hoarding	Reaction formation against this could be feeling compelled to give things away or lose them through gambling or speculation on the stock market.
Phallic (3–5/6)		1 Homosexuality 2 Curiosity 3 Exhibitionism 4 Exploitation of others	5 Excessive displays of masculinity/femininity 6 Extreme self-centredness 7 Excessive ambition 8 Narcissism (self love)	A surgeon may be sublimating hostile feelings toward a same-sex parent. A writer of pornography may be sublimating sexual preoccupations.
Latency (5/6–puberty)		1 Never feeling comfortable with members of the opposite sex; may avoid heterosexual relationships. 2 May perform sexual activities in an emotionally-detached or aggressive way.		

TABLE 21.2 *Relationship between fixation at psychosexual stages and adult personality*

these personality variables are related to early oral/anal experiences?

Fisher and Greenberg (1977) found that the evidence is often contradictory. For example, some studies have found a correlation between orality and length of breastfeeding and others that dependency is related to severity of weaning. However, still others have found no relationship between dependency and duration of breastfeeding. However, the measures of feeding styles used in these studies do not do justice to the complexities of mother-infant interaction and when these are taken into account, the evidence tends to be favourable to Freud. As to the anal character, most studies have failed to verify that the anal person differs from other types in age of initiation or completion of toilet training or in severity of training procedures.

DEVELOPMENT OF THE SELF-CONCEPT

As we noted in the introduction and overview, self-awareness is what allows us to (try to) see ourselves as others see us and the self-concept can be thought of as the individual's beliefs about his/her personality – how the individual perceives his/her personality.

● Consciousness and self-consciousness

When you look in the mirror at your face, you are both the person who is looking and that which is looked at. Similarly, when you think about the kind of person you are or something you have done, you are both the person doing the thinking and what is being thought about. In other words, you are both subject (the thinker or looker) and object (what is being looked at or thought about). We use the personal pronoun 'I' to refer to us as subject and 'me' to refer to us as object and this represents a rather special relationship that we have with ourselves, namely *self-consciousness/self-awareness.*

While other animal species have consciousness (i.e. they have sensations of cold, heat, hunger, thirst and can feel pleasure, pain, fear, sexual arousal, etc.), only humans have self-consciousness. The term 'self-conscious' is often used to mean embarrassment or shyness and certainly we do feel like this in situations where we are made to feel object-like or exposed in some way, e.g. if we get on the bus in the

morning to discover that our sweater is on back-to-front. But this is a secondary meaning – the primary meaning refers to this unique relationship whereby the same person, the same self, is both subject and object.

● What is the self?

There are many 'self' terms, which are often used interchangeably but which have fairly distinct meanings (e.g. 'self-image', 'self-esteem', 'ideal self', 'self-identity'). 'Self' and 'self-concept' are used interchangeably to refer to an individual's overall self-awareness. According to Murphy (1947), 'the self is the individual as known to the individual' and Burns (1980) defines it as 'the set of attitudes a person holds towards himself'.

● Components of the self-concept

The self-concept is a general term that traditionally refers to three major components:

1 self-image;
2 self-esteem;
3 ideal self.

Self-image refers to the way in which we describe ourselves, the kind of person we think we are (whether we like what we are or not). One way of investigating self-image is to ask people to answer the question 'Who am I?' 20 times (Kuhn and McPartland, 1954). This typically produces two main categories of answers – social roles and personality traits. *Social roles* are usually quite objective aspects of our self-image (e.g. son, daughter, brother, sister, student, etc.); they are 'facts' and can be verified by others. *Personality traits,* on the other hand, are more a matter of opinion and judgement and what we think we are like may be different from how others see us (e.g. we may think we are quite friendly but others may see us as cold or a little aloof). But we shall see below that how others behave towards us has an important influence on our self-perception.

As well as social roles and personality traits, people often make reference to their physical characteristics in response to the 'Who am I?' question, such as tall, short, fat, thin, blue-eyed, brown-haired, etc. These are part of our *body image* or *bodily self,* the bodily *me* which also includes bodily sensations (usually temporary states) of pain, cold, hunger and so on. A more permanent feature of our body image is concerned with what we count as part of our body (and hence belonging to us) and what we do not. Gordon Allport (1955), an eminent self-theorist, gives two rather dramatic and vivid examples of how intimate our bodily sense is and just where we draw the boundaries between 'me' and 'not me':

- Imagine swallowing your saliva – or actually do it! Now imagine spitting it into a cup and drinking it! Clearly, once we have spat out our saliva, we have disowned it – it no longer belongs to us.
- Imagine sucking blood from a cut in your finger (something we do quite automatically, assuming the cut is relatively slight). Now imagine sucking the blood from a plaster on your finger! Again, once it has soaked into the plaster it has ceased to be part of ourselves.

This 'rule' does not always apply, however. For example, we might feel we have lost part of ourselves when we have very long hair cut off and lovers often keep a lock of each other's hair as a constant (and tangible) reminder that the other exists. Clearly, whenever our body changes in some way, so our body image changes. In extreme cases, where a limb is lost, a person is scarred due to an accident or undergoes cosmetic surgery, we would expect a correspondingly dramatic change in body image, sometimes favourable, sometimes not.

Throughout our lives, as part of the normal process of maturation and ageing, we all experience growth spurts, changes in height, weight and the general appearance and 'feel' of our body and each time we have to make an adjustment to our body image. Later, we shall see how the bodily changes involved in puberty affect the adolescent's body image and, hence, self-concept. Another fundamental aspect of body image is to do with our biological sex. As we will see in Chapter 23, gender is the social equivalent or the social interpretation of sex and our gender, or gender identity, is another part of the central core of our self-image.

While the self-image is essentially descriptive, *self-esteem* (or *self-regard*) is essentially evaluative: it refers to the extent to which we like and accept or approve of ourselves, how worthwhile a person we think we are. Coopersmith (1967) defined it as 'a personal judgement of worthiness, that is expressed in the attitudes the individual holds towards himself'.

How much we like or value ourselves can be an overall judgement or it can relate to specific areas of our lives. For example, we can have a generally high opinion of ourselves and yet not like certain of our characteristics or attributes, such as our wavy or curly hair (when we want it straight) or our lack of assertiveness (when we want to be more assertive). Alternatively, it may be impossible or certainly very difficult to have high overall esteem if we are very badly disfigured or are desperately shy. Our self-esteem can be regarded as how we evaluate our self-image, i.e. how much we like the kind of person we think we are. Clearly, certain characteristics or abilities have a greater value in society generally and so are likely to influence our self-esteem accordingly, for example, being physically attractive as opposed to unattractive (see Chapters 15 and 16). The value attached to particular characteristics will also depend on culture, gender, age, social background and so on.

Our self-esteem will also be partly determined by how much our self-image differs from our ideal self, the third component of the self-concept. If our self-image is the kind of person we think we are, then our *ideal self* (*ego-ideal* or *idealized self-image*) is the kind of person we would like to be. Again, this can vary in extent and degree – we may want to be different in certain aspects or we may want to be a totally different person. (We may even wish we were someone else!) We might be very dissatisfied with what we are like and want to be different for this reason or we may basically like ourselves and want to develop and extend ourselves along essentially the same lines. Generally, the greater the gap between our self-image and our ideal self, the lower our self-esteem (see Rogers' self theory in Chapter 29).

● Self-schemata

Just as we represent and store information about other people, so we represent and store information about ourselves (see Chapter 12), but in a more complex and varied way; this information about self constitutes the self-concept. We tend to have very clear conceptions of ourselves (i.e. *self-schemata*) on some dimensions (such as those that are very important to us), but not others. For example, if you think of yourself as athletic, as definitely not unathletic and being athletic is important to you, then you are self-schematic on that dimension (i.e. it is part of your self-concept) (Hogg and Vaughan, 1995).

Most people have a complex self-concept with a relatively large number of self-schemata; these include an array of possible selves, future-oriented schemata of what we would like to become (ideal self) (Markus and Nurius, 1986); visions of future possible selves may influence how we make important life decisions, such as career choice . The idea of multiple selves raises the question of whether there is any one self that is more real or authentic than the others; for example, perhaps we feel most real (most 'ourselves') when with someone we believe sees us as we wish to be seen. While personality theorists tend to assume that the person has a single, unitary self (for example, typical instructions at the top of a personality questionnaire do not specify which self the respondent should describe) (Hampson, 1995), social psychologists recognize the possibility that the self refers to a complex set of perceptions, composed of a number of schemata relating both to what we are like and how we could be.

THEORIES OF SELF

A major theoretical approach to the self is *symbolic interactionism,* which is mainly associated with Mead (1934) who was influenced by the earlier theories of both James (1890) and Cooley (1902). According to symbolic interactionism, human beings act towards things in terms of their meanings; people exist in a symbolic as well as a physical environment, such that the importance of a social interaction is derived from the meaning it holds for the participants. The 'interaction' refers specifically to the fact that people communicate with each other, which provides the opportunity for meanings to be learned. Because we share a common language and have the ability for symbolic thought, we can (at least in principle) look at the world from the point of view of other perceivers, i.e. take the role of the other; according to Mead (1934) , this is essentially the process by which the self develops (see below).

- It was James (1890) who first made the distinction between self-as-subject or knower ('I') and self-as-object or known ('me'); the 'I' represents the principal form of the self, lying at the centre of our state (or 'stream') of consciousness. We have as many selves as we have social relationships, i.e. the self is multifaceted. This is consistent with the widely shared view that we modify our behaviour to some extent depending on whom we are with: different others bring out different aspects of our personalities (Hampson, 1995). It is also consistent with Goffman's (e.g.

1959) account of *self-presentation* which he defined as the creation and maintenance of a public self. By analogy with the theatre, each participant in a social interaction is engaged in a performance designed as much for its effect on the audience as it is for honest and open expression of the self (see the discussion of impression management and self-monitoring in Chapter 15). Indeed, according to this *dramaturgical approach,* personality is equated with the various roles the person plays in life. But the Jamesian idea of multiple selves goes much further than this by suggesting that different personalities are constructed in the context of every relationship one has (Hampson, 1995).

- Cooley's theory of the *looking-glass self* maintains that the self is reflected in the reactions of other people, who are the 'looking-glass' for oneself, i.e. in order to understand what we are like, we need to see how others see us and this is how children gradually build up an impression of what they are like. What is reflected back to us are judgements and evaluations of our behaviour and appearance, which produce some form of self-feeling (such as pride or shame). Consistent with the notion of multiple selves, Cooley claims that the looking-glass is not a 'mere mechanical reflection' because it will differ depending on whose view we take. The individual and society are opposite sides of the same coin (Denzin, 1995).

- Mead turned James and Cooley on their heads: the self is not mentalistic (i.e. something privately going on inside the individual) but, like mind, is a cognitive process lodged in the ongoing social world. However, like Cooley, he saw self and society as two terms in a reciprocal process of interaction (Denzin, 1995); knowledge of self and others develops simultaneously, both being dependent on social interaction, and self and society represent a common whole and neither can exist without the other. The human being is an organism with a self and this converts him into a special kind of actor, transforms his relation to the world and gives his actions a unique character. The human being is an object to himself, that is, he can perceive himself, have conceptions about himself, communicate with himself and so on. In sum, he can interact with himself and this self-interaction is a great influence upon his transactions with the world in general and with other people in particular. Self-interaction is a reflexive process, which is Mead's way of making the 'I'/'me' distinction –

BOX 21.4 Mead's developmental theory of the self

According to symbolic interactionism, an important feature of interaction is language, which represents a fundamental means by which we come to represent ourselves to ourselves. But the key process by which we come to represent ourselves to ourselves (i.e. develop a concept of self) is *role taking*. By placing ourselves in the position of others we can look back on ourselves. The idea of self can only develop if the individual can 'get outside himself (experientially) in such a way as to become an object to himself' (Mead, 1934), i.e. to see ourselves from the standpoint of others.

Initially, the child thinks about his conduct as 'good or bad only as he reacts to his own acts in the remembered words of his parents' (Mead, 1934); 'me' at this stage is a combination of the child's memory of his own actions and the kind of reaction they received. In the next stage, the child's pretend play, in particular 'playing at mummies and daddies' or 'doctors or nurses', helps the child to understand and incorporate adult attitudes and behaviour. Here, the child is not merely imitating but also 'calls out in himself the same response as he calls out in the other', i.e. he is being, say, the child *and* the parent and, as the parent, is responding to himself as the child. So, in playing with a doll, the child 'responds in tone of voice and in attitudes as his parents respond to his cries and chortles' (Mead, 1934). Play is distinguished from *games,* which involve *rules:* '...The child must not only take the role of the other, as he does in the play, but he must assume the various roles of all the participants in the game, and govern his action accordingly ...' (Mead, 1934). Games are a later development than play (see Piaget's theory; Chapter 25).

In this way, the child acquires a variety of social viewpoints or 'perspectives' (mother, father, nurse, doctor, etc.) which are then used to accompany, direct and evaluate its own behaviour. This is how the socialized part of the self (Mead's 'me') expands and develops. At first, these viewpoints or perspectives are based upon specific adults but, in time, the child comes to react to itself and its behaviour from the viewpoint of a 'typical mother', a 'typical nurse' or 'people in general'. Mead called these the perspectives of the generalized other and the incorporation of the generalized other marks the final, qualitative change in the 'me'. 'It is this *generalized other* in his experience which provides him with a self' (Mead, 1934).

Grammatically, our 'me' is third person (like 'she' or 'he') and it is an image of self seen from the perspective of a judgmental, non-participant observer. By its very nature, 'me' is social, because it grows out of this role playing, whereby the child is being the other person.

---

the experiencing 'I' cannot be an object, it cannot itself be experienced, since it is the very act of experiencing; what we experience and interact with is our 'me'. Mead's theory of how the self develops is summarized in Box 21.4.

Influenced by Mead, many sociologists and social psychologists see the role of language as fundamental to the construction and maintenance of the self. What we say about ourselves often depends on who is listening: in selecting what to say and not to say, we are actively constructing a self in relation to the other person, we are constantly 'making a self'. The self is not a static, internal entity but a process that is constantly changing (Petkova, 1995).

According to Harré (1985, 1989), our understanding and experience of ourselves as human beings, our subjective experience of selfhood, is laid down by the beliefs about being a person that are implicit in our language. The structure of our language implies certain assumptions/beliefs about human nature, which we live out in our daily interactions with others. For example, the words 'I' and 'me' mislead us into believing that each of us is represented by a coherent, unified self which operates mechanisms and processes (the subject matter of psychology) that are responsible for our actions. But 'self', 'ego', 'mind' and so on do not refer to anything that exists objectively in the world; they are hypothetical constructs which perform the very important function of helping us to organize and structure our world (Burr, 1995).

Similarly, Potter and Wetherell (1987) argue that the very experience of being a person, the kind of mental life one can have, perhaps even how we experience sensory information, are dependent on the particular representations of selfhood, the particular ways of accounting for/talking about ourselves, that are available to us in our culture. These 'stories' or accounts, whose meaning is shared by members of a culture, are called *discourses;* since these differ from culture to culture, it follows that members of different cultures will experience being human ('selves') in different ways (see Box 21.5)

BOX 21.5	Critical discussion: The self-concept as a cultural phenomenon

According to Potter and Wetherell (1987), in Maori culture, the person is invested with a particular kind of power (*mana*), given by the gods in accordance with the person's family status and birth circumstances. This is what enables the person to be effective, whether in battle or everyday dealings with others. But this power is not a stable resource; it can be increased or decreased by the person's day-to-day conduct – for example, it could be reduced by forgetting a ritual observance or committing some misdemeanour. People's social standing and successes and failures, etc. are seen as dependent on external forces, not internal states (such as personality or level of motivation); in fact, *mana* is only one of these external forces which inhabit the individual.

People living in such a culture would necessarily experience themselves quite differently from what we are used to in Western culture. Instead of representing themselves as the centre and origin of their actions, which is crucial to the Western concept of the self, '...The individual Maori does not own experiences such as the emotions of fear, anger, love, grief; rather they are visitations governed by the unseen world of powers and forces ...' (Potter and Wetherell, 1987).

According to Moscovici (1985), 'the individual' is the greatest invention of modern times; only in recent times has the idea of the autonomous, self-regulating, free-standing individual become dominant and this has fundamental implications for the debate about free will and determinism (see Chapter 32). Smith and Bond (1993) argue that we need to distinguish between the independent and the interdependent self; the former is what is stressed in Western, individualist cultures and the latter by non-Western, collectivist cultures (see Chapter 15).

FACTORS INFLUENCING THE DEVELOPMENT OF THE SELF-CONCEPT

Much of the research into factors that influence the self-concept can be understood in relation to the symbolic interactionist position. But the importance of these factors extends beyond childhood –

our self-concept is constantly being revised – but probably the most significant 'change' is the time when it is originally being formed.

Argyle (1969, 1983) believes that there are four major influences:

1 the reaction of others;
2 comparison with others;
3 social roles;
4 identification (which we have already discussed in relation to Freud's psychosexual stages of personality development and will return to in Chapters 23 and 27).

● Reaction of others

We have already seen in the theories of Cooley and Mead how central the reactions of others are in the formulation of our self-concept. Any attempt to explain how we come to be what we are and how we change involves us in the question of what kind of evidence we use. Kelly (1955), in a similar vein to Cooley and Mead, believes that we derive our picture of ourselves through what we learn of other people's picture of us (see Chapter 29). So the central evidence is the reaction of others to us, both what they say of us and the implications of their behaviour towards us; we filter others' views of us through our view of them. We build up a continuous and changing picture of ourselves out of our interaction with others.

Guthrie (1938) tells the famous story of a female student, a dull and unattractive girl. Some of her classmates decided to play a trick on her by pretending she was the most desirable girl in the college and drawing lots to decide who would take her out first, second and so on. By the fifth or sixth date, she was no longer regarded as dull and unattractive – by being treated as attractive she had, in a sense, *become* attractive (perhaps by wearing different clothes and smiling more, etc.) and her self-image had clearly changed; for the boys who dated her later, it was no longer a chore! 'Before the year was over, she had developed an easy manner and a confident assumption that she was popular' (Guthrie, 1938).

During the preschool years, children are extremely concerned with how adults view them and few things are more relevant than how significant others react to them, i.e. parents, older siblings and other people whose opinions the child values. Strictly speaking, it is the child's *perception* of others' reactions that makes such an important contribution to how the child comes to perceive itself. After all, the child has no frame of reference for evaluating parental reactions – parents are all-powerful figures as far as the preschooler is concerned, so what they say is 'fact'. If a child is consistently told how beautiful she is, she will come to believe it, it will become part of her self-image; similarly, if a child is repeatedly told how stupid or clumsy he is, this too will become accepted as the 'truth' and the child will tend to act accordingly. The first child is likely to develop high self-esteem and the second low self-esteem. Argyle explains this in terms of *introjection* (a process very similar to identification) whereby we come to incorporate into our own personalities the perceptions, attitudes and reactions to ourselves of our parents and it is through the reactions of others that the child learns its *conditions of worth,* i.e. which behaviours will produce positive regard and which will not (see Rogers' theory; Chapter 29).

When the child starts school, the number and variety of significant others increase to include teachers and peers. At the same time, the child's self-image is becoming more differentiated and significant others then become important in relation to different parts of the self-image. For example, the teacher is important as far as the child's academic ability is concerned, parents as far as how loveable the child is and so on.

A good deal of research has been conducted in connection with self-esteem and the reaction of others and an influential study is that of Coopersmith (1967); this is described in Box 21.6.

Coopersmith's data are only correlational, so we cannot be sure that how the boys were raised was actually responsible for their level of self-esteem. Remember, too, that the boys were white middle-class and therefore not representative of the American population as a whole – what about working-class, black and female children?

Girls, generally, have lower self-esteem than boys. For instance, when paired with boys in problem-solving tasks, they sometimes artificially depress their performance so as not to outshine their male partners (boys very rarely do this!). Some girls seem to feel uncomfortable in the superior role, as if this is inconsistent with their 'true' position in life (see Chapters 6 and 15). They also tend to rate themselves less highly than boys on written tests of self-esteem, set themselves lower goals in life and are more inclined to underestimate their abilities than boys, even in primary school, where in reading and language skills they often tend to surpass boys. (See Chapter 23)

BOX 21.6 Key study: Coopersmith's study of self-esteem

From an original sample of hundreds of nine- and ten-year-old white, middle-class boys, Coopersmith selected five groups, including those who scored high on each of three measures of self-esteem (his Self-Esteem Inventory, teachers' evaluations of the boys' reactions to failure, self-confidence in new situations etc., and scores on the Thematic Apperception Test (TAT); see Chapter 5) and those who scored low on the three measures (17 per group). They were studied in depth, using a variety of tests, and it was found that the high-esteem boys were confident about their own perceptions and judgements, expected to succeed at new tasks and to influence others and readily expressed their opinions. They were also doing better in school and were more often chosen as friends by other children than the low-esteem boys; they had a realistic view of themselves and their abilities, were not unduly worried by criticism and enjoyed participating in things. By contrast, the low-esteem boys were a 'sad little group', isolated, fearful, reluctant to join in, self-conscious, oversensitive to criticism, consistently under-rated themselves, tended to underachieve in class and were preoccupied with their own problems. Interestingly, there were no measurably significant differences in intelligence or physical attractiveness between the two groups; they were all white and from middle-class homes and were free from any obvious emotional disturbance.

So how did Coopersmith account for their differences in self-esteem? Based on a questionnaire and in-depth interviews with the mothers, plus interviews with the boys about their parents' childrearing methods, he found significant differences between the two sets of parents. The optimum conditions for the development of high self-esteem seem to involve a combination of firm enforcement of limits on the child's behaviour, plus a good deal of acceptance of the child's autonomy and freedom within those limits. Firm management helps the child to develop firm inner controls and a predictable and structured social environment helps the child to deal effectively with the environment and hence to feel 'in control' of the world (rather than controlled by it).

Coopersmith followed the boys through into adulthood and found that the high-esteem boys consistently outperformed the low-esteem boys and proved more successful educationally and vocationally.

An interesting contrast with the parents of high-esteem boys in Coopersmith's study is the study of interaction between parents and their schizophrenic children. These parents tend to deny communicative support to the child and often do not respond to the child's statements and demands for recognition of its opinions. When the parents do communicate with the child it is often in the form of an interruption or an intrusion, rather than a response to the child. In fact, they respond selectively to those of the child's utterances which they themselves have initiated rather than those initiated by the child. Laing (1971) suggests that these kinds of communication patterns within the family make the development of ego boundaries in the child very difficult, i.e. there is a confusion between self and not-self (me and not-me). This impaired autonomy of the self (or self-identity) and impaired appreciation of external reality are often found to be fundamental characteristics of schizophrenic adolescents and adults (see Chapter 30).

Comparison with others

According to Bannister and Agnew (1976), the personal construct of 'self' is intrinsically bipolar, i.e. having a concept of self implies a concept of not-self. (This is similar to Cooley and Mead's view that self and society are really two sides of the same coin.) So one way in which we come to form a picture of what we are like is to see how we compare with others. Indeed, there are certain parts of our self-image which only take on any significance at all through comparison with others. For example, 'tall' and 'fat' are not absolute characteristics (like, say, 'blue-eyed') and we are only tall or fat in comparison with others who are shorter or thinner than ourselves. This is true of many other characteristics, including intelligence.

Parents and other adults often react to a children by comparing them with other siblings (or unrelated children). If a child is told repeatedly that she is 'less clever than your big sister', she will come to incorporate this as part of her self-image and will probably have lower self-esteem as a result; this could adversely affect her academic performance so that she does not achieve in line with her true ability. A child of above average intelligence who has grown up in the shadow of a brilliant brother or sister may be less successful academically than an average or even below average child who has not had to face these unfavourable comparisons.

Rosenburg (1965) studied large numbers of adolescents and found that those with the highest self-esteem tended to be of higher social class, to have done better at school and to have been leaders in their clubs, all of which represent the basis for a favourable comparison between self and others.

Social roles

As we noted earlier, social roles are what people commonly regard as part of 'who they are'. Kuhn (1960) asked seven-year-olds and undergraduate students to give 20 different answers to the question, 'Who am I?'. The seven-year-olds gave an average of five answers relating to roles, while the undergraduates gave an average of ten. As we get older, we incorporate more and more roles into our self-image; this is what we would expect since, as we get older we assume an increasing number and variety of roles. The preschooler is a son or daughter, perhaps a brother or sister, has other familial roles and may also be a friend to another child, but the number and range of roles are limited compared with the older child or adult. As we grow up and venture into the 'big wide world', our duties and responsibilities, as well as our choices, involve us in all kinds of roles and relationships with others (e.g. occupational roles, groups and organizations we belong to and so on).

DEVELOPMENTAL CHANGES IN THE SELF-CONCEPT

How do we get to know ourselves?

According to Lewis (1990), achieving identity, in the sense of acquiring a set of beliefs about the self (a self-schema), is one of the central developmental tasks of a social being. It progresses through several levels of complexity and continues to develop through the lifespan (see Chapter 24). During the first few months, the baby gradually distinguishes itself from its environment and from other people and related to this is a sense of continuity through time (the *existential self*). But at this stage, the infant's self-knowledge is comparable to that of other species (e.g. monkeys); what makes human self-knowledge distinctive is becoming aware that we have it – we are conscious of our existence and uniqueness (Buss, 1992).

According to Maccoby (1980), babies are able to distinguish between themselves and others on two counts:

1 Their own fingers hurt when bitten (but they do not have any such sensations when they are biting their rattle or their mother's fingers).
2 Probably quite early in life, they begin to associate feelings from their own body movements with the sight of their own limbs and the sounds of their own cries. These sense impressions are bound together into a cluster that defines the bodily self, so this is probably the first aspect of the self-concept to develop.

Other aspects of the self-concept develop by degrees, but there do seem to be fairly clearly defined stages of development. Young children may know their own names, understand the limits of their own bodies and yet be unable to think about themselves as coherent entities, so self-awareness or self-consciousness develops very gradually. According to Piaget, an awareness of self comes through the gradual process of adaptation to the environment (see Chapter 25). As the child explores objects and accommodates to them (thus developing new sensorimotor schemas) it simultaneously discovers aspects of its self; for example, trying to put a large block into its mouth and finding that it will not fit is a lesson in selfhood as well as a lesson about the world of objects.

● Self-recognition

One way in which the development of bodily self has been studied is through *self-recognition* and this involves more than just a simple discrimination of bodily features. To determine that the person in a photograph or a film or the reflection in a mirror is oneself, certain knowledge seems to be necessary : (a) at least a rudimentary knowledge of oneself as continuous through time (necessary for recognizing ourselves in a photograph or movie) and space (necessary for recognizing ourselves in mirrors); and (b) knowledge of particular features (what we look like). Although other kinds of self-recognition are possible (e.g. one's voice or feelings), only visual self-recognition has been studied extensively, both in animals and humans.

Many non-human animals (including fish, birds, chickens and monkeys) react to their mirror-images as if they were other animals, i.e. they do not seem to recognize it as their reflection at all. But self-recognition has been observed in the higher primates –

chimpanzees and other great apes. Gallup's famous 'red dot' study with chimps is described in Box 21. 7.

A number of researchers (e.g. Lewis and Brooks-Gunn, 1979) have used modified forms of Gallup's technique with 6–24-month-olds. The mother applies a dot of rouge to the child's nose (while pretending to wipe the baby's face) and the baby is observed to see how often it touches its nose. It is then placed in front of a mirror and again the number of times it touches its nose is recorded. At about 18 months, there is a significant change: touching the dot was never seen before 15 months; between 15 and 18 months, 5–25 percent of infants touched it, while 75 percent of the 18–20–month-olds did.

BOX 21.7   Key study: It's not just people who have a 'red nose' day

Gallup (1977), working with preadolescent, wild-born chimps, placed a full-length mirror on the wall of each animal's cage. At first they reacted as if another chimp had appeared – they threatened, vocalized or made conciliatory gestures – but this quickly faded out and by the end of three days had almost disappeared. They then used the image to explore themselves, e.g. they would pick up a piece of food and place it on their face, which could not be seen without the mirror.

After ten days exposure, each chimp was anaesthetized and a bright red spot was painted on the uppermost part of one eyebrow ridge and a second spot on the top of the opposite ear, using an odourless, non-irritating dye. When the chimp had recovered from the anaesthetic, it was returned to its cage, from which the mirror had been removed, and it was observed to see how often it touched the marked parts of its body. The mirror was then replaced and each chimp began to explore the marked spots 25 times more often than it had done before.

The procedure was repeated with chimps which had never seen themselves in the mirror and they reacted to the mirror-image as if it were another chimp (they did not touch the spots). So it seems that the first group had learned to recognize themselves, supporting Cooley's and Mead's theories which stress interaction with others and the reactions of others as crucial to the development of self-concept. Lower primates (monkeys, gibbons and baboons) are unable to learn to recognize their mirror-image, whether they are raised in isolation or normally.

In order to use the mirror-image to touch the dot on its nose, the baby must also have built up a schema of how its face should look in the mirror before it can notice the discrepancy created by the dot and it seems this does not develop before about 18 months. This is also about the time when, according to Piaget, object permanence is completed, so *object permanence* would seem to be a necessary condition for the development of self-recognition (see Chapter 25).

Self-definition

Piaget, Mead and many others have pointed to the importance of language in consolidating the early development of self-awareness by providing labels which permit distinctions between self and not-self ('I', 'you', 'me', 'it' and so on). These labels can, of course, then be used by the toddler to communicate notions of selfhood to others. One important kind of label is the child's name.

Names are not usually chosen arbitrarily – either the parents particularly like the name or they want to name the child after a relative or famous person and so on; certainly, names are not neutral labels in terms of how people respond to them and what they associate with them. Indeed, they can be used as the basis for stereotyping (see Chapter 15.) Jahoda (1954) described the naming practices of the Ashanti tribe of West Africa. Children born on different days of the week are given names accordingly, because of the belief that they have different personalities. Police records showed that among juvenile delinquents, there was a very low percentage of boys born on Monday (believed to have a quiet and calm personality) but a very high rate of Wednesday-born boys (thought to be naturally aggressive).

This demonstrates the *self-fulfilling prophecy*. It is reasonable to believe that these Ashanti boys were treated in a way consistent with the name given to them and that, as a result, they 'became' what their name indicated they were 'really' like. In English-speaking countries, days of the week (e.g. Tuesday) and months of the year (April, May and June) are used as names and they have associations which may influence others' reactions (for example, 'Monday's child is fair of face, Tuesday's child is full of grace ...').

When children refer to themselves as 'I' (or 'me') and others as 'you', they are having to reverse the labels that are normally used to refer to them by others ('you', 'he', 'she'). Also, of course, they hear others refer to themselves as 'I' and not as 'you', 'he', 'she'; this is a problem of *shifting reference*. Despite this, most children do not invert 'I' and 'you', but two interesting exceptions are autistic and blind children, who often use 'I' for others and 'you' for self. (This may be associated with the abnormal interactions and relationships that these children experience which, in turn, would further support Cooley and Mead.)

The psychological self

Maccoby (1980) has asked what exactly children mean when they refer to themselves as 'I' or 'me'. Are they referring to anything more than a physical entity enclosed by an envelope of skin?

Flavell *et al.* (1978, cited in Maccoby, 1980) investigated development of the psychological self in 2½–5-year-olds. In one study, he placed a doll on the table in front of the child and explained that dolls are like people in some ways – arms, legs, hands and so on (pointing as he did so). Then the child was asked how dolls are different from people, whether they know their names and think about things, etc. Most children said a doll does not know its name and cannot think about things, but people can. They were then asked, 'Where is the part of you that knows your name and thinks about things?' and 'Where do you do your thinking and knowing?' Fourteen out of 22 children gave fairly clear localization for the thinking self, namely 'in their heads', while others found it very difficult. The experimenters then looked directly into the child's eyes and asked, 'Can I see you thinking in there?'. Most children thought not.

These answers suggest that by 3½–4 years, children have a rudimentary concept of a private, thinking self that is not visible even to someone looking directly into their eyes; they can distinguish this from the bodily self which they know is visible to others. In other words, by about age four, children begin to develop a *theory of mind,* the awareness that they – and other people – have mental processes (e.g. Leekam, 1993; Shatz, 1994; Wellman, 1990). However, one group of children who fail to develop a theory of mind are those suffering from autism; see Chapter 25.

The categorical self

Age and gender are both part of the central core of the self-image; they represent two of the categories regarding the self which are also used to perceive and interpret the behaviour of others.

Age is probably the first social category to be acquired by the child (and is so even before a concept of number develops). Lewis and Brooks-Gunn (1979) found that 6–12-month-olds can distinguish between photographs, slides and papier-mâché heads of adults and babies. By 12 months, they prefer interacting with strange babies to strange adults. Also, as soon as they have acquired labels like 'mummy' and 'daddy' and 'baby', they almost never make age-related mistakes. (Gender is discussed in Chapter 23.)

Before the age of seven, children tend to define the self in physical terms – hair colour, height, favourite activities and possessions – while inner, psychological experiences and characteristics are not described as being distinct from overt behaviour and external, physical characteristics. During middle childhood through to adolescence, self-descriptions now include many more references to internal, psychological characteristics, such as competencies, knowledge, emotions, values and personal traits (Damon and Hart, 1988). However, Damon and Hart also report important cultural differences in how the self-concept develops.

School highlights others' expectations about how the self should develop; it also provides a social context in which new goals are set and comparisons with others (peers) are prompted. This makes evaluation of the self all the more important (Durkin, 1995).

ADOLESCENCE AND THE SELF-CONCEPT

● Body image

Just as the bodily self is the first aspect of the self-concept that emerges in the baby, so the bodily self undergoes a dramatic change with the onset of puberty, which marks the beginning of adolescence. Prior to the onset of puberty, most children have been relatively unconcerned with what their bodies are like (and how they look) and more concerned with what their bodies enable them to do. But the growth spurt of puberty, the dramatic changes in the shape and appearance of the body, plus the new sexual feelings and other sensations that accompany these changes, change all that! Inevitably, it seems, the adolescent has a much stronger and more clearly defined body image.

According to Coleman (1995), the development of identity requires not only feeling separate and different from others, but also knowing how one appears to the rest of the world. Dramatic bodily changes seriously affect these aspects of identity and represent a considerable challenge in adaptation for even the most well-adjusted young person. Consequently, the timing of the adolescent growth spurt may have an important effect on the adolescent's self-concept, especially self-esteem.

The behavioural and emotional effects of early and late maturation on the self-concept seem to be different for boys and girls. Jones and Bayley (1950) compared early and late maturers among 14–18-year-old boys. Early maturers were usually seen as more attractive, less childish and less talkative than the late maturers, they showed more interest in girls at 15 and were more likely to be popular and hold positions of responsibility; the later maturers were more childish and attention seeking. At 17, the early maturers were still more self-confident and less dependent; the later maturers had very strong desires for contact with girls and were more aggressive.

Probably because of the subjective meaning of bodily change, puberty seems to be a more difficult transition for girls than boys. For example, there is a greater increase in body fat composition for girls than for boys (who gain muscle mass) and Western society has developed increasingly stringent norms for thinness in women; girls' dissatisfaction with their appearance begins during puberty, along with a decline in self-esteem (Crawford and Unger, 1995). Comparisons between early- and late-maturing girls indicate that dissatisfaction with looks is associated with the rapid and normal weight gain that is part of growing up (Attie and Brooks-Gunn, 1989, cited in Crawford and Unger, 1995). Early-maturing girls have less positive body images, despite the fact that they date more and earlier; menstruation is an undeniable sign of maturation but it is also negatively associated with blood and physical discomfort. This paradox highlights the contradictions produced by the different meaning of mature physical development in females compared with males: an attractive appearance is stressed more for young women despite the fact that excessive thinness is physiologically more abnormal for them. Sexual activity is also more problematic for women, because of still existing double standards and differential responsibility in relation to pregnancy. For males, early maturation offers unambiguous social advantages, including opportunities for enhanced athletic achievement, leadership roles and expectations of occupational success (Crawford and Unger, 1995).

Davies and Furnham (1986), in a study of 182 11–18-year-olds, reported that, although comparatively few at any age were actually overweight, nearly half in each age group wished to lose weight – and considerably fewer wished to put on weight. Dissatisfaction with their weight was also found to increase with age and this was particularly marked between 14 and 16. Further, the numbers wishing to lose weight (at all ages) far exceeded the numbers classifying themselves as overweight, which seems to represent very powerful evidence of the influence of cultural pressures. Indeed, Davies and Furnham noted a trend towards exercising as against dieting as a way of losing weight, reflecting the recent 'aerobics revolution'. The pressure to conform to ideal bodily types may partly account for the illness anorexia nervosa (literally, 'nervous lack of appetite'), which is suffered mainly by 16–19-year-old girls.

What all anorexics seem to have in common is a distorted body image, a belief that they look and are greatly overweight when, in fact, they are severely underweight. They are also particularly vulnerable to ordinary life events, have rather obsessive personalities and tend to avoid situations they fear. They have low self-esteem and seem incapable or afraid of managing their own lives as an adult – it is easier to remain a child and they both want and fear autonomy. Some anorexics cannot control their desperate need to eat and find a solution in starving, then going on a binge of eating and then finally making themselves vomit (this is known as 'secondary anorexia' or bulimia nervosa; see Chapters 5 and 30).

ERIKSON'S PSYCHOSOCIAL THEORY OF DEVELOPMENT

As well as a significant contribution to psychological theory in its own right, Erikson's theory represents an important way of assessing Freud's theory and putting it into perspective.

● Brief biographical sketch

Born in Germany in 1902 to Danish parents, Erikson (Fig. 21.4) trained as a Montessori teacher and took a teaching post in Vienna in 1927, where he undertook psychoanalytic training with Anna Freud,

FIGURE 21.4 *Erik Erikson (1902–1994). (Olive Pierce: Black Star)*

Sigmund Freud's daughter. She was much more interested in child analysis than her father had been and this influenced Erikson. He fled from the Nazis in 1933 and went to the USA, setting up private practice as a child analyst in Boston, where he came into contact with such famous anthropologists as Ruth Benedict and Margaret Mead, whose discipline was to have such an impact on his theory. Some of the important similarities and differences between Erikson's and Freud's theories are summarized in Table 21.3.

Both agreed that there is a biological basis to development, i.e. the sequence of stages is genetically determined and so is universal, the same for members of all cultures. However, whereas for Freud, the baby begins life as a 'bundle of id' and only gradually becomes socialized, acquiring in turn an ego and superego, for Erikson, the human being is at all times an organism (id), an ego and a member of society (superego) and the individual must be biologically, psychologically and socially ready to move from one stage to the next. This, in turn, is matched by society's readiness. Although the order of stages is biologically based, the stages constitute the ego's timetable and mirror the structure of the relevant social institutions; in this sense, individuals and society are interdependent.

Erikson's belief in the fixed, predetermined sequence of the stages is expressed in his *epigenetic principle*, based on embryology, which maintains that the entire pattern of development is governed

Similarities

- Erikson accepted Freud's tripartite theory of the structure of personality (id, ego and superego).
- He accepted Freud's three levels of consciousness (conscious, preconscious and unconscious; see Chapter 29).
- He accepted Freud's psychosexual stages as basically valid, as far as they went (but he thought that, as they stood, they did not go far enough).

Differences

- Erikson sees development as proceeding throughout the lifecycle, with Freud's last stage – the genital – constituting the preadult (adolescent) stage and a subsequent three stages spanning adulthood (early, middle and late). (*His Eight Ages of Man* were first proposed in 1950.)
- Erikson believes (as do many other neo-Freudians) that Freud underemphasized the role of socialization of the individual, particularly the various patterns of behaviour which different cultures consider desirable and which individuals need to adopt in order to be accepted by their cultural or subcultural group.
- Erikson believes that the interaction between the individual and the social environment produces eight psycho*social stages* (as opposed to Freud's psycho*sexual* stages), each of which centres around a developmental crisis, involving a struggle between two opposing or conflicting personality characteristics.
- Erikson was much more concerned than was Freud with mental health. This is reflected in his concept of *ego identity* which is achieved by resolving the specified psychological crisis at each developmental stage.
- Erikson is an *ego* psychologist (whereas Freud is an *id* psychologist), believing, for example, that conflict within the ego itself (as against conflict between the ego and the id or superego) could produce emotional disturbance and this, in turn, is related to his greater emphasis on social and cultural factors. Indeed, the individual (psychological) aspect of each developmental stage is inseparable from the social and cultural – they are opposite sides of the same coin. At each stage, a new dimension of 'social interaction' becomes possible and this denotes the person's interaction both with the self and the social environment.

Table 21.3 *Similarities and differences between Erikson and Freud*

by a genetic structure common to all humans, whereby the genes dictate a timetable for the growth of each part of the unborn baby. Erikson extended this principle to social and psychological growth: it is human nature to pass through a predetermined sequence of psychosocial stages which are genetically determined. However, the social-cultural environment has a significant influence on the psychosocial modalities (dominant modes of acting and being), 'the radius of significant individuals and institutions' with which the individual interacts and the nature of the crisis which arises at each stage (Table 21.4).

● Stages of psychosocial development

Each stage is named by reference to two opposed outcomes, the first referring to the positive or functional (*adaptive*) outcome, e.g. trust, and the second referring to the negative or dysfunctional (*maladaptive*) outcome, e.g. mistrust. However, these are *not* either/or alternatives; every personality represents some mixture of trust and mistrust (and similarly for the other seven stages). Trust and mistrust, etc. are *relative* qualities and healthy development involves the adaptive quality outweighing the maladaptive.

Although the optimum time for developing a sense of trust is during infancy, Erikson believes it is possible to make up for unsatisfactory early experiences at a later stage, although it becomes increasingly difficult to do so. Conversely, a sense of trust developed during infancy could be shattered or at least shaken if later deprivation is experienced. Either way, Erikson presents a much less deterministic view than Freud: the issue of trust-mistrust is not resolved once and for all during the first year but recurs at each successive stage of development, so there are 'second chances' as well as the danger of positive early outcomes turning out badly later on.

● Basic trust versus basic mistrust (0–1)

The quality of care the baby receives determines how it comes to view its mother in particular and the world (including other people) in general (see Chapter 22) – is it a safe, predictable, comfortable place to be or is it full of danger and uncertainty? This is linked to the infant's sense of its ability to influence what happens to it and hence to its trust in itself. If the infant's needs are met as they arise and its discomforts quickly removed, if it is cuddled and fondled, played with and talked to, it develops a

Number of stage	Name of stage (psycho-social crisis)	Psycho-social modalities (dominant modes of being and acting)	Radius of significant relation-ships	Human virtues (qualities of strength)	Freud's psycho-sexual stages	Approximate ages
1	Basic trust versus Basic mistrust	To get, To give in return	Mother or mother figure	Hope	Oral – Respiratory Sensory – Kinaesthetic	0–1
2	Autonomy versus Shame and doubt	To hold on, To let go	Parents	Willpower	Anal- Urethral Muscular	1–3
3	Initiative versus Guilt	To make (going after) To 'make like' (playing)	Basic family	Purpose	Phallic Locomotor	3–6
4	Industry versus Inferiority	To make things (completing), To make things together	Neighbourhood and school	Competence	Latency	6–12
5	Identity versus Role confusion	To be oneself (or not to be), To share being oneself	Peer groups, and outgroups, models of leadership	Fidelity	Genital	12–18
6	Intimacy versus Isolation	To lose and find oneself in another	Partners in friendship, sex competition, co-operation	Love		20s
7	Generativity versus Stagnation	To make be, To take care of	Divided labour and shared household	Care		Late 20s–50s
8	Ego integrity versus Despair	To be, through having been, To face not being	'Humankind', 'my kind'	Wisdom		50s and beyond

TABLE 21.4 *Comparison between Erikson's and Freud's stages of development. (Based on Thomas, 1985/Erikson, 1959)*

sense of the world as a safe place to be and of people as helpful and dependable (*trust*). However, if its care is inconsistent, it develops a sense of *mistrust, fear and suspicion* which reveal themselves as apathetic or withdrawn behaviour, a sense of being controlled rather than being able to control. A sense of trust allows the baby to accept fear of the unknown as part and parcel of having new experiences.

● Autonomy versus shame and doubt (1–3)

The child's cognitive and muscle systems are maturing and it is becoming more mobile so that its range of experience and choices is expanding. The child is beginning to think of itself as a person in its own right, separate from the parents, and this new sense of power is the basis for its growing sense of *autonomy* and independence. The child wants to do everything (for) itself and parents have to allow it

BOX 21.8 Erikson's theory of play

The great emphasis given to play by psychotherapists is based on their recognition that young children are limited in their ability to communicate their problems in the way adults may. So in therapy, play situations are opportunities for the child to externalize its problems, work them through and come to terms with them; they are also, of course, opportunities for the therapist to observe and understand those problems.

Play deals with life experiences which the child attempts to repeat, master or negate in order to organize its inner world in relation to the outer one. It also involves self-teaching and self-healing:

> The child uses play to make up for defeats, sufferings and frustrations, especially those resulting from a technically and culturally limited use of language. (Erikson, 1950)

'Playing it out' becomes the child's means of reasoning and allows the child to free itself from the ego boundaries of time, space and reality but maintain a reality orientation because it and others know it is 'just play'. Play, too, is an important form of self-expression for the ego and helps the child towards new mastery and new

developmental stages. For example, play provides a safe island where the child can develop a sense of autonomy within its own boundaries or laws. Doubt and shame can be conquered here.

Just as Freud defined sexuality in a very broad way, so Erikson defined play very broadly. In *Toys and Reasons* (1977), he makes it clear that play is not limited to childhood but is pursued throughout the lifecycle. Play is not simply what we do when we are not working, not just a non-serious pastime or diversion, but rather is often an attempt to resolve a current psychosocial crisis. So, for Erikson, the child is playing when it builds a structure with bricks or when it acts out the family drama with dolls and the physicist, too, is playing when putting forward a model of the universe.

Erikson believes that anatomical differences contribute to personality differences between males and females. The 'inner space' or a woman's ability to bear children is a pervasive force in female gender identity. This is based on observations of the miniature play constructions of boys and girls from ten to 12 years: typically, girls construct an interior scene, while boys construct an exterior scene with elaborate walls or facades and protrusions or high towers (contrast the internal and external sex organs of females and males respectively).

to exercise these new abilities while simultaneously ensuring that the child does not 'bite off more than it can chew' – repeated failures and ridicule from others can lead to a sense of *shame* and *doubt*. The child must be allowed to do things at its own pace and in its own time; parents should not impatiently do things for it 'to save time' or criticize the child for its failures and the inevitable accidents. These 'accidents' (and the stage as a whole) may become focused on toilet training; if this is too strict or starts too early, the child may be faced with a 'double rebellion and a double defeat', feeling powerless to control its bowels and its parents' actions. This may result in regression to oral activities (e.g. thumb sucking), attention seeking or a pretending to have become autonomous by rejecting the help of others and becoming very strong-willed. But firm and considerate training helps the child to develop a sense of 'self-control without a loss of self-esteem'.

● Initiative versus guilt (3–5/6)

Physical, intellectual and social development are all happening very rapidly and the child is keen to try

out its developing abilities and skills to achieve all sorts of new goals. If the child is encouraged to ask questions and in other ways express its natural curiosity and is given the freedom to engage in physical activity, as well as to indulge in fantasy and other kinds of play, its sense of *initiative* will be reinforced. However, if parents tend to find the child's questions embarrassing, difficult intellectually or a nuisance, its motor activity dangerous and its fantasy play silly, then the child may come to feel *guilty* about intruding into others' lives and activities, which may inhibit its initiative and curiosity. This guilt can be exaggerated by the Oedipus complex, but whereas for Freud this is the central feature of this stage, for Erikson it is but one feature of a much wider theme.

● Industry versus inferiority (7–12)

Industry refers to the child's concern with how things work, how they are made and their own efforts to make things. This is reinforced when the child is encouraged by adults, who now are no longer confined to the parents. Teachers begin to assume a very real significance in the child's life and society requires them to help the child to develop all sorts of new skills valued by society. The peer group also assumes increasing importance relative to that of adults and is a major source of self-esteem; children begin to compare themselves with other children as a way of assessing their own achievements. Unfavourable comparisons, the unsuccessful completion of realistic tasks, not being allowed to make things and receiving the necessary guidance and encouragement from adults can contribute to a sense of *inferiority*.

Identity versus role confusion (12–18)

Throughout life, the individual has to try to maintain a balance between the constant (or invariant) and the changing (or variant) aspects of the self. But across the lifespan there are periods when the self-concept undergoes quite dramatic and extensive change, for example during toddlerhood or the 'terrible twos' (1½–3 years), when starting school (4–5) and adolescence (starting with puberty), and at these times the balance is much more difficult to maintain.

Remember that at all stages, Erikson believes that the individual exists and develops on three planes and levels simultaneously:

1 the biological (organism);
2 the social (member of society);
3 the psychological (individual).

We have already looked at how the *body image* changes in adolescence but a few of Erikson's observations are worth noting. He says that the rapid body growth disturbs the previous trust in the body and mastery of its functions that were enjoyed in childhood. So adolescents have to learn to 'grow into' their new body, but for a long time it will not feel comfortable and will not seem to 'fit' properly. Sexual maturity implies the need for other people to fulfil new sexual needs and feelings. Masturbation is very common, especially among boys, in early adolescence and is often accompanied by sexual fantasy, but it can never be totally fulfilling. The social and psychological counterpart of this is having to decide on a sexual identity, that is, deciding about one's sexual preference/orientation, i.e. whether to be heterosexual or homosexual.

At the *social* level, Western culture has invented adolescence as a moratorium, an authorized delay of adulthood (in the form of extended formal education, certain laws relating to marriage, voting and so on) which is aimed at helping the young person to make the difficult transition from childhood to adulthood.

Yet this delay often creates confusion and conflict at the same time as it reduces them. For example, social and biological abilities and status may not be compatible, as in the case of the 'gym-slip mother' or the teenager who is married and still at school. Teenagers are expected to make decisions about their future (by parents and teachers) but are not allowed to vote and generally they are being kept dependent on adults while being expected to behave like adults, in an independent and responsible way. If adolescents ask 'When do I become an adult?', they are likely to receive a different answer from a police officer, doctor, teacher, social worker and parent (Coleman, 1995).

If adolescents make their choices too early (what Erikson calls a *premature foreclosure* of the moratorium), this may be regretted and they become especially vulnerable to identity confusion in later life. Religious 'initiations', such as the Catholic confirmation and the Jewish bar-mitzvah, and any unquestioning adoption of parents' attitudes, values and lifestyle may limit young people, forcing them into a narrow identity, without having explored possible alternatives.

Marcia (1966, 1980), inspired by Erikson and based on his own research, identified four *statuses* of adolescent identity formation. To achieve a mature identity, the individual must: (a) experience several *crises* in exploring and choosing between life's alternatives; and (b) finally arrive at a *commitment*, an investment of the self in those choices. The four statuses are:

1 *Identity diffusion.* The person is in crisis and is unable to formulate clear self-definition, goals and commitments; it represents an inability to 'take hold' of some kind of adult identity.
2 *Identity foreclosure.* The person has avoided the uncertainties and anxieties of crisis by rapidly committing themselves to safe and conventional goals without exploring the many options open to the self.
3 *Identity moratorium.* Decisions about identity are postponed while the person tries out alternative identities without being committed to any particular one.
4 *Identity achievement.* The person has experienced a crisis but has emerged successfully with firm commitments, goals and ideology (see Fig. 21.5).

Unlike Erikson's eight stages, these four statuses are not sequential (they are not stages), with the exception that identity moratorium is a prerequisite for identity achievement. However, one American study

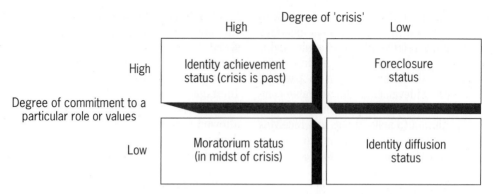

FIGURE 21.5 *The four identity statuses proposed by Marcia (based on Erikson's theory). To fully achieve identity, the young person must both examine his or her values or goals and reach a firm commitment. (Based on Marcia, 1980)*

by Meilman (1979, cited in Durkin, 1995) found that among 12–24-year-old males, these statuses were broadly age-related, i.e. younger men (12–18) tended to be classified as experiencing diffusion or foreclosure, while those over 18 were increasingly likely to be identity achievers. However, at all ages, only small proportions were experiencing moratorium, which is meant to represent the peak of the crisis. Marcia (1980) acknowledges that, when applied to females, his model and the identity status approach work 'only more or less'; this mirrors a criticism made of Erikson's claim that the sequence of stages applies equally to males and females (especially the transition from adolescence to young adulthood), namely that male experience is being taken as the standard (see Chapter 24).

Quite clearly, there is no well-defined initiation into adulthood in our culture as there is in many non-Western cultures where, at a certain age, ritualized puberty rites or initiation ceremonies take place, marking the end of childhood and the start of adulthood. For example, among some African hunter-gatherer peoples, adulthood is attained for males once they can participate successfully in the hunt and for females once they menstruate or become pregnant (Turnbull, 1989). In others, there may be a period of adolescence but its beginning or end may be clearly marked; an example of the former is nose-bleeding rites for males of the Sambia of Papua-New Guinea (Savin-Williams and Berndt, 1990, cited in Durkin, 1995) and the latter is illustrated among some Aboriginal communities by marriage and having children, often in the late teens (Burbank, 1988, cited in Durkin, 1995) While puberty is a biological fact, adolescence is very much a socially constructed phenomenon (see the discussion of adolescence below).

At the *psychological* level, the adolescent re-experiences the conflicts of early childhood, particularly the early encounter with parents as authority figures (focused around toilet training) and the Oedipus complex. Related to this are the typical adolescent mood swings and ambivalence, whereby they are sometimes very co-operative with parents and other adults and at other times 'dig in their heels' and disobey, almost for the sake of it (this ambivalence is also typical of the three-year-old). This is very difficult for parents to cope with, especially when they need to remain stable, firm and predictable for the sake of their adolescents.

As we shall see when discussing Piaget's theory of cognitive development in Chapter 25, adolescents, having obtained formal operational thought, can think in abstract and hypothetical terms about what might be (and not just about what exists), about other people's thinking and, particularly, what others think about them. They can conceive of ideal families, religions and societies, which can then be compared with what they have themselves experienced. They can also construct theories and philosophies designed to bring all the varied and conflicting aspects of society into a working, harmonious and peaceful whole. According to Elkind (1970), the adolescent is 'an impatient idealist, who believes that it is as easy to realize an ideal as it is to imagine it'.

Elkind also draws an intriguing parallel between the child and the adolescent in terms of *egocentrism*: even though adolescents are cognitively able to understand that their view of things is not the only possible way of things:

> Since he fails to differentiate between what others are thinking about and his own mental preoccupations ... he assumes that other people are as obsessed with his behaviour and appearance as he is himself. It is this belief that others are preoccupied

with his appearance and behaviour that constitutes the egocentrism of the adolescent. (Elkind, 1967)

He goes on to say that adolescents are forever playing to (imaginary) audiences, think they are special, have a sense of immortality and 'personal fable', a story which they tell themselves but which is not true.

The major developmental task of adolescence is to develop a sense of identity, i.e. to bring together all the things we have learned about ourselves as a son/daughter, brother/sister, friend, student and so on, plus all our past experiences, thoughts and feelings, to integrate these varied images of ourselves into a whole which makes sense and which has continuity with the past while preparing for the future. If young people are successful, they will emerge from this developmental stage with a sense of *psychosocial identity* (the positive component), a sense of who they are, where they have been and where they are going. The influence of parents is much more indirect than it has been in previous stages; it is more a question of how they influenced earlier stages rather than how they directly influence the search for identity. So, the more positive the outcome of the earlier stages, the more likely it is that the adolescent will achieve an integrated psychosocial identity.

Elkind (1970) points out that this will also depend on the social milieu in which the adolescent grows up. For example, in a society where women are second-class citizens, it may be more difficult for females to arrive at a sense of psychosocial identity (see Chapter 24). Likewise, at times of rapid social and technological change, such as the present, where there is a breakdown of many traditional values, it may be more difficult for young people to find continuity between what they learned and experienced as children and what they learn and experience as adolescents. This may lead them to seek causes (political, religious, humanistic) which give meaning and direction to their lives.

Typically, the adolescent will experiment with several different identities which may involve taking very extreme views on certain issues: whereas children merely play at social roles, the adolescent actually tries them out. *Identity confusion* (or *diffusion*, the negative component) has four major aspects:

1 *Intimacy*. Fear of commitment to, or involvement in, close relationships out of fear of losing one's own identity. This can result in stereotyped, formalized relationships or isolation.
2 *Time perspective*. Inability to plan for the future or retain any sense of time, associated with anxieties about change and becoming an adult.
3 *Industry*. Difficulty in channelling resources in a realistic way in work or study, both of which require commitment. As a defence, the adolescent may find it impossible to concentrate or become frenetically engaged in a single activity to the exclusion of all others.
4 *Negative identity*. Not knowing what you are, where you belong or to whom you belong. A negative identity (e.g. delinquent, punk), although clearly the exact opposite of what parents and other important adults would approve of, is not an act of rebellion but a way of achieving some identity – a negative identity may be better than having no identity at all.

Whatever the final outcome of this stage, Erikson believes that some form of stress or turmoil or disturbance of identity is inevitable: the adolescent identity crisis is a *normative crisis*. He says, 'At no other phase of the lifecycle are the pressures of finding oneself and the threat of losing oneself so closely allied'.

Erikson stresses that life is constant change and that confronting problems at one stage of life is no guarantee against the reappearance of these problems at later stages or against the finding of new solutions to them. As far as a sense of identity is concerned, the optimum time to achieve it is during adolescence. To have a sense of self-identity is to have a 'feeling of being at home in one's body, a sense of knowing where one is going and an inner assurance of anticipated recognition from those who count'.

● Work as a source of identity

Traditionally, the 'world of work' and the 'adult' world have been virtually synonymous and this is what most young people aim at, either through gaining relevant qualifications or by wanting to leave school at the earliest opportunity in order to assume adult status and to earn money and become self-supporting. At times of high unemployment, the purpose of schooling and young people's expectations regarding their entry into the adult world become much more blurred. Erikson (1968) believes that the jobs people choose play a major role in their representation of themselves to society and Durkin (1995) claims that of all the transitions of adolescence, preparation for adult work roles is particularly crucial to the direction and quality of the individual's future life.

According to Kelvin (1981), if work is crucial to an individual's self-concept, it will also be crucial to their relationships with others; as Brown (1978 cited in Kelvin, 1981) says, a person's work (or the fact that they do not or cannot work) tells us so much else about their social situation and likely life experiences.

Erikson claims that a state of acute identity confusion usually manifests itself at a time when the young person is faced with a combination of experiences which demand simultaneous commitment, including occupational choice. If such a choice is denied the school-leaver, the opportunity to engage in other activities vital to the development of a sense of personal identity may be denied as well. Failure to achieve identity may prevent the development of intimacy (along with work, the other major criterion of adulthood).

According to Hill (1977), one of the main problems for the young person out of work might be that unemployment extends the period of stay at home and increases dependence on parents at a time when the main psychosocial task is to achieve independence. For many young people, therefore, unemployment may represent an enforced and prolonged moratorium. What are the psychological consequences?

Jahoda (1979) believes that a change of economic status is not the only consequence of unemployment; a loss of structured activity, social contacts and a sense of identity and purpose are also suffered. Indeed, the young school-leaver is unlikely to experience a significant change of economic status at all (if anything they will be better off by becoming eligible for social security benefits) and yet their distress may be as great as that of any adult faced with redundancy. This lack of structure, etc. is, according to Kelvin (1981), a problem of 'not being in work' (as opposed to being unemployed as such) and its ill-effects are also found amongst the retired (see Chapter 24). Leisure activities are usually no substitute for the interdependence, on a continuing basis, which is the essence of most work relationships (Kelvin, 1981).

Stafford *et al.* (1980) studied school-leavers in the North of England and found that those who did not find work showed higher levels of minor psychiatric problems. Similar results were found by Banks and Jackson (1982). Youngsters were studied while still at school and after leaving and finding (or not finding) work and, while there were no significant differences between them prior to leaving school, the experience of unemployment increased symptoms. Similarly, Donovan *et al.* (1985) compared 800 15-year-olds while still at school and then again 6–8 months after leaving school and found that those who were unemployed showed the greatest number of psychological symptoms, had the lowest degree of satisfaction with their lives and experienced poorer family and social relationships; these differences held good after allowance was made for individual differences, gender, socioeconomic status and educational attainment.

● Evaluation of Erikson's theory

As we saw earlier, Erikson has emphasized the healthy personality in contrast to Freud, who stressed conflict and the neurotic personality. This difference stems largely from the importance of the ego and id in their respective theories (see Table 21.3).

In 1964, Erikson expanded his basic, 1959 picture of positive ego development by describing a set of human virtues or qualities of strength, representing an integration of psychosexual and psychosocial growth schedules. As can be seen from Table 21.4, they are based on the positive outcomes of each of the eight stages of development.

The criticisms made of Freud's methods of study and his biased and limited samples (see Chapter 29) cannot be made so easily against Erikson; he did not confine his studies to small numbers of neurotic adults from one particular culture but included much larger numbers of both disturbed and healthy individuals of all ages from a variety of cultures. Erikson was a psychoanalyst and teacher in Europe, a child analyst in Boston, he studied normal adolescents in California and spent time living among the Sioux Indians of South Dakota and the Yurok Indians of Northern California.

It was while working with the Indians that Erikson began to notice syndromes which he could not explain within the terms of Freudian theory. Central to many of the Indians' emotional problems was their sense of being uprooted and a lack of continuity between their present lifestyle and the one portrayed in the tribal history. This sense of a break with the past, and an inability to identify with a future requiring assimilation of white cultural values, is an ego-related and culture-related conflict and has little to do with sexual drives. These impressions were reinforced during the Second World War when Erikson worked at a war veterans' rehabilitation centre. He saw many soldiers who did not seem to fit the traditional 'shell shock' or 'malingerer' cases of the First World War; instead they seemed to have lost a sense of who and what they were. They suffered an 'identity confusion' – they could not reconcile what they had felt and done as soldiers with what they had known before the war.

One of Erikson's major innovations is his method of *psychohistory*, in which he applies his theory of the human lifecycle to the study of famous historical figures; after essays on Gorky, Shaw and Freud, he devoted whole books to Martin Luther (*Young Man Luther*, 1958) and Gandhi (*Gandhi's Truth*, 1969). According to Elkind (1970), teaching of Erikson's concepts is on the increase in psychology, psychiatry, education and social work. However, although researchers have found his theory rather difficult to test and not everyone agrees with the details of the theory, it is generally agreed that Erikson has inspired the 'lifespan' approach in developmental psychology.

OTHER THEORIES OF ADOLESCENCE

● What is adolescence?

The word 'adolescence' comes from the Latin *adolescere* meaning 'to grow into maturity'. Traditionally, this stage has been regarded as a prelude to and a preparation for adulthood, a transitional period of life between immaturity and maturity. While adolescence is usually taken to begin with puberty, the considerable individual variation in the timing of these physical changes makes it very difficult to define it in terms of chronological age (such as 'the teenage years'). Coleman (1995) believes that the difficulties involved in defining adolescence reflect an important feature of the phenomenon, namely, is it a stage that is to some extent artificially created?

In *Coming of Age in Samoa* (1928), Margaret Mead describes a society in which individuals pass from childhood to adulthood with no trauma or stress. Rites of passage enable boys and girls to be clear about when and how they should assume adult roles and responsibilities and there is no long transitional period or ambiguity of status. Although it is generally agreed that she viewed Samoan society through rose-coloured glasses, the feeling continues that Western society, through its emphasis on continued education and prolonged financial dependence on parents, encourages adolescence as a distinct period.

● Is adolescence something new?

Not only is adolescence seen by many as a creation of Western culture, but it is also thought to be a very recent 'invention' of Western capitalist society. For example, it is often claimed that the concept of the 'teenage years' was invented only after the end of the Second World War and came to public attention in the 1950s through films such as James Dean's 'Rebel Without a Cause'. Coleman (1995) disputes this, pointing out that adolescence has existed in one form or another since the ancient Greeks, such as Plato: 2000 years ago, the young were seen as the political force most likely to challenge the existing order. According to Shakespeare, the young were more likely to be 'wronging the ancientry' and 'getting wenches with child' than doing anything useful. Montemayor (1983, in Coleman) analysed parent-adolescent relationships from the 1920s to the 1980s and concluded that both the issues over which there was disagreement and the overall levels of conflict remained remarkably similar.

In spite of enormous social and economic changes in the 20th century, the phenomenon of adolescence has changed very little. While the term 'teenager' may have entered our vocabulary during the 1950s, adolescence itself has been around for very much longer; indeed, as we shall see below, the first formal psychological theory of adolescence appeared in 1904, so adolescence itself must have existed before that! While social and economic factors are clearly important and while adolescence may manifest itself differently according to cultural and historical context, some form of transitional stage is common to most societies (Coleman, 1995).

● Hall's recapitulation theory

Probably the earliest theory of adolescence was that of G. Stanley Hall in his book *Adolescence* (1904) and he is generally regarded as the father of adolescent psychology; he was also one of the pioneers of developmental psychology as a whole. Heavily influenced by Darwin's evolutionary theory, Hall believed that each individual's psychological development recapitulates the evolution of the human species, both biological and cultural. In the case of adolescence (12 to 25 years), he saw it as a time of storm and stress (or *Sturm und Drang*) which mirrors the volatile history of the human race during the past 2000 years. Although the theory is only of historical interest, it has become part of popular culture (Durkin, 1995), as well as contributing to the 'classical' theory of adolescence, both of which portray it as a 'problem age' (see below).

● Psychoanalytic theories

Both Sigmund Freud and his daughter, Anna, saw adolescence as a stage in which the balance within the personality of the child becomes disturbed. During the latency period, the id, ego and superego are in relative harmony, but the new id urges which arise at the genital stage (starting with puberty) are very powerful and the superego is 'in the melting pot', that is, there is a bid for independence (whereby the identification with the same-sex parent is weakened) but at the same time there is a renewed dependence on the opposite-sex parent. Adolescence involves a 'detachment from parental authority, a process that alone makes possible the opposition, which is so important for the progress of civilization, between the new generation and the old' (Freud, 1905). He observed that girls are less able to separate, persisting in their 'childish love far beyond puberty', which he later (1908) attributed to society's double standard by which young men are able to express their sexuality, while young women have theirs suppressed (Jacobs, 1992).

Anna Freud (in *The Ego and the Mechanisms of Defence*, 1937) believed that her father had overemphasized the development of sexuality early in life and neglected its adolescent manifestation. She also regarded the ego defence mechanisms (see Chapter 29) which were used prior to puberty as no longer adequate to deal with the upsurge of instincts. She identified two new adolescent defences: *asceticism,* whereby adolescents deprive themselves of pleasurable experiences and activities (particularly sexual ones); and *intellectualization,* whereby anxiety-provoking subjects are discussed and read about at great length (typically, adolescents spend more time talking about sex than enjoying it).

More recently, Blos (1967) has described adolescence as a 'second individuation process', i.e. the process of becoming a separate person (the first individuation process having occurred at the end of the child's third year). Adolescents disengage, i.e. renounce their dependency on the family and loosen early childhood ties which, until puberty, were the main source of emotional sustenance. This, in turn, produces 'affect and object hunger', a means of coping with the 'inner emptiness' which results from the breaking of childhood ties. Affect and object hunger are satisfied by group experiences (a family substitute); doing exciting things 'just for kicks'; frequent

and abrupt changes in relationships; and drug-induced and mystical experiences.

Disengagement also produces regression, which can take the form of 'hero worship' (of rock stars, sporting personalities, etc.) and the 'homosexual crush' (on a same-sex teacher or friend of the parents – both involving the search for substitute parents), absorption in politics, religion and philosophy, etc., and ambivalence. Ambivalence underlies relationships with parents in early childhood and involves a fluctuation between loving and hating, dependence and independence, co-operation and non-co-operation and so on. Ambivalence is reactivated in adolescence in an extreme form and accounts for much of the aggressive, negative and generally unpredictable behaviour which parents in particular, and adults in general, find so hard to understand. One form this may take is what Baittle and Offer (1971) call 'negative dependence', in which adolescents do the opposite of what the parents want, showing that they are still dependent on their parents but in a negative way. So although the behaviour is overtly an act of rebellion against the parents, at the same time it reveals that passive dependency longings are still in force (Coleman, 1995).

Blos believes that regression is actually necessary for progress to take place and the non-conformity of adolescents is, in fact, a very adaptive defence against the temptation to become dependent again on the parents and other adults. He also sees transient maladaptive behaviour (what Erikson calls the 'psychopathology of everyday adolescence') as inevitable.

● Does attachment to peers necessarily imply detachment from parents?

Based on Blos's theory, Steinberg and Silverberg (1986) devised a measure of *emotional autonomy* (defined in terms of the giving up of childish dependency on parents) and, based on a large sample of American 10–16-year-olds, found that as this increased, so resistance to peer pressure decreased, i.e. peers become a more powerful influence, especially between 11 and 13. The 'two social worlds' of home and peer group seemed to be inversely related, such that emotional dependency on parents is 'traded' for dependency on peers. Contrary to stereotypical expectations, girls are more autonomous with respect to their parents, but also more resistant to peer pressure, than boys.

However, Ryan and Lynch (1989) suggest that the emotional autonomy scale may be measuring emotional detachment and a subjective sense of parental rejection, rather than true independence: the higher individuals score, the *less* secure and connected they feel with their family. Rather than 'trading' parental dependency for peer dependency, those who become particularly dependent on peers are actually compensating for lack of emotional support at home. They found that the adolescents who were more securely attached to their parents also reported more emotional security with their friends: this group did not seem to be seeking compensation in their peer relationships. Ryan and Lynch concluded that 'Individuation is not something that happens from parents but rather with them' (see Chapter 21).

According to Hill (1993), the transition from childhood to adolescence reflects a subtle transformation of parent-child relationships rather than a revolution. Although some minor squabbles over everyday issues are quite common, '... changes in the way parents and adolescents relate and the achievement of autonomy take place against a backdrop of emotional closeness rather than emotional distancing ...'.

● Cultural relativism: the contribution of cultural anthropology

The theories of Ruth Benedict (1934, 1954) and Margaret Mead (1942, 1944, 1961) were partly a reaction against the instinct theories of Freud; any conflict, stress or problem experienced by young people cannot usefully be understood in isolation from the cultural norms and institutions to which they are related.

While it is universal for children to move from a state of dependence upon older people to relative independence, how this takes place varies greatly from one society to another. In some (such as the Cheyenne Indians studied by Benedict in 1934) the transition is smooth, gradual and continuous, e.g. a Cheyenne boy's hunting prowess is recognized by adults and his contribution to the feast is valued alongside the father's. However, in Western culture, many adult activities are forbidden to children and a great deal of behaviour which is thought appropriate for children must be 'unlearned' when we 'grow up'. We make fairly sharp distinctions between 'being mature' and 'being immature' and the unlearning which this involves produces inevitable strain which lies at the root of adolescent difficulties. Specifically, there are three types of discontinuity in Western culture, namely those centring around:

- *responsible and non-responsible roles*: this involves unlearning play attitudes when moving into the world of work;
- *dominant and submissive roles:* this involves unlearning submissive attitudes when assuming positions of authority;
- *sexual roles:* this involves unlearning the taboo on sex when moving into sexual relationships.

Although Mead (like Erikson) acknowledged the part played by biological changes at puberty, she believed that adolescent problems are mainly due to social factors, in particular the wide range of choices open to the individual in a rapidly changing world. If the primary task of adolescence is to establish a meaningful identity, the obstacles to doing this are greater now than ever before; there is no enduring frame of reference, no single set of values (religious, political, ideological, etc.) by which the adolescent can make sense of the world.

● Sociological theory (or the social psychological approach)

As summarized by Coleman (1995), sociologists see *role change* as an integral feature of adolescent development. Changing schools, leaving school to go to university, leaving home and starting a job all involve a new set of role relationships, producing different and often greater expectations; these, in turn, demand a substantial reassessment of the self-concept and speed up the process of socialization. This can be problematic because the adolescent is exposed to a wide variety of competing socialization agencies (family, school, peer group, mass media, etc.) representing often conflicting values and demands.

Sociologists commonly assume that young people's socialization depends more on the generation than on the family or other social institutions, what Marsland (1987) calls 'auto-socialization'.

> The crucial social meaning of youth is withdrawal from adult control and influence compared with childhood. Peer groups are the milieu into which young people withdraw ... this withdrawal ... is, within limits, legitimated by the adult world ...'
> (Marsland, 1987, quoted in Coleman, 1995)

What Marsland is describing is the 'generation gap'.

● The 'classical' theory of adolescence

All the theories we have considered so far, including Erikson's, have contributed to the 'classical' picture of adolescence; this has three main components:

1 storm and stress;
2 identity crisis;
3 the generation gap.

We shall now consider the evidence relevant to each of these three components.

Storm and stress

Several studies have concluded that adolescence is not a period which typically involves stress, tension and emotional turmoil. One such study is summarized in Box 21.9.

The National Children's Bureau study (1976) of all the 16-year-olds born in a single week in 1958 in England, Scotland and Wales (over 14,000 of them) concluded that it is a 'difficult' age, at least for parents. Parents most often described their 16-year-olds as solitary, then came irritable ('quick to fly off the handle'), then 'fussy or overparticular'. Very few were described as destructive or aggressive to others or frequently disobedient; 12 percent were thought to be untruthful on some occasions; 2 percent still sucked their thumbs; 3 percent suffered emotional problems; 15 percent were nail-biters; 11 percent suffered from migraine or recurrent headaches; 3 percent had a stammer or stutter and 1 percent were still wetting the bed (Fogelman, 1976).

According to Offer (1969), the large majority of adolescents adjust well to the transition of adolescence, are in touch with their feelings and develop meaningful relationships with significant others; they lack the turmoil of the disturbed adolescent precisely because their ego is strong enough to withstand the pressures. Similarly, Siddique and D'arcy (1984) found that 33.5 percent of adolescents surveyed

reported no symptoms of psychological distress and another 39 percent reported five or fewer symptoms (a mild level of distress). While for a minority it does indeed appear to be a period of stress and turmoil (27.5 percent reported higher levels of psychological distress), for the majority, the adolescent transition will be relatively smooth.

Identity crisis

Many of Erikson's ideas surrounding identity crisis are difficult to test empirically, but many researchers have used measures of the self-concept (in particular, self-esteem) as indicators of crisis.

We have already discussed self-esteem in relation to body image, including early and late maturation and satisfaction with body weight, particularly in girls; we have also discussed the effects of being out of work on self-esteem and general mental health.

Simmons and Rosenberg (1975) found that lowered self-esteem is more common during early adolescence than either late childhood or later adolescence and this was more evident in girls than boys. For example, 32 percent of 12–14-year-old girls had lower self-esteem (26 percent of boys) and 43 percent of girls had a more unstable self-image (30 percent of boys). (The sample comprised nearly 2000 school-age children.) Half the prepubescent girls were satisfied with their physical appearance, compared with only one-quarter of the early adolescents.

However, most studies seem to paint a rather different picture. For example, based on the use of the Offer Self-Image Questionnaire, Offer *et al.* (1981) concluded that there seems to be no increase in the disturbance of the self-image during early adolescence.

Coleman and Hendry (1990) take the view that while such disturbance is more likely in the early adolescent years (around puberty) than later on in adolescence, only a relatively small proportion of the total adolescent population are likely to have a negative self-image or to have very low self-esteem.

The generation gap

In the National Children's Bureau study, the majority of parents and 16-year-olds reported harmonious family relationships; only 3 percent of the teenagers were totally against marriage and the vast majority believed the ideal age for getting married is between 20 and 25 with two children as the ideal family. Parents were given a list of issues on which it is commonly thought that adults and 16-year-olds might

---

BOX 21.9   Key study: Growing up sane on the Isle of Wight

In a study of adolescents on the Isle of Wight, Rutter et al. (1976) found hardly any difference in the number of ten-year-olds, 14-year-olds and adults who were judged as having psychiatric disorders (10.9 percent, 12.5 percent and 11.9 percent, respectively) and a substantial proportion of those 14-year-olds with problems had had them since childhood. Again, when difficulties did first appear during adolescence, they were mainly associated with stressful situations, such as parents' marital discord. Only 20 percent of teenagers agreed with the statement 'I often feel miserable or depressed'.

	OFTEN %	SOMETIMES %	NEVER OR HARDLY EVER %
Choice of same -sex friends	3	16	81
Choice of opposite-sex friends	2	9	89
Dress or hairstyle	11	35	54
Time of coming in at night or going to bed	8	26	66
Places visited in own time	2	9	89
Doing homework	6	18	76
Smoking	6	9	85
Drinking	1	5	94

TABLE 21.5 *Disagreement between parents and study child (parents' report) (N=11,521)*

disagree. The results indicated a situation which was, from the parents' point of view, a harmonious one (Table 21.5). The 16-year-olds confirmed their parents' attitudes – appearance and evening activities were sometimes issues of disagreement in the home, but otherwise the atmosphere was free from major conflict (Table 21.6).

About two-thirds of those with siblings said they quarrelled between themselves, yet many wrote a qualifying note to the effect that although they might often quarrel with a brother or sister or disagree with their parents, this did not mean there was anything wrong with the underlying relationship (Fogelman, 1976).

In a large cross-cultural study (conducted in Australia, Bangladesh, Hungary, Israel, Taiwan, Italy, Turkey, the US and the former West Germany), Offer *et al.* (1988) found that over 91 percent of teenagers in each country denied holding grudges against their parents and similar proportions rejected the idea that parents were ashamed of them or would be disappointed in them in the future.

There seems to be little doubt that the extreme view of a generation gap involving a 'war' between the generations or a separate adolescent subculture is basically a myth. However, it would be just as inaccurate to deny that there is any conflict: adolescents could not grow into adults unless they were able to test out the boundaries of authority, nor could they discover what they believe unless given the opportunity to push hard against the beliefs of others (Coleman, 1995).

● So what conclusions can we draw about the 'classical' theory in the light of the evidence?

According to Coleman and Hendry (1990), research provides little support for the 'classical' account: while there is certainly some change in the self-concept, there is no evidence to show that any but a small minority experience a serious identity crisis. In most cases, relationships with parents are positive and constructive and young people do not reject adult values in favour of those espoused by the peer group. In fact, in most situations, peer group values appear to be consistent with those of important adults, rather than in conflict with them. Fears of promiscuity among the young are not borne out by the research findings, nor do studies support the belief that the peer group encourages antisocial behaviour. Nor is there any evidence to suggest that during the adolescent years there is a higher level of psychopathology than at other times: although a small minority may show disturbance, the great majority of teenagers seem to cope well and to show no undue signs of turmoil or stress.

So if the 'classical' view and empirical data present two contradictory pictures, how can we reconcile them? Coleman and Hendry's solution, essentially, is to see the truth as lying somewhere between these two versions:

● Psychoanalytic theories have tended to be based upon clinical data, so that a distorted picture of

	VERY TRUE %	TRUE %	UNCERTAIN %	UNTRUE %	VERY UNTRUE %
I get on well with my mother	41	45	8	4	1
I get on well with my father	35	45	13	5	2
I often quarrel with a brother or sister	23	43	10	19	5
My parents have strong views about my appearance (e.g. dress, hairstyle, etc.)	15	33	19	27	6
My parents want to know where I go in the evening	27	51	8	11	3
My parents disapprove of some of my male friends	9	19	18	37	16
My parents disapprove of some of my female friends	5	15	18	40	22

TABLE 21.6 *Family relationships (children's report) (N = 11,045)*

the 'typical' adolescent emerges from an atypical sample of emotionally disturbed patients, specifically, an overestimation of the degree of distress experienced by young people.

- Sociologists must disentangle the concepts of 'youth'/the youth movement from notions about young people themselves: youth should not be used as a metaphor for social change and we must not confuse radical forces in society with the beliefs of ordinary young people.
- Certain adolescent behaviours (e.g. vandalism/drugs/hooliganism, etc.) are extremely threatening to adults; the minority involved in such activities, therefore, attain undue prominence in the public eye, especially through the mass media. This sensationalism makes those behaviours seem very much more common than they really are.
- Large-scale surveys tend to neglect the possibility that individual adolescents may be either unwilling or unable to reveal their innermost feelings. It

is very difficult for a shy, resentful or anxious teenager to share fears, worries or conflicts with a strange interviewer. This kind of inhibition may result in an underestimation of the degree of stress experienced by young people. So there may be methodological causes of the widening of the gap between theory and research, i.e. research workers are missing more subtle indications of emotional tension.

Coleman and Hendry (1990) go on to discuss the *need* for a theory of adolescence. Both psychoanalysis and sociology have contributed theories which are still relevant: they have provided the foundation for an understanding of young people with serious problems and of those who belong to minority or deviant groups. However, adolescence needs a theory not of abnormality but of normality; it must account for the fact that, although for some young people adolescence may be a difficult time, for the majority it is a period of relative stability. The transition from childhood and adulthood cannot be achieved without substantial adjustments of both a psychological and social nature and yet most young people appear to cope without undue stress. How do they do it? One answer is Coleman's focal theory.

● Coleman's focal theory

The *focal theory* (1974, 1978, 1979, 1980) was based on a study of 800 boys and girls at ages 11, 13, 15 and 17. They were given a set of identical tests dealing with self-image, being alone, heterosexual relationships, parental relationships, friendships and large group situations. Attitudes towards all these issues changed as a function of age but, more importantly, concerns about different issues reached a peak at different ages for both sexes (Figure 21.6 only shows data for boys).

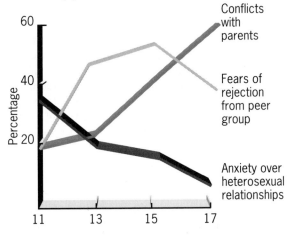

FIGURE 21.6 *Peak ages for the expression of different themes (boys only). (From Coleman & Hendry, 1990).*

At different ages, particular sorts of relationship patterns come into focus (i.e. they are the most prominent), but no pattern is specific to one age only. Patterns overlap and there will also be individual differences, so that just because an issue is not the predominant feature of a particular age does not mean that it will not be critical for some individuals. In order to adjust to so much potentially stressful change and at the same time to do this with relative stability, the adolescent copes by dealing with one issue at a time: they spread the process of adaptation over a span of years, attempting to resolve first one issue and then the next. Different problems and relationship issues come into focus and are tackled at different stages, so that the stresses resulting from the need to adapt to new modes of behaviour are

rarely concentrated all at one time. It follows from this that it is precisely in those who, for whatever reason, do have more than one issue to cope with at a time that problems are most likely to occur (Coleman and Hendry, 1990).

● Evaluation of focal theory

It is directly based on empirical evidence and helps to reconcile the apparent contradiction between the 'classical' and empirical views. While it needs further testing, some writers regard it as an important contribution to the theoretical understanding of adolescence (Siddique and D'arcy, 1984; Meadows, 1986). Kroger (1985) replicated Coleman's (1974) research on large US and New Zealand samples and found almost identical patterns of development in the three countries.

Simmons and Blyth (1987) tested the hypothesis that those who adjust less well during adolescence are likely to be those facing more than one interpersonal issue at a time and found strong support for focal theory, especially if change occurs at too young an age, if it causes the individual to be extremely off-time in development, if change is marked by sharp discontinuity and if many significant changes accumulate and occur close together in time.

A way of coping is to see certain issues as residing in the future, so that they do not have to be dealt with now. Porteous (1984) showed that for 12–16-year-olds living in the North of England and Eire, problems which are prevalent in early adolescence (e.g. about rules, permissiveness, adult criticism, bullying and friendships) decline and are replaced by worries about employment and, in some cases, worries about their worth as an individual. Coleman and Hendry (1990) conclude by saying that:

> ... most young people pace themselves through the adolescent transition. Most of them hold back on one issue, while they are grappling with another. Most sense what they can and cannot cope with, and will, in the real sense of the term, be an active agent in their own development.

CHAPTER SUMMARY

● Freud's theory of psychosexual development is closely related to the rest of his psychoanalytic theory as well as to psychoanalysis. Freud, who was trained as a neurologist, was influenced by Helmholtz, Brücke, Charcot and Breuer in his search for psychological explanations of his patients' symptoms.

- According to Freud, the psychic apparatus consists of the id, ego and superego.

- The id represents the biologically determined , presocialized part of the personality, which is governed by the pleasure principle. It is capable of primary process thinking, which underlies all forms of fantasy and wish fulfilment.

- The ego is the rational, decision-making 'executive' of the personality, which uses secondary process thinking and is governed by the reality principle. Like the id, it is amoral but, unlike the id, it is capable of deferred gratification, taking into account the consequences of the act.

- The superego is the moral or judicial branch of the personality, comprising the conscience and the ego-ideal; these are the source of guilt and self-esteem respectively.

- Freud believed that conflict is inevitable; this may be between the ego and external reality (external/reality conflict), the ego and the id (neurotic conflict) or the ego and the superego (moral conflict).

- Although Freud's theory is called an instinct theory, it would be more accurate to call it a 'drive' theory; he also stressed the role played by the reactions of significant others. He distinguished between *eros* (the life instincts), including sexuality, and *thanatos* (the death instincts), including aggression.

- Freud's theory of infantile sexuality conflicts with the Victorian view of sexuality in terms of the source, impetus, aim and object of sexual feelings; for Freud, these are present at birth and pass through a series of predetermined, psychosexual stages, i.e. the oral, anal, phallic, latency and genital. At each stage , sexual needs become focused on a different erogenous zone.

- Freud defined sexuality in an unusually broad way, taking into account adult perversions and observations of normal adult and infant sexual behaviours.

- Early experience will affect later personality and behaviour through fixation; the form it takes will depend on whether the child experienced extreme gratification or deprivation and at what particular stage.

- The most important aspect of psychosexual development is the Oedipus complex, which occurs during the phallic stage. With boys, fear of castration/castration anxiety helps resolve the complex through identification with the aggressor (the father), but girls believe they have already been castrated and experience penis envy; tentatively, Freud proposed that they identify with the mother through anaclitic identification.

- Freud's Oedipal theory has been criticized on the grounds that it is not universal but there is some empirical support, as well as indirect evidence, such as the interpretation of fairy tales. Freud's own evidence includes his case studies, but only one of these, little Hans, involved a child. The importance of this case is matched by its flaws and it has been subjected to alternative interpretations by Fromm and Bowlby.

- There is considerable controversy surrounding the seduction theory, which predated the theory of infantile sexuality. Instead of ditching the former for the latter out of cowardice, it seems that Freud doubted its validity, partly because of the way he elicited memories of abuse from his patients.

- Self-awareness allows us to see ourselves as others see us. Our self-concept refers to our perception of our personality; it consists of the self-image (including social roles, personality traits and body image/bodily self), self-esteem and ideal self. It can also be defined in terms of a complex set of self-schemata, which themselves include an array of possible selves.

- A major theoretical approach to the self is symbolic interactionism, associated mainly with Mead. He was influenced by James's 'I'/'me' distinction and belief in multiple selves and by Cooley's theory of the 'looking-glass self', but he denied that the self is mentalistic, seeing it as a process of social interaction. It develops through role taking, in particular, taking the perspective of the 'generalized other' in the context of the child's play.

- Based on Mead, many sociologists and social psychologists see language as fundamental to how the self is constructed. Our language provides stories or accounts of what being a person is like ('discourses') and these differ between cultures; the view of people as independent, self-contained individuals is a relatively recent invention of Western, individualist cultures.

- Two major influences on the development of the self-concept are the reaction of others and comparison with others. Much of the relevant research is consistent with the theories of James, Cooley and Mead.

- The self-concept develops in fairly regular, predictable ways. During the first few months, the existential self emerges, but the bodily self is probably the first aspect of the self-concept to develop. This has been studied through self-recognition, particularly visual, as in mirror recognition, which appears at about 18 months; this ability is also found in chimps.

- Self-definition is related to the use of language, including the use of labels, such as names. By 3½–4, children seem to have a basic understanding of a psychological self (or 'theory of mind'). Age and gender are two basic features of the categorical self; this changes from being described in physical to more psychological terms during middle childhood through to adolescence.

- With puberty, body image changes dramatically and the timing of the adolescent growth spurt can have an important effect on self-esteem. In boys, early maturers have a distinct advantage, while early-maturing girls have less positive body images. Girls in general are more dissatisfied with their physical appearance, reflecting normal weight gain and society's norms for thinness and physical attractiveness. Anorexia nervosa is suffered mainly by 16–19-year-old girls.

- Erikson's psychosocial theory has much in common with Freud's theory, but he saw development as continuing throughout the life cycle, and was more concerned with ego development. Despite his epigenetic principle, the social-cultural environment has a significant influence on development.

- Each psychosocial stage centres around a crisis, involving a struggle between two conflicting personality outcomes, one positive (adaptive), the other negative (maladaptive), e.g. basic trust versus basic mistrust; healthy development involves the former outweighing the latter. Each stage represents the optimum time for the development of the associated personality quality.

- Trust versus mistrust is followed by autonomy versus shame and doubt, initiative versus guilt, industry versus inferiority and identity versus role confusion. At all stages, the individual is an organism, member of society and individual; this corresponds to the biological, social and psychological level respectively.

- At the social level, Western culture has invented adolescence as a moratorium, designed to help with the transition to adulthood. But this can cause confusion and adolescents may be forced into making a 'premature foreclosure'. This is one of four statuses of adolescent identity formation which, according to Marcia, relate to the dimensions of crisis and commitment.

- Adolescents typically experience ambivalence, are able to think about things they have not actually experienced and display a form of egocentrism. Their main developmental task is to form an integrated sense of themselves as an individual, i.e. to achieve a greater sense of identity than identity diffusion.

- Work represents a major source of identity; being out of work extends the adolescent's dependence on the parents, represents a lack of structured time and increases the risk of psychiatric problems.

- Compared with Freud, Erikson used a much wider range of methods with a much more representative sample of human beings in formulating his lifespan developmental theory.

- There is considerable debate as to whether adolescence is a recent invention of Western capitalist society. But even if reference to 'teenagers' is recent, it seems that 'the youth' have always been considered a distinct social group and adolescence has changed very little during the 20th century, despite major social and economic changes.

- The first formal psychological theory of adolescence was Hall's recapitulation theory, which portrayed it as a period of storm and stress.

- Psychoanalytic theory stresses the powerful sexual urges of puberty at the start of the genital stage. The psychic balance of latency is disrupted and new ego defences are needed to deal with the upsurge of instincts.

- Blos sees it as a second individuation process, in which adolescents disengage from their emotional dependency on parents. This implies a 'trading' of parental dependency for dependency on the peer group, the 'two social worlds' being seen as opposed, but this may only be true of those who lack emotional support at home.

- Benedict sees adulthood in Western cultures as involving the unlearning of much of what is learned as a child; this discontinuity lies at the root of adolescent problems. Mead stresses the rapid social change in Western culture and the resulting lack of an enduring value system.

- Sociologists focus on the role change that is part and parcel of adolescence; this brings the adolescent into contact with competing demands, including those made by the peer group, and one 'solution' is the creation of the 'generation gap'.

- Storm and stress, identity crisis and the generation gap together constitute the 'classical' theory of adolescence. However, the empirical evidence fails to support this picture. Although a small minority may experience lower self-esteem and emotional disturbance, the large majority enjoy positive relationships with parents and manage the transition without major crisis.

● Psychoanalysis and sociology may help to account for young people with serious problems or who belong to deviant groups, but they cannot do justice to the normal majority. Focal theory explains why most adolescents cope without undue stress by seeing different issues peaking at different times during adolescence, so that the process of adaptation is spread over a number of years. Empirical evidence shows that those who adjust less well are having to face a number of changes all at the same time.

GLOSSARY

Ambivalence Opposed feelings of love/hate, co-operation/rebellion, etc. typical of both adolescents and 2–3-year-olds. In adolescents, can be seen as 'negative dependence'.

Anaclitic identification Becoming what someone else wishes you to be in order to keep them 'alive' inside yourself. Girls identify with their mothers to ensure that she continues to love them.

Auto-eroticism Directing one's sexual drive towards one's own body (as in masturbation).

Discourses 'Stories' or accounts used for talking about what it is like to be a human being, widely shared within a culture and shaping the way we experience ourselves as people.

Ego The conscious part of the personality, referred to by 'I'/'me', which plans, decides, thinks logically and rationally, taking into account the consequences of actions. Governed by the reality principle. Capable of deferred gratification.

Epigenetic principle Based on embryology, Erikson's belief that it is human nature to pass through a genetically predetermined sequence of psychosocial stages.

Erogenous zones Parts of the body which become particularly sexually sensitive at different psychosexual stages. Also called erotogenic zones.

External conflict Conflict created when the ego is threatened by something in the outside world (e.g. a falling tree). Also called reality conflict.

Fixation Getting 'stuck' at a particular psychosexual stage, either as a result of excessive overindulgence or extreme deprivation. May manifest itself as a particular personality type (e.g. the 'anal personality') or particular behaviours (e.g. smoking).

Focal theory Coleman's theory, according to which adolescents spread the process of adaptation over a number of years, thereby avoiding crisis.

Id The biologically determined, presocialized part of the personality, present at birth, governed by the pleasure principle. Demands immediate gratification.

Ideal self The kind of person we would like to be. Also called ego-ideal/idealized self-image.

Identification with the aggressor Making someone else's personality, values, etc. part of oneself, motivated by fear of that person. Boys identify with their fathers from fear of castration.

Infantile sexuality The theory that babies and young children have sexual needs and are capable of experiencing sexual pleasure.

Looking-glass self Cooley's theory, according to which the self is reflected in the reactions of others, i.e. their judgements and evaluations of our behaviour and appearance.

Moral conflict Conflict created when the ego feels threatened by punishment from the superego.

Moratorium Erikson's view of adolescence as an authorized delay of adulthood.

Neurotic conflict Conflict created when the ego fears being overwhelmed by the id's demands for gratification.

Oedipus complex The young child's intense attraction towards the opposite-sex parent and the resulting jealousy and hatred of the same-sex parent. This happens during the phallic stage.

Primary process The only form of thinking that the id is capable of, in which an image of a desired object is formed; the image cannot be distinguished from the real object.

Psychic apparatus Freud's term for the personality as a whole, comprising the id, ego and superego (the tripartite theory of personality structure).

Psychological self The private, thinking part of the person which is not visible to others, as distinct from the bodily self, which is. Relates to 'theory of mind'.

Recapitulation theory Hall's view that every individual's psychological development retraces the evolution of the human species; adolescence is a time of storm and stress, mirroring the volatile history of the human race.

Second individuation process Blos's theory of adolescence in which the adolescent becomes a separate person by disengaging from emotional dependency on the parents.

Secondary process A form of thinking by the ego, which corresponds roughly to the cognitive processes of perception, memory, attention, reasoning and problem solving.

Seduction theory Freud's original contention that adult neurosis is caused by actual child sexual abuse; predecessor to the Oedipal theory.

Self-concept All the ways in which an individual perceives his or her personality. Comprises self-image, self-esteem and ideal self.

Self-esteem How worthwhile a person we think we are, how much we value ourselves. Also called self-worth/self-regard.

Self-image The kind of person we think we are. Includes bodily self/body image, personality traits and social roles.

Self-schemata Stored representations of ourselves, which together make up the self-concept. Include possible selves.

Superego The moral or 'judicial' part of the personality, comprising the conscience (source of guilt) and the ego-ideal (source of pride/self-esteem). The 'heir' to the Oedipus complex.

Symbolic interactionism Mead's theory of self, according to which humans act towards things in terms of their meanings, which are learned through communication. Sharing a common language helps us to look at the world from others' perspectives (i.e. role taking).

FURTHER READING

Durkin, K. (1995) *Developmental Social Psychology: From Infancy to Old Age*. Oxford; Blackwell. An extremely lucid and often witty as well as thorough textbook that brings together social and developmental psychology, from lifespan perspective. Chapters 9, 15 and 16 are especially relevant here.

22

ATTACHMENT AND SEPARATION: THE EFFECTS OF EARLY EXPERIENCE

INTRODUCTION AND OVERVIEW

The study of attachments and their loss or disruption is an important way of trying to understand how early experience can affect later experience. Although a central assumption in Freud's psychoanalytic theory is that experience in the first five years largely determines the kind of adult we become (see Chapters 21 and 29), it is really only since the 1950s that developmental psychologists have systematically studied the nature and importance of the child's tie to its mother.

A common assumption made about children is that they have a fundamental need for parents/parent figures, especially a mother (-figure). But children can be attachment figures for each other

Probably the single most influential figure in the area of attachment theory and research is the English psychiatrist John Bowlby. He was commissioned by the World Health Organization (WHO) to investigate the effects on children's development of being brought up in orphanages and other institutions (in the aftermath of the Second World War) and he published his findings in *Maternal Care and Mental Health* in 1951. The central concept of his report was that of *maternal deprivation* which is actually a misnomer (Rutter, 1981) but which has become almost synonymous with all the harmful effects of growing up outside a family context.

Bowlby's WHO report was popularized as *Child Care and the Growth of Love* (1953), which Holmes (1993) claims is not just a scientific work but is also a landmark social document: what marks it out in the history of social reform is its emphasis on psychological as opposed to economic, nutritional, medical or housing difficulties as a root cause of social unhappiness. Although many of his claims of the importance of the mother-child relationship are criticized for being at best exaggerated, and at worst false and politically very reactionary, they need to be understood in the context of postwar Europe and America, just as the world was horrified in the 1990s by the revelation of the squalor and emotional deprivation in the Romanian orphanages (Holmes, 1993).

Bowlby's work has had an enormous impact on social work policy, legislation relating to children, psychiatry and psychology. He was trained as a psychoanalyst but was enormously influenced in his attachment theory by the work of the ethologists, especially in their study of imprinting. In recent years, the 'rediscovery' of fathers as attachment figures has been made by developmental psychologists and, more recently still, attachment theory has been applied to adult sexual relationships, which is ironic, given that it was always meant to apply across the lifecycle. Relating adult attachment style to parenting received as a child represents another way of investigating the effects of early experience.

WHAT DO WE MEAN BY ATTACHMENTS AND WHY ARE THEY SO IMPORTANT?

According to Ainsworth (1989), who, along with Bowlby, is probably the key figure in the field, an attachment is an affectional bond that is a '... relatively long-enduring tie in which the partner is important as a unique individual and is interchange-able with none other'. While this definition applies whenever in the lifecycle an attachment is formed, the first relationship is generally regarded as crucial for healthy development because it acts as a model (or prototype) of all later relationships. For example, Freud (1938, 1969) declared the mother's status as 'unique, without parallel, established unalterably for a whole lifetime as the first and strongest love-object as the prototype of all later love-relations'. Erikson (1950) believes that what the infant learns through its interaction with its mother is a sense of basic trust or basic mistrust of the world in general and other people in particular.

Bowlby (1951) maintained that 'mother love in infancy and childhood is as important for mental health as are vitamins and proteins for physical health'. More recently (1969, 1973), he has gone so far as to suggest that individuals with any kind of psychiatric disorder *always* show a disturbance in their social relationships (affectional bonding) and that, in many cases, this has been caused by disturbed bonding (selective attachment) in childhood. While all affectional bonds have in common the desire to maintain closeness to the partner, a unique feature of attachments is that the attachment figure provides a sense of security and comfort (a safe/secure base) for approaching what is unfamiliar, unknown and even threatening (Ainsworth, 1989).

Some of the key questions that we shall be asking in the rest of this chapter are :

- Do attachments always and inevitably develop between every mother and child or does it depend, at least to some extent, on the quality of the mothering the child receives?
- When attachments are formed, does it happen immediately or over a period of time?
- Can a child be attached to only one person at a time (i.e. the mother) or can it have multiple attachments, and how important are fathers as attachment figures?
- How do psychologists explain the formation of attachments?
- Is there a critical or sensitive period for the development of attachments and what are the effects of failing to develop an attachment?
- What are the short- and long-term effects of separation from attachment figures?
- How does attachment theory help us understand our adult sexual relationships?

THE GRADUAL DEVELOPMENT OF ATTACHMENTS

According to Schaffer (1977, 1989), social development in infancy may be thought of in terms of three basic steps:

1 From about six weeks, babies develop an attraction to other human beings in preference to inanimate features of the environment. As we saw in Chapter 10, it is initially the complexity of a stimulus which attracts babies rather than its 'human-ness', but then they begin to smile more at human faces and voices,. The first 'social smile', therefore, occurs at about six weeks and this stage continues until about three months.

2 Starting at about three months, infants begin to distinguish different human beings, so that the parent is recognized as familiar and strangers as unfamiliar, as shown by its smiling, for example. However, the baby still allows other people to handle and look after it without becoming noticeably upset; people are still largely interchangeable (i.e. equivalent) so long as they provide adequate care. This stage of *indiscriminate attachment* lasts until about seven or eight months.

3 Starting at about seven or eight months, the baby actively seeks the proximity of certain individuals and becomes distressed when separated from them (the baby 'misses' them) (Schaffer and Emerson, 1964). At around the same time, the baby avoids proximity with other, unfamiliar people and displays the fear response to strangers (Schaffer, 1966). However, the mere presence of a stranger is not usually sufficient to induce this fear response – some direct contact is usually necessary. (By contrast, the mere presence of the mother may offer the young child enough security for it to explore and investigate a strange environment; see below.) This sensitivity to what the stranger is doing could be seen as indicating an evolved, preprogrammed defence mechanism, whereby the more energetic the approach of a stranger, the greater the risk that some threat is entailed (Durkin, 1995). This is the stage of *specific attachment.*

So while the developmental course of attachment formation takes place over quite a prolonged period, the actual onset of separation distress and fear of strangers is usually quite rapid (Schaffer, 1989).

● Attachments and attachment behaviour

As we have seen, starting at about six weeks, babies show a general tendency to want to be close to people and at first this is directed towards anyone who happens to be around; if familiar figures are absent, babies will soon seek new attachments to other people (Robertson and Robertson, 1971). In infancy and early childhood, attachment is shown primarily by four kinds of behaviour:

1 seeking to be near the other person;
2 showing distress on separation from that person;
3 showing joy or relief on reunion;

4 being generally oriented towards the person, even when not in close proximity (through listening for the person's voice, watching what they do, getting their attention by showing them toys and so on).

So an attachment can be thought of as directing attachment behaviours to a particular individual (or individuals) fairly consistently and regularly over a period of time.

This distinction between attachments and attachment behaviours is important for understanding how attachments can differ. The *strength* of an attachment refers to the intensity with which attachment behaviours are displayed, while the *security* of an attachment refers to how confident the child is of the attachment figure being there when needed and being able to use her (or him) as a safe base from which to explore in a strange environment. How are strength and security related?

Sometimes they are inversely related. For example, Tizard and Rees (1974) found that four-year-old children reared in institutions showed more clinging and following behaviour than family-reared children but were less likely to show selective attachment or deep relationships: although they seemed to be closely attached to someone, they did not seem to care at all when the person left, which seemed to be a defensive reaction to many experiences of loss. When these children were two (Tizard and Tizard, 1971), they were very clinging, would run and climb on the lap of anybody they knew even slightly and in this respect were much more like 12–18-month-olds. When first meeting strangers, they were very shy and frightened but were much more affectionate to a much wider range of people whom they knew just a little compared with most two-year-olds.

Rosenblum and Harlow (1963) found that rejected infant monkeys showed very strong attachments to rejecting 'mothers' – the monkeys were isolated at birth and reared in a cage with a 'cloth mother' which at random intervals blasted the clinging baby with a strong current of compressed air. These 'blasted' infants spent more time clinging to the surrogate (substitute) mother than controls whose cloth mothers did not abuse them in this way. Similar results were found when infant monkeys were abused by their mothers (who themselves had been 'reared' from birth with surrogate mothers). Harlow's experiments are discussed further below.

It seems that the very act of 'rejection' results in more clinging which, in turn, results in more rejection and this pattern of interaction can be seen in the strength of attachment and loyalty of many abused children. Anxiety appears to increase attachment behaviour regardless of the response of the attachment object.

There are also examples of a positive relationship between strength and security. For instance, Stayton and Ainsworth (1973) found that children of sensitive, responsive mothers showed more positive greeting on reunion and following (suggesting stronger attachments) than those shown by children of insensitive, unresponsive mothers, but that the former showed less crying and distress on separation (suggesting more secure attachments; see below).

As we noted earlier, the whole purpose of attachment is to enable the child to feel secure in strange environments, to move further away from the mother, both literally and emotionally, so that attachment behaviours are reduced and exploration and independence increase; this is known as *detachment*. Normally, we would expect attachment behaviour to be at its peak between 12 and 18 months (although, according to Maccoby (1980), it is quite common up to 24 months) and to decline gradually after that. According to Rutter (1981), the aim of attachment is detachment, but for this to happen the bonds must be secure.

● The study of attachments: the 'Strange Situation'

Ainsworth and her colleagues (Ainsworth *et al.*, 1971, 1978) devised a method of studying attachments called the 'Strange Situation', which allows for the collection of multiple measures in the course of a standarized series of events. It consists of a sequence of eight episodes in which the mother (and/or the father) and a stranger come and go from the room, each episode lasting about three minutes. The sequence of comings and goings is predetermined and is the same for all the children and so involves controlled observation: one or more trained observers record the child's attachment behaviour in the mother's presence, when she leaves, when she returns, how the child responds to the stranger and how the child's play is affected throughout. The whole sequence is summarized in Box 22.1.

According to Ainsworth *et al.*, the crucial feature of the mother's behaviour towards her child which is associated with different attachment styles in the child is her sensitivity. The sensitive mother can see things from her baby's point of view and correctly

<table>
<tr><td>

BOX 22.1

The eight episodes involved in the 'Strange Situation' (based on Ainsworth et al., 1978)

Episode 1 The mother and baby are shown into an observation room.

Episode 2 The mother is inactive; the baby is free to explore.

Episode 3 A female adult stranger enters the room. She is silent at first; after one minute, she begins to speak to the mother. After another minute, she approaches the baby. The mother leaves.

Episode 4 The stranger and baby are left alone together.

Episode 5 The mother returns and the stranger leaves. She tries to resettle the baby, then she leaves.

Episode 6 The baby is left alone in the room.

Episode 7 The stranger returns and begins to interact with the baby.

Episode 8 The mother returns again and the stranger leaves again.

</td></tr>
</table>

interpret its signals, she responds to her baby's needs and wishes as and when they arise; she is also accepting of the baby, co-operative with it and accessible or available for it. By contrast, the insensitive mother interacts with the baby almost exclusively in terms of her own wishes, moods and activities. She may distort the implications of the baby's signals and communications or may even ignore them altogether.

Based on the Strange Situation, Ainsworth *et al.* have concluded that: (i) sensitive mothers have secure babies who can explore strange environments, using the mother as a safe base and who can also tolerate brief, occasional separations from her; and (ii) babies of insensitive mothers are so insecure that either they become very angry when she leaves or they seem almost indifferent to her presence or absence and do not use her as a safe base (see Table 22.1).

In general, then, attachments probably develop most readily to people (not just mothers) who can adapt their behaviour to the specific needs – and personality – of the individual child; parental apathy and lack of responsiveness tend to inhibit the bonding process (see below).

Category	Name	% of sample	Typical behaviour
Type A	**Anxious-avoidant**	15	Baby largely ignores mother, because of indifference towards her: play is little affected by whether she is present or absent. No or few signs of distress when mother leaves and actively ignores or avoids her on her return. Distress is caused by being alone, rather than being left by the mother; can be as easily comforted by the stranger as by the mother. In fact, both adults are treated in a very similar way.
Type B	**Securely attached**	70	Baby plays happily while the mother is present, whether the stranger is present or not. Mother is largely 'ignored' because she can be trusted to be there if needed. Clearly distressed when mother leaves and play is considerably reduced. Seeks immediate contact with mother on her return, is quickly calmed down in her arms and resumes play. The distress is caused by the mother's absence, not being alone. Although the stranger can provide some comfort, she and the mother are treated very differently.
Type C	**Anxious-resistant**	15	Baby is fussy and wary while the mother is present; cries a lot more and explores much less than types A and B and has difficulty using mother as a safe base. Very distressed when mother leaves, seeks contact with her on her return but simultaneously shows anger and resists contact; e.g. may approach her and reach out to be picked up, but then struggles to get down again. This demonstrate the baby's ambivalence towards her. Doesn't return readily to play. Actively resists stranger's efforts to make contact.

Table 22.1 *Behaviour associated with three types of attachment in one-year-olds using the 'Strange Situation' (based on Ainsworth et al., 1978)*

● Evaluation of the 'Strange Situation'

According to Lamb *et al.* (1985), the Strange Situation is '... the most powerful and useful procedure ever available for the study of socioemotional development in infancy'. Ainsworth *et al.*'s classification system is generally regarded as very reliable and has been used in a large number of studies in which attachment has been the major dependent variable.

Several studies have shown this pattern of attachment to be a **stable characteristic**; however, a particular child's attachment style may change, as demonstrated by Vaughn *et al.* (1979); see Box 22.2. Also, these are not the only attachment types that have been identified. Main (1991) reports that in a series of more recent studies (e.g. Main *et al.*, 1985), many babies (about 13 percent in the Main *et al.* study) proved unclassifiable in terms of types A, B or C. They show a diverse array of 'disorganized and/or disoriented behaviours', failing to use a clear-cut strategy for dealing with attachment-related stress (unlike the other three types). They act as if it is not just the environmental threat that is fear-inducing but also the attachment figure herself: to increase attachment behaviour would lead to closer proximity to one of the sources of fear, thus producing a conflict between two quite incompatible behaviours (i.e. to both seek and avoid proximity). This type is called *insecure-disorganized/disoriented* (type D) (Main, 1991).

Cross-cultural studies have also revealed important differences both within and between cultures. In an early study (not using the Strange Situation), Ainsworth (1967) found very similar patterns of infant distress on separation from the mother among the Ganda people of Uganda and among American infants. Van IJzendoorn and Kroonenberg (1988, cited in Durkin, 1995) carried out a major review of 32 worldwide studies using the Strange Situation, involving over 2000 infants, and reached three main conclusions :

1 There are marked intracultural differences in the distribution of types A, B and C. For example, in one of two Japanese studies, there was a complete absence of type A but a high proportion of type C, while the other was much more consistent with the Ainsworth *et al.* pattern.
2 The aggregated total pattern was very close to the Ainsworth *et al.* 'standard', as was the aggregated US pattern; but even within the US, there was considerable variability between samples.
3 There seems to be a pattern of cross-cultural differences, whereby while type B is the most common, type A is relatively more common in Western European countries and type C is relatively more common in Israel and Japan.

These findings, especially the last, may be due to differences in the meaning that the Strange Situation has for participants in different cultural settings which, in turn, account for the different causes of distress. For example, Japanese children are rarely separated from their mothers, so that her departure is the most upsetting episode, while for children raised on Israeli kibbutzim (small, closeknit groups), the entrance of a stranger was the main source of distress. Also, different studies have not always used an identical, standard procedure, as when episodes 3 and 5 were omitted in one Japanese study, because the mothers were so uneasy (Durkin, 1995).

Lamb *et al.* (1984) have criticized the Strange Situation for being highly artificial, for being extremely limited in terms of the amount of data that is actually gathered and for failing to take account of the mother's behaviour. We should also point out its ethical status: it is designed in order to see how young children react to stress, which is deliberately produced, in the form of (a) an unfamiliar physical environment, (b) separation from the mother, and (c) contact with a stranger which becomes more

---

BOX 22.2	Key study: Attachment behaviour as a reflection of family circumstances

Vaughn *et al.* (1979) studied mother-infant pairs living in poverty and experiencing frequent changes of accommodation; they were all single-parent families. At 12 months, 55 percent were assessed as securely attached (the rest evenly distributed between types A and C) while at 18 months, 66 percent were securely attached. Significantly, 38 percent were classified differently on the two occasions and this seemed to be related to changes in the family's circumstances. For example, those who were securely attached at first, but were anxiously attached by 18 months, had the most stressed mothers and those who shifted from anxious to secure or who were anxious on both occasions had mothers who experienced an intermediate amount of stress.

Children's early attachment patterns, then, are not necessarily permanent characteristics; if important aspects of their life situation change, children can shift from secure to insecure attachments or vice-versa.

intrusive (in episode 3 she approaches the child prior to the mother leaving and in episode 7, she interacts with the child in the mother's absence). How can this type of research be justified (see Chapter 32)?

THEORIES OF ATTACHMENT

● 'Cupboard love' theories

Until the early 1950s, the dominant theory of attachment was that babies become attached to the mother who feeds them (i.e. cupboard love)! There are two strands to this theory, which normally are diametrically opposed, namely Freud's psychoanalytic theory and learning theory.

According to Freud (1926), 'The reason why the infant in arms wants to perceive the presence of its mother is only because it already knows by experience that she satisfies all its needs without delay'. And again, ' Love has its origin in attachment to the satisfied need for nourishment' (Freud, 1940). So the primary drive is for food and through associating the mother with satisfaction of this primary drive, the baby acquires a secondary drive for the mother – she eventually becomes desired in her own right. It is in these terms (*drive reduction* or *secondary drive theory*) that Dollard and Miller (1950), Sears *et al.* (1957) and other learning theorists explain the development of attachments. The baby's primary hunger drive is reduced (satisfied) by the mother and, through a process of classical conditioning, the baby acquires a secondary (dependency) drive for the mother herself. While food is a primary reinforcer, the mother is a secondary reinforcer (see Chapter 7).

How adequate is the cupboard love explanation of attachment? A number of studies and theoretical developments have helped to expose its shortcomings:

● In some very famous but ethically very dubious experiments, Harlow and Zimmerman (1959) raised rhesus monkeys from birth with two surrogate mothers – a wire 'mother' and a 'mother' covered in terry-towelling. Half the infants were supplied with milk by the wire mother and the other half by the cloth mother. Regardless of who fed them, all the infants became attached to the cloth mother – they used her as a safe base for exploring a new cage and would seek comfort from her when they were frightened by a mechanical

FIGURE 22.1 *Harlow's rhesus monkeys*

toy. The warmth and 'contact comfort' provided by the cloth mother seemed to be a more powerful contributor to the attachment than the milk she supplied (although the cloth mother who also supplied milk represented an even more powerful combination; Fig. 22.1).

● In a longitudinal study of Scottish infants, Schaffer and Emerson (1964) (see Box 22.3) found that infants become attached to people who do not perform caretaking activities (notably the father) and, conversely, in 39 percent of cases, the person who usually fed, bathed and changed the child (typically the mother) was not the child's primary attachment object. Schaffer and Emerson concluded that the two features of an attachment figure's behaviour which best predicted the character of the infant's attachment to them were: (i) responsiveness to the infant's behaviour; and (ii) the total amount of stimulation provided (e.g. talking, touching and playing) (see Box 22.3).

● Schaffer (1971) sees the infant as an active seeker of stimulation and not a passive recipient of food and drink (which is the image portrayed by the cupboard love approach). Much of the infant's social interaction, even in the first few months, takes place when it is fed, clean and generally free from obvious 'biological' needs. As we saw earlier, the need for stimulation, which Schaffer believes is inborn, becomes selective (the infant comes to prefer human sources of stimulation) and eventually focuses on particular individuals (the infant comes to prefer specific attachment figures). According to this view, babies do not 'live to eat' but 'eat to live'.

● The work of ethologists, beginning with Lorenz's famous studies of imprinting in goslings (1935), found that attachment of young birds (and various mammals too) takes place through mere exposure, without any feeding taking place. Although there is no direct comparison between imprinting and human attachments, Bowlby (1969) was greatly influenced by the ethological approach. We shall take a closer look at the relevant aspects of ethological theory before describing how Bowlby applied them to human infant attachments.

Ethological theory

Central to ethological explanations of behaviour is the concept of *instinct*. Essentially, an instinct is an inherited behaviour pattern which is common to all members of a species, i.e. universal (hence, it is often used synonymously with species-specific behaviour); it is innate as opposed to learnt (i.e. independent of an animal's experience) and it tends to be stereotyped, i.e. it appears in the same form every time it is displayed. An instinct is what motivates behaviour and makes it purposeful and goal-directed. As we saw in Chapter 5, a major problem with a term like 'instinct' is that it sounds deceptively like an explanation for behaviour when, in fact, it is nothing more than a label, a description.

Partly for this reason and partly because it is impossible to investigate an instinct without investigating particular manifestations of it, Tinbergen, Lorenz and other ethologists define instincts in terms of *fixed action patterns* (FAPs). These are readily identifiable units of behaviour which break up the stream of behaviour; every species has a repertoire of FAPs which are as characteristic of the species as its structural aspects (Hinde, 1982), i.e. FAPs are species specific. A famous example is the begging response in herring-gull chicks (Tinbergen and Perdeck, 1950). Herring-gulls nest on the ground and the parents go off to find food at sea or on local rubbish tips. When they return, they land on their small nesting territory and stand close to the chick (or even over it), pointing their beaks at the ground. The chick then pecks at the red spot on the parent's beak which stimulates the parent to regurgitate the food it has collected, allowing the chick to be fed. In addition to the characteristics of instincts that we have already considered, Lea (1984), based on Lorenz, states that all FAPs are triggered by specific stimuli, which constitute the immediate cause of the FAP. These trigger stimuli can be considered both a necessary and sufficient condition for the appearance of the FAP, so that the herring-gull chick will only peck at the red spot and will always do so; the red spot is an example of a *sign stimulus*.

Attachment and imprinting

A large number of instinctive behaviour patterns are concerned with interactions between parents and their young who need to 'know', for instance, what to do in order to elicit food (as in herring-gull chicks). It may also be vital for the young animal's survival that it stay close to its parent(s) if they belong to a *precocial* species in which the newborn are capable of locomotion and possess well-developed sense organs. A mobile young animal needs to stay close to its parents and, if it has to learn to recognize them, this learning needs to be rapid and this is one of the characteristics of a form of learning which Lorenz (1935) called *imprinting*.

Lorenz defined imprinting as the learning which occurs in a young bird when following a moving object. Specifically, what the bird learns is the characteristics of the object (which, in the wild, will usually be the mother) so that it discriminates the object from others and, in this way, becomes attached to the imprinted object. This attachment is manifested as a tendency to follow the familiar object, so that following is both a cause and effect of imprinting. This tendency to become imprinted (*imprintability*) is genetically determined (and species-specific) and the following response is an FAP: the sign stimuli include movement, size and general conspicuousness and since young birds do not innately recognize their mothers, any object which combines these properties can be a potential 'target' for imprinting. Lea (1984) maintains that instinct gives the chick a 'concept' or 'template' of the mother, but the environment has to supply the details.

Indeed, in a very famous ethological experiment, Lorenz took a large clutch of goose eggs and kept them until they were about to hatch out. Half were then placed under the goose mother and the other half Lorenz kept beside him for several hours. After hatching, the first group followed the mother and the second group followed Lorenz. He then put them all together under an upturned box to allow them to mix and, when the box was removed, the two groups separated to go to their respective guardians (Fig. 22.2).

Lorenz believed that imprinting is unique for a number of reasons, including the fact that it only occurs during a brief critical period early in the bird's life and once it has occurred, it is irreversible.

Critical and sensitive periods

Lorenz borrowed the term *critical period* from embryology, implying that there are periods in development during which the individual is especially

FIGURE 22.2 *Konrad Lorenz with one of his devoted Greylag geese*

never occur (it also conveys the second major characteristic of imprinting, namely irreversibility). Imprintability, according to Lorenz, is genetically 'switched on' and then 'switched off' again at the end of the period; for example, in the case of mallard ducklings the critical period lasts for the first few hours after hatching (Lorenz, 1935) and, more precisely, between five and 24 hours after hatching, with a peak between 13 and 16 hours (Ramsay and Hess, 1954).

However, many researchers have shown that if a young bird is kept in isolation, it remains unimprinted (and still imprintable) beyond the end of the normal critical period (for example, Sluckin (1961) and Bateson (1964) with ducklings). This and other evidence that the young bird's experience can extend the period of imprintability cast serious doubt on Lorenz's claim that the termination (as well as the onset) of the critical period is under genetic control. This led Sluckin (1965) to coin the term *sensitive period* instead. A sensitive period is one during which learning is most likely to happen and will happen most easily, but it is not as 'critical' or 'once and for all' as the critical period concept suggests. As far as reversibility is concerned, Lorenz believed that once imprinting had taken place, it could not be 'undone' or reversed. However, there are many experimental demonstrations of reversibility, although these are mainly laboratory studies: irreversibility is probably more a feature of imprinting in natural settings than in the laboratory.

As originally defined by Lorenz, imprinting was confined to a few species of precocial birds. However, according to Suomi (1982), since the early 1970s there has been a substantial change in how ethologists (and developmental psychologists) have come to view imprinting. It is now considered to be a very common phenomenon in many species (including fish, sheep, deer, buffalo, dogs and goats, higher primates and human beings). For example, a human infant will respond selectively to its own mother's breastpads by three days after birth (MacFarlane, 1975) and to her voice by 30 days at the latest (Mehler *et al.*, 1978; both cited in Lea, 1984; see Chapter 10). Lea (1984) suggests that imprinting-like processes may be involved in this rapid learning (and may be further examples of the instinctive 'concept' which requires specific experience to 'flesh it out'; see above). However, imprinting is no longer seen as confined to attachment behaviours but can apply to choice of habitat, preferences for specific foods, learning communications, signals, choice of sexual partner and control of aggression. 'As such,

impressionable or vulnerable, that is, when particular experiences exert a profound and lasting influence on later behaviour. In relation to imprinting, 'critical' implies that unless learning occurs during a particular period after hatching, it will

the existence of sensitive phases most likely represents a general psychological principle of development' (Suomi, 1982).

● Bonding: the other side of attachment

While psychologists (including Bowlby) have studied attachment almost exclusively from the point of view of the child, ethological theory, and later, sociobiological theory, has interesting implications for the role of parents. Bowlby (1988) argues that parenting behaviour, like attachment behaviour (see below), has strong biological roots and this is why such strong emotions are associated with it. Consistent with Bowlby's theory of *monotropy* and the central importance of the mother, sociobiologists have proposed *parental investment theory* (Kenrick, 1994; Low, 1989, cited in Durkin, 1995), according to which the cost of reproduction is greater for the female. She only has one egg per cycle and can produce only a very small number of children at once. When she does have a child, her commitment is already high (nine months of pregnancy, etc.), so instead of wasting all this effort, she is oriented naturally to take every care of the baby, spending a lot of time with it and becoming emotionally bonded to it.

Consistent with this theory is the observation that even in unconventional domestic arrangements, such as communes, it is mothers who tend to undertake primary childcare responsibilities. This is not surprising, given that about 90 percent of human history was spent as hunter-gatherers, with hunting and childcare allocated along strict male/female lines; this heritage has left females 'intrinsically better prepared than males for childrearing and attachment to their offspring' (Porter and Laney, 1980, cited in Durkin, 1995). According to Klaus and Kennell (1976), based on studies of premature babies, the amount of physical contact ('skin to skin') between mothers and their newborn babies is important, but even more crucial is the timing of such contact; they propose that 6–12 hours after birth constitutes a critical period for the mother's emotional bonding to her infant, i.e. the contact must take place during that time or the attachment may fail to develop!

However, others disagree. For example, Rutter (1979) stresses that the bonding process builds up slowly over a period of months (rather than hours) just as the baby's does: the idea of a 'maternal instinct' can blind us to the gradual development of the mother's attachment to her infant, which is by no means automatic or immediate. Durkin (1995) points out that pregnancy and birth in humans are not simply biological occurrences, but major life events (see Chapter 24): the meanings that parents impose upon the event, how they explain their emotions and their expectations of the relationship with the child may well have substantial influence over how that relationship develops. The idea of a critical or sensitive period for maternal bonding is not widely accepted.

● Bowlby's theory of attachment

According to Schaffer (1989), Bowlby's theory is the most comprehensive theoretical account of attachment formation and has become the most widely used conceptual framework within which research on attachment has been conducted in recent years. As we have noted above, Bowlby was very much influenced by ethological theory in general, but especially Lorenz's study of imprinting. In particular, Bowlby emphasized (a) the instinctive nature of attachment, including the concept of monotropy; and (b) the importance of the timing of attachment formation, i.e. the existence of a critical period.

Attachment behaviour is *instinctive*. Babies are born with the tendency to display certain behaviours which help ensure proximity and contact with the mother or mother-figure (e.g. crying, smiling, crawling, etc.); these are *species-specific* behaviours. During the evolution of the human species, it would have been the babies who stayed close to their mothers who would have survived to have children of their own and Bowlby hypothesized that both infants and mothers have evolved a biological need to stay in constant contact with each other; each of these attachment behaviours initially functions like an FAP and all share this same function.

In the course of development, two changes in particular happen to the system: firstly, there is a progressive narrowing down in the range of sign stimuli. For example, smiling is initially elicited by just two dots (equivalent to the red dot on the herring-gull's beak that triggers the pecking response). By stages, the dots must become more eyelike, they must be accompanied by other facial features, the whole face must be presented, until eventually only the actual face of familiar individuals will produce smiling. This and other FAPs are no longer independent of each other, but become integrated by being focused on one particular individual, usually the mother (Schaffer, 1989). Bowlby (1969) claimed that the infant displays a strong innate tendency to become attached to one particular individual (*monotropy*), although this need not be the natural or biological mother, and also that this attachment is different in kind (qualitatively different) from any subsequent attachments. Bowlby seems to be arguing that the relationship with the mother is, somehow, of a different order altogether from other relationships.

Secondly, the attachment system becomes an organized whole which increasingly functions in a 'goal-corrected' way; for example, the young baby does not vary its cry according to whether the mother is nearby or further away, coming or going, while the older infant continuously adjusts its behaviour in the light of prevailing circumstances, noting the discrepancy between stimulus conditions and its set goal, namely proximity. Attachment behaviours will be activated by any conditions that seem to threaten the achievement of proximity, such as separation, insecurity and fear; the baby is using feedback to control its actions that are becoming flexible and purposive and organized in accordance with 'plans'.

We should note that just as attachment behaviours are instinctive, so Bowlby also believes (1969, 1988) that fear of strangers represents a rudimentary survival mechanism, built in by nature. The emergence of some kind of fear system would be an adaptive counterbalance to the attachment system which, if unconstrained, could lead to the infant responding positively to strangers who may not always have friendly intentions.

In general, mothering is almost useless if delayed until after 2½–3 years and, for most children, if delayed till after 12 months, i.e. there is a critical period for the development of attachments (Bowlby, 1951).

An evaluation of Bowlby's attachment theory

Much of the discussion – and controversy – of Bowlby's theory has focused on the claim that there is a critical period and monotropy. Here, we shall consider evidence relating to monotropy; discussion of the critical period and the related maternal deprivation hypothesis will come later in the chapter.

The display of attachment behaviour

Rutter (1981) points out that each of several indicators of attachment (protest or distress if the attached person leaves the child, reduction of anxiety and increase in exploration in a strange situation when the attachment figure is present and following or seeking contact with the person) has been shown for a variety of attachment figures: siblings, peers, fathers and even inanimate objects (as in Harlow and Zimmermann's cloth mothers), as well as mothers. Significantly, these attachment responses to others occur even in children who are attached to their mothers – but they are not shown towards strangers.

Attachments with more than one person

Although Bowlby may not dispute that young children develop multiple attachments, he still contends that the attachment to the mother is unique in that it is the first to appear and remains the strongest of all. However, on both these counts, the evidence seems to suggest otherwise. A very important study in this context is the Schaffer and Emerson (1964) study, described in Box 22.3.

BOX 22.3   Key study: Mothers don't have the monopoly on attachments

Schaffer and Emerson (1964) made four-weekly visits to the family home during the baby's first year, followed by another visit at 18 months. As their measure of attachment they used the amount of protest the baby showed when separated from a familiar person; they also asked mothers whether the baby cried or fussed when left in its crib, outside a shop in its pram or in a room by itself.

At about seven months, 29 percent had already formed several attachments simultaneously; in fact, 10 percent had formed five or more. At ten months, 59 percent had developed more than one attachment and by 18 months, 87 percent had done so (a third had formed five or more). Although there was usually one particularly strong attachment, the majority of the children showed multiple attachments of varying intensity and only half of the 18-month-olds were principally attached to the mother; in nearly a third of cases, the main attachment was to the father and 75 percent were attached to the father at 18 months. Although the infants, when young, tended to protest more when the mother left than when the father left, this tendency was shortlived and by 18 months, most children protested equally at the departure of either parent.

Although the evidence supports the view that not all the child's attachments are of equal strength or intensity, i.e. that there is a persisting hierarchy, multiple attachments seem to be the rule rather than the exception and the mother is not always or necessarily the main attachment figure.

Fathers as attachment figures

The Schaffer and Emerson findings suggest that there is more to 'parenting' than 'mothering'. However, both Bowlby and Freud believed that the father is a less important and secondary attachment figure than the 'primary' mother. Bowlby argued that the father is of no direct (emotional) significance to the young child but is only of indirect value as an emotional and economic support for the mother. Margaret Mead, the anthropologist, regarded the father as a 'biological necessity but a social accident' (1949), again implying the relative unimportance of the father as an attachment figure.

Traditionally, the influence of parenting on the child's development has been equated with the influence of 'mothering', hence the term 'maternal deprivation' (see below). It is very unusual to hear psychologists discuss 'paternal' or even 'parental' deprivation and the notion of a 'paternal instinct' is even more improbable. However, a number of studies (in addition to the Schaffer and Emerson study) reveal a very real role that fathers play in the social and emotional development of their young children. However, despite the increasing involvement of fathers in childcare, they seem to make a different kind of contribution from mothers and the attachments that develop are correspondingly different (although not in the way or for the reasons that Bowlby suggests). In studies using the Strange Situation (e.g. Main and Weston, 1981), it has been found that infants may be securely attached to one parent but not to the other, securely attached to both or insecurely attached to both. Those securely attached to both parents reacted more positively to a novel social situation (interacting with a clown) (Main and Weston, 1981).

Clarke-Stewart (1978) found that most children between seven and 30 months chose their fathers as playmates in preference to their mothers. Parke (1981) reports that even when the mother's and father's style of play are compared, there are important differences. The father usually engages in more vigorous, physically stimulating games or unusual and unpredictable types of play (which babies seem to enjoy the most), while the mother plays more conventional games (e.g. pat-a-cake), joins in the child's play with toys and reads to the child. Similar results were found by Lamb (1977) who observed 7–13-month-olds at home. Mothers and fathers hold their babies for basically different reasons, mothers for caretaking and restricting, fathers for playful purposes or because the baby wants to be held. Mothers seem to be preferred as sources of comfort when the infant is distressed, although this is more likely in unfamiliar surroundings (e.g. the Strange Situation); fathers are preferred as playmates and someone to have fun with!

According to Parke (1981), ' Both mother and father are important attachment objects for their infants, but the circumstances that lead to selecting mum or dad may differ'. The father is not just a poor substitute for the mother – he makes his own unique contribution to the care and development of infants and young children. This is true, of course, in situations where both parents are available to the child. Mothers and fathers may be more comparable as single parents. Men are capable of providing adequate parenting and becoming attachment figures for their young children to the extent that :

- there is no foundation for the belief that the biological mother is uniquely capable of caring for her child (the 'blood bond' myth);
- the 'mother' does not even have to be female;
- multiple attachments, rather than a distinct preference for a mother-figure, are the rule rather than the exception for even young infants; and
- attachment is unrelated to the amount of physical caretaking the baby receives from the attachment figure.

BOWLBY'S MATERNAL DEPRIVATION HYPOTHESIS

As we have seen, Bowlby argued that there is a critical period for the formation of attachments. This, together with his theory of monotropy, led him to claim that the attachment to the mother could not be broken in the first few years of life without serious and permanent damage to social, emotional and intellectual development. This is the *maternal deprivation hypothesis* (1951) which was based largely on studies during the 1930s and 1940s of children brought up in orphanages, residential nurseries and other large institutions. Goldfarb's 1943 study is described in Box 22.4.

Classic studies by Spitz (1945, 1946) and Spitz and Wolf (1946) concentrated more on the emotional effects of institutionalization. Spitz visited some very poor orphanages in South America where infants, who received only irregular attention from the staff, became extremely apathetic and displayed high rates

BOX 22.4   Key study: The effects of an institutional upbringing

Goldfarb (1943) compared one group of 15 children raised in institutions from about six months until 3½ years of age, when they were fostered (the institution group), with another group of 15 children who had gone straight from their mothers to foster homes (the fostered group). Although they were matched for genetic factors, mothers' education and occupational status, they might have differed in other important respects which may have determined whether they were fostered or placed in an institution initially, for example, how bright or easygoing they seemed, how withdrawn or prone to illness they were. Clearly, they were not assigned randomly.

The institutions were very clean but lacked human contact or stimulation. Babies below nine months were kept in separate cubicles, intended to prevent the spread of infection, and their only contact with other people occurred during feeding and changing. After nine months, they were put into groups of 15–20 and were supervised by a single nurse. They lived 'in almost complete social isolation during the first year of life' and their experience in the following two years was only slightly better.

At the age of three they were given intelligence tests, tests of abstract thinking and social maturity and their ability to follow rules and make friends was also assessed. Not surprisingly, the institution group fell behind the fostered group on all these measures. For example, all 15 in the fostered group were average in language development compared with only three in the institution group and the latter were characterized by an inability to keep the rules, a lack of guilt, craving for affection and an inability to make lasting relationships. When they were assessed later, between the ages of ten and 14, the institution group performed more poorly on tests of intelligence (average IQ was 72 compared with 95 for the fostered group), social maturity, speech and ability to form relationships. Goldfarb attributed all these differences to the time spent in the institutions.

---

of *anaclitic depression*, a severe disturbance which involves symptoms such as poor appetite and morbidity. After three months of unbroken deprivation, recovery is rarely, if ever, complete. A similar syndrome, which Spitz called *hospitalism*, involving physical and mental deterioration, is caused by prolonged hospitalization, when separation from the mother takes place.

What both these studies, and Bowlby himself, failed to recognize is that the institutions, which were clearly of a very poor quality, not only failed to provide adequate maternal care but they were also extremely unstimulating environments in which to grow up. Consequently, we cannot conclude that it was 'maternal deprivation' that was responsible for the developmental retardation – we must distinguish between different kinds of deprivation and try to relate these to different kinds of retardation (Rutter, 1981).

Also, by using the general term 'maternal deprivation', Bowlby failed to distinguish between (a) the effects of being separated from an attachment figure, and (b) the effects of never having formed an attachment to begin with. As Rutter (1981) points out, the term *deprivation* (de-privation) refers to the loss (through separation) of the mother-figure; the effects are usually short term and can be summarized as distress. However, the effects can also be long term, as we shall see below. Bowlby's theory, and much of his own research, was concerned mainly with depriva-

tion. *Privation*, by contrast, refers to the absence of any attachment; the effects are usually long term and can be summarized as developmental retardation.

● Short-term effects of deprivation (separation)

Typical examples of a short-term separation is a child going into a residential nursery while its mother goes into hospital to have another baby or a child itself having to go into hospital. It is difficult to define precisely how short a short-term separation is but, as a rough guide, it is days or weeks rather than months. Bowlby has found that the term *distress* characterizes the kind of response which young children typically manifest when they go into hospital; it comprises three components or stages:

1 *Protest.* The initial and immediate reaction takes the form of crying, screaming, kicking and generally struggling to escape or clinging to the mother to prevent her leaving. This is an outward and direct expression of everything the child feels – anger, fear, bitterness, bewilderment, etc.

2 *Despair.* The struggling and protest eventually give way to calmer behaviour. The child may seem to have become apathetic but internally still feels all the anger and fear that were previously displayed to the world; these are now kept locked inside and the child wants nothing to do with

other people, appearing depressed and sad. The child may no longer anticipate the mother's return, barely reacting to offers of comfort from others and preferring to comfort itself – by rocking, thumb sucking, etc.

3 *Detachment.* If the separation continues, the child begins to respond to people again but will tend to treat everybody alike and rather superficially. However, if reunited with the mother at this stage, the child may well have to 'relearn' the relationship with her and may even 'reject' her (as she 'rejected' her child).

However, not every child goes through these stages of distress and the degree of distress is not the same for all children. So what factors determine the kind of experience the separation is for a child?

Separations are likely to be more distressing between seven and eight months (when attachments have just developed) and three years, reaching a peak between 12 and 18 months (Maccoby, 1980). One of the crucial variables associated with age is the ability to hold in the mind an image of the absent mother (i.e. to think of her). Also, the child's limited under-

standing of language, especially concepts like 'tomorrow' and 'only for a few days', makes it very difficult to explain to the child that the separation is only temporary (and why it has to take place). Young children, therefore, may believe that they have been abandoned altogether, that their mother no longer loves them and that they may in some way be to blame for what has happened ('Because I'm naughty').

Despite wide variations within gender groups, boys are generally more distressed and vulnerable than girls. For both genders, any behaviour problems existing prior to separation are likely to become accentuated. For example, those who make poor relationships (with adults and/or children) or who are socially inhibited, uncommunicative or aggressive are the most likely to be disturbed by admission to hospital. In general, the more stable and less tense the relationship with the mother before separation, the better the child appears to cope. For example, there is less chance that the child will blame itself in any way for the separation taking place. On the other hand, an extremely close and protective relationship, where the child is rarely out of its mother's sight for more than a few minutes and

---

BOX 22.5   Critical discussion: The effects of daycare on attachment

A number of American studies have compared the attachments of children (both working and middle-class, from one- and two-parent families) who have experienced daycare (usually a daycare centre) with those of children who have not. There seems to be general agreement that what matters is not whether or not the child experiences daycare but: (i) the quality of that substitute care, e.g. how well staffed the institutions are; and (ii) the stability of the arrangement.

Infants in daycare are somewhat more likely to avoid their mothers following a brief separation and later on they will be more disobedient and more likely to bully their peers. However, they also gain knowledge and self-confidence from their experience (Clarke-Stewart, 1989).

In one of the biggest longitudinal studies, Kagan *et al.* (1980) studied children who experienced daycare for seven hours a day, five days a week, over five years. They were thoroughly tested from 3½ to 29 months for intellectual growth (e.g. language development), social development (e.g. relationships with other children) and attachment to the mother and were compared with children raised at home. No significant differences were found between the two groups in any aspect of

development, provided that the daycare facility was well staffed and well equipped; but poor centres can be harmful.

Another crucial factor is the role of work in the mother's life as a whole and whether she enjoys what she is doing. Hoffman (1974) reviewed 122 studies of working mothers and concluded that the dissatisfied mother, whether working or not and regardless of social class, is less likely to be an adequate mother. Working mothers who enjoy their job are more affectionate and less likely to lose their tempers and their children are likely to have higher self-esteem.

Studies of childminders (Mayall and Petrie, 1977; Bryant *et al.*, 1980) and day nurseries in Britain (Garland and White, 1980) tend to confirm the American findings, especially in relation to quality and stability of the substitute care. However, the variety of quality of care, especially among childminders, and the different beliefs about their function, especially among day nurseries, are perhaps greater than the American studies reveal and direct comparisons with children who do not receive regular substitute care have not been made.

According to Clarke-Stewart (1989), given the reality of maternal employment, the issue is not whether infants should be in daycare, but how to make their experiences there and at home supportive of their development and of their parents' peace of mind.

where it is unused to meeting new people (children or adults), may cushion the child against separations to its disadvantage, i.e. the present separation will be more traumatic because the child has never experienced anything like it before!

Indeed, there is evidence that 'good' previous separations may not only help the child cope with subsequent separations but that they help the child become more independent and self-sufficient generally. For example, Stacey *et al.* (1970) studied four-year-old children in Wales who went into hospital to have their tonsils removed. They stayed four days and their parents were not able to stay overnight. Some coped very well and it was discovered that they had experienced separations before, mostly staying overnight with their grandparents or a friend.

Multiple attachments should also make any separation less stressful because the child is, by definition, not totally dependent upon any one individual. Kotelchuck (1976), using the Strange Situation, found that when fathers are actively involved as caretakers, children are more comfortable when left alone with strangers and the period during which children strongly protested at separation was shorter if they were cared for by both parents (as opposed to mainly the mother).

Even institutions can provide high-quality substitute care, a famous example being the Hampstead nursery run by Burlingham and Anna Freud (1942–44), where stability, affection and active involvement were encouraged. However, many institutions are run in such a way that it is virtually impossible for any kind of substitute attachment to develop, such as the residential nurseries studied by Tizard and Rees (1974) (see below). A more general issue is the effects of day care on attachment, which is discussed in Box 22.5.

● Long-term effects of separation

Long-term separation includes the permanent separation resulting from the death of a parent and the increasingly common separation caused by divorce. Possibly the most common effect of long-term separation is what Bowlby calls separation anxiety, namely the fear that separations will occur again in the future. *Separation anxiety* may manifest itself as:

- psychosomatic (psychophysiological) reactions (see Chapter 6);
- increased aggressive behaviour and greater demands towards the mother;

- clinging behaviour – the child will not let the mother out of its sight. This may generalize to relationships in general, so that a man who experienced 'bad' separations in childhood may be very dependent on and demanding of his wife;
- detachment – the child becomes apparently self-sufficient because it cannot afford to be let down again;
- some fluctuation between clinging and detachment.

Bowlby regards *school phobia/refusal* as an expression of separation anxiety – the child fears that something dreadful will happen to its mother while it is at school and stays home in order to prevent it. Two major sources of such fears are: (i) actual events (e.g. the recent illness of the mother or the death of a relative); and (ii) threats by the mother that she will leave home or 'go mad' or 'kill herself' if things do not improve. (Recall that Bowlby interpreted little Hans' fear of horses in terms of separation anxiety; see Chapter 21.)

● The effects of death and divorce

The total number of children under 16 affected by divorce in England and Wales increased steadily during the 1970s and 1980s, so that in 1986, 20 percent of children were affected before their 19th birthday. About 60 percent of all divorces involve children and of those affected, 25 percent are under four years old. More than half of them will lose touch with the non-custodial parent within two years.

Both death and divorce are most usefully thought of as processes (as opposed to events), but as Richards (1987) points out, research shows that the consequences of divorce are more serious than those following the death of the father (children are much more likely to lose their father than their mother this way). From the perspective of attachment theories like Bowlby's (which see the mother-child relationship as the critical one), this is a rather puzzling finding. Richards attempts to answer this by comparing the two situations as processes:

- It is commonly found that children experiencing parental divorce show separation anxiety (e.g. by refusing to be left at nursery or school, insisting on having their bedroom light left on at night) – it is not surprising that they may begin to question the security of their remaining relationship, since if the father can leave, why not the mother too? (This could occur after a parent's death too but is less likely given the other differences below.)

- Children usually deeply resent their parents' separation and may retain fantasies of reunion for many years to come. They experience the separation as a course that has been chosen by the parents in the knowledge that they (the children) do not want it. This makes them feel powerless, disregarded and angry. By contrast, when a parent dies, the child does not have to contemplate an act which was chosen by others against the child's wishes.

- It is, sadly, commonplace for children to be given a very negative picture of the departing parent by the one who remains. When the father dies, however, he is often idealized. Also, the custodial parent is less likely to visit school to discuss the child's progress, etc., while widows usually become more involved. And, not surprisingly, divorce has a far greater negative effect on the child's school work than the death of a parent.

- Especially if the departing parent loses regular touch with the child, the child may also lose contact with all the relatives on that side of the family. The opposite seems to happen following a death – usually members of the whole kinship network are expected to play an active part in the funeral and grieving process. After divorce, however, there is a tendency to take sides and in-laws may cut off (or be cut off from) all future relationships.

- Re marriage is more likely after divorce and the interval is much briefer. This can create new stresses for children (e.g. having to get used to a step-parent and maybe step-siblings too), although it can also produce financial benefits (financial problems are usually more severe following divorce).

As a result of all these factors, the relationship between the child and the custodial parent is bound to suffer, at least temporarily. Hetherington *et al.* (1979) studied four-year-olds living with their mothers following divorce and who were in regular contact with their fathers. During the first year, mothers became more authoritarian, increasing the number of demands and restrictions and becoming less affectionate. The children (especially boys) became more aggressive and inflexible. Domestic routines became disrupted. Fathers tended to become less disciplinarian and more indulgent, treating the child and buying presents more often (the *crisis phase*). By two years after the divorce, the balance was beginning to be restored – mother had become more patient and communicative and

domestic life was more structured with both parents. The children's behaviour settled down accordingly (the *adjustment phase*).

Richards (1987) concludes that the best arrangement as far as the child's short- and long-term psychological well-being is concerned is a good relationship with both parents following the divorce. The essential point of difference between death and divorce is the degree of conflict which is typically involved – it is this, rather than divorce as such, which seems to be damaging. This is consistent with the view that a bad marriage is worse for the children than divorce.

Rutter (1970) studied 9–12-year-old boys living on the Isle of Wight and in London. He found several who had been separated from their mothers when young but who seemed quite well adjusted. Although they had suffered difficulties at the time, they had overcome them when family life returned to normal; however, some were later rated as maladjusted. Rutter discovered that those who became maladjusted had been separated due to family discord caused, for instance, by the psychiatric illness of one or both parents. Those who did not become maladjusted had been separated because of physical illness, housing problems or holidays and not disturbance of social relationships as such – even the death of a parent had little lasting effect. Clearly, it is not separation as such which is harmful but the *reasons* for the separation and the longer the family disharmony lasts, the greater the risk for the child.

THE EFFECTS OF PRIVATION

As we noted earlier, *privation* refers to the failure to develop an attachment to any individual and is usually, but not necessarily, associated with children reared from birth (or shortly after) in institutions. Dwarfism (failure to grow properly), for example, may result from inadequate diet, but also from maternal rejection (privation in a family setting). As we noted earlier, the studies of Spitz and Goldfarb confused the effects of maternal and other kinds of privation, namely sensory and intellectual (all of which are normally referred to as forms of deprivation). Prior to these studies, Skeels and Dye (1939) had shown the dramatic effect on intellectual functioning of being raised in an institution (see Box 22.6).

BOX 22.6	Key study: Long-term effects of early intellectual privation (Skeels and Dye, 1939)

Twenty five children were raised in an orphanage in the USA, where they experienced a minimum of social interaction and stimulation, until they were almost two years old; 13 (average IQ 64.3) were then transferred to a school for the mentally retarded where they received individual care from older, sub-normal girls. They also enjoyed far superior play facilities, intellectual stimulation, staff-child ratios and so on (and constituted the experimental group). The other 12 children (average IQ 86.7) stayed behind (the control group).

When they were about 3½ years old, the experimental group either returned to the orphanage or were adopted; their average IQ had risen to 92.8 while that for the control group had dropped to 60.5. When they were seven years old, the average gain for the experimental group was 36 IQ points and the average loss for the control group was 21 points.

Skeels (1966) followed them up into adulthood. All the participants in the experimental group had had more education than the controls, they had all finished high school, about one-third had gone to college, had married, had children of normal intelligence and had been self-supporting through their adult lives. The control participants had mostly remained in institutions and were unable to earn enough to be self-supporting; they were still mentally retarded.

● Affectionless psychopathy

In the light of what we said earlier about the importance of the child's first relationship, it would not be unreasonable to expect that a failure to develop an attachment of any kind early on in life would adversely affect all subsequent relationships.

The Harlow 'socially deprived' infant monkeys, especially if they were brought up only with surrogate mothers (and not with other infants), were very disturbed in their later sexual behaviour and unmothered females themselves become very inadequate mothers. (They have to be artificially inseminated because they will not mate naturally.) But what about human infants?

Bowlby's original contention was that maternal deprivation caused affectionless psychopathy, i.e. the inability to have deep feelings for other people and the consequent lack of meaningful interpersonal relationships. One source of evidence he gives

in support of this claim is a very unconvincing 1946 study of 44 juvenile delinquents who had committed theft. Of the 44 thieves, 14 (but none in a control group of emotionally disturbed juveniles not guilty of crime) showed many characteristics of the affectionless character (including an inability to experience guilt) and seven of them had suffered complete and prolonged separation from their mothers, or established foster mothers, for six months or more during the first five years of life; another two had spent nine months in hospital, unvisited, during their second year (when attachments are normally being consolidated). Only three of the 30 other, non-affectionless thieves had suffered comparable separations. Bowlby claimed that affectionless psychopathy was strongly linked to separation experiences in early childhood

However, a more accurate interpretation would seem to be that privation, rather than deprivation, was the major cause of the affectionless character: the general picture is of multiple changes of mother-figure and home during the early years, making the establishment of attachments very difficult (Rutter, 1981). Also, apart from the retrospective nature of the study (the delinquents and their mothers had to remember past events), how does Bowlby account for the remainder of the juvenile thieves (the majority) who had not suffered complete and prolonged separations?

A further study carried out by Bowlby *et al.* (1956) involved 60 children (41 boys and 19 girls) aged seven to 13, who had spent between five months and two years in a tuberculosis sanatorium, at various ages up to age four; about half of them had been separated from their parents before they were two. No substitute mothering was provided in the sanatorium. Compared with a group of non-separated control children from the same classes at school, there were few significant differences in terms of either IQ score or teachers' ratings. Although the separated children did more daydreaming, showed less initiative, got overexcited, were rougher in their play, less able to concentrate and less competitive, the overall picture was of two groups who were more similar than different. There was certainly no evidence of the sanatorium children showing more signs of affectionless psychopathy than the controls, regardless of whether the separation had occurred before or after two years of age. Referring to the fact that illness and death were common in the families of the sanatorium children (10 percent of the mothers had died by the time of follow-up), Bowlby *et al.* themselves admit that '... part of the emotional disturbance can be attributed to factors other than separation' (Bowlby *et al.*, 1956)

Therefore, Bowlby's claim for a link between affectionless psychopathy and separation (attachment disruption) seems largely unsupported but indirectly he may have provided evidence to support the view that privation (failure to form attachments) may be associated with the affectionless character. Rutter (1981) supports this latter view.

● Developmental retardation

The Skeels and Dye (1939) and Skeels (1966) studies suggest that a crucial variable for intellectual development is the amount of intellectual stimulation the child receives and not the amount of mothering (as Spitz, Goldfarb and Bowlby claimed). In general, poor, unstimulating environments are associated with mental subnormality and retarded linguistic development (language is crucial for intellectual development generally).

One difficulty in trying to identify the effects of privation is to be able to pinpoint which type of privation (e.g. sensory, intellectual, social or emotional) produces which particular long-term effect. A possible solution is to try to identify critical or sensitive periods.

● Are there critical or sensitive periods for the effects of privation?

It seems that the first 6–8 months are critical for the rhesus monkey's social development and, according to Bowlby, the first three years for the development of affectionless psychopathy in humans; as we noted earlier, he went even further and said that mothering is useless for most children after 12 months. Dennis (1960), based on his study of orphanages in Iran, concluded that there is a critical period for intellectual development before two years of age: children adopted from orphanages after two years, unlike those adopted earlier, seemed to be incapable of closing the gap in average IQ between themselves and the average child. Postnatal brain growth is most rapid in the first two years of life and susceptibility to damage is greatest during periods of most rapid development (see Chapter 4).

So what is the evidence that critical or sensitive periods actually exist? In general, the more difficult it is to reverse the effects of privation, the stronger the belief in such crucial early developmental periods. According to Clarke and Clarke (1976), in a major review of the relevant studies, the effects of early privation are much more easily reversible than has been traditionally thought. For example, as far as Dennis's critical period for intellectual development is concerned, they argue that a later age of adoption makes adapting to the new home a totally different process from that experienced by the early-adopted child. Also, the child has had longer in which to develop habits which may interfere with adjustment; the child may be more withdrawn and disturbed and this may have a reciprocal effect on the family. Looked at in this way, the time spent in the institution has not had a direct, irreversible effect on intellectual functioning, but has had effects which may interfere with future learning and development. Again, though, the early-adopted child may have been brighter to begin with, which may have influenced their selection!

Studies of adoption

Barbara Tizard in *Adoption – A Second Chance* (1977) and Tizard and Hodges (1978) report their findings on children in care throughout their early years who, on leaving care, were either adopted or returned to their own families ('the 'restored' group).

The children (whose behaviour at age two (Tizard and Tizard, 1971) and at age four (Tizard and Rees, 1974) was described above, page 551) received good physical care in their institutions, which also appeared to provide adequately for their cognitive development. However, staff turnover and an explicit policy against allowing too strong an attachment to develop between the children and the staff had given the children little opportunity to form close, continuous relationships with an adult. By the age of two, an average of 24 different caregivers had looked after them for at least a week; by age four, the average was 50. (This fits Bowlby's (1951) description of maternal deprivation very closely.) As a result, the children's attachment behaviour was very unusual (see page 551). It seems likely that generally the children's first opportunity for a close reciprocal long-term attachment came when they left the institutions and were placed in families, at ages between two and seven years.

By age eight (Hodges and Tizard, 1978), the majority of adopted children and some of the restored children had formed close attachments to their parents, despite their lack of early attachments in the institutions. The adoptive parents very much wanted a child and put much time and energy into building up a relationship. The biological parents, by contrast, were more likely to be ambivalent about having the child back and often had other children, plus material difficulties, competing for their attention. According to their parents, the ex-institutional children did not present more problems than a comparison group who had never been in care; but according to their teachers more of them showed problems, notably attention-seeking behaviour, especially from adults, restlessness, disobedience and poor peer relationships – they were quarrelsome and unpopular (as they had been at age four) (Tizard and Hodges, 1978).

Hodges and Tizard (1989) followed these children up again at age 16. The family relationships of most of the adopted 16-year-olds seemed satisfactory, both for them and their parents, and differed little from non-adopted comparisons who had never been in care. Early institutional care had not necessarily led to a later inability to form a close attachment to parents and to become as much a part of the family as any other child. In contrast, the restored group still suffered difficulties and poor family relationships (including mutual difficulty in showing affection and parents feeling closer to siblings than to the restored child) much more often than either the adoptees or their own comparison group.

However, both ex-institution groups showed very similar relationships to peers and adults *outside* the family. They were still more often oriented towards adult affection and approval than comparison adolescents and they were also more likely to have difficulties in peer relations, less likely to have a special friend or to see peers as a source of emotional support and more likely to be friendly to any peer, rather than choosing their friends. The findings suggest that children who are deprived of close and lasting attachments to adults in their first years of life can make such attachments later. But these do not arise automatically if the child is placed in a family, but depend on the adults concerned and how much they nurture such attachments. Yet despite these attachments, certain differences and difficulties in social relationships are found over 12 years after the child has joined a family; these are not related to the kind of family, but seem to originate in the children's early institutional experience. Since they affect relationships with peers, as well as with adults outside the family, they may have implications for the future adult relationships (Hodges and Tizard, 1989).

If their major relationship difficulties are with peers, would we expect this to apply to heterosexual relationships as much as to same-sex friendships? We need to know whether the ex-institution adolescents will be able to form stable, long-term relationships

(Erikson's *intimacy*) and, in turn, be able to nurture children of their own (*generativity*). Ideally, follow-up for another 20–30 years should be carried out (Gross, 1994).

Kadushin (1970) in the USA followed up 91 children adopted between the ages of five and 12. The vast majority were perfectly successful when studied at age 14 and the outcome was much better than expected on the basis of their early history of neglect, multiple changes of foster parents and late age of adoption. Triseliotis (1980) followed up 40 people born during 1956 and 1957 who had experienced long-term fostering (between seven and 15 years in a single foster home before the age of 16) and interviewed them when they were 20–21 years old. He concluded that if the quality and continuity of care and relationships are adequate, the effects of earlier disruptions and suffering can be reversed and normal development can be achieved.

● Can the effects of extreme early privation be reversed?

Some very dramatic evidence comes in the form of studies of children who have been discovered after enduring years of extreme privation and isolation. Among the most famous are Anna (Davis, 1940, 1947), Isabelle (Mason, 1942), the Czech twins (Koluchova, 1972, 1976), Genie (Curtiss, 1977) and the concentration camp survivors (Freud and Dann, 1951). Less well known is the study by Skuse (1984) of Mary and Louise (see Gross, 1994).

Genie is briefly described in Chapter 26. Here, we shall look in some detail at the Freud and Dann study (Box 22.6), the case of the Czech twins (Box 22.7) and at Mary and Louise (Box 22.8).

CONCLUSIONS: EARLY EXPERIENCE AND LATER DEVELOPMENT

Studies of maternal (de-)privation should be seen in the wider context of the effect of early experience on later behaviour and development. According to Rutter (1989), in recent years there has been something of a return to the view that development involves both *continuities* (consistencies of personality and behaviour) and *discontinuities* (inconsistencies). The process of development is concerned with change and it is not reasonable to suppose that the pattern will be set in early life. Physiological changes (e.g. puberty)

BOX 22.7 | Childhood survivors of the Holocaust

Anna Freud and Sophie Dann (1951) studied six German-Jewish orphans rescued from a concentration camp at the end of the Second World War. They had all been orphaned when a few months old and thereafter kept together as a group in a deportation camp (Tereszin) and cared for by camp inmates who were successively deported to Auschwitz. One of the inmates who survived later said, 'We looked after the bodily welfare of the children as much as possible ... but it was not possible to attend their other needs' (Moskovitz, 1985, cited in Tizard, 1986).

They had been subjected to many terrifying experiences, including witnessing camp hangings. On release, at age three, all were severely malnourished, normal speech had hardly developed and they had developed the same kind of intense attachment to each other that children normally have for their parents and an absence of the jealousy and rivalry usually found among siblings. They refused to be separated even for a moment and were extremely considerate and generous to each other. Towards adults they showed cold indifference or fearful hostility. A month after the liberation of the camp by the Russians they were flown to England to a special reception camp in Windermere, in the Lake District. Subsequently they were moved to Bulldogs Bank.

The children's positive feelings were centred exclusively on each other; they obviously cared greatly for each other and not at all for anybody or anything else. Their insistence on being inseparable made it impossible at first to treat them as individuals. But gradually they began to form attachments to specific adult caretakers and, despite being jealous and possessive of each other's relationships, this lessened and they showed a spurt in social and language development. Within the next two years, all but one of the children was adopted. The exception was Berli, who was a very mischievous child, often getting into trouble at school and the children's home until early adolescence, when he began to settle down. At 18 he went to live with an uncle in the USA. He spent a year in Vietnam, was a sergeant and teacher in the National Guard and had a long and troubled marriage.

Judith married and had children, as did Jack, a London taxi-driver, who talked of great feelings of aloneness which came in bursts every so often.

Leah married and had four children. She had migraines since childhood, very low self-esteem and was unsuccessful at school. She became a devout Christian. She had a fear of hospitals, had trouble sleeping and had received psychiatric care from age 7½.

Gadi was a history teacher in the USA, having obtained a Master's degree in education. He had trouble adjusting to school and was prone to temper tantrums and locking himself in the bathroom. He died in 1980.

Finally, Bella married and had children, having met her husband while training to be a (Hebrew) Sunday class teacher. She believes strongly that '...If children come from good [group] homes, where they have the companionship of other children, I think sometimes they're better off [there] than being isolated individually into families that don't really know how to cope with them'.

All six were traced and interviewed by Sarah Moskovitz during 1979 and 1980 and described in her book *Love Despite Hate – Child Survivors of the Holocaust and their Adult Lives* (1983). The Freud and Dann study suggests that it is attachment formation per se which is important for the development of social and emotional relationships in later childhood and adulthood, rather than with whom the bond is formed.

and new experiences will both serve to shape psychological functioning. But continuities will also occur because children carry with them the results of earlier learning and of earlier structural and functional change (Rutter, 1989).

The studies of adoption and extreme privation that we have discussed represent a major source of data regarding the whole continuity-discontinuity debate. What they seem to demonstrate is that theories which stress the overriding importance of early experience for later growth (i.e. critical periods) are inadequate (Clarke, 1972). Adverse early life experiences may, but not necessarily will, have serious lasting effects on development in some circumstances (Rutter, 1981). Individuals can show great resilience, some being much more resilient than others, and there is no straightforward connection between cause and effect in most cases. Further, according to Skuse (1984), there is an increasing tendency to see the child as part of a social system in which they are in a mutually modifying relationship, with the mother no longer playing such a pivotal role. 'Maternal deprivation' is too general and heterogeneous and its effects too varied to be of continuing value (Rutter, 1981).

Skuse (1984) believes that there is a characteristic clinical picture of the victim of extreme privation when first discovered, namely motor retardation,

BOX 22.8 The case of the Czech twins

Koluchova (1972) reported the case of identical twin boys in (the former) Czechoslovakia, who were cruelly treated by their stepmother and found in 1967 at about seven years of age. They had grown up in a small, unheated closet, had often been locked in the cellar and were often harshly beaten. After their discovery, they spent time in a children's home and a school for the mentally retarded, before being fostered in 1969. At first they were terrified of many aspects of their new environment and communicated largely by gestures; they had little spontaneous speech. They made steady progress, both socially and intellectually.

A follow-up in 1976 reported that, at 14 (seven years after discovery), the twins showed no psychopathological symptoms or unusual behaviour. In a personal communication to Clarke (reported in Skuse, 1984), Koluchova reported that by 20 they had completed quite a demanding apprenticeship (in the maintenance of office machinery), were above average intelligence, still had very good relationships with their foster mother and her relatives and their adopted sisters and they had developed normal heterosexual relationships, both recently experiencing their first love affairs.

Like the study of the Holocaust survivors, the case of the Czech twins seems to highlight the fundamental importance of having somebody (not necessarily a mother-figure) with whom to form an emotional bond, as well as showing that the effects of long-term, extreme privation can be reversed. According to Tizard (1986), '... This study provides ... evidence of the protective function of attachments in development, even when they are not directed to the mother, or indeed to an adult'.

BOX 22.9 The case of Mary and Louise (Skuse, 1984)

In 1977, Mary, almost nine, was referred to the Children's Department at a large postgraduate teaching hospital. During the previous year she had shown increasingly disruptive behaviour in the small children's hospital where she had lived for the previous six years with her sister Louise (14 months older). Their early lives were spent in a remarkably deprived environment with a mentally retarded mother, who may have also been schizophrenic. Upon their discovery by the Social Services, they were described as '... very strange creatures indeed'.

Aged 3½ and 2⅓, they took no notice of anyone, except to scamper up and sniff strangers, grunting and snuffling like animals. Both still sucked dummies and no attempt had been made to toilet train them (so they were still in nappies). Neither had any constructive play but picked up objects, handled, smelt and felt them. Mary had no speech at all and made no hearing responses – she made just a few high-pitched sounds. It later came to light that they had been tied on leashes to the bed, partly as a way their mother could ensure the flat stayed spotless and partly to ensure they would not fall off the balcony. If they became too noisy or active, they were put onto a mattress and covered with a blanket. They were subsequently taken into care.

absent or very rudimentary vocal and symbolic language, grossly retarded perceptuomotor skills, poor emotional expression, lack of attachment behaviour and social withdrawal. (This combination is unlikely to be found in any other condition, except perhaps profound mental retardation and childhood autism.) Language is undoubtedly the most vulnerable cognitive faculty – it was profoundly retarded at first in all cases (even where other features of mental development are apparently unaffected). The early combination of profound language deficit and apathy/withdrawal from social contact leads to special difficulties in developing a normal range and quality of relationships later on.

The evidence suggests that if recovery of normal ability in a particular faculty is going to occur, rapid progress is the rule. However, further progress may be made several years after discovery, even in cases where the obstacles to success were thought to be genetic/congenital – in the case of Mary and Louise, both received speech therapy after discovery but this was abandoned with Mary due to poor progress. Her relative lack of social communication and language at age nine were reminiscent of autism. But four years later, a remarkable transformation had occurred – she had made tremendous progress in both areas and such autistic features vanished. Despite having been placed in a variety of children's homes over that period, she did receive some consistent, intensive speech therapy. Skuse (1984) concludes by saying that the evidence suggests that, in the absence of genetic or congenital abnormalities, victims of such privation have an excellent prognosis.

ADULT–ADULT ATTACHMENTS

According to Bartholomew (1993), attachment theory, as developed by Bowlby , Ainsworth and others, predicts that (a) attachment behaviour characterizes human beings throughout life ('Attachment behaviour is held to characterize human beings from the cradle to the grave'; Bowlby, 1977), and (b) patterns established in childhood parent–child relationships tend to structure the quality of later adult–adult relationships. As far as (a) is concerned, any adult relationship potentially could meet the criteria for an attachment, namely (i) a desire for proximity with the attachment figure, especially under stressful conditions; (ii) a sense of security derived from contact with the attachment figure; and (iii) distress or protest when threatened with loss or separation from the attachment figure (Bartholomew, 1993). Some evidence in support of

(ii) and (iii) can be found in Chapter 24. (Further discussion can be found in Gross, 1995.)

As far as (b) is concerned, this represents another way of considering the effects of early on later experience. A ground-breaking study is that by Hazan and Shaver (1987), described in Box 22.10.

Hazan and Shaver's findings have been replicated and extended in several studies. For example, Bartholomew and Horowitz (1991) proposed a model based on Bowlby's (1977) suggestion that children, over time, internalize early attachment experiences and use these inner working models to judge '(a) whether or not the attachment figure is ... the sort of person who ... responds to calls for support and protection; [and] (b) whether or not the self is...the sort of person towards whom anyone, and the attachment figure in particular, is likely to respond in a helpful way'. The former concerns the child's image of other people, while the latter concerns the child's image of the self. This can be represented in a 2×2 matrix with four prototypic forms of adult attachment (Bartholomew, 1990; Bartholomew and Horowitz, 1991; Horowitz et al., 1993). This is shown in Figure 22.3.

As shown in Figure 22.3, the person's image of the self can be either positive or negative (the self is or is not worthy of love and support) and the person's image of other people is also positive or negative (others are seen as either trustworthy and available or unreliable and rejecting). This produces four attachment styles :

- Cell I indicates a sense of worthiness (lovability) plus an expectation that other people are generally accepting and responsive. This corresponds to Hazan and Shaver's securely attached type or simply secure.
- Cell II indicates a sense of unworthiness (unlovability) combined with a positive evaluation of others, leading the person to strive for self-acceptance by gaining the acceptance of valued others. It corresponds to Hazan and Shaver's anxious-ambivalent style, what Horowitz et al. call preoccupied.
- Cell III indicates a sense of unworthiness (unlovability) combined with an expectation that others will be negatively disposed (untrustworthy, rejecting). By avoiding close involvement with others, people using this style are able to protect themselves against anticipated rejection. It corresponds partly to Hazan and Shaver's anxious-avoidant style; Horowitz et al. call it fearful-avoidant.

| **BOX 22.10** | **Key study: Romantic love conceptualized as an attachment process** |

Hazan and Shaver (1987) made the first attempt to apply the three basic attachment styles identified by Ainsworth et al. to adult–adult sexual relationships. When describing the three styles, Ainsworth et al. refer to the child's expectations regarding the mother's availability and responsiveness. This is similar to Bowlby's claim that older infants and young children construct inner working models (internal representations or *mental models,* to use Hazan and Shaver's term) of themselves and their major social-interaction partners. These working models become integrated into the individual's personality structure, thereby providing a prototype for later relationships, which represents a vital source of continuity between early and later feelings and behaviours.

The attachment styles were 'translated' into three descriptions of adult sexual relationships, from which the participant had to choose one in response to the question 'Which of the following best describes your feelings?'. This formed part of a 'Love Quiz' which also included an adjective checklist describing their childhood relationships with their parents. The correlation between the attachment style which participants chose and their recollections of the kind of parenting they received mirrored Ainsworth et al.'s findings using the Strange Situation with one-year-olds remarkably closely.

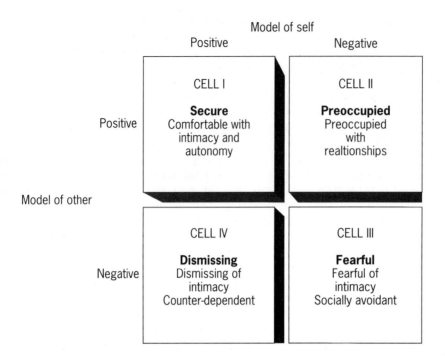

FIGURE 22.3 *Four theoretical adult attachment styles. (From Horowitz et al., 1993)*

● Cell IV indicates a sense of love-worthiness combined with a negative disposition toward others. Such people protect themselves against disappointment by avoiding close relationships and maintaining a sense of independence and invulnerability. This is a dismissive-avoidant style.

Horowitz *et al.* found evidence for the prediction that different attachment styles will be associated with different kinds of interpersonal problems.

CHAPTER SUMMARY

● Attachments represent an important feature of early experience; despite Freud's emphasis on what happens during our first five years, it was only with Bowlby's report on maternal deprivation in 1951 that the systematic study of attachments started.
● Attachments are relatively permanent emotional ties to particular individuals who provide a safe base in situations that are unfamiliar and frightening. They are especially important because they act as a prototype for all later relationships.
● From six weeks to about three months, babies come to prefer people to inanimate aspects of the

environment. Then until about 7–8 months, they learn to recognize familiar people but are happy to be taken care of by strangers. But after this, they actively seek proximity with familiar people and miss them if separated from them and they also show a fear of strangers, both indications that attachments have started to develop.
● The distinction between attachments and attachment behaviours is important for understanding how attachments can differ in terms of their strength and security. These can be inversely related, as in the institution-reared children studied by Tizard and in infant rhesus monkeys blasted with air from a rejecting mother, but they can also be positively related.
● The aim of attachment is detachment, but this requires the attachment to be secure.
● The most widely used, standardized procedure for studying attachment in babies and young children is Ainsworth *et al.*'s Strange Situation, which consists of eight predetermined episodes involving the child, mother and a female stranger. The child's play, together with its response to the mother's leavings and returns, and those of the stranger, are observed.
● Ainsworth *et al.* have identified three main types of attachment: type A (anxious-avoidant), type B (securely attached) and type C (anxious-resistant).

These are associated with the mother's sensitivity to the baby's needs.

- Although attachment styles are generally stable, they can change if the mother's circumstances and related stress levels change. Also, not all children fit Ainsworth *et al.*'s categories and Main has identified a fourth type, type D (disorganized/disoriented).

- Cross-cultural studies have revealed important differences both within and between cultures. These can be explained partly in terms of the different meaning that the Strange Situation has in different cultures and partly in terms of the failure of some studies to use the standardized procedure.

- The Strange Situation has been criticized on scientific grounds but its ethics are also dubious, given that it is designed to see how young children react to stress that is deliberately produced.

- 'Cupboard love' theories explain attachment in terms of the mother's satisfaction of the baby's biological need for food. Freud adopted this view, as did learning theorists, such as Dollard and Miller's drive reduction/ secondary drive theory.

- Harlow's experiments with rhesus monkeys showed that 'contact comfort' is more important than food and Schaffer and Emerson's longitudinal study found that babies are often attached to people who do not look after their physical needs. Responding to the baby's behaviour in a stimulating way seems to be much more important than feeding.

- The work of the ethologists, in particular Lorenz's study of imprinting, showed the importance of instinctive aspects of attachment behaviour. Instincts have been studied in the form of fixed action patterns (FAPs), which are universal, species specific, stereotyped and triggered by specific stimuli called sign stimuli.

- Lorenz saw imprintability as confined to a few species of precocial birds and as genetically determined; imprinting only occurs during a brief critical period early in the bird's life. Once it has occurred, it is irreversible.

- Subsequent research has shown that the period of imprintability can be extended, leading to Sluckin's proposal of a sensitive period. It is also accepted that imprinting occurs in a wide range of species, including humans, and that it is not confined to attachment behaviours.

- Ethological theory sees parental behaviour, as well as attachment behaviour in infants, as having strong biological roots. Sociobiologists stress the greater investment in parenting of the mother, which explains why females are naturally better parents, and Klaus and Kennell claim that there is a critical period for the bonding of a mother to her baby. However, bonds take time to develop and birth and pregnancy are much more than just biological events.

- Bowlby's attachment theory was very much influenced by ethological theory. In particular, he emphasized the instinctive nature of attachment, including his theory of monotropy, and the existence of a critical period for attachment formation; for most babies, this lasts until the end of the first year.

- Babies' attachment behaviours initially function like FAPs. Over time, they are triggered by a much narrower range of stimuli and become focused on one particular individual; this is related to monotropy. The attachment system also increasingly functions in a 'goal-corrected' way. Fear of strangers is also instinctive and serves as a counterbalance to the attachment system.

- All attachment behaviours are displayed towards all attachment figures – not just to mothers. Also, multiple attachments seem to be the rule rather than the exception and the mother is not always or necessarily the main attachment figure.

- In recent years, there has been growing recognition of the role of fathers as attachment figures in their own right. They are no longer seen as mere biological necessities or substitutes for the mother in her absence, but they seem to make a different kind of contribution from her, especially as 'playmate'. As the sole parent, fathers may be just as adequate as mothers.

- Bowlby's maternal deprivation hypothesis was based largely on studies of orphanages and other large institutions, such as those by Golfarb, Spitz and Wolf in the 1930s and 1940s, in which babies suffered anaclitic depression, hospitalism and general retardation. Not only is it impossible to separate the effects of 'maternal deprivation' from those of the general lack of stimulation, but the children raised in these institutions suffered privation (not 'deprivation' at all).

- The effects of deprivation (separation) are usually short term and typically take the form of distress. This can be mediated by the child's age, gender, existing relationships with attachment figures, multiple attachments, previous experience of separations and intellectual development.

- Daycare is not in itself harmful but depends on the quality and stability of the care that is provided. It can even work to the child's advantage, especially if the mother is more satisfied by being able to work.

- A major long-term effect of separation is separation anxiety, which can manifest itself in various ways, including school phobia. The death of a parent and divorce represent two permanent forms of separation which should be seen as processes. In general, the effects of divorce are likely to be more harmful to the child, primarily because of the conflict that is typically involved. It is not separation itself that is harmful, but the reasons for it.
- The effects of privation are usually long term, are often associated with an institutional upbringing and take the form of developmental retardation, such as the mental retardation demonstrated by Skeels and Dye. It is important to link particular forms of retardation to particular kinds of privation.
- One way of trying to identify critical or sensitive periods for the effects of privation is to study their reversibility; this has been done through studies of adoption, such as the longitudinal study of Tizard involving children raised in care. While the adopted children had close attachments to their parents, those who returned to their natural families had difficult relationships, but all of them had difficult peer relationships and relationships with adults outside the home.
- Other studies of adoption also suggest that attachments can be formed long after Bowlby's critical period.
- Studies of children who have experienced extreme privation, such as the Czech twins studied by Koluchova and the child survivors of the Holocaust studied by Freud and Dann, suggest that it is attachment formation with somebody that matters, rather than attachment with a mother-figure, as Bowlby argued. Adverse early experience does not necessarily and inevitably have lasting, harmful effects and individuals vary greatly in their susceptibility to such experience.
- Attachment theory sees adult attachments as essentially the same as childhood attachments and Hazan and Shaver applied Ainsworth *et al.*'s three attachment styles to the study of adult sexual relationships. They found a correlation between adults' choice of attachment style and recollections of the kind of parenting they received which mirrored Ainsworth *et al.*'s findings remarkably closely.
- Bartholomew has extended Hazan and Shaver's research, identifying four attachment styles based

on positive or negative images of the self and of other people.

GLOSSARY

Affectionless psychopathy The inability to have deep feelings for others, the lack of meaningful interpersonal relationships. Often accompanied by lack of guilt feelings.

Anaclitic depression A severe emotional disturbance, associated with the loss of a love-object, in which the baby becomes extremely apathetic, withdrawn, loses appetite, etc. Similar to *hospitalism.*

Anxious-avoidant (type A) An attachment style, in which the baby is largely indifferent towards the mother; her absence causes little distress and she and the stranger are treated very much alike.

Anxious-resistant (type C) An attachment style, in which the baby is very distressed when the mother leaves but shows ambivalence towards her when she returns: seeks contact but also shows anger and resists contact.

Attachment A relatively permanent emotional/ affectional tie to a particular individual, who provides a sense of security and comfort at times of stress.

Critical period Time in development during which particular experiences exert a profound and lasting influence on later behaviour (i.e. the effects are irreversible).

'Cupboard love' A view of attachment, proposed by both Freud and learning theorists as arising from the mother's satisfaction of the baby's primary drive for food; the baby acquires a secondary drive for the mother.

Deprivation The loss (through separation) of the mother-figure, usually associated with short-term effects (distress), but permanent separation (e.g. through death) can produce long-term effects, such as separation anxiety.

Fixed action pattern (FAP) Ethologists' way of defining and investigating instincts, through identifying units of behaviour which are only triggered by specific stimuli (sign stimuli), e.g. the begging response in herring-gull chicks, and the following response involved in imprinting.

Imprinting In precocial birds, the rapid learning to recognize the parents, which occurs as a result of the innate following response triggered during a critical period after hatching.

Insecure-disorganized (type D) An attachment style, in which the baby fails to show a clear-cut strategy for dealing with stress. Seems to involve a conflict between seeking and avoiding proximity with the mother, who is herself a source of fear. Also called insecure-disoriented

Maternal deprivation hypothesis Bowlby's claim that attachment to the mother/mother-figure cannot be broken in the early years of life without serious and permanent damage to the child's social, emotional and intellectual development.

Monotropy Bowlby's theory that babies have an innate tendency to become attached to one particular person, i.e. the mother/mother-figure. This attachment is different in kind from any later attachments.

Privation The absence of any attachment figure or lack of opportunity to form an attachment. More generally, lack of particular kinds of stimulation. Usually associated with long-term developmental retardation.

Securely attached (type B) An attachment style, in which the baby uses the mother as a safe base for exploring an unfamiliar environment. The baby is distressed by her departure and seeks immediate contact when she returns. She and the stranger are treated very differently.

Sensitive period Time in development during which learning is most likely to occur and will happen most easily.

Separation anxiety The fear of future separations, based on some previous separation. Can be manifested as school phobia.

Species specific Behaviour that is unique to a particular species and which is found in every member of that species (universal). Relates to the concept of instinct.

'Strange Situation' A standardized , controlled observational procedure, devised by Ainsworth, for studying attachments in 12-month-olds, comprising a sequence of eight episodes, involving the mother and an adult female stranger leaving and entering an observation room.

FURTHER READING

Parkes, C.M., Stevenson-Hinde, J. and Marris, P. (eds (1991) *Attachment Across The Life Cycle.* London: Routledge. A collection of original articles by some of the leading figures in the field, including Ainsworth, Main and Parkes, ending with a postscript by Bowlby, written shortly before his death.

Hazan, C. and Shaver, P.R. (1987) Conceptualizing romantic love as an attachment process. *Journal of Personality and Social Psychology,* 52, 511–24. The landmark study in adult attachment research.

23 SEX AND GENDER

INTRODUCTION AND OVERVIEW

Often the first thing we notice about someone is whether they are male or female; it is as if we need to have this information about a person if we are to be able to interact with them appropriately. We also expect people to be able to identify us correctly as male or female and if they cannot, or do not, we would probably be most offended. Our name, age and sex are standard pieces of information on all official forms and our sex is one of the facts which appears on our birth certificate.

The importance of sexual identity to our self-concept and our interactions with others (see Chapter 21) is a reflection of the fact that every known culture in the world makes a distinction between male and female and, in turn, this distinction is accompanied by a widely and deeply held belief that males and females are substantially different as regards psychological make up and behaviour. The particular characteristics and behaviours thought to be typical of males and females in specific cultures are called *stereotypes* (see Chapter 15) and the study of psychological sex differences is really an attempt to see how accurate these stereotypes are.

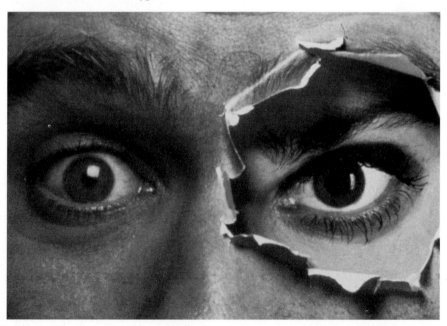

At the turn of the century (particularly in the US), many of the first generation of scientifically trained women psychologists devoted their research efforts to the extent and nature of sex differences. While a few achieved some professional success, as a group they failed to either legitimize or institutionalize the study of women and gender and psychology's interest in sex differences and gender waned with the rise of behaviourism (Crawford and Unger, 1995). Interest was revived in the 1970s, driven largely by feminist psychologists, although this label covers a wide range of theoretical positions and shades of opinion, i.e. there are many feminist interpretations of sex differences. What they tend to have in common is the belief that social, political, economic and cultural factors are fundamental in determining gender itself (and hence male/female differences), in contrast to the beliefs of sociobiologists (e.g. Wilson, 1975) (and the related, very recent field of evolutionary psychology, e.g. Buss, 1994) who argue that male/female differences have evolved as part of the more general adaptation of the human species to its environment and hence are 'natural'.

These two approaches (feminist psychology and sociobiology) can be seen as adopting diametrically opposed views regarding the *nature/nurture* or heredity/environment debate. Other explanations of sex differences that we shall be discussing in this chapter include the biological approach (e.g. Hutt, 1972) which obviously falls close to the sociobiological end, while cultural relativism (e.g. Mead, 1935) is in many ways as extreme as many feminist approaches. Somewhat less extreme are biosocial theory (Money and Ehrhardt, 1972), Freud's psychoanalytic theory, social learning theory (e.g. Bandura, 1977) and the cognitive-developmental approach (e.g. Kohlberg, 1966), all of which stress the interaction between biological and environmental influences, but in quite different ways. We shall also be discussing Bem's concept of androgyny and her gender schema theory. Much of the content of this chapter is 'social' in nature, much is developmental and much is to do with individual differences, so there is considerable overlap with other chapters in other parts of the book.

TERMS RELATING TO SEX AND GENDER

Feminist psychologists such as Unger (1979) distinguish between sex and gender. *Sex* refers to some biological fact about a person, namely having a particular genetic make-up and reproductive anatomy and functioning; it is usually denoted by the terms 'male' and 'female'. (However, as we shall see below, it is much more complex than it is often taken to be.) *Gender* is what culture makes out of the 'raw material' of biological sex, the social equivalent, or the social interpretation, of sex. Sexual identity is an alternative way of referring to our biological status as male or female and corresponding to our gender is our gender identity, which refers to our classification of ourselves (and others) as male or female, boy or girl, etc. While for most of us, sexual identity and gender identity correspond, an important exception is the transsexual (see below).

Gender role (often called sex role) refers to the behaviours, attitudes, values, beliefs and so on which a particular society expects from, or considers appropriate to, males and females on the basis of their biological sex. So to be masculine, a male must conform to the male gender role; similarly, for a female to be feminine, she must conform to the female gender role. As we saw earlier, *gender* (often called sex) *stereotypes* represent widely held beliefs about psychological differences between males and females (often reflecting gender roles). *Gender role identity* (or sex role identity) refers to the understanding and acceptance of gender roles, i.e. understanding and accepting that males and females are expected to be different from each other and to behave in different ways.

Sexual orientation or *preference* refers to an individual's tastes or preferences in sexual partners: this can be heterosexual (preference for a partner of the opposite sex, *hetero* meaning different), homosexual (preference for a partner of the same sex, *homo* meaning same) or bisexual (a choice of both kinds of partner, although there may be a stronger preference for one or the other). Homosexuals are anatomically normal males or females whose gender identity is, usually, quite consistent with their biological sex and sex of rearing. The transsexual is an anatomically normal person who genuinely and very firmly believes that he or she is a member of the opposite sex ('trapped' inside an 'alien' body); consequently, there is a fundamental inconsistency between their biological sexual identity and their gender identity.

● Biological categories

Biologically, sex is not a unidimensional variable, i.e. there are at least five separate biological categories which can be distinguished, each constituting a (partial) definition:

1 *Chromosomal sex*. A normal female has inherited two X chromosomes, one from each parent (XX), while a normal male has inherited one X from the mother and a Y from the father (XY).
2 *Gonadal sex*. This refers to the sexual or reproductive organs (ovaries in females and testes in males).
3 *Hormonal sex*. The male hormones are the androgens, the most important of which is testosterone (secreted by the testes); the ovaries secrete two distinct types of female hormone, namely oestrogen and progesterone. While the number and range of hormones produced by males and females are virtually the same, females usually produce a greater amount of oestrogen and progesterone, while males usually produce a greater amount of testosterone and androgen, i.e. we all produce both male and female hormones, but males usually produce more male hormones and females more female hormones.
4 *Sex of the internal accessory organs*. The Wolffian ducts in males and the Mullerian ducts in females are the embryonic forerunners of the reproductive structures (namely, the prostate gland, sperm ducts, seminal vesicles and testes in males and the fallopian tubes, womb and ovaries in females).
5 *Function and appearance of the external genitalia*. Theses are the penis and scrotum in males, and the outer lips of the vagina (labia majora) in females (Fig. 23.1).

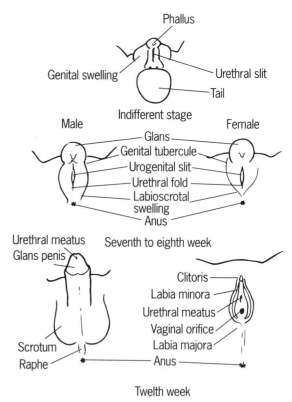

FIGURE 23.1 *Prenatal differentiation of male and female genitalia. From a relatively undifferentiated state, development proceeds by means of the relative enlargement of structures that have analogues in members of the other sex. (From Unger, R.K (1979) Female and Male, New York: Harper and Row)*

All five of these sexual categories are usually highly correlated, i.e. an individual tends to be either male in all respects or female in all respects. They also tend to be correlated with non-biological aspects of sex, including the sex to which the baby is assigned at birth, how the child is brought up, gender identity, gender role identity and so on. However, there are certain disorders which arise during pre- and postnatal development resulting in an inconsistency or lack of correlation between the five sexual categories. From these we can learn a great deal about the development of gender identity, gender role and gender role identity; collectively, individuals with such disorders are known as hermaphrodites.

● Hermaphroditism

This term is currently used to refer to any discrepancy or inconsistency between any of the various components of sexual anatomy and physiology, although strictly the term hermaphrodite (from the mythical Greek god/goddess who had attributes of both sexes) denotes a person who has functioning organs of both sexes (either simultaneously or sequentially). So included under this heading are:

1 *chromosome abnormalities*, where there is a discrepancy between chromosomal sex and external appearance, including the genitalia (the best known are Turner's syndrome (XO) and Klinefelter's syndrome (XXY));

2 *testosterone insensitivity* or testicular feminizing

syndrome (see Box 23.4 – the Batista family);

3 *adrenogenital syndrome*;

4 *true hermaphroditism* (the others are, strictly, pseudo-hermaphrodites) (see Box 23.1).

Both 2 and 3 are the effects of hormones (or lack of them) on the process of sexual differentiation.

Testosterone insensitivity (testicular feminizing syndrome)

For many individuals, the route to maleness is never completed and they end up as neither fully male nor fully female. Goldwyn (1979) describes the case of Daphne Went, a motherly-looking woman, who possessed two testes where most women have ovaries. She is one of 500 or so 'women' in Britain who have this condition called testosterone insensitivity (or testicular feminizing syndrome).

This woman's development began along the male route but it was never finished. The egg was fertilized by a Y sperm and two normal testes developed. They secreted their first hormone, which absorbed the

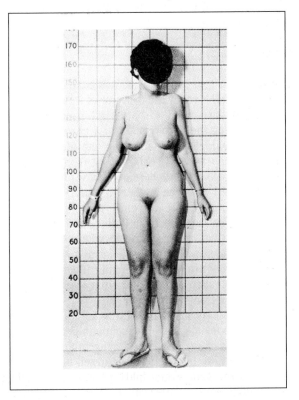

FIGURE 23.2 *Adult with testicular feminization (XY but with an insensitivity to androgen). These individuals are usually taller than the average female and tend to have an attractive 'female' physique. (From Money and Ehrhardt, 1972, reprinted with permission)*

BOX 23.1   The case of Mr Blackwell

In an article called 'The Fight to be Male' (1979), Edward Goldwyn cites the case of Mr Blackwell, only the 303rd patient in all of medical history to be a true hermaphrodite. He is described as a handsome and rather shy 18-year-old Bantu. Although he had a small vaginal opening as well as a penis, he was taken to be a boy and brought up as such. But when he was 14 he developed breasts and was sent to hospital to discover why this had happened. It was found that he had an active ovary on one side of his body and an active testicle on the other. He expressed the wish to remain male and so his female parts were removed.

Goldwyn points out that if his internal ducts had been differently connected, Mr Blackwell could have actually fertilized himself without being able to control it.

female parts, but when they produced testosterone her body did not respond to it. So, apart from the womb, which had gone, everything developed along female lines. When at puberty she developed no pubic hair and did not menstruate (despite breast development and female contours – as a result of the action of oestrogen), there was clearly something wrong! Hormones did not bring on her periods because she had no womb. Chromosomally, Mrs Went is male, in terms of her gonads she is also male (she has testes), but her external appearance is female. She is married, has adopted two children and leads an active and successful life as a woman.

This insensitivity to testosterone is due to a recessive gene and is often diagnosed when a hernia (lump in the abdomen) turns out to be a testis. There is a high probability that the testes will become malignant and so these are usually removed surgically. A 'blind' (very short) vagina is present so that little or no plastic surgery is needed for the adoption of a female appearance and gender role. The Y chromosome tends to give these individuals extra height, which is more typical of males than females (Fig. 23.2).

Adrenogenital syndrome

This is more common than the testicular feminizing syndrome and is really the converse of it. It is caused by an excessive amount of a testosterone-like substance during the development of a chromosomally normal female. It can happen in one of two ways: either *endogenously* (originating from within), where androgens (male hormones) are produced by excessive activity of the mother's adrenal glands during pregnancy (the adrenal glands produce oestrogens and androgens in both sexes); or *exogenously* (originating from without), where the mother takes progesterone (which is chemically very similar to testosterone) in the form of an artificial hormone preparation called progestin or other steroids, in an attempt to prevent miscarriage.

However it is caused, the adrenogenital syndrome involves the female's external genitalia bearing varying degrees of resemblance to the male external genitalia. There is usually an enlarged clitoris and fusion of the labioscrotal folds, producing a rather ambiguous genital appearance. Some individuals have even had a complete closure of the urethral groove and a penis capable of becoming erect. The internal organs do not appear to be affected, however. Until fairly recently, sex at birth was assigned on the basis of inspection of the genitalia, so that two

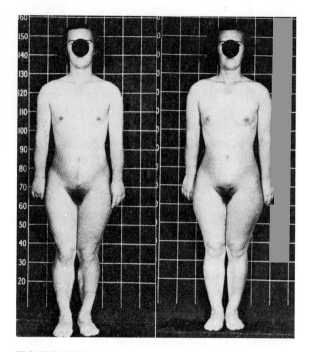

FIGURE 23.3 *(Left) The masculinized body contours of a female with untreated adrenogenital syndrome. (Right) The beginning of feminization induced by treatment. (From Money, J. and Ehrhardt, A. (1972) Man and Woman, Boy and Girl. Baltimore, Johns Hopkins Press © 1972 Johns Hopkins Press. Reprinted with permission)*

individuals with equivalent ambiguities might have been classified differently. More recently, information about the structure of the gonads and the chromosomal make-up of the individual has been acquired, so that females with the syndrome are usually raised as females. The internal structure is usually female and many such individuals are fertile. Therefore, a relatively small amount of cosmetic surgery is all that is required to bring their external appearance into line with other components of their sexual identity (Fig. 23.3).

PSYCHOLOGICAL SEX DIFFERENCES: WILL BOYS BE BOYS AND GIRLS BE GIRLS?

As Edley and Wetherell (1995) point out, the whole enterprise of sex difference research hangs on the assumption that there is a fundamental, irreducible, biological difference between males and females; without it, such studies become meaningless. To the extent that the five categories of sex

BOX
23.2

BOX 23.2 Critical discussion: The politics of sex difference research

An issue that applies to the study of individual differences in general, and arguably to sex differences in particular, is the wider socioeconomic and political context in which the research is carried out. The view of psychology as a value-free, objective science is at best naive and at worst misleading, since its findings can be taken as reflecting 'the way things are', rather than 'the way things look' from a particular political or ideological perspective (see Chapters 2 and 32).

According to Edley and Wetherell (1995), debates in the 19th century about which sex is more intelligent were clearly more than just academic: early attempts to prove that men's brains are larger and more powerful were just as much about justifying men's dominant social position as about trying to discover the 'natural' order of things. Similarly, the argument over inherent or natural sex differences is often part and parcel of a more general political debate about how society should be organized. For example, the claim that women are naturally more subjective, empathic and emotional leads very neatly to the decision that they are best suited to childcare and other domestic tasks which are devalued, by men, precisely because they are typically performed by women.

More specifically, within psychology as a whole but perhaps in the study of gender in particular, there is a strong bias towards publishing studies that have produced 'positive' results, i.e. where statistically significant sex differences have been found. When sex differences are not found, the findings tend to remain unreported; the far more convincing evidence for 'sex similarity', therefore, is ignored, creating the very powerful impression that differences between men and women are real, widespread and 'the rule'. Indeed, the very term 'sex similarities' sounds very odd (Jackson, 1992; Tavris, 1993; Unger, 1979). According to Denmark *et al.* (1988), ignoring studies which fail to produce non-significant sex differences represents a form of sexism or gender bias in psychological research.

---

that we considered above are normally correlated, then this assumption is correct, providing the logical basis for sex difference research. But before we discuss the evidence, we should consider some of the political and methodological issues surrounding sex difference research (see Box 23. 2).

● Gender stereotypes: how common are they?

As we noted earlier, sex difference research attempts to test out gender stereotypes, so it is important to know more about the latter before discussing the former. According to Williams and Best (1994), gender stereotypes represent one of three related but distinct ways in which women and men are viewed; the other two are *self-perceptions* (the degree to which gender stereotypes are incorporated into men's and women's self-concepts; see Chapter 21) and *gender role ideology* (beliefs about proper role relationships between men and women). Studying all three cross-culturally provides a greater range of beliefs and roles than single-culture studies can do, which can in turn suggest possible causes of gender differences.

During the 1980s and 1990s, Williams and Best conducted studies in over 30 countries, on every continent, asking university students to indicate, for each of 300 adjectives, whether they are more often associated with women, men or both genders equally.

The results show a high degree of agreement across all the countries studied regarding the characteristics most commonly associated with each gender group; these are shown in Table 23.1.

Despite this high degree of similarity in gender stereotypes, there were also systematic cultural variations; for example, stereotypes were much more differentiated in Protestant compared with Catholic countries. Also, in 25 of the countries, five- and eight-year-old children were studied; five-year-olds showed at least the beginning of adult stereotypes (most clearly in Pakistan, least in Brazil) and in all countries, there was an increase in gender stereotyping between five and eight, which seems to go on increasing through the teenage years and into young adulthood. Diversity between cultures decreases as children get older, i.e. stereotypes become more similar across cultures with age.

The degree of differentiation of men's and women's self-concepts was related to a large number of cultural variables: the lower the level of socioeconomic development, the lower the percentage of women working outside the home or attending university, the lower the percentage of the population identified as Christian and the more rural the environment, the greater the differentiation. This was true also for gender role ideology: the most modern, egalitarian ideologies were found in The Netherlands, Germany and Finland (with England

Male-associated				
Active	Courageous	Individualistic	Precise	Sharp-witted
Adventurous	Cruel	Initiative	Progressive	Show-off
Aggressive	Cynical	Interests wide	Quick	Steady
Arrogant	Determined	Inventive	Rational	Stern
Autocratic	Disorderly	Lazy	Realistic	Stingy
Bossy	Enterprising	Loud	Reckless	Stolid
Capable	Greedy	Obnoxious	Resourceful	Tough
Coarse	Hardheaded	Opinionated	Rigid	Unfriendly
Conceited	Humourous	Opportunistic	Robust	Unscrupulous
Confident	Indifferent	Pleasure-seeking	Serious	Witty
Female-associated				
Affected	Dependent	Fussy	Self-pitying	Timid
Affectionate	Dreamy	Gentle	Sensitive	Touchy
Appreciative	Emotional	Imaginative	Sentimental	Unambitious
Cautious	Excitable	Kind	Sexy	Unintelligent
Changeable	Fault-finding	Mild	Shy	Unstable
Charming	Fearful	Modest	Softhearted	Warm
Complaining	Fickle	Nervous	Sophisticated	Weak
Complicated	Foolish	Patient	Submissive	Worrying
Confused	Forgiving	Pleasant	Suggestible	Understanding
Curious	Frivolous	Prudish	Talkative	Superstitious

TABLE 23.1 *The 100 items most commonly associated with males and females in over 30 countries. (Based on Williams and Best, 1994)*

coming fourth), while the most traditional, male-dominated ideologies were found in Nigeria, Pakistan and India. The US fell roughly in the middle.

● So what is the evidence for psychological sex differences?

According to Edley and Wetherell (1995), it has proved notoriously difficult to find clear empirical support for most stereotypes (despite the politics of sex difference research; see Box 23.2).

In one of the largest reviews of the literature, Maccoby and Jacklin (1974) set out to show that many of the popular stereotypes about males and females are not borne out by the evidence and concluded that there is a great deal of myth in both popular and scientific views regarding male-female differences (as well as some degree of truth). They found no consistent sex differences in traits such as achievement motivation, sociability, suggestibility, self-esteem and cognitive style; the most convincing evidence related to verbal and spatial ability, mathematical reasoning and aggressiveness.

Are males more aggressive than females?

According to Maccoby and Jacklin, in all cultures where aggression has been observed, boys are more

aggressive than girls, both physically and verbally; they engage in mock-fighting and aggressive fantasies, as well as in direct forms of aggression more often than girls. The difference manifests itself as soon as social play begins, at about 2½ years, and usually the primary victims of male aggression are other males, not females. Although both sexes become less aggressive with age, boys and men remain more aggressive during the college years. Weisfeld (1994) confirms this general picture, claiming that sex differences are present throughout development.

However, the findings are mixed: according to Durkin (1995), females sometimes score higher for certain kinds of indirect, non-physical aggression. In some cross-cultural studies, no sex difference is reported, sometimes because there is so little aggression observed at all in particular cultures. Another problem is that some studies do not specify the type of aggression being observed, but whenever significant differences are found, it is males who have proved to be the more aggressive (Weisfeld, 1994). It is also well established that males are much more likely to be involved in delinquency, criminality and violence in general (Hoffmann *et al.*, 1994), although Campbell and Muncer (1994) report that national surveys of violence between spouses show that men and women admit to similar numbers of aggressive acts towards their spouses.

Do girls have greater verbal ability than boys?

According to Maccoby and Jacklin, girls' verbal abilities probably mature somewhat more rapidly in early life, although a number of studies have found no sex differences. From preschool to adolescence, the sexes are very similar in their verbal abilities, but at about 11, they begin to diverge and female superiority increases during adolescence and possibly beyond. Female superiority relates both to 'high level' verbal tasks (analogies, comprehension of difficult written material, creative writing) and 'lower level' measures (fluency and spelling).

However, Durkin (1995) notes that, as with aggression, the evidence is far from conclusive. He cites a meta-analysis (see below) by Hyde and Lynn (1988) which concludes that any difference is so small that it can effectively be considered to be zero.

Do boys have greater spatial abilities than girls?

This involves the visual perception of figures or objects in space and how they are related to each other; for example, jigsaw puzzles require this sort of ability, as do mental rotation tasks and the embedded figure test. Maccoby and Jacklin reported that male superiority does not appear in childhood but is fairly consistent in adolescence and adulthood and according to Hyde (1981, cited in Edley and Wetherell, 1995), about 25 percent of women score higher than the average (mean) male. Durkin (1995) again is much more cautious: while there is some superiority in male ability in some spatial tasks, within-sex variability is large and when significant between-sex differences are found, they are usually small.

Do boys have greater mathematical ability than girls?

According to Maccoby and Jacklin, the sexes are similar in the early acquisition of number concepts and the mastery of arithmetic during the primary school years. But beginning at about 12 or 13, boys' mathematical skills increase faster than girls. Different studies tend to reveal differences of varying sizes, but overall they are not as great as for spatial ability. Indeed, according to a meta-analysis carried out by Hyde *et al.* (1990, cited in Durkin, 1995), based on millions of participants, sex differences are quite small: among the general population (as opposed to students), there is a significant difference, but in the opposite direction to the stereotype. Hyde *et al.* confirmed the developmental picture whereby up to late childhood, there are no differences, but during adolescence they become detectable in certain areas. This relatively late developmental change suggests that factors other than genetic ones (i.e. 'natural' differences) are involved (Durkin, 1995).

● What conclusions can we draw about sex differences?

According to Durkin (1995), 'The overwhelming conclusion to be drawn from the literature on sex differences is that it is highly controversial...'. There is no doubt that the whole debate generates a lot of heat and that the results are open to many interpretations. For example, there is a misapprehension that a statistically significant difference implies a large difference; in fact, what determines a significant result is the *consistency* of differences between groups, such that if all the girls in a school scored 0.5 percent higher than all the boys on some test, this would produce a small but highly significant result (Edley and Wetherell, 1995).

According to Eagly (1983), where significant differences are found, the size of the difference is often quite substantial. She argues that by adding together the results of several compatible studies (i.e. those measuring the same variable), it is sometimes the case that the overall (or composite) picture that is produced is of significant differences; this is the basic method of meta-analysis (a 'study of studies'). Using meta-analysis, Eagly and Carli (1981) claim to have 'established' that women are more easily influenced than men. Eagly (1983) argues that, if anything, research has tended to conceal, rather than exaggerate, sex differences and that stereotypes are mainly confirmed by the available research. By contrast, Maccoby (1980) argues that even if group gender differences are found in a given area of behaviour (physical, cognitive, emotional or social), the differences within each gender are at least as great as the differences between them.

THEORIES OF PSYCHOLOGICAL SEX DIFFERENCES

● The sociobiological approach

According to sociobiologists, gender roles have taken shape gradually in the course of human evolution as part of our broader adaptation to the environment;

each sex is equipped with instincts and physical attributes for particular types of activity and responsibility (Durkin, 1995). Wilson (1975, 1978), for example, argues that males and females have developed different roles as a function of their respective contributions to reproduction and domestic labour: males' relative physical strength, greater lung power, etc. made them better suited to hunting, defending territory and family, while females' childbearing and milk-producing capacities make them ideally suited to childcare and other nurturant roles.

Related to this is the difference in the relative costs of reproduction between males and females. According to *parental investment theory* (Kenrick, 1994; Trivers, 1972, 1985; Wilson, 1978), reproduction is inexpensive for the male but costly for the female: the human family emerged as males and females struggled to establish an uneasy compromise, whereby she trades her reproductive capacity for his protection. The female has a clear advantage here, namely that while she can be certain that any offspring she produces is genetically related, the male cannot be sure of this; he needs to prevent his mate from mating with other males, which helps to explain why, in almost all societies, men try to control female

sexuality (Archer, 1992). The mother needs to know that the father will stay around to provide for her and the offspring (see Chapter 22).

As a result of these respective needs, society came to be organized in sexually exclusive domestic partnerships (or *polygynous* arrangements), which gave rise to different courtship roles: the female dresses up and decorates herself but also displays coyness and 'plays hard to get', because she needs time to assess her potential mate's commitment, while he, the hunter in pursuit of a conquest and keen to demonstrate his potential as a protector, displays aggressive and commanding postures. Sociobiologists point to the widespread patterns of contemporary sexual relationships; in Western and many other societies, women do dress up and wear make-up and both sexes place great emphasis on female physical attractiveness. Buss (1987, 1994), an evolutionary psychologist, argues that universally, what females find attractive in men are characteristics associated with the provision of resources, while males see physical beauty as most important (see Chapter 16). The 'unbridgeable gap' between males and females is discussed further in Box 23.3.

BOX 23.3	Critical discussion: Evolutionary psychology, sexual dimorphism and rape

The Human Behaviour and Evolution Society (HBES), founded in 1988, is the society of the new social Darwinists (or 'neo-Darwinists'), some of whom, while acknowledging their debt to sociobiologists such as Wilson, contend that sociobiologists often ignore the mind's role in mediating the links between genes and human behaviour. To reflect this emphasis on the mind, they call themselves *evolutionary psychologists* (Horgan, 1995).

According to Cosmides and Tooby (cited in Horgan, 1995), the mind consists of a number of specialized mechanisms or modules, designed by natural selection to solve problems that faced our hunter-gatherer ancestors, such as acquiring a mate, raising children and dealing with rivals; the solutions often involve emotions such as lust, fear, affection, jealousy and anger. Evolutionary psychology is mainly concerned with universal features of the mind but insofar as individual differences exist, they are seen as the expression of the same universal human nature as it encounters different environments.

However, the crucial exception to this rule is gender: natural selection has constructed the mental modules of men and women very differently as a result of their divergent reproductive roles. Buss's *The Evolution of Desire* (1994) claims that there is a distinct gender gap in 'mate choice' and according to Thornhill and Wilmsen Thornhill (1992, cited in Edley and Wetherell, 1995), human sexual psychology is *dimorphic*, i.e. the respective adaptations differ in men and women. The sexes differ in their feelings about whether, when and how often it is in their interests to mate: because women are more selective about their mates and more interested in evaluating them and delaying intercourse, men, to get sexual access, must often break through female resistance. According to Thornhill and Wilmsen-Thornhill's 'rape adaptation hypothesis', during human evolutionary history there was enough directional selection on males in favour of traits that solved the problem of forcing sex on a reluctant partner to produce a psychological tendency specifically towards rape.

In other words, not only does this hypothesis recast an oppressive form of behaviour in a much more positive light (it is 'adaptive'), but it also represents it as a natural characteristic of men ('they can't help it'). Not surprisingly, it has been condemned as not simply trying to explain men's sexual coercion, but justifying it (Edley and Wetherell, 1995).

Evaluation of the sociobiological approach

Sociobiologists assume that promiscuity increases the male's prospects of ensuring survival of his genes. But the 'love-'em-and-leave-'em' male who moves on after mating leaves behind a partner who could then mate with and be impregnated by someone else which , in sociobiological terms, seems to be maladaptive (Sternglanz and Nash, 1988, cited in Durkin, 1995).

According to Sayers (1982, cited in Durkin, 1995), animal behaviour, including dominance patterns, may be learned and is not always associated with greater strength and aggression. In the case of humans, dominance is often centred around 'status-seeking' – prestige, reputation and so on, and status presupposes values, which are culturally determined; culture is also unique to humans. Similarly, Bem (1993) criticizes sociobiological theories for overlooking one of the most remarkable features of human evolution, namely our ability to transform our environments and hence, arguably, ourselves. (See Chapters 16 and 17 for more general criticisms of sociobiological theories.)

● The biological approach

This does not represent a unitary theory, but is a way of trying to account for gender differences by concentrating directly on biological aspects of sex differences, such as:

- genetic differences,
- the process of sexual differentiation, and
- hormonal differences.

As far as *sexual differentiation* is concerned, Alfred Jost proposed (1970 a and b) that the natural form of the human is female. This was based on his observation (in rats and later in rabbits) that even if the ovaries are removed at the earliest stage of embryonic development, growth still follows a female route, while if the testicles are removed early on, development reverts to the female route. So Jost saw male development as the result of interference with the natural (female) developmental course; if a Y chromosome is present, the gonad becomes the testis and male development proceeds, while in the absence of a Y chromosome, an ovary is produced and the embryo becomes a female (see Fig. 23.1).

Not only does the presence or absence of a Y chromosome determine the course of sexual differentiation, it also seems to be correlated with the *biological vulnerability* of the sexes, both before and

after birth. Although in theory there is a 50:50 chance of a male or female being conceived, in fact there is a preponderance of males: approximately 120 males are conceived for every 100 females, but this ratio reduces to 110:100 for foetuses that survive to full term (40 weeks of pregnancy) and reduces still further to 106:100 for live births. This means that more male foetuses are spontaneously aborted and more of them are stillborn or die of birth trauma (including congenital deformities). In fact, throughout life, the male is more vulnerable than the female and more women survive to older ages, i.e. their average life expectancy is higher (see Chapter 24). Males are also more susceptible to asphyxiation, cerebral palsy, convulsions, virus infections, ulcers, heart disease and some kinds of cancer and the smaller Y chromosome makes the male more vulnerable to various kinds of inherited diseases and disorders (e.g. haemophilia). There is no doubt that males are, biologically, the weaker sex!

BOX 23.4	The case of the Batista family: an overnight sex change?

Imperato-McGinley *et al.* (1974) studied a remarkable family who live in Santo Domingo in the Dominican Republic (in the Caribbean). Of the ten children in the Batista family, four of the sons have changed from being born and growing up as girls into muscular men : they were born with normal female genitalia and body shape but when they were 12, their vaginas healed over, two testicles descended and they grew full-size penises.

The Batistas are just one of 23 affected families in their village in which 37 children have undergone this change. All these families had a common ancestor, Attagracia Carrasco, who lived in the mid-18th century. She passed on a mutant gene which only shows when carried by both parents.

What happens to these children in the womb? The egg is fertilized by a Y sperm and it first develops into a foetus with normal testes. The female parts are absorbed in the normal way and testosterone preserves the male ducts. But the body misses a critical chemical step and so the external anatomy does not change. The step that is missed is the production of the hormone dihydrotestosterone which, it is now known, is responsible for creating the male external anatomy. The change that occurs at puberty is due to the flood of testosterone which, in turn, produces enough dihydrotestosterone to give the normal male appearance (which would normally happen 10–12 years earlier).

Genetic and hormonal differences are responsible for a number of sex-linked characteristics which are apparent at birth or shortly after. Could it be that, if these sex differences are innate, males and females are biologically programmed for certain kinds of activities that are compatible with male and female roles? For instance, might boys be predisposed towards aggression, assertiveness, rough-and-tumble play, etc. by virtue of higher pain thresholds, higher activity levels, a more muscular physique and their more irritable and demanding temperament? And might docile, undemanding and highly verbal females be ideally suited for adopting nurturant, co-operative, compliant roles? Is there any evidence to support the biological view?

The case of the four Batista boys (Box 23.4), who were raised as girls from birth and who at puberty suddenly 'became' males, seems to support the bio-logical view: inside each female body was a brain which had been masculinized by the testosterone present before birth and which was then activated by another surge at puberty. They have all taken on male roles, do men's jobs, have married women and are accepted as men in spite of the fact that they were reared as girls and, presumably, thought of themselves as girls for the first ten years or so of their lives (i.e. had a female gender identity). However, they may have made the transition as easily as they did because their environment supported their new identity.

The claim that the Batista boys could so easily assume male roles because the testosterone had pre-programmed masculinity into their brains itself implies that male and female brains are different. Is there any evidence that they are?

Dorner (1968) thinks so. He identified a sex cen-tre in the rat's brain such that when a small part of this was destroyed in a newborn male, it would behave as a female. In his terms, it became homosex-ual. Dorner argues that the same basic differences exist in human brains and that male homosexuals have a female brain, due to unusually low levels of testosterone in the womb. In turn, low levels of the male hormone can be induced by high levels of stress in the pregnant mother. But again, this relationship is based on studies of rats. What about the human evidence?

The case of Mrs Went (see page 577) certainly does nothing to support Dorner's hypothesis, nor is there any convincing evidence that there are hor-monal differences between homosexual and heterosexual adults. The case of Mr Blackwell (see Box 23.1) also detracts from the biological view. He has a female brain – his hormones used to go through a complete female menstrual cycle and he used to ovulate once a month. Yet, despite his female brain, he wanted to remain a male and does not dis-play the female behaviour predicted by Dorner's theory.

A different kind of evidence relating to brain dif-ferences is to do with *hemispheric specialization* (see Chapter 3). As measured by brainwave patterns, it appears that men have a greater degree of such specialization than women. For example, when per-forming spatial tasks, a man's right hemisphere tends to be more active while with women both hemispheres are activated. In fact, the right hemi-sphere is generally the dominant one in men and the left in women, which could explain why men are gen-erally superior at spatial and mathematical tasks and women at verbal tasks (see above).

Ornstein (1986) refers to the work of de Lacoste and her colleagues, who are beginning to be able to identify the male and female corpus callosum by sight alone. They are, it seems, as 'dimorphic' as are male and female arms: women's are larger overall and longer towards the back of the brain. However, according to Kimura (1992), the evidence regarding this alleged difference is far from conclusive; this may be due partly to variations in the shape of the corpus callosum associated with age, as well as dif-ferent methods of measurement. The assumption made is that the larger the corpus callosum, the greater the number of fibres connecting the two hemispheres and the more efficient the communica-tion between them. However, it is not clear whether it is the number of fibres which is the crucial male-female difference and sex differences in cognitive functioning have yet to be related to a difference in callosal size (Kimura, 1992).

Evaluation of the biological approach

Although those who emphasize the biological causes of sex differences usually do not deny the role of environmental factors (and even sociobiologists, such as Wilson, acknowledge the importance of cul-ture and society in the development of the human species), the biological approach assumes an 'addi-tional' model of influence, i.e. nature and nurture can be separated out and measured against each other to see which is the more important (Edley and Wetherell, 1995).

Probably the most common version of this model is the one that sees biology as defining the limits or parameters of human behaviour (e.g. Hutt, 1972), such that, for example, men are naturally potentially more aggressive, but whether or not they display it depends on the environment. While not denying the role of biology, Edley and Wetherell (1995) believe that to ask 'What is the biological basis of masculinity?' (and, by the same token, femininity) is to pose a false question: '...It requires us to separate what cannot be separated: men are the product of a complex system of factors and forces which combine in a variety of ways to produce a whole range of different masculinities...'. This is a theme which is central to cultural relativism and feminist accounts of gender differences (see below).

● Biosocial theory

Biosocial theory, as the name suggests, takes social factors into account in relation to biological ones. Specifically, it focuses on how babies of different temperaments contribute to their own development by influencing how others treat them; it is the *interaction* between biological and social factors that is important rather than the influence of biology directly. Intuitively, it is easy to see how these constitutional differences can be reinforced by interaction with adults: adults prefer to spend time with babies who respond to them in 'rewarding' ways and more demonstrative babies (or 'demanding' ones) tend to receive the adult attention they seek while the more passive baby is more easily 'forgotten'.

However, the baby's sex is just as important as its temperament as far as others are concerned; if people have stereotyped expectations regarding the differences between boys and girls, then these are likely to be expressed through different ways of relating to boys and girls, simply because they are male or female. This was demonstrated in the 'baby X' experiments (Smith and Lloyd, 1978, cited in Rutter and Rutter, 1992), in which toddlers were dressed in unisex snowsuits and then given names to indicate gender, half the time in line with their true gender, half the time not. When adults played with them, they treated them differently, according to which gender they believed the toddler to be.

What the 'baby X' experiments show is that a person's (perceived) biological make-up becomes part of his or her social environment through the process of others' reactions to it. Money and Ehrhardt (1972) have concentrated on the very fact of a child's sexual identity; for them, 'anatomy is destiny' in the sense that how the infant is labelled sexually determines how the infant is raised or socialized. This, in turn, determines the child's gender identity

and from this follow gender role, gender role identity and sexual orientation. Money and Ehrhardt believe that at first there is considerable flexibility in the process by which the child categorizes itself as a boy or girl: the sex of rearing can be changed within the first 2½–3 years without any undue psychological harm being done. However, once a child has developed a gender identity, being reassigned to the opposite sex can result in extreme psychological disturbance. Thus the first 2½–3 years of life represent a critical or sensitive period for the development of gender identity.

Money and Ehrhardt (1972) studied girls with the adrenogenital syndrome and who were raised as boys. When the mistake was discovered, their genitals were surgically corrected and they were reassigned and reared as girls before the age of three, they easily accepted the gender change; but when this happened after three years, there were many adjustment problems. Money *et al.* (1957) studied matched pairs of individuals with the adrenogenital syndrome, the members of each pair having a very similar external genital appearance. The crucial difference between them was that they had been assigned to a different sex. They concluded that psychosexual identity is established more in accordance with the sex of rearing than on the basis of any biological factors.

Money and Ehrhardt (1972) also studied ten individuals with the testicular feminizing syndrome (who, remember, are genetically male but who are invariably reared as female because of their female external appearance); they showed a strong preference for the female role. The case of Mrs Went, discussed earlier, also tends to support the view that sex of rearing is more important than biological sex.

Money and Ehrhardt, and others, conclude that, despite disparities between an individual's genetic sex, hormonal sex, internal and external organs and the sex of rearing, in the vast majority of cases the individual assumes the gender role consistent with the sex of rearing. In their view, psychologically, sexuality is undifferentiated at birth and it becomes differentiated as masculine or feminine in the course of various experiences of growing up: the human central nervous system is so amenable to the effects of learning that biological contributions to psychosexual identity can be moulded and even reversed by the social influences of early childhood. Money (1971) pointed out that requests for sexual reassignment are very rare amongst such individuals. The conformity of most hermaphrodites to their early sex of assignment is so strong that it can withstand ugly virilization in a 'girl' at puberty or breast development and difficulties in having an erection in a 'boy'.

Evaluation of biosocial theory

Diamond (1978) points out that to demonstrate that human beings are flexible in their psychosexual identity does not in itself disprove that 'built-in biases' still have to be overcome. Money *et al.*'s participants have been hermaphrodites and, therefore, atypical, not representative of the population as a whole. Is it valid to generalize from an abnormal sample to the 'normal' population? The fact that individuals of ambiguous sex are flexible in their psychosexual ori-

---

> ## BOX 23.5
>
> ## The circumcision that went wrong (Money, 1974)
>
> An accident occurred during circumcision (by cautery) of a pair of monozygotic (identical) twins whose embryonic and foetal development were those of a normal male: one of the twins lost his penis. Assuming that gender is primarily a social phenomenon and that identity is learned, it was decided to raise the unfortunate 'penectomized' boy as a girl. This would seem to be a decisive way of choosing between the learning versus biological arguments, by letting rearing 'compete' with biology, and it would have been a true test case had not as much as possible been done to 'defeat' the male biological realities and to enhance female biological maturation.
>
> At 17 months, 'he' was castrated, i.e. the androgen-secreting testes were removed, and was given oestrogen (female hormone); a vaginal canal was constructed at this time. Much earlier than this, the parents changed 'his' clothes and hairstyle. By the age of four, 'he' preferred dresses to trousers, took pride in 'his' long hair and was much neater and cleaner than 'his' brother. 'He' sat while urinating, in the usual female fashion, and was modest about exposing 'his' genitals (in contrast to the other twin, for whom an incident of public urination was described by the mother with amusement). 'He' was encouraged to help the mother with the housework, while the brother 'couldn't care less about it'.
>
> At five years, 'he' had many tomboyish traits, but was encouraged to be less rough and tough than the other twin and was generally quieter and more 'lady-like', while the normal twin was physically protective of his 'sister'. At nine years, although 'he' had been the dominant one since birth, 'he' expressed this by being a 'fussy little mother' to 'his' brother. The brother continued to play the traditional protective, male role.

entation and identity does not necessarily mean that the same is true of people in general. How could we settle the controversy? A classic piece of evidence relevant to the issue was reported by Money (1974) and is described in Box 23.5.

The case described in Box 23.5 seems to support the view that gender identity (and gender role) is learned. The reversal of original sexual assignment is possible if it takes place early enough and is consistent in all respects, which includes the external genitalia conforming well enough to the new sex. However, the castration and use of oestrogen clearly contributed to the ease of reassignment and probably also accounts for the normal twin being taller. Significantly, follow-up research with the 'girl' when she reached her teens (Diamond, 1982) found that she was an unhappy adolescent, with few friends, uncertain about her gender, maintaining that boys have a better life. She also looked rather masculine. Diamond concluded that biology had ultimately proven irrepressible.

● Freud's psychoanalytic theory

We have discussed Freud's theory of psychosexual development in great detail in Chapter 21. You will recall that, according to Freud, sexual identity and sex role are acquired (along with a superego) when the Oedipus complex is resolved, at 5-6 years of age. The role of the traditional mother and father family unit (two-parent family) is, therefore, of crucial importance in Freud's theory of sexual development, whereby the child must identify with the same-sex parent.

So what would Freud have predicted about the psychosexual development of a child who grows up in an 'abnormal', atypical family, which is becoming increasingly commonplace in contemporary society: for example, single-parent families, including lesbian and heterosexual women who have become pregnant by artificial insemination, and lesbian couples with children? Indeed, according to Rutter (1979), the non-traditional family may have become the norm. Is there any evidence that psychosexual development is adversely affected as a result of growing up in an 'un-Freudian' family?

According to Lamb (1977, 1979), fathers, at the beginning of the child's second year, begin to pay special attention to their sons and withdraw from their daughters. As this happens, boys channel their attention towards their father's behaviour and girls towards their mother's. Through this channelling, children prefer to interact with the same-sex parent

| BOX 23.6 | Key study: The effects of being raised by homosexual or transsexual parents |

Green (1978) studied 37 children (18 males, 19 females), aged between three and 20 (average age 11), all of whom were being raised by either a lesbian (21) or by parents who had undergone sex reassignments (16); most of the children of the latter were aware that their parents had at one time been a member of the opposite sex.

The study was conducted over a two-year period. Green evaluated the younger children's sexual preferences by asking them what toys and games they preferred, about their peer preferences, the roles they chose during fantasy play, their clothing preferences and vocational desires. They were also given the draw-a-person test – children usually draw a person of their own gender before one of the opposite gender. For the adolescents, Green obtained information about their sexual desires and their fantasies about sexual partners as well as about their overt sexual behaviour.

All 37 (with the questionable exception of one child) developed heterosexual preferences and showed a marked desire to conform to the gender roles provided by their culture. None had homosexual or transsexual fantasies. All the young children wanted to play with others of the same gender. Boys wanted to be doctors, firemen, policemen, engineers or scientists, while the girls wanted to be nurses, teachers, mothers or housewives.

The biggest single fear expressed in relation to unconventional families is that if the children are exposed to any combination other than a 'feminine' mother and a 'masculine' father, then they are considerably more 'at risk' of becoming homosexual. However, just as exposure to heterosexual relationships between parents does not prevent the child becoming homosexual (indeed, the vast majority of homosexuals grow up in heterosexual families), so exposure to homosexual models seems unlikely to have a decisive impact on sexual orientation either. The evidence suggests that homosexuality, in so far as it is shaped by early life experience, is more likely to be influenced by poor relationships with parents, perhaps especially with the same-sex parent.

Hoeffer (1981) and Kirkpatrick et al. (1981) (both cited in Golombok et al. 1983) compared children raised in homosexual and heterosexual single-mother households and found normal levels of heterosexual development in both groups. An important study by Green (1978) is described in Box 23.6.

Finally, Golombok et al. (1983) compared 37 5–17-year-olds reared in 27 lesbian households (i.e. lesbian couples) with 38 of the same age range raised in 27 heterosexual single-parent households. There were systematic, standardized interviews with the children and the mothers, plus questionnaires given to teachers and the mothers. The two groups did not differ in terms of gender identity, sex role behaviour or sexual orientation, nor did they differ on most measures of emotions, behaviour and relationships (although there was some indication of more frequent psychiatric problems in the single-parent group). It was concluded that rearing in a lesbian household as such did not lead to atypical psychosexual development or constitute a psychiatric risk factor.

and this makes it more likely that identification will occur. So preference for the same-sex parent does seem to be a major factor in the child's acquisition of gender role identity.

Research on father absence, for example by Hetherington (1966, 1972), supports the idea that gender role identity develops within the first 2–3 years and that fathers are important in this process. If the father is absent before the boy's fourth birthday, he is likely to be less 'masculine', in the sense of being more dependent on his peers, less assertive and less involved in competitive and physical contact sports. However, after the age of four, absence of the father has little effect on the boy's gender role identity. In the case of girls, the effect does not usually show up until adolescence; the most common outcome of father absence for girls is difficulty in adjusting to the female role and in interacting with men.

● Social learning theory

As we have seen elsewhere (Chapter 7), social learning theory (SLT) emphasizes the crucial role played by observational learning (learning from models) and reinforcement. Bandura et al. (1961) found that boys were more likely to imitate aggressive male models than girls were (based on perceived similarity and relevance; see Chapter 27). But how representative are these findings? Are children more likely to imitate same-sex models and are boys and girls socialized along stereotyped lines?

Imitation and modelling

Overall, the evidence is inconclusive. Maccoby and Jacklin (1974), for example, concluded that there is very little evidence that children do actually imitate same-sex models more than opposite-sex models. It is sometimes found that children are more likely to imitate a same-sex model than an opposite-sex model even if the behaviour is sex-inappropriate. But other studies have found the reverse to be true, namely, that children preferred to imitate behaviour that is appropriate to their own sex, regardless of the sex of the model!

Perhaps children imitate same-sex models more than opposite-sex ones when there is no information regarding the sex-appropriateness of the modelled behaviour. However, when there is such information, then the sex of the model seems to become relatively unimportant. It could be that children attend equally to all models but imitate same-sex models more because they are reinforced for doing so. However, while it does appear that children recall more of a model's behaviour when they have previously been reinforced for imitating that model, there is little evidence that children are actually rewarded for imitating models of the same sex (see Chapter 27). Starting at about six or seven years, children do begin to pay more attention to same-sex models; significantly, this is when *gender constancy* develops (see Kohlberg's cognitive developmental theory below).

Effects of the media on gender role stereotypes

Parents, of course, are not the only models that children are exposed to and social learning theorists are particularly interested in the way that males and females are portrayed on TV, in books, films, etc. *Gender role stereotyping* is the belief that it is only natural and fitting for males and females to adhere to traditional gender role patterns.

There is a great deal of evidence that gender role stereotypes are held by parents, preschool teachers and the media, including both TV and books. For example, a recent British survey (Wober *et al.*, 1987) explored children's perceptions of whether on TV different occupational activities were seen to be done primarily by males or by females. The children were 334 members of a national UK viewing panel, aged between five and 12. From a list of 14 jobs, 'serving customers in a shop', 'attending to patients in a hospital', 'taking care of baby children' and 'typing in an office' were principally done by girls or women on TV, while 'working a big machine in an office', 'piloting

an aeroplane', 'laying bricks to build a house', 'manning a fire engine and putting out a fire' and 'repairing TVs and electric machines' were very much male occupations. Some were seen as being done by both males and females (e.g. 'being in charge of curing a sick animal' and 'driving a police car').

Before we can properly evaluate studies of the effects of TV watching, it is important to adopt a valid view of the person who is watching (see Chapter 17). To assume that television can impact upon a passively receptive child audience with messages about sex stereotyping, thus moulding innocent young viewers' conceptions of gender, is largely accepted as an oversimplistic picture of what really goes on. Viewers exhibit a degree of activity in selecting what to watch, what to pay attention to and what to remember of the things they see. Even children respond in a selective fashion to particular characters and events and their perceptions, memories and understanding of what they have seen may often be mediated by dispositions they bring with them to the viewing situation (Gunter and McAleer, 1990).

Gunter (1986) cites a small number of surveys which report significant links between personal or parental estimates of children's TV viewing and their sex role perceptions – these have been taken as evidence for a TV influence; youngsters who were categorized as heavy viewers were found to hold stronger stereotyped beliefs than lighter viewers. However, much of this research failed to produce precise measures of what programmes were actually watched (Gunter and McAleer, 1990).

Frueh and McGhee (1975) interviewed 4–12-year-olds (40 boys and 40 girls) about their viewing, along with their parents, and then gave the children a projective measure of sex stereotyping (a paper and pencil test which examined choice of sex-typed toys). A clear relationship was found between the amount of reported TV viewing and choice of toys – the heaviest viewers were the ones who chose toys in the most stereotyped way. But what role did parents play, not only in teaching children about sex roles but also in helping them to interpret what they watched? How accurate was parental monitoring of actual viewing among the youngest children? Was the sample representative? Was the projective test valid? Gunter and McAleer (1990) believe that these and other critical questions remain unanswered about the Frueh and McGhee study. An important study by Williams (1986), which was discussed in Chapter 17 in relation to aggression, is discussed further here, in Box 23.7.

BOX 23.7	Key study: There's no Tel-ing the impact that television can have

A study in Canada (Williams, 1986) investigated the effects of the introduction of TV on an essentially TV-naïve community (i.e. one which previously had not had TV reception). Three towns were compared ('Notel', 'Unitel' and 'Multitel') which at the start of the study had no TV, one channel only and four channels, respectively. By the end of the study (two years later), Notel had one channel, Unitel had two and Multitel still had four. Children in Notel were assessed for their sex role attitudes at the start of the study and then two years later.

Initially, children in Unitel and Multitel were found to be much more stereotyped in terms of how appropriate or frequent they believed certain behaviours are for their peer group. Two years later, Notel children had become significantly more stereotyped but the change did not extend to how they rated their own parents' frequency of performing certain tasks.

Williams concluded that, in the longer term, TV had the potential to shape children's sex role attitudes and recommended that special attention should be given to how women are presented on TV. It appeared that any sex-stereotyped messages that were being broadcast were being absorbed, especially by boys.

Do parents raise their sons and daughters differently?

Social learning theorists are also interested in child-rearing methods and how differences in these may contribute to gender differences. An important dimension of childrearing is how parents (and other adults) treat and react to the child by virtue of the child's biological sex, i.e. *sex typing*.

Sears *et al.* (1957) found that the greatest and most consistent differences between boys and girls was in the area of aggression, with boys being allowed more aggression in their relationships with other children, while this was discouraged in girls. Boys were also allowed to express aggression towards their parents more than girls were. For some mothers, being 'boylike' meant being aggressive and boys were often encouraged to fight back.

However, Maccoby and Jacklin (1974), in their major review, found no consistent differences in the extent to which boys and girls are reinforced for aggressiveness or encouraged to be autonomous, etc. In fact, contrary to expectations, the picture they painted was one of remarkable uniformity in the socialization of the two sexes. This was largely confirmed in a more recent meta-analysis of a large number of studies by Lytton and Romney (1991, cited in Durkin, 1995): they found very few sex differences in terms of parental warmth, overall amount of interaction, encouragement of achievement or dependency, restrictiveness and discipline or clarity of communication.

● Cultural relativism

This really represents the most direct challenge to the biological approach. If gender differences do reflect biological differences, then we would expect to find the same differences occurring in different cultures; any differences that exist between different cultures in relation to gender roles (*cultural relativism*) would tend to support the view that gender role is culturally determined.

The famous anthropologist Margaret Mead (who died in 1980), in *Sex and Temperament in Three Primitive Societies* (1935), claimed that the traits which we call masculine and feminine are completely unrelated to biological sex. Just as the clothing, manner and head-dress that are considered to be appropriate in a particular society, at a particular time, are not determined by sex, so temperament and gender role are not biologically but culturally determined. She studied three New Guinea tribes, who lived quite separately from each other within about a 100-mile radius:

● The Arapesh, who lived on hillsides, she described as gentle, loving and co-operative; boys and girls were reared in order to develop these qualities, which in Western society are stereotypically feminine ones. Both parents were said to 'bear a child' and men took to bed while the child was born.

● The Mundugumor were riverside dwellers and ex-cannibals. Both males and females were self-assertive, arrogant, fierce and continually quarrelling and they both detested the whole business of pregnancy and child rearing. Sleeping babies were hung in rough-textured baskets in a dark place against the wall and when they cried, someone would scratch gratingly on the outside of the basket.

● The Tchambuli, who lived on the lakeside, represented the reversal of traditional Western gender roles. Girls were encouraged to take an interest in the tribe's economic affairs while the boys were not. The women took care of trading and food gathering while the men, considered sentimental, emotional and incapable of making serious decisions, spent much of the day sitting around in groups, gossiping and 'preening' themselves.

Booth (1975) believes that the conclusions which Mead drew from her research may have been influenced by things going on in her private life, in particular, her perception of the aggressive, child-hating Mundugumor may have been coloured by her own sadness and frustration at not being able to have children. Also, she described the Arapesh after the colonial period (before colonization, the Arapesh had been quite warlike), yet referred to the Mundugumor as if they still practised their old forms of warfare – this exaggerated the differences between them.

By 1949 (*in Male and Female – a Study of the Sexes in a Changing World*), after she had studied four other cultures (Samoa, Manus, Iatmul and Bali), Mead had rather dramatically changed her views about gender roles. From a rather extreme 'cultural determinism' in the original 1935 book, she now concluded that women were 'naturally' more nurturing than men, expressing their creativity through childbearing and childbirth, and are superior in intellectual abilities requiring intuition. While motherhood is a 'biological inclination', fatherhood is a 'social invention': the implication is that societies which encourage a gender role division other than that in which dominant, sexually energetic men live with passive, nurturant women are 'going against nature'. Significantly, by this time she had given birth to a child of her own!

Is there any evidence for cultural universals and what do they mean?

A finding which may seem to support Mead in her search for 'natural' differences is that there is no known society in which the female does the fighting in warfare and this includes the Tchambuli and the Arapesh (Fortune, 1939 in Booth 1975). However, to define aggression in this way is extremely limited – aggression can be expressed in many, more subtle ways which it is often difficult to measure (see Chapter 17). More to the point, Malinowski (1929), studying the Trobriand Islanders, reported that, in order to foster their tribe's reputation for virility, groups of women would catch a man from another tribe, arouse him to erection and rape him! This 'gang rape' was carried out in a brutal manner and the women often boasted about their achievement.

Yet even if it is shown that men are, universally, the hunters and war-makers, does this necessarily mean that males are naturally more aggressive than females? Is there something 'essential' about the sexes, beneath the veneer of culture, which is immutable and eternal (Wade and Tavris, 1994)? According to Archer (1976) and Gilmore (1990), for example, universal patterns of gendered behaviour may represent common practical solutions to universal problems and Wade and Tavris (1994) note that, because early researchers assumed that men are naturally aggressive (and women are naturally nurturant), they often defined nurturing in a way that excluded the altruistic, caring activities of men, as in nurturing the family by providing food for mother and child and sometimes by going off to fight in faraway places, sacrificing their lives if necessary, in order to provide a safe haven for their people.

While most cultures distinguish between 'men's' and 'women's work' and while biological factors undoubtedly play some part in the sexual division of labour, the content of this work varies enormously between cultures. In some cultures, '...men weave and women make pots, whereas in others these roles are reversed; in some parts of the world women are

---

BOX 23.8 | Critical discussion: Are there more than two genders?

Among the Sakalavas in Madagascar, boys who are thought to be pretty are raised as girls and readily adopt the female gender role. Similarly, the Alentian Islanders in Alaska raise handsome boys as girls; their beards are plucked at puberty and they are later married to rich men and they too seem to adapt quite readily to their assigned gender role.

Studies of certain North American Indian tribes reveal the possibility of more than two basic gender roles. For example, the 'berdache', a biological male of the Crow tribe, simply chooses not to follow the ideal role of warrior. Instead, he might become the 'wife' of a warrior but he is never scorned or ridiculed by his fellow Crows. (Little Horse in the film *Little Big Man*, starring Dustin Hoffman, was a 'berdache').

The Mohave Indians recognized four distinct gender roles: (i) traditional male; (ii) traditional female; (iii) 'alyha'; and (iv) 'hwame'. The 'alyha' was a male who chose to live as a woman (to the extent of mimicking menstruation by cutting his upper thigh and undergoing a ritualistic pregnancy) and the 'hwame' was a female who chose to become a man.

the major agricultural producers, and in others they are prohibited from agricultural activity' (Hargreaves, 1986).

The picture emerging is that while anatomical sex is universal and unchangeable, gender, which refers to all the duties, rights and behaviours a culture considers appropriate for males and females, is a social invention and it is gender that gives us a sense of personal identity as male or female (Wade and Tavris, 1994). An even stronger argument for the social construction of gender comes from studies of societies in which gender reversal is relatively commonplace or, more importantly, where there are more than two genders (see Box 23.8).

● The cognitive-developmental approach

We could sum up the SLT approach in this way: I want rewards, I am rewarded for doing boy/girl things, *therefore* I want to be a boy/girl. Using the same form of argument, we could sum up Kohlberg's cognitive-developmental theory like this: I am a boy/girl, I want to do boy/girl things, *therefore* the opportunity to do boy/girl things (and gain approval) is rewarding.

For Kohlberg (1966, 1969), the child first comes to categorize itself as a boy or girl and only then will it selectively attend to (or identify with) same-sex models, i.e. the child first develops a gender identity which determines who it will imitate (which is the reverse of the SLT account). The child actively constructs its own conception of gender, based on both physical and social sources; once it has acquired its gender label, it comes to value behaviours, objects and activities which are consistent with it – rewards stem from behaving consistently with one's gender label rather than from what other people consider appropriate.

● The development of gender identity

Gender labelling or basic gender identity (2–3½ years)

Children of this age are gradually becoming aware of being a member of a particular gender, but at first this is little more than a label, equivalent to a personal name. They are also beginning to discover which other individuals fall into the same category and their use of labels extends to 'man' and 'woman', as well as 'boy' and 'girl'. Kohlberg (1966) found that a 2–3-year-old boy may be able to tell you that he is a boy, but that he believes he could become a girl, or a mummy, if he wanted to, e.g. by playing girls' games or wearing dresses or growing his hair long.

Gender stability (3½–4½ years)

This involves understanding that you stay the same gender throughout your life, i.e. basic gender identity is seen as stable over time, as reflected in the answers to questions such as 'When you were a little baby, were you a little boy or a little girl?' and 'When you grow up will you be a mummy or a daddy?' However, their understanding of gender is limited to external, 'social' definitions, so that while all the three-year-olds could identify the gender of dolls on the basis of hair and clothing cues, only 12 percent could do so on the basis of genitals. However, 31 percent of four-year-olds, 51 percent of five-year-olds and 70 percent of six-year-olds could use genital differences to classify male and female dolls (Marcus and Overton, 1978; Slaby and Frey, 1975). Also, the child still believes that a change in appearance implies a change in gender (reflecting lack of conservation; see below and Chapter 25).

Gender constancy or consistency (4½–7 years)

The child now grasps that gender identity is stable over time and across situations, e.g. someone remains the same gender even though they may appear to change by wearing different clothes or a different hairstyle. Gender constancy represents a kind of conservation which, significantly, appears shortly after the child has mastered conservation of quantity (Marcus and Overton, 1978). The child has to learn that gender is not like other personal characteristics that do change, such as age and size.

Evaluation of Kohlberg's theory

Slaby and Frey (1975) divided 2–5-year-olds into high and low gender constancy and showed them a silent film of adult models simultaneously performing a series of simple activities, using a split screen, with male and female models on opposite sides. Those children rated as being high in gender constancy showed a more marked same-sex bias, as measured by the amount of visual attention they gave to each side of the screen. This supports Kohlberg's belief that gender constancy is a cause of imitation of same-sex models rather than an effect: children actively construct their gender role knowledge through purposeful monitoring of the social environment. However, while Kohlberg believes that processing of gender-related information begins when the child attains gender constancy, according to *gender schematic processing theory* (e.g. Martin, 1991, cited in Durkin, 1995) this begins at the gender-labelling stage (i.e. when it first discovers its own sex).

A major problem for Kohlberg's theory is that sex typing is already well underway before the child acquires a mature gender identity. For example, two-year-old boys prefer masculine toys before they have even become aware that these are more appropriate for boys and Kuhn *et al.* (1978) and Maccoby (1980) found that three-year-olds have learned many gender role stereotypes and already prefer same-sex activities or playmates long before they begin to attend selectively to same-sex models. Maccoby also concluded that boys are more likely to avoid 'sissy' behaviours than girls are to avoid 'tomboy' behaviours.

Finally, Money and Ehrhardt's claim (1972) that gender reassignment is very difficult after three years of age (which is when, according to Kohlberg, the child is only just beginning to develop a stable and constant sense of its status as boy or girl) seems to pose serious problems for Kohlberg's theory.

ANDROGYNY

This represents a convenient way of drawing together many of the findings and controversies regarding how gender roles are determined and the stereotypes which reflect them.

In *Fluffy Women and Chesty Men* (1975), Sandra Bem points out that the masculine-feminine pair of opposites had traditionally been taken as evidence of psychological health. This is reflected in psychological tests of masculinity and femininity, where a person scores as either one or the other – they do not permit a person to say that he or she is both. The word 'androgynous' (from *andro* meaning male and *gyne* meaning female) is used to refer to the possession and expression of characteristics, behaviours, abilities, values, etc. that are both 'masculine' and feminine' by the same person, regardless of biological sex.

Bem, together with a growing number of psychologists and feminists, believes that we need a new standard of psychological health, one that frees us from the straitjacket of stereotypes and which allows people to be more flexible in meeting new situations, in what they can do and how they do it. Usually, we tend to suppress parts of our personality which might be thought 'unmasculine' or 'unfeminine', e.g. men being afraid to be gentle or to cry and women being afraid to be assertive. In brief, men are reluctant to do 'women's work' and women are afraid to enter the 'man's world'. Bem believes that there is considerable evidence that traditional sex typing is unhealthy.

In order to 'discover' androgyny, it was necessary to see masculinity and femininity as not mutually exclusive but as two independent dimensions and to incorporate this into a new sort of test which would produce two logically independent scores. Bem developed such a test (1974), the Bem Sex Role Inventory (BSRI), which consists of a list of 60 personality characteristics, 20 traditionally masculine, 20 traditionally feminine and 20 neutral; the participant has to rate each of the 60 characteristics in terms of the extent to which they apply to them personally. If masculinity and femininity scores are approximately equal, the individual is judged to be androgynous.

The BSRI is the most widely used measure of sex role stereotyping in adults (Hargreaves, 1986) but is not the only fairly recent test of androgyny. Quite independently of Bem, Spence *et al.* (1975) devised the Personal Attributes Questionnaire (PAQ), which comprises instrumental (masculine) and expressive (feminine) trait terms and produces two essentially independent scores. However, the PAQ did not assess androgyny in the same way as the BSRI , highlighting a major problem with the BSRI to do with the very concept of androgyny itself. By defining androgyny as the similarity between a person's masculinity and femininity scores, Bem (unwittingly, of course) allowed for the same androgyny score to be obtained in two very different ways – by an individual who scores high on both scales or low on both. But surely two such individuals are likely to be very different kinds of persons, in which case what do their same androgyny scores mean?

By contrast, the PAQ allowed for four categories of person:

1 the highly sex-typed male – high masculinity, low femininity;
2 the highly sex-typed female – low masculinity, high femininity;
3 the androgynous person – high masculinity and high femininity;
4 the 'undifferentiated' person – low masculinity and low femininity.

The crucial difference is that Bem confounded 3 and 4. Consequently, she compared her original (1974) results with those of Spence *et al.* and concluded that the four categories (2×2) were superior; androgyny was now defined as only high in both masculinity and femininity (not low in both too). Her revised, and shortened, version of the BSRI (1977) is considered to be equivalent to the PAQ.

One of the major predictions made on the basis of the BSRI is that androgyny is a good predictor of psychological well-being/mental health. Does the evidence support the prediction? Lubinski *et al.* (1981) reported that androgynous individuals express greater subjective feelings of emotional well-being and Spence *et al.* (1975) found that they show higher levels of self-esteem. However, a review by Taylor and Hall (1982) suggests that masculinity in both males and females may be a better predictor than certain measures of androgyny and Taylor (1986) makes the point that traditional sex roles are, on the whole, advantageous for men but disadvantageous for women. According to Hefner *et al.* (1975, quoted in Taylor, 1986), '... both men and women are trapped in the prisons of gender ... but the situation is far from symmetrical; men are the oppressors and women are the oppressed'.

Psychological well-being (measured by, for example, self-esteem, adjustment, relative absence of anxiety, depression, psychophysiological symptoms) is generally more strongly related to masculinity than femininity on the BSRI and seems not to distinguish reliably between sex-typed and androgenous individuals (Taylor, 1986). As might be predicted, samples of homosexual male students (at the University of Texas), when compared with unselected male students, were found to be significantly lower on masculinity and higher on femininity and the reverse pattern was found for lesbians, using the PAQ (Spence and Helmreich, 1978). Larson (1981) found similar results using the BSRI.

Bem (1984) has reformulated her ideas as *gender schema theory*. She believes that the BSRI and the PAQ are adequate measures of sex typing and androgyny, despite criticisms that they are measuring characteristics rather more narrow than 'masculinity' and 'femininity'. Sex typing essentially involves spontaneously thinking of things in sex-typed terms, whereas androgyny is a disposition to process information in accordance with relatively non-sex principles; the essential difference here is between two kinds of cognitive style.

She revised her views further during the 1980s, taking account of the social institutions that push women and men into different and unequal roles and the fact that, because most societies are male-domi-

nated, women are much more constrained by these social institutions than men are. In *The Lenses of Gender* (1993), she argues that there are hidden assumptions embedded in cultural discourses, social institutions and the minds of individuals, which shape both perceptions of reality and material reality itself. These assumptions take the form of three kinds of lens:

1 *androcentrism* or male-centredness (see above and Chapters 2 and 32);
2 *gender polarization*, by which a male-female dichotomy is superimposed on almost every aspect of human experience;
3 *biological essentialism*, which rationalizes and legitimizes the other two lenses by treating them as the inevitable consequences of the inherent, 'natural' (i.e. biological) make-up of women and men.

Bem's *encultured lens theory* tries to explain how we either acquire the culture's lenses and construct a conventional gender identity or we construct a gender-subversive identity: 'We must reframe the debate on sexual inequality so that it focuses not on the differences between women and men but on how male-centred discourses and institutions transform male–female differences into female disadvantage' (Bem, 1993).

CHAPTER SUMMARY

- Every known culture distinguishes between male and female, which is reflected in stereotypes regarding typical male and female characteristics and behaviour.
- Many of the first women psychologists studied psychological sex differences, but psychology's interest in the topic declined until its revival in the 1970s, inspired by feminist psychologists.
- Feminist psychologists distinguish between biological sex and gender, which is the social equivalent of sex.
- Masculinity and femininity refer to conformity with male and female gender roles respectively.
- Biologically, sex refers to at least five separate categories, namely chromosomal sex, gonadal sex, hormonal sex, sex of the internal accessory organs and the function and appearance of the external genitalia. These are usually highly correlated with each other, as well as with non-biological aspects

of sex, such as sex of rearing and gender identity.

- Hermaphroditism refers to a physical disorder in which there is a discrepancy or inconsistency between any of the five sexual categories; these include testosterone insensitivity and adrenogenital syndrome.
- People with testosterone insensitivity (testicular feminizing syndrome) are chromosomally and in terms of their gonads male, but their external appearance is female. Adrenogenital syndrome refers to a chromosomally normal female whose external genitalia resemble those of a male; the internal organs are usually female.
- The study of psycholgical sex differences assumes that males and females are biologically distinct; normally, the five sexual categories are correlated.
- Underlying much of the scientific study of psychological sex differences are value judgements about the way that society should be organized and attempts to justify men's social dominance. This is reflected in the bias towards publishing evidence of sex differences, which gives the misleading impression that differences are much greater than they actually are.
- Cross-cultural research shows a high degree of agreement regarding the characteristics most commonly associated with each gender group. As there is an increase in stereotyping within a culture as individuals get older, so the stereotypes become more similar across cultures with age.
- The differentiation of men's and women's self-concepts and gender role ideology are both related to a large number of cultural variables.
- Despite bias towards reporting sex differences, there is little clear-cut evidence for most stereotypes. In Maccoby and Levin's large-scale review, the most convincing evidence related to aggressiveness, verbal and spatial ability and mathematical reasoning.
- Although boys are more aggressive throughout development, some studies fail to specify the type of aggression and others show that females display more indirect aggression. Although males are more likely to be involved in violent crime, wives and husbands are equally involved in domestic violence.
- Despite some evidence that females' verbal ability starts to become superior at adolescence, the overall evidence suggests that any differences can be disregarded.
- A similar developmental change has been claimed for boys' spatial and mathematical abilities; while the evidence for the former is greater, in both cases it is far from conclusive. Among the general population, it is females who show superior mathematical ability.
- Small differences can be highly significant and some reported differences are substantial. Meta-analysis can reveal an overall picture of significant differences, leading to the suggestion that sex differences have been underestimated, rather than exaggerated.
- Sociobiologists see gender roles as part of the wider human adaptation to the environment. Males and females have evolved instincts and physical attributes which equip them for hunting and childcare respectively.
- This relates to parental investment theory, according to which the female invests much more in reproduction than the male. Society came to be organized in sexually exclusive (polygynous) domestic partnerships as a way of meeting the female's needs for protection and the male's need for preventing his mate from mating with other males. This gave rise to different courtship roles, which are still evident in many Western and other cultures.
- Sociobiological theories have been criticized for mistakenly equating dominance with greater aggression, in both humans and non-human animals. In humans, dominance often relates to status seeking, which implies the role of culturally determined values.
- Evolutionary psychologists stress the role of the mind in mediating between genes and behaviour. Men and women have evolved dimorphic mental models regarding reproduction and, according to the rape adaptation hypothesis, men inherit an adaptive tendency towards rape.
- It is thought that the natural form of the human is female; it is the Y chromosome that determines the course of sexual differentiation. It is also correlated with the greater biological vulnerability of males.
- Genetic and hormonal differences are responsible for many sex-linked characteristics present at birth, which might predispose towards certain kinds of behaviour. The case of the Batista family supports the biological view and could be explained in terms of their brains having been masculinized by testosterone.
- Evidence for a difference between male and female brains comes mainly from rats. The human evidence is much weaker, including study of hormonal differences between homosexuals and heterosexuals, hemispheric specialization

and differences in the corpus callosum.

- The biological approach assumes an additive model of the influence of nature and nurture, but this in turn assumes that they can be separated, which many feminist and other critics believe is impossible.

- Biosocial theory stresses the interaction between biological and social factors: a child's sexual identity becomes part of its environment through how others react to it.

- Based on studies of individuals with the adrenogenital syndrome and testicular femininizing syndrome, Money and Ehrhardt claim that sexuality is undifferentiated at birth: the sex of rearing can be changed within the first 2½–3 years without any undue psychological harm to the child but not after this time. Sex of rearing seems to be the single most crucial factor involved in gender identity.

- It might not be valid to generalize from hermaphrodites to the normal population. The case of the identical twin who lost his penis and was raised as a girl is not conclusive, partly because of the medical changes that followed the accident and as revealed by a follow-up into adolescence.

- According to Freud's psychoanalytic theory, it is essential that the child is able to identify with the same-sex parent. Boys whose fathers are absent up to the age of four seem to be less masculine and, during adolescence, girls have difficulties with their gender role and relating to men.

- Studies of children raised by lesbian, transsexual or heterosexual single parents show that their psychosexual development is similar to those raised in traditional families.

- The evidence that children imitate same-sex models, or that they are rewarded for doing so, is very mixed, but they do start paying more attention to same-sex models at age six or seven.

- There is considerable evidence that the media portray gender role stereotypes. Although we should not assume that the media have a simple, one-way influence on a passive child viewer, there is evidence which suggests that the media are a major source of learning of such stereotypes.

- Overall, there is little evidence that parents consistently treat their sons and daughters differently (i.e. sex typing).

- According to cultural relativism, any differences in gender roles between cultures are likely to be culturally determined. Mead, based on the study of three New Guinea peoples (the Arapesh, Mundugumor and Tchambuli), claimed that masculine and feminine traits are completely unrelated to biological sex. Mead later changed her views, claiming that motherhood is natural, while fatherhood is a social invention.

- If it is true that men are the universal hunters and war-makers, this does not necessarily mean that they are naturally more aggressive or that they cannot be nurturant. Similarly, the enormous cultural diversity of the content of men's and women's work, together with the existence of more than two genders in some native American peoples, strongly suggests that gender is socially constructed.

- According to Kohlberg's cognitive-developmental theory, the child will only selectively attend to same-sex models once it has constructed its gender identity. This develops through three stages: gender labelling, gender stability and gender constancy.

- According to gender schematic processing theory, children start to process gender-related information at the gender labelling stage, rather than at the gender constancy stage (as Kohlberg believes). Also, sex typing begins long before the child's gender identity has developed.

- Bem's concept of androgyny represents a way of freeing ourselves from the straitjacket of gender stereotypes and assumes that masculinity and femininity are independent dimensions. These are measured by the BSRI, which defined the androgynous person as someone scoring equally on both dimensions. The PAQ defines the androgynous person as a high scorer on both masculinity and femininity.

- The evidence does not tend to support the prediction that androgyny is a good indicator of mental health, which seems to be more closely related to masculinity for both men and women.

- Bem's gender schema theory sees androgynous individuals as displaying a different kind of cognitive style from sex-typed individuals. Her later enculturated lens theory tries to explain how sex differences are transformed into female disadvantage by identifying the hidden assumptions (or 'lenses') that are part of society and of individual minds.

GLOSSARY

Adrenogenital syndrome Caused by excessive amounts of testosterone-like substance during the development of a chromosomally normal female.

External genitalia become more or less like a male's, producing an ambiguous genital appearance. Internal organs are usually female and many such people are fertile.

Androgynous (*Andro* = male/*gyne* = female). The possession/ expression by the same individual of characteristics/ behaviours/values, etc. which are both masculine and feminine.

Biological essentialism Justifying androcentrism (male-centredness) and gender polarization (imposing a male-female dichotomy on all experience) by treating them as the inevitable consequences of the inherent, 'natural ' make-up of women and men.

Biosocial theory The belief that the interaction between biological and social factors is crucial: temperament and especially gender become part of the child's environment through how others react to them.

Cultural relativism The view that gender roles differ between cultures and that these differences (and gender roles generally) are culturally determined.

Evolutionary psychology Derived from sociobiology, the view that the mind mediates between genes and human behaviour. The mind comprises a number of specialized mechanisms/ modules, designed by natural selection to solve problems faced by our hunter-gatherer ancestors, such as acquiring a mate and raising children.

Gender What culture makes out of the 'raw material' of biological sex; the social equivalent or interpretation of sex.

Gender identity How we classify ourselves (or others) as male or female. This develops through three stages: gender labelling. gender stability and gender constancy.

Gender role The behaviours, attitudes and values which a particular society expects from/considers appropriate for males and females, based on biological sex. Conforming to male/female gender roles is called masculinity and femininity respectively.

Gender role identity The understanding and acceptance of gender roles.

Gender role ideology Beliefs about the proper role relationships between men and women.

Gender role stereotyping The belief that it is natural and fitting for males and females to adhere to traditional gender role patterns.

Gender schema theory Bem's view that the difference between androgynous and sex-typed people is one of cognitive style, i.e. how information is processed in sex-relevant terms or not.

Gender stereotypes Widely held beliefs about psychological sex differences.

Hermaphrodite Strictly, someone with functioning organs of both sexes. More commonly, any discrepancy/inconsistency between any of the categories of sexual anatomy/physiology.

Meta-analysis A statistical method for combining the outcomes of a large number of individual studies measuring the same variable, in order to obtain some overall (composite) outcome.

Polygyny The social arrangement whereby one male/husband has access to a number of females/wives.

Sex Biological facts about a person's chromosomal make-up, reproductive organs (gonads), hormones and external genitalia. Also called sexual identity.

Sex-typing Treating and reacting to a child according to its biological sex. More generally, any classification/description/interpretation of activities, clothes, toys, etc. in sex-related terms.

Sexual differentiation The process by which biological sex develops in the embryo; for male development to take place, a Y chromosome must be present to interfere with the natural female route.

Sexual orientation An individual's tastes in sexual partners. Also called sexual preference.

Testosterone insensitivity A condition in which a chromosomally normal male foetus fails to respond to testosterone, producing the outward appearance of a female. The testes are present but removed and the person lives as a woman. Also called testicular feminizing syndrome.

Transsexual An anatomically normal male or female who believes he/she is a member of the opposite sex. (Often used to refer to someone who has undergone the surgical and medical transformation from one sex to the other.)

FURTHER READING

Unger, R. K. (1979) *Female and Male: Psychological Perspectives.* New York: Harper and Row. An excellent review of the study of psychological sex differences by a leading feminist psychologist.

24 ADULTHOOD AND OLD AGE: DEVELOPMENT OF PERSONALITY AND THE SELF-CONCEPT

INTRODUCTION AND OVERVIEW

According to Levinson *et al.* (1978) adulthood is '... one of the best kept secrets in our society and probably in human history generally'. By this they mean that, while adulthood is the longest phase of the lifecycle (i.e. we spend most of our lives as adults – assuming we enjoy a normal lifespan), until recently very little was known about it in terms of psychological theory and research.

Traditionally, the focus of developmental psychology has been on infancy and childhood and Freud's emphasis on the formative nature of the first five years of life has probably had much to do with the neglect of the study of adulthood. Equally, Erikson has had much to do with the

reversal of that trend or at least with the view that development is a lifelong process (the *lifespan approach* or 'womb to tomb'). The mere fact of devoting a whole chapter to adulthood and old age reflects the growing importance of this approach (especially during the last 20 years or so).

However, while there is not usually any need to define what we mean by 'childhood' or 'adolescence', this is not true in the case of adulthood and we shall begin the chapter by discussing the criteria that have been proposed for defining this longest period of our lives. There is also controversy surrounding the appropriateness of trying to understand adult development in terms of a series of predictable stages; while this approach is not without its critics as applied to child development (see Chapter 25), it raises particular problems in the context of adulthood, particularly in relation to the so-called 'midlife crisis'. A major alternative to the 'stage' approach is to explain adult development in terms of the impact of critical life events. We shall consider both approaches.

If 'growing up' has positive connotations, for most people 'growing old' definitely has negative ones and although there are stereotyped images of adolescence and middle age, we normally understand ageism to refer to prejudice and discrimination against the elderly (rather than against any age group). This prejudice can be seen in psychological theories of ageing, as well as in social stereotypes and policies, perhaps because of the association between being old and death.

WHAT DOES IT MEAN TO BE AN ADULT?

● The concept of maturity

One criterion of psychological adulthood is the concept of *maturity* which, according to Whitbourne and Weinstock (1979), involves the ability to shoulder responsibilities, make logical decisions, empathize with others, cope with minor frustrations and accept one's social role. Turner and Helms (1989) define it as '... a state that promotes physical and psychological well being ...'. In most cases, they say, a mature person possesses a well-developed value system, an accurate self-concept, stable emotional behaviour, satisfying social relationships, intellectual insight and a realistic assessment of future goals. This might sound like a rather tall order, something which most of us would not expect

to achieve. But maturity is not a unitary concept (there are many features which comprise maturity) nor is it an all-or-none phenomenon, i.e. we can achieve varying degrees of maturity. What many writers agree about is that being mature means being able to deal with failures and frustrations as well as accepting triumphs and successes. Maturity also implies accepting responsibility for one's choices and decisions.

● Erikson's stages of young and middle adulthood

A second way of trying to define adulthood is in terms of successful handling of the developmental tasks which characterize adulthood. When discussing adolescence in Chapter 21, we noted that, for Erikson, intimacy is a criterion of having attained the psychosocial state of adulthood; the attainment of identity by the end of adolescence is a prerequisite for the ability to become intimate with another person. By this, he means not simply making love but the ability to share with and care about another person, 'without fear of losing oneself in the process' (Elkind, 1970). According to Dacey (1982), it refers to the essential ability to relate our deepest hopes and fears to another person and to accept another's need for intimacy in turn; indeed, intimacy need not involve sexuality at all and describes the relationship between friends as much as that between husband and wife. Our personal identity only becomes fully realized and consolidated through sharing ourselves with another and if a sense of intimacy is not established with friends or a marriage partner, the result, in Erikson's view, is a sense of *isolation*, of being alone without anyone to share with or care for.

Intimacy is normally achieved in our 20s (young adulthood), after which we enter middle age (our 30s, 40s and 50s) which brings with it either generativity or stagnation (self-absorption). *Generativity* means that the person begins to be concerned with others beyond the immediate family, with future generations and the nature of the society and world in which those generations will live. Generativity is not confined to parents but is displayed by anyone who is actively concerned with the welfare of young people and with making the world a better place for them to live and work in, such as teachers, youth workers, community workers and so on. Failure to establish a sense of generativity results in a sense of *stagnation* in which the individual becomes preoccupied with their personal needs and comforts. Such people indulge themselves as if they were their own (or another's) only child. Many writers believe that most adults never attain generativity and that men get 'stuck' in Erikson's industry stage (7–12) and women in the adolescent stage.

An evaluation of Erikson's stages

According to Gould (1978), the major task of women during their mid-40s is to deal with the persisting assumption that they need a 'protector' to survive; it is a time for women to reach full independence for the first time. Sanguiliano (1978, cited in Bee and Mitchell, 1980) interviewed women in depth and concluded that they achieve identity and intimacy in reverse order. Agreeing with Gould, she found that a full occupational identity is not achieved until much later than is typical for men. Indeed, the typical life course for women is to pass directly into a stage of intimacy without achieving personal identity; most women submerge their identity into that of their partner and only at midlife do they emerge from this to search for their own, separate identity.

However, Sanguiliano's sample was very small and unrepresentative and important qualifications need to be made to her conclusions, particularly in relation to social class differences, which interact with gender. Working-class men and women tend to marry earlier and their careers may 'top out' sooner; this may change the pace of the sequence of stages compared with middle-class men and women. Neugarten (1975) found that working-class men see an early marriage as part of the normal or 'good' life pattern. Their young adulthood (20s) is a time for settling down, having a family and working steadily. In contrast, middle-class men and women see their 20s as a time for explorations, trying out different occupations; marriage comes later and settling down is postponed until the 30s. Bee (1994) cites a study by Hodgson and Fischer (1979) which found a different pattern between male and female undergraduates in the relationship between identity and intimacy. Nineteen out of 21 women rated as identity achievers were also rated as showing intimacy in their relationships, but 15 out of 29 not rated as identity achievers were also rated as showing intimacy. For men, on the other hand, only three showed intimacy without identity.

These findings suggest that it is necessary to describe developmental patterns for gender and social class groups separately, illustrating how it is more difficult to describe universal stages for adults than it is for children and even adolescents. While his *Eight Ages of Man* (1950, 1968) were meant to be universal, applying to men and women in different cultures equally, Erikson himself acknowledges (1968) that the sequence of stages is different for the female: she suspends her identity as she prepares to attract the man who will marry her. While men achieve identity before achieving intimacy with a sexual partner, for women these developmental tasks seem to be fused: 'The female comes to know herself as she is known, through her relationships with others' (Gilligan, 1982).

● Levinson *et al.'s Seasons of a Man's Life*

Erikson's theory highlights a qualitatively different developmental task that becomes the focus of successive stages of development. Other 'stage' theories are concerned with the question 'How is adulthood experienced?' (Sugarman, 1986), representing a third approach to defining adulthood, and the most influential example of this type of theory is Levinson *et al.'s* (1978) *life structure theory* reported in their book entitled *Seasons of a Man's Life* and again in Levinson (1986).

During 1969, 40 men (business executives, university biologists, industrial workers and novelists) aged between 35 and 45 were studied primarily through 'biographical interviewing'; 5–10 interviews per participant were conducted, each lasting 1–2 hours, over a 2–3 month period. These were tape-recorded and then transcribed (producing an average of 300 pages per participant).

The pivotal concept is the individual's life structure – 'the underlying pattern or design of a person's life at a given time'. It is used to explore '... the interrelationships of self and world – to see how the self is in the world and the world is in the self'. Life structure evolves through a series of alternating *stable* (structure-building) and *transitional* (structure-changing) phases or periods which give overall shape to the course of adult development ('the seasons of a man's life'). Each developmental phase involves interrelated biological, psychological and social adjustments (compare this with Erikson's psychosocial theory; see Chapter 21), but central to the life structure at any point are family and work roles and individual development is fundamentally interwoven with changes in these roles (Durkin, 1995).

Figure 24.1 shows the life-cycle as comprising a sequence of eras (pre-adulthood, early adulthood, middle adulthood and late adulthood), which overlap in the form of cross-era transitions, each lasting about five years and terminating the outgoing era and initiating the next.

Era of early adulthood

The early adult transition (17–22) represents the developmental bridge between the adolescent (preadult) and adult worlds. One key theme is *separation* (especially from the family of origin) which is both external (moving out of the family home, increasing financial independence, entering more independent and responsible roles and living arrangements) and internal (increasing differentiation between self and parents, greater psychological distance from family, less emotional dependence on parental support and authority). The process of separation from the parents continues throughout life and is never completed. A second theme is the formation of initial *attachments* to the adult world – exploring its possibilities, imagining oneself as a participant in it, making and testing some preliminary identities and choices for living in the adult world before becoming fully part of it. The major task is to reappraise the sense of self developed during adolescence and to obtain further training and to learn more about the self and world in general.

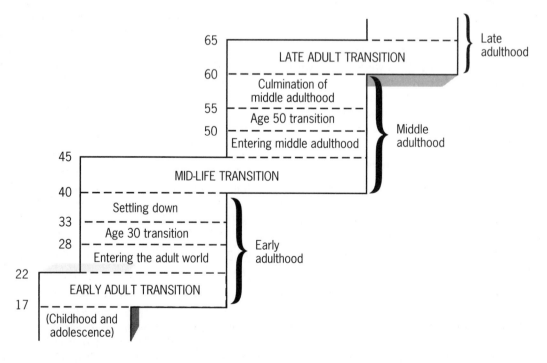

Figure 24.1 *Developmental periods in early and middle adulthood. (Based on Levinson et al., 1978)*

Entering the adult world (22–28) represents the first structure-*building* (as opposed to *changing*) phase and the overall goal is '...to fashion a provisional structure that provides a workable link between the valued self and adult society' (Levinson *et al.,* 1978). The young person enters a *novice phase,* in which he must begin to define himself as an adult and make and live with initial choices regarding occupation, love relationships, peer relationships, lifestyle and values. However, there needs to be a balance between exploring possibilities and not committing himself prematurely to a given course ('keeping one's options open') and creating a stable life structure ('putting down some roots'). These decisions are made within the context of one's *dream,* 'a vague sense of the self in the adult world', what one wants to do with one's life. The young adult must overcome disappointments and setbacks and learn to accept and profit from successes so that the 'thread' of the dream isn't lost in the course of 'moving up the ladder' and revising the life structure. Looking to older, more experienced others for guidance and direction (*mentors*; see below) helps young adults in their efforts at self-definition.

The age 30 transition (28–33) '... provides an opportunity to work on the flaws and limitations of the first life structure and to create the basis for a more satisfactory structure with which to complete the era of young adulthood' (Levinson *et al.,* 1978). Most participants experienced an 'age 30 crisis', involving high or moderate stress, considerable self-doubt, feelings that life is losing its provisional quality, is becoming more serious, of time pressure, i.e. if we want to change, we must do so now! But a minority experienced a 'smooth process of change', without crisis, in which relationships with family and friends remained satisfactory and occupational pursuits progressed quickly.

Settling down (33–40) represents consolidation of the second life structure. There is a shift away from tentative choices regarding family and career towards a strong sense of commitment to a personal, familial and occupational future. The individual begins to map out a path for success in work, husband and father roles. ('I am a responsible adult now' as opposed to 'I'm just beginning to find out what's important to me or what my opinions are'.) There are two substages:

1 Early settling down (33–36), which involves establishing a niche in society, a 'digging in', 'building a nest'. This contributes to the stability of a defined structure.
2 Becoming one's own man (BOOM) (36–40), which involves advancement and striving to succeed,

building a better life, improving and using one's skills, becoming more creative and in general contributing to society. We want recognition, affirmation from society, but we also want to be self-sufficient and free of social pressure and control; this may produce a 'boy–man' conflict but can represent a step forward.

We may assume a *mentor* role for someone younger who is just beginning to work on his own life structure. Mentors can fulfil a formal, more external guiding and teaching function in helping the novice to define his dream or a more informal, internal, advisory, emotionally supportive function (like a parent). Like active parenting, the mentor role will be shed (willingly or not) as the young adult reaches his own BOOM period (where he will serve as someone else's mentor).

Era of middle adulthood

The three main tasks of the midlife transition (40–45) are (i) termination of one life structure; (ii) initiation of another; and (iii) continuation of the process of individuation started during BOOM. It is a time of soul searching, questioning and assessing the real meaning of the achievements of the life structure ('midlife crisis'). For some, the change is gradual and fairly painless, for others it is full of uncertainties: 'They question nearly every aspect of their lives and feel that they cannot go on as before. They will need several years to form a new path or modify the old one'. The age 50 midlife crisis stems from the unconscious tensions between attachment and separation, resurfacing of the need for creativity which is often repressed in order to achieve in one's career and retrospective comparisons between one's dream and the reality of one's life .

Most of Levinson *et al.'s* participants had not reached the age of 45. Follow-up interviews were conducted with most two years later and four men were chosen for more intensive study. Altogether, data were obtained on their lives after 45 for 15 men aged 42–45 at the start of the study (but none was actually in his 50s). Consequently, the evidence for the remaining phases is much sketchier than that for earlier ones; we shall consider only the first structure-building phase of middle adulthood.

In entering middle adulthood (45–50), having resolved (more or less satisfactorily) whether what one has committed oneself to is really worthwhile, choices must again be made regarding a new life structure. Sometimes these choices are defined by *marker events* (divorce, illness, change in occupation, death of someone close), sometimes by less obvious but significant changes such as subtle shifts in enthusiasm for work or in the quality of one's marriage. As before, the resulting life structure varies in how satisfying it is, how connected it is to the self – it may or may not be intrinsically happy and fulfilling. The restructuring comprises many steps and may face many setbacks; options may have to be abandoned ('back to the drawing board').

● Evaluation of Levinson et al.'s theory

Is there a midlife crisis and is it a developmental stage?

Just as Erikson made the idea of an 'identity crisis' part of the popular stereotype of adolescence, so Levinson et al. have helped to make the 'midlife crisis' part of the 'commonsense' understanding of adult development. (We should note that, although they talked about 'crisis' during the midlife transition – see above – they themselves did not use the term 'midlife crisis').

Another interesting parallel between Erikson and Levinson et al. is that they both see crisis as not only inevitable ('... It is not possible to get through middle adulthood without having at least a moderate crisis in either the midlife transition or the age 50 transition'; Levinson et al., 1978) but necessary (men who do very little soul searching 'will pay the price in a later developmental crisis or in a progressive withering of the self and a life structure minimally connected to the self'). This view of midlife crisis as normative (to use Erikson's term), i.e. both inevitable and desirable/ necessary, represents the most controversial component. Given that people of all ages suffer occasional depression, self-doubt, sexual uncertainty and concerns about the future, are these more prevalent and intense during middle age (Durkin, 1995) and are those who 'get off lightly' bound to suffer later on in life?

Several studies show that substantial proportions of middle-aged people actually feel more positive about this phase of their life than earlier ones, with only about 12 percent feeling that they have experienced a crisis:

> ... In short, the midlife crisis does not appear to be as universal as Levinson's data first indicated, and it may be that the time and the extent to which people experience uncomfortable self-assessments is subject to variability as a function of personality, social context, and cohort. (Durkin, 1995)

According to Rutter and Rutter (1992) , although the available data are sparse, it seems that going through

BOX 24.1	**Gould's (1978, 1980) theory of the evolution of adult consciousness**

Gould's ideas derived from his work as a psychiatrist but were tested on over 500 non-patients aged 16–50. They represent perhaps the most significant extension of Freud's theory to adulthood. Gould sees growth and maturity as essentially a complete resolution of separation anxiety in childhood.

While Levinson et al. talk about evolving life structures, Gould talks about 'the evolution of adult consciousness as we release ourselves from the constraints and ties of childhood consciousness'. The thrust of adult development is towards the realization and acceptance of ourselves as creators of our own lives and away from the false assumption that the rules and standards of childhood determine our destiny. We have to free ourselves of the *illusion of absolute safety*; this involves transformations, giving up the security of the past to form our own ideas, something that we inevitably find very difficult to do.

These false assumptions often embody the concept of dependency on parents and this must be replaced by a sense of personal autonomy, of owning one's self.

But this is very hard because these ideas are a normal feature of childhood – indeed, they represent beliefs ('convenient fictions') which keep children secure and without which childhood might resemble a nightmare! But to 'grow up', you have to 'give up' these basic assumptions about the self and the world. This is a gradual process and continues throughout adulthood (at least up to age 50), both intellectually and emotionally.

Alongside the shedding of childhood consciousness, there is change in the individual's sense of time. From our mid-30s to mid-40s, there develops a sense of urgency that time is running out. We also have an emotional awareness of our own mortality which, once attained, is never far from consciousness. How time is spent becomes a matter of great importance. We also begin to question whether our 'prize' (freedom from restrictions by the persons who have formed us – our parents) has been worth it (or even if it exists). (This is similar to Levinson's 'dream'.)

Old people who haven't made this contact with their inner core have no recourse against the feeling that they are losing the battle with life – finding no meaning in their own life, they attack life itself as meaningless (in Erikson's terms, they've lost the battle between integrity and despair).

middle age in a relatively peaceful, untroubled way is actually a favourable indicator of future development, i.e. lack of emotional disturbance predicts better, not worse, functioning later in life.

FIGURE 24.2 *Fathers' involvement in child care, though on the increase, is still not seen as 'men's work', but is more of a bonus – for child and father alike. Nor does it seem to reduce any of the mother's burden of responsibility*

What are much less contentious are two other components of midlife crisis: (a) a wide range of adaptations in the life pattern, some stemming from role changes that produce fairly drastic consequences, such as divorce, remarriage, major occupational change, redundancy and serious, debilitating illness, and others that are more subtle, such as the 'empty nest syndrome', the ageing (and likely death) of one's parents and the new role of grandparent. Some of these (and other) critical life events (or marker events) will be discussed further below; (b) significant changes in the internal aspects of a person's life structure (regardless of external events), i.e. a reappraisal of our achievements and remaining ambitions, in particular those regarding work and relationships (especially with our sexual partner). A fundamental development at this time is the realization that the final authority for life rests with the individual; this relates to another major theory of adult development, namely Gould's (1978, 1980) theory of the *evolution of adult consciousness* (see Box 24.1).

In *Passages – Predictable Crises of Adult Life* (1976), Gail Sheehy describes a shift in our 40s when men begin to explore and develop their more 'feminine' selves (e.g. they become more nurturant, affiliative and intimate) while women are discovering their more 'masculine' selves (e.g. they become more action-oriented, assertive and ambitious). This passing-by, in opposite directions, produces distress and pain which is the 'midlife crisis'. However, Hopson and Scally (1980) argue that it is not a stage through which everyone must pass; it can stem from a number of sources, including ineffective adjustment to the normal stresses of growth and transition in middle age and the reaction of a particularly vulnerable person to these stresses. Because of the diversity of adult experience, terms like 'stage' or 'seasons' are too restrictive and instead they describe *themes;* these include the changing nature of roles, adaptation to life transitions, adjustment to biological ageing and so on.

Bee and Mitchell (1980) suggest that, in any particular society, there are particular ages at which a large number of stressful life changes (biological, social and psychological) are likely to happen together, so that most people will experience a transition or crisis at roughly the same time in their life-cycle. Individuals will differ in how much stress they can tolerate before a 'crisis' is experienced and in how they respond to it when it does occur. One potential response is personal growth, so that another piece of 'childhood consciousness' is removed (in Gould's terms); another response is to change major 'external' aspects of one's life, such as change jobs, get divorced or move house (which are emphasized by Levinson *et al.*).

The seasons of a woman's life

A glaringly obvious limitation of Levinson *et al.*'s theory is that the sample is unrepresentative of human beings in general. In 1986, Levinson refers to 45 women being interviewed as part of an ongoing study and in 1990, he presented his preliminary findings at the 98th Annual Convention of the American Psychological Association; these are summarized by Craig (1992). Roberts and Newton (1987) also review the findings of four (unpublished) PhD dissertations, involving 39 women in all. Although there are broad similarities between these female samples and

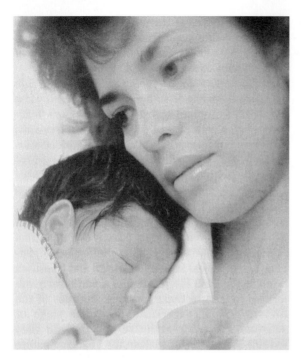

FIGURE 24.3 *While child care is still regarded as predominantly 'woman's work', mothers are increasingly likely to have a 'second career' outside of the home. Whether her paid employment is full- or part-time, this is likely to be additional to her domestic duties*

Levinson *et al.*'s men, one important difference stands out, namely the different dreams of women and men.

According to Levinson, there is a 'gender splitting' phenomenon in adult development, whereby men have a fairly unified vision of their future, which is focused on their career, while women's dreams are more likely to be split between career and marriage. Although this was true of both academics and business women, the former were less ambitious and more willing to forego their careers, while the latter wanted to maintain their careers but on a reduced level. Only the 'homemakers' had a unified dream – to be full-time wives and mothers (much as their own mothers had been). Similarly, Roberts and Newton saw the family as playing a 'supportive' role for men, while women constructed their dreams around relationships with their husband and family and subordinating their personal needs: part of *her* dream is *his* success. This difference in women's and men's priorities may put women at greater risk of '...disappointment and developmental tension as their investments in others' goals conflict with their personal needs' (Durkin, 1995).

The age 30 transition is as important for the women as for the men: women who gave marriage and motherhood top priority in their 20s tended to develop more individualistic goals for their 30s, while those who had been career-oriented earlier on tended to focus more on marriage and family concerns. Generally, the transitory instability of the early 30s lasted longer for women than for men, with much less clear-cut 'settling down'. Trying to integrate career and marriage/family responsibilities proved very difficult for most women, who experience greater conflict than their husbands are likely to.

Women, work and the division of labour

In a review of several American studies, Craig (1992) concludes that, although the pattern of career development for women is far more varied than that for men, most women still interrupt their careers, at least temporarily, to take care of children, while men rarely do. Nicholson (1993) finds a similar picture in the UK. A woman's decision to have children usually results in a significant gap in her career; on average, this will be seven years. At the same time, there has been a dramatic increase in the number of women in the workforce, making the phenomenon of 'dual earner couples/marriages' (where the husband works full-time and the wife works at least 20 hours per week) quite common in the US (Craig, 1992) and probably in the UK too. Compared with more 'traditional' couples, these husbands report more marital dissatisfaction and conflicts over family and work responsibilities and the wives, similarly, report higher levels of conflict as well as a very realistic work overload.

Despite some evidence that domestic tasks (especially childcare) are more equally shared in some dual earner families, it is nearly always the woman who is still primarily responsible for both housework and childcare, regardless of the age of the children and whether she is working full- or part-time. When there are no children, working wives still do the bulk of the shopping, etc., and when there are, the husband's contribution to running the house actually *declines* with each child, such that hers increases by 5–10 percent per child. (This is based on studies in Eastern and Western Europe and North and South America, reported by Nicholson, 1993.) Although there do not appear to be any social class differences in men's contributions to the domestic division of labour, there are cultural ones, with Swedish men doing much more than their American counterparts (Wright *et al.*, 1992, cited in Durkin, 1995). These findings seem to confirm the 'gender splitting' reported by Levinson (see above).

IS ADULT DEVELOPMENT STAGE-LIKE?

As we saw above when discussing the midlife crisis, views are divided as to the validity of seeing adult development as a ladderlike progression through an inevitable, universal series of stages. Although Levinson prefers to talk about age-linked 'periods' than stages, Rutter and Rutter (1992) criticize his and other 'stage' theories on the grounds that this approach underestimates the degree of *individual variability*, which itself can stem from a variety of sources, i.e. stage theories imply that there is just one developmental path that everyone takes. They and others also see considerable continuity of personality during adult life, while 'stages' imply discontinuity of development.

According to Craig (1992), '... Changes in adult thought, behaviour and personality are less a result of chronological age or specific biological changes and are more a result of personal, social and cultural events or forces ...'. As we noted at the beginning of the chapter, many theorists see adulthood as characterized by maturity, a hallmark of which is the ability to respond to change and adapt successfully to new conditions. Craig believes that positive resolution of contradictions and difficulties is the basis of adult activity and this gradual (re-)structuring of social understanding and behaviour does not lend itself easily to a stage theory approach.

CRITICAL LIFE EVENTS

Baltes (1987) and Hetherington and Baltes (1988) offer a way of integrating these apparently conflicting views as to the predictability of changes in adult life. They identify three kinds of factors whose interaction can help to explain adult development :

1 *Normative, age-graded influences*, which refer to biological and social changes which normally occur at predictable ages, such as puberty, the menopause, marriage and retirement. To these we could add parenthood, the 'empty nest syndrome' and the death of one's parents.
2 *Normative, history-graded influences*, which refer to historical events, such as wars, reces-

sions, and epidemics (e.g. AIDS) which affect a whole generation or cohort at about the same time.
3 *Non-normative influences*, which refer to idiosyncratic transitions, such as divorce, unemployment and illness (and, in addition, death of spouse, change of job and moving house).

According to this classification, some major life changes (or *psychobiosocial* transitions – Levinson, 1986) are fairly predictable, both in the sense that they will happen to the vast majority of people and at fairly predictable ages (normative, age-graded), while others are much less predictable in both these senses (non-normative). Related to age-graded influences is Schlossberg *et al.*'s (1978) suggestion that a 'social clock' is used by adults to judge whether or not they are 'on time' with respect to a particular life event (marriage, having children, etc.). To be 'off-time' (either early or late) is to be an age deviant and, like other forms of deviancy, this can result in social penalties.

Contained within the age-graded and non-normative categories are what are often called *critical life events* (Levinson's marker events), although some of these are more accurately thought of as processes (rather than events), such as marriage, divorce and retirement. However, it is interesting to note that of the ten highest ranked life events on Holmes and Rahé's (1967) Social Readjustment Rating Scale measure of stress, three are age-graded influences (death of close family member, marriage, and retirement) and three are non-normative influences (death of spouse, divorce and marital separation) (see Chapter 6). The study of the impact of critical life events (or what Parkes (1993) calls *psychosocial transitions*) represents an alternative (but not necessarily incompatible) approach to stage theories in the explanation of adult development.

In taking a closer look at some of these critical life events, it is useful to relate them to different eras of adulthood. According to Bee (1994):

> If the biological clock is all but inaudible during the years of early adulthood, the social clock is all but deafening. In early adulthood, each of us takes our place in society. For nearly all of us, this means acquiring, learning and performing the three roles central to adult life: worker, spouse and parent.

So marriage and parenthood tend to happen in early adulthood, the 'empty nest syndrome' in middle adulthood and retirement can be seen as marking the entry into late adulthood. While death of loved ones can happen at any age, we shall discuss bereavement and grief in relation to ageing at the end of the chapter, but we shall begin this section by discussing unemployment, which can also occur at any time during our adult lives, and comparing its effects with those of retirement.

● The effects of unemployment

Raphael (1984) distinguishes between sudden, unanticipated loss of work (unemployment) and anticipated loss of work (retirement). She claims that loss of work is in many ways similar to other kinds of loss, such as bereavement. The initial response may be shock, numbness, disbelief. If other similar work is easily available, these feelings may be transient and soon replaced by rationalizations that it was 'all for the best anyway' and blame directed at the employer. Even so, there is likely to be some sense of loss – of workmates, security, self-esteem. Where the job was valued and cannot be easily replaced, the bereavement response is likely to be much more intense.

According to Argyle (1989), the unemployed have higher rates of mental ill health and distress of several kinds :

- Depression is usually higher among the unemployed and the level increases with the period of unemployment (Warr, 1984). After a long period of unemployment, people increasingly blame themselves, get into a state of 'learned helplessness' where aspects of themselves are seen as the main cause of their unemployment and can't be changed. (They make an internal (self-) attribution in a situation that has gone badly, which is a fairly typical 'depressive' response; see Chapter 15.)
- Depression (together with poverty, reduced social support and alcoholism) is a factor contributing to suicide, which is more common among the unemployed.
- General emotional disturbance is lower for those at work than for all categories of unemployed (including retired people); it usually takes some time for the effects of unemployment on mental health to appear (Argyle, 1989).
- According to Argyle (1989), physical health usually suffers as a result of unemployment (rather than being a cause). However, Warr (1984) studied 954 British unemployed men and found that although 27 percent said their health deteriorated, 11 percent said it actually improved (due to less work strain and more relaxation and exercise). The mortality rate is higher for the unemployed.

What specific factors related to unemployment cause distress?

In addition to the material hardships of low income, there is loss of self-esteem through ceasing to be the breadwinner and through becoming the recipient of unemployment benefit. Financial strain is likely to be greater when there are dependent children and financial problems are a major source of emotional distress (Warr, 1984, cited in Argyle, 1989). In addition to the financial effects of unemployment, Argyle (1989) identifies five major causes of distress: length of unemployment, commitment to work, social support from the family, level of activity and perceived causes of unemployment.

Some claim that, depending on the length of unemployment, there is a series of regular reactions to loss of a job (as it is claimed there is to bereavement; Kelvin and Jarrett, 1985):

1 the initial response is *shock,* anger and incomprehension;
2 the first stage is followed by *optimism,* a feeling of being between jobs, a kind of holiday with active job searching;
3 this is replaced by *pessimism* as job searching fails – people see themselves as unemployed and become worried about money and the future;
4 *fatalism* – hopelessness and apathy set in and job hunting is abandoned. But there are many exceptions to this sequence, as there are to the sequence of 'stages' of bereavement; see page 620).

Those most attached or committed to their jobs are more distressed by losing them; this probably explains why unemployment is more distressing for middle-aged men than for young people or married women (Warr, 1987). Social support, especially from the family, 'buffers' the stressful effects of unemployment, a major feature of which is loss of social relationships, i.e. loss of a co-operative network of friendships. At work, people are part of a complex set of complementary relationships which convey identity and status, both of which are lost in unemployment; unemployed people may feel inferior and stigmatized and even ostracized by their employed friends. The bonds between unemployed people are weak: it is a group to which they do not want to belong (Argyle, 1989).

Level of activity refers to how structured or organized a pattern of life unemployed people create for themselves. A minority undertake unpaid work, pursue hobbies, do gardening and keep active in other ways (Argyle, 1989); General Health Questionnaire scores are worse for those whose time is not fully occupied or have problems filling time, with correlations as high as 0.55 (Warr, 1984). After a long period out of work, some individuals adapt by staying in bed late, killing time, watching a lot of TV and they give up bothering to look for work.

Even during an economic recession, to be out of work may still be seen as a sign of failure – it is a social stigma, a form of deviance (Kelvin, 1981). However, one feature of the current recession is that it affects people from all sections of society, including many highly qualified professionals and those who have held responsible jobs in the past: no one is 'immune' any longer. In certain parts of the country where there is mass unemployment, very large proportions of all age groups cannot find work. The result is that many of the unemployed now feel less responsible for their plight and more accepting of it. If you know many other people who are also out of work, this part of the identity problem is greatly eased. Research has shown that satisfaction with the self is higher when the local level of unemployment is high (Warr, 1984, cited in Argyle, 1989).

● Retirement

Retirement is an anticipated loss of work and '... many make this transition in a careful, measured way without undue psychological upheaval ...' (Raphael, 1984). But even in the most positive of situations, some losses are inevitable, including those of finances, personal identity, meaning to life and sources of gratification, Even though it is seen as inevitable by most people, retirement may feel very unacceptable at a particular stage in life when, for instance, a person sees himself as 'too young' to stop work (Raphael, 1984).

Perhaps the most serious loss is of everyday, regular, ritualized patterns of behaviour. The comfortable familiarity of the workplace and colleagues, the times of day spent there and the tasks all contribute to the fabric of the individual's existence. When these are gone, there will be a great emptiness, at least for a while, '... the work and all it meant will be gradually mourned...' (Raphael, 1984). While shock and disbelief are uncommon, some people use denial and realize what retirement means only on the first days at home – its full meaning 'hits' them only then. For most, the early weeks are full, freedom is celebrated and only as the months go by do frustration and a sense of 'uselessness' set in. There may be an angry and irritable response to the world.

Many couples face the problem of adjusting to increased time together; many compound the crisis of retirement by moving to a new house which involves loss of familiar surroundings, friendships and neighbourhood networks. Retirement entails the transition from an economically productive role, which is clearly defined, to an economically non-productive role, which is often vague and ambiguous. This ambiguity partly reflects its relative newness as a social role: in the past, people worked for almost their entire lives (and this is still true in many traditional cultures; see below) (Harris and Cole, 1980, cited in Turner and Helms, 1989). Similarly, Turner and Helms (1989) maintain that 'Since retirement as a stage of life is such a new developmental phenomenon ... our culture has yet to prescribe suitable behaviour for this period. Consequently, each of us may react differently'.

Leaving the world of work and relinquishing a significant part of one's identity is a difficult psychological adjustment. For many, such a transition brings about a major loss of self-esteem. The ability to deal with this stage of life depends to a considerable extent on past adjustment patterns. Those who adjust well to retirement are typically able to develop a lifestyle that provides continuity with the past and meets their long-term needs (Turner and Helms, 1989). Atchley (1982, 1985) and Atchley and Robinson (1982) see retirement as a process and a social role which unfold through a series of six phases, at each of which an adjustment is required. These phases are difficult to relate to chronological age, occur in no fixed order and are not necessarily all experienced by every individual (see Box 24.2).

An important distinction here is between *voluntary* and *involuntary* retirement. Those who retire voluntarily usually have little or no difficulty adjusting, but those forced to because they have reached compulsory retirement age tend to be dissatisfied at first (but eventually adapt). The least satisfied are those whose health is poor (though health very often improves after retirement). According to Argyle (1989), satisfaction with and adjustment to retirement depends on a number of factors (although several are predictors of satisfaction for everybody): (i) health; (ii) finance; (iii) purpose in life; (iv) having strong interests; (v) education and social class; (vi) voluntary and planned retirement; (vii) gender – married women have the least difficulty in adjusting to retirement. Given reasonable physical health and financial resources, the average retired man or woman soon adapts to the changed circumstances and shows an improvement in physical health and outlook. It is the transition that creates problems of

BOX 24.2	The six phases in the process of retirement (based on Atchley, 1982, 1985; Atchley and Robinson, 1982)

1 *Pre-retirement phase*: (i) in the remote subphase, retirement is seen as in a reasonably distant future; (ii) the near subphase may be initiated by the retirement of older friends/colleagues and there may be much anxiety about how lifestyle will change, especially financially.
2 *Honeymoon phase* (immediate post-retirement): typical euphoria, partly due to newfound freedom, often a busy period (which may be long or short).
3 *Disenchantment phase*: involves a slowing down after the honeymoon phase, feelings of being let down and even depressed. The degree of disenchantment is related to declining health and finances. Eagerly anticipated post-retirement activities (e.g. travel) may have lost their original appeal. Disenchantment may be produced by unrealistic pre-retirement fantasies or inadequate anticipatory socialization (i.e. preparation for retirement).
4 *Reorientation phase*: time to develop a more realistic view of life alternatives. May involve exploring new avenues of involvement, sometimes with the help of community groups (e.g. special voluntary/paid jobs for the retired); this helps to decrease feelings of role loss and is a means of achieving self-actualization.
5 *Stability phase*: involves the establishment of criteria for making choices, allowing the individual to deal with life in a fairly comfortable and orderly way. They know what's expected of them, what their strengths and weaknesses are, allowing mastery of the retirement role.
6 *Termination phase*: usually illness and disability make housework and self-care difficult or impossible, leading to the assumption of a sick or disabled (as opposed to retirement) role.

adjustment (Bromley, 1988). The people who are most satisfied in retirement are scientists, writers and other academics who can simply carry on working with little loss of continuity from very satisfying jobs. Another group are those who discover really satisfying leisure activities, which in most cases have some of the characteristics of work (Argyle, 1989).

We can no longer think of retirement as a sudden enforced dislocation of a working life, almost inevitably causing feelings of rejection and physical and mental ill health. For example, a substantial proportion of men choose early retirement and, although a majority of women work only part-time, they represent about 40 percent of the total workforce and about 50 percent of adult women are in paid employment. Until recently, it has been unusual to think of women as 'retired', as their social condition was defined in terms of their marital status and continuing domestic activities. However, a large number of older women are retired from paid employment and so have to face not only that problem but also their husband's retirement and, for many, widowhood. But home and family still occupy a major part of a working woman's time – so retirement is seen as less of a change in lifestyle compared with men (Bromley, 1988).

Are the effects of retirement and unemployment different?

Argyle (1989) compares the effects of retirement and unemployment and these are summarized in Table 24.1. The differences can be explained at least partly in terms of the fact that '...retirement is an accepted and honourable social status, while unemployment is not. Retirement is seen as a proper reward for a hard life's work, while unemployment has the implication of failure, being unwanted, a scrounger living on charity...' (Argyle, 1989).

● Marriage

In contemporary Western societies, over 90 percent of adults marry at least once (Perlmutter and Hall,

Similarities	Differences
1 Both involve being out of work	1 The retired don't go job hunting
2 Both involve a drop in income	2 The retired get out and about less
3 Both involve increased leisure time	3 The retired are happier. Some feel bored, lonely and useless, but the unemployed are depressed and generally in poor mental health.
	4 The unemployed are in poor general health

Table 24.1 *Comparison of the effects of retirement and unemployment. (Based on Argyle, 1989)*

1992), showing it to be a normative, age-graded influence (see above). However, while young people are forming intimate partnerships as early and as often as they always have, there is a growing tendency to live together (and to have children outside marriage) (e.g. Bumpass *et al.*, 1991).

Marriage, or some very similar arrangement, is crucial to societal and personal life for most adults in most societies (Durkin, 1995) and clearly represents an important transition for many young adults, because it involves a lasting personal commitment to another person, as well as financial and potentially also family responsibilities. However, as Rutter and Rutter (1992) point out, it cannot be viewed as representing the same type of transition for everyone:

● In some cultures, the individual may have little choice as to who their partner will be (i.e. arranged marriages).
● At the opposite extreme is the love marriage following a long engagement, that used to be 'normal' in the UK and other Western countries.
● For some, this major life change can prove very stressful. Davies (1956) described cases of psychiatric disorder occurring for the first time in those engaged to be married (especially anxiety and depression). Typically, this began in connection with some event which hinged on the marriage date (e.g. booking the reception/finding a place to live) and, usually, either breaking off the engagement or going ahead with the wedding led to an improvement, clearly indicating that the stress did not lie in being married, but rather in the decision to make the commitment.

The couples studied by Davies included those who had lived together happily for some years; even so, the decision to marry produced stress and psychological disturbance. Indeed, couples who live together before marriage are actually more likely to divorce later and be less satisfied with their marriage than those who marry without living together first. It is also known that about 40 percent of couples who cohabit don't marry, which is a higher proportion compared with previous generations. So cohabitation may indeed be preventing some divorces but at the same time, cohabitees who do marry are more likely to divorce. Why?

According to Bee (1994), the most likely explanation is that it is not cohabiting itself that 'spoils' people for marriage (or marriage for people?), but that people who choose to cohabit are different to begin with. As a group, they seem more willing to

flout tradition in many ways, including less traditional sex roles, less religious and less likely to agree that one should stick with a marriage partner no matter what. Those who don't cohabit include a large percentage of more traditional individuals.

What are the psychological effects of marriage itself?

It is not so much being married as such but rather the qualities and pattern of the relationship, characteristics of the partner and the consequences of marriage for the individual's lifestyle that matter. It seems that married young adults (and those who are cohabiting) are happier, healthier, live longer and have lower rates of various psychiatric disorders than those without a partner. Those who seem to benefit most are married men (compared with single, divorced and widowed men, and women), while unmarried men are the worst off. Married women are slightly better off than unmarried women, but unmarried women are considerably healthier and happier than unmarried men. Why?

According to Bee (1994), married adults are less vulnerable to both disease and emotional distress because they are buffered by support from their attachment to their partner. Men seem to benefit most of all from the protective nature of marriage, partly because they are less likely to have close confidants outside marriage and because wives (more than husbands) provide emotional warmth/support to their spouse. For women, marriage isn't so obviously psychologically protective as it is for men, not because a close, confiding, harmonious relationship is any less important for women (indeed, if anything it is more important) but because many marriages don't provide such a relationship and because other consequences of marriage differ between the sexes. Despite major changes in attitudes to education and women's careers:

> ... for females, the potential benefits of a harmonious marriage relationship may be counterbalanced by the stresses involved in giving up their job or being handicapped in a career progression or promotion through having to combine a career and parenthood ... (Rutter and Rutter, 1992)

This, of course, supports what we said earlier about the difference in the dreams of women and men.

What are the psychological effects of divorce?

Reasons for marriage breakdown were discussed in Chapter 16. Although divorce rates are highest during the first five years, they peak again at around 15 and 25 years (Turnbull, 1995). Like death, whenever it takes place, divorce involves loss of one's major attachment figure and source of emotional support; this is a stressor, for both men and women, but men are likely to experience this loss as more stressful (see above). For women, divorce tends to be associated with both loss of income and increased parental responsibilities, while neither change applies so much to men (Rutter and Rutter, 1992).

Most of the research into the effects of divorce have focused on the children/adolescents (see Chapter 22), but divorcing parents also experience great distress and disruption. They may show wide mood swings, experience problems at work and poor health (Hetherington, 1989). Parenting style becomes much less authoritative (as distinct from authoritarian), almost neglectful.

● Parenthood

Parenthood and childrearing represent key transitions for most people (nine out of ten adults will become parents, most in their 20s and 30s; Bee, 1994). However, it varies in meaning and impact more than any other life transition (Rutter and Rutter, 1992). It may take place at any time from early adolescence to middle age, it may be planned/unplanned, wanted/unwanted and the motives for wanting children are many and various. Pregnancy may involve a single woman, a lesbian couple, a cohabiting couple, as well as a traditional married couple, adoption and fostering (see Box 24.3).

Other changes to traditional patterns involve deciding when to become pregnant. Since the 1950s, the greater acceptability of sexuality among young people was accompanied by a marked rise in teenage pregnancies, which is now declining. The increasing importance of work careers for women has led more couples to postpone starting a family until the woman's 30s so that she can become better established in her career. (Again, this relates to women's dream.) This postponement of parenthood has produced a new class of middle-aged parents with young children (Turnbull, 1995). According to Jones (1995), 20 percent of women in the UK born between 1960 and 1990 are unlikely to ever become mothers. They are likely to be well-educated, middle-class women, not necessarily pursuing a career, but realizing that '...it's OK to go through life without having children' (Root Cartwright, in charge of the British Organization of Non-Parents – BON).

BOX 24.3 Critical discussion: Homosexual parents in a heterosexual society

In the context of advocating that psychologists should study homosexual relationships in their own terms (and not by comparison with heterosexual ones), Kitzinger and Coyle (1995) suggest that we might want to ask how the children of lesbian/gay couples understand and talk about their parent's relationship and how they can develop positive views about homosexuality in a heterosexual culture. Given the recent increase in fostering/adoption of children by gay men and the ongoing 'lesbian baby boom', other key questions include decision making around parenthood, co-parenting arrangements and how homosexual couple relationships change with the birth/adoption of children.

Differences between homosexual and heterosexual relationships are discussed in Chapter 16.

What psychological adaptations must be made in parenthood?

Many women worry that the baby (especially with the first pregnancy) may be abnormal, about the physical changes in their bodies, how they'll cope with childbirth and how their relationship with their husband/partner will be affected. While pregnancy undoubtedly brings many couples closer together, most men take longer than women to become emotionally involved in the pregnancy and some feel decidedly left out. This feeling of exclusion may continue after the baby is born, with the mother being preoccupied with the baby; if the father doesn't wish or is unable to share in this, the baby may pull them further apart.

As we saw in Chapter 16, a common pattern is that marital satisfaction is highest before children arrive, then it drops and remains relatively low as long as there are dependent children at home, finally rising again during the 'postparental' and retirement stages. New parents discover that parent and spouse roles are at least partially incompatible; they report that they have much less time for each other, be it conversation, sex, simple affection or routine chores that used to be done together (Bee, 1994).

Parents, of course, are now attachment figures for their dependent children and, unlike the relationship with their partner, the parent-child relationship is asymmetrical. This new form of responsibility can be very stressful in itself and the couple's relationship prior to the baby's arrival has implications for how they adapt to these new role demands and the quality of their interactions with the child (Durkin, 1995). Unhappy couples sometimes stay together not just 'for the kids' but because the parental role has sufficient meaning and value for each partner that it outweighs the dissatisfaction with the marriage (Levinson *et al.*, 1978).

The 'empty nest' (syndrome) refers to grown-up children leaving home and the resulting sense of loss experienced by the now middle-aged parents. However, consistent with what we have said above about patterns in marital satisfaction (and see Chapter 16), research shows that most do not find this a distressing time; on the contrary, many find the conclusion of childrearing responsibilities liberating and welcome the new opportunities for a closer relationship with the partner and for personal fulfilment through work, return to education, etc. The extent to which women report empty nest distress may be cohort related, i.e. it is more typical of women who reach maturity during historical periods when traditional roles are stressed (Durkin, 1995).

What can be a source of strain and stress is the 'crowded nest' (Datan, 1980, cited in Durkin, 1995), where grown-up children opt not to leave home; this defies the demands of the social clock established by preceding generations. Also, although the parent-child relationship has (in Hartup's 1989 terms) been getting less vertical since adolescence, it is difficult for parents to adjust to virtual horizontal equality that comes with an 'adult child' living at home – especially if the parents are still doing much of the material providing (see Fig. 24.4).

LATE ADULTHOOD AND AGEING

We noted earlier that while 'growing up' is normally taken to be something desirable and almost an end in itself, 'growing old' has, traditionally, had very negative connotations. This negative view of ageing is based on the *decrement model,* which sees ageing as a process of decay or decline of our physical and mental health, our intellectual abilities and our social relationships. In contrast, the *personal*

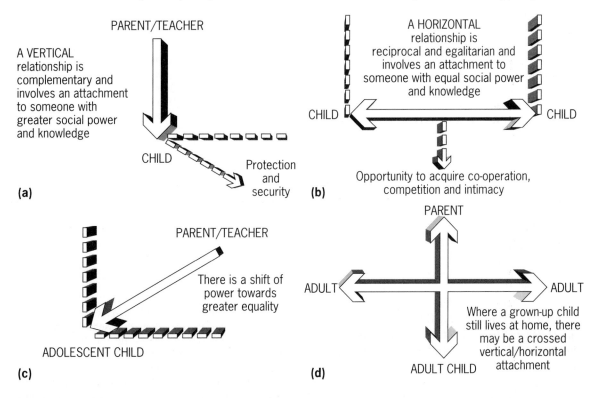

FIGURE 24.4 *Different kinds of relationships based on Hartup's (1989) distinction between vertical and horizontal relationships. While (a) and (b) are clear-cut in terms of this distinction, (c) involves a change from vertical to horizontal, while (d) involves both dimensions simultaneously. Both (c) and (d) may involve conflict – but for different reasons*

growth model stresses the potential advantages of old age and this much more positive attitude is the way in which ageing is studied within the lifespan approach. For example, Kalish (1979, 1982) emphasizes the increase in leisure time, the reduction in many day-to-day responsibilities and the ability to pay attention only to matters of high priority among the elderly. Older people respond to the reality of a finite and limited future by ignoring many of the inconsequential details of life and channelling their energies into what is really important.

● Ageism

As Durkin (1995) observes, becoming old is considered such a liability that from about the age of 30, we take it as a compliment if someone tells us we are not looking our age. Our prejudice against elderly people runs very deep (reflecting, perhaps, our deep-seated fear of death) and is mirrored in our language and our behaviour (*ageism*). In an article called '"Old" is not a four-letter word' (1978), Anderson claims that old people face a painful wall of discrimination that they are often too polite or too timid to attack. Even those psychologists who study ageing and try to present the positive features of growing old may, inadvertently, be guilty of ageism. For example, Kalish (1975) defines 'successful ageing' as continuing to behave as we did when we were younger (i.e. middle-aged); this assumes that one age group's pattern of behaviour is somehow inherently superior to that of another and is, therefore, a value judgement (rather than an objective observation) which merely reinforces the idea of 'younger' being more desirable than 'older'.

Our prejudices against the elderly are reflected in *stereotypes* (as are our racial, religious and gender-related prejudices) and expressions such as 'dirty old man' and 'old hag', which we often use without being aware of the attitudes on which they are based. Goldman and Goldman (1981) interviewed over 800 children aged 5–15 in Australia, England, Sweden and the US and found that children of all ages were more likely to say negative than positive things about the elderly, a tendency that became even stronger with age. Nor were negative comments limited to physical attributes, but also applied to both psychological and social/emotional attributes.

Despite the existence of some very positive images of the elderly person, such as the 'perfect grandparent' and 'sage' or 'wise old man'(Schmidt and Boland, 1986, cited in Durkin, 1995), the elderly enjoy a very low status compared with both children and younger adults and this inevitably influences the self-concept of elderly people which in turn may partly determine their behaviour. But how much are changes we associate with being old an inherent part of the ageing process itself?

This is one of the major questions investigated by *gerontology* (from the Greek words *geron* and *ontos*, meaning 'old man') which is a multidisciplinary field of scientific research concerned with the ageing process. It is interesting to note that *geriatrics* (from the Greek words *geras* meaning 'old age' and *iatros* meaning 'physician'), which is the branch of

---

BOX 24.4   The Ages of Me

Robert Kastenbaum, in *Growing Old – Years of Fulfilment* (1979), has devised a questionnaire (called 'The Ages of Me') which assesses how we see ourselves at the present moment in relation to our age.

● My *chronological* age is my actual or official age, dated from the time of my birth. (Interestingly, this is not a universal method – in some cultures, a year is added on so that we are one when we are born.) Again, different people (according to their actual age) will define what is chronologically old very differently; children will probably see anyone over 16 as old, while the 70-year-old will regard those over 80 as old and not themselves! Chronological age itself, therefore, is a very unreliable measure of 'old-ness'; what is old is a very relative matter!

● My *biological* age refers to the state and appearance of my face and body (on the questionnaire, this is indicated by the items (i) 'In other people's eyes, I look as though I am about ___ years of age'; and (ii) 'In my own eyes, I judge my body to be like that of a person of about ____ years of age').

● *Subjective* age is indicated by 'Deep down inside, I really feel like a person of about ____ years of age'. This corresponds, of course, to the popular expression 'you're as old as you feel'.

● My *functional* age, which is closely related to my *social* age, is the kind of life I lead, what I am able to do, the status I believe I have, whether I work, have dependent children, live in my own home, etc. Thus (i) 'My thoughts and interests are like those of a person of about ____ years of age'; and (ii) 'My position in society is like that of a person of about ____ years of age'.

The young old (60–69)	Marks a major transition. Most adults must adapt to a new role structure in an effort to cope with the losses and gains of the decade (Havighurst, 1972). Income is reduced due to retirement, friends and colleagues start to disappear. Although physical strength wanes somewhat, a great many have surplus energy and seek out new and different activities.
The middle-aged old (70–79)	Often marked by loss/ illness: friends/family may die at an increased rate. Must also cope with reduced participation in formal organizations. Often show restlessness/irritability. Own health problems become more severe. Major developmental task = to maintain the personality reintegration achieved in the 60s.
The old-old (80–90)	Increased difficulty in adapting to/interacting with their surroundings. Need help in maintaining social/cultural contacts.
The very old-old (90–99)	Less data available. Although health problems become more acute, can successfully alter their activities to make the most of what they have. Major advantage of old age = freedom from responsibilities. If previous crises have been resolved satisfactorily, this decade may be joyful, serene and fulfilling.

Table 24.2 *Description of 'the elderly', decade by decade. (Based on Burnside et al., 1979/Craig 1992)*

medicine concerned with the diseases and care of the elderly, is more recent, has much less money spent on it and is generally less attractive and respected than paediatrics, which is concerned with the diseases of childhood. (This is another example of ageism.)

● Who is old?

Can 'age' have more than one meaning? Can we be more than one age at the same time? These may seem rather strange questions to ask until you begin to think about them a little more carefully. If age is an important part of our self-concept and if society generally seems to value 'younger' much more positively than 'older', then how old (or young) we perceive ourselves as being is going to have a significant effect on how we value ourselves (i.e. our self-esteem) (see Box 24.4).

Because of official retirement, society makes it very difficult for people over 60 or 65 to be in work, even if they are fit and willing to go on working. This contributes to what is probably a fairly high correlation between functional, social and chronological age (i.e. the older we are – at least beyond 60 or 65 – the lower our social status, for example). If people were allowed to go on working until they decided to stop or until they became physically unfit to do so, the correlation would be much lower.

In practice, few people, at any chronological age, describe themselves consistently (i.e. give the same answer to all the items). One of the most typical differences occurs between subjective and chronological age: people in their 20s and above usually feel younger than their official age (and this includes many in their 70s and 80s) and also prefer to be younger, that is to say, they consider themselves to be too old. Very few people say they want to be older, which seems to confirm the aversion to old age that we have already discussed.

Two people of the same chronological age may behave quite differently and have very different subjective, biological, functional and social ages. The range of individual differences between people in their 60s and above is probably as great as that between children and younger adults and knowing a person's chronological age tells us really very little about them. Yet one of the dangerous aspects of ageism is that actual age is taken as an accurate indicator of all the others, so that we tend to infer that people over 60 all have certain characteristics which, together, make up the decrement model ('past it', 'over the hill', etc.). Recognizing the different 'ages of me' should help us to break down this idea of ageing as decaying and to look more analytically and more positively at old age.

Related to the stereotyping of the elderly is Burnside *et al.*'s (1979) classification of 'old', as summarized in Table 24.2.

As Craig (1992) says, 'the aged' are not one cohesive group but rather a collection of subgroups, ranging from the active, newly retired 65-year-old to the frail, perhaps incontinent 90-year-old. Each group has unique problems and capabilities but also share to some extent the age-related difficulties of reduced income, failing health and loss of loved ones.

'...But having a problem is not the same as being a problem. The all-too-popular view of those over age 65 as needy, non-productive and unhappy needs revision.' According to Dietch (1995), 'Life's final stage is surrounded by more myths, stereotypes and misinformation than any other developmental phase...'.

Lifespan and life expectancy

People are living longer, that is, life expectancy is increasing; this is shown in Table 24.3.

What this increase in life expectancy means is that the elderly represent an increasingly large proportion of the population (see Table 24.4). In the UK, there were one million people aged 80 and over in 1961 (representing 2 percent of the population), 1.6 million in 1981 (representing 3 percent of the population) and (an expected) 2.2 million in 1991 (representing almost 4 percent of the population). The projected figure for 2001 is 2.5 million (representing 4 percent of the population)

	Male	Female
1920	53.6	54.6
1930	58.1	61.6
1940	60.8	65.2
1950	65.6	71.1
1960	66.6	73.1
1970	67.1	74.8
1980	70.0	77.4
1989	71.8	78.5

Table 24.3 *Increase in average life expectancy in the US. (Based on Craig, 1992)*

But is there an upper limit to how long a human being can live? This is the question of lifespan (as distinct from life expectancy). All forms of life have some upper limit to how long they live; for example, 10–20 days for the house-fly and up to 2000 years for some trees. Our increasing longevity (long life) reflects the fact that we are now able to live out a greater portion of our intrinsic lifespan, i.e. our life expectancy has increased and has moved close to the lifespan of our species. Lifespan itself – the inherent length of life of a particular species – has remained unchanged for humans during this century and, apparently, throughout recorded history. Humans live longer than other mammals; Medvedev (1975) estimates a maximum lifespan of 110 years.

1950	8.1
1960	9.2
1970	9.8
1980	11.3
1988	12.3
2000	13.0
2010	13.9

Table 24.4 *Percentage of the population (US) 65 years/over. (Based on Craig, 1992)*

COGNITIVE CHANGES IN OLD AGE

Intelligence, IQ and ageing

Until recently, psychologists believed that our intellectual capacity reaches a peak in our late teens or early 20s, levels off (reaches a plateau) in our 20s and 30s and then starts to decline fairly steadily during middle age and more rapidly in old age. This general picture of decline seems to be based upon a number of factors, in particular:

- the way that intelligence is defined;
- the type of tests used to measure intelligence and the way the results are analysed;
- the kind of study used to compare intelligence at different ages (cross-sectional versus longitudinal).

Trying to define intelligence has always been a matter of disagreement and controversy among psychologists and will be looked at in detail in Chapter 28. Intelligence (at any age) is best understood as *multidimensional*, that is, it is composed of a number of different abilities and each of us has a different pattern or profile, so that we are better at some than at others (compared with ourselves and with others). Also, this pattern may change over time, both for individuals and for age groups as a whole. This way of thinking about intelligence makes it possible that, as far as certain abilities are concerned, the traditional picture of decline may be fairly accurate, but as far as others are concerned intelligence may actually go on increasing.

One way of classifying these various abilities is in terms of fluid and crystallized intelligence (Cattell, 1963; Horn, 1982). *Fluid intelligence* refers to the ability to solve novel and unusual problems (ones which the individual has not come across before) and involves memory span and mental agility, i.e. the

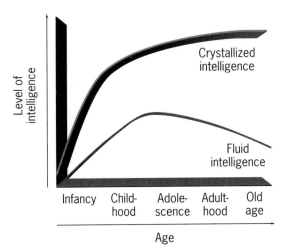

Figure 24.5 *Changes in fluid and crystallized intelligence with age*

speed of thought needed, for example, to find the pattern in a string of letters, visualizing an object in space or doing jigsaws. So it is not based on specific knowledge or any particular previous learning. It can also be thought of as the capacity or aptitude to learn. *Crystallized intelligence,* on the other hand, refers to knowledge and skills acquired through living in society and includes the ability to define words, verbal skills in general and the effective use of the skills and knowledge which formal education is primarily concerned with.

Since fluid intelligence is thought to be more sensitive to changes in the central nervous system and since ageing involves such changes, we might expect it to decline with age, and since crystallized intelligence is more dependent on ongoing experience, we might expect that it will go on improving. This is exactly what has been found. Botwinick (1978), for example, found that fluid intelligence begins a gradual decline in middle age and may drop more sharply for many people in later adulthood, while Nesselroade *et al.* (1972) found that crystallized intelligence remains the same or actually improves, at least until the early 80s (see Fig. 24.5).

A test which attempts to measure these two different kinds of intelligence is the Primary Mental Abilities (PMA) test, based on the work of Thurstone (1938). Fluid intelligence is measured by response speed (for example, writing down, within a specific time limit, all words beginning with a particular letter), memory span and non-verbal reasoning. These do show a decline with age. Crystallized intelligence is measured by reading

comprehension and vocabulary and these show no decline with age. However, the most widely used test of adult intelligence is the Wechsler Adult Intelligence Scale (WAIS), first designed by Wechsler in 1958. It consists of two separate scales, a verbal scale and a performance scale, and each of these produces a separate IQ (Intelligence Quotient); the scales can be combined to produce a third, total or overall IQ (see Chapter 28).

The test was originally standardized on 2000 men and women, aged 16 to 75 years, i.e. it was given to these participants in order to determine how people typically score at different ages. The pattern that emerged was that while total IQ seems to decline with age, verbal IQ does not (at least not until after 60); performance IQ seems to follow the pattern for total IQ. (This is equivalent to the findings for fluid and crystallized intelligence.) However, there are certain important differences within each scale; for example, as far as digit span (one of the verbal subtests) is concerned, while there is very little deterioration for recalling digits in the order in which they are presented, there is more when they have to be remembered in reverse order (especially in people over 45) and there is usually more decline for mental arithmetic, where marks are given for speed and accuracy.

These findings for the WAIS (and those referred to earlier for the PMA) are based mainly on *cross-sectional* studies, which involve studying different age groups at the same time so that, say, 20-year-olds are a different group from the 50-year-olds, who are a different group from the 70-year-olds, and so on. The traditional view of intelligence as declining steadily with age has emerged from these cross-sectional studies, in which an overall IQ on the WAIS or the PMA is compared for different age groups or where group tests (pencil-and-paper tests, often computer-marked, giving just an overall IQ) have been used. But there are serious problems associated with this method of study, in particular, what is known as the *cohort effect*, i.e. differences between, say, 20-year-olds and 80-year-olds, is not confined merely to age, but includes all those features of their upbringing and experience, such as wars, poverty and education (people born in the 1930s did not have computers as part of their educational experience; Labouvie-Vief, 1985). The two age groups represent different cohorts and so we cannot draw any conclusions about how intelligence changes with age simply on the basis of differences in IQ between the two groups – we know how a whole range of environmental and social factors can influence the development of intelligence and hence of IQ (including familiarity with doing IQ tests, confidence and motivation).

Longitudinal studies do not face this difficulty: since the same individuals are tested and retested at various times during their lifetime, we are always comparing them with themselves (i.e. there is only one cohort involved). However, it is practically very difficult to carry them out: the study has to last at least 60 years in the case of intelligence and ageing and so, not surprisingly, there are very few covering the full adult lifespan. However, those that have been conducted, according to Botwinick (1978),

show less decline in intelligence with age than cross-sectional studies and the decline tends to occur late in life. However, there is a kind of compromise method of study (the *cross-longitudinal method*), which attempts to combine the advantages of both while reducing the disadvantages; groups of participants, of different ages, are followed up over as long a period of time as possible (see Box 24. 5).

● Piagetian research

As we shall see in Chapter 25, Piaget argued that, although adults may become increasingly knowledgeable and skillful in the use of logical thinking, there is no new kind of thinking that develops after about 15 years of age. Indeed, many adults never attain formal operational thinking at all and, of those who do, many do so only in relation to their own particular area of expertise and experience.

But many psychologists have pointed out that the mental abilities related to formal operational thought are all focused on problem solving of one kind or another, whereby several pieces of information must be brought together to find the solution to a problem; this is known as *convergent thinking* (it is the kind of thinking assessed by IQ tests). Yet many problem situations in real life require *divergent thinking* whereby, for example, a solution is found by approaching the problem in an original and unconventional way and where a number of possible solutions may be required and not just one. This kind of approach is not covered by Piaget's theory.

Patricia Arlin (1975, 1977) has suggested that there is a fifth stage of development, corresponding to this ability to think divergently, which she calls *problem finding*. Similarly, Riegel (1973) advocated that we should de-emphasize formal thought and study mature thought in adults instead: *mature thought* is the acceptance that some things can be both true and not true at the same time. For example, to the person using *concrete operations*, it would mean understanding that two lumps of plasticine are simultaneously the same (quantity) *and* different (shape). But in Piaget's *conservation tasks*, only one or the other can be true. In Piaget's theory, the emphasis is on how the child tries to resolve this (apparent) contradiction by building new cognitive structures, but Riegel suggests that, instead of resolving the contradiction, the child needs to learn to accept it – concrete operations can be used skillfully and flexibly.

BOX 24.5	Key study: Studying adult intelligence the cross-longitudinal way

Starting in 1956, Schaie gave the PMA test to a large group of participants aged 20 to 70, and in 1963 and again in 1970 as many as possible were retested (161 in all). They were divided into age groups (on the basis of their age at the start of the study) ranging from 25, 32, 39 and so on up to 67. Each group was a cohort and test scores for each cohort can be viewed as a small longitudinal study of a particular 14-year-long 'slice' of adulthood. These overlapping slices could then be combined.

Number, word fluency, word meaning, inductive reasoning and spatial ability were tested. On word meaning, scores for the 25- and 32-year-old groups actually got better; for 50–60-year-olds, there was a minimal decline, but for the 60–67-year-olds changes were large enough for individuals to notice the difference in everyday life .This pattern was more or less repeated for overall scores. Fluid intelligence (measured by, for example, word fluency) showed a decline for all age groups (Schaie and Hertzog, 1983).

But are these normative declines in fluid intelligence inevitable or due to lack of practice, i.e. do they reflect changes in cognitive demands placed on adults as opposed to being an inevitable part of the ageing process (Cavanaugh, 1995)? Baltes and Willis (1982) began a series of studies in 1979 (Project ADEPT) involving the training of adults on PMAs that show that decline over time. People's performance improved significantly after training and after 'booster sessions' in 1981 and 1986, these improvements were maintained, even among 70 and 80-year-olds (Willis and Nesselroade, 1990, in Cavanaugh, 1995).

● Memory

This represents the most extensively researched aspect of adult cognition (see Chapter 12). The capacity and efficiency of *working memory* declines somewhat with age, resulting in poorer quality information being passed along the system. Because these changes may potentially affect many other aspects of information processing, they may underlie cognitive changes in general (Salthouse, 1991, cited in Cavanaugh, 1995). Also, STM in the elderly is likely to be hindered by a task requiring a division of attention; for example, they have more difficulty performing two tasks at the same time (where you have to keep a lot of information in your head at the same time; see Chapter 11), as when having to sort triangles according to colour, say, and circles according to size.

As far as LTM is concerned, older adults tend to perform worse than younger adults on recall tests, but these differences are less apparent or may disappear when recognition tests are used instead. Older adults also tend to be less efficient at spontaneously using strategies (such as putting items into categories), but when instructed to do so, they perform better.

As far as *everyday memory* is concerned, the popular belief that the elderly have little trouble recalling events from their youth and early adult life has some empirical support. But Warrington and Sanders (1971), for example, found that older adults had rather more difficulty recalling news events from the distant past compared with younger adults, although the differences were not dramatic. Older adults perform better at locating objects in familiar settings than younger adults; they are also consistently superior in remembering to remember (e.g. to post a card on a certain day). Because memory is used by many older adults to judge their own overall cognitive competence, it is important to know whether their evaluations are accurate. In memory self-evaluation studies, older adults tend to rate their memory as poorer than young adults rate theirs; the former tend to see memory as less stable, expect their memory to deteriorate with age and perceive themselves as having less control over memory. While reporting forgetting names as a particular problem, they report no more problems with remembering appointments and errands than do younger adults (Cavanaugh, 1995).

Significant memory deficits are one feature of dementia, the most common form of which is Alzheimer's disease; this is discussed further in Chapter 30.

SOCIAL CHANGES IN OLD AGE

● Social disengagement theory

Social disengagement theory (Cumming and Henry, 1961, *Growing Old – The Process of Disengagement*; Cumming, 1975) is perhaps the most influential account of what happens to us socially as we grow old. It was based on a five-year study of 275 50–90-year-olds in Kansas City. *Social disengagement* refers to the mutual withdrawal of society from the individual (compulsory retirement, children growing up and leaving home and starting families of their own, the death of spouse and friends, etc.) and of the individual from society (reduced social activities and a more solitary life). According to Cumming's (1975) version, disengagement has three aspects:

1 *Shrinkage of life space*: as we age, we interact with fewer and fewer others and occupy fewer and fewer roles.
2 *Increased individuality*: in the roles that remain, older individuals are less and less governed by strict rules and expectations.
3 *Acceptance – even embrace – of these changes*: the healthy older adult actively disengages from roles and relationships, turning more and more inward and away from interactions with others, i.e. withdrawal is the most appropriate and successful way to age. The disengaging person retreats from the social world as if preparing for their eventual death and it is a process resulting from both external (economic and social) and internal (physical and developmental) factors, including increased preoccupation with the self and decreased emotional investment in other people and objects and, to this extent, disengagement is a natural process rather than an imposed one. The older person who has a sense of psychological well-being will usually have attained a new equilibrium characterized by greater psychological distance, altered types of relationships and decreased social interaction.

According to Bee (1994), while the first two aspects are largely beyond dispute, it is the third that has proved most controversial. Is this process of disengagement inevitable and is it the one which most accurately describes and accounts for what happens? Bromley (1988) proposes three main criticisms of the theory, practical, theoretical and empirical. The practical criticism is that such a view of ageing encourages a policy of segregation, even indifference to the elderly and a very destructive belief that old age has no value. The theoretical criticism claims that disengagement is not a true theory but more of a 'proto-theory': a collection of loosely related arguments and assumptions. The most serious is the empirical criticism; this is the one which Bromley and other critics have focused their objections on.

Does everyone disengage?

While there are losses in social relationships following retirement, children leaving home, death of spouse and so on, relationships with other relatives (in particular, grandchildren), friends and neighbours go some way to replace these losses. The activities and relationships of later life may be more important in nature (quality may become more important than quantity). Contrary to expectations, engagement and activity are more likely to be sought by older people.

Havighurst *et al.* (1968) followed up the 1961 sample, although only 55 percent of the original 275 were included. They showed that although increasing age is accompanied by increasing disengagement, some elderly people who remained active and engaged reported relatively high levels of contentment; on the whole, the most active were the happiest. While the theory assumes that the tendency to withdraw from mainstream society is natural, that it is an inherent part of the ageing process, all the evidence suggests that those who disengage the least are the happiest, have the highest morale and live longest. Although this effect is small, it is consistent and contradicts the claim that isolation and withdrawal is the healthier choice (Bee, 1994).

However, there is also some evidence that older adults seem to be more content with solitude than at earlier ages; they are the least likely to describe themselves as lonely (while young adults are the most likely). Also, every indepth study of lifestyles of older adults identifies at least a few who lead contented, socially isolated lives, sometimes revolving around some all-consuming hobby. So, although it is possible to choose a highly disengaged lifestyle and to find satisfaction in it and although roles and relationships may rule our lives less in late adulthood that at earlier ages, such disengagement is not necessary for overall mental health in old age; indeed, for the majority, the opposite is true: roles and relationships still seem to be essential ingredients for emotional balance (Bee, 1994).

Bromley (1988) points out that the disposition to disengage is a *personality dimension* as well as a characteristic of ageing. The Havighurst *et al.* (1968) follow-up identified a number of different personality types, including *reorganizers,* who are involved in a wide range of activities and re-organize their lives to substitute for lost activities, and the *disengaged,* who have voluntarily moved away from role commitments and so have low activity levels but have high life satisfaction (thus consistent with disengagement theory).

Bromley (1988) believes that it is generally more accurate to speak of 'industrial disengagement and increased socioeconomic dependence' than of 'social disengagement'; in this way, the origins and circumstances of retirement are kept in focus and the theory ties in more closely with the empirical evidence and commonsense impressions.

● Activity (or re-engagement) theory

The major alternative to disengagement theory is *activity theory* (Havighurst, 1964; Maddox, 1964), according to which, except for the inevitable changes in biology and health, older people are the same as middle-aged people, with essentially the same psychological and social needs. Decreased social interaction in old age results from the withdrawal by society from the ageing person and happens against the wishes of most elderly people – so the withdrawal is not mutual, as maintained by social disengagement theory.

Optimal ageing, therefore, involves staying active and managing to resist the 'shrinkage' of the social world by maintaining the activities of middle age for as long as possible and then finding substitutes for work or retirement and for spouse and friends upon their deaths. In particular, it is important for older adults to maintain their 'role count', i.e. to ensure that they always have several different roles to play. While activity theory represents a counterbalance to disengagement theory (preventing the consequences of disengagement from going too far in the direction of isolation, apathy and inaction; Bromley, 1988), it also presents another 'blanket' view of the 'best' way to age and so is open to the same criticism as is disengagement theory, i.e. it does not take account of individual differences.

Not only has activity theory oversimplified the issues involved but there is little empirical support for it – as we saw above, activity can decline without adversely affecting morale and a more leisurely lifestyle, with fewer responsibilities, etc. can be seen as one of the rewards of old age. This idea is at the centre of social exchange theory (not to be confused with the theory of human relationships and helping behaviour discussed in Chapters 16 and 17).

Social exchange theory

Dyson (1980) has criticized both disengagement and activity theories for not taking sufficient account of the physical and economic factors which might limit individuals' choice as to how they age. Both theories are, therefore, *prescriptive*, i.e. they say what the elderly should be doing during this stage of life rather than accounting for how most people do, in fact, age. They also involve value judgements about what it is to age successfully (Hayslip and Panek, 1989).

Dyson suggests that a more useful approach is to see the process of adjusting to retirement in particular, and ageing in general, as a sort of contract between the individual and society. Dowd (1975), for instance, proposed that we give up our role as an economically active member of society when we retire but, in exchange, we receive increased leisure time, less responsibility and so on. The contract is, for the most part, unwritten and not enforceable, but most people will probably conform to the expectations about being elderly which are built in to social institutions and stereotypes.

An evaluation of theories of ageing

According to Hayslip and Panek (1989), each theory may refer to a legitimate process by which some individuals come to terms with a multitude of changes which may accompany ageing. In this sense, they are options. Just as disengagement may be involuntary (for instance, through poor health or having to move house), so an individual may face involuntarily high levels of activity (for example, through having to work or look after grandchildren) and both may be equally maladaptive. Arguably, disengagement theory underestimates and activity theory overestimates the degree of control people have over the 'reconstruction' of their lives and both see ageing as being essentially the same for all elderly people. However, '... personality is the pivotal factor in determining whether an individual will age successfully, and ... activity and disengagement theories, alone, are inadequate to explain successful ageing ...' (Turner and Helms, 1989).

Increasingly, theories tend to see development as a lifespan phenomenon (Baltes, 1987) and so see adjustment to old age as an extension of earlier personality styles, i.e. the stress is on the continuity between earlier and later phases of our lives (Craig, 1992). According to Reedy (1983, quoted in Turner and Helms, 1989):

> ... Satisfaction, morale, and adaptations in later life generally appear to be closely related to a person's lifelong personality style and general way of dealing with stress and change. In this sense, the past is prologue to the future. While the personality changes somewhat in response to various life events and changes, it generally remains stable throughout all of adult life.

Erikson's psychosocial theory

Perhaps a more valid and useful way of looking at what all elderly people have in common is to look at the psychological importance of old age as a stage of development, albeit the last that we shall go through; indeed, this is precisely where its importance lies. This brings us, almost full circle, to the personal growth model, which stresses the advantages and positive aspects of ageing. According to Erikson, in old age ('maturity') there is a conflict between ego integrity (the positive force) and despair (the negative force) and the individual's task is to end the stage, and hence his/her life, with greater ego integrity than despair. The achievement of this represents successful ageing.

What exactly does Erikson mean by ego integrity?

- The conviction that, in the long-term view, life does have a purpose and a meaning and does make sense.
- The conclusion that, within the context of one's life as a whole, what happened was somehow inevitable and could only have happened when and how it did.
- The belief that all life's experiences offer something of value, i.e. there is something to be learned from everything that happens to us, including the bad times. Looking back, we are able to see how we have grown psychologically as a result of life's ups and downs, triumphs and failures, calm and crisis.
- Coming to see our own parents in a new light and being able to understand them better because we have lived through our own adulthood and probably have raised children of our own.
- Coming to see that what we share with all other human beings, past, present and future, is the inevitable cycle of birth and death. Whatever the differences, historically, culturally, economically,

etc., all human beings have this much in common; in the light of this, 'death loses its sting'.

Lack or loss of this ego integrity is signified by a fear of death, which is the most conspicuous symptom of despair. Despair expresses the feeling that it is too late to undo the past, to put back the clock, in order to do what one has omitted to do or to put right the wrongs. Life is almost over and it is the only chance you get! This despair is, in fact, a form of basic mistrust, a fear of the unknown which follows death (see Chapter 21).

DEATH, GRIEF AND BEREAVEMENT

As we have seen, a feature of growing old is that it becomes increasingly likely that we will suffer the loss, through death, of loved ones, parents, husbands and wives, siblings and friends, even children. Suffering such losses is referred to as *bereavement,* while *grief* is the complex set of psychological and bodily reactions commonly found in people who suffer bereavement. Parkes and Weiss (1983) define grief as 'a normal reaction to overwhelming loss, albeit a reaction in which normal functioning no longer holds'; they distinguish between grief and mourning, the latter being the 'observable expression of grief'. (Mourning is also used in a different sense to refer to the social customs and conventions surrounding death, such as funerals, wearing dark clothes, cancelling social engagements and so on; we talk about a 'period of mourning' in which grieving is 'official' and largely public.)

● Is there a normal pattern of grieving?

A number of writers (including Freud, Engel and Parkes) have described the characteristic stages or phases of the grieving process. Engel (1962), for example, uses the concept of grief work to refer to the process of mourning through which a bereaved person readjusts to loss; it comprises three phases:

1 *Disbelief* and *shock:* the initial reaction to the loss, which can last for up to a few days and involves the refusal to accept the truth of what has happened.
2 *Developing awareness:* the gradual realization and acknowledgement of what has happened, often accompanied by pangs of grief and guilt. Apathy, exhaustion and anger are also common,

the last being closely related to self-blame and guilt; at this time it is important that there are people around who are willing simply to listen and tolerate the expression of all these feelings.
3 *Resolution:* the establishment of a new identity, the full acceptance of what has happened, marking the completion of grief work. The bereaved person takes a realistic view of their situation and resolves to cope without the loved one and begin a new life.

All grief theorists agree that grief must be worked through – there is some sort of natural progression and blending of feelings which must be experienced if a healthy adjustment to the loss is to be achieved. However, some prefer to talk about *components of grief* instead of stages: the latter implies a clear-cut, orderly, predetermined set of events which is the same for everyone. Yet this is not the case – the 'stages' are not separate, may not be successive and it is not certain that everyone has to experience each and every one of them. For example, Ramsay and de Groot (1977) describe nine components, some of which tend to appear earlier in the grief process, some of which come later (see Table 24.5).

● Normal and abnormal grieving

One problem involved in trying to distinguish normal from abnormal or pathological grief is the enormous individual variations in grieving patterns (even though the components may be similar). Grief is not a simple, universal process involving fixed stages (Stroebe *et al.*, 1993).

Some researchers deny that emotional distress is inevitable following a major loss, although most would say it is usual, at least in Western cultures. Some people probably do not grieve intensely and there can be positive consequences following loss of a close relative (such as relief, the end of suffering, etc.), which need not necessarily indicate pathology (Stroebe *et al.*, 1993).

Parkes believes that prolonged, incapacitating grief ('chronic grief') is the most common variant of the usual pattern of grieving and that people who at first do not show their grief may later show this disturbed, chronic form of mourning. Hinton (1975) identifies three other abnormal patterns:

1 exaggeration of the numbness associated with the shock of the loss;
2 shading of some of the more immediate responses into neurotic forms of emotional distress.

1. Shock:	usually the first response, most often described as a feeling of 'numbness'. Can also include pain, calm, apathy, depersonalization and derealization. It is as if the feelings are so strong that they are 'turned off'; can last from a few seconds to several weeks.
2. Disorganization:	the inability to do the simplest thing or, alternatively, organizing the entire funeral and then collapsing.
3. Denial:	behaving as if the deceased were still alive, a defence against feeling too much pain, usually an early feature of grief but one that can recur any time. A common form of denial is searching behaviour, e.g. waiting for the deceased to come home, or having hallucinations of them.
4. Depression:	emerges as the denial breaks down but can occur, usually less frequently and intensely, at any point during the grieving process. Either 'desolate pining' (a yearning and longing, an emptiness 'interspersed with waves of intense psychic pain') or 'despair' (feeling of helplessness, the blackness of the realization of powerlessness to bring back the dead).
5. Guilt:	can be both real and imagined, for actual neglect of the deceased when they were alive or for angry thoughts and feelings.
6. Anxiety:	fear of losing control of one's feelings, of going mad or more general apprehension about the future (changed roles, increased responsibilities, financial worries, etc.).
7. Aggression:	irritability towards family and friends, outbursts of anger towards God or fate, doctors and nurses, the clergy or even the person who has died.
8. Resolution:	an emerging acceptance of the death, a 'taking leave of the dead and an acceptance that life must go on'.
9. Reintegration:	putting acceptance into practice by reorganizing one's life in which the deceased has no place. (However, pining and despair, etc. may reappear on anniversaries, birthdays, etc.)

Table 24.5 *Ramsay and de Groot's nine components of grief*

According to Parkes (1970), occasional feelings of panic are so commonplace that it could be considered a normal reaction. Other illogical fears may include being alone, claustrophobia, dirt and death. Feelings of depersonalization among the bereaved, a sense of being unreal or unfamiliar to oneself, and obsessions too may become more likely;

3 the appearance of physical symptoms, sometimes merely accompanying, sometimes overshadowing the emotional disturbance. Fatigue, insomnia, loss of appetite, weight loss, headaches, breathlessness, palpitations, blurred vision and exhaustion are among the many physical symptoms about which widows complain to their doctors. Parkes (1964) found that widows needed to consult their GPs much more often than usual during the first six months of widowhood, both for physical and psychological symptoms. Elderly people who suffer bereavement are especially likely to experience their distress as predominantly physical.

Widows and widowers, for some time after the death of their spouse, in fact run a greater risk of suffering serious illness and themselves dying than married people of similar age, with widowers being at a relatively greater risk. Parkes *et al.* (1969) believe this risk is largely confined to the first six months after the bereavement and identify three main factors that are responsible: (i) self-neglect; (ii) suicide; and (iii) cardiac disease ('broken heart') and (in the case of widowers) death through a disease similar to that of the wife. It is younger adults (up to their mid-30s), especially men, who are most at risk.

● Can we talk of 'recovery' from grief?

According to Lieberman (1993), traditional measures used in bereavement research, such as symptoms, variations of grief and social adjustment, represent a homeostatic model in which the underlying assumption is that bereavement is a stressor that upsets the person's equilibrium and a return to a normal balanced state is desirable. He sees this as a very limited perspective, as does Weiss (1993), for whom 'recovery' is not a simple 'return to baseline' level of functioning. Do we ever 'get over it'? Should we substitute 'adaptation' or 'degree of damage' for 'recovery'?

According to Stroebe *et al.* (1993), the majority of bereaved people do cease to grieve intensely after a year or two, but a minority continue to do so for longer. Some aspects of grief may never end for a proportion of otherwise normally adjusted bereaved individuals; '...if there has been a strong attachment to a lost loved one, emotional involvement is likely to continue, even for a lifetime...' (Stroebe *et al.*, 1993).

DEATH OF THE SELF

Much of what we have said about ageing has been to do with loss of various kinds – loss of work, loss of financial status, loss of social status, loss of relationships through death and so on. According to Raphael (1984), 'As life draws to its end, the ageing person faces another death. He experiences even more clearly the knowledge of his own death – the death of the "self". There may be many partial deaths along the way. The loss of sexuality may seem the death of a vital part of the self ...'.

The older person becomes increasingly preoccupied with death, which starts to be thought of personally – when and how will it come? There is an ambivalence in attitudes to death – sometimes shutting it out and trying to deny it, sometimes desperately wanting to talk about it, share one's fears and find out more about the unknown. This is a process of *anticipatory grief,* a term coined by Kübler-Ross (1969) to describe how the terminally ill come to terms with their own imminent death. A common feature of anticipatory grief is *reminiscing.* According to Butler (1963), much of the reminiscing common in later life may be a valuable way of 'sorting out' the past and the present. Prompted by the recognition of impending death, the elderly re-examine old conflicts, consider how they have treated others and come to some conclusion about themselves and their lives. This *life review* may result in a new sense of accomplishment, satisfaction and peace (Erikson's ego integrity).

It represents, at least partly, grieving for the life and the self which will be relinquished with death. Coming to terms with our own death is a crucial task of old age (what Peck (1968) calls *ego transcendence* versus *ego preoccupation*). Some individuals review their lives privately or internally, others share their memories and reflections with others. For the latter, this serves a double purpose: (i) it helps them to organize a final perspective on their lives for themselves; (ii) it leaves a record that will live on with others after their death. Clearly, however we may go

about it, one task of life, especially during our 'twilight years', is to prepare for death.

CHAPTER SUMMARY

- It is only in the last 20 years or so that developmental psychologists have taken adulthood seriously, reflecting the lifespan approach inspired by Erikson.
- One criterion for defining psychological adulthood is maturity, conveying the ability to deal with failures, accept successes and take responsibility for decisions and choices.
- A second way of trying to define adulthood is in terms of developmental tasks, such as intimacy versus isolation (young adulthood) and generativity versus stagnation (middle adulthood). This sequence of development, together with the achievement of identity during adolescence, may not apply equally to women and men or to different social class groups.
- Asking 'How is adulthood experienced?' is a third way of trying to define adulthood and Levinson *et al.*'s *Seasons of a Man's Life* is a major example of this approach. Life structure theory proposes a series of structure-building and structure-changing (transitional) phases or periods, each involving biological, psychological and social adjustments; work and family roles are always central.
- According to Levinson *et al.*, the lifecycle comprises the eras of pre-adulthood, early, middle and late adulthood, which overlap in the form of cross-era transitions. The early adult transition involves separation from the pre-adult world and initial attachments to the adult world.
- Entering the adult world involves the establishing of one's dream, with mentors playing a crucial role. The age 30 transition typically brings an 'age 30 crisis ', followed by settling down, the later part of which involves becoming one's own man.
- The most famous and controversial part of Levinson *et al.*'s theory is the 'midlife crisis' (during the midlife transition), which they see as a normative crisis, i.e. both inevitable and necessary. The evidence fails to support either its inevitability (it is not a 'stage' that everyone goes through) or its desirability (crisis isn't necessary for healthy later development), but it is widely accepted that middle age does involve adapting

to changes brought about by marker events and a reappraisal of our achievements and ambitions.

- Gould's theory of the evolution of adult consciousness claims that in order to achieve adulthood, we must free ourselves of the illusion of absolute safety derived from our childhood. This painful process requires us to relinquish our dependency on our parents and to accept ourselves as creators of our own lives.

- One of the obvious limitations of Levinson *et al.*'s theory is the use of an all-male sample. More recent research of women's lives reveals general similarities with men's life structure, but a major difference concerns women's dream, which is typically split between family and career. Despite changes in their role in the labour force and an increasing number of 'dual earner couples', women still have the major responsibility for childcare and domestic affairs as a whole.

- Stage theories of adulthood greatly underestimate both individual variability in adult experience and the continuity of personality during adult life. An alternative approach is to study the impact of critical life events/psychosocial transitions, which can be classified according to whether they represent normative, age-graded/normative, history-graded/ non-normative influences.

- Unemployment represents a sudden, unanticipated loss of work and reactions to it may be very similar to other kinds of loss. Compared with those in work, the unemployed suffer higher rates of both mental illness, including depression, and physical illness, including mortality rate.

- Apart from the financial hardships and related loss of self-esteem, the harmful effects of unemployment are likely to be greater if it continues for a long period of time, if the person has been very committed to their job, lacks social support, especially from family, fails to replace work with some structured activity and blames themselves for their situation.

- Retirement involves loss of regular, ritualized patterns of behaviour, the familiarity of workplace and colleagues and the transition to an economically non-productive role. The ambiguity of the role reflects its newness as a social role in Western culture.

- Retirement can be seen as a process involving phases, each requiring an adjustment. People who adjust best are those who are able to establish continuity with their past, retire voluntarily, are in good health and discover satisfying leisure activities.

- A substantial proportion of men choose early retirement and, as women become a larger proportion of the workforce, they become more likely to experience retirement – as well as their husband's.

- Marriage is a normative, age-graded influence that represents a major transition. The decision to commit oneself through marriage can be very stressful and couples who have lived together are actually more likely to divorce later and be less satisfied than those who haven't.

- Married couples or those who are cohabiting are generally happier, physically and mentally healthier and live longer than those without a partner; married men seem to benefit the most. Men are also likely to experience divorce as more stressful than women.

- Parenthood varies in meaning more than any other major life transition. The timing of pregnancy is affected by women's career involvement, with an increasing trend towards postponing parenthood, producing a new class of middle-aged parents with young children. There is also a trend towards not having children at all.

- There are many anxieties involved in pregnancy, especially with a first child. There may be conflict between spouse and parent roles and marital satisfaction is likely to decrease while there are still dependent children.

- The marital relationship prior to the baby's arrival is related to how they adjust to their new role. Satisfaction provided by the parental role may outweigh marital dissatisfaction.

- The 'empty nest' (syndrome) usually marks the beginning of improved marital satisfaction and is not a stressful time for parents, unlike the 'crowded nest'.

- Two major views of the ageing process are the decrement model and the personal growth model, with the former being the more influential, both within and outside psychology.

- Ageism is linked to the decrement model and is reflected in negative stereotypes of the elderly which are learned from an early age; being old is considered undesirable by society at large and is the basis for discrimination of many kinds.

- Defining who is old is not straightforward. Kastenbaum distinguishes between chronological, biological, subjective and functional/social age, which are typically different for the same individual. Society tends to stereotype everyone over a certain chronological age as 'the same', ignoring the variability between them, and considerable changes occur during the decades from 60 onwards.

- With the increase in life expectancy, the elderly represent an increasingly large proportion of the population.
- The traditional view of steady decline in intelligence from middle age onwards was based on particular definitions of intelligence, the type of tests used and the kind of study used to compare different age groups.
- While fluid intelligence may gradually decline with age, crystallized intelligence remains stable or even improves in old age. These are tested by the Primary Mental Abilities test, although the most widely used test of adult intelligence is the Wechsler Adult Intelligence Scale.
- The most widely used method of comparing intelligence at different ages is the cross-sectional method, which suffers from the cohort effect. The main alternative, the longitudinal method, is practically very difficult but a compromise method is the cross-longitudinal method, which combines features of the other two.
- An alternative view of adult intelligence is based on Piaget's theory of cognitive development. Research suggests that there is a form of thinking beyond formal operations, in which the adult thinks divergently and is able to tolerate contradictions.
- Working memory seems to become less efficient with age and having to perform two tasks at a time becomes more difficult. But in certain aspects of everyday memory, older adults outperform younger adults, even though they may evaluate their memory as being poorer than younger adults evaluate theirs.
- According to social disengagement theory, there is a mutual withdrawal of society from the individual and of the individual from society. However, the evidence does not support this view. Although some may prefer a solitary lifestyle, this is not true of the majority; those who disengage the least seem to be the happiest.
- Activity/re-engagement theory stresses the continuity between late and middle adulthood and rejects the view that disengagement is what the elderly want and that it is 'natural'. But both theories overlook individual differences and the influence of personality on the ageing process.
- Social exchange theory sees ageing as involving a kind of contract between the individual and society, in which certain roles are given up in exchange for others.

- For Erikson, old age involves a conflict between ego integrity and despair; the former involves an acceptance of death, while the latter is a form of basic mistrust.
- While it is generally agreed that grieving is a normal reaction to loss and that it is essential for people to grieve, there is much less agreement as to whether there are universal stages of grief and how normal and pathological grieving can be distinguished. Some prefer to identify components of grief rather than stages.
- Individual differences make it very difficult to define normal/abnormal grieving and it may be inappropriate to think of people 'recovering' from grief.
- In old age, we must face 'death of the self' and anticipatory grief is a way of trying to come to terms with our death. This commonly involves reminiscing, part of the life review which helps foster ego integrity or ego transcendence.

GLOSSARY

Activity theory Theory of ageing which sees older people as essentially having the same psychological and social needs as middle-aged people; any disengagement that occurs is involuntary and optimal ageing involves staying as active as possible. Also called re-engagement theory.

Ageism Prejudiced attitudes and discriminatory behaviour against the elderly, reflected in negative stereotypes and the generally low status of the elderly in society.

Anticipatory grief The process by which the terminally ill and elderly come to terms with their own, imminent death.

Cohort effect In cross-sectional studies, differences in experience between age groups (who constitute different generations) that could account for the age difference over and above the effects of age itself.

Cross-longitudinal method Method for studying developmental change in which groups of participants, of different ages, are followed up over as long a time period as possible.

Cross-sectional method Method for studying developmental change in which different age groups are compared at the same point in time.

Decrement model view of ageing as a process of decay/decline in our physical and mental health, intellectual abilities and social relationships.

Ego integrity The acceptance of one's life as it has turned out and, therefore, an ability to accept death. Its opposite is despair.

Generativity Being concerned with, helping to nurture, the next generation, either through parenting or work with young people. Its opposite is stagnation.

Geriatrics Branch of medicine concerned with diseases and care of the elderly (from the Greek *geras* = 'old age' and *iatros* = 'physician').

Gerontology A multidisciplinary scientific study of the ageing process (from the Greek *geron* and *ontos* = 'old man').

Grief The complex set of psychological and bodily reactions to bereavement, i.e. suffering loss, such as the death of a loved one.

Intimacy The capacity to share with and care about another person, usually through commitments such as marriage. But it can also be expressed through close friendships. Its opposite is isolation.

Life expectancy the average length of life that people can expect. Differs for men and women and has increased steadily over the last 100 years or so.

Lifespan The upper limit to how long members of a species can live. Estimated at 110 years for humans.

Lifespan approach The view that psychological development is a lifelong process ('womb to tomb'), pioneered by Erikson.

Life structure theory Levinson *et al.*'s theory of adulthood which sees the lifecycle comprising the eras of pre-, young, middle and late adulthood, which overlap in the form of transitions (structure-changing) and consist of structure-building phases/periods.

Longitudinal method Method for studying developmental change in which the same individuals (a single cohort) are tested/re-tested at various points in their lives.

Maturity A criterion for defining adulthood, denoting the ability to deal with failures and frustrations and to accept successes and responsibility for one's choices and decisions.

Midlife crisis A period of inevitable (and necessary) emotional distress, occurring during the midlife transition (40–45), due to soul searching about one's past achievements and future goals.

Mourning The observable, public expression of grief.

Non-normative influences Idiosyncratic transitions, such as divorce, unemployment, illness and death of spouse, which can happen at any time during adulthood.

Normative, age-graded influences Biological and social changes which usually occur at predictable ages, such as puberty, menopause, marriage, retirement, parenthood and the 'empty nest' syndrome.

Normative, history-graded influences Historical events, such as wars, recessions and epidemics, which affect a whole generation/cohort at about the same time.

Personal growth model View of ageing which stresses the advantages of old age; relates to the lifespan approach.

Psychosocial transitions Parkes' term for critical life events/marker events which require us to make major adjustments.

Reminiscing A common feature of anticipatory grief, involving a sorting out of the past and present. Part of the life review, a re-examination of old conflicts and treatment of others in a bid to achieve ego integrity.

Social disengagement theory Theory of ageing which sees a voluntary withdrawal of the individual from society as the 'natural' and healthy way to age, mirrored by society's withdrawal from the individual.

Social exchange theory Theory of ageing, according to which there is a 'contract' between the individual and society, whereby certain roles are given up in exchange for increased leisure time, reduced responsibilities, etc.

FURTHER READING

Levinson, D.J., Darrow, D.N., Klein, E.B., Levinson, M.H. and McKee, B. (1978) *The Seasons of a Man's Life.* New York: A.A.Knopf. One of the classics in this relatively recent field of adult development research.

Stroebe, M.S., Stroebe, W. and Hansson, R.O. (eds) (1993) *Handbook of Bereavement: Theory, Research, and Intervention.* New York: Cambridge University Press. A collection of original articles by leading researchers and practitioners, including Colin Murray Parkes, Robert Weiss and Beverley Raphael.

25 COGNITIVE DEVELOPMENT

INTRODUCTION AND OVERVIEW

According to Meadows (1993, 1995), in studying cognitive development we are concerned with 'the child as thinker'. However, different theoretical accounts of how the child's thinking develops rest on very different images of what the child is like:

- Piaget sees the child as an organism adapting to its environment, as well as a scientist constructing its own understanding of the world;
- according to the information-processing approach, the child (like adults) is a manipulator of symbols;
- Vygotsky, in contrast with both the first two approaches, sees the child as a participant in an interactive process by which socially and culturally determined knowledge and understanding gradually become individualized. Bruner, like Vygotsky, emphasizes the social aspects of the child's cognitive development.

Some years ago, Piaget's theory was regarded as the major framework or paradigm within child development. However, despite remaining a vital source of influence and inspiration, both in education and psychology generally, today there are hardly any 'orthodox' Piagetians left (Dasen, 1994); many fundamental aspects of Piaget's theory have been challenged and fewer and fewer developmental psychologists now subscribe to his or other 'hard' *stage theories* (Durkin, 1995).

In this chapter, we shall be discussing all of these approaches but we shall be concentrating on the work of Piaget and Vygotsky, some of whose ideas, along with Bruner's, were considered in Chapter 13 on the relationship between language and thought. Piaget's theory will be discussed again in Chapter 27 on moral development.

PIAGET'S THEORY

● Biographical sketch

FIGURE 25.1 *Jean Piaget (1896–1980). (Yves de Braine from Black Star)*

Born in Neuchâtel, Switzerland, Piaget (1896–1980; Fig. 25.1) was trained as a zoologist and as such, he was especially interested in the question of how animals adapt to their environment; it was in this context that he become involved in the study of human intelligence. He was also very interested in philosophy, particularly the branch that deals with general questions about the nature of knowledge, called epistemology. He combined these two areas of interest in the form of *genetic epistemology*, the study of how knowledge develops in human beings: for Piaget, developmental psychology is the best method for studying how scientific reasoning came about in Western culture (Dasen, 1994).

● Intelligence: trait or process?

Ironically, Piaget's early involvement with intelligence tests, which attempt to compare individuals on what is assumed to be a fixed trait, was to lead him towards his lifelong study of intelligence as a process, something which changes over time. He was not concerned with individual differences but with what is common to all individuals as they pass through the same stages of intellectual or cognitive development.

While working in Binet's Paris laboratory (Binet developed the first recognized intelligence test) on the standardization of Burt's IQ test for use with French children (see Chapter 28), Piaget became intrigued by the unusual and unexpected replies that children often gave and wanted to discover the processes by which these wrong answers were arrived at. He believed that children's mistakes were a much better indicator of how they think than their correct answers ever could be; he also became convinced that their errors were not random but systematic, that there was a pattern to them which revealed the underlying mental structures that generated them. Whereas IQ tests are concerned with the *what* of the child's answers (how many are right or wrong), Piaget was concerned with the *how* (especially as suggested by their mistakes).

● The nature of intellectual development

Intelligence, for Piaget, is the means by which human beings adapt to their environment. It is a process which essentially involves the individual trying to construct an understanding of reality through interacting with it; knowledge does not come 'ready-made' but has to be discovered actively (or even 'invented'). It consists:

> ... neither of a simple copy of external objects nor of a mere unfolding of structures preformed inside the subject, but rather ... a set of structures progressively constructed by continuous interaction between the subject and the external world. (Piaget, 1970)

The view of knowledge as a 'simple copy' of the external world or the passive registration of associations is known as *associationism* (the basis of stimulus–response psychology and closely associated with *empiricism*; see Chapter 2) and the 'mere unfolding of preformed structures' refers to the process of *maturation* (which relates to *nativism*, the view that knowledge and ability are innate; see Chapter 10). Piaget's theory of knowledge, known as *constructivism*, differs from both of these.

The structures develop in a predictable fashion and can be summarized as four stages which all children pass through in the same sequence. Underlying these changes are certain functional invariants, i.e. fundamental aspects of the developmental process which remain the same and work in the same way throughout the various stages, in particular, *assimilation*, *accommodation* and *equilibration*. But before we can properly understand these unchanging features of development, we need to understand exactly what it is that changes, namely schemas (or schemata; see Chapters 9 and 12).

A *schema* (or scheme) can be thought of as the basic unit or building block of intelligent behaviour. More formally, it is a way of organizing experience which makes the world more simple, more predictable and more 'know-able'. The baby's schemas are largely confined to inborn reflexes, such as sucking, and they tend to operate quite independently of other reflexes; a sucking schema is also a physical, overt action. But in the course of development, individual schemas become co-ordinated and integrated into more inclusive structures and it is these larger structures which constitute the typical abilities and understanding of each developmental stage: 'Each stage is characterized by an overall structure in terms of which the main behaviour patterns can be explained' (Piaget and Inhelder, 1969).

Also, the baby's physical (motor) behaviour comes more and more under its voluntary control and schemas gradually become more and more internal or 'interiorized', i.e. they become mental and the child starts to think in something like the adult sense of the word. But if at birth we are limited to a few, simple, unrelated reflexes, how do our schemas change in these ways? This is where assimilation, accommodation and equilibration come in.

At first, the baby will suck anything that touches its lips or is put into its mouth, whether this is its mother's nipple (which produces nourishment) or its father's finger (which does not). The baby is applying a schema that it already possesses by (in this case, literally) fitting objects into it, sucking them in more or less the same way, i.e. *assimilating* them. However, while the baby is still very young, it will gradually change the shape of its lips according to whether it is sucking a nipple or a finger. Later on, when it is given a cup to feed from, it must change the way it sucks (and swallows) yet again; this will not occur without a lot of spilt milk but eventually a 'drinking-out-of-a-cup' schema will have developed and this illustrates *accommodation*. So in assimilation we apply the schemas we already possess and try to fit the environment into them; it can be thought of as a generalized use of what we can already do. Schemas are not just physical actions or skills but include ideas, concepts, bits of knowledge, verbal labels and so on. In accommodation, we change already-existing schemas to match the requirements of the environment, which brings us to equilibration.

As long as the child is able to deal with all (or most) new experiences by assimilating them, it will be in a comfortable state of balance or equilibrium (brought about by *equilibration*). However, if already-existing schemas are inadequate to cope with new situations, the child is pushed into a less comfortable state of disequilibrium and, to restore the balance, it must change one or more of its schemas, i.e. it must accommodate. So it is through this process of equilibration that development proceeds, a continuous series of assimilations and accommodations, equilibrium and disequilibrium, an ongoing process throughout life but with the most significant developments taking place during the first 15 years or so (Fig. 25.2).

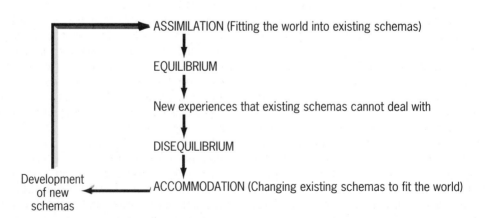

FIGURE 25.2 *Relationship between assimilation, equilibrium, disequilibrium and accommodation in the development of schemas*

When a schema has recently developed, assimilation ensures that the new learning (which the schema represents) is consolidated, i.e. it is practised repeatedly until it can be used easily and even automatically. But assimilation alone would make behaviour very rigid and inflexible and, indeed, very little development would actually take place – this can only happen through accommodation. So assimilation and accommodation are both necessary and complementary and together they constitute the fundamental process of *adaptation* (adaptation = assimilation + accommodation).

● Stages of cognitive development

Having discussed how schemas change and develop in general, we are in a position to look at the characteristic changes that take place during the four major stages that Piaget describes, namely:

1 *the sensorimotor* (0–2 years);
2 *the preoperational* (2–7 years);
3 *the concrete operational* (7–11 years);
4 *the formal operational* (11–15 years).

Each represents a stage in the development of intelligence (hence 'sensorimotor intelligence', 'preoperational intelligence' and so on) and is really a way of summarizing the various schemas the individual has at any particular time. But two notes of caution are necessary:

1 The ages corresponding to each stage are only approximations or averages. Children move through the stages at different speeds, often due to environmental factors, although the sequence of stages is invariant (the order is fixed and stages cannot be skipped) and universal (the same for all human beings) and is based on biological maturation.
2 The concept of a 'stage' of development is often interpreted to indicate that development is discontinuous, i.e. not a gradual process of change but broken up into 'segments' (the stages). This was not the impression Piaget wanted to create and, from 1970, he preferred to think of development as a spiral, implying a continuous process. However, later stages build on earlier ones (which is why the sequence is invariant) and entail reconstructing at a new level what was achieved at the earlier stage. (We shall discuss the concept of a stage again when we evaluate Piaget's theory; see below.)

The sensorimotor stage (0–2)

The baby's intelligence is essentially practical, i.e. its interactions with the environment consist of overt actions, either sensory (seeing, hearing, etc.) or motor (grasping, pulling, etc.). The baby 'thinks' through acting upon objects and/or perceiving them – a rattle *is* its colour when looked at, its texture when touched or sucked, its sound when shaken – and when it is not being perceived or acted upon in any of these ways, it no longer exists as far as the baby is concerned: the baby lacks *object permanence*. The development of object permanence is one of the major achievements of the sensorimotor period so we shall discuss it in some detail (also see Chapter 10).

Object permanence

Between one and four months, when the baby sees its bottle, for example, it begins to suck, apparently for the pleasure of it, even if the teat does not touch its lips. This suggests that the baby has learned to recognize its bottle but this hardly constitutes understanding that the bottle exists independently of the baby itself. The infant will look at a toy if it is within visual range, follow it with its eyes and, between three and four months, try to grasp it, but as soon as it has moved out of sight, the baby acts as if it had ceased to exist; there is no attempt to search for it, with eyes or hands ('out of sight, out of mind').

However, some psychologists believe that Piaget may have been misjudging what babies can do. For example, Bower and Wishart (1972) found that the way an object is made to disappear influences a baby's response, while Piaget believed that it should not make any difference at all. If babies were looking at an object and reaching for it when the lights were turned off, Bower and Wishart found that they would continue to reach for it for up to 1½ minutes (they used infrared cameras to observe the babies in the dark). This strongly suggests that the baby remembers that the object is still there and Bower (1977) believes that the baby's initial difficulty is to do with understanding concepts of location and movement and not object permanence as such.

Also during this stage, according to Piaget, the whole object must be visible if the baby is to respond to it at all. However, Bower (1977) claims that if a month-old baby is shown a toy, then a screen is put between the baby and the toy and the toy is removed and then the screen, the baby shows some surprise or even a startle response, indicating that it expected the toy still to be there. Piaget may have been observing immature motor skills in the infant's failure to 'search' rather than immature object permanence.

1. Baby sees ball placed under cloth on her left (A).

A

2. She retrieves it and the sequences is repeated.

A

3. Baby sees ball placed under cloth on her right (B) but continues to search under cloth on her left (A).

B   A

FIGURE 25.3 *Piaget's demonstration of the limited object permanence of babies between eight and 12 months. They can retrieve a hidden object only from its original hiding place, not where it was last hidden. Not until about 12 months will they search under the cushion where they last saw the object hidden; they can do this even when three or four cushions are used. (Others have suggested that this ability appears as early as nine months.) (From Barnes-Gutteridge, 1974)*

By 6–7 months, the baby will reach for a familiar object if only a part of it is visible, suggesting that it realizes that the rest of it is attached to the part that is showing. (Bower (1977) believes this will happen as early as four months.) However, if you cover up the object completely, even if the baby sees you do it, it will not search for it. A good illustration of this is one

of the many accounts Piaget gives of his own three children (see Box 25.1).

Not until eight months will the baby search for a completely hidden object but even then, and for a few months after that, the baby will still be 'deceived' by the physical conditions of the search (see Fig. 25.3). Not until about 12 months will the baby search where

BOX 25.1 An illustration of lack of object permanence (Piaget, 1963)

At 0,7 (28) [7 months, 28 days] Jacqueline tries to grasp a celluloid duck on top of her quilt. She almost catches it, shakes herself and the duck slides down beside her. It falls very close to her hand but behind a fold in the sheet. Jacqueline's eyes have followed the movement, she has even followed it with her out-stretched hand. But as soon as the duck has disappeared – nothing more! It does not occur to her to search behind the fold of the sheet, which would be very easy to do (she twists it mechanically with-out searching at all) ... I try showing it to her a few times. Each time she tries to grasp it, but when she is about to touch it I replace it very obviously under the sheet. Jacqueline immediately withdraws her hand and gives up ... Everything occurs as though the child believed that the object is alternately made and unmade ...

it last saw the toy hidden. (Others have suggested that this ability appears as early as nine months.) Another way of testing object permanence is to observe the baby's eye movements to see if it follows a moving object and continues to look along its path even after it has vanished, for example behind a screen. If the baby looks at the other side of the screen where the object would reappear, the visual search suggests that the baby expects it to reappear which, in turn, indicates object permanence. (Bower *et al.* (1971) found that this visual tracking of objects begins between four and eight months.)

Between eight and twelve months, the concept of a person as a permanent 'object' develops rapidly and, according to Bell (1970), 'person permanence' may develop at a faster rate than 'physical object perma-nence', especially in babies whose mothers spend a great deal of time with them in a warm and close relationship; see Chapter 22.

Even when the baby can successfully retrieve a hidden object from where it was last hidden, object permanence is still not fully developed. For instance, the baby watches you place a toy in a matchbox, after which you place the matchbox under a pillow. When the baby isn't looking, you slip the toy out of the box and leave it under the pillow. Next, you put the now empty box in front of the baby who quickly searches it; on finding no toy inside, it does not search for the missing toy under the pillow. Before about eighteen months, the young child cannot take into account the

possibility that something might have happened that it has not actually seen; Piaget refers to this as a *fail-ure to infer invisible displacements* and, once the child can do this, the development of object perma-nence is complete.

The general symbolic function

Apart from object permanence, the sensorimotor stage is important mainly for the development of the *general symbolic function*, one manifestation of which is language. But rather than regarding lan-guage as the source of thought, Piaget saw it as reflecting thought that originates in action. (We shall return to the issue of the relationship between lan-guage and thought later, but also see Chapter 13.)

Piaget distinguishes between *symbols*, which resemble the things they represent (e.g. mental images), and *signs*, which stand for things in a quite arbitrary way and are merely conventional; language in fact falls into the latter category. When the child begins to represent objects to itself in the form of mental images, it is no longer so dependent on physi-cal exploration and the manipulation of objects; it is now beginning to think, working things out in its head. Schemas are now 'interiorized' and this can lead to sudden, insightful solutions. For example, the child might put a cup down on the floor in order to have both hands free to open a door. After looking at the door and then at the cup, it 'realizes', through a mental image of the door opening, that the cup is in the way. So it decides to move the cup to a safer place before trying to open the door.

The other major manifestations of the general symbolic function are:

- *deferred imitation*, the ability to imitate or repro-duce something seen or heard when the 'model' is no longer present, indicating an important advance in the child's capacity to remember;
- *representational or make-believe play*, where one object is used as if it were another and this too depends on the child's growing ability to form mental images of things and people in their absence. These developments usually become apparent between 18 and 24 months.

The pre-operational stage (2–7)

Probably the main difference between this and the sensorimotor stage is the continued development and use of internal images, symbols and language, which is especially important for the child's develop-ing sense of self-awareness. At the same time, the child's world is still fundamentally concrete and

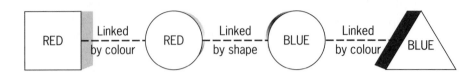

FIGURE 25.4 *Simple example of syncretic thought*

absolute – things are very much as they *seem* and the child tends to be influenced by how things look rather than by logical principles or operations (hence 'preoperational': the child lacks the logical operations characteristic of later stages). Piaget in fact subdivided the stage into two: (i) the preconceptual (2–4); and (ii) the intuitive (4–7).

Pre-conceptual

The absolute nature of the child's thinking makes it very difficult for it to understand relative terms such as 'bigger' or 'stronger' and things tend to be 'biggest' or just 'big'. As far as classification is concerned, if you ask a 2–4-year-old to divide apples into 'big red apples' and 'small green apples', the child will *either* put all the red apples together or all the green apples together (regardless of size) *or* all the big ones together or all the small ones together (regardless of colour), i.e. a child of this age can only classify things on the basis of a single attribute at a time – in our example, either colour or size but not both at the same time. Piaget called this *centration*; until it can decentre, the child will be unable to classify things in any kind of logical or systematic way.

This is well illustrated by what Piaget calls *syncretic thought* (what Vygotsky called 'complexive thinking'), i.e. the tendency to link together any neighbouring objects or events on the basis of what individual instances have in common. For example, if a three-year-old is given a box of wooden shapes of different colours and asked to pick out four that are alike, the child might pick the shapes shown in Figure 25.4. Here, the characteristic the child focuses on changes with each second shape that is chosen: a red square is followed by a red circle which is followed by a blue circle which is followed by a blue triangle, so that only the first and second, second and third, and third and fourth objects have anything in common – there is no one characteristic that all four have in common. A five-year-old would be able to select four of the same shape or four of the same colour and say what they have in common.

In *transductive reasoning*, the child draws an inference about the relationship between two objects based on a single attribute. For example, if A has four legs and B has four legs, then A must be B. If A happens to be a cat and B a dog, the child will call

> **BOX 25.2** Examples of children's animism during the pre-operational stage (from Piaget, 1973)

Cli (3 years 9 months) speaking of a motor in a garage: *'The motor's gone to bye-byes. It doesn't go out because of the rain* [elle fait dodo, elle sort pas ...].

Bad (3 years): *'The bells have woken up, haven't they?'*

Nel (2 years 9 months) seeing a hollow chestnut tree: *'Didn't it cry when the hole was made?'* To a stone: *'Don't touch my garden! ... My garden would cry.'* Nel, after throwing a stone on to a sloping bank, watching the stone rolling down said: *'Look at the stone. It's afraid of the grass.'*

Nel scratched herself against a wall. Looking at her hand: *'Who made that mark? ... It hurts where the wall hit me.'*

Dar (1 year 8 months to 2 years 5 months) bringing his toy motor to the window: *'Motor see the snow.'* Dar stood up in bed, crying and calling out: *'The mummies (the ladies) all on the ground, hurt!'* Dar was watching the grey clouds. He was told that it was going to rain. *'Oh, look at the wind! Naughty wind, smack wind.'*

'Do you think that would hurt the wind?'

'Yes.' A few days later: *'Bad wind. No, not naughty – rain naughty. Wind good.'*

'Why is the rain naughty?'

'Because Mummy pushes the pram and the pram all wet.' Dar couldn't go to sleep, so the light was left on at his demand: *'Nice light'* [gentile]. On a morning in winter when the sun shone into the room: *'Oh, good! The sun's come to make the radiator warm.'*

FIGURE 25.5 *The falling-stick card test*

both cats and dogs by the one name with which it is most familiar. This kind of reasoning can lead to what Piaget calls *animism,* the belief that inanimate objects are alive. For example, because the sun (seems to) follow us when we walk, it must be alive, the reasoning being that if people move and if the sun moves, then the sun is the same as people, i.e. they are both alive (see Box 25.2).

The preconceptual child also has difficulty with *seriation,* i.e. arranging objects on the basis of a particular dimension, such as increasing height. Piaget and Szeminska (1941, 1952) asked children to put a number of sticks in order of decreasing length and found that even five- and six-year-olds tended to do this by trial and error. They had particular difficulty understanding that a stick (B) can be both smaller than one stick (A) and larger than another stick (C) and once they have completed the series they are unable to insert an extra stick. The 2–4-year-old also cannot easily perceive actions as following a particular order or sequence through time, as in the falling-stick card test shown in Figure 25.5.

Intuitive

While 4–7-year-olds may have developed the kinds of thinking described above, they are still very limited in their ability to think logically. Let us look at classification again, this time at what are known as *class-inclusion tasks.*

Imagine a child is presented with several wooden beads, mostly brown but a few white, and is then asked:

● 'Are they all wooden?' The child will answer 'Yes'.
● 'Are there more brown or more white beads?' 'Brown.'
● 'Are there more brown beads or more beads?' 'Brown.'

According to Piaget, what the child is failing to understand is the relationship between the whole (the class of wooden beads) and the parts (the classes of brown and white beads); these are referred to as the superordinate and the subordinate class(es) respectively. The child is still influenced by what it perceives; it can see the brown beads, which are more numerous than the white, in a more immediate and

BOX 25.3	Key study: Never mind the number, feel the fullness

Donaldson and McGarrigle (1974) used toy cars and garages, arranged on two shelves, one above the other (Fig. 25.6). At first, 4–6-year-old children saw the cars without garages and were asked 'Are there more cars on this shelf or more cars on this shelf?'; most answered readily and correctly. When the garages were placed

over the cars and the question repeated , about one-third of the children changed their judgements, saying that now the shelf with four cars had more cars than the shelf with five! Why? Donaldson (1978) suggests that, when the garages are present, the children tend to interpret the situation in terms of the full set of cars which would be appropriate to the garages, so that the row of five cars with six garages is seen as lacking a car, i.e. the children seem to think they are meant to attend to *fullness.*

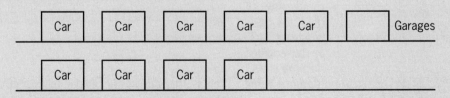

FIGURE 25.6 *Toy cars and garages as used by Donaldson and McGarrigle (1974)*

BOX
25.4

Key study: The 'Swiss mountain scene' test of egocentrism (Piaget and Inhelder, 1956)

The three mountains were of different colours with snow on top of one, a house on another and a red cross on the third. The child could walk round and explore the model and then sat on one side while a doll was placed at some different location: the child was shown a set of ten pictures showing different views of the model and asked to choose the one that represented how the doll saw it.

Four-year-olds were totally unaware of different perspectives from their own and always chose a picture which matched how they themselves saw the model; six-year-olds showed some awareness but often chose the wrong picture and only 7–8-year-olds consistently chose the one that represented the doll's view. According to Piaget, children below seven are bound by the *egocentric illusion*; they fail to understand that what they see is relative to their own position and instead take it to represent 'the world as it really is'.

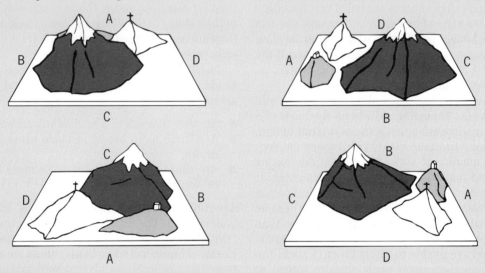

FIGURE 25.7 *Piaget and Inhelder's three-mountain scene, seen from four different sides. (From Smith and Cowie, 1988)*

direct way than the wooden beads (despite being able to answer the first question correctly).

Piaget took this to be another example of the child's inability to decentre, but others have challenged his interpretation. Donaldson (1978), for example, asks if the difficulty the child experiences is to do with what is expected of it and how the task is presented. She cites a study by McGarrigle *et al.* which involved four toy cows, three black and one white; they were laid on their sides and children (average age of six) were told they were 'sleeping'. Of those children asked the standard form of the question ('Are there more black cows or more cows?'), 25 percent answered correctly; while of those asked 'Are there more black cows or more *sleeping* cows?' 48 percent answered correctly, the difference being statistically significant.

Piaget's interpretation of his own findings assumes that the child's understanding of 'more' is

the same as an adult's. But is it? Donaldson and McGarrigle (1974) carried out a study which suggests it is not; this is described in Box 25. 3.

Although not a class-inclusion study, Donaldson and McGarrigle's cars and garage experiment underlines the importance of making the experimental situation as unambiguous for the child as possible – both linguistic and social factors will affect the child's performance over and above the child's actual abilities and Piaget has been criticized for underestimating their influence. This criticism probably applies most clearly in his study of egocentrism and conservation.

Egocentrism

This represents another major feature of the whole pre-operational period. The child, according to Piaget, is literally self-centred, i.e. sees the world totally from its own standpoint and cannot under-

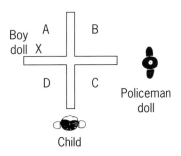

FIGURE 25.8 *Apparatus used by Hughes to test egocentrism. (From Donaldson, 1978)*

stand that other people might see things differently. Essentially, what the child is unable to do is put itself, psychologically, in other people's shoes in order to realize that they do not know or perceive everything that it knows or perceives. One amusing example (Phillips, 1969) is of a four-year-old who is asked 'Do you have a brother?' to which he replies 'Yes'. Then he is asked 'What's his name?' to which he replies 'Jim'. Finally, in response to the question 'Does Jim have a brother?', he says 'No'. One of Piaget's most famous demonstrations of egocentrism involved a three-dimensional model of a Swiss mountain scene (Piaget and Inhelder, 1956; see Box 25.4 and Fig. 25.7).

Several more recent studies have disputed Piaget's conclusion that children below seven are egocentric. Borke (1975), for instance, believes that the three-mountain scene is an unusually difficult way of presenting the problem. She allowed the child to move a second model on a turntable and, under these conditions, even three-year-olds (42 percent of the time) and four-year-olds (67 percent of the time) were able to see things as the doll 'saw' them (the doll was *Grover*, a character from *Sesame Street*). Borke demonstrated clearly that the task itself has a crucial influence on the child's performance of perspective-taking skills.

Donaldson (1978) cites a study by Hughes using a piece of apparatus meant to be equivalent to the three-mountain scene, comprising two 'walls' intersecting to form a cross (Fig. 25.8). At first, the policeman doll is placed where he could 'see' areas B and D but not A and C (he isn't tall enough to 'see' over the wall). Then the boy doll is put into area A and the child is asked if the policeman can see him, and this is repeated by putting the boy doll in areas B, C and D. Next the policeman is placed where he could see A and C and the child is asked to 'hide the boy so that the policeman can't see him'. If the child

makes any mistakes at this stage they are pointed out and the question repeated until the correct answer is given; but very few mistakes were made. The test proper begins with the introduction of a second policeman and the child is now asked to hide the boy from both policemen; this is repeated three times so that each time a different area becomes the only possible hiding place left. For example, with one policeman at the right end of the cross and the other at the top end, the only hiding place for the boy is C.

Piaget would predict that children would hide the boy from themselves, i.e. where they, the child, could not see him. However, 3½–5-year-olds hid the boy successfully 90 percent of the time (including 88 percent of the 3½–4-year-olds), even when this meant the boy doll being clearly visible to the child. Even when Hughes used up to six sections of wall and a third policeman, four-year-olds were successful 90 percent of the time and even three-year-olds managed 60 percent success.

How can we account for this discrepancy between Hughes' results and those of Piaget? According to Donaldson, the policeman and boy doll situation enables the child to understand what is being asked of it because there is a meaningful context: it makes 'human sense', even to a three-year-old, because the child can relate to the idea of 'hiding from someone'. By contrast, she thinks the three-mountain situation has no meaningful context, is 'disembedded' (taken out of context), does not make 'human sense' and is 'coldblooded'. Donaldson compares this situation with that in which an American Indian was asked to translate into his native tongue 'The white man shot six bears today'. 'How can I do that?' he protested, 'No white man could shoot six bears in a day.' It just did not make 'human sense'.

Finally, an intriguing study by Flavell (1978) tested Piaget's egocentric interpretation of the young child who, with its hands covering its eyes, says, 'Now you can't see me'. According to Flavell, children may think of their eyes as 'the window of the soul', so that when somebody is not looking directly into their eyes, they cannot see the child's real self (see Chapter 21). Flavell tested these two hypotheses by giving 2½–5-year-olds a series of tests concerning what they thought others could see. The experimenter and the child sat on opposite sides of a table on which sat a Snoopy doll. In the simplest procedure, the child was asked to close or cover both eyes and the experimenter said 'Now your eyes are closed and mine are open' and then asked a series of questions – 'Do I see you?', 'Do I see Snoopy?', 'Do I see your head?' and so on.

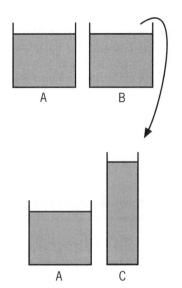

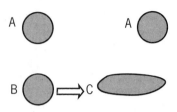

FIGURE 25.11 *Substance or quantity conservation using plasticine. Two equal-sized balls of plasticine are used. B is rolled into a sausage shape (C); the pre-operational child typically thinks there is more plasticine in C than A, having originally agreed that A and B have the same amount*

FIGURE 25.9 *The conservation of liquid quantity. Although the child agrees that there is the same amount of liquid in A and B, when the contents of B are poured into C, the appearance of C sways the child's judgement so that C is now judged to contain more liquid than A ('it looks more' or 'it's taller'). Although the child has seen the liquid poured from B into C and agrees that none has been spilled or added in the process (what Piaget calls 'identity'), the appearance of the higher level of liquid in the taller, thinner beaker C is compelling.*

The youngest children (below 3½) often said that the experimenter could not see them but, without exception, they said that he could see Snoopy and most believed that he could see their head or arm. So the egocentric explanation was ruled out – the children understood that the experimenter could see something which they themselves could not.

Conservation
The pre-operational child, according to Piaget, is unable to *conserve*: the child fails to understand that things remain the same (constant) despite changes in their appearance (how they look). The perceptual

appearance of things still dominates – things are what they seem and this is what 'intuitive' is meant to convey. Piaget's conservation experiments are probably his most famous and have been replicated many times. Let us start with the conservation of liquid (or continuous) quantity (which incidentally is often referred to, incorrectly, as *volume* conservation) (see Fig. 25.9).

According to Piaget, the child's inability to conserve is yet another example of centration; here the pre-seven-year-old is centring on just one dimension of the beaker C, usually its height, and so fails to take width into account. What the concrete operational child will be able to understand is that as C gets taller it also gets narrower and that these cancel each other out. Piaget calls this *compensation*. If the water is poured back from C into B, the child will again say that there are equal amounts in A and B; but what it cannot do (which the concrete operational child can) is perform this operation mentally, in its head. This ability to mentally return a situation to what it was like at the beginning is called *reversibility*.

Other kinds of conservation include number (Fig. 25.10), quantity or substance (discrete or discontinuous quantity) (Fig. 25.11), weight and volume. Weight conservation is tested by putting two balls of plas-

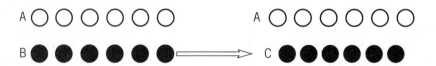

FIGURE 25.10 *Number conservation using counters. Two rows of counters are put in a one-to-one correspondence and then one row is pushed together. The pre-operational child usually thinks there are more counters in A than in C because A is 'longer', despite being able to count correctly and agreeing that A and B have equal numbers.*

ticine on measuring scales and then transforming one of them as in conservation of quantity; and volume conservation involves dropping plasticine into water and seeing how much is displaced before and after transformation.

As with Piaget's test of egocentrism, many other psychologists have been critical of his methods and, consequently, of his conclusions regarding the preoperational child's lack of conservation. For example, Donaldson (1978) has argued that the experimenter may be unwittingly forcing children to produce the wrong answer against their better judgement by the mere fact that they ask the same question twice, once before and once after the transformation. 'If the experimenter pours the liquid from one beaker into another or pushes one row of counters together, they must be doing it for a reason and probably want me to give a different answer' is how the child's reasoning might run, suggesting that 'contextual cues might override purely linguistic ones'. How could we test these hypotheses?

One method, used by Rose and Blank (1974), was to drop the pre-transformation question and only ask the child to compare two rows of counters after the transformation: under these conditions, six-year-olds often succeeded compared with those tested on the standard form of the task. Significantly, they made fewer errors on the standard task when re-tested a week later. Samuel and Bryant (1984), testing 252 boys and girls aged 5–8½, confirmed Rose and Blank's findings for conservation of number, quantity and volume (the latter tested by different sized beakers of liquid so, strictly, liquid quantity). Another alternative to Piaget's method was devised by McGarrigle and Donaldson (1974) (see Box 25.5).

Light *et al.* (1979) replicated the 'Naughty Teddy' experiment (using only conservation of length) with five-year-olds. The overall conservation rates were lower than McGarrigle and Donaldson had found in both conditions, but their findings confirmed a significantly higher success rate in the 'Naughty Teddy' condition. However, they were at the same time critical of the basic assumption made in the original study, namely that Naughty Teddy represents an accidental transformation of the materials – while the children were clearly willing to play along with the experimenter in attributing responsibility (agency) to the teddy, they clearly also knew that it was the experimenter who was responsible for both introducing and manipulating it (Light, 1986).

So Light *et al.* (1979) created an incidental condition in which five- and six-year-olds were tested in pairs.

BOX 25.5 Key study: Conservation accidents, or Naughty Teddy strikes again

McGarrigle and Donaldson (1974) were concerned with conservation of number and length. In the case of number conservation, the procedure begins in the usual way up to the point where the child agreed that there is an equal number of counters in the two rows. Then 'Naughty Teddy' emerges from a hiding place and sweeps over one of the rows and disarranges it, so that the one-to-one correspondence is disrupted. The child is invited to put Teddy back in his box (usually accepted with glee) and the questioning resumes: 'Now, where were we? Ah, yes, is the number in this row the same as the number in that row?' and so on.

Fifty out of 80 4–6-year-olds conserved, compared with 13 out of 80 tested using the standard (Piagetian) version. According to Piaget, it should not matter who rearranges the counters (or how it happens) but it seems to be relevant to the child. The point is that the transformation caused by Naughty Teddy is meant to be seen as accidental (not intentionally made by the experimenter). Children tested with Naughty Teddy before the standard version performed significantly better than those tested in the reverse order.

- In the standard condition, they watched as two identical beakers were filled to the same level with pasta shells. When both the children had judged the quantities to be equal, the experimenter introduced a further, larger container and tipped into it the contents of one of the beakers. The children were then asked (in turn) to judge whether or not the amounts of shells were still the same.

- In the incidental condition, the pairs of children were first shown grids into which the pasta shells could be inserted, one per cell, and it was explained to them that they would be playing a game in which the first child to get all his or her shells into the grid would be the winner. So when the shells were put into the two identical beakers, the children understood this to be a preparation for the competitive game. When they had judged the two beakers to contain equal amounts (i.e. the game was fair), as the second child was about to receive his/her beaker, the experimenter 'noticed' with some alarm that the rim was chipped, making it too dangerous to use and 'found' another container which was then filled with the shells from the chipped beaker. The usual conservation question followed.

The results were that 5 percent of the children conserved in the standard condition compared with 70 percent in the incidental condition.

This finding has been replicated by others, including Hargreaves *et al.* (1982), using five-year-olds and number conservation. They had an accidental condition (featuring a naughty monkey glove puppet and also two experimenters, one of whom controlled the monkey while the other asked the questions, etc.), thereby replicating the Naughty Teddy experiment, and an incidental condition, in which a second adult came into the room to 'borrow' some of the counters, taking them from the table. The experimenter protested that the counters were needed and they were duly returned, but of course they had become disarranged. Conservation rates under this condition were close to 90 percent.

In both the Light *et al.* and the Hargreaves *et al.* studies, the transformation was successfully embedded within a socially intelligible sequence of events. Children who fail on the standard version of the task certainly do seem to be able to conserve under these more meaningful conditions.

However, is it possible that in the accidental and incidental conditions the child is being (unwittingly) misled into making the correct judgement (i.e. being right for the wrong reasons) just as Donaldson believes that the child is being led to make the incorrect judgement in the standard condition? In Piaget's version, there may be an implicit message: 'Take note of the transformation – it is relevant' (i.e. give a different answer), while in the accidental/incidental conditions, the implicit message might be: 'This transformation makes no difference – ignore it' (i.e. give the same answer; Light, 1986). It follows that if some change actually takes place, the implicit message to ignore the transformation would make children give an incorrect conservation answer. The standard Piaget task involves an irrelevant perceptual change (nothing is being added or taken away), but where a relevant perceptual change occurs, children tested under the accidental or incidental condition should do worse than those tested in the standard way. This prediction was supported by Light and Gilmour (1983) and Moore and Fry (1986).

Other criticisms of Piaget deal with the actual words used in the conservation task questions. For example, when the liquid is poured from beaker B to beaker C and the child is asked 'Which contains more or are they the same?', how does the preoperational child interpret 'more'?

Berko and Brown (1960) and Bruner *et al.* (1966) found that some children used 'more' or 'less' when they were really referring to height and length, so in the conservation task they might be quite correct in pointing to beaker C because it is 'taller' than beaker A. As Dworetzky (1981) points out, when a child asks for 'more milk', it observes the level in the glass rise and there may be other similar examples which explain why 'more' is understood as 'tall' or 'taller'. Another relevant study here is the Donaldson and McGarrigle (1974) study using toy cars and garages (see Box 25.3).

The concrete operational stage (7–11)

In this stage, children develop the mental structure called an *operation* which is, essentially, an action, performed mentally, comprising *compensation, reversibility* and *identity* and is best seen in the ability to conserve (see above). However, they can only perform the operation in the presence of actual objects – they must be looking at or manipulating the materials (beakers of water, counters, etc.), hence the name of the stage (i.e. *concrete*).

Also, some types of conservation are mastered before others and the order in which they appear tends to be invariant (as in the order of the four major stages), namely: number and liquid quantity (at 6–7); substance/quantity and length (at 7–8); weight (at 8–10); and volume (at 11–12).

This step-by-step acquisition of new operations is called *décalage* (displacement or 'slips in level of performance'); in the case of conservation it is horizontal (e.g. a seven-year-old can conserve number but not weight), so that inconsistencies exist *within* the same kind of ability or operation. Vertical décalage refers to inconsistencies *between* different abilities or operations, e.g. a child may have mastered all kinds of classification but not all kinds of conservation.

With regard to classification, the concrete operational child can now understand the relationship between super- and subordinate classes, i.e. the part–whole relationship. This is closely related to addition and subtraction, e.g. adding the parts to make the whole and then subtracting the parts (a form of reversibility). Further examples of the child's growing ability to decentre include: (i) sorting objects on the basis of two or more attributes; and (ii) a significant decline in egocentrism and the growing relativism of the child's viewpoint.

One remaining problem for the child is concerned with *transitivity* tasks. For example, 'If John is taller than Susan and Susan is taller than Charlie, who is taller, John or Charlie?' Not until the age of 11 or so will the child be able to solve this entirely in its head; the concrete operational child is usually limited to solving the problem using real objects (e.g. dolls).

The formal operational stage (11–15)

While the concrete operational child is still concerned with manipulating things (even if this is done 'in the mind'), the formal operational thinker can manipulate ideas or propositions and can reason solely on the basis of verbal statements ('first order' and 'second order' operations, respectively). 'Formal' refers to the ability to follow the form of an argument without reference to its particular content. In the case of transitivity problems, for example, 'If A is taller than B, and B is taller than C, then A is taller than C' is a form of argument such that the conclusion is logically true and will always be true, regardless of what A, B or C might refer to.

Adolescents can also think hypothetically, i.e. think about situations they have not actually experienced before or about things which nobody has experienced

---

BOX 25.6 **Piaget's theory of play**

Piaget (1951) saw play as an adaptive activity, which begins early in the sensorimotor period when infants start to repeat actions which they find satisfying or pleasurable. He called these repetitions of actions *circular reactions* and distinguished three major kinds corresponding to three *sub-stages* of the sensorimotor period: (i) primary circular reactions (1–4 months) which are centred on the baby's own body; (ii) secondary circular reactions (4–8 months) which are centred on external objects; and (iii) tertiary circular reactions (12–18 months) where the child experiments in order to find new ways to solve problems or to reproduce interesting outcomes.

As an adaptive activity, play involves both assimilation and accommodation. However, assimilation is often the more important and evident of the two processes; a great deal of play (especially up to the end of the preoperational period) is 'pure assimilation', whereby the child attempts to fit the world of reality into its own needs and experience. (By contrast, imitation is an action of almost 'pure' accommodation.)

Piaget distinguished between play and 'strictly intellectual activity'. In the latter, there is 'adaptation of the schemas to an external reality which constitutes a problem', i.e. there is an external aim or purpose. But in play, the child 'repeats his behaviour not in any further effort to learn or investigate but for the mere joy of mastering it and of showing off to himself his own power of subduing reality' (Piaget, 1951), i.e. it is done for its own sake, allowing children to practise their competencies in a relaxed and carefree way.

This distinction between play and intellectual activity applies to all three major kinds of play, although it is arguably more difficult to make in the case of mastery play than it is in the other two.

- In *mastery* (or *practice*) play, the child repeats new motor schemas in one new context after another and, in a sense, this theme of 'play as mastery' runs through the other kinds of play too: whenever a new skill has been acquired, it tends to be used at almost every opportunity, for the sheer pleasure of doing so, and represents 'pure assimilation'. So play involves the repetition of a schema that has already been mastered, while investigation or exploration involve accommodation to reality and constitute ways in which new schemas develop. This is the predominant form of play during the sensorimotor stage.
- In *symbolic* (or *make-believe*) play, the child transforms itself or some object into somebody or something else. An important feature is role taking (or role play) which may help the child to cope with emotional crises and reduce interpersonal conflicts, e.g. having rules which it does not fully understand imposed by parents. Piaget and Inhelder (1969) observe that a child may discipline its doll or teddy as the child itself had been disciplined (so inverting or reversing roles) or it might re-enact a scene and produce a happy ending. So through make-believe play the child can change the world, internally, into what it wants it to be. (Compare this with Freud's theory of play; see Chapter 21.)

  Many psychologists (Garvey, 1977) have pointed out the vital role of language in the development of symbolic play. This is shown when children speak to their doll in the way their parents talk to them and (usually from four onwards) when 'collective symbolism' appears, e.g. children playing together and all assuming complementary roles (e.g. 'mummies and daddies'). It begins between 1½ and two years and is usually at its height up until about the age of five.
- As the child's thinking becomes more logical, so its games begin to incorporate and be governed by rules. But the child's understanding of rules itself goes through certain developmental changes (see Chapter 27 on moral development).

before. For example, Dworetzky (1981) notes that if you asked formal operational individuals what it would be like if people had tails, they might tell you:

'Lovers could secretly hold tails under the table.'
'People would leave lifts in a great hurry.'
'Dogs would know when you were happy.'

By contrast, a concrete operational child might tell you not to be so silly or would tell you where on the body a tail might be or how funny it would look, showing its dependence upon what has actually been seen.

This ability to imagine and discuss what has never been encountered before is evidence of the continued decentration that occurs beyond concrete operations. The formal operational person can, therefore, deal with possibilities and not just with actualities, with alternatives to existing (concrete) reality as well as inconsistencies and contradictions in other people's behaviour (especially that of their parents). Similarly, adolescents can ask questions about themselves which would have been impossible earlier, such as 'What or who can I become?'. These kinds of questions form part of the 'identity crisis' of adolescence discussed by Erikson (see Chapter 21).

Finally, adolescents can experiment and search systematically and methodically in order to find the solution to a problem. They can consider all the possible combinations of factors likely to have an effect and through careful reasoning eliminate the irrelevant ones. For example, in the beaker problem (Inhelder and Piaget, 1958), there are four beakers of colourless, odourless liquid (1, 2, 3 and 4) plus a smaller bottle (g) also containing a colourless, odourless liquid; the problem is to find the liquid, or combination of liquids, which will turn yellow when a few drops from bottle g are added to it (the actual combination is 1 plus 3 plus g). Concrete operational children often begin randomly, trying various combinations of pairs of liquids, while adolescents systematically consider all the possible combinations; they are displaying *hypothetico-deductive reasoning* (see Chapter 2).

Is formal operations a universal stage?

Several studies have found that even well-educated adults make all sorts of mistakes on formal reasoning problems and that only about one-third of average adolescents and adults ever attain formal operations. According to Dasen (1994), the hypothetico-deductive reasoning of formal operations does not appear at all in some cultures and even where it does occur, it may not be the typical mode of thought. It is not what is most valued in every community, not even within Western societies; it seems to be strongly dependent on secondary schooling. Similarly, Flavell (1977) concludes that, while formal operational thinking may emerge during adolescence, it cannot be regarded as the 'characteristic mode of thought for that developmental period'.

Piaget (1972) himself suggests that all normal individuals attain formal operations, if not by the age of 15 then by 20, but they do so in different areas according to their aptitudes and areas of experience and expertise. He seems to be saying that the specific knowledge and training people have are as important to their cognitive performance as is their general level of cognitive development, which seems to be a rather different position from the one he adopts regarding the first three stages.

● Evaluation of Piaget's theory

How valid is the concept of a stage?

We saw earlier that from 1970 Piaget proposed that development should be thought of as a spiral (implying a continuous process) rather than as a step-by-step, discontinuous process (as implied by a stage theory proper). Indeed, the individual may 'straddle' more than one stage at any one time (décalage), which means that cognitive structures do not have to change all at the same time (and to the same extent), which again is implied by a stage theory. Clearly, intellectual development may not be as 'stage-like' as Piaget first thought.

There is no doubt that the concept of 'stage' implies a degree of consistency of thought and understanding across a range of different content areas. However, some inconsistency is to be expected, particularly while concrete or formal operations are in the process of developing (i.e. during 'transitional' periods). For example, some new ability usually appears first in the content areas most familiar to the child and only later in more unfamiliar, abstract areas. But the question then arises: how much consistency is needed to warrant categorizing a child as, say, 'pre-operational' or 'concrete operational'?

According to Meadows (1988), the research tends to show less consistency between different aspects of concrete operations than Piaget's theory would predict and, although he did acknowledge the existence of décalages, he was more interested in how children manage the general principle underlying operational thought. Even though Flavell (1971), for example, argues that it is not necessary in a stage theory to predict abrupt, all-or-nothing changes, Sternberg (1990) wonders whether it might be better to abandon (at least temporarily) the idea of stages and to focus instead on the development of individual processes and strategies. He believes that we cannot just assume that there is only one strategy for solving a particular problem (as Piaget does, e.g. children give correct answers in conservation tasks because they have mastered reversibility and compensation); what is needed is an analysis of the information-processing requirements of the task (i.e. exactly what cognitive processes are involved/needed to succeed; see below).

These have been ignored by Piaget, as have differences in ability between children within a common stage, and Sternberg believes that this reduces the value of Piaget's theory in explaining and predicting many aspects of performance. Piaget acknowledged that the rate of progress through the stages does vary to some extent between individuals (due to differences in environmental stimulation) but Meadows (1988) says that he was concerned with the idealized 'normal' individual (i.e. with common structures of knowledge) rather than with individual differences. In all these ways, he has been criticized for not offering an explanation but an elaborate description of cognitive development.

A different way of evaluating the stage concept is to look at attempts to train children; i.e. can the rate of development be deliberately speeded up? According to Piaget this should not be possible – the child's current level of cognitive functioning will set limits on learning, since:

> The child cannot assimilate or accommodate to events which are too incompatible with his or her whole coherent system of understanding, and instructions can at best produce only a limited and possibly temporary advance isolated in the area being trained. (Meadows, 1988)

However, Meadows (1988) argues that, contrary to Piaget's predictions, training *does* produce improvement in performance which can be considerable, long-lasting and pervasive. For example, preschoolers have successfully been trained on concrete operational tasks (the focus of most such attempts), three or four years ahead of 'schedule' and their performance following training seems to be as competent as that of untrained eight-year-olds (Brainerd, 1983). Any speeding up of development which might occur would, according to Piagetians, have to involve the use of learning experiences which resemble those which occur outside the experimental training situation, namely active self-discovery. This is contrasted with the traditional methods of teaching whereby the teacher imparts information ('ready-made knowledge') to a passively receptive child ('tutorial' training). However, the successful attempts at training

which Meadows and Brainerd refer to have all used some kind of 'tutorial' method. Since the early 1970s, studies have shown that ' ... although self-discovery training can produce learning, it is generally less effective than tutorial training' (Brainerd, 1983). (The question of whether there are any stages of cognitive development beyond formal operations was discussed in Chapter 24.)

How has Piaget contributed to educational theory and practice?

Brainerd (1983) believes that there are three main

BOX 25.7 The role of the teacher in the Piagetian classroom

- It is essential for the teacher to assess very carefully each individual child's current stage of cognitive development. (This relates to the concept of readiness.) The child can then be set tasks which are tailored to its needs and so are intrinsically motivating.
- The teacher must provide the child with learning opportunities which enable the child to advance to the next developmental step. This is done by creating disequilibrium, whereby the child's current schemas are not quite sufficient to deal with the reality it is confronted with, leading to accommodation and equilibrium. This means that the teacher does not just provide the appropriate materials and equipment and let the child 'get on with it'; instead, the teacher is expected to achieve a proper balance between actively guiding and directing children's thinking patterns and providing opportunities for children to explore by themselves (Thomas, 1985).
- The teacher is concerned with the process rather than the end-product of learning. This entails encouraging the child to ask questions, experiment, explore and so on, looking for the reasoning behind the child's answers, particularly the child's mistakes.
- The teacher's role is also to encourage children to learn from each other, to hear other (often conflicting) views, which can help break down egocentrism. Peer interaction can have cognitive, as well as social value, so small-group activity is as important as individual work.
- The teacher is the guide in the child's process of discovery and the curriculum is adapted to each child's individual needs and intellectual level (Smith and Cowie, 1991).

implications of Piaget's theory for education, which should be seen not as explicit recommendations but more as how others have interpreted Piaget's relevance for education (particularly preschool and primary). (Piaget himself had no 'theory of instruction'; Ginsberg, 1981.) These are: (i) the concept of *readiness;* (ii) curriculum (what to teach); and (iii) teaching methods (how to teach).

As far as (i) is concerned, much of what we said above about limits set on learning by the child's current stage of development relates to the concept of readiness. The apparent success of attempts to train concepts suggests that this is not a particularly helpful or valid concept.

Regarding (ii), appropriate concepts to teach will be logic (e.g. transitive inference), maths (e.g. numbers), science (e.g. conservation) and space (e.g. Euclidean geometry). Whatever the particular concepts, teaching materials should comprise concrete objects of some sort that can be easily manipulated. However, Ginsberg (1981) believes that attempting to base education on the teaching of Piagetian stages

is an unfortunate misapplication of the theory. A more useful approach is the modification of the curriculum in line with knowledge of the Piagetian stages, without placing undue emphasis on them and without allowing them to limit one's approach; yet Piaget's theory seems to suggest that certain concepts should be tackled in a definite sequence. For example, conservation of substance naturally precedes conservation of weight, which naturally precedes conservation of volume, but traditional schools often do not base their teaching on such sequences in development (Elkind, 1976).

As far as (iii) is concerned, we saw earlier that central to Piaget's view of the educational process is active self-discovery (or discovery learning) whereby the child is at the centre of its learning and not the teacher. From the Piagetian standpoint, children learn from actions rather than from passive observations; the teacher must recognize that each child needs to construct knowledge for itself and that active learning results in deeper understanding (Smith and Cowie, 1991).

BOX 25.8   Critical discussion: Cultural influences on cognitive development

Dasen (1994) refers to studies that he conducted in remote parts of the central Australian desert with 8–14-year-old Aborigines. He gave them conservation of liquid, weight and volume tasks (used as tests of quantification), plus a task that tested understanding of spatial relationships: either (a) two landscape models were used, one of which could be turned round through 180°: the participants had to locate an object (doll or sheep) on one model and then find the same location on the second model; or (b) a bottle was half-filled with water, then tilted into various positions, with a screen hiding the water level: participants were shown outline drawings of the bottle and they had to draw in the water level.

As far as conservation is concerned, the same shift from pre-operational to concrete operational thought was found as with Swiss children; but it took place between ten and 13 (instead of five and seven). A fairly large proportion of adolescents and adults also gave non-conservation answers. On the spatial tasks, again the same shift from pre- to concrete operational thought as for Swiss children occurred, but they found the spatial task easier than the conservation tasks (i.e. operational thinking develops earlier in the spatial domain than in the area of quantification), which is the reverse of what is found for Swiss children.

According to Dasen, this makes good sense in terms of Aboriginal culture, where things are not quantified: water is vital for survival but the exact quantity matters little. Counting things is unusual and number words only go up to five (after which everything is 'many'). By contrast, finding one's way around is crucial: water holes must be found at the end of each journey and family members meet up at the end of the day after having split up in order to search for water. The acquisition of a vast array of spatial knowledge is helped by the mythology, such as the 'dream time' stories that attribute a meaning to each feature of the landscape and to routes travelled by ancestral spirits.

This, together with Dasen's studies of Inuit (Eskimo) children and the Ebri and Baude peoples of the Ivory Coast, points to the importance of the context in which development takes place, what the culture values, what is needed and adaptive. While the sequence of Piaget's stages may be universal, rates of development in various cognitive domains vary between cultures:

> ... the *deep* structures, the basic cognitive processes, are indeed universal, while at the *surface* level, the way these basic processes are brought to bear on specific contents, in specific contexts, is influenced by culture. Universality and cultural diversity are not opposites, but are complementary aspects of all human behaviour and development. (Dasen, 1994)

So what is the teacher's role in the Piagetian classroom? Some answers are provided in Box 25.7.

In evaluating the Piagetian contribution to education, Ginsberg (1981) believes that the two great deficiencies are: (i) ignoring individual differences (referred to earlier); and (ii) the emphasis on discovery learning to the exclusion of academic or school knowledge.

Are Piaget's stages universal?

There is a great deal of cross-cultural evidence (mostly using conservation tasks) to support Piaget's claim that the stages are invariant and universal, at least up to and including the concrete operational stage. For instance, Flavell (1977), Fishbein (1984) and Dasen (1994) all conclude that the order of stages originally observed in Piaget's Swiss sample also describes the course and content for children in hundreds of countries, cultures and subcultures. These include the Meru of Tanzania, the Themne of Sierra Leone, the Kamba of Kenya, the Micmac Canadian Indians, Australian Aborigines, Inuit (Eskimo) people and the Ebri and Baude peoples of the Ivory Coast in Africa.

However, the picture is more complicated than this summary suggests: see Box 25.8.

How valid are Piaget's methods?

We have already seen how many of his basic ways of testing children's abilities (e.g. classification, egocentrism, conservation) have been criticized and seem to have resulted in the underestimation of what children can do at particular ages. We shall treat this separately below.

His general clinical method comprises a question-and-answer technique: the child is presented with a problem of some sort and then invited to respond; once the child answers, the investigator will ask a second question or introduce a variation of the original problem in order to clarify the child's reasoning. All children are asked the same questions to begin with, but how each child responds to these initial probes determines what the investigator does next. The essential problem with this approach is that if the questions and tasks are tailored to individuals, how can we compare the answers of different children to identify general trends? How reliable are the data when the procedures are basically unstandardized (i.e. different for different participants)? Additional criticisms are that Piaget often did not give details regarding the numbers and ages of his participants and usually did not present any kind of statistical analysis.

Although aware of some of these shortcomings, Piaget did stress the need for a flexible methodology, i.e. one which enables investigators to probe the child's thinking without distorting it by imposing their own views on the child. According to Ginsberg (1981), Piaget's clinical method is deliberately unstandardized since that is a superior way to explore the subtleties of the child's cognitive structure; tapping the child's competence requires subtle and sensitive procedures, tailored to the peculiarities of each individual child. Similarly, Dasen (1994) claims that the clinical method provides a dynamic description of the child's thinking processes, as opposed to a simple, static, IQ test score (see Chapter 28).

Some critics claim that Piaget overemphasized cognitive aspects of development to the exclusion of the emotional (and others would say the reverse is true for Freud). But he was familiar with Freud's work and thought it provided valuable clues as to the content of children's thinking if not about how they think, which was Piaget's prime concern. However, he claimed (1972) that there will be a time when ' ... the psychology of the cognitive functions and psychoanalysis will have to blend into a general theory which will improve both by correcting each'. Elkind (1971) draws an interesting parallel between Piaget and Freud by remarking how they both stressed the qualitative differences between children and adults. Elkind says that, relative to adults, the child is a 'cognitive alien' (Piaget) and an 'emotional alien' (Freud).

As we have seen, Donaldson (1978) has been one of the major critics of Piaget's methods, such as his classification tasks and tests of conservation and egocentrism. Essentially, when children are confronted with a task or problem, they have to decide what is required of them and they do this from two sources: the spoken words and the setting in which the words are spoken; the former are interpreted according to how they interpret the latter. In Piaget's conservation task, for example, these two sources of information can conflict:

> ... before the child has developed a full awareness of language, language is embedded for him in the flow of events which accompany it. So long as this is the case, the child does not interpret words in isolation – he interprets situations. He is more concerned to make sense of what people do when they talk and act than to decide what words mean. (After all, he may not be aware of language, but he is keenly aware of other people). (Donaldson, 1978)

What Donaldson is arguing is that intellectual development cannot be properly understood without examining the development of *social understanding*:

by trying to investigate cognitive development in isolation, Piaget has systematically underestimated children's logical abilities.

By focusing on the child's understanding of the physical world, Piaget largely ignored understanding of the social world (moral development being the major exception; see Chapter 27). For Piaget, social understanding is simply a manifestation of cognitive development, while for Donaldson (and others), development of the former is actually more important.

A parallel criticism is that, by emphasizing the child's construction of knowledge and understanding (of the physical world), Piaget implied a view of the child as a largely independent, isolated individual, thus excluding the contribution of other people to the child's cognitive development (e.g. Meadows, 1995). The two other major developmental theorists, Bruner and Vygotsky (especially Vygotsky), corrected this 'cognitive individualist' view by stressing the social nature of knowledge and thought.

VYGOTSKY'S DEVELOPMENTAL THEORY

● Biographical sketch

Vygotsky (1896–1934) (Fig. 25.12) is, arguably the greatest Russian psychologist of all time and one of the greatest psychologists of any country (Sternberg, 1990). Born in the same year as Piaget, he died of tuberculosis at the age of 38, but not before he had made a considerable and lasting contribution to psychology. His major works were first published in the 1920s and 1930s but were not translated into English until the early 1960s.

We discussed his views on the relationship between language and thought in Chapter 13. Remember that one of the major differences between his ideas and those of Piaget was to do with the origins of language – for Vygotsky, all speech is social in nature, i.e. it is about communication and human interaction. This theme runs right through his developmental theory.

Our ability to think and reason by ourselves and for ourselves (inner speech or verbal thought) is the result of a fundamentally social process. We begin life as social beings, capable of interacting with others but able to do little by or for ourselves (either practically or intellectually) and gradually move towards self-sufficiency and independence. Through participation in social activity, the individual's capabilities gradually become transformed: cognitive

FIGURE 25.12 *L.S. Vygotsky (1896–1934). (From Vygotsky, 1978)*

development involves an active internalization of problem-solving processes that initially take place between people, usually the child and an adult. This process of internalization is the reverse of how Piaget (originally) saw things. Piaget's 'child as scientist' is replaced by Vygotsky's 'child as apprentice' (Rogoff, 1990, cited in Durkin, 1995), acquiring the knowledge and skills of the culture through guided collaboration with those who already possess them. 'Any function in the child's cultural development appears twice, or on two planes. First it appears on the social plane, and then on the psychological plane' (Vygotsky, 1981).

Vygotsky (1978) gives the specific example of pointing. Initially, pointing is nothing more than an unsuccessful attempt to grasp something beyond the baby's reach. When the mother sees the baby trying to grasp it, she takes it as a sign that the baby wants it (an indicatory gesture) and she comes to its aid, probably pointing to the object herself. Gradually, the baby comes to use the gesture deliberately; the 'reaching' becomes reduced to movements which could not themselves achieve the desired object even if it were in reach and is accompanied by cries, looks at the mother, and eventually words. The gesture is now directed towards the mother (it has become a gesture 'for others') rather than towards the object itself (it is no longer a gesture 'in itself') (Meadows, 1995).

The transformation of an *inter*personal process into an *intra*personal one, the internalization of socially based and historically developed activities, represents the essential difference between human and animal intelligence.

● Other people as tutors/instructors, scaffolding and the zone of proximal development

If children are 'apprentices', they need more experienced and skilled teachers to 'tutor' and guide them. The more expert person, who may be an adult or a more experienced peer, provides a context or *scaffolding* (Wood *et al.*, 1976, cited in Durkin, 1995) within which the child can act as though competent to solve the problem. As the task becomes more familiar and more of it is within the child's competence, the tutor can leave more and more for the child to do until it can perform the whole task successfully. In this way, the developing thinker does not have to create cognition 'from scratch' (as Piaget's 'scientist' image of the child implies), because there are others available who have already served their own apprenticeship when they were children (see Box 25.9).

The internalized cognitive skills remain social, both in the sense that as mature learners we can 'scaffold' ourselves through difficult tasks by 'instructing ourselves' as our teachers once scaffolded our earlier attempts, and in the sense that for most individuals the only cognitive skills practised to a high level of competence are those that their culture offers: cognitive potential may be universal, but cognitive expertise is culturally determined. ' ... Culturally given ways of thinking, remembering, categorizing, reading and so forth build on and may supersede the biologically based ways we begin with' (Meadows, 1995) (see Box 25.8 and Box 12.9).

Meadows (1995) points out that since the 1980s, research has stressed the role of social interaction in language development, especially the facilitating effects of the use of child-contingent language by adults talking with children. This 'fit' between adult and child language closely resembles Vygotsky's concept of 'scaffolding' (see Chapter 26).

Another way of looking at the collaborative nature of the child's cognitive development is by reference to Vygotsky's famous concept of the *zone of proximal* (or *potential*) *development* (ZPD). Since children move from being able to do things with others to being able to do them by themselves, the development of this ability is seen in terms of what the child could do under adult guidance or in collaboration with more capable peers:

The zone of proximal development defines those functions that have not yet matured but are in the

---

BOX 25.9 Key study: Collaborative learning and ZPD, or individual abilities are built on social support

Wertsch *et al.* (1980, cited in Durkin, 1995) tested Vygotsky's hypothesis that the order of emergence of a new function is first social, then psychological (individual). Two-, three- and four-year-olds and their mothers completed a reconstruction task which involved building a replica of a model truck, using a set of pieces of different shapes and colours. At certain stages it was essential to consult the model: several looks by the child to the model were preceded by maternal looks to the model and in about 90 percent of cases, when the mother looked, so did the child. The frequency of mother-guided looks declined with age, supporting Vygotsky's idea of a shift from other- toward self-regulation; older children seemed to extract the relevant information from the maternal looks more efficiently.

Vygotsky did not actually spell out in any detail how the more expert adult or peer assists the child's cognitive development. The term *scaffolding* was coined by Wood *et al.* (1976) to 'flesh out' the process of collaborative learning and refers to the ways that teachers organize their interventions around the child's progress, guiding its attention towards relevant aspects of the task and so on. Wood *et al.* found that in a construction task with 4–5-year-olds, different mothers used instructional strategies of varying levels of specificity, from general verbal encouragement to direct demonstration of a relevant action. No single strategy guaranteed learning, but the most efficient maternal instructors were those who combined general and specific interventions according to the child's progress; the most useful help is that which adapts itself to the learner's successes and failures (Bruner, 1983). For example, begin with a general instruction, until the child runs into difficulties, at which point a more specific instruction or demonstration is given. This style allows the child considerable autonomy but also provides carefully planned guidance at the boundaries of its abilities (i.e. at the edges of the child's ZPD).

As would be predicted from Vygotsky's theory, there is also evidence of scaffolding processes in everyday, naturalistic contexts; these are often linked to the transmission across generations of culturally valued skills, such as weaving among the Zinacauteco Mexicans and American mothers' involvement in their preschoolers' development of number (Durkin, 1995).

process of maturation, functions that will mature tomorrow but are currently in an embryonic state. These functions could be termed the 'buds' or 'flowers' of development rather than the 'fruits' of development. The actual developmental level characterizes mental development retrospectively, while the zone of proximal development characterizes mental development prospectively. (Vygotsky, 1978)

Consider the investigation of two ten-year-olds, both with a mental age of eight; can we necessarily be sure that they will subsequently develop and succeed academically to the same degree? Of course not, because there are non-intellectual factors which influence school achievement. But what if we assume these are comparable for the two children – could we now make comparable predictions about each child? The predictive validity of IQ tests is based on this very assumption (see Chapter 28) but Vygotsky believes it is a mistaken view.

Suppose a teacher-examiner provides guided assistance to each child in order to help them solve a given problem. With this help child A can deal with the problem up to a 12-year-old level but child B can only go up to a nine-year-old level. Would we still want to say that they are mentally the same? No, because child A's ZPD is the difference between a mental age of 12 and eight, while child B's is the difference between nine and eight: ' ... what is the zone of proximal development today will be the actual developmental level tomorrow – that is, what a child can do with assistance today she will be able to do by herself tomorrow' (Vygotsky, 1978).

● Is there any evidence for the ZPD?

According to Durkin (1995), there is a growing body of research into the effects of collaborative learning and the nature of the ZPD. Some of this research is summarized in Box 25.9.

BRUNER'S DEVELOPMENTAL THEORY

In discussing Vygotsky's ideas, we have seen that Bruner has helped to extend them and to apply them in the context of education; one important example of this is the concept of scaffolding, reflecting the influence of Vygotsky on Bruner's thinking. However, Bruner has also been influenced by Piaget and they share certain basic beliefs, in particular:

- Children are born with a biological organization that helps them to understand their world and their underlying cognitive structure matures over time, so that they can think about and organize their world in an increasingly complex way.
- Children are actively curious and explorative , capable of adapting to their environment through interacting with it. Abstract thinking grows out of action; competence in any area of knowledge is rooted in active experience and concrete mental operations.

However, there are also some basic areas of disagreement between them, stemming from Vygotsky's influence. In particular, Bruner stresses the role of language and interpersonal communication and the need for active involvement by expert adults (or more knowledgeable peers) in helping the child to develop as a thinker and problem solver; language plays a crucial part in the scaffolding process. He also sees instruction as an essential part of the learning process, both in naturalistic settings and in educational ones; we shall have more to say about both language and instruction below.

Also unlike Piaget's theory, Bruner's (1966b) theory is not about stages of development as such but rather about three ways or modes of representing the world, i.e. forms that our knowledge and understanding can take, and so he is not concerned exclusively with cognitive growth but also with knowledge in general. The three modes are the *enactive, iconic* and *symbolic* and they develop in this order in the child.

● The enactive mode

At first, babies represent the world through actions; any knowledge they have is based upon what they have experienced through their own behaviour (this corresponds to Piaget's sensorimotor stage). Past events are represented through appropriate motor responses; many of our motor schemas, e.g. 'bicycle riding, tying knots, aspects of driving, get represented in our muscles, so to speak,' and even when we have the use of language, it is often extremely difficult to describe in words how we do certain things. Through repeated encounters with the regularities of the environment (i.e. recurrent events and conditions), we build up virtually automatic patterns of motor activity which we 'run off' as units in the appropriate situation. Like Piaget, Bruner sees the onset of object permanence as a major qualitative change in the young child's cognitive development.

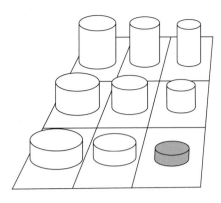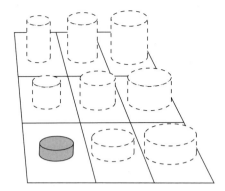

FIGURE 25.13 *The two arrangements of glasses used by Bruner and Kenney (1966)*

● The iconic mode

An icon is an image, so this form of representation involves building up a mental image of things we have experienced. Such images are normally composite, i.e. made up of a number of past encounters with similar objects or situations. This mode, therefore, corresponds to the last six months of the sensorimotor stage (where schemas become interiorized) and the whole of the preoperational stage, where the child is at the mercy of what it perceives in drawing intuitive conclusions about the nature of reality, i.e. things are as they look.

● The symbolic mode

Bruner's main interest was in the transition from the iconic to the symbolic mode. He and Piaget agree that a very important cognitive change occurs at around 6–7 years: while Piaget describes it as the start of logical operations (albeit tied to concrete reality), Bruner sees it as the appearance of the symbolic mode, with language coming into its own as an influence on thought. The child is now freed from the immediate context and is beginning to be able to 'go beyond the information given' (Bruner, 1957).

The transition from iconic to symbolic modes was demonstrated by Bruner and Kenney (1966). They arranged nine plastic glasses on a 3×3 matrix, as shown in Figure 25.13; 3–7-year-olds were familiarized with the matrix. The glasses were then scrambled and the children were asked to put them back the way they had been before (the *reproduction task*). In the *transposition task*, the glasses were removed from the matrix and the glass which had been in the bottom right-hand square was placed in the bottom left-hand square; the child had to rebuild the matrix in this transposed manner.

Children generally could reproduce it earlier than they could transpose it: the reproduction task involved the iconic mode (60 percent of the five-year-olds could do this, 72 percent of the six-year-olds and 80 percent of the seven-year-olds); while the transposition task involved the symbolic mode (the results were nil, 27 percent and 79 percent, respectively). Clearly, the five-year-olds were dominated by the visual image of the original matrix, while the 6–7-year-olds translated their visual information into the symbolic mode. They relied upon verbal rules to guide them, such as, 'It gets fatter going one way and taller going the other'. So a child using images but not symbols can reproduce but not restructure.

However, the major difference between Bruner and Piaget is to do with the role that language plays in cognitive development.

● Language and cognitive development

Bruner believes that the leap from the iconic to the symbolic mode is due to the development of language; Piaget, on the other hand, believes that the development of logical thought is due to the acquisition of operations–language is not the cause of cognitive development but a tool to be used in the course of operational thinking. So for Bruner, language and logical thinking are inseparable; without language, human thought would be limited to what could be learned through actions or images; for Piaget, language merely reflects and builds on cognitive structures which have already developed through interaction with the environment. It follows that Bruner believes that cognitive development can be significantly speeded up by training children in the use of symbols, while as far as Piaget is concerned, it would make no difference.

In a study of conservation of liquid quantity, Bruner (1966a) gave 4–7-year-olds the orthodox Piagetian task (pre-test): almost all the 4–5-year-olds said that there was more liquid in the taller, thinner beaker, as did about half the 6–7-year-olds. They were then shown two standard beakers and a third, wider beaker and all three were screened, so that when the contents of one of the standard beakers was poured into the wider one, the children could not see the level of the liquid but only the tops of the beakers. They were asked which had the most liquid with the screen still covering the liquid level and almost all the 5–7-year-olds answered correctly, as did about half the four-year-olds. When the screen was removed, all the four-year-olds reverted to their pre-screening answer but all the others stuck to the answer given while the screen was in place.

Finally, in the post-test, two standard beakers and a taller, thinner one were used in the orthodox Piagetian way (without a screen): the four-year-olds were unaffected by having seen the beakers screened but the five-year-olds' success rate rose from 20 per cent (pre-test) to 70 percent (post-test) and for the 6–7-year-olds,the figures were 50 percent (pre-test) and 90 percent (post-test). What do these results mean?

Activating their speech (symbolic mode) by having them 'say' their judgement when the screen was covering the liquid levels prevented the children of five and over (who normally fail to conserve on the standard Piagetian task) being dominated by the iconic mode. However, the four-year-olds were clearly not ready to benefit from this symbolic training and, to this extent, Piaget's view that the mental structures must have already developed before training can help seems to have been supported. Yet the five-year-olds did benefit, contrary to what Piaget would have predicted, and so this finding also seems to support Bruner.

Attempts by Sinclair-de-Zwart (1969) to train children in the use of language seem to support Piaget's prediction that unless children understand the concept of conservation, teaching them relevant words like 'bigger', 'more', 'as much as' and 'same' would have little effect on their performance on conservation tasks. As far as formal operational thought is concerned, Piaget himself seems to take the view that while language might be necessary, it is not sufficient; indeed, the language of the formal operational individual does not seem to differ significantly from what it was at some earlier stage.

● The 'spiral curriculum'

Bruner's modes of representation lie at the heart of the 'spiral curriculum', according to which the principles of a subject come to be understood at increasingly more complex levels of difficulty. Like Vygotsky, Bruner was unhappy with Piaget's concept of 'readiness' and proposed a much more active policy of intervention, based on the belief that 'any subject can be taught effectively in some intellectually honest form to any child at any stage of development' (1963). Educators need to provide learners with the means of grasping the structure of a discipline, i.e. the underlying principles and concepts (rather than just mastering factual information); this enables learners to go beyond the information given and develop ideas of their own. Teachers also need to encourage learners to make links and to understand the relationships within and between subjects (Smith and Cowie, 1991).

THE INFORMATION-PROCESSING APPROACH

When evaluating Piaget's stage concept earlier in the chapter, we referred to Sternberg's (1990) argument that we need to analyse the exact cognitive processes that are involved – or required – to successfully carry out tasks such as conservation. What Sternberg is advocating is an *information-processing approach* to cognitive development, which shares with Piaget's theory the assumption that there are psychological structures in people's minds that explain their behaviour and which are essentially independent of the individual's social relationships, social practices and cultural environment (Meadows, 1995).

The central metaphor underlying this approach is 'people as manipulators of symbols' (see Chapter 14). Cognition involves the use of a fairly small number of basic cognitive processes in a structured way over a period of time; the same basic processes (such as recognition, categorization, association) are used to solve all types of problem, though in different combinations and sequences. While these basic processes appear in a rudimentary form even in the very youngest children, during development the processes that people use to 'manipulate symbols' become more complex, faster, more flexible and generally more efficient, with a more deliberate use of strategies for problem-solving. These changes are comparable to the move from novice to expert (Meadows, 1986).

Pascual-Leone (1970) and Case (1978, 1984, 1985) (both cited in Meadows, 1986) have proposed neo-Piagetian models of cognitive development couched in information-processing terms. They claim that what develops are (a) a series of distinct executive strategies for problem-solving, and (b) the size of working memory (WM), the amount of mental 'space' ('M-space') available for information-processing strategies to work in (see Chapter 12). The number of things that we can do at the same time increases as we get older or more expert in a task and more information can be handled automatically, without conscious processing (see Chapter 11). (We saw in Chapter 24 that the elderly find it increasingly difficult to manage more than one thing at a time.) Pascual-Leone believes that improvement within a stage reflects changes in strategies, while movement between stages is due to increases in M-space.

DOMAINS OF COGNITIVE DEVELOPMENT, THEORY OF MIND AND AUTISM

A 'domain' refers to a fairly coherent set of processes and concepts which constitute a whole, distinct from other domains (Meadows, 1995). These are sometimes called *modules*, thought to be genetically programmed, operating with minimal environmental support, such as the specialized capacity for language and language acquisition (Chomsky, 1968; Fodor, 1983; see Chapter 26).

Another example is the 'naive', common sense theories that divide our complex experience of the world into fundamental categories, such as people, other living things and inanimate objects. One form of this is what has been called the *theory of mind mechanism* (ToMM), a specialized module, appearing between 12–18 months and 3–4 years, which processes information in the form of *metarepresentations*, i.e. it is a highly specialized mechanism for representing mental representations (Leslie, 1987; Leslie and Roth, 1993). It is more generally referred to as the child's 'theory of mind' (Premack and Woodruff, 1978), the understanding that people (and not objects) have desires, beliefs and other mental states, some of which (such as beliefs) can be false (see Chapter 21).

We use our theory of mind to explain other people's behaviour (see the discussion of the attribution process in Chapter 15) and it also helps social inter-action and interpersonal communication. Given its importance for social life, anyone who lacked a theory of mind (or whose theory was deficient in some way) would be seriously handicapped; this core inability to appreciate others' mental states is called *mind-blindness* (Baron-Cohen, 1990). In all cases of *autism,* the child fails to develop normal social relationships and according to the mind-blindness theory, this is an inevitable consequence of the inability to understand mental states and how these influence behaviour, i.e. people with autism lack a theory of mind (Baron-Cohen, 1995).

CHAPTER SUMMARY

- Different theoretical accounts of cognitive development are based on very different images of what the child is like, such as Piaget's organism adapting to its environment, the information-processing approach's manipulator of symbols and Vygotsky's participant in an interactive, collaborative process.
- Despite the enormous influence of Piaget, many of his basic assumptions have been challenged, including the concept of developmental stages.
- Piaget's interest in zoology and philosophy were combined in his genetic epistemology. He saw intelligence as a process of adaptation and was interested in how children think and how their thinking changes as they mature.
- Intelligence involves the construction of the individual's understanding of reality, in contrast with both associationism/empiricism and maturation/nativism. What is constructed are structures that can be summarized as four stages (sensorimotor, 0–2; pre-operational, 2–7; concrete operational, 7–11; formal operational, 11–15) which develop in an invariant sequence; each stage is characterized by an overall structure.
- What changes between stages and what structures consist of are schemas. Initially, these are inborn reflexes, which gradually become co-ordinated and less tied to overt action (more interiorized), i.e. more mental.
- Schemas change through an ongoing process of adaptation, consisting of the complementary processes of assimilation and accommodation. The need for accommodation is brought about when assimilation is no longer adequate and disequilibrium is experienced.
- Sensorimotor intelligence is essentially practical.

The baby lacks object permanence which develops through a number of substages up to 18 months. At first, what cannot be directly perceived seems not to exist and the whole object must be visible if the baby is to respond to it. Later, the baby will search for a completely hidden object but only where it was first hidden. It is complete when the child can infer invisible displacements.

- The other major change in the sensorimotor stage is development of the general symbolic function, which refers to language, deferred imitation and representational/make-believe play.

- The pre-operational stage is divided into the pre-conceptual (2–4) and intuitive (4–7) substages. On classification tasks, the pre-conceptual child can only sort objects in terms of a single attribute at a time, as in syncretic thought and transductive reasoning, which can lead to animism. The younger child also has difficulty with seriation.

- On class-inclusion tasks, the intuitive child fails to understand the relationship between superordinate and subordinate classes. This may reflect a difference between adults and young children in their understanding of basic terms such as 'more', rather than a basic inability of the child to think logically.

- Piaget saw many of the limitations in the pre-operational child's thinking as stemming from the inability to decentre; other important manifestations of this are egocentrism and lack of conservation. Donaldson and others have criticized Piaget's methods of testing egocentrism, claiming that he made it difficult for children to demonstrate their ability to see things from other people's viewpoint. These claims have been empirically supported.

- Piaget's studies of conservation show that the pre-operational child believes that things are as they look; they demonstrate identity, but not compensation and reversibility, all of which are necessary for conservation. Alternative , more meaningful methods, such as dropping the pre-transformation question and using accidental transformation and incidental transformation conditions, show that children are very likely to conserve when they would fail using standard, Piagetian methods.

- Children in the concrete operational stage can perform logical operations, such as conservation, but only in concrete situations. Different types of conservation develop in sequence, illustrating horizontal décalage. They are no longer egocentric and can manage most types of classification, but

they cannot perform transitivity tasks without real objects.

- Formal operational thought involves the manipulation of ideas, the ability to follow the form of an argument regardless of its content, the ability to think about possibilities and systematic problem solving as shown in hypothetico-deductive reasoning.

- Only a minority of adolescents and adults in Western samples attain formal operations and it is absent altogether in some cultures. When it is attained, it may only be manifest in areas of experience and expertise.

- Piaget saw play as an adaptive activity, which is initially seen in the infant's circular reactions. It involves both assimilation and accommodation and is distinct from intellectual activity. The three main types of play are mastery/practice, symbolic/make-believe and play with rules.

- There has been considerable criticism of the stage concept and much debate about how much consistency is necessary in order to classify a child as belonging to a particular stage. Related to this is the issue of training, i.e. deliberately trying to speed up the rate of development.

- Piaget sees active self-discovery/discovery learning as crucial to the learning process, with readiness setting limits on learning. The teacher's role involves assessing the child's current stage of development, creating disequilibrium, encouraging the children's curiosity and learning from each other.

- Although there is considerable cross-cultural support for Piaget's stages up to and including concrete operations, there is also evidence for different rates of development in different cultures, as well as different patterns in the development of different abilities; this reflects what abilities are adaptive and valued in different cultural contexts.

- Piaget's clinical method has been criticized for being unstandardized, but this was a deliberate attempt to explore the more subtle aspects of the child's thinking.

- By focusing on the child's understanding of the physical world, Piaget largely ignored understanding of the social world; this is reflected in his failure to appreciate the influence of the testing situation as social and his attempt to study cognitive development in isolation. By contrast, Vygotsky stressed the social nature of knowledge and thought.

- For Vygotsky, human beings are social creatures from birth and the child is an apprentice in a collaborative learning process. Through interaction and communication with others, problem-solving processes that are initially interpersonal become intrapersonal through internalization. This is illustrated in the act of pointing.

- Adults and more experienced peers act as tutors, providing a context or scaffolding within which the child can be helped to become more competent by gradually doing more and more for itself. Another form of the collaborative nature of cognitive development is the zone of proximal development.

- Bruner shared Piaget's belief that children's inborn biological structure matures over time and that abstract thinking grows out of action. He was also influenced by Vygotsky's ideas and stressed the role of language in the scaffolding process, the need for the active involvement of more expert others and instruction in both formal and informal settings. Both Bruner and Vygotsky rejected Piaget's concept of readiness.

- Also unlike Piaget, Bruner does not identify stages of development but three modes of representation, namely the enactive, iconic and symbolic, which develop in this order. He stressed the transition from iconic to symbolic at age 6–7, seeing logical thought as dependent on language; this implies that language training can speed up cognitive development. This contrasts with Piaget's view that language merely reflects cognitive structures that have already developed.

- The information-processing approach sees people as symbol manipulators and cognition as the use of a small number of basic cognitive processes used to solve all types of problem. These basic processes become more flexible, faster and more efficient as the child develops; for example, the size of WM increases, providing greater mental 'space' in which information-processing strategies can operate.

- Dividing the world into fundamental categories reflects cognitive domains or modules. One example is the theory of mind mechanism, which represents mental representations (metarepresentations). According to the mind-blindness theory, people with autism do not have a theory of mind.

GLOSSARY

Accommodation Modifying already-existing schemas in order to meet the demands of new experiences/ situations.

Adaptation The complementary processes of assimilation and accommodation.

Animism The belief that inanimate objects are alive; attributing to them feelings, motives and other mental states.

Assimilation Applying the schemas we already possess, in a generalized way, by trying to fit new experiences into what we can already do/what we already know.

Centration Focusing on a single attribute of an object/situation at a time, to the exclusion of others, as in syncretic thought, transductive reasoning, egocentrism and failure to conserve.

Clinical method Piaget's way of probing children's thinking, by presenting them with a problem, then asking a series of questions. Initially, every child is asked the same questions; subsequent questions differ for each child depending on answers to previous questions.

Conservation Understanding that things remain constant (their quantity, weight, volume, etc.) despite changes in their appearance.

Constructivism Piaget's theory which sees each individual actively discovering what the world is like; contrasted with both empiricism and nativism.

Décalage An inconsistency in performance, either within the same ability (e.g. conservation: horizontal) or between different abilities (e.g. conservation and classification: vertical).

Egocentrism Seeing the world exclusively from one's own perspective, such that others are attributed with the same perceptions, knowledge, feelings, etc. as oneself. Literally = self-centred.

Equilibration The ongoing process of assimilation, accommodation, equilibrium and disequilibrium.

Functional invariants Fundamental aspects of development which remain the same/work in the same way throughout the changing developmental stages, e.g. assimilation, accommodation, equilibration.

General symbolic function The use of mental images, words and other symbols to represent objects (as in object permanence, deferred imitation and representational/make-believe play). (Strictly, words are signs not symbols, since symbols, according to Piaget, resemble what they represent.)

Genetic epistemology Piaget's term for the study of how knowledge develops in human beings.

Mind-blindness The lack of a theory of mind; thought to be the underlying cause of the difficulties that all autistic individuals have in forming normal social relationships.

Modes of representation Bruner's term for forms of

knowledge/understanding: enactive (based on action), iconic (based on images), symbolic (based on symbols, especially language).

Object permanence The understanding that objects continue to exist even when they are not being perceived or manipulated in some way.

Reversibility The ability to mentally return a situation to its starting point.

Scaffolding Providing a context in which a child is helped to become more competent in problem-solving abilities by adults or more experienced peers.

Schema A way of organizing experience, making the world more simple and predictable; basic unit of intelligent behaviour.

Seriation Arranging objects on the basis of specific dimensions, such as increasing height.

Syncretic thought The tendency to categorize together any neighbouring objects/events on the basis of what individual instances have in common; similar to complexive thinking.

Theory of mind The understanding that people (and not objects) have desires, beliefs and other mental states, which can sometimes be mistaken.

Theory of mind mechanism (ToMM) A specialized cognitive domain or module for processing information in the form of metarepresentations, i.e. representing mental representations.

Transductive reasoning Drawing an inference about the relationship between two things based on a single attribute that they have in common.

Zone of proximal development Those abilities which have not yet developed, but are in the process of maturing: what the child could do with the help of more expert others.

FURTHER READING

Meadows, S. (1993) *The Child as Thinker*. London: Routledge. An extremely thorough review of recent theory and research, including physical and social influences on children's cognition, individual differences and applied areas, such as reading and writing.

Piaget, J. (1973) *The Child's Conception of the World*. London: Paladin. This provides a good insight into Piaget's whole approach to the study of cognitive development, including the clinical method as an investigative tool.

26 THE DEVELOPMENT OF LANGUAGE

INTRODUCTION AND OVERVIEW

So many of our interactions with other people, so much of our learning, so much of our belief and knowledge of the world goes on through the medium of language (spoken and written) that it is almost impossible to discuss any aspect of human behaviour without taking the role of language into account (see Chapter 13).

As our brains seem specially designed to enable us to use speech (see Chapter 3), it is perhaps not surprising that language should play such a central part in our lives. Many psychologists and philosophers have claimed that it is language which makes us unique as a species – that it is almost what makes us human. There are a number of separate but inter-related questions that we shall be asking in this chapter:

- What is language? How can it be defined and what are its major components?
- How can we best describe the course of language development, e.g. are there distinct stages that all children go through?
- Why does language develop in the way it does, i.e. what are the major theories of language acquisition?
- What can we conclude about language as a unique human ability from attempts to teach language to non-humans, particularly chimpanzees?

According to Durkin (1995), while developmental psychologists have always been interested in language, during the mid-20th century it became peripheral. Piaget's stress on the development of logical structures and his view of language as merely reflecting these – a lens through which to inspect the child's thought (see Chapter 25) – seemed to reinforce the behaviourists' earlier rejection of anything 'mental' (such as grammar and meaning) (see Chapters 2 and 7).

However, there has been a revival of interest in language since the 1960s, inspired very largely by Chomsky's (1959) rejection of Skinner's (1957) *operant conditioning* account of language acquisition and his alternative nativist theory in the form of an innate language acquisition device (LAD). Chomsky's theory is probably the clearest, and most extreme, example of a *nativist* approach in the whole of psychology, just as Skinner's is 'pure empiricism'; so the language controversy is a very important example of the *nature–nurture debate*. Attempts to teach language to non-human animals have very important implications for Chomsky's claim that language is a unique human ability.

While LAD was seen as a language-specific part of the child's biological make-up, many psychologists (such as Cromer, 1974) began to consider the relationship between language and the child's cognitive development (the *cognition hypothesis*). Others (such as Bruner, 1983) began to study the contexts of language development, especially children's interactions with other language users who help to structure the situations in which language is used; language acquisition theory and research have become increasingly social. We shall discuss all these theoretical approaches in this chapter.

WHAT IS LANGUAGE?

In order to understand language development and to discuss whether language is unique to human beings, we must first ask what language is, what precisely it is which develops in the child and which only appears spontaneously in our species.

Until fairly recently, the study of language was undertaken largely by linguists, who are concerned primarily with the *structure* of language – the sounds that compose it, how these relate to words and sentences and the rules which govern the relationships between all of these. But in the last 20 years or so, psychologists have become interested in language not so much for its own sake but for how it is acquired, whether it is a human species-specific behaviour, how it affects learning, memory, thinking in general and

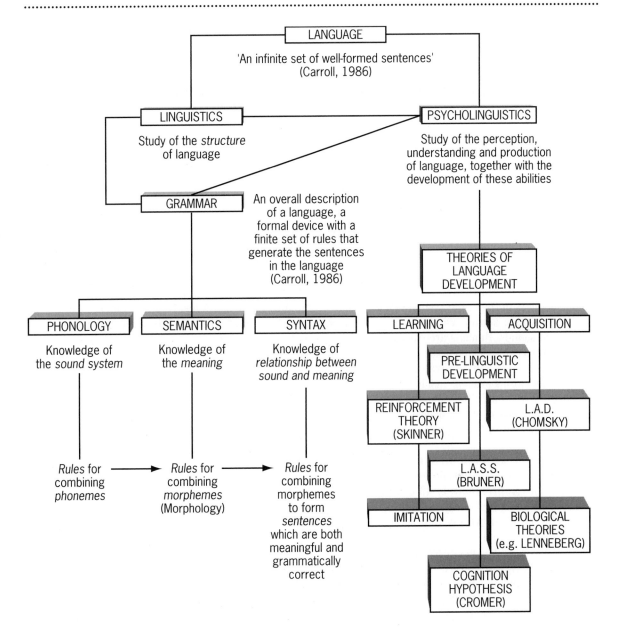

FIGURE 26.1 *The major components of grammar and the relationship between linguistics and psycholinguistics*

so on. The 'marriage' of psychology and linguistics is called *psycholinguistics*, which can be defined as the study of how language is acquired, perceived, understood and produced.

Roger Brown (1965), an eminent American psycholinguist, defines language as an arbitrary system of symbols ' ... which taken together make it possible for a creature with limited powers of discrimination and a limited memory to transmit and understand an infinite variety of messages and to do this in spite of noise and distraction'. It is, perhaps, this 'infinite

variety of messages' that makes human language unique; other species may be able to communicate with each other but only in a very limited way. For example, even wild chimpanzees, which use about 36 different vocalizations to convey about the same number of meanings, may repeat a sound to intensify its meaning, but they do not string sounds together to make new 'words' (Calvin, 1994). As we shall see later in the chapter, claims that chimps are capable of language are based largely, and until recently, on deliberate training; contrast this with children's spontaneous and quite easy mastery of human language within about five years after birth.

In another definition of language, Brown (1973) points out that people do not simply learn a repertoire of sentences but 'acquire a rule system that makes it possible to generate a literally infinite variety of sentences, most of them never heard from anyone else'. This rule system is what psycholinguists call *grammar* (or *mental grammar*), but grammar is much more than the parts of speech that we learn about in English at school. It is concerned with the description of language, the rules which determine how a language works, what governs our patterns of speech (Jackendoff, 1993); it comprises *phonology, semantics* and *syntax* (see Fig. 26.1).

● Phonology

Phonology refers to the sound system of a language – what counts as a sound, what is an acceptable sequence of sounds. Humans are capable of producing many different speech sounds (called *phones* or *phonetic segments*). By convention, phones are denoted by enclosing symbols inside square brackets, for example [p] is the initial phone in the word 'pin'. The linguistic analysis of a language typically begins with a description of the phones used in that language.

Different languages consist of different numbers and combinations of these basic sounds. English, for example, uses approximately 40 distinguishable sounds, some languages use as few as 15 and others as many as 85. When we say that someone speaks English with a foreign accent, we are really saying that they have not yet mastered all the phones of English. Similarly, when we recognize a foreign language as, say, French without being able to speak it or even understand it ourselves, we are recognizing the phones as those which 'define' French.

Although all phones are different only some of the differences matter, namely those which affect the meaning of what is being said. For example, the [p] phone can be articulated (pronounced) slightly differently each time it is uttered without changing the perception of 'pin'. But the difference between [p] and [d] does matter because that difference alone can lead to two words with different meanings (e.g. 'pin' and 'din', 'pot' and 'dot'). So [p] and [d] cannot be interchanged without changing the meaning of the words, so that they belong to different functional classes of phones. The classes of phones which are functionally important in a language are called *phonemes* (phonological

segments). So [p] and [d] belong to the different phonemes /p/ and /d/. Just as languages differ with respect to phones, so they differ in terms of their phonemes, e.g. [l] and [r] belong to different phonemes in English but not in Japanese. Phonological rules also constrain the permitted sequences of phonemes, e.g. 'port' is an *actual* sequence, 'plort' is a *possible* sequence, but 'pbort' is an *impossible/prohibited* (ungrammatical) sequence in English.

These examples show that phonemes in themselves have no meaning – they are just sounds. They correspond roughly to the vowels and consonants of the alphabet but, as there are only 26 of these in English, the same vowel, for example, can represent more than one phoneme (e.g. the 'o' in 'hop' is pronounced very differently from the 'o' in 'hope' and so constitutes a different phoneme). However, although meaningless in themselves, phonemes are, as we have seen, important for meaning, which brings us onto semantics.

● Semantics

Semantics is the study of the meaning of language and can be analysed at the level of *morphemes* and at the level of sentences (which is where syntax comes in). Morphology refers to the rules for combining phonemes into morphemes which are the basic units of meaning in a language and consist mainly of words. Other morphemes are prefixes (letters attached to the beginning of a word, such as 'de' or 're') and suffixes (letters attached to the end of a word, such as 's' to make a plural – adding 's' to 'dog' clearly changes the meaning, since we now know there is more than one animal). Some morphemes are 'bound' (like the plural 's'), i.e. they only take on meaning when attached to other morphemes. But most morphemes are 'free', i.e. they have meaning when they stand alone, as most words have. However, single words have only a limited meaning and we usually combine them into longer strings of phrases and sentences.

● Syntax

Syntax refers to the rules for combining words into phrases and sentences (and is often taken to be the same as grammar but, as we have seen, syntax is only one part of grammar). For example, in the sentence 'The dog chased the ___' , we know that only a noun can complete it; this is an example of a *syntactic rule*.

Another important syntactic rule is word order, which has great significance for understanding language development and for evaluating studies which claim that chimps and other non-human primates can be taught language. Clearly, 'John loves Mary' has a very different meaning from 'Mary loves John'. Again 'The academic lecture attracted a limited audience' and 'The academic liquid became an odourless audience' are both equally correct (syntactically) but it is difficult to know what the second one means. 'Liquid the an became audience odourless academic' breaks all the rules of syntax and is also incomprehensible. These examples show that syntax and semantics are very closely inter-related but they are distinct. We should also note that sentences have sounds *and* meanings and syntax refers to the *structure* which relates the two.

● Psycholinguistics

As shown in Figure 26.1, while both linguists and psycholinguists are interested in the structure of language and the rules which govern that structure (i.e. grammar), linguists are interested largely in language itself (almost disembodied from the human beings who use it), while psycholinguists attempt to understand language as it is used by people (the language-user rather than the language itself).

Psychologists are interested in the grammars proposed by linguists because 'Grammars represent the tacit knowledge that native speakers have about their language, which includes knowing how to form

grammatically acceptable sentences, knowing what they mean and knowing how to pronounce them ... ' (Carroll, 1986). Psycholinguists want to know whether grammatical rules have any 'psychological reality', i.e. do people actually use the linguist's rules when producing and understanding everyday language (Plunkett, 1981)? An adequate psychological model of language will need to represent the language user's knowledge of the language and to specify the process by which this knowledge is translated into actual performance (Carroll, 1986). Also, it must be consistent with what is known about cognitive processes in general; although language is a very special skill, it is only one of the ways in which we get things done in the world (Plunkett, 1981). As far as the present chapter is concerned, the most important criterion is that any adequate psychological model of language must be able to account for how children acquire complex linguistic skills.

A linguist whose model of language promised to meet these criteria is Noam Chomsky, who has undoubtedly had the greatest impact on psychology in recent times. His *Syntactic Structure* (1957) caused a revolution in thinking about language. In that book he outlined his theory of *transformational grammar* (TG), at the heart of which is a set of rules called *phrase structure rules*. When applied systematically, these rules generate sentences in English or any other language. Some examples are given in Figure 26.2. Applied to a particular example, a tree diagram can be drawn to represent the structure of the sentence, as in Figure 26.3.

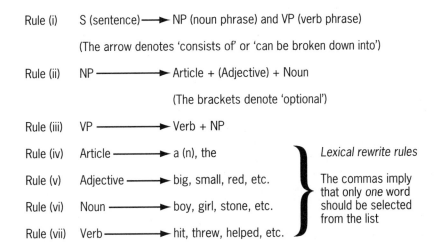

FIGURE 26.2 *Examples of Chomsky's phase structure rules*

While phrase structure rules replace single symbols by different sets of symbols, transformational rules rearrange strings of symbols and often add to them: the sentence in Figure 26.3 is an active sentence and from it, using transformational rules, more complex sentence forms can be derived (e.g. passive, interrogative and negative). If we take the original sentence:

A		small		boy
(Article)	+	(adjective)	+	(noun)

helped		the		girl
+(verb)	+	(article)	+	(noun)

and now apply a transformational rule (rule viii), we obtain the passive form of the sentence:

Article	+	noun	+	was	+	verb
The		girl		was		helped

+ by	+	article	+	adjective +	noun
by		a		small	boy

If the above account is correct, then simple active sentences occupy a special place in the language: they are the only ones where phrase structures do not undergo any transformation (they are called *kernel sentences*) and should therefore be the easiest sentences for native speakers to produce and understand. We would also expect them to appear earlier developmentally than more complex sentences (see below).

Chomsky not only proposed a grammar which is one of the most adequate ever written (Plunkett, 1981) but he proposed how such an extremely complex grammar could be acquired by the child, in the form of *universal grammar, linguistic universals* and a *language acquisition device* (LAD).

DESCRIBING LANGUAGE DEVELOPMENT

Many psychologists believe that there is a universal timetable for language development, i.e. all children pass through the same predictable sequence of stages, regardless of the particular language or culture, and at more or less the same age, although the rate of development may differ from child to child. So *maturation* seems to play a very important part but, of course, environment is equally necessary – the child comes to speak the language it does because that is the one it is exposed to. Children seem to be programmed by nature to learn language if they are exposed to it and, as we shall see later, sometimes even when they are not (for example, children of deaf-mute parents or congenitally deaf children), they still seem to create some kind of non-verbal language.

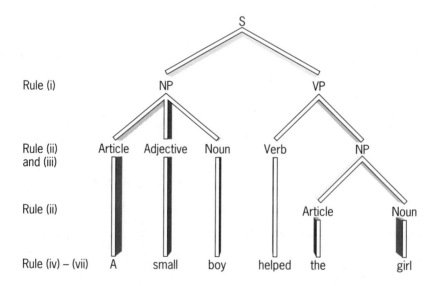

FIGURE 26.3 *A sentence produced by Chomsky's phrase structure rules*

The major stages are:

1 the pre-linguistic (0–12 months);
2 the one-word stage (12–18 months); and
3 the stage of two-word sentences, which comprises two substages, stage 1 grammar (18–30 months) and stage 2 grammar (from 30 months).

● Pre-linguistic stage (0–12 months)

The first year of life is really a pre-linguistic phase; the baby makes various sounds with its vocal organs, including crying, long before it can talk. Crying tends to dominate the first month or so, with the baby having different kinds of cries, which the parents learn to discriminate.

At about six weeks, babies begin to coo, producing sounds which seem to be associated with pleasurable states. The vowel sounds that are produced during these early weeks are different from those that will later be made and out of which the first words will be built. During the first six months, the baby's oral cavity and nervous system are not sufficiently mature to enable it to produce the sounds necessary for speech.

The major development to occur during the first year is *babbling,* which usually begins somewhere between six and nine months; the baby now produces phonemes, which take the form of combinations of vowels and consonants (e.g. *ma, ba, ga, da*). Sometimes these are repeated to produce reduplicated monosyllables (*mama, gaga*) and although very different from the earliest cooing sounds, these babbled sounds still have no meaning. Two of the main differences between babbling and pre-babbling vocalization are: (i) the baby spends more time making noises, especially when alone in its cot, and seems to enjoy exercising its voice for the sake of it; (ii) babbling has intonational patterns, like speech, with rising inflections and speechlike rhythm. By 11–12 months, the baby often repeats syllables over and over again (*dadadada*) and this is called *echolalia*; the baby seems to be echoing itself. (The term is also used to refer to the repeating back of other people's speech, in autistic children for example.)

At first, only a few phonemes are produced, but then *phonemic* (or phonetic) *expansion* occurs, whereby almost every available phoneme is produced. The onset of babbling and phonemic expansion both seem to be based on maturation, independent of experience or learning. Babbling occurs roughly at the same time all over the world and even deaf babies or those born to deaf-mute parents (and who therefore hear very little speech, if any) babble and, on average, at the same time as normal babies. However, by 9–10 months, *phonemic contraction* begins to take place, whereby phonemes become restricted to those used in the baby's native tongue, which seems to be based on the baby's sampling of the phonemes used in its language environment. At this age, therefore, it would be possible to distinguish babies of different nationalities – English, Chinese and French babies would no longer all sound alike. Significantly, deaf babies normally stop babbling at around 9–10 months, presumably because of lack of feedback from their own voice.

Although the baby is now only using phonemes which are 'useful' (those necessary for speech) it won't be until seven years that most English-speaking children will have mastered them all. For example, by 2½ years, most children have mastered 27 of the 40 or so phonemes of English (all the vowels and about two-thirds of the consonants); three-, four- and five-year-olds commonly have trouble pronouncing at least one phoneme.

It seems that the ability to perceive the difference between speech sounds is innate (see Box 26.1).

Eimas's study shows that babies do not need to learn the 'p'/'b' difference and similarly, with 'd'/'t' and 'g'/'k'. Without such inborn abilities, the sound of language would seem very confusing. In Chomsky's terms, these phonetic discriminations may be thought of as the first linguistic universals

---

BOX 26.1 Key study: Using conditioning to show VOT newborns can do

Eimas (1975) conditioned two-day-old infants to suck a dummy in order to operate the repeated presentation of 'ba'. Habituation occurred after about 30 seconds (i.e. the baby stopped sucking). If a new sound was presented (e.g. 'pa'), sucking picked up to its original rate. He also systematically varied the *voice onset time* (VOT) of 'b' in 'ba' as it was repeated; VOT refers to the interval between the time the lips move and the time the vocal cords are set in motion, so that for 'b' VOT is 0 milliseconds (there is no measurable delay) while for 'p' it is 40 milliseconds. The babies' sucking continued to drop off as 'ba' was repeated until VOT reached about 30 milliseconds, when it picked up again, indicating that the baby had perceived a different sound.

which the baby discovers, i.e. the first grammatical rules to be acquired are phonetic rather than syntactic.

Pre-linguistic communication

One of the influences which Chomsky's theory had on the study of language development was to focus on the emergence of syntactic rules, which do not usually appear before 18 months, with the beginning of the two-word stage. But during the 1970s, there was a shift in the study of language development to what goes on during the first 12–18 months, which is clearly a great deal: the basic skills acquired during the first 18 months of life may contribute substantially to the syntactic skills characteristic of adult language (Plunkett, 1981)

How do children 'discover' their language, i.e. how do they learn that there is such a thing as language which can be used for communicating, categorizing, problem-solving and so on? A purely syntactic analysis cannot possibly provide answers to these kinds of questions. According to Smith and Cowie (1991), the *language and social interaction approach* sees language as being used to communicate needs and intentions and as an enjoyable means of entering into a community – the baby initially masters a social world onto which it later 'maps' language. How is this achieved?

Snow (1977), for example, observes that adults tend to attach meaning to the baby's sounds and utterances – burps, gurgles, grunts, etc. are interpreted as expressions of intent and feeling, as are their non-verbal communication (smiling, eye contact, etc.). This represents a kind of primitive conversation (*proto-conversation*) which has a rather one-sided quality: it requires a 'generous' adult attributing some kind of intended meaning to the baby's sounds and non-verbal behaviour. From this perspective, the infant is an inadequate conversational partner.

Much more two-way exchanges are 'visual co-orientation' or joint attention and formats. *Visual co-orientation* (Collins and Schaffer, 1975, cited in Schaffer, 1989) refers to the process whereby two individuals come to focus on some common object; it puts the infant's environmental explorations into a social context, such that an infant–object situation is converted into an infant–object–mother situation (Schaffer, 1989). The joint attention that this entails provides opportunities for learning how to do things; as parents and infants develop their mutual patterns of interaction and share attention to objects, some of

their activities recur, as in joint picture-book reading and peekaboo.

Bruner (1975, 1978) refers to these rule-bound activity routines as *formats*, in which the infant has many opportunities to relate language to familiar play (for example, the mother inserts name labels into the game or activity, initially in indicating formats, later in requesting formats). These ritualized exchanges stress the need for turn taking and so help the baby to discover the social function of communication; the infant can learn about the structures and demands of social interaction, preparing and rehearsing the skills that will eventually become essential to successful interchanges such as conversation.

LASS: the active adult

According to Bruner (1983), formats are what the *language acquisition support system* (LASS) is composed of. He takes a pragmatic, functional approach to language development, i.e. he is concerned with what language is used for:

> ... entry into language is entry into discourse that requires both members of a dialogue pair to interpret a communication and its intent. Learning a language ... consists of learning not only the grammar of a particular language but also learning how to realize one's intentions by the appropriate use of that grammar.

This emphasis on intent requires a far more active role on the part of the adult in helping the child's language acquisition than that of just being a 'model', i.e. simply providing the input for the child's LAD (see below). According to Moerk (1989, cited in Durkin, 1995), 'The LAD was a lady', i.e. the lady who does most of the talking to the child (the mother); she not only simplifies linguistic input but also breaks it down into helpful illustrative segments for the child to practise and build on. According to this view, language acquisition is a very sophisticated extension of the processes of meaningful interaction that the caregiver and child have constructed over several months (Durkin, 1995).

The emergence of communicative intentionality: the active child

So far, we have looked at the 'partnership' between adult and infant mainly from the adult's point of view or, at least, with the adult being portrayed as the 'senior partner'. Another way of looking at things, with the baby as a more 'active' partner, is the view of language as a *cause–effect analytic device*. According to Gauker (1990), ' ... the fundamental function of words is to bring about changes in the speaker's environment and ... linguistic understanding consists in a grasp of these causal relations'.

Bates *et al.* (1979) stress that language should be viewed as a form of tool use, a tool being a symbol or set of symbols whose use results in a change of behaviour in the listener. This use of words as a communicative tool can be seen during the 'emergence of communicative intentionality' (Bates *et al.*, 1979; Bruner, 1983). During the pre-linguistic stage, the child at first has no awareness that one can gain a desired effect indirectly by changing somebody else's behaviour (through behaviours such as words, gestures or glances) – he/she may cry and reach for something but not look back at the caretaker nor direct the cry towards the caretaker. The cry is a mere expression of frustration, not a communicative signal designed to affect the other's behaviour. (This 'analysis' of means–end relationships, i.e. what causes what, solely as the product of one's own actions, is called *first order causality.*)

However, the emergence of communicative intentionality involves *second order causality,* the awareness that it is possible to bring about a desired goal by using another person as a tool. Pointing gestures and glances now rapidly proliferate as a means of asking others to look at or act upon an object (see Chapter 25 for Vygotsky's analysis of pointing). The child is beginning to understand in a general sense ' ... that it is possible to "cause" others to engage in desired actions, through the mechanism of communications about these actions' (Savage-Rumbaugh, 1990). This use of animate tools (other people) parallels the child's use of inanimate tools (physical objects) which is an important feature of sensorimotor intelligence (see Chapter 25); some kind of *instrumental understanding* (what leads to what) seems to underlie both activities.

However, it is more difficult to analyse language *comprehension* in terms of a cause–effect analysis than language *production* (the former preceding and outstripping the latter) – what is one causing to happen by understanding the things said to one? Based on work with chimps, Savage-Rumbaugh (1990) concludes that language comprehension is clearly becoming the driving force underlying the language acquisition process; under normal circumstances, language production is just one outcome of the development of language comprehension.

● One-word stage (12–18 months)

While there is considerable variability in the age at which infants produce their very first word (anywhere from nine to 16 months), on average it occurs at 12 months. (The word 'infant' comes from the Latin word *infans,* which means 'without speech' or 'not speaking'; so perhaps when individuals begin to use words for the first time, they can no longer be considered babies.)

Of course, the baby does not wake up on its first birthday and decide that it is about time it stopped babbling like a baby and started speaking like a child: babbling merges and overlaps with patterned speech (words). Non-word sounds continue for up to another six months (and are called *jargon*, what we often criticize experts in various fields for using such that no one outside their field of expertise can understand them).

Lenneberg (1967) believes that the shift from babbling to words occurs as a result of fundamental developments in the brain; certainly the one-word stage is universal. Since the baby's first words (or articulate sounds) come soon after phonemic contraction, it is not surprising that they involve only a few phonemes. They are often 'invented', not very much like 'adult words' at all to begin with. For example, Scollon (1976) studied the first words of Brenda, a one-year-old. 'Da' was used only when referring to a doll; 'awa', though used in several different situations, always meant something like 'I don't want'; and 'nene' was used to refer to a whole collection of objects or people who had something to do with nurturing or comfort.

Scollon defines a word as 'a systematic matching of form and meaning' – the baby consistently uses the same sound to label the same thing or kind of thing and there is now a clear intent to communicate. However, this does not necessarily imply that the words are being used referentially (to refer to the same thing regardless of the context); indeed, the infant's earliest words are usually context bound in nature, their predominant characteristic being that they are produced only in very limited and specific situations or contexts in which particular actions or events occur (Barrett, 1989). For example, Bloom (1973) reports the case of one child who initially began to use the word 'car' at nine months only while she was looking out of the living room window at cars moving on the street below; it was not used to refer to stationary cars, pictures of cars or while actually sitting in a car. Similarly, Bates *et al.* (1979) reported on one infant who only ever said 'bye' (when it was first acquired) while putting a telephone receiver down and Barrett (1986) found that 'duck' was produced (at first) by one infant only while hitting a toy duck off the edge of the bath and never in any other context.

What all these examples have in common is that the words, when first used, are tied to a specific situation or context characterized by a frequently occurring event which involves behaviours which have often acquired a ritualized or standardized format (which relates to what we said earlier about pre-linguistic conversation). These context-bound words are typically used simply as accompaniments to the occurrence of particular actions or events and, to this extent, they are not serving a communicative purpose as such; they function as pure 'performatives', i.e. their utterance is more like the performance of a ritualized action than the expression of a lexical meaning to another person (Barrett, 1989). However, some of the infant's first words do seem to be concerned with communicating either internal states, such as pleasure or distress, or reactions to objects, such as surprise, recognition or rejection (the *expressive function*) or with directing the behaviour of other people (the *directive function*), such as ordering, requesting, obtaining attention and directing their attention (e.g. 'see' and 'go'; this is a further development of second order causality; see above).

These two functions of speech are mirrored by the infant's pre-linguistic gestures, for example, arm waving, hand flapping and object rejection are often used to express internal states, while open-handed reaching, arm raising, pointing and direct physical contact are often used to direct others' behaviour. This supports what we said earlier about there being considerable functional continuity between pre-linguistic and very early linguistic communication (Barrett, 1989).

Another characteristic of this stage is that single words are often used to convey a much more complex message, sometimes a whole sentence, in which case they are known as *holophrases*. So, 'milk' might, on one occasion, mean 'I want some more milk', on another occasion 'I don't want to finish my milk' and on a third 'I've just spilt my milk'. Greenfield and Smith (1976) see holophrases as precursors of later, more complex sentences: the child uses gestures, tone of voice and the situation to add the full meaning to the individual word. Of course, they are still very much dependent on the adult or perhaps older siblings making the 'correct' interpretation.

Nelson (1973) studied 18 babies and found that it took anywhere from 13 to 19 months to acquire a ten-word vocabulary (the average being 15 months) but after that vocabulary builds quite quickly, so that by 19–20 months, babies had a 50-word vocabulary. Despite individual differences, all 18 babies showed this 'vocabulary explosion' after the initial ten words. What kinds of words are they? Nelson identified six categories and calculated the percentage of the babies' first 50 words that each category represented in her sample; these are summarized in Table 26.1.

So the nouns (specific and general nominals) comprise 65 percent and action words another 13 percent, making 78 percent altogether. Interestingly, even the nouns were related in some way to things the child could do, for example the names of toys and food. It seems that it is not just the amount of exposure to objects and words that matters but whether the child can play with it, manipulate it, eat it and so on; active involvement with its environment will help determine many of the child's first words.

While the child is continuing to acquire new context-bound words, it is at the same time beginning to

---

1 *Specific numerals.* Names for unique objects, people or animals (14 percent).

2 *General nominals.* Names for classes of objects, people or animals, e.g. 'ball', 'car', 'milk', 'doggie', 'girl', 'he', 'that' (51 percent).

3 *Action words.* Describe or accompany actions or express or demand attention, e.g. 'bye-bye', 'up', 'look', 'hi', (13 percent).

4 *Modifiers.* Refers to properties or qualities of things, E.g. 'big', 'red'. 'pretty', hot', all gone', 'there', 'mine' (9 percent).

5 *Personal-social words.* Say something about a child's feelings or social relationships. e.g. 'ouch', 'please', 'no', 'yes', 'want', (8 percent).

6 *Function words.* Have only grammatical function, e.g. 'what', 'is', 'to', for', (4 percent).

TABLE 26.1 *The percentage of children's first 50 words falling into six categories (Nelson, 1973)*

de-contextualize many of these words as the single-word stage progresses (but this occurs at different times for different words). In addition, the child acquires many new *referential* words for labelling objects, i.e. words which are used from the start in a de-contextualized way (Barrett, 1989). Finally, as the single-word stage progresses, new communicative functions begin to emerge, namely answering and asking questions and providing comments on the people and objects in the child's immediate environment. These abilities enable children to participate in very simple conversations with other people.

● Two-word stage

This stage, like the earlier one, is universal but individual differences in the rate of development become more marked. Like the transition from babbling to one-word sentences, the move from the one-word to the two-word stage is also gradual. Initially, two-word sentences are produced relatively infrequently and children still rely primarily on single-word utterances. Multi-word utterances begin to predominate only at about 24 months.

Bee and Mitchell (1980) point out that as well as the continued development of the child's vocabulary, what becomes important now is the growth of understanding of grammar. They subdivide this third stage into two: stage 1 grammar (18–30 months) and stage 2 grammar (from 30 months).

Stage 1 grammar (18–30 months)

The child's speech is typically *telegraphic* (Brown, 1965). The essence of a telegram is that as much information as possible is conveyed in as few words as possible, so the words must be very economical and this is exactly what the child's speech is like:

● Only key words are used, those that contain the most information (Brown calls these *contentives*).
● Purely grammatical terms, e.g. the verb *to be*, plurals, possessives, are omitted (these are known as functional words or *functors*).
● There is a rigid word order, which seems to preserve the grammatically correct order and so helps preserve the meaning of the sentence. For example, if a child is asked 'Does Tanya want to go to sleep?' she might say, 'Tanya sleep' (or, later on, 'Tanya go sleep').

By contrast, adults do not rely exclusively on word order to express meaning; the passive form of a sentence is a good example ('Joelle ate the banana' and 'The banana was eaten by Joelle' both convey the same meaning, although the word order of each sentence is different).

Similarly, the child's imitations of adult sentences are simple but retain the word order of the original sentence, e.g. 'Jessica is playing with the dog' is imitated as 'Play dog' (*imitation by reduction*). Complementary to this is *imitation with expansion*, which is the adult's imitation of the child's utterances and involves inserting the 'missing' functors, e.g. 'Baby highchair' becomes 'Baby is in the highchair'. The rigid word order of the child's utterances make it easier to interpret their meaning, but gestures and the context still provide important clues (as in the one-word stage).

Several studies have shown that, compared with adult–adult speech, adults talking to children tend to use much shorter sentences, simplify the syntax, raise the pitch of their voice for emphasis and repeat or paraphrase much of what they say (*motherese* or *baby-talk register*) in order to achieve a mutual understanding with children who have not yet mastered the full complexity of language. Sensitivity to a child's vocabulary and intellectual and social knowledge is an example of a pragmatic rule for ensuring a degree of shared understanding (Greene, 1990) (this further supports the social interaction approach).

Clearly, the child's two-word utterances are not random combinations of words, but are systematic expressions of specific semantic relations. Some examples are shown in Table 26.2.

Brown (1970) distinguishes two main types of semantic relations:

1 those expressed by combining a single constant term or pivot word (e.g. 'more', 'all gone') with another word which refers to an object, action or attribute;
2 those which do not involve the use of constant or pivot words.

The appearance of two-word utterances can, therefore, be attributed to the child's acquisition of two different types of combinatorial rule, namely *pivotal* and *categorical rules*. There is considerable individual variation in the type of two-word utterances which different children produce, with some relying largely on pivotal rules and others relying primarily on categorical rules instead (Barrett, 1989).

Word order in two-word utterances seems to reflect the child's pre-linguistic knowledge. According to the *cognition hypothesis* (Cromer, 1974), language structures can only be used correctly when our

Two-word utterance	Semantic relation expressed	Combinatorial rules involved
That book	Nomination (of object, action or attribute)	
Hi belt	Notice (of object, action or attribute)	
More milk	Recurrence (of object, action or attribute)	Pivotal rules
All gone juice	Non-existence (of object, action or attribute)	
Big train	Attribute-object	
Mummy lunch	Possessor-possessed	
Book table	Object-location	
Walk street	Action-location	
Adam put	Agent-action	Categorical rules
Mummy sock	Agent-object	
Hit ball	Action-object	

TABLE 26.2 *Examples of two-word utterances and the semantic relations expressed by them. (Based on Barrett, 1989; Brown, 1970)*

cognitive structures enable us to do so. Children form schemas to understand the world and then talk about them; for example, object permanence is a necessary prerequisite for understanding that words can represent things – if the child didn't already understand the relationships between objects, people and events in the real world, its first words would be like random, unconnected lists. These are important concepts in Piaget's developmental theory and are consistent with his view of language development reflecting the child's stage of cognitive development (see Chapters 13 and 25).

Stage 2 grammar (from about 30 months)

This lasts until about four or five years of age and although it may be different for different languages, the rule-governed behaviour in language development is universal. Vocabulary grows rapidly but sentences also become longer and more complex. The increase in *mean length of utterance* (MLU) is due largely to the gradual inclusion of the functors that are left out of the telegraphic speech of stage 1 grammar. So stage 2 grammar really begins with the first use of purely grammatical words and continues for several years.

Brown (1973) has found that there is a distinct regularity among English-speaking children in the order in which the grammatical complexities are added. Similarly, de Villiers and de Villiers (1973) found that children the world over seem to acquire functional words in the same general order but at different rates. Each function word corresponds to a syntactic rule but when children begin to apply these rules, for example plurals, how do we know that they have actually learned a rule and are not just imitating what they have heard others say?

One demonstration of children's rule-learning ability was carried out by Berko (1958) (see Fig. 26.4). In their spontaneous speech, children show that they apply rules that they have inferred or deduced from all the speech going on around then. It is often

This is a wug

Now there is another one.
There are two of them.
There are two ———

FIGURE 26.4 *Berko's (1958) method of testing children's use of the rule for forming plurals. Children were shown a picture of a fictitious creature called a wug and were told 'This is a wug'. They were then shown a second picture in which there were two of these creatures and were told 'Now there is another one. There are two of them'. They were asked to complete the sentence 'There are two_____'. Three- and four-year-olds were able to answer correctly despite never having seen a wug before. They could not have been imitating anybody else's speech but were applying a rule about how to form plurals*

through their grammatical mistakes that children demonstrate this rule-governed behaviour, e.g. 'sheeps', 'geeses', 'mans', 'goed', 'wented'. Since it is extremely unlikely that the child has actually heard these words spoken (by adults), the child could not be simply imitating them. What the child seems to be doing is *overgeneralizing* the rule or *over-regularizing* the English language. Significantly, the child is not consciously aware that it has acquired these rules and could not say what they are; nor have they been deliberately taught by parents and yet they govern the child's speech.

By the age of four or five, basic grammatical rules have been learned and by five or six a child's language is remarkably like that of an adult. But typically, a five-year-old will have difficulty understanding passive sentences (e.g. if asked to act out 'The horse is kissed by the cow', the child will reverse the meaning, making the horse do the kissing). There are also a great number of irregular words still to be learned and this aspect of grammatical development will take several more years. However, all the basic skills have been acquired.

THEORIES OF LANGUAGE DEVELOPMENT

As we noted at the beginning of the chapter, trying to answer the question of why children develop language in the way they do involves the *nature–nurture* issue. Skinner's theory regards language as being learned through essentially the same processes as other behaviour, namely selective reinforcement, shaping and imitation (see Chapter 7), while according to Chomsky, language is an inherent, biologically determined capacity of human beings and the process of language development is essentially one of *acquisition* (as distinct from learning).

● Skinner's operant conditioning theory

In *Verbal Behaviour* (1957), Skinner applied the principles of operant conditioning to explain language development in children. In essence, he claimed that adults shape the baby's sounds into words and its words into sentences (i.e. correct grammar is reinforced and incorrect grammar is not) through *selective reinforcement*. Sometimes, the positive reinforcement comes in the form of the child

getting what it asks for; 'May I have some water?' produces a drink which then reinforces that form of words ('*mands*'):

Parents may provide reinforcement by becoming excited, poking, touching, patting and feeding children when they vocalize. A mother's delight upon hearing her child's first real word is exciting for the child and so acquiring language becomes reinforcing in itself. Skinner also refers to the imitation (*echoic responses*) of verbal labels ('*tacts*') which receive immediate reinforcement in the form of the approval of parents, etc. to the extent that they resemble the correct word.

But what is the evidence that parents do actually shape their children's speech? And even if parents are found to reinforce selectively in the way Skinner claims, does it necessarily have any influence on the child's grammar?

Brown *et al.* (1969) wanted to discover whether mothers' responses to their children's language depended on its grammatical correctness or on its presumed meaning. In most cases it was the truth value and not the grammatical correctness or complexity which the mothers responded to: they extract meaning from and interpret the child's incomplete and sometimes primitive sentences. Braine (1971) and Tizard *et al.* (1972) found that trying to correct grammatical mistakes or teach grammar has very little effect. Indeed, Nelson (1973) found that the children of mothers who systematically corrected their child's poor word pronunciation and rewarded good pronunciation actually developed vocabulary more slowly.

Slobin (1975) found that children learn grammatical rules despite their parents, who usually pay little attention to the grammatical structure of their child's speech and often, in fact, reinforce incorrect grammar. He claims that 'A mother is too engaged in interacting with a child to pay attention to the linguistic form of his utterance'. So, while parents usually respond to (reinforce) true statements and criticize or correct false ones, they pay little regard to their grammatical correctness and even if they did it would have little effect.

As for the role of imitation, it clearly has to be involved in the learning of accent and vocabulary. But when it comes to the complex aspects of language, namely syntax and semantics, the role played by imitation is much less obvious. As we saw earlier, when children do imitate adult sentences, they tend to reduce or convert them to their own, currently operating grammar: between 18 and 30 months the child's imitations are as telegraphic as its spontaneous speech (imitation by reduction). Again, a good deal of adult language is, in fact, ungrammatical, so that imitation alone could not explain how we ever learn 'correct' English. Even if we do not always speak grammatically ourselves, we still know what is good grammar and what is not.

Lenneberg (1967) cites the case of a boy who was totally dumb but who could hear and was quite normal mentally; he could understand language and obey verbal instructions, etc. but, of course, he could not imitate.

An evaluation of Skinner's theory

What selective reinforcement and imitation both fail to explain are:

- why native speakers of a language have the capacity to produce and understand an indefinitely large number of sentences that they have never heard before and which, indeed, may never have been uttered before by anyone. This is referred to as the *creativity of language* (or its 'open-endedness'), in contrast to the 'closed' nature of the vast majority of animal communication;(see above). As Chomsky (1968) says, 'The normal use of language is innovative, in the sense that much of what we say in the course of normal language use is entirely new, not a repetition of anything that we have heard before ... ';
- the distinction between *competence* (implicit knowledge or understanding of the rules of language) and *performance* (actual use of language on particular occasions); for Skinner, there is only performance. In an important sense, we are all linguists: we may not be able to describe the structures of our language in technical terms and our performance is sometimes less than perfect (we make grammatical mistakes, stumble over our words and so on), but we can distinguish between mistakes and well-formed sentences (by reference to our competence);
- the spontaneous use of grammatical rules, which have never been explicitly heard or taught. These rules, as we have seen, are often overgeneralized, resulting in linguistic mistakes, but they are clearly not the product of imitation or reinforcement. Indeed, we have also seen that children are largely impervious to parental attempts to correct their grammatical errors.
- the child's ability to understand the meaning of sentences, as opposed to word meaning: the meaning of a sentence is not simply the sum of the meanings of individual words. As Neisser

(1967) points out, the structure of language is comparable to the structure of perception as described by the Gestalt psychologists (see Chapter 9). Skinner may be able to account for how the child learns the meaning of individual nouns and verbs (since they have an obvious reference), but what about the meaning of grammatical terms (functors)?

- the universal sequence of stages of language development.

● Chomsky's LAD and the biological approach

The major alternative to Skinner's operant conditioning account has two main strands: (i) Chomsky's (1965, 1968) and McNeill's (1970) innate *language acquisition device* (LAD); and (ii) biological aspects of language.

Chomsky's central idea is that children are born already programmed in some way to learn language. LAD is a hypothetical model (i.e. an attempt to explain language development by inferring what must be going on in the child's brain but without being able to observe it directly). It is based on the theory that individuals are born with the ability to formulate and understand all types of sentences even though they have never heard them before.

To understand properly what Chomsky is proposing, let us look at one of the major criticisms he made of Skinner's theory. He argued that Skinner fundamentally misunderstands the nature of language; it is infinitely more complex and less predictable than Skinner believes. For example, it uses *structure-dependent operations*. Aitchison (1983) points out that sometimes language does involve simple slot-filling operations (which corresponds to Skinner's simplistic view); for example:

a Bees/love/honey.
b I/want/my/tea.
c My brother/has hit/me.

In these examples, each sentence is allocated a number of 'slots' and then units are slotted into each hole. But there is a lot more going on than this: 'It is evident that more is involved in sentence structure than insertion of lexical items in grammatical frames' (Chomsky, 1959). For example:

d Performing fleas/can be/amusing.
e Playing tiddlywinks/can be/amusing.

have the same superficial structure but rather different meanings. In (d) 'performing' describes the fleas, but in (e), 'playing' is a verb. As soon as we try to find other words to fit into the second slot, we run into problems: 'are' fits in with (d), but not (e) and vice versa with 'is'. Even more ambiguous are the following:

f Cleaning ladies can be delightful.
g The missionary was ready to eat.

It was examples like these which led Chomsky to distinguish between the deep and surface structure of a sentence.

When we hear a spoken sentence, we do not 'process' or retain the grammatical structure, the actual words or phrases used (i.e. the *surface structure*) but instead we transform it into another form, which more or less corresponds to the meaning of the sentence (i.e. *deep structure*). This understanding or knowledge of how to transform the meaning of a sentence into the words that make up the sentence and vice versa (i.e. *transformational grammar*) is what Chomsky believes is innate and it is this innate ability which enables us to produce an infinite number of meaningful sentences.

For example, the same surface structure can have different deep structures, as in examples (f) and (g). Can you work out the two meanings of each sentence? Conversely, different surface structures can have the same deep structure, for example:

h The dog chased the cat.
i The cat was chased by the dog.

Our ability to understand both meanings of (f) and (g) and the single meaning of (h) and (i) is based on transformational grammar, which is essentially what LAD comprises. Children are equipped with the ability to learn the rules that transform deep structure into various surface structures (transformations). This is done by looking for certain kinds of linguistic features (linguistic universals) which are common to all languages. For example, all known languages make use of consonants and vowels, syllables, subject-predicate, modifier and noun, verb and object. Collectively, these universals provide the deep structure.

Chomsky argues that these features must be universal because all children can learn any language to which they are exposed with equal ease: a child born in England of English parents, if flown over to China soon after birth and brought up by a Chinese family, will learn to speak Chinese just as efficiently as any native-born Chinese (and just as efficiently as it would have learnt English). Only some kind of LAD, Chomsky argues, can account for the child's

learning and knowledge of grammatical rules, in view of the limited and often ungrammatical and incomplete samples of speech that a child hears. (Lyons (1970) notes that transformational grammar is not intended as a psychological model of how people construct and understand utterances. The grammar of a language, as seen by Chomsky, is an idealized description of the linguistic competence of native speakers of the language; any model of how this competence is applied in actual performance must take into account certain psychologically relevant facts such as memory, attention, the workings of the nervous system and so on.)

Is there any evidence to support Chomsky?

Much of the supporting evidence which does exist comes from study of the biological aspects of language.

We have already seen that many of the stages of language development are universal, which suggests the role of maturation. We also saw that deaf babies babble at the same time and in the same way as hearing babies – this too implies a maturational underpinning. The ability to discriminate different speech sounds also seems to be innate. Our vocal organs, breathing apparatus, auditory systems and brain are all highly specialized for spoken communication.

As we noted above, adult languages all over the world have certain important features in common (linguistic universals) and transformational grammar is acquired in some form by all human beings, regardless of culture. This universality of language features may reflect the fact that all human brains are 'built' in a certain way and this matching of language structures and brain structure could account for the ease with which babies learn their native tongue.

Lenneberg (1964, 1967) studied normal and Down's syndrome children and found a consistently strong correlation between motor milestones (e.g. sitting, crawling, standing, walking) and language milestones (e.g. babbling, one-word sentences, two-word sentences). Although the rate of motor and language development is much slower in Down's syndrome children, the correlation between them is as high as it is for normal children. This again strongly suggests the role of maturation in language development, which Lenneberg says is much more like learning to walk than learning to read.

The built-in tendency to develop language in some form or other is dramatically illustrated by the case

BOX 26.2 Key study: Using language in a silent, signless world

Goldin-Meadow and Feldman (1977) studied four congenitally deaf children who developed what looked like stage 1 grammar in their gestures, although their parents did not know how to use sign language, they were not exposed to any sign language and they could hear no speech. They were observed from the time they were 18 months old and it was found that they created a sign language, first for individual objects and actions (comparable to holophrases) and then later combined them into two-gesture sentences. Although confined to things that were immediately present, they were beginning to use the language process on their own with no encouragement or training from parents. So it seems that LAD may be applied to gestural language as well as to speech. Language is very difficult to suppress, even in adverse environmental circumstances.

BOX 26.3 The case of Genie (Curtiss, 1977; based on Skuse, 1984)

One of the most extraordinary cases of severe deprivation yet reported is that of Genie, who was born in the USA in April 1957. She was found aged 13 years 7 months, a painfully thin child who appeared 6–7 years old. From the age of 20 months she had been confined to a small room under conditions of extreme physical restraint. In this room she received minimal care from a mother who was herself rapidly losing her sight. Genie was physically punished by her father if she made any sound. Most of the time she was kept harnessed into an infant's potty-chair, but at night she was confined in a homemade sleeping bag fashioned like a straitjacket and lay in an infant's crib covered with wire mesh. She was fed only infant food. Genie's father was so convinced that she would die, he promised that the mother could seek help for the child if she lived beyond 12, but when this age had come and gone and she survived, he reneged on his promise. It was not for another 18 months that her mother managed to escape, leaving home and husband to seek help for the child.

At this time, Genie could not stand erect and could walk only with difficulty, shuffling her feet and swaying from side to side. Having been beaten for making any noise, she had learned to suppress almost all vocalization save a whimper. She salivated copiously, spitting onto anything at hand, and was doubly incontinent. Curtiss comments: 'Genie was unsocialized, primitive, hardly human'.

On her discovery, she could understand a few words ('rattle', 'bunny', 'red', 'blue', 'green' and 'brown') to which she always responded in the same way. But essentially she had to learn her first language at 13½ years of age and she never developed normal language. At age 18, her sentences were short and lacked important aspects of grammar, such as auxiliary verbs, question formation and use of pronouns and she had difficulty understanding complex syntax. Her vocabulary expanded and she could hold a conversation, but her use of intonation was poor and only those who knew her well could understand much of what she said. The fact that it was possible for Genie to learn any language at all tends to detract from Lenneberg's idea of a critical period, but the obvious retardation of her speech is consistent with at least a 'sensitive period' hypothesis.

of four congenitally deaf children (Goldin-Meadow and Feldman, 1977); see Box 26.2.

Lenneberg also points out that almost all human beings acquire language, regardless of IQ. The only exceptions (apart from individuals who are severely retarded) are 'wild' or 'wolf' children, who are thought to have been raised by wild animals. However, it has been suggested that such children may have been abandoned at birth because they were brain damaged in some way.

Lenneberg believes that the years leading to puberty (10–11) constitute a critical period for language development. His argument centres around the relative lack of specialization of the brain while it is still developing, so that brain-damaged children who lose their language abilities can relearn at least some of them as other, non-damaged parts of the brain seem to take over the language function. By contrast, adults or adolescents suffering an equivalent amount of damage will be unable to regain abilities corresponding to the site of the injury because their brains have already 'set', i.e. become specialized. For most of us, our left hemisphere is dominant for language (see Chapter 3). However, many of these claims have been disputed. For example, several researchers have suggested that specialization or localization of brain function may be present at birth.

Studies of children reared in conditions of extreme (de)privation also suggest that the first ten years or so may not necessarily be the critical period that Lenneberg maintains (Box 26.3).

An evaluation of Chomsky's theory

According to Aitchison (1983), Chomsky is substantially correct when he assumes that children are 'wired' with an innate hypothesis-making device. They automatically 'know' that language is rule governed and they make a succession of hypotheses about the rules underlying the speech they hear around them. However, he goes on to claim that a child's brain naturally contains a considerable amount of specific information about language (transformational grammar) – LAD comprises both a hypothesis-making device and transformational grammar.

Aitchison rejects this second claim (what she calls 'Content Cuthbert') and, in preference, opts for 'Process Peggy', a process approach whereby children are seen as having an inbuilt puzzle-solving equipment which enables them to process linguistic data. She cites Sampson (1980), according to whom no special advance knowledge of what language is like is necessary because children are highly efficient puzzle-solvers in all areas of human behaviour – language is just one type of puzzle which their high level of general intelligence enables them to solve fast and well.

By contrast, Chomsky believes that an innate language ability exists independently of other innate abilities – the mind is 'constituted of "mental organs" just as specialized and differentiated as those of the body' (1979) and 'Language is a system ... easy to isolate among the various mental faculties' (1979; see Gardner's theory of multiple intelligences; Chapter 28).

An alternative explanation of the rule-bound nature of children's speech is that it arises from the child's pre-linguistic knowledge, which we discussed earlier on; this represents a move away from the grammatical competence approach inspired by Chomsky and McNeill.

TEACHING LANGUAGE TO NON-HUMAN ANIMALS

Another way of investigating the nature–nurture issue is to look at attempts that have been made to teach language to non-human animals. Until recently, it was generally believed that language ability is confined to humans: Lenneberg claims that it represents a species-specific behaviour, common to all humans and found only in humans. But clearly, if non-humans can be taught to use language, then they have the capacity for language (although it does not appear spontaneously, it must be latent in them) and so we would have to revise our ideas as to what makes us different from other species. (Chomsky, as we have seen, also believes that language is unique to human beings.)

The obvious subjects for such language training are our closest evolutionary relatives, chimpanzees and gorillas, the non-human primates. But before considering the findings, we should look again at what defines language. Clearly, speech and language are not identical (although we often equate them) – parrots can 'talk' but they are not capable of language because there is no meaning or understanding in the sounds they produce. (This is why we call rote learning 'parrot-fashion' learning, because it does not require understanding, just recall.) In Chomsky's terms, the parrot displays no linguistic competence.

So how can we define language in a way that will prove useful for evaluating the results of studies where humans have tried to teach it to non-humans (who do not speak)? Hockett (1960) proposed 13 'design features' of language (Fig. 26.5). Based on these, Aitchison (1983) proposes that ten criteria should be sufficient (not all of these are included in Hockett's list); these are shown in Table 26.3.

By analysing human and animal language in terms of all ten criteria, Aitchison concludes that four are unique to humans, namely 3, 8, 9 and 10. It is in terms of these criteria that we shall evaluate attempts to teach language to non-human primates.

Early attempts to teach chimpanzees to speak were almost totally unsuccessful. Kellogg and Kellogg (1933) raised Gua with their own child and treated them exactly alike. Although she could understand a total of 70 words or commands, Gua failed to utter a single word. Hayes and Hayes (1951) used operant conditioning in what was the first deliberate attempt to teach human language to a non-human – Viki, a baby chimp. By age three, she could say 'up' and 'cup' and (less convincingly) 'mama' and 'papa'. It became obvious that chimps' vocal apparatus is unsuited to making English speech sounds, but this does not rule out the possibility that they may still be capable of learning language in some non-spoken form. This is precisely what several psychologists have tried to demonstrate since the 1960s (see Table 26.4).

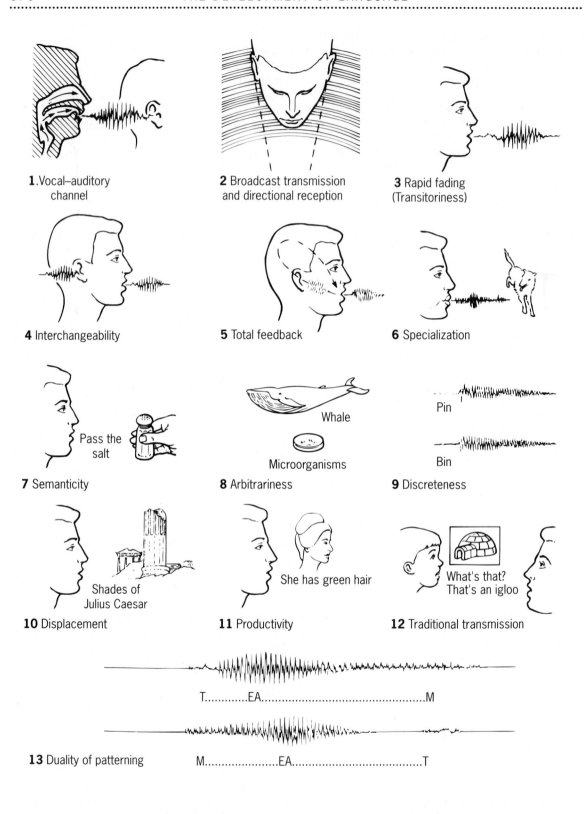

FIGURE 26.5 *Thirteen design features of language (Hockett, 1960)*

1 Use of the vocal–auditory channel
2 Arbitrariness (use of neutral symbols – words – to denote objects, etc.)
3 Semanticity (use of symbols to mean or refer to objects/actions, etc.)
4 Cultural transmission (handing down the language from generation to generation)
5 Spontaneous usage (freely initiating speech, etc.)
6 Turn taking (conversation is a two-way process)
7 Duality (organization into basic sounds plus combinations/sequences of these)
8 Displacement (reference to things not present in time or space)
9 Structure dependence (the patterned nature of language and use of 'structured chunks, e.g. word order)
10 Creativity (what Brown (1972) calls productivity – the ability to produce and understand an infinite number of novel utterances)

TABLE 26.3 *Ten criteria for language proposed by Aitchison (1983, based on Hockett, 1960)*

● Washoe and American Sign Language

Gardner and Gardner (1969) took advantage of the fact that chimps are extremely nimble-fingered (they can groom themselves and others, peel fruit, make simple tools, use a screwdriver, wind watches, thread needles and so on) to teach Washoe American sign language (ASL or Ameslan). This is the sign language used by many deaf people in the USA and is based on a series of gestures, each of which corresponds to a word; many gestures visually represent aspects of the word's meaning. ASL also has devices for signalling verb tense and other grammatical structures and it is fully adequate for expressing everything that can be spoken.

Washoe's training began when she was about one year old. The Gardners created for her as human an environment as possible (her 'house' was a house trailer), with social companions, objects and daily play activities, including word or sign games. They signed to Washoe and to one another in her presence (just as deaf parents might) and whenever she made a correct sign, she was positively reinforced. Sometimes her natural gestures were close enough to the correct signs to permit shaping and her fingers were placed in the correct position. After four years of training, Washoe had about 130 signs.

In many ways her progress was similar to a young child learning spoken language. Once she had learned a particular sign, she quickly generalized it

Study	Subject	Method of language training
Gardner & Gardner (1969)	Washoe (female chimp)	American sign language (ASL or Ameslan). Based on a series of gestures, each corresponding to a word. Many gestures visually represent aspects of the word's meaning
Premack (1971)	Sarah (female chimp)	Small plastic symbols of various shapes and colours, each symbol standing for a word; they could be arranged on a special magnetized board. E.g. a mauve △ = 'apple'; a pale blue ◇ =' insert'; a red ☐ = 'banana'
Rumbaugh *et al.* (1977)/Savage-Rumbaugh *et al.* (1980)	Lana (female chimp)	Special typewriter controlled by a computer. Machine had 50 keys each displaying a geometric pattern representing a word in a specially devised language ('Yerkish'). When Lana typed, the pattern appeared on the screen in front of her ◈ 'Lana' ◉ 'Eat'
Patterson (1978, 1979, 1980)	Koko (female gorilla)	American sign language
Terrace (1979)	Nim Chimpsky (male chimp)	American sign language

Operant conditioning is used in all these studies when signs, etc. are correctly used.

TABLE 26.4 *The major studies which have attempted to teach language to non-human primates*

to appropriate activities or objects. For example, 'more' was signed to request more tickling, more hair brushing, more swinging and a second helping of food; she also overgeneralized, as we have seen young children typically do.

Significantly, as soon as Washoe had learned 8–10 signs, she spontaneously began to combine them, forming sentences such as 'more sweet', 'listen dog' and 'Roger come'; later she combined three or more. By age five, her command of language was roughly equivalent to that of a three-year-old child. It seemed that she did acquire syntax and could combine signs in various ways. But in other respects, Washoe's progress was quite different from a child's. She was not exposed to sign language until she was a year old and the Gardners had only just acquired ASL as a 'second language'. More recently, they have been working with chimps that have been exposed since birth to people who are fluent in ASL and the chimps seem to be learning much faster.

Fouts (1972), one of the Gardners' former assistants, has been trying to study how chimps might use ASL with each other and whether chimp mothers teach it to their offspring. It was hoped that Washoe might spontaneously teach her own babies but, unfortunately, they both died soon after birth. Since then, Washoe has adopted a baby chimp called Loulis. Experiments began in 1979 and Washoe began signing to Loulis daily. Loulis has imitated a number of Washoe's signs, but it is not yet clear if he understands what they mean.

● Alternatives to ASL

Premack (1971) taught Sarah a language based on small plastic symbols of varying shapes and colours; each plastic symbol stood for a word. She learned to construct sentences by arranging symbols on a special magnetized board. (This is easier than learning ASL because the symbols were all in front of her and so she did not have to remember them; but she was 'mute' when she did not have her symbols with her.) Sarah was raised in a cage and had much less contact with humans than Washoe. Once again, operant conditioning was used, e.g. if she correctly chose the symbol for a banana, she would receive the banana as a reinforcement. In this way, she developed a small but impressive vocabulary, making compound sentences and answering simple questions; however, she was unable to generate new sentences of her own.

Rumbaugh *et al.* (1977) used a different kind of approach again with Lana. They taught her to operate a special typewriter controlled by a computer. The machine had 50 keys, each displaying a geometric configuration or pattern representing a word in a specially devised language called Yerkish. When Lana typed a configuration it appeared on a screen in front of her. She spontaneously learned to correct herself by checking the sequence of configurations on the screen – she learned to read! Not only did Lana respond to humans who 'conversed' with her via the computer, but she initiated some of the conversations and when confronted with an object for which she had not been taught a word, she created one. For example, when seeing a ring for the first time she labelled it as a 'finger bracelet' (combining two words she already knew).

Finally, Patterson (1978, 1979, 1980) trained Koko, a female gorilla. She used ASL and, after seven years of training, Koko has mastered almost 400 signs. She also understands many equivalent English words for these signs. She has developed syntax and a number of novel sentences; she has also invented 20 of her own combinations of signs for 'nail file', 'eye make-up', 'runny nose' and 'obnoxious'! Koko's hearing is excellent and she can make subtle auditory language discriminations. For example, one day in a 'discussion' about time, she signed 'lemon'. Her thumb is too short to make the sign for 'eleven', so instead she signed 'lemon o'clock', a like-sounding word: 11 o'clock happens to be the time she has her morning snack!

● An evaluation

Dworetzky (1981) claims that speaking to a gorilla is like glimpsing inside the mind of an alien who sees some things in a different way, sometimes a metaphorically beautiful way (see Table 26.5). Koko can use language to express anger ('red mad gorilla') and she has even lied by blaming others, claiming events which never happened and deliberately describing acts differently from how they were. This represents a quite sophisticated use of language.

Terrace (1979), after five years of working with his own chimp, Nim Chimpsky, concludes that although chimps can acquire a large vocabulary, they are not capable of producing original sentences. He argues that the great apes have been operantly conditioned to make certain signs in order to get what they want and that they are often inadvertently cued by their trainers to produce these signs in sequence; the apes are not really aware of what the signs mean.

Subject of study	Criteria of language			
	Semanticity	**Displacement**	**Structure dependence**	**Creativity (productivity)**
Washoe	After 4 years, about 130 signs Could generalize from one situation to another (e.g. 'more')	Some evidence of this e.g. could ask for or refer to absent objects/ people ('more milk', 'all gone cup')	Didn't always care about sign order e.g. as likely to sign 'sweet go' as 'go sweet'. But in later reports (1971/ 75/78) it's claimed she eventually became consistent	Once 8–10 signs learned, spontaneously began to combine them e.g. 'gimme tickle' (come and tickle me), 'listen eat' (listen to the dinner gong), 'go sweet' (take me to the raspberry bushes), 'open food drink' (open the fridge),'hurry gimme tooth-brush' 'Roger Washoe tickle'
Sarah	Over 100 words including complex ideas, e.g. 'colour of', 'some', 'different', 'if ... then'	No evidence	Trained to use fixed word order, no reward if order incorrect. Could obey instructions and answer simple questions	Could reproduce compound sentences previously rewarded but couldn't spontaneously produce new sentences. Didn't hold 'conversa-tions' like Washoe
Lana	Over 100 symbols. Could generalize	Had been taught 'put' and 'in' in connection with putting a ball into a box. Soon after, one of her trainers, Tim, was late with her morning milk. She spontaneously requested: 'Tim put milk in machine'	Trained to use fixed word order (as with Sarah). But could distinguish between 'Lana groom Tim' and 'Tim groom Lana'	'Apple which is orange' (orange).'Banana which is green' (cucumber)
Koko	After 7 years training, nearly 400 signs (also understands many English words for those signs). Generalizations e.g. 'straw' (drinking straw) generalized to cigarettes/ plastic tubing/ car radio aerial	She supposedly apologized for a biting incident 3 days before. When shown bite mark on Penny's arm, she signed: 'Sorry bite scratch wrong bite'. (Penny) 'Why bite?' (Koko) 'Because mad' (Penny) 'Why mad?' (Koko) 'Don't know	No evidence	'Cookie rock' (sweet or roll) 'Penny toilet dirty devil (when angry with her trainer) 'Bottle match' (cigarette lighter) 'White tiger' (zebra) 'Quiet chase' (hide and seek) 'Look mask' (view master) 'False mouth' (nose) 'Elephant baby' (Pinocchio doll) 'Eye-hat' (mask)
Nim Chimpsky	Acquired many signs but not used to make longer sentences as time passed	No evidence	Had a statistical preference for putting certain words in certain order (e.g. 'more' verb taking an object) No evidence of rules	Only 12 percent of utterances were spontaneous

TABLE 26.5 *Summary of major findings of primate studies in relation to four criteria of language*

Looking at Table 26.5, the most consistent evidence seems to be for semanticity and creativity, while the least convincing evidence relates to displacement and structure dependence. As for Washoe's apparent failure to show structure dependence, Aitchison (1983) suggests four reasons:

1 the Gardners' overeagerness may have led them to reward her every time she signed correctly (regardless of order), so that the idea that order was important may never have been learnt;
2 it may be easier to preserve order with words than with signs, e.g. deaf adults are also inconsistent in their word order;
3 this may have been a temporary, intermediate stage before she eventually learnt to keep to a fixed order (the Gardners in fact claim (1971, 1975, 1978, 1980) that she did so);
4 she did not and could not understand the essentially patterned nature of language.

Both Sarah and Lana were trained to use a fixed order (and were not rewarded if they deviated from this). However, Sarah could obey instructions and answer simple instructions, while Lana could distinguish between 'Lana groom Tim' and 'Tim groom Lana'. Koko does not seem to have kept to any particular sign order, while Nim Chimpsky showed a statistical preference for putting certain words in a certain order (i.e. they were more likely to appear in one position rather than another) but no evidence of understanding any rules.

Petitto and Seidenberg (1979) conclude that 'Repetitive, inconsistently structured strings are in fact characteristic of ape signing': Nim's longest recorded utterance is: 'Eat drink eat drink, eat Nim eat Nim, drink eat drink eat, Nim eat Nim eat, me eat me eat.'

● Is the language of children and chimps qualitatively different?

If we evaluate these studies by comparing chimps with children, then even semanticity turns out to be problematical. Is the correct use of signs to refer to things a sufficient criterion of semanticity? Savage-Rumbaugh et al. (1980) seriously doubt whether any of the apes (including their own, Lana) used the individual elements of their vocabularies as words. Terrace (1987) suggests that a strong case can be made for the hypothesis that the deceptively simple ability to use a symbol as a name required a cognitive advance in the evolution of human intelligence at

least as significant as the advances that led to grammatical competence.

The function of much of a child's initial vocabulary of names is to inform another person (usually the adult) that it has noticed something (MacNamara, 1980); often the child refers to the object spontaneously, showing obvious delight from the sheer act of naming, something which has not been observed in apes. Could any amount of training produce an ape with such ability? MacNamara thinks not, for the simple reason that the act of referring is not learnt but is a 'primitive of cognitive psychology' (and is a necessary precursor of naming). By contrast, chimps usually try to 'acquire' an object (approach it, explore it, etc.) and show no signs of trying to communicate the fact that they have noticed an object as an end in itself (Terrace, 1987).

This, in turn, relates to something we discussed earlier regarding the pre-linguistic stage of development, namely the 'emergence of communicative intentionality' and second order causality. Remember that this is to do with the child's learning to bring about changes in its environment through influencing the behaviour of other people (via the child's use of gesture, etc.). This is a view of communication as having an instrumental function (i.e. it helps to get things done).

Several critics have claimed that the linguistic abilities of chimps amount to a wholly 'instrumental use' of symbols. Referring to Savage-Rumbaugh's work with Kanzi (a pygmy chimp, supposedly spectacularly intelligent), Seidenberg and Petitto (1986) claim that Kanzi 'may not know what the symbols mean' but only 'how to produce behaviours that others can interpret'. However, Gauker (1990) argues that ' ... we might do well to view "knowing what symbols mean" as nothing other than an understanding of more or less sophisticated instrumental uses of symbols ... even in human beings linguistic understanding consists in a grasp of the causal relations into which linguistic signs may enter ... '. As we saw earlier, the use of words as a communicative tool can be seen during the 'emergence of communicative intentionality'.

● Helping chimps be more like children

Since the 1980s, Savage-Rumbaugh, at the Yerkes Primate Centre and Georgia State University, has been working with chimps in a way which is much more like how children acquire language (and in certain respects more like the pioneers in this field, the

Kelloggs' and the Hayes'). Instead of putting the chimps through rote learning of symbols, gradually building up a vocabulary a symbol at a time (production-based training), she aimed to use a large vocabulary of symbols from the start, using them as language is used around human children. This way, they might pick up language as children do. This represents a move away from an emphasis on grammatical structure (at least in the beginning) and towards comprehension:

> It seemed reasonable to me – obvious even – that comprehension was an important element of language, that language is first acquired through comprehension, and that production flows from that. (Savage-Rumbaugh, quoted in Lewin, 1991)

This new approach was applied on a limited scale with Austin and Sherman, two common chimps. But it really got going with some pygmy chimps (bonobos), which are slightly smaller than common chimps and said to be more vocal and more communicative through facial expressions and gestures.

Work with Matata began in 1981. But Matata did not come alone – six months earlier she had kidnapped a newborn infant and kept it as her own. This was Kanzi. While Savage-Rumbaugh and her colleagues were working with Matata, Kanzi ran around, generally playing about and getting into mischief. Instead of ASL, Savage-Rumbaugh used an extensive 'lexigram', a matrix of 256 geometrical shapes on a board. Instructors touch the symbols, which represent verbs and nouns, to create simple requests or commands. At the same time, the sentence is spoken, with the aim of testing comprehension of spoken English.

Although she was clearly intelligent in many ways, Matata was a poor learner and only used about six symbols. However, despite no attempt to teach Kanzi anything, he had picked up the symbols Matata knew, as naturally as human children do. From that point onwards, an even greater effort was made to place language learning in a naturalistic context. Kanzi acquired a sister, Mulika, when he was 2½ years old and they grew up together.

By age ten (1991), Kanzi has a vocabulary of some 200 words, but it is not the size of his vocabulary but what the words apparently mean to him that is impressive. He was given verbal requests to do things, in sentence form, by someone out of his sight. Savage-Rumbaugh's assistants in the same room with Kanzi wore earphones so they could not hear the instructions and so could not cue Kanzi, even unconsciously. None of the sentences was practised and

each one was different. 'Can you put the raisins in the bowl?' and 'Can you give the cereal to Karen?' posed no problems for Kanzi. Nor did 'Can you go to the colony room and get the telephone?' (there were four or five objects in the colony room, which were not normally there). Already, these kinds of abilities went beyond what Austin and Sherman could do; for one thing, they had been unable to learn and understand spoken English.

More testing still was the instruction 'Go to the colony room and get the orange' with an orange in front of Kanzi. This caused him confusion about 90 percent of the time. But if asked to 'Get the orange that's in the colony room', he did so without hesitation, suggesting that the syntactically more complex phrase is producing better comprehension than the simple one (Savage-Rumbaugh, cited in Lewin, 1991). Kanzi showed this level of comprehension when he was nine years old, but not when he was younger than six; he also showed understanding of the syntactic rule that in two-word utterances, action precedes object and, significantly, he went from a random ordering initially to a clear, consistent preference:

> Language training that is production-based as was the case for Sherman and Austin, is sufficiently detrimental that it may be said to disrupt the 'normal course' of language acquisition in the ape.
>
> When the environment is structured in a way that makes it possible for the chimpanzee to acquire language much as does the normal child, by coming to understand what is said to it before it elects to produce utterances, the perspective of language acquisition and function that emerges is very different from that seen by Sherman and Austin. (Savage-Rumbaugh, 1990)

Kanzi was the first to demonstrate that observational exposure is sufficient for the acquisition of lexical and vocal symbols. Three other chimps (two pygmy and one common) have also learned symbols without training (so Kanzi's ability is neither unique to him nor his species). According to Savage-Rumbaugh (1990), observational learning is a more powerful method of language acquisition than is symbol training, given that the ape can manage to imitate the movements required to produce the symbols. When words are learned observationally, it is difficult to offer an explanation of how the behaviour was acquired and what served as the reward; for example, how can a chimp (or a child, for that matter) know where one word ends and the next begins, i.e. what the units are, if it is only 'exposed to language' and not deliberately taught it? Savage-Rumbaugh's answer is through the learning of routines which emerge out of daily life that has been constructed for the chimpanzees.

● A day in the life of a chimp exposed to language

A typical day (for Kanzi and two other chimps, Panbanisha and Panpanzee) is like a field-based pre-school for apes. Food can be found throughout a 50-acre forest. They have much time off for social play with different companions, interesting places to visit, plus time devoted to structured testing, during which the chimp is asked to sit quietly and apply itself as fully as possible. Caretakers' only instructions are to communicate with them much as one would with very young children, except that they must accompany their speech with pointing to lexical symbols. They talk about things which are concrete and immediate and clarify their intent with gestures and actions. More input focuses on where they and the chimps are going, what they're both going to do next and what just happened to them. There is no insistence that the chimps 'talk' but they respond if they do so spontaneously. 'Conversations' move from topic to topic with the natural flow of the day and routines include nappy changing, getting ready to go outside, bathing, riding in the car, looking at a book, blowing bubbles, putting things in the backpack, visiting other apes, playing games of tickle and travelling down various forest trails.

Apes move from passive observer of routine towards active participant, to primitive initiator to a communicator symbolically announcing its intentions to another party. At first, symbols are only understood within an established routine; later it will be understood and used beyond the routine itself. The driving force that moves the ape from symbol comprehension to symbol production is the desire to exert some control over what happens next (Savage-Rumbaugh, 1990).

● Conclusions: is language uniquely human after all?

According to Aitchison (1983), even though intelligent animals seem capable of coping with some of the basic features of human language, they do not seem predisposed to cope with them; by contrast, the apparent ease with which humans acquire language, compared with apes, supports the suggestion that they are innately programmed to do so. Similarly, although these chimps have grasped some of the rudiments of human language, what they have learned

and the speed at which they learn it is qualitatively different from those of human beings (Carroll, 1986).

Aitchison and Carroll seem to be talking for a majority of psychologists. However, the criticisms of ape studies and the conclusions that have been drawn from them are based on the production-based studies (as summarized in Tables 26.2 and 26.3). Savage-Rumbaugh believes that there is only a quantitative difference (i.e. one of degree) between ape and human language. Referring to criticisms by Terrace that Kanzi still only uses his symbols to get things done, to ask for things, rather than to share his perception of the world, she acknowledges that Kanzi uses his symbols for these purposes, but so do young children. In fact, the predominant symbol use of normal children is 'requesting': while Kanzi's percentage is higher,' ... he can reliably tell you some things, such as when is he going to be "good" or "bad", when he has just eaten or where he is headed while travelling. Terrace has consistently refused to acknowledge this' (Savage-Rumbaugh, quoted in Lewin, 1991).

Kanzi's capacity for comprehension far outstrips his capacity for producing language using the lexigram and this makes him extremely frustrated, at which times he often becomes very vocal, making high-pitched squeaks. Is he trying to speak?

> And if Kanzi were to talk, what would he say? Maybe the first thing he'd say is that he is fed up with Terrace claiming that apes don't have language. (Lewin, 1991)

CHAPTER SUMMARY

- Language plays a central part in our lives and many, including Chomsky, believe that it is the distinctive characteristic of the human species.
- Explanations of language development range from Skinner's extreme empiricist operant conditioning to Chomsky's nativism, in the form of an innate language acquisition device (LAD).
- Linguists are concerned with the structure of language, while psycholinguists study how language is acquired, perceived, understood and produced, its relationship to other abilities and so on.
- The communication systems of non-human species are extremely limited compared with human language, which allows us to transmit and understand an infinite variety of messages; what makes this possible is the rule system called grammar/mental grammar, which comprises phonology, semantics and syntax.

- Phonology refers to the sound system of a language; phonological rules constrain the permitted sequences of phonemes. Semantics is the study of meaning; it includes morphology, the rules for combining morphemes. Syntax refers to the rules for combining words into phrases and sentences; one important syntactic rule is word order.

- Psycholinguists see grammars as representing the implicit knowledge that native speakers have about their language and study how this knowledge is related to actual language use, including how children acquire complex linguistic skills.

- Chomsky's theory of transformational grammar (TG) has had a tremendous impact on the psychology of language. Central to TG are phrase structure rules and transformational rules. In addition, universal grammar, linguistic universals and a language acquisition device (LAD) help explain how the child acquires a complex grammar.

- Children seem to be programmed by nature to learn language, with maturation playing a crucial role. The first year of life is a pre-linguistic phase. Babbling involves the production of phonemes; phonemic expansion is followed by phonemic contraction. The ability to discriminate between speech sounds seems to be innate.

- It seems that the first 12–18 months is a time when pre-linguistic communication prepares the child for acquiring complex syntactic rules. Language is 'mapped' onto a social world through proto-conversations, visual co-orientation and joint attention and formats which are what Bruner's language acquisition support system (LASS) consists of.

- The use of words as a communicative tool can be seen during the 'emergence of communicative intentionality', which involves second order causality.

- The one-word stage usually begins at 12 months. The baby's first words are often 'invented' and context-bound (non-referential). Some early words serve the expressive or directive function, which are mirrored by the infant's pre-linguistic gestures. Single words are often used to convey a more complex message or whole sentence (holophrase).

- There is a vocabulary explosion after the first few words appear, most falling into the categories of specific and general nominals and action words. Early words are becoming de-contextualized and more new words are being used referentially from the start.

- The two-word stage is divided into stage 1 grammar and stage 2 grammar. In stage 1 grammar, speech is typically telegraphic (comprising contentives and omitting functors) and there is a rigid word order. The child's imitation by reduction is complemented by the adult's imitation with expansion. Adults also use motherese/baby-talk register.

- The child's two-word utterances are based on pivotal and categorical rules. According to the cognition hypothesis, word order reflects the child's pre-linguistic knowledge and the development of cognitive structures and schemas, such as object permanence.

- During stage 2 grammar, there is an increase in mean length of utterance (MLU), largely due to the inclusion of functors, each of which corresponds to a syntactic rule. Grammatical mistakes often involve the child overgeneralizing a rule, demonstrating that simple imitation is not involved.

- According to Skinner, adults shape the baby's speech sounds into words and its words into sentences through selective reinforcement; imitation (echoic responses) of verbal labels are immediately reinforced.

- The evidence suggests that parents respond to the truth value of the child's speech, not its grammatical correctness, and even if they did, it would have little beneficial effect. Children's imitation of adult speech reflects their currently operating grammar.

- Selective reinforcement cannot account for the creativity/open-endedness of language, the distinction between competence and performance, the child's spontaneous use of grammatical rules, the child's ability to understand the meaning of sentences (as opposed to single words) or the universal sequence of stages of language development.

- According to Chomsky, Skinner misunderstood the nature of language, such as its structure-dependent operations (as opposed to simple slot-filling operations) and the fundamental distinction between deep and surface structure.

- Knowing how to transform deep structure into surface structure (and vice-versa) is made possible by transformational grammar, which is essentially what the innate LAD comprises. It enables the child to identify linguistic universals, which collectively provide the deep structure.

- The universal timetable of language development, plus other biological aspects of language, the existence of linguistic universals, the strong inbuilt tendency to develop language in some form, despite lack of exposure to language, and the observation that language development is not related to IQ, all support Chomsky's theory.

- Lenneberg's argument for the existence of a critical period for language development is controversial; the case of Genie suggests that a 'sensitive period' hypothesis may be more valid.

- Although it is widely accepted that children have an inborn ability to formulate hypotheses about the rules of language, Chomsky's claim that they also have specific knowledge about language is much more controversial; their puzzle-solving abilities allow them to infer syntactic rules without any specialized knowledge of language being necessary.

- Lenneberg's claim that language is a human species-specific behaviour has been tested by attempts to teach language to non-human primates, mainly chimpanzees. The most useful criteria of language for assessing these attempts are semanticity, displacement, structure dependence and creativity/productivity.

- Early attempts to teach chimps to speak failed because their vocal apparatus is unsuited to making speech sounds. Since the 1960s, American sign language (ASL) (Washoe – Gardner and Gardner, 1969; Koko – Patterson, 1978–1980), plastic symbols on a magnetized board (Sarah – Premack, 1971) and a computer-controlled typewriter which printed symbols of a specially devised language (Lana – Rumbaugh *et al.*, 1977) have all been used in different production-based training studies.

- The most consistent evidence is for semanticity and creativity; the least convincing is for displacement and structure dependence. For example, while chimps may show a statistical preference for certain word orders, there is little evidence of any following of rules.

- Compared with children, chimps show little spontaneous naming of objects and they seem to use symbols in a purely instrumental way.

- Since the 1980s, Savage-Rumbaugh has been using a comprehension-based approach, with Kanzi and other pygmy chimps and a 'lexigram' board combined with speech. This approach structures the environment in a way that allows the chimp to acquire language through observational learning, much like a child, by exposing it to language in the course of daily life routines.

- Kanzi seems to have demonstrated understanding of certain syntactic rules, including word order,

and Savage-Rumbaugh believes that there is only a quantitative difference between ape and human language. Rejection of the claim that chimps are capable of language has arisen from the earlier, production-based studies.

GLOSSARY

Babbling The baby's spontaneous production of phonemes, between six and nine months. At first, this involves phonemic expansion followed, between nine and ten months, by phonemic contraction.

Cause–effect analytic device A view of the function of words as bringing about changes in the speaker's environment. Relates to the view of language as a communicative tool.

Cognition hypothesis The theory (of Piaget, Cromer) that language can only be used correctly when appropriate cognitive structures have already developed.

Creativity The ability to produce/understand an infinite number of novel utterances. Also called productivity/openendedness.

Deep structure The meaning of sentences, provided by linguistic universals, linguistic features common to all languages (such as consonants/vowels, noun/verb/object). Surface structure refers to the actual words and phrases used.

Emergence of communicative intentionality The awareness that it is possible to bring about a desired goal by using another person as a tool (second order causality).

Formats Rule-bound, ritualized activity routines, such as peekaboo and joint picture-book reading, which involve turn taking.

Grammar A set of rules which determine how a language works and what governs our patterns of speech. It consists of phonology, semantics and syntax.

Holophrase The use of single words, during the one-word stage (12–18 months), to convey a much more complex message.

Imitation by reduction The child's imitation of adult speech (in line with its telegraphic speech), in contrast with the adult's imitation with expansion of the child's speech.

Language acquisition device (LAD) Chomsky's hypothetical model of an innate ability to formulate/understand all types of sentences never heard before. Consists essentially of transformational grammar, the rules for converting deep structure into surface structure and vice-versa.

Language acquisition support system (LASS)

Bruner's term for the active role that adults play in helping the child's language acquisition; consists of a number of formats.

Linguistic competence The implicit knowledge/ understanding of the rules of language, contrasted with performance.

Morphology Part of semantics, rules for combining phonemes into morphemes, the basic units of meaning in a language.

Motherese The simplified speech that adults use when talking to children, involving shorter sentences, simplified syntax, raised pitch, repetition, etc. Also called baby-talk register.

Phonology The sound system of a language; phonological rules determine the permitted sequence of phonemes.

Phrase structure rules Rules for replacing single symbols by different sets of symbols; a central part of Chomsky's theory of transformational grammar.

Production-based training Method used in most attempts to teach language to non-human animals, in which rote learning is used to gradually build up a vocabulary of symbols, one at a time.

Proto-conversation An early form of social interaction, in which the adult attributes meaning/intent to the baby's sounds and utterances and non-verbal behaviour.

Psycholinguistics The study of how language is acquired, perceived, understood and produced.

Semanticity The use of symbols to mean/refer to objects/actions, etc.

Semantics The meaning of language; can be analysed at the level of morphemes or sentences.

Structure dependence The patterned nature of language and use of 'structured chunks', such as word order.

Syntax The rules for combining words into phrases and sentences; an important syntactic rule is word order.

Telegraphic speech Typical speech of a child in the two-word stage (18–30 months), involving words that contain the maximum information (contentives) and omitting purely grammatical terms (functors). Also characterized by rigid word order.

Transformational rules Rules for rearranging strings of symbols (and often adding to them), as in converting an active sentence to a passive; part of Chomsky's theory of transformational grammar.

Visual co-orientation The process whereby two individuals come to focus on some common object; involves joint attention.

FURTHER READING

Barrett, M. (1989) *Early language development.* In A. Slater and G. Bremner (eds) Infant Development. Hillsdale, NJ: Erlbaum. An excellent review of the emergence of early vocabulary and syntactic rules.

Jackendoff, R. (1993) *Patterns in the Mind: Language and Human Nature*. Hemel Hempstead: Harvester Wheatsheaf. An extremely readable, yet informative and challenging introduction to psycholinguistics, which examines what language and language acquisition can tell us about the human mind and human nature.

27 MORAL DEVELOPMENT

INTRODUCTION AND OVERVIEW

As scientists, psychologists who study moral development are not interested in morality as such (i.e. those rules and principles for distinguishing right from wrong) or in particular moralities or moral codes, but in the *process* by which the individual acquires those rules; this is assumed to be the same for all, regardless of the particular moral code the individual acquires.

Brown (1965) compared a morality with the grammar of language, the latter being a set of rules for forming well-formed as opposed to badly-formed sentences (see Chapter 26). For Maccoby (1980), moral development is the child's acquisition of rules which govern behaviour in the social world and, in particular, the development of a sense of right and wrong, how the child begins to understand the values that guide and regulate behaviour within a given social system.

As implied by Maccoby's definition, morality has more than one dimension: it is not merely a matter of acquiring an intellectual understanding of society's rules, i.e. knowing what is right and wrong (*cognitive* component), but also of behaving in accordance with those rules, i.e. our actual moral conduct (*behavioural* component). Clearly, we often say one thing and behave in a contradictory way – we may know what is right or wrong but we do not necessarily translate this into action. There is also a third component, the feeling aspect, i.e. guilt, shame, pride and so on (*affective* component): we may behave in a way that most people would judge to be immoral and yet feel no guilt or remorse or, conversely, we may be troubled by a guilty conscience and yet be a law-abiding citizen.

These examples suggest that the three components of morality are, indeed, distinct and that the exact relationship between them is complex and worthy of empirical investigation by psychologists. In practice, psychologists have tended to concentrate on one of the three components, often to the exclusion of the other two, resulting in four major theoretical approaches, each of which we shall discuss in this chapter:

1 Freud's psychoanalytic theory focuses on the affective component; in particular, guilt or moral anxiety on the one hand and pride or self-esteem on the other.

2 Learning theory, based on classical and operant conditioning, emphasizes the behavioural component (but one version – Eysenck's – is concerned with the acquisition of guilt).

3 Social learning theory is also concerned largely with the behavioural component.

4 The cognitive–developmental theories of Piaget and Kohlberg concentrate on the cognitive component, i.e. moral knowledge, understanding and reasoning. Under this heading, we shall also consider Eisenberg's model of prosocial moral reasoning.

According to Durkin (1995), psychologists have tended to investigate the transmission and reinvention of morality in new generations, asking how morality is acquired and how it changes. This largely ignores the broader picture, which is the concern of sociobiologists, who ask why human communities have found it advantageous to develop moral standards. Sociobiologists, such as Wilson (1975), see morality as an involuntary function of species' adaptation and genetic survival: behaviours appear and recur because they maximize *inclusive fitness* (see Chapter 17). From this perspective, we may like to believe that our actions are governed by higher moral principles but the reality is that 'The genes hold culture on a leash' (Wilson, 1975, cited in Durkin, 1995).

The relationship between morality and human nature has been a topic of philosophical debate for thousands of years. According to Rousseau (1762), humans are 'naturally' good, but this natural goodness may be constrained and distorted by external factors. Only sociobiologists, among modern-day scientists, agree with this view of morality as innate, part of our biological make-up; common to all four psychological approaches that we shall be discussing is the assumption that the acquisition of morality is part of the wider process of socialization, i.e. it develops according to the same principles which govern the development of other aspects of socialized behaviour.

FREUD'S PSYCHOANALYTIC THEORY

According to Freud, our moral behaviour is controlled by the superego, which comprises the *conscience* and the *ego-ideal*. As we saw in Chapter 21, the conscience is that part of our personality which punishes us when we have committed some wrong-doing and so is the source of feelings of guilt; it represents the 'punishing parent' within our personality and is composed of all the prohibitions imposed on us by our parents, the 'thou shalt nots'. The ego-ideal rewards us when we have behaved in accordance with our basic moral values ('thou shalts'); it is the source of our feelings of pride and self-satisfaction and represents the 'rewarding parent' within our personality.

Each part of the superego is acquired through a different process of identification (the conscience through identification with the aggressor, the ego-ideal through anaclitic identification) and the process is completed by the age of 5–6.

Psychosexual and moral development – and gender differences

To appreciate Freud's theory of moral development, it must be seen in the context of personality development which, you will remember from Chapter 21, proceeds through five psychosexual stages: it is the third of these – the phallic stage – which is the important one as far as moral development is concerned because it is during this stage that the Oedipus complex occurs and the outcome of this is the acquisition of the superego, through the process of identification.

Freud admitted he was much less clear about the girl's motive for identifying with the mother than he was about the boy's motive for identifying with the father: the boy's fear of castration is a very powerful motive but 'The fear of castration being thus excluded in the little girl, a powerful motive also drops out for the setting up of a superego … ' (Freud, 1924). He was quite sure, however, that whatever the girl's motive may be, her identification with her mother is bound to be weaker than that of the boy's with his father. For boys ' … the authority of the father … is introjected into the ego and there it forms the nucleus of the superego, which takes over the severity of the father and perpetuates his prohibition against incest' (Freud, 1924).

However, this only happens partially in the girl to whom, in any case, the father is something less of an authority figure. He has always been more interested in 'seducing' her affection ('daddy's little girl') and so she remains in a state of hostile attachment to her mother. The girl's love for her father does not have to be as thoroughly abandoned (repressed) as the boy's for his mother – she does not have to shatter her Oedipus complex so completely (Mitchell, 1974).

Are males morally superior to females?

If we follow Freud's account through, it would seem that the boy's conscience will be stronger than the girl's because:

- the conscience represents the punishing parent;
- it is acquired through identification with the aggressor; and

- the boy's motive for identifying is much stronger than the girl's (i.e. the fear of castration).

Similarly, we would expect a girl's ego-ideal to be more pronounced than a boy's since:

- the ego-ideal represents the rewarding parent;
- it is acquired through anaclitic identification; and
- the girl's motive for identifying is stronger than the boy's (i.e. fear of loss of mother's love).

Freud did, in fact, maintain that women have weaker superegos than men (although he did not specifically differentiate between the conscience and ego-ideal in this context). Because her identification with the mother is less complete, the girl relies more on external authority figures throughout her childhood, has to be more compliant, less 'naughty' (there is no equivalent of 'boys will be boys'). It is through his strong identification with the father that the boy achieves independence which the girl will have to try to achieve in adolescence: ' … Many women, though nominally they leave home, understandably, never make it … ' (Mitchell, 1974).

However, there is no evidence to support this view. For example, Hoffman (1975) reviewed a number of studies where children are left alone and tempted to violate a prohibition. There are not usually any overall gender differences but where they are found, they tend to show that it is girls who are better able to resist temptation.

Freud also saw females as being sexually inferior – they have to make do with babies as a poor substitute for a penis. Not surprisingly, many feminists, including psychologists, regard his whole account of development as 'phallocentric', which Grosz (1987, cited in Wilkinson, 1989) defines as 'the use of general or universal models to represent the two sexes according to the interests and terms of one, the male'. Many feminist writers (including Karen Horney (1924) and Clara Thompson (1943), two eminent psychoanalysts) have pointed out that what girls (and women) envy is not the penis but the superior status that men enjoy in our society: it is the penis as a *symbol* for that superior status which is envied, not literally the penis as such, and it is men, not women, who equate lack of a penis with inferiority. Horney and Sherman (1971) both report 'womb envy' in men.

There is little evidence that women have more difficulty achieving gender identity than men or that they have an inferiority complex about their bodies, although Horney (1924) 'concedes' that since the woman's genitals are hidden and so cannot be displayed, she later displays her whole body instead and is liable to turn inward on herself in greater subjectivity.

● Is a guilty conscience the sign of a moral or an immoral person?

Turning now to the relationship between our moral behaviour and our experience of guilt (which has its source in the conscience), Freud's view is counter-intuitive. The commonsense view is that the more wrong-doing we do, the more reason we have to feel guilty. But Freud claims that the greater the wrong-doing, the less the guilt or the less the wrong-doing, the greater the guilt, i.e. they are *inversely* related. How can this be?

The conscience causes us to renounce many of our basic impulses or instinctual wishes, especially our aggressive and sexual urges, and the energy from these renounced desires then becomes available to the conscience. Aggression that is not expressed and directed outwards towards others is instead directed inwards, against the self, a form of self-punishment which is experienced as guilt. So a severe, punitive conscience is one which has a lot of energy at its disposal to keep in check our basic impulses. A study

that is relevant here is that of MacKinnon (1938), which is described in Box 27.1.

MacKinnon's data are, of course, only correlational so we cannot be sure that the differences in the strength of conscience were caused by differences in childrearing. For instance, parents who used psychological methods may have differed in other important respects from those who preferred physical methods and these other differences may have been the critical ones. In fact, the direction of causation could have been the other way round – the children may have forced their parents to use physical methods as a last resort when more psychological methods failed. For instance, it is probably easier to use psychological methods of discipline with children who are relatively passive, placid or 'undemanding' by nature. Also, MacKinnon's participants had to recall their childhood experiences and make judgements about how to classify the kinds of punishment used by their parents; memory is notoriously unreliable, particularly with regard to such emotionally salient matters as this. Finally, can we be sure that the behaviour of MacKinnon's participants was typical of their moral behaviour in general? This is an issue which we shall return to shortly.

BOX 27.1	Key study: The more guilty you are, the less guilty you feel

MacKinnon (1938) gave 93 participants a series of problems to solve, working alone in a room which contained answer books, some of which they were allowed to use, others not. It was found that 43 cheated, the other 50 did not.

Four weeks later, those who had cheated (and who did not know they had been found out) were asked if they had, in fact, cheated; about 50 percent of them confessed, while the rest denied it. Those who confessed were asked if they felt guilty about what they had done and those who denied were asked if they would have felt guilty – 25 percent said they did or would have felt guilty. Of those who had not cheated, 84 percent said they would have felt guilty.

They were also asked, 'Do you in everyday life often feel guilty about things you have done or not done?'

Seventy five percent of the non-cheats said 'Yes', compared with 29 percent of the cheats. MacKinnon also recorded the incidental behaviour of participants when they were working on the original problems: nine of the cheats swore out loud or otherwise cursed the problem (e.g. 'You bastard' or 'These are the God-damnedest things I ever saw') but none of the non-cheats did this. Of the cheats, 31 percent also did things such as pound their fists or kick the leg of the table, compared with only 4 percent of the non-cheats.

Some time after the original experiment, MacKinnon managed to track down 28 of the original participants, all males, 13 of the cheats and 15 of the non-cheats. They were asked to check on a list of common forms of punishment those most often used by their parents and the findings are shown in the table below. Physical punishments included beatings and loss of privileges, while psychological punishments included making the child feel that it had fallen short of some standard or had hurt the parents and lost some of their love.

Type of punishment		
	Physical	**Psychological**
Cheats (13)	78 percent	22 percent
Non-cheats (15)	48 percent	52 percent

● Childrearing methods and the development of conscience

There is, in fact, a good deal of additional evidence which supports the view that a strong conscience and psychological methods of punishment are positively correlated. For example, Sears *et al.* (1957) interviewed 379 mothers of five-year-olds in Boston, USA, both middle and working class. Two main kinds of childrearing techniques emerged:

1 *love-oriented,* more psychological techniques, which used praise and affection as rewards for good behaviour and isolation and love withdrawal as punishments for bad behaviour;
2 *object-oriented,* more physical techniques, which used tangible rewards, deprivation of privileges and actual physical punishment.

The love-oriented parents tended to have children with a more highly developed conscience compared with the children of object-oriented parents. However, the associations were not strong; the strongest were with physical punishment, so that of parents who used it a great deal, 15 percent had children with a strong conscience compared with 32 percent of those who used it very little. The mothers most likely to have children with a strong conscience were generally warm and used love withdrawal as a major disciplinary technique. This is consistent with Danziger's (1971) claim that it may be fear of loss of love, rather than love itself, which motivates the child to behave in socially approved ways (and hence with Freud's notion of anaclitic identification).

According to Hoffman (1970), excessive use of power-assertive techniques of punishment (physical punishment, withdrawal of privileges or the threat of either) is associated with low levels of moral development. Reasoning or explaining tends to be associated with high levels of moral development (as measured by consideration for others, moral reasoning and guilt), verbal explanations are more effective than physical punishment and children seem to learn best how to control their own behaviour if parents explain what they have done wrong, what led up to the misdeed or what the consequences of the misdeed were for the child and others.

Glueck and Glueck (1950) found that severe punishment is one of the major factors associated with delinquency in young boys. Similarly, Bandura and Walters (1959) compared the attitudes of parents of 26 highly aggressive boys with those of 26 normal boys, matched for intelligence and socioeconomic status. Most of the former had been in trouble with the law, felt less guilt and had parents who used physical punishment, compared with the latter; the aggressive boys were also more likely to have been rejected by their parents.

If it is method of punishment which determines the strength of conscience, how does it actually work to produce the effect it does? One suggestion is that different responses are required in the child in order to end the punishment:

● In the case of psychological methods, there must be some kind of *symbolic renunciation* – an apology, a promise not to do it again, etc. In time, these responses become organized into what is normally called conscience.
● When the child is punished physically, the response is often more aggression or, at least, feelings of hostility and the parent may in fact be unwittingly providing the child with a model of aggressive behaviour to imitate; this does not encourage the inner control implied by conscience (see Chapter 7).

● An evaluation of Freud's account of conscience

According to Freud (1938), 'This new psychical agency [the superego] continues to carry on the functions which have hitherto been performed by the people in the external world: it observes the ego, gives it orders, judges it and threatens it with punishments, exactly like the parents whose place it has taken'.

This way of characterizing the superego serves to reinforce a common way of referring to it in everyday language (or, at least, to a part of it, the conscience). White (1975) points out that we usually tend to personalize conscience (e.g. we say 'My conscience would not let me do it' or 'My conscience got the better of me') as if it had an independent life of its own and existed in its own right. The word 'conscience' (*con* plus *sciens*) means 'knowing with someone else' and it is often used as if it were an independent witness of our behaviour, an internal judge (as Freud says) of whether our behaviour conforms with our moral code.

Many psychologists have become dissatisfied with the term in recent years, partly for the reasons outlined above and partly also because of the particular form it takes in Freud's theory. One major criticism (Kohlberg, 1969; Hoffman, 1976) has been that conscience does not suddenly come into existence at 5–6 years old, but rather moral development is a gradual process which begins in childhood and extends into adulthood.

Another criticism is that the belief in an internalized conscience implies that moral behaviour should be consistent across different situations, that is, if our moral conduct is determined by a part of our personality which is unchanging, then the details of the moral situation should be largely irrelevant as far as how we act is concerned. People will display moral traits, such as honesty, whereby someone who is honest on one occasion, in one type of situation, will be honest on another occasion in other types of situation. But is this what people are like? Are we consistent in our moral behaviour? The classic study which set out to investigate this issue was the Character Education Inquiry, begun in 1928 by Hartshorne and May (see Box 27.2).

However, subsequent re-analysis of the data showed a significant, if small, tendency for children who were honest on one test to be so on others and subsequent studies of different measures have tended to confirm that they are positively correlated, including resistance to temptation and altruism. The most valid conclusion, therefore, would seem to be that personality (i.e. an individual's strength of conscience), as well as the situation, determines several important aspects of moral behaviour and this represents some measure of support for Freud's concept of the superego. (The consistency of moral behaviour relates to the more general 'trait–situation' debate as an explanation of behaviour; see Chapter 29.)

Freud's approach also sees the child's moral learning as confined to the family which, admittedly, was a much greater influence on the child at the turn of the century, when Freud was first formulating his theories, than it is now. Today's child is exposed to many moral influences in addition to the family, both before and after starting school, including the media, teachers and peers. Other criticisms have come from learning theorists who, as well as being generally critical of Freud's theories, believe that conscience can be accounted for in terms of the principles of conditioning.

THE LEARNING THEORY APPROACH

The learning theory (or S–R) approach maintains that moral behaviour is learned according to exactly the same principles of classical and operant conditioning as any other behaviour (see Chapter 7).

● The contribution of classical conditioning

Psychologists such as Eysenck believe that what we normally call conscience is no more and no less than a conditioned emotional response (CER) or, more precisely, a collection of such CERs. How might these CERs come about? The short answer is, by exactly the same procedure by which salivation becomes a conditioned response (CR) to a bell. If, for example,

---

| **BOX 27.2** | Key study: Moral inconsistency rules, OK! |

Hartshorne and May (1928) studied 12,000 11–14-year-olds who were given the opportunity to cheat, lie and steal under conditions in which they were confident of not being found out.

They were observed in a variety of situations – in the classroom, playground, after-school activities, in sports, during party games and at home. They were also given 20 pencil-and-paper tests designed to measure moral knowledge (where the questions had correct answers) and moral opinions (where they did not). These tests were sometimes scored against adult consensus (what a majority of adults believed) and sometimes against a kind of ideal code supplied by the researchers.

It came as quite a surprise to Hartshorne and May that the results were very inconsistent, so that a child

who, say, cheated in one situation (e.g. an arithmetic test) would often not cheat in another (e.g. a spelling test). The overall correlation between bad behaviour in one setting and bad behaviour in another situation was 0.34, much lower than had been expected. Even within the same situation (e.g. school tests in the classroom) children behaved inconsistently, although the consistency was relatively higher than it was between situations (e.g. playground and classroom). So it would appear that a child does not have a uniform, generalized code of morals to determine behaviour in a variety of situations, but rather the situation is at least as much responsible for the child's moral actions as conscience.

Hartshorne and May concluded that honesty was largely situation-specific and not a general personality trait, i.e. we cannot say that some people are more honest than others, because this implies consistency across situations which they did not find (*doctrine of specificity*).

a child is frequently disciplined for being naughty, the negative feelings (mainly anxiety) which the child associates with punishment become associated with the wrong-doing. So the child comes to feel anxious when contemplating doing something naughty and this eventually happens even when the parents are not present.

For instance, if the child is smacked for stealing (unconditioned stimulus, UCS), which produces pain and anxiety (unconditioned response, UCR), and the child is told 'You must not steal' (conditioned stimulus, CS) just before it is smacked, eventually the words 'You must not steal' will come to produce anxiety in the child (conditioned response, CR) and, finally, when the child even thinks about stealing, this CR will be produced. This anxiety builds up at the thought of doing wrong and reaches a climax just before the wrong-doing and is a far more effective deterrent than the thought of being caught (which may or may not happen), hence Hamlet's 'Thus conscience does make cowards of us all'. In this sense, the self is generally a better deterrent against law breaking than police or magistrates.

These CERs represent our ability to resist temptation. But conscience, according to Eysenck, also refers to our susceptibility to feelings of guilt, i.e. what we feel after we have committed some wrong-doing. It is the timing of the punishment which determines whether the resistance to temptation component or the guilt component of conscience is affected and this was demonstrated in a famous experiment by Solomon *et al.* (1968) with puppies (see Box 27.3).

The Solomon *et al.* experiment shows that 'punishment' that is consistently given before a misdeed will result in high resistance to temptation but weak guilt when wrong-doing does occur, and the reverse will be true when punishment consistently follows the misdeed. (We should note that the anxiety experienced when contemplating some misdeed is reduced if the temptation is actually resisted; in this way, through *negative reinforcement*, resistance to temptation can be strengthened through operant conditioning.) Several studies involving children have found similar effects to those found with puppies. For example, Aronfreed (1963) punished a group of young boys verbally for touching attractive toys while still in the act of reaching (as the transgression was about to occur), while boys in a second group were punished a few moments after picking up the toys; they were then left in a room with the toys and told not to touch them. As predicted, the first group were better able to resist than the second group.

BOX 27.3   Key study: Food, newspapers and 'doggy guilt'

In an experiment by Solomon *et al.* (1968), puppies were 'punished' (swatted with a newspaper) either just before they began to eat forbidden food or just after they had started to eat it. After being trained in one of these two ways, they were all tested by being made hungry and left alone in a room with the forbidden food. Those puppies punished just before eating held out much longer against the temptation to eat than those punished just after they had eaten a little during training sessions.

However, once the early-punished puppies had started to eat, they showed little sign of anxiety, in sharp contrast to the second group which showed all the usual signs of 'doggy guilt'. These differences are explained by assuming that the first group were classically conditioned to respond with anxiety to all those stimuli which occurred during the approach to food, while the second group were conditioned to those stimuli occurring after food had been eaten.

However, even in the relatively simple case of a child who is conditioned to feel anxiety when about to steal, cognitive factors are clearly involved. For example, if children are given a rationale for not touching a particular toy (it is fragile and might break or it belongs to another child who did not want them to touch it), together with a mild punishment, they are significantly less likely to touch it than if given just punishment. Equally important is the finding that, when reasons are given, the timing of punishment becomes irrelevant. Parke, in a review of several studies (1972, 1977), concluded that when a rationale accompanies punishment:

● mild forms of punishment become just as effective as severe punishment at producing resistance to temptation;
● delayed punishment becomes as effective as early punishment;
● punishment from an aloof and impersonal adult becomes as effective as that from a warm, friendly adult;
● resistance to temptation is much more stable over time.

There are also interesting developmental factors involved. For instance, Parke (1974) found that three-year-olds were quite effectively inhibited from touching by being told the toy was fragile and might break (*object-oriented rationale*) but telling them it belonged to another child (*person-oriented rationale*) had very little effect. However, five-year-olds did respond to appeals based on property rights. Parke concludes that long-term (internalized) moral controls may require cognitively-oriented training procedures as opposed to those which rely solely on the conditioning of anxiety responses.

● The contribution of operant conditioning

Operant conditioning takes a more active view of the learner; what is being conditioned is not an automatic, physiological response like anxiety but some behaviour of the child which is essentially voluntary. So, while classical conditioning is concerned primarily with the affective or emotional components of morality, operant conditioning is concerned with trying to explain how moral behaviour is acquired. Like all other operant behaviour, it is assumed that moral behaviour can be made more or less likely to occur depending on its *consequences,* i.e. whether it is reinforced or punished. Let us look at some of the evidence.

The role of positive reinforcement and punishment

Several studies have used a variety of positive reinforcements for increasing a range of morally desirable behaviours, including bubblegum, praise, hugs and sharing marbles, giving sweets to other children and co-operating with others. However, several researchers have also pointed out that reward cannot be applied mechanically: if a parent is not warmly attached to their child, then reward may be of little value in altering the child's behaviour. (This parallels the point we made earlier that the threat of withdrawal of love is only effective if

---

● Positive reinforcement (or reward) provides information about which of the many alternatives for action are likely to bring pleasant outcomes, but punishment only tells us what we should *not* do, not what we should (or may). So while reward can produce morally acceptable behaviour, punishment, at best, produces an inhibition of morally unacceptable behaviour.

● Children quickly learn to suppress the punishable behaviour in the presence of the punisher, but tend to be all the more prone to engage in it again when no longer under 'surveillance' (Walters and Grusec, 1977).

● Punishment often produces hostility and resentment, as well as fear and avoidance of the punisher, instead of moral concern (Parke and Collmer, 1975).

● The punisher may underestimate the severity and intensity of the punishment and thus abuse it. This is especially likely to occur when an adult physically punishes a child; 'I didn't know my own strength' may be used as an excuse (and sometimes, perhaps, a genuine reason) for a case of child abuse. Also the child may well get used to certain levels of physical punishment, so that the adult has to step up the intensity of the punishment ('smack a bit harder') for it to have any effect.

● Each time the child is punished (either by an adult or an older child) it is witnessing the meaning of 'social power'. The punisher, by virtue of age, gender, strength or status, is seen as having the right to define what is and what is not 'desirable behaviour' and to perform acts against the powerless child (which, in turn, are condoned by society). So the child learns to follow this model and may well use punishing strategies for controlling the behaviour of others.

● Punishment often occurs in a social situation involving people other than the punisher and the punished. The presence of these others may add to the humiliation felt by the person being punished and they may even 'join in' (as when both parents tell the child off, one after the other). Alternatively, the presence of others may bias the behaviour of the punisher who may be concerned about their image and use punishment to impress the onlookers in some way or to 'keep up appearances'. O'Leary *et al.* (1970) found that when teachers reprimanded disruptive children publicly (loud enough to be heard by the rest of the class), there was little effect on the disruptive behaviour. When they were asked to use soft reprimands, audible only to the child being disruptive, the disruptive behaviour almost always decreased .

● Punishments may, inadvertently, increase the very behaviour they are intended to stop. For example, if children find that adults will pay attention to them only when they are being naughty, then they are more, rather than less, likely to be naughty, since even a smack or a telling off is preferable to being ignored! So what may be intended as a punishment by the adult may be a reinforcement as far as the child is concerned.

TABLE 27.1 *The relative effectiveness of positive reinforcement and punishment*

BOX 27.4	Key study: Not all rewards are the same or, children can't be bribed so easily

Lepper *et al.* (1973) studied children in nursery school who spent most of their time in a large room with tables set out with a variety of toys (e.g. puzzles, clay, picture books, letter games and beads). They had free choice and could spend as much time as they wished with each one. For several days before the experiment, a set of magic markers (which the children did not previously have access to in the school) was put on one of the tables; records were kept of how long each child spent using them. The children were then individually taken into an adjoining room where they participated in one of three experimental conditions.

● Group one sat at a table with a set of magic markers. They were shown an impressive-looking 'good player award' and were told they could earn it if they did a good job of drawing with the markers. When they had worked on drawings for a standard length of time, they were given the award.

● Group two worked with the markers for a time equal to the first group, but they were not shown the reward before they started drawing and nothing was said about a reward. At the end of the session, however, they received an award and were told they had done well.

● Group three spent an equivalent time using the markers but were neither promised an award nor given one.

About two weeks later, the markers were set out in the classroom again and the researchers recorded the children's spontaneous interest in them. It was found that the first group had lost interest compared with the other two groups. Lepper *et al.'s* explanation is that an expected reward robs an activity of its intrinsic interest value and makes it seem like a means to an end (not an end in itself). To support this, they showed that, although the first group of children produced more pictures, the pictures were of lower quality (less detailed, thoughtful and original) than those produced by the children in the other two groups.

---

the relationship between parent and child is a warm and close one.) The effect of punishment also seems to depend on the relationship between the punisher and the child; if there is already a warm and affectionate relationship between them, the child is much more likely to inhibit unacceptable behaviour than if the same punishment is given by a cold, unaffectionate agent (Sears *et al.*, 1957; Parke, 1969). Table 27.1 considers the relative effectiveness of positive reinforcement and punishment.

Is it possible for rewards to decrease the behaviour being rewarded?

The answer is 'yes', when extrinsic (external) rewards are offered for activities which are already intrinsically rewarding, that is, activities which are rewarding in themselves. This is known as the *paradox of reward*. Extrinsic rewards may cause people to change their explanation (or *attribution*) for their own behaviour: for example, 'I do it because I enjoy it' may become 'I do it for the compliments that people pay me' and if those are then withdrawn, they may decide that the activity is no longer worth doing (Bem, 1972; Lepper and Greene, 1978) (see Chapter 15). An important demonstration of the paradox of reward is the study by Lepper *et al.* (1973) summarized in Box 27.4.

SOCIAL LEARNING THEORY

We discussed in Chapter 7 some of the major differences between social learning theory (SLT) and orthodox learning theory (classical and operant conditioning), one of them being the importance of *observational learning* (or *modelling*), another being the role of cognitive factors intervening between stimulus and response. We also said that SLT arose partly as an attempt to 'translate' Freud's theories, in particular his concept of identification, into learning theory terms and has been studied largely through the laboratory study of imitation (see Chapter 17).

Bandura (1977) believes that the development of self-control is heavily influenced by the models children observe and by patterns of direct reinforcement they encounter (i.e. the disciplinary measures used by adults).

● What kinds of models are most likely to be imitated?

Evidence from everyday observation tells us that it is not necessary for the model to be known personally, to the child: older children and adolescents imitate pop stars, sporting personalities, film stars and other 'remote' people as models, although for most children it is parents and siblings who are the most important and frequently imitated models. Research has tried to identify the specific behaviour of models that make them most likely to be imitated. These include:

- its appropriateness;
- its relevance;
- the similarity between the child and model;
- its consistency.

The impact of the *appropriateness* of the model's behaviour, as perceived by the child, was demonstrated in an experiment by Bandura *et al.* (1961), who found that aggressive male models were more readily imitated than aggressive female models. One probable reason for this is to do with gender roles: it is more acceptable in Western culture for men to be aggressive than for women and even by 3–4 years of age, children are learning the dominant stereotypes that relate to gender-role differences (see Chapter 23). So aggressive male models are more likely to be imitated since this is seen by the child as more fitting or appropriate for men (in general) than for women (in general).

In the same experiment, Bandura *et al.* showed that the *relevance* of the model's behaviour, again as perceived by the child, is another important variable. Boys were more likely to imitate the aggressive male model than were girls: the greater relevance of the male model's behaviour for boys lies in the fact that boys perceive the *similarity* between themselves and the model. Perception of this similarity is based upon development of the child's gender identity, i.e. the ability to classify itself (and others) as a boy or girl, male or female (see Chapters 21 and 23). The first stage of this ability is not usually reached until 2½–3-years of age and certainly before that there is no preferential imitation of same-sex models.

The *consistency* of a model's behaviour also seems to be a factor that will determine how likely they are to be imitated, both inside and outside the laboratory. Many psychologists have observed that inconsistency is one of the consistent characteristics of human behaviour and parents may be as guilty of this as anybody. So what happens when they do not practise what they preach, when they tell their children to behave one way (e.g. 'You must not shout') and then behave themselves in a contradictory way (e.g. raising their own voices while telling their children not to shout)? (This is an example of how we can, inadvertently, model the very behaviour which we wish to discourage in others.) Research suggests that talking is not enough: children tend to imitate adults exactly, in a rather 'literal' way. So 'do as I say, not as I do' (parent) becomes 'I'll say as you say and do as you do' (child). If the adult's behaviour is at odds with their preaching, then children's behaviour tends to copy this inconsistency.

● Learning versus performance and the role of reinforcement

We saw in Chapter 7 that Tolman, working with rats in mazes, demonstrated that reinforcement is not necessary for learning to take place but is necessary for the learning to be displayed in the rats' behaviour. This means that learning and the demonstration of learning (i.e. performance) are not the same. This distinction was demonstrated by Bandura (1965) in an experiment with young children, described in Box 27.5.

What Bandura's experiment shows is that reinforcing the child for imitating the model merely brought out what the child had already learned through earlier observation of the model – it was not the agent or cause of the original learning (as Skinner would maintain). This means that it is possible for learning to occur but not actually to show up in the child's overt behaviour at the time. For learning to occur, mere exposure to the model is sufficient, but whether this learning actually reveals itself in the child's behaviour depends upon factors such as the consequences of the behaviour (both for the model and the child), the child's anticipation of reward or punishment, whether the child is instructed or encouraged to produce the model's behaviour and so on. This, in turn, suggests that children may learn equally from all kinds of models but are more likely to imitate models who possess certain characteristics.

● Evaluation of experimental studies of imitation

Bronfenbrenner (1973) has been one of the most outspoken critics of laboratory studies of imitation. He points out that the basic situation involves the child and an adult model, which is a rather limited social situation and is treated as if it existed in isolation from all other social relationships. Also, there is usually no actual interaction between the child and the model at any point; certainly, the child has no chance to influence the model in any way. Also, the model and the child are complete strangers and the model is often seen on film and not in the flesh at all.

**BOX
27.5** Key study: Rewarding the
learning that has already taken
place

Bandura (1965) showed three groups of children a film
of an adult behaving aggressively towards a bobo doll:

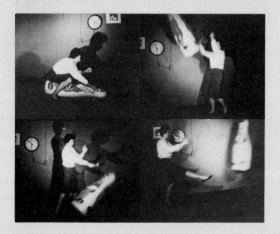

- Group A (the control group) saw the adult kicking,
  pummelling and punching the bobo doll.
- Group B (the model-rewarded group) saw the same
  adult performing exactly the same aggressive acts,
  but this time a second adult entered the scene,
  towards the end of the film, complimented the
  model on his aggressive behaviour and gave him
  helpings of sweets and lemonade to restore his lost
  energy.
- Group C (the model-punished group) saw the same
  aggressive model as the other two groups, but this
  time a second adult came on at the end of the film
  and scolded the model and warned him not to be
  aggressive again.

Thus, the only difference between the three groups was
the consequences of the model's behaviour: for group A
nothing happened (neither reward nor punishment),
for group B the model was rewarded and for group C the
model was punished.

After the film, all the children (one by one) went into
a playroom which contained a great number of toys,
many of which had not been seen in the film, but which
included a bobo doll and a mallet. They were left for ten
minutes in order to see how many acts of imitative
aggression each performed (Fig. 27.1). As might be
expected, group C children showed significantly less imitative aggression than those in the other two groups;
however, there was no difference between groups A and
B. According to the principle of *vicarious reinforcement*, group B children, who had seen the model
rewarded, should have shown much more imitative

aggression than group A children, who saw the model
neither rewarded nor punished. So it appears that seeing someone else being reinforced is much less powerful
an influence than seeing someone else being punished.

But more significant still are the findings from a second stage of the experiment. Each child (from all three
groups) was asked to reproduce as much as possible of
the model's behaviour and was directly rewarded for each
act of imitative aggression. Under these conditions, there
was no difference between any of the three groups – they
all showed the same high level of imitative aggression.
What this means, of course, is that the children in the
model-punished group had attended to and remembered
the model's behaviour (i.e. learned from the model) to
the same extent as those in the other two groups; however, this had not been manifested in their behaviour at
first. So the original difference between group C and the
other two groups was one of *performance* (imitation) and
not one of *learning* (acquisition).

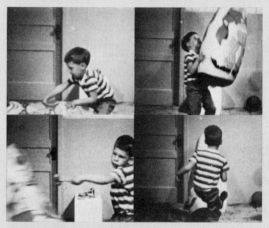

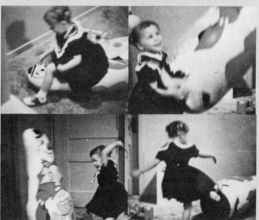

FIGURE 27.1 *After watching films of an aggressive
model who punched, pummelled and hurled a bobo
doll, these children spontaneously imitated the model's
aggression*

Similarities
• They both involve the reproduction of someone else's behaviour (the model).
• They are both examples of observational learning.

Differences	
Imitation	**Identification**
• Involves fairly specific and overt aspects of the model's behaviour	• Involves the child coming to think, feel and act as if it were the model, so is not confined to overt behaviour but includes attitudes, values, beliefs, likes and dislikes etc.
• Usually occurs shortly after observation of the model's behaviour (minutes/hours, rather than days/weeks)	• A process that takes place over an extended period of time, usually years
• Does not require prior interaction or familiarity with the model, who may be a total stranger	• Requires a personal relationship between the child and the model, based on previous interaction, often involving a strong emotional tie between them (as in parent and child)
• Involves positional modelling. The model represents a social role (e.g. men in general), with the emphasis on the model's behaviour, rather than the model as a person	• Involves personal modelling. The model is a unique individual and the child is trying to be (like) the model, imitating the model's personal characteristics
• May be conscious or unconscious	• An unconscious process

TABLE 27.2 *Major similarities and differences between imitation and identification*

This, of course, is quite unlike 'normal' modelling which takes place within the family.

Bandura would probably reply that television, movie and sporting stars are often important models and are also complete strangers, at least in the sense that there is no interpersonal contact between the child and the model (see Chapter 17). This relates to a distinction made by Danziger (1971) between two kinds of models: *personal models are* imitated because of their personal qualities or characteristics, while *positional models are* imitated because of the social role that they represent (e.g. gender, age, occupation).

In the kind of laboratory experiment that Bandura and his colleagues have conducted, a male model represents not only himself but men in general. So, not surprisingly, the aggressive behaviour of a male model is more readily imitated than that of a female model. (We have already discussed this as an example of the appropriateness factor.) Taking over aggressiveness from a female model would involve a more personal kind of imitation and is much less likely to occur in the laboratory where there is no familiarity with the model as a person. Familiarity, based on previous interaction with the model, may be crucial for personal modelling but is not needed for positional modelling, where the child need only be familiar with the social role in general. Clearly, personal modelling is much more

closely related to the process of *identification* than it is to imitation.

The relationship between imitation and identification

Baer and Sherman (1964) found that when children are directly rewarded for imitating a model's behaviour, imitation often generalizes to other aspects of the model's behaviour; such *generalized imitation* may play an important part in the learning processes included under the concept of identification. This generalized (spontaneous) imitation may be seen as an important area of overlap between the two concepts of imitation and identification. The major similarities and differences between imitation and identification are summarized in Table 27.2.

The role of cognitive variables

As we saw in Chapter 7, SLT represents an S–O–R approach to learning, where 'O' stands for 'organism'; it recognizes the role of cognitive and other intervening variables (between stimulus and response), such as attention and memory. Identification can also be seen as one of these intervening variables which ' ... very early in life enables the child to learn without the parents having to teach and which creates a self-reinforcing mechanism that competes effectively in some instances with external sources of reinforcement' (Sears *et al.*, 1965).

Sears *et al.* (1965) derived a series of hypotheses about how different sorts of parents might influence children through the models they provide and they tested these through the study of childrearing practices. We considered some of these when discussing Freud's theory earlier in the chapter and we have also seen the importance of the child's perception of the model and how the model's behaviour is interpreted by the child.

Mischel (1973) (Fig. 27.2) describes five kinds of cognitive or *person variables,* namely:

1 *Competencies:* intellectual abilities, social skills, physical skills and other special abilities.
2 *Cognitive strategies*: habitual ways of selectively attending to information and organizing it into meaningful categories.

FIGURE 27.2 *Walter Mischel*

3 *Expectancies* about the consequences of different behaviours, about the meaning of different stimuli and about the efficacy of one's own behaviour.
4 *Subjective outcome variables*: the value we place on the expected outcome or consequences of our behaviour. For example, what may be a punishment for one child may actually be reinforcing for another (as in the attention-seeking child for whom a smack represents the giving of attention). So rewards and punishments cannot be defined 'objectively', independently of the individual concerned.
5 *Self-regulatory systems and plans*: self-imposed standards or rules which people adopt for regulating their own behaviour. This relates to an important distinction that SLT makes between external and internal reinforcement and punishment (for Skinner, they are external only; see Fig. 27.3).

Internal reinforcement and punishment can be seen as the SLT equivalent of Freud's superego (ego-ideal and conscience respectively). Both theories agree that, eventually, the child no longer needs an outside agency (parents or other adults) to administer rewards and punishments – the child can reward itself (through feelings of pride) and punish itself (through guilt). Just as both parts of the superego develop through identification, so *self-reinforcement* and *self-punishment* are acquired through observation and imitation of the parents' rewards and punishments. The child's own actions, previously rewarded or punished by the parents, can be reinforced or punished when performed alone by the child's own *imitative self-approval* ('good girl') and *imitative self-disapproval* ('bad boy').

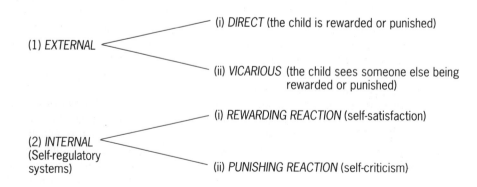

FIGURE 27.3 *Different sources of reinforcement and punishment as seen by social learning theory*

We set our own standards of conduct and evaluate our behaviour in the light of these; external reinforcement (social approval) may only be effective when it is consistent with self-reinforcement (behaviour which the individual already values highly). This idea of self-regulation is very similar to that of conscience as an internal judge or policeman, making sure that we 'keep to the straight and narrow'. The ability to reward or punish oneself is an important kind of cognitive or mediating variable.

Whatever the advantages of SLT compared with orthodox learning theory, one limitation of both approaches is the fact that they say nothing about moral *progress*. Although social learning theorists accept that children learn more as they get older and in that sense become 'more' moral, they do not see development as having certain laws of its own and so do not see children as changing in similar ways as they get older – the changes that occur are quantitative rather than qualitative. Although they take cognitive factors (including cognitive development) into account, they represent but one set of factors amongst several (including the situation itself) which determine the child's moral behaviour and it is still primarily behaviour which is of interest.

THE COGNITIVE–DEVELOPMENTAL APPROACH

This fourth and final major approach is the only one which focuses on the cognitive aspect of morality and hence on moral development as such, since moral development and overall cognitive development go very much hand in hand. The cognitive–developmental approach, therefore, is the only one which does offer a progressive view of morality: disagreeing with Freud, it sees morality as developing gradually during childhood and adolescence into adulthood and, disagreeing with the learning theory and SLT approaches, it maintains that there are stages of moral development which, like all developmental stages, are qualitatively different (different in kind). The two major figures are Jean Piaget and Lawrence Kohlberg.

● Piaget's theory

Just as Piaget's theory of cognitive development is concerned with how the child's knowledge and understanding change with age (see Chapter 25), so his theory of moral development is concerned with how the child's moral knowledge and understanding change with age. More specifically, in *The Moral Judgement of the Child* (1932), Piaget investigated:

- the child's ideas about the rules of the game of marbles;
- the child's moral judgements; and
- the child's conception of punishment and justice.

Rules

According to Piaget (1932):

> Children's games constitute the most admirable social institutions. The game of marbles, for instance, as played by boys, contains an extremely complex system of rules, that is to say, a code of laws, a jurisprudence of its own ... All morality consists in a system of rules, and the essence of all morality is to be sought in the respect which the individual acquires for these rules.

So, for Piaget, morality is any system of rules which governs interaction between people and that includes the game of marbles. By studying how moral knowledge is acquired in games, he believed he could discover how children's moral knowledge in general develops. He also thought that by studying rules in the context of a game, he could by-pass the influence of adult teaching and study the child's spontaneous thought directly.

He played the game with a child and pretended not to know the rules. He asked the child to explain them to him and in the course of the game he probed the child's understanding by asking questions such as: 'Where do rules come from?', 'Who made them?' and 'Can we change them?'. The idea was to pose the child a problem which it had not had to face before and so throw the child on its own resources. What were his findings?

Children of 5–9/10 years of age tended to believe that rules came from the semi-mystical authority of older children, adults or even God; they are sacred, have always existed in their present form and cannot be changed in any way (an 'external law'). But in their actual play, children unashamedly bent the rules to suit themselves and saw nothing contradictory in the idea of both players winning. Children of ten years and over understood that the rules are invented by children themselves, so that they can be changed. However, as rules are needed to make a game possible and to prevent quarrelling and to ensure fair play, they can only be changed if all the players agree to the change. At the same time, the older children kept meticulously to the rules, becoming 'lawyers' of the game, discussing the finer points and the implications of any changes that might be made.

Moral judgements

Piaget told children pairs of stories about hypothetical children who tell lies or steal or break something. For example:

> A little boy called John is in his room. He is called to dinner. He goes into the dining room. But behind the door there is a chair and on the chair there is a tray with fifteen cups on it. John couldn't have known that there was all this behind the door. He goes in, the door knocks against the tray, bang go the fifteen cups, and they all get broken.

and:

> Once there was a little boy called Henry. One day, when his mother was out, he tried to get some jam out of the cupboard. He climbed up onto a chair and stretched out his arm. But the jam was too high up and he couldn't reach it and have any. But while he was trying to get it he knocked over a cup. The cup fell down and broke.

or:

> There was once a little girl who was called Marie. She wanted to give her mother a nice surprise and cut out a piece of sewing for her. But she didn't know how to use the scissors properly and cut a big hole in her dress.

and:

> A little girl called Margaret went and took her mother's scissors one day when her mother was out. She played with them for a bit. Then, as she didn't know how to use them properly, she made a little hole in her dress.

The child is asked 'Who is naughtier?' and 'Who should be punished more?'.

Piaget was interested in the *reasons* the children gave for their answers, rather than the answers themselves. Typically, 5–9/10-year-olds said that John or Marie were naughtier, because John broke 15 cups (compared with Henry's one) and Marie made a big hole in her dress (compared with Margaret's little one). Although able to distinguish between intentional and unintentional actions, younger children based their judgement on the severity of the outcome, the sheer amount of damage done (*objective* or *external responsibility*). Children of ten years and over, on the other hand, chose Henry and Margaret, because they were both doing something they should not have been and, although the damage

done was not deliberate in either case, older children based their judgement on the motive or intention behind the act that resulted in the damage (*internal responsibility*).

However, Piaget's stories confound two independent variables – the nature of the character's intentions and the extent of the consequences. What happens when they are manipulated separately? Constanzo *et al.* (1973) read stories to six-, eight- and ten-year-olds about a boy who emptied a box of toys on the floor either so he could sort them out (good motive/intention) or to make a mess (bad intention). His mother, not knowing his intentions, entered the room and either approved or disapproved (this was their measure of the consequences). When she disapproved, the six-year-olds (but not the others) judged him naughty regardless of his actual intention (thereby confirming Piaget's results), but when she approved, the six-year-olds were just as likely to judge him according to his intentions as were the older children. The former could be explained in terms of parents' tendency to punish on the basis of how much damage is done, which teaches children that the amount of damage and the amount of wrong-doing are connected (and which has a bigger impact on younger children); the latter could be explained in terms of parents' tendency to be more concerned with inhibiting undesirable behaviour than with promoting commendable behaviour, making them more likely to punish than reward. Since ill-intended acts are likely to lead to punishment and well-intended acts are less likely to be rewarded, children – of all ages – will have greater experience with the social consequences of the former than of the latter (Karniol, 1978).

Nelson (1980) found that even three-year-olds can make judgements about intentions regardless of consequences if the information about intentions is made explicit; in Piaget's stories, it was the consequences that were made explicit. Nelson found that in this kind of story, three-year-olds assume that actors who bring about negative consequences must have had negative motives (consistent with the first of Constanzo *et al.*'s findings); in this way they are less proficient than older children at discriminating intentions from consequences and using these separate pieces of information to make moral judgements.

What happens when children are asked to make a judgement between a small amount of deliberate damage and a large amount of accidental damage? Armsby (1971) found that even six-year-olds say that a small amount of deliberate damage is naughtier. However, the answers depend partly on the extent and nature of the damage. For example, if the choice is between the deliberate breakage of a cup and the accidental damage of a television set, 40 percent of six-year-olds and fewer than 10 percent of ten-year-olds said the latter was more deserving of punishment. This suggests that young children can understand intention (in the sense of deliberate naughtiness) and are aware that damage to valued objects is something to be avoided, but also that as we get older, it becomes easier to weigh up the relative importance of intentions and the damage done, as it does to infer what others' intentions actually are.

All of these studies suggest not only that children's understanding of intention is much more complex than Piaget believed, but that they are able to bring it to bear in moral decision making, something that should not be possible according to Piaget: the pre-school child is not a-moral (Durkin, 1995).

What do children understand by a lie? Piaget found that an unintentional falsehood which has serious consequences is judged as naughtier by younger children than a deliberate lie that does not. This too suggests the difficulty that younger children have in weighing up the relative importance of intention on the one hand and damage or consequences on the other. For younger children, the seriousness of a lie is measured by the degree of literal departure from the truth. So, for example, a child who claims to have seen a 'dog as big as an elephant' is naughtier than one who claims to have seen a 'dog as big as a horse' (since elephants are bigger than horses). For the younger child, lies are wrong because they are punished by adults and lying to adults is worse than lying to other children. For the older child, lying is wrong because it betrays the trust without which fruitful and worthwhile social interaction is impossible; lying to adults is not necessarily worse than lying to one's peers.

Punishment and justice

The young child feels the need for misdeeds to be punished in some way, but the form of the punishment can be quite arbitrary: what matters is that people should pay for their crime with some kind of suffering and, generally, the greater suffering the better (Piaget called this *expiatory punishment*, 'expiatory' meaning 'making amends for' or 'paying the penalty of'). Punishment is decreed by authority and is accepted as just because of its source. So, for example, it is acceptable for a whole class of children to be punished for the misdeed of a single child

if the latter does not own up and the others refuse to identify the offender.

If someone suffers a misfortune shortly after committing a misdeed that has gone undetected or unpunished, young children will often construe the misfortune as a punishment, as if God (or some equivalent force) is 'in league' with people in authority to ensure that 'the guilty will always be caught in the end' (this is known as *immanent justice*, 'immanent' meaning 'inherent'). So, if a child tells a lie and gets away with it, then later trips and breaks an arm, this is taken by the younger child as a punishment. The older child, by contrast, sees punishment as bringing home to the offender the nature of the offence and as a deterrent against future misdeeds. Also the 'punishment should fit the crime'. For example, if one child takes another's sweets, the former should be deprived of their sweets or should make it up to the victim in some other appropriate way (the principle of *reciprocity*). (Part of the philosophy behind community service is a 'giving back' to society in a practically useful way, such as making good the damage done during a crime, instead of simply sending the offender to prison.) Justice is no longer tied to authority, there is less belief in immanent justice and punishing innocent persons for the misdeeds of only one is now thought to always be wrong.

Summary of Piaget's theory

The morality of the 5–9/10-year-old is *heteronomous* ('being subject to another's laws or rules'), which is associated with moral realism, and that of the child of ten and over is *autonomous* ('being subject to one's own laws or rules'), associated with moral relativism (see Table 27.3).

However, the moral thinking of any child is always a mixture of heteronomous morality/moral reality and autonomous morality/moral relativism – it is a matter of which one predominates and they are not mutually exclusive. Also, many elements of the former can be detected in adults' moral thinking (see the discussion of errors in the attribution process in Chapter 15). How did Piaget account for the shift from heteronomous to autonomous morality?

● It happens partly because of the move from egocentric to operational thought (see Chapter 25), which enables the child to see things from the point of view of others. According to Piaget, this decline of egocentrism usually happens at around the age of seven, so cognitive development seems to be a necessary condition for moral development, but not a sufficient condition. Moral

Heteronomous morality (5–9/10 years);	Autonomous morality (10+ years);
Associated with *moral realism*: moral knowledge and understanding are objective and absolute : laws, rules, punishment, right and wrong etc. emanate form external sources (God, adults) and obedience is good in itself	Associated with *moral relativism*: morality is not a matter of obeying external authorities; rather, moral rules grow out of human relationships and we must respect people's differing points of view
External responsibility	Internal responsibility
Expiatory punishment; immanent justice	Reciprocity; much reduced belief in immanent justice

Table 27.3 *Summary of Piaget's theory of moral development*

development lags at least a year or two behind cognitive development and the latter is no guarantee of the former. So what else is involved?

- There is also a progressive change in social relationships from *unilateral respect* (i.e. unconditional, absolute and one-way obedience to parents and other adults) to *mutual respect* within the peer group, where disagreements and disputes between equals have to be negotiated and resolved and a compromise reached. Although they must appear in this order, mutual respect can be delayed or prevented, either by slow cognitive development or by social experience in which unilateral respect predominates.

An evaluation of Piaget's theory

Until very recently, Piaget's claim regarding the crucial importance of disagreements and their resolution among children had not been empirically tested. However, a study by Kruger (1992) provides support for Piaget (see Box 27.6).

While there is quite a lot of cross-cultural support for the existence of general age trends as Piaget described them (i.e. a general shift from heteronomous to autonomous morality at about nine or ten years), Kohlberg (1963) concluded that, overall, the evidence regarding the association between heteronomous morality and unilateral respect on the one hand, and autonomous morality and mutual respect on the other, is very inconclusive.

According to Wright (1971), Piaget's theory is really intended to explain how practical morality develops, i.e. how we conceive those situations in which we are actively involved and which demand a moral response or decision. Yet the evidence which Piaget drew on were samples of the child's theoretical morality, i.e. how an individual thinks about moral problems, real and hypothetical, one's own and others', when not immediately or directly

BOX 27.6   **Key study: Criticizing your mates can aid your moral development**

Kruger (1992) paired 48 'focal' female participants (mean age 8.6 years) either with a female age-mate or her mother. All the focal participants were pre- and post-tested for moral reasoning abilities. In the intervention, the pairs were asked to try to reach agreement about two moral dilemmas. As predicted, those focal participants who were paired with an agemate showed significantly more sophisticated moral reasoning after the discussions than those who were paired with an adult. The former used more active discussion styles (more egalitarian, more two-way and more critical) which were positively correlated with post-test scores whether or not the participant was paired with an age-mate. These results indicate that the advantage of being paired with an age-mate is attributable to the greater use of active discussion styles (rather than the mere fact of being paired with an equal).

involved. So how are the two related? According to Piaget, they are related via the concept of conscious realization – theory is the *conscious realization* of the moral principles on which we actually operate, i.e. we can already do things by the time we come to think about them and reflect on them. (A good example is the fact that a child learns to talk according to the rules of grammar long before the realization that there are such things as grammatical rules – as we saw in Chapter 26.)

It follows that there is always a time-lag between practical and theoretical morality, a delay before a developmental change at the practical level is registered at the theoretical level; this implies that theoretical morality is shaped by practical morality (and not the other way round). It follows that adult theorizing (tuition) will not affect the child's practical morality. At best, it can only help theoretical morality to catch up with practical morality (Wright, 1971).

Finally, Piaget felt that popular girls' games (such as 'you're it' and a form of hopscotch) were so simple compared with marbles (the most popular game among boys) as to hardly merit research effort. Although he believed that girls eventually achieved similar moral levels to boys, he thought that they are less concerned with 'legal elaborations': the possibility of gender bias in Piaget's theory is a theme we shall return to when discussing Kohlberg's theory.

● Kohlberg's theory

Kohlberg was critical of both the concept of a superego or conscience and of the learning theory and SLT approaches to morality. He believed that the learning theory approach in particular (which emphasizes overt behaviour) largely ignores or underplays the importance of the way the individual construes the situation and thinks about the issues raised by it, as well as how these cognitive processes change with age. SLT also fails to show developmental changes which even common sense suggests do, in fact, occur.

Kohlberg also believes that research has failed to show any consistent relationship between different patterns of child-rearing and different kinds of moral behaviour. The only way to find any underlying consistency in an individual's moral behaviour and any evidence of developmental trends is to study the philosophy, logic or reasoning implicit in the cognitive structure which underlies both an individual's thinking and acting (corresponding to Piaget's theoretical and practical morality, respectively). He believes that only the cognitive–developmental approach provides a satisfactory conceptual integration of such phenomena as resistance to temptation, prosocial behaviour and so on.

The way Kohlberg has studied moral development is to present participants with moral dilemmas (ten in all), each involving a conflict between two (or more) moral principles; the participant has to choose between them. Like Piaget, he is interested not in the actual judgement or choice itself but in the reasons the person gives for making the choice – *how* people think rather than what they think. The reasons represent the structure of the judgement and centre around ten universal moral issues or values, namely punishment, property, law, roles and concerns of affection, roles and concerns of author-

ity, life, liberty, distributive justice, truth and sex.

The most famous of the Kohlberg dilemmas is the one involving Heinz, whose central conflict is between preserving life and upholding the law:

> In Europe, a woman was near death from a special kind of cancer. There was one drug that the doctors thought might save her. It was a form of radium that a druggist in the same town had recently discovered. The drug was expensive to make but the druggist was charging ten times what the drug cost him to make. He paid $200 for the radium and charged $2000 for a small dose of it. The sick woman's husband, Heinz, went to everyone he knew to borrow the money, but he could only get together about $1000, which is half of what it cost. He told the druggist that his wife was dying and asked him to sell it cheaper or let him pay later. But the druggist said 'No. I discovered the drug and I'm going to make money from it' . Heinz got desperate and broke into the man's store to steal the drug for his wife.

- Should the husband have done it? Why?
- Was it actually right or wrong? Why?
- What if he didn't love his wife – would that change anything?
- Is it a husband's duty to steal the drug for his wife if he can get it no other way?
- Would a good husband do it?
- Did the druggist have the right to charge that much where there is no law actually setting a price limit? Why?
- What if the dying person were a stranger? Should he have stolen the drug anyway?

Based on the logic or reasoning revealed by their answers, participants are classified according to their level of moral development (i.e. which of the six stages their answers best illustrate; see Table 27.4). Two people at the same level and stage could still give two opposing answers: one could say 'Yes, Heinz should have stolen the drug', the other could say 'No, Heinz should not have stolen it'. Remember, it is the underlying reasons that determine how mature is a person's moral development. Let us see how Kohlberg's stages would apply to a particular moral dilemma (not one of Kohlberg's):

> John is seven and has recently been beaten up by an older boy who attends his brother Alan's school. Alan is a very protective older brother and they are very close; Alan decides to avenge John's victimization and to beat up the older boy. But his parents strongly disapprove of physical aggression and he could get into serious trouble with them (as well as the school authorities). One day, after school, Alan waited for the boy and gave him a thorough beating.

Level 1:
Pre-conventional

Stage 1 (Punishment and obedience orientation)
What is right and wrong is determined by what is punishable and what is not – if stealing is wrong , it is because authority figures say so and because they will punish it ('might makes right'). Moral action is essentially the avoidance of punishment.

Stage 2 (Instrumental relativist orientation)
What is right and wrong is determined by what brings rewards and what people want Other people's needs and wants come into the picture, but only in a reciprocal sense ('You scratch my back, I'll scratch yours').

Level 2:
Conventional

Stage 3 (Interpersonal concordance or 'good boy-nice girl' orientation)
Good behaviour is whatever pleases and helps others and doing what they approve of. Being moral is being 'a good person in your own eyes . and those of others'. What the majority thinks is right is right by definition.

Stage 4 ('Law and order' orientation)
Being good means 'doing one's duty' – showing respect for authority and maintaining the social order (status quo) for its own sake. Concern for the common good goes beyond the Stage 3 concern for the welfare of one's family: society protects the rights of individuals, so society must be protected by the individual. Laws are unquestionably accepted and obeyed.

Level 3:
Post-conventional

Stage 5 (Social contract–legalistic orientation)
Since laws are established by mutual agreement, they can be changed by the same democratic process. Although laws and rules should be respected, since they protect individual rights as well as those of society as a whole, individual rights can sometimes supersede these laws if they become too destructive or restrictive. The law should not be obeyed at all costs, e.g. life is more 'sacred' than any legal principle.

Stage 6 (Universal–ethical principle orientation)
Moral action is determined by our inner conscience and may/may not be in agreement with public opinion or society's laws. What is right or wrong is based upon self-chosen, ethical principles which we arrive at through reflection – they are not demanded by society as such. These principles are abstract and universal, such as justice, equality, the sacredness of human life and respect for human dignity; only if we act in accordance with them can we attain full moral responsibility.

TABLE 27.4 *Kohlberg's three levels (six stages) of moral development*

Should he have done it? Why?

Table 27.5 shows some typical pro and con answers at each of the six stages. Can you identify the central conflict involved?

The relationship between cognitive and moral development

Like Piaget, Kohlberg believes that cognitive development is a necessary but not a sufficient condition of moral development, i.e. cognitive development sets a limit on maturity of moral reasoning, with moral development usually lagging behind cognitive development. Table 27.6 shows the relationship between these two aspects of development.

When discussing cognitive development in Chapter 25, we noted that many adults do not attain formal operations (about 50 percent in fact) and if this is a necessary condition for reaching Kohlberg's stages 5 and 6, then it is not surprising that only about 10 percent (Kohlberg, 1975) to 15 percent (Colby *et al.*, 1983) of adults attain the highest level of moral reasoning (according to the latter, not before their mid-30s).

What evidence is there to support Kohlberg?

Kohlberg (1963) reported his findings from a cross-sectional study of 58 boys, both working class and middle class, in Chicago; they were aged seven, ten, 13, and 16. Each boy was given a two-hour interview based on ten dilemmas. There was a reasonable

Pro	Anti
Stage 1 It isn't really bad to beat him up – so long as he doesn't suffer any serious injury. After all, he's only doing what the boy did to John and no one else need find out. He might be called a coward if he didn't do it.	**Stage 1** You can't go round beating people up – he might suffer serious injury. If he gets caught he'll be in real trouble: he could be expelled. Even if he's not caught, he'll always be afraid of being beaten up himself or of John being picked on again.
Stage 2 If he wants to show he really cares for John and can look after him, then he should have beaten the boy up. Wouldn't the punishment be worth it if you've proved you can play 'big brother'?	**Stage 2** The boy must have had his reasons for beating up John – perhaps he was provoked. What good would it do John anyway ? He might prefer Alan to do nothing.
Stage 3 Physical violence is bad – but the whole situation is a bad one. He's doing what is natural for a good older brother. You can't blame him for doing something out of caring for his younger brother and wanting to protect him. He would have been blamed if he hadn't done it.	**Stage 3** If your younger brother gets beaten up, you can't blame yourself for it. Alan showed he cared by wanting to beat the boy up – it's the older boy who is the guilty one, not Alan. Alan couldn't have prevented what happened to John and if he gets expelled, this will bring disgrace on the whole family.
Stage 4 The older boy can't be allowed to get away with bullying . It's Alan's duty to look after John and he would always reproach himself for not doing so. But nor can Alan go round beating people up and he must accept the consequences of his actions, even if this means being expelled. Two wrongs don't make a right.	**Stage 4** It is natural for Alan to want to avenge John, but it is always wrong to be violent. You have to follow the rules, regardless of your feelings or special circumstances.
Stage 5 Before you say what Alan did was wrong, you must consider the whole situation. Of course, if an adult were to commit the same act of violence as Alan, they could be prosecuted for assault – the law is quite clear. But it would be quite reasonable for anyone in Alan's situation to do what he did; people will respect him for it.	**Stage 5** Alan would feel better, and so would John, if the culprit was punished for what he did. But it's not Alan's place to do the punishing – the end doesn't justify the means. You can't say categorically it's wrong, but even in the circumstances, you can't (fully) condone it either. Alan might reproach himself later for acting impulsively.
Stage 6 When you have to choose between acting in a caring and protective way towards someone close to you and behaving in a violent way towards a person who was aggressive to them, the higher principle of caring and protecting makes it morally right to behave violently – the end justifies the means.	**Stage 6** The only correct course of action is one that is 'right' or everyone concerned. Alan's behaviour is the same as the behaviour he is avenging. Others might understand his behaviour, but he might condemn himself later on. His behaviour should be determined by what he thinks an 'ideally just person' would do in the situation.

Table 27.5 *Responses to a moral dilemma at each of Kohlberg's six stages*

degree of within-stage consistency (each boy tended to display the same level of moral reasoning for different dilemmas, with the rest being at the next adjacent stage – up or down); the younger ones tended to perform at stages 1 and 2, with higher proportions of stages 3 and 4 among the older boys . Some of the boys were followed up and re-tested at three-yearly intervals up to age 30–36 (Colby *et al.*, 1983); these longitudinal data broadly confirmed the cross-sectional pattern.

Kohlberg (1969) also studied children in Britain, Mexico, Taiwan, Turkey, USA and Yucatan, and found a similar pattern of development in all these countries, although those in non-industrialized countries tended to progress through the stages more slowly (see below).

Rest (1983), in a 20-year longitudinal study of men from early adolescence to their mid-30s, found that the stages do occur in the order Kohlberg described, but change is very gradual. Over the 20-

Kohlberg's levels of moral development	Age group included within Kohlberg's levels	Corresponding stage of moral development (Piaget)	Corresponding stage of cognitive development (Piaget)
1 Pre-conventional (Stages 1 and 2)	Most 9-year-olds and below. Some over 9	Heteronomous (5–9/10)	Preoperational (2–7)
2 Conventional (Stages 3 and 4)	Most adolescents and adults	Heteronomous (e.g. respect for the law and authority figures) plus autonomous (e.g. taking intentions into account)	Concrete operational (7–11)
3 Post-conventional (Stages 5 and 6)	10–15 percent of adults, not before mid-30s	Autonomous (10 and above)	Formal operational (11 and above)

Table 27.6 *The relationship between Kohlberg's and Piaget's stages of moral development and Piaget's stages of cognitive development*

year period, these men changed, on average, less than two stages.

Researchers, including Kohlberg himself, have failed to uncover any stage 6 reasoning in the responses of 'ordinary' participants and considerably less stage 5 reasoning than Kohlberg originally reported. In 1978, he reviewed his theory and concluded that there may not after all be a separate stage 6. It seems that universal ethical principles guide the reasoning of only a few very exceptional individuals, such as Martin Luther King, who devote their lives to humanistic causes. Only 10–15 percent of adults show level 3 reasoning as we have seen, and according to Atkinson *et al.* (1990), it cannot be considered part of the normal or expected course of development but a philosophical ideal. However, Colby *et al.* (1983) argue that although the dilemmas and interviewing techniques may be unable to differentiate between stages 5 and 6, stage 6 may still exist as a 'natural psychological stage in the moral developmental sequence'.

An evaluation of Kohlberg's theory

1 Some critics have pointed out that the dilemma stories are unfamiliar to most participants – children might show more mature reasoning if asked about issues relevant to their day-to-day experience. They are also hypothetical and do not involve any serious personal consequences. Would participants reason at the same level if they had to think about practical moral issues that could have negative implications for themselves? Sobesky (1983) presented the Heinz dilemma to high school and college students who were told either that the consequences of stealing the drug were severe (Heinz would definitely be caught

and sent to prison) or mild (Heinz could take such a small amount it would not be missed). They were asked to imagine themselves in Heinz's position and describe what they would do and why; in the severe condition, they were less likely to advocate stealing and levels of reasoning were lower.

2 Underlying the dilemmas is what is called *ethical rule theory*, which places universal principles at the centre of moral judgement – for Kohlberg justice is the fundamental principle underlying moral development. This theory assumes that one must have a moral rule in order to make a justified moral judgement and this rule is needed for identifying the relevant facts of a case before the judgement is made. An alternative view is *ethical act theory* – relevant facts may be identified without moral rules and may over-ride moral generalizations. Moral rules are 'summaries' to which there may be exceptions and so morality is situation-specific. For example, Rosen (1980) asks us to suppose that Heinz's wife has contemplated suicide for years and wants to die with dignity now. What if Heinz wants to keep her alive because they live off interest from a trust fund in her name? Again, suppose the druggist is the wife's brother, knows her wishes and prices the drug so that Heinz will not be able to afford it. Do these details of the case change it from a moral point of view? Meadows (1986), for one, thinks they do: moral dilemmas are real problems, faced by people in a real setting. It is no test of an ethical theory or of the moral reasoning of people to pose artificial problems. Kohlberg's dilemmas are artificial not primarily because they are fictional (hypothetical), but

because they do not represent realistic situations with all their complexity.

3 Some critics, notably Carol Gilligan (1977, 1982), believe that Kohlberg has overemphasized justice to the exclusion of other aspects of morality and by doing so has built a *sexist bias* into his theory of moral development (see Box 27.7).

4 According to Turiel (1978), Kohlberg has failed to make a basic distinction between *social rules or conventions* (arbitrary rules about behaviour which serve to co-ordinate social behaviour, applicable only within certain cultures as a matter of custom and tradition), such as eating with a knife and fork, and *moral rules* (general principles relating to justice, fairness and the welfare of others), e.g. 'thou shalt not commit murder'. At least within a given culture, social conventions can be changed by agreement, but moral rules cannot – the latter seem to be right in themselves. Turiel goes as far as to claim that social and conventional thinking are two distinct conceptual systems.

Weston and Turiel (1980) found that 4–6-year-olds could recognize the difference. They also read 5–11-year-olds two kinds of hypothetical stories, one about a school in which there were no rules about hitting (representing a moral rule) and the other about a school where children were allowed to take their clothes off (representing a social convention); a majority of children at all ages said a school should not allow hitting but it could allow undressing. These findings contradict Piaget's view of early morality as heteronomous and Kohlberg's view that principles outweigh conventions only in the more advanced stages (Durkin, 1995).

5. Kohlberg's theory has stimulated a great deal of research, especially cross-cultural research. A number of reviews of studies using Kohlberg's dilemmas have been carried out, including those of Snarey (1985) and Eckensberger (1994). Snarey reviewed 44 studies in 26 countries and reported strong support for the universality of the stages. Eckensberger reviewed over 50 studies, carried out in an impressive range of cultures, including many in Africa, Asia, East and Western Europe, the Near East and Mediterranean, the Caribbean and Latin America, the USA and Canada. The findings from cross-cultural research are discussed further in Box 27. 8.

BOX 27.7 Critical discussion: Gender and morality – is Kohlberg's theory sexist?

According to Carol Gilligan (1977, 1982) , the essence of morality for women is not the same as for men. Different upbringings produce different moral orientations: (a) males are socialized to be independent and achievement orientated, so that they become preoccupied with issues such as fair return, equality of treatment and the application of abstract principles to resolve conflicts of interest; (b) females are socialized to be caring and nurturant and to maintain a sense of responsibility towards others. In terms of Kohlberg's theory, these are stages 4 and 3 respectively, which he has taken to mean that females' moral development is typically 'lower' than males' .

However, this comparison is fundamentally flawed because it is based on a male concept of morality (i.e. where justice is paramount). Not only was much of Kohlberg's early research done with male samples, but most of the dilemmas involve males as the principal characters (such as Heinz), possibly making it easier for males to relate to them.

Again, Kohlberg sees the ability to detach oneself from the situation one is judging as a measure of advanced morality, while the female role is organized around attachment and concern for others' welfare. Ironically, it seems that the very traits which have traditionally defined 'goodness' for women (their care for, sensitivity to and responsibility towards others) make them inferior to men in moral development. Instead of seeing females' moral reasoning as deficient, Gilligan sees it as different (hence the title of her 1982 book, In a Different Voice) but largely ignored in the male-dominated research into moral development.

In her own research, Gilligan interviewed 29 females, aged 15–33, all facing a significant, real-life dilemma, namely whether or not to continue with a pregnancy. The decision involved a conflict between (a) the right to personal choice and (b) the traditional association between femininity and self-sacrifice and caring for others. She identified three levels: self-interest, self-sacrifice, and care as a universal obligation; the last represents a balance between care for others and the well-being of the self. It is this care-oriented voice that Kohlberg's theory fails to hear. According to Durkin (1995), if Piaget had regarded relating to others as more central to morality than relating to rules, the field of moral development would have progressed quite differently.

BOX 27.8	Critical discussion: Is Kohlberg's theory universal?

According to Eckensberger (1994), while stages 1 and 5 are rare (as is stage 6, as we noted earlier), stages 2, 3 and 4 are found in many cultures. The highest stages have been found in Israeli kibbutzim, followed by Germany, together with upper class groups from the US, Taiwan and India; the lowest scores are found in the Bahamas, Kenya, Papua and Turkey. In all these studies, level of moral reasoning was assessed using Kohlberg's interview method. However, an alternative method has been used in some more recent studies, in which 'pencil-and-paper' tests, designed for speedy use with groups, present a number of predefined arguments from which participants are asked to choose the one they prefer or think most appropriate. Using this alternative method, people from South Korea, Taiwan and Greece score highest, while those from Belize, Sudan and Trinidad-and-Tobago tend to score lower.

While there is substantial – though by no means complete – cross-cultural support for the stages (i.e. the form of the moral arguments presented in the interviews), Kohlberg also claimed that the moral issues (or content) contained in the dilemmas are universal and complete, i.e. the material in his official scoring manual is sufficient to score all kinds of responses from all over the world. However, recent studies show that this is not so; there are cultural differences in moral themes that are difficult to score. For example, data from India show that non-violence and sacredness of (all) life are not moral principles restricted to human beings, but apply to all forms of life (including animals); this reflects the inseparable unity of religion and morality in India and other Buddhist and Hindu cultures.

According to Shweder (1991), Kohlberg's research strategies impose stage classifications upon members of non-Western cultures that distort the meaning of what they say and fail to take account of implicit structures in their views of their own social order.

Stage 1: Hedonistic, pragmatic orientation.
Concern with selfish, pragmatic consequences rather than moral considerations. What's 'right' is whatever is instrumental in achieving the actor's own needs/desires. Reasons for helping or not include direct gain to the self, future reciprocity and concern for others whom the individual needs and/or likes.

Stage 2: Needs of others orientation.
Concern for the physical, material and psychological needs of others, even though these conflict with one's own needs. This concern is expressed in the simplest terms, without clear evidence of role taking (e.g. 'He's hungry' or 'She needs it').

Stage 3: Approval and interpersonal orientation and/or stereotyped orientation.
Stereotyped images of good and bad persons and behaviour and/or considerations of others' approval/acceptance are used in justifying prosocial or non-helping behaviours (e.g. 'It's nice to help' or 'He'd like him more if he helped').

Stage 4a: Empathic orientation.
Some evidence of sympathetic responding, role taking, concern with others' humanness and/or guilt or positive affect related to the consequences of one's actions (e.g. 'He knows how he feels', 'She cares about people' and 'I'd feel bad if I didn't help because he'd be in pain').

Stage 4b: Transitional stage.
Justifications for helping or not involve internalized values, norms, duties or responsibilities or refer to the need to protect the rights and dignity of others. But these are not clearly or strongly stated (e.g. 'It's just something I've learned and feel').

Stage 5: Strongly internalized stage.
As 4b, but internalized values etc. are much more strongly stated. Additional justifications for helping include the desire to honour individual and societal contractual obligations and belief in the dignity, rights and equality of all human beings, the wish to maintain self-respect and live up to one's own values and accepted norms.(e.g. 'She'd feel a responsibility to help other people in need' or 'I would feel bad if I didn't help because I'd know that I didn't live up to my values').

Table 27.7 *Stages of prosocial moral reasoning (based on Eisenberg, 1982)*

THE DEVELOPMENT OF PROSOCIAL MORAL REASONING

Kohlberg's dilemmas involve a conflict between some law or rule and the individual's sense of right and wrong, but not all 'moral conflicts' are like this. Nancy Eisenberg (previously Eisenberg-Berg) (1982, 1986) argues that if we want to understand developmental changes in helping or altruism (see Chapter 17), we need to examine children's reasoning when there is a conflict between their own needs and wants and those of others, in a context where the role of laws, rules, the dictates of authority or formal obligations are minimal, i.e. *prosocial moral reasoning* (Eisenberg *et al.*, 1991). She presented children with prosocial moral dilemmas, such as the one involving Mary:

> A girl named Mary was going to a friend's birthday party. On her way, she saw a girl who had fallen down and hurt her leg. The girl asked Mary to go to her home and get her parents so the parents could take her to the doctor. But if Mary did run and get the child's parents, she would be late for the birthday party and miss the ice cream, cake and all the games. What should Mary do? Why?

Based on children's responses to this and other similar dilemmas, Eisenberg identified six stages of prosocial moral reasoning, which are summarized in Table 27.7.

Longitudinal studies carried out to test the model have found overall support (Eisenberg *et al.*, 1987, 1991). Boys at adolescence may regress to more hedonistic kinds of reasoning, but in later adolescence both boys and girls begin to display higher levels.

How do these changes relate to actual changes in helping behaviour? While the relationship is far from perfect (as is true for moral reasoning and moral behaviour), as children move towards more mature, sophisticated forms of reasoning, so their tendency to display sympathy and empathy and to spontaneously help others also increases (Eisenberg *et al.*, 1987, 1991). According to Schroeder *et al.* (1995), the content of prosocial moral reasoning (i.e. the specific kinds of actions judged as good or bad) is probably influenced by cultural factors, but the basic patterns of changes in what motivates helping (and the reasoning involved) seem to be universal.

CHAPTER SUMMARY

- Developmental psychologists study the process by which the individual acquires the rules and principles used to distinguish right from wrong, i.e. how morality is acquired and how it changes. By contrast, sociobiologists ask what is the adaptive function of morality in the evolution of the human species.

- Morality consists of three distinct, but interrelated, components, namely cognitive, behavioural and affective; Freud's psychoanalytic theory focuses on the affective component, learning theory and social learning theory are mainly concerned with the behavioural component, while Piaget and Kohlberg's cognitive – developmental theories concentrate on the cognitive component.

- While sociobiologists believe that morality is part of our genetic make-up as a species, all psychologists see it as part of the wider process of socialization.

- According to Freud, the conscience and ego-ideal represent the punishing and rewarding parent respectively; they become part of the child's personality through identification, which takes place at the end of the phallic stage with the resolution of the Oedipus complex.

- The girl's resolution of her Oedipus complex is much less complete than the boy's, with the result that her conscience is weaker and her ego-ideal stronger than his. This leaves females much more dependent on others, as well as the morally weaker sex, according to Freud. However, there is no evidence to support this view of females, nor that they are sexually inferior; penis envy represents envy of men's superior social status.

- Freud claims that guilt and wrong-doing are inversely related. Support for this comes from the study by MacKinnon of cheats and non-cheats, which also found that cheats are more likely to have received physical than psychological punishment.

- Several other studies have shown a positive correlation between strength of conscience and psychological methods of punishment, as in Sears *et al.*'s love-oriented childrearing techniques. While object-oriented methods, including the use of physical punishment, are associated with low levels of moral development (as well as actual delinquent behaviour), reasoning/explaining and other psychological methods are associated with high levels.

- Freud's concept of the superego reflects the commonsense personalization of conscience, but it fails to capture the long-term nature of moral development. Also, belief in an internalized conscience implies the consistency of moral behaviour, a claim that has been challenged by Hartshorne and May's doctrine of specificity.

- Eysenck explains conscience in terms of classically conditioned emotional responses (CERs), taking the form of anxiety that builds up and reaches a climax just before some wrong-doing. If sufficiently strong, this anxiety will prevent the act from being committed, so CERs represent our ability to resist temptation. They also represent feelings of guilt following a misdeed.

- The classical conditioning account underestimates the role of cognitive factors, such as a rationale that accompanies punishment. There is evidence of developmental changes in the effectiveness of different types of rationale, such as object oriented and person oriented.

- The effect of reinforcements and punishments will depend on the relationship with the person who is rewarding/punishing. Only rewards can produce morally acceptable behaviour, while punishments, at best, inhibit morally unacceptable behaviour; more seriously, punishment often produces hostility and resentment and may model the very behaviour it is trying to discourage.

- Extrinsic rewards can actually decrease intrinsically rewarding behaviour; this is called the paradox of reward. One explanation for this is to do with the kind of attribution people make about their behaviour.

- Social learning theorists differ from learning theorists by stressing the influence of observational learning (or modelling) and the role of cognitive factors intervening between stimulus and response. SLT, therefore, represents an S–O–R approach to learning.

- Children are most likely to imitate models who display socially appropriate behaviour, whose behaviour is relevant for the child in terms of perceived similarity with the model and who behave consistently.

- There is a crucial distinction between learning and performance. Merely observing a model's behaviour may be sufficient for the child to learn, but whether that behaviour will be imitated depends on several factors, including the consequences for the child of doing so and the consequences for the model of the original behaviour.

- Laboratory studies of imitation have been criticized for the artificial relationship between the model and the child. However, the distinction between positional and personal modelling shows that different models can have different kinds of influence, depending on what the model represents and the nature of the relationship. Personal modelling is much closer to the process of identification, with generalized imitation overlapping imitation and identification.

- Apart from attention, perception and memory, person variables are important cognitive variables that come in between stimulus and response. These include self-reinforcement/self-punishment, which are acquired through imitative self-approval/self-disapproval respectively.

- Only the cognitive developmental approach focuses on moral progress as such, identifying universal, qualitatively different stages of moral development. Piaget studied children's understanding of rules (of marbles, seeing all morality as consisting of rules), their moral judgements (about naughtiness, based on pairs of stories) and their conceptions of punishment and justice.

- Children from 5–9/10 display (predominantly) heteronomous morality, comprising moral realism, external responsibility and a belief in expiatory punishment and immanent justice; the child of ten and over displays autonomous morality, involving moral relativism, internal responsibility and belief in reciprocity and much less belief in immanent justice.

- Although Piaget recognized that younger children can tell the difference between deliberate and accidental naughtiness, he seems to have underestimated their ability to take intention into account when making moral judgements. His stories tended to emphasize the consequences of the character's behaviour and to confound this with the character's intentions; children become better able to weigh up their relative importance as they get older.

- The change from heteronomous to autonomous morality occurs partly because of changes in cognitive development and partly because of a change in social relationships from unilateral to mutual respect.

- While Piaget's theory is meant to explain how practical morality develops, he sampled the child's theoretical morality; these are linked through conscious realization. Adult theorizing will not affect the child's practical morality, which shapes, and is in advance of, theoretical morality.

- Kohlberg's cognitive developmental theory is an extension of Piaget's, comprising three levels (pre-conventional, conventional, post-conventional) with two stages at each level; these six stages span childhood, adolescence and adulthood.
- Kohlberg presented participants with moral dilemmas (the most famous being the Heinz dilemma) involving a conflict between two or more moral principles; the reasons given for choosing between these principles determine the stage of moral development to which participants are assigned.
- Evidence from both cross-sectional and longitudinal studies, both Kohlberg's own and those of others, supports the sequence and the invariance of stages. However, there seems to be no distinct stage 6, and only 10–15 percent of adults show any post-conventional reasoning at all.
- The dilemmas themselves have been criticized, together with Kohlberg's emphasis on justice which, according to Gilligan, is a primarily male concept of morality. Females are socialized to be caring and nurturant, which is reflected in stage 3 reasoning, while males typically reach stage 4; his theory is, therefore, inherently sex biased. Kohlberg also fails to distinguish between moral rules and social rules/conventions; children as young as four can tell the difference.
- Kohlberg's theory has generated considerable cross-cultural research, which reveals differences in the stages that are typically reached in different countries. However, results vary according to whether interviews or a pencil-and-paper alternative are used. While there is considerable support for stages 2, 3 and 4 in all cultures, there are cultural differences in moral content that are difficult to score using the standard manual.
- Prosocial moral reasoning involves conflicts between what different people need and want, but where the law or rules are not relevant. Eisenberg has identified six stages of this kind of reasoning, which are positively correlated with helping behaviour and which seem to be universal.

GLOSSARY

Autonomous morality The ten-year-old and over's morality, incorporating moral relativism, internal responsibility, and much weaker belief in immanent justice ('autonomous' = 'subject to one's own laws').

Doctrine of specificity The view that honesty is largely situation-specific and not a general personality trait, i.e. people's honesty is not consistent across situations.

Expiatory punishment The young child's belief that people should be punished for their misdeeds through some kind of suffering; generally, the greater the suffering, the better. The punishment needn't fit the crime.

External responsibility The young child's judgement of behaviour as good or bad based on the severity of the outcome/amount of damage, rather than the motive/intention behind the act. Also called objective responsibility.

Generalized imitation In a laboratory experiment, the spontaneous imitation of aspects of the model's behaviour for which there has been no direct reinforcement.

Heteronomous morality The 5–9/10-year-old's morality, incorporating moral realism, external responsibility, immanent justice and expiatory punishment ('heteronomous' = 'subject to another's laws').

Imitative self-(dis)approval The process by which the child's own actions, previously rewarded (punished) by the parents, can be reinforced (punished) by the child itself in their absence.

Immanent justice The young child's belief that God (or some similar force) is in league with authority figures to ensure that 'the guilty will always get caught in the end'.

Internal responsibility The older child's judgement of behaviour as good or bad based on the motive/intention, rather than the damage done.

Moral realism The young child's belief that laws, rules, punishment, right and wrong emanate from external sources (such as God, adults); obedience is good in itself.

Moral relativism The older child's belief that morality is not just a matter of obeying external authorities, but moral rules grow out of human relationships and we must respect people's differing points of view.

Mutual respect Negotiating and resolving disagreements and disputes between one's peers (equals) and reaching a compromise.

Paradox of reward The finding that extrinsic (external) rewards offered for activities that are already intrinsically rewarding can actually reduce behaviour relating to those activities.

Personal model A person whose behaviour is imitated because of his/her personal qualities. Related to identification.

Positional model A person whose behaviour is imitated because of the social role that he/she represents (e.g. gender, age, occupation).

Prosocial moral reasoning Reasoning about situations in which there is a conflict between the needs/wants of two or more individuals, rather than a conflict between some law/rule and the individual's sense of right and wrong.

Reciprocity The older child's belief that punishment should fit the crime, as when criminals compensate their victims in some appropriate way.

Self-regulatory systems and plans Self-imposed standards or rules which we adopt for regulating our own behaviour. Relates to the distinction between external and internal (self-) reinforcement and punishment; one of Mischel's person variables.

Subjective outcome variables The value we place on the expected consequences of our behaviour; one of Mischel's person variables.

Unilateral respect Unconditional, absolute, one-way obedience of parents and other adults.

FURTHER READING

Gilligan, C. (1993) *In A Different Voice: Psychological Theory and Women's Development.* Cambridge, MA: Harvard University Press. A modern classic, this is about much more than moral development. A feminist critique of male-centred psychology.

Individual Differences

28 INTELLIGENCE

INTRODUCTION AND OVERVIEW

The concept of intelligence is probably one of the most elusive in the whole of psychology: to try to pin it down and provide a definition which all (or even most) psychologists can agree on seems almost impossible and attempts to measure it are fraught with difficulties (not least of which is not knowing what it is).

Intelligence represents one of the most intensively researched sources of individual differences but it is not just of academic interest. The intelligence test (in one form or another) has impinged on the lives of most of us, whether it is for educational selection, occupational selection or selection for Mensa, the high IQ society. According to Vernon (1979), over 2000 million tests of intelligence or achievement are given every year in the USA alone.

 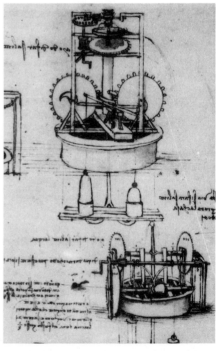

Leonardo da Vinci. His 'intelligence' was extremely versatile and multiple, as he was seemingly an expert in all areas from art to engineering through to anatomy.

In this chapter, we shall begin by trying to define the concept of intelligence, before discussing the major theories of intelligence, in particular the *psychometric* theories of Spearman, Burt and Vernon, Thurstone and Guilford, Sternberg's *information-processing approach* (which forms part of his *triarchic theory*) and finally Gardner's *theory of multiple intelligences*.

At the heart of the psychometric approach lie the statistical technique called *factor analysis* and the use of *intelligence (IQ) tests*; we shall look at the two most widely used tests, the Stanford–Binet and the Wechsler, in the light of the criteria used for evaluating psychometric tests in general, in particular *validity*. One aspect of the issue of validity is the debate about whether IQ tests are 'culture fair', which raises many fundamental methodological as well as political and ethical questions.

The near-obsession of Western culture with measuring and categorizing people is highly emotionally charged and politically sensitive, particularly in relation to the question of racial differences in intelligence, which represents another instance of the heredity–environment/nature–nurture issue. We shall discuss the use of twin and adoption studies to measure the relative influences of genetics and environment before considering the 'race and IQ' debate as an aspect of this wider controversy. Unlike other cases, the nature–nurture debate in intelligence has become equated with extremes of political viewpoints and the issue highlights the impossibility of completely divorcing the social from the scientific functions of psychology.

DEFINITIONS OF INTELLIGENCE

So diverse are the definitions of intelligence that Vernon (1960) thought it necessary to identify three broad groups of definition, namely biological, psychological and operational.

Biological definitions see intelligence as related to adaptation to the environment. As we saw in Chapter 25, Piaget studied intelligence as a process and not as a set of capacities, so that he was not interested in how individuals differ from one another but rather in what stages of development all individuals go through. For Piaget (1950), intelligence is:

> ... essentially a system of living and acting operations, i.e. a state of balance or equilibrium achieved by the person when he is able to deal adequately with the data before him. But it is not a static state, it is dynamic in that it continually adapts itself to new environmental stimuli.

So Piaget represents the *qualitative* approach to intelligence, where the focus is on intelligence itself and not differences in intelligence between individuals.

Psychological definitions, by contrast, represent the *quantitative* or *psychometric* approach, where the emphasis is very much on the measurement of intelligence to compare and differentiate between individuals. There are many psychological definitions and some of the best known and most influential are shown in Table 28.1.

The definitions of Terman, Burt and Vernon all stress the purely intellectual aspects of the concept, while Binet's and Wechsler's definitions are much broader and perhaps closer to commonsense understanding. According to Heim, however intelligence may be defined, 'it is complex and not simple, facets are many and varied' and, consequently, to speak of an individual's 'true' intelligence is meaningless. (We shall take up this point again later when we discuss intelligence tests.)

| It seems to us that in intelligence there is a fundamental faculty, the impairment of which is of the utmost importance for practical life. This faculty is called judgement, otherwise called good sense, practical sense, initiative, the faculty of adapting one's self to circumstances. To judge well, to comprehend well, to reason well ... (Binet, 1905) |
| An individual is intelligent in proportion as he is able to carry on abstract thinking. (Terman, 1921) |
| Innate, general, cognitive ability. (Burt, 1955) |
| The aggregate of the global capacity to act purposefully, think rationally, to deal effectively with the environment. (Wechsler, 1944) |
| The effective all-round cognitive abilities to comprehend, to grasp relations and reason. (Vernon, 1969) |
| Intelligent activity consists in grasping the essentials in a situation and responding appropriately to them. (Heim, 1970) |

TABLE 28.1 *Some psychological definitions of intelligence*

Heim objects to the use of intelligence as a noun because, she says, it smacks of an 'insoluble entity or thing', which is opposed to her belief that intelligence should be regarded as part of personality as a whole (combining cognitive, affective and conative dimensions, the last referring to the 'striving, doing, aspect of experience'), which is an integrated unit. Consequently, she prefers to talk about 'intelligent activity' rather than 'intelligence'.

An *operational* definition simply defines intelligence in terms of tests designed to measure it, i.e. 'Intelligence is what intelligence tests measure' (Boring, 1923). While such a definition is intended to get round the problem of the multiplicity of definitions that exists, it fails to tell us exactly what it is that intelligence tests measure and is circular, i.e. the concept being defined is part of the definition itself. Miles (1957) argues that if we substitute the names of particular tests, then we can break into the circle but Heim is not convinced, pointing out that this merely decreases the circumference of the circle! Like Heim, Ryle (1949) believes that 'intelligence' does not denote an entity or an engine inside us causing us to act in particular ways; instead, he argues that any action can be performed more or less intelligently, so it should be used as an adjective and not as a noun. One attempt to 'solve' the problem of defining intelligence was made by Neisser (1979):

> There are no definitive criteria of intelligence, just as there are none for 'chairness', it is a fuzzy-edged concept to which many features are relevant. Two people may both be quite intelligent and yet have very few traits in common – they resemble the prototype along different dimensions ... [Intelligence] is a resemblance between two individuals, one real and the other prototypical.

Perhaps most of our concepts are like this and trying to define something so precisely that it accommodates every single instance is doomed to failure – intelligence is a 'natural' concept which is too 'loose' to be adequately defined by any single definition. Neisser advocates that intelligence should be viewed in terms of *prototypes* ('best instances' or ideal cases) – we imagine a prototypically intelligent person and compare particular individuals with the imagined person.

However, different social groups may have somewhat different prototypes and while Neisser's approach seems to be an excellent way of discovering what people mean by 'intelligence', it does not help us discover what 'intelligence' means – for Neisser there is no difference, but for Sternberg (1987), for example, there is.

FACTOR ANALYTIC THEORIES OF INTELLIGENCE: ONE FACTOR OR MANY?

Having looked at some of the major definitions of intelligence, we now turn to more detailed accounts of the nature of intelligence. Not surprisingly, there are sharp divisions of opinion here too, but they all have in common the basic assumption that intelligence is a characteristic of a person that can be measured by intelligence tests which, in turn, implies that individuals differ with respect to that characteristic. This describes the *psychometric* ('mental measurement') approach.

We shall be discussing tests later in the chapter and all we need to understand for the moment is that theories of intelligence are based upon analysis

Sub test	Infor-mation	Digit span	Voca-bulary	Arith-metic	Compre-hension	Simil-arities	Picture comple-tion	Picture arrange-ment	Block design	Object assem-bly	Digit symbol
Information	–										
Digit span	0.46	–									
Vocabulary	0.81	0.52	–								
Arithmetic	0.61	0.56	0.63	–							
Comprehension	0.68	0.45	0.74	0.57	–						
Similarities	0.66	0.45	0.72	0.56	0.68	–					
Picture completion	0.52	0.37	0.55	0.48	0.52	0.54	–				
Picture arrangement	0.50	0.37	0.51	0.46	0.48	0.50	0.51	–			
Block design	0.50	0.43	0.52	0.56	0.48	0.51	0.54	0.47		–	
Object assembly	0.39	0.33	0.41	0.42	0.40	0.43	0.52	0.40	0.63	–	
Digit symbol	0.44	0.42	0.47	0.45	0.44	0.46	0.42	0.39	0.47	0.38	–

(Source: data adapted from Wechsler, 1981.)
(from Colman, (1990) in Roth, I. (ed.) *Introduction to Psychology*, Open University and LEA.)

Table 28.2 *Average correlations between WAIS–R subtests*

of scores of large numbers of individuals on various intelligence tests using a statistical technique called *factor analysis* (FA) (see Chapter 29). This involves correlating the scores of a large sample of participants to determine whether scores on certain tests are related to scores on certain other tests, i.e. whether some, or any, of the tests have something in common. The basic assumption is that the more similar the scores on two or more tests (i.e. the higher the correlation), the more likely it is that these tests are tapping the same basic ability (or factor).

If we find, for example, that people's scores on tests A, B, C, D and E are highly correlated (i.e. if they score high on one they tend to score high on the others) then it could be inferred that all five tests are measuring the same ability and individuals differ according to how much or how little of that particular ability they have. However, if there is very little relationship between scores on the five tests, then each test may be measuring a distinct ability and when comparing individuals we would have to look at each ability separately (Table 28.2).

These two hypothetical outcomes roughly correspond to two theories of intelligence, the first of which is sometimes referred to as the 'London Line' and is associated with Spearman (1904, 1967), Burt (1949, 1955) and Vernon (1950), in contrast with the mainly American approach of Thurstone (1938) and Guilford (1959). However, as we shall see, there are important differences within each of these approaches.

● Spearman's two-factor theory

Spearman factor-analysed the results of children's performance on various tests and found that many tests were moderately positively correlated, concluding that all the tests had something in common (a general factor) as well as something specific to each test (a specific factor). Spearman believed that every intellectual activity involves both a general factor (which he called *g* or general intelligence) and a specific factor (*s*) and differences between individuals are largely attributable to differences in their . (This *g* is, in fact, an abbreviation for neogenesis, which refers to the ability to 'educe relations', as in a common kind of test item which asks 'A is to Y as B is to ?'). Although *g* accounts for why people who are good at one mental ability also tend to be good at others, people also differ according to their specific abilities. *g* is entirely innate.

Spearman himself believed that he had discovered the elusive entity that would make psychology a true science. He had found, he thought, the innate essence of intelligence, the reality underlying all the superficial and inadequate measures devised to search for it:

Spearman's *g* would be the philosopher's stone of psychology, its hard, quantifiable 'thing' – a fundamental particle that would pave the way for an exact science as firm and as basic as physics. (Gould, 1981)

If this was to prove to be a rather exaggerated claim, it was still a major landmark in psychometrics: according to Guilford (1936, quoted in Gould, 1981), 'No single event in the history of mental testing has proved to be of such momentous importance as Spearman's proposal of his famous two-factor theory'.

● Burt and Vernon's hierarchical model

Burt (who was a student of Spearman) agreed that there is a *g* factor common to all tests but also thought that the two-factor model was too simple. He and Vernon elaborated and extended Spearman's model by identifying a series of *group factors* (major and minor) in between *g* and *s* factors (Fig. 28.1). *g* is what all the tests are measuring, the *major* group factors (v:ed and k:m) are what some tests are measuring (some to a greater extent than others), the *minor* group factors are what particular tests measure whenever they are given, while specific factors are what particular tests measure on *specific* occasions (Vernon, 1971).

An important educational implication of this view is that, given the dominance of *g* in the hierarchy, each child can be ranked on a single scale of (innate) intelligence; general ability can be measured early in life and children sorted according to their intellectual promise. (This is the thinking behind the 11-plus examination.)

● Thurstone's primary mental abilities

Using 14-year-olds and college students as his participants, Thurstone (1938, 1947) found that not all mental tests correlate equally but appear to form seven distinct factors or groupings, which he called *primary mental abilities* (or PMAs), namely:

1   spatial (S) – the ability to recognize spatial relationships;
2   perceptual speed (P) – the quick and accurate detection of visual detail;
3   numerical reasoning (N) – the ability to perform arithmetical operations quickly and accurately;
4   verbal meaning (V) – understanding the meaning of words and verbal concepts;
5   word fluency (W) – speed in recognizing single and isolated words;
6   memory (M) – the ability to recall a list of words, numbers or other material;
7   inductive reasoning (I) – the ability to generate a rule or relationship that describes a set of observations.

Thurstone sometimes referred to these mental abilities as 'mental faculties' or 'the vectors of mind' (the title of his 1935 book). He saw *g* as a grand average of positive correlations for a particular battery of tests. This means that *g* can change according to the particular battery of tests used and so it ' ... has no fundamental psychological significance beyond the

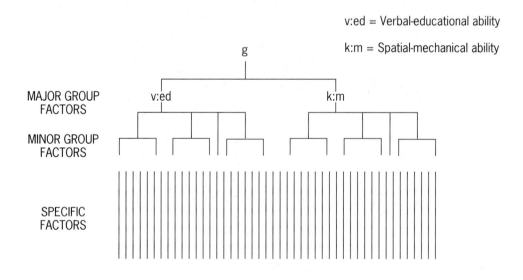

FIGURE 28.1 *The hierarchical model of intelligence. (After Vernon, 1950)*

arbitrary collection of tests that anyone happens to put together ... We cannot be interested in a general factor which is only the average of any random collection of tests' (Thurstone, 1940, quoted in Gould, 1981).

So the PMAs are independent and uncorrelated; they corresponded to the group factors in the hierarchical model but there was no general factor to which they were all related. As there is no general ability, the overall ranking of pupils is inappropriate; some children will be good at some things, others at other things. He advocated the use of individual *profiles* of all PMAs.

Many researchers have questioned Thurstone's conclusions, pointing out that people who score high on a test of one PMA also tend to score high on most of the others. Indeed, Thurstone himself later (1947) admitted that *g* seems to be involved in all PMAs (having carried out a 'second-order' factor analysis on the results of the first; see Chapter 29).

Jensen (1980), a key figure amongst the psychologists who argue that intelligence differences are largely genetic, believes that this change of mind by Thurstone proves that Spearman and Burt were right all along. Jensen is a 'pure Spearman-ian' (Gould, 1981); he based his 800-page defence of IQ (*Bias in Mental Testing*) on the reliability of *g*. Intelligence is 'the *g* factor of an indefinitely large and varied battery of mental tests'; 'We identify intelligence with *g*' and 'To the extent that a test orders individuals on *g*, it can be said to be a test of intelligence' (Jensen, 1980).

However, Gould (1981) disagrees that Thurstone eventually came to accept *g*. It was still of secondary importance to the PMAs and, mathematically, he seems to have been correct – a 'second-order' *g* rarely accounts for more than a small percentage of the total information in a matrix of tests (compared with Spearman's *g*, which often accounts for more than half). Even after he admitted a second-order *g* (when he revised his *Vectors of Mind* in 1947), Thurstone continued to contrast himself with the British school.

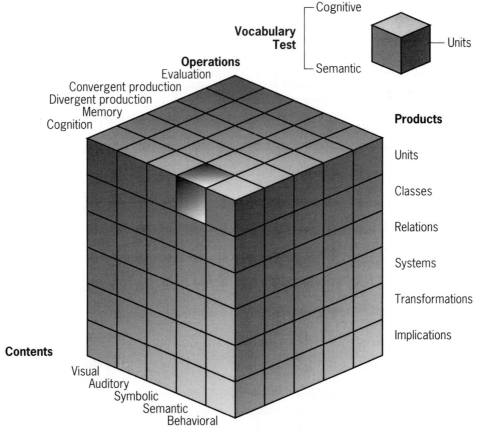

FIGURE 28.2 *Guilford's (1967, 1982) structure of intellect model. (From Zimbardo P.G, (1992) Psychology and Life 13th ed. New York, Harper Collins Publishers. (Originally, Guilford identified 120 abilities, but he later distinguished between Visual and Auditory Content (previously included under 'Figural') giving 5 × 5 × 6 = 150).*

● Guilford's 'structure of intellect' model

This represents the most extreme alternative to Spearman's two-factor theory and totally rejects the notion of a general intelligence factor. Guilford first classified a cognitive task along three major dimensions:

1 *content* (what must the participant think about?);
2 *operations* (what kind of thinking is the participant being asked to perform?); and
3 *products* (what kind of answer is required?).

He identified five kinds of content, five kinds of operation and six kinds of product which, multiplied together, yields a total of 150 distinct mental abilities. Guilford's model is presented in more detail in Figure 28.2. Guilford set out to construct tests to measure each of the 150 abilities; according to Shaffer, writing in 1985, tests have been devised to assess more than 70. However, the scores people get are often correlated, which suggests that the number of basic mental abilities is much smaller than Guilford assumed (Brody and Brody, 1976).

However, the multifactorial approach of Guilford (and to a lesser extent that of Thurstone) represents an important counterbalance to the much more restricted model of Spearman. Vernon (1950, 1971) concluded that intelligence is neither a single general mental ability nor a number of more specific, independent abilities but both; general intelligence plays a part in all mental activities but more specific abilities are also involved in producing performance. Sternberg (1995) believes that this combined, hierarchical approach is probably the most widely accepted factorial description of intelligence.

● Criticisms of factor analysis

How can we account for the conflicting models of intelligence which have emerged from the work of different psychologists, all of whom have used factor analysis?

1 The simple answer is that there is more than one way of factor-analysing a set of data and there is no 'best' way. As we have seen above, Thurstone reanalysed his original data by using a 'second-order' FA which produced a very different pattern of factors. Originally, he had used a form of FA which gives a 'simple structure' solution in contrast to the 'principal component' solutions resulting from Spearman's and Burt's analyses. Shackleton and Fletcher (1984) say that these two alternatives are mathematically equivalent and the same data from the same sample can produce a number of different patterns of factors depending on which alternative is used. (But doesn't this contradict what Gould says about Thurstone being correct?)

2 In practice, however, it seems that the split between the British and American models of intelligence is as much a reflection of the type of participants used as of the form of FA employed. Thurstone and Guilford used mainly college students, while Spearman, Burt and Vernon used mainly schoolchildren. The former are much more alike in terms of their all-round intelligence than the latter and are a much more self-selected and therefore homogeneous group, and so differences between them are likely to reflect differences in particular abilities which are relatively independent of each other.

3 The type and number of tests used (in conjunction with type of participants) can also determine the pattern of factors that emerges. Shackleton and Fletcher (1984) maintain that if a few, similar tests are used with participants who vary widely in age, education, cognitive abilities and so on, a picture of intelligence comprising one dominant, general ability is likely to emerge, while a large number of different types of tests given to a homogeneous sample is likely to produce a larger number of independent factors without a general intelligence factor being involved.

4 Even without these problems, there is still the fundamental issue of interpreting the factors which do emerge. All that FA achieves is a cluster of intercorrelations between different tests and parts of tests – it is then up to the researcher to scan these patterns of intercorrelations and to label them. As Radford (1980) says, factors do not come 'ready-labelled' and the labels that are attached to the factors are only 'best guesses' about the psychological meaning of the factors – they may or may not reflect 'psychological reality'. (This could be compared with the debate in artificial intelligence about whether computers really think and have intelligence: if computers manipulate symbols but symbols are meaningless in themselves, it needs a human to give them meanings (see Chapter 14). In the same way, clusters of intercorrelations (the product of FA) are meaningless until they are given an interpretation by the psychologist.)

5 Surely a technique that leaves so much room for subjective interpretation and, hence, disagreement amongst different researchers is hardly very objective and several writers have questioned the relevance of the whole technique in providing an account of the structure of intelligence.

6 Once a factor has been labelled (e.g. 'verbal ability') there is the danger of believing that it exists in some objective way (this is called reification), whereas a factor is merely a statistic. In Gould's (1981) terms they are ' ... by themselves, ... neither things nor causes; they are mathematical abstractions ... '. Similarly, according to Gillham (1978):

> Factors, like human beings, are born with no name although there is usually one waiting for them, which may not fit their character very well. But as with their human counterparts they soon become assimilated to their name ...
>
> Human beings, however, have the advantage over factors in that their meaning does not reside just in their name. Factors, like correlation coefficients, have no intrinsic psychological significance: meaning is ascribed to them by a psychologist with his preferences and presuppositions ...

ALTERNATIVE MODELS OF INTELLIGENCE

Here we shall consider Cattell and Horn's fluid/crystallized intelligence, Sternberg's information-processing approach, which forms part of his triarchic theory, and Gardner's theory of multiple intelligences.

● Fluid and crystallized intelligence

Working within the FA approach, Cattell (1963) and Horn and Cattell (1967, 1982) have proposed a model which can to some degree reconcile the different models discussed above. They argue that the *g* factor can be subdivided into two major dimensions – *fluid* and *crystallized* intelligence.

Fluid intelligence ('gf') is the ability to solve abstract relational problems of the sort that are not taught and which are relatively free of cultural influences. It increases gradually throughout childhood and adolescence as the nervous system matures, then levels off during young adulthood and after that begins a steady decline. By contrast, *crystallized intelligence* ('gc') increases throughout the lifespan and is primarily a reflection of one's cumulative learning experience. It involves understanding relations or solving problems which depend on knowledge acquired as a result of schooling and other life experiences (e.g. general knowledge, word comprehension and numerical abilities) (see Chapter 24).

● Information-processing approach

Apart from Piaget's qualitative approach, the other major theoretical approach to the study of intelligence is the information-processing approach. According to Fishbein (1984), this approach sees intelligence as the steps or processes people go through in solving problems; one person may be more intelligent than another because they move through the same steps more quickly or efficiently or are more familiar with the required problem-solving steps.

Advocates of this view (e.g. Sternberg, 1979) focus on: (i) how information is internally represented; (ii) the kinds of strategies people use in processing that information; (iii) the nature of the components (e.g. memory, inference, comparison) used in carrying out those strategies; and (iv) how decisions are made as to which strategies to use. Regarding (iii), Sternberg (1987) identifies five major kinds of components:

1 *meta-components* – higher-order control processes used in planning how a problem should be solved, in making decisions regarding alternative courses of action during problem solving and in monitoring one's progress during the course of problem solution;

2 *performance components* – processes used in the actual execution of a problem-solving strategy;

3 *acquisition components* – processes used in learning (acquisition of knowledge);

4 *retention components* – processes used in remembering (retrieval of previously acquired information);

5 *transfer components* – processes used in generalizing (transfer of knowledge from one task or task context to another).

He gives the example of how these five kinds of components might be applied in the solution of an arithmetical problem:

> *Mrs Smith decided to impress Mrs Jones. She went to a costume jewellery shop and bought three imitation diamonds of equal value. She received £4 in change from the £10 note she gave the assistant. (But as Mrs Smith was receiving her change, Mrs Jones walked into the shop!) How much did each imitation diamond cost?*

Meta-components would be used in setting up the equations for solving the problem, e.g. in deciding that the problem can be solved by subtracting £4 from £10 and dividing the difference by 3. They must also decide what information is relevant and what is not. *Performance* components would be used in the actual solution of these equations to obtain first £6 as the price of the imitation diamonds and, then, £2 as the price of each item. *Acquisition* components were used in the problem solver's past to learn how to set up the equation, how to subtract, divide and so on. *Retention* components are used to retrieve this information from memory when it is needed and *transfer* components are used to draw an analogy between this problem and previous ones of a similar kind.

How does this relate to the various factorial theories of intelligence (such as Spearman's and Thurstone's)? According to Sternberg, the *g* factor results from the operations of components which are general across the range of tasks represented on IQ tests. These are mainly meta-components; for example, deciding which particular components to use in the solution of a problem, deciding on a strategy for solving it and monitoring whether the chosen strategy is leading to a solution, plus deciding how quickly the strategy can be executed and still achieve a satisfactory result. Burt and Vernon's major group factors and Thurstone's PMAs are the result of the operation of the other four kinds of component.

We noted earlier that Sternberg believes Neisser's 'prototype' view of intelligence is unsatisfactory partly because different social groups will have different prototypes. While the components involved in the solution of the 'same' problem would overlap regardless of the particular culture, the kinds of problems needing solution will differ widely from one culture to another:

> Hence, the kinds of persons who are considered intelligent may vary widely from one culture to another, as a function of the components that are important for adaptation to the requirements of living in the various cultures. (Sternberg, 1987)

(We shall return later in the chapter to the issue of the cultural nature of intelligence.)

Like Piaget, those who adopt an information-processing approach are trying to develop a theory of intelligence which is universal (and so which applies equally to everyone), but like the factor-analytic theorists, they are interested in individual differences in information processing. As Fishbein (1984) puts it, they see intelligence as neither an 'it' (for example *g*) nor a 'them' (for example, primary mental abilities) but as everything the mind does in processing information.

● Triarchic theory of human intelligence

Sternberg's (1985, 1988) triarchic theory incorporates the components involved in information processing but is far broader. It comprises three subtheories which attempt to explain, in an integrative way, the relationship between:

- intelligence and the *internal* world of the individual, i.e. the mental mechanisms which underlie intelligent behaviour (the *componential sub-theory*);
- intelligence and the *external* world of the individual, i.e. how these mechanisms are used in everyday life in order to attain an intelligent fit with the environment (the *contextual sub-theory*);
- intelligence and experience, i.e. ' ... the mediating role of one's passage through life between the individual's internal and external worlds' (the *experiential sub-theory*).

As far as the first is concerned, one of the most interesting classes of performance components are those found in inductive reasoning, the kind of thinking required in series completion tasks and analogies; for example, 'A is to B as Y is to ?'. Sternberg believes that identifying these performance components can provide insight into the nature of *g*; however:

> ... understanding the nature of the components of intelligence is not, in itself, sufficient to understand the nature of intelligence, because there is more to intelligence than a set of information-processing components. One could scarcely understand all of what it is that makes one person more intelligent than another by understanding the components of processing on, say, an intelligence test ... (Sternberg, 1990)

The other two sub-theories address some of the other aspects of intelligence which contribute to individual differences in observed performance – both inside and outside test situations.

Intelligent thought is not aimless or random mental activity but is directed towards one or more of three behavioural goals: *adaptation* to an environment, *shaping* of an environment and *selection* of an environment. As far as adaptation is concerned, ' ... what is intelligent in one culture may be viewed as unintelligent in another' and ' ... To understand intelligence, one must understand it ... in terms of how thought is intellectually translated into action in a variety of different contextual settings ... ' (Sternberg, 1990).

Sternberg believes that shaping may represent the essence of intelligent thought and behaviour:

> ... Perhaps it is this skill that has enabled human kind to reach its current level of scientific, technological, and cultural advancement ... In science, the

greatest scientists are those who set the paradigms (shaping), rather than those who merely follow them (adaptation) ...

According to the experiential subtheory, intelligence is best measured at those regions of the experiential continuum that involve tasks or situations that are either relatively novel, on the one hand, or in the process of becoming automatized, on the other. To test how far children's understanding extends, you might give them problems which are just at the limits of their current understanding (this relates to Vygotsky's *zone of proximal development*; see Chapter 25). Several sources of evidence suggest that the *ability to deal with relative novelty* is a good way of measuring intelligence (and is a characteristic of intellectually gifted children). (Compare this with Cattell's fluid intelligence.)

Equally, a key aspect of intelligence is the ability to automatize information processing (e.g. as in a skilled reader), because this makes more resources available for dealing with novelty. (This relates to the distinction between controlled and automatic processing; see Chapter 11.)

According to Bee (1989), standard IQ tests have omitted many of the kinds of abilities included under the contextual and experiential subtheories; in the world outside school, these may be required at least as much as those included under the componential sub-theory. Clearly, traditional IQ tests do not measure all significant aspects of intellectual skill.

● Theory of multiple intelligences

Gardner proposed his theory of multiple intelligences in his book *Frames of Mind* (1983). It is based on three fundamental principles:

1 intelligence is not a single, unitary, thing but a collection of multiple intelligences, each one a system in its own right (as opposed to merely separate aspects of a larger system, i.e. 'intelligence');
2 each intelligence is independent of all the others;
3 the intelligences interact, otherwise nothing could be achieved.

An intelligence is defined as ' ... an ability or set of abilities that permits an individual to solve problems or fashion products that are of consequence in a particular cultural setting' (Walters and Gardner, 1986, quoted in Sternberg, 1990). Gardner's seven intelligences are summarized in Table 28.3.

Gardner identifies eight different criteria for distinguishing an independent intelligence, including:

● potential isolation by brain damage (he believes that each intelligence resides in a separate region of the brain, so that a given intelligence should be isolable by studying brain-damaged patients);
● an identifiable core operation or set of operations;
● support from psychometric findings (patterns of intercorrelations/FA);
● the existence of idiots savants, prodigies and other exceptional individuals. A discussion of studies of idiots savants appears in Box 28.1.

Intelligence	Description
1 Linguistic	Includes skills involved in reading, writing, listening and talking.
2 Logical-mathematical	Involved in numerical computation, deriving proofs, solving logical puzzles and most scientific thinking.
3 Spatial	Used in marine navigation, piloting a plane, driving a car, working out how to get from A to B, figuring out one's orientation in space. Also important in the visual arts and playing chess, recognizing faces and scenes.
4 Musical	Includes singing, playing an instrument, conducting, composing and, to some extent, musical appreciation.
5 Bodily-kinaesthetic	Involves the use of one's whole body or parts of it, to solve problems, construct products and displays. Used in dance, athletics, acting, surgery.
6 Interpersonal	Includes understanding and acting upon one's understanding of others – noticing differences between people, reading their moods, temperaments, intentions, etc. Especially important in politics, sales, psychotherapy and teaching.
7 Intrapersonal	Self-understanding – symbolized in the world of dreams.

TABLE 28.3 *Gardner's theory of multiple intelligences (1983)*

BOX
28.1 The study of idiots savants (based on Howe, 1989, and O'Connor and Hermelin, 1988)

'Idiots savants' is a term applied to certain mentally retarded individuals who, despite their disabilities, are capable of remarkable feats. But how is it possible for certain people to possess abilities which seem to demand high levels of intelligence which they obviously do not have? Such cases certainly challenge the view that human intelligence is unitary or controlled by some general factor. A substantial minority of idiots savants are also autistic but they constitute a very varied group with little in common.

Harriet (Viscott, 1970) was a mentally retarded woman with an overall IQ of 73; she had very poor general knowledge and was also strikingly socially inadequate. But she was a superb pianist. She could transcribe from memory, make different key changes in the middle of playing a piece, fill in parts from the full orchestra version not included in her piano score and could name each of the component notes of a four-note chord held for just half a second. When talking about music she often used words that she never otherwise used and had an encyclopaedic knowledge of classical music. There are other cases similar to hers.

Sacks (in *The Man Who Mistook His Wife For a Hat*, 1985) described a profoundly retarded, autistic man with no speech who made realistic drawings of natural objects, showing humour and imagination not otherwise even glimpsed.

Other cases of extraordinary artistic abilities include a young autistic boy, Stephen Wiltshire, who draws buildings and has sold some of his drawings and has been commissioned by large corporations to do drawings for them.

Nadia (Selfe, 1977), a young autistic girl who had no speech and was profoundly retarded, produced, from the age of three, drawings of animals of an outstanding technical standard. Selfe (1983) reports on 11 others with similar talents, all abnormal in some way, mostly mentally retarded.

About one-third of all published cases are of calendar counting – at its simplest, the ability to state the day of the week on which a specified date falls; some calendar counters can solve problems of this kind for spans of dates extending several 100 years into the past and future. Clearly, calendar counting makes substantial demands on memory and many of the accomplishments of idiots savants are essentially memory feats. But how are these skills acquired? Case studies are largely descriptive and no serious attempt is made to answer this question. However such abilities develop, these cases show that it is quite possible for complex intellectual skills to exist in relative isolation and that different abilities in people of all ability levels may be largely autonomous, thus supporting theories such as Gardner's multiple intelligences.

INTELLIGENCE TESTS

● A brief history of intelligence tests

In 1904, Binet and Simon were commissioned by the French government to devise a test which would identify those children who would not benefit from ordinary schooling because of their inferior intelligence. The result was the *Simon–Binet test* (1905), generally accepted as the first intelligence test. The sample of children used for the development of the test (the standardization sample) was very small and it was subsequently revised twice, in 1908 and 1911, with much larger samples.

In 1910, Terman began adapting the Simon–Binet test for use in the USA and, as he was working at Stanford University, the test became known as the *Stanford–Binet* test and is still referred to in this way. The first revision was published in 1916 and was designed to measure normal and superior intelligence as well as subnormal. In 1937, the Terman–Merrill revision appeared, comprising two equivalent forms of the test (L and M) and in 1960 the most useful questions from the 1937 revision were combined into a single form (L–M) and an improved scoring system was used. Prior to 1960, the Stanford–Binet test was designed for individuals up to age 16 (starting at 2½–3) but this was extended to 18 in the 1960 revision; a further revision was published in 1973 and the most recent in 1986.

Another major figure in intelligence testing is Wechsler, who developed the most widely used test of adult intelligence, the *Wechsler Adult Intelligence Scale* (WAIS; 1944), revised in 1958 and again in 1981 (WAIS-R). (It was originally published in 1939 as the Wechsler–Bellvue Intelligence Scale.) Wechsler has also constructed the *Wechsler Intelligence Scale for Children* (WISC), first published in 1949 and revised in 1974 (WISC–R), designed for children between five and 15 years, and the *Wechsler Pre-School Primary Scale of Intelligence* (WPPSI) first published in 1963 and designed for 4–6½-year-olds.

An important impetus to the development of intelligence testing was America's involvement in the First World War; a fairly quick and easy method of selecting over 1 million recruits for suitable tasks was needed and the result was the Army Alpha and Army Beta tests.

The most recent new individual British test is the *British Ability Scales* (BAS) (Elliot *et al.*, 1979), which consists of 24 subscales designed to measure 24 distinct aspects of intelligence in 2½–17-year-olds, relating to five major 'mental processes', including retrieval and application of knowledge and speed of information processing. The latter is meant to underlie performance on all the other sub-scales and is one of the novel features of the test, reflecting the influence of the information-processing approach. One way of testing this is to present a page of a 5×5 block of numbers: the child has to strike out the largest number in each row and total time is measured. Difficulty is increased from item to item by increasing the number of digits in each number (from three to five).

Like the Wechsler scales, the BAS gives three IQ scores – a verbal, a visual and an overall (general) IQ. In keeping with Thurstone's PMA model, 'From the start ... the original research team had in mind the construction of an intelligence scale which would provide a profile of special abilities rather than merely produce an overall IQ figure ... ' (Elliot, 1975, quoted in Richardson, 1991).

Individual and group tests

Although all the tests mentioned above are tests of intelligence, an important difference between them is that some are given to one person at a time (e.g. the Stanford–Binet and Wechsler tests and the BAS) and so are known as *individual tests*, while others are given to groups of people at a time (e.g. the Army Alpha and Beta tests) and so are referred to as *group tests*. Related to this distinction are other important differences:

- Individual tests are used primarily as diagnostic tests in a clinical setting; for example, they are used to assess the ability of a child who has learning difficulties in school and the Stanford–Binet and Wechsler are the tests most widely used by educational psychologists both in the UK and the USA. Group tests, by contrast, are used primarily for purposes of selection and research; for example, in Britain until the mid-1960s, all children aged 11 sat an examination (the 11-plus), which would determine the kind of secondary schooling they would receive and this consisted largely of a group test of intelligence. (It was designed largely to assess *g*.) (Despite the introduction of comprehensive schools, there are many parts of the UK where selection at 11 still takes place.) Again, when large groups of people are being studied as part of a research project, it is very likely that their intelligence will be assessed by using one or other group test.

- Because the individual test involves a one-to-one situation, it is clearly more time consuming than a group test which, in theory, can be given to as many individuals as can be comfortably accommodated in a particular room.

- Although individual tests require that instructions are standardized (the same for all testees) and that the same questions are asked and in the same sequence, there is some degree of leeway on the part of the tester as to exactly how the test is conducted; for example, the child must be put at its ease before the test proper can begin and it is important that a good rapport be established between the child and the tester. How the tester achieves this will probably vary on each occasion; no face-to-face situation can be made totally uniform or predictable and the psychologist's training will help prepare them for this. Groups tests, on the other hand, are presented in the form of written questions, a set of standardized instructions is read out to the group and the test is timed. The person administering the test need not be a psychologist and, indeed, may have no special training or familiarity with the particular test; the marking can be done by using a special marking key or by computer. In this respect, then, group tests are more objective, that is, only one answer is accepted as correct and there is no room for interpretation on the part of the marker.

- Individual tests usually involve some *performance items*, i.e. the testee has to do something (e.g. a jigsaw puzzle) as well as answer questions about the meaning of words and do some mental arithmetic, etc. By contrast, group tests are 'pencil-and-paper' tests and in that respect are much like other written exams.

Mental age and IQ

The Stanford–Binet test is based on the assumption that mental ability is developmental, i.e. it increases with age through childhood and so consists of a number of age-related scales; each scale comprises a series of questions which are normally answered correctly by a majority of children of that age. So, for example, the five-year-old scale is what

Stanford–Binet	Wechsler Adult Intelligence Scale (WAIS-R)
Children of three should be able to: Point to objects that serve various functions (e.g. 'goes on your feet'). Repeat a list of two words or digits (e.g. 'can' and 'dog'). *Children of four should be able to:* Discriminate visual forms (e.g. squares, circles and triangles). Define words (e.g. 'ball' and 'bat'). Repeat ten-word sentences, count up to four objects, solve problems (e.g. 'In daytime it is light, at night it is … .'). *Children of nine should be able to:* Solve verbal problems (e.g. 'tell me a number that rhymes with tree'). Solve simple arithmetical problems and repeat four digits in reverse order. *Children of 12 should be able to:* Define words (e.g. 'skill' and 'muzzle'). Repeat five digits in reverse order. Solve verbal absurdities (e.g. 'One day we saw several icebergs that had been entirely melted by the warmth of the Gulf Stream'. What is foolish about that?)	*Verbal Scale* (none of these sub-tests is timed) 1 Information – general knowledge. 2 Comprehension – ability to use knowledge in practical settings (e.g. 'What would you do if you were lost in a large, strange town?'). 3 Arithmetic. 4 Similarities – conceptual and analogical reasoning (e.g. 'In what ways are a book and TV alike?'). 5 Digit span – STM (e.g. repeating a string of digits in the same/reverse order). 6 Vocabulary – word meaning. *Performance Scale* (all sub-tests are timed) 1 Picture completion – assessment of visual efficiency and memory by spotting missing items in drawings. 2 Picture arrangement – assessment of sequential understanding by arranging a series of pictures to tell a story. 3 Block design – ability to perceive/analyse patterns by copying pictures using multicoloured blocks. 4 Object assembly – jigsaw puzzles 5 Digit symbol – ability to memorize and order abstract visual patterns.

Table 28.4 *Some items from the Stanford–Binet (1973) and the two scales of the WAIS-R (1981)*

most five-year-olds could pass comfortably (as well as all children over five) but which most four-year-olds could not. Hence, a child passing the five-year-old scale has a *mental age* of five, that is, the child can do what the average five-year-old can do (some examples of questions from different age scales are given in Table 28.4).

In practice, a child is started off on the scale immediately below its chronological (actual) age (CA) (to determine its *basal age*) and then the scale corresponding to its CA and so on, until the child fails to answer any questions correctly on a particular scale.

The concept of mental age (MA) is useful in that it gives an absolute assessment of the child's level of intellectual development, but by itself it does not tell us how bright, average or dull the child is; to establish this we must compare the child's MA with its CA. Imagine two children, both of whom do equally well on the test and attain a MA of ten; can we regard them as equally intelligent? The answer is 'No', because one of them is ten years old while the other is only nine and nine-year-olds are not expected to do as well on the test as ten-year-olds. So, when we take CA into account, we are making a comparison with other children.

For these reasons, Stern (1912) introduced the notion of an *intelligence quotient* (IQ), in which the MA is expressed as a ratio of CA, multiplied by 100 to produce a whole number. The first IQ was therefore a *ratio* IQ, such that where MA and CA are the same, IQ is 100 (which, by definition, is average), where MA is greater than CA, IQ is over 100 (and therefore above average) and where CA is greater than MA, IQ is below 100 (and therefore below average).

It should be clear from these examples that for IQ to remain stable over time, the MA must increase in step with the CA. However, the concept of MA does not apply beyond 18, since intellectual ability is usually fully developed by that time (according to the 1960 version of the Stanford–Binet, anyway) and consequently, the test IQ is not meaningful beyond a chronological age of 18. (The measurement of adult IQ was discussed in Chapter 24.)

The WAIS-R is the most widely used test of adult intelligence (16–74-year-olds) and is structured in a similar way to the WISC-R. The test comprises two separate scales (a verbal scale and a performance scale), each comprising a number of sub-tests and each producing a separate IQ, which can then be combined to yield an overall IQ. By contrast, the Stanford–Binet test includes performance items only

Test A

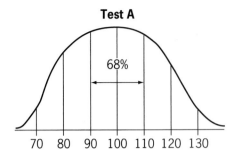

68%

70 80 90 100 110 120 130

Test B

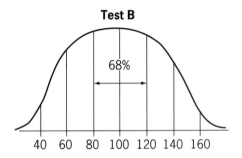

68%

40   60   80   100 120 140 160

FIGURE 28.3 *Normal curves of two hypothetical IQ tests, each with a different standard deviation.*

for the youngest children (up to age 4–5) when verbal abilities are still relatively underdeveloped (see Table 28.4).

A second important difference between them is that the same items are given to all children (or adults) on the Wechsler tests, so that age-related scales are not used. The questions become progressively more difficult and the testing usually continues until the testee has failed on a pre-determined number of items in succession.

In the 1986 revision of the Stanford–Binet, items are grouped into four broad areas of intellectual ability: (i) verbal reasoning; (ii) abstract/visual reasoning; (iii) quantitative reasoning; and (iv) short-term memory. A separate score is obtained for each area (whereas previously a single overall IQ score was given).

● The relationship between intelligence and IQ

The Wechsler tests do not use the concept of MA in the way that the Stanford–Binet test did but instead uses a *deviation IQ*, which expresses the test result as a standard score, i.e. it tells the tester how many

standard deviations (SDs) above or below the mean of the testee's age group the score lies.

Before 1960, it was very difficult to compare scores on the two tests because of the difference in the way the IQ was calculated – the ratio IQ of the Stanford–Binet and the deviation IQ of the Wechsler test are not equivalent. However, in the 1960 revision of the Stanford–Binet, the ratio IQ was replaced by the deviation IQ, making scores on the two tests more comparable. However, although all tests are designed in such a way as to produce a normal curve, i.e. a symmetrical distribution of IQ scores with a mean of 100, the SD (or dispersal of the scores around the mean) can differ from test to test.

Fontana (1981b) gives the example of two tests, A and B, test A having a SD of ten and test B having a SD of 20. In both cases, 68% (approximately) of children would be expected to have scores one SD below or above the mean (i.e. between 90 and 110 in test A and between 80 and 120 in test B). So a particular child might have a score of 110 on test A and 120 on test B and yet the scores would be telling us the same thing (Fig. 28.3). This suggests that while intelligence is a *psychological concept*, IQ is a purely *statistical concept*: if it is possible for the same characteristic (intelligence) to be assigned different values according to which test is used to measure it, then instead of asking 'How intelligent is this individual?', we should ask 'How intelligent is this individual as measured by this particular test?'. Since the IQ score of the same individual can vary according to the SD of the particular test being used, we cannot equate 'IQ' with 'intelligence'.

The very relationship between 'intelligence' and 'IQ' is problematic in a way that the one between 'height' and 'metres and centimetres' is not. Normally, we are prepared to accept an *operational definition* of someone's height (height is the number of metres and centimetres as measured by a tape measure) and there is no debate as to the 'true nature of height'. However, as we have seen, an operational definition of intelligence is not satisfactory precisely because there is such a variety of definitions: IQ is an unwarranted 'reduction' of intelligence, something very diverse and complex, to a single number (see Chapter 32). In agreeing with Heim that to name the particular test used is merely to reduce the circumference of the circle represented by an operational definition, we could perhaps take this a step further by saying that for each separate test there exists a separate circle.

In *IQ – The Illusion of Objectivity* (1972), Joanna Ryan points out that because intelligence is expressed as a number, the impression is created that IQ tells us in some absolute way about an individual's intellectual ability (in the same way as metres and centimetres tell us about someone's height). However, there is a fundamental difference between the two measuring scales being used. IQ scores are not 'free-standing' scores in the way that somebody's height is: we can measure a person's height without having to take anybody else's height into account, but IQ only derives its meaning as a comparison with other people's scores. This is because intelligence is measured on an *ordinal scale,* which tells us whether one person is more or less intelligent than another but little else. For instance, the difference between an IQ of 100 and 105 appears to be the same as the difference between scores of 105 and 110 and leads some to argue that intelligence tests involve an *interval scale* (as in temperature); however, Ryan (1972) argues that this sort of arithmetical move is unjustified.

Interestingly enough, the BAS claims to give 'direct estimates of ability' (as opposed to a mere relative ordering of participants), as if by a dipstick or linear rule; Richardson (1991) is doubtful that this claim to interval scaling is valid.

● The criteria of an intelligence test. What makes a test a 'good' test?

According to Kline (1982), all psychological tests must fulfil three criteria if they are to be considered good or efficient tests:

1 discriminatory power;
2 reliability;
3 validity.

To these we can add a fourth – standardization.

Discriminatory power and standardization

Good psychological tests should be *discriminating,* i.e. they should produce a wide distribution of scores. If everyone scored equally well (or badly) on a particular test it would not be discriminating, i.e. it would not reveal differences between people with respect to the characteristic or ability being measured. This requirement is a practical and a statistical one, but it is not a logical one. For example, we want tests to be discriminating because we want to use test scores as a basis for categorizing and selecting people and if our society did not run this way, there would be no problem involved in most people scoring very high; indeed, in such a society,

there might be no need for tests at all. Quite clearly, what is considered a 'good' test depends to a very large extent on its *purposes.*

The statistical side of the requirement that a good test be discriminating is related to the kind of distribution of scores that is expected and here we return to the normal curve and the SD. It is assumed that intelligence is normally distributed, so that fixed proportions of the population will score so many SDs above or below the mean. (This idea is based on the further assumption that intelligence is largely biologically determined; since other characteristics such as height and weight, which are also largely biologically determined, are found to be normally distributed, then it is expected that intelligence will also be. This assumption has itself been challenged.)

Starting out with this assumption, when testers are standardizing their tests, i.e. trying to establish a set of norms for a particular population against which any individual's score can be compared, they modify the test items to fit the requirements of a normal distribution. For example, if a particular item is passed by all testees it would be considered too easy and probably dropped from the test; similarly, if an item is so difficult that it is passed by nobody, then it too will be dropped. The items that are retained should then discriminate between testees so as to conform with the normal curve. Of course, once a test has been standardized so as to produce a normal distribution, the tester can use this as evidence that intelligence is, indeed, a biological property.

Standardization also requires testing a large, representative sample of the population for whom the test is intended, otherwise the resulting norms cannot be used legitimately for certain groups of individuals. Classic examples of improper standardization involve the two most widely used individual tests of intelligence, the Stanford–Binet and the Wechsler scales, both of which were originally standardized in the USA. In the 1960 revision of the Stanford–Binet, Terman and Merrill took only the population included in the census as their reference group, which excluded many migrant and unemployed workers. More seriously, both tests were standardized on whites only (without any explanation for this from the authors) and yet they would be used with both black and white children. As Ryan (1972) says, these tests are therefore tests of white abilities and although we can still compare black and white children, we must be aware that in doing so we are not comparing black and white intelligence 'but instead how blacks do on tests of white intelligence'. In the 1973 revision of the Stanford–Binet, the 2100-

strong standardization sample did include black children, but it remains to be seen how this will affect the race and IQ controversy in the future (see below).

Heather (1976) also points out the ideological significance of IQ as illustrated by *re-standardization* of tests. Before 1937, the mean score of women on the Stanford–Binet was ten points lower than that of men and it was decided to eliminate this discrepancy by modifying the items so that average scores for men and women were the same. Heather asks why this has not been done with blacks and answers his own question in terms of the *predictive efficiency* (a measure of validity) of the test: tests are meant to predict future education and occupational success, so changing a test so as to eliminate racial differences, while not at the same time changing social inequalities (a much longer process, of course), would render the test a less efficient predictive tool. As Heather notes, removing the male–female bias did, in fact, make the test less efficient as a predictor of gender differences in educational and occupational success.

Reliability

This refers to how consistently the test measures whatever it is measuring. Consistency can refer either to the test itself (*internal consistency*) or consistency over time (*stability*). If a test is internally consistent, each item on the test should be measuring the same variable and to the same extent, i.e. they should all contribute equally to the overall test score. One way of assessing internal reliability is the *split-half method* where, for example, scores on the odd-numbered questions are correlated with scores on the even-numbered questions. If the test is reliable, there should be a significant, positive correlation. These two sets of scores can be thought of as two forms of the same test and, indeed, there is a method of assessing reliability called *alternate or parallel forms* (as in the 1937 version of the Stanford–Binet) where scores on one form should correlate very highly with scores on the other.

Consistency over time/stability is most commonly assessed using *test–retest reliability*, where the same participants are given the same test on more than one occasion; a reliable test is one which produces very similar scores when repeated. IQ is expected to be stable across time, not just because a good test must be reliable but also because the predominant view of intelligence underlying most tests is that it is largely genetically determined and, hence, unlikely

to fluctuate in an individual over time (see below).

Reliability is not only important in itself but is a prerequisite for validity: if a test is unreliable, it cannot possibly be valid, yet a test's reliability is no guarantee of its validity.

Validity

A test is valid if it measures what it claims to measure and there are several ways of assessing it. In relation to intelligence tests, the question is 'Do they measure intelligence?'.

- *Face* (or *content*) *validity* is a rather superficial type of validity which refers to whether or not the test seems to be testing what it claims to test by looking at the kind of questions it contains. In a sense, this begs the question of just what intelligence is. Whereas we can fairly easily determine whether a test measures knowledge of history, for example, and know that it is not a valid history test if the questions deal with geography, the situation is far more complex in the case of intelligence tests precisely because of the failure of psychologists to agree on what intelligence is.

- *Concurrent validity* involves trying to correlate scores on an intelligence test with some other, independent measure or criterion at the same point in time. One method is to correlate scores on a new test with scores on another, well-established test (in practice, this is very often the Stanford–Binet). The circularity of this attempt should be obvious: what independent proof do we have that the well-established test is itself a valid test of intelligence? Even if we could get around this problem, we should want to know what value the new test has, since, if the correlation between the two tests is very high, they would seem to be measuring the same thing! (Kline, 1982). Other criteria that might be used include teachers' ratings and the child's current academic performance, both of which seem to create as many problems as they solve and which are most usefully discussed in relation to predictive validity.

- *Predictive validity* refers to the correlation of a test with some future criterion measure and is the more commonly used method of establishing validity. (Concurrent and predictive validity are collectively referred to as **external validity**.) Probably the most common and powerful external criterion is educability or educational success and Binet started the trend by establishing that scores on his test differentiated between children thought to be bright or dull based on classroom performance. Many studies show that well-established tests do, in fact, predict school achievement with considerable accuracy.

Many writers have pointed out that all the variables (including cognitive ability) that contribute to school success also contribute to performance on IQ tests and a high correlation would be expected for this reason. Heather (1976), for example, argues that 'general intelligence' can be called 'school intelligence', the ability to do well at school. Similarly, Richardson (1991) asks whether the correlation with school performance makes IQ tests valid tests of educational prediction rather than valid tests of intelligence. Ryan (1972) maintains that to the extent that tests do measure educability, they are measuring something which is influenced to a considerable extent by various social and motivational factors; this conflicts with the test's purpose, i.e. to measure only cognitive ability or potential. Heim (1970), who advocates a view of intelligence as a part of personality as a whole, would agree.

As we saw when discussing standardization, the predictive validity of tests is closely related to the practical and social purposes to which they are put so validation is not a purely objective, scientific process.

The other major external criterion used is *occupational success*. According to Jensen (1975), 'Intelligence tests have more than proved themselves as valid predictors of scholastic performance and occupational level'. But this is precisely what they are designed to predict, so might not predictive correlations be self-fulfilling? (Richardson, 1991).

- *Construct validity* involves ' ... taking a large set of results obtained with the test and seeing how well they fit in with our notion of the psychological nature of the variable which the test claims to measure' (Kline, 1982). So it embraces both concurrent and predictive validity and normally involves formulating hypotheses about what kind of test results we would expect if the test really does measure intelligence. For example: (i) scores on the test will correlate highly with educational attainment (both currently and in the future); and (ii) scores on the test will correlate highly with scores on other, well-established tests (concurrent validity).

  To the extent that such hypotheses are supported, the construct validity of the test has been demonstrated and Kline (1982) concludes that most well-known tests of intelligence 'have now

accumulated so much evidence relating to validity that there is no dispute about them'. Similarly, Heim (1970) concludes that 'A reputable test is still the best single means of assessing an individual's intelligence, whatever definition is used. It is more objective, consistent and valid as a first approximation than any of the validatory criteria against which tests may be calibrated'.

However, we should also remind ourselves of the diversity of definitions and (perhaps more importantly) theories of intelligence which

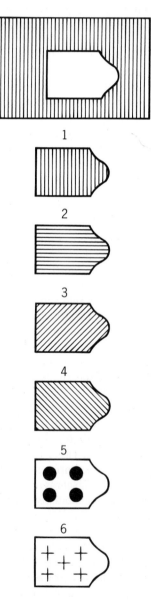

FIGURE 28.4 *A sample item from Raven's progressive matrices test*

BOX 28.2 Critical discussion: intelligence as a cultural phenomenon

If the construction of culture-fair tests has proved so problematical, a major reason could be that the very notion of intelligence is itself culturally defined. For example, Bruner maintains that 'The culture-free test is the intelligence-free test, for intelligence is a cultural concept' (quoted by Gillham, 1975). Similarly, Gillham (1975) argues that any attempts to 'define' intelligence which do not involve identifying 'specially valued cultural attainments' must fail. The concept of intelligence only derives its meaning within a particular cultural and social context (see Sternberg's criticism of Neisser and his contextual sub-theory).

Something which can never be 'built-in' to a test's construction (or translation) is the meaning of the experience of taking an intelligence test. Taking tests of various kinds is a familiar experience for members of Western culture, both within and outside the educational context, but what about cultures in which there is no generally available schooling? How can we measure intelligence independently of people's responses to taking the test itself?

The very nature or form of the tasks involved in an intelligence test (as distinct from the content) is something that has a cultural meaning, as illustrated by Glick's report of research with the Kpelle people (1975, cited in Rogoff and Morelli, 1989). Participants were asked to sort 20 familiar objects into groups. They did this by using *functional* groupings, such as knife with orange, potato with hoe, rather than *taxonomic* groups, which the researcher thought more appropriate. When their way of classifying the objects was challenged, they often explained that this was how a wise man would do it. When the exasperated researcher finally asked 'How would a fool do it?', the objects were immediately arranged into four neat piles of foods, tools, clothing and utensils (i.e. taxonomic groups!). The Kpelle participants and the American researcher differed in their beliefs about the intelligent way of doing things.

Different cultures may also promote the development of different abilities. For example, Serpell (1979) predicted that Zambian children would perform better than English children on a task in which they were required to copy objects using bits of wire; this was based on the observation that children all over central and southern Africa are very skilled at constructing wire cars from scraps of wire as a popular form of play. He also predicted that the English children would perform better when asked to draw the objects. Both predictions were supported, demonstrating that the abstract psychological function of pattern reproduction can be manifested in different ways according to the demands of the eco-cultural niche to which participants' behaviour is adapted (Serpell, 1994).

We need to take culture into account when considering both the nature and the assessment of intelligence (Sternberg, 1995).

---

abound in psychology and the logical problem of measuring something if we cannot first agree what it is that we are measuring; as Richardson (1991) says, ' ... the absence of a clear theory about the intelligence we claim to be measuring [makes] construct validity ... not one of the strengths of most IQ tests ... '.

● IQ tests: tests of aptitude or attainment?

One of the major criticisms of intelligence tests has been that they are biased in favour of white middle-class children and adults; it follows that it is both unfair and meaningless to compare groups which differ substantially in their social and cultural experience.

However, defenders of tests would appeal to the distinction between attainment and aptitude tests, i.e. two kinds of ability tests. *Attainment* (or *achievement*) *tests* are concerned with how much a person knows about a specific subject (e.g. geography) or with a person's current level of performance (e.g. reading) and are unambiguously related to actual learning and educational experiences. By contrast, *aptitude tests* are intended to measure somebody's capacity or potential ability to succeed in a particular task or job of work or academic subject and are designed to reduce to a minimum the influence of specific learning and experience. Test constructors have always maintained that IQ tests are aptitude tests and, to this extent, they are said to be *culture free/culture fair*.

But is the attainment–aptitude distinction a valid one and is it possible to design a test which is completely culture free? Aren't aptitude tests merely attainment tests in disguise? Group tests, in particular, rely on reading and arithmetic which are taught in all schools and so, in practice at least, it is very difficult to separate aptitude from attainment. It is somewhat easier to distinguish between them in terms of their purpose and ways of trying to validate them; aptitude tests, by definition, are trying to assess some future performance and so involve predictive validity, but we have already seen the problems that this entails.

According to Ryan (1972), it is logically impossible to measure potential separately from some actual behaviour, i.e. some of the skills that individuals have developed during their lifetime must be used when they do an intelligence test. 'There is nothing extra "behind" the behaviour corresponding to potential that could be observed independently of the behaviour itself.' She concludes that the notion of 'innate potential' itself makes no sense.

What is meant by a culture-fair test and is a culture-free test possible?

According to Frijda and Jahoda (1966, cited in Segall *et al.*, 1990), a culture-fair test (a) could be a set of items which are equally unfamiliar to all possible persons in all possible cultures, so that everyone has an equal chance of passing (or failing) them (this is what is often called a culture-free test); or (b) could comprise multiple sets of items, modified for use in each culture to ensure that each version would contain the same degree of familiarity. This would give members of each culture about the same chance of being successful with their respective version. The first option is virtually impossible and usually, when the issue is being discussed, it is the second option that is in question (whichever term – 'free' or 'fair' – is used).

According to Segall *et al.* (1990), while the second option is a theoretical possibility, in practice it is very difficult to construct. A number of attempts have been made to produce culture-free tests, which usually consist of non-verbal questions; traditionally, the emphasis on language has been one of the more obvious sources of bias in intelligence tests. An example of the kind of questions involved is shown in Figure 28.4 and is based on Raven's progressive matrices, one of the most widely cited examples of a culture-free test.

Even without any written instructions, you can probably infer what you have to do. However, the very nature of the task is something which is likely to reflect particular cultural experiences: questions must be formulated in words or symbols of some kind and the testee's familiarity with these will depend on their life experience. According to Simon (1971), 'The suggestion that human intelligence might be measurable by the development of a new kind of test which actually eliminates all words and symbols is an absurdity' and Owen and Stoneman (1972) believe that because the influence of language is so pervasive, any attempt to devise a culture-fair test by removing 'overt language structures' is doomed to failure. Vernon (1968) rejects the idea of a culture-fair test (see Box 28.2).

● Psychophysiological approaches to measuring intelligence

A fairly recent attempt to avoid some of the difficulties discussed above (although not usually discussed in the context of 'culture-free' tests) is to correlate IQ test scores with certain physiological measures, such as electroencephalograms (EEGs), evoked potentials (EPs) and reaction time (RT). Some of the early investigators found only moderate correlations between average evoked potentials (AEPs) and IQ but more recently much higher correlations have been reported. For example, McCarthy and Donchin (1981, cited in Sternberg, 1995) found that one EP (P300) seems to reflect the allocation of cognitive resources to a given task; it seems to increase in strength with the amount of surprise a participant experiences as a result of the presentation of a stimulus.

Schafer (1982, cited in Sternberg, 1995) proposes that a functionally efficient brain will use fewer neurons to process a stimulus that is familiar and more to process a novel stimulus, i.e. more intelligent individuals should show greater P300 responses to unfamiliar stimuli, as well as smaller P300 responses to expected stimuli, than less intelligent individuals. Schafer reported correlations of 0.82 between an individual-differences measure of EP and IQ: the higher the IQ, the greater the difference in EP amplitude between expected and unexpected stimuli.

But how should such findings be interpreted? Do the EPs somehow *cause* intelligent cognition? Equally plausible is the claim that intelligent cognition produces certain patterns of EP. Despite the striking magnitude of some correlations, we are far from understanding the neural mechanisms that are actually responsible for them and until we understand the relationship better, we should not use EPs as some kind of 'culture-free' intelligence test (Sternberg, 1990). Also, despite these promising findings, the use of IQ tests as a validating criterion throws up all the difficulties which we have already encountered.

THE HEREDITY–ENVIRONMENT ISSUE. WHY ARE SOME PEOPLE MORE INTELLIGENT THAN OTHERS?

Along with gender differences, the debate about the source of intelligence differences must be the most controversial and divisive in the whole of psychology.

Before we begin to consider the relevant evidence, there are a number of preliminary points that should be made.

- Intelligence tests are, in practice, assumed to be valid measures of intelligence, so 'IQ' is used synonymously with 'intelligence' in discussion of the heredity–environment issue.
- The heredity–environment issue is about how we account for intelligence differences *between individuals* (and, even more controversially, between groups, particularly working-class, middle-class and black–white differences), not about how much of an individual's intelligence is determined by genetic factors and how much by environmental factors (which is logically absurd anyway: Hebb (1949) likened it to asking how much of the area of a rectangle is contributed by its width, a meaningless question, since area, by definition, is width times length).

According to McGurk (1975), there are four interrelated propositions which seem to follow from the *genetic theory* (the belief that IQ differences are largely determined by genetic factors), namely:

- *Proposition 1* The closer the genetic relationship between any two individuals, the greater should be the correspondence (concordance) between them with respect to intelligence.
- *Proposition 2* As the genetic inheritance of each individual is a constant, there should be a high degree of continuity in IQ throughout an individual's lifespan.
- *Proposition 3* Individual differences in early experience should have no fundamental effect on the development of individual differences in intelligence.
- *Proposition 4* Deliberate attempts to increase the level of intelligence by special enrichment experience should have no effect.

What is the evidence for and against these propositions?

Proposition 1

Table 28.5 shows the results of Bouchard and McGue's (1981) review of 111 studies of IQ correlations between relatives from the world literature. It updates the Erlenmeyer-Kimling and Jarvik (1963) review and the findings are generally consistent with it.

First, we need to understand the difference between MZ and DZ twins. MZ stands for 'monozygotic' meaning 'one egg' so MZs are *identical* twins who have developed from the same, single, fertilized

	No. of correlations	No. of pairings	Median correlation	Weighted average
Monozygotic twins reared together	34	4672	0.85	0.86
Monozygotic twins reared apart	3	65	0.67	0.72
Midparent–midoffspring reared together	3	410	0.73	0.72
Midparent–offspring reared together	8	992	0.475	0.50
Dizygotic twins reared together	41	5546	0.58	0.60
Siblings reared together	69	26 473	0.45	0.47
Siblings reared apart	2	203	0.24	0.24
Single parent–offspring reared together	32	8433	0.385	0.42
Single parent–offspring reared apart	4	814	0.22	0.22
Half-siblings	2	200	0.35	0.31
Cousins	4	1176	0.145	0.15
Non-biological sibling pairs (adopted/natural pairings)	5	345	0.29	0.29
Non-biological sibling pairs (adopted/adopted pairings)	6	369	0.31	0.34
Adopting midparent–offspring	6	758	0.19	0.24
Adopting parent–offspring	6	1397	0.18	0.19
Assortative mating	16	3817	0.365	0.33

TABLE 28.5 *Familial correlations for IQ. The vertical bar on each distribution indicates the median correlation; the arrow, the correlation predicted by a simple polygenic model. From Bouchard and McGue (1981)*

ovum and are genetically identical and are, by definition, of the same sex. DZ stands for 'dizygotic', meaning 'two-egg', so DZs are *non-identical* (or fraternal) twins who have developed from two quite separately fertilized ova; they are no more alike than ordinary siblings (i.e. they have roughly 50% of their genes in common) and can be either of the same or different sex.

Secondly, it is fairly easy to see that the closer the kinship relation (and, hence, the greater the genetic similarity), the higher the correlation for IQ; this seems to support the genetic theory. Unfortunately, the situation is not as simple as this , because as the genetic similarity increases, so the environments are also becoming more similar!

Take the case of MZs reared together: not only are they as similar genetically as any two humans can get, but they are much more likely to be treated in the same way than DZs or ordinary siblings. Kamin (1981), for example, points out that even MZs vary in their physical likeness and this seems to be a factor in determining how similarly they are treated; significantly, the more alike physically they are, the more similar their IQ. He also claims that DZs of the same sex are treated more alike than opposite-sex DZs and both are treated more alike than ordinary siblings; even though all these groups are similar genetically, same-sex DZs are most alike in IQ scores.

This is borne out by the Bouchard and McGue data. Table 28.5 does not give separate figures for DZs of same and different sex but they were, in fact, 0.62 and 0.57 respectively. (The figure used here is the *weighted average*, i.e. a figure which takes sample size into account to make different studies more comparable). However, there is also evidence to support the *equal environments assumption,* which is discussed in Chapter 30 in relation to schizophrenia: the conclusion reached there is that the greater similarity of MZs is a *cause* of their more similar parental treatment, rather than an effect (Lilienfeld, 1995).

So it is difficult to draw any conclusions from the fact that MZs reared together are most alike in IQ (0.86) since this would be predicted from both a genetic theory and an environmentalist theory. Yet how would an environmentalist explain the finding that separated MZs are more alike than same-sex DZs reared together (0.72 and 0.60, respectively)? Taken at face value, this would certainly seem to support the genetic argument and, indeed, is generally regarded as the strongest single piece of evidence. But we need to look at studies of separated twins in more detail.

The rationale of twin studies

As we have seen, MZs reared together do not tell us about the relative importance of genetic and environmental factors, although even here environmental factors must be playing some role, since if only genetic factors were involved in IQ, the correlation would be perfect (i.e. 1.00). If the differences in IQ due to environmental difference (MZs reared apart) are smaller (i.e. the correlation is higher) than IQ differences due to genetic differences (DZs of the same sex reared together), then we can conclude that environmental factors are less important than genetic factors in causing differences in IQ. The study of twins who have been separated represents an important kind of *natural experiment* (see Chapter 2), but the 'design' is complex: in the case of MZs reared apart, genetic factors are held constant while environmental factors vary, while when DZs of the same sex are reared together, environmental factors are held constant and genetic factors vary (i.e. there are two 'independent variables').

The four best known studies of separated MZs are Newman *et al.* (1937), Burt (1955, 1958, 1966), Shields (1962) and Juel-Nielsen (1965); a summary of the main findings appears in Table 28.6. The most recently reported study, the Minnesota twin study (Bouchard *et al.*, 1990), has been going on since 1979, accumulating pairs of separated MZs during that time, with the latest figure standing at 56 (including two sets of male triplets); they have also studied 30 pairs of separated DZs but the data are presented almost exclusively in terms of separated MZs compared with MZs reared together. Bouchard *et al.* are interested in a wide range of characteristics, of which intelligence is just one. They also refer to a large-scale Finnish twin study (Langainvaimio *et al.*, 1984).

As Table 28.6 shows, MZs reared apart turn out to be more alike than DZs of like sex brought up together (and in the Shields study, they were actually more alike than MZs reared together – a rather strange finding which neither theory would predict). The Bouchard *et al.* (1990) data are consistent with those of the earlier studies. So is the genetic theory proven? According to Kamin (1977, 1981) the answer is a resounding 'No'. Why?

Problems with twin studies

Perhaps the most damaging criticism is that the 'separated' MZs often turn out not to be separated at all. For instance, in the Shields study, the criterion of separation was that the twins should have been

Study	IQ correlations (numbers of pairs are shown in brackets)		
	MZs reared together	MZs reared apart	DZs (same sex) reared together
Newman et al. (1937)	0.91 (50)	0.67 (19)	0.64 (50)
Burt (1955) *	0.944 (83)	0.771 (21)	
Burt (1958)	0.944 (?)	0.771 ('over 30')	
Conway (1958)	0.936 (?)	0.778 (42)	
Burt (1966)	0.944 (95)	0.771 (53)	0.552 (127)
Shields (1962)	0.76 (34)	0.77 (40)	0.51
Juel-Nielsen (1965)		0.62 (12)	

* The Burt data are not included in the Bouchard and McGue (1981) review (see text).

TABLE 28.6 *Findings from the four 'standard' studies involving separated identical (MZ) twins*

reared in different homes for at least five years, even though in some cases the separation did not occur until age seven, eight or nine (and very few separations occurred at birth). Out of 40 separated pairs, 27 were actually raised in related branches of the parents' families and attended the same school. The most common arrangement was for one twin to stay with the natural mother and the other to go to the maternal grandmother or aunt; the correlation for these 27 pairs was 0.83. The remaining 13 pairs were, in fact, raised in unrelated families (although these often were friends of the mother) and their correlation was 0.51.

Jessie and Winifred were eight years old when studied and had been 'separated' at three months, but they were brought up within a few hundred yards of each other, told they were twins after the girls discovered it for themselves, having gravitated to one another at school at the age of five. They played together quite a lot: ' ... Jessie often goes to tea with Winifred ... They were never apart and wanted to sit at the same desk' (Shields, 1962).

Similar cases are reported in the Juel-Nielsen (1965) study and Kamin (cited in Horgan, 1993) questions the amount of contact the separated MZs in the Bouchard et al. (1990) study had with each other while growing up and has repeatedly drawn a blank when requesting detailed case histories. He claims that the twins themselves have strong motives for playing down any previous contacts and for exaggerating similarities between them. The study has attracted considerable media coverage, both in the US and in other parts of the world, and some of the twins have acquired agents and been paid for TV appearances; indeed, one pair has sold their life story to a Hollywood film producer (Horgan, 1993).

When twins have to be split up, the agencies responsible for placing them will try to match the

respective families as closely as possible, which can account for much of the similarity found between the separated MZs. However, when the environments are substantially different, very marked IQ differences are found. For example, one of the pairs in the Newman et al. (1937) study experienced very contrasting upbringings: one girl was raised in a good farming region, went to college and became a teacher and her IQ was 116; her sister was reared in the backwoods, had only two years of regular schooling and, although she later worked in a big city as a general assistant in a printing firm, her IQ was only 92. This 24-point difference was the largest difference found for any of the 19 pairs, which also included differences of 19 and 17 points. Three other pairs had very different educational experiences and the average difference for these was 13 IQ points. Using a rating scale to estimate the educational difference between all 19 pairs, there was an overall correlation of 0.79 between educational difference and IQ difference. These findings also demonstrate the large *absolute differences* which may exist between pairs of separated MZs; this is important because the use of correlation coefficients tends to emphasize the *relative similarities* of MZs compared with DZs.

Experimenter bias is another problem, especially in the Newman et al. and Shields studies. In the Newman et al. study, when the twins were tested, the investigators knew which were MZs and which were not. Similarly, Shields tested both members of 35 out of the 40 pairs of separated MZs himself and the overall correlation was 0.84 (with a mean difference of 8.5 points); this compared with 0.11 (and a mean difference of 22.4 points) for the remaining five pairs (one member of which was tested by Shields and the other by another tester).

The twin samples were often biased. For instance, in the Newman et al. study, volunteers responded to newspaper and radio appeals and then had to send in a questionnaire and a photograph of themselves. When a pair who looked so alike that they were mistaken for each other gave very different answers on the questionnaire, they were judged not to be MZs and were excluded from the study; so it is possible that amongst those who were excluded were MZs who happened to have developed very different personalities. This is a particularly serious criticism since, in 1937, there was no reliable medical test of zygosity (i.e. whether twins are MZ or DZ) and the reliability of the case histories is very dubious (e.g. regarding when they were separated).

In the Finnish study (Langainvaimio *et al.*, 1984), researchers combed the birth registers and sent questionnaires to MZs, but in the Bouchard *et al.* study, great use was made of media coverage to recruit, with 'self-referrals' or relatives and friends telling twins about the study. According to Kaprio (one of the Finnish researchers, cited by Horgan, 1993), the study has attracted people who like publicity, making them an atypical sample of twins (let alone typical of people in general).

The intelligence tests used differed from study to study, which makes it very difficult to compare different studies. There are also problems with the tests used in particular studies; for example, Newman *et al.* used the 1916 version of the Stanford–Binet which, as we have seen, was designed for people up to the age of 16 and, since the 19 pairs of MZs were mostly adults (age range 11–59), the similarity of their IQs was artificially increased.

Similarly, Shields used the dominoes test (a test of non-verbal intelligence) and the Mill Hill Vocabulary Scale, neither of which had been standardized on females, a significant fact when you consider that two-thirds of his sample of MZs were female! The Danish translation of the WAIS used by Juel-Nielsen had never been standardized on a Danish sample.

As can be seen from Table 28.6, the largest number of separated MZs was gathered by Burt, and Eysenck and Jensen have based their genetic theory largely on Burt's findings. However, there is a serious question mark over the status of Burt's data, since Kamin (1977) first pointed out 'a number of puzzling inconsistencies' as well as 'a number of astonishing consistencies' (there are correlation coefficients expressed to three decimal places, despite differences in the number of twin pairs). Some of his data were published under the names of fictitious co-workers (e.g. the Conway (1958) paper) and Kamin

(1977) concludes that 'The numbers left behind by Professor Burt are simply not worthy of our current scientific attention'. However, Kamin's claims have themselves been criticized and there is an ongoing debate about the 'Burt affair'.

An evaluation of twin studies

Based on twin studies in general, and Burt's study in particular, Eysenck and Jensen have proposed that 80% of the variance between the IQ scores of individuals is attributable to genetic differences; this is referred to as a *heritability estimate* (of 80%).

In view of all the shortcomings of twin studies, they would appear to be an extremely unreliable basis for drawing such a conclusion, particularly (as pointed out by Kamin and others) when a heritability estimate applies only to a particular population at a particular time. What does this mean? All the twin studies used white middle-class Americans, Britons or Danes and so we are not justified in applying the heritability estimate to blacks or to working-class populations (something of which both Eysenck and Jensen are guilty); if they tell us anything at all, they tell us about differences within the white middle-class population of those particular countries. We have also seen that where environmental differences between separated MZs are quite substantial, there is a correspondingly large difference in their IQs, which means the heritability will be smaller and, indeed, different studies produce different heritability estimates. Bouchard *et al.* (1990) claim a heritability estimate of 0.70 (based solely on twin data), which is higher than the 0.47–0.58 proposed by Bouchard and McGue (1981) in their comprehensive review and by Loehlin (1989) and Plomin and Loehlin (1989).

Even within the white middle-class populations that have been studied, Kamin argues that twin studies could be used as a basis for a heritability estimate only if:

● the twins were genetically representative of the population;
● the range of environments to which the twins were exposed was also representative;
● there was no tendency for the environments to be systematically correlated (or matched).

According to Bodmer (1972), for example, the difference between members of a DZ pair represents only a fraction of the genetic difference that can exist between any two individuals taken at random; like siblings, they have half their genes in common. MZs, of course, have all their genes in common and so are even less representative of the population as a whole.

As far as their environments are concerned, Bodmer again argues that the environmental differences between members of a twin pair represent only a fraction of the total environmental differences that can exist between two individuals chosen at random. Even within the same family, the environment of twins (MZ or DZ) will be more similar than for ordinary siblings, as we have seen. We have also seen how similar the environments of separated MZs were, partly because of deliberate matching by the agencies responsible and partly because of the more informal arrangements made by the family.

In the light of this, Kamin concludes that none of the three conditions has been met and so twin studies are not a reliable source of data regarding a heritability estimate for intelligence. Regarding the exposure of Burt's fabrication of his results, Jensen (1974) claims that there is other evidence which is equally supportive of the genetic theory, Scarr and Weinberg (1977) believe that estimates of heritability should be scaled downwards, but not drastically, and Vernon (1979) agrees. The other evidence which Jensen alludes to are fostering and adoption studies.

Fostering and adoption studies

The average correlation of 0.19 between fostered/adopted children and their foster/adoptive parents compared with 0.50 between natural children and their parents suggests a strong genetic component.

The early studies (Burks, 1928; Leahy, 1935; Skodak and Skeels, 1949) have been criticized on methodological grounds. Both Burks and Leahy found a correlation of 0.15 between adoptive parents and adopted children, compared with a correlation of 0.48 between biological parents and biological children in a 'matched control group' of ordinary families. But how were they matched?

The two groups of children were matched for age and sex and the two groups of families were matched for parental occupation, educational levels and 'type of neighbourhood'. But the adoptive parents were considerably older (having tried to have a child of their own for some time before adopting, so there were also fewer siblings in the adoptive families), had incomes that were 50% higher, larger and more expensive homes and, like all adoptive parents, actively wanted children and were carefully screened by the adoption agencies for their suitability as parents. So not only did they turn out to be more

'successful' as a group than the control group, but they also represent a more homogeneous group and there was very little variation in the richness of the environment they provided; the statistical consequence of this is that there cannot be a very high correlation between adopted children's IQ and environmental measures, such as the adoptive parents' IQ (Rose et al., 1984).

McGurk (1975) and others also point out that in terms of absolute level of IQ, adopted children move towards the level of the adoptive parents and, on average, they score significantly above those of the natural parents, i.e. the adoptive environment raises the child's IQ above what it probably would have been if the child had remained with the natural parents.

The obvious improvement on this 'classic' design is to study adoptive parents who also have a biological child of their own: the two children will have been reared in the same environment by the same parents but are genetically unrelated to each other. Two such studies are those of Scarr and Weinberg (1977, 1983) and Horn et al. (1979). Scarr and Weinberg studied *transracial adoptions*, i.e. in almost all cases the mother and her biological child were white while the adopted child was black. In both studies, there was no significant difference between: (i) the correlation of the mother's IQ and her biological child's IQ; and (ii) the correlation of her IQ with the adopted child's IQ (although Horn et al. found a slightly greater correlation between the mother and adopted child while for Scarr and Weinberg it was slightly greater with the natural child). According to Rose et al. (1984), the child's race, like its adoptive status, had no effect on the degree of parent–child resemblance in IQ. These results appear to inflict fatal damage on the notion that IQ is highly heritable; children reared by the same mother resemble her in IQ to the same degree, whether or not they share her genes.

Many of these black children (and many of those in the Skodak and Skeels study) came from disadvantaged homes where the biological parents were poorly educated and were below average in IQ. By age 4–7, the adopted children were scoring well above average on IQ tests (about 110 in the Scarr and Weinberg study and 112 in Skodak and Skeels), scores that are considerably higher than would have been expected on the basis of the natural parents' IQ and education levels or the IQs of other children from disadvantaged backgrounds. Since the adoptive parents are known to be highly educated and above average in IQ, it seems reasonable to assume that

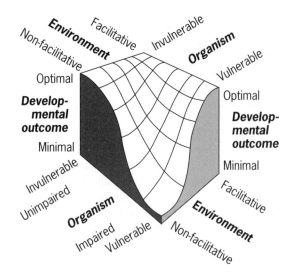

FIGURE 28.5 *Horowitz's model of the interaction of a child's environment with protective factors and vulnerabilities. The surface of the curve illustrates the level of a developmental stage, such as IQ or social skills. According to this model, if a low-birthweight child is reared in a poor environment then it is likely that the child will do less well than other children reared with a different combination of vulnerabilities and environment*

they provide an enriched, intellectually stimulating home environment which facilitates the cognitive development of the adopted children.

Finally, Schiff *et al.* (1978), in France, studied 32 children, born to parents of low social status, who were adopted before they were six months old by parents of high social status. Compared with the IQs of their biological siblings reared by the natural mother, the average IQ of the adopted children was far superior (95 and 111, respectively).

Gene–environment interaction

A way of summarizing the adoption studies of Scarr and Weinberg, Horn *et al.* and Schiff *et al.* is by reference to the concept of *reaction range*. This refers to the range of possible responses by an individual to the particular environment he or she encounters; it is unique to that individual and is related to genetic make-up. So, for instance, your genes might dictate that you grow to be six feet tall but this will only happen if you receive an adequate diet.

As far as IQ is concerned, Scarr-Salapatek (1971) maintains that, assuming the individual is not severely retarded, he or she has a reaction range of 20–25 IQ points, i.e. any individual's IQ score can vary by as

> **BOX 28.3**   Key study: children of the Garden Island
>
> Starting in 1955, Werner and her colleagues studied all the children (nearly 700 of them) born on the Hawaiian island of Kauai in a given period, following them up when they were one, two, ten, 18 and 31–32 years old.
>
> Werner became interested in a number of 'high risk' or 'vulnerable' children who, despite exposure before the age of two to four or more of the following – reproductive stress (difficulties during pregnancy and/or during labour and delivery), discordant and impoverished home lives, including divorce, uneducated, alcoholic or mentally disturbed parents – went on to develop healthy personalities, stable careers and strong interpersonal relationships.
>
> There were two main kinds of protective factors which contributed to their resilience, constitutional and environmental factors. *Constitutional* factors included temperamental characteristics which elicit positive responses from family and strangers, such as low excitability and high sociability. *Environmental* factors included being brought up in a family with four or fewer children, with two or more years between the resilient child and the next child, attachment to at least one carer (older sibling, grandparent, etc.) and seeing school as a refuge from a disordered household.
>
> Of the 72 children classified as resilient, 62 were studied after reaching their 30s. As a group, they seemed to be coping well with the demands of adult life, three-quarters had had some college education, nearly all had full-time jobs and were satisfied with their work.
>
> As long as the balance between stressful life events and protective factors is favourable, successful adaptation is possible. When stressful events outweigh the protective factors, however, even the most resilient child can have problems. (Werner, 1989)

much as 25 points (almost two SDs) depending on the kind of environment to which the person is exposed.

Related to reaction range is the concept of *facilitativeness* (Horowitz, 1987, 1990, cited in Bee, 1994). A highly facilitative environment is one in which the child has loving and responsive parents and is provided with a rich array of stimulation. When different levels of facilitativeness are combined with a child's initial vulnerabilities, there is an interaction effect. For example, a resilient child (one with many protective factors and few vulnerabilities) may do quite well in a poor environment; equally, a vulnerable child may do quite well in a highly facilitative environment. Only the vulnerable child in a poor environment will do really poorly (see Fig. 28. 5).

This interactionist view is illustrated in a 30-year longitudinal study which took place in Hawaii and is described in Box 28.3.

Another classic example of gene–environment interaction is the disease *phenylketonuria* (PKU), which involves the inheritance of two recessive genes, one from each parent, which prevent the body's production of an enzyme whose function is to metabolize phenylalanine (a common constituent of many foodstuffs, particularly dairy produce). If untreated, phenylalanine builds up in the bloodstream and poisons the nervous system, causing severe mental retardation and, eventually, death. However, by putting the child on a low-protein diet (for at least its first 10–12 years), these effects can be prevented and normal intelligence will develop. This suggests that any talk of 'high or low IQ genes' is meaningless; how particular genes contribute to high or low intelligence depends upon the environment in which they express themselves; in themselves they are neither 'bright' nor 'dull'.

● Proposition 2

To evaluate studies of the stability of IQ, we should note that IQ is not normally used as a measure of intelligence below two years of age. Instead a *developmental quotient* (DQ) is used, such as the Bayley Scales of Infant Development (Bayley, 1969); designed for 2–30-month-olds, these assess a child's rate of development compared with the 'average' child of the same age.

Generally, the younger a child is when given a developmental test, the lower the correlation between its DQ and its later performance on an IQ test (Anderson, 1939; Honzik, 1976). Once IQ begins to be measurable, it becomes a better predictor of adult IQ (compared with DQ). However, the evidence is still very mixed. Honzik *et al.* (1948) studied over 250 children in California, testing them at regular intervals between two and 18 years. Some of the

important findings are shown in Table 28.7.

Clearly, the closer in time the IQ scores are taken, the higher the correlation and the overall picture is one of little fluctuation over time. However, there were many fluctuations in the short term, often related to disturbing factors in the child's life, and the 'stability coefficients' are based on large groups of participants, obscuring important individual differences.

The Fels Longitudinal Study of Development (McCall, 1973) studied 140 middle-class children from 2½ to 17 years. The average change in IQ during that period was 28 points and even the 'most stable' changed an average of ten points; about 15% shifted 50 points or more (in either direction) and one child increased by 74 points!

BOX 28.4 Key study: Kagan *et al.*'s study (1977) of Guatemalan children

Kagan *et al.* (1977, cited in Kagen *et al.*, 1980) conducted some research in a small, remote, farming village in Guatemala, where infants typically spend their first year in an isolated state, in a dark and tiny hut. They are not played with or spoken to and are poorly nourished, experiencing continuous gastrointestinal and respiratory illness; compared with American babies of the same age, they are mentally retarded.

By their second year, conditions change; they are allowed to move about outside the hut and they begin to develop an interest in people, animals and objects. By 4–5 years they are playing with other children and at 8–9 assume some responsibilities in the family farm and domestic chores. Yet until ten they remain inferior intellectually to their American counterparts; they also do more poorly on tests of perception, memory and reasoning compared with other Indian children from a nearby village who are not so completely isolated during their first year. However, by the time they reach adolescence, they do almost as well as Americans on intelligence tests; any remaining differences are likely to be due to relatively poor schooling and general cultural deprivation.

Age of child	Correlation with IQ at age 10	Correlation with IQ at age 18
4	0.66	0.42
6	0.76	0.61
8	0.88	0.70
10		0.76
12	0.87	0.76

TABLE 28. 7 *Correlations for IQ at ages 4–18 for the same individuals (after Honzik et al., 1948)*

IQ tests	Infant scores (Bayley DQ)	
	12 months	24 months
Four years (Stanford–Binet)	0.21 *	0.53 *
Eight years (WISC-R)	0.15 *	0.39 *

* Statistically significant

TABLE 28.8 *Correlations between IQ scores at 12 and 24 months and four and eight years. (From Bee, 1989)*

Bee *et al.* (1982) studied 193 families from before the birth of their first child until the child was eight. The Bayley Infant Development Scales were given at one and two years, the Stanford–Binet at four and the WISC–R at eight. The results are shown in Table 28.8. They are consistent with previous studies in showing that the closer in time the two measures are taken, the higher the correlations will be. However, fluctuations in score seem to be much greater than a simple genetic theory would predict and Rebok (1987) warns that caution is needed when drawing conclusions about later-life IQ from early performance data because intelligence is not as fixed as the original theories assumed.

A different approach to studying the continuity of IQ is Kagan *et al.*'s study of a Guatemalan village (Box 28.4).

● Proposition 3

A much-cited study (which could just as easily be discussed in relation to proposition 4) is that of Skeels and Dye (1939) and the follow-up by Skeels (1966); these were described in detail in Chapter 22. Perhaps the most directly relevant studies here are those which are concerned with factors which adversely affect intellectual development. Table 28.9 summarizes some of the major variables.

● Proposition 4

Two books which first appeared in the early 1960s contributed to the deliberate attempt in the USA to close the educational gap between white middle-class children and those from socially disadvantaged backgrounds, particularly those from black and other ethnic minorities.

J. McVicker Hunt's *Intelligence and Experience* (1961) summarized all the evidence showing that intelligence was not a fixed attribute of a person but depended very heavily on environmental experience. Bloom's 1964 *Stability and Change in Human Characteristics* also argued that intellectual ability could be increased by circumstances

Genetic	Environmental	
Down's syndrome (extra 21st chromosome) Klinefelter's syndrome (apparent males) XXY Turner's syndrome ('apparent females' XO) Phenylketonuria (see text)	*Biological (pre-natal)* Maternal diseases (e.g. rubella, syphilis). Rh incompatibility X-rays and other radiation. Toxic agents (e.g. lead poisoning, carbon monoxide). Drugs (e.g. cigarettes, alcohol, barbiturates, heroin). Maternal stress during pregnancy. Mother's age. Multiple pregnancies. ──────→ Birth order. Birth difficulties. Prematurity. Poor maternal nutrition during pregnancy.	*Socio-cultural (post-natal)* Many of these pre-natal variables are correlated with socio-economic status (SES) and race. In the USA, SES and race are more highly correlated than in the UK. Family size

TABLE 28.9 *Major variables, genetic and environmental, which adversely influence intellectual development*

BOX
28.5 Key study: intensive
intervention in Milwaukee

One of the most intensive pre-school intervention programmes was the Milwaukee Project (Garber and Haber, 1977; Garber, 1988), in which the mothers received remedial education, home management and job training, and the children participated in a structured education programme up to age six. All the mothers had an IQ of 75 or below and the families were markedly socially disadvantaged; 20 children entered the experimental programme, while another 20 served as controls.

The initial findings were dramatic, with the experimental group greatly outperforming the controls during the pre-school years. The follow-up results continued to show benefits but they diminished progressively over time: an IQ advantage of 28 ponts at age four reduced to ten points at age 14. More disappointing still were the very modest academic benefits: while the experimental group did have somewhat better scores than the controls in reading, there was little difference in maths, in which both groups were performing poorly.

The results show that a vigorous and relatively prolonged intervention makes a substantial difference to the cognitive performance of severely disadvantaged children, but they also show that much of the gain is lost in the years following the end of the programme (at the time of starting school) (Rutter and Rutter, 1992) (Fig. 28.6).

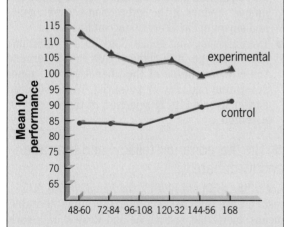

FIGURE 28.6 *IQ performance with increasing age of severely disadvantaged children participating in a broad-ranging intensive intervention programme in the preschool years. Data from Garber. (From Rutter M. and Rutter M. (1992) Developing Minds. Harmondsworth, Penguin)*

and that it was essential to give disadvantaged children enriched opportunities early in life.

The first of these compensatory pre-school programmes was Operation Headstart, begun in 1965. Initially this took the form of an eight-week summer programme and shortly afterwards became a full year's pre-school project. The aim was, literally, to give an educational headstart, but the first follow-up studies (conducted 1–2 years after starting school) were discouraging: IQ gains, when they did occur, were short-lived and educational improvement was minimal.

However, Hunt (1969, 1972) was critical of Headstart, claiming that it was inappropriate to the needs of the children involved, not providing them with the skills that they had failed to develop at home during their first four years and which are developed by most middle-class children. There was also too much emphasis on IQ as a criterion of success.

Yet these criticisms were themselves to prove premature, since the impact of early intervention has been shown to be cumulative, not showing up for several years. One major follow-up of Headstart by Collins (1983) suggests there is a 'sleeper effect'. Compared with non-participants:

- participants tend to score somewhat higher on tests of reading, language and maths and this 'achievement gap' tends to widen between the ages of six and 14;
- participants are more likely to meet the school's basic requirements, i.e. they are less likely to be assigned to special education/remedial classes, to repeat a year in the same grade or to drop out of high school;
- participants are more likely to want to succeed academically;
- participants' mothers are more satisfied with their children's school performance and hold higher occupational aspirations for their children.

The gains in IQ, which lasted for up to four years after the programme ended, were not sustained and by age 11–12 there were no differences between those who participated and those who had not . However, the academic benefits were longer lasting (Lazar and Darlington, 1982). The reverse result was found by Garber and Haber (1977) and Garber (1988) in the Milwaukee Project, although as Box 28. 5 shows, the gains in IQ declined over time.

CONCLUSIONS: NATURE, NURTURE OR AN INTERACTION?

Much of what we have discussed in relation to each of the four propositions implied by the genetic theory seems to suggest that environmental factors are considerably more important than a heritability estimate of 80:20 suggests.

As long ago as 1949, Hebb suggested that the whole nature–nurture controversy was a result of the 'double reference' of the term 'intelligence'. One meaning of the term (*intelligence A*) is an 'innate potential, the capacity for development, a fully innate property that amounts to the possession of a good brain and a good neural metabolism'; in this sense, intelligence is not measurable. *Intelligence B* is a product of the interaction between intelligence A and the environment and is defined as 'the functioning of a brain in which development has gone on, determining an average level of performance or comprehension by the partly grown or mature person'. To ask about differences in intelligence is to ask about intelligence B; we can never, in principle, compare people's intelligence A or know how much of their innate potential is reflected in their intelligence B.

However, despite Hebb, the controversy has raged on, particularly since the mid to late 1960s. Vernon, who in 1969 added intelligence C to Hebb's A and B (to refer to IQ test scores, really a sample of B), believes that there are certain observed phenomena which represent very strong arguments in favour of the genetic theory:

- the difference in IQ between siblings, sometimes of up to 30 points;
- very bright children being born to relatively dull parents;
- very dull children being born to highly intelligent parents.

He believes that an environmentalist would find it very difficult to explain these, while they are exactly what a genetic theorist would predict. Reviewing the evidence in all its forms, Vernon (1979) concludes that it demonstrates a strong genetic component in the development of individual differences in intelligence. Although environment has an important role to play, measurable IQ seems to 'depend more on genetic endowment than on favourable or unfavourable environmental opportunities and learning, at least within white culture'. However, both heredity and environment 'are essential and neither

can be neglected if we are to plan children's upbringing and education wisely'.

The idea that differences in IQ are inherited is deeply built into the theory of IQ testing itself because of its commitment to the measurement of something intrinsic and unchangeable. From the very beginning of the American and British mental testing movement, it was assumed that IQ was biologically heritable (Rose *et al.*, 1984). Spearman, for example, believed that *g* is a physical property of the brain, a form of mental energy pervading the entire brain: the strength of a person's *g* reflects heredity alone (while *s* factors reflect the influence of education). So IQ, as a measure of *g*, records an innate general intelligence.

However, according to Rose *et al.* (1984), psychometricians often use the term 'heritable' mistakenly compared with how the geneticist uses it and this contributes to false conclusions about the consequences of heritability:

- Genes do not determine intelligence: there is no one-to-one correspondence between the genes inherited from one's parents and even physical characteristics. What we inherit is the *genotype*, the genes which are involved in the development of a particular trait, while the *phenotype* is the actual trait itself as it manifests itself in the organism. While the former is fixed, the latter develops and changes constantly. The first principle of developmental genetics is that every organism is a unique product of the interaction between genes and environment at every stage of life.
- Even allowing that genes alone do not determine the phenotype, it is claimed that they determine the effective limits of the phenotype, i.e. genes determine capacity or potential. We considered earlier Ryan's (1972) rejection of the concept of potential.

● The 'hereditarian fallacy' and the race and IQ debate

According to Gould (1981), the *hereditarian fallacy* rests on two false assumptions: first, that 'heritable' means 'inevitable' (which he and Rose *et al.* clearly believe it does not); and second, that within-group heredity can be applied to between-group heredity. The fallacy, especially the second assumption, is central to the claim that certain racial groups are genetically inferior to others.

The figure at the centre of the race and IQ controversy is the American psychologist Arthur Jensen. In 1969, in the *Harvard Educational Review*, he published an article called 'How much can we boost IQ and scholastic achievement?', in which he reviewed all the literature which compared black and white IQ scores. The basic finding, that 'On average, Negroes test about one standard deviation (15 IQ points) below the average of the white population in IQ' is not itself a matter of dispute; it is Jensen's explanation of these findings that constitutes the controversy:

> Genetic factors are strongly implicated in the average Negro–white intelligence differences. The preponderance of the evidence is, in my opinion, less consistent with a strictly environmental hypothesis than with a genetic hypothesis ... (Jensen, 1969)

Eysenck (1971) and Hernstein (1971) agree with Jensen.

Some of the evidence upon which Jensen based his genetic theory was the apparent failure of compensatory pre-school programmes such as Headstart, which, as we have seen, was a rather premature conclusion. Perhaps the most fundamental criticism of Jensen is that he bases his view of black–white differences (*between-group* differences) on the heritability estimate of 80:20 which, as we have seen, is based on studies of the white population (and is about *within-group* differences). Several writers, including many biologists (e.g. Bodmer, 1972) have pointed out the illegitimacy of making this logical jump.

Suppose we take a bag of seed collected from a wheat field and sow one handful on barren ground and another on fertile ground. Those sown on fertile ground will clearly grow taller and give a much higher yield per plant than those sown on barren ground. Within each crop there will be differences, which clearly must be related to genetic differences but which have nothing to do with the overall differences between the two crops, which have grown in two very different environments (Bodmer, 1972).

Relating this to intelligence, it is perfectly possible that individual differences in IQ (within-group differences) are heavily influenced by genetic factors, while group differences (between-group differences) are largely or entirely the result of environmental factors.

Jensen's response to this criticism is to appeal to studies in which environmental factors are controlled. For example, Shuey (1966) compared middle- and working-class blacks and whites and found the same average 15-point difference. But is social class (measured largely in terms of occupation and income) a sufficiently sensitive measure of 'environment' to be very helpful? Should we expect the

experience of working-class and middle-class blacks to be equivalent to that of their white counterparts, given the history of slavery and continuing prejudice and discrimination? According to Bodmer (1972), 'Measuring the environment only by standard socioeconomic parameters is a little bit like trying to assess the character of an individual by his height, weight and eye colour'.

Tobias (1974) points out a further problem with Jensen's argument; when he says that environment has been controlled, he means controlled at the moment in time when the investigation began. Yet the study of a ten-year-old child, for example, when the family may have attained a reasonable status, tells us nothing about the family's position when the child was passing through its critical, formative period (both pre- and post-natally), such as mother's diet, illnesses, emotional stress and other adverse influences on intellectual development (see Table 28.9).

● Race-fair IQ tests?

We have already discussed the cultural nature of IQ tests, which represents another stumbling block to Jensen's argument: it is certainly easier to devise tests which are biased than to construct a culture-fair or culture-free test. This was demonstrated by Dove, a black American sociologist, who in 1968 published the Dove Counterbalance General Intelligence Test ('Chitling Test'), a parody of the white bias in traditional tests. It draws freely on black language and culture and whites would be expected to emerge as inferior to blacks on such a test. (See Chapter 13 for a discussion of Black English.) Significantly, the gap between American whites and blacks is almost nonexistent in the pre-school years (using, for example, the Gesell Developmental Test for 0–2-year-olds). Both African and American black children show the highest mean scores of any group tested, while Western whites score lowest of all. It is only at school age, when IQ tests come to rely much more heavily on verbal items, that the gap begins to widen – in the opposite direction.

● What is this thing called race?

Finally, the whole concept of race itself is problematic. Like intelligence, there are various definitions and criteria, but whichever is used (e.g. blood types) the extent of genetic variation within any population is usually far greater than the average difference between populations (e.g. Bodmer, 1972). The same is true of IQ scores and to emphasize average group differences (as Jensen does) is to overlook the considerable overlap between whites and blacks as well as the even greater differences within each population:

> ... *Homo sapiens* is tens of thousands, or at most a few hundred thousand, years old, and all modern human races probably split from a common ancestral stock only tens of thousands of years ago. A few outstanding traits of external appearance lead to our subjective judgement of important differences. But biologists have recently affirmed – as long suspected – that the overall genetic differences among human races are astonishingly small. Although frequencies for different states of gene differ among races, we have found no 'race genes' – that is, states fixed in certain races and absent from all others ... (Gould, 1981)

CHAPTER SUMMARY

- The concept of intelligence is extremely difficult to define, despite being one of the most intensively researched aspects of individual differences and having such practical significance.
- Biological definitions of intelligence see it as related to adaptation to the environment; the best example of this approach is Piaget, who was not interested in individual differences but in the nature of intelligence itself and the qualitative changes that everyone goes through.
- Psychological definitions are linked to the psychometric approach, which is concerned with quantitative differences between individuals. Many stress the purely intellectual aspects of intelligence, while others are broader and include more practical aspects.
- An operational definition is circular and so does not solve the problem of the multiplicity of definitions. Another attempted solution is Neisser's concept of prototypes, but different social groups may have different prototypes and this only tells us about people's understanding of the term rather than what it actually means.
- The psychometric approach assumes that intelligence is an individual characteristic that varies between individuals and which can be measured by intelligence tests. Scores of large numbers of participants on different tests are factor-analysed to determine, through patterns of correlation, whether they are tapping the same or different factors or abilities.

- According to Spearman's two-factor theory, every intellectual activity involves both a general factor (*g* or general intelligence) and a specific factor (*s*); differences between individuals are largely due to differences in their *g*, which is entirely innate.
- Burt and Vernon extended Spearman's model by identifying major group factors (*v:ed* and *k:m*) and minor group factors in between *g* and *s*. Because *g* is still at the top of the hierarchy, children can be ranked on a single scale of innate intelligence early in life.
- Thurstone identified seven distinct primary mental abilities (PMAs) ('mental faculties' or 'vectors'), namely spatial, perceptual speed, numerical reasoning, verbal meaning, word fluency, memory and inductive reasoning. These correspond to the group factors in the hierarchical model; *g* is simply the grand average of correlations for a particular battery of tests and so has no psychological significance. No overall ranking of individuals is possible; instead, individuals should be profiled on all PMAs. Although Thurstone later acknowledged the existence of *g*, there is disagreement as to the significance of this change.
- Guilford's 'structure of intellect' model totally rejects the idea of *g*. Any cognitive task can be classified in terms of content, operations (including convergent and divergent thinking) and products, making 150 distinct mental abilities. Correlations are found, however, suggesting a smaller number of basic abilities.
- The hierarchical approach, which sees *g* as involved in all mental activities as well as more specific abilities, is probably the most widely accepted factorial description of intelligence.
- There are different forms of factor analysis (FA) which are mathematically equivalent but which produce different patterns of factors. Differences between British and American models also reflect differences in the kind of participants and the type and number of tests used.
- Quite apart from these differences, the resulting factors still have to be given a psychological interpretation; this cannot be an objective process and there is the danger of reification of factors, which are just mathematical abstractions, once they have been labelled.
- According to Cattell and Horn, *g* can be subdivided into fluid intelligence ('*gf* '), which is relatively free of cultural influences and reflects the maturity of the nervous system, and crystallized

intelligence ('gc') which reflects cumulative learning and knowledge and goes on increasing throughout the lifespan.

- The information-processing approach sees intelligence as the steps people go through in solving problems. People differ according to how quickly or efficiently they move through the steps or their familiarity with them.

- Sternberg identifies five components used in carrying out information-processing strategies, namely meta-components, performance, acquisition, retention and transfer. g results from the operation of components which are general across the range of tasks represented on IQ tests and are mainly meta-components. Operation of the other four kinds of component produces Burt and Vernon's major group factors and Thurstone's PMAs.

- Sternberg's information-processing model comprises one part of his triarchic theory, namely the componential sub-theory, which is concerned with the internal, mental mechanisms underlying intelligent behaviour. The contextual sub-theory deals with how these mechanisms are used in everyday life to fit the external world and the experiential sub-theory is concerned with the relationship between intelligence and experience.

- Sternberg maintains that there is more to intelligence than a set of information-processing components, since different cultures define intelligence in different ways (adaptation); shaping and selection of an environment are the other behavioural goals of intelligence.

- Both the ability to deal with novelty and to automatize information processing are useful ways of assessing intelligence, neither of which is included in standard IQ tests.

- Gardner's theory of multiple intelligences sees intelligence as a collection of separate, independent but interacting systems, namely linguistic, logical-mathematical, spatial, musical, bodily-kinaesthetic, interpersonal and intrapersonal. Criteria for distinguishing an independent intelligence include potential isolation by brain damage, an identifiable core operation, support from psychometric findings and the existence of idiots savants (such as Harriet, Nadia, Stephen Wiltshire and calendar counters) and other exceptional individuals.

- The original Simon–Binet intelligence test was adapted for use in the USA and became known as the Stanford–Binet test; it has been revised several times. Wechsler has devised a number of tests, both for children (WISC-R and WPPSI) and adults (WAIS-R); the WAIS-R is the most widely used test of adult intelligence. The recent British Ability Scales (BAS) have been influenced by the information-processing approach. These are all individual tests. The Army Alpha and Beta tests were the earliest group tests of intelligence.

- Individual tests are mainly used as diagnostic tests in clinical settings, while group tests are mainly used for educational selection (as in the 11-plus examination) and research. There needs to be a good rapport between the tester and testee in an individual test, which usually includes some performance items, whereas a group test is much like any written examination.

- The Stanford–Binet comprises a number of age-related scales, based on the assumption that mental ability is developmental. A child is usually started off on the scale immediately below its chronological age (CA) to determine its basal age, then works through the scales to determine its mental age (MA) which provides an absolute assessment of its intellectual development. But we want to know how the child compares with others of the same age and this is done by the intelligence quotient (IQ).

- The Stanford–Binet MA only goes up to 18, while the WAIS-R is designed for 16–74-year-olds. Both the WAIS-R and WISC-R comprise a verbal and a performance scale, each comprising sub-tests and each producing a separate IQ, which can be combined to give an overall IQ; they don't use age-related scales. The Stanford–Binet only uses performance items for children up to 4–5 but the latest edition gives separate scores for verbal reasoning, abstract/visual reasoning, quantitative reasoning and short-term memory.

- The Wechsler tests use a deviation IQ as opposed to the ratio IQ of the Stanford–Binet. Since 1960, the Stanford-Binet has used a deviation IQ, making scores on the two tests more comparable; however, standard deviations (SDs) can still differ between tests. While intelligence is a psychological concept, IQ is a statistical concept, so that they cannot be equated. We cannot simply reduce intelligence to an IQ score, whereas an operational definition of height is perfectly acceptable.

- By definition, IQ involves a comparison with others and so is measured on an ordinal scale; because it is expressed as a number, it appears to be an interval measurement.

- Good psychological tests should have discriminatory power; they are designed to produce a normal distribution of scores, which is based on the assumption that intelligence is largely biologically determined. This requirement guides the standardization process, whereby norms are established for various groups allowing the scores of individuals to be meaningfully compared.

- Both the Stanford–Binet and Wechsler scales were originally standardized on whites only and the re-standardization of the former so as to equalize the mean scores of women and men reveals the ideological significance of IQ. This adjustment changes the test's predictive efficiency.

- Tests must also be reliable. Reliability can refer to the test itself (internal consistency, measured by the split-half method or alternate/parallel forms) or consistency over time (stability, measured by the test–retest method). Reliability is a prerequisite for validity.

- The weakest form of validity is face/content validity. Both concurrent and predictive validity correlate scores on an IQ test with some independent, external criterion, which may be scores on another test or, most commonly, educability/school success or occupational success. The well-established correlations between IQ scores and both school and occupational success do not in themselves demonstrate the validity of IQ tests.

- Construct validity embraces both predictive and concurrent validity. While there is considerable evidence in support of construct validity, there remains the problem of psychologists not being able to agree about what it is that IQ tests are actually measuring.

- Constructors of IQ tests claim that they represent tests of aptitude rather than attainment/achievement, making them culture-free/culture-fair. However, this distinction is controversial and Ryan rejects the very notion of potential, which is what aptitude tests claim to measure.

- A strictly culture-free test is impossible, while a culture-fair test is possible but very difficult to construct in practice. An example is Raven's progressive matrices, but it is impossible to construct a test that doesn't involve symbols of some kind or other and these, by definition, are bound up with cultural experience. The very concept of intelligence is cultural and no test can assess the meaning that the experience of taking an intelligence test has for the testee.

- Attempts to correlate IQ scores with various psychophysiological measures, such as EEGs, EPs and RT, can be seen as attempts to resolve some of the problems surrounding culture-fair tests. Although there is evidence of high correlations between IQ scores and individual differences in measures of P300, for example, interpretation of these findings is problematical.

- The nature–nurture debate in relation to differences in intelligence between individuals and groups is extremely controversial and divisive; it is assumed that IQ tests are valid measures of intelligence.

- According to the genetic theory, the more genetically similar two individuals are, the more similar their IQ scores should be. While the correlations are very much in line with this prediction, they are also consistent with the environmentalist theory, since increasing genetic similarity is associated with increasing similarity of environments. This is especially clear in the case of MZs reared together and also applies to same-sex DZs compared with opposite-sex DZs and ordinary siblings.

- Studies involving MZs reared apart and adoption studies attempt to separate the effects of genetic and environmental factors. The finding that separated MZs are more alike than same-sex DZs reared together is very strong supporting evidence for the genetic theory, but there are serious problems with the way that twin studies have been carried out.

- The so-called separated twins often turn out not to be truly separated at all, i.e. the criteria for separation are very suspect, especially in the Shields study. When they are separated, the agencies responsible for placing them try to match the respective families, although when the environments are substantially different, very marked IQ differences are found, as in the Newman *et al.* study.

- The use of correlation tends to exaggerate the relative similarities of MZs compared with DZs, obscuring sometimes large absolute differences between pairs of separated MZs. Experimenter bias, bias in the twin samples themselves and methods of recruitment and the use of different IQ tests in different studies all make the data less convincing than they otherwise would be. In addition, there is ongoing controversy over Burt's data.

- Twin studies have been used to derive a heritability estimate of 80 percent (Eysenck and Jensen). But even without all the methodological problems, a heritability estimate can only tell us about a particular population at a particular time and even then, twins would need to be representative of the population, their environments would also have to be representative and they would have to be randomly allocated to their adoptive families. Kamin argues that none of these conditions has been met.

- Adoption studies also appear to support the genetic theory, but they too have been criticized on methodological grounds, especially the 'classic' design of the early studies (Burks and Leahy), e.g. involving the matching of the adoptive/adopted group with a biological control group. In terms of absolute level of IQ, adopted children become more like the adoptive parents and score well above what they probably would have scored had they stayed in their disadvantaged natural families.
- An improved design involves adoptive parents who also have a biological child of their own; this was used in Scarr and Weinberg's transracial adoption study and Horn *et al.*'s study. Both studies found that children reared by the same mother resemble her IQ to the same degree, whether or not they share her genes; this strongly challenges the genetic theory.
- The findings of these more recent adoption studies can be explained by reference to the concept of reaction range, which is itself related to facilitativeness; both these concepts highlight the interaction between genetic and environmental influences. Facilitativeness is illustrated by Werner's 30-year longitudinal study of children in Hawaii. Interaction is also illustrated by the disease phenylketonuria (PKU).
- The genetic theory predicts that IQ scores will remain stable across an individual's lifetime. Before age two, a developmental quotient (DQ) is used rather than IQ; generally, the younger a child is when given a developmental test, the lower the correlation between its DQ and later IQ scores. Large changes in IQ are often found beyond what a simple genetic theory would predict. Kagan's study of Guatemalan children also suggests that stability may not be the rule.
- According to the genetic theory, individual differences in early experience should have no fundamental effect on the development of individual differences in intelligence; linked to this is the prediction that deliberate attempts to increase the level of intelligence by special enrichment experience should have no effect.
- There has been considerable debate concerning the effectiveness of compensatory pre-school programmes for disadvantaged children in the USA, starting with Operation Headstart. The initial follow-up suggested short-lived gains in IQ and minimal educational improvement, but then a 'sleeper effect' was discovered, although the academic benefits were longer lasting than the IQ gains. The reverse pattern was found in the Milwaukee Project.
- Hebb's distinction between intelligence A and B was meant to settle the nature–nurture controversy, since differences in intelligence could only refer to B, as A is impossible to estimate. Vernon added intelligence C to refer to IQ test scores (a sample of B).
- Intelligence testing has always been founded on the belief that IQ is biologically heritable, but the term is often used mistakenly, what Gould calls the hereditarian fallacy. Part of this is the belief that heritability estimates based on within-group differences (such as are found in twin studies) can be applied to between-group differences (such as between blacks and whites). Jensen explains the average 15-point difference between blacks and whites in terms of the genetic inferiority of blacks, based on twin studies which have used samples from the white population only.
- Trying to equate the environments of blacks and whites in terms of social class is invalid and any study in which black–white comparisons in IQ are made use tests that are racially biased. The whole race and IQ controversy is complicated by the fact that the overall genetic differences between human races are astonishingly small; there are no 'race genes'.

GLOSSARY

Crystallized intelligence One dimension of Spearman's *g* ('gc'); understanding relations and solving problems which depend on knowledge gained as a result of schooling and other life experiences. Increases throughout the lifespan.

Deviation IQ Expressing a test result (i.e. an individual's score) as a standard score, i.e. how many standard deviations above/below the mean of the individual's age group.

Discriminatory power A requirement of a psychological test, whereby it should produce a wide distribution of scores; usually, this means a normal distribution.

Face validity A crude way of assessing the validity of a psychological test by looking at the test items to see if they 'look' right. Also called content validity.

Fluid intelligence One dimension of Spearman's g ('gf '); the ability to solve abstract problems of the kind not taught and which are relatively free of cultural influences. Related to maturation of the nervous system. Declines, steadily in adulthood.

Hereditarian fallacy Two mistaken beliefs about the meaning of 'heritable' : (i) heritable = inevitable; (ii) within-group heredity can be applied to between-group heredity.

Idiots savants Term used to refer to certain mentally handicapped individuals who, despite low overall intelligence, show exceptional abilities, such as drawing and calendar counting.

Information-processing approach Defining intelligence as the processes/strategies people use in solving problems, the components involved in those strategies and decisions taken as to which strategies to use.

Intelligence quotient (IQ) The ratio of mental age (MA) to chronological age (CA) multiplied by 100 to give a whole number. Introduced by Stern and used in the Stanford–Binet test until 1960.

Mental age (MA) How well an individual performs on a test compared with others of a particular chronological age; for example, doing as well as the average five-year-old means a MA of five. Used in the original Simon–Binet test.

Reliability The consistency with which a psychological test measures whatever it measures; internal consistency refers to the test itself, stability refers to consistency over time.

Split-half method A way of measuring internal consistency, by splitting the test in half (e.g. all the odd/even numbered items), then correlating scores on the two halves. They can be thought of as two forms of the same test (alternate/parallel forms).

Standardization Testing a large, representative sample of the population for which a particular test is designed in order to obtain a set of norms against which individual scores can be compared.

Test–retest reliability A way of measuring consistency over time by giving the same participants the same test on more than one occasion and correlating the scores.

Validity The requirement that a psychological test measures what it claims to measure.

Construct validity Formulating hypotheses about what kind of test results would be expected if the test really does measure what it claims to measure. Involves both concurrent and predictive validity.

Concurrent validity Correlating the scores on a psychological test with some other independent measure (criterion) at the same point in time. Predictive validity is the same, except the criterion measure is made at some future time. Together, they form external validity.

Attainment tests Tests concerned with how much a person knows about a specific subject or with current level of performance (e.g. reading age); also called achievement tests.

Aptitude tests Tests concerned with a person's capacity or potential for succeeding in a particular academic subject or occupation.

Culture-fair test A test modified for use in a variety of cultural settings, to ensure that each version contains the same degree of familiarity with test items, so that each cultural group has an equal chance of success.

Heritability estimate (In the case of intelligence) the proportion of the variance in IQ scores between individuals which can be attributed to genetic differences.

Reaction range The range of possible responses by an individual to the particular environment they encounter; it is unique to that individual and is linked to genetic make-up.

Intelligence A Innate potential; the possession of a good brain and neural metabolism (Hebb); cannot be measured separately from intelligence B.

Intelligence B Product of the interaction between intelligence A and the environment; the only sense in which intelligence can be measured (Hebb).

Intelligence C Scores on an IQ test; really a sample of intelligence B (Vernon).

FURTHER READING

Sternberg, R.J. (1990) *Metaphors of Mind: Conceptions of the Nature of Intelligence.* Cambridge: Cambridge University Press. An extremely wide-ranging discussion of intelligence, from a variety of psychological perspectives, as well as anthropology and sociology.

29 PERSONALITY

INTRODUCTION AND OVERVIEW

Most personality theories, however different they may be in other respects, share the basic assumption that personality is something that 'belongs' to the individual so that the appropriate unit of analysis for personality psychology is the person (Hampson, 1995). Much of this chapter will be devoted to discussing some of the major theories of personality, in particular Allport's trait theory, Cattell's and Eysenck's psychometric theories, Kelly's personal construct theory, Rogers' self theory and the psychoanalytic theories of Freud, Jung and Adler.

To the extent that every individual 'has' a personality that is stable and relatively permanent, behaviour will be consistent from one situation to another; an alternative view (originally proposed by Mischel) is that behaviour is largely determined by situational factors and that behaviour will show considerable inconsistency across situations. This is sometimes referred to as the *trait versus situation* debate or the *consistency controversy*.

Personality theories differ from each other with respect to whether they are trying to compare individuals in terms of a specified number of traits or dimensions common to everyone (*nomothetic*) or whether they are trying to identify individuals' unique characteristics and qualities (*idiographic*).

'Personality' is one of those terms which, while commonly used in everyday language, has been given a special technical meaning by psychologists which is why, in any psychological discussion, it makes no sense to say that a person has 'lots of personality'. 'Personality' is also a *hypothetical construct*, something which cannot be directly observed but only inferred from behaviour in order to make sense of it (see Chapter 1).

In Chapter 15 we discussed the ways in which our perception of other people is influenced by 'implicit personality theories' or informal theories about the way that personality traits cluster together in individuals. If our informal theories influence how we expect others to behave and if they influence how we behave towards them, then this suggests that personality is not merely an abstraction which helps to explain an individual's behaviour in isolation but a concept which has real meaning in the context of interpersonal behaviour. Again, personality is not something a person 'has' (it is not a 'thing') but rather is to do with how we relate to other people and generally deal with the world. We also discussed how individuals engage in self-presentation in an attempt to influence the impression that others form of their personality and ability.

You will remember from Chapter 21 that one of the major categories to emerge from studies of people's *self-concept* is personality traits. Also, when participants are given self-report measures of personality, such as personality questionnaires, they are in fact being asked to report on their self-concept, i.e. how they perceive their own personality.

According to the *constructionist approach* (Hampson, 1995), personality is constructed, in the course of social interaction, from a person's self-presentation (the actor), the perception of this presentation by an audience (observer) and self-awareness (the self-observer). This approach represents a meta-theory, i.e. a theory about theories, and is an attempt to integrate (a) the great variety of personality theories and (b) aspects of social psychology that have been studied independently of the former but which are closely related to it.

HOW DO THEORIES OF PERSONALITY DIFFER?

Because of the diversity of theories, it is virtually impossible to find a definition which all psychologists would accept. However, if our aim is to highlight some of the dimensions along which various theories differ, then a useful definition of personality would be:

> ... those relatively stable and enduring aspects of individuals which distinguish them from other people, making them unique, but which at the same time allow people to be compared with each other.

This definition brings into focus two central issues:

1 Does personality consist of permanent traits or characteristics?
2 Is the study of personality the study of unique individuals or is it aimed at comparing individuals and discovering the factors which constitute personality in general? (Table 29.1).

- Those psychologists who answer 'yes' to the first question and who are interested in personality in general belong to the *psychometric* tradition and are known as *type* and *trait* theorists; the major

figures are Eysenck and Cattell. They make great use of personality questionnaires and the results from these are analysed using a statistical technique called factor analysis. In trying to establish factors in terms of which everyone can be compared, they adopt a *nomothetic* approach.
- Those who believe in the uniqueness of every individual represent the *idiographic* approach, but beyond this it is not easy to say what else they have in common. For example, they may or may not see personality as permanent or may differ as to how much or what kind of change is possible. But they are concerned with the *whole person*, whereas psychometric theorists want to rank or order individuals with respect to particular aspects of personality. Allport is probably the most ardent advocate of the idiographic approach, although, paradoxically, he puts forward a trait theory of personality (but one that is very different from that of Cattell, for example).
- Kelly's *personal construct theory* is idiographic but is also perhaps the most radical of all theories, either idiographic or nomothetic, in so far as it is not so much a theory of personality as a total psychology. According to Fransella (1981), 'Kelly sought to incorporate within the same theoretical framework those areas in psychology

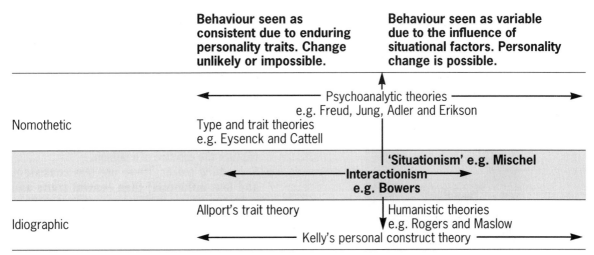

	Behaviour seen as consistent due to enduring personality traits. Change unlikely or impossible.	Behaviour seen as variable due to the influence of situational factors. Personality change is possible.
Nomothetic	◄——— Psychoanalytic theories ———► e.g. Freud, Jung, Adler and Erikson Type and trait theories e.g. Eysenck and Cattell	
	◄——————— Interactionism ——► e.g. Bowers	'Situationism' e.g. Mischel
Idiographic	Allport's trait theory ◄——————— Kelly's personal construct theory ———————►	Humanistic theories ▼ e.g. Rogers and Maslow

TABLE 29.1 *A classification of personality theories*

usually coming under separate chapter headings' (learning, cognition, motivation, emotion, psychophysiology) and, to this extent, the theory provides a total psychology about the total person.

- The other major representatives of the idiographic approach are the *humanistic* psychologists, in particular Maslow (whose hierarchy of needs was discussed in Chapter 5) and Rogers. What they share is a concern for those characteristics of people which make us distinctively human, including our experience of ourselves as persons.

- The *psychoanalytic* theories of Freud, Jung and Adler are clearly idiographic in that they are based on case studies of patients in the clinical context of psychotherapy and they are not attempting to measure personality in any sense. However, they are concerned with the nature of personality in general; Freud was trying to discover general laws of the psyche/personality and both he and Jung were also trying to account for individual differences. It was Jung, for example, who first distinguished between introverts and extroverts, which Eysenck later investigated in depth and measured in his personality questionnaires. As far as the enduring nature of personality is concerned, the psychoanalytic theorists all allow for the possibility of change, primarily through psychotherapy, although at any point in time behaviour is essentially the reflection of a person's characteristics and habitual ways of dealing with the world.

NOMOTHETIC VERSUS IDIOGRAPHIC APPROACHES: INDIVIDUAL DIFFERENCES OR UNIQUE INDIVIDUALS?

According to Kluckhohn and Murray (1953), 'Every man is in certain respects like all other men, like some other men and like no other men'. What we have in common with *all* other human beings is the subject matter of experimental or 'general' psychology, which studies cognitive and physiological processes and learning; much of developmental and social psychology too are concerned with discovering 'universal norms' which apply equally to all individuals.

What we have in common with *some* other human beings is the subject matter of individual differences (or differential psychology); personality differences represent one kind of 'group norm', others being age, gender, ethnic and cultural background and intelligence. It is the study of 'how and how much a particular individual is similar to or differs from others' (Shackleton and Fletcher, 1984) which constitutes the *factor-analytic/psychometric* approach; as we have seen, this is also a nomothetic approach.

Finally, what we have in common with *no* other human beings is what makes us unique and, of course, this is an expression of the idiographic approach which attempts to discover 'individual/ idiosyncratic norms'.

● Allport's trait theory (1961)

Allport (1961) (Fig. 29.1) defined personality as: ' ... The dynamic organization within the individual of those psychophysical systems that determine his characteristic behaviour and thoughts'.

FIGURE 29.1 *Gordon W. Allport (1897–1967). (UPI/Bettmann Archive)*

Allport and Odbert (1936) found over 18,000 terms describing personal characteristics and, even after omitting evaluative terms and transient states, there remained 4–5000. Allport believed that this large number of trait words could be reduced further; in fact, to two basic kinds:

1 *Common traits.* These are basic modes of adjustment which are applicable to all members of a particular cultural, ethnic or linguistic background. For instance, since we must all interact in a competitive world, we must each develop our own most suitable level of aggression and each of us can be placed somewhere along a scale of aggressiveness. Clearly, these are the subject matter of the nomothetic approach.

2 *Individual traits.* These are a unique set of personal dispositions based on unique life experiences and are unique ways of organizing the world; they are not dimensions which can be applied to all people. They cannot be measured by a standardized test and can be discovered only by careful and detailed study of individuals; they are the subject matter of the idiographic approach. Individual traits can take one of three forms:

● *Cardinal traits.* These are so all-pervading that almost all of an individual's behaviour is dictated and directed by a cardinal trait; for instance, someone who is consumed by greed,

ambition or lust. However, such traits are quite rare and most people do not have one predominant trait.

● *Central traits.* These are the basic building blocks which make up the core of personality and which constitute the individual's characteristic ways of dealing with the world (e.g. honest, loving, happy-go-lucky). A surprisingly small number of these is usually sufficient to capture the essence of a person.

● *Secondary traits.* These are less consistent and less influential than central traits and refer to tastes, preferences, political persuasions, reactions to particular situations and so on.

Individual traits are peculiar (idiosyncratic) to each person in at least three senses:

1 A trait that is central for one person may only be a secondary trait for another person and irrelevant for a third. What makes a trait central or secondary is not what it is, but how often and how strongly it influences the person's behaviour (Carver and Scheier, 1992).

2 Some traits are possessed by only one person; indeed, there may be as many separate traits as people to have them.

3 Even if two different people are given (for convenience) the same descriptive label (such as 'helpful'), it may not mean the same for the individuals concerned and, to that extent, it is not the same trait. For Allport, since personality dispositions reflect the subtle shadings that distinguish a particular individual from all others, they must often be described at length ('Little Susan has a peculiar anxious helpfulness all her own'), instead of by a single label ('helpful'). This makes it very difficult to compare people:

> ... [Any given individual] is a unique creation of the forces of nature. There was never a person just like him and there never will be again ... (Allport, 1961).

Yet comparing people in terms of a specified number of traits or dimensions (in order to determine individual differences) is precisely what the nomothetic approach involves: traits have the same psychological meaning for everyone, so that people only differ in the extent to which the trait is present. For example, in Eysenck's terms, everyone is more or less extroverted, i.e. everyone will score somewhere on the extroversion (E) scale and the difference between individuals is one of degree only (i.e. a quantitative difference). By contrast, the idiographic approach sees differences between people as qualitative, i.e. differences in kind.

Allport believed that comparisons between people can be made only, as we saw above, in terms of common traits; at best, these can only provide a rough approximation to any particular personality. For example, many individuals are predominantly outgoing or shy, yet 'There are endless varieties of dominators, leaders, aggressors, followers, yielders, and timid souls ... When we designate Tom and Ted both as *aggressive*, we do not mean that their aggression is identical in kind. Common speech is a poor guide to psychological subtleties' (Allport, 1961). The nomothetic approach, for Allport, can only portray human personality in an oversimplified way: even the traits that people seem to share with one another always have a personal flavour which differs from individual to individual.

● Does the wholly unique individual exist?

Holt (1967) argues that the idiographic–nomothetic issue is based on a false dichotomy: all description involves some degree of generalization, so that to imagine that we can describe an individual in terms which make no reference to any other individual is a fallacy. To describe *this* person, we must already have a concept of *a* person, i.e. some schema about people in general. As Kirby and Radford (1976) argue, a 'truly unique individual would be incomprehensible, in fact not recognizable as an individual'.

Disagreement between Allport and nomothetic theorists is not so much to do with whether or not they believe in the idea of uniqueness, but rather the way it is defined. Eysenck, for example, sees uniqueness as reflecting a unique combination of levels on trait dimensions, with the dimensions themselves being the same for all: 'To the scientist, the unique individual is simply the point of intersection between a number of quantitative variables' (Eysenck, 1953, quoted in Carver and Scheier, 1992). For Allport, as we have seen, this is a definition of uniqueness based on common traits and is a contradiction in terms: only individual traits capture the individuality of individuals.

According to Krahé (1992), the idiographic claim that there are unique traits that apply to only one individual is undoubtedly false, if taken literally: traits are defined as differential constructs referring to a person's position on a trait dimension relative to that of other people. But she also believes that, at the opposite extreme, the nomothetic view of traits as explanatory constructs which apply to everyone is equally misguided.

Holt (1967) also argues that Allport's so-called idiographic methods are just more or less nomothetic ones applied to individual cases. Conversely, Kline (1981b) believes that the existence of personality scales or questionnaires is not incompatible with the notion of uniqueness: in any one sample individuals will have very different *profiles* across a range of scales, but this does not mean that they will not share certain characteristics or groups of characteristics in common with other members of the sample. (This sounds very similar to Eysenck's definition of uniqueness in terms of a unique combination of scores on common dimensions.)

● Is a science of unique individuals possible?

As shown in Figure 29.2, the distinction between idiographic and nomothetic approaches is related to a distinction made, independently, by two 19th century German philosophers, Dilthey and Windelband, between two kinds of science. The *Naturwissenschaften* (natural sciences), such as physics and chemistry, aim to establish general laws about the natural world ('laws of nature') allowing predictions based on statements about cause-and-effect relationships and dividing nature into elements, while the *Geisteswissenschaften* ('moral' or 'human sciences'), such as philosophy, the humanities, history, biography and literary criticism and 'social science', involve *Verstehen*, an intuitive, empathic understanding of human mental activity (i.e. consciousness), stressing the inner unity of individual life and the person as an articulated whole (Valentine, 1992). While the natural sciences stress the general, Windelband, together with another German Rickert, argued that the human sciences should not – and by their very nature cannot – generalize, but must devote themselves to understanding particular cases (Holt, 1967). So where does psychology fit in?

As we saw above, Holt (1967) believes that the whole idiographic–nomothetic distinction is based on a false dichotomy and that the study of particular cases and the drawing of general conclusions are quite compatible with each other. In fact, psychologists today are increasingly coming to believe that the two approaches, far from being opposed and mutually exclusive, are complementary and interdependent (Krahé, 1992). Even Allport did not reject the nomothetic approach completely; for example, when discussing the nature of psychology as a science, he says that :

FIGURE 29.2 *John Major and Margaret Thatcher: both British Prime Ministers but very different individuals. Are there enduring traits which influence their respective behaviour in systematic and predictable ways?*

Science aims to achieve powers of understanding, prediction and control above the level of unaided common sense. From this point of view it becomes apparent that only by taking adequate account of the individual's total pattern of life can we achieve the *aims* of science. Knowledge of general laws ... quantitative assessments and correlational procedures are all helpful: but with this conceptual (nomothetic) knowledge must be blended a shrewd diagnosis of trends within an individual ... Unless such idiographic (particular) knowledge is fused with nomothetic (universal) knowledge, we shall not achieve the *aims* of science, however closely we imitate the methods of the natural and mathematical sciences. (Allport, 1960)

Jaccard and Dittus (1990, cited in Krahé, 1992) argue that it is untrue that a strictly idiographic approach is directly opposed to the identification and development of universal laws of human behaviour. The idiographic researcher, like the nomothetic, is interested in explaining behaviour and to do this, both seek a general theoretical framework that specifies the constructs that should be focused upon and the types of relationships expected among these concepts. The essential difference between them is that one applies the framework to a single person, while the other applies it to people in general: they share the same scientific aim. (For a more detailed discussion of the whole idiographic–nomothetic issue, see Gross, 1995; see also Chapter 2.)

BEHAVIOUR. IS IT THE PRODUCT OF PERSONALITY OR THE SITUATION OR BOTH?

Most definitions of traits focus on their stability and permanency which, in turn, implies that an individual's behaviour is consistent over time and from one situation to another. Indeed, Baron and Byrne (1991) define personality as ' ... The combination of those relatively enduring traits which influence behaviour in a predictable way in a variety of situations'.

Guilford (1959) defined a trait as 'any relatively enduring way in which one individual differs from another' and Hall and Lindzey (1957) defined it as 'a determining tendency or predisposition to respond'.

When discussing the attribution process (Chapter 15) we noted that there is a tendency to attribute other people's behaviour primarily to their dispositional qualities (including personality traits) as opposed to situational factors *(fundamental attribution error)* while we tend to see our own behaviour primarily as a response to the situation *(actor–observer effect)*. It follows from this that we are likely to regard the behaviour of others as more consistent (and, hence, more predictable) and to regard our own as more variable from situation to situation (and, hence, less predictable).

Seeing behaviour as primarily caused by personality traits (the *trait approach*) is usually opposed to what has become known as *situationism* (Mischel, 1968), the view that behaviour is largely determined by situational factors.

Mischel, a social learning theorist (see Chapters 7 and 27), sparked the 'consistency controversy' in 1968 by declaring that his review of a wide range of personality domains provided very little support for the concept of intraindividual consistency. He argued that the average correlation between different behavioural measures designed to tap the same personality trait was typically between 0.1 and 0.2, often lower, while correlations between scores on personality tests designed to measure a given trait and measures of behaviour in various situations meant to tap the same trait rarely exceeded 0.3. This lack of cross-situation consistency was taken by Mischel to indicate the importance of the situation in determining behaviour. According to personality theorists, it is the possession of traits which accounts for the consistency and predictability of behaviour, but if these are lacking, the usefulness of the trait concept disappears and we are left only with situational influences to account for the inconsistency of individual behaviour: the same person behaves differently in different situations because different situations require different behaviour and are associated with different kinds of reinforcements. So, from this (rather extreme) situationist perspective, intraindividual *inconsistency* is exactly what you would expect!

However, intuitively there seems to be something wrong with situationism, at least in its extreme form. Surely different people behave differently even within the same situation and, conversely, are we not recognizably the same person from one situation to another?

Eysenck and Eysenck (1980) and Kline (1983) cite a number of studies which demonstrate consistency between scores on questionnaires and rating scales on the one hand and behaviour on the other, with average correlations of around 0.8, and Bowers (1973) criticized the social learning theorists for favouring an experimental design which is intended to emphasize the role of situational determinants of behaviour (situation specificity) relative to behavioural consistency or stability.

A number of writers have pointed out that to regard behaviour as being caused either by situational factors or by personality traits is an oversimplification of a complex issue. Bowers (1973), Endler (1975) and Pervin and Lewis (1978) all advocate an *interactionist* position, which stresses the mutual influence of situational and dispositional variables:

$$\text{Behaviour} = \text{Person} \times \text{Situation}$$

Bowers, for instance, reviewed 11 studies covering a wide range of behaviour including aggression in young boys, anxiety in students and resistance to temptation in children and concluded that 13 percent of the variance in participants' behaviour was due to person variables, 10 percent to situational variables and 20 percent to an interaction between the two. While this kind of research cannot determine whether personality or situation is more important, the results nevertheless clearly favour the interactionist position (Argyle, 1983).

Mischel has himself moved towards a more interactionist position (e.g. 1973) but prefers to talk about 'person' variables (as we saw in Chapter 27) as opposed to traits, the former being more cognitive, the latter being more related to temperament. Mischel believes that the 'same' situation can have different meanings for different individuals, depending on past learning experiences; this determines how we select, evaluate and interpret stimuli and, in turn, how particular stimuli will affect behaviour. It follows that situational factors cannot account adequately for human behaviour on their own because they do not exist objectively, independently of the actor. Based on a study of children's ability to resist temptation when looking at attractive sweets, Mischel (1973) concluded that 'The results clearly show that what is in the children's heads – not what is physically in front of them – determines their ability to delay'.

Similarly, rather than trying to define the situation independently of the actors involved, it is the *psychological situation* which constitutes a critical determinant of behaviour: the psychological meaning of a situation for the individual (how it is perceived) is a crucial factor in predicting behaviour and accounting for regularities in behaviour across situations (Krahé, 1992). (Another sense in which the influence of situations cannot be defined objectively is that personality traits, in particular introversion – extroversion, dictate the choice of situations that people expose themselves to (Eysenck and Eysenck, 1985; see below).

Reference to the psychological situation suggests at least a partial explanation for the lack of behavioural consistency originally claimed by Mischel: if people fail to show consistent behaviour across situations, might this be because those situations don't

BOX 29.1 Key study: you can predict some of the people some of the time

Bem and Allen (1974), while recognizing the validity of Mischel's criticisms of trait theory, also stressed the considerable importance of it. They argued that our intuitions are not entirely wrong – instead of claiming that everyone is more or less equally consistent and predictable according to whichever traits one chooses to measure, most people will show consistent behaviour as far as a few traits are concerned but which traits they are will vary from person to person.

The traditional trait approach (the target of Mischel's attack) adopts a nomothetic approach, assuming that every person can be meaningfully assigned a score on every personality dimension, while Bem and Allen were advocating an idiographic approach, focusing on the unique aspects of a given individual's personality pattern (Ross and Nisbett, 1991); to do this, one must first identify the particular traits that 'apply' for the individual in question. However, their test of this hypothesis adopted an essentially nomothetic approach: they stipulated two specific traits, friendliness and conscientiousness.

Students were asked to rate themselves on their consistency for these two traits and for each trait they were divided into two groups, one which rated themselves as consistent and one which rated themselves as quite inconsistent. These self-ratings were then compared with ratings from their parents and friends and with the ratings of two independent observers who rated their behaviour in group discussions and other situations.

For both traits, the high-consistency participants were rated in a similar way by friends and parents (the average correlation coefficient was 0.61 for friendliness and 0.48 for conscientiousness and the correlations between these ratings and the relevant behavioural measures were 0.47 and 0.36 respectively). In all cases, correlations for the low-consistency individuals were lower. As far as correlations between the relevant behavioural measures were concerned, for friendliness the high-consistency and low-consistency individuals scored 0.73 and 0.30 respectively (in line with predictions), while for conscientiousness the results were –0.04 and –0.19 respectively (not in line with predictions).

those situations in an objective way)? In other words, only if the perceptions of actors and researchers coincide can there be any possibility of finding consistency. A 'solution' to this problem was proposed by Bem and Allen (1974); this is discussed in Box 29.1.

Hilgard *et al.* (1979) point out that if a random selection of participants is taken in an attempt to demonstrate high cross-situational consistency (as would be predicted by a trait theorist), this is bound to fail, because some will be highly consistent on that trait while others will be low on consistency. The claim that some people behave consistently with respect to certain traits while other people behave consistently on others is called the *metatrait hypothesis* (Baron and Byrne, 1991). (We should also note that those traits on which individuals rate themselves as consistent – and on which they are consistent as rated by others – are likely to be an important part of their self-image and, in Allport's terms, are likely to be central traits.)

Bem and Allen (1974) conclude that we must take internal and external forces into account, the former including the person's perception of the situation. Carver and Scheier (1992) point out that attempts to replicate Bem and Allen's findings have met with very mixed fortunes. However, what their view of consistency represents is an important *moderator variable*, i.e. something which links personal dispositions and actual behaviour and which can account for the very low levels of consistency found in earlier studies and on which Mischel based his attack of the trait approach. Another such moderator variable is *self-monitoring* (Snyder, 1987) which relates to the 'self-observer' in the constructionist approach (see Chapter 15).

When situational factors are very powerful, personality factors are relatively weak in explaining people's behaviour. Milgram's classic study of obedience and Zimbardo *et al.*'s prison simulation experiment (see Chapter 20) are good examples of how the 'demands of the situation' can largely 'override' individual traits and dispositions, so that knowing what these demands are is a fairly accurate predictor of how people will behave. However, even here not all participants behave in an identical way. In general, when situational factors are numerous and complex or weak, personality variables are more likely to operate and knowing how particular individuals usually behave in a variety of situations will be a much better predictor of how they will behave in the current situation (see Sources of Error in the Attribution Process, Chapter 15).

all have the same meaning for the individuals concerned (which they 'should' have – and need to have – according to the researchers who define

THE PSYCHOMETRIC APPROACH – EYSENCK AND CATTELL

To understand the similarities and differences between these two psychometric theorists, we need to say something about factor analysis (FA) which is an essential part of this approach.

● The criteria of a good psychometric test

As we saw in Chapter 28 in relation to intelligence tests, a 'good' psychological/psychometric test should :

● have *discriminatory power*, i.e. it should produce a wide distribution of scores;
● be properly *standardized,* i.e. it should have been tried out with a large, representative sample of the population for whom the test is intended so that the resulting norms (typical scores or distribution for the groups) can be legitimately used when assessing an individual's score;
● be *reliable,* i.e. it should consistently measure the variable it addresses;
● be *valid,* i.e. it should actually measure what it claims to measure.

● Factor analysis (FA)

FA is a statistical technique, based on correlation, which attempts to reduce a large amount of data (scores on personality questionnaires, objective tests and other measuring devices) to a much smaller amount. Essentially, the aim is to discover which test items correlate with one another and which do not and then to identify the resulting correlation clusters (or factors). Put another way, what is the smallest number of factors which can adequately account for the variance between participants on the measures in question? Assuming that the tests are 'good' tests, the researcher is trying to discover the fundamental components of personality which apply to everyone and in terms of which everyone can be compared; as measured by the tests, individuals will differ in the degree to which they display these components.

Just as there are different kinds of reliability and validity, so there are different kinds of FA. One of the most important distinctions is between orthogonal and oblique methods. An *orthogonal* method aims to identify a small number of powerful factors which are independent of each other (uncorrelated), and this is the method preferred by Eysenck; an oblique method aims to identify a larger number of less powerful factors which are not independent (i.e. they are correlated to some degree), and this is the method preferred by Cattell.

Since it is possible to carry out a further FA of oblique factors, they are referred to *as first-order factors* and the resulting re-grouping of the oblique factors as *second-order factors*. In fact, Cattell has discovered a small number of second-order factors which correspond closely to Eysenck's three major second-order factors (see below). Eysenck's second-order factors are referred to as *types* (what Cattell calls surface traits) and Cattell's first-order factors as traits (or *source traits*). The differences between the two theorists are summarized in Table 29.2.

Ultimately, the method used depends on the taste or preference of the researchers. Both Cattell and Eysenck believe that their method best reflects the psychological reality of personality, but there is no objective way of establishing that one is right and the other wrong.

Because there is an infinite number of possible solutions, Heim (1975) believes that FA should not be used at all. However, Thurstone (1947) had argued that *rotation to simple structure* could overcome this difficulty and Cattell (1966) and Cattell and Kline (1977) support this view. *Simple structure* means that each factor will have a few high loadings (i.e. correlate quite highly with a few other factors) and a large number of low or nil loadings (very little or no correlation with a large number of factors), making each factor simple to interpret. The rationale behind simple structure is

	Eysenck	Cattell
Preferred method of FA	Orthogonal	Oblique
Level of analysis	Second order	First order
Description of factors	Types ('surface traits')	Traits ('source traits')

TABLE 29.2 *Differences in the type of factor analysis preferred by Eysenck and Cattell*

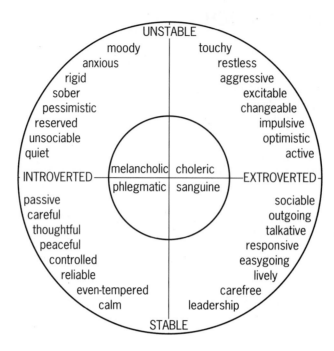

FIGURE 29.3 *Dimensions of personality. (From Eysenck, 1965)*

the law of parsimony, i.e the most economical solution to the problem. As Kline (1981b) suggests, if each FA solution is regarded as a hypothesis accounting for the correlations, the most simple is to be preferred. Cattell argues that an orthogonal technique prevents the attainment of simple structure.

Guilford (1959), on the other hand, believes that a set of uncorrelated factors is more simple than a set of oblique or correlated ones, which is why Eysenck opts for an orthogonal technique (see Chapter 28). According to Kline (1981b), most factor analysts, in practice, prefer oblique factors.

● Eysenck's type theory

The term 'type' was formerly used to describe people who belonged to one *or* other group or category, such that a particular individual could only be counted as a member of one or another. For example, in the ancient Greek theory of the 'Four Temperaments' or 'Four Humours' (Galen, second century AD), one of the earliest type theories (and, indeed, one of the first theories of personality of any kind), a person was either choleric (due to an excess of yellow bile), sanguine (due to an excess of blood), melancholic (due to an excess of black bile) or phlegmatic (due

to an excess of phlegm). These four humours are included in the inner circle of Eysenck's diagram, shown in Figure 29.3.

According to Eysenck (1995), today, 'type' is either not used at all or is reserved for combinations of traits that are found to correlate; for example, extroversion is a type concept based on the observed correlations of sociability, liveliness, activity and so on. The search for a reliable and valid measurement of personality traits is only a first step: the traits we find are not independent of each other but are correlated in certain patterns that suggest more complex entities that might be called types (Eysenck, 1995). However, unlike Galen's four humours, Eysenck's types are personality *dimensions* which represent continuums along which everyone can be placed.

Eysenck's dimensions in fact constitute the highest level of a *hierarchy* (Cattell's 'surface traits') with a number of traits at the next level down (Cattell's 'source traits') and below that a set of habitual responses (typical ways of behaving) linked to a particular trait. At the lowest level is a specific response (a response on one particular occasion; see Fig. 29.4). This hierarchical model is similar to Vernon's (1950) model of intelligence, to which Eysenck subscribes (see Chapter 28).

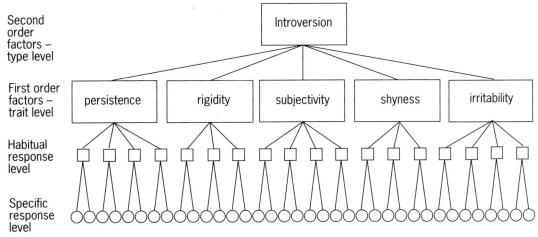

FIGURE 29.4 *Eysenck's hierarchical model of personality in relation to the introversion dimension. (After Eysenck, 1953)*

● Extroversion (E), neuroticism (N) and psychoticism (P)

Eysenck (1947) factor-analysed 39 items of personal data for each of 700 neurotic soldiers, screening them for brain damage and physical illness; the items included personality ratings. Two orthogonal (uncorrelated) factors emerged, *introversion–extroversion* (E) and *neuroticism* (emotionality)–*stability* (N). These two dimensions are assumed to be normally distributed so that most people will score somewhere in the middle of the scale and very few at either extreme. Box 29.2 contains descriptions of 'typical' introverts and extroverts, which are 'idealized extremes' (or ideal types).

As regards neuroticism, the typical high N scorer could be described as:

> ... an anxious, worrying individual, moody and frequently depressed; he is likely to sleep badly and to suffer from various psychosomatic disorders. He is overly emotional, reacting too strongly to all sorts of stimuli and finds it difficult to get back on an even keel after each emotionally arousing experience. (Eysenck, 1965)

By contrast, the typical low N scorer (stable) individual:

> ... tends to respond emotionally only slowly and generally weakly and to return to baseline quickly after emotional arousal; he is usually calm, even-tempered, controlled and unworried. (Eysenck, 1965)

Since the original 1947 study, the existence of E and N has been supported by further research involving literally thousands of participants. Exhaustive research in many parts of the world, by many different researchers, has confirmed the existence of E and N, as well as a third dimension, *psychoticism*

BOX 29.2 Typical introverts and extroverts (from Eysenck, 1965)

The *typical introvert* is a quiet, retiring sort of person, introspective, fond of books rather than people; he is reserved and distant except to intimate friends. He tends to plan ahead, 'looks before he leaps' and distrusts the impulse of the moment. He does not like excitement, takes matters of everyday life with proper seriousness and likes a well-ordered mode of life. He keeps his feelings under close control, seldom behaves in an aggressive manner and does not lose his temper easily. He is reliable, somewhat pessimistic and places great importance on ethical standards.

The *typical extrovert* is sociable, likes parties, has many friends, needs to have people to talk to and does not like reading or studying by himself. He craves excitement, takes chances, often sticks his neck out, acts on the spur of the moment and is generally an impulsive individual. He is fond of practical jokes, always has a ready answer and generally likes change; he is carefree, easy-going, optimistic and likes to 'laugh and be merry'. He prefers to keep moving and doing things, tends to be aggressive and lose his temper quickly; altogether his feelings are not kept under tight control and he is not always a reliable person.

(P) (Eysenck and Eysenck, 1985). This was originally uncovered in a 1952 study of psychiatric patients but is less well established than the other two dimensions. Just as E and N are unrelated to each other, so they are both unrelated to P. According to Eysenck and Eysenck (1975):

> A high scorer ... may be described as being solitary, not caring for people; he is often troublesome, not fitting in anywhere. He may be cruel and inhumane, lacking in feelings and empathy, and altogether insensitive. He is hostile to others, even his own kith and kin, and aggressive, even to loved ones. He has a liking for odd and unusual things, and a disregard for danger; he likes to make fools of other people, and to upset them.

Unlike E and N, P is not normally distributed – both normals and neurotics score low on P. Eysenck also believes that P overlaps with (other) psychiatric labels, in particular with 'schizoid', 'psychopathic' and 'behaviour disorders'. However, there is only a quantitative difference (i.e. a difference of degree) between normals and psychotics (and this applies equally to differences between normals and neurotics). However, Eysenck (1995) stresses that the personality dimensions N and P only represent a predisposition ('diathesis'), unlike neurosis and psychosis which are actual psychological disorders; however, under extreme stress, the predisposition can become a psychiatric illness (Claridge, 1985) (see Chapter 30).

Personality questionnaires

The original questionnaire was the Maudsley Medical Questionnaire (MMQ), first used in 1952, which only measured N. This was replaced in 1959 by the Maudsley Personality Inventory (MPI), which measured both E and N. The Eysenck Personality Inventory (EPI) added a Lie Scale, which measures a person's tendency to give socially desirable answers and which Eysenck believes is a stable personality dimension (Eysenck and Eysenck, 1964). Finally, the Eysenck Personality Questionnaire (EPQ) added a P scale (Eysenck and Eysenck, 1975). There are also junior versions of these questionnaires for use with nine-year-olds and over.

The scales all comprise items of a 'yes/no' variety. They are essentially intended as research tools (as opposed to diagnostic tools for use in clinical settings) and, as such, they are generally regarded as acceptable, reliable and valid (Kline, 1981a; Shackleton and Fletcher, 1984), the main exception

being the P scale, which Eysenck himself admits is psychometrically inferior to other scales.

An important way in which Eysenck has attempted to validate his scales is through *criterion analysis*. This involves giving the questionnaires to groups of individuals who are known to differ on the dimensions in question. For example, although the test is not meant to diagnose neurosis, we would still expect diagnosed neurotics to score very high on N compared with non-neurotics and generally this is found to be the case. Eysenck also believes that criterion analysis overcomes the problem of the arbitrary nature of the labels given to the factors that emerge from FA (see Chapter 28).

The biological basis of personality

Eysenck's theory attempts to explain personality differences in terms of the kinds of nervous system that individuals possess; in turn, these nervous system differences are inherited.

As far as E is concerned, it is the balance between *excitation* and *inhibition* processes in the central nervous system that is crucial, specifically the ascending reticular activating system (ARAS; see Chapter 3). The ARAS is located in the central core of the brain-stem and its main function is to maintain an optimum level of alertness or 'arousal': it can do this by enhancing the incoming sensory data to the cortex through the excitation of neural impulses or it can 'damp them down' through inhibition.

In these terms, extroverts have a 'strong nervous system'; their ARAS is biased towards the inhibition of impulses, inhibition builds up quickly and strongly and it dissipates only slowly, with the effect of reducing the intensity of any sensory stimulation reaching the cortex (they are chronically under-aroused). For introverts, the bias is in the opposite direction; for them, excitation builds up strongly and rapidly and inhibition develops slowly and weakly, with the effect of increasing the intensity of any sensory stimulation reaching the cortex (they are chronically over-aroused).

As far as N is concerned, it is the reactivity (or lability) of the autonomic nervous system (ANS) that determines a person's standing on the scale and, in particular, differences in the limbic system, which controls the ANS. Especially important is the sympathetic branch of the ANS, which is activated by frightening or stressful experiences ('fight or flight syndrome'), resulting in increases in heart rate, breathing rate, blood pressure, sweating, adrenaline production and so on (see Chapter 3). The person who scores high on N has an ANS which reacts particularly strongly and quickly to stressful situations compared with less emotional or more stable individuals.

Finally, regarding P, the biological basis is much more uncertain but Eysenck (1980) has suggested that it may be related to levels of the male hormone, androgen, and/or other hormones.

Is there any evidence to support this part of Eysenck's theory?

Eysenck (1967) linked the concepts of inhibition and excitation to psychical fatigue, so that extroverts 'tire' more easily (e.g. become bored more easily and persevere less) than introverts. According to Kline (1983), there should be clear differences between introverts and extroverts on long and tedious jobs: extroverts should start better than introverts, do worse in the middle and then improve again towards the end, while introverts would work much more steadily throughout. Evidence to support these hypotheses comes from Eysenck (1967, 1971) and Harkins and Green (1975), who found that introverts do better at vigilance tasks, which require prolonged periods of concentration.

The low arousal of extreme extroverts leads them to seek constant change, as existing stimuli lose their arousal value. In the laboratory, their vigilance, which is low, or their desire for change can be tested by giving them a chance to alter the stimuli offered. In real life, it is found (in line with predictions) that, compared with introverts, extroverts change jobs and sexual partners more frequently, are more likely to divorce, show less brand loyalty in shopping behaviour and move house more often. (Eysenck, 1965; Eysenck and Eysenck, 1985).

According to Eysenck (1970), the greater sensitivity of introverts to stimuli is matched by their relative dislike of strong stimuli; everyone has an optimum level of stimulation but this is lower for the more highly aroused introvert. Introverts have lower pain thresholds and extroverts are more susceptible to the adverse effects of sensory deprivation. For example, one demonstration of the 'stimulus hunger' of extroverts is their willingness to go to great lengths to obtain a 'reward' of loud music or bright lights which introverts work hard to avoid.

However, Claridge (1967) could not find a simple relationship between E and physiological arousal;

instead, there seems to be a complex interconnection between arousal and the individual's position on E and N (as shown by a study by Claridge and Herrington (1963); see below). According to Hampson (1995), evidence for the role of the ARAS and arousal mechanisms in E is inconclusive, but great advances have been made since the mid-1980s in understanding the genetics of personality. As a result of large-scale twin, adoption and family resemblance studies, it is now widely concluded that about 50 percent of the variation in self-report personality measures may be due to heredity (Loehlin *et al.*, 1988) (see Chapters 28 and 30).

Drugs and personality

Wilson (1976) points out that we would expect introverts to be more difficult to sedate using a drug such as sodium amytal because they are supposed to be more aroused. He cites a study by Claridge and Herrington (1963)(cited in Claridge, 1967) in which

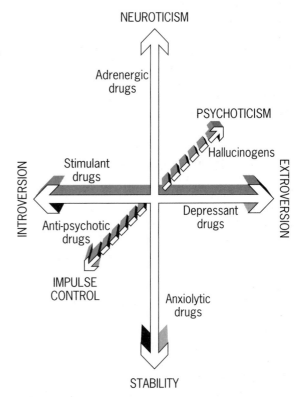

FIGURE 29.5 *Drug addiction and personality (Eysenck, 1983). Source Eysenck, H.J. (1995) Trait theories of personality. In S.E. Hampson & A.M. Coleman (Eds) Individual Differences and Personality. London, Longman*

introverted neurotics (*dysthymics*) were more diffi-cult to sedate than extroverted neurotics (*hysterics*), the latter being more easily sedated than normal participants. For the same reasons, regardless of an individual's normal position on the scale, stimulant drugs should shift behaviour in an introverted direc-tion while depressant drugs (such as alcohol) should have the opposite effect, pushing behaviour in an extroverted direction.

Anxiolytic (anti-anxiety) drugs should increase emotional stability, adrenergic drugs (those which mimic the effects of adrenaline) should decrease it, hallucinogens should increase psychotic behaviour and anti-psychotic drugs (narcoleptics) should decrease it (see Chapter 31). According to Eysenck (1995), empirical studies have, on the whole, sup-ported these causal hypotheses (see Fig. 29.5).

● Personality and conditionability

From a strictly psychological point of view, the importance of the biological aspects of Eysenck's theory is how they are related to individual differ-ences in conditionability. Because extroverts require a stronger stimulus to make an impact (they are 'stimulus hungry'), compared with the more easily stimulated introvert, and because the learning of S–R connections is best achieved by a strong and rapid build-up of excitation in the nervous system (which is characteristic of introverts), introverts should be more easily conditioned than extroverts. Does the evidence support Eysenck?

Despite Eysenck's strong claims to the contrary, the evidence is equivocal; for instance, about half the studies he reviewed in 1967 support his predictions while the other half do not. Eysenck seems to regard conditionability as a unitary trait, i.e. if an introvert is easily conditioned to one kind of stimulus, they will also condition easily to a range of other stimuli. However, such a general trait has never been demon-strated and the experimental evidence mainly involves three conditioned responses – the GSR (gal-vanic skin response), the eye blink and simple verbal conditioning. According to Kline (1983), until such a general dimension is discovered, this part of the the-ory remains weak and, in addition, extrapolation from laboratory studies to real-life situations is a dangerous business.

● Personality and criminality

In view of the criticisms of conditionability, it becomes all the more important to 'test' the theory in the 'real world' and one way in which Eysenck has done this is by advancing a theory of criminality. For Eysenck, the criminal is a *neurotic extrovert:* because the extrovert is more difficult to condition and because 'conscience' is nothing more than a series of conditioned anxiety responses (see Chapter 27), the neurotic extrovert is undersocial-ized and has an underdeveloped conscience.

Cochrane (1974) reviewed a number of studies in which prisoners and control groups were given EPI questionnaires. Although prisoners are generally higher on N, they are not higher on E and, indeed, several studies have shown criminals to be less extroverted (and so more introverted) than con-trols. Given the crucial part played by conditionability in Eysenck's theory, these findings would appear to seriously undermine it. However, Eysenck (1974) retorted by claiming that the EPI largely measures the 'sociability' component of extroversion rather than the 'impulsivity' compo-nent, which is more relevant to conditionability; here, he is certainly changing his earlier position whereby he equated 'sociability' (i.e. capacity for socialization) and 'conditionability'. Cochrane con-cludes that, at least in its original form, the theory has been discredited.

Even if prisoners were uniformly more extro-verted and neurotic than non-prisoners, it could still be possible to explain these differences by ref-erence to factors other than personality. For example, offenders who are caught (or found guilty) might differ in certain significant ways from those who are not (or who are not found guilty), such as the nature of the offence and the 'offender's' social status.

Hampson (1982), in a review of the research, concludes that, although there is some evidence that criminals are highly neurotic, the neurotic extrovert theory is not supported (thus agreeing with Cochrane) and any attempt to identify any per-sonality trait or dimension which differentiates criminals from non-criminals has been singularly unsuccessful.

A final criticism comes from Heather (1976), who argues that 'The notion that such a complex and meaningful *social* phenomenon as crime can ever be explained by appealing to the activity of individual nervous systems would be laughable were it not so insidious'. What makes the theory insidi-ous, he says, is that it 'places the fault inside individuals rather than in the social system where it almost always belongs' (see the discussion of reduc-tionism in Chapter 32).

● An evaluation of Eysenck's theory as a whole

- One of the most serious weaknesses seems to be the failure to produce any convincing evidence that introverts do, in fact, condition more easily than extroverts. Conditionability is a vital part of the overall theory because it 'points inwards' towards the biological (including genetic) basis of personality and 'outwards' towards the socialization experiences of different individuals (behaviour always being the product of an interaction between a nervous system and an environment).
- Heim (1970) has criticized the EPI (and, by implication, the EPQ) because of its forced-choice ('yes/no') form; she argues that a few, simple yes/no questions can hardly be expected to do justice to the complexities of human personality and she has criticized the Lie Scale for its lack of subtlety (see Chapter 2).
- Validation of the scales, as we have seen, has involved the use of criterion groups, for instance, groups of neurotics who tend to score at the extreme ends of the scale. But can we assume that the scale is 'valid' for the majority of people who lie somewhere in the middle? This is something that needs to be empirically tested, rather than simply assumed.
- Shackleton and Fletcher (1984) have pointed out the vast amount of research Eysenck's theory has generated: 'Whilst the theory as it now stands is not adequate, some aspects of it, maybe even most, may well survive the test of time'. Indeed, E and N seem to have stood the test of time, in that they are both included in the 'Big Five' personality factors (see below).

● Cattell's trait theory

As we have seen, Cattell's factors are first-order, oblique, source traits, which he believed to be the fundamental dimensions of personality, the underlying roots or causes of clusters of behaviour that are surface traits. Whereas surface traits may correspond to commonsense ways of describing behaviour and may sometimes be measured by simple observation, they are, in fact, the result of interactions among the source traits; valid explanations of behaviour must concentrate on source traits as the structural factors which determine personality.

Cattell identified three sources of data relevant to personality: L-data (L for 'Life'), Q-data (Q for 'Questionnaire') and T-data (T for 'Tests').

1 *L-data* refer to *ratings by observers* which Cattell regarded as the best source but which he also recognized are notoriously difficult to make; great skill and time are needed to make accurate ratings. His research began by identifying all the words in the English language which describe behaviour (trait elements), including the more technical terms from psychology and psychiatry, and after removing all the synonyms, a small sample of students was intensively studied for six months by trained personnel who rated each student on all the trait elements. The resulting data were factor-analysed, producing 15 first-order traits or source traits (also called *primary traits* by Cattell).

2 *Q-data* refer to scores on *personality questionnaires*. Based on the original 15 source traits, a large number of questionnaire items were assembled and given to large numbers of participants. When their scores were factor-analysed, 16 source traits emerged (12 of the original L-data factors plus four new ones). These 16 factors were measured by the widely used Cattell 16PF (Personality Factor) Questionnaire, which is intended for adults. As shown in Table 29.3, the first 12 factors are found in L-data and Q-data, while the last four (Q1–Q4) are based on Q-data only. There are versions of the 16PF designed for children as young as four.

Unlike Eysenck's questionnaires, Cattell's scales are not exclusively of the 'yes/no' variety; for instance, there may be three choices – yes/occasionally/no. However, there is the problem of social desirability (which Eysenck tries to measure by inclusion of an L-scale) and also acquiescence, a kind of 'response set' in which the participant tends to put 'yes' rather than 'no' or to agree with the questionnaire items (see Chapter 18). Although intended mainly as a research instrument, the 16PF has been used in clinical work, as well as occupational selection and assessment; however, its validity as a diagnostic tool in a clinical setting has been seriously questioned.

3 *T-data* refer to *objective tests* specially devised to measure personality; for instance, the Objective–Analytic (O–A) test battery measures, amongst other things, GSR, reaction time, body sway and suggestibility. T-data are objective primarily in the sense that the purpose of the test is concealed from the participant. Factor analysis of these has yielded 21 factors altogether (the O–A battery measuring just 12 of these) and some of these correspond to a number of second-order factors obtained from Q-data.

Description	Name of trait	Description
Warm-hearted, outgoing, easygoing, sociable	**A** Affectia v. Sizia	Reserved, cool, detached, aloof
High score: abstract thinker, intellectual interests	**B** Intelligence	Low score: concrete thinker, practically minded
Emotionally stable, calm, mature, stable	**C** Ego strength v. Dissatisfied emotionality	Emotionally unstable, easily upset, immature
Assertive, aggressive dominant, competitive	**E** Dominance v. Submissiveness	Submissive, modest, mild, accommodating
Happy-go-lucky, enthusiastic, unworrying	**F** Surgency v. Desurgency	Pessimistic, subdued, sober, cautious, serious, taciturn
Persevering, conscientious, moralistic, strait-laced } High score	**G** Superego strength	Expedient, disregards rules, feels few obligations, law unto oneself } Low score
Adventurous, gregarious, uninhibited, socially bold	**H** Parmia v. Threctia	Shy, restrained, timid, diffident, inhibited
Tender-minded, sensitive, gentle, clinging	**I** Premsia v. Harria	Tough-minded, self-reliant, practical, realistic, no nonsense
Suspicious, jealous, self-opinionated	**L** Protension v. Alexia	Trusting, understanding, adaptable, easy to get along with
Unconventional, imaginative, strong subjective life, bohemian	**M** Autia v. Praxernia	Conformist, conventional, influenced by external realities
Shrewd, calculating, worldly, penetrating	**N** Shrewdness v. Naivety	Simple, artless, natural, unpretentious, lacking insight
Insecure, worrying, self-reproaching	**O** Guilt Proneness	Self-assured, confident, complacent, spirited
Liberal, free thinking	**Q1** Radicalism v. Conservatism	Conservative, traditional
Prefers own decisions	**Q2** Self-sufficiency v. Group dependence	Group dependent, a follower
High score: controlled, socially precise	**Q3** Self-sentiment Strength	Low score: undisciplined, careless of social rules
High score: relaxed, composed	**Q4** Ergic tension	Low score: overwrought, tense, frustrated

TABLE 29.3 *The sixteen source traits measured by Cattell's 16PF questionnaire. (After Cattell, 1965)*

● First- and second-order factors: Cattell and Eysenck compared

As we have seen, first-order (oblique) factors correlate with each other to some degree and, indeed, Cattell argues that overlapping factors are what would be expected since, for example, an intelligent person (B-factor) is also likely to be shrewd and worldly (N-factor). We should note here that whereas Eysenck does not include intelligence amongst his three major personality dimensions, Cattell does include it in his 16 primary factors, although it assumes a rather different meaning in the 16PF than it does in his distinction between fluid and crystallized intelligence (see Chapters 24 and 28).

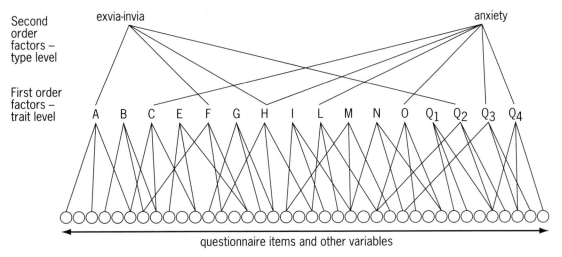

FIGURE 29.6 *The hierarchical organization of personality resulting from a second-order analysis of the first-order 'source traits'. (After Cattell, 1965)*

However, Cattell has carried out a second-order factor analysis of his 16 primary factors which yields a number of surface traits, the two most important being *exvia–invia* and *anxiety,* which seem to correspond to Eysenck's E and N respectively (Fig. 29.6). Others include *radicalism* (aggressive and independent), *tendermindedness* (sensitivity, frustration and emotionality) and *superego* (conscientious, conforming and preserving).

Another important difference is that Cattell believes that there is a fundamental discontinuity between normals and, say, schizophrenics, i.e. there is a qualitative difference and not merely a quantitative one, as Eysenck maintains. For instance, Q-data used with psychiatric patients produce 12 factors which discriminate psychotics as a group (e.g. paranoia, suicidal disgust, schizophrenia and high general psychosis), who score very high on these compared with normals. A second-order FA of Q-data from psychiatric patients yields three factors, one of which resembles Eysenck's P.

● Evaluation of the 16PF

As far as test–retest reliability is concerned, no data are presented, as Cattell assumes that normal variations in traits occur over time and so low test–retest correlations are only to be expected.

As for its validity, this has been challenged by several researchers, including Eysenck and Eysenck (1969) and Browne and Howarth (1977), all of whom found a smaller number of source traits than Cattell. However, Kline (1981a) has pointed out that different investigators have used different techniques and

so it is not always possible to make meaningful comparisons.

As we have already seen, the agreement between Cattell and Eysenck as far as certain second-order factors are concerned tends to enhance the validity of the 16PF and Cattell believes that many of these criticisms no longer apply to the improved 1974 version of the questionnaire.

● Personality and behaviour

Although seeing behaviour as reflecting a relatively enduring personality (see Table 29.1), Cattell, much more than Eysenck, acknowledges the way that behaviour can fluctuate in response to situational factors. His definition of personality as 'what determines behaviour in a defined situation and a defined mood' (Cattell, 1965) implies that behaviour is never totally determined by source traits: although personality factors remain fairly stable over time, they constitute only one kind of variable influencing overt behaviour. So what other kinds are there?

Cattell distinguishes between: (i) *mood and state factors* (e.g. depression, arousal, anxiety, fatigue and intoxication); and (ii) *motivational factors*. He distinguishes two kinds of motivational factors: (i) *ergs,* which are the innate, biological drives (the ten so far identified are food-seeking, gregariousness, mating, narcissism, acquisitiveness, parental, pugnacity, security, exploration and assertiveness); and (ii) *sentiments,* which are culturally acquired drives.

Cattell also identifies seven main components of a motive, three of which are *alpha,* the 'id' component (corresponding to 'I want'), *beta,* the 'ego' component (concerned with knowledge and information) and *gamma*, the 'superego' component (corresponding to 'I ought'). Although an ardent behaviourist, Cattell was influenced by Freud's psychoanalytic theory, at least to the extent that three of the 16PF names are derived from Freudian terminology (C – ego strength, G – superego strength and Q4 – ergic or id tension) together with the three components of a motive which we have just discussed.

We shall discuss the relationship between Freud's theory and factor-analytic concepts later in the chapter.

● Single trait theories, multi-trait theories and the 'Big Five'

As we have seen, the concept of a personality trait has assumed central importance in personality theory. Eysenck's and Cattell's theories are examples of multi-trait theories, but an influential single trait theory is Rotter's (1966) *locus of control* (see Chapter 5). For a single trait theory to be useful, it must identify a trait that determines a wide range of important behaviours (Hampson, 1995).

Multi-trait theories try to include all aspects of personality and assume that individual differences can be described in terms of a particular profile on the same set of traits. According to Krahé (1992), despite its troubled history, 'The trait concept presents itself in remarkably good shape at the beginning of the '90s'. Since the 1980s, there has been a vast amount of research involving a search for a small but comprehensive number of basic trait dimensions which can account for the structure of personality and individual differences and there is growing consensus that personality can be adequately described by five broad constructs or factors, commonly referred to as the 'Big Five' (McCrae and Costa, 1989; Digman, 1990; Goldberg, 1992); they are summarized in Table 29. 4.

While different versions of the 'Big Five' have been proposed, the five-factor model has provided a unified framework for trait research (Costa and McCrae, 1993). Although Eysenck (1991) continues to argue for a 'Giant Three' (E, N and P – a combination of factors II and III), the differences seem quite trivial now compared with, say, the disagreement between Eysenck and Cattell's 16 source traits (Hampson, 1995). Nevertheless, there remains the fundamental problem of the meaning of the factors that are extracted (Kline, 1993; Krahé, 1992).

Ultimately, personality factors, however many or

Factor I Extroversion (or surgency)	This corresponds to Eysenck's construct.
Factor II Agreeableness agreeable – –disagreeable kind – – – – –unkind generous – – –stingy warm – – – – –cold unselfish – – –selfish	High scorers tend to obey rules and adopt the conventions of the society they live in, while low scorers are the opposite. It may be related to tough-mindedness (see Chapter 19).
Factor III Conscientiousness organized – –disorganized hardworking –lazy reliable – – – –unreliable thorough – – –careless practical – – –impractical	
Factor IV Neuroticism (or emotional stability)	This corresponds to Eysenck's construct. This trait anxiety must be distinguished from state anxiety, which fluctuates according to our experiences (Kline, 1995).
Factor V Openness to experience (or culture or experience) intelligent – – –unintelligent sophisticated – –unsophisticated creative – – – – –uncreative curious – – – –uninquisitive analytical – – –unanalytical	Basically, this refers to receptivity to new ideas and approaches.

TABLE 29.4 *The 'Big Five' personality factors*

few, must be identified from their correlations with external criteria (Kline, 1993); according to Eysenck (1995), the system is still too new (except for E and N) for there to have been enough research to allow a proper evaluation.

KELLY'S PERSONAL CONSTRUCT THEORY (1955)

As Table 29.1 shows, Kelly's *personal construct theory* (PCT) is an idiographic approach, stressing the uniqueness of each individual; it is also a *phenomenological* approach, in that it attempts to understand the person in terms of his/her experience and perception of the world, a view of the world through the person's own eyes and not an observer's interpretation or analysis which is imposed on the person.

Kelly's dissatisfaction with both Freudian and behaviourist theories led him to propose a model of the human being which was radically different from any model previously put forward, namely *man the scientist*. (This was a notion we discussed in relation to interpersonal perception; see Chapter 15.) What does Kelly mean?

We are all scientists in the sense that we put our own interpretation (or theories) on the world of events and from these personal theories we produce hypotheses, which are predictions about future events. Every time we act, we are putting our hypotheses to the test and, in this sense, behaviour is the independent variable – it is the experiment. Depending on the outcome, our hypotheses are either validated or not and this will determine the nature of our subsequent behavioural experiments (Fransella, 1981). But what exactly are these personal theories from which we derive our hypotheses?

To answer this question, we need to discuss Kelly's philosophy of *constructive alternativism*. Although a real world of physical objects and events does exist, no one organism has the privilege of 'knowing' it; all we can do is place our personal constructs upon it. The better our constructs 'fit' the world, the better will be our control over our own, personal world. To quote Kelly (1955) :

> Man looks at his world through transparent patterns or templates which he creates and then attempts to fit over the realities of which the world is composed. The fit is not always very good. Yet without such patterns the world appears to be such an undifferentiated homogeneity that man is unable to make any sense of it.

In other words, there is no way of getting 'behind' our interpretation of the world to check if it matches what the world is really like: all we have are our own interpretations (compare this with Gregory's definition of perception; see Chapter 9) and so we necessarily see the world 'through goggles', which cannot be removed. However, these goggles or *constructs* are not fixed once and for all; the person as scientist is constantly engaged in testing, checking, modifying and revising his/her unique set of constructs which represent these working hypotheses.

Each person's construct system is organized in a hierarchical way, with some broad constructs (superordinate) subsuming other, narrow constructs (subordinate). The theory basically comprises a *fundamental postulate* ('A person's processes are psychologically channelized by the ways in which he anticipates events') plus 11 corollaries, meant to explain how we use our personal constructs to predict the future.

● The repertory grid technique

The original test used for eliciting personal constructs was the Role Construct Repertory Test ('Rep Test'), which was designed for individual use by a clinical psychologist. This has been succeeded by the Repertory Grid Test ('Rep Grid') which is used as a major research instrument (Box 29.3).

The Rep Grid is a very flexible instrument and can be used in different ways. Kelly himself suggested that 24 role titles (elements) might provide a representative sample of 'significant others' and eight different ways in which triads of role titles can be compiled. However this may be done, the Rep Grid is an attempt to help individuals discover the fundamental constructs they use for perceiving and relating to others.

The grid can be factor-analysed and this often reveals that many constructs overlap, i.e. they mean more or less the same thing: probably between 3–6 major constructs cover most people's construct system. It can be used nomothetically, as Bannister and Fransella have done with thought-disordered schizophrenics. Their Grid Test of Thought Disorder (Bannister and Fransella, 1966, 1967) contains standardized elements and constructs (i.e. they are supplied by the researcher) and the test has been standardized on large numbers of similar patients so that an individual score can be compared with group norms. However, this is probably rather far removed from how Kelly intended the technique to be used. It has also been used to study how patients participating

BOX 29.3	Constructing a repertory grid (based on Kelly, 1955)

The basic method involves the following steps:

(a) Write a list of the most important people in your life (*elements*).
(b) Choose three of these elements.
(c) Ask yourself, 'In what ways are two of these alike and different from the third?' The descriptions given (e.g. 'My mother and girlfriend are affectionate, my father is not') constitute a construct which is expressed in a bipolar way, i.e. 'affectionate–not affectionate'.
(d) This construct is applied to all the remaining ele-

ments. Remember, constructs are bipolar opposites (either affectionate or not affectionate).

(e) Then another set of three elements is selected and the whole process is repeated. It continues until either you have produced all the constructs you can (which is usually no more than 25 with one set of elements) or until a sufficient number has been produced as judged by the investigator.

All this information can be collated in the form of a grid, with the elements across the top and the constructs down the side and a tick or cross indicating which pole of the construct is applicable (for example, a tick indicates 'affectionate' and a cross indicates 'not affectionate').

Constructs	Elements						
	Mother	**Father**	**Brother**	**Sister**	**Boyfriend**	**Girlfriend**	**Psychology etc. lecturer**
Affectionate (✓) Non-affectionate (✗)	✓	✗	✗	✓	✗	✓	✓
Intelligent (✓) Unintelligent (✗)							
Sense of humour (✓) No sense of humour (✗)							
etc.							

in group psychotherapy change their perception of each other (and themselves) during the period of therapy, where the group members themselves are the elements and a number of constructs are supplied (Fransella, 1970). Fransella (1972) has used it extensively with people being treated for severe stuttering.

However, its uses are not confined to clinical situations. Elements need not be people at all but could be occupations, religions, cars and so on and Shackleton and Fletcher (1984) argue that the Rep Grid stands on its own as a technique, that is, you do not have to believe in Kelly's PCT in order to use it.

● An evaluation of PCT

Some of the most common criticisms have been to do with the reliability and validity of the Rep Grid. Gathercole *et al.* (1970), for example, studied 'parallel-form' reliability (in which different persons were put into the same role titles) as well as test–retest reliability of various types of Rep Grid in general use. They concluded that generalizations about individuals based on single grids, especially if

the constructs are elicited from the participant, should only be made with extreme caution because the results are likely to be unreliable. However, Bannister and Mair (1968) believe that the concepts of reliability and validity are not strictly relevant or applicable since the Rep Grid is primarily a methodology rather than a standardized test.

Unfortunately, we have only been able to scratch the surface of Kelly's very complex and challenging theory. An excellent summary is Bannister and Fransella's *Inquiring Man* (1980) and Fransella (1981). They point out that the theory is deliberately stated in very abstract terms so as to avoid the limitations of a particular time and culture; it is an attempt to redefine psychology as a psychology of persons and is 'content free'. As we noted earlier, PCT is not so much a personality theory, more a total psychology: Kelly is not concerned with separate subdivisions of psychology as dealt with in most textbooks because he believes these can all be dealt with by the fundamental postulate and 11 corollaries.

For instance, Kelly believes that the traditional concept of motivation can be dispensed with. We do not need concepts like drives or needs or psychic energy (see Chapters 5 and 21) to explain what makes people 'get up and go' – man is a form of motion and a basic assumption about life is that 'it goes on': 'It isn't that something *makes* you go on, the going on is the *thing itself*' (Kelly, 1962).

However, he implicitly assumes that we all seek a sense of order and predictability in our dealings with the external world – the over-riding goal of anticipating the future represents a basic form of motivation. We achieve this through (as we have already seen) behaving much like a research scientist. 'The scientist's ultimate aim is to predict and control ...'

Various aspects of emotion are dealt with in terms of how an individual's construct system is organized and how it changes; for instance, 'anxiety' is the awareness that what you are confronted with is not within the framework of your existing construct system – you do not know how to construe it (this is discussed in Chapter 31). For some, this is far too cognitive and rational an approach; what about the subjective experience (the gut feeling) that we call anxiety? It is almost as if emotional experiences and 'behaviour' itself are being drowned in a sea of constructs.

Peck and Whitlow (1975) believe that Kelly trivializes important aspects of behaviour, including learning, emotion and motivation, as well as neglecting situational influences on behaviour; PCT, they say, appears to place the person in an 'empty world'. However, they conclude by saying that 'Personal Construct Theory constitutes a brave and imaginative attempt to create a comprehensive, cognitive, theory of personality' (Peck and Whitlow, 1975).

HUMANISTIC THEORIES

'Humanistic' is an umbrella term referring to a group of theories which all share the belief that scientific attempts to study human beings are misplaced and inappropriate, because ' ... to see man at second hand through his behaviour as against his experience is ultimately to see ourselves at second hand and never be ourselves' (Evans, 1975). The term was coined by the British psychologist John Cohen in a book called *Humanistic Psychology* in 1958 (Graham, 1986), the same year in which Abraham Maslow introduced the notion of a 'third force' in psychology – behaviourism ('ratomorphic robotic psychology' – Cohen, 1958) and psychoanalytic theory being the first and second

forces – and it is he and Rogers who are the best known humanistic psychologists.

Humanistic theories (and Kelly's PCT) have their philosophical roots in phenomenology and existentialism and, some would say, they warrant the label 'philosophical' more than the label 'psychological'. They are concerned with characteristics that are distinctively and uniquely human, in particular, experience, uniqueness, meaning, freedom and choice; we have first-hand experience of ourselves as persons and Rogers' particular theory is centred around the self-concept.

What Rogers and Maslow have in common is their positive evaluation of human nature, a belief in the individual's potential for personal growth, what they call *self-actualization*. However, Maslow's theory is commonly referred to as a 'psychology of being' (self-actualization is an end in itself and lies at the peak of his hierarchy of needs; see Chapter 5), while that of Rogers is a 'psychology of becoming' (it is the *process* of becoming a 'fully functioning person' that is of major importance and interest).

● Rogers's self theory

Rogers, like Maslow, rejected the deterministic nature of psychoanalysis (behaviour is a response to unconscious forces) and behaviourism (behaviour is a response to environmental stimuli), believing rather that behaviour is a response to the individual's perception/interpretation of external stimuli. As no one else can know how we perceive, we are the best experts on ourselves.

Related to this emphasis on how we perceive and interpret reality is the importance of a person's current, moment-to-moment experience, what we are thinking and feeling now, in contrast to Freud's belief that our present behaviour is largely determined by our past, in the form of repressed childhood experiences. Freud also believed that human nature is fundamentally destructive and irrational and he took a very pessimistic view of human beings. Rogers (like Maslow), on the other hand, sees human nature in a very positive and optimistic light: 'There is no beast in man; there is only man in man'. This positive view of human beings is illustrated in Rogers' description of the process of becoming a fully functioning person (1961, but originally proposed in 1947):

> The individual has within him the capacity and tendency, latent if not evident, to move forward to maturity. In a suitable psychological climate, this

tendency is realized, and becomes actual rather than potential. It is evident in the capacity of the individual to understand those aspects of his life and of himself which are causing pain and dissatisfaction, an understanding which probes beneath his conscious knowledge of himself into those experiences which he has hidden from himself because of their threatening nature

... Whether one calls it a growth tendency, a drive toward self-actualization, or a forward- moving directional tendency, it is the mainspring of life ... It is the urge which is evident in all organic and human life – to expand, extend, become autonomous, develop, mature.

Central to Rogers' theory (and to his form of psychotherapy, known as *client-centred therapy*) is the concept of *self*. The self is an 'organized, consistent set of perceptions and beliefs about oneself'. It includes my awareness of 'what I am and what I can do' and influences both my perception of the world and my behaviour. We evaluate every experience in terms of it and most human behaviour can be understood as an attempt to maintain consistency between our self-image and our actions (see Chapter 21).

However, this consistency is not always achieved and our self-image (and related self-esteem) may differ quite radically from our actual behaviour and from how others see us. For example, a person may be highly successful and respected by others and yet regard himself as a failure! This would be an example of what Rogers calls *incongruence* – being told you are successful is incongruent or inconsistent with the fact that you do not hold this view of your self. Incongruent experiences, feelings, actions and so on, because they conflict with our (conscious) self-image and because we prefer to act and feel in ways that are consistent with our self-image, may be threatening and so are denied access to awareness (they may remain *unsymbolized*) through actual denial, distortion or blocking.

These defence mechanisms prevent the self from growing and changing and widen the gulf between our self-image and reality (i.e. our actual behaviour or our true feelings). As the self-image becomes more and more unrealistic, so the incongruent person becomes more and more confused, vulnerable, dissatisfied and, eventually, seriously maladjusted. The self-image of the congruent person is flexible and realistically changes as new experiences occur; the opposite is true of the incongruent person. When your self-image matches what you really think and feel and do, you are in the best position to realize your potential (self-actualize); the greater the gap between self-image and reality, the greater the

likelihood of anxiety and emotional disturbance. Similarly, the greater the gap between self-image and ideal self, the less fulfilled the individual will be.

To show how two different examples of a rigid and inflexible self-image may work, let us suppose that a young man's self-image requires that every woman he meets will find him irresistible and fall head-over-heels in love with him. He meets a woman whom he finds attractive but she shows no interest in him; this represents an incongruence between his self-image and his experience. How does he deal with the threat this represents for him? He might say 'She's just playing hard to get' or 'She has no taste' or 'She must be crazy – thank goodness I found out before she fell hopelessly in love with me'. At the opposite extreme is a young man who believes that he is totally unattractive to women. If an attractive woman shows an interest in him, this will produce incongruence and hence threat and he might deal with it by rationalizing that 'She's just feeling sorry for me' or he might deliberately do something (e.g. be rude to her) to sabotage the relationship and so remove the threat.

Of course, most of us will not have such an extreme self-image as these two hypothetical young men, whether positive or negative, and most of us are sufficiently flexible and realistic to recognize that just as we are not 'God's gift to the opposite sex' nor are we sexually hopeless cases; indeed, our self-image regarding our sexual appeal has been learned from our past successes and failures ('you win some, you lose some').

● How does our self-concept develop?

Many of Rogers' therapeutic clients had trouble accepting their own feelings and experiences; they seemed to have learned during childhood that in order to obtain the love and acceptance of others (particularly their parents), they have to feel and act in distorted or dishonest ways, i.e. they had to deny certain parts of themselves. Rogers calls this *conditional positive regard*.

This applies, in varying degrees, to almost every child – love and praise are withheld until the child conforms to parental and social standards of conduct. So the child (and later the adult) learns to act and feel in ways that earn approval from others, rather than in ways which may be more intrinsically satisfying and more 'real'. To maintain conditional positive regard, we suppress actions and feelings that are unacceptable to others who are important to us (significant others), instead of using our own spontaneous perceptions and feelings as guides to our behaviour. Rogers says that we develop *conditions of worth* (those conditions under which positive regard will be forthcoming) which become internalized; we perceive and are aware of those experiences that coincide with the conditions of worth but distort or deny those that do not. This denial and distortion leads to a distinction between the *organism* and the *self*, whereby the organism is the whole of one's possible experience (everything we do and feel and think) and the self is the recognized, accepted and acknowledged part of a person's experience. Ideally, the two would refer to one and the same thing but, for most of us, they do not.

Corresponding to the need for positive regard (the universal wish to be loved and accepted by significant others) is the need for positive self-regard, the internalization of those values and behaviour of which others approve, so that we think of ourselves as good and lovable and worthy. (This corresponds to high self-esteem, while negative self-regard corresponds to low self-esteem.)

To experience positive self-regard, our behaviour and experience must match our conditions of worth; the problem here is that this can produce incongruence through the denial of our true thoughts and feelings. But since the need for positive regard and positive self-regard is so strong, these conditions of worth can supersede the values associated with self-actualization. Consequently, we come to behave and think and feel in particular ways because others want us to and many adult adjustment problems are bound up with an attempt to live by other people's standards instead of one's own.

Congruence and self-actualization are enhanced by substituting *organismic values* for conditions of worth, so that the distinction between the self and organism becomes more and more blurred. The greater the unconditional positive regard, the greater the congruence between: (i) self-image and reality; and (ii) self-image and ideal self. It is precisely this *unconditional positive regard* that the therapist offers the client in Rogers' client-centred therapy, i.e. the therapist creates an atmosphere of total acceptance and support regardless of what the client says or does, which is non-judgemental, so that the client in turn comes to accept certain feelings and thoughts as their own, instead of denying, distorting and disowning them (illustrated by such responses as 'I don't know why I did that' or 'I wasn't feeling myself'). Finally, positive self-regard is no longer dependent upon conditions of worth (see Chapter 31).

PSYCHOANALYTIC THEORIES

We have already discussed at length the developmental aspects of Freud's theory (Chapters 21, 23 and 27) as well as some of the more general features, such as the structure of the personality (id, ego, superego). We have also discussed Erikson's psychosocial theory in Chapters 21, 22 and 24. Two of the other major psychoanalytic or *psychodynamic* theories are those of Jung and Adler.

'Psychodynamic' implies the active forces within the personality that motivate behaviour, the inner causes of behaviour, in particular the unconscious conflict between the id, ego and superego. Freud's was the first of this kind of theory and all psychodynamic theories stem, more or less directly, from Freud's work; collectively, they are known as *depth psychology.*

● Freud's psychoanalytic theory

You will recall from Chapter 21 that Freud believed that conflict within the personality is unavoidable, because the ego is being 'pulled' in two opposing directions: on one side is the id, wanting immediate satisfaction of its instinctual wishes, on the other is the superego, which threatens the ego with punishment (in the form of guilt) if it gives in to the id. So what is the ego to do? Freud's answer is to describe three forms of compromise, namely dreams, neurotic symptoms and defence mechanisms.

Dreams

'A dream is a (disguised) fulfilment of a (suppressed or repressed) wish' (Freud, 1900; 1976) and so is another example of the id's primary process thinking; it represents a compromise between forbidden urges and their repression. What we dream about and are conscious of upon waking (what we report) is called the *manifest content*, while the meaning of the dream (the wish being fulfilled) is the *latent content*. The manifest content is often the product of the weaving together of certain fragments from that day's events (*day residues*) and the forbidden wish and is, essentially, a hallucinatory experience (predominantly visual for most people). It often appears disjointed, fragmentary and sometimes bizarre and nonsensical. Dream interpretation (a major technique involved in psychoanalysis) aims to make sense of the manifest content by 'translating' it into the underlying wish fulfilment.

BOX
29.4 Dreams reported by two of Freud's patients (from *The Interpretation of Dreams,1900; 1976a)*

1 A young woman who had been orphaned at an early age spent her adolescence in the home of her older sister, who had two sons, Otto and Charles. The patient adored Otto and treated him like her own son. To her great sadness, Otto died. She eventually went to live on her own. When in therapy with Freud she dreamt:

> ... That I saw Charles lying dead before me. He was lying in his little coffin, his hands folded; there were candles all about; and, in short, it was just as it was at the time of little Otto's death, which gave me such a shock. Now tell me, what does this mean? You know me – am I really so bad as to wish that my sister should lose the only child she has left? Or does the dream mean that I wish that Charles had died rather than Otto, who I liked so much better?

Freud knew that when the patient was living with her sister, she had fallen in love with a friend of the family, a professor of literature. For various reasons, the courtship ended and thereafter he avoided the house. She turned her affections to Otto but she continued to be in love with the professor and she found various ways of seeing him without his knowing (for example, she would attend his public lectures). When asked if she connected the professor in any way with Otto's death, she said, 'Of course, the professor returned then after a long absence and I saw him once more beside little Otto's coffin'. This was just as Freud expected and he interpreted the dream as follows:

> ... if now the other boy were to die, the same thing would happen again. You would spend the day with your sister, the professor would certainly come to offer his condolences and you would see him once more under the same circumstances as before. The dream signifies nothing more than this wish of yours to see him again – a wish against which you are fighting inwardly.

The scene of death is the ego's way of 'slipping' the erotic wish fulfilment past the superego. A child's funeral is the last thing one would (consciously) associate with sexual yearning and so it offered excellent 'cover' or disguise.

2 A 'typical example of a disguised Oedipus dream' is that of a man who dreamt that he had a secret liaison with a lady whom someone else wanted to marry. He was worried in case this other man might discover the liaison and the proposed marriage come to nothing. He, therefore, behaved in a very affectionate way to the man. He embraced him and kissed him (see Chapter 21).

Dreams come into being through dream work, which converts the underlying (latent) wish into the manifest content and comprises displacement, condensation and concrete representation; it is controlled by the ego.

- *Displacement* refers to the substitution for the real target of the dreamer's feelings a person or object that becomes the target for those feelings. The substitute is symbolically (unconsciously) linked to the true target (which is true also of neurotic symptoms; see below and Chapter 31), as in the example of one of Freud's patients who dreamed of strangling a little white dog which represented her sister-in-law, who had a very pale complexion and whom the dreamer had previously called 'a dog who bites' (Stevens, 1995); this is a crucial part of the disguise that conceals from the dreamer the true meaning of the dream. The sister-in-law/dog example shows how certain symbols will be peculiar to individual dreamers, but many dream symbols have a conventional meaning within a culture, particularly those that represent the penis (e.g. snakes, trees, trains, daggers, umbrellas), the vagina (e.g. small boxes, cupboards, ships and other vessels) and sexual intercourse (e.g. climbing ladders or stairs and entering tunnels).

- *Condensation* involves the same part of the manifest dream representing different parts of the latent wish. For example, a king may represent not only the dreamer's father but authority figures in general or very wealthy and powerful people. So more than one dream idea may be 'condensed' into a single manifest image and Freud would say the manifest image is 'overdetermined' (see below).

- *Concrete representation* refers to the expression of some abstract idea in a very concrete way; the concrete image of a king, for example, could represent the abstract notion of authority, power or wealth. This is sometimes called *dramatization* and is related to the use of symbols.

The importance of dream work as a whole is that it permits the expression of a repressed (and, therefore, forbidden and disturbing) wish and at the same time allows the dreamer to go on sleeping. The compromise involved in dreaming takes the form of disguising the true nature of the dream (i.e. wish fulfilment) for if the wish were not disguised, the dreamer would wake up in a state of shock and distress. Hence, 'the dream is the guardian of sleep'.

Dream interpretation is also the 'royal road to the unconscious'; reversing the dream work and unravelling the wish from the manifest content can provide invaluable information about the unconscious mind in general and about the dreamer's in particular. (Interpreting his own dreams was a major part of Freud's self-analysis.) Two examples of dreams as diagnosed wish fulfilment are given in Box 29.4.

So what happens when we have a nightmare (or 'anxiety dream')? Freud says that the ego normally acts as a 'censor' of what is consciously experienced but is less alert and on guard when we are asleep. Occasionally, the dream work is less effective than usual in disguising the repressed wish so that it becomes too clear and, therefore, too dangerous; consequently, the dream awakens the sleeping ego and brings the undisguised wish fulfilment to an abrupt end.

Neurotic symptoms

Symptoms have much in common with dreams; they are essentially the expression of a repressed wish (or memory) that has become disguised in ways that are very similar to those involved in dream work.

- The symptom in some way symbolizes the wish to which it is linked. For example, one of Freud's patients (cited by Wollheim, 1971) suffered from hysterical hand-twitching, which was related to her memories of being badly frightened while playing the piano (*displacement*).
- A symptom can be overdetermined; for example, this same patient's hand-twitching was traced to two other memories –receiving a disciplinary strapping on the hands as a schoolgirl and being forced to massage the back of a detested uncle (*condensation*).
- The symptom is often something 'physical', while the underlying cause is something 'mental' (*concrete representation*).

Most of Freud's patients were suffering from 'hysterical conversion neurosis' (or 'somatoform' disorders in current terminology), whereby emotional energy is converted into physical energy so that the manifest problem is paralysis, blindness, deafness, headaches and a whole variety of other 'physical' symptoms (see Chapter 30). Through displacement and concrete representation in particular, the symptom deflects the patient's attention (and that of others) away from the repressed material – it is

acceptable to consult a doctor about the symptom but not about the unconscious wish. It is in this way that symptoms, like dreams, are compromises – every symptom must comply with the demands of the ego or it too would be repressed. Freud and Breuer (1895) called these underlying wishes and memories *pathogenic* ('disease-producing') *ideas* and Freud later reached the conclusion that all symptoms are caused by pathogenic ideas of a sexual nature (although not every dream).

Defence mechanisms

These represent the third major form of compromise used by the ego in the face of inevitable conflict. The defence mechanisms of the ego are, by definition, unconscious and this is partly how they derive their effectiveness: if we knew about them (at the time), we would in most cases be unable to go on using them. They also share the characteristic of involving some degree of self-deception (which is linked to their being unconscious) and this, in turn, is related to their distortion of 'reality', both the internal reality of feelings, etc. and the external reality of other people and the physical world.

Partly because of this distortion and deception and partly despite it, the defences help us deal with anxiety; they prevent us from being overwhelmed by temporary threats or traumas and can provide 'breathing space' in which to come to terms with conflict or find alternative ways of coping. As short-term measures, they are advantageous, necessary and 'normal', but as long-term solutions to life's problems they are usually regarded as unhealthy and undesirable. Some of the major defence mechanisms are shown in Table 29.5; many of these, as well as some that are not included, were originally proposed or implied by Freud and later elaborated by his daughter, Anna, in *The Ego and Mechanisms of Defence* (1936).

Freud's theory of mind: three levels of consciousness

Freud believed that thoughts, ideas, memories and other psychic material could operate at one of three levels: conscious, preconscious and unconscious. These levels of consciousness do not correspond to areas or layers of the mind or brain but refer to how accessible the thought, etc. is to the thinker.

What we are consciously aware of at any one time represents the mere tip of an iceberg – most of our thoughts and ideas are either not accessible at that moment (*pre-conscious*) or are totally inaccessible (*unconscious*), at least without the use of special

Name of defence	Description	Example(s)
1 **Repression**	Forcing a dangerous/threatening memory/idea/feeling/wish out of consciousness and making it unconscious. Often used in conjunction with one or more other defences; one of the earliest used by the child.	A 5–6-year-old child repressing its incestuous desire for the opposite-sex parent as part of its attempt to resolve the Oedipus complex (see Chapter 21). Motivated forgetting is discussed in Chapter 12.
2 **Displacement**	Choosing a substitute object for the expression of your feelings because you cannot express them openly towards their real target. You transfer your feelings onto something quite harmless or innocent that will not retaliate ('kicking the cat').	Anger with your boy/girlfriend is taken out on your parents or brother/sister; frustration caused by lack of power and influence at work is expressed as violence towards spouse and children. Prejudice/discrimination (see Chapter 19). Phobias (see Chapters 30 and 31)
3 **Denial**	Refusing to acknowledge certain aspects of reality; refusing to perceive something because it is painful, distressing or threatening.	Refusing to accept that you have a serious illness or that a relationship is 'on the rocks' – or that you have an exam tomorrow! A common component of grieving (see Chapter 24).
4 **Rationalization**	Finding an acceptable excuse for something which is really quite unacceptable; a 'cover story' which preserves your self-image/that of someone close to you. Justifying your own/others' actions to yourself – and believing it!	'Being cruel to be kind. 'I only did it for you.' 'It was in your best interests.' 'I did so badly because I didn't revise properly.'A feature of cognitive dissonance theory (see Chapter 18).
5. **Reaction formation**	Consciously feeling/thinking the very opposite of what you truly (unconsciously) feel/think; the conscious feelings/thoughts are experienced as quite genuine.	Being considerate/polite to someone you strongly dislike, even going out of your way to be nice to them. This 'display' may be 'overdone' but this will only be obvious to an observer, not to the actor.Obsessive –compulsive disorder, e.g. compulsive hand-washing (see Chapter 30).
6. **Sublimation**	A form of displacement in which a substitute activity is found to express an unacceptable impulse. The activity is usually socially acceptable, if not desirable. One of the most positive/ constructive of all defences.	Playing sport to re-direct aggressive impulses (see Chapter 17). Doing sculpture /pottery/gardening to satisfy (unconscious) desire to play with faeces.All artistic and cultural activities.
7. **Identification**	The incorporation/introjection of an external object (usually another person) into one's own personality, making them a part of oneself. Coming to think/act/ feel as if one were that person.	Involves imitation and modelling (see Chapter 27). A young boy's identification with his father in order to avoid castration (identification with the aggressor) (see Chapters 21 and 27).
8. **Projection**	Displacing your own unwanted feelings and characteristics onto someone else; often involves a reversal of the subject/ object of the feelings.	Suspecting/accusing someone of dishonourable motives based on your own (unconscious) dishonourable motives/intentions. 'I hate you' becomes 'You hate me'; this is the basis of paranoia (see Chapter 30).

TABLE 29.5 *Some of the major ego defence mechanisms*

Name of defence	Description	Example(s)
9 Regression	Engaging in behaviour characteristic of an earlier stage of development. We normally regress to the point of fixation (see Chapter 21).	Taking to your bed when upset, crying, los ing your temper, eating when depressed, wetting yourself if extremely frightened.
10 Isolation	Separating contradictory thoughts/feelings into 'logic-tight' compartments, so that no conflict is experienced. Separating thoughts and emotions that usually go together. A form of dissociation.	Calmly and clinically talking about a very traumatic experience without showing any emotion – or even giggling about it, as in hebephrenic schizophrenia (see Chapter 30).

TABLE 29.5 (continued)

techniques such as free association and dream interpretation (see Chapter 31). The ego represents the *conscious* part of the mind, together with some aspects of the superego, namely those moral rules and values that we are able to express in words.

The ego also controls the *pre-conscious*, a kind of 'anteroom', an extension of the conscious, whereby things we are not fully aware of right now can become so fairly easily if our attention is directed to them. For example, you suddenly realize that you have been in pain for some time or you notice a ticking clock that has been ticking away all the time. The pre-conscious also processes ill-defined id urges into perceptible images and part of the superego may also function at a pre-conscious level.

The *unconscious* (the most contentious part of Freud's theory of the mind) comprises: (i) id impulses; (ii) all repressed material; (iii) the unconscious part of the ego (the part which is involved in dream work, neurotic symptoms and defence mechanisms); and (iv) part of the superego, for example, the free-floating or vague feelings of guilt or shame which are difficult to account for and behaving in ways which seem to reflect parental standards but not being able to say what these standards are. Freud depicted the unconscious as a dynamic force and not a mere 'dustbin' for all those thoughts, etc. which are too weak to force themselves into awareness; this is best illustrated by the process of repression, whereby what is threatening is actively forced out of consciousness by the ego (Thomas, 1985) (see Table 29.5).

'Our reasons' versus 'the reasons'

Earlier, we discussed overdetermination in relation to dream work and neurotic symptoms. Freud also used the term in a more general way to refer to the fact that much of our behaviour (and our thoughts and feelings)

has multiple causes, some conscious, some unconscious. By definition, we only know about the conscious causes and these are what we normally take to be the reasons for our actions. However, if the causes also include unconscious factors, then the reasons we give for our behaviour can never tell the whole story and, indeed, the unconscious causes may be the more important. This view of the individual as never being fully aware of all the reasons for his/her behaviour is one of *irrational man* – we do not know ourselves as well as we would like or as well as we think we do.

Overdetermination is one aspect of *psychic determinism*, the view that all behaviour is purposive or goal-directed and that everything we do, think and feel has a cause (often unconscious). It follows that what we often call 'accidents' (implying a chance occurrence, something which 'just happens') do have a cause after all and, taking this a step further, that the cause (or a contributory cause) may actually turn out to be the 'victim'. For instance, the 'accident-prone' person is not, according to Freud, an unfortunate victim of circumstances but is unconsciously bringing about the accidents – perhaps in an attempt to punish themselves in some way. Freud did not deny the existence of events which lie beyond the control of the victim, but these are rare occurrences; it is more common for an 'accident' to be the consequence of our own, unconscious wishes and motives.

The psychopathology of everyday life

We have seen how the unconscious reveals itself through dreams and neurotic symptoms and the major aim of psychoanalysis is to make the unconscious conscious. But Freud believed that there is another important way in which our everyday behaviour provides us with glimpses of the unconscious at work and that is what he called *Fehlleistungen*

BOX 29.5 Some examples of parapraxes ('Freudian slips') (from *The Psychopathology of Everyday Life*, 1901, 1976b)

1 A patient consulted me for the first time and from her history it became apparent that the cause of her nervousness was largely an unhappy married life. Without any encouragement she went into details about her marital troubles. She had not lived with her husband for about six months and she saw him last at the theatre, when she saw the play 'Officer 606'. I called her attention to the mistake and she immediately corrected herself, saying that she meant to say 'Officer 666' (the name of a recent popular play). I decided to find out the reason for the mistake, and as the patient came to me for analytic treatment, I discovered that the immediate cause of the rupture between herself and her husband was the disease which is treated by '606' [i.e. venereal disease].

2 I was to give a lecture to a woman. Her husband, upon whose request this was done, stood behind the door listening. At the end of my sermonizing, which had made a visible impression, I said, 'Good-bye, sir!'. To the experienced person I thus betrayed the fact that the words were directed towards the husband; that I had spoken to oblige him.

3 While writing a prescription for a woman who was especially weighted down by the financial burden of the treatment, I was interested to hear her say suddenly, 'Please do not give me *big bills*, because I cannot swallow them'. Of course she meant to say *pills*.

('faulty achievements'; Bettelheim, 1985), the all too common slips of the tongue ('Freudian slips'), slips of the pen, forgetting things (including words and people's names), leaving things behind and 'accidents'. Freud's translators used the term *parapraxes* and some examples are given in Box 29.5.

● An evaluation of Freud's theory

Empirical studies

There have been literally thousands of empirical studies of various aspects of Freud's theories. Two of the major reviews of this research have been carried out by Kline (1972, 1982) and Fisher and Greenberg (1977), the latter being perhaps the most comprehensive to date. They conclude that Freud was right

in some areas, wrong in others and too vague to be tested at all in still others. Psychoanalytic theory cannot be accepted or rejected as a total package: 'It is a complex structure consisting of many parts, some of which should be accepted, others rejected and the rest at least partially re-shaped' (Fisher and Greenberg, 1977).

Three basic kinds of study have been carried out:

1 *validational*, which try to test directly various parts of the theory, mainly in the laboratory;
2 those which try to investigate some of the *underlying mechanisms* involved but which are not direct tests of the theory. Again mainly laboratory experiments;
3 those which study the *effects of psychoanalysis* as therapy (these will be discussed in Chapter 31).

Fonagy (1981) asks whether it is conceivable that laboratory studies could 're-create' the clinical concepts and experience that Freud describes and, therefore, questions the usefulness of validational studies. He also queries the relevance of studies of treatment effectiveness as a way of 'testing' the theory – he says it is equivalent to the relevance of the effectiveness of aspirin to a theory of headaches!

Many validational studies have been concerned with Freud's theory of personality types, especially the oral and anal (see Chapter 21) and defence mechanisms, including repression, which was discussed in relation to theories of forgetting, in Chapter 12. While the experimental evidence for repression is weak, rather stronger evidence in support of Freud comes from the study by Speisman *et al.* (1964) who demonstrated intellectualization by measuring participants' GSR as they watched a stressful film with commentaries intended either to increase or decrease stress (see Chapter 6).

However, Fonagy (1981) points out that in some of these studies, the thinking and feeling involved were conscious, while defence mechanisms, as Freud defined them, are unconscious. But these difficulties aside, he believes that much more relevant is the second kind of study, namely those that go beyond trying to replicate clinical phenomena and which instead attempt to identify basic mechanisms or processes which may underlie unconscious phenomena.

Relationship between Freudian and factor-analytic concepts

Although not validation studies as such, the factor-analytic studies of Eysenck and Cattell provide some indirect support for Freud. In a review of these, Kline

(1983) argues that studies of Eysenck's N, showing a continuum, indirectly support Freud's view that neurotics are only different in degree from non-neurotics.

As far as psychotics are concerned, Freud (1924) argued that they deny reality and obey their instinctual urges compared with neurotics who deny their urges and obey reality; in other words, there is a discontinuity between psychotics on the one hand and neurotics and normals on the other (hence, a qualitative difference) but only a quantitative difference between normals and neurotics. Eysenck's findings that both normals and neurotics score low on P is consistent with Freud's view, but since P is dimensional (like E and N), everyone appears on the scale (including normals and neurotics).

As far as Cattell is concerned, we noted that he was influenced by Freud in the labels he attached to some of his primary factors: factor C (ego strength), factor G (superego) and factor Q4 (id tension). According to Freud, neurotics have weak egos: either they feel threatened by id impulses (neurotic conflict) or they have a very strong superego (moral conflict) and this picture has been confirmed by Cattell. For example, on the 16PF, diagnosed neurotics score low on C and high on Q4 and as far as factor O is concerned (guilt proneness), neurotics also score high.

Fonagy (1981) believes that much more relevant is the second kind of study, namely those that go beyond trying to replicate clinical phenomena and which instead attempt to identify basic mechanisms or processes which may underlie unconscious phenomena. A concept which is closely related to that of repression is *perceptual defence*, whereby stimuli which are threatening or anxiety-provoking in some way are more difficult to perceive at a conscious level (than those which are not). In turn, perceptual defence is linked to the more general – and less defence-oriented – concept of *subliminal perception*, i.e. perception which takes place below the threshold of conscious awareness. In Chapter 9 we discussed a number of relevant studies and found considerable support for both concepts.

Neurophysiological studies

A further source of evidence is neurophysiological psychology. Penfield (1958) directly stimulated the temporal cortex and patients reported phenomenal experiences of 'bygone days', including the entire spectrum of emotions and visual/acoustic components. The central nervous system seems to preserve a record of past experience and perceptions of astonishing detail, which is not normally available to consciousness. Perhaps these perceptions, encoded as memories, form the basis of pre-conscious and unconscious systems.

Bogen (1969), Galin (1974) and McKinnon (1979) have all equated the function of the dominant hemisphere of the brain (the left for most people) with secondary process thinking and that of the minor hemisphere with primary process thinking. These conclusions are partly based on studies of split-brain patients (whose left and right hemispheres are no longer physically connected; see Chapters 3 and 4). Several studies have found that, as the ability to speak is localized in the left (dominant) hemisphere, all phenomenal experiences these patients report refer to the left hemisphere: their dreams are free from primary process distortions and bizarreness and lie much closer to ordinary modes of thinking of awake adults. This suggests that dreams and primary process thinking as a whole are normally controlled by the right side of the brain.

Is the theory scientific?

We have seen how much research Freud's theories have generated and, in the light of this, it seems very difficult to accept Popper's criticism (see Chapter 2) that they are unfalsifiable and, therefore, unscientific. The theory as a whole (or, at least, many parts of it) does seem testable (even if it is not always shown to be true), although we should note Fonagy's (1981) warning that many validational studies may not be very relevant to an understanding of the clinical phenomena as Freud described them. Perhaps more relevant to Popper's criticism are rather specific parts of the theory, in particular, the defence mechanism of reaction formation. Box 29.6 describes research which illustrates Popper's criticism very well. The problem here, from a scientific point of view, is that the same psychological phenomenon (in this case, preference for big-breasted women) can have two opposite manifestations (preference for large or small breasts): Freud cannot lose.

The converse of this problem is where very different or opposed experiences can produce the same behaviour; for example, fixation at a particular stage of psychosexual development can be caused by either deprivation or overindulgence (see Chapter 21). This is partly an issue of falsifiability and partly to do with the ability to predict particular outcomes, which Freud's theory is very bad at; it is very good, however, at accounting for what has already happened in the past. Is there, at least in

BOX 29.6 Key study: like it or not, dependent men prefer big-breasted women

Scodel (1957) predicted, based on Freud's theories, that highly dependent men would prefer big-breasted women. (Dependency is an oral trait and the breast can be regarded as a symbol of a state of dependency.) Scodel in fact found the opposite to be true – dependent men tended to prefer small-breasted women, so Freud's theory, in this respect, seems to have been falsified (on this occasion, at least). However, Kline (1972) invoked the concept of reaction formation in order to show that Scodel had confirmed the theory, since a fixation (unconscious) with big breasts may show up as a preference (conscious) for small breasts! According to Kline then, either outcome (preference for big- or small-breasted women) would have shown Freud to be right!

principle, any way of testing the hypothesis that someone's affection for another person is actually a reaction formation against their repressed hostility? At the worst, the Freudian would only have to concede (if it was somehow shown that the affection was genuine) that the person's behaviour was 'overdetermined' (i.e. motivated by conscious affection and unconscious hostility). Eysenck (1973) also points to reaction formation to demonstrate the low status of psychoanalytic theory as a scientific theory: he argues that for the Freudian all behaviour can be explained, even if none can be predicted, and this is largely because of the retrospective nature of data collection involved in the case study method which Freud used (see below).

However, it would be a serious mistake to regard reaction formation as typifying Freudian theory; the sheer volume of research suggests that it cannot be dismissed as lightly as Popper and Eysenck would like on the grounds of being 'unscientific'. According to Kline (1989), the view adopted by almost all experimental psychologists involved in the study of Freud's theory is that it should be seen as a collection of hypotheses. Agreeing with Fisher and Greenberg (1977), this view holds that some of these will turn out to be true, others false, when put to Popper's test of falsifiability. Some hypotheses are undoubtedly more critical to the overall theory than others; for example, if no evidence could be found for repression, this would alter considerably the nature

of psychoanalysis, but if it was found that the Oedipus complex was more pronounced in small as opposed to large families, this would not radically affect the theory (Kline, 1989).

How valid is the case study method?

Although Freud often states or implies that his theories have been derived from his observations of his patients, he left us no direct record of the original data. He deliberately made no notes during therapy sessions, since this might interfere with the therapeutic relationship (see Chapter 31) and wrote them up several hours later, so that his case studies are reconstructions of what happened. He also reported on very few patients; only 12 are reported in depth and in some of these the details are incomplete (Stevens, 1995). Relying as it does on the reconstruction of childhood events, the case study, as used by Freud, is generally considered to be the least scientific of all empirical methods used by psychologists; it is open to many types of distortion and uncontrolled influences.

Fisher and Greenberg (1977) point out the tendency to select or emphasize material which supported particular interpretations and nowhere is this more clearly illustrated than in the case of Little Hans. As we saw in Chapter 21, Freud recognized that there was a problem of objectivity because it was little Hans' father actually conducting the psychoanalysis. But he goes on to say that this case was no different from the analysis of adults, ' ... For a psychoanalysis is not an impartial scientific investigation, but a therapeutic measure. Its essence is not to prove anything but merely to alter something' (Freud, 1909).

But doesn't this condemn the whole of Freud's work to the realm of 'non-science', since his theories are all constructed from his case studies? Isn't the consulting room his 'laboratory', his patients his 'participants', what they say about themselves (especially their childhood) the data?

This point is answered by Storr (1987), a leading popularizer of psychoanalytic theory and himself a trained psychoanalyst. He claims that although some of the hypotheses of psychoanalytic theory can be tested scientifically (i.e. are refutable), this applies only to a minority; the majority are based on observations made in the course of psychoanalytic treatment, which cannot be regarded as a scientific procedure. Such observations are inevitably contaminated by the subjective experience and prejudice of the observer, however detached he/she tries to be, and so cannot be regarded in the same light as observations made during, say, a chemistry or physics experiment. It is certainly possible, he goes on, to study human beings as if they were objects merely responding to the stimuli impinging on them (i.e. experimental psychology) but it is not possible to conduct psychoanalysis (or any form of psychotherapy) in this way.

So do we have to accept Storr's conclusion that psychoanalytic theory can never be thought of as scientific? One defence of Freud may be that to study people as objects responding to stimuli is not truly scientific because that is not what people are actually like and so to study them in this way is not only unethical but inaccurate. Perhaps Freud is much closer to treating people as people and, to that extent, perhaps more of a scientist than most experimental psychologists! (This relates to the *hermeneutical* nature of Freud's theory; see below.)

Some critics have gone further and claimed that Freud, rather than deriving or developing his ideas by his observations of his patients, actually imposed his interpretations on them, distorting and fabricating evidence to fit his theories (e.g. Esterson, 1993). An example of this is Freud's seduction theory (the forerunner of the Oedipus complex); see Chapter 21 for a discussion of seduction theory and child sexual abuse.

How representative were Freud's patients?

One of the standard criticisms made of Freud's database is that his patients were mainly wealthy, middle-class Jewish females, living in Vienna at the turn of the century, and therefore hardly representative of the population to whom his theories were generalized. If these people were also neurotic, how can we be sure that what Freud discovered about them is true of normal individuals? However, as we have seen, Freud regarded neurosis as continuous with normal behaviour; that is, neurotics are suffering only from more extreme versions of problems experienced by all of us.

More serious, perhaps, is the criticism that Freud studied only adults (with the very dubious exception of little Hans) and yet he put forward a theory of personality development. How many steps removed were his data from his theory? According to Thomas (1985), the analyst interprets, through his theoretical 'lens', ostensibly symbolic material derived from the reported dreams/memories, etc. of neurotics about ostensible experiences stemming from their childhood one or more decades earlier. However, this

in itself does not invalidate the theory, it merely makes the study of children all the more necessary.

Significantly, although Freud described most of his patients as neurotics, many writers have subsequently concluded that many of them would today be diagnosed as psychotic (see Chapter 30).

The role of biological factors

A key issue which divides Freudians and other psychodynamic theorists is the role of biological factors in personality development. While none of the neo-Freudians (Fromm, Horney and Erikson, for example) denied that biological factors are important or that all psychic energy must ultimately be rooted in the body, they did deny that all behaviour is directed towards the satisfaction of biological needs in the way Freud believed. For example, although it may be true that hoarding is a trait associated with the anal stage, it is absurd to claim that hoarding is always the manifestation of anal fixation (Brown, 1963; see Chapter 21).

It was Freud's emphasis on the role of sexuality which ultimately led to the split with Jung and Adler (see below) and Erikson stressed the role of sociocultural influences almost as a counterbalance to Freud's preoccupation with biological factors (see Chapter 21).

Reification

Several writers have criticized terms like the id, ego and superego as bad metaphors; they do not correspond to any aspect of psychology or neurophysiology and they encourage reification, i.e. treating metaphorical terms as if they were 'things' or entities.

However, Bettelheim (1985) points out that much of Freud's terminology was mistranslated and this has led to a misrepresentation of those parts of his theory. For example, Freud himself never used the Latin words *id*, *ego* and *superego*; he used the German *das Es* ('the it'), *das Ich* ('the I') and *das Über-Ich* (the 'over-I'), which were intended to capture how the individual relates to different aspects of the self, whereas the Latin terms tend to depersonalize these and give the impression that there are three separate 'selves' which we all possess! The Latin words (chosen by his American translator to give greater scientific credibility) turn the concepts into cold technical terms which arouse no personal associations; whereas the 'I' can only be studied from the inside (through introspection), the 'ego' can be studied from the outside (as behaviour). In translation, Freud's 'soul' became scientific psychology's 'psyche' or 'personality' (Bettelheim, 1985).

The nature of Freudian theory

According to Stevens (1995), Freud's theory has great *hermeneutic strength*, i.e. it provides methods and concepts which enable us to interpret and 'unpack' underlying meanings. Instead of seeing the criticisms of Eysenck and Popper and others that we discussed above as detracting from the value of the theory, what they do is alert us to the nature of human behaviour and personality as a subject matter and to the kind of understanding that is possible or appropriate in this area. Specifically, it leads to the realization that personality and behaviour are constituted by meanings (both conscious and unconscious); these aren't measurable in any precise way and are constructed, i.e. we actively make sense of the world in terms of our past experiences and the concepts we have acquired and developed. Stevens claims that:

> ... Although Freud wanted to create a nomothetic theory ... in effect he finished up with a set of 'hermeneutic tools' – concepts and techniques that help us to interpret underlying meanings ...

These tools can become part of our own way of explaining our motives and those of others and to this extent they are very powerful. But hermeneutic theories offer a different form of understanding from those expressed in observable and testable form, which leads to their rejection by some as 'unscientific'; yet they may actually be more appropriate for capturing the nature of human experience and action.

There is no doubting the tremendous impact that Freud has had, both within psychology and outside. The fertility of psychoanalytic theory, in terms of the debate, research and theorizing it has generated, makes it one of the richest in the whole of psychology:

> He [Freud] has provided us with a set of ideas and concepts which, both in literature and everyday conversation, have helped us to formulate questions about ourselves, our inner experience and our social conditioning. He helped explode the myth of 'rational Man' and has brought us face to face with our irrational selves, a new image of ourselves as least as valid as any other major image-of-man that Social Science has offered and perhaps as challenging and disturbing as any it is ever likely to offer. (Clift, 1984)

According to Kline (1989):

> ... Freudian theory is still a powerful intellectual force. To claim that it is dead, as do many experimental psychologists – at least by implication for it rarely influences their thinking – must be either ignorance or wishful thinking.

● Jung's analytical psychology

Jung 'broke ranks' with Freud in 1913 to form his 'analytical psychology'. He disagreed with Freud over a number of fundamental issues and it is these disagreements that we shall emphasize here.

Structure of the personality and levels of consciousness

For Jung , the personality as a whole is the psyche, the totality of all *psychic* processes, conscious and unconscious. It embraces all thought, feeling and behaviour and helps the individual adapt to the social and physical environment; the term psyche also includes what is normally called 'soul'. The person is seen as a whole almost from the moment of birth: personality is not acquired piece by piece (the 'jigsaw' concept) through learning and experience but it is already there, so that instead of striving to achieve wholeness, our aim in life is to maintain it and to prevent the splitting or dissociation of the psyche into separate and conflicting parts. Jung saw the role of therapy as helping the patient recover this lost wholeness and to strengthen the psyche so as to resist future dissociation.

The psyche comprises three major, interacting levels: (i) consciousness, (ii) the personal unconscious and (iii) the collective unconscious. The distinction between (ii) and (iii) represents one of the major differences between Jung and Freud.

Consciousness

This is the only part of the mind known directly by the individual; it appears early in life through the operation of four basic *functions*:

1 *thinking*, which tries to understand the world through cognition;
2 *feeling*, which tries to evaluate things in terms of 'pleasant–unpleasant', 'acceptable–unacceptable';
3 *sensing*, which comprises all conscious experiences produced by stimulation of the sense organs, internal and external;
4 *intuiting*, which is 'knowing something without knowing how you know it' or 'perception via the unconscious'.

While all four functions are constitutionally present in each person, they are not all used to the same degree and one usually predominates; this is what makes the basic character of one person different from that of another.

In addition to these four functions there are two *attitudes* which determine the orientation of the conscious mind: *extroversion* and *introversion*. The extrovert's *libido* (Jung's term for psychic energy as a whole or life-force) is directed outwards towards the external, objective world of physical objects, people, customs and conventions, social institutions and so on; extroverts are preoccupied with interpersonal relationships and are generally more active and outgoing. By contrast, the introvert's libido is directed inwards towards the internal, subjective world of thoughts, feelings and so on and they are preoccupied with intrapersonal matters, are introspective and withdrawn and may be seen by others as aloof, reserved and antisocial. Jung believed that a person is predominantly one or the other throughout life, although there may be occasional inconsistencies in different situations. So for Jung, extroversion–introversion represents a typology of the 'either/or' variety while, as we saw above, Eysenck's 'adoption' of Jung's terms took the form of personality dimensions, with extreme extroversion at one end and extreme introversion at the other.

Jung believed that the development of consciousness is also the beginning of *individuation*, the process by which a person becomes psychologically 'in-dividual', i.e. a separate, indivisible unity or whole, and from this process emerges the *ego*. The ego refers to how the conscious mind is organized and consists of conscious perceptions, memories, thoughts and feelings. Although it represents only a small part of the psyche as a whole, it plays the essential role of 'gatekeeper to consciousness', i.e. it selects important sensations, feelings, ideas, etc. and allows them through into conscious awareness (much as Freud's pre-conscious does); this prevents us from becoming overwhelmed by the mass of stimulation going on around (and inside) us. The ego provides a sense of identity and continuity for the individual and it is the central core of the personality.

The personal unconscious

The Freudian unconscious, in Jung's terms, is predominantly 'personal', i.e. composed of the individual's particular and unique experiences which have been made unconscious through repression. For Jung, repressed material represents only one kind of unconscious content. The personal unconscious also includes things we have forgotten because they were irrelevant (or seemed unimportant) at the time or because they have lost some of their 'energetic value' since they happened, as well as all those things which we think of as being 'stored in memory' and things which may not be accessible to conscious recall at a particular time but which are available and could become accessible (see Chapter 12). In these respects, Jung's personal unconscious resembles Freud's pre-conscious.

A major feature of the personal unconscious is that associated groups of feelings, thoughts and memories may cluster together to form a *complex,* which represents a quite autonomous and powerful 'mini-personality' within the total psyche. It is from Jung that the term has been 'borrowed' and become a commonly used one in everyday language, together with synonyms such as 'hang-up' (Hall and Nordby, 1973) and Freud's Oedipus complex illustrates this constellation of thoughts and feelings. Although not necessarily detrimental, complexes often prevent the complete individuation of a person from taking place and one aim of therapy is to free the patient from the grip of such complexes. In looking for the origin of complexes, Jung eventually turned to the collective unconscious.

The collective unconscious

This part of Jung's theory sets him apart from Freud probably more than any other, as Jung was acknowledging the role of evolution and heredity in providing a blueprint for the psyche just as they do for the body. Freud's id is, of course, part of each individual's 'personal' unconscious and represents our biological inheritance. (Ironically, in view of the criticism of Freud that he overemphasized the role of biological factors, Jung could be seen as having given inherited factors an even greater role than Freud by virtue of his collective unconscious.) According to Jung, the mind (through the brain) has inherited characteristics which determine how a person will react to life experiences and what type of experiences these will be.

Whereas for Freud our childhood is of critical importance in making us what we are as adults, Jung attached relatively little importance to our individual past in relation to the personal unconscious but saw the evolutionary history of human beings as a species as being all-important in relation to the collective (or *racial*) unconscious.

The collective unconscious can be thought of as a reservoir of latent images, called *primordial images*, which relate to the 'first' or 'original' development of the psyche, stemming from our ancestral past, human, pre-human and animal (Hall and Nordby, 1973). These images are not literally pictures in the mind but predispositions or potentialities for experiencing and responding to the world in the same way that our ancestors did. For example, we do not have to learn to fear the dark or snakes through direct experience because we are naturally predisposed to develop such fears through the inheritance of our ancestors' fears. (Interestingly, support for Jung comes from studies of conditioning which, as we saw in Chapter 7, show that it is much easier to induce a fear of snakes, for example, than to induce a fear of flowers. Similarly, clinical psychology shows that naturally acquired phobias of snakes and spiders are the most common amongst adults and of the dark in children; see Chapters 30 and 31.)

These primordial images are also known as *archetypes* (a prototype or 'original model or pattern') which, according to Hall and Nordby (1973), are more like a negative (which has to be developed through experience) than an already developed and clearly recognizable photograph; they are 'forms without content', potential ways of perceiving and feeling and acting. Jung identified a large number of archetypes, including birth, rebirth, death, power, magic, the hero, the child, the trickster, God, the demon, the wise old man, earth mother and the giant. Although universal, archetypes are expressed differently by different individuals, within and between racial and cultural groups; they also form the nucleus of a complex. Jung paid special attention to four archetypes – the persona, the anima/animus, the shadow and the self – and these are featured in Box 29.7.

What is the evidence for Jung's theory of archetypes?

According to Brown (1963), there are three major sources of evidence:

BOX 29.7 The four major archetypes of the collective unconscious

The persona ('mask')
This is the outward face we present to the world, both revealing and concealing the real self; it allows us to play our part in social interaction and to be accepted by others. It is the 'packaging' of the ego, the ego's PR man or woman, a kind of cloak between the ego and the objective world. It is very similar to the notion of a social role, which refers to the expectations and obligations associated with a particular social position; Jung describes it as the 'conformity' archetype.

Normally, we play a variety of roles and personality as a whole cannot be reduced to any one of them or to the entire set. However, we sometimes become dominated by a particular role, which can take over our entire personality; when the ego identifies with the persona, Jung says that *inflation* is happening.

Anima/animus
This refers to the unconscious mirror-image of our conscious ('official') sex – if we are male, our *anima* is our unconscious female side and if we are female, our *animus* is our unconscious male side. We all have qualities of the opposite sex – both biologically and psychologically – and in a well-adjusted person both sides must be allowed to express themselves in thought and behaviour.

The anima has a preference for all things vain, helpless, uncertain and unintentional; the animus prefers the heroic, the intellectual, the artistic and athletic.

These would be expressed in different ways in different cultures but are universal characteristics (compare them with gender role stereotypes as discussed in Chapter 23). Jung believed that repression of the anima/animus is very common in Western culture, where the persona predominates. (This relates to androgyny; again see Chapter 23.)

The shadow
This contains more of our basic animal nature than any other archetype and is similar to Freud's id. Like the id, it must be kept in check if we are to live in society but this is not achieved easily and is always at the expense of our creativity and spontaneity, depth of feeling and insight. So the shadow represents the source of our creative impulses, but also of our destructive urges; if it is too severely repressed it will seek revenge, as in war. When the ego and shadow work harmoniously, the person is full of energy, both mentally and physically. The shadow of the highly creative person may occasionally overwhelm the ego, causing temporary insanity (confirming the popular belief that genius is akin to madness).

The self
This is the central archetype ('the archetype of archetypes') which unites the personality, giving it a sense of 'oneness' and firmness. The ultimate aim of every personality is to achieve a state of selfhood and individuation (similar to self-actualization); this is a lifelong process, attained by very few individuals, Jesus and Buddha being notable exceptions. It is commonly represented as a *mandala*, an age-old symbol of wholeness and totality, found all over the world.

1 the 'extraordinary' similarity of themes in the mythologies of various cultures;

2 the recurring appearance, in therapy, of symbols which have become divorced from any of the patient's personal experiences and which become more and more like the primitive and universal symbols found in myths and legends;

3 the content of fantasies of psychotics (especially schizophrenics) which are full of themes such as death and rebirth, which are similar to those found in mythology.

Many writers do not accept the theory of a collective unconscious. For example, Brown (1963) argues that members of all cultures share certain common experiences and so it is not surprising that they dream or create myths about archetypal themes. The deeper the interpretation, he says, the more likely we are to come up with universal explanations which seem to have an innate or biological basis. Less deep, ego interpretations, however, are more likely to reveal the specific features of different cultures, i.e. cultural differences (Brown, 1963; see Fig. 29.7 for a diagrammatic representation of the psyche as a whole).

Other similarities and differences between Jung and Freud

Dream theory
Jung shared Freud's belief that dreams are the 'royal road to the unconscious'. However, he certainly disagreed with Freud that all dreams are wish fulfilments; rather, Jung saw dreams as an important way of attaining self-knowledge which, in turn (together with religious or spiritual experiences), is a path to achieving individuation. However, not all dreams are equally significant in this respect.

The great function of dreams is to restore our psychological balance and to re-establish 'the total psychic equilibrium' and they are just as likely to point to the future (e.g. by suggesting a solution to a conflict) as to the past. He also believed that Freud's 'disguise' was far too elaborate and preferred to take the dream at face value. Dream symbols do not have a fixed meaning (as they very largely did for Freud) and he also advocated the study of dream series, i.e. several dreams recorded over a period of time by the same individual.

Neurosis and therapy
Repression plays very little part in Jung's theory of neurosis; more important is the conflict between different parts of the personality which have developed

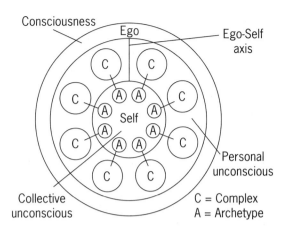

FIGURE 29.7 *Schematic diagram of Jung's model of the psyche. (Based on Stevens, 1990)*

unequally. Jungian therapy is much more concerned with future goals than past history and the present situation is the key to neurosis; therapy aims to bring the patient into contact with the healing collective unconscious, largely through dream interpretation. Free association is also important but the Jungian analyst, compared with the Freudian, plays a much more active role and therapy is seen as a co-operative venture between patient and therapist (see Chapter 31).

● Adler's individual psychology

Adler broke from Freud two years earlier than Jung, in 1911. Although he agreed with Freud about the importance of unconscious forces, he, like Jung, rejected Freud's emphasis on sexuality as the major influence on the personality and instead saw people as being motivated primarily by the drive towards affirmation of their personality, the tendency towards self-preservation, the will to power or striving for superiority. Adler was much more interested than Freud in the social nature of human beings and, like Jung, he saw the individual as an indivisible unity or whole; any event must be considered in the light of its effect on the whole person if we are to understand it properly.

Adler was impressed by the body's capacity to compensate for organic damage; for example, damage to a kidney or lung may be followed by increased compensatory functioning of the undamaged one and an undamaged part of the brain may take over the job normally carried out by the damaged area (see Chapter 3). To this extent, the strictly biological basis of Freud's theory was attractive to Adler and he believed that similar processes could be observed in the psychological sphere; for example, painters with imperfect vision, musicians and composers who are deaf, might be compensating for their defect in such a way that their inferiority actually becomes transformed into superiority. Adler saw feelings of inferiority as not only inevitable but as the key to understanding the whole of mental life.

The origins of inferiority

Every child spends its early years in a state of dependence on others and experiences all kinds of desires which cannot be satisfied; by comparison, adults seem happier and have more power. As a result, children come to experience their dependence and powerlessness as a state of inferiority relative to adults and, in reaction to this, an unconscious drive emerges towards superiority, the will to power. Against this common background of inferiority, Adler identified several factors which could influence the degree of inferiority an individual might experience:

1 Any kind of *physical deformity*, either congenital (e.g. harelip) or environmental (scarring as the result of an accident), to the extent that it is experienced psychologically.
2 *Gender.* Adler recognized the inequality of men and women in society and believed that the equation between 'masculine' and 'strong and superior' and 'feminine' and 'weak and inferior' is made at an early age. Some boys may be unable to live up to these gender role stereotypes, especially if their fathers attribute them with masculine qualities which they do not possess, and this may be at the root of homosexuality and other sexual 'deviations'. The Don Juan character, for example, is continually trying to convince himself of his masculinity (which he equates with sexual prowess); it is usually the 'conquest' rather than the actual sexual experience that matters – his behaviour is motivated not by an insatiable sexual appetite as such but by his underlying sense of inferiority. Women may try to compensate for their inferiority by wishing to be a man (the 'masculine protest') or by exploiting their 'weakness' and their feminine charms.
3 *Birth order*, the *social and economic status* of the family and the length and quality of *education* can all contribute to a sense of inferiority.
4 The way parents in particular, and adults in general, react to the child's *successes and failures* is vitally important; pressure to succeed may be too great and unrealistic for a particular child and its failures can produce anxiety in the parents which,

in turn, causes extra pressure and anxiety in the child (compare this with Erikson's stage of 'initiative versus doubt and shame'; see Chapter 21).
5 A *neglected, spoilt* or *hated child* is likely to have very low self-esteem.

How do people cope with inferiority?

In general, the more the original feelings of inferiority develop into the unconscious form of an inferiority complex, the greater the drive towards compensation. Each child develops early on in life its own particular strategy for dealing with the family situation as it is perceived; this strategy essentially comprises a set of attitudes which, collectively, form the 'lifestyle' upon which the adult personality is based. The traits we adopt had functional value for us in the earliest days – they were the traits which seemed to give us the best results in terms of power.

In addition, Adler identified three major techniques by which people try to overcome inferiority:

1 *Successful compensation* involves compensating in a positive and constructive way which is socially advantageous for the individual, for example, intellectual achievement as a compensation for some physical disability. In general, it refers to a successful adjustment to life's three challenges – society, work and sex.
2 *Overcompensation* involves trying too hard, so that the underlying motive becomes obvious, i.e. aiming for extraordinary achievements and settling for nothing less. Such goals may be achievable only in fantasy and this can result in maladjustment. Less extreme examples are the bumptious little man, the small man who smokes a huge cigar or drives an enormous car or lives in an enormous house or the coward who becomes a bully.
3 *Escape from combat* is essentially a way of ensuring that failure is impossible (or is reduced to a minimum) but at the price of any real success. For example, physical symptoms can be 'used' to deflect attention away from the real reasons for opting out, which may be fear of failure (very often the fear of failing to achieve impossibly high standards). This retreat into illness or adoption of the sick role can become a way of life and a means of gaining power over others.

Neurosis and therapy

According to Adler, 'Every neurosis can be understood as an attempt to free oneself from a feeling of inferiority in order to gain a feeling of superiority'. The neurotic is a person who is unable to gain superiority by legitimate means and so develops symptoms, either as an excuse to avoid situations in which they might be exposed as a failure or as a means of gaining control over others by a sort of emotional blackmail (as we saw in escape from combat).

The essential aim of therapy is to help patients to understand their secret psychic processes and to gain the courage and self-confidence necessary to exist and develop in a normal way; the analyst points out the patient's style of life with its *fictive goals* (unrealistic goals) and gives some practical advice regarding a more sensible future lifestyle.

● An evaluation of Adler's theory

Adler's emphasis on social factors in personality development, his view of the person as a unity, the de-emphasis on sexual influences and his relative emphasis on the conscious ego (as opposed to unconscious forces) are all significant modifications of Freud's theory which helped to inspire the theories of the neo-Freudians, such as Erikson (1902–1994), Horney (1885–1952) and Fromm (born 1900).

However, he seems to have overemphasized the role of inferiority; as Brown (1963) points out, it is difficult to believe that all the non-organic nervous disorders (neuroses) are produced by a 'feeling of inferiority' or that psychoses are the result of complete failure to conquer inferiority, which leads the psychotic to 'refuse to play' the game of life. According to Brown (1963), Adler's individual psychology has almost ceased to exist as a distinct, independent theory but its influence lives on (although this is not always acknowledged) in the theories of neo-Freudians.

CHAPTER SUMMARY

- Most personality theories assume that personality is something that the individual 'has', although it refers to a hypothetical construct which can only be inferred from behaviour.
- Implicit personality theories are important in impression formation and also influence interpersonal behaviour; to this extent, personality refers to how we relate to other people. Personality traits also constitute an important part of the self-concept.
- The constructionist approach sees personality as constructed in the course of social interaction, involving the actor's self-presentation, the

observer's perception of the actor and the self-observer (the actor's self-awareness).

- Two central issues underlying different theories are (a) does personality consist of permanent traits/characteristics? and (b) is the study of personality concerned with unique individuals (the idiographic approach) or personality in general (the nomothetic approach)?
- Psychometric theories, such as those of Eysenck and Cattell, see personality as comprising permanent traits and are nomothetic. Idiographic theories are concerned with the whole person; some may see personality as composed of permanent traits (e.g. Allport), while others take a very different view of the person, such as Kelly's personal construct theory and humanistic theories (e.g. Rogers). Psychoanalytic theories (e.g. Freud, Jung, Adler) can be seen as both idiographic and nomothetic and allow for personality change.
- Experimental/'general' psychology is concerned with those psychological processes common to all human beings ('universal norms'). Personality differences represent one kind of 'group norm' and belong to individual differences/differential psychology which is nomothetic. The idiographic approach is concerned with discovering individual/idiosyncratic norms.
- Allport distinguished between common traits, which are the subject matter of the nomothetic approach, and individual traits, which are the subject matter of the idiographic approach; the latter consist of cardinal, central and secondary. Most people possess a small number of central traits which compose the core of the personality.
- Allport believes that the same individual trait label has a different meaning for every individual to whom it is applied (a qualitative difference), whereas nomothetic theories assume that it has the same meaning but individuals differ in the extent to which it is present (a quantitative difference).
- There has been much controversy over Allport's claim that individuals are unique. The nomothetic–idiographic distinction is based on a false dichotomy and traits are defined in terms of relative positions on a dimension. However, Eysenck accepts that individuals are unique, although he defines it very differently from Allport (i.e. in terms of common traits).
- The nomothetic–idiographic distinction is related to the distinction between *Naturwissenschaften* (natural sciences) and *Geisteswissenschaften* (moral/human sciences), which were seen as deal-

ing with the general and the particular respectively. However, these are increasingly being seen as complementary and interdependent approaches; even Allport argued that both should be used together in order to achieve the aims of science.

- Defining personality traits as permanent implies the consistency of behaviour and seeing behaviour as primarily caused by traits (the trait approach) was challenged by Mischel's situationism, the view that behaviour is largely determined by situational factors. He claimed to have found very little support for intraindividual consistency which seemed to undermine the trait concept.

- Critics of situationism cite evidence for consistency and interactionists argue that not only is all behaviour the product of both personality and situational variables, but more of the variance in behaviour can be accounted for by an interaction between the two than by either on its own.

- Situations cannot be defined objectively, i.e. independently of the actor; it is the psychological situation that influences behaviour, since this takes account of the meaning that the situation has for the actor. The influential study by Bem and Allen supports the metatrait hypothesis, according to which different people behave consistently with respect to different traits; this represents an important moderator variable, another being self-monitoring.

- Situations differ in terms of how powerful they are in influencing behaviour and allowing the expression of individual personality; many famous social psychological experiments demonstrate the demands of the situation over-riding individual traits.

- A good psychometric test should have discriminatory power and be properly standardized, reliable and valid. Assuming these criteria are met, factor analysis (FA) is then applied to identify the fundamental components or factors of personality.

- Orthogonal FA aims to identify a small number of powerful, uncorrelated factors (the method preferred by Eysenck) while oblique FA aims to identify a larger number of less powerful, correlated factors (preferred by Cattell). Oblique factors are referred to as first-order factors (traits/'source traits'), while orthogonal factors are second-order factors (types/surface traits').

- There is no objective way of establishing which type of FA is superior and even the principle of simple structure does not help resolve the debate, although oblique FA is generally more popular.

- One of the first personality theories was Galen's

'Four Humours' which saw people as belonging to one or other category or type. Eysenck uses the term 'type' for sets of correlated traits or personality dimensions, specifically introversion–extroversion (E), neuroticism–stability (N), which are both normally distributed, and psychoticism (P), which is not normally distributed.

- Differences between normals and neurotics, and between normals and psychotics, are quantitative only. N and P represent predispositions to develop neurosis and psychosis respectively.

- E, N and P are measured by the Eysenck Personality Questionnaire (EPQ), which also contains a Lie Scale. The scales are designed primarily as research tools; E and N are widely accepted as being reliable and valid, but there is much more doubt about P. Eysenck uses criterion analysis as a way of validating the scales.

- Extroverts have a strong nervous system; their ARAS is biased towards inhibition, resulting in the reduction of intensity of sensory stimulation reaching the cortex (they are chronically underaroused). The ARAS of introverts is biased towards excitation, resulting in the increase of intensity of sensory stimulation reaching the cortex (they are chronically over-aroused).

- High N scorers have an ANS that reacts particularly strongly and quickly to stressful situations, so it is the sympathetic branch that is especially important in distinguishing between them and low scorers. The biological basis of P is much more uncertain, but male hormones may be involved.

- Extroverts should display greater psychical fatigue when performing long and tedious tasks, such as vigilance tasks, than introverts, who do appear to work more steadily and maintain concentration for longer. Both in the laboratory and in real life, extroverts seek constant change, due to stimuli quickly losing their arousal value, while more highly aroused introverts have a lower optimum level of stimulation.

- There seems to be a complex interaction between arousal and the individual's position on E and N and evidence for the role of the ARAS/arousal mechanisms in E is inconclusive. However, the role of genetic influences on self-report personality measures is strong.

- Introverted neurotics are more difficult to sedate than extroverted neurotics, who are easier to sedate than normals. In general, stimulant drugs make behaviour more introverted, while depressant drugs make it more extroverted. Anxiolytic drugs increase emotional stability, adrenergic drugs decrease it, while hallucinogens increase psychotic behaviour and anti-psychotic drugs decrease it.

- Introverts should be more easily conditioned than extroverts, but the evidence is equivocal. Eysenck assumes that conditionability is a unitary trait, but this has never been demonstrated and represents a weakness of the theory.
- Eysenck claims that the criminal is a neurotic extrovert, but although prisoners are generally higher on N, they are no higher on E and generally attempts to differentiate criminals from non-criminals in terms of personality have failed. Eysenck's theory is also reductionist and has political implications.
- According to Cattell, surface traits are the result of interactions between source traits which are the structural factors which determine personality. Three sources of data relevant to personality are L-data, which are ratings by observers requiring great skill and time, Q-data, which refer to scores on personality questionnaires, including the Cattell 16 PF (Personality Factor) Questionnaire, and T-data, which refer to scores on specially devised objective tests.
- Despite the differences between Cattell and Eysenck regarding the best form of FA, Cattell has identified a number of second-order, surface traits, including exvia–invia and anxiety, corresponding to E and N respectively. Cattell claims that Q-data with psychiatric patients reveals a qualitative difference between normals and psychotics.
- Compared with Eysenck, Cattell acknowledges the influence of situational factors on behaviour, as well as mood and state factors and motivational factors (ergs and sentiments). Three components of a motive are the 'id', 'ego' and 'superego' components, reflecting the influence of Freudian theory.
- Eysenck's and Cattell's theories are multitrait theories. An influential single trait theory is Rotter's locus of control. There is a growing consensus that personality can be adequately described by five broad constructs/factors (the 'Big Five'), namely extroversion/surgency, agreeableness, conscientiousness, neuroticism/emotional stability and openness to experience/culture/experience. Although the 'Big Five' has provided a unified framework for trait research, the problem remains of the meaning of the factors that are extracted.
- Kelly's personal construct theory (PCT) is both idiographic and phenomenological. The underlying model is man the scientist: each time we act we are testing hypotheses derived from our personal theories, which take the form of personal constructs, designed to make the world more predictable and controllable.
- Each person's construct system is organized hierarchically and each construct is expressed as a pair of bipolar adjectives; these are elicited by constructing a repertory grid, which is used as a major research tool. It can be factor-analysed and has been used nomothetically with schizophrenics, as well as with stutterers and in psychotherapy research.
- The reliability and validity of the Rep Grid have been questioned but it represents a methodology rather than a standardized test. PCT is not so much a personality theory, more a total psychology, so that traditional sub-divisions, such as motivation and emotion, can be accommodated by the fundamental postulate and the 11 corollaries.
- PCT is often called a cognitive theory of personality and has been criticized for denying the subjective reality of emotional experience, as well as neglecting situational influences on behaviour.
- Humanistic theories share a rejection of the scientific study of behaviour rather than experience; like PCT, they are rooted in phenomenology and existentialism and are concerned with uniquely human characteristics, including self-actualization. This lies at the top of Maslow's hierarchy of needs, while Rogers is more concerned with the process of becoming a 'fully functioning person'.
- Rogers rejected the deterministic nature of both psychoanalysis and behaviourism; instead he focuses on the person's current experience. He also rejected Freud's pessimistic view of human beings, arguing that we have a natural drive towards self-actualization.
- The central concept in Rogers' theory is the self; most human behaviour is an attempt to maintain consistency between our self-image and our actions. When this fails to happen, incongruence results, which may be experienced as threatening; defence mechanisms may then be used. But defences prevent the self from growing and changing, widening the gap between self-image and reality and making the self-image inflexible; this can lead to anxiety and emotional disturbance.
- Almost every child experiences conditional positive regard as they are growing up; related to this is the internalization of conditions of worth (those conditions under which conditional positive regard

will be obtained). Through denial and distortion of experiences which don't match our conditions of worth, there is a separation between the self and the organism.

- To experience positive self-regard, our behaviour and experience must match our conditions of worth, but this can produce incongruence. The need for positive regard and positive self-regard are so strong that conditions of worth can supersede the values associated with self-actualization.

- In client-centred therapy, the therapist provides unconditional positive regard, which enables the client to accept certain feelings/thoughts that are usually denied/distorted/disowned; in this way, organismic values gradually replace conditions of worth.

- Freud's psychoanalytic theory was the original psychodynamic theory, in which unconscious motivating forces play a central role. Dreams, neurotic symptoms and defence mechanisms represent three types of compromise through which the ego tries to meet the conflicting demands of the id and superego.

- Dreams consist of the manifest content (a blend of a forbidden wish and day residues) and the latent content (the meaning of the dream, namely, a disguised wish fulfilment). Dreams are created through dream work (displacement, condensation and concrete representation/dramatization), with symbols playing a central role. The disguise allows the dreamer to carry on sleeping, while dream interpretation provides invaluable insights into the unconscious mind.

- Neurotic symptoms have a similar structure to dreams: displacement and concrete representation deflect the patient's attention away from the pathogenic ideas underlying the symptom.

- Defence mechanisms involve some degree of self-deception and distortion of reality which, in the short term, prevent us from being overwhelmed by anxiety but as long-term solutions, they are unhealthy and undesirable. Major examples are repression, displacement, denial, rationalization, reaction formation, sublimation, identification, projection, regression and isolation.

- What we are consciously aware of is merely the tip of an iceberg: most of our thoughts and feelings, etc. are either not accessible at that moment (pre-conscious) or completely inaccessible (unconscious). The unconscious is made up of id impulses, all repressed material, part of the superego and the part of the ego that controls dreams, neurotic symptoms and defence mecha-

nisms; it is a dynamic force, best illustrated by repression.

- Our thoughts/feelings, etc. are overdetermined, which means that the reasons we are aware of for our behaviour may not be the important reasons (i.e. we are not rational); this is one aspect of psychic determinism. The unconscious is revealed through parapraxes, including slips of the tongue ('Freudian slips').

- Freud's theories have generated a huge amount of empirical research; this has taken the form of validational studies, studies of underlying mechanisms and those which assess the effects of psychotherapy. While some support for Freud comes from studies of personality types and certain defence mechanisms, the value of validational studies is questionable. Some support for Freud comes from Eysenck's and Cattell's psychometric theories.

- The most relevant studies are likely to be those which try to identify mechanisms/processes that may underlie unconscious phenomena, such as perceptual defence and subliminal perception, and neurophysiological studies, including those involving split-brain patients, which suggest that dreams and primary process thinking are usually controlled by the right hemisphere.

- One major criticism made of Freud's theories is that they are unfalsifiable, as in the case of reaction formation, which seems to be able to account for two contradictory outcomes. They also seem to be very poor at predicting specific outcomes. However, psychoanalysis should be seen as a collection of hypotheses, some of which are more critical to the overall theory than others.

- Freud's use of the case study method has been criticized for several reasons; he reconstructed the therapy session several hours later and he acknowledged that psychoanalysis is not an impartial scientific investigation. He has also been accused of imposing interpretations on his patients and even distorting evidence to fit his theories.

- His patients are considered to have been unrepresentative of people in general, making generalization very dubious; the fact that they were almost all adults makes his theory of development less valid than if it had been based on the study of children.

- A key issue which divides Freudians from other psychodynamic theorists is the former's emphasis on sexuality; this led to the split between Freud, Jung and Adler.

- Although Freud intended to produce a nomothetic theory, his work can be thought of as a set of hermeneutic tools – concepts and techniques that help to interpret underlying meanings. Although this kind of theory is difficult to test and measure empirically, it has influenced our everyday understanding of ourselves.

- In Jung's analytical psychology, consciousness operates through the four basic functions of thinking, feeling, sensing and intuiting, together with extroversion and introversion, which determine the orientation of the conscious mind; people are predominantly one or the other. The development of consciousness marks the beginning of individuation, from which the ego emerges.

- In Jung's terms, the Freudian unconscious is largely personal; it comprises much more than repressed material, including complexes, which constitute separate 'mini-personalities' within the total psyche. In his search for the origin of complexes, Jung turned to the collective/racial unconscious, a reservoir of primordial images or archetypes, stemming from our ancestral past.

- Jung identified several archetypes which, although universal, are expressed differently by different individuals, both within and between cultures. The most important are the persona, anima/animus, the shadow and the self (the 'archetype of archetypes').

- As well as being controversial, the collective unconscious represents the major difference between Freud and Jung. Jung also rejected Freud's theory of dreams as wish fulfilments and advocated the study of dream series. Jungian therapy aims to bring the patient into contact with the healing collective unconscious, largely through dream interpretation.

- In Adler's individual psychology, people are motivated primarily by the will to power, a striving for superiority as compensation for the inevitable feelings of inferiority that we all experience. These inferiority feelings originate in the child's dependence and powerlessness but are compounded by several factors, including physical deformity, gender, birth order and parental reaction to the child's successes and failures.

- Three major techniques for overcoming inferiority are successful compensation, overcompensation and escape from combat. Therapy aims to help the neurotic person to understand his or her fictive goals and to develop a more sensible, realistic lifestyle.

- Adler's theory was influential in the theories of the neo-Freudians, such as Erikson, Fromm and Horney, especially his emphasis on social factors relative to sexuality and on the conscious ego relative to unconscious forces.

GLOSSARY

Archetype The contents of the collective unconscious; primordial/latent images which represent predispositions to experience/respond to the world in the same way as our ancestors, e.g. persona, anima/animus, shadow, self.

Common traits Basic modes of adjustment applicable to all members of a particular cultural/ethnic/linguistic group; related to the nomothetic approach.

Conditional positive regard Feeling/acting/ in dishonest/distorted ways in order to obtain the love/approval of others (particularly children and parents).

Conditions of worth Those conditions under which positive regard will become available.

Constructionist approach The view that personality is constructed in the course of social interaction, from a person's self-presentation (actor), perception of this by an audience (observer) and self-awareness (self-observer).

Dream work The process by which the latent content is converted into the manifest content; involves displacement, condensation, concrete representation/dramatization.

Factor analysis (FA) A statistical technique, based on correlation, which attempts to reduce a large amount of test data to a much smaller amount; the aim is to identify the smallest number of components/factors which can account for variance in test performance. Orthogonal methods aim for a small number of independent (second-order) factors; oblique methods aim for a larger number of first-order factors that are correlated to some degree.

Hermeneutic Pertaining to the interpretation of meanings.

Idiographic approach The study of the unique personality characteristics of individuals (individual/idiosyncratic norms).

Incongruence Inconsistency between our self-image and our actual behaviour or others' perceptions of us.

Individual traits A unique set of personality dispositions/ways of organizing the world based on unique life experiences: cardinal/central/secondary. Related to the idiographic approach.

Manifest content The consciously experienced dream; a blend of a forbidden wish (the latent content) and day residues.

Metatrait hypothesis The belief that different people behave consistently with regard to different traits.

Nomothetic approach The attempt to identify personality factors which apply to people in general (group norms), allowing personality to be measured and people compared in terms of the degree to which these factors are displayed.

Phenomenology The study of the world through the eyes of the perceiver, rather than from the perspective of an observer.

Psychic determinism The view that all behaviour/thought/feeling is caused; overdetermination refers to the multiple causes, conscious and unconscious, of behaviour, etc.

Psychodynamic The active forces within the personality that motivate behaviour, in particular the unconscious conflicts between the id/ego/superego. Psychodynamic theories stem from Freud's psychoanalytic theory; also called depth psychology.

Situationism The view that behaviour is largely determined by situational factors, as opposed to personality factors (the trait approach).

Unconditional positive regard The creation, by a therapist in client-centred therapy, of an atmosphere of total acceptance/support, enabling the client to accept previously disowned feelings/thoughts.

FURTHER READING

Carver, C.S. and Scheier, M.F. (1992) *Perspectives on Personality*, 2nd edn. Boston: Allyn and Bacon. A thorough, readable, comprehensive text covering all the major approaches.

Freud, S. (1976) *The Interpretation of Dreams.* Harmondsworth: Penguin (Pelican Freud Library). Generally regarded as Freud's finest work, originally published in 1900.

PSYCHOLOGICAL ABNORMALITY

INTRODUCTION AND OVERVIEW

So far, the emphasis in this book has been on normal psychological processes and development. However, we have also had occasion to qualify what we have said in two ways: first, by considering examples of abnormality (which often serve to illuminate the normal); and secondly, by considering individual differences. In this chapter, these two issues are brought together, since mental disorders represent a major source of individual differences.

The study of mental disorders also constitutes the point of contact between psychiatry (a branch of medicine) and psychology, most clearly and importantly in the shape of abnormal psychology (see Chapter 1). Here and in Chapter 31, we shall be looking at the contributions of both disciplines to the understanding and alleviation of psychological disorders and we shall see how radically different their theories and methods are, reflecting the very different training each discipline provides.

However, within abnormal psychology itself there are various approaches which correspond to the major psychological theories that we have discussed throughout the book (the psychoanalytic, behavioural, humanistic–existential, neurobiological/biogenic and cognitive); each defines psychological abnormality differently and, accordingly, favours a different way of dealing with it (see Table 1.1, p.12).These will be discussed in detail in Chapter 31; here, we shall concentrate on the concept of abnormality itself, as far as possible without reference to any particular theoretical view. However, we shall be discussing the *medical model,* which sees abnormality as mental illness and is the view taken by a majority of psychiatrists; in turn, it is closely related to the biogenic approach. An integral part of the medical model is the classification of mental disorders, which has proved extremely controversial, both scientifically (in terms of the reliability and validity of the major classification systems – *DSM* and *ICD*) and as regards accusations of gender, racial, and sexual orientation bias.

We shall look at some of the major mental disorders, including schizophrenia and depression, both the major symptoms associated with each and some major theories of their aetiology.

THE CONCEPT OF ABNORMALITY

Implicit within each psychological theory of abnormality is the assumption that it is possible, and meaningful, to draw the line between normal and abnormal. How, if at all, can the line be drawn?

● The statistical criterion (or deviation from the average)

This represents the literal sense of abnormality, whereby any behaviour which is not typical or usual (i.e. infrequent) is, by definition, abnormal: 'normal' is 'average'. However, this does not help to distinguish between atypical behaviour which is desirable (or, at least, acceptable) and that which is undesirable and unacceptable. For example, creative genius (such as Picasso's) and megalomania (such as Hitler's) are both statistically rare (and according to this criterion abnormal) but the former would be rated as much more desirable than the latter.

Again, there are certain types of behaviour and experience which are so common as to be normal in the statistical sense but which are regarded as constituting psychological disorders, such as anxiety and depression. So the statistical criterion would seem to be neither necessary nor sufficient as a way of defining abnormality.

● Deviation from the norm criterion

If the statistical criterion is insufficient, it is because it is essentially neutral, i.e. deviation from the average is neither good nor bad, desirable nor undesirable. Deviation from the norm, however, implies not behaving or feeling as one should: 'norm' has an 'oughtness' about it whereby particular behaviours are expected from us at particular times and in particular situations and if those expectations are not met or are positively 'transgressed', we and/or our behaviour, may be judged 'bad' or 'sick'.

For example, as far as many people are concerned, homosexuality is abnormal not because it is statistically less common than heterosexuality but because the 'normal' or 'natural' form of sexual behaviour in human beings is heterosexual. From a religious or moral perspective, homosexuality might be judged as 'bad', 'wicked', 'sinful', etc. (implying, perhaps, the element of choice) while from a more biological or scientific perspective, it might be labelled 'sick', 'perverse', 'deviant', etc. (implying perhaps lack of choice

and responsibility). Either way, even if it was found that a majority of men and women engaged in homosexual relationships (making heterosexuality abnormal according to the statistical criterion), this would still be considered a deviation from the norm and, therefore, abnormal. (This point is discussed further in relation to the next criterion of mental health.) There is a further implication, which is that what is 'normal' is also 'desirable'; unlike the statistical criterion, deviation from the norm does not allow for deviations which are also desirable.

Within the same culture or society, a particular instance of behaviour may be considered normal or abnormal depending on the situation or context. For example, taking your clothes off is fine if you are about to step into a bath but not in the middle of a supermarket and what determines judgements of normality/abnormality are the norms (expectations) associated with those situations. However, situational norms are not the only ones used to judge behaviour: *developmental* norms dictate that, for instance, temper tantrums are perfectly normal in a two-year-old regardless of where they occur, but decidedly abnormal in a 32-year-old (even in the privacy of their own home).

Yet it is often far from obvious what norms are being broken when someone displays mental disorder: there is no law against being schizophrenic or having a panic attack, or being depressed, nor is it obvious what moral law or ethical principle is being broken in such cases. The kind of rule-breaking involved is discussed below in relation to the concept of mental illness.

● The adequacy or mental health criterion

One way of 'fleshing out' the notion of desirability is to identify characteristics and abilities which people should possess for them to be considered normal; by implication, any lack or impoverishment of these characteristics and abilities constitutes abnormality or disorder.

Jahoda (1958) identified several ways in which mental health has been (or might be) defined, including:

● the absence of mental illness (clearly, a very negative definition);
● being able to introspect about ourselves, being aware of what we are doing and why;
● growth, development and self-actualization (as emphasized by Rogers and Maslow; see Chapters 5 and 29);

- integration of all the processes and attributes of the individual (e.g. balance between the id, ego and superego in Freud's theory and the achievement of ego identity in Erikson's theory; see Chapters 21 and 24);
- the ability to cope with stress (see Chapter 6);
- autonomy (a concept which appears in many theories; e.g. Maslow and Erikson);
- seeing the world as it really is (part of Erikson's concept of ego identity);
- environmental mastery – the ability to love, work and play, to be satisfactory in our interpersonal relationships and to have the capacity for adaptation and adjustment (Erikson's ego identity again, Adler's belief in the need for an adjustment in the areas of love, work and society and Freud's *lieben und arbeiten* – love and work).

While many or all these criteria of mental health may seem valid and are intuitively appealing, their claim to be universal and absolute raises three serious problems:

1 According to these criteria, most of us would be considered maladjusted or disordered; for example,

Maslow himself argues that most of us do not achieve self-actualization and so there is a fundamental discrepancy between these criteria and the statistical criterion (Mackay, 1975).

2 Although many psychologists would accept these criteria, they are essentially *value judgements*, reflecting what is considered to be an ideal state of being human. By contrast, there is little dispute as to the precise nature of physical health. According to Szasz (1960), 'The norm is the structural and functional integrity of the human body' and if there are no abnormalities present, the person is considered to be in good health. Judgements about physical health do not involve making moral or philosophical decisions, 'What health is can be stated in anatomical and physical terms' (Szasz, 1960) and ideal and statistical criteria tend to be roughly equivalent (Mackay, 1975).

3 It follows from 2 that what is considered to be psychologically normal (and, hence, abnormal) depends upon the society and culture in which a person lives; psychological normality and abnormality are culturally defined (unlike physical

---

BOX 30.1 | **Critical discussion: homosexuality – shifting definitions of abnormality**

DSM-II (the second edition of the American Psychiatric Association's (APA) official classification of mental disorders, published in 1968) included homosexuality as a sexual deviation. In 1973, the APA Nomenclature Committee, under pressure from many professionals and gay activist groups, recommended to the general membership that the category should be removed and replaced with *sexual orientation disturbance*. This was to be applied to gay men and women who are 'disturbed by, in conflict with, or wish to change their sexual orientation'. The change was approved but not without fierce protests from several eminent psychiatrists who maintained the 'orthodox' view that homosexuality is inherently abnormal.

When *DSM-III* was published in 1980, another new term, *ego-dystonic homosexuality* (EDH) was used to refer to someone who is homosexually aroused, finds this arousal to be a persistent source of distress and wishes to become heterosexual. Since homosexuality itself was no longer a mental disorder, there was no inclusion in *DSM-III* of predisposing factors (as there was for all disorders), but they were included for EDH, namely, the individual homosexual's internalization of society's negative attitudes (homophobia – fear of

homosexuals – and heterosexism – anti-homosexual prejudice and discrimination). So, according to *DSM-III*, a homosexual is abnormal if he or she has been persuaded by society's prejudices that homosexuality is inherently abnormal, but at the same time it denied that homosexuality in itself abnormal! (Davison and Neale, 1994).

For whatever reasons, very little use was made of the EDH category; less surprisingly, no such category as 'ego-dystonic heterosexuality' has ever been used (Kitzinger, 1990). When *DSM-III* was revised (*DSM-III-R*, 1987), the APA decided to drop EDH. However, one of the many 'dustbin' categories, 'Sexual Disorder Not Otherwise Specified', includes 'persistent and marked distress about one's sexual orientation'; this has been retained in *DSM-IV* (1994). *ICD-10* (1992), the latest edition of the World Health Organization's classification of diseases, also includes 'ego-dystonic sexual orientation' under 'Disorders of adult personality and behaviour'.

In the UK up until the 1960s, homosexuality among consenting adults was illegal; in 1995 the age of consent was lowered to 18. Clearly, nothing has happened to homosexuality itself during the last 30 years or so; what has changed are attitudes towards it, which then became reflected in its official psychiatric and legal status. Homosexuality in itself is neither normal nor abnormal, desirable nor undesirable, and this can be extended to behaviour in general.

normality and abnormality which, Szasz believes, can be defined in universally applicable ways); see Box 30.1.

● Abnormality as personal distress

From the perspective of the individual, abnormality is the subjective experience of intense anxiety, unhappiness, depression or a whole host of other forms that personal distress/suffering can take. While this may often be the only indication that anything is wrong (and may not necessarily be obvious to others), it may be a sufficient reason for seeking professional help. As Miller and Morley (1986) say, 'People do not come to clinics because they feel they have met some abstract definition of abnormality. For the most part they come because their feelings or behaviour cause them distress'. However, the converse is also sometimes true: someone whose behaviour is obviously 'mad' as far as others are concerned may be oblivious of how others see them and may experience no subjective distress. This is sometimes referred to as lack of insight and is a feature of psychotic illness; see below.

● Abnormality as others' distress

If the person seen by others as behaving abnormally is the last to recognize that there is a problem, then others' concern may act as a counterbalance to their lack of insight. This suggests, as with all behaviour, that abnormality is interpersonal and not simply intrapersonal/intrapsychic, i.e. it takes place between people, in social situations, and is not merely a reflection of an individual actor's personal qualities or characteristics.

From a practical and ethical perspective, this is a double-edged sword: others' distress may be both a 'blessing' (literally a life-saver, as in the case of someone who is unaware of the self-destructive nature of their drug abuse) and a curse (such as when a parent is distressed about a son or daughter's homosexuality, with which they may feel perfectly comfortable). The former could be called *empathic concern*, where the 'helper' has an altruistic desire to reduce the other's distress, while in the latter, the helper's personal distress produces an *egoistic desire* to reduce their own distress (see Chapter 17). The question is, whose distress is the main focus of the attempt to intervene?

● Abnormality as maladaptiveness

When people's behaviour prevents them from pursuing and achieving their goals or does not contribute to their personal sense of well-being or prevents them from functioning as they would wish in their personal, sexual, social, intellectual and occupational life, it may be seen as abnormal for that reason. For example, drug abuse (or substance-related disorder) is defined mainly by how it produces social and occupational disability, such as poor work performance and serious marital arguments; a fear of flying might prevent someone from taking a job promotion (Davison and Neale, 1994). Although the emphasis here is on the consequences of the behaviour, such behaviours may be very distressing for the person concerned; for example, phobias, by their nature, are negative experiences because they involve intense fear, regardless of any practical effects brought about by the fear.

● Abnormality as unexpected behaviour

According to Davison and Neale (1994), it is abnormal to react to a situation or event in ways that could not be (reasonably) predicted, given what we know about human behaviour. For example, anxiety disorders are diagnosed when the anxiety is 'out of proportion to the situation'. The problem with this criterion is: Who makes the decision about what is 'in proportion'? Is it just another form of deviation from the average, whereby what is reasonable or acceptable is simply how most people would be expected to behave? By this definition, under-reacting is just as abnormal as over-reacting and yet only the latter is usually seen as a problem.

● Abnormality as highly consistent or inconsistent behaviour

If we have generalized expectations about people's typical reactions to particular kinds of situation, then a person's behaviour is predictable to the extent that we know about the situation. However, not all situations are equally powerful influences on behaviour and so cannot be used equally to predict a person's behaviour. It follows that it is normal for any individual's behaviour to be only partially predictable or consistent and, in turn, that it is abnormal for a person to display either extremely predictable or extremely unpredictable behaviour.

If someone acts so consistently that they seem to be unaffected by the situation, including the other people involved, it is almost as if we are dealing with a machine rather than a person. For example, someone suffering from paranoid delusions may see the world entirely in terms of others' harmful intentions towards them; this may, in turn, elicit certain kinds of responses in others, which may reinforce the delusions. According to Smith *et al.* (1986), people with behaviour disorders are unable to modify their behaviour in response to changing environmental requirements; their behaviour is maladaptive because it is inflexible and unrealistic. Equally, someone whose behaviour is very unpredictable is very difficult to interact with; people with schizophrenia are often perceived as embodying this kind of unpredictability, which is unnerving and unsettling. In both these extreme cases, the assessment being made is as much a reflection of the perceiver making the judgement as it is of the person whose behaviour is being judged: as we saw in Chapter 29, many psychologists believe that behaviour is always the product of an interaction between the actor's personal qualities and the situation (including other people).

● Abnormality as mental illness

Many writers (e.g. Maher, 1966) have pointed out that the vocabulary we use to refer to psychological disorder is borrowed from medical terminology: deviant behaviour is referred to as psychopathology, is classified on the basis of symptoms, the classification being called a diagnosis, the methods used to try to change the behaviour are called therapies and these are often carried out in mental or psychiatric hospitals. If the deviant behaviour ceases, the patient is described as cured.

This way of talking about psychological abnormality reflects the pervasiveness of a 'sickness' model, the *medical model* (together with terms such as 'syndrome', 'prognosis', 'in remission' and so on); i.e. whether we realize it or not, when we think about abnormal behaviour we think about it as if it were indicative of some underlying illness.

How valid is the medical model and does mental illness exist?

Many defenders of the medical model have argued that it is more humane to regard a psychologically disturbed person as sick (or mad) than plain bad, i.e. it is more stigmatizing to be regarded as morally defective (Blaney, 1975). However, when we label someone as sick or ill we are removing all responsibility from them for their behaviour; just as we do not normally hold someone responsible for having cancer or a broken leg, so 'mental illness' implies that something has happened to the person who is a victim and who is, accordingly, put in the care (and often the

custody) of doctors and nurses who will take over responsibility. (The attribution of blame and responsibility is relevant to understanding why certain types of victim are more or less likely to be helped; see Chapter 17).

It could be argued that the stigma attached to mental illness is actually greater than that attached to labels of 'bad' because our fear of mental illness is even greater than our fear of becoming involved in crime or other immoral activities, based on our belief that the former is something that 'happens to people' (i.e. we have no control over it) while the latter is chosen in some way.

While it may be considered more humanitarian to care for people in hospitals than to torture them for witchcraft, exorcize their evil spirits or lock them up in prisons, there is a sense in which these past practices were more honest than some of the current abuses of psychiatry. When people were imprisoned, society was saying quite unambiguously 'We do not approve of your behaviour and will not tolerate it', making its values clear but also not removing responsibility from the person whose behaviour was being condemned. However, when (until recently) Soviet political dissidents were diagnosed as suffering from schizophrenia (the most 'serious' form of mental illness), society was saying 'No one in their right mind could hold the views you express, so you must be out of your mind', thereby by-passing the actual issues raised by the dissident's beliefs and removing responsibility for those beliefs from the 'patient'.

As we have seen in discussing the criteria of normality and abnormality, defining psychological health is much more problematic than defining physical health; not only do norms differ between cultures but they change within the same culture over time (see Box 30.1) and, for this reason, Heather (1976) believes that the criteria used by psychiatry to judge abnormality must be seen in a moral context, not a medical one. The fact of cultural relativity, he argues, makes psychiatry an entirely different kind of enterprise from legitimate medicine: psychiatry's claim to be an orthodox part of medical science rests upon the concept of mental illness, but far from being another medical speciality, psychiatry is a 'quasi-medical illusion' (Heather, 1976).

Similarly, in trying to describe the norms from which the mentally ill are thought to deviate, Szasz (1962) found that they have to be stated in psychological, ethical and legal terms, and yet the remedy is sought in terms of medical measures. For this reason, Szasz believes that the concept of mental illness has replaced beliefs in demonology and witchcraft ('Mental illness thus exists or is "real" in exactly the same sense in which witches existed or were real' (Szasz, 1962)) and serves the same political purposes. What might these be? In *Ideology and Insanity* (1974), Szasz argues that whenever people wish to exclude others from their midst, they attach to them stigmatizing labels (e.g. 'foreigner', 'criminal', 'mentally ill'). Unlike people suffering from physical illness, most people considered to be mentally ill (especially those 'certified' or 'sectioned' and so legally mentally ill) are so defined by others (relatives, friends, employers, police, etc.), not by themselves. They have upset the social order (by violating or ignoring social laws and conventions) and so society labels them as mentally ill and (in many cases) punishes them by commitment to a mental hospital.

However, punishment is the last thing that psychiatrists would admit to giving their patients. As doctors, they must believe that what they give is help, care, treatment, etc., which are all in the patient's best interest. Patients soon learn that until they change their behaviour (in the way required by the hospital) they will remain segregated from society. However, even if this happens and the patient is 'let out', their 'record' goes with them (much like a criminal record); stigmatizing labels become very firmly attached! (see Box 30.3).

Underlying the labelling process, according to Szasz, is the need to predict other people's behaviour: people who are labelled 'mentally ill' are far less easy to predict and others find this disturbing. Attaching a diagnostic label represents a *symbolic recapture* and this may be followed by a physical capture (hospitalization, drugs, etc.). (Laing also observes that it is usually others who are disturbed by the patient's behaviour, rarely the patient.) While medical diagnosis usually focuses only on the damaged or diseased parts of the body (e.g. someone has a broken leg or lung cancer), psychiatric diagnosis describes the whole person – someone does not have schizophrenia but is *schizophrenic.* This represents a new and total identity, which describes not only the person but also how they should be regarded and treated by others; psychiatric diagnosis, therefore, is a form of action. (We should note here that *DSM-IV* explicitly rejects the use of labels such as 'schizophrenia'; instead, it recommends 'an individual with schizophrenia'.)

But in what ways are schizophrenics unpredictable and what kinds of rules are they breaking? According to Scheff (1966), they are breaking *residual rules*, the 'unnameable' expectations we have regarding such things as 'decency' and 'reality'.

Because these rules are themselves implicit, taken for granted and not articulated, behaviour that violates them is not easily understood and is also difficult to articulate; hence, it is found strange and frightening. According to Becker (1963), psychiatric intervention is based, generally speaking, on middle-class values regarding decent, reasonable, proper behaviour and experience; these are applied to working-class patients, who constitute the vast majority of the inmates of psychiatric hospitals.

Szasz is probably the most radical critic of the concept of mental illness. In books such as *The Myth of Mental Illness* (1962), he argues that the basic assumption made by psychiatrists is that 'mental illness' is caused by diseases or disorders of the nervous system (in particular, the brain) which are revealed in abnormal thinking and behaviour. If this is the case, it would be better to call them 'diseases of the brain' or neurophysiological disorders; this would then get rid of the confusion between any physical, organic defect (which must be seen in an anatomical and physiological context) and any 'problems in living' the person may have (which must be seen in an ethical and social context).

The vast majority of cases of 'mental illness' are, according to Szasz, actually cases of problems of living and they should be referred to as such. It is the exception to the rule to find a 'mentally ill' person who is actually suffering from some organic brain disease (as in Alzheimer's disease, alcoholic poisoning, etc.) and this fact is recognized by psychiatrists themselves when they distinguish between *organic psychosis* and *functional psychosis;* 'functional' means that there is no demonstrable physical basis for the abnormal behaviour and that something has gone wrong with the way the person functions in the network of relationships which make up their world (Bailey, 1979). However, organic psychiatrists believe that medical science will, in time, identify the physical causes of functional disorders (which include schizophrenia and psychotic depression); indeed, many claim that this point has already been reached (see below). Yet according to Heather (1976), even if such evidence were available, it would still leave major categories of mental disorder (in particular, neurosis and personality disorder) which even the organicists admit are not bodily diseases in any sense!

If it is not the brain which is diseased, we are left asking in what sense can we think of the mind as being diseased? For Szasz , it is only in a *metaphorical* sense that we can attribute disease to the mind; in a literal sense, it is logically impossible for a non-spatial, non-physical mind to be suffering from a disorder of a physicochemical nature (unless, of course, we identify the mind with the brain; see the discussion of reductionism in Chapter 32). It is important to make it clear that Szasz does not deny that the problem behaviours that mental health professionals see as indicative of mental illness are often strange, irritating and deviant; they may also be distressing for the person concerned, but they are not a symptom of underlying brain disease.

According to Bailey (1979), medicine began by classifying such things as syphilis and tuberculosis as illnesses, all sharing the common feature of reference to a state of disordered structure and/or functioning of the human body as a physicochemical machine; the mistake was to keep adding to this list additional items which are not illnesses in this sense. Agreeing with Szasz, Bailey maintains that: (i) organic mental illnesses are not mental illnesses at all but physical illnesses in which mental symptoms are manifested and which aid diagnosis and treatment; (ii) functional mental illnesses are not illnesses but disorders of psychosocial or interpersonal functioning (Szasz's 'problems in living') in which mental symptoms are important in deciding the type of therapy the patient requires.

An important difference between diagnosis in general medicine and psychiatry is to do with the role of signs and symptoms. While a doctor looks for *signs* of disease (i.e. the results of objective tests, such as blood tests and X-rays, as well as physical examination) and *symptoms* (the patient's report of pain, etc.), they tend to attach more weight to the former when forming a diagnosis. (This has implications for classification; see later.) By contrast, the psychiatrist is much more at the mercy of symptoms; although psychological tests are the psychiatric equivalent of blood tests and X-rays, they are nothing like as reliable and valid (see Chapters 28 and 29) and, in practice, the psychiatrist will rely to a large extent on the patient's own description of the problem.

However, observation of the patient's behaviour, talking to relatives and others about the patient's behaviour and, increasingly, the use of brain-scanning techniques such as CAT and PET (see below and Chapter 3) also contribute data regarding the signs of the illness, especially in the case of serious disorders, such as schizophrenia. Nevertheless, the two major classification systems used by psychiatrists today, *DSM* and *ICD*, are based largely on the abnormal experiences and beliefs reported by patients, because we have no objective or biological markers for most neurotic or psychotic disorders (Frith and Cahill, 1995).

According to Lilienfeld (1995), during the late 1970s, the APA considered including a formal statement in *DSM-III* to the effect that mental disorders are a subset of medical diseases. While this proposal was eventually rejected, it sparked a storm of protests from psychologists, as well as many psychiatrists; the implication of the proposal was that the distinction between organic and functional disorders is invalid and that all disorders are organic. The controversy resurfaced in the mid 1980s and early 1990s over whether to include syndromes such as premenstrual dysphoric disorder (premenstrual syndrome), self-defeating personality disorder and sadistic personality disorder in *DSM-III-R* (1987) and *DSM-IV* (1994).

A major change that took place in *DSM-IV* from *DSM-III-R* was the removal of the category of 'Organic Mental Disorders' and its replacement with 'Delirium, Dementia, Amnestic and Other Cognitive Disorders' (see Table 30.1). According to Davison and Neale (1994), the thinking behind this change is that the term 'organic' implies that the other major categories do not have a biological basis; since research has shown the influence of biological factors through a whole range of disorders, it is now considered misleading to use the term 'organic'. To this extent, the concept of psychological abnormality is even more medicalized than it has ever been. However, we should note that ICD retains a separate category for organic disorders.

THE CLASSIFICATION OF MENTAL DISORDERS

An integral part of the medical model is the classification of mental disorder and the related process of *diagnosis*. All systems of classification stem from the work of Emil Kraepelin, who published the first recognized textbook of psychiatry in 1883. Kraepelin claimed that certain groups of symptoms occur together sufficiently often for them to be called a 'disease' or syndrome; i.e. there is an underlying physical cause, just as a physical disease may be attributed to a physiological dysfunction (Davison and Neale, 1994). He regarded each mental illness as distinct from all others, with its own origins, symptoms, course and outcome; even though cures had not been found, at least the course of the disease could be predicted.

DSM-IV	ICD-10
1 Delirium, dementia, amnestic and other cognitive disorders	1 Organic, including symptomatic, mental disorders
2 Schizophrenic and other psychotic disorders	2 Schizophrenia, schizotypal and delusional disorders
3 Substance related disorders	3 Mental and behavioural disorders due to psychoactive substance use
4 Mood disorders	4 Mood (affective) disorders
5 Anxiety disorders	5 Neurotic, stress-related and somatoform disorders
6 Somatoform disorders	
7 Dissociative disorders	
8 Adjustment disorders	
9 Disorders usually first diagnosed in infancy, childhood or adolescence (including mental retardation – Axis II)*	6 Behavioural and emotional disorders with onset usually occurring in childhood and adolescence
	7 Disorders of psychological development
	8 Mental retardation
10 Personality disorders (Axis II)*	9 Disorders of adult personality and behaviour
11 Sexual and gender identity disorders	
12 Impulse control disorders not elsewhere classified	
13 Factitious disorders	
14 Sleep disorders	10 Behavioural syndromes associated with physiological disturbances and physical factors
15 Eating disorders	
16 Other conditions that may be a focus of clinical attention	11 Unspecified mental disorder

* See Table 30.3

TABLE 30.1 *The major categories of mental disorder as identified by DSM-IV and ICD-10*

Kraepelin (1896) proposed two major groups of serious mental diseases: *dementia praecox,* the original term for schizophrenia (caused by a chemical imbalance), and *manic-depressive psychosis* (caused by a faulty metabolism). His classification helped to establish the organic nature of mental disorders, as well as forming the basis for the *Diagnostic and Statistical Manual of Mental Disorders (DSM),* which, as we have seen, is the APA's official classification system, and the *International Classification of Diseases (ICD)* (Chapter 5: Mental and Behavioural Disorders) published by the World Health Organization.

DSM-I was published in 1952, *DSM-II* in 1968, followed by *DSM-III* (1980), *DSM-III-R* (1987) and *DSM-IV* (1994). Mental disorders were included in *ICD* for the first time in 1948 (*ICD-6*) and *ICD-10* was published in 1992. Table 30.1 shows the major categories of both *ICD-10* and *DSM-IV*; Table 30.2 shows ten major categories, with examples of specific disorders based on both classification schemes.

Kraepelin's classification is also embodied in the 1983 Mental Health Act (in England and Wales); the Act identifies three major categories of mental disturbance/disorder, namely, mental illness (neurosis and psychosis, the latter subdivided into organic and functional), personality disorder (including psychopathy) and mental impairment. (We shall discuss the important distinction between neurosis and psychosis below.)

Organic mental disorders Delirium. Dementia due to: Alzheimer's disease; Creutzfeld-Jakob disease (human version of BSE- 'mad cow disease'); HIV; Huntington's chorea; Parkinson's disease. Brain infections. Brain tumours. Brain damage.

Schizophrenia and related psychotic disorders Schizophrenia: paranoid;hebephrenic (disorganized); catatonic; simple; undifferentiated. Schizotypal disorder. Delusional disorder (paranoia). Schizophreniform disorder. Schizoaffective disorder. Brief reactive psychosis.

Psychoactive substance use disorders Intoxication,harmful use/abuse, dependence, withdrawal state re : alcohol; amphetamines; caffeine (and other stimulants);cannabis (cannabinoids); cocaine; hallucinogens; inhalants/volatile solvents; tobacco (nicotine); opioids; sedatives/hypnotics/anxiolytics; phencyclidine.

Mood (Affective) disorders Depressive disorder (unipolar); manic disorder (bipolar 1); bipolar (2) disorders; mood disorder with seasonal pattern (seasonal affective disorder/SAD); mood disorder with post-partum onset (post-natal depression); pre-menstrual dysphoric disorder (pre-menstrual disorder/PMD); dysthymic disorder; cyclothymic disorder.

Neurotic disorders Anxiety disorders. Phobic anxiety disorders. Obsessive-compulsive disorders. Panic disorder. Dissociative disorders : dissociative amnesia (psychogenic amnesia); dissociative fugue (psychogenic fugue); dissociative identity disorder (multiple personality disorder); depersonalization. Somatoform disorders. Hypochondriasis. Post-traumatic stress disorder.

Disorders of infancy, childhood and adolescence Autistic disorder. Attention-deficit/disruptive behaviour disorders : hyperkinetic disorder; conduct disorder. Separation anxiety disorder. Elective mutism. Tic disorders (e.g. Tourette's disorder). Enuresis. Encopresis. Stuttering. Disorders of speech and language. Specific developmental disorders of scholastic skills. Learning disorders.

Mental retardation Mild/Moderate/Severe/ Profound. Associated with : genetic (e.g. chromosome) abnormalities; gross disease of the brain; Ante-natal damage; perinatal damage; post-natal damage; Malnutrition.

Personality disorders (disorders of adult personality) Antisocial (psychopathic). Paranoid. Schizoid (schizotypal). Anxious/avoidant. Dependent. Obsessive-compulsive. Emotionally unstable. Histrionic. Narcissistic. Pathological gambling. Pyromania. Kleptomania.Trichotillomania. Factitious disorder.

Eating and sleeping disorders Anorexia nervosa. Bulimia nervosa. Insomnia. Hypersomnia. Sleepwalking (somnambulism). Sleep (night) terrors.

Sexual and gender identity disorders Sexual desire disorders. Sexual arousal disorders. Paraphilias : exhibitionism; fetishism; voyeurism; paedophilia; frotteurism; transvestism; sexual sadism; sexual masochism. Transsexualism.

TABLE 30.2 *Major categories of mental disorder, with specific examples, based on DSM-IV and ICD-10*

● Comparison between DSM-IV and ICD-10

Broad similarities and differences between DSM-IV and ICD-10

Table 30.1 shows how the two systems overlap. One of the major differences between them is the number of major categories; most differences arise because *DSM-IV* uses a larger number of discrete categories to classify disorders that appear under a smaller number of more general categories in *ICD-10*. Two such differences are shown in Figure 30.1. However, this is also reversed in one instance, as shown in Figure 30.2.

Neither system uses the term 'mental illness'; instead, they use the term *mental disorder*, which is defined by *DSM-IV* as:

A clinically significant behaviour or psychological syndrome or pattern that occurs in a person and that is associated with present distress (a painful symptom) or disability (impairment of one or more important areas of functioning) or with a significantly increased risk of suffering death, pain, disability, or an important loss of freedom. In addition, this syndrome or pattern must not be merely an expectable response to a particular event, for example, the death of a loved one. (APA, 1994)

and is used by *ICD-10*:

... to imply the existence of a clinically recognizable set of symptoms or behaviour associated in most cases with distress and with interference with personal functions.. (WHO, 1992)

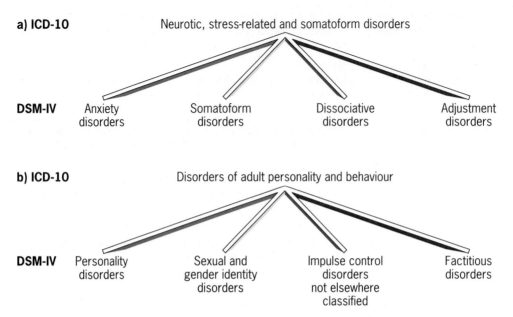

FIGURE 30.1 *Two examples of how a general ICD-10 category incorporates three or more DSM-IV categories*

While we noted earlier that *DSM-IV* has become more organic in its approach, Cooper (1994) argues that only a few psychiatric diagnoses are associated with disturbed anatomy or physiology. Use of the term 'disorder' avoids the need to debate the meaning or value of 'disease' or 'illness'.

Multi-axial classification

One of the major changes which was made in *DSM-III* (1980) compared with *DSM-II* (1968) was the introduction of a multi-axial system of classification. Whereas *DSM-II* required only a simple diagnostic label (e.g. 'schizophrenia' or 'anxiety neurosis'), *DSM-III* (and, similarly, *DSM-III-R* and *DSM-IV*) instructed the psychiatrist to evaluate the patient on

five different *axes*, which represent different areas of functioning; these are shown in Table 30.3. The inclusion of the axes reflects the assumption that most disorders are caused by the interaction of biological, psychological and sociological factors. Instead of simply placing someone in a single clinical category (e.g. schizophrenia), the patient is assessed much more broadly, giving a more global and in-depth picture. However, while axes 1–3 are compulsory, 4 and 5 are optional. An important change made in DSM-IV compared with DSM-III-R was the 'return' of most developmental disorders to Axis I, with the exception of Mental Retardation.

According to Cooper (1994), it is often assumed that *ICD-10* has only a single axis. However, although

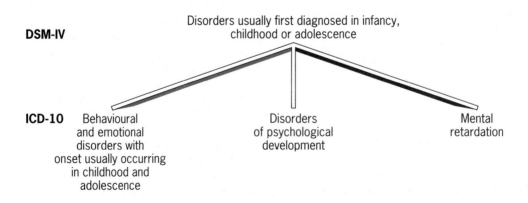

FIGURE 30.2 *An example of how a general DSM-IV category incorporates three ICD-10 categories*

Axis I: Clinical Disorders (diagnostic category); Other Conditions That May Be a Focus of Clinical Attention	This lists all mental disorders and the criteria for rating them, except personality disorders and mental retardation. 'Other Conditions' may include problems related to abuse or neglect, academic problems and 'phase of life' problems.
Axis II: Personality Disorders;w Mental Retardation	These life-long, deeply ingrained, inflexible and maladaptive traits and behaviours may occur quite independently of Axis I clinical disorders.
Axis III: General Medical Conditions	Any medical problem that could affect the patient's mental state. How might heart disease/diabetes/cancer affect mood and cognitive abilities, as well as response to treatment?
Axis IV: Psychosocial and Environmental Problems	Stressful events which have occurred within a year of the current problem (e.g. divorce, death of parent or spouse), which could be a contributory factor and/or which might influence the course of treatment. Rated on a scale of 1–7 (non–catastrophic).
Axis V: Global Assessment of Functioning	How well has the patient performed, during the last year, in social relationships, in leisure time and at work? On the Global Assessment of Functioning Scale, 0 denotes 'persistent danger' and 100 denotes 'superior functioning'.

TABLE 30.3 *The five axes of DSM-IV*

it does not have separate axes in the way that DSM has (as in Table 30.3), built into the groupings of the disorders are broad types of aetiology (causal factors), such as organic causes, substance use and stress. When ICD-10 was being constructed, it was agreed that, because of the incomplete and often controversial state of knowledge about the *aetiology* of most psychiatric disorders, the classification would be, as far as possible, worked out on a *descriptive* basis. This implies, strictly, that disorders should be grouped according to similarities and differences of symptoms and signs, so that a particular disorder should only occur in one place. But it soon became clear that this would not appeal to clinicians, who like to be able to give prominence to aetiology wherever possible; hence, the inclusion of the broad types of aetiology within the categories. Although this makes ICD-10 impure from a taxonomic (classificatory) point of view, it is much more likely to be used by clinicians (Cooper, 1994). In DSM-IV, assumptions about causation are not used in making a diagnosis, i.e. it is *a-theoretical* (see section on Neurosis and Psychosis below).

Neurosis and psychosis

Both systems have dropped the traditional distinction between *neurosis* and *psychosis*, although ICD-10 retains the term 'neurotic' and DSM-IV retains the term 'psychotic'. According to Gelder *et al.* (1989), there are four major reasons for getting rid of the distinction:

1 there are exceptions to all the criteria used to distinguish them (Table 30.4);

2 disorders included under the broad categories of 'neurosis' or 'psychosis' have little in common;

3 it is less informative to classify a disorder as neurotic or psychotic than it is to classify it as a particular disorder within that very broad category (e.g. 'schizophrenic' is more informative than 'psychotic');

4 DSM-III wanted to remove the psychoanalytic influence in the way 'neurotic' was used and understood (based on Freud's theories). However, Gelder *et al.* say that in everyday psychiatric practice they are convenient terms for disorders which cannot be given a more precise diagnosis and also the terms are still in general use (as in 'antipsychotic drugs' and when referring to symptoms).

What Table 30.4 implies is that psychosis is a very much more serious form of mental disorder than neurosis. According to Frith and Cahill (1995), *psychosis* is the technical term for what the layperson calls madness. In contrast to the symptoms of neurosis, psychotic symptoms (in particular delusions, hallucinations, passivity experiences and thought disorder) are categorically outside the normal realm of experience and, as such, are outside our commonsense powers of understanding and empathy. It is these aspects of psychotic symptoms that isolate the person having them in 'a world of their own'. Schizophrenia is by far the commonest of the psychoses: the lifetime risk of having a schizophrenic breakdown is 0.5–2

Neurosis	Psychosis
Only a part of the personality is involved/affected.	The whole personality is involved/affected.
Contact with reality is maintained.	Contact with reality is lost: hallucinations and delusions represent the inability to distinguish between subjective experience and external reality.
The neurotic has insight (i.e. recognizes that they have a problem).	The psychotic lacks insight.
Neurotic symptoms/behaviour can be seen as an exaggeration of 'normal' symptoms/behaviour (i.e. there is only a quantitative difference).	Neurotic symptoms/behaviour are discontinuous with 'normal' symptoms/behaviour (i.e. there is a qualitative difference).
Often begins as a response to a stressor.	There is usually no precipitating cause.
The neurotic disturbance is related to the patient's personality prior to their 'illness' (the premorbid personality).	The psychotic disturbance is not related to the premorbid personality.
Treated mainly by psychological methods.	Treated mainly by physical methods (especially early on).

TABLE 30.4 *The major criteria for making the traditional distinction between neurosis and psychosis*

percent, compared with 0.6–1.1 percent for affective psychosis, and, despite powerful drugs, about two-thirds of schizophrenics suffer recurring episodes. Delusions are by far the commonest of the psychotic symptoms; according to Jasper (1962, quoted in Frith and Cahill, 1995), 'Since time immemorial, delusion has been taken as the basic characteristic of madness. To be mad was to be deluded'.

The use of diagnostic criteria

The idea of specifying diagnostic criteria for research purposes is not new (e.g. Cooper, 1967; Feighner *et al.*, 1972; Spitzer *et al.*, 1978), but their use in comprehensive classification systems is more recent. Both DSM and ICD have introduced explicit operational criteria for diagnosis (based on Spitzer *et al.*'s (1978) *Research Diagnostic Criteria*). For each disorder, there is a specified list of symptoms, all or some of which must be present, for a specified period of time, in relation to age and gender, stipulation as to what other diagnoses must be present and the personal and social consequences of the disorder. The aim is to make diagnosis more reliable and more valid (see below) by laying down rules for the inclusion or exclusion of cases.

The policy of the WHO has been to provide 'clinical guidelines' for general psychiatric use (1992) and a separate but compatible set of diagnostic criteria for research purposes (1993). Cooper (1994) asks whether the social consequences should be included among the defining features of a disorder itself, especially within an internationally used system such as

ICD, since the social environment of individuals varies so widely between cultures: ' ... The same symptoms and behaviour that are tolerated in one culture may cause severe social problems in another culture, and it is clearly undesirable for diagnostic decisions to be determined by cultural and social definitions'.

What Cooper seems to be saying is that definitions of normality/abnormality are *culturally relative* (see the earlier discussion of the deviation from the norm criterion), but he is at the same time implying that it is possible to diagnose mental disorders independently of cultural norms, values and worldviews. This raises the fundamental question as to whether mental disorders exist in some objective sense; just as modern medicine is based on the assumption that physical illness is the same throughout the world and that definition, classification, causation and diagnosis are largely unaffected by cultural factors, so biologically orientated psychiatrists argue that organic psychoses, in particular schizophrenia and depression, are also 'culture free' (see Box 30.2).

PROBLEMS WITH THE CLASSIFICATION OF MENTAL DISORDER

One of the most famous studies criticizing basic psychiatric concepts and practices is that of Rosenhan (1973), which is described in Box 30.3.

| BOX 30.2 | Critical discussion: is schizophrenia culture free? |

During the 1970s and 1980s, psychiatrists and clinical psychologists became increasingly interested in 'cultural psychiatry'. The central issue in the cross-cultural study of mental disorder is whether phenomena such as schizophrenia are (i) absolute (found in all cultures in precisely the same form); (ii) universal (present in some form in all cultures, but subject to cultural influence); (iii) culturally relative (unique to particular cultures and understandable only in terms of those cultures) (Berry *et al.*, 1992).

Of these three possibilities, only (i) corresponds to a 'culture-free' view of abnormality; Berry *et al.* reject this view of abnormality, on the grounds that ' ... cultural factors appear to affect at least some aspects of mental disorders, even those that are so closely linked to human biology'. Universality is a more likely candidate for capturing the objective (biological) nature of mental disorder; schizophrenia is the most commonly diagnosed mental disorder in the world and of the major disorders, the largest number of culture-general symptoms has been reported for schizophrenia (WHO, 1973, 1979; Draguns, 1980, 1990).

However, according to Brislin (1993), there are at least three possible ways in which culture-specific factors can influence schizophrenia: (a) the form that symptoms will take, (b) the specific reasons for the onset of the illness, and (c) the prognosis.

When schizophrenics complain that their minds are being invaded by unseen forces, in North America and Europe these forces keep up to date with technological developments. So, in the 1920s, these were often voices from the radio, in the 1950s, they often came from the television, in the 1960s it was satellites in space and in the 1970s and 1980s spirits were transmitted through microwave ovens. In cultures where witchcraft is considered common, the voices or spirits would be directed by unseen forces under the control of demons.

Day *et al.* (1987, cited in Brislin, 1993) studied schizophrenia in nine different locations in the USA, Asia, Europe and South America. Acute schizophrenic attacks were associated with stressful events 'external' to the patients (such as losing one's job, unexpected death of spouse), which tended to cluster within a 2–3-week period before the onset of obvious symptoms. Some events could only be understood as stressful if the researchers had considerable information about the cultural background of the sample.

Lin and Kleinman (1988, cited in Brislin, 1993) found that the prognosis for successful treatment of schizophrenia was better in non-industrialized than industrialized societies. The former provide more structured, stable, predictable and socially supportive environments that allow schizophrenic patients to recover at their own pace and to be reintegrated into society.

Finally, a large number of studies have found that, in a wide range of non-Western cultures, there are apparently unique ways of 'being mad' (Berry *et al.*, 1992), i.e. there are forms of abnormality that are not easily accommodated by the categories of ICD or DSM. These *culture-bound syndromes* (CBSs) or 'exotic' disorders are first described in, and then closely or exclusively associated with, a particular population or cultural area, with the local, indigenous name being used. For example, *Koro, jinjin bemar, suk yeong, suoyang* refers to an acute panic/anxiety reaction in which men become convinced that the penis will suddenly withdraw into the abdomen and women sense that their breasts, labia or vulva will retract into their bodies. This is reported in southeast Asia, south China and India (Finerman, 1994). These disorders are 'outside' the mainstream of abnormality as defined by, and 'enshrined' within, the classification systems of Western psychiatry, which determines the standard; the underlying assumption is that mental disorders in the West are culturally neutral, i.e. they can be defined and diagnosed objectively (while only CBSs show the influence of culture) (Fernando, 1991).

Rosenhan's study was intended to test the hypothesis that psychiatrists cannot reliably tell the difference between people who are genuinely mentally ill and those who are not. Since reliability is a necessary prerequisite for validity (see Chapter 28), the implications of Rosenhan's results for the traditional psychiatric classification of mental disorders are very serious indeed.

● Reliability

Diagnosis is the process of identifying a disease and allocating it to a category on the basis of symptoms and signs. Clearly, any system of classification will be of little value unless psychiatrists can agree with one another when trying to reach a diagnosis (Gelder *et al.*, 1989); this is *inter-rater/inter-judge reliability* and represents a fundamental requirement of any classification system.

Early studies consistently showed poor diagnostic reliability: psychiatrists varied widely in the amount of information they elicit at interview and in their interpretation of that information and variations were found between groups of psychiatrists trained in different countries. For example, the US–UK Diagnostic Project (Cooper *et al.*, 1972) showed

| BOX 30.3 | On being sane in insane places (Rosenhan, 1973) |

Eight psychiatrically 'normal' people (a psychology student, three psychologists, a paediatrician, a psychiatrist, a painter–decorator and a housewife) presented themselves at the admissions offices of 12 different psychiatric hospitals in the USA, complaining of hearing voices saying 'empty', 'hollow' and 'thud' (auditory hallucinations). These symptoms, together with their name and occupation, were the only falsification of the truth that was involved at any stage of the study.

All eight pseudo-patients were admitted (in 11 cases with a diagnosis of 'schizophrenia', in the other 'manic depression') and once this had occurred, they stopped claiming to hear voices; they were eventually discharged with a diagnosis of 'schizophrenia (or manic depression) in remission' (i.e. without signs of illness). The only people to have been suspicious of their true identity were some of their 'fellow' patients. It took between seven and 52 days (average 19) for them to convince the staff that they were well enough to be discharged.

In a second experiment, members of a teaching hospital were told about the findings of the original study and were warned that some pseudo-patients would be trying to gain admission during a particular three-month period. Each member of staff was asked to rate every new patient as an impostor or not. During the experimental period, 193 patients were admitted, of whom 41 were confidently alleged to be impostors by at least one member of staff, 23 were suspected by one psychiatrist and a further 19 were suspected by one psychiatrist and one other staff member. All were genuine patients.

American and British psychiatrists the same video-taped clinical interviews and asked them to make a diagnosis. New York psychiatrists diagnosed schizophrenia twice as often, while the London psychiatrists diagnosed mania and depression twice as often. (This led some wit to recommend that American schizophrenics should cross the Atlantic for a cure – presumably, the same advice should be given to British manic-depressives! However, New York was thought not to be typical of North America.)

The International Pilot Study of Schizophrenia (WHO, 1973) compared psychiatrists in nine countries – Columbia, the former Czechoslovakia, Denmark, England, India, Nigeria, Taiwan, USA and the former USSR – and found substantial agreement between seven of them, the exceptions being the USA and the USSR which both seemed to have unusually broad concepts of schizophrenia (thus confirming, after all, the Cooper *et al.* results).

Agreement between psychiatrists can be improved if they are trained to use standardized interview schedules, such as the Present State Examination (PSE; Wing *et al.*, 1974) and Endicott and Spitzer's (1978) Schedule of Affective Disorders and Schizophrenia (SADS). These are intended to: (i) specify sets of symptoms which must be enquired about; and (ii) define the symptoms precisely and give instructions on rating their severity. As we noted earlier, both DSM and ICD use explicit operational criteria (based on the Research Diagnostic Criteria, Spitzer *et al.*, 1978; Williams and Spitzer, 1982) in making a diagnosis, so that diagnosis may be more objective and hence more reliable. These are basically rules for deciding whether a particular patient is to be included within a particular diagnostic category or excluded from it.

Despite the undoubted improvements in reliability since the publication of DSM-III (1980), aided by the use of 'decision trees' and computer programs that lead the psychiatrist through the tree (Holmes, 1994), problems remain. For example, specifying a particular number of symptoms from a longer list that must be evident before a particular diagnosis can be made (see Table 30.5.) seems very arbitrary and the reliability of Axes 1 and 2 may not always be as high in everyday practice as they are when psychiatrists know that they are taking part in a formal reliability study (Davison and Neale, 1994). Also, there is still room for subjective interpretation on the part of the psychiatrist, as when the elevated mood must be 'abnormally and persistently elevated' when diagnosing mania and when assessment on Axis 5 requires comparison between the patient and an 'average person'. These examples beg all sorts of questions (Davison and Neale, 1994).

As far as ICD-10 is concerned, Okasha *et al.* (1993, cited in Costello *et al.*, 1995) found higher reliability compared with both ICD-9 and DSM-III-R and Sartorious *et al.* (1993) concluded that ICD-10 clinical guidelines were suitable for widespread international use and showed good reliability. ICD-10 is expected to remain in use for about 20 years (twice as long as its predecessors) (Costello *et al.*, 1995).

● Validity

This is much more difficult to assess than reliability, because for most disorders there is no absolute standard against which we can compare our diagnosis;

however much we improve reliability, this is no guarantee that the patient has received the 'correct' diagnosis (Holmes, 1994).

The primary purpose of making a diagnosis is, surely, to enable a suitable programme of treatment to be chosen; treatment cannot be selected randomly but is aimed at eliminating the underlying cause of the disorder (where it is known). However, in psychiatry, as Heather (1976) argues, there is only a 50 percent chance of correctly predicting what treatment a patient will receive on the basis of diagnosis. Bannister *et al.* (1964) statistically analysed the relationship between diagnosis and treatment in 1000 cases and found that there simply was no clear-cut connection. One reason for this seems to be that factors other than diagnosis may be equally important in deciding on a particular treatment.

If the label applied to a patient does not allow the psychiatrist to make a judgement about the causes of the disorder or a prediction regarding prognosis and response to treatment, how can that diagnostic process be valid? According to Mackay (1975):

> The notion of illness implies a relatively discrete disease entity with associated signs and symptoms, which has a specific cause, a certain probability of recovery and its own treatments. The various states of unhappiness, anxiety and confusion which we term 'mental illness' fall far short of these criteria in most cases.

However, to put psychiatric diagnosis into perspective, we should compare it with medical diagnosis in general. In one survey, Falek and Moser (1975) found that agreement between doctors regarding angina, emphysema and tonsillitis (diagnosed without a definitive laboratory test) was no better (and sometimes actually worse) than that for schizophrenia. Clare (1980) argues that the nature of physical illness is not as clear-cut as the critics of the medical model claim; while agreeing with criticisms of psychiatric diagnosis, he believes they should be directed at psychiatrists and not the process of diagnosis in general.

Clare (1980) and Clarke (1975) agree that there is a false dichotomy between body and mind: physical suffering is never without psychological aspects and psychological suffering is often expressed physically. Clarke (1975) also argues that treatment does not always aspire to 'cure' the patient but often aims simply to alleviate the suffering. Knowledge of the cause does not always or necessarily determine treatment and disorders rarely have single causes; people are neither mindless bodies not bodyless minds, he says, and many organic illnesses require psychological treatment.

● Conclusions: to classify or not to classify?

According to Gelder *et al.* (1989), classifications are needed in psychiatry, as in medicine, in order that doctors and others can communicate easily about the nature of patients' problems and about prognosis and treatment and so that research can be conducted with comparable groups of patients. They believe that critics of psychiatric classification are usually psychotherapists who believe that: (i) allocating a patient to a diagnostic category detracts from understanding his/her unique personality difficulty and (ii) individual patients do not fit neatly into the available categories.

The critics seem to be saying that psychiatrists are using a nomothetic approach when an idiographic approach is more appropriate (see Chapter 29). Davison and Neale (1994) and Holmes (1994) agree that whenever we classify, we lose information about the uniqueness of the individual; this seems to be an inevitable consequence of emphasizing the similarities between people. What matters is whether the lost information is relevant which, in turn, depends on the purposes of the classification system (Davison and Neale, 1994).

For Gelder *et al.* (1989), psychiatric classification attempts to bring some order into the great diversity of phenomena encountered in clinical practice; its purpose is to identify groups of patients who share similar clinical features, so that suitable treatment can be planned and the likely outcome predicted. Also, the anti-classification arguments are only arguments against the improper use of classification (rather than classification per se): ' ... The use of classification can certainly be combined with consideration of a patient's unique qualities, indeed it is important to combine the two because these qualities can modify prognosis and need to be taken into account in treatment'. The multi-axial approach of DSM can be regarded as a way of providing a much more detailed and rounded picture of the patient than was ever possible prior to 1980.

As fundamental as the questions raised by Rosenhan's (1973) study might be, the study itself has been criticized, notably by Spitzer (1976). As a professor of law and psychology, Rosenhan should know that the terms 'sane' and 'insane' are legal, not psychiatric, concepts and that no psychiatrist makes a diagnosis of 'sanity' or 'insanity'. Perhaps more seriously, Spitzer notes that the diagnosis 'schizophrenia in remission' is extremely rare; in addition to his own New York hospital, he examined the records of discharged schizophrenic patients for 12 other US hospitals and found that in 11 cases, 'in remission' was either never used or used for only a handful of patients each year. Spitzer concluded from this that the psychiatrists involved successfully recognized that the pseudo-patients were not in fact genuine, which is why they were given a discharge label that is rarely used with most real schizophrenics.

Further, there is a serious problem in generalizing from these eight pseudo-patients to genuine psychiatric patients in general; as Spitzer argues, they are two different populations and if Rosenhan's pseudo-patients had tried to get themselves admitted once DSM-III (1980) had been introduced, they would almost certainly have failed. Finally, evidence regarding the unreliability of medical diagnosis, even when tests are used, does not mean that medical diagnosis is of no value; similarly, with psychiatric diagnosis (Spitzer, 1976).

SOME MAJOR MENTAL DISORDERS

● Phobic disorders

A phobia is defined as an extreme, irrational fear of some specific object or situation. Typically, the patient acknowledges that the object of fear is harmless but the fear is nevertheless experienced (this is the *irrational* element); trying to hide the phobia from others may induce further anxiety, guilt and shame. Trying to avoid the feared object or situation at all costs can interfere with the person's normal functioning and distinguishes a phobia from a milder fear or mere dislike of something.

Almost anything may become the object of a phobia but some phobias are much more common than others. The most common of all is *agoraphobia* (a collection of fears, centring on open spaces and travelling or leaving home unaccompanied; see below), accounting for about 60 percent of all phobic patients (and about six per 1000 of the general population). This is followed by *social phobias*, including fear of having to eat or drink in public, talking to members of the opposite sex or having to speak or write in front of others (8 percent), and *animal* phobias (*zoophobia*), with some much more common than others, e.g. snakes and spiders (3 percent) (Marks, 1970). (See Chapters 7 and 31 for a discussion of 'preparedness').

Marks (1970) conducted a ten-year retrospective study of outpatients seen at the Maudsley Hospital in London and found that phobic disorders represented 5 percent of all cases seen. According to Mitchell (1982), although some patients are terrified of being alone in wide open spaces (such as fields, deserted moorland and so on), what all agoraphobics share is a fear of being alone anywhere and they are probably suffering from a form of separation anxiety, fearing that something unpleasant will happen to them because there is no one there who could come to their assistance (see Chapter 24). The *primary* fear is leaving the safety and security of home and/or companions; fear of being in public places (shops, on buses, in the street, etc.) represents a *secondary* fear but, significantly, the patient is usually aware only of the latter.

Agoraphobia occurs predominantly in women, while most other phobias tend to be fairly evenly divided between the sexes. Other phobias include *acrophobia* (fear of heights), *school phobia* or 'school refusal' (see Chapter 22), *algophobia* (fear of pain), *astraphobia* (fear of thunder and/or lightning), *hydrophobia* (fear of water), *nyctophobia* (fear of darkness, which is quite normal in young children), *xenophobia* (fear of strangers/foreigners) (see Chapter 19) and, would you believe, *phobophobia* (fear of fear!).

● Obsessive–compulsive disorder

Obsessions are recurring irrational thoughts or ideas over which the person has no control, while compulsions are actions which the victim feels compelled to repeat over and over again (a common example being compulsive hand-washing). Obsessions and compulsions are often related, the latter representing an attempt to counteract the former; for example, compulsive hand-washing may be an attempt to remove the obsessive preoccupation with contamination by dirt or germs, either as agent or victim (hence 'obsessive–compulsive' disorder).The millionaire Howard Hughes displayed this kind of disorder.

An example of an obsession occurring without compulsive behaviour is sexual jealousy, an extreme case of which is described by Stuart Sutherland in *Breakdown* (1976). Sutherland was a well-known British experimental psychologist who had been happily married for several years when his wife suddenly revealed that she had been having an affair (but had no wish to end their marriage). At first, he was able to accept the situation and, indeed, found that the increased honesty and communication actually improved their marriage. However, after asking his wife for further details of the affair, he became obsessed with vivid images of his wife in moments of sexual passion with her lover and he could not remove these thoughts from his mind, day or night. Finally, he had to leave his teaching and research duties and it was only after several months of trying various forms of therapy that he managed to reduce the obsessive thoughts sufficiently to be able to return to work.

Somatoform disorders

In the *conversion type* of what was commonly called 'hysterical neurosis' (which was the 'model' of neurosis on which Freud based his psychoanalytic theory), a simulation of physical symptoms occurs, i.e. the person experiences physical symptoms for which there is no detectable physical or bodily cause. According to Mackay (1975), these are usually one of three kinds:

1 *sensory symptoms*: anaesthesia (complete loss of sensation to pain) or paraesthesia (tingling or other unusual sensation), hysterical blindness or deafness;
2 *motor symptoms*: paralysis, aphonia (inability to talk above a whisper) and mutism (complete inability to talk);
3 *visceral symptoms*: pseudo-appendicitis, malaria, tuberculosis, pregnancy, coughing fits, black-outs, severe headaches.

There are usually three 'tell-tale' signs: (a) a lack of concern about the symptoms ('la belle indifférence'); (b) the selective nature of the dysfunction (for example, the patient is mute only in the presence of certain people); and (c) the inconsistency in the symptomatology (for example, the paralysed arm which does not atrophy or wither). Symptoms can also appear and disappear quite suddenly (unlike genuine symptoms). These apparently physical symptoms will still demand a great deal of attention from doctors and relatives and they may also ensure that the person will avoid certain unpleasant situations; these advantages of being 'ill' are known as 'secondary gain' (see Chapter 31).

Dissociative disorders

In the *dissociative type* of 'hysterical neurosis', psychological rather than physical dysfunction occurs and takes the form of a separation, or dissociation, of one part of the self from the other parts. (This has led to the common confusion between dissociative identity disorder or multiple personality disorder (MPD) and schizophrenia; see below).

Dissociative (psychogenic) *amnesia* often appears 'out of the blue' (with nothing to account for it, such as a blow to the head) and may disappear just as suddenly. The forgetting is very selective and the forgotten material can often be recovered under hypnosis or will be recognized when presented (which would not be true of a brain-damaged patient). *Dissociative* (psychogenic) *fugue* ('flight') may be thought of as an extension of amnesia, in which the patient flees from home and self by wandering off on a journey, not knowing how they got there and unable to recall their true identity. The person assumes a new identity but, unlike many amnesic patients, does not experience confusion and disorientation. It is usually a brief episode, lasting from hours to days rather than weeks. Like amnesia, it may often be triggered by severe psychological stress and in both cases recovery is usually rapid and complete and recurrence is rare.

Dissociative identity disorder (multiple personality disorder) involves two or more integrated personalities 'residing' within the same body, each dominating at different times. The 'host' personality is usually not aware of the other(s), but they may be (at least partly) aware of the host. Often, the other personalities embody parts of the first personality which have become repressed and so have remained unexpressed; for example, a shy and sexually inhibited person may develop a second personality who is flirtatious and sexually promiscuous. Shifts from one to the other may be sudden and dramatic and multiple personality may be accompanied by fugue.

The 'original' case was Robert Louis Stevenson's fictional *Dr Jekyll and Mr Hyde*. True-life cases (which are very rare) include *The Three Faces of Eve* (Thigpen *et al.*, 1957) and the truly staggering *'Sybil'* (Schreiber, 1973) who had 16 separate personalities – the case must be read to be believed! (For a detailed discussion of 'Eve', see Gross, 1994.)

Mood (affective) disorders

Manic disorder (mania)

Mania is a sense of intense euphoria or elation, which may manifest as anything from infectious humour to wild excitement. A characteristic symptom is a 'flight of ideas': ideas come rushing into the person's mind with little apparent logical connection and there is a tendency to pun and play with words. Manics have a great deal of energy and rush around, usually achieving little and not putting their energies to good use; they have little need for sleep and may appear excessively conceited ('grandiose ideas'). They display *disinhibition*, which may take the form of a vastly increased sexual appetite (usually out of keeping with their 'normal' personality) or going on spending sprees and building up large debts.

Mania usually occurs in conjunction with depression, in which case it is referred to as *bipolar disorder*; however, in the rare cases in which mania occurs alone,'bipolar' is also used (as opposed to *unipolar*, which refers to the patient who has episodes of depression alone). 'Manic-depressive' refers to both the unipolar and bipolar forms of affective disorder.

Depressive disorder

Depression represents the complete reverse of mania: the depressed person experiences a general slowing down and loss of energy and enthusiasm for life. There may be delusions of physical decay, an expectation of severe punishment and suicide may seem the only way out of a hopeless situation (see Table 30.5).

A distinction that is deeply embedded within psychiatric thinking is that between *endogenous* ('from the inside') and *reactive* (or 'exogenous', from the outside) depression. The former was meant to denote depression arising from biochemical disturbances in the brain, while the latter was seen as being caused by stressful life experiences. These were also classified as *psychotic* and *neurotic* depression respectively, implying that the former is much more serious. However, the distinction is controversial and 'endogenous' is now used to describe a certain cluster of symptoms and not to refer to how the depression was caused (Williams and Hargreaves, 1995). (Depression is not included within the ICD category of 'Neurotic, stress-related and somatoform disorders' but only under 'Mood (affective) disorders'.)

Another controversial feature of depressive disorder relates to sex differences. In England, a woman is about 40 percent more likely to be admitted to a psychiatric hospital than a man. However, as in other countries, rates of hospitalization rise rapidly among the elderly and women outnumber men by 2:1 in the elderly population (75 and over). When admission rates for other categories of disorder are taken into account (such as the very similar rates between males and females for schizophrenia), it is depression that contributes most to the high overall rate of treated mental illness among women (Cochrane, 1995); they are 2–3 times more likely to become clinically depressed than men (Williams and Hargreaves, 1995). Williams and Hargreaves cite evidence which suggests that sex differences arise because women are much more likely than men to experience a *recurrence* of depressive illness. Several explanations have been proposed for the sex difference, but they do not directly address this difference in vulnerability to recurrence (see Box 30.4).

In order to be said to be suffering from clinical depression, a person should have experienced a number of the following symptoms together over a period of time.

A Persistent low mood (for at least two weeks)

plus

B At least five of the following symptoms:

1 Poor appetite or weight loss or increased appetite or weight gain (change of 1lb a week over several weeks or 10lb in a year when not dieting).
2 Sleep difficulty or sleeping too much.
3 Loss of energy, fatiguability or tiredness.
4 Body slowed down or agitated (not mere subjective feeling of restlessness or being slowed down but observable by others).
5 Loss of interest or pleasure in usual activities, including social contact or sex.
6 Feelings of self-reproach, excessive or inappropriate guilt.
7 Complaints or evidence of diminished ability to think or concentrate such as slowed thinking or indecisiveness.
8 Recurrent thoughts of death or suicide or any suicidal behaviour.

TABLE 30.5 *Symptoms of clinical depression (based on Spitzer et al., 1978)*

BOX 30.4 Critical discussion: are women naturally disposed towards depression?

A popular and widely held view is that women are naturally more emotional than men and so are more vulnerable to emotional upsets; hormonal fluctuations associated with the menstrual cycle, childbirth, the menopause and oral contraceptives have all been proposed as the mechanism which might account for the sex difference (Cochrane, 1995). Cochrane believes that there is no evidence that biochemical or physiological changes involved in the menopause, for example, have any direct effect on psychological functioning. However, while the hormonal changes of the menstrual cycle may not be sufficient on their own to cause clinical depression, they may tend to reactivate memories and feelings from a previous period of major depression (caused by other factors) (Williams and Hargreaves, 1995).

According to Callaghan and O'Carroll (1993), there is some evidence that one in ten women who have just given birth is sufficiently depressed to need medical or psychological help (mood disorder with post-partum onset/post-natal depression). However, no specific causal hormonal abnormality has been identified and social factors may be just as important as physical ones, such as her adjustment to a new role and the attention being diverted from her to the baby. Again, hormonal changes cannot explain why the discrepancy in the female/male rates of depression is so large or why only some women are affected and one study found that when women who have recently given birth are compared with a sample of non-pregnant women of the same age, depression rates were very similar (8.7 and 9.9 percent respectively) (Cooper *et al.*, 1988, cited in Cochrane, 1995). Not only does the risk of depression not increase following childbirth, it seems to be good for you!

Cochrane points out a number of non-biological explanations of women's greater susceptibility to depression:

- Girls are very much more likely to be abused, particularly sexually, than boys and victims of abuse are at least twice as likely to suffer clinical depression in adulthood as non-victims. Abuse alone could account for the female–male difference in depression.
- A woman's acceptance of the traditional female gender role involves accepting that she will have relatively little control over her life (see Chapter 23), which may contribute to learned helplessness which has been used to account for the development of depression (see Chapter 15).
- The female–male difference in the rate of depression is at its greatest between the ages of 20 and 50; it is during these years, of course, that marriage, childbearing, motherhood and the 'empty nest' syndrome will be experienced by a majority of women. Although, as we saw in Chapter 24, women are increasingly becoming part of the labour force, being a full-time mother (especially of young children) and wife and not having paid employment outside the home are increasingly being seen as risk factors for depression, especially if they lack an intimate, confiding relationship (Brown and Harris, 1978).
- In *The Social Creation of Mental Illness* (1983), Cochrane argues that depression may be seen as a *coping strategy* that is available to women, in contrast to those of men (including alcohol and drugs and their work). Not only is it more acceptable for women to admit to psychological symptoms, but they may represent a means of changing an intolerable situation.

Unhappiness about their domestic, social, and political circumstances lies at the root of many women's concerns. This unhappiness must not be medicalized and regarded as a 'female malady' ... (Callaghan and O'Carroll, 1993)

● Personality disorders

Antisocial (psychopathic/sociopathic) personality

Psychopaths are often of above average intelligence and are charming and socially skilled; their charm can be very disarming and enables them to manipulate and exploit others for their own gain. Whether or not they engage in criminal activities, they are amoral (cannot experience guilt), insensitive to others' feelings, impulsive, stimulus seeking (needing excitement) and have a low tolerance of frustration. They are unable to develop or maintain meaningful interpersonal relationships because they are incapable of giving or receiving love and affection (affectionless psychopathy; see Chapter 22). Sexual activity is carried on without evidence of tenderness. Marriage is often marked by lack of concern for the partner and sometimes by physical violence. The characteristic impulsiveness often leads to frequent dismissals from jobs and is often reflected in a lack of any overall purpose in life. The combination of impulsiveness and lack of guilt is often associated with repeated crime, which may be violent and usually shows a callous lack of concern for others.

Obsessive–compulsive personality

Such people are unable to adapt to new situations, are rigid in their views and inflexible in their approach to problems. They are upset by change and prefer a safe and familiar routine. They are inhibited by their perfectionism which makes ordinary work a burden and gets them bogged down in trivial detail. Exaggerated moral standards become painful and result in a guilty preoccupation with wrong-doing, which prevents enjoyment. They are also often humourless, judgmental, mean, indecisive and sensitive to criticism.

Paranoid personality

The central traits are suspiciousness and sensitivity. Such people may be constantly on the lookout for attempts by others to get the better of them, deceive them or play tricks on them and they doubt others' loyalty and trustworthiness. They do not make friends easily and may avoid involvement with groups. They may be perceived by others as secretive, devious and self-sufficient to a fault, as well as argumentative and stubborn. But they also show a strong sense of self-importance, a powerful inner conviction of being unusually talented and capable of great things – but others have prevented them from realizing their potential! They are easily made to feel ashamed and humiliated; they take offence easily and appear prickly, unreasonable and 'difficult'.

Schizoid personality

Such people are introspective and prone to engage in fantasy rather than take action, emotionally cold, self-sufficient and detached from others. The term was originally used by Kretschmer (1936) who believed that schizoids were likely to become schizophrenic, but this is certainly not always so and the term does not imply a causal relationship with schizophrenia (Gelder et al., 1989). They seem incapable of expressing affection or tenderness or making intimate friendships and often remain unmarried. They pursue a lonely course through life and their usually solitary habits tend to be intellectual rather than practical.

● Mental retardation

The 1959 Mental Health Act (England and Wales) introduced the terms 'subnormality' and 'severe subnormality' to replace the terms 'idiocy', 'imbecility' and 'feeble-mindedness' (used by the 1944 Education Act). Severe subnormality is usually associated with brain damage (genetic, e.g. Down's syndrome, or otherwise), while subnormality is usually associated with gross understimulation during infancy and childhood. However, according to the 1983 Mental Health Act, the distinction is ultimately one of clinical judgement (Gelder et al., 1989).

Mild retardation (IQ 50–70)

This accounts for 80 percent of all mentally retarded people. Their appearance is usually normal and any sensory or motor deficits are slight. Most develop more or less normal language and social behaviour during the pre-school years and their retardation may never be formally identified. As adults, most can live independently but they may need help with housing and employment or when under some unusual stress.

Moderate retardation (IQ 35–49)

This accounts for about 12 percent of all mentally retarded people. Most can talk or at least communicate and most can learn to care for themselves with supervision. As adults, they can usually undertake simple routine work and find their way around.

Severe retardation (IQ 20–34)

This accounts for about 7 percent of all mentally retarded people. In the pre-school years their development is usually very slow. Eventually many can be trained to look after themselves with close supervision and to communicate simply (see the discussion of 'idiots savants' in Chapter 28.)

Profound retardation (IQ below 20)

This accounts for less than 1 percent of all mentally retarded people. Few learn to care for themselves completely but some achieve some simple speech and social behaviour.

● Schizophrenia

As we saw earlier, what we now call schizophrenia was originally called dementia praecox ('senility of youth') by Kraepelin (1896), who believed that the typical symptoms (namely, delusions, hallucinations, attention deficits and bizarre motor activity) were due to a form of mental deterioration which began in adolescence. Bleuler (1911) observed, however, that many patients displaying these symptoms did not go on deteriorating and that illness often begins much

1 *Passivity experiences and thought disturbances* include *thought insertion* (thoughts are inserted into one's mind from outside and are under external influence), *thought withdrawal* (thoughts are removed from one's mind and are under external control) and *thought broadcasting* (thoughts are broadcast to/otherwise made known to others). External forces may include the Martians, the Communists and the 'Government'.

2 *Auditory hallucinations (in the third person)*. Hallucinatory voices are heard discussing one's thoughts or behaviour as they occur (a kind of 'running commentary') or they are heard arguing about one in the third person (or using one's name) or repeating one's thoughts out loud/anticipating one's thoughts. They are often accusatory, obscene and derogatory and may demand that the patient commit extreme acts of violence. 'True' hallucinations involve the voices being experienced as alien or under the influence of some external source. (The hallucinations of patients with organic psychoses are predominantly visual.) They may be experienced in the light of concurrent delusions (e.g. as the voice of God or the devil; see below).

3 *Primary delusions*. Delusions are false beliefs. According to Jasper (1962, cited in Frith and Cahill, 1995), they are held with extraordinary conviction, are impervious to other experiences or compelling counterargument/contradictory evidence and their content is incompatible with reality. The patient may be so convinced of their truth that they act on the strength of their belief, even if this involves murder, as in the case of Peter Sutcliffe, the 'Yorkshire Ripper'.
Most common are delusions of *persecution* (e.g. 'My wife is trying to poison me'); also common are delusions of *grandeur* (e.g. 'I am Napoleon'/'I am Jesus'). A 'primary' delusion appears suddenly and in a moment of clear consciousness.

TABLE 30.6 *Schneider's (1959) first rank symptoms of schizophrenia*

later than adolescence. Consequently, he introduced the term *schizophrenia* instead (literally 'split mind' or 'divided self') to describe an illness in which 'the personality loses its unity'.

According to Clare (1976), the diagnosis of schizophrenia in the UK relies greatly on what Schneider (1959) called *first rank symptoms*; in the presence of one or more of these (and in the absence of brain disease, etc.) a diagnosis of schizophrenia is usually made. Schneider's first rank symptoms are shown in Table 30.6.

Schneider's first rank symptoms are subjective experiences which can only be inferred on the basis of the patient's verbal report. Slater and Roth (1969) regard hallucinations as the least important of all the major symptoms because they are not exclusive to schizophrenia (this is also true of delusions; see below); they identify four additional symptoms, which are described in Table 30.7. These are directly observable from the patient's behaviour.

As shown in Table 30.2, both DSM and ICD distinguish between different kinds of schizophrenia and reference is often made to 'the schizophrenias'.

1 *Thought process disorder*. The inability to keep to the point, being easily distracted/side-tracked, especially in the form of *clang associations* (e.g. 'big', 'pig', 'twig'), where words are 'thrown' together based on their sound rather than their meaning; this produces an apparently incoherent jumble of words ('word salad'). The inability to finish a sentence, sometimes stopping in the middle of a word ('thought blocking'). Also, making up new words (neologisms) and interpreting language (e.g. proverbs) very literally.

2 *Disturbances of affect*. *Blunting* refers to an apparent lack of emotional sensitivity; events or situations do not elicit the usual emotional response. *Flattening of affect* refers to a more pervasive, general absence of emotional expression: the patient appears devoid of emotional tone, showing minimal inflection in their speech and a lack of the normal variation of facial or bodily movements used to convey feelings or emotions. *Incongruity of affect* refers to a loss of appropriate emotional responses (such as laughing or getting angry for no apparent reason, changing mood very suddenly, giggling when given bad news or describing some tragic incident).

3 *Psychomotor disorders*. *Catelepsy* (muscles in a state of semi-rigidity), grimacing of facial muscles, limb twitching, stereotyped behaviours (such as constant pacing up and down) or *catatonic stupor* (assuming a fixed position for long periods of time, several years in extreme cases).

4 *Lack of volition*. Inability to make decisions or carry out a particular activity, loss of will power or drive, loss of interest in the environment and loss of affection for friends and relatives.

TABLE 30.7 *Major symptoms of schizophrenia (additional to Schneider's). (Based on Slater and Roth, 1969)*

Simple schizophrenia

This often appears during late adolescence and has a slow, gradual onset. The main symptoms are gradual social withdrawal and difficulty in making friends, aimlessness and idleness, blunting of affect, loss of volition and drive and a decline in academic or occupational performance. Such people may become drifters or tramps and are often regarded by others as idle and 'layabouts', but there are no major psychotic symptoms as in the other types of schizophrenia. Only ICD actually distinguishes this type; while acknowledging that it is controversial, it is retained because it is still used in some countries.

Hebephrenic (disorganized) schizophrenia

This is probably the nearest thing to many people's beliefs about what a 'mad' or 'crazy' person is like and is normally diagnosed only in adolescents and young adults. Mood is shallow and inappropriate, thought is disorganized and speech is incoherent. Delusions and hallucinations are fleeting and fragmentary and behaviour is irresponsible, unpredictable, silly or mischievous, childish or bizarre and sometimes may be violent (if, for example, the patient is approached while hallucinating).

Catatonic schizophrenia

This is dominated by conspicuous psychomotor disturbances These may alternate between extremes such as *hyperkinesis* (hyperactivity) and *stupor* (a marked decrease in responsiveness to the environment and a reduction of spontaneous movements and activity) or *automatic obedience* ('command automatism') and *negativism* (apparently motiveless resistance to all instructions/attempts to be moved or doing the opposite of what is asked). There may be episodes of violent excitement (apparently purposeless motor activity) combined with a dreamlike (*oneroid*) state with vivid scenic hallucinations. Other characteristics are mutism, posturing (the voluntary assumption of inappropriate and bizarre postures) and *waxy flexibility* (maintenance of the limbs and body in externally imposed positions).

Paranoid (paraphrenic) schizophrenia

This is dominated by relatively stable, often paranoid delusions (although delusions of grandeur are also quite common). These are usually accompanied by hallucinations (especially auditory) and perceptual disturbances but in other respects, the patient is less disturbed (the personality is better preserved) than in the other kinds. It is the most homogeneous type, i.e. paranoid schizophrenics are more alike than are catatonics, etc.

Undifferentiated (atypical)

This is meant to accommodate patients who cannot be easily placed elsewhere, i.e. psychotic conditions that meet the general diagnostic criteria for schizophrenia but which do not conform to any of the sub-types, due to either insufficient or overlapping symptoms.

With the possible exception of paranoid, these 'sub-categories' are of doubtful validity. Some patients present symptoms of one sub-group at one time then those of another sub-group later and catatonic symptoms are much less common now than 50 years ago (perhaps because of improvement in the social environment in which patients are treated). The four sub-groups cannot be clearly distinguished in clinical practice (Gelder *et al.*, 1989), which relates to the issue of reliability and validity of psychiatric diagnosis (see above).

Related disorders

Brief reactive psychosis refers to a syndrome which does not last more than a month; it is apparently precipitated by stress with prominent emotional turmoil. *Schizophreniform psychosis* is a syndrome similar to schizophrenia, lasting less than six months. *Schizotypal disorder* refers to eccentric behaviour and unusual thinking and affect which resemble those seen in schizophrenia but without definite and characteristic schizophrenic abnormalities. *Schizoaffective disorder* involves episodes in which both affective and schizophrenic symptoms are prominent but which do not justify a diagnosis of either schizophrenia or depressive or manic psychosis. *Persistent delusional disorder* (paranoia) is characterized by persistent single or multiple delusions without other symptoms.

Is schizophrenia a disease?

Not only is schizophrenia one of the most serious forms of mental disorder but , as we have seen throughout much of this chapter, it has become the focus for the whole controversy surrounding the medical model; many of its most articulate critics, such as Szasz and Laing, have directed their criticism towards schizophrenia as the example par excellence of what the medical model sees as mental illness.

What's different about the brains of schizophrenics?

When Kraepelin first identified dementia praecox, he was convinced that it was a physical disease like any other; the neuropathological changes associated with general paralysis of the insane (caused by syphilis) and Alzheimer's disease had just been discovered and he expected that similar 'markers' would be found for schizophrenia and manic-depressive illness. However, schizophrenia was categorized as a functional psychosis up until 1978 when, according to Gershon and Rieder (1992), the then new CT scan (see Chapter 3) was used for the first time to study the brains of chronic schizophrenics (by Johnstone *et al.* at the Clinical Research Centre in Middlesex, England). It revealed that chronic schizophrenics show an increase in the size of the lateral cerebral ventricles (the fluid-filled spaces in the middle of the brain) and other X-ray evidence confirmed that there was *less* brain tissue (especially in the medial temporal lobe). This was subsequently confirmed by MRI scans which, along with postmortem examinations, also revealed that schizophrenics have a smaller hippocampus and part of the limbic system is also smaller.

Gershon and Rieder (1992) also refer to research which has shown reduced blood flow in the frontal cortex of schizophrenics, implying decreased neuronal activity. For example, compared with normal participants who show increased blood flow while taking the Wisconsin Card Sort, a test of working memory and abstract thinking, schizophrenics show less of an increase (as well as doing worse on the test); those with the smallest hippocampus show the greatest deficit in blood flow. Postmortems also show that certain groups of neurons are organized in an abnormal way or are connected differently compared with non-schizophrenics.

All these differences are found when patients first develop symptoms (and may even precede the onset of symptoms), which suggests that they are not the result of being ill for a long time or of medication (Harrison, 1995). Also, these differences do not progress over time, nor is there any evidence of neural scar tissue (gliosis) that is normally found in degenerative disorders (such as Alzheimer's and Huntington's), suggesting a neurodevelopmental disorder, i.e. a failure of brain tissue to develop normally, such as failure of neuronal growth or neuronal connections or a disturbance in the 'pruning' of neurons that normally takes place between three and 15 years of age (Gershon and Rieder, 1992).

However, the differences are only apparent if a group of schizophrenics is compared with a group of non-schizophrenics, i.e. no one can yet diagnose schizophrenia in an individual based solely on a brain scan or looking down a microscope (Harrison, 1995). Also, all the studies which have reported differences have taken 'schizophrenia' to be a homogeneous diagnosis, i.e. they have not distinguished between different sub-types of schizophrenia. A way of testing the validity of this particular aspect of ICD and DSM classification would be to identify different neuropathology for each of the sub-types.

The biochemical theory of schizophrenia

It has been proposed that what directly causes schizophrenic symptoms is an excess of the neurotransmitter dopamine (the *dopamine hypothesis*). The evidence for this hypothesis comes from three main sources:

1 postmortems on schizophrenics show unusually high levels of dopamine, especially in the limbic system (Iversen, 1979);
2 the belief that anti-schizophrenic drugs (such as chlorpromazine) work by binding to dopamine receptor sites. Chlorpromazine was developed in the 1950s as a surgical anaesthetic and its effectiveness as an anti-psychotic drug was discovered quite by chance;
3 the observation that high doses of amphetamines and L-dopa (used in the treatment of Parkinson's disease), both of which enhance the activity of dopamine, can sometimes produce symptoms very similar to the psychomotor disorders seen in certain types of schizophrenia (see Table 3.2). Dopamine-containing neurons are concentrated in the basal ganglia and frontal cortex, which are concerned with the initiation and control of movement; degeneration of the dopamine system produces Parkinson's disease.

Although there is strong evidence that dopamine is central to the action of anti-psychotic drugs, the evidence that dopamine metabolism is abnormal in schizophrenia is weak. PET scans provide a way of studying dopamine receptor binding in the brain of living patients (untreated), but the evidence to date is very inconclusive and more work is needed before definite conclusions can be reached (Gelder *et al.*, 1989; see Chapter 3).

According to Carlsson and Carlsson (1990, cited in Gershon and Rieder, 1992), schizophrenia involves an imbalance between dopamine neurons originating in the midbrain and glutamate neurons in the cortex; this might involve an excess of dopamine, a deficit in glutamate or both. A reduction in glutamate neurons is consistent with the reduced brain tissue and with the action of phencyclidine (PCP), a hallucinogen, which blocks glutamate receptors and which can produce psychosis; amphetamines, which can also induce psychosis, cause the release of dopamine.

A word of caution: even if schizophrenics do have higher natural levels of dopamine, this could as easily be a *result* of schizophrenia as its *cause*. Even if dopamine were found to be a causative factor, this could turn out to be indirect, such that abnormal family circumstances give rise to high levels of dopamine which, in turn, trigger the symptoms (Lloyd *et al.*, 1984). Similarly, even if brain differences were large and reliable enough to enable psychiatrists/neurologists to diagnose schizophrenia on the strength of them alone and even if some kind of neurodevelopmental account were generally accepted, this would still leave unanswered the more fundamental question

as to why some people develop these disorders and others do not. The cognitive and affective abnormalities involved in psychosis are so severe that it is reasonable to expect brain abnormalities to be involved (Frith and Cahill, 1995), but the data are largely correlational. However, even if it could be shown that the former are actually caused by the latter, we still want to know how the latter come about. The main explanation is the genetic theory.

The genetic theory of schizophrenia

A great deal of research has gone into trying to demonstrate a genetic component in schizophrenia. As with intelligence (Chapter 28), one type of *behaviour-genetic design* that has been used, family resemblance studies, confounds genetic and environmental influences, i.e. there is no way of telling whether the correlation between the risk of developing schizophrenia and degree of family resemblance/blood tie is due to the greater genetic

Study	'Narrow' concordance *		'Broad' concordance *	
	% MZs	% DZs	% MZs	% DZs
Rosanoff *et al.* (1934) USA (41 MZs, 53 DZs)	44	9	61	13
Kallmann (1946) USA (174 MZs, 296 DZs)	59	11	69	11-14
Slater (1953) England (37 MZs, 58 DZs)	65	14	65	14
Gottesman and Shields (1966); England (24 MZs, 33 DZs)	42	15	54	18
Kringlen (1968) Norway (55 MZs, 90 DZs)	25	7	38	10
Allen *et al.* (1972) USA (95 MZs, 125 DZs)	14	4	27	5
Fischer (1973) Denmark (21 MZs, 41 DZs)	24	10	48	20

* 'Narrow' based on attempt to apply a relatively strict set of criteria when diagnosing schizophrenia. 'Broad' includes 'borderline schizophrenia', 'schizoaffective psychosis', 'paranoid with schizophrenia-like features'.

TABLE 30.8 *Concordance rates for schizophrenia for identical (MZ) and non-identical (DZ) twins. (Based on Rose et al., 1984)*

similarity or the greater similarity of environments.

The two major alternative designs, *twins studies* and *adoption studies*, both face problems of their own. Just as those studies discussed in Chapter 28 presuppose that IQ tests are a valid measure of intelligence, so twin and adoption studies presuppose that schizophrenia is a distinct syndrome which can be reliably diagnosed by different psychiatrists; this presupposition has been seriously questioned (see below).

Some of the major twin studies are summarized in Table 30.8. It can be seen that there is a wide variation in the concordance rate for schizophrenia in different studies, for both MZs and DZs ,which suggests that different countries use different criteria for diagnosing schizophrenia (and there is evidence that they do; see below). By the same token, if the highest concordance rate for MZs is 69 percent (and that is when a 'broad' criterion is used), this still leaves plenty of scope for the role of environmental factors. If schizophrenia were totally genetically determined, then we would expect to find 100 percent concordance rate for MZs, i.e. if one member of an MZ pair has schizophrenia, the other twin should also have it in every single case. In fact, most diagnosed cases do not report a family history (Frith and Cahill, 1995).

However, the average concordance rate for MZs is five times higher than that for DZs (50 percent and 10 percent, respectively; Shields, 1976, 1978). A more precise estimate for the relative importance of genetic and environmental factors comes from studies where MZs reared apart are compared with MZs reared together; according to Shields (1976, 1978), the concordance rates are quite similar for the two groups, suggesting a major genetic contribution.

Twin studies are based on the important *equal environments assumption*: (a) MZs are not treated more similarly than same-sex DZs or, (b) if they are, this does not increase MZs' similarity for the characteristic in question relative to same-sex DZs. (This assumption therefore applies to the study of intelligence too). According to Lilienfeld (1995), this assumption has stood up surprisingly well to careful empirical scrutiny. For example, researchers have identified MZs and DZs whose zygosity has been misclassified (i.e. MZs mistaken for DZs and vice-versa). If similarity of rearing were the key factor underlying the greater concordance for MZs, then *perceived* zygosity (as opposed to actual zygosity) should be the best predictor of concordance. However, twin similarity in personality and cognitive ability is related much more closely to actual than perceived zygosity (Scarr and Carter-Saltzman, 1979). Again, the greater similarity in parental rearing for MZs seems to be due largely or entirely to the fact that MZs elicit more similar reactions from their parents (Lytton, 1977). It seems, therefore, that the greater similarity of MZs is a cause, rather than an effect, of their more similar parental treatment.

In adoption studies, children born to parents of whom one or both are schizophrenic are adopted early in life into a normal family and these children are compared either with biological children of the adoptive parents or other adopted children whose biological parents are not schizophrenic. In many ways, adoption studies provide the most unequivocal test of genetic influence because they allow the clearest separation of genetic and environmental factors.

In one such study, Heston (1966) studied 47 adults who had been born to schizophrenic mothers and separated from them within three days of birth. As children, they had been reared in a variety of circumstances, though not by the mother's family. They were compared (average age 36) with controls who were matched for circumstances of upbringing, but where mothers had not been schizophrenic: five of the experimental group but none of the controls were diagnosed as schizophrenic. There was also an excess of antisocial personality and neurotic disorders among the children of schizophrenic mothers, i.e. children of schizophrenic parents run a greater risk of developing some kind of mental disorder even if it is not schizophrenia. Rosenthal *et al.* (1971) began a series of studies in 1965 in Denmark, which has national registers of psychiatric cases and adoptions; they confirmed Heston's findings, using children separated from schizophrenic mothers, on average at six months.

The major study (Kety *et al.*, 1975) uses a different design. Two groups of adoptees were identified, 33 who had schizophrenia and a matched group who did not. Rates of disorder were compared in the biological and adoptive families of the two groups of adoptees – the rate was greater among the biological relatives of the schizophrenic adoptees than among those of the controls, a finding which supports the genetic hypothesis. Further, the rate of schizophrenia was not increased among couples who adopted the schizophrenic adoptees, suggesting that environmental factors were not of crucial importance (Gelder *et al.*, 1989). The reverse situation was studied by Wender *et al.* (1974), who found no increase among adoptees with normal biological parents but with a schizophrenic adoptive parent.

Gottesman and Shields (1976, 1982), reviewing adoption studies, conclude that they show a major role for heredity.

A crucial assumption made when evaluating the results of adoption studies is *random placement* (which, as with the equal environments assumption, also applies to adoption studies in relation to intelligence), i.e. adoptees are placed with parents who are no more similar to their biological parents than by chance. While Rose *et al.* (1984) consider selective placement to be the rule (rather than random placement) and so a major, if not fatal, stumbling block of adoption studies, Straube and Oades (1992, cited in Lilienfield, 1995) believe the random placement assumption is largely or entirely warranted.

Conclusions: The nature and nurture of schizophrenia

Perhaps the most reasonable conclusion that can be drawn is that, although the evidence is far from flawless, converging evidence from multiple sources implicates genetic factors in the aetiology of schizophrenia. Its heritability seems to be comparable to that of any medical condition known to have a major genetic component, such as diabetes, hypertension, coronary artery disease and breast cancer (Lilienfield, 1995). However, the precise mode of inheritance remains controversial (Frith and Cahill, 1995; Lilienfield, 1995). While some researchers propose a single (*monogenic*), dominant gene located on chromosome 5, attempts to replicate it have so far failed. The most popular current view is the 'multifactorial' (*polygenic*) model, i.e. a number of genes are involved which determine a predisposition, which then requires environmental factors to trigger the symptoms of the illness; this is consistent with the view of schizophrenia as denoting a number of different disorders/sub-types (see above), as originally proposed by Bleuler. This is referred to as a *diathesis-* (i.e. predisposition) *stress model.*

Zubin and Spring (1977), for example, claim that what we probably inherit is a degree of vulnerability to exhibit schizophrenic symptoms; whether or not we do will depend on environmental stresses which may include viral infections during pregnancy (especially influenza A), severe malnourishment during pregnancy, birth injury or difficult birth, being born in winter, as well as 'critical life events' (see Chapters 6 and 24). This relates to the important distinction between reactive and process schizophrenia: *reactive* schizophrenia appears quite suddenly and usually later in life (not before adolescence) and is normally

seen as a response to extreme stress, while in *process* schizophrenia, pathological symptoms have been evident for many years before the 'breakdown' occurs and genetic factors seem to play a relatively greater role (Rosenthal *et al.*, 1971).

Laing and existential psychiatry

During the 1950s and 1960s, several British psychiatrists, notably R. D. Laing, David Cooper and Aaron Esterson, united in their opposition to existing conditions in state mental hospitals. They rejected the medical model of mental disorder and were hostile to the exclusively organic and genetic explanations of schizophrenia. Like Szasz, they denied the existence of schizophrenia as a disease entity and instead saw it as a metaphor for dealing with people whose behaviour and experience fail to conform to the dominant model of social reality; they thus spearheaded the *antipsychiatry movement* (Graham, 1986). Heather (1976) identifies three major landmarks in the development of Laing's thought, corresponding to the publication of three major books.

In *The Divided Self* (1959), Laing tried to make sense of schizophrenia by 'getting inside the head' of a schizophrenic, by trying to see the world as the schizophrenic sees it. This *existentialist* analysis retained the categories of classic psychiatry but proceeded from the assumption that what the schizophrenic says and does are intelligible if you listen carefully enough and relate to their 'being in the world'. What Laing found was a split in the patient's relationship with the world and with the self. The schizophrenic experiences an intense form of *ontological insecurity* and everyday events may threaten the schizophrenic's very existence.

Specifically, ontological insecurity comprises engulfment, implosion and *petrification* or depersonalization. *Engulfment* refers to the dread of being swallowed up by others if involvement becomes too close and common expressions of this are 'being buried, drowned, caught and dragged down into quicksand', being 'on fire, bodies being burned up', feeling 'cold and dry – dreads fire or water'. To be loved is more threatening than to be hated; indeed, all love is a form of hate. *Implosion* refers to the fear that the world, at any moment, will come crashing in and obliterate their identity. Schizophrenics feel empty, like a vacuum, and they are the vacuum; anything ('reality') can threaten that empty space which must be protected at all costs. *Petrification* or *depersonalization* involves fear of being turned to stone (catatonia), fear of being turned into a robot or automaton (thought control) and fear of turning others into stone. To consider another person as a free agent can be threatening, because you can become an it for them; in order to prevent the other depersonalizing you, you may have to depersonalize the other.

In *Self and Others* (1961), Laing maintained that 'schizophrenia' does not refer to any kind of entity (clinical, existential or otherwise) but rather refers to an *interpersonal ploy* used by some people (parents, doctors, psychiatrists, etc.) in their interactions with others (the schizophrenic). According to the *family interaction model*, schizophrenia can only be understood as something which takes place between people (and not inside them, as maintained by the psychoanalytic model of *The Divided Self*). To understand individuals we must study not individuals but interactions between individuals and this is the subject matter of *social phenomenology* (see Chapter 15). The family interaction model was consistent with research in America, especially that of Bateson *et al.* (1956), which showed that schizophrenia arises within families which use 'pathological' forms of communication, in particular contradictory messages (double-binds) in which, for example, a mother induces her son to give her a hug but when he does so tells him 'not to be such a baby'.

In *Sanity, Madness and the Family* (1964), Laing and Esterson presented 11 family case histories (in all of which one member becomes a diagnosed schizophrenic) in order to make schizophrenia intelligible in the context of what happens within the patient's family and, in so doing, to further undermine the disease model of schizophrenia.

Finally, in *The Politics of Experience* (1967), two new models emerged, the conspiratorial and the psychedelic. The *conspiratorial model* maintains that schizophrenia is a label, a form of violence perpetrated by some people on others. The family, GP and psychiatrists conspire against schizophrenics to keep them in check; to maintain their definition of reality (the status quo) they treat schizophrenics as if they were sick, imprison them in a mental hospital where they are degraded and invalidated as human beings.

According to the *psychedelic model*, the schizophrenic is seen as an exceptionally eloquent critic of society and schizophrenia is 'itself a natural way of healing our own appalling state of alienation called normality'. Again, 'Madness need not be all breakdown ... it may also be breakthrough'; in Bateson's words, the 'patient embarks on a voyage of discovery (death) and returns (rebirth) to the normal world with new insights'. Schizophrenia is seen as a voyage into 'inner space', a 'natural healing process'. Unfortunately, the 'natural sequence' of schizophrenia is very rarely allowed to occur because, says Laing, we are too busy treating the patient.

CHAPTER SUMMARY

- Different psychological theories of abnormality assume that the line can be drawn between normal and abnormal.
- The statistical criterion/deviation from the average defines abnormality as what most people do, but this fails to distinguish between atypical behaviour that is desirable and undesirable.
- Deviation from the norm defines abnormality as not behaving or feeling as one is expected to in particular situations/contexts or according to one's stage of development; normality implies 'desirable', even 'natural'. But it is not obvious what norms are being broken in the case of mental disorder.
- The adequacy/mental health criterion identifies several definitions of mental health, including absence of mental illness, being able to introspect, self-actualization, integration, ability to cope with stress, autonomy, seeing the world realistically and environmental mastery. But this involves value judgements about ideal states that are culturally defined (unlike physical health).
- Official psychiatric classification of mental disorder used to include homosexuality as a sexual deviation. The change to 'sexual orientation disturbance', then to 'ego-dystonic homosexuality/sexual orientation' and the change in the law regarding homosexuality in the UK reflect changes in social/political attitudes, not in homosexuality itself.
- Abnormality as personal distress/suffering defines abnormality in terms of subjective experiences. Abnormality as the distress of others may act as a counterbalance to the lack of insight shown by some people with a mental disorder, but this can reflect either empathic concern or egoistic motives.
- Abnormality as maladaptiveness focuses on the consequences of abnormal behaviour for the individual, especially being prevented from achieving their goals or functioning in the way they wish.
- Abnormality as unexpected behaviour means reacting in an extreme way to something, but under-reacting could be considered just as

abnormal as over-reacting. Highly consistent/predictable behaviour, as well as highly inconsistent/unpredictable behaviour, may be considered abnormal.

- The way we talk about psychological disorder reflects the medical model, i.e. we think about abnormal behaviour as if it were indicative of some underlying illness.

- Although it may be more humane to treat psychologically disturbed people as sick rather than bad, it also removes responsibility from them and the stigma attached to mental illness may be greater than that associated with crime.

- According to Szasz and Heather, the norms from which the mentally ill are thought to deviate are expressed in moral, psychological and legal terms, not medical ones, yet the solution takes the form of medical treatment. Psychiatric diagnoses represent stigmatizing labels used to exclude those who are unwanted because they have upset the social order; mental illness has replaced beliefs in demonology and witchcraft.

- Attaching a diagnostic label makes the person's behaviour seem more predictable and represents a symbolic recapture, often followed by a physical capture; labels like 'schizophrenic' also describe the whole person and so confer a new identity .

- According to Scheff, schizophrenics are breaking residual rules, which tend to reflect middle-class values regarding 'decency' and 'reality'.

- Szasz rejects the concept of mental illness, cases of which turn out to be either neurophysiological disorders or, more often, problems in living or disorders of psychosocial/interpersonal functioning; this corresponds to the distinction between organic and functional psychosis. While DSM-IV no longer has a separate category for organic disorders, ICD-10 does.

- Compared with doctors in general medicine, psychiatrists are much more dependent on reported symptoms as opposed to signs of illness; there are no objective markers for most mental disorders.

- An integral part of the medical model is the classification of mental disorder and the related process of diagnosis. All systems of classification stem from Kraepelin's identification of two major groups of mental diseases or syndromes, namely dementia praecox (schizophrenia) and manic-depressive psychosis.

- Kraepelin's classification helped to establish both DSM and ICD and is embodied in the Mental Health Act, which distinguishes three major categories of mental disturbance/disorder.

- DSM-IV uses a larger number of discrete categories to classify mental disorders that appear under a smaller number of wider categories in ICD-10.

- DSM uses a multi-axial system of classification; these represent different areas of functioning and comprise: clinical disorders (Axis I); personality disorders/mental retardation (Axis II); general medical conditions (Axis III); psychosocial and environmental problems (Axis IV); global assessment of functioning (Axis V). This provides a much broader assessment than a single axis would allow.

- ICD does not have separate axes in the way that DSM does, but broad types of aetiology are built into the categories of mental disorder. DSM-IV makes no assumptions about aetiology and is a-theoretical.

- Both DSM and ICD have dropped the traditional distinction between neurosis and psychosis, partly because of the exceptions to all the criteria used to distinguish between them. Psychosis is a much more serious form of mental disorder, by virtue of the loss of contact with reality; it is qualitatively different from 'normal' behaviour and major symptoms are delusions, hallucinations, passivity experiences and thought disorder.

- Both DSM and ICD use explicit diagnostic operational criteria, intended to make diagnosis more reliable and valid; these include the social consequences of the disorder. This relates to the fundamental question of whether mental disorders exist objectively, independently of social and cultural norms and values.

- The cross-cultural study of schizophrenia tries to determine whether it is absolute ('culture free'), universal or culturally relative. While a number of culture-general symptoms have been reported for schizophrenia, culture can influence the form of symptoms, specific reasons for onset of symptoms and prognosis. Culture-bound syndromes (CBSs) are seen as falling outside mainstream classifications of disorder, implying that Western mental disorders are objective and uninfluenced by cultural factors.

- Rosenhan's study of pseudo-patients claimed to show the unreliability of psychiatric diagnosis. Early studies showed poor international inter-rater/inter-judge reliability, particularly for schizophrenia. This has been improved in more recent versions of both DSM and ICD by the use of standardized interview schedules and explicit diagnostic criteria; however, there is still room for subjective interpretation.

- Validity is more difficult to assess in the absence of absolute standards. For a diagnosis to be considered valid, it should allow prediction of treatment and recovery, as well as implying the cause(s) of the disorder. While there is reason to doubt that these criteria are always fulfilled, the situation may not be very different from general medicine.

- Classification is needed by psychiatrists as a means of communicating about patients, to bring some order to a great diversity of problem behaviours and to enable research to be carried out. Psychotherapists from an idiographic perspective criticize the use of classification, but this more nomothetic approach and a focus on the individual's unique qualities are not mutually exclusive.

- Rosenhan's study has been criticized for several reasons; for example, the discharge label of 'schizophrenia in remission' suggests that the psychiatrists did recognize that the pseudopatients were not real.

- A phobia is an extreme, irrational fear. Most common is agoraphobia, followed by social phobias and animal phobias, with fear of certain animals being much more common than others.

- Obsessions are recurrent irrational thoughts/ideas which are often accompanied by compulsions, which are attempts to counteract the obsessions.

- Somatoform disorders refer to what used to be called conversion type hysterical neurosis, involving a simulation of physical/bodily symptoms, usually sensory, motor or visceral. These differ from genuine physical symptoms in several important ways.

- Dissociative disorders involve a separation between different parts of the self, as in amnesia, fugue and dissociative identity disorder (multiple personality disorder).

- Mood (affective) disorders include mania, a sense of intense euphoria or elation, which usually occurs in conjunction with depression (bipolar disorder), which refers to a general loss of energy and enthusiasm for life. Both mania and depression often involve delusions.

- The traditional distinction between endogenous/psychotic and reactive/neurotic depression is controversial and causation is no longer implied when a diagnosis of clinical depression is made.

- Also controversial are the very significant sex differences in rates of diagnosed and treated depression. There is only weak evidence to support the theory that the higher rate of depression among women is due to hormonal factors; much stronger evidence is found for non-biological explanations, such as child sexual abuse, learned helplessness linked to gender roles and depression as a coping strategy.

- There are several distinct types of personality disorder, including antisocial/psychopathic, obsessive–compulsive, paranoid and schizoid.

- Mental retardation is classified as mild, moderate, severe and profound, accounting for 80 percent, 12 percent, 7 percent and 1 percent of all mentally retarded people respectively.

- In schizophrenia, the personality loses its unity. Schneider's first rank symptoms involve passivity experiences and thought disturbances (thought insertion/withdrawal/broadcasting), auditory hallucinations and primary delusions, mainly delusions of persecution or grandeur.

- Slater and Roth identify four additional symptoms, directly observable from the patient's behaviour, namely thought process disorder (e.g. clang associations/word salad/thought blocking/neologisms), disturbances of affect (blunting/flattening of affect/incongruity of affect), psychomotor disorders (catelepsy/catatonic stupor) and lack of volition.

- Distinct subtypes of schizophrenia include simple, hebephrenic/disorganized, catatonic, paranoid/paraphrenic and undifferentiated/atypical. There is some doubt about the ability to distinguish between these in clinical practice, with the possible exception of paranoid.

- Other related disorders include brief reactive disorder, schizophreniform psychosis, schizotypal disorder, schizoaffective disorder and persistent delusional disorder.

- Despite Kraepelin's original belief that schizophrenia was a physical disease, it wasn't until new imaging techniques such as CT and PET started to be used in the 1970s to investigate the brain that neuropathological markers were found. Evidence shows that the brains of schizophrenics have enlarged ventricles and smaller medial temporal lobes and hippocampuses and part of the limbic system is also smaller. There is also reduced blood flow in the brains of schizophrenics when engaged in cognitive tasks.

- These brain differences do not appear to be the result of being ill or of taking medication and in the absence of neural scarring, they seem to be the product of a failure to develop properly.

However, the differences are not sufficient on their own to allow diagnosis.

- According to the dopamine hypothesis, schizophrenic symptoms are caused directly by an excess of dopamine. The hypothesis is based on postmortems, beliefs about how drugs like chlorpromazine work and the observed effects of amphetamines and L-dopa, the latter used in the treatment of Parkinson's disease. However, PET scans suggest that dopamine metabolism may not be abnormal. A deficit in glutamate neurons in the cortex has also been implicated.

- Even if the evidence of structural and functional differences were conclusive and even if it could be shown that these differences actually cause the symptoms, we still wouldn't know how these differences come about. The main explanation is the genetic theory, which is tested using three types of behaviour-genetic design, namely family resemblance studies, twin studies and adoption studies.

- Family resemblance studies confound genetic and environmental factors. Twin studies point towards a major genetic contribution, although the concordance rate for MZs is far from 100 percent. A crucial feature of twin studies is the equal environments assumption, which appears to be justified.

- Adoption studies use different designs, but they too support the genetic theory. They assume random placement of children who are adopted and there is some controversy as to whether this is the exception or the rule.

- On balance, schizophrenia is seen as being influenced by genetic factors as much as many medical disorders are; the mode of inheritance is likely to be polygenic, whereby several genes determine a predisposition, which then requires environmental factors to trigger the symptoms (the diathesis-stress model). There is no clear-cut evidence as to what the environmental triggers are.

- Laing, together with Cooper and Esterson, spearheaded the antipsychiatry movement in the 1960s. Laing proposed a number of models of schizophrenia, the existentialist analysis (according to which the person experiences ontological insecurity), the family interaction model (based on social phenomenology), the conspiratorial model (which sees labelling as central) and the psychedelic model.

GLOSSARY

Agoraphobia The most common phobia, comprising a collection of fears: primarily, fear of leaving the safety/security of home or familiar people; secondarily, fear of open/public places/spaces.

Bipolar mood/affective disorder Either alternating episodes of mania and depression (the most common) or mania alone (very rare).

Culture-bound syndromes (CBSs) Forms of mental disorder thought to be unique to particular cultural populations and which fall outside the mainstream classification systems. Seen as culturally determined (unlike Western mental disorders). Also called 'exotic' disorders.

Dementia praecox Kraepelin's original term for what Bleuler later called 'schizophrenia'.

Diathesis-stress model A theory of schizophrenia, according to which a predisposition is inherited which requires environmental factors to act as a trigger for the symptoms ('diathesis'= predisposition).

Dopamine hypothesis A theory of schizophrenia according to which symptoms are directly caused by an excess of dopamine in the brain.

Double bind Bateson's term for contradictory messages that form part of the pathological forms of communication commonly used in schizophrenic families.

DSM Diagnostic and Statistical Manual of Mental Disorders, the official classification system of the American Psychiatric Association. Currently in its fourth edition (DSM-IV, 1994).

Ego-dystonic homosexuality Term introduced into DSM-III to refer to someone who is homosexually aroused, finds this arousal distressing and wishes to become heterosexual. Replaced 'homosexuality' as a mental disorder. ICD-10 includes 'ego-dystonic sexual orientation'.

Equal environments assumption The belief that identical twins (MZs) are not treated more similarly than non-identical twins (DZs) of the same sex.

Functional psychosis A serious psychological disturbance for which there is no demonstrable physical basis. Something has gone wrong with the way the person functions socially and interpersonally (Szasz's 'problem in living').

ICD International Classification of Diseases (Mental and Behavioural Disorders; Chapter 5), published by the World Health Organization (WHO). Currently in its tenth edition (ICD-10).

Insight The recognition that one has a problem, something lacking in the case of psychosis.

Ontological insecurity Term used by Laing to describe the schizophrenic person's experience of feeling overwhelmed, so that their very existence is under threat. Involves engulfment, implosion and petrification/depersonalization.

Organic psychosis A serious psychological disturbance which has a demonstrable physical basis.

Process schizophrenia A form of schizophrenia, in which symptoms have been evident for many years before the 'breakdown' occurs; genetic factors seem to play a greater role than in reactive schizophrenia.

Random placement assumption The belief that children being adopted are placed with parents who are no more like their biological parents than by chance.

Reactive schizophrenia A form of schizophrenia in which symptoms appear quite suddenly, usually later in life, as a response to extreme stress.

Residual rules Scheff's term for the 'unnameable' expectations or unarticulated rules concerning 'decency' and 'reality', which schizophrenics are seen as breaking, making their behaviour seem strange and frightening.

Symptoms The patient's description/report of feelings, sensations, perceptions, thoughts, etc. Distinguished from the signs of an illness, based on physical examination, objective tests, observation of the patient's behaviour, etc.

Unipolar mood/affective disorder Episodes of depression. 'Manic depression' refers to both unipolar and bipolar disorders.

FURTHER READING

Davison, G.C. and Neale, J.M. (1994) *Abnormal Psychology*, 6th edn. New York: John Wiley and Sons. An excellent reference text, as well as adopting a critical approach to all aspects of abnormal psychology; it is equally relevant to Chapter 31.

Lilienfeld, S.O. (1995) *Seeing Both Sides: Classic Controversies in Abnormal Psychology.* Pacific Grove, CA: Brooks/Cole Publishing Company. A unique approach in which each of 19 controversial issues is represented by two readings that present opposing viewpoints, with the author previewing and discussing the debate and offering a balanced synthesis. An exceptional book.

31 TREATMENTS AND THERAPIES

INTRODUCTION AND OVERVIEW

We saw in the previous chapter that the study of psychological abnormality involves a convergence of psychiatry and abnormal psychology, the latter being defined as the scientific study of the causes of abnormal behaviour and mental disorders. In this chapter, we are more concerned with the application of psychological knowledge and understanding of abnormality; this is the concern of *clinical psychology*, as well as the more recent *counselling psychology,* the two professional branches of the discipline of psychology whose goals are the maintenance of mental and physical health and the generation of psychological well-being (Powell, 1995).

There is considerable overlap between clinical and counselling psychology: they both draw on the same research findings and the same range of theoretical approaches that have recurred throughout this book (the psychoanalytic, humanistic-existential, behavioural, cognitive and neurobiological/biogenic) and they both adopt the scientist-practitioner model of helping, according to which the professional helper is guided by, and operates within the framework of, general scientific method, i.e. clear descriptions of problems, the formation of alternative hypotheses guided by psychological knowledge and the testing of the hypotheses by observation, monitoring and other forms of assessment of alternative treatments (Dallos and Cullen, 1990).

However, clinical psychologists have traditionally been more influenced by *behavioural* approaches, based on classical and operant conditioning (see Chapter 7), while counselling psychologists (and the trained counsellor who may not be a psychologist) have been more influenced by the *humanistic* approach, especially that of Carl Rogers. A third, overlapping professional group are *psychotherapists,* who are trained to use one or other form of psychotherapy, all deriving originally from Freud's psychoanalysis.

We shall begin the chapter by trying to classify the great diversity of therapies and treatments. Then we shall discuss all the major theoretical approaches in terms of their model of psychological abnormality and the main techniques and procedures they use to try to change people's behaviour, thoughts and feelings. Finally, we shall consider the highly controversial but very important question: is therapy effective?

A CLASSIFICATION OF TREATMENTS AND THERAPIES

As you can see from Figure 31.1, all the major theoretical approaches which have been discussed throughout this book are represented. Table 1.1 (p.12) shows that the way each approach defines abnormality is logically related to how it defines normality; however, the relationship between theory and therapy is not quite so straightforward.

Where theory has grown out of clinical practice (i.e. work with psychiatric patients), theory and therapy are intimately connected (e.g. Freud's psychoanalysis and Rogers' client-centred therapy). By contrast, behavioural therapies (of which there are many different kinds) are not always directly derived from learning theory, which is sometimes unable to account for therapeutic outcomes and certain aspects of abnormal behaviour. (This is especially true in the case of phobias, which we shall discuss in detail.) Some forms of therapy are not directly related to any particular theory (e.g. psychodrama and transactional analysis) and, in practice, treatment is often 'eclectic', i.e. it combines different techniques from different approaches.

Three important dimensions along which treatments and therapies can be placed are physical/organic vs. psychological, directive vs. non-directive and individual vs group.

- What *psychological* treatments (the vast majority) all have in common is a rejection of the medical model (which, as the basis of psychiatry, involves the use of physical/organic or biogenic treatments). For example, although Freud distinguished between 'symptoms' and 'underlying pathology', the latter is conceived in psychological terms (not genetic or biochemical) and he was concerned with the individual and not the 'disorder'. Although he used diagnostic labels, he did so as linguistic conveniences rather than as an integral part of his theories and he focused on understanding his patients' problems in their life context rather than on clinical labelling (Mackay, 1975).

- One aspect of 'technique' which is profoundly important in the therapeutic relationship is whether or not the therapist makes suggestions and gives advice to the patient (or client). In *directive* therapies, concrete suggestions are made and clients are often instructed to do certain things; for example, they may be given 'homework' in between sessions or may have to perform specific exercises under the therapist's supervision – the best examples are behaviour therapy, cognitive behaviour therapy and personal construct therapy. These differ in terms of what they suggest the client does and how this leads to the desired change (which in turn, of course, depends upon what the therapist sees as 'the problem' in the first place). For example, behaviour therapy concentrates directly upon changing people's behaviour (and any desired changes in thoughts and feelings will 'look after themselves') while cognitive behaviour therapy is aimed directly at thoughts and feelings, so that clients are instructed to talk to themselves in different ways, to give themselves instructions for behaviour, to write down their distressing and negative thought patterns and so on.

Non-directive therapies, on the other hand, concentrate on making sense of what is going on in the relationship between therapist and client and on understanding the meanings of the client's experience; the best examples are psychoanalysis and client-centred therapy. These are more difficult to describe than directive therapies because the therapist plays a more passive role and generally does not suggest things to the client but, 'rather listens and takes part with the client in exploring and experiencing what is going on between them' (Oatley, 1984). But as with directive therapies, there are important differences, in particular how the therapist contributes to that process of exploring and experiencing which, in turn, reflect the therapist's theoretical assumptions about what is wrong.

- *Individual* therapies are conducted between a therapist and a client, while *group* therapies involve several clients at a time, with one or more therapists or leaders ; most of the major approaches described in this chapter are individual

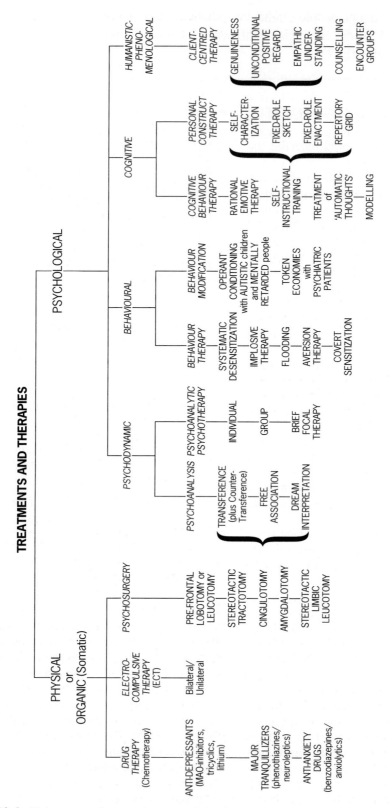

FIGURE 31.1 *Major approaches to treatment and therapy*

but some less well-known therapies are, by definition, group therapies (e.g. psychodrama, encounter
groups and therapeutic communities). We should
also note that psychodynamic and client-centred
therapies may be individual or group but they will
be described here in their individual form.

A major development in psychotherapy in the late
1970s and early 1980s was the emergence of *family
therapies* and *marital/couple therapy*, reflecting the
growing awareness by therapists of the important
role played by the client's relationships in the development and maintenance of their problems (Dryden,
1984). This change seems to have been inspired by
Laing's *family interaction model* of schizophrenia
(see Chapter 30), which has been applied to less
'serious' problems that commonly occur in families
and between partners. Generally, where the problem
is seen as interpersonal, family, marital/couple or
group therapy is likely to be recommended. However,
where the problem is seen as 'residing' within the
client (*intrapsychic*), individual therapy would be
recommended. While intrapsychic and interpersonal
processes are always mutually influencing one
another, Dryden (1984) sees them as separate, independent dimensions; it is not unusual for a client to
be involved in some form of individual and group,
family or marital/couple therapy at the same time.

● What is psychotherapy?

The term 'psychotherapy' is sometimes used to refer
to all psychological treatments (as opposed to physi-
cal/organic ones):

> The systematic use of a relationship between thera-
> pist and patient – as opposed to pharmacological or
> social methods – to produce changes in cognition,
> feelings and behaviour. (Holmes and Lindley, 1989)

Similarly:

> ... Psychotherapy is distinguished from such other
> forms of psychiatric treatment as the use of drugs,
> surgery, electric shock treatment and insulin coma
> treatment. (Freedman *et al.*, 1975)

'Psychotherapy' is also used to refer to those methods which are based, directly or indirectly, on
Freud's psychoanalysis. A more general term than
'psychoanalytic' is 'psychodynamic', which includes
the approaches of Jung, Adler, Klein, etc.(see
Chapter 29); this approach is also known as *insight
therapies* (or 'talking cures').

In the UK, the tradition has been to contrast 'psychotherapy' with 'behaviour therapy', while in the US

'psychotherapy' is used more broadly to include
'behavioural psychotherapy' as well as 'psychodynamic
therapy'. However, the UK Council for Psychotherapy
(UKCP), which changed its name in 1993 from the UK
Standing Conference for Psychotherapy, has a behavioural psychotherapy section (members of which
include the British Association for Behavioural and
Cognitive Psychotherapy) as well as a psychoanalytic
and psychodynamic psychotherapy section (members
of which include the British Association of
Psychotherapists (BAP) and the Women's Therapy
Centre). Other sections include humanistic and integrative psychotherapy and family, marital, and sexual
therapy. In 1994, there were 73 member organizations;
special members include the British Psychological
Society (BPS) and the Royal College of Psychiatrists,
and the British Association for Counselling is an affili-
ated organization (Pokorny, 1994).

THE PHYSICAL/ORGANIC
APPROACH

● Drug therapy (chemotherapy/pharma-
cological therapy)

Table 3.2 (p.49) shows the three major groups of psychoactive drugs used in the treatment of mental
illness:

1 the *anti-depressants* (comprising the MAO
   inhibitors, tricyclics and lithium);
2 the *major tranquillizers* (phenothiazines ,'anti-
   schizophrenic drugs' or neuroleptics); and
3 the *anti-anxiety drugs* (minor tranquillizers,
   benzodiazepines or anxiolytics).

Anti-depressants

Anti-depressants were discovered accidentally in
1952; tuberculosis patients who were being treated
with a new drug called iproniazid seemed to be making a remarkable recovery but it was soon discovered
that while their disease remained unaffected, their
understandable depressed mood was being lifted by
the drug. It was later learned that iproniazid and
related drugs (e.g. phenelzine or Nardil) inhibit the
activity of an enzyme known as *monoamine oxidase*
(MAO) and tend to gradually raise the levels of activity of neurons that utilize dopamine or noradrenaline
(the *monoamines*). This group of drugs is therefore
known as *MAO inhibitors*.

The search for better and safer drugs for depression led to the discovery of the *tricyclic anti-depressants* (so named because their basic chemical structure includes three carbon rings), such as imipramine (Tofranil),which is the most studied and is often used as a standard for comparing other anti-depressants. They seem to act by blocking the reuptake of dopamine and noradrenaline, but some also block the re-uptake of serotonin, some block serotonin alone and some have no known effect on any of these systems (Hamilton and Timmons, 1995).

The MAO inhibitors are less effective than the tricyclics and can cause cerebral haemorrhage by promoting the bodily accumulation of amine chemicals. Newer, 'second generation' drugs have been developed, such as buproprion and fluoxetine, which is marketed as Prozac. Prozac has stirred great controversy, largely because of claimed side-effects which, as yet, have not been scientifically verified; it has rapidly become the most commonly prescribed anti-depressant medication (Costello *et al.*, 1995).

Lithium carbonate (Lithane or Lithonate) is used to treat bipolar mood disorder (see Chapter 30); it tends to stabilize the neurons, preventing the development of mania, although the precise mechanism remains unclear.

Anti-anxiety drugs

The anti-anxiety drugs are designed to treat 'everyday' anxieties, rather than the extreme symptoms of psychotic illness, in particular schizophrenia; see below. Barbiturates (and alcohol) had been used with some success, but dosages that reduced anxiety also produced troublesome side-effects of sedation. This led to the marketing of *meprobamate*, which became very popular even though it was in fact just a mild barbiturate that had as many sedative effects as other similar drugs. By the early 1960s two drugs had been discovered which claimed to be able to reduce anxiety without sedation, namely *chlordiazepoxide* (marketed as Librium) and *diazepam* (Valium); these quickly became the most widely prescribed drugs of their time. In 1989, for example, there were 21 million prescriptions in the UK alone (Rassool and Winnington, 1993).

Chlordiazepoxide and related *benzodiazepine* compounds were initially called minor tranquillizers (as opposed to the anti-psychotic, major tranquillizers), but this terminology became unpopular and they are now known simply as anti-anxiety drugs. They act by facilitating the activity of GABA (see Chapter 3) and there is growing evidence that the brain produces its own anti-anxiety compounds that are released during periods of stress (Hamilton and Timmons, 1995).

Major tranquillizers

Major tranquillizers such as *chlorpromazine* were originally developed in order to calm patients facing surgery and they proved highly effective in reducing the incidence of death from surgical shock. Chlorpromazine (Largactil) and related *phenothiazine* drugs were soon used with psychiatric patients, starting in the early 1950s, and are considered to have revolutionized psychiatry by allowing the most disturbed schizophrenic patients to live outside a psychiatric hospital or to reduce their average length of stay. However, many critics have called these drugs 'pharmacological straitjackets', replacing the kind with straps with the 'zombie-like' state which they produce.

Chlorpromazine becomes concentrated in the brainstem and is secreted only very slowly, so that the effect on the brain is prolonged. At first there is a striking sedation effect, which wears off after a few days; it reduces responsiveness to external stimulation and gross motor activity but without reducing motor power or co-ordination. It has been shown to be superior to placebos in controlling hallucinations, excitement, thought disorder and delusions and it seems to produce its beneficial effects by blocking the *D2 receptor* for dopamine. However, this is often at the expense of a dry mouth, blurred vision, low blood pressure (which may cause fainting attacks) and neuromuscular effects (identical to those seen in Parkinson's disease), most serious being *tardive dyskinesia*, whose existence 'should be a deterrent to the long-term prescribing of anti-psychotic drugs in large doses' (Gelder *et al.*, 1989).

Many believe that the combination of these drugs with psychotherapy is the most productive way of treating severely disturbed patients; drugs cannot produce a 'cure' but can only alleviate some of the symptoms which may enable the patient to benefit from other forms of treatment or therapy.

● Electroconvulsive therapy

It was commonly believed during the 1920s and 1930s that schizophrenia and epilepsy do not occur together in the same person, i.e. each somehow buffers the individual against developing the other. Based on this belief, Nyiro, in the early 1930s, transfused schizophrenic patients with blood from epileptics, but in vain (pun intended!). Sakel induced epileptic-like seizures in schizophrenics using *insulin coma therapy*, which involves inducing hypoglycaemic coma by administering increasing doses of insulin over a 2–4-week period (see Chapter 5); each coma was typically followed by seizures.

In 1938, Cerletti and Bini, two Italian doctors, first gave an electric shock to the brain of a psychiatric patient (the process being described by an eyewitness as barbaric – Lilienfeld, 1995) on the assumption that if a grand mal epileptic fit is induced (artificially), this should reduce or eliminate the symptoms of schizophrenia. It started to be used widely in the US from the early 1940s but, ironically, it was found to be more effective for severe depression than schizophrenia and is now used mainly with depressive patients. What happens?

First, the patient is made comfortable on a bed, clothes loosened and shoes and dentures removed; atropine is given as a routine pre-anaesthetic medication (to dry up salivary and bronchial secretions) and then thiopentone, a quick-acting anaesthetic, followed by a muscle relaxant. A 70–150 volt shock lasting 0.04–1.00 seconds is then given through electrodes placed on the temples, producing a generalized convulsion which lasts for up to a minute (and is detected by facial and limb twitching). Typically, 2–3 treatments per week are given for 3–4 weeks.

Many psychiatrists believe that for severe depression, *bilateral* ECT (one electrode on each side of the head) is preferable as it acts more quickly and fewer treatments are needed. In *unilateral* ECT, an electrode is applied to the non-dominant hemisphere side (the right side for most people) and is intended to reduce the side-effects, particularly memory disruption (Benton, 1981). Memory disruption includes retrograde amnesia and impaired ability to acquire new memories (see Chapter 12); however, depression is associated with impaired memory function and so it is not clear how much ECT itself is responsible (Benton, 1981). The patient is normally confused for up to 40 minutes following treatment but recall of events prior to treatment gradually returns, although some degree of memory loss may persist for several weeks.

The mortality rate is now quite low, somewhere between 3.6 and 9 per 100,000 treatments (a figure very similar to that resulting from anaesthesia for minor surgery). This makes it one of the safest medical treatments there is and when the number of suicides resulting from depression are taken into account (one estimate being that, without treatment, 11 percent of depressives will die from suicide or other causes over a five-year period), ECT emerges as very low-risk indeed.

However, the possibility of death is only one of the objections made to ECT by, for example, MIND (the National Association for Mental Health) and PROMPT (Protect the Rights of Mental Patients in Therapy) in the UK and NAPA (Network Against Psychiatric Assault) in the USA. The main objections are ethical, one of them being that since we do not know how it works (and *if* it works) it should not be used; another relates to the issue of consent (see Chapter 32). Despite all the objections, ECT seems to be currently enjoying a revival (Twombly, 1994).

Just how effective is ECT?

One problem with trying to measure its effectiveness experimentally is, ironically, also ethical, namely, the problem of the placebo effect or simulated (sham or 'dummy') ECT in which the patient undergoes all aspects of the ECT procedure except that no electrical current is passed through the brain (so no seizure is produced).

Sackeim (1989) reviewed controlled comparisons of real and sham ECT and concluded that real ECT is significantly more effective; although bilateral is slightly more effective than unilateral, this is outweighed by the greater memory deficits produced by bilateral. He also concluded that ECT is probably the most effective available treatment for depression (including anti-depressant drugs), but use of medication following ECT can help to prevent relapse.

One of the most outspoken critics of all physical treatments, the American psychiatrist Peter Breggin (1991), presents two case histories to support his claim that ECT is capable of producing profound brain damage and points out that elderly women are the most likely to receive it. It almost invariably causes acute organic brain syndrome or delirium and severe, long-term deficits in cognitive and emotional functioning. He argues that, to the extent that it 'works', it does so by causing brain damage: the patient suffers *anosognosia*, a condition in which patients deny their psychological and physical difficulties (which is like 'treating' prolonged depression by being permanently drunk). Any beneficial effects are short-lived and the evidence that it reduces suicide risks is weak.

How does ECT work?

Benton (1981) identifies the following proposed explanations:

● Patients learn that treatment is recommended because of their pathological behaviour and so ECT is seen as a *punishment* which extinguishes the undesirable behaviour. However, equally unpleasant but *sub*-convulsive shocks (i.e. which do not produce a convulsion) are not effective, which seems inconsistent with the punishment explanation.

- *Memory loss* allows the restructuring of the patient's view of life. However, unilateral ECT is intended to minimize memory disruption and so it seems possible to dissociate memory loss from therapeutic advantage.
- The shock produces a wide range of *biochemical changes* in the brain (e.g. the stimulation of neurotransmitters, including noradrenaline(and endorphins; Lilienfeld, 1995)) and this effect is more widespread than that produced by anti-depressant drugs.

There is no generally accepted explanation, only very tentative hypotheses; however, Benton (1981) believes that this does not constitute a reason for not using it since many medical treatments fall into this category (e.g. aspirin getting rid of headaches). Clare (1980) argues that, because it is relatively quick and easy to administer, ECT is much abused and overused: psychiatrists who persist in so abusing it have only themselves to blame if the public conclude that the treatment is a fraud and an anachronism and demand its abolition. Clare, himself a psychiatrist, observes that 'It is easier for a psychiatrist, overwhelmed by the sheer number of patients, to reach for the ECT machine than to use more time-consuming and different approaches'.

● Psychosurgery

Psychosurgery was pioneered by Moniz, a Portuguese professor of neurology, who was so impressed by the tranquilizing effects of lesions to the frontal lobes of monkeys that he performed the first *pre-frontal lobotomies* (or *leucotomies*) on human schizophrenics in 1935. Between 1935 and 1949, Moniz performed about 100 such operations in which tissue connecting the frontal lobes of the cortex with subcortical brain areas is cut on both sides of the cortex. (Moniz was awarded the Nobel Price for Medicine in 1949 and was later shot in the spine by one of his lobotomized patients, confining him to a wheelchair for the rest of his life.)

Freeman and Watts (1942) pioneered psychosurgery in the USA and it has been estimated that 40,000–50,000 pre-frontal lobotomies have been performed in that country alone since the late 1930s. They modified Moniz's technique by inserting a scalpel either into burr holes drilled through the patient's temple or through the eye socket (see Fig. 31.2). Although their so-called 'standard leucotomy' was far from standardized anatomically and despite unacceptable side-effects, the procedure was widely used in the UK and other countries (Gelder *et al.*, 1989). For example, in the UK, about 10,000 operations were carried out between 1942 and 1952, two-thirds of which involved schizophrenics and about one-quarter depressives, with the latter responding much more favourably.

Side-effects included apathy, lethargy, epilepsy, intellectual impairment, aggressiveness and personality changes, as well as death. As it became clear that the frontal cortex has complex connections with the hypothalamus, temporal cortex, hippocampus, amygdala and mammillary bodies, the surgical approach became directed to some of these connections, rather than to the frontal lobe itself. Today, the older 'blind' operations have been replaced by *stereotactic procedures*, which allow only very small amounts of brain tissue to be destroyed in very precise locations ('fractional operations'). Some of these include:

- *stereotactic tractotomy*, in which the lesion is produced by implanting radioactive yttrium 'seeds';
- *stereotactic limbic leucotomy*, in which small bilateral lesions are made on a particular part of the frontal lobe, in order to interrupt two of the frontolimbic pathways, and in the cingulum, which is located near the corpus callosum. A *cingulotomy* is occasionally used for obsessions and compulsions, in which 2–3 cm of white matter are destroyed;
- *amygdalotomy*, involving bilateral lesions in the amygdala (destroying the neural circuit connecting the amygdala and the hypothalamus, based on Kluver and Bucy's work with cats; see Chapter 3), usually in the treatment of abnormal, intractable aggression (Gelder *et al.*, 1989). This is perhaps the most controversial of all psychosurgical techniques, partly because the patient is not usually suffering, partly because it is often used with subnormal aggressive patients (so informed consent is unlikely to be given) and partly because, although the surgery has a 'marked calming effect' in 95 percent of cases, it cannot entirely eliminate episodes of terror and outbursts of violence.

The abuse of psychosurgery

Balasubramanian (1970, cited in Taylor, 1992) performed 115 operations on hyperactive children (three aged under five and 36 under 11), using how quiet and well-behaved they became as the criterion of success.

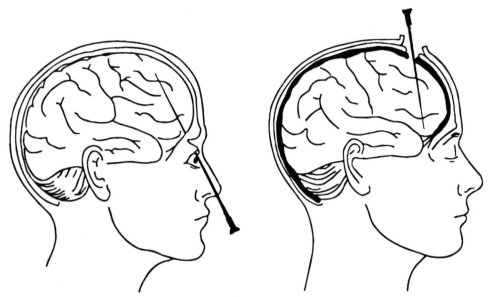

FIGURE 31.2 *The drawing on the left shows the technique used by Freeman and Watts (transorbital leucotomy), a modification of Moniz's classical pre-frontal lobotomy/leucotomy (shown on the right)*

Sargent and Slater, two major British enthusiasts of psychosurgery, operated on a woman who was extremely depressed; her husband was a psychopath but she felt unable to leave him because of the children. Despite feeling that drugs might help her, they opted for a leucotomy (Taylor, 1992). Finally, Taylor refers to the views of two American neurosurgeons, Mark and Sweet, and a psychiatrist, Ervin, who believed that the rise in urban violence in the USA in the early 1970s could be slowed if more leucotomies were performed. They began a series of government-funded studies to pinpoint, diagnose and treat those with a low violence threshold; specifically, their goal was to detect and treat limbic dysfunctions.

Does it work and should it ever be used?

In 1968, there were 38,000 leucotomies performed worldwide, but this figure dropped substantially during the 1970s. In England, the 500 operations in 1970 dropped to 62 in 1980 and a mere 18 in 1991 (Taylor, 1992). Since the 1950s and the widespread use of anti-schizophrenic drugs, schizophrenics have rarely been treated in this way. In England and Wales, its use is governed by the 1983 Mental Health Act which endorses it only as a last resort, requiring the patient's consent. Though rare in the U.K., it is still used and is more common in Australia and the US (Taylor, 1992).

Because no adequate controlled evaluations have been carried out, judgements as to the effectiveness of psychosurgery have to be based on follow-up studies of patients who have undergone the procedure; lack of proper controls makes it impossible to determine how much improvement would have taken place without surgery (Gelder *et al.*, 1989). While some improvements have been reported, ' ... this intervention is rightfully viewed as a treatment of very last resort, given the permanence of psychosurgery and the poorly understood ways in which it works' (Davison and Neale, 1994). Even with modern stereotactic procedures, serious side-effects occur and they should only ever be used if all other forms of treatment have been tried (Gelder *et al.*, 1989).

PSYCHOANALYSIS AND OTHER PSYCHODYNAMIC APPROACHES

● Freud's model of psychological disorder

In Chapter 29, neurotic symptoms were described as compromises (as were dreams and defence mechanisms) between the opposing demands made on the ego by the id and the superego; symptoms, dreams and defences are all expressions of the inevitable conflict which arises from these opposing demands and are, at the same time, attempts to deal with it.

When the person experiences anxiety, the ego is signalling that it fears being overwhelmed by an all-powerful id (*neurotic anxiety*) or superego (*moral anxiety*) and so must mobilize its defences. Anxiety is the hallmark of most neurotic disorders but, except in 'free-floating anxiety' it becomes redirected or transformed in some way (depending on which particular defence is used), so that the resulting symptom makes it even less likely that the true nature of the problem (i.e. the underlying conflict) will be spotted. Phobias, for example, involve repression (as do all neuroses) plus displacement and projection. Little Hans (see Chapter 21) had a phobia of being bitten by a horse, which could be explained in terms of:

- *repressing* his jealous anger and hatred felt towards his father;
- *projecting* these feelings onto his father, thus seeing him as a threatening, murderous man; and
- *displacing* this perception of his father onto a 'safer' target, namely, horses.

Phobic objects, according to Freud, are not arbitrarily chosen but in some way symbolically represent the object for which they are a substitute.

Neuroses, therefore, are maladaptive solutions to the problems faced by the person; that is, they do not help resolve the conflict but merely help to avoid it (both in thought and behaviour). So neurotics adopt self-defeating strategies; far from solving problems, the neurotic's behaviour usually creates its own distress and unhappiness (the *neurotic paradox*). How can we account for such paradoxical behaviour? One answer is that it permits immediate tension release, even if it only adds to the neurotic's problems in the long term. (This is an explanation that easily fits the learning theory principle of reinforcement, which we shall discuss in detail in the next section.)

Psychoneurotic symptoms, therefore, are indicative of deep-seated, unresolved, unconscious conflicts, usually of a sexual and/or aggressive nature, which stem from childhood feelings, memories, wishes and experiences which have been repressed and defended against in other ways. However, these defences are not effective ways of dealing with the conflict and they create their own distress and anxiety.

● The aims of psychoanalysis

There are many ways in which the goals of psychoanalysis have been defined. These can be stated in very broad, abstract terms, such as ' ... a far-reaching and radical restructuring of the personality ... ' (Fonagy, 1995) and as attempts to provide the client with insight, self-knowledge and self-understanding. (This is a different sense of the term 'insight' from that given in Chapter 30 when distinguishing neurosis and psychosis; there, it meant the patient's recognition that there is a problem while here, it means understanding the true nature of the problem. Patients would not be coming for psychoanalysis in the first place unless they thought something was wrong.) A little more specifically, the basic goal of psychoanalysis is to make 'the unconscious conscious', to undo unsatisfactory defences and through a 'therapeutic regression' (Winnicott, 1958) to re-experience repressed feelings and wishes, which have been frustrated in childhood, in a safe context and to express them, as an adult, in a more appropriate way, 'with a new ending' (Alexander and French, 1946).

FIGURE 31.3 *Sigmund Freud's couch. (©Freud Museum Publications Ltd)*

● Therapeutic techniques: How are the aims achieved?

In classic psychoanalysis, the analyst is meant to remain faceless and 'anonymous', i.e. he/she should not show any emotion or reveal any personal information. Instead, ' ... The doctor should be opaque to his patients and, like a mirror, should show them nothing but what is shown to him' (Freud, 1912, quoted in Jacobs, 1992). With the analyst as an 'ambiguous object' or 'blank screen', the patient is able to project and displace repressed feelings onto them , in particular, those concerning parents (*transference*), and the process is aided by the client lying on a couch with the analyst sitting behind, out of the client's (*analysand's*) field of vision (Fig. 31.2). (Jacobs notes that, in practice, Freud often became personally involved in the therapeutic conversation and would explain his thinking to the patient; see below).

Transference typically goes through a positive phase of emotional attachment to the analyst followed by a negative and critical phase; according to Freud, this reflects working through the ambivalence experienced in the child's relationship with their parents (Stevens, 1995). According to Thomas (1990), transference has become so central to theory and practice that many, though not all, analysts believe that making interpretations about transference is what distinguishes psychoanalysis from other forms of psychotherapy. When attention is focused on the transference and what is happening in the here and now, the historical reconstruction of childhood events and the search for the childhood origins of conflicts may take second place.

There is also the related process of *counter-transference*, which refers to the therapist's feelings of irritation, dislike or sexual attraction towards the client:

> ... In Freud's time, counter-transference feelings ... were considered to be a failing on the part of the analyst. These feelings were to be controlled absolutely ... Now, counter-transference is considered an unavoidable outcome of the analytic process, irrespective of how well prepared the analyst is by analytic training and its years of required personal analysis ... most modern analysts are trained to observe their own counter-transference feelings and to *use* these to increase their understanding of the patients' transference and defences. (Thomas, 1990)

To enable the client to understand the transference and how it relates to childhood conflicts, the analyst must *interpret* it, i.e. tell the client what it means, its significance in terms of what has already been revealed about the client's childhood experiences. Because this is likely to be painful and distressing clients use another form of defence called *resistance*, an attempt to escape from or avoid these self-revelations. It may take the form of 'drying up' when talking, changing the subject, dismissing some emotionally significant event in a very flippant way, even falling asleep or arriving late for therapy. All forms of resistance are extremely significant items and themselves require interpretation.

Despite what we have said about the analyst's anonymity, it is essential that there is a 'working alliance' with the client, whereby the client's ego is strengthened sufficiently to be able to cope with the anxiety caused by the return to consciousness of repressed feelings and memories. According to Jacobs (1984), the working alliance consists of two adults co-operating to understand the 'child' in the client; the analyst adopts a quiet, reflective style, intervening when they judge the client to be ready to make use of a particular interpretation. This is an art, says Jacobs, and does not involve fitting the client into psychoanalytic theory, as some critics suggest.

Two other major techniques used to reveal the client's unconscious mind are *dream interpretation* (which we discussed in Chapter 29) and *free association*, in which the client says whatever comes to mind, no matter how silly, irrelevant or embarrassing it may seem. (These may both lead to resistance which, like transference, will in turn be interpreted by the analyst.)

● The concept of cure: How do you know when to stop?

According to Jacobs (1984), the goals of therapy are limited by what clients consciously want to achieve and are capable of achieving, together with their motivation, ego strength, capacity for insight, ability to tolerate the frustration of gradual change, financial cost and so on. These factors, in turn, will determine how a cure is to be defined and assessed.

In practice, psychoanalysis ranges from psychoanalytical first aid (Guntrip, 1968) or symptom relief to different levels of more intense work. However, Storr (1966) believes that a quick, complete 'cure' is very much the exception rather than the rule and the majority of people who present themselves for psychoanalysis cannot expect that their symptoms will easily disappear or, even if this should happen, that they will be freed of emotional problems. This is because neurotic symptoms are merely the outward and visible signs of an inner, less visible distortion of the client's total personality and exploration and analysis of the symptoms inevitably lead to an analysis of the whole person.

In trying to assess the effectiveness of psychoanalysis, the usual practice is to assess the extent to which clients experience relief of their symptoms, but Storr believes this is an inappropriate way of thinking of 'cure', partly because symptom analysis is only the start of the analytic process and also because a majority of clients do not have clear-cut symptoms anyway. (We shall return later on to the debate about the effectiveness of psychoanalysis compared with other approaches). Freud himself was aware of the limitations of psychoanalysis. It is only likely to be successful if the patient is voluntary, open to change, acknowledges that there is a problem and is neurotic rather than psychotic; the latter displays an extreme form of the turning away from reality shown by the former and is unable to form a positive transference. Even if the patient possesses these characteristics, fresh neurosis or even the return of the original one cannot be ruled out; analysis never really ends and even those which end satisfactorily are, in some sense, unfinished. 'What analysis achieves for neurotics is nothing other than what normal people bring about for themselves without its help' (Freud, 1937, quoted in Jacobs, 1992).

● Psychoanalytic psychotherapy

In the UK, classic psychoanalysis requires the client to attend five 50-minute sessions per week for several years which, for many people, is far too expensive, as well as too time-consuming.

In a modified form of analysis, therapist and client meet once or twice a week for a limited period; there may be a 'contract' for a specified number of weeks as opposed to the open-ended arrangement of classic analysis. For example, Malan (1976) at the Tavistock Clinic in London uses *brief focal therapy* (one session per week for about 30 weeks), in which the focus is on fairly specific psychological problems such as a single conflict area or relationship in the client's current life. Although all the basic techniques of psychoanalysis may be used, there is considerably less emphasis on the client's past and client and therapist usually sit in armchairs face to face; this form of psychotherapy is practised by many clinical psychologists (as well as psychiatrists and social workers) without receiving a full-blown psychoanalytic training (Fonagy, 1995; Fonagy and Higgitt, 1984).

BEHAVIOURAL APPROACHES

Treatment methods based on classic learning theory (i.e. conditioning) are often referred to interchangeably as 'behaviour therapy' and 'behaviour modification'. However, I shall distinguish between them in the way proposed by Walker (1984), namely:

● Behaviour *therapy* refers to techniques based on *classical conditioning* developed by psychologists such as Wolpe and Eysenck in order to extinguish maladaptive behaviours and substitute adaptive ones.
● Behaviour *modification* refers to techniques based on *operant conditioning* developed by psychologists such as Ayllon and Azrin to build up appropriate behaviour (where it did not previously exist) or to increase the frequency of certain responses and decrease the frequency of others.

● Models of psychological disorder

Both behaviour therapy and modification regard all behaviour, whether adaptive or maladaptive, as acquired by the same principles of classical and operant conditioning respectively (see Chapter 7).

The medical model is completely rejected, including any distinction between 'symptoms' and underlying pathology; according to Eysenck (1960), if you 'get rid of the symptom ... you have eliminated the neurosis', i.e. what you see is what there is! The focus for the often heated disagreement between 'Freudians' and 'behaviourists' has been *symptom substitution*: according to psychoanalysts, if the underlying, unconscious conflict is not dealt with (but only the symptoms, as in behaviour therapy), new neurotic symptoms will replace those which are successfully removed. However, this is increasingly being seen as an oversimplification and misunderstanding of what behaviour therapy involves. Wachtel (1989), for example, argues that in some ways all theories and therapies make assumptions about 'symptoms as manifestations of some underlying problem'; what distinguishes different approaches is the view taken of the nature of those underlying problems and how much change is needed in the organism in order for the problem to be remedied. He calls for an integration between the two approaches which, in practice, is already happening.

According to Mackay (1975), some behaviour therapists make use of the formal diagnostic categories or 'syndromes' and try to discover which techniques are most effective with particular diagnostic groups; key figures in this nomothetic approach are Eysenck, Rachman and Marks (*behavioural technology*). Others, however, believe that therapists should isolate the stimuli and consequences that are maintaining the inappropriate behaviour in each individual case and that, accordingly, any treatment programme should be derived from such a 'behavioural analysis' (or 'functional analysis'). Key figures in this idiographic approach are Yates and Meyer (*behavioural psychotherapy*).

Part of the functional analysis is an emphasis on current behaviour–environment relations, in contrast to the Freudian emphasis on past events (particularly early childhood ones) and unconscious (and other internal) factors. Psychological problems are behavioural problems which need to be *operationalized* (i.e. described in terms of observable behaviours) before we attempt to change them.

According to Eysenck and Rachman (1965), the case of little Albert (Chapter 7) exemplifies how all abnormal fears are acquired (i.e. through classical conditioning):

> Any neutral stimulus, simple or complex, that happens to make an impact on an individual at about the time a fear reaction is evoked, acquires the ability to evoke fear subsequently ... there will be generalization of fear reactions to stimuli resembling the conditioned stimulus. (Wolpe and Rachman, 1960)

Evidence to support this view comes from many sources; for example, phobics often recall an earlier traumatic experience associated with the onset of their phobia (e.g. a dog phobic recalling being attacked by a large Alsatian) and laboratory studies with humans and animals have shown that if the UCS is highly traumatic, a single pairing of the CS and UCS may be sufficient to induce a long-lasting CR (e.g. Garcia's taste aversion studies; see Chapter 7).

However, there is also considerable evidence against Eysenck and Rachman. Several studies have shown that phobics are often unable to recall any traumatic experience involving the object of their fear and, conversely, people may experience profound traumas without developing any obvious phobias (e.g. the concentration camp survivors, studied by Freud and Dann, 1951; see Chapter 22, and evidence from civilians who were continually bombed during the Second World War).

We noted in Chapter 7 that some phobias are easier to induce in the laboratory (in participants who do not already have them) and it is well known that certain naturally occurring phobias are more common than others. For example, rats, jellyfish, cockroaches, spiders and slugs are consistently rated as frightening and rabbits, ladybirds, cats and lambs as non-frightening and the crucial perceptual qualities seem to be ugliness, sliminess, speed and suddenness of movement (Bennett-Levy and Marteau, 1984). These and similar findings are consistent with the concept of preparedness (Seligman, 1970), which was discussed in Chapter 7. However, these findings have not always been replicated. For example, induced phobias of snakes and corpses are no harder to extinguish through treatment than phobias of chocolate and, in a review of the literature, McNally and Reiss (1982) concluded that there is little evidence to support the concept of preparedness.

Rachman (1977) himself now believes that direct conditioning of any kind accounts for relatively few phobias. Instead, he claims that many phobias are acquired on the basis of information transmitted through observation and instruction. Some support for this comes from a study by Murray and Foote (1979) who conclude by saying that although preparedness for direct conditioning does not seem to be relevant, a preparedness for observational and instructional learning is possible. Baddeley (1990) also takes the view that phobias are not acquired by the chance association of a stimulus with a fearful situation, but can be learned by imitation and tend to be associated with certain objects rather than others.

It is the persistence of naturally occurring phobias (i.e. their failure to extinguish) that poses one of the greatest difficulties for the classical conditioning explanation; the major theoretical attempt to account for this phenomenon has been the two-process/two-factor model, whereby the reduction of fear brought about by escaping or avoiding the feared object or situation negatively reinforces the escape or avoidance behaviour so that it tends to be repeated (this is the operant conditioning factor). The fear may have been acquired initially through classical conditioning (the other 'factor') but, on its own, classical conditioning cannot explain its persistence (see Chapter 7).

The persistence of neurotic behaviour may also be accounted for in terms of what Freud (1926) called *secondary gain*, whereby other people may, inadvertently, positively reinforce it; because of the role of positive and negative reinforcement in maintaining neurotic behaviour, Ullman and Krasner (1975) refused to accept that neurosis is, in any sense, paradoxical. The two-process/factor model has itself come in for criticism; an important alternative to it is the safety signal hypothesis, which maintains that avoidance is motivated not by the reduction of anxiety but by the positive feeling of safety. According to Rachman (1984), agoraphobia is motivated by seeking signals of safety and the *safety signal hypothesis* provides a better explanation of why agoraphobics find it easier to go out with, or be driven by, someone they trust and to take certain routes to their destination than the two-process/factor model – perhaps trusted individuals and certain streets and situations, etc. act as safety signals. It may also explain why the loss of a close relative so often marks the onset of a phobia (Fonagy and Higgitt, 1984) (see Chapters 24 and 30)

● Behaviour therapy

Systematic desensitization

As we saw in Chapter 7, the case of little Peter represents perhaps the earliest attempt to remove a phobia using systematic desensitization (SD) (and, indeed, the earliest attempt at any kind of behavioural treatment); it represents a form of *counterconditioning*.

Wolpe (1958) defined behaviour therapy as a whole as 'the use of experimentally established principles of learning for the purpose of changing unadaptive behaviour' and he is perhaps best known for his use and development of SD. Wolpe was very much influenced by the theory of Hull (see Chapter 5) and the key principle in SD is that of *reciprocal inhibition*, according to which:

> ... if a response inhibitory of anxiety can be made to occur in the presence of anxiety-evoking stimuli it will weaken the bond between these stimuli and the anxiety. (Wolpe, 1965)

In other words, it is impossible for two opposite emotions (e.g. anxiety and relaxation) to exist together at the same time. Accordingly, a patient with, for example, a spider phobia is taught to relax through deep muscle relaxation in which different muscle groups are alternately relaxed and tensed (alternatively, hypnosis or tranquillizers might be used) so that relaxation and fear of the object or situation 'cancel each other out' (this is the 'desensitization' part of the procedure).

The 'systematic' part of the procedure involves a graded series of contacts with the phobic object (usually by imagining it) based on a hierarchy of possible forms of contact from the least to the most frightening. Starting with the least feared contact, the patient, while relaxing, imagines it until this can be done without feeling any anxiety at all; then, and only then, will the next most feared contact be dealt with, in the same way, until the most frightening contact

can be imagined with no anxiety. For example, imagining the word 'spider' on a printed page may cause very little anxiety while imagining a large, hairy spider running all over your body might be very frightening indeed!

An evaluation of SD

Wolpe used imagination because some of his patients' fears were so abstract (e.g. fear of criticism or failure) that it was impractical to confront them with real-life situations that would evoke these fears. He also believed that the ability to tolerate stressful imagery is generally followed by a reduction in anxiety in related real-life situations. Between sessions, patients are usually instructed to put themselves in progressively more frightening real-life situations; these 'homework assignments' help to move their adjustment from imagination to reality (Davison and Neale, 1994).

Rachman and Wilson (1980) and McGlynn *et al.* (1981) believe that SD is definitely effective, although it is most effective for the treatment of minor phobias (e.g. animal phobias) as opposed to say, agoraphobia and for patients who are able to learn relaxation skills and have sufficiently vivid imaginations to be able to conjure up the sources of their fear. Another limitation of SD is that some patients may have difficulty transferring from the imaginary stimulus to real-life situations.

There is some debate as to whether or not either relaxation or the use of a hierarchy is actually necessary at all. According to Wilson and Davison (1971), for example, relaxation might be merely a useful way of encouraging a frightened person to confront what they are afraid of, which would otherwise be avoided. According to Marks (1973), SD works not because of the inhibiting effect of relaxation on anxiety (reciprocal inhibition) but because of the exposure to the feared situation; this seems to represent the generally accepted view among psychologists. Exposure is especially effective if it allows the person to disprove any predictions that something awful will happen if they come into contact with the feared object or situation and graded exposure helps to build up the person's confidence to cope with the exposure (Williams and Hargreaves, 1995).

Implosive therapy (implosion) and flooding

The essence of *implosion* is to expose the patient to what, in SD, would be at the top of the hierarchy; there is no gradual exposure accompanied by relaxation but the patient is 'thrown in at the deep end' right from the start. This is done by getting the patient to imagine their most terrifying form of contact (the big, hairy spider let loose, again) with vivid verbal descriptions by the therapist (*stimulus augmentation*) to supplement the patient's vivid imagery. How is it meant to work?

1 The patient's anxiety is maintained at such a high level that eventually some process of exhaustion or stimulus satiation takes place – the anxiety level can only go down!

2 Extinction occurs by preventing the patient from making their usual escape or avoidance response (Mowrer, 1960) and so implosion (and flooding) represent 'a form of forced reality testing' (Yates, 1970).

Flooding is exposure that takes place *in vivo* (e.g. with an actual spider). Marks *et al.* (1971) compared SD with flooding and found flooding to be superior and Gelder *et al.* (1973) compared SD with implosion and found no difference. These findings suggest that it is *in vivo* exposure which is crucial, and several writers consider flooding to be more effective than implosion (Emmelkamp and Wessels, 1975). Emmelkamp and Wessels (1975) and Marks *et al.* (1981) used flooding with agoraphobics very successfully and other studies have reported continued improvement for up to nine years after treatment without the appearance of 'substitute' problems. Wolpe (1960) forced an adolescent girl with a fear of cars into the back of a car and drove her around continuously for four hours; her fear reached hysterical heights but then receded and, by the end of the journey, had completely disappeared.

Marks (1981), in a review of flooding studies, found it to be the most universally effective of all the techniques used to treat fear.

Aversion therapy and covert sensitization

In *aversion therapy* some undesirable response to a particular stimulus is removed by associating the stimulus with another, aversive, stimulus. So, for example, alcohol is paired with an emetic drug (which induces severe nausea and vomiting) so that nausea and vomiting become a conditioned response to alcohol, i.e.:

$$\text{(UCS)} \longrightarrow \text{(UCR)}$$
Emetic drug (Antabuse   Nausea/vomiting
or apomorphine)

$$\text{(CS)} + \text{(UCS)} \longrightarrow \text{(UCR)}$$
Alcohol + emetic drug   Nausea/vomiting

$$\text{(CS)} \longrightarrow \text{(CR)}$$
Alcohol   Nausea/vomiting

BOX 31.1	Critical discussion: aversion therapy as a form of heterosexism

According to Davison and Neale (1994), several psychologists have argued that the social pressures on homosexuals to become 'straight' make it difficult to believe that the small minority of people who consult therapists for help in changing sexual preference are acting from choice.

The very fact that change-of-orientation treatments exist can be seen as condoning heterosexism. Clinicians work to develop procedures and study their effects only if they are concerned about the problem which their techniques are intended to remedy. The therapeutic literature contains relatively little material on helping homosexuals develop as individuals without this involving a change of sexual orientation; this contrasts with the many books and articles on how best to discourage homosexual behaviour and replace it by heterosexuality.

One very radical proposal is that therapists should not help homosexuals become straight even when such treatment is requested. But this, in turn, raises basic questions about limiting the options available to clients and, in refusing such treatment, aren't therapists making value judgements, just as they are when they agree to it? Again, isn't it the professional responsibility of therapists to meet the needs expressed by their clients? However, a client's request for a certain kind of treatment has never been sufficient justification for providing it (Davison and Neale, 1994).

There has, in fact, been a dramatic reduction in the use of aversion therapy with homosexuals since the mid-1970s. (See Chapter 32 for a discussion of more general ethical issues relating to therapies.)

The patient would, typically, be given warm saline solution containing the emetic drug; immediately before the vomiting begins, they are given a four-ounce glass of whisky which they are required to smell, taste and swill around in the mouth before swallowing. (If vomiting has not occurred, another straight whisky is given and, to prolong nausea, the patient is given a glass of beer containing emetic.) Subsequent treatments involve larger doses of injected emetic or increases in the length of treatment time or a widening range of hard liquors (Kleinmuntz, 1980). (Between trials, the patient may sip soft drinks to prevent generalization to all drinking behaviour and to promote the use of alcohol substitutes.)

Meyer and Chesser (1970) found that about half their alcoholic patients abstained for at least one year following treatment and that aversion therapy is better than no treatment.

More controversially, aversion therapy has been used with homosexuals, fetishists, male transvestites and sadomasochists and Marks *et al.* (1970) reported desired changes for up to two years after treatment. In a typical treatment, slides of nude males are presented to male homosexuals and then quickly followed by electric shocks; the conditioned response to the slides is intended to generalize to homosexual fantasies and activities outside the treatment sessions. More recently, attempts have been made to replace homosexual responses with heterosexual ones by showing slides of naked females; any sexual response will terminate the shock (see Box 31.1).

Covert sensitization (Cautela, 1967) is a variant of aversion therapy which also includes elements of SD. 'Covert' refers to the fact that both the behaviour to be removed and the aversive stimulus to be associated with it are imagined by the patient, who has to visualize the events leading up to the initiation of the undesirable behaviour: just as this happens they have to imagine nausea or some other aversive sensation. 'Sensitization' is achieved by associating the undesirable act with an exceedingly disagreeable consequence (Kleinmuntz, 1980). The patient may also be instructed to rehearse an alternative 'relief' scene in which, for example, the decision not to drink is accompanied by pleasurable sensations. This is generally preferred to aversion therapy on humanitarian grounds, but is no more effective than aversion therapy (Gelder *et al.*, 1989).

● Behaviour modification

Accordingly to Baddeley (1990), most behavioural programmes follow a broadly similar pattern involving a series of steps:

- *Step 1*. Specify the behaviour to be changed. It is important to choose small, measurable, achievable goals.
- *Step 2*. The goal should be stated as specifically as possible.
- *Step 3*. A baseline rate should be measured over a period of several days – i.e. how the person 'normally' behaves with respect to the selected behaviour. This may involve detailed observation which can suggest hypotheses as to what is maintaining that behaviour.
- *Step 4*. Decide on a strategy; for example, selectively reinforce non-yelling behaviour (through

---

BOX 31.2 Self-mutilation treated by operant conditioning (Bull and LaVecchio, 1978)

A boy suffering from Lesch–Nyhan syndrome, a rare genetic disorder which involves neurological disorders, psychomotor retardation and often self-mutilation, began showing self-injurious behaviour at about age three. He was eventually confined to a wheelchair, his arms were constrained by splints, he wore a helmet and shoulder pads. At night, he slept in a jacket and safety straps to stop him biting. He held his breath, removed his finger and toe nails, spat, displayed projectile vomiting and head-banging, screamed and used foul language. Despite the restraints, he could still inflict wounds on various parts of his body and while doing so, would often shout 'I hate myself'. His abnormal behaviour seemed to be associated with periods of anxiety and agitation and was sometimes provoked by the removal of his restraining devices about which he felt very ambivalent (he didn't want them on but nor did he want them off!).

Treatment was aimed at: (i) allowing him to tolerate being without his restraints; and (ii) extinguishing the self-injurious behaviour. Initially, removal of even a peripheral part of the protective equipment could only be achieved using nitrous oxide as a relaxant. It was also observed that treating his self-inflicted wounds was reinforcing so this was then done under anaesthetic to avoid any association between self-injury and reward.

He was then put in a room on his own (containing a one-way mirror) and his self-injurious behaviour stopped, suggesting it was motivated by the need for attention. Consequently, attention was used as a reinforcer, being withheld during self-mutilation and given at other times.

Over the course of 15 one-hour sessions, withdrawal of attention during self-injury led to the reduction and ultimate extinction of biting behaviour. The process was repeated for the other abnormal behaviours. Eighteen months later, the improvement had clearly been maintained. He had no restraints, could feed himself, was learning to walk with crutches, was attending a special class in a normal school and was interacting and communicating with other children.

---

attention) and ensure that yelling behaviour is ignored.
- *Step 5*. Plan treatment. It is essential that everyone coming into contact with the patient behaves in accordance with the chosen strategy.

A design which is commonly used to check the effectiveness of treatment is the AB–AB design, where A is the baseline condition and B is the experimental treatment. So, if treatment is working, the level of yelling should be reduced during the initial B-phase (compared with the initial A-phase) and should increase again when treatment is stopped (the second A-phase); when treatment is re-introduced (second B-phase), yelling should once more reduce.

- *Step 6.* Begin treatment.
- *Step 7.* Monitor progress.
- *Step 8.* Change the programme if necessary.

Operant conditioning with autistic children and the mentally retarded

Lovaas *et al.* (1967) pioneered operant conditioning with autistic children who normally have little or no normal speech. They used a shaping technique:

1. The first step was to pair verbal approval with a bit of food whenever the child made eye contact or merely attended to the therapist's speech or behaviour (which is also unusual for autistic children); this reinforces attention and associates a positive social gesture with food so that verbal approval eventually becomes a conditioned reinforcer.
2. The next step was to reinforce the child with food and praise whenever it made any kind of speech sound or even tried to imitate the therapist's actions.
3. Once this occurred without prompting, the therapist gradually withheld reinforcement until the child successfully imitated complete actions or uttered particular vowel or consonant sounds, then syllables, then words and, finally, combinations of words.

Sometimes hundreds or even thousands of reinforcements were necessary before the child began to label objects appropriately or imitate simple phrases and even when children have received extensive training they are likely to regress if returned to a non-supportive institutional setting. Even under optimum conditions, they never achieve the creative use of language and broad range of social skills of normal children (Thomas, 1985). However, Lovaas *et al.* (1976 in Shaffer, 1985) believe that many therapeutic gains can be retained (and even some modest improvements shown) at home if parents have been trained to use the shaping techniques.

There are many striking examples of successful modification programmes with the mentally retarded, both adults and children. In one large-scale study, Matson *et al.* (1980) reported substantial improvements in the eating behaviour of profoundly impaired adults; they used peer and therapist modelling (see below), social reinforcement, verbal prompts to shape eating, the use of utensils, table manners, etc. Reinforcers included going to meals early and having one's own table-mat and there was a significant improvement in the treated group even four months after the end of treatment, compared with an untreated control group.

Azrin and Foxx (1971) and Foxx and Azrin (1973) produced a toilet-training 'package' in which: (i) the client is taken to the toilet every half hour and given extra fluids, sweets, biscuits, praise and attention when it is used successfully; (ii) the client is strapped into a chair for half an hour, away from other people, if they have an accident (this is not a punishment procedure but 'time out', i.e. a time away from positive reinforcement). As with speech training in autistic children, there are problems of generalizing from hospital-based improvement to the home situation, but if parents continue the programme at home, there can be short- and long-term benefits.

A form of behaviour often displayed by autistic and mentally retarded individuals is self-mutilation by biting, scratching, head-banging and so on, all of which can be life-threatening. Baddeley (1990) describes a case of self-mutilation which was successfully treated by use of operant techniques (Box 31.2).

The token economy

The *token economy* (TE) is based on the principle of *secondary reinforcement*, whereby tokens (conditioned reinforcers) are given for socially desirable/acceptable behaviours as they occur; the tokens can then be exchanged for certain 'primary' reinforcers.

The 'pioneers' of the TE, Ayllon and Azrin (1968), set aside an entire ward of a psychiatric hospital for a series of experiments in which reinforcements were provided for activities such as making beds and combing hair and withheld for withdrawn or bizarre behaviour. Forty-five female patients, who were chronic schizophrenics with an average 16 years of hospitalization, are the most severely debilitated, institutionalized adults ever studied systematically; some screamed for long periods, some were mute, many were incontinent and a few were assaultive. Most no longer ate with cutlery and some buried their faces in the food.

They were systematically reinforced for their ward work and self-care by receiving plastic tokens that

BOX 31.3	Key study: how effective is the token economy?

Eighty-four chronic psychiatric patients, matched for age, gender, socioeconomic status, symptoms and length of hospitalization, were randomly assigned to one of three treatment situations:

Social learning/token economy
While acceptable behaviour was reinforced by giving the patient tokens, learning took place, specifically through modelling, shaping, prompting and instructions. Inappropriate behaviour would not be reinforced (e.g. 'You don't earn your appearance token this morning,——, your hair is all tangled'). This regime embraced all aspects of patients' lives. Like money, the tokens were a necessity – they bought meals. They could also be used to rent better sleeping quarters (a four-bed dorm room cost ten tokens per week and a furnished single room, 22 tokens), obtain passes to leave the hospital, buy recreation time (e.g. TV, piano),and various luxuries/privileges (e.g. staying up later); all of these had to be 'earned'.

In addition to living by the rules of the TE, individuals received behavioural treatments tailored to their needs. They were kept busy for 85 percent of their waking hours 'learning how to behave better' (Davison and Neale, 1994).

Milieu therapy
The entire hospital became a 'therapeutic community' (Jones, 1953), with all its ongoing activities and personnel a part of the treatment programme. Social interaction and group activities were encouraged, so that through group pressure, patients were directed towards normal functioning. They were treated as responsible human beings, expected to participate in their own readjustment, as well as that of fellow patients; this includes participating in decision making about the running of the ward. Staff impressed on them their positive expectations and praised them for doing well. When they behaved symptomatically, staff stayed with them and impressed on them their expectation that they'd soon behave more appropriately. Like the TE, this regime occupied 85 percent of their waking hours.

Custodial care (routine hospital management)
This included the use of heavy anti-psychotic drugs. Patients were alone for all but 5 percent of their waking hours, with only occasional recreational, occupational, individual and group therapies.

The study lasted for 4½ years, with an 18-month follow-up. Throughout the entire six-year period, patients were assessed at regular six-monthly intervals, using structured interviews and meticulous behavioural observation. The objectives of both the TE and milieu therapy were to teach self-care, housekeeping, communication and vocational skills, to reduce symptomatic behaviour and to release patients into the community.

could later be exchanged for special privileges (e.g. listening to records, going to movies, renting a private room, extra visits to the canteen). The entire life of each patient was, as far as possible, controlled by this regime.

If the introduction of chlorpromazine and other anti-schizophrenic drugs (neuro-leptics) in the 1950s marked a revolution in psychiatry, the introduction of token economy programmes during the 1960s was, in its way, equally revolutionary, partly because it drew attention to the ways in which nursing (and other) staff were inadvertently maintaining the psychotic, 'mad' behaviour of many chronic schizophrenics by giving them attention, thus reinforcing unwanted behaviour.

Two main advantages of the TE are:

● Tokens can be given immediately after some desirable behaviour occurs and 'cashed in' at a later time for a primary reinforcer; i.e. they can be used to 'bridge' very long delays between the target response and the primary reinforcer. This is especially important when it is impractical or impossible to deliver the primary reinforcer immediately following the behaviour.

● Tokens make it easier to give consistent and effective reinforcers when dealing with a group of individuals.

According to Davison and Neale (1994):

... These regimes have demonstrated how even markedly regressed adult hospitalized patients can be significantly affected by systematic manipulation of reinforcement contingencies, that is, rewarding some behaviour to increase its frequency or ignoring other behaviour to reduce its frequency ...

Since the 1960s, hundreds of carefully controlled experiments have shown that various psychiatric patient behaviours can be brought under control by manipulating reward and punishment contingencies. According to Holmes (1994), one of the most impressive tests of the effectiveness of the TE is the study by Paul and Lentz (1977); the three treatment conditions are described in Box 31.3.

What were the results of the Paul and Lentz study?
Both social learning/token economy and milieu ther-

apy reduced some symptoms, with the former achieving better results on several measures, such as bizarre motor behaviours (e.g. rocking, other repetitive movements and blank staring). But both were equally unsuccessful in reducing cognitive distortions (delusions, hallucinations and incoherent speech) and hostile behaviour, such as screaming and cursing. They were also both successful with interpersonal skills (co-operativeness, helpfulness and social activity), instrumental role performance (vocational and housekeeping skills) and self-care skills (grooming, care of belongings, appropriate meal-time behaviour); again, the TE was the more successful.

Over 10 percent of patients in the TE and 7 percent of those in milieu therapy achieved release to live independently, compared with none in custodial care. Many more patients from all three groups were discharged to community placements (e.g. boarding houses, halfway houses), but those from the TE did significantly better at staying there. About 90 percent of patients in all three groups were receiving neuroleptics at the outset; this figure reduced to 18 percent for the milieu therapy and 11 percent for the TE; the figure rose to 100 percent for those in custodial care

What conclusions can we draw?

- According to Davison and Neale (1994), considering how poorly these patients had been functioning before the study began, the results are remarkable. They also point out that the overall superiority of the TE compared with milieu therapy is significant, since the latter is used in many, perhaps most, psychiatric hospitals. Patients in milieu therapy actually received more attention than those in the TE, which would seem to control well for any placebo effect involved in the TE (see below).
- The results shouldn't be accepted as demonstrating the effectiveness of the TE as such. This condition contained elements that went beyond the operant conditioning of overt motor behaviour. Indeed, the TE was relegated to a secondary, though not trivial role, i.e. a useful means of getting the attention of severely regressed patients in the initial stages of treatment. The TE created the opportunity for patients to acquire new information ('to get good things into their head'; Paul, 1981, quoted in Davison and Neale, 1994).
- Paul and Lentz never claimed that any one of their patients was cured. Despite some being able to live outside the hospital, most continued to manifest many signs of mental disorder, failed to

gain employment or participate in 'normal' social activities. However, many learning theorists would respond by saying, 'So what? The patient's happy, and so is everyone else' (Holmes, 1994).

- At the present time, it is generally acknowledged among mental health professionals that therapy programmes with a learning framework are the most effective psychological procedures for helping schizophrenics function better. Although the changes brought about do not represent a cure, behavioural interventions do help to reverse the effects of institutionalization, fostering social skills such as assertiveness in people who have been reinforced by hospital staff for passiveness and compliance.(Davison and Neale, 1994).
- Despite the success of the study, it has had little impact on the care of hospitalized patients. According to Paul and Menditto (1992), there has been very little increase in the use of TEs, despite continuing evidence of their effectiveness.
- The useful changes that are produced in the hospital setting tend to disappear when the patient moves to new surroundings, at work or in the family. Relapse probably occurs because the patient starts meeting people who respond to them just as the staff originally did in hospital, taking more notice of abnormal (symptomatic) behaviour. Such a setback can be avoided by training these other people to respond appropriately (Gelder *et al.*, 1989). The control of behaviours has to be transferred from tokens to social reinforcers, both within and, ultimately, outside the hospital; the former is normally achieved by gradually 'weaning' patients off the tokens and the latter by transferring patients to halfway houses and other community live-in arrangements. However, there tends to be a high re-hospitalization rate for such patients.
- Do tokens have any specific effect? If they do, it may be that they encourage *staff* to observe behaviour systematically – not because they act as reinforcers of the patient's behaviour (Gelder *et al.*, 1989). Indeed, the use of behaviour modification to change staff behaviour can be very effective; for example, Burgio *et al.* (1983) found that selectively reinforcing staff for verbal interaction with residents produced a reliable improvement in the residents' behaviour. Feedback that staff receive about their own effectiveness seems to be another crucial factor. For instance, if ward staff know how well they are doing with their patients' behaviour, then they will tend to keep up the kind of interaction with these patients which will maintain the acceptable behaviours.

- These studies suggest that although token economies work, this does not in itself prove that they work because of reinforcement; other, confounding variables may include improvement in nurse:patient ratio, increase in staff morale and a generally more optimistic and enthusiastic approach to patients. Any one of these could, on its own, account for at least some of the improvements commonly found, so that, as with other successful behavioural interventions, the reason for the effectiveness of token economy programmes may be quite unrelated to learning theory principles (Fonagy and Higgitt, 1984). This relates to what is called *process research* (as opposed to *outcome research*; see below).

Ethical considerations

Ethical problems arise with TEs because it is often necessary to deprive patients of some amenity before it can be earned with tokens. If this amenity is something that the patient should have by right (e.g. food), there is clearly an ethical difficulty. With some amenities (e.g. watching TV), it is difficult to decide whether they are a right or a privilege (Gelder *et al.*, 1989).

As a precaution against the possibility of abusing the techniques, the system should be made completely open to public scrutiny, with the approval of the clients or their advocates. Confidentiality must be ensured. Ayllon and Azrin even adopted the policy of giving visitors conducted tours, with the clients as guides. Such an open-door policy will help not only to ensure high ethical standards, but also to allay the fears and suspicions about behaviour modification techniques. Some TEs provide clients with the option of leaving without penalty and suggesting or negotiating changes in the contingencies used.

Another precaution is to inform clients clearly of their legal and moral rights and to instruct clients and staff to report any infringements of those rights. According to Martin and Pear (1992), the 'acid test' of the ethics of a TE are the ends and the suitability to those ends of the means for obtaining them . Thus, the ethics of a TE will ultimately be judged on the basis of how effectively and humanely the transfer to the natural environment is carried out.

Baddeley (1990) argues that when used in an educational setting (e.g. in a home for emotionally disturbed children), a TE can produce a very mercenary approach to learning (token economies lead to token learning), i.e. children may only read or indulge in any educational activity if directly rewarded for it. This may be effective within the confines of the TE itself, but will be quite unproductive outside, where it is necessary to learn to operate on a more subtle and less immediate reward system.

COGNITIVE APPROACHES

● Cognitive behaviour therapy

Model of psychological disorder

According to Mahoney (1974) and Meichenbaum (1977), many (if not the majority) of clinical problems are best described as disorders of thought and feeling and since behaviour is to a large extent controlled by the way we think, the most logical and effective way of trying to change maladaptive behaviour is to change the maladaptive thinking which lies behind it.

Wessler (1986) defines *cognitive behaviour therapy* (CBT) as a 'collection of assumptions about disturbance and a set of treatment interventions in which human cognitions are assigned a central role'. It is derived from various theoretical and therapeutic sources and the way that cognition is defined and operationalized differs according to particular approaches. However, Wessler stresses that the attempt to change cognition (*cognitive restructuring*) is always a means to an end, that end being the 'lasting changes in target emotions and behaviour' (Wessler, 1986).

Rational emotive therapy (Ellis, 1962, 1973)

Ellis believes that *irrational thoughts* are the main cause of all types of emotional distress and behaviour disorders. Irrational thinking leads to a self-defeating internal dialogue of negative self-statements and these are seen as 'covert' behaviours which are subject to the same principles of learning as overt behaviour. Phobias, for example, are linked to catastrophizing self-statements and, as with other disorders, the aim of therapy is to replace these irrational, unreasonable beliefs and ideas with more reasonable and realistic ones.

In its simplest form, patients are told to look on the bright side, stop worrying, pull themselves together and so on. As Walker (1984) observes, 'rational' should not be taken too literally as sometimes counterproductive thoughts and beliefs may be replaced by more positive and helpful but equally irrational ones. For instance, it is not necessarily more rational to be an optimist than a pessimist but it is usually more productive and should be encouraged in depressed patients (Walker, 1984).

Ellis (1962) identified 11 basic irrational beliefs or ideas which tend to be emotionally self-defeating and which are commonly associated with psychological problems, including, 'I must be loved and accepted by absolutely everybody', 'I must be excellent in all possible respects and never make mistakes – otherwise I'm worthless' and 'I am unable to control my emotions'. In rational emotive therapy (RET), the patient is challenged to prove that they are worthless because they make mistakes, etc. or to say exactly how making mistakes makes one a worthless person. Patients may be explicitly directed to practise certain positive/optimistic statements and are generally urged to 'look for the "musts" when they experience inappropriate emotions' (Wessler, 1986).

Self-instructional training (Meichenbaum, 1973)

Meichenbaum believes that neurotic behaviour is due, at least partly, to *faulty internal dialogues* (internal speech), in which the patient is failing to *self-instruct* successfully. The underlying rationale for self-instructional therapy (SIT) is a study by Meichenbaum and Goodman (1971) in which impulsive and hyperactive children were trained to administer self-instructions for tasks on which they had previously made frequent errors, first by talking aloud, then covertly, without talking, but still moving their lips and, finally, without any lip movements. This 'silent speech' is the essence of verbal thought (see Chapter 13).

Patients are made aware of the maladaptive nature of their self-statements and are then helped to develop coping skills in the form of coping self-statements, relaxation and plans for behaviour change. For instance, a patient might write down a strategy for dealing with a particular social interaction (e.g. asking someone to dance at a disco) and then role-play it with a continuous commentary on self-statements before actually doing it 'for real'; as well as these advance preparations, the patient may give on-the-spot self-warnings and self-debriefings once it is over.

Wolpe (1978) argues that these techniques are not very useful in cases of severe anxiety because many strong neurotic fears are triggered by objects and situations which the patient *knows* are harmless – this is why phobias are irrational! So Wolpe has used a technique called *thought stopping* (mainly with obsessive–compulsive patients) in which the patient is told to dwell on their obsessive thoughts and, while this is happening, the therapist shouts

'Stop!'. The patient then repeats the command out loud and eventually repeats it subvocally (in thought only). (Covert sensitization, which we discussed above, is a form of self-instruction or self-training.)

Treatment of 'automatic thoughts' (Beck, 1963)

Beck believed that depressives see themselves as victims. The key elements in depression are negative thought about oneself, the world and the future (the *cognitive triad* of depression) and these thoughts seem to come automatically and involuntarily. The source of such thoughts are logical errors based on faulty 'data' and, once negative thinking has been identified, it can be replaced by collecting evidence against it. Accordingly, Beck sees the client as a colleague of the therapist who researches verifiable reality (Wessler, 1986).

For example, if a client expresses the negative thought, 'I'm a poor father because my children are not better disciplined', Beck would take the second part of the statement and seek factual evidence about its truth; he would also focus on the evaluative conclusion that one is a poor father because one's children sometimes misbehave. In these and other ways, clients are trained to distance themselves from

---

BOX 31.4 Key study: learning not to be afraid by seeing how others do it

Bandura and Menlove (1968) divided 48 nursery school children with dog phobias into three groups:

Group 1 (*the single model condition*) saw eight three-minute films (two per day for four days) in which a five-year-old boy engaged in progressively bolder interactions with a cocker spaniel.
Group 2 (*the multiple model condition*) saw similar films, but several boys and girls were seen interacting with a number of dogs ranging in size from very small to quite large.
Group 3 (*the control group*) saw a film about Disneyland and Marineland.

The day after the final film, the children were asked to perform 14 acts as a test of their fear of dogs. Compared with a pre-test performance, the control group showed no fear reduction, but groups 1 and 2 were much more willing to approach and interact with a real dog and, one month later, the differences remained. Group 2 children were much more willing to initiate very intimate contact than group 1 children.

things, to be more objective, to distinguish fact from fiction and fact from evaluation, to see things in proportion and not to see things in such extreme terms.

Beck's *cognitive therapy* is less confrontational than RET and its use has been extended to anxiety and personality disorders, amongst others.

Modelling (Bandura, 1968, 1977)

Modelling, of course, is a direct application of social learning theory (see Chapters 7 and 27). A famous demonstration of therapeutic modelling is described in Box 31.4.

Bandura argues that: (i) modelling is more effective for treating phobias than counter-conditioning (based on classical conditioning); (ii) symbolic modelling (films) is less powerful than live demonstrations; and (iii) the age of the model seems to be irrelevant. Bandura (1969) claimed a 90 percent success rate in curing snake phobias and similar success for dog phobias. However, it seems to be mainly effective with children (although it may form part of behaviour therapy with adults) and with simple (e.g. animal) phobias; it may work simply by persuading the child to expose itself to the object of its fear (Marks, 1978).

● Personal construct therapy (Kelly, 1955)

Model of psychological disorder

Kelly's concept of disorder is directly related to his view of normality (his personal construct theory was discussed in Chapter 29). He completely rejects the medical model and with it all notions of 'illness' and 'health'. Instead, he uses the concept of *functioning*: a person who is functioning fully is able to construe the world in such a way that predictions are, most of the time, confirmed or validated but, when they are not validated, the person can change his/ her personal construct system accordingly (things are put down to 'experience'; Fransella, 1984).

If our constructs are repeatedly invalidated, we may consider we have 'a problem' and a psychological disorder is defined as 'any personal construction which is used repeatedly in spite of consistent invalidation' (Kelly, 1955). Symptoms serve to give structure and meaning to the chaotic experience which arises out of the use of invalidated constructs. For instance, anxiety is an indication that an individual's personal construct systems are inadequate for, or inappropriate to, the events to which they are applied, i.e. those events lie outside its *range of convenience*. One response to anxiety is to loosen our constructs, so that more events can be accommodated by them – our predictions become less specific and so there is less chance of our being wrong.

According to Bannister (1963, 1965), schizophrenia represents an extreme form of loosening – constructs which are normally interlinked come to 'hang together' in an almost random way. Obsessive–compulsive symptoms represent the opposite way of dealing with anxiety, namely an extreme tightening of the construct system, an attempt to ensure that predictions are never invalidated.

The aims of therapy

The basic aim of personal construct therapy (PCT) is to change the client's way of construing the world in order to make better sense of it and predict it more accurately: the constructs of a loose construer need to be tightened and those of a tight construer loosened.

Therapeutic techniques

It is much more difficult to identify specific techniques than it is in most other approaches and the therapist may well use techniques from other approaches. For example, if a client is a tight construer, free association, dream interpretation and some aspects of Rogers' client-centred therapy may be used (see below) while a loose construer may undergo behaviour therapy (Mackay, 1975). More specifically, the client–therapist relationship, self-characterization and fixed role therapy (sketch and enactment) constitute the basic ingredients of PCT.

1   The relationship between client and therapist is seen, essentially, as comparable to that between a PhD student and their supervisor; together, they struggle to understand why one of them is failing to solve the problems that they encounter in life. The therapy room is a laboratory and the therapist is a *validator* of the client's behavioural experiments who can help the client to see alternative ways of construing the world (Fransella, 1984).

2   A client's problem is that his/ he construct system has not adapted to deal with certain vital aspects of life; therefore, 'diagnosis' involves trying to understand the problem as the client sees it and a method of trying to achieve this is *self-characterization* (which, together with fixed role therapy, is the only really original treatment device, according to Mackay, 1975). The client is asked to write a character sketch about themselves, in the third person ' ... just as if she were the principal character in a play. Write it as if it

might be written by a friend who knew her *intimately* and very *sympathetically*, perhaps better than anyone ever really could know her ... ' (Fransella, 1984).

3   The therapist then writes a second version of the client's original self-characterization (called a *fixed role sketch*) which, ideally, lies somewhere between the client's self-portrait and its exact opposite, e.g. if the client uses the construct 'aggressive–submissive' in relation to their boss, the therapist will use 'respectful' (Fransella, 1984). The client and therapist discuss the fixed role sketch together and modify it until it describes a person the client feels it is possible to be. The client then goes away and lives the life of that person for a few weeks (*fixed role enactment*) with frequent meetings during this period in the prescribed role. The purpose of fixed role enactment is to show the client that we can, indeed, change ourselves.

4   The repertory grid (see Chapter 29) may be used in a variety of ways: (i) to measure the client's construct system; (ii) to measure the therapist's construct system, e.g. how they construe the client; and (iii) to monitor the therapeutic process, for example, the client can provide a series of self-ratings and the selves as rated can form the elements of a grid which can then be combined to make a grid which can provide a summary of the change, through time, of the therapeutic process (Ryle, 1975).

HUMANISTIC–PHENOMENOLOGICAL APPROACHES

● Client-centred therapy (Rogers, 1942, 1951)

Model of psychological disorder

As we saw in Chapter 29, when a person is aware of a lack of congruence between their experience and self-concept, threat, anxiety or depression is experienced. Because of our need for positive regard, we may behave in ways which are discordant with the values of our self and feeling threatened, anxious or depressed is the price we pay. As defences against these unpleasant feelings, we use *denial* and *distortion*, whereby part of reality is prevented from entering consciousness and is, consequently, unable to contribute to our self-concept. As a result, our self-concept becomes increasingly incongruent with reality which, in turn, increases anxiety and makes the need for defences all the greater – a vicious circle has been created.

Where the incongruence is severe and/or persistent, the resulting threat, anxiety or depression may interfere with the person's life in a neurotic way; where it is so great as to defy denial and distortion, the incongruent experience is accurately symbolized at a conscious level and this leads to the disintegration of personality (characterized by bizarre, crazy, behaviour) which is commonly called *psychotic*. However, Rogers regards individuals as unique and human personality is so complex that no diagnostic labelling of persons can ever be fully justified; indeed, Rogers rejects all diagnostic labelling.

The aims of therapy

Client-centred therapy (CCT) is a process where individuals have the opportunity to reorganize their subjective world so as to integrate and actualize the self. The key process, therefore, is facilitation of the experience of becoming a more autonomous, spontaneous and confident person (Graham, 1986).

People have within themselves an inherent capacity for, and tendency towards, self-understanding and self-actualization, but the conditions for facilitating its development reside in the relationship between the client and the therapist. The word 'client' is used to emphasize the person's self-responsibility (while 'patient' implies the opposite) and 'client-centred' implies that the client is encouraged to direct the whole therapeutic process – any changes which occur during therapy are brought about by the client.

The therapeutic process

The therapist's main task is to create a *therapeutic atmosphere* in which clients can become fully integrated again; this can only be achieved if clients reduce their conditions of worth and increase their unconditional positive self-regard. The therapist's job is to create a situation in which clients can change themselves and this is aided by an emotionally warm, accepting, understanding and non-evaluative relationship in which the person is free from threat and has the freedom to be 'the self that he really is' (Graham, 1986).

There are three particularly significant qualities to the relationship or *attitudes* on the part of the therapist who must effectively communicate them to the client as both a necessary and sufficient condition for therapeutic change:

- *Genuineness* (authenticity or congruence). The therapist must show themselves to be a real person, with feelings which should be expressed where appropriate. The client needs to feel that the therapist is emotionally involved and not hiding behind a facade of professional impersonality; the therapist must be 'transparent'. This is the most important of the three qualities or attitudes.

- *Unconditional positive regard*. The therapist must show complete acceptance of, and regard for, the client as a separate person in his/her own right. The therapist must have a deep and genuine caring for clients *as they are now* in a non-judgemental way.

- *Empathic understanding*. The therapist must try to enter the client's inner world through a genuine, attentive listening, which involves intense concentration. This may involve restating what the client says as a way of trying to clarify its emotional significance (rather than its verbal content) and this requires the therapist to be sensitive to what is currently going on in the client and to meanings which are just below the level of awareness. Thorne (1984) believes that this is the most 'trainable' of the three therapist attitudes but is at the same time remarkably rare. He also suggests that a fourth attitude, *tenderness*, could be added to Rogers' three.

If these therapeutic conditions are established, clients will talk about themselves more honestly and this will bring about a re-establishment of congruence which will be sufficient to produce changes in behaviour (Fonagy and Higgitt, 1984).

Unlike most other humanistic therapists, Rogers has attempted to validate his therapy empirically (and has encouraged others to do so). A form of assessment used by Rogers is the *Q-sort*, which comprises a number of cards with statements referring to the self (e.g. 'I am a domineering person'); the client is asked to arrange them in a series of ten piles ranging from 'very characteristic of me' to 'not at all characteristic of me' (describing the self-image) and the process is repeated so as to describe the ideal self. The two Q-sorts are then correlated to determine the discrepancy between self-image and ideal self – the lower the correlations, the greater the discrepancy. The whole procedure is repeated at various intervals during the course of therapy (in a similar way to the use of the repertory grid in Kelly's PCT).

One way of assessing the importance of the three qualities or attitudes of the therapist is to give trained judges transcripts or tape-recordings of therapy sessions which they have to rate. Truax and Mitchell (1971) found that therapists who were rated high were much more likely to be associated with desirable changes in their clients and low-rated therapists actually worsened their clients' condition. But others have found that the therapist's personal characteristics are likely to be no more important than any specific techniques used.

CCT and counselling

Despite their questionable empirical basis, Rogers' ideas about ideal therapeutic relationships and attitudes have become part of the accepted clinical wisdom of psychologists of all theoretical orientations. Essentially, Rogerian therapy provides a situation in which the client learns to be free and, as such, it is an educational process, which Rogers believes can be as effective in the classroom as in the clinic (*Freedom to Learn*, 1969). He is generally regarded as having inspired the counselling movement, especially in the UK, which is a product of his involvement with therapy and education (Graham, 1986).

Encounter groups

Another spin-off of CCT is the *encounter* or *personal growth movement*, very much an American (particularly Californian) phenomenon of the 1960s and 1970s. Encounter groups were originally developed by Rogers 'as a means whereby people can break through the barriers erected by themselves and others in order to react openly and freely with one another' (Graham, 1986). Participants (not 'clients') are encouraged to act out their emotions (not just talk about them) through body contact and structured activities and 'games'. The leader (or facilitator) attempts to create a climate of mutual trust in which people (usually 8–18 in number) feel free to express their true feelings – both positive and negative – thereby reducing defensiveness and promoting self-actualization (Rogers, 1973).

AN EVALUATION OF THERAPY: IS IT EFFECTIVE?

This deceptively simple-sounding question really comprises two inter-related questions:

1 Does it work? This is related to what is called *outcome research*.

2 How does it work? This is related to what is called *process research.*

Each question, in turn, comprises several other overlapping questions. Outcome questions can be:

● Is psychotherapy (in general) effective?
● Is any one kind of psychotherapy more effective than another?
● What constitutes a satisfactory outcome?
● How should change be measured (and for how long after the end of treatment)?
● How much and what kind of change are necessary for a judgement of improvement to be made?

Process questions can be:

● What are the necessary components of effective therapy?
● What are the mechanisms by which change is brought about, i.e. what are the 'active ingredients' ?
● Are different therapies effective because of the particular techniques and tools that they use or are there common factors that apply to all therapies?

Despite the close connection between them, researchers tend to focus on either outcome or process questions. Psychotherapy research began by concentrating on outcome, in the form of Eysenck's much-cited 1952 article in which he challenged what had up to that time been taken for granted about the effectiveness of psychoanalysis (see Box 31.5).

BOX 31.5 Key study: Eysenck's (1952) review of the effectiveness of psychotherapy

Eysenck reviewed five studies of the effectiveness of psychoanalysis and 19 studies of the effectiveness of 'eclectic'(mixed) psychotherapy. He concluded that only 44 percent of psychoanalytic patients and 64 percent of those who received the 'mixed' therapy improved. However, since roughly 66 percent of patients improve without any treatment (*spontaneous remission*), Eysenck concluded that psychoanalysis in particular, and psychotherapy in general, simply do not work – they achieve nothing which would not have happened anyway without therapy!

● Outcome research: Does therapy work?

According to Eysenck (1992), the outcome problem had never been properly addressed by clinical psychologists prior to his article, which showed only that the available evidence was not sufficient to prove that psychoanalysis (and psychotherapy in general, which is largely based on Freudian assumptions) was instrumental in bringing about recovery; it did not suggest that they are ineffective (which is how many others interpreted his conclusions). Nevertheless, if it can be shown that psychoanalysis does no better than placebo treatments (see below) or no treatment at all (which the 1952 article showed):

> ... then clearly the theory on which it is based was wrong. Similarly, if there were no positive effects of psychoanalysis as a therapy, then it would be completely unethical to apply this method to patients, to charge them money for such treatment, or to train therapists in these unsuccessful methods ... (Eysenck, 1992)

By 1960, Eysenck was arguing that behaviour therapy is the only kind of therapy worth rational consideration and he inspired an enormous amount of research on therapy outcomes (Oatley, 1984).

But are Eysenck's conclusions justified?

● If the many patients who drop out of psychoanalysis are excluded from the 44 percent quoted by Eysenck (they cannot legitimately be counted as 'failures' or 'not cured'), the figure rises to 66 percent.
● Bergin (1971) reviewed some of the papers included in Eysenck's review and concluded that, by choosing different criteria of 'improvement', the success rate of psychoanalysis could be raised to 83 percent. He also cited studies which showed only a 30 percent spontaneous remission rate.
● The two studies which Eysenck used to establish his spontaneous remission rate of 66 percent were Landis (1938) and Denker (1946). Basically, Landis compared patients who had received psychotherapy ('experimental group') with a control group who had been hospitalized for 'neurosis' in state mental hospitals, while Denker's control group had been treated only by their GPs with sedatives, tonics, suggestion and reassurance. Landis himself pointed out a number of differences between his psychotherapy group and the hospital patient controls and concluded that these differences 'all argue against the acceptance of

[this] figure ... as a truly satisfactory baseline, but in the absence of any other better figure this must serve'.

- Bergin and Lambert (1978) reviewed 17 studies of untreated 'neurotics' and found a median spontaneous remission rate of 43 percent. They also found that the rate of spontaneous remission varies a great deal depending on the disorder: generalized anxiety and depression, for example, are much more likely to 'cure themselves' than phobias or obsessive–compulsive disorders. This is supported by Rachman and Wilson (1980) who, while agreeing with Eysenck's spontaneous remission rate of roughly two-thirds within two years of onset (based on a review of evidence for the period 1952–1977), argue that there is a strong case for refining this estimate for each of a group of different neurotic disorders: ' ... the early assumption of uniformity of spontaneous remission rates among different disorders is increasingly difficult to defend' (Rachman and Wilson, 1980).
- Garfield (1992) argues that both the quantity and quality of psychotherapy research have increased since the time of Eysenck's 1952 article, especially since the 1970s, but Eysenck does not refer to this in his 1992 article. For example, Lambert et al. (1986) not only evaluated the recent literature but included a table summarizing almost all of the meta-analytic reviews (see below); the overall pattern of results is relatively clear and clearly positive, in favour of the benefits of a range of psychotherapies.

Other outcome research

A review by Luborsky et al. (1975) concluded that 'Everyone has won, and all must have prizes', i.e. all types of therapy are equally effective. Smith and Glass (1977) reviewed 400 studies of a wide variety of therapies (including psychodynamic, Gestalt, CCT, SD and eclectic) and concluded that all were more effective than no treatment. For example, the 'average' client who had received therapy scored more favourably on the outcome measures than 75 percent of those in the untreated control groups.

Smith et al. (1980) extended the 1977 study to include 475 studies (an estimated 75 percent of the published literature). Strict criteria for accepting a study included the comparison between a treated group (given a specified form of therapy) with a second group (drawn from the same population) either given no therapy, put on a waiting list or given some alternative form of therapy. As with the 1977 results,

the effectiveness of therapy was shown to be highly significant – the average client was better off than 80 percent of the control groups on the outcome measures.

Different therapies had different kinds of effects:

- the largest overall effects were produced by cognitive therapies and cognitive behaviour therapies, which were particularly effective with single, simple phobias, fear and anxiety;
- CCT did best with low self-esteem clients;
- dynamic eclectic therapy did best with work and school adjustment;
- neither behaviour therapy nor psychodynamic therapy emerged as superior to the other.

However, overall, 'Different types of psychotherapy (verbal or behavioural, psychodynamic, client-centred, or systematic desensitization) do not produce different types or degrees of benefit' (Smith et al., 1980).

A distinctive feature of these last two studies is their use of meta-analysis (MA). This was defined by Glass (1976, cited in Smith and Glass, 1977) as '... the integration of research through statistical analysis of the analyses of individual studies', i.e. a 'study of studies'. More fully, MA is:

> ... a procedure for aggregating and averaging the results of a large number of studies. Unlike the 'voting' method, meta-analysis allows researchers to consider the magnitude of findings and yield an overall measure of effect size – that is, an index of the magnitude of the effects of a treatment ... averaged across all studies ... (Lilienfeld, 1995)

Effect size is essentially an indicator of the extent to which people who receive psychotherapy improve relative to those who do not; the greater the difference between these two groups, the greater the effect size. The 'voting method' that Lilienfeld refers to (a term coined by Smith and Glass) simply involves adding up all the studies that support the effectiveness of psychotherapy and all those that do not; a result is counted as a 'hit' as long as the difference between the two totals is statistically significant. However, some statistically significant results are very large, while others are very small; the 'voting method' obscures these distinctions by lumping together all positive findings and all the negative findings regardless of their size. As a result, it provides only a crude and often misleading summary of a body of literature (Lilienfeld, 1995); all outcome studies prior to Smith and Glass (1977) used the 'voting method'.

Another advantage of MA is that it allows researchers to examine whether certain variables are correlated with effect size, such as how experienced the therapists is and the age of clients; in this way, they can determine not only the overall effectiveness of psychotherapy (outcome research) but what factors, if any, influence its effectiveness (process research).

● Process research: How does therapy work?

When discussing the various approaches to therapy earlier in the chapter, we asked several times if changes in behaviour of the kind predicted by that approach were necessarily due to the specific techniques used. For example, are the relaxation and graded exposure to the feared object/situation what make SD an effective means of removing phobias, are the tokens an essential part of the TE which successfully reduces the psychotic behaviour of schizophrenic patients and are the three therapist attitudes necessary if clients are to develop positive self-regard and to achieve congruence?

These are all questions about process, i.e. what are the 'active ingredients' involved in therapeutic effectiveness.

According to Kazdin and Wilcoxin (1976), the crucial ingredients of therapy (whatever techniques are involved) are: (i) the patient is influenced to expect success; and (ii) the patient's self-concept changes, whereby they come to believe (through supervised practice) that the previously feared object or situation can be coped with. The first of these, i.e. the patient's expectations of success, relates to the crucial and controversial issue of the *placebo effect*.

The purpose of a control group is to be able to compare the experimental manipulation (here, a particular therapeutic intervention) with patients who don't receive this (or any other) therapeutic intervention. A placebo, as used in drug trials, denotes an inactive/inert substance (usually a sugar pill), which takes account of the psychological (as opposed to pharmacological) influences on physiological change (e.g. the expectation of improvement). So, in drug trials, the placebo condition *is* the control condition.

Why aren't things as straightforward in psychotherapy research?

When we call a change a placebo effect, we usually mean that it was brought about by some means other than that intended in a particular treatment. While it is quite appropriate in drug trials to use an intentional placebo (as opposed to an inadvertent one), i.e. a treatment designed to have no effect, in itself, on a particular disorder, using intentional placebos in psychotherapy research is a misapplication of drug trial methods: in psychotherapy, the expectancy is part of the treatment (Mair, 1992). This makes 'placebo' an unfortunate term, since it clearly doesn't denote something inactive/inert. Indeed, is it possible to devise a placebo control which is inactive in a way that's equivalent to taking a sugar pill? Even non-placebo controls (such as delayed treatment or no treatment conditions) will produce expectations specific to that particular condition (e.g. disappointment and rejection respectively) (Barkham and Shapiro, 1992).

If a placebo's capacity to inspire client expectations is one of the main 'active ingredients' or components involved in psychotherapeutic success, making psychotherapy–placebo comparisons may underestimate the actual effectiveness of psychotherapy (Lilienfeld, 1995). Indeed, according to Frank (1989), if therapy effects don't exceed those of placebos (a conclusion drawn by, for example, Prioleau *et al.*, 1983), this is because the placebo is psychotherapy: 'As a symbolic communication that combats demoralization by inspiring the patient's hopes for relief, administration of a placebo *is* a form of psychotherapy. It is therefore not surprising that placebos can provide marked relief in patients who seek psychotherapy' (Mair, 1989, quoted in Mair, 1992).

But if therapy effects don't exceed those of placebos, ' ... Why make lavish claims for the effectiveness of psychotherapy when much or all of this effectiveness could more easily and cheaply be accomplished by a sugar pill, a priest, or perhaps even a friend?' (Lilienfeld, 1995).

Cordray and Bootzin (1983) argue that perhaps one of the major ingredients involved in psychotherapy effectiveness are the non-specific factors shared by most, or even all, therapies. The main 'champion' of this view is Frank (1973). He argues that psychotherapy has much in common with faith healing and other similar techniques. Far from being a derogatory comparison, Frank believes that the success of psychotherapy can be traced largely or entirely to four non-specific factors/components, summarized in Box 31.6.

These components give the client new opportunities for learning, problem solving and reality testing, the hope of relief, the experience of success (Mair, 1992). Above all, they help to combat *demoralization*, the universal malady that brings people to

<table>
<tr><td>

BOX 31.6

Frank's (1973) four non-specific factors/components involved in therapy

According to Frank, all psychotherapies:

1 prescribe clearly delineated roles for therapist and client, with the former defined as 'expert' possessing unique healing skills. This lifts the client's hopes that help will be forthcoming;

2 involve settings (e.g. carpeted rooms with scholarly books and journals and prominently displayed diplomas) designed to be associated with the alleviation of psychological distress (a 'designated place of healing');

3 provide a convincing theoretical rationale for making sense of the client's problems; this instills a sense of confidence in clients and reassures them that their problems aren't incomprehensible or unique;

4 include *therapeutic rituals* (prescribed tasks or procedures) (e.g. SD, free association) that further enhance the client's faith in the therapist and the therapeutic rationale. These are akin to the ceremonial rituals of faith healers; they cultivate the impression that something deeply significant and mysterious is taking place.

</td></tr>
</table>

therapy, i.e. essentially all individuals who voluntarily seek treatment experience low self-esteem, despair, helplessness, alienation and a profound sense of incompetence. All psychotherapies alleviate demoralization by raising hopes and expectations of improvement and by instilling feelings of confidence and self-worth.

Bandura (1977) has integrated a number of findings into the proposal that the central element in psychological therapy is the cognitive change towards *self-efficacy*, i.e. the 'conviction that one can successfully execute a behaviour to produce a specified outcome' and this is brought about best through actual experience in facing previously feared or avoided situations.

The results of meta-analytic studies, like those of Smith and Glass (1977) and Smith *et al.* (1980), which claimed that differences in the effectiveness of different therapies are negligible, support Frank's argument. But other outcome studies have shown that the more active, structured, directive therapies work best (at least for certain types of disorder); these can be seen as more heavily 'saturated' with Frank's non-specific factors than are other psychotherapies (Lilienfeld, 1995).

CONCLUSIONS

The whole concept of 'cure' is highly complex and is itself defined differently from different theoretical and therapeutic perspectives. The crux of Eysenck's (1952) review is how the effectiveness of psychotherapy should be assessed: he used Denker's criteria, namely: (i) return to work and ability to carry on well in economic adjustments for at least five years; (ii) complaint of no further or very slight difficulties; and (iii) making successful social adjustments.

These are all fairly tangible indicators of improvement and even more so is the behaviour therapist's criterion that cure is achieved when patients no longer manifest the original maladaptive behaviour (e.g. the fear of spiders is eliminated). If these more stringent (or more easily measured) criteria of actual behaviour change are required before the therapist can be viewed as successful, then behaviour therapists do seem to be more effective than psychoanalysts or humanistic therapists (with cognitive approaches in between) (Rachman and Wilson, 1980; Shapiro and Shapiro, 1982).

But are those kinds of criteria necessarily appropriate for assessing 'cure' or improvement as applied to psychoanalysis? Psychoanalytic therapists may answer the question 'Does therapy work?' by saying it is a misleading question, like asking whether friendship 'works'. It is an activity that people take part in, which is important to them, affects, moves, even transforms them (Oatley, 1984).

But for Eysenck, if it cannot be empirically demonstrated that it has well-defined beneficial effects, then it is worthless. Because he is interested in comparing recovery rates (measured statistically), his assessment of the effects of therapy is purely quantitative, while psychoanalysts and those from other non-behavioural approaches (e.g. Rogers' client-centred therapy) are likely to be much more concerned with the qualitative aspects of therapy – how does it work, what is the nature of the therapeutic process, the role of the relationship between client and therapist, important qualities of the therapist, etc.? There are different kinds of questions one can ask when trying to assess the effects of psychotherapy.

Outcome studies in general indicate the effectiveness of both specific factors due to the particular form of therapy used and some non-specific factors, the most important of which might well be the relationship with the therapist and the expectation of improvement (Oatley, 1984).

According to Lilienfeld (1995), it could be argued that the question 'Is psychotherapy effective?', although remarkably complex in some respects, is actually too simple in others. As Paul (1966) observes, what we need to ask is '*What* treatment, by *whom*, is most effective for *this* individual, with that specific problem, and under *which* set of circumstances?'. This is to do with the matching of client, therapy and setting and, according to Wilson and Barkham (1994), this question still haunts psychotherapy research and disturbs therapists.

CHAPTER SUMMARY

- Both clinical and counselling psychology draw on the same theory and research findings in an attempt to promote mental health and both adopt the scientist-practitioner model of helping, but they have been more influenced by behavioural and humanistic approaches respectively.
- Psychotherapists are trained to use one of several forms of psychotherapy, all stemming from Freud's psychoanalysis.
- Where theory has developed from clinical practice, as in psychoanalysis and client-centred therapy, theory and therapy are very closely related, but this is often not the case, as in certain forms of behaviour therapy. In practice, treatment is often eclectic.
- Treatments and therapies differ according to whether they are physical/organic (as used by psychiatrists as part of the medical model) or psychological, directive or non-directive, individual or group.
- Most therapies are psychological (and individual) and involve a rejection of the medical model. Behaviour therapy, cognitive behaviour therapy and personal construct therapy are the best examples of directive therapies, while psychoanalysis and client-centred therapy are non-directive.
- Family and marital/couple therapies reflect the influence of Laing's family interaction model of schizophrenia and are likely to be recommended when the problem is interpersonal. Individual therapy is likely to be recommended for intrapsychic problems, but the two approaches may be used in conjunction.
- The term 'psychotherapy' is sometimes used to refer to all non-organic treatments, sometimes to refer to psychodynamic approaches/insight therapies. The UKCP has separate sections for behavioural psychotherapy and psychoanalytic and psychodynamic psychotherapy.
- Drug therapy/chemotherapy involves the use of anti-depressants, major tranquillizers and anti-anxiety drugs.
- Iproniazid and related drugs (e.g. phenelzine-/Nardil) inhibit the activity of MAO and raise levels of monoamines (MAO inhibitors); these are less effective than the tricyclic anti-depressants (such as imipramine/Tofranil) and can cause cerebral haemorrhage. The much newer fluoxetine/Prozac is the most commonly prescribed anti-depressant medication.
- Lithium carbonate/Lithane/Lithonate is used to treat bipolar mood disorder.
- Chlordiazepoxide/Librium and diazepam/Valium are widely prescribed anti-anxiety drugs, which reduce anxiety without sedation, unlike the previously widely used meprobamate. The benzodiazepines facilitate the activity of GABA.
- Chlorpromazine and other phenothiazines are major tranquillizers/neuroleptics which revolutionized the treatment of schizophrenia and other psychotic disorders, but they have been called pharmacological straitjackets.
- Chlorpromazine reduces hallucinations, delusions and other psychotic symptoms by blocking the D2 receptor for dopamine. However, this doesn't constitute a cure and there are several side-effects, the most serious neuromuscular effect being tardive dyskinesia.
- The belief that schizophrenia and epilepsy cannot coexist led to a number of treatments for schizophrenia, such as blood transfusions from epileptics, insulin coma therapy and electroconvulsive therapy (ECT). ECT is now used mainly with depressive patients.
- The ECT procedure involves pre-anaesthetic medication, followed by a fast-acting anaesthetic and muscle relaxant, then a brief 70–140 volt shock, either bilateral, which is more effective but has greater side-effects, or unilateral.
- Memory disruption includes retrograde amnesia and impaired ability to acquire new memories and deaths have been known to occur. But compared with other medical treatments, ECT is very safe, especially when suicide rates among depressives are taken into account. The main objections to its use are ethical, in particular, the issue of consent.
- Controlled comparisons of real and sham ECT suggest that real ECT is significantly more effective and it is probably more effective than anti-depressant drugs. However, its effects may

reflect profound brain damage and anosognosia; while cognitive and emotional deficits may be long term, the benefits are only short term. Its simplicity and speed as a treatment make it open to abuse and overuse.

- A number of explanations have been proposed for how ECT works; it may be seen as a punishment, memory loss allows restructuring of the patient's view of life and the shock stimulates noradrenaline and endorphins in the brain.

- Moniz was the pioneer of psychosurgery, performing the first prefrontal lobotomy/leucotomy in 1935 on schizophrenic patients. Freeman and Watts' 'standard leucotomy' involved inserting a scalpel either into burr holes in the temple or through the eye socket. Large numbers of operations were performed in the USA and UK during the 1940s and 1950s.

- Modern stereotactic procedures are directed more to the connections between the frontal lobe and other brain structures (such as the hypothalamus, temporal lobe and amygdala) rather than the frontal lobe itself ; they are 'fractional operations', such as stereotactic tractotomy, limbic leucotomy, cingulotomy and amygdalotomy.

- The use of psychosurgery is extremely controversial; not only is it irreversible, but the patient may not be suffering, informed consent is not always obtained, it has been used with very young children and has been seen as a means of social control. It is much less common than it used to be and in the UK is only used as a last resort.

- According to Freud, anxiety is at the core of neurotic symptoms, reflecting the conflict arising from demands made on the ego by the id (neurotic anxiety) or superego (moral anxiety). Neuroses involve defences (such as repression, displacement and projection) in an attempt to combat the anxiety, but they are self-defeating, creating their own distress.

- The aims of psychoanalysis include the restructuring of personality and providing insight, through making the unconscious conscious, undoing unsatisfactory defences and re-experiencing repressed feelings and wishes.

- In classic psychoanalysis, the analyst remains anonymous, a blank screen, which facilitates transference, which can be positive and negative. Interpreting transference is now considered to be a distinctive feature of psychoanalysis, as is the analyst's counter-transference. The client's resistance to interpretations of transference must itself be interpreted. Free association and dream interpretation are other major techniques.

- Psychoanalysis requires there to be a working alliance between analyst and client. Trying to define a cure is very complex and may be different for different clients. But quick and complete cures are the exception: symptom relief is usually only the start of the analytic process, since these are clues to the client's total personality which needs to be explored.

- Freud acknowledged the limitations of psychoanalysis; new problems may develop after therapy has finished, although it never really ends.

- Psychoanalytic psychotherapy represents a modified form of psychoanalysis, such as brief focal therapy, in which therapy focuses on a specific area of difficulty and is dealt with in a much shorter period of time. This is practised by many clinical psychologists and other professionals without a full-blown psychoanalytic training.

- Behaviour therapy and behaviour modification refer to techniques based on classical and operant conditioning respectively. Both see adaptive and maladaptive behaviour as being acquired in the same way and both reject the medical model. Although Freud also rejected the medical model, controversy between Freudians and behaviour therapists, such as Eysenck, has been fierce, especially over the symptom substitution issue, but there is a growing integration between the two approaches.

- Behavioural technology involves a nomothetic approach and makes use of formal diagnostic categories, while behavioural psychotherapy involves an idiographic approach , based on a behavioural/functional analysis of individual cases. The latter stresses current behaviour–environment relations which need to be operationalized before they can be changed.

- Eysenck and Rachman see the case of little Albert as a model of how all phobias are acquired. While there is both experimental (e.g. taste aversion studies) and non-experimental evidence to support this view, there is other evidence against it, including the fact that some phobias are much more common than others, which is consistent with Seligman's concept of preparedness. Instead of direct conditioning, many phobias are probably acquired through observational and instructional learning.

- The two-process/factor model can account for both the initial learning of phobias (through classical conditioning) and their persistence (through negative reinforcement, i.e. operant conditioning). An alternative account is the safety signal hypothesis. The persistence of neurotic symptoms can also be explained in terms of positive reinforcement, what Freud called secondary gain.

- Systematic desensitization (SD) represents a form of counter-conditioning. According to Wolpe, the key principle in SD is reciprocal inhibition, which relates to the 'desensitization' of fear by combining it with relaxation. 'Systematic' refers to the use of a hierarchy of fear which is worked through, starting with the least frightening contact that can be imagined. Homework assignments are intended to help the patient bridge the gap between imagination and reality.

- SD seems to be most effective with minor phobias and with patients able to learn relaxation skills and with vivid imaginations. It is now commonly believed that neither the relaxation nor the use of a hierarchy is necessary; the 'active ingredient' seems to be exposure to the feared object/situation.

- Implosion begins with the patient imagining their most feared form of contact with the feared object, supplemented by the therapist's stimulus augmentation. High anxiety levels lead to exhaustion and both implosion and flooding (which involves *in vivo* exposure) represent forms of 'forced reality testing'. Flooding is thought to be the most effective of all treatments for phobias.

- Aversion therapy involves the removal of an undesirable response to a particular stimulus (such as alcohol) by associating it with another, aversive stimulus (such as an emetic drug, like Antabuse/apomorphine). It is particularly controversial when used with homosexuals; the very existence of techniques for changing sexual orientation can be seen as condoning heterosexism.

- Covert sensitization is aversion therapy that takes place in the patient's imagination and is preferable on humanitarian grounds.

- A commonly used design for assessing the effectiveness of behaviour modification programmes is the AB–AB design, where A is the baseline condition and B is the experimental treatment.

- Lovaas pioneered operant conditioning with autistic children in an attempt to teach them to use speech. He used shaping so that verbal responses became gradually more speech-like, but parents need to use the same shaping techniques at home outside the treatment sessions.

- Behaviour modification has been successfully used with mentally retarded adults and children,

both to reduce self-mutilation and to teach toilet training (e.g. Azrin and Foxx); as with the autistic children, there needs to be continuity between the institution and home.

- Ayllon and Azrin were the pioneers of the token economy (TE), first used with chronic schizophrenics in the 1960s. In its own way, it was as revolutionary as the introduction of anti-schizophrenic drugs in the 1950s.

- The TE is based on the principle of secondary reinforcement, with tokens (conditioned reinforcers) being given immediately for socially desirable behaviours; these tokens can later be exchanged for a range of treats and privileges.

- A major demonstration of the effectiveness of TE is the study by Paul and Lentz, which compared social learning/TE, milieu therapy and a custodial care condition to which patients were randomly assigned. Both the first two conditions produced marked improvements in many aspects of behaviour, with the former proving superior in certain areas, such as reducing bizarre motor behaviours and improving interpersonal and self-care skills, as well as the numbers of patients being released from/staying out of hospital and no longer taking neuroleptics.

- Despite these remarkable results, TE played a secondary role in the treatment programme, so that they do not demonstrate the effectiveness of TE as such. Nevertheless, behavioural interventions seem to be the most effective way of reversing the effects of institutionalization, even if they do not produce 'cures'.

- One of the problems with TE is the lack of generalization of improved behaviours from the hospital to other settings outside. Patients need to be weaned off the tokens and onto social reinforcers, both within the hospital and outside; halfway houses, etc. can help with this.

- Tokens may be effective because of the way they change staff behaviour and attitudes; this suggests that TEs may not be successful because of the learning theory principles on which they are based.

- TEs raise some very basic ethical issues, such as patients' access by right to certain amenities, such as food. Patients should be informed of their legal and moral rights and TEs need to be open to public scrutiny.

- Cognitive behaviour therapy is based on the view that clinical disorders involve faulty thoughts/cognitions, which then produce maladaptive behaviour; cognitive restructuring is a means to the end of changing emotions and behaviour.

- According to Ellis's rational emotive therapy, irrational thoughts (such as the catastrophizing self-statements involved in phobias) are the main cause of all types of emotional/behaviour disorders. By challenging patients about their irrational thoughts, therapy aims to replace them with more reasonable /realistic ones.

- According to Meichenbaum's self-instructional training, neurotic behaviour is due to faulty internal dialogues, indicating improper self-instruction. Patients are helped to develop coping self-statements, relaxation and plans for behaviour change. Where patients recognize the harmless nature of the things they fear, thought stopping (Wolpe) is used.

- Beck's cognitive therapy aims to help clients to understand the illogical nature of their negative thoughts (the cognitive triad of depression) which usually occur automatically and involuntarily . Therapy involves training in being more objective, separating fact from evaluation and seeing things in less extreme ways.

- Modelling as a form of therapy is a direct application of Bandura's research into observational learning. It seems to be effective mainly with children with simple phobias and may represent a form of exposure to the feared object.

- According to Kelly's personal construct therapy (PCT), psychological disorders arise when a person continues to use personal constructs which are repeatedly invalidated. For example, if a construct is applied to events which lie outside its range of convenience, anxiety will be produced. The basic aim of therapy is to help the person loosen or tighten their constructs so that they explain and predict events more accurately.

- PCT may use techniques from other approaches as appropriate, in addition to self-characterization and fixed role therapy (fixed role sketch and fixed role enactment). The relationship between client and therapist is a central feature of the therapy and is comparable to that between student and supervisor, who validates the former's behavioural experiments. The repertory grid can be used in various ways during therapy.

- According to Rogers, threat, anxiety and depression are responses to a lack of congruence between our experience and self-concept; this may arise because of our need for positive regard. We may defend against these feelings by using denial and distortion, setting up a vicious circle, which may manifest in a neurotic or psychotic way.

- The aim of client-centred therapy (CCT) is to enable the individual to become a more independent, confident person by creating a therapeutic atmosphere in which the natural tendency towards self-understanding and self-actualization is allowed to develop. The therapist's task is to help the client to increase their positive self-regard and to become fully integrated again. This is achieved through the therapist's genuineness/authenticity, unconditional positive regard and empathic understanding.

- There is mixed evidence as to the importance of therapists actually possessing these three attitudes/qualities as far as benefit to clients is concerned. Rogers uses the Q-sort in order to assess the validity of CCT; it can be used at various stages during therapy.

- CCT forms the basis of counselling, especially in the UK, reflecting Rogers' involvement with both therapy and education. CCT also helped to inspire the encounter/personal growth movement, especially in the US.

- To ask if therapy is effective is to ask 'Does it work?' (outcome research) and 'How does it work?' (process research). Each question comprises several other overlapping questions. Psychotherapy research began by asking about the outcome of psychoanalysis and therapies based on Freud's theories compared with patients who receive no therapy.

- Eysenck's landmark 1952 article claimed that recovery from neurosis following psychotherapy is no greater than the rate of spontaneous remission. However, there were a number of methodological problems with his study, including the control groups used to establish the spontaneous remission rate, which it is now widely accepted varies considerably between disorders.

- Since the 1970s especially, both the quantity and quality of outcome research have increased, showing psychodynamic therapies in a much more favourable light than Eysenck's early study. One important improvement is the use of meta-analysis, which gives an average of the results of a large number of individual studies, instead of the much cruder results provided by the earlier 'voting method'.

- According to Kazdin and Wilcoxin, the crucial ingredients of any therapy are the patient's expectations of improvement and changes in the patient's self-concept. The former relates to the placebo effect. As used in drug trials, a placebo is an inert/inactive substance that has no effect in itself, but in psychotherapy, it may be impossible to devise a placebo control which is inactive in an equivalent way. Even non-placebo controls will produce expectations.

- If therapy effects don't exceed those of placebos, this is not because psychotherapy is not effective, but because the placebo is a form of psychotherapy, i.e. it raises hopes of improvement.
- Frank identifies four non-specific factors which are responsible for the success of psychotherapy and which make it similar to faith healing and other similar techniques. They help to combat demoralization, the common factor shared by all those who seek therapeutic help. Related to this is Bandura's concept of self-efficacy.
- Different therapeutic approaches define 'cure' in different ways; Eysenck assessed cure using quantitative criteria, while those who use non-directive approaches will be more concerned with the qualitative aspects of therapy, especially the therapeutic relationship. Simply asking 'Is psychotherapy effective?' is, in many ways, too simple.

GLOSSARY

Anti-anxiety drugs Benzodiazepines, such as chlordiazepoxide/Librium and diazepam/Valium, used for 'everyday anxieties'. Also called anxiolytics; used to be called minor tranquillizers.

Cognitive triad Beck's view of depression, in which the person has negative, automatic thoughts about self, the world and the future.

Directive therapies Therapies, such as behaviour therapy, cognitive behaviour therapy and personal construct therapy, in which the therapist gives direct/concrete instructions to the client, both within the session and as 'homework assignments'.

Electroconvulsive therapy (ECT) The delivery of a brief, 70–140 volt shock via electrodes to the temple, either on both sides of the head (bilateral) or on the non-dominant hemisphere side (unilateral).

Frontal lobotomy The cutting of tissue connecting the frontal lobes of the cortex with subcortical areas, on both sides of the cortex. Also called leucotomy.

Major tranquillizers Phenothiazines, such as chlorpromazine/Largactil, used for psychotic symptoms. Also called neuroleptics, anti-schizophrenic drugs.

MAO inhibitors Anti-depressant drugs (such as iproniazid, phenelzine/Nardil) which inhibit monoamine oxidase (MAO) and raise levels of monoamines (dopamine and noradrenaline).

Neurotic paradox Freud's observation that, while neurotic symptoms represent an attempt to solve an unconscious conflict, they at the same time create their own distress and unhappiness.

Outcome research The study of psychotherapy in order to see if it is effective, if it works, as distinct from process research, which is concerned with why/how it works.

Placebo In drug trials, an inert/inactive substance (sugar pill, for instance) used to control for the psychological (as opposed to pharmacological) influence on physiological changes. In this context, it is an intentional placebo.

Reciprocal inhibition The central principle involved in systematic desensitization, according to Wolpe, whereby two opposed emotions (such as anxiety and relaxation) cannot coexist (they 'cancel each other out').

Resistance A form of defence, seen in psychoanalysis, against the painful revelations concerning childhood conflicts that are made through transference.

Scientist-practitioner model Model of helping, used in clinical and counselling psychology, according to which the professional helper is guided by/operates within the framework of general scientific method.

Secondary gain Other people's inadvertent rewarding of neurotic behaviour (e.g. through attention, sympathy), making it more likely to persist.

Self-efficacy The cognitive change that, according to Bandura, all therapies are trying to achieve, namely the client's belief that they can successfully carry out a particular behaviour in order to achieve a particular goal.

Spontaneous remission Improvement/recovery from neurotic symptoms without having received any form of treatment.

Stereotactic psychosurgery The destruction of small areas of brain tissue in very precise locations ('fractional operations'), such as stereotactic tractotomy, stereotaxic limbic leucotomy and amygdalotomy.

Symptom substitution The spontaneous replacement of one neurotic symptom with another, which Freudians believe will happen if only the symptomatic behaviour (e.g. phobia) is treated and not the underlying, unconscious conflict.

Transference In psychoanalysis, the patient's (*analysand*) displacement and projection of repressed feelings about parents onto the analyst. Counter-transference refers to the analyst's feelings of dislike and sexual attraction towards the analysand.

Tricyclic anti-depressants Drugs, such as imipramine/Tofranil, which block the re-uptake of dopamine, noradrenaline and possibly serotonin.

Two-process/factor model An account of phobias, whereby they are initially acquired by classical conditioning, but they persist due to negative reinforcement of the escape/avoidance behaviour (i.e. operant conditioning).

FURTHER READING

Dryden, W. and Feltham, C. (eds) (1992) *Psychotherapy and its Discontents.* Buckingham: Open University Press. A collection of original articles, in which eight distinguished critics of psychotherapy outline their views, with a response from eight psychotherapists, followed by a rebuttal of the response; the critics include Eysenck, Sutherland and Masson.

Dryden, W. and Rentoul, R. (eds) (1991) Adult *Clinical Problems: A Cognitive-Behavioural Approach.* London: Routledge. A detailed account of how cognitive-behavioural therapies, currently the most influential and popular among clinical psychologists, can be applied to anxiety, depression, eating disorders, schizophrenia and many other disorders.

Ethical and Philosophical Issues

32 ETHICS, REDUCTIONISM AND FREE WILL VERSUS DETERMINISM

INTRODUCTION AND OVERVIEW

In discussing psychology as a science in Chapter 2, we noted that one of its unique features is that the subject matter (what is being studied) is essentially the same kind of thing as those carrying out the study – people in both cases. Compared with physics or chemistry, this means that the 'things' being studied in a psychological investigation are capable of thoughts and feelings, whereby they try to understand what is going on and respond emotionally to what is going on, either positively or negatively. Biologists and scientists working in medical research share with psychologists the problem of subjecting living, sentient things to what are often painful, stressful or simply strange and unusual experiences, i.e. they face questions about the *ethics* of what they do.

Just as Orne (1962) regards every psychology experiment as primarily a social situation (which, as we saw in Chapter 2, raises questions of objectivity), we could also regard every psychological investigation as an *ethical situation* (raising questions of propriety and responsibility). Just as methodological issues permeate every area of psychology, so do ethical issues; in fact, it is very difficult to keep them apart, as many of the preceding 31 chapters have shown. For example, when discussing the aims of psychology as a science in Chapter 2, we were raising issues about what is appropriate as much as about what is possible: these are really two sides of the same coin which may conflict with each other on occasions. The issue of the aims of psychology resurfaced in Chapter 29 in relation to theories of personality, namely in the debate about nomothetic vs idiographic approaches. The use of stooges in social psychology as part of often very elaborate attempts to deceive the naive participant (Chapters 15–20) and the surgical manipulations of animals' brains in biopsychology (Chapters 3–6) are just two further examples of the essential difference between the study of the physical world and the world of people and non-human animals. What the psychologist does cannot be determined simply by what they want to find out but also by the effects of the research on those being studied.

However, psychologists are not just scientists or investigators, they are also practitioners; that is, they work in practical and clinical settings in which people with psychological problems require help, i.e. something needs to be changed (see Chapters 1, 30 and 31). Whenever the possibility of changing people arises, ethical issues also arise, just as they do in medicine and psychiatry (and, to some degree, in teaching). In this chapter, we shall look at the psychologist as a scientist/-investigator, both of humans and animals, and as practitioner.

We also saw in Chapter 2 that discussing psychology as science raises some fundamental questions about the nature of human beings or, at least, the image of the person that underlies major psychological theories and which is implicit in much of the experimental study of human behaviour. One major issue is the extent to which people's behaviour is determined by influences over which they have no control (*free will* vs *determinism*), another is *reductionism*, the attempt to explain some complex whole in terms of its basic parts, and one form of this debate is the relationship between the mind or consciousness and the brain (the 'mind–body' issue). Both of these, especially the former, may be thought of as ethical in a broad sense of the term.

PSYCHOLOGY AND ETHICS

While all psychologists have responsibilities and obligations towards those they 'work' with, which are common to both the scientist and practitioner roles, there are also some important differences arising from the different roles. These differences are reflected in the various codes of conduct and ethical guidelines which are published by the major professional bodies for psychologists – the British Psychological Society (BPS) and the American Psychological Association (APA).

As shown in Figure 32.1, the *Code of Conduct for Psychologists* (BPS, 1983) applies to both of the main areas of research and practice, while there are additional documents designed for the two areas separately. The *Ethical Principles for Conducting Research with Human Participants* (BPS, 1990, 1993) and the *Guidelines for the Use of Animals in Research* (BPS and the Committee of the Experimental Psychological Society, 1985) obviously apply to the former while, for example, the

Guidelines for the Professional Practice of Clinical Psychology (BPS, 1983) apply to the latter.

Clinical psychologists are by far the largest single group of psychologists: more than one-third classify themselves as clinical and a further 10 percent call themselves 'counselling psychologists' (see Chapters 1 and 31). Both groups deal with people with psychological problems and, in this respect, they have much in common, in terms of therapeutic methods and techniques used, with psychotherapists, and ethically, with both psychotherapists and psychiatrists. (Unless otherwise stated, quotes will be from the BPS's *Ethical Principles for Conducting Research with Human Participants*).

● The psychologist as scientist /investigator

According to Gale (1995), the problem of ethics in psychological research is daunting; guidelines prove difficult to apply in any hard and fast way in any particular research context and are nothing more than guidelines. Most journals assume that ethical issues

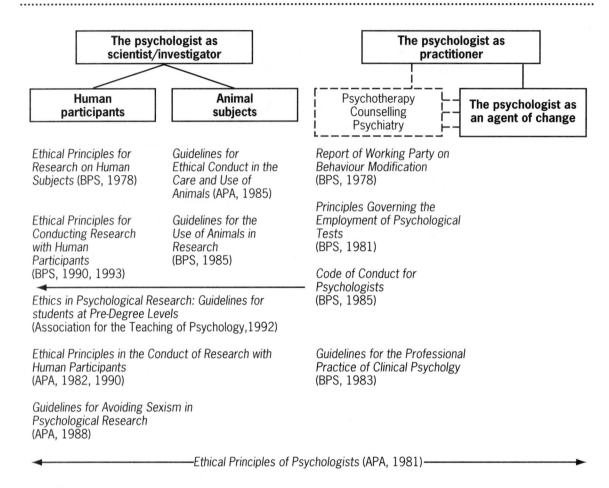

FIGURE 32.1 *Major codes of conduct/ethical guidelines published by the British Psychological Society (BPS) and the American Psychological Association (APA).*

have been considered by the researcher, rather than requiring a formal statement to that effect.

He also notes that the fact that both BPS and APA codes are periodically reviewed and revised indicates that at least some aspects do not depend on absolute or universal ethical truths. Guidelines need to be updated in the light of the changing social and political context of psychological research; for example, new issues, such as sexual behaviour in the context of AIDS, might highlight new ethical problems and, more importantly, changing views about the nature of individual rights will call into question the extent to which psychological research respects or is insensitive to such rights.

● Human participants

Figure 32.1 shows that in the 1978 *Ethical Guidelines*, the term 'subject' is used, while later documents, as well as the APA *Ethical Principles*,

use 'participant'. Gale believes that this reflects a genuine shift in how the individual is perceived within psychology, from object (a more appropriate term than 'subject') to person. This change can be attributed at least in part to the influence of feminist psychologists (see Chapter 2 and Gross, 1995), who have also helped to bring about the removal of sexist language from BPS and APA journals as a matter of policy. (We should note, however, that most psychologists persist in using 'subject', a case of old habits dying hard; but I have deliberately used 'participant' throughout this book.)

The introduction to the *Ethical Principles for Conducting Research with Human Participants* (BPS, 1990) states that:

Participants in psychological research should have confidence in the investigators. Good psychological research is possible only if there is mutual respect and confidence between investigators and participants. Psychological investigators are potentially interested in all aspects of human behaviour and conscious experience. However, for ethical reasons, some areas of human experience and behaviour may be beyond the reach of experiment, observation or other form of psychological investigation. Ethical guidelines are necessary to clarify the conditions under which psychological research is acceptable. (paragraph 1.2)

Psychologists are urged to encourage their colleagues to adopt the Principles and to ensure that they are followed by all researchers whom they supervise (including all students, GCSE, A/AS level, undergraduate and beyond):

In all circumstances, investigators must consider the ethical implications and psychological consequences for the participants in their research. The essential principle is that the investigation should be considered from the standpoint of all participants; foreseeable threats to their psychological well-being, health, values or dignity should be eliminated ... (paragraph 2.1)

This may require consulting with members of various ethnic, racial, sex, age or social class populations.

Consent, informed consent and the right to withdraw

Participants should be informed of the objectives of the investigation and all other aspects of the research which might reasonably be expected to influence their willingness to participate – only such information allows *informed consent* to be given. (paragraph 3.1) If this is not possible, additional safeguards are needed to protect the welfare and dignity of the participants, especially in the case of children and those with psychological impairments (e.g. mental retardation) which limit understanding and/or communication. (paragraph 3.2) But even here, real (informed) consent should be obtained and, in addition, all below-16-year-olds should have parental consent (or consent from those in *loco parentis*). (paragraph 3.3) Special care needs to be taken when research is conducted with detained persons (those in prison, psychiatric hospital, etc.), whose ability to give free informed consent may be affected by their special circumstances. (paragraph 3.5)

Investigators must realize that they often have influence over participants, who may be their students, employees or clients: this relationship must not be allowed to pressurize the participants to take part or remain in the investigation. (paragraph 3.6) Nor must payment be used to induce participants to risk harm beyond that which they risk without payment in their normal lifestyle. (paragraph 3.7)

We should note in relation to paragraph 3.6 that it is standard practice in American universities for psychology students to participate in research as part of their course requirements. (They receive payment and credits, which go towards their final grade, and are free to choose which research to participate in but they are not free to refuse to participate.)

If harm, unusual discomfort or other negative consequences for the individual's future life might occur the investigator must obtain the disinterested approval of independent advisors, inform the participants and obtain informed, real consent, from each of them. (paragraph 3.8)

A study which is invariably (almost inevitably) cited in relation to ethical issues is Milgram's obedience experiment, which is discussed in detail in Chapter 20. This is summarized briefly in Box 32.1.

BOX 32.1 Key study: Milgram's shocking study of obedience – a brief reminder

Participants initially volunteered for a study of memory, which then turned out to be a study of the effects of punishment on learning. Each participant was paired with a confederate who always 'chose' the role of learner, which left the participant as the teacher who had to punish the learner with increasingly strong electric shocks each time he made a mistake on the learning task. Milgram wanted to see how obedient participants were as measured by the shock level they were prepared to go to.

One of Milgram's critics, Baumrind (1964), expressed concern for the welfare of the participants: were adequate measures taken to protect them from the undoubted stress and emotional conflict which they experienced? Milgram replied that this presupposes that the outcome of the experiment was expected – Baumrind is confusing the (unanticipated) outcome with the basic experimental procedure. The production of stress was not an intended and deliberate effect of the manipulation; it was discussed with colleagues beforehand and none anticipated the reactions which occurred. He asked some of his students and a group of psychiatrists to predict when, on average, participants would stop obeying the experimenter: they estimated that most would stop at the point when the learner began to protest, thus implying that participants would experience very little conflict.

According to Milgram (1974), 'Understanding grows because we examine situations in which the end is unknown. An investigator unwilling to accept this degree of risk must give up the idea of scientific inquiry', i.e. you cannot know your results in advance!

However, while this might meet Baumrind's original criticism, it does not get rid of the charge of *deception* (which is a feature of much psychological research); if participants are deceived as to the true purpose of the study, they cannot give informed consent (see below).

Another famous and controversial study (also discussed in detail in Chapter 20) is the prison simulation experiment (Zimbardo *et al.*, 1973), summarized in Box 32.2.

BOX 32.2 | **Key study: a mock prison but real brutality – a brief reminder**

Participants volunteered for a study of the psychological effects of imprisonment and were randomly allocated to the role of prisoner or prison guard. Some of the prisoners experienced (largely) unanticipated distress but there was little in the way of deception and informed consent was obtained for this study which took place in a specially converted basement at Stanford University.

The legal counsel of Stanford University was consulted, drew up a formal 'informed consent' statement and told us of work, fire, safety and insurance requirements we had to satisfy (which we did). The 'informed consent' statement, signed by every participant, specified that there would be an invasion of privacy, loss of some civil rights and harassment. Neither they, nor we, however, could have predicted in advance the intensity and extent of these aspects of the prison experience. We did not, however, inform them of the police arrests, in part, because we did not secure final approval from the police until minutes before they decided to participate and, in part, because we did want the mock arrests to come as a surprise. This was a breach, by omission, of the ethics of our informed consent contract. The staff of the university's Student Health Department was alerted to our study and prior arrangements made for any medical care which might be required.

Approval was officially sought and received in writing from the sponsoring agency ONR, the Psychology Department and the University Committee of Human Experimentation ... (Zimbardo, 1973)

The study was planned to last for two weeks but was abandoned after six days because of the distress the prisoners were suffering. By contrast, once Milgram saw the degree of distress his 'teachers' were experiencing, why didn't he call a halt to the experiments there and then? This relates to the question of *withdrawal from the investigation*.

> Along with the provision of information, which forms the basis of informed consent, investigators should make plain to the participants their right to withdraw from the study at any time, regardless of any payment or other inducement offered. This may be difficult in certain observational or organizational settings but must be an aim and applies to children as much as to adults. (paragraph 6.1) In the light of experience of the investigation, or as a result of debriefing (see below), participants have the right to withdraw their consent retrospectively and to require their own data (including any recordings) to be destroyed. (paragraph 6.2)

(In longitudinal research, consent may need to be obtained on more than one occasion and so retrospective withdrawal of consent could involve a considerable amount of data collected over a substantial period of time.)

Coolican (1990) believes that Milgram flagrantly contravened all principles regarding the right to withdraw at any point and to terminate proceedings when distress levels are substantially higher than anticipated or than is acceptable. Each time a participant expressed the wish to stop giving shocks, he was ordered to continue, with the prods and prompts becoming increasingly harsh. Coolican points out that the APA (1987) stresses special vigilance when the investigator is in a position of power over the participant, a position that was, of course, very forcefully exploited by Milgram. So why did Milgram allow the experiments to continue?

He acknowledges that he could have stopped them but felt that 'momentary excitement is not the same as harm' and he did not feel that the stress was sufficiently intense to warrant abandoning the research. (He was largely vindicated by the results of his debriefing; see below.)

At a more abstract level, Milgram started out with the belief that every person who came to the laboratory was free to accept or reject the dictates of authority: far from being passive creatures, participants are active, choosing adults. If some were able to defy the experimenter, then surely others were free to do the same. Indeed, the final prod 'You have no other choice, you *must* go on!' was often the occasion for the participant to break off and say something like 'That's where you're wrong, I do have a choice!'.

Colman (1987) points out that an ethical committee of the APA investigated Milgram's research not long after its first publication (during which time Milgram's APA membership was suspended) and eventually found it ethically acceptable. In 1965 he was awarded the prize for outstanding contribution to social psychological research by the American Association for the Advancement of Science.

Is there more to informed consent than being informed?

Although, clearly, informed consent requires that the participant be informed of the procedure, a participant will not have full knowledge of it until they have experienced it; indeed, there is no guarantee that the investigators fully appreciate the procedure without undergoing the experience themselves (Gale and Chapman, 1984, cited in Gale, 1995). In this sense, it is difficult to argue that full prior knowledge can ever be guaranteed: how much information should be given beforehand, how much information can young children, elderly people, infirm or disabled people or those in emotional distress be expected to absorb? Even if a potential participant fulfils this 'informational' criterion of consent, the status of the experimenter, people's desire to please others and not let them down, the desire not to look foolish by insisting on withdrawing when an experiment is already underway, all seem to detract from the idea that the participant is truly choosing freely in a way that is assumed by the *Ethical Principles* (Gale, 1995). The interpersonal nature of the experimental situation is, of course, what Orne (1962) was interested in (see Chapter 2).

Deception

Intentional deception of the participants over the purpose and general nature of the investigation should be avoided whenever possible. Participants should never be deliberately misled without extremely strong scientific or medical justification. Even then there should be strict controls and the disinterested approval of independent advisors. (paragraph 4.2)

The decision that deception is necessary should only be taken after determining that alternative procedures avoiding concealment or deception are not available, ensuring that the participants will be debriefed at the earliest opportunity and consulting

on how the withholding of information and deliberate deception will be received.

Coolican (1990) cites a study by Menges (1973) who reviewed about 1000 American studies and found that 80 percent involved giving participants less than complete information. In only 3 percent were they given complete information about the independent variable and only in 25 percent of cases was complete information given about the dependent variable.

In terms of the likely harm to the participant, clearly some cases of deception are less serious than others. Perhaps most serious are those likely to affect the participant's self-image, particularly self-esteem; this is why studies like Milgram's and that of Zimbardo *et al.* have proved so controversial. It could be argued that it is in social psychology generally that the most potentially damaging deception goes on, since it is in this kind of research that people are most likely to learn things about themselves as a person, things which will be of much greater emotional significance than, say, one's ability to perceive, remember or solve problems (the concern of cognitive psychology).

A form of deception used almost exclusively in social psychology is the confederate (or stooge) who (usually) pretends to be another participant (as in Milgram's experiments); this involves an elaborate 'staging' of events into which the naive participant has to fit without realizing that there is any pretence being staged, but at least debriefing (see below) allows confederates to be revealed for what they really are. However, in field experiments of bystander intervention (see Chapter 17), emergencies are staged in real-life situations which do not permit any debriefing to occur (e.g. actors pretending to collapse in the New York subway – Piliavin *et al.*, 1969). This means that such unsuspecting participants never find out that they were participating in an experiment at all and so never find out that they have been deceived – a double deception!

Can deception ever be justified?

Aronson (1988) defends Milgram on the grounds that if he had not used deception, he would have found results: ' ... which simply do not reflect how people behave when led to believe they are in real situations': deception may be the best and (perhaps) the only way to get useful information about how people behave in most complex and important situations. Each year Aronson asks his psychology students how they would have behaved if they had been one of

Milgram's participants: about 1 percent each year say they'd go all the way. Does this mean they are nicer people than Milgram's participants? Aronson doesn't think so. It means that if given half a chance, most people will try to 'look good'.

Assuming that we believe it is important to understand the processes involved in obedience (the end), can we then justify deception as a *means* of studying it, and even if we can, is it a sufficient justification?

If participants themselves don't mind being deceived, does that make it all right?

What if we found that, despite expecting to be deceived, people still volunteered or that, not expecting to be deceived, they say that the deception did not particularly bother them? Would this change the ethical 'status' of deception? A number of points need to be made in response to this question.

Mannucci (1977, cited in Milgram, 1992) asked 192 laypeople about ethical aspects of psychology experiments. They regarded deception as a relatively minor issue and were far more concerned about the quality of the experience they would undergo as participants.

Most of the actual participants who were deceived in Asch's conformity experiments (see Chapter 20) were very enthusiastic and expressed their admiration for the elegance and significance of the experimental procedure (Milgram, 1992).

In defence of his own obedience experiments, Milgram (1974) reports that, as part of the very thorough debriefing of his participants, they all received a comprehensive report when all the experiments were over, detailing the procedure and the results, as well as a follow-up questionnaire concerning their participation. Of the 92 percent who returned the questionnaires (an unusually high response rate), almost 84 percent said they were glad or very glad to have participated, while fewer than 2 percent said they were sorry or very sorry. Eight per cent said they felt that more experiments of this kind should be carried out and 74 percent said they had learned something of personal importance. More specifically, the 'technical illusions' (a morally neutral term which he prefers to the morally biased or loaded 'deception') are justified for one reason only: they are in the end accepted and endorsed by those who are exposed to them:

> The central moral justification for allowing a procedure of the sort used in my experiment is that it is judged acceptable by those who have taken part in it. Moreover, it was the salience of this fact throughout that constituted the chief moral warrant for the continuation of the experiments.

He goes on to say that any criticism of the experiment (or any other, for that matter) which does not take account of the tolerant reactions of the participants is hollow. ' ... Again, the participant, rather than the external critic, must be the ultimate source of judgement' (Milgram, 1974).

In a review of several studies focusing on the ethical acceptability of deception experiments, Christensen (1988, cited in Krupat and Garonzik, 1994) reports that, as long as deception is not extreme, participants don't seem to mind. He suggests that the widespread use of mild forms of deception is justified, firstly, because apparently no one is harmed and secondly, because there seem to be few, if any, acceptable alternatives.

Krupat and Garonzik (1994) found that, among 255 university psychology students, those who had had at least one experience of being deceived while participating in some psychological research, compared with those who had not been deceived, were significantly more likely to expect to be deceived again. But the experience of being deceived does not have a significant impact on the students' evaluation of other aspects of participation, such as enjoyment and interest, and, consistent with the findings of Christensen and Mannucci, previously deceived participants were not terribly upset at the prospect of being deceived again. Indeed, those who had been deceived at least once said they would be less upset at being lied to or misled again. According to Krupat and Garonzik (1994), ' ... It almost seems that these people are accepting deception as par for the course and, therefore, not worthy of becoming upset about ... '

Protection of participants

> Investigators have a primary responsibility to protect participants from physical and mental harm during the investigation. Normally, the risk of harm must be no greater than in ordinary life, i.e. participants should not be exposed to risks greater than or additional to those encountered in their normal life styles .
>
> Participants must be asked about any factors in the procedure that might create a risk, such as pre-existing medical conditions, and must be advised of any special action they should take to avoid risk. (paragraph 8.1).

Fortunately, there are relatively few cases in which actual physical harm (e.g. pain) comes to participants, although little Albert (who was made to fear a white rat through the association of the rat with a hammer smashing down on a steel bar right behind his head) is a notable exception (see Chapter 7) and many experiments have involved electric shock, extreme noise levels, food and sleep deprivation, anxiety or nausea, etc. (Coolican, 1990). But in many of these cases, the adult participants give informed consent, especially in sleep and food deprivation (see Chapters 4 and 5), where there is often no need for deception and the right to withdraw at any time acts as an additional safeguard (at least in theory).

However, little Albert was too young to give consent (informed or otherwise) although his mother presumably did (it's actually not clear what she knew in advance) and she certainly exercised her right to withdraw her son from the experiment to save him any more 'punishment'. There is also no doubt that having a hammer crash down on a four-foot steel bar right behind your ear is very painful (Albert may have suffered permanent hearing loss as a result) but equally worrying is the distress – the 'mental harm'. The point of the experiment was to induce a phobia of rats (and other 'furry' things) and this was undoubtedly achieved.

Debriefing (along with confidentiality and the right to withdraw) can be regarded as a major means of protecting participants where emotional suffering has occurred – with or without deception. Participants must also be protected from the stress that might be produced by disclosing highly personal and private information; they must be reassured that they are not obliged to answer such questions.

Debriefing

According to Aronson (1988):

> The experimenter must take steps to ensure that subjects leave the experimental situation in a frame of mind that is at least as sound as it was when they entered. This frequently requires post-experimental 'debriefing' procedures that require more time and effort than the main body of the experiment.

Where no undue suffering is experienced but participants are deceived regarding the real purpose of the experiment:

> ... the investigator should provide the participant with any necessary information to complete their understanding of the nature of the research. The investigator should discuss with the participants their experience of the research in order to monitor any unforseen negative effects or misconceptions. (paragraph 5.1)

However:

> ... some effects which may be produced by an

experiment will not be negated by a verbal description following the research. Investigators have a responsibility to ensure that participants receive any necessary de-briefing in the form of active intervention before they leave the research setting. (paragraph 5.3)

This is more like a 'therapeutic' measure than it is a matter of 'good manners'. Examples of this second kind of debriefing (which also incorporates the first) can be found in both the Zimbardo *et al.* and Milgram experiments:

> Following the study, we held a group and individual de-briefing session, had all the subjects return post-experimental questionnaires several weeks later, several months later, and at yearly intervals. Many submitted retrospective diaries and personal analyses of the effects of their participation. We have met with most of the subjects since the termination of the study singly or in small groups, or where that was not possible, have discussed their reactions in telephone conversations. We are sufficiently convinced that the suffering we observed and were responsible for, was stimulus-bound and did not extend beyond the confines of the basement prison. (Zimbardo, 1973).

In Milgram's experiments, a very thorough debriefing ('dehoax') was carefully carried out with all participants during which:

● they were reunited with the unharmed actor-victim;

● they were assured that no shock had been delivered; and

● Milgram and the participant had an extended discussion. Obedient participants were assured that their behaviour was entirely normal and their feelings of conflict and tension were shared by others, while defiant participants were supported in their decision to disobey the experimenter. They were all told they would receive (and did) a comprehensive report when all the experiments were over, detailing the procedure and the results. They were also sent a follow-up questionnaire regarding their participation (see above).

One year after the completion of the experiments, an impartial psychiatrist interviewed 40 participants, several of whom had experienced extreme stress; none showed any signs of having been psychologically harmed or having suffered any traumatic reactions.

According to Aronson (1988), not only is debriefing valuable as a means of undoing any discomfort or deception which might have occurred during the experimental session, but it also provides the experimenter with an opportunity to provide additional information about the topic under investigation, so the experiment can become an educational experience for participants. In addition, the experimenter can determine to what extent the procedure worked:

> ... and find out from the one person who knows best (the subject) how the procedure might be improved. In short, the prudent experimenter regards subjects as colleagues – not as objects ...

(This touches on the more general issue of the mechanistic nature of psychology; see Chapter 2.) However:

> Debriefing does not provide a justification for unethical aspects of an investigation. (paragraph 5.2)

Confidentiality

> Subject to the requirements of legislation, including the Data Protection Act, information obtained about a participant during an investigation is confidential unless otherwise agreed in advance ... Participants in psychological research have a right to expect that information they provide will be treated confidentially, and, if published, will not be identifiable as theirs. In the event that confidentiality and/or anonymity cannot be guaranteed, the participant must be warned of this in advance of agreeing to participate. (paragraph 7.1)

Apart from the ethical considerations, a purely pragmatic argument for guaranteeing anonymity is that members of the public would soon stop volunteering if their identity was disclosed without their permission. If participants have been seriously deceived, they have the right to witness destruction of any such records they don't wish to be kept. Results are usually made anonymous as early as possible by use of a letter/number instead of name (Coolican, 1994).

Are there special circumstances in which the investigator might contravene the confidentiality rule? Yes, namely where there are clear dangers to human life; for example, participant observation of gang life where a serious crime is planned or a psychiatrist's patient plans to kill themselves, etc.: '...The ethical principles involved here are broader than those involved in conducting scientific research' (Coolican, 1994).

Involuntary participation and observational research

> Studies based upon observation must respect the privacy and psychological well-being of the individuals studied. Unless those observed give their consent to being observed, observational research is only acceptable in situations where those observed would expect to be observed by strangers. Additionally, particular account should be taken of local cultural values and of the possibility of intruding upon the privacy of individuals who, even while in a normally public space, may believe they are unobserved. (paragraph 9.1)

In the case of *naturalistic observation*, the essential ethical issue is one of consent – not only can informed consent not be given, *no consent at all* can be given. At the same time, the possibility of any kind of debriefing is virtually nil, from a practical point of view. Even more serious is participant observation, where people's private lives may be invaded. Coolican (1994) cites a study by Humphreys (1971) of the behaviour of consenting homosexuals; he acted as public washroom 'lookout'. Those being studied were completely unaware of the scrutiny and of the fact that their car registration numbers were recorded in order to obtain more background information later on.

We mentioned earlier the case of *field experiments*, where people are unwitting, unsolicited participants in an experiment and where, implicitly, demands are made on them, for instance in the form of an actor pretending to collapse in a public place. This puts them under some degree of obligation and, depending on their participation or otherwise, they may experience a range of feelings, including guilt/embarrassment/disgust/helplessness, etc. There may be twice the amount of deception involved, but instead of receiving twice the amount of debriefing, they don't receive any!

Publication and access to data

The APA (1981) states explicitly that psychologists, as scientists, must accept primary responsibility for the selection of research topics, research methods, analysis and reporting. Data must not be suppressed, alternative hypotheses and explanations must be acknowledged. Researchers must only take credit for what they have done so those who have made equal or unequal contributions must be named, either as a co-author or in footnotes or elsewhere (including research assistants, who often do much of the 'donkey work', clerical assistants, etc.). A basic requirement of research papers, etc. is to provide a sufficiently detailed account to enable other researchers to test the hypothesis for themselves (*replication*). In the light of this, perhaps the greatest sin that can be committed by a scientist is what it is widely (but not universally) agreed was done by Burt, namely inventing data for his twin studies to support the genetic theory of intelligence (see Chapter 28).

Protecting the individual vs. benefiting society

The debate about the ethics of psychological research usually focuses on the vulnerability of individual participants and the responsibility of the psychologists towards their participants to ensure that they do not suffer in any way from their experience of participating.

Wider issues about the 'morality' of the questions which the researcher is trying to answer through the research are much less commonly discussed, but these would include the fundamental issue of the values which are, often unconsciously, helping to shape the research questions (see Chapter 2). If the questions themselves are limited and shaped by the values of the individual researcher, they are also limited and shaped by considerations of methodology, i.e. what it is possible to do, practically, when investigating human behaviour and experience. For example, in the context of interpersonal attraction, Brehm (1992) claims that, by its nature, the laboratory experiment is extremely limited in the kinds of questions that it will allow psychologists to investigate (see Chapter 16).

Conversely, and just as importantly, there are certain aspects of behaviour and experience which could be studied experimentally, but it would be unethical to do so. Brehm (1992) gives 'jealousy between partners participating in laboratory research' as an example. Indeed:

> ... all types of research in this area [intimate relationships] involve important ethical dilemmas. Even if all we do is to ask subjects to fill out questionnaires describing their relationships, we need to think carefully about how this research experience might affect them and their partner ...

So the research that psychologists do is partly constrained by practical (methodological) considerations and also partly by ethical considerations: what it is possible to do may be unacceptable but equally, what may be acceptable may not be possible. As shown in Figure 32.2, the *what* of research is constrained by both the *how* and the *should*.

As we have seen, ethical debates (the 'should') are usually confined to protecting the integrity and welfare of the individual participant; this is what the various Codes of Conduct and Ethical Principles are designed to try and ensure. But there is a wider ethical issue involved: as important as it surely is to protect individuals, psychologists are also obliged to

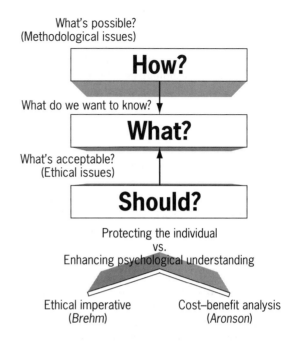

FIGURE 32.2 *Ethical and methodological constraints on the questions that psychologists can try to answer through the research process.*

gain more understanding of important areas of human behaviour (Brehm, 1992), to carry out socially meaningful research, i.e. research which potentially may improve the quality of people's lives. Social psychologists in particular have a two-fold ethical obligation – to individual participants *and* to society at large (Myers, 1994). Psychologists respect the dignity and worth of the individual and strive for the preservation of fundamental human rights. They are committed to increasing knowledge of human behaviour and of people's understanding of themselves and others and to the utilization of such knowledge for the promotion of human welfare (APA, 1981). (This is very relevant to discussion of the aims of psychology as a science; see Chapter 2.)

This general statement is echoed by Aronson (1992) who argues that, in a real sense, social psychologists are ' ... obligated to use their research skills to advance our knowledge and understanding of human behaviour for the ultimate aim of human betterment. In short, social psychologists have an ethical responsibility to the society as a whole ... '

In talking about the aim of 'human betterment', we are, of course, raising many important questions to do with basic values, but at least it opens out the ethical debate in such a way that values must be addressed and recognized as part of the research process (something that feminist psychologists advocate very strongly; see Chapter 2).

The short-term deception of individual participants (and the distress which this might cause) may be necessary if psychologists are to learn things about human behaviour and experience which can then be used to benefit people in general. What form might such benefits take?

In some of the early, and very famous, studies of bystander intervention (see Chapter 17), people were deceived as to the 'emergency' that was supposedly taking place. In the Latané and Darley (1968) experiment, steam, which was meant to resemble smoke, poured into the room where the participants were filling out questionnaires, and in a second study (Darley and Latané, 1968), participants believed that another participant, who was supposedly in another part of the building and could only be heard via an intercom system (really a stooge), was having an epileptic fit. Many participants were very distressed by their experience, especially those in the latter experiment. Yet when asked to complete a post-experiment questionnaire (which followed a very careful debriefing), all said that they believed the deception was justified and that they would be willing to participate in similar experiments again. None reported any feelings of anger towards the experimenter.

A later study, by Beaman et al. (1978, cited in Myers, 1994) built on these earlier experiments. They used a lecture to inform some students about how bystanders' refusal to help can influence both one's interpretation of an emergency and one's feelings of responsibility. Two other groups of students heard either a different lecture or no lecture at all. Two weeks later, as part of a different experiment in a different location, the participants found themselves (accompanied by an unresponsive confederate) walking past someone who was slumped over or sprawled under a bike. Of those who had heard the lecture about helping behaviour, 50 percent stopped to offer help, compared with 25 percent who had not.

What this suggests, of course, is that the results of psychological research can be used to make people more aware of the influences that affect our behaviour, making it more likely that we will act differently armed with that knowledge from how we might otherwise have done. In the case of bystander intervention, this 'consciousness raising' is beneficial in a very tangible way to the person who is helped; as for the helper, being more sensitive to the needs of others and the feeling of satisfaction from actually having helped another person may be seen as benefits too. (The participants in the Beaman et al.

experiment were, of course, being deceived, both as to the identity of the unresponsive confederate and the apparent 'victim'.)

Judging the methodology in terms of the outcome

Our judgement about the ethics of any experiment, i.e. the acceptability of the procedure (including any deception involved), may be (unconsciously) influenced by the results that are obtained. If the results tell us something pleasant or flattering about human nature, the procedure is less likely to be criticized as unethical, while the reverse is true if the results tell us ' ... something we'd rather not know' (Aronson, 1992). But this is to confuse the procedure with the outcome, when they need to be assessed independently before being weighed against each other.

There is little doubt that Milgram's experiments told us something about ourselves that 'we'd rather not know'. Aronson agrees with Milgram himself, who is convinced that ' ... much of the criticism [of his obedience experiments], whether people know it or not, stems from the results of the experiment. If everyone had broken off at slight shock or mild shock, this would be a very reassuring finding and who would protest? (Milgram, 1992).

Consistent with this argument is Aronson's observation that the dilemma faced by social psychologists (regarding their obligations to society and to their individual participants) is greatest when investigating such important areas as conformity, obedience and bystander intervention. In general, the more important the issue:

- the greater the potential benefit for society; and
- the more likely that an individual participant will experience distress and discomfort, etc.

The 'missing middle' from this observation is that the more important the issue, the more essential it becomes that deception (or 'technical illusion') is used. Why? Because the psychologist wants to know how people are likely to behave when they find themselves in that situation outside the laboratory (or, at least, outside the experimental situation). While this raises a number of crucial methodological questions (such as experimental realism, external validity or mundane realism; see Chapter 2), the key ethical issue hinges on the fact that the use of deception both contributes enormously (and perhaps irreplaceably) to our understanding of human behaviour (helping to satisfy the obligation to society) and at the same time significantly increases the distress of individual participants (detracting from the responsibility to protect individuals). So what is the psychologist to do?

Some suggested solutions to the 'double obligation' dilemma

1 Having accepted that, under certain circumstances, deception is permissible, most psychologists still advocate that it should not be used unless it is considered to be *essential* to do so (Milgram, 1992; Aronson, 1992). This is consistent with the BPS *Ethical Principles*.

2 While accepting the principle involved in 1, Milgram (1992) believes that if we excluded, on principle, the experimental creation of stress or conflict and only allowed studies which produced positive emotions, ' ... such a stricture would lead to a very lopsided psychology, one that caricatured rather than accurately reflected human experience'.

Historically, the most informative experiments in social psychology include those which examine how participants resolve conflicts of one kind or another, such as the Asch studies of conformity (truth vs. conformity; see Chapter 20), the Latané and Darley bystander intervention studies (getting involved in another's troubles vs not getting involved; see Chapter 17) and Milgram's own obedience experiments (internal conscience vs external authority; see Chapter 20). If we exclude the study of such core human issues, we would be causing an 'irreparable loss' to any science of human behaviour.

But what about the accusation that Milgram's experiment may produce diminished self-esteem, or sense of self-worth, in those participants who obey the experimenter all the way up to 450 volts? Milgram's reply is to agree that it is the experimenter's responsibility to make the laboratory session as constructive an experience as possible and to explain the experiment in a way that allows participants to integrate their performance into their self-concept in an insightful way. However, if the experimenter were to hide the truth from the participant, even if this is negative, this would set the experiment completely apart from other life experiences (and, we could add, would simply be dishonest).

3 Two compromise solutions to the problem of not being able to obtain informed consent are (i) *presumptive consent* (of 'reasonable people') and (ii) *prior general consent*. In the former, the views of a large number of people are obtained about the acceptability of an experimental procedure. These people would not participate in the actual experiment (if it went ahead), but their views could be taken as evidence of how people in general would react to participation. In the latter, prior general consent could be obtained from people who might, subsequently, serve as experimental participants. Before joining a pool of volunteers to serve in psychological research, people would be explicitly told that sometimes participants are misinformed about the true purpose of the study and sometimes experience emotional stress. Only those agreeing, in the light of this knowledge, would be chosen for a particular study (Milgram, 1992). This is a compromise solution because people would be giving their 'informed consent' (a) well in advance of the actual experiment, (b) only in a very general way, and (c) without knowing what specific manipulations/deceptions will be used in the particular experiment in which they participate. This seems to fall somewhere between 'mere' consent and full 'informed consent'; perhaps this should be called *semi-* or *partially informed consent*.

● Animal subjects

The Scientific Affairs Board of the BPS published their *Guidelines for the Use of Animals in Research* (1985), in conjunction with the Committee of the Experimental Psychological Society. They offered a checklist of points which investigators should carefully consider when planning experiments with living animals. Researchers have a general obligation to:

> ... avoid, or at least to minimize, discomfort to living animals ... discuss any future research with their local Home Office Inspector and colleagues who are experts in the topic ... seek ... Widespread advice as to whether the likely scientific contribution of the work ... justifies the use of living animals, and whether the scientific point they wish to make may not be made without the use of living animals ... (BPS, 1985)

This raises two fundamental questions:

1 How do we know animals suffer?
2 What (goal) can ever justify the subjection of animals to pain?

How do we know that animals suffer?

According to Dawkins (1980), the question of how much we know regarding the suffering of an animal of another species is fundamental to many of the current debates about animal welfare.

What criteria should be used to judge animal suffering?

- Are the animals physically healthy? Disease and injury are generally acknowledged to be major causes of suffering. For this reason, experiments like the executive monkey experiments (in which pairs of monkeys were attached to an apparatus which gave electric shocks, such that the 'executive' could prevent the shock by pressing a lever but the other could not, with the effect that the former developed ulcers and eventually died) would be unlikely even to be debated in the current climate (Mapstone, 1991) (see Chapter 6). It is self-evident that these monkeys were suffering and the experiments were quite rightly condemned by the scientific community.

- Even if we are sure that they are not suffering, we would still have to decide whether their confinement imposed mental suffering which did not affect their external condition (Dawkins, 1980). Apparently healthy zoo and farm animals often show bizarre behaviour (bobbing up and down, eating faeces, etc.). An animal may also suffer intensely but too transiently for any overt signs of injury to make themselves obvious (transporting food animals may produce subtle physiological effects, e.g. changes in the ammonia content of the muscles or hormone levels).

- The biggest difficulty is not being able to ask animals what they are feeling but with greater knowledge of the animals themselves, the lack of words may not turn out to be such a formidable barrier. The animals' behaviour may provide evidence enough, e.g. a fairly direct way of getting animals to express what they feel by their behaviour is to give them access to switches which control their environment in some way. For example, what happens when pigs are given the opportunity to adjust their own levels of illumination? Work at the Agricultural Research Council has shown that pigs quickly learn what light switches are for and can be effectively asked what sort of lighting they like and when they like the lights to go on and off.

- We must find out about animal suffering by careful observation and experimentation:

  > ... Because different species have different requirements, different lifestyles, and, for all we know, different kinds of emotions, we cannot assume that we know about their suffering or well being without taking the trouble to study them species by species ...
  > (Dawkins, 1980)

To build up a picture of what an animal might be feeling, we need a great deal of factual information about its biology.

According to the Institute of Medical Ethics (IME) Working Party (Haworth, 1992), some of the long-term benefits (and, therefore, justifications) of animal research include :

- improvements in animal husbandry;
- contributions to animal welfare on farms and zoos;
- wildlife conservation; and
- the general challenge to science of increasing our understanding of the 'how and why of animal behaviour'.

Drawing on the IME Working Party's report, Bateson (1986, 1992) has proposed criteria for assessing animal suffering, including :

- possessing receptors sensitive to noxious or painful stimulation; and
- having brain structures comparable to the human cerebral cortex.

Based on how an animal's nervous system works and its behaviour in the face of noxious stimuli, Bateson (1992) tentatively concludes that insects probably do not experience pain, whereas fish and octopuses probably do; but the boundaries between the presence and absence of pain are 'fuzzy'.

How can we justify animal experiments?

The question of suffering wouldn't arise if animals were not being used in experiments in the first place. According to Gray (1987), the main justifications for animal experimentation are: (i) the pursuit of scientific knowledge; and (ii) the advancement of medicine.

To justify the use of animals, especially when the procedures used are likely to be very stressful, the research must be rigorously designed and the potential results must represent a significant contribution to our knowledge of medicine, pharmacology, biopsychology or psychology as a whole: this is a safeguard against distressing research being carried out for its own sake or at the whim of the researcher.

The guidelines state that if the animals are confined, constrained, harmed or stressed in any way, the experimenter must consider whether the knowledge to be gained justifies the procedure – some knowledge is trivial and experiments must not be done simply because it is possible to do them. To take the example of the executive monkeys again, the medical justification (to discover why business executives develop ulcers) was insufficient to justify the continuation of these experiments – the monkeys' obvious suffering superseded even the combination of scientific and medical justification. But there are other cases where, while the scientific justification may be apparent, the medical justification is much less so, such as experiments where animals' brains are stimulated via implantation of a permanent electrode (electrical self-stimulation of the brain – ESB; e.g. Olds and Milner, 1954; see Chapter 5).

Safeguards for animal subjects

Whatever practical application Olds and Milner's ESB experiments may have subsequently had (e.g. pain/anxiety relief in psychotics, epileptics and cancer patients), they don't seem to have been conducted with such human applications in mind. Can the scientific knowledge gained about ESB as a very powerful positive reinforcer justify, on its own, the fact that the rats were eventually 'sacrificed' (i.e. killed)? The very least that can be required of researchers is that every step is taken to ensure the minimum of suffering is caused, both during and following any surgical procedure and by any electric shock or food deprivation, which are such common features of laboratory experiments.

Gray (1987) claims that rats are the most commonly used experimental subjects in psychology, with food deprivation and electric shock being the most objected-to treatments. He claims that food deprivation is not a source of suffering and that the rats are either fed once a day when the day's experimentation is over or are maintained at 85 percent of their free-feeding (*ad lib*) body weight and that both are actually healthier than allowing them to eat ad lib. Regarding shock, Gray claims this may cause some pain but not extreme pain (based on observations of the animals' behaviour). The level permitted is controlled by the Home Office (HO) inspectors – the average level used in the UK is 0.68 milliamperes, for an average of 0.57 seconds. This usually produces an unpleasant tickling sensation in humans.

The Guidelines point out that procedures causing pain or distress are illegal unless the experimenter holds an HO licence and relevant certificates; even then, there should be no alternative ways of conducting the experiment without the use of aversive stimulation. Similarly, it is illegal in the UK to perform any surgical or pharmacological procedure on vertebrates without an HO licence and relevant certification. Such procedures must be performed by

| BOX 32.3 | Critical discussion: the dilemma of studying animals in the wild – knowing when to sit back and let nature take its course |

Cayo Santiago (the oldest continuously maintained primate colony in the world, established in 1939) is a Caribbean island that is almost literally a laboratory in the field ('open-air laboratory'). The rhesus monkeys which inhabit the island are given provisions, so that some aspects of their feeding ecology cannot be studied. But it is possible to follow the behaviour, development and population dynamics of a species over many generations. Each year the monkeys are trapped and the youngsters born that year are tattooed and blood samples are taken – the colony is still used partly for medical research, but these are the only interventions. Without this, the age, sex and maternal genealogy of every individual (plus a detailed biography) would not be known (Rawlins, 1979).

Prior to 1970, Cayo's primary purpose was to supply monkeys for medical research (having already deprived them of their natural habitats) and behavioural studies were not allowed to interfere with this. Since 1970, no animal has been captured and the developmental study of the free-ranging monkeys is at least as important as the medical research. But if, for example, there were an outbreak of some infectious disease which threatened the colony, this would pose a dilemma between practical and moral considerations. Interference to save the monkeys could be both defended and attacked on moral grounds. The scientists' moral duty is to save them if they have the power to do so; however, they are also bound to retain and preserve the naturalness of Cayo. So should the monkeys be free to die? This dilemma seems to underline and reflect the dual nature of Cayo both as natural and human-made, 'field' and laboratory (Gross, 1994).

experienced staff and it is a particular responsibility of senior staff to train and supervise others. Experimenters must be familiar with the technical aspects of anaesthesia and appropriate steps should be taken to prevent post-operative infection in chronic experiments.

Throughout the Guidelines, the importance of understanding *species differences* is emphasized in relation to: (i) caging and social environment; (ii) the stress involved in marking wild animals for identification or attaching radio transmitters to them; and (iii) the duration of food/drink deprivation. Paragraph 8 also states that field workers should disturb animals as little as possible, pointing out that even simple observation of wild animals can have marked effects on their breeding and survival. A case in point is the Cayo Santiago primate colony described in Box 32.3.

The medical justification argument

The strongest argument for animal experiments is undoubtedly the advancement of medical knowledge and treatments. Green (1994) points out that many drugs used in the treatment of human diseases have been developed using animals and could not have been developed otherwise, including anaesthetics, anti-cancer drugs, anti-AIDS treatments, anti-epilepsy, anti-anxiety and anti-depressant drugs. He believes that the potential benefits of animal experiments are sufficient to justify their use, as do many other biopsychologists, such as Carlson (1992).

Gray (1991) extends the medical justification argument by claiming that, while most people (both experimenters and animal rights activists) would accept the ethical principle that inflicting pain is wrong, we are sometimes faced with having to choose between different ethical principles (i.e. we have to make moral choices), which may mean having to choose between human and animal suffering. He believes that *speciesism* (discriminating against and exploiting animals because they belong to a particular (non-human) species; Ryder, 1990) is justified and argues that ' ... not only is it not wrong to give preference to the interests of one's own species, one has a duty to do so ... '

Such a moral choice involves establishing a calculus (Dawkins, 1990) which pits the suffering of the animals against the human suffering which the use of animals will alleviate:

> In many cases the decision not to carry out certain experiments with animals (even if they would inflict pain or suffering) is likely to have the consequence that more people will undergo pain or suffering that might otherwise be avoided ... (Gray, 1991)

One of the problems associated with the pro-speciesism argument, according to Gray, is that medical advance may only become possible after extensive development of knowledge and scientific understanding in a particular field; in the meantime, scientific understanding may be the only specific objective that the experiment can readily attain. It is at this interim stage that the suffering imposed on the animals in experiments will far outweigh any (lesser) suffering eventually avoided by people – this is at the core of the decisions that must be made by scientists and ethical committees.

Gray has been criticized by Ryder (1991) for being inconsistent between declared ethical principles and action. If Gray believes his own principle that 'If it is wrong to inflict pain unnecessarily, it is equally wrong whether the pain is inflicted upon a human being, a rat or a spider', then he should abandon painful research upon animals, i.e. there can be no exceptions. But this seems to assume that Gray's distinction between ethical principles and moral choices is false which, in turn, seems to hinge upon the interpretation of 'unnecessarily'. Surely Gray's argument is about what are *justifiable exceptions* to the general ethical rule that inflicting suffering is wrong – if the animal's suffering is a means to an end (i.e. the prevention of human suffering) then it is not unnecessary.

● The psychologist as practitioner

According to Fairbairn and Fairbairn (1987), the *Guidelines for the Professional Practice of Clinical Psychology* (1983) attempt to spell out in detail sound practice as well as ethical advice: (i) the need to maintain professional competence; (ii) not allowing the false impression of competence to be entertained by others; (iii) safeguards for the work of trainees; (iv) the need to obtain valid consent for treatment; and (v) the problems of privacy and confidentiality.

Paragraph 1 states that psychologists ' ... shall hold the interests and welfare of those in receipt of their services to be paramount at all times ... '. But psychologists may face split loyalties – as part of an interdisciplinary team they may have obligations to both the client and, say, the psychiatrist in charge. The Guidelines make it clear that, in cases of conflict, it is the psychologist's responsibility to ensure that ' ... the client receives the care that he or she is considered to require ... ', i.e. loyalty to the client predominates over any loyalty to colleagues.

The Guidelines also state that psychologists must not unreasonably impose their values (nor those of the institution) on their clients, nor should they ' ... condone, use or participate in the application of psychological knowledge or technology in any way that infringes human rights' (paragraph 13.1).

Psychologists as agents of change

Unlike the psychologist as researcher, the clinical psychologist (like educational psychologists, psychotherapists, psychiatrists, social workers, nurses, counsellors and special needs teachers) is involved with bringing about psychological change (although the physical benefits to the client may often be the primary aim, as in the treatment of severely self-mutilating clients). It is in their capacity as *agents of change* that clinical psychologists, etc. face their greatest ethical challenges. For example:

> ... They must decide how they will interact with those who seek their help; for example, whether in general they will regard them as autonomous beings with rights and responsibilities, or rather as helpless individuals, incapable of rational choice ... All ... face the problems of confidentiality that being in possession of privileged information causes. And all face the problem of deciding how much of themselves to give to their professional work and how much to keep for themselves, their families and friends ... (Fairbairn and Fairbairn, 1987)

Fairbairn and Fairbairn (1987) believe that ethics has received relatively little attention in psychology as compared with other caring professions, such as medicine, nursing and social work, yet ' ... a consideration of the ethical dimensions of psychological change is fundamental to the development of practice ... '. They argue that two quite common beliefs which are likely to lead away from an explicit consideration of professional ethics and values in psychological practice are that:

1 psychology is a value-free science; and
2 therapists should be value neutral or 'non-directive'.

Psychology as value-free science

As we noted in Chapter 31, clinical (and counselling) psychologists adopt the scientist-practitioner model of helping which, according to Dallos and Cullen (1990), has become central for clinical psychology; this sees clinical psychology as being guided by, and operating within, the framework of general scientific method.

> ... Psychological science has traditionally been thought of as developing through careful, value-free investigations. The notion of an objective (and hence, so it is thought, value-free) clinical psychology, favoured by many psychologists, rests on the possibility of a foundation in a positivist science ... (Fairbairn and Fairbairn, 1987).

(This raises the debate about the nature of psychology as a whole. According to Shotter (1975), psychology as a discipline should be thought of as a 'moral science of action' as opposed to a 'natural science of behaviour'; see Chapter 2.)

According to Fairbairn and Fairbairn (1987), the greater the emphasis on the scientific credibility of research, the less likely interpersonal or professional values or ethics are to be widely and seriously debated. If clinical psychologists view clinical psychology as having firm foundations in positivist science, they may disregard ethics because these are not amenable to objective consideration. However, even if the psychological knowledge used in clinical practice was always the result of the application of an objective scientific method, moral questions of an interpersonal kind are bound to arise at the point at which it is applied.

This distinction between possession of knowledge and application of that knowledge ('science' versus 'technology') is fundamental to any discussion of ethics because it is related to the notion of *responsibility*. Presumably, the clinical psychologist chooses which techniques to use with clients and how these are to be used: the mere existence (and even the demonstrated effectiveness) of certain techniques does not in itself mean that they must be used. Similarly, the kind of research which clinical psychologists consider worth doing (and which, then, provides the scientific basis for the use of particular techniques) is a matter of choice and reflects views as to the nature of human beings and how people can be changed. In this respect, perhaps, the clinical psychologist is different from the atomic physicist or geneticist, whose discoveries may be abused (in the form of atomic bombs or genetic engineering) by others (governments, dictators, etc.) with greater power and authority: the clinical psychologist is both researcher and practitioner, scientist and technocrat.

What is the view of the person underlying the practice of a scientifically based clinical psychology?

According to Trower (1987), the two major criticisms of scientific behaviour therapy or modification are that:

1 Because of (rather than despite) its espoused status as a value-free, applied science, it tends to devalue and thereby dehumanize its clients and it does this by treating people for 'scientific' purposes as if they were 'organisms' as opposed to 'agents' who are helpless victims of forces outside their control. This criticism also applies to medical psychiatry and classical psychoanalysis,

except that both see the controlling forces as being internal (organic abnormalities or intrapsychic forces, respectively) as opposed to environmental contingencies.

2　Clients (soon come to) believe (given the overwhelming 'scientific' ethos) that they are abnormal organisms (deficient, ill, etc.) and that they are not only helpless but also worthless, because this is part of the culture-wide stereotype of 'mental illness' and related terms (see Chapter 30).

Negative self-evaluation and passivity characterize many, if not the majority of, mental health clients, i.e. clients think and behave like passive organisms and this is precisely the problem. Trower believes that the solution lies in helping people recover or discover their agency.

Therapists as value neutral and non-directive

If psychology as a value-free science involves not regarding or treating clients fully as human beings, this second major issue is about the therapist or psychologist functioning as something less than a complete person in the context of the therapeutic situation.

According to Fairbairn and Fairbairn (1987), providing help and support in a non-directive, value-free way is a tradition for psychotherapists and counsellors. But this may seem to require remaining aloof and distant from the client which, in turn, may entail not treating the client with respect as a person, since this requires the therapist to recognize that the client is a person like themselves.

The influence of the therapist

Adopting what is thought to be a value-free position in therapy may lead the therapist to deny the importance or influence of their own moral values, which are often hidden in therapy. This kind of influence is much more subtle and covert than the subtle coercion that can operate on hospitalized psychiatric patients, even voluntary ones. The in-patient is subjected to strong persuasion to accept the treatment recommendations of professional staff and ' ... even a "voluntary" and informed decision to take psychotropic medication or to participate in any other therapy regimen is often (maybe usually) less than free ... (Davison and Neale, 1994).

The issue of the influence of the therapist on the patient/client has been central to a long-standing debate between traditional (psychodynamic) psychotherapists and behaviour therapists (who are usually clinical psychologists by training) (see

Chapters 30 and 31). In the opinion of many psychotherapists, behaviour therapy is unacceptable (even if it works) because it is seen as manipulative and demeaning of human dignity. By contrast, their own methods are seen as fostering the autonomous development of the patient's inherent potential, helping the patient to express their true self, and so on. Instead of an influencer, they see themselves as a kind of psychological midwife, present during the birth, possessing useful skills, but there primarily to make sure that a natural process goes smoothly (Wachtel, 1977).

But this, according to Wachtel, is an exaggeration and misrepresentation of both approaches: for many patients, the 'birth' would probably not happen at all without the therapist's intervention and they undoubtedly do influence the patient's behaviour. Conversely, behaviour therapists are at least partly successful because they establish an active, co-operative relationship with the patient who plays a much more active role in the therapy than psychotherapists believe. Wachtel argues that all therapists, of whatever persuasion, if they are at all effective, influence their patients: both approaches comprise a situation in which one human being (the therapist) tries to act in such a way as to enable another human being to act and feel differently and this is as true of psychoanalysis as it is of behaviour therapy.

The crucial issue is the *nature* of this influence (and not whether or not it occurs) and there are four crucial questions that need to be asked:

1　Is the influence exerted in a direction that is in the patient's interest or in the service of the therapist's needs?

2　Are some good ends (e.g. reduction in anxiety) being achieved at the expense of others (e.g. the patient's enhanced vision of the possibilities that life can offer or an increased sense of self-directedness)?

3　Is the patient fully informed about the kind of influence that the therapist wishes to exert and the kind of ends being sought? (This, of course, relates to informed consent.)

4　Is the patient's choice being excessively influenced by a fear of displeasing the therapist, rather than by what they would really prefer?

The neutrality of therapists is a myth. They influence their clients in subtle yet powerful ways:

> ... Unlike a technician, a psychiatrist cannot avoid communicating and at times imposing his own values upon his patients. The patient usually has consider-

able difficulty in finding the way in which he would wish to change his behaviour, but as he talks to the psychiatrist his wants and needs become clearer. In the very process of defining his needs in the presence of a figure who is viewed as wise and authoritarian, the patient is profoundly influenced. He ends up wanting some of the things the psychiatrist thinks he should want. (Davison and Neale, 1994)

In the above quotation, we can add 'psychologist' and 'psychotherapist' to 'psychiatrist'.

Behavioural control

While a behavioural technique such as systematic desensitization is largely limited to the reduction of anxiety, this can at least be seen as enhancing the patient's freedom, since anxiety is one of the greatest restrictions on freedom. By contrast, methods based on operant conditioning can be applied to almost any aspect of a person's life (largely because they are applied to voluntary as opposed to reflex or autonomic behaviour). Those who use operant methods, such as the token economy, often describe their work rather exclusively in terms of behavioural control and they subscribe to Skinner's (1971) view that freedom is an illusion. (See discussion of free will and determinism below.)

Wachtel (1977) believes that, when used in institutional settings (as with long-term schizophrenic patients in psychiatric hospitals; see Chapter 31), the token economy is so subject to abuse that its use is highly questionable. It may be justifiable (a) if it works, and (b) if there is clearly no alternative way of rescuing the patient from an empty and destructive existence, but as a routine part of how society deals with deviant behaviour, this approach raises very serious ethical questions. One of these relates to the question of *power*: like the experimental 'subject' relative to the experimenter, the patient is powerless relative to the institutional staff responsible for operating the token economy programme:

> ... reinforcement is viewed by many – proponents and opponents alike – as somehow having an inexorable controlling effect upon the person's behaviour and rendering him incapable of choice, reducing him to an automaton or duly wound mechanism ... (Wachtel, 1977)

It is the reinforcing agent's power to physically deprive unco-operative patients of 'privileges' that is the alarming feature of the token economy.

The abuse of patients by therapists

In recent years, there has been a wave of criticism of psychotherapy (especially of the Freudian variety) from a number of directions, including its ethical shortcomings. One of the most outspoken critics is an American ex-Freudian psychoanalyst, Jeffrey Masson, who also believes that there is an imbalance of power involved in the therapeutic relationship and individuals who seek therapy need protection from the constant temptation to abuse, misuse, profit from and bully on the part of the therapist. The therapist has almost absolute emotional power over the patient and in his *Against Therapy: Emotional Tyranny and the Myth of Psychological Healing* (1988), Masson catalogues example after example of patients' abuse – emotional, sexual, financial- at the hands of their therapists.

Naturally enough, Masson's attack has stirred up an enormous controversy . Holmes (1992) agrees with the core of Masson's argument, namely that '...no therapist, however experienced or distinguished, is above the laws of the unconscious, and all should have access to supervision and work within a framework of proper professional practice' (Masson, 1992), But in defence of psychotherapy, he points out that exploitation and abuse are by no means confined to psychotherapy: lawyers, university teachers, priests and doctors are also sometimes guilty. All these professional groups have ethical standards and codes of practice (often far more stringent than the law of the land) with disciplinary bodies which impose severe punishments, usually expulsion from the profession. We should not condemn an entire profession because of the transgressions of a small minority.

● Conclusions: what is psychology for?

Hawks (1981) (cited in Fairbairn and Fairbairn, 1987) believes that prevention rather than cure should be a primary aim of psychology, enabling people to cope by themselves without professional help, thus 'giving psychology away' to the people/client. (This was the theme of George Miller's 1969 Presidential Address to the American Psychological Association; see Chapter 2.)

> The value of understanding human functioning does not inhere in its application in the usual sense but in its possession ... In order to help a person who is in psychological difficulties we work to enhance his understanding of himself and of his relationships to others. If we think in terms of traditional roles, then

the significant place in society of the psychologist will be more that of the teacher than expert or technician. (Bakan, 1967, quoted in Fairbairn and Fairbairn, 1987)

REDUCTIONISM

Imagine a very powerful and versatile satellite camera in space, showing the planet earth, then moving closer towards Europe and then the British Isles, then closer still towards England, then the city or village in which you live, then your particular part of the city or village, then your particular street, then your actual house, then your room, with you in it, then inside your body, travelling inside your brain, focusing on your cortex, then a particular region of your cortex, then one particular nerve cell, then the

atoms and molecules of which that nerve cell is composed, then the sub-atomic particles which make up the atoms and molecules ... We've come a long way. If we know everything there is to know about your nerve cells, do we know everything about you? Or is the whole greater than the sum of its parts?

● What is reductionism?

Along with mechanism, positivism, determinism, empiricism and objectivity, reductionism represents part of 'classical' science (see Chapter 2). Luria (1987) traces the origins of reductionism to the mid-19th century view within biology that the organism is a complex of organs and the organs are a complex of cells. In order to explain the basic laws of the living organism, we have to study as carefully as possible the features of separate cells. From its biological origins, reductionism was extended to science in

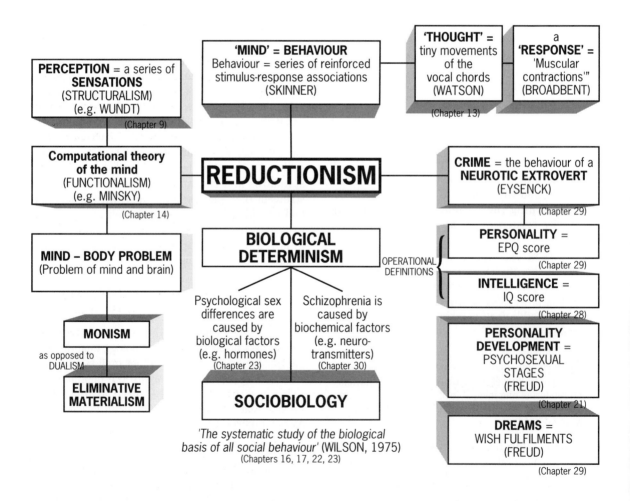

FIGURE 32.3 *Examples of reductionism relating to various topic areas within psychology as a whole.*

In favour of reductionism	Against reductionism
The sciences of biology and psychology ... .are an application of physics and chemistry to natural history ... .[and] ... organisms are simply very complicated physico-chemical mechanisms. (Smart, 1959, quoted in Teichman, 1988).	... There can be no descent into a physiological universe of discourse. Of course, it is possible to study the human physiology by the scientific method, but this is not studying personality or psychology. Even if physiology is studied alongside behaviour it adds nothing to our understanding of psychology. Suppose that cortical cells A and B always fired when I saw red and at no other time. What does this tell us about my experience of red? Indeed, it is banal because it goes without saying that there must be neural, bio-chemical or electrical changes underlying experience, for there can be no others. (Kline, 1988)
You, your joys and your sorrows, your memories and your ambitions, your sense of personality and free will, are in fact no more than the behaviour of a vast assembly of nerve cells and their associated molecules. (Crick, 1994, quoted in Smith, 1994)	Garnham (1991) gives the example of evolutionary biology and biochemistry. Breakthroughs in biochemistry in the 1950s and since have uncovered in increasing detail the mechanisms by which offspring inherit their parents' characteristics. We can now see how, in principle, a theory of evolution fits together with a biochemical account of inheritance. But: ... a scientific theory of evolution still needs concepts such as gene pool and evolutionary stable strategy which cannot be defined in biological terms. Similarly, although a scientific approach to cognition assumes that perceiving and thinking depend on brain functioning, there will always be a need for a level of explanation in which cognitive concepts play a role. Cognitive science will no more be replaced by physiology than the theory of evolution has been replaced by biochemistry. (Garnham, 1991)
	... the mind is never replaced by the brain. Instead, we have two distinct and legitimate languages, each describing the same unitary phenomena of the material world. (Rose, 1992)

TABLE 32.1 *Views for and against reductionism*

general. For example, the properties of a protein molecule could be uniquely determined or predicted in terms of properties of the electrons or protons making up its atoms, and 'society' could be explained in terms of its individual members.

Although ultimately, the aim (according to supporters of reductionism) is to account for all phenomena in terms of microphysics, any attempt to explain something in terms of its component parts may be thought of as reductionist (see Fig. 32.3). According to Rose *et al.* (1984), for example, reductionism is:

> ... the name given to a set of general methods and modes of explanation both of the world of physical objects and of human societies. Broadly, reductionists

try to explain the properties of complex wholes ... in terms of the units of which ... [they] are composed.

But is a reductionist approach acceptable or even meaningful? Can a thorough knowledge of the primary sciences (in particular, physics) ever replace the need for psychological explanations? Table 32.1 presents the views of some psychologists, philosophers and biologists both in favour and opposed to reductionism.

Legge (1975) gives the example of signing our name. Although this could, in principle, be explained in terms of nerve activity and muscle movement, the real importance of a signature is its *social* (psychological) *meaning*. In trying to give an objective definition of a response (as 'muscular contractions'),

Broadbent (1961) is replacing something which has meaning for something which does not: 'muscular contractions' have no meaning in themselves, they only become meaningful when they form part of a series of movements that is intended to achieve some goal (in which case we call them *actions*). It is very difficult trying to describe (let alone explain) behaviour without relating it to what we are trying to achieve by doing it, whether it is scratching our back, writing an essay or eating our supper. The further we go in trying to break these actions down into their component parts (i.e. *reduce* them), the further removed we become from the categories we normally use to describe behaviour and the less meaningful the descriptions become.

Even if we could reduce signing our name to nerve activity and muscle movement, we would only be specifying what nerve activity and muscle movements are involved in a particular instance of name signing, not every possible instance, i.e. we could sign our name in many different ways apart from the conventional use of pen on paper, such as holding the pen in our mouth, using a stick in the sand or chalk on a wall. While each of these involves a very different combination of brain and muscle activity, what they all have in common is the social meaning of the act, which is largely independent of any particular neurophysiological activity that may accompany it.

Even if we knew everything there is to know about what is going on neurophysiologically when we act, isn't a psychological description/explanation more useful – and more valid – under most circumstances than a neurophysiological one? According to Rose (1976), the controversy over reductionism stems from a semantic confusion (i.e. a confusion over word meaning), namely between 'explaining' and 'explaining away'. If we try to get rid of psychological explanations altogether and replace them with neurophysiological ones, this represents the 'unacceptable face' of reductionism ('explaining away'). But if an explanation of brain and nerve activity is used to enhance or complement our psychological explanation, then this is perfectly acceptable and is not a threat to psychology ('explaining').

Rose believes that this confusion can be removed through the concept of a *hierarchy of levels of explanation*, as shown in Figure 32.4. The different levels in the hierarchy correspond to different scientific disciplines: as you move up the hierarchy, the size of the unit of explanation increases (*holistic*) and as you move down, the units become smaller (*reductionist*). Also, the fundamental explanations in a particular discipline can be found at some lower or more basic level. For example, what physics can tell us about atoms can provide explanations relevant to chemistry (e.g. how atoms combine to form molecules) and psychology can be seen as providing 'basic' explanations for sociology (e.g. how memory and perception work).

Rose's major argument is that each level involves a different *universe of discourse*, i.e. a different set of concepts and terminology, a different way of conceptualizing the 'same' phenomena; because they are different, one cannot be substituted for the other. Levels lower down in the hierarchy cannot replace those higher up because they are doing essentially different jobs; each is valid in its own right and what makes one level the 'right' one depends on the purpose

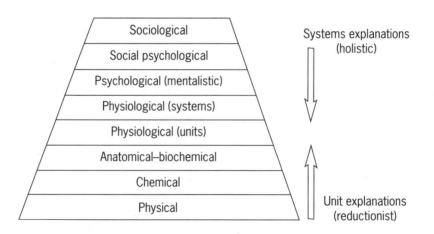

FIGURE 32.4 *Hierarchical levels of explanation. (From Rose, 1976)*

of the explanation. The more holistic, higher-level explanations are more 'economical' than the reductionist, lower-level ones; for example, it is easier, faster and generally more effective to talk about 'signing our name' than to describe all the brain and muscle activity which accompanies it. Kline (1988) also argues for the independence of different universes of discourse.

In Chapter 3, biopsychology was defined as the study of the biological bases, or physiological correlates, of behaviour, i.e. biopsychologists are concerned with what is going on in the nervous system when behaviour takes place, but this does not mean that the biopsychologist sees the former as somehow the 'real' or 'true' account and is aiming to replace psychological with physiological explanations. For example, when discussing split-brain patients (see Chapters 3 and 4), we considered the claim that such patients have, effectively, two minds or two distinct types of consciousness which, in normal people, work together and so are not easily distinguishable: mind and brain are correlated inseparably and the focus is on the cognitive and emotional characteristics of each hemisphere as much as on the neurophysiology of the brain. Biopsychology is not, in itself, reductionist, although there are neuroscientists, such as Crick (see Table 32.1), who are.

One argument against reductionism in relation to biopsychology specifically is given by Penrose (1990). When discussing connectionism in Chapter 14, we noted that there is a built-in indeterminacy in the way that individual neurons and their synaptic connections work, i.e. their responses are inherently unpredictable. Yet, despite this unpredictability at the level of the individual units/components, the system as a whole is predictable, i.e. the 'nervous system' (or sub-systems within it) does not operate randomly but in a highly organized, structured way. Consciousness, intelligence and memory are properties of the brain as a system, not properties of the individual units, and they could not possibly be predicted from analysing the units. Instead, they 'emerge' from interactions between the units that compose the system (and so are called *emergent properties*): the whole is truly greater than the sum of its parts.

In the context of the debate about the mind–brain relationship, Rose (1992) claims that we should learn how to translate between 'mind language' and 'brain language' and not try to replace the former with the latter. The mind–brain relationship (or the mind–body problem) has traditionally been the focus of the debate over reductionism.

● The mind–body problem. What is the relationship between mind and brain?

Many neurophysiogists, biologists and philosophers, as well as psychologists, take the view that the mind (or consciousness) is real, i.e. it is a property of human beings, along with having a particular type of body and brain and walking upright on two legs. It is also widely agreed that, without the human brain, there would be no consciousness: the two seem to have evolved together.

But does this mean that the mind is synonymous with the brain?

The 'problem' of the mind–brain relationship is really two-fold:

1 How can two 'things' be related when one of them is physical (the brain has size, weight, shape, location in space and time) and the other apparently lacks all these characteristics (e.g. can you weigh the mind or point to it?). This is the logical or philosophical component of the problem.
2 How can something that is non-physical/non-material (the mind) influence or produce changes in something that is physical (the brain/body)?

The 'classic' example given by philosophers to illustrate the problem is the commonplace, taken-for-granted act of deciding to lift my arm: how can a non-physical event (my *deciding* to lift my arm) bring about a physical event (the lifting of my arm)? From a strictly scientific perspective, this kind of causation should be impossible; science, including psychology and neurophysiology, has traditionally rejected any brand of *philosophical dualism*, which stems from Descartes' belief in the essential difference between the physical and the mental (or non-physical).

However, if consciousness evolved because of its survival value, could it have equipped human beings with such survival value unless it had causal properties (Gregory, 1981), i.e. unless it could actually bring about changes in behaviour? This seems to be one of the more psychologically relevant questions to ask about the mind–brain relationship. There is little doubt that our subjective experience tells us that our mind does affect our behaviour, i.e. that consciousness does have causal properties (just try lifting your arm), but philosophers and many scientists from a variety of disciplines have not always shared the layperson's commonsense understanding.

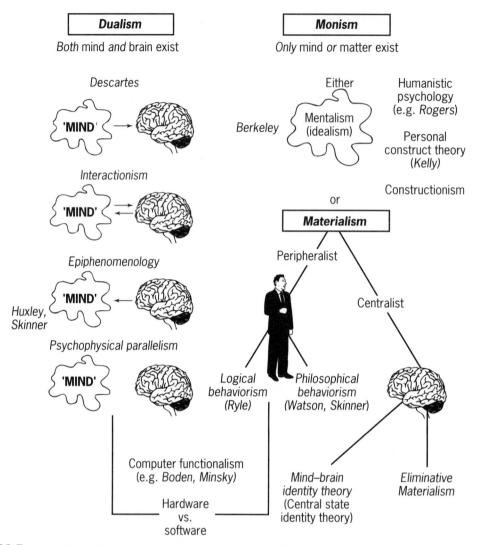

FIGURE 32.5 *An outline of the major theories of the mind–brain relationship*

● An overview of some of the major theories of the mind–brain relationship

As shown in Figure 32.5, there are two broad types of theory: *dualist* theories, which see both mind and matter (brain) as real and as existing in their own right, and *monist* theories, according to which only mind or matter (brain) is real.

Dualist theories

It was Descartes' 17th century distinction between the physical body and the non-physical mind which introduced the mind–body problem into philosophy for the first time. For Descartes, the mind has its own separate existence from the body and has causal powers to control the body, and hence, behaviour.

This represents a 'pure' or extreme form of dualism, in the sense that the mind can influence the body (through the operation of the pineal gland in the brain), whereas the body cannot influence the mind. By contrast, *interactionists* believe that body and mind influence each other, which seems to sit much better with the commonsense view that both mental and physical events have causal powers. For example, we talk about 'mind over matter', and there seems to be some medical support for this view, as in the case of cancer patients who beat their disease through their determination to get better. Again, psychosomatic (or psychophysiological) ('mind' and 'body') illness is usually defined as caused by stress or other psychological factors, although the symptoms are very real (e.g. stomach ulcers) (see Chapter 6). Conversely, we often attribute changes in perception to the action of 'mind-changing' drugs (e.g. the hallucinogens) through their effect on brain chemicals or changes in intelligence or personality to brain damage or surgery (see Chapters 3 and 31).

Like Descartes, *epiphenomenologists* believe that the influence is one-way only but unlike him, they maintain that the influence works in the opposite direction, i.e. the brain influences the mind; although the independent reality of mental events is acknowledged, it is the brain that is the controlling influence. An *epiphenomenon* is an accompanying event, outside the chain of causation, and was first proposed by T.H. Huxley. This is sometimes construed as behaviour affecting mind and in this respect, Skinner can be seen as an epiphenomenologist since he at times seemed to accept the existence of mental phenomena but denied their influence on behaviour, which is controlled entirely by environmental contingencies of reinforcement. Most of the time, however, he denied their existence altogether (see Chapter 7).

Parallelists (or psychophysical parallelists) are dualists who believe that there is no interaction between mind and brain, in either direction. This was first proposed by the philosopher Leibnitz in 1714. In psychology, Wundt was an early advocate of this view, as were the Gestalt psychologists, who argued that there is a one-to-one correspondence between how a stimulus is perceived and the pattern of brain cells which accompanies the perception (*isomorphism*) (see Chapter 9). Clearly, any simple correlation between mental and physical events is often missing; for example, depression can be associated with a variety of physical states (such as alcohol consumption, physical illness, lack of sleep) and, conversely, physiological arousal may be associated with fear or sexual excitement (see Chapter 5).

Monist theories

According to *mentalism* (or *idealism*), only mental phenomena are real. Although most psychologists (and philosophers) reject such an extreme view, the theories of Rogers and Kelly may be seen as 'mentalist' in flavour. In Rogers' *phenomenological* approach, experience is of central importance and in Kelly's *personal construct theory* the world 'is' how it is defined and interpreted by the individual (see Chapter 29).

The vast majority of monists are *materialists*, who believe that the only kind of reality is physical.

Ironically, this view was inspired by Descartes, when he claimed that human and animal bodies are simply machines (or 'physicochemical mechanisms'), controlled by precisely the same laws of physics as control the non-organic world. Armstrong (1987) divides materialism into *peripheralist* and *centralist*.

The *peripheralist* version is better known as *logical* or *philosophical behaviourism*, according to which the mind is reduced to behaviour. Watson, for example, claimed that all thought processes are really no more than the sensations produced by tiny movements of the vocal cords which are too small to produce audible sounds. In fact, he was trying to deny the existence of thought altogether by reducing it to 'silent speech' (see Fig. 32.5).

For Skinner, all mentalistic terms are 'explanatory fictions', i.e. there is nothing to which they refer; instead, he advocated *radical behaviourism*, according to which only overt behaviour exists. But after 1945, he modified his views, now seeing mental events as made of the same (physical) stuff and obeying the same sorts of laws (i.e. those of operant and classical conditioning) as overt behavioural events; in other words, he now distinguished between internal (covert) and external (overt) actions, the former simply being less accessible than the former (Flanagan, 1984).

Ryle's *logical behaviourism*, which is consistent with Watson's views and the early, radical behaviourism of Skinner, claims that mentalistic terms are simply a grammatical alternative to terms which describe behaviour, so that sentences about the mind can be translated into sentences about behaviour, without anything being 'left over'. For Ryle (1949), there is no 'ghost in the machine' (or mind), just behaviour, and it is the way we sometimes talk about behaviour (e.g. 'intelligence' rather than 'intelligent behaviour') that creates the false impression that the mind is somehow distinct from behaviour.

Centralist materialism (mind–brain identity theory/central state identity theory) identifies mental processes with purely physical processes in the central nervous system. This represents an example of *contingent identity*, i.e. according to Place (1956) and Smart (1959), it just happens to be true, as a matter of fact, that mental states are identical with states of the nervous system (and it could be otherwise). However, Smith (1994) believes that the mind–brain problem is radically different from other cases of contingent identity with which it is usually compared, such as: (a) heat is mean kinetic energy, and (b) a gene is a section of the DNA molecule.

What is different is reductionism and the related issue of exactly what is meant by *identity*.

Although we cannot have a mind without a brain, mind states and brain states are not systematically correlated (as we noted earlier), i.e. the neurophysiological and neurological evidence points towards *token identity*. By contrast, it has generally been assumed that mind–brain identity implies *type identity*, whereby whenever a mind state of a certain type occurs, a brain state of a certain type occurs (Harre *et al.*, 1985). For example, Broadbent (1981, cited in Harré *et al.*, 1985) has shown that we cannot just assume that the same neurophysiological mechanisms will be used by two different people both engaged in the 'same' activity of reading: there are many ways that 'the brain' can perform the same task.

The views of Place, Smart and Crick (see Table 32.1) represent *eliminative materialism*. This is an extreme reductionist form of materialism, according to which a psychological account of behaviour can, and should, be replaced by a neurophysiological description of brain function. But if the available evidence suggests only token identity (rather than type identity), then 'explaining away' psychological accounts simply cannot be defended.

This relates to the hierarchy of levels of explanation that we discussed earlier. Is it possible to be a materialist and at the same time to be anti-reductionist? Rose is certainly one example of a scientist who holds both beliefs simultaneously (see Table 32.6) and Freud is another; he was a materialist who believed that no single scientific vocabulary (e.g. anatomy) could adequately describe, let alone explain, all facets of the material world. He upheld the thesis of the autonomy of psychological explanation.

Are there any alternatives to dualism and monism?

According to Eiser (1994), it is irrelevant, from a psychological point of view, to establish exactly how, in physical terms, the brain goes about being a mind. This view is similar to that of *computer functionalists*, such as Boden and Minsky, who stress the importance of the processes carried out by the brain to the exclusion of what the brain is actually made of. They attempt to solve the mind–brain problem by distinguishing between *software* and *hardware*: the mind is to software as the brain is to hardware. Since it is the software/mind that is important (i.e. logical operations involving the manipulation of symbols),

the problem of the relationship between it and the hardware/brain disappears. This view is called the *computational theory of the mind* (CTM) (see Chapter 14).

However, as Rose (1992) points out, this separation of the mind from its actual material base is in some ways a reversion to Cartesian dualism. But at the same time, by treating the brain as a sort of black box whose internal biological mechanisms and processes are irrelevant and insisting that all that matters is matching inputs to outputs, it is also behaviouristic. It therefore seems to (re)create some of the problems it was designed to solve and to face the same objections as other attempted solutions.

FREE WILL VERSUS DETERMINISM

Like the mind–body issue, free will versus determinism is one of the most intractable philosophical problems that still 'haunts' psychology. It also seems to capture the basic conflict between the commonsense view of ourselves and the view that is offered by scientific psychology.

Our everyday, intuitive, commonsense understanding is that people have the ability to choose their own course of action, to determine their behaviour and, to this extent, have free will. At the same time, this freedom is exercised only within certain limits set by physical, political, sociological and other environmental factors. Yet the positivistic/mechanistic nature of scientific psychology implies a very different view, namely that behaviour is determined by external events or stimuli and that people are passive responders and, to this extent, are not free. Determinism also implies that behaviour occurs in a regular, orderly manner which is totally predictable (at least in principle) and that every human action has a cause.

● What reasons are there for believing in free will?

Tim is 14 and shows a variety of twitches and tics. His head sometimes jerks and he often blinks and grimaces. Most surprising is that occasionally he blurts out words, usually vulgarities. He does not mean to do it, and he is embarrassed by it, but he cannot control it. Because of his strange behaviour, most other children avoid him. His isolation and embarrassment are interfering with his social development. Tim suffers from a rare disorder known as Tourette's disorder. (Holmes, 1994)

Cases of disorders such as Tourette's disorder/syndrome, together with other mental disorders, can be seen as involving the partial or complete breakdown of the control over our behaviour, emotions and thinking which we usually have. Things seem to happen to the patient, i.e. these are exceptions to the general rule that we are in control or exercise our will (see Chapter 30).

We normally think of people as being morally responsible for what they do – *they* are the cause of their behaviour, not some powerful internal or external force. The whole legal/criminal justice system is built on this notion of responsibility which in turn rests on the assumption of free will: unless we believed in free will, we could not hold people responsible. The legal defences of diminished criminal responsibility or unfit to plead because of insanity represent further exceptions to the general rule.

William James (1890) proposed a compromise between the extreme rejection of free will (as with Freud and Skinner) and its unqualified acceptance. According to *soft determinism*, the question of free will depends on the type(s) of cause(s) our behaviour has, not whether it is caused or not caused. (In fact, the opposite of 'caused', strictly speaking, is 'random' and it would be very difficult to reconcile moral responsibility with the idea of randomness.) James argues that, if our actions have, as their proximate, immediate cause, something like *conscious mental life* (CML) (which includes consciousness itself, purposefulness, personality and personal continuity), then they can be considered free, rational, voluntary, purposive actions. Free acts are free from coercion or compulsion, but this is consistent with them being determined.

According to Popper (1950), for example, total predictability is impossible (see Chapter 2): the past does not logically guarantee the future and if this is true of classical physics, how much more true is it of human behaviour? So if determinism's main requirement is that behaviour should be completely predictable, it does not seem to pose the same 'threat' to the free will view after all.

Heather (1976) points out that we can describe human behaviour in lawful terms and still 'give man his freedom'. How? By thinking of the person as a *rule-following animal*. Much of our social behaviour is highly predictable and there is a great deal of regularity about it; for instance, 'Would you pass the salt, please?', followed by, 'Yes certainly'. Although the response is very predictable it is far from being inevitable, nor is it 'caused' by the initial request; in principle, at least, we are free to ignore the request or we may give an unexpected reply, such as 'Why, what's wrong with my cooking?'. The 'rules' of social interaction are, of course, often implicit and should not be equated with the formal or explicit rules of a game of football. But seeing human behaviour as governed by rules allows us to: (i) predict it, within certain limits; and (ii) continue to think of humans as fundamentally free.

● Skinner's rejection of free will

Apart from Freud, whose psychic determinism theory is discussed in Chapter 29, probably the most outspoken advocate of the view that the person is not free is Skinner (see Chapters 7 and 31). In *Beyond Freedom and Dignity* (1971) he argues that behavioural freedom is an illusion. Just as Freud believed that freedom is an illusion to the extent that we are unaware of the unconscious causes of our feelings and behaviours, so Skinner claimed that it is only because the causes of human behaviour are often hidden from us in the environment that the myth or illusion of free will survives.

When negative reinforcers (i.e. consequences that an organism will work to escape from or avoid) are considered along with positive ones ('rewards'), then almost all behaviour is controlled by the contingencies of reinforcement which occur constantly in the environment. When we believe we are behaving 'freely', we are merely free of negative reinforcement or its threat; our behaviour is still determined by the pursuit of things that have been positively reinforcing in the past and consists of responses that have previously been positively reinforced. When we perceive others as behaving 'freely', we are merely unaware of their reinforcement histories and the contingencies that govern their behaviour. So, for Skinner, the doctrine of 'autonomous man', upon which so many social institutions are based, is illusory.

Based on his work with rats and pigeons, which shows that behaviour is more efficiently controlled through the use of positive reinforcement (rather than negative reinforcement or punishment), Skinner advocates that we should abandon our illusory beliefs in behavioural freedom, accept the inevitability of control and design an environment in which behaviour will be directed towards socially desirable ends exclusively through the use of positive reinforcement. This is the key to Skinner's imaginary utopia described in his 1948 novel *Walden Two*.

If Skinner is advocating positive reinforcement as a means to achieving a socially desirable goal, the question still remains as to who is to say what those goals should be. Skinner urges psychologists themselves not to be shy about participating in the shaping of policies of control but in so doing, would they not be exercising their free will? For Skinner, there seems to be no contradiction in the idea of a few powerful individuals deciding to create a totalitarian society in which the majority is controlled, externally, through conditioning techniques, which is what he describes in *Walden Two* and subsequently advocated for the 'real' world.

CHAPTER SUMMARY

- The subject matter of psychology is itself capable of thoughts, feelings and emotional responses; along with biologists and medical scientists, psychologists have to confront the ethics of exposing humans and animals to unpleasant experiences.

- Every psychological investigation may be seen as an ethical, as well as a social situation; discussion of the aims of psychology shows that it is also very difficult to separate the methodological from the ethical issues that permeate psychology.

- The distinction between psychologists as scientists/investigators and practitioners is important from an ethical point of view, because the latter role is concerned with bringing about psychological change in people with psychological problems; clinical psychologists therefore have much in common with psychotherapists and psychiatrists.

- The BPS and APA both publish various codes of conduct/ethical guidelines, some of which apply to both the scientist and practitioner roles, others which apply to one or the other. These are reviewed periodically, in the light of new ethical problems produced by social change and changing views about individual rights.

- The gradual replacement of 'subject' with 'participant' reflects a shift towards perceiving the individual as a person; this, together with the removal of sexist language from psychology journals, is largely attributable to the influence of feminist psychologists.

- Milgram's obedience experiment highlights many basic ethical principles, including informed consent, the right to withdraw and the protection of participants from distress and other negative consequences. Zimbardo *et al.*'s prison simulation experiment is also very controversial, despite every participant signing an informed consent statement and approval being granted by various organizations.

- The distress experienced by Milgram's and Zimbardo *et al.*'s participants was neither intended nor anticipated, either by the researchers themselves or others who were consulted. However, while the prison study was abandoned less than halfway through, Milgram allowed his to continue.

- The question of informed consent is complicated by the fact that participants may need to experience the procedure in order to have full knowledge of it and this may also apply to the researchers. Even if the informational criterion is satisfied, the interpersonal nature of the experimental situation detracts from the participant's freedom.

- Deception should only be used 'as a last resort' and if it is, the participant should be debriefed as soon as possible afterwards. Deception is potentially most damaging in social psychological research, because of its likely impact on self-image and self-esteem. However, in field experiments of bystander intervention and naturalistic observation studies, neither consent nor informed consent can be obtained and debriefing is not possible.

- Deception is necessary if the psychologist is to gain insights into how people behave in real situations. If participants themselves are not particularly bothered when they learn that they have been deceived or they volunteer expecting to be deceived, then this may make deception ethically more acceptable.

- As far as Milgram is concerned, 'technical illusions' are justified if they are accepted/endorsed by those who are exposed to them; however, since they prevent participants from giving informed consent, they should only be used if absolutely essential.

- Participants are rarely exposed to actual physical harm, such as pain, without their informed consent (such as in sleep and food deprivation studies), one exception being little Albert.

- Debriefing is not only one means of trying to protect participants from emotional suffering in the short term (before they leave the laboratory), but it may also take the form of long-term follow-up, as in both the Milgram and Zimbardo *et al.* experiments. Its therapeutic value can be combined with its role of informing both the participant and

- the researcher about the procedure.
- Confidentiality represents another basic ethical principle intended to protect the rights of the participant; however, there are certain circumstances in which the investigator may be obliged to contravene this principle.
- Research data must not be suppressed and researchers must only take credit for what they have done, acknowledging the contributions of everyone else involved. Research papers must be sufficiently detailed to allow others to replicate the research.
- The questions that psychologists try to answer through their research are shaped partly by their values and partly by methodological considerations. The research itself is constrained by what is possible and what is ethically acceptable.
- Ethical debates usually concentrate on the need to protect the integrity and welfare of the individual participant. But psychologists are also obliged to carry out socially meaningful research, for the ultimate aim of 'human betterment', i.e. improving the quality of people's lives; this opens up the ethical debate to include discussion of values. The benefits of research may include making it more likely that people will act in a prosocial way, as in bystander intervention studies, to the advantage of both helper and helped.
- The two-fold obligation to individual participants and society at large can present psychologists with a dilemma: if deception (and the related distress) is sometimes justifiable, researchers must weigh up the possible benefits to society against the possible costs to individual participants.
- There is the danger of judging the ethics of an experimental procedure in terms of the nature of the results, when these should be assessed independently. Milgram's obedience experiments are a good illustration of this confusion.
- Generally, the more socially significant the issue, the greater the need for deception (such as obedience, conformity and bystander intervention) and the more likely that an individual participant will experience conflict and consequent distress. Possible solutions to this dilemma include using deception only if the scientific/medical justification is extremely strong, and the use of presumptive consent and prior general consent.
- BPS Guidelines for using animal subjects require that animal discomfort should be at least minimized, if not avoided. This raises the questions of how we assess animal suffering and how this can ever be justified.

- Assessment of suffering will depend on the animals' physical health, observation of any bizarre or abnormal behaviour, allowing animals to change environmental conditions in some way and research to learn about the biology of different species. If an animal possesses receptors sensitive to painful stimulation and brain structures comparable to the human cerebral cortex, then it is likely to experience pain, but this is impossible to assess with any certainty.
- Rats are the most commonly used research species; food deprivation may actually be healthier than ad lib feeding and electric shock never causes extreme pain. Research is supervised by Home Office inspectors and only those holding a Home Office licence and certificates are allowed to perform surgical and other painful/distressing procedures.
- The Guidelines also stress the importance of understanding species differences and point out that even simple observation of animals in the wild can affect their breeding and survival. Field researchers may face dilemmas concerning the issue of intervention, as in the Cayo Santiago rhesus monkey colony in the Caribbean.
- The main justifications for using animals are the pursuit of scientific knowledge and, particularly, the advancement of medical knowledge and treatments.
- Many drugs used in the treatment of human diseases could not have been developed without animal research and this may be seen as a sufficient justification for the use of animals. According to Gray, not only is speciesism justified, but it is our duty to carry out animal research if this may result in the alleviation of human suffering. There may be an interim period during which animal suffering may outweigh the reduction of human suffering.
- BPS Guidelines for clinical psychologists stipulate that the psychologist's paramount loyalty is to clients and that they must not impose values on the client or in any way infringe human rights.
- As agents of change, clinical psychologists (along with educational psychologists, psychotherapists, counsellors and other professionals) face ethical decisions about their basic attitude towards their clients, confidentiality and the nature of the relationship with the client.
- Ethics have been relatively neglected in psychology because of the claim that psychology is a value-free science and the belief that therapists should be value neutral/'non-directive'.

- Clinical and counselling psychologists adopt the practitioner model of helping, reflecting belief in a value-free, objective, positivist science. However, even if the psychological knowledge used in clinical practice was based on objective research, there is a crucial distinction between possession and application of knowledge.

- Adopting a value-neutral/non-directive position in therapy may lead therapists to deny the often subtle influence of their own moral values, which are often less obvious than the subtle coercion seen in psychiatric hospitals.

- Many psychotherapists see behaviour therapy and modification as manipulative and demeaning of human dignity, devaluing and dehumanizing their clients (although psychiatry and classical psychoanalysis have been similarly criticized) and see their own methods as helping people to become autonomous, to express their true selves, etc. But this exaggerates and misrepresents both approaches: all therapists influence their patients and it is the kind of influence that is in question. There is no such thing as a neutral therapist.

- The token economy, as a form of behavioural control, is ethically highly dubious, at least as a routine way of dealing with deviant behaviour. One objection is the powerlessness of patients relative to staff who are operating the programme; another is the patient's reduction to an automaton, who lacks choice.

- Masson condemns psychotherapists for abusing the power that they have over their clients. But exploitation and abuse can be found in all professions and we should not condemn the whole profession for the sins of a small minority.

- Psychology should aim at helping people to solve their own psychological difficulties; the appropriate role for the psychologist is teacher, rather than expert or technician.

- Reductionism is part of 'classical' science; it originated in mid-19th century biology and was then extended to science in general. Although the ultimate goal of reductionists is to explain all phenomena in terms of microphysics, any attempt to explain the properties of some complex whole in terms of its basic units may be considered reductionist.

- Trying to explain the act of signing our name as nerve activity or a series of muscle movements may be possible, but while the former has a social meaning, the latter have no meaning in themselves at all. There are also many different ways of performing the same act, each of which involves a different combination of brain and muscle activity. The social meaning of the act and any accompanying neurophysiological activity are independent.

- Reductionists are trying to 'explain away' psychological accounts and replace them with neurophysiological ones, instead of using facts about brain and nerve activity to enhance psychological explanations. This confusion can be removed through the concept of a hierarchy of levels of explanation, with each level involving a different universe of discourse; each is valid in its own right and none can be substituted for any other.

- An argument against reductionism is that the brain as a system has emergent properties, such as consciousness, intelligence and memory, which cannot be predicted from analysis of individual neurons; the whole is greater than the sum of its parts.

- The debate about reductionism has traditionally focused on the mind–body problem/mind–brain relationship. Different theories of the mind–brain relationship are trying to solve two major 'puzzles': (i) how something physical (the brain) can be related to something non-physical (the mind/consciousness); (ii) how something non-physical can influence and produce changes in something physical.

- Belief in the non-physical mind, as a reality distinct from the physical brain/body, is called philosophical dualism, first proposed by Descartes; he believed that the mind can influence the body but not vice-versa. In contrast, epiphenomenologists argue that the brain influences the mind and not vice-versa. According to interactionism, there is some form of interaction between mind and brain.

- Psychophysical parallelists are dualists who maintain that there is no mind–brain interaction.

- Any theory which is not dualist is monist. According to mentalism/idealism, only mental phenomena are real: phenomenological theories, such as that of Rogers and Kelly's personal construct theory, can be seen as having a mentalist 'flavour'.

- Most monists are materialists, who can be divided into peripheralists and centralists. The peripheralist version is better known as logical/philosophical behaviourism; Skinner's radical behaviourism at first obliged him to deny the existence of 'subjective entities' altogether, but he later 'reduced' thoughts to covert/internal behaviour.

- According to Ryle's logical behaviourism, the mind–brain problem is a pseudo-problem resulting from a purely grammatical confusion.
- Centralist materialism (mind–brain identity theory/central state identity theory) identifies mental states with purely physical processes in the central nervous system. One of the difficulties with identity theory is that it is generally assumed to imply type identity, while the available evidence points instead towards token identity: 'brain talk' can never displace/replace 'mind talk'.
- Eliminative materialism represents an extreme reductionist form of materialism. Even type identity would not be a sufficient reason for rejecting psychological accounts of thought and action in favour of a neurophysiological account.
- It is possible to be both a materialist and an antireductionist (such as Freud and Rose), because of the independent existence of different levels of description.
- An alternative to both dualism and monism is the computational theory of mind (CTM), according to which it is the software (the mind) that is important, so that its relationship to the hardware (the brain) becomes irrelevant. But this can be seen as having ingredients of both dualism and behaviourism.
- The free will vs. determinism issue captures the conflict between the commonsense view of ourselves, which regards individuals as being free to choose how they act (within certain constraints), and the deterministic account of behaviour provided by positivistic/mechanistic psychological approaches.
- We normally think of people as being in control of their behaviour, with mental disorders representing an important exception to this general rule. Also, the whole legal/criminal justice system assumes that people are responsible for their actions which, in turn, assumes free will.
- Provided that we are not coerced or compelled into behaving in a particular way and that our actions are caused by conscious mental life, they can said to be free; according to soft determinism, it is the type of cause that is crucial, not whether they are caused or not.
- Nothing in the physical world is totally predictable and that applies to behaviour too; this means that one basic requirement of determinism simply cannot be met. Much of the predictability and regularity of social behaviour can be explained by reference to people as rule-following animals.

- Both Freud and Skinner argued that free will is an illusion, although for very different reasons. Skinner claimed that most of the time it is not obvious what the environmental causes of our behaviour are : all behaviour is in fact determined by past reinforcements. In his utopian *Walden Two*, socially desirable behaviour will be controlled by psychologists applying the principles of operant conditioning: but in deciding what is socially desirable, aren't the controllers exercising their free will?

GLOSSARY

Debriefing Revealing to a participant, following initial deception, the experiment's true purpose. It may involve attempts to reverse or prevent any harmful psychological effects produced by the procedure and may extend long after the participant has left the laboratory.

Dualism The philosophical belief in the existence of two essentially different kinds of substance, the physical (body or *res extensa*) and non-physical (mind or *res cogitans*). Originally proposed by Descartes, who believed that mind can influence the body but not vice-versa.

Eliminative materialism An extreme reductionist form of materialism, according to which a psychological account of behaviour can, and should, be replaced by a neurophysiological description of brain function.

Emergent properties Properties of the brain as a system, such as consciousness and intelligence, which cannot be predicted from the properties of individual neurons.

Epiphenomenology a form of dualism, according to which only the brain can influence the mind and not vice-versa.

Informed consent An individual's agreement to participate in an investigation based on knowledge of the objectives and nature of the procedure involved.

Interactionism A form of dualism, according to which there is a two-way influence between mind

Materialism A form of monism, according to which only physical phenomena are real. Can be peripheralist (logical/philosophical behaviourism) or centralist (mind–brain identity theory/central state identity theory).and brain.

Mentalism A form of monism, according to which only mental phenomena are real. Also called idealism.

Monism The philosophical belief that only mind or matter exists.

Presumptive consent A compromise solution to not obtaining informed consent, in which the views are obtained of a large number of 'reasonable' people ('people in general') as to the acceptability of a particular experimental procedure.

Prior general consent A compromise solution to not obtaining informed consent, in which people are informed about the deception and emotional stress that are sometimes involved in experiments; only those who agree are accepted as members of a 'pool' of participants for future studies.

Psychophysical parallelism A form of dualism, according to which there is no interaction between mind and brain.

Reductionism Any attempt to explain the properties of some complex whole in terms of its basic units/components; for example, trying to explain behaviour in terms of the activity of neurons/brain processes.

Soft determinism James's theory that human behaviour is free if it is caused by conscious mental life, rather than external forces as in coercion or compulsion

Speciesism Discrimination against and exploitation of animals because they belong to a particular (non-human) species.

Type identity The co-occurrence of a particular type of mind state and a particular type of brain state, i.e. they are systematically correlated (assumed by eliminative materialism). Contrasted with token identity, in which mind and brain states are not systematically correlated, although we need a brain in order to have a mind.

Universe of discourse A set of concepts and terminology, a way of conceptualizing phenomena, corresponding to the different levels in a hierarchy of explanations (i.e. to different scientific disciplines).

FURTHER READING

Milgram, S. (1992) *The Individual in a Social World: Essays and Experiments*, 2nd edn. New York: McGraw-Hill. A collection of articles, reprinted from a variety of sources, with Chapters 10, 12 and 15 particularly relevant to a discussion of ethical issues.

Humphrey, N. (1986) *The Inner Eye*. London: Vintage. A short but rich exploration of the nature of consciousness.

REFERENCES

Abernathy, E.M. (1940) The effect of changed environmental conditions upon the results of college examinations. *Journal of Psychology, 10,* 293–301.

Abrams, D., Wetherell, M., Cochrane, S., Hogg, M.A. & Turner, J.C. (1990) Knowing what to think by knowing who you are: Self-categorization and the nature of norm formation, conformity and group polarization. *British Journal of Social Psychology, 29* (part 2), 97–119.

Abramson, L.Y. & Martin, D.J. (1981) Depression and the causal inference process. In J.H. Harvey, J. Ickes & R.F. Kidd (Eds.), *New directions in attitude research, Vol. 3.* Hillsdale, New Jersey: Lawrence Erlbaum Associates Inc.

Abramson, L.Y., Seligman, M.E.P. & Teasdale, J.D. (1978) Learned helplessness in humans: Critique and reformulation. *Journal of Abnormal Psychology, 87,* 49–74.

Adler, A. (1927) *The practice and theory of individual psychology.* New York: Harcourt Brace Jovanovich.

Adler, A. (1936) The neurotic's picture of the world. *International Journal of Individual Psychology, 2,* 3–10.

Adorno, T.W., Frenkel-Brunswick, E., Levinson, D.J. & Sanford, R.N. (1950) *The authoritarian personality.* New York: Harper & Row.

Ainsworth, M.D.S. (1967) *Infancy in Uganda: infant care and the growth of love.* Baltimore: John Hopkins University Press.

Ainsworth, M.D.S. (1989) Attachments beyond infancy. *American Psychologist* 44 (4), 709–16.

Ainsworth, M.D.S., Bell, S.M.V. & Stayton, D.J. (1971) Individual differences in strange-situation behaviour of one-year-olds. In H.R. Schaffer (Ed.), *The origins of human social relations.* New York: Academic Press.

Ainsworth, M.D.S., Blehar, M.C., Waters, E. & Wall, S. (1978) *Patterns of attachment: A psychological study of the strange situation.* Hillsdale, New Jersey: Lawrence Erlbaum Associates Inc.

Aitchison, J. (1983) *The articulate mammal* (2nd ed.) London: Hutchinson.

Ajzen, I. (1988) *Attitudes, personality and behaviour.* Milton Keynes: Open University Press.

Ajzen, I. & Fishbein, M. (1977) Attitude–behaviour relations: A theoretical analysis and review of empirical research. *Psychological Bulletin, 84,* 888–918.

Ajzen, I. & Fishbein, M. (1980) *Understanding attitiudes and predicting social behaviour.* Englewood Cliffs, NJ: Prentice-Hall.

Allen, V. & Levine, J.M. (1968) Social support, dissent and conformity. *Sociometry,* 31, 138–49.

Alexander, F. & French, T.M. (1946) *Psychoanalytic therapy.* New York: Ronald Press.

Allport, D.A. (1980a) Patterns and actions: Cognitive mechanisms are content specific. In G. Claxton (Ed.), *Cognitive psychology: New directions.* London: Routlege, Kegan Paul.

Allport, D.A. (1980b) Attention and performance: In G. Claxton (Ed.), *Cognitive psychology: New directions.* London: Routledge, Kegan Paul.

Allport, D.A. (1989) Visual attention. In M.I. Posner (Ed.) *Foundations of cognitive science.* Cambridge, MA: MIT Press.

Allport, D.A., Antonis, B. & Reynolds, P. (1972) On the division of attention: A disproof of the single channel hypothesis. *Quarterly Journal of Experimental Psychology, 24,* 225–35.

Allport, F.H. (1924) *Social psychology.* Boston: Houghton Mifflin.

Allport, G.W. (1935) Attitudes. In C.M. Murchison (Ed.) *Handbook of Social Psychology.* Worchester, MA: Clark University Press.

Allport, G.W. (1937) *Personality: A psychological interpretation.* New York: Holt, Rinehart & Winston.

Allport, G.W. (1947) *The Use of Personal Documents in Psychological Science.* London: Holt, Rinehart & Winston.

Allport, G.W. (1954) *The nature of prejudice.* Reading, Massachusetts: Addison-Wesley.

Allport, G.W. (1955) *Becoming – basic considerations for a psychology of personality.* New Haven, Connecticut: Yale University Press.

Allport, G.W. (1960) *Personality and Social Encounter.* Boston: Beacon Press.

Allport, G.W. (1961) *Pattern and growth in personality.* New York: Holt Rinehart Winston.

Allport, G.W. (1968) The historical background of modern psychology. In G. Lindzey & E. Aronson (Eds.) *Handbook of Social Psychology, Vol.* 1 (2nd ed.). Reading, Mass.: Adison-Wesley.

Allport, G.W. & Odbert, H.S. (1936) Trait names: A psycho-lexical study. *Psychological Monographs: General and Applied, 47,* (Whole No. 211).

Allport, G.W. & Pettigrew, T.F. (1957) Cultural influences on the perception of movement: The trapezoidal illusion among Zulus. *Journal of Abnormal and Social Psychology, 55,* 104–13.

Allport, G.W., Vernon, P.G. & Lindzey, G. (1951) *Study of values.* Boston: Houghton-Mifflin.

Altman, I. & Taylor, D.A. (1973) Social penetration: The development of interpersonal relationships. New York: Holt, Rinehart & Winston.

Anand, B.K. & Brobeck, J.R. (1951) Hypothalamic control of food intake in rats and cats. *Yale Journal of Biological Medicine,* 24, 123–40.

American Psychiatric Association (1980) *Diagnostic and statistical manual of mental disorders* (3rd ed.). Washington, DC: American Psychiatric Association.

American Psychiatric Association (1987) *Diagnostic and statistical manual of mental disorders* (3rd ed. revised). Washington, DC: American Psychiatric Association.

American Psychiatric Association (1994) *Diagnostic and statistical manual of mental disorders* (4th ed.). Washington, DC: American Psychiatric Association.

American Psychological Association (1981) *Ethical Principles of Psychologists*. Washington, D.C.: American Psychological Association.

American Psychological Association (1982) *Ethical Principles in the Conduct of Research with Human Participants*. Washington, D.C.: American Psychological Association.

American Psychological Association (1985) *Guidelines for Ethical Conduct in the Care and Use of Animals*. Washington, D.C.: American Psychological Association.

Amir, Y. (1969) Contact hypothesis in ethnic relations. *Psychological Bulletin*, 71, 319–42.

Amir, Y. (1994) The contact hypothesis in intergroup relations. In W.J.Lonner & R.S. Malpass (Eds.) *Psychology and Culture*. Boston: Allyn & Bacon.

Anderson, A. (1978) 'Old' is not a four-letter word. *Across the Board*, May.

Anderson, J.R. (1983) *The architecure of cognition* (2nd ed.). Cambridge, Massachusetts: Harvard University Press.

Anderson, J.R. (1985) *Cognitive psychology and its implications*. New York: Freeman.

Anderson, J.R. (1995) *Learning and memory: An integrated approach*. New York: John Wiley & Sons, Inc.

Anderson, J.R. & Reder, L. (1979) An elaborate processing explanation of depth of processing. In L.S. Cermak & F.I.M. Craik (Eds.), *Levels of processing in human memory*. Hillsdale, New Jersey: Lawrence Erlbaum Associates Inc.

Anderson, L.P. (1991) Acculturative stress: A theory of relevance to black Americans. *Clinical Psychology Review*, 11, 685–702.

Anderson, N.H. (1974) Cognitive algebra: Integration theory applied to social attribution. In L. Berkowitz (Ed.), *Advances in experimental social psychology, Vol. 7*. New York: Academic Press.

Annett, M. (1991) Laterality and cerebral dominance. *Journal of Child Psychology and Psychiatry*, 32(2), 219–32.

Antaki, C. (1984) Core concepts in attribution theory. In J. Nicholson & H. Beloff (Eds.), *Psychology Survey 5*. Leicester: British Psychological Society.

Archer, J. (1976) Biological explanations of psychological sex differences. In B. Lloyd & J. Archer (Eds.) *Exploring sex differences*. London: Academic Press.

Archer, J. (1992) Childhood gender roles: social context and organization. In H. McGurk (Ed.) *Childhood Social Development: contemporary perspectivs*. Hove: Erlbaum.

Archer, J. & Lloyd, B. (1985) *Sex and gender*. New York: Cambridge University Press.

Ardrey, R. (1966) *The territorial imperative*. New York: Atheneum.

Arendt, H. (1965) *Eichmann in Jerusalem: A report on the banality of evil*. New York: Viking.

Argyle, M. (1983) *The psychology of interpersonal behaviour* (4th ed.) Harmondsworth; Penguin.

Argyle, M. (1987) *The psychology of happiness*. London: Methuen.

Argyle, M. (1988) *Bodily communication* (2nd ed.). London: Methuen.

Argyle, M. (1989) *The social psychology of work* (2nd ed.). Harmondsworth, Middlesex: Penguin.

Argyle, M. Alkema, F. & Gilmour, R. (1972) The communication of friendly and hostile attitudes by verbal and non-verbal signals. *European Journal of Social Psychology*, 1, 385–402.

Argyle, M. & Dean, J. (1965) Eye contact, distance and affiliation. *Sociometry*, 28, 289–364.

Argyle, M. & Henderson, M. (1984) The rules of friendship. *Journal of Social and Personal Relationships*, 1, 211–37.

Argyle, M., Henderson, M. & Furnham, A. (1985) The rules of social relationships. *British Journal of Social Psychology, 24*, 125–9.

Arlin, P.K. (1975) Cognitive development in adulthood: A fifth stage? *Developmental Psychology*, 11, 602–6.

Arlin, P.K. (1977) Piagetian operations in problem finding. *Developmental Psychology*, 13, 297–8.

Armsby, R.E. (1971) A re-examination of the development of moral judgement in children. *Child Development, 42*, 1241–8.

Armstrong, D.M. (1987) Mind-body problem: Philosophical theories. In R.L. Gregory (Ed.) *The Oxford companion to the mind*. Oxford: Oxford University Press.

Aronfreed, J. (1963) The effects of experimental socialization: paradigms upon two moral responses to transgression. *Journal of Abnormal & Social Psychology, 66*, 437–8.

Aronfreed, J. (1969) The concept of internalization. In D.A. Goslin (Ed.), *Handbook of socialization theory and research*. Chicago: Rand McNally.

Aronfreed, J. & Reber, A. (1965) Internalized behavioural suppression and the timing of social punishment. *Journal of Personality & Social Psychology*, 1, 3–17.

Aronson, E. (1968) The process of dissonance. In N. Warren & M. Jahoda (Eds.), *Attitudes*. Harmondsworth, Middlesex: Penguin.

Aronson, E. (1980) *The social animal* (3rd. ed.). San Fransisco: W.H. Freeman.

Aronson, E. (1988) *The social animal* (5th ed.). New York: Freeman.

Aronson, E. (1992) *The social animal* (6th. ed.) New York: W.H. Freeman & Co.

Aronson, E. & Carlsmith, J.M. (1963) Effect of the severity of threat on the devaluation of forbidden behaviour. *Journal of Abnormal and Social Psychology, 6*, 584–8.

Aronson, E. & Linder, D. (1965) Gain and loss of esteem as determinants of interpersonal attractiveness. *Journal of Experimental & Social Psychology*, 1, 156–71.

Aronson, E. & Mills, J. (1959) The effect of severity of initiation on liking for a group. *Journal of Abnormal and Social Psychology*, 59, 177–81.

Aronson, E. & Osherow, N. (1980) Co-operation, prosocial behaviour and academic performance: Experiments in the desegregated classroom. In L. Bickman (Ed.), *Applied social psychology annual, Vol. 1*. Beverly Hills, California: Sage Publications.

Aronson, E., Bridgeman, D.L. & Geffner, R. (1978) The effects of a co-operative classroom structure on student behaviour and attitudes. In D. Bar-Tal & L. Saxe (Eds.), *Social psychology of education*. New York: Wiley.

Asch, S.E. (1946) Forming impressions of personality. *Journal of Abnormal and Social Psychology, 4*, 258–90.

Asch, S.E. (1951) Effect of group pressure upon the modification and distortion of judgements. In H. Guetzkow (Ed.), *Groups, leadership and men*. Pittsburg, Pennsylvania: Carnegie Press.

Asch, S.E. (1952) *Social psychology*. Englewood Cliffs, New Jersey: Prentice Hall.

Asch, S.E. (1955) Opinions and social pressure. *Scientific American*, 193 (5), 31–35.

Asch, S.E. (1956) Studies of independence and submission to group pressure: 1: A minority of one against a unanimous majority. *Psychological Monographs, 70*, (9) (Whole No. 416).

Aserinsky, E. & Kleitman, N. (1953) Regularly occurring periods of eye mobility and concomitant phenomena during sleep. *Science, 118*, 273.

Association for the Teaching of Psychology (1992) Ethics in psychological research: Guidelines for students at pre-degree levels. *Psychology Teaching*, 4–10, New Series, No 1.

Atchley, R.C. (1982) Retirement: leaving the world of work. *Annals of the American Academy of Political and Social Science*, *464*, 120–31.

Atchley, R.C. (1985) *Social forces and ageing: An introduction to social gerontology*. Belmont, California: Wadsworth.

Atchley, R.C. & Robinson, J.L. (1982) Attitudes towards retirement and distance from the event. *Research on Ageing, 4 (3)*, 288–313.

Atkinson, R.C. & Shiffrin, R.M. (1968) Human memory: A proposed system and its control processes. In K.W. Spence & J.T. Spence (Eds.), *The psychology of learning & motivation, Vol. 2*. London: Academic Press.

Atkinson, R.C. & Shiffrin, R.M. (1971) The control of short-term memory. *Scientific American*, *224*, 82–90.

Atkinson, R.L., Atkinson, R.C., Smith, E.E. & Bem, D.J. (1990) *Introduction to psychology* (10th ed.). New York: Harcourt Brace Jovanovich.

Attneave, F. (1954) Some informational aspects of visual perception. *Psychological Review*, *61*, 183–93.

Averill, J.R. (1994) In the eyes of the beholder. In P. Ekman & R.J. Davidson (Eds.) *The nature of emotion: Fundamental questions*. New York: Oxford University Press.

Ax, A.F. (1953) The physiological differentiation between fear and anger in humans. *Psychosomatic Medicine*, 15, 433–42.

Ayllon, J. & Azrin, N.H. (1968) *The token economy*. New York: Appleton-Century-Crofts.

Azrin, N. H. & Foxx, R.M. (1971) A rapid method of toilet training the institutionalized retraded. *Journal of Applied Behaviour Analysis, 4*, 89–99.

Azrin, N.H. & Holz, W.C. (1966) Punishment. In W.K. Honig (Ed.) *Operant behaviour: Areas of research and application*. New York: Appleton-Century-Crofts.

Baddeley, A.D. (1966) The influence of acoustic and semantic similarity on long term memory for word sequences. *Quarterly Journal of Experimental Psychology*, *18*, 302–9.

Baddeley, A.D. (1978) The trouble with levels: A re-examination of Craik and Lockharts' 'Framework for memory research'. *Psychological Review*, *85*, 139–52.

Baddeley, A.D. (1981) The concept of working memory: A view of its current state and probable future development. *Cognition*, *10*, 17–23.

Baddeley, A.D. (1982) Domains of recollection. *Psychological Review*, *89*, 708–29.

Baddeley, A.D. (1984) Neuropsychological evidence and the semantic/episodic distinction. *Behavioural & Brain Sciences*, *7*, 238–9.

Baddeley, A.D. (1986) *Working memory*. Oxford: Oxford University Press.

Baddeley, A.D. (1990) *Human memory*. Hove, East Sussex: Lawrence Erlbaum Associates Ltd.

Baddeley, A.D. (1995) Memory. In C.C. French & A.M. Colman (Eds.) *Cognitive Psychology*. London: Longman.

Baddeley, A.D. & Hitch, G. (1974) Working memory. In G.A. Bower (Ed.), *Recent advances in learning and motivation, Vol. 8*. New York: Academic Press.

Baddeley, A.D. & Warrington, E.H. (1970) Amnesia and the distinction between long- and short-term memory. *Journal of Verbal Learning & Verbal Behaviour*, *9*, 176–89.

Baer, D.M. & Sherman, J.A. (1964) Reinforcement control of generalized imitation in young children. *Journal of Experimental Child Psychology*, *1*, 37–49.

Bailey, C.L. (1979) Mental illness – a logical misrepresentation? *Nursing Times*, *May*, 761–2.

Baittle, B. & Offer, D. (1971) On the nature of adolescent rebellion. In F.C. Feinstein, P. Giovacchini & A. Miller (Eds.) *Annals of adolescent psychiatry*. New York: Basic Books.

Bales, R.F. (1950) *Interaction Process Analysis: a method for the study of small groups*. Reading, Mass.: Addison-Wesley.

Baltes, P.B. (1987) Theoretical propositions of life-span developmental psychology: on the dynamics of growth and decline. *Developmental Psychology, 23*, 611–26.

Baltes, P.B. & Willis, S.L. (1982) Plasticity and enhancement of intellectual functioning in old age: Penn State's Adult Development and Enrichment Program (ADEPT). In F.I.M. Craik & S.E. Trehub (Eds.) *Ageing and cognitive processes*. New York: Plenum.

Banks, M.H. & Jackson, P.R. (1982) Unemployment and risk of minor psychiatric disorder in young people: cross-sectional and longitudinal evidence. *Psychological Medicine, 12*, 789–98.

Bandura, A. (1965) Influence of model's reinforcement contingencies on the acquisition of imitative responses. *Journal of Personality and Social Psychology*, *1*, 589–95.

Bandura, A. (1973) *Aggression: A social learning analysis*. London: Prentice Hall.

Bandura, A. (1974) Behaviour theory and models of man. *American Psychologist*, *29*, 859–69.

Bandura, A. (1977) Self-efficacy: Toward a unifying theory of behaviour change. *Psychological Review*, *84*, 191–215.

Bandura, A. & Menlove, F.L. (1968) Factors determining vicarious extinction of avoidance behaviour through symbolic modelling. *Journal of Personality & Social Psychology*, 8, 99–108.

Bandura, A., Ross, D. & Ross, S.A. (1961) Transmission of aggression through imitation of aggressive models. *Journal of Abnormal & Social Psychology, 63*, 575–82.

Bandura, A., Ross, D. & Ross, S.A. (1963) Imitation of film-mediated aggressive models. *Journal of Abnormal and Social Psychology*, *66*, 3–11.

Bandura, A. & Walters, R. (1959) *Social learning and personality development*. New York: Holt.

Bandura, A. & Walters, R. (1963) *Adolescent aggression*. New York: Ronald Press.

Bannister, D. (1963) The genesis of schizophrenic thought disorder: A serial invalidation hypothesis. *British Journal of Psychiatry, 109*, 680–8.

Bannister, D. (1965) The genesis of schizophrenic thought disorder: A retest of the serial invalidation hypothesis. *British Journal of Psychiatry, 111*, 377–82.

Bannister, D. & Agnew, J. (1976) The child's construing of self. In J.K. Coal & A.W. Landfield (Eds.), *Nebraska Symposium on Motivation*. Lincoln, Nebraska: University of Nebraska Press.

Bannister, D. & Fransella, F. (1967) *A grid test of schizophrenic thought disorder*. Barnstaple: Psychological Test Publications. Also in *British Journal of Social & Clinical Psychology*, *5*, 95–102.

Bannister, D. & Fransella, F. (1980) *Inquiring Man: The Psychology of Personal Constructs* (2nd ed.). Harmondsworth: Penguin.

Bannister, D. & Mair, M.J.M. (1968) *The evaluation of personal constructs*. London: Academic Press.

Bannister, D., Salmon, P. & Leiberman, D.M. (1964) Diagnosis – treatment relationships in psychiatry: a statistical analysis. *British Journal of Psychiatry, 110*, 726–32.

Barber, T.X. (1969) *Hypnosis: A scientific approach*. New York: Van Nostrand.

Barkham, M. & Shapiro, D. (1992) Response to Paul Kline. In W. Dryden & C. Feltham (Eds.) *Psychotherapy and its discontents*. Buckingham: Open University Press.

Baron, R.A. (1977) *Human aggression*. New York: Plenum.

Baron, R.A. & Byrne, D. (1991) *Social psychology* (6th ed.). Boston: Allyn and Bacon.

Baron-Cohen, S. (1990) Autism: A specific cognitive disorder of 'mind-blindness'. *International Review of Psychiatry, 2,* 79–88.

Baron-Cohen, S. (1995) Infantile autism. In A.A. Lazarus & A.M. Colman (Eds.) *Abnormal psychology*. London: Longman.

Barrett, M.D. (1986) Early semantic representations and early word usage. In S.A. Kuczaj & M.D. Barrett (Eds.), *The development of word meaning*. New York: Springer Verlag.

Barrett, M. (1989) Early language development. In A. Slater & G. Bremmer (Eds.), *Infant development*. Hove, East Sussex: Lawrence Erlbaum Associates Ltd.

Bar-Tal, D. & Saxe, L. (1976) Perception of similarity and dissimilarity in attractive couples and individuals. *Journal of Personality and Social Psychology, 33,* 772–81.

Bartlett, F.C. (1932) *Remembering*. Cambridge: Cambridge University Press.

Bartlett, F.C. (1958) *Thinking*. New York: Basic Books.

Bartholomew, K. (1990) Avoidance of intimacy: An attachment perspective. *Journal of Social and Personal Relationships, 7,* 147–178.

Bartholomew, K. (1993) From childhood to adult relationships: Attachment theory and research. In S. Duck (Ed.), *Learning about relationships*. Newbury Park, Ca: Sage Publications.

Bartholomew, K. & Horowitz, L.M. (1991) Attachment styles among young adults: A test of a model. *Journal of Personality & Social Psychology, 61,* 226–244.

Bates, E., Benigni, L., Bretherton, I., Camaioni, L. & Volterra, V. (1979) *The emergence of symbols: Cognition and communication in infancy*. New York: Academic Press.

Bateson, G., Jackson, D., Haley, J. & Weakland, J. (1956) Toward a theory of schizophrenia. *Behavioural Science, 1,* 251–64.

Bateson, P. (1986) When to experiment on animals. *New Scientist, 109* (14960), 30–2.

Bateson, P. (1992) Do animals feel pain? *New Scientist, 134* (1818), 30–3.

Bateson, P.P.G. (1964) Effect of similarity between rearing and testing conditions on chicks' following and avoidance responses. *Journal of Comparative and Physiological Psychology, 57,* 100–3.

Batson, C.D. & Oleson, K.C. (1991) Current status of the empathy–altruism hypothesis. In M.S. Clark (Ed.), *Prosocial behaviour, review of personality and social psychology, 12.* Newbury Park, California: Sage Publications.

Baumrind, D. (1964) Some thoughts on ethics of research: after reading Milgram's behavioural study of obedience. *American Psychologist, 19,* 421–3.

Bayley, N. (1969) *Bayley scale of infant development*. New York: Psychological Corporation.

Beaumont, J.G. (1988) *Understanding neuropsychology*. Oxford: Blackwell.

Beck, A.T. (1963) Thinking and depression. *Archives of General Psychiatry, 9,* 324–33.

Becker, H.S. (1963) *Outsiders: Studies in the sociology of deviance*. New York: Free Press.

Bee, H. (1989) *The developing child* (5th ed.). New York: Harper & Row.

Bee, H. (1994) *Lifespan development* New York: HarperCollins.

Bee, H., Barnard, K.E., Eyres, S.J., Gray, C.A., Hammond, M.A., Spietz, A.L., Snyder, C. & Clark B. (1982) Prediction of IQ and language skill from perinatal status, child performance, family characteristics and mother–infant interaction. *Child Development, 53,* 1135–56.

Bee, H. & Mitchell, S.K. (1980) *The developing person: A lifespan approach*. New York: Harper & Row.

Bekerian, D.A. & Bowers, J.M. (1983) Eye-witness testimony: Were we misled? *Journal of Experimental Psychology, Learning, Memory, and Cognition, 9,* 139–45.

Bell, S. (1970) The development of the concept of object as related to infant–mother attachment. *Child Development, 41,* 291–311.

Belson, W.A. (1978) *Television violence and the adolescent boy*. Farnborough: Saxon House.

Bem, D.J. (1965) An experimental analysis of self-persuasion. *Journal of Experimental and Social Psychology, 1,* 199–218.

Bem, D.J. (1967) Self-perception: An alternative interpretation of cognitive dissonance phenomena. *Psychological Review, 74,* 183–200.

Bem, D.J. (1970) *Beliefs, attitudes and human affairs*. Belmont, California: Brooks Cole.

Bem, D.J. (1972) Self-perception theory. In L. Berkowitz (Ed.), *Advances in experimental social psychology;* Vol. 6. New York: Academic Press.

Bem, D.J. & Allen, A. (1974) On predicting some of the people some of the time: A search for cross-situational consistencies in behaviour. *Psychological Review, 81,* 506–20.

Bem, S.L. (1974) The measurement of psychological androgyny. *Journal of Consulting and Clinical Psychology, 42* (2), 155–62.

Bem, S.L. (1975) Sex role adaptability: One consequence of psychological androgyny. *Journal of Personality & Social psychology, 31,* 634–43.

Bem, S.L. (1977) On the utility of alternative procedures for assessing psychological androgyny. *Journal of Consulting & Clinical Psychology, 45,* 196–205.

Bem, S.L. (1984) Androgyny and gender schema theory: a conceptual and empirical integration. In R.A. Dienstbier (Ed.), *Nebraska Symposium on Motivation*. Lincoln, Nebraska: University of Nebraska Press.

Bem, S.L. (1993) Is there a place in psychology for a feminist analysis of the social context? *Feminism & Psychology, 3* (2), 230–4.

Benedict, R. (1934) *Patterns of culture*. Boston: Houghton Mifflin.

Benedict, R. (1954) Continuities and discontinuities in cultural conditioning. In W.E. Martin & C.B. Stendler (Eds.), *Readings in child development*. New York: Harcourt Brace Jovanovich.

Bennett-Levy, J. & Marteau, T. (1984) Fear of animals: What is prepared? *British Journal of Psychology, 75,* 37–42.

Benson, P.L., Karabenick, S.A. & Lerner, R.M. (1976) Pretty pleases: The effects of physical attractiveness, race and sex on receiving help. *Journal of Experimental and Social Psychology, 12,* 409–15.

Benton, D. (1981) ECT. Can the system take the shock. *Community Care,* 12 March, 15–17.

Bereiter, C. & Engelman, S. (1966) *Teaching disadvantaged children in pre-school*. Englewood Cliffs, New Jersey: Prentice Hall.

Bergin, A.E. (1971) The evaluation of therapeutic outcomes. In A. Bergin & S.L. Garfield (Eds.), *Handbook of psychotherapy and behaviour change: An empirical analysis*. New York: Wiley.

Bergin, A.E. & Lambert, M.J. (1978) The evaluation of therapeutic outcomes. In A.E. Bergin & S.L. Garfield (Eds.), *Handbook of psychotherapy and behaviour change (2nd ed.): An empirical analysis*. New York: Wiley.

Berko, J. (1958) The child's learning of English morphology. *Word, 14,* 150–77.

Berko, J. & Brown, R. (1960) Psycholinguistic research methods. In P.H. Mussen (Ed.) *Handbook of research methods in child development.* New York: Wiley.

Berkowitz, L. (1962) *Aggression: A social psychological analysis.* New York: McGraw Hill.

Berkowitz, L. (1966) On not being able to aggress. *British Journal of Clinical & Social Psychology,* 5, 130–9.

Berkowitz, L. (1968) Impulse, aggression and the gun. *Psychology Today,* September, 18–22.

Berkowitz, L. (1969) The frustration–aggression hypothesis revisited. In L. Berkowitz (Ed.), *Roots of aggression: A re-examination of the frustration–aggression hypothesis.* New York: Atherton Press.

Berkowitz, L. (1993) *Aggression: Its causes, consequences and control.* New York: McGraw-Hill.

Berkowitz, L. (1995) A career on aggression. In G.G. Brannigan & M.R. Merrens (Eds.) *The social psychologists: Research adventures.* New York: McGraw-Hill.

Berkowitz, L. & Geen, R.G. (1966) Film violence and the cue properties of available targets. *Journal of Personality & Social Psychology,* , 3, 525–30.

Berkowitz, L. & LePage, A. (1967) Weapons as aggression-eliciting stimuli. *Journal of Personality and Social Psychology,* 7, 202–7.

Berlin, B. & Kay, P. (1969) *Basic Colour Terms: Their Universality and Evolution.* Berkeley, CA: University of California Press.

Berlyne, D.E. (1960) *Conflict, Arousal and Curiosity.* London: McGraw-Hill.

Bernstein, B. (1961) Social class and linguistic development. In A.H. Halsey, J. Flaud & C.A. Anderson (Eds.), *Education, economy and society.* London: Collier–Macmillan Ltd.

Berry, J.W., Poortinga, Y.H., Segall, M.H. & Dasen, P.R. (1992) *Cross-cultural psychology: Research and applications.* New York: Cambridge University Press.

Berscheid, E. & Walster, E.M. (1974) Physical attractiveness. In L. Berkowitz (Ed.), *Advances in experimental social psychology, Vol. 7.* New York: Academic Press.

Berscheid, E. & Walster, E. (1978) *Interpersonal attraction* (2nd ed.). Reading, Massachusetts: Adison-Wesley.

Berscheid, E., Dion, K., Hatfield, E. & Walster, G.W. (1971) Physical attractiveness and dating choice: A test of the matching hypothesis. *Journal of Experimental and Social Psychology,* 7, 173–89.

Bettelheim, B. (1976) *The uses of enchantment: The meaning and importance of fairy tales.* London: Thames & Hudson.

Bettelheim, B. (1985) *Freud and man's soul.* London: Flamingo.

Bexton, W.H., Heron, W. & Scott, T.H. (1954) Effects of decreased variation in the sensory environment. *Canadian Journal of Psychology,* 8, 70.

Bickman, L. (1971) The effect of another bystander's ability to help on bystander intervention in an emergency. *Journal of Experimental Social Psychology,* 7, 367–79.

Bickman, L. (1974) The social power of a uniform. *Journal of Applied Social Psychology,* 1, 47–61.

Biederman, I. (1987) Recognition-by-components: A theory of human image understanding. *Psychological Review,* 94, 115–47.

Bierhoff, H.W. & Klein, R. (1988) Prosocial behaviour. In M. Hewstone, W. Stroebe, J.P. Codol & G.M. Stephenson (Eds.), *Introduction to social psychology.* Oxford: Basil Blackwell.

Billig, M.G. (1976) *Social psychology and intergroup relations.* London: Academic Press.

Billig, M. & Tajfel, H. (1973) Social categorization and similarity in intergroup behaviour. *European Journal of Social Psychology,* 3, 27–52.

Blakemore, C. (1988) *The mind machine.* London: BBC Publications.

Blakemore, C. & Cooper, G.F. (1970) Development of the brain depends on the visual environment. *Nature,* 228, 477–8.

Blaney, P. (1975) Implications of the medical model and its alternatives. *American Journal of Psychiatry* 132, 911–14.

Blank, M. & Solomon, F. (1968) A tutorial language programme to develop abstract thinking in socially disadvantaged pre-school children. *Child Development,* 39, 379–89.

Blau, P.M. (1964) *Exchange and power in social life.* New York: John Wiley & Sons.

Bleuler, E. (1911) *Dementia praecox or the group of schizophrenias.* (J. Avikin, trans.). New York: International University Press.

Block, N.J. & Dworkin, G. (1974) I.Q.: Heritability and inequality. *Philosophy and Public Affairs,* 3, 331–407.

Bloom, B.S. (1964) *Stability and change in human characteristics.* New York: Harcourt Brace Jovanovich.

Bloom, L. (1973) *One word at a time.* The Hague: Mouton.

Blos, P. (1967) The second individuation process of adolescence. *The psychoanalytic study of the child, Vol. 22.* New York: International University Press.

Blundell, J.E. & Hill, A.J. (1995) Hunger and appetite. In B. Parkinson & A.M.Colman (Eds.) *Emotion and Motivation.* London: Longman.

Boas, F. (1927) *Primitive art.* Oslo: Institute for Sammenlignende Kulturforskning.

Boden, M. (1972) *Purposive explanation in psychology.* Cambridge, Massachusetts: Harvard University Press.

Boden, M. (1980) Artificial intelligence and intellectual imperialism. In A.J. Chapman and D.M. Jones (Eds.) *Models of man* Leicester: British Psychological Society.

Boden, M. (1987a) *Artificial intelligence and natural man* (2nd ed.). Cambridge, Massachusetts: Harvard University Press.

Boden, M. (1987b) Artificial intelligence. In R. Gregory (Ed.), *Oxford companion to the mind.* Oxford: Oxford University Press.

Boden, M. (1993) The impact on philosophy. In D. Broadbent (Ed.) *The simulation of human intelligence.* Oxford: Blackwell.

Bodmer, W.F. (1972) Race and I.Q.: The genetic background. In K. Richardson & D. Spears (Eds.), *Race, culture and intelligence.* Harmondsworth, Middlesex: Penguin.

Bogardus, E.S. (1925) Measuring social distance. *Journal of Applied Sociology,* 9, 299–308.

Bogdonoff, M.D., Klein, R.F., Estes, E.H., Shaw, D.M. & Back, K. (1961) The modifying effect of conforming behaviour upon lipid responses accompanying CNS arousal. *Clinical Research,* 9, 135.

Bogen, J.E. (1969) The other side of the brain. In R. Ornstein (Ed.), *The psychology of consciousness* (2nd ed., revised 1986). Harmondsworth, Middlesex: Penguin.

Bolles, R.C. (1967) *Theory of motivation.* New York: Harper & Row.

Bolles, R.C. (1980) Ethological learning theory. In G.M. Gazda & R.J. Corsini (Eds.), *Theories of learning: A comparative approach.* Itaska, Illinois: Free Press.

Booth, T. (1975) *Growing up in society.* London: Methuen.

Borke, H. (1975) Piaget's mountains revisited: Changes in the egocentric landscape. *Developmental Psychology,* 11, 240–3.

Bornstein, M.H. (1976) Infants are trichromats. *Journal of Experimental Child Psychology,* 19, 401–19.

Bornstein, M.H. (1988) Perceptual development across the life cycle. In M.H. Bornstein & M.E. Lamb (Eds.), *Perceptual, cognitive and linguistic development.* Hove, East Sussex: Lawrence Erlbaum Associates Ltd.

Botwinick, J. (1978) *Aging and behaviour* (2nd ed.). New York: Springer.

Bouchard, T.J., Lykken, D.T., McGue, M., Segal, N.L.,& Tellegen, A.(1990) Sources of human psychological differences: the Minnesota study of twins reared apart. *Science, 250,* 223–8.

Bouchard, T.J. & McGue, M. (1981) Familial studies of intelligence: A review. *Science, 22,* 1055–9.

Bousfield, W.A. (1953) The occurrence of clustering in the recall of randomly arranged associates. *Journal of General Psychology, 49,* 229–40.

Bower, G.H. (1972) Mental imagery and associative learning. In L. Gregg (Ed.), *Cognition in learning and memory.* New York: Wiley.

Bower, G.H. (1975) Cognitive psychology: An introduction. In W. Estes (Ed.), *Handbook of learning and cognitive processes, Vol 1.* Hillsdale, New Jersey: Lawrence Erlbaum Associates Inc.

Bower, G.H. & Karlin, M.B. (1974) Depth of processing pictures of faces and recognition memory. *Journal of Experimental Psychology, 103,* 751–7.

Bower, G.H., Clark, M., Lesgold, A. & Winzenz, D. (1969) Hierarchical retrieval schemes in recall of categorized word lists. *Journal of Verbal Learning and Verbal Behaviour, 8,* 323–43.

Bower, G.H., Black, J.B. & Turner, T.J. (1979) Scripts in memory for text. *Cognitive Psychology, 11,* 177–220.

Bower, G.H. & Springston, F. (1970) Pauses as recoding points in letter series. *Journal of Experimental Psychology, 83,* 421–30.

Bower, T.G.R. (1966) The visual world of infants. *Scientific American, 215* (6), 80–92.

Bower, T.G.R. (1971) The object in the world of the infant. *Scientific American, 225* (4), 30–8.

Bower, T.G.R. (1976) Repetitive processes in child development. *Scientific American, 235* (5), 38–47.

Bower, T.G.R. (1977) *The Perceptual World of the Child.* London: Fontana Paperbacks.

Bower, T.G.R. (1979) *Human development.* San Francisco: W.H. Freeman.

Bower, T.G.R., Broughton, J.M. & Moore, M.K. (1970) Infant responses to approaching objects: An indicator of response to distal variables. *Perception and Psychophysics, 9,* 193–6.

Bower, T.G.R. & Wishart, J.G. (1972) The effects of motor skill on object permanence. *Cognition, 1* (2), 28–35.

Bowers, K. (1973) Situationism in psychology: An analysis and critique. *Psychological Review, 80,* 307–36.

Bowlby, J. (1946) *Forty-four juvenile thieves.* London: Balliére, Tindall and Cox.

Bowlby, J. (1951) *Maternal care and mental health.* Geneva: World Health Organization.

Bowlby, J. (1953) *Child Care and the Growth of Love.* Harmondsworth: Penguin.

Bowlby, J. (1969) *Attachment and loss. Vol. 1: Attachment.* Harmondsworth, Middlesex: Penguin.

Bowlby, J. (1973) *Attachment and loss. Vol. 2: Separation.* Harmondsworth, Middlesex: Penguin.

Bowlby, J. (1977) The making and breaking of affactional bonds: 1. Aetiology and psychopathology in the light of attachment theory. *British Journal of Psychiatry, 130,* 201–10.

Bowlby, J. (1988) *A Secure Base: Clinical Applications of Attachment Theory.* London: Tavistock/Routledge.

Bowlby, J., Ainsworth, M., Boston, M. & Rosenbluth, D. (1956) The effects of mother-child separation: a follow-up study. *British Journal of Medical Psychology* 24 (3 and 4), 211–47.

Bradbury, T.N. & Fincham, F.D. (1990) Attributions in marriage: Review and critique. *Psychological Bulletin,* 107, 3–33.

Bradley, L.A. (1995) Chronic Benign Pain. In D. Wedding (Ed.) *Behaviour and Medicine* (2nd ed.) St. Louis, MO: Mosby-Year Book Inc.

Brady, J.V. (1958) Ulcers in 'executive monkeys'. *Scientific American, 199,* 95–100.

Braine, M.D.S. (1971) On two types of models of the internalization of grammars. In D.I.Slobin (Ed.) *The Ontogenesis of Grammar.* New York: Academic Press.

Brainerd, C.J. (1978) Learning research and Piagetian theory. In L. Siegel & C.J. Brainerd (Eds.), *Alternatives to Piaget: Critical essays on the theory.* New York: Academic Press.

Brainerd, C.J. (1983) Modifiability of cognitive development. In S. Meadows (Ed.), *Development thinking.* London: Methuen.

Bransford, J.D., Franks, J.J., Morris, C.D. & Stein, B.S. (1979) Some general constraints on learning and memory research. In L.S. Cerack & F.I.M. Craik (Eds.), *Levels of processing in human memory.* Hillsdale, New Jersey: Lawrence Erlbaum Associates Inc.

Breggin, P. (1991) *Toxic Psychiatry.* London: HarperCollins

Brehm, J.W. (1956) Post-decision changes in the desirability of alternatives. *Journal of Abnormal and Social Psychology, 52,* 384–9.

Brehm, J.W. (1966) *Theory of psychological reactance.* New York: Academic Press.

Brehm, J.W. & Cohen, A.R. (1962) *Explorations in cognitive dissonance.* New York: Wiley.

Brehm, S.S. (1992) *Intimate Relationships* (2nd ed.) New York: McGraw-Hill.

Breuer, J. & Freud, S. (1895) *Studies on hysteria.* In J. Strachey (Ed. and trans.) *Standard edition of the complete psychological works of Sigmund Freud* (vol. 2) London:Hogarth.

Brislin, R. (1981) *Cross-cultural encounters: Face-to-face interaction.* Elmsford, NY: Pergamon.

Brislin, R. (1993) *Understanding Culture's Influence on Behaviour.* Orlando Fla.: Harcourt Brace Jovanovich.

British Broadcasting Corporation (1972) *Violence on television: Programme content and viewer perceptions.* London: BBC Publications.

British Psychological Society (1978) Ethical principles for research with human subjects. *Bulletin of the British Psychological Society, 31,* 48–9.

British Psychological Society (1983) *Guidelines for the professional practice of clinical psychology.* Leicester: British Psychological Society.

British Psychological Society (1985) A code of conduct for psychologists. *Bulletin of the British Psychological Society, 38,* 41–3.

British Psychological Society (1990) Ethical principles for conducting research with human participants. *The Psychologist, 3* (6), 269–72.

British Psychological Society (1993) Ethical principles for conducting research with human participants (revised). *The Psychologist,* 6 (1), 33–5.

British Psychological Society (1995) *Recovered memories ; The report of the Working Party of the British Psychological Society.* Leicester: British Psychological Society.

British Psychological Society and Committee of the Experimental Psychological Society (1985) *Guidelines for the use of animals in research.* Leicester: British Psychological Society.

British Psychological Society Scientific Affairs Board (1985) Guidelines for the use of animals in research. *Bulletin of the British Psychological Society,* 38, 289–91.

Broadbent, D.E. (1954) The role of auditory localization in

attention and memory span. *Journal of Experimental Psychology*, *47*, 191–6.

Broadbent, D.E. (1958) *Perception and communication*. London: Pergamon.

Broadbent, D.E. (1961) *Behaviour*. London: Eyre & Spottiswoode.

Brody, E.B. & Brody, N. (1976) *Intelligence: Nature, determinants and consequences*. New York: Academic Press.

Broca, P.P. (1864/1970) Cited in M. Critchley, *Aphasiology and other aspects of language*. London: Edward Arnold.

Bradley, L.A. (1995) Chronic benign pain. In D. Wedding (Ed.) *Behaviour and Medicine* (2nd ed.). St. Louis, MO: Mosby-Year Book.

Brody, H. (1995) The placebo response. In D. Wedding (Ed.) *Behaviour and Medicine* (2nd ed.). St. Louis, MO: Mosby-Year Book.

Bromley, D.B. (1988) *Human ageing: An introduction to gerontology* (3rd ed.). Harmondsworth, Middlesex: Penguin.

Bronfenbrenner, U. (1960) Freudian theories of identification and their derivatives. *Child Development*, *31*, 15–40.

Brown, G.W. & Harris, T.O. (1978) *Social origins of depression: A Study of psychiatric disorder in women*. London: Tavistock.

Brown, H. (1985) *People, groups and society*. Milton Keynes: Open University Press.

Brown, J.A. (1958) Some tests of the decay theory of immediate memory. *Quarterly Journal of Experimental Psychology*, *10*, 12–21.

Brown, J.A.C. (1963) *Freud and the post-Freudians*. Harmondsworth, Middlesex: Penguin.

Brown, R. (1958) *Words and things*. Glencoe, Illinois: Free Press.

Brown, R. (1965) *Social psychology*. New York: Free Press.

Brown, R. (1970) The first sentences of child and chimpanzee. In R. Brown, *Psycholinguistics*. New York: Free Press.

Brown, R. (1973) *A first language: The early stages*. Cambridge, MA.: Harvard University Press.

Brown, R. (1986) *Social psychology: The second edition*. New York: Free Press.

Brown, R., Cazden, C.B. & Bellugi, U. (1969) The child's grammar from 1 to 3. In J.P. Hill (Ed.) *Minnesota Symposium on Child Psychology*, Vol. 2. Minneapolis: University of Minnesota Press.

Brown, R. & Kulik, J. (1977) Flashbulb memories. *Cognition*, *5*, 73–99.

Brown, R. & Lenneberg, E.H. (1954) A study in language and cognition. *Journal of Abnormal & Clinical Psychology*, *49*, 454–62.

Brown, R. (1988) Intergroup relations. In M. Hewstone, W. Stroebe, J.P. Codol & G.M. Stephenson (Eds.), *Introduction to social psychology*. Oxford: Basil Blackwell.

Brown, R.J. & Turner, J.C. (1981) Interpersonal and intergroup behaviour. In J.C. Turner & H. Giles (Eds.), *Intergroup behaviour*. Oxford: Basil Blackwell.

Browne, J.A. & Howarth, E. (1977) A comprehensive factor analysis of personality questionnaire items: a test of twenty putative factor hypotheses. *Multivariate Behavioural Research*, *12*, 399–427.

Bruce, V. & Green, P.R. (1990) *Visual perception* (2nd ed.). Hove, East Sussex: Lawrence Erlbaum Associates Ltd.

Bruner, J. S. (1957) On perceptual readiness. *Psychological Review*, 64, 123–52.

Bruner, J.S. (1966a) On the conservation of liquids. In J.S. Bruner, R.R. Olver & P.M. Greenfield (Eds.), *Studies in cognitive growth*. New York: Wiley.

Bruner, J.S. (1966b) *Towards a theory of instruction*. Cambridge, Massachussets: Harvard University Press.

Bruner, J.S. (1975) The ontogenesis of speech acts. *Journal of Child Language*, *2*, 1–21.

Bruner, J.S. (1978) Acquiring the uses of language. *Canadian Journal of Psychology*, 32 (4), 204–18.

Bruner, J.S. (1983) *Child's talk: Learning to use language*. Oxford: Oxford University Press.

Bruner, J.S. & Goodman, C.C. (1947) Value and need as organizing factors in perception. *Journal of Abnormal and Social Psychology*, *42*, 33–44.

Bruner, J.S., Goodnow, J.J. & Austin, G.A. (1956) *A study of thinking*. New York: Wiley.

Bruner, J.S. & Kenney, H. (1966) *The development of the concepts of order and proportion in children*. New York: Wiley.

Bruner, J.S., Oliver, R.R. & Greenfield, P.M. (Eds.) (1966) *Studies in cognitive growth*. New York: Wiley.

Bruner, J.S. & Postman, L. (1949) On the perception of incongruity: A paradigm. *Journal of Personality*, *18*, 206–23.

Bruner, J.S. & Tagiuri, R. (1954) The perception of people. In G. Lindzey (Ed.), *Handbook of social psychology*, *Vol. 2*. Reading, Massachusetts: Addison-Wesley.

Brunswik, E. (1952) The conceptual framework of psychology. In *The international encyclopaedia of unified science*, *1*, 10. Chicago, ILL: University of Chicago Press.

Brunswik, E. (1955) Representative design and probabilistic theory in a functional psychology. *Psychological Review*, *62*, 193–217.

Brunswick, E. (1956) *Perception and the representative design of psychological experiments*. Berkeley, California: University of California Press.

Bryant, B., Harris, M. D.Newton (1980) *Children and Minders*. London ; Grant McIntyre.

Buckhout, R. (1974) Eyewitness testimony. *Scientific American*, December, 23–31.

Bumpass, L.L., Sweet, J.A. & Cherlin, A. (1991) The role of cohabitation in declining rates of marriage. *Journal of Marriage and the Family*, *53*, 913–27.

Burgio, L.D., Whitman, T.I. & Reid, D.H. (1983) A participative management approach for improving direct-care staff performance in an institutional setting. *Journal of Applied Behaviour Analysis*, *16*, 37–52.

Burks, B.S. (1928) The relative influence of nature and nurture upon mental development: A comparative study of foster parent–foster child resemblance and true parent–true child resemblance. *Yearbook of the National Society for the Study of Education*, *27*, 219–316.

Burns, R.B. (1980) *Essential Psychology*. Lancaster: MTP Press.

Burns, R.B. & Dobson, C.B. (1984) *Introductory psychology*. Lancaster: MTP Press.

Burnside, I.M., Ebersole, P. & Monea, H.E. (Eds.) (1979) *Psychosocial caring throughout the lifespan*. New York: McGraw-Hill.

Burr, V. (1995) *An introduction to social constructionism*. London: Routledge.

Burt, C.L. (1949) The structure of the mind: A review of the results of factor analysis. *British Journal of Eduactional Psychology*, 19, 110–11, 176–99.

Burt, C. L. (1955) The evidence for the concept of intelligence. *British Journal of Eduactional Psychology*, 25, 158–77.

Burt, C. (1958) The inheritance of mental ability. *American Psychologist*, *13*, 1–15.

Burt, C.L. (1966) The genetic determination of differences in intelligence: A study of monozygotic twins reared together and apart. *British Journal of Psychology*, *57*, 137–53.

Burton, R.V. (1963) Generality of honesty reconsidered. *Psychological Review*, *70*, 481–99.

Buss, A.H. (1961) *The psychology of aggression*. New York: Wiley.

Buss, A.H. (1963) Physical aggression in relation to different frustrations. *Journal of Abnormal and Social Psychology*, *67*, 1–7.

Buss, A.H. (1966) Instrumentality of aggression, feedback and frustration and determinants of physical aggression. *Journal of Personality and Social Psychology*, *3*, 153–62.

Buss, D.M. (1987) Sex differences in human mate selection criteria: an evolutionary perspective. In C. Crawford, M. Smith & D. Krebs (Eds.) *Sociobiology and Psychology: ideas, issues and applications.* Hillsdale, NJ: Erlbaum.

Buss, D.M. (1988) The evolutionary biology of love. In R.J.Sternberg & M.L. Barnes (Eds.) *The psychology of love.* New Haven, CT: Yale University Press.

Buss, D.M. (1989) Sex differences in human mate preferences: Evolutionary hypotheses tested in 37 cultures. *Behavioural and Brain Sciences*, 12, 1–49.

Buss, D.M. (1994) Mate preference in 37 cultures. In W.J. Lonner & R.S. Malpass (Eds.) *Psychology and Culture.* Boston: Allyn & Bacon.

Butler, R. (1963) The life review: An interpretation of reminiscence in the aged. *Psychiatry*, *26*, 65–76.

Butler, R.A. (1954) Curiosity in monkeys. *Scientific American*, February, 70–5.

Byrne, D. (1971) *The attraction paradigm.* New York: Academic Press.

Byrne, D. & Buehler, J.A. (1965) A note on the influence of propinquity upon acquaintanceships. *Journal of Abnormal and Social Psychology*, *51*, 147–8.

Bryne, D. & Griffitt, W. (1973) Interpersonal attraction. *Annual Review of Psychology*, *24*, 317–36.

Callaghan. P. & O'Carroll, M. (1993) Making women mad. *Nursing Times, 89 (27)*, 26–9.

Calvin, W. H. (1994) The emergence of language. *Scientific American*, October, 79–85.

Campbell, A & Muncer, S. (1994) Men and the meaning of violence. In J. Archer (Ed.) *Male violence.* London: Routledge.

Campbell, B.A. & Church, R.M. (1969), (Eds.) *Punishment and aversive behaviour.* New York: Appleton-Century-Crofts.

Campbell, D.T. (1967) Stereotypes and the perception of group differences. *American Psychologist*, *22*, 817–29.

Campos. J.J., Langer, A. & Krowitz, A. (1970) Cardiac responses on the cliff in pre-locomotor human infants. *Science*, *170*, 196–7.

Cannon, W.B. (1927) The James–Lange theory of emotions: A critical examination and an alternative. *American Journal of Psychology*, *39*, 106–24.

Cannon, W.B. (1928) Neural organization for emotional expression. In M.L. Reymert (Ed.) *Feelings and emotions: The Wittenberg symposium.* Worcester, MA: Clark University Press.

Cannon. W.B. (1929) *Bodily changes in pain, hunger, fear and rage.* New York: Appleton-Century-Crofts.

Cannon, W.B. & Washburn, A.L. (1912) An explanation of hunger. *American Journal of Psychology*, *29*, 441–54.

Carlsmith, J.M., Collins, B.E. & Helmreich, R.L. (1966) Studies in forced compliance: 1. The effect of pressure for compliance on attitude change produced by face-to-face role playing and anonymous essay writing. *Journal of Personality and Social Psychology*, *4*, 1–13.

Carlson, N.R. (1992) *Foundations of Physiological Psychology* (2nd ed.). Boston: Allyn & Bacon.

Carmichael, L., Hogan, P. & Walter, A. (1932) An experimental study of the effect of language on the reproduction of visually perceived forms. *Journal of Experimental Psychology*, *15*, 1–22.

Carroll, D.W. (1986) *Psychology of language.* Monterey, California: Brooks/Cole Publishing Co.

Carroll, J.B. & Casagrande, J.B. (1958) The function of language classifications in behaviour. In E.E. Maccoby, T.M. Newcombe & E.L. Hartley (Eds.), *Readings in social psychology* (3rd ed.). New York: Holt, Rinehart & Winston.

Carver, C.S. & Scheier, M.F. (1992) *Perspectives on Personality* (2nd ed.) Boston: Allyn & Bacon.

Cattell, R.B. (1963) Theory of fluid and crystallized intelligence: A critical experiment. *Journal of Educational Psychology*, *54*, 1–22.

Cattell, R.B. (1965) *The scientific analysis of personality.* Harmondsworth, Middlesex: Penguin.

Cattell, R.B. (1966) The scree test for the number of factors. *Multivariate Behavioural Research, 1,* 140–61.

Cattell, R.B. & Kline, P. (1977) *The scientific study of personality and motivation.* London: Academic Press.

Cautela, J.R. (1967) Covert sensitization. *Psychology Reports*, *20*, 459–68.

Cavanaugh, J.C. (1995) Ageing. In P.E. Bryant & A.M.Colman (Eds.) *Developmental psychology.* London: Longman.

Cernoch, J.M. & Porter, R.H. (1985) Recognition of maternal axillary odors by infants. *Child Development*, *56*, 1593–8.

Chaiken, S. (1987) The heuristic model of persuasion. In M.P. Zanna, J.M. Olsen & C.P. Herman (Eds.), *Social influence: The Ontario symposium, Vol 5.* Hillsdale, New Jersey: Lawrence Erlbaum Associates Inc.

Chaikin, A.L. & Darley, J.M. (1973) Victim or perpetrator? Defensive attribution of responsibility and the need for order and justice. *Journal of Personality and Social Psychology*, *25*, 268–75.

Chase, W.G. & Simon, H.A. (1973) Perception in chess. *Cognitive Psychology*, *4*, 55–81.

Cheng, P.W. (1985) Restructuring versus automaticity: Alternative accounts of skill acquisition. *Psychological Review*, *92*, 414–23.

Cherry, E.C. (1953) Some experiments on the recognition of speech with one and two ears. *Journal of the Acoustical Society of America*, *25*, 975–9.

Chomsky, N. (1957) *Syntactic structures.* The Hague: Mouton.

Chomsky, N. (1959) Review of Skinner's *Verbal Behaviour. Language*, *35*, 26–58.

Chomsky, N. (1965) *Aspects of the theory of syntax.* Cambridge, Massachusetts: MIT Press.

Chomsky, N. (1968) *Language and mind.* New York: Harcourt Brace Jovanovich.

Chomsky, N. (1979) *Language and responsibility.* Sussex: Harvester Press.

Chapanis, N.P. & Chapanis, A. (1964) Cognitive dissonance – 5 years later. *Psychological Bulletin*, *61* (1), 1–22.

Chapman, L.J. (1967) Illusory correlation in observational report. *Journal of Verbal Learning & Verbal Behaviour, 6,* 151–55.

Cialdini, R.B. (1988) *Influence: Science and practice.* Glenview, IL: Scott, Foresman.

Cioffi, F. (1974) Was Freud a liar? *The Listener*, February, 172–4.

Clare, A. (1976) What is schizophrenia? *New Society*, *May 20*, 410–12.

Clare, A. (1980) *Psychiatry in dissent.* London: Tavistock.

Claridge, G.S. (1967) *Personality and arousal.* Oxford: Pergamon Press.

Claridge, G.S. & Chappa, H.J. (1973) Psychoticism: A study of its biological basis in normal subjects. *British Journal of Social and Clinical Psychology*, *12*, 175–87.

Clark, K.E. & Miller, G. A. (1970), (Eds.) *Psychology: Behavioural and social sciences survey committee.* Englewood Cliffs, N.J.: Prentice Hall.

Clark, M.S., Mills, J. & Corcoran, D. (1989) Keeping track of needs and inputs of friends and strangers. *Journal of Personality & Social Psychology, 15,* 533–42.

Clark, R.D. & Maass, A. (1988) The role of social categorization and perceived source credibility in minority influence. *European Journal of Social Psychology,* 18, 381–94.

Clarke, A.D.B. (1972) Comment on Koluchova's 'Severe deprivation in twins: a case study'. *Journal of Child Psychology & Psychiatry, 13,* 103–6.

Clarke, A.M. & Clarke, A.D.B. (1976) *Early experience: Myth and evidence.* London: Open Books.

Clarke, P.R.F. (1975) The medical model defended. *New Society, January 9,* 64–5.

Clarke, R. (1979) Assessment in psychiatric hospitals. *Nursing Times, April 5,* 590–2.

Clarke-Stewart, K.A. (1973) Interactions between mothers and their young children: Characteristics and consequences. *Monograph of the Society for Research into Child Development, 38* (6–7, Serial No. 153).

Clarke-Stewart, K.A. (1978) And daddy makes three: The father's impact on mother and young child. *Child Development, 49,* 446–78.

Clarke-Stewart, K.A. (1989) Infant day care: Maligned or malignant? *American Psychologist,* 44, 266–73.

Clift, S.M. (1984) Should we still teach Freud? *Psychology Teaching, December,* 8–14.

Clore, G.L. (1994) Why emotions require cognition. In P. Ekman & R.J. Davidson (Eds.) *The nature of emotion: Fundamental questions.* New York: Oxford University Press.

Clore, G.L. & Byrne, D. (1974) A reinforcement-affect model of attraction. In T.L. Huston (Ed.) *Foundations of interpersonal attraction.* New York: Academic Press.

Cochrane, R. (1974) Circadian variations in mental efficiency. In W.P. Colquhoun (Ed.), *Biological rhythms and human performance.* London: Academic Press.

Cochrane, R. (1974) Crime and personality: theory and evidence. *Bulletin of the British Psychological Society, 27,* 19–22.

Cochrane, R. (1983) *The social creation of mental illness.* London: Longman.

Cochrane, R. (1995) Women and Depression. *Psychology Review,* 2 (1), 20–4.

Cohen, F. & Lazarus, R. (1979) Coping with the stresses of illness. In G.C. Stone, F. Cohen & N.E. Ader (Eds.) *Health psychology: A handbook.* San Francisco, CA: Jossey-Bass.

Cohen, G. (1975) Cerebral apartheid: A fanciful notion? *New Behaviour, 18,* 458–61.

Cohen, G. (1986) Everyday memory. In G. Cohen, M.W. Eysenck & M.E. Le Voi (Eds.), *Memory: A cognitive approach.* Milton Keynes: Open University Press.

Cohen, G. (1990) Memory. In I. Roth (Ed.), *Introduction to psychology, Vol. 2.* Hove, E.Sussex/Milton Keynes: Open University/Lawrence Erlbaum Associates Ltd.

Cohen, G. (1993) Everyday memory, and memory systems: The experimental approach. In G. Cohen, G. Kiss & M. Le Voi, *Memory:Current issues* (2nd ed.) Buckingham: Open University Press.

Cohen, N.J. & Squire, L.R. (1980) Preserved learning and retention of pattern-analyzing skills in amnesia: Dissociation of knowing how from knowing that. *Science, 210,* 207–10.

Cohen, S. & Taylor, L. (1972) *Psychological survival: The experience of long-term imprisonment.* Harmodsworth: Penguin.

Colby, A., Kohlberg, L., Gibbs, J. & Lieberman, M. (1983) A longitudinal study of moral develoment. *Monographs of the Society for Research in Child Development, 48* (1–2 Serial No. 200).

Colman, A.M. (1987) *Facts, fallacies and frauds in psychology.* London: Unwin Hyman.

Coleman, J.C. (1974) *Realtionships in adolescence.* London: Routledge & Kegan Paul.

Coleman, J.C. (1978) Current contradictions in adolescent theory. *Journal of Youth & Adolescence. 7,* 1–11.

Coleman, J.C. (Ed.) (1979) *The school years.* London: Methuen.

Coleman, J.C. (1980) *The nature of adolescence.* London: Methuen.

Coleman, J. C. (1995) Adolescence. In P.E. Bryant & A.M. Colman (Eds.) *Developmental Psychology.* London: Longman.

Coleman, J.C. & Hendry, L. (1990) *The nature of adolescence* (2nd ed.). London: Routledge.

Collins. A.M. & Loftus, E.F. (1975) A spreading-activation theory of semantic processing. *Psychological Review, 82,* 407–28.

Collins, A.M. & Quillian, M. (1969) Retrieval time for semantic memory. *Journal of Verbal Learning and Verbal Behaviour, 8,* 240–7.

Collins, A.M. & Quillian, M. R. (1972) How to make a language user. In E. Tulving & W. Donaldson (Eds.) *Organization of memory.* New York: Academic Press.

Collins, H. (1994) *Times Higher Education Supplement,* September 30, 18.

Collins, R.C. (1983) Head start: An update on program effects. *Newsletter of the Society for Research in Child Development,* Summer, 1–2.

Condry, J. & Condry, S. (1976) Sex differences: A study in the eye of the beholder. *Child Development, 47,* 812–19.

Conrad, C. (1972) Cognitive economy in semantic memory. *Journal of Experimental Psychology, 92,* 148–54.

Conrad, R. (1963) Acoustic confusions and memory span for words. *Nature, 197,* 1029–30.

Conrad, R. (1964) Acoustic confusion in immediate memory. *British Journal of Psychology, 55,* 75–84.

Constanzo, P.R., Coie, J.D., Grumet, J.F. & Farnill, D. (1973) Re-examination of the effects of intent and consequence on children's moral judgements. *Child Development, 44,* 154–61.

Cook, M. (1971) *Interpersonal perception.* Harmondsworth, Middlesex: Penguin.

Cook, S.W. & Selltiz, C.A.(1964) A multiple indicator approach to attitude measurement. *Psychological Bulletin, 62,* 36–55.

Cooley, C.H. (1902) *Human nature and social order.* New York: Shocken.

Coolican, H. (1990) *Research methods and statistics in psychology.* Sevenoaks: Hodder & Stoughton.

Coolican, H. (1994) *Research methods and statistics in psychology* (2nd ed.). London: Hodder & Stoughton.

Coon, D. (1983) *Introduction to psychology* (3rd ed.). St Paul, Minnesota: West Publishing Co.

Cooper, J.E. (1994) Notes on unsolved problems. In *Pocket guide to the ICD-10 classification of mental and behavioural disorders.* London: Churchill Livingstone.

Cooper, J.E., Kendall, R.E., Gurland, B.J., Sharple, L., Copeland, J.R.M. & Simon, R. (1972) Psychiatric diagnosis in New York and London. *Maudsley monograph No. 20.* London: Oxford University Press.

Cooper, J. & Fazio, R.H. (1984) A new look at dissonance theory. In L. Berkowitz (Ed.), *Advances in experimental social psychology, Vol. 15.* New York: Academic Press.

Cooper, P.J. (1995) Eating disorders. In A.A. Lazarus & A.M. Colman (Eds.) *Abnormal psychology.* London: Longman.

Coopersmith, S. (1967) *The antecedents of self esteem.* San Francisco: Freeman.

Cordray, D.S. & Bootzin, R.R. (1983) Placebo control conditions: Tests of theory or of effectiveness. *Behavioural and Brain Sciences, 6,* 286–7.

Cornsweet, T.N. (1970) *Visual perception*. New York: Academic Press.

Corteen, R.S. & Wood, B. (1972) Autonomic responses to shock-associated words in an unattended channel. *Journal of Experimental Psychology*, 94, 308–13.

Corteen, R.S. & Dunn, D. (1974) Shock-associated words in a non-attended message: A test for momentary awareness. *Journal of Experimental Psychology*, 102, 1143–4.

Corter, C.M. (1973) A comparison of the mother's and a stranger's control over the behaviour of infants. *Child Development*, 44, 705–13.

Costa, P.T. & McCrae, R.R. (1993) Bullish on personality psychology. *The Psychologist*, 6 (7), 302–3.

Costello, T.W., Costello, J.T. & Holmes, D.A. (adapting author) (1995) *Abnormal psychology*. London: HarperCollins.

Cox, T. (1975) The nature and management of stress. *New Behaviour, September 25*, 493–5.

Cox, T. (1978) *Stress* London: Macmillan Education.

Craig, G.J. (1992) *Human development* (6th ed.). Englewood Cliffs, NJ: Prentice-Hall.

Craik, F. & Lockhart, R. (1972) Levels of processing. *Journal of Verbal Learning and Verbal Behaviour*, 11, 671–84.

Craik, F. & Tulving, E. (1975) Depth of processing and the retention of words in episodic memory. *Journal of Experimental Psychology: General*, 104, 268–94.

Craik, F.I.M. & Watkins, M.J. (1972) The role of rehearsal in short-term memory. *Journal of Verbal Learning & Verbal Behaviour*, 12, 599–607.

Crawford, M. & Unger, R.K. (1995) Gender issues in psychology. In A.M. Colman (Ed.) *Controversies in psychology*. London: Longman.

Crick, F. & Mitchison, G. (1983) The function of REM sleep. *Nature*, 304, 111–14.

Cromer, R.F. (1974) The development of language and cognition: The cognition hypothesis. In B. Foss (Ed.), *New perspectives in child development*. Harmondsworth, Middlesex: Penguin.

Cromer, R.F. (1980) Normal language development: Recent progress. In L.A. Hersov, M. Berger & A.R. Nicol (Eds.), *Language and language disorders*. Oxford: Pergamon Press.

Crosby, F., Bromley, S. and Saxe, L. (1980) Recent unobtrusive studies of black and white discriminations and prejudice: A literature review. *Psychological Bulletin*, 87, 546–63.

Croyle, R.T. & Cooper, J. (1983) Dissonance arousal: Physiological evidence. *Journal of Personality and Social Psychology*, 45, 782–91.

Crutchfield, R.S. (1954) A new technique for measuring individual differences in conformity to group judgement. *Proceedings of the Invitational Conference on Testing Problems* (pp. 69–74).

Crutchfield, R.S. (1955) Conformity and character. *American Psychologist*, 10, 191–8.

Cumberbatch, G. (1987) *The portrayal of violence on British television*. London: BBC Publications.

Cumming, E. (1975) Engagement with an old theory. *International Journal of Ageing & Human Development*, 6, 187–91.

Cumming, E. & Henry, W.E. (1961) *Growing old: The process of disengagement*. New York: Basic.

Cummins, M.S. & Suomi, S.J. (1976) Long-term effects of social rehabilitation in rhesus monkeys. *Primates*, 17, 43–51.

Curtiss, S. (1977) *Genie: A psycholinguistic study of a modern-day 'wild child'*. London: Academic Press.

Dacey, J.S. (1982) *Adolescents today* (2nd ed.). Glenview, Illinois: Scott, Foresman & Co.

Dallos, R. & Cullen, C. (1990) Clinical psychology. In I. Roth (Ed.), *Introduction to psychology, Vol. 2*. Hove, E.Sussex/Milton Keynes: Open University Press/Lawrence Erlbaum Associates Ltd.

Damon, W. & Hart, D. (1988) *Self-understanding in childhood and adolescence*. Cambridge: Cambridge University Press.

Danziger, K. (1971) *Socialization*. Harmondsworth, Middlesex: Penguin.

Darley, J.M. (1991) Altruism and prosocial behaviour research: Reflections and prospects. In M.S. Clark (Ed.), *Prosocial behaviour, review of personality and social psychology, 12*. Newbury Park, California: Sage Publications.

Darley, J.M. & Batson, C.D. (1973) From Jerusalem to Jericho: A study of situational and dispositional variables in helping behaviour. *Journal of Personality and Social Psychology*, 27, 100–8.

Darley, J.M. & Huff, C.W. (1990) Heightened damage assessment as a result of the intentionality of the damage-causing act. *British Journal of Social Psychology*, 29 (2), 181–8.

Darley, J.M. & Latané, B. (1968) Bystander intervention in emergencies: Diffusion of responsibility. *Journal of Personality and Social Psychology*, 8, 377–83.

Darwin, C.R (1859) *The origin of species by means of natural selection*. London: John Murray.

Darwin, C. R. (1972) *The expression of the emotions in animal and man*. London: John Murray.

Dasen, P.R. (1977) *Piagetian psychology: Cross-cultural contributions*. New York: Gardner Press.

Dasen, P.R. (1994) Culture and cognitive development from a Piagetian perspective. In W.J. Lonner & R.S. Malpass (Eds.) *Psychology and culture*. Boston: Allyn & Bacon.

Dashiell, J.F. (1935) Experimental studies of the influence of social situations on the behaviour of individual human adults. In C. Murchison (Ed.) *Handbook of social psychology*. Worcester, Mass.: Clark University Press.

Davidson, A.R. & Jaccard, J. (1979) Variables that moderate the attitude–behaviour relation: Results of a longitudinal survey. *Journal of Personality and Social Psychology*, 37, 1364–76.

Davies, D.L. (1956) Psychiatric illness in those engaged to be married. *British Journal of Preventive and Social Medicine*, 10, 123–7.

Davies, E. & Furnham, A. (1986) The dieting and body shape concerns of adolescent females. *Journal of Child Psychology & Psychiatry* 27 (3) 417–28.

Davis, J.A. (1959) A formal interpretation of the theory of relative deprivation. *Sociometry*, 22, 280–96.

Davis, K. (1940) Extreme isolation of a child. *American Journal of Sociology*, 45, 554–65.

Davis, K. (1947) Final note on a case of extreme isolation. *American Journal of Sociology*, 52, 432–7.

Davison, G.C. & Neale, J.M. (1994) *Abnormal psychology* (6th ed.) New York: John Wiley & Sons.

Davidson, R.J. & Ekman, P. (1994) Afterword: What Are The Minimal Cognitive Prerequisites for Emotion. In P. Ekman & R.J. Davidson (Eds.) *The Nature of Emotion: Fundamental Questions*. New York: Oxford University Press.

Dawkins, M.S. (1980) The many faces of animal suffering. *New Scientist*, November 20.

Dawkins, M.S. (1990) From an animal's point of view: Motivation, fitness and animal welfare. *Behavioural and Brain Sciences*, 13, 1–9.

Dawkins, R. (1976) *The selfish gene*. Oxford: Oxford University Press.

de Bono, E. (1967) *The use of lateral thinking*. Harmondsworth, Middlesex: Penguin.

Deese, J. (1972) *Psychology as a science and art*. New York:

Harcourt Brace Jovanovich.

de Groot, A.D. (1965) *Thought and choice in chess*. The Hague: Mouton.

de Groot, A.D. (1966) Perception and memory versus thought: Some old ideas and recent findings. In B. Kleinmuntz (Ed.) *Problem solving: Research, method and theory*. New York: Wiley.

Dement, W. (1960) The effect of dream deprivation. *Science, 131*, 1705–7.

Dement, W. (1972) *Some must watch while some must sleep*. Stanford, California: Stanford Alumni Association.

Dement, W. & Kleitman, N. (1957) The relation of eye movements during sleep to dream activity: An objective method for the study of dreaming. *Journal of Experimental Psychology, 53* (5), 339–46.

Denker, R. (1946) Results of treatment of psychoneuroses by the general practitioner. A follow-up study of 500 cases. *New York State Journal of Medicine, 46*, 356–64.

Denmark, F., Russo, N.F., Frieze, I.H. & Sechzer, J.A. (1988) Guidelines for avoiding sexism in psychological research: A report of the *ad hoc* committee on non-sexist research. *American Psychologist, 43* (7), 582–5.

Dennis, W. (1960) Causes of retardation among institutional children: Iran. *Journal of Genetic Psychology, 96*, 47–59.

Denzin, N.K. (1995) Symbolic interactionism. In J.A. Smith, R. Harré, & L.V. Langenhove (Eds.) *Rethinking psychology*. London: Sage.

Department of Health and Social Security (1983) *Mental Health Act, 1983*. London: HMSO.

Deregowski, J. (1968) Pictorial recognition in subjects from a relatively pictureless environment. *African Social Research, 5*, 356–64.

Deregowski, J. (1969) Preference for chain-type drawings in Zambian domestic servants and primary school children. *Psychologia Africana, 82*, 9–13.

Deregowski, J. (1970) A note on the possible determinants of split representation as an artistic style. *International Journal of Psychology, 5*, 21–6.

Deregowski, J. (1972) Pictorial perception and culture. *Scientific American, 227*, 82–8.

Deregowski, J., Muldrow, E.S. & Muldrow, W.F. (1972) Pictorial recognition in a remote Ethiopian population. *Perception, 1*, 417–25.

Dermer, M. & Thiel, D.L. (1975) When beauty may fail. *Journal of Personality and Social Psychology, 31*, 1168–76.

Deutsch, J.A. & Deutsch, D. (1963) Attention: Some theoretical considerations. *Psychological Review, 70*, 80–90.

Deutsch, M. & Collins, M.E. (1951) *Interracial housing: A psychological evaluation of a social experiment*. Minneapolis, Minnesota: University of Minnesota Press.

Deutsch, M. & Gerard, H.B. (1955) A study of normative and informational social influences upon individual judgement. *Journal of Abnormal and Social Psychology, 51*, 629–36.

de Villiers, P.A. & de Villiers, J.G. (1979) *Early language*. Cambridge, Massachusetts: Harvard University Press.

Devine, P.G. (1989) Stereotypes and prejudice: Their automatic and controlled components. *Journal of Personality & Social Psychology, 56*, 5–18.

Devine, P.G. & Zuwerink, J.R. (1994) Prejudice and guilt: The internal struggle to control prejudice. In W.J. Lonner & R.S.Malpass (Eds.) *Psychology and culture*. Boston: Allyn & Bacon.

Devlin Report (1976) Report to the Secretary of State for the Home Department of the Departmental Committee on Evidence of Identification in Criminal Cases. London: HMSO.

Dewey, J. (1922) *Human nature and conduct: An introduction to social psychology*. New York: Modern Library (1957).

Diagram Group (1982) *The brain – a user's manual*. New York: G.P. Putnams & Son.

Diamond, M. (1978) Sexual identity and sex roles. *The Humanist, March/April*.

Diamond, M. (1982) Sexual identity, monozygotic twins reared in discordant sex roles and a BBC follow-up. *Archives of Sexual Behaviour, 11*, 181–6.

Dicara, L.V. & Miller, N.E. (1968) Changes in heart rate instrumentally learned by curarised rats as avoidance responses. *Journal of Comparative and Physiological Psychology, 65*, 8–12.

Diener, E., Fraser, S.C., Beaman, A.L. & Kelem, R.T. (1976) Effects of deindividuation variables on stealing among Halloween trick-or-treaters. *Journal of Personality & Social Psychology, 33*, 178–83.

Dietch, J.T. (1995) Old Age. In D. Wedding (Ed.) *Behaviour and Medicine* (2nd ed.). St. Louis, MO: Mosby-Year Book.

Dion, K.K. (1972) Physical attractiveness and evaluation of children's transgressions. *Journal of Personality and Social Psychology, 24*, 207–13.

Dion, K.K. & Berscheid, E. (1974) Physical attractiveness and peer perception among children. *Sociometry, 37*, 1–12.

Dion, K.K., Berscheid, E. & Walster, E. (1972) What is beautiful is good. *Journal of Personality and Social Psychology, 24*, 285–90.

Dion, K.K. & Dion, K.L. (1995) On the love of beauty and the beauty of love: Two psychologists study attraction. In G.G. Brannigan & M.R. Merrens (Eds.) *The social psychologists: research adventures*. New York: McGraw-Hill.

Dixon, N.F. (1971) *Subliminal perception: The nature of the controversy*. London: McGraw Hill.

Dixon, N.F. (1981) *Preconscious processing*. London: Wiley.

Dodwell, P.C. (1995) Fundamental processes in vision. In R.L. Gregory & A.M. Colman (Eds.) *Sensation and perception*. London: Longman.

Dollard, J. & Miller, N.E. (1950) *Personality and psychotherapy*. New York: McGraw Hill.

Dollard, J., Doob, L.W., Miller, N.E., Mowrer, O.H. & Sears, R.R. (1939) *Frustration and aggression*. New Haven, Connecticut: Harvard University Press.

Donaldson, M. (1978) *Childrens' minds*. London: Fontana.

Donaldson, M. & McGarrigle, J.(1974) Some clues to the nature of semantic development. *Journal of Child Language, 1*, 185–94.

Donaldson, M. & Wales, R.J. (1970) On the acquisition of some relational terms. In J.R. Hayes (Ed.), *Cognition and the development of language*. New York: Wiley.

Donovan, A., Oddy, M., Pardoe, R. & Ades, A. (1986) Employment status and psychological well-being: A longitudinal study of 16-year-old school leavers. *Journal of Child Psychology and Psychiatry, 27(1)*, 65–76.

Dorner, G. (1976) *Hormones and brain differentiation*. Amsterdam: Elsevier.

Douvan, E.A. & Adelson, J. (1966) *The adolescent experience*. New York: Wiley.

Dovidio, J.F. (1995) With a little help from my friends. In G.G. Brannigan & M.R. Merrens (Eds.) *The social psychologists: research adventures*. New York: McGraw-Hill.

Dovidio, J.F., Piliavin, J.A., Gaertner, S.L., Schroeder, D.A. & Clark, R.D. (1991) The arousal: Cost–reward model and the process of intervention. In M.S. Clark (Ed.), *Prosocial behaviour: Review of personality and social psychology, 12*. Newbury Park, California: Sage Publications.

Downing, D. (1988) *Day-light robbery*. London: Arrow Books.

Drabman, R.S. & Thomas, M.H. (1974) Does media violence increase children's toleration of real-life aggression? *Developmental Psychology*, *10*, 418–21.

Draguns,. J. (1980) Psycological disorders of clinical severity. In H.C. Triandis & J. Draguns (Eds.) *Handbook of cross-cultural psychology:* Vol. 6. Psychopathology. Boston: Allyn & Bacon.

Draguns, J. (1990) Applications of cross-cultural psychology in the field of mental health. In R. Brislin (Ed.) *Applied cross-cultural psychology*. Newbury Park, CA: Sage.

Dryden, W. (1984) Therapeutic arenas. In W. Dryden (Ed.), *Individual therapy in Britain*. London: Harper & Row.

Duchenne, P. (1990) Using biofeedback for childbirth pain. *Nursing Times, 86 (25),* 56.

Duck, S. (Ed.) (1982) *Personal relationships 4: dissolving personal relationships*. London: Academic Press.

Duck, S. (1988) *Relating to others*. Milton Keynes: Open University Press.

Duck, S. (1992) *Human relationships* (2nd ed.). London: Sage.

Duncan, H.F., Gourlay, N. & Hudson, W. (1973) *A study of pictorial perception among Bantu and white primary school children in South Africa*. Johannesburg: Witwatersrand University Press.

Duncan, J. (1979) Divided attention: The whole is more than the sum of its parts. *Journal of Experimental Psychology: Human Perception, 5*, 216–28.

Duncan, S.L. (1976) Differential social perception and attribution of intergroup violence: Testing the lower limits of stereotyping of blacks. *Journal of Personality and Social Psychology, 34*, 590–8.

Duncker, K. (1926) A qualitative (experimental and theoretical) study of productive thinking (solving of comprehensible problems). *Journal of Genetic Psychology, 68*, 97–116.

Duncker. K. (1939) The influence of past experience upon perceptual properties. *American Journal of Psychology, 52*, 255–65.

Duncker, K. (1945) On problem solving. *Psychological Monographs, 58* (Whole No. 270).

Durkin, K. (1985) *Television, sex roles and children*. Milton Keynes: Open University Press.

Durkin, K. (1995) *Developmental social psychology: From infancy to old age*. Oxford: Blackwell.

Dutton, D.C. & Aron, A.P. (1974) Some evidence for heightened sexual attraction under conditions of high anxiety. *Journal of Personality and Social Psychology, 30*, 510–17.

Dutton, D.C. & Aron, A.P. (1989) Romantic attraction and generalized liking for others who are sources of conflict-based arousal. *Canadian Journal of Behavioural Science*, 21, 246–57.

Dworetzky, J.P. (1981) *Introduction to child development*. St Paul, Minnesota: West Publishing Co.

Eagly, A.H. (1983) Gender and social influence: a social psychological analysis. *American Psychologist*, September.

Eagly, A.H. (1987) *Sex differences in social behaviour: A social-role interpretation*. London: Lawrence Erlbaum Associates Ltd.

Eagly, A.H. & Carli, L.L. (1981) Sex of researchers and sex-typed communication as determinants of sex differences in influencability: a meta-analysis of social influence studies. *Psychological Bulletin, 90*, 1–20.

Eagly, A.H. & Crowley, M. (1986) Gender and helping behaviour: A meta-analytic review of the social psychological literature. *Psychological Bulletin, 100*, 282–308.

Eaton, N. (1991) Expert systems in nursing. *Nursing Standard, 5* (38), 32–5.

Ebbinghaus, H. (1885) *On memory*. Leipzig: Duncker.

Eckensberger, L.H. (1994) Moral development and its measurement across cultures. In W.J. Lonner & R.S.Malpass (Eds.) *Psychology and Culture*. Boston: Allyn & Bacon.

Edley, N. & Wetherell, M. (1995) *Men in perspective: Practice, power and identity*. Hemel Hempstead: Prentice Hall/Harvester Wheatsheaf.

Edwards, D. & Potter, J. (1992) *Discursive psychology*. London: Sage.

Efran, M.G. (1974) The effect of physical appearance on the judgement of guilt, interpersonal attraction and severity of recommended punishment in a simulated jury task. *Journal of Experimental Research in Personality, 8*, 45–54.

Eimas, P.D. (1975) Speech perception in early infancy. In L.B. Cohen & P. Salapatek (Eds.), *Infant perception: From sensation to cognition, Vol. 2*. New York: Academic Press.

Eisenberg, N. (1982) The development of reasoning regarding prosocial behaviour. In N. Eisenberg (Ed.) *The development of prosocial behaviour*. New York: Academic Press.

Eisenberg, N. (1986) *Altruistic emotion, cognition and behaviour*. Hillsdale, NJ: Erlbaum.

Eisenberg, N., Miller, P., Shell, R., McNally, S. & Shea, C. (1991) Prosocial development in adolescence: A longitudinal study. *Developmental Psychology, 27*, 849–57.

Eisenberg, N., Shell, R. Pasternack, J., Lennon, R. , Beller, R. & Mathy, R.M. (1987) Prosocial development in middle childhood: A longitudinal study. *Developmental Psychology, 23*, 712–18.

Eiser, J.R. (1994) *Attitudes, chaos and the connectionist mind* Oxford: Blackwell.

Eiser, J.R. & van der Pligt, J. (1988) *Attitudes and decisions*. London: Routledge.

Ekman, P. (1994) All emotions are basic. In P. Ekman & R.J. Davidson (Eds.) *The nature of emotion: Fundamental questions*. New York: Oxford University Press.

Ekman, P. & Friesen, W.V. (1975) *Unmasking the face*. Englewood Cliffs, NJ: Prentice-Hall.

Ekman, P., Friesen, W.V. & Ellsworth, P. (1972) *Emotion in the human face: Guidelines for research and an integration of findings*. New York: Pergamon.

Ekman, P., Friesen, W.V. & Simons, R.C. (1985) Is the startle reaction an emotion? *Journal of Personality and Social Psychology, 49*, 1416–26.

Elkind. D. (1967) Egocentrism in adolescence. *Child Development*, 38, 1025–1034.

Elkind, D. (1970) Erik Erikson's eight ages of man. *New York Times Magazine, April 5*.

Elkind, D. (1971) *Children and adolescents: Interpretative essays on Jean Piaget*. New York: Oxford University Press.

Elkind, D. (1976) *Child development and education: A Piagetian perspective*. New York: Oxford University Press.

Elliot, C. D., Murray, D.J. & Pearson, L.S. (1979) *British ability scales*. Slough: National Foundation for Educational Research.

Ellis, A. (1962) *Reason and emotion in psychotherapy*. Secausus, New Jersey: Lyle Stuart.

Ellis, A. (1973) *Humanistic psychotherapy*. New York: McGraw Hill.

Ellsworth , P.C. (1994) Levels of thought and levels of emotion. In P. Ekman & R.J. Davidson (Eds.) *The nature of emotion: Fundamental questions*. New York: Oxford University Press.

Elms, A.C. (1976) *Attitudes*. Milton Keynes: Open University Press.

Emmelkamp, P.M.G. (1982) *Phobic and obsessive–compulsive disorders*. New York: Plenum.

Emmelkamp, P.M.G. & Wessels, H. (1975) Flooding in imagination versus flooding in vivo: A comparison with agoraphobics.

Behaviour Research and Therapy, 13, 7–15.

Empson, J. (1989) *Sleep and dreaming*. London: Faber & Faber.

Empson, J. (1993) *Sleep and dreaming* (2nd, revised ed.) Hemel Hempstead: Harvester Wheatsheaf.

Endicott, J. & Spitzer, R.L. (1978) A diagnostic interview: The schedule for affective disorders and schizophrenia. Archives of General Psychiatry, *35*, 837–44.

Engel, G. (1962) *Psychological development in health and Disease*. Philadelphia: Saunders.

Erdelyi, M.H. (1974) A new look at the new look: Perceptual defence and vigilance. *Psychological Review, 81*, 1–24.

Erikson, E.H. (1950) *Childhood and society*.New York: Norton.

Erikson, E.H. (1963) *Childhood and society*.(2nd ed.) New York: Norton.

Erikson, E.H. (1964) *Insight and responsibility* London: Faber.

Erikson, E.H. (1968) *Identity: Youth and crisis*. New York: Norton.

Erikson, E.H. (1977) *Toys and reasons: Stages in the ritualization of experience*. London: Marion Boyars.

Erikson, E.H. (1980) *Identity and the life cycle*. New York: Norton.

Erikson, M. (1968) The inhumanity of ordinary people. *International Journal of Psychiatry, 6*, 278–9.

Erlenmeyer-Kimling, L. & Jarvik, L.F. (1963) Genetics and intelligence: A review. *Science, 142*, 1477–9.

Esterson, A. (1993) *Seductive mirage: An exploration of the work of Sigmund Freud*. Chicago and La Salle, Ill.: Open Court.

Estes, W.K. (1970) *Learning theory and mental development*. New York: Academic Press.

Etzioni, A. (1968) A model of significant research. *International Journal of Psychiatry, 6*, 279–80.

Evans, P. (1975) *Motivation*. London: Methuen.

Evans, P. (1980) Ethiological studies I and II, In J. Radford & E. Govier (Eds.), *A textbook of psychology*. London: Sheldon Press.

Evans, P.D. (1990) Type A behaviour and coronary heart disease: When will the jury return? *British Journal of Psychology, 81* (2), 147–57.

Eysenck, H.J. (1952) The effects of psychotherapy: An evaluation. *Journal of Consulting Psychology, 16*, 319–24.

Eysenck, H.J. (1954) *The psychology of politics*. London: Routledge & Kegan Paul.

Eysenck, H. J. (1965) *Fact and fiction in psychology* Harmondsworth: Penguin.

Eysenck, H. J. (1967) *The biological basis of personality*. Springfield, Ill.: C.C. Thomas.

Eysenck, H.J. (1970) *Crime and personality*. London: Paladin.

Eysenck, H.J. (1971) *Race, intelligence and education*. London: Temple-Smith.

Eysenck, H.J. (1973) Personality and the maintenance of the smoking habit. In W. Dunn (Ed.) *Smoking Behaviour*. Washington , DC: Winston.

Eysenck, H.J. (1974) Crime and personality reconsidered. *Bulletin of the British Psychological Society, 27*, 23–4.

Eysenck, H.J. (1976) The learning theory model of neurosis: A new approach. *Behaviour Research and Therapy, 14*, 251–67.

Eysenck, H.J. (1980) The biosocial model of man and the unification of psychology. In A.J.Chapman & D.M. Jones (Eds.) *Models of man*. Leicester: British Psychological Society.

Eysenck, H.J. (1985) *Decline and fall of the Freudian empire*. Harmondsworth: Penguin.

Eysenck, H.J. (1992) The outcome problem in psychotherapy. In W. Dryden & C. Feltham (Eds.) *Psychotherapy and its Discontents*. Buckingham: Open University Press.

Eysenck, H.J. (1995) Trait Theories of Personality. In S.E. Hampson & A.M. Colman (Eds.) *Individual differences and personality*. London: Longman.

Eysenck,H.J. & Eysenck, S.B.G. (1969) *Personality structure and measurement*. London: Routledge & Kegan Paul.

Eysenck, H.J. & Eysenck, S.B.G. (1975) *Manual of the Eysenck personality questionnaire*. London: Hodder & Stoughton.

Eysenck, H.J. & Eysenck, M.W. (1985) *Personality and individual differences: A natural science approach*. New York: Plenum.

Eysenck, H.J. & Rachman, S. (1965) *The cause and cure of neurosis*. London: Routledge & Kegan Paul.

Eysenck, H.J. & Wilson, G.D. (Eds.), (1973) *The experimental study of Freudian theories*. London: Methuen.

Eysenck, M.W. (1979) Depth, elaboration and distinctiveness. In L.S. Cermak & F.I.M. Craik (Eds.), *Levels of processing in human memory*. Hillsdale, New Jersey: Lawrence Erlbaum Associates Inc.

Eysenck, M.W. (1984) *A handbook of cognitive psychology*. London: Lawrence Erlbaum Associates Ltd.

Eysenck, M.W. (1986) Working memory. In G. Cohen, M.W. Eysenck & M.A. Le Voi, *Memory: A cognitive approach*. Milton Keynes: Open University Press.

Eysenck, M.W. & Eysenck, H. J.(1980) Mischel and the concept of personality. *British Journal of Psychology, 71*, 191–204.

Eysenck, M.W. & Eysenck, M.C. (1980) Effects of processing depth, distinctiveness and word frequency on retention. *British Journal of Psychology, 71*, 263–74.

Eysenck, M.W. & Keane, M.J. (1990) *Cognitive psychology: A Student's Handbook*. Hove, East Sussex: Lawrence Erlbaum Associates Ltd.

Eysenck, M.W. & Keane, M.J. (1995) *Cognitive psychology: A Student's Handbook* (2nd. ed). Hove: Lawrence Erlbaum Associates.

Fairbairn, G. & Fairbairn, S. (1987) Introduction: Psychology, ethics and change. In S. Fairbairn & G. Fairbairn (Eds.), *Psychology, ethics and change*. London: Routledge & Kegan Paul.

Falek, A. & Moser, H.M. (1975) Classification on schizophrenia. *Archives of General Psychiatry* 32 59–67.

Fancher, R.E. (1979) *Pioneers of psychology: Studies of the great figures who paved the way for the contemporary science of behaviour*. New York: Norton.

Fantz, R.L. (1961) The origin of form perception. *Scientific American, 204* (5), 66–72.

Faraday, A. (1973) *Dream power*. London: Pan Books.

Faris, J.C. (1972) *Nuba personal art*. London: Temple Smith.

Fazio, R.H. (1986) How do attitudes guide behaviour ? In R.M. Sorrentino & E.T. Higgins (Eds.) *Handbook of motivation and cognition: Foundations of social behaviour*. New York: Guilford.

Fazio, R.H. & Zanna, M.D. (1978) Attitudinal qualities relating to the strength of the attitude-behaviour relation. *Journal of Experimental Social Psychology* 14, 398–408.

Fazio, R.H. & Zanna, M.D. (1981) Direct experience and attitude-behaviour consistency. In L. Berkowitz (Ed.), *Advances in experimental social psychology, Vol. 14*. New York: Academic Press.

Fazio, R.H., Zanna, M.P. & Cooper, J. (1977) Dissonance and self-perception: An integrative view of each theory's major domain of application. *Journal of Experimental and Social Psychology, 13*, 464–79.

Feighner, J.P., Robins, E., Guze, S.B., Woodruff, R.A., Winokur, G. & Munz, R. (1972) Diagnostic criteria for use in psychiatric research. *Archives of General Psychiatry, 26*, 57–63.

Felipe, N.J. & Sommer, R. (1966) Invasion of personal space. *Social Problems*, *14*, 206–14.

Fernando, S. (1991) *Mental health, race and culture*. London: Macmillan, in conjunction with MIND Publications.

Ferster, C.B. & Skinner, B.F. (1957) *Schedules of reinforcement*. New York: Appleton-Century-Crofts.

Feshbach, S. (1964) The function of aggression and the regulation of aggressive drive. *Psychological Review*, *71*, 257–72.

Festinger, L. (1954) A theory of social comparison processes. *Human Relations*, *7*, 117–40.

Festinger, L. (1957) *A theory of cognitive dissonance*. New York: Harper & Row.

Festinger, L. & Carlsmith, J.M. (1959) Cognitive consequences of forced compliance. *Journal of Abnormal and Social Psychology*, *58*, 203–10.

Festinger, L., Schachter, S. & Back, K. (1950) *Social pressures in informal groups: A study of human factors in housing*. Stanford, California: Stanford University Press.

Fielder, F.E. (1965) A contingency model of leadership effectiveness. In L. Berkowitz (Ed.) *Advances in experimental social psychology*, vol 1. New York: Academic Press.

Fiedler, F.E. (1967) *A theory of leadership effectiveness*. New York: McGraw Hill.

Fiedler, F.E. (1968) Personality and situational determinants of leadership effectiveness. In D. Cartwright & A. Zander (Eds.), *Group dynamics*. New York: Harper & Row.

Fiedler, F.E. (1971) Validation and extension of the contingency model of leadership effectiveness: A review of empirical findings. *Psychological Bulletin*, *76*, 128–48.

Fiedler, F.E. (1972) Personality motivational systems and the behaviour of high and low LPC. *Human Relations*, *25*, 391–2.

Fielder, F.E. (1981) Leadership effectiveness. *American Behavioural Scientist*, *24*, 619–32.

Fishbein, H.D. (1984) *The psychology of infancy and childhood-evolutionary and cross-cultural perspectives*. Hillsdale, New Jersey: Lawrence Erlbaum Associates Inc.

Fishbein, M & Ajzen, I. (1974) Attitudes towards objects as predictors of single and multiple behavioural criteria. *Psychological Review*, *81*, 59–74.

Fishbein, M. & Ajzen, I. (1975) *Belief, attitude, intention and behaviour: An introduction to theory and research*. Reading, MA: Addison-Wesley.

Fisher, S. (1978) Dirt-anality and attitudes towards negros. A test of Kubie's hypothesis. *Journal of Nervous and Mental Disease*, *166*, 280–91.

Fisher, S. & Greenberg, R.P. (1977) *The scientific credibility of Freud's theories and therapy*. New York: Basic Books.

Fiske, S.T. & Neuberg, S.L. (1980) A continuum of impression formation, from category-based to individuating processes: influences of information and motivation on attention and interpretation. In L. Berkowitz (Ed.) *Advances in experimental social psychology*, vol. 23. New York: Academic Press.

Fiske, S.T. & Taylor, S.E. (1991) *Social cognition*.(2nd ed.). New York: McGraw-Hill.

Flanagan, O.J. (1984) *The science of the mind*. London: MIT Press.

Flavell, J.H. (1971) First discussant's comments: What is memory development the development of? *Human Development*, *14*, 272–8.

Flavell, J.H. (1977) *Cognitive development*. Englewood Cliffs, New Jersey: Prentice-Hall.

Fleischman, E.A. (1973) Twenty years of consideration and structure. In E.A. Fleischman & J.F. Hunt (Eds.) *Current developments in the study of leadership*. Carbondale, IL: South Illinois University Press.

Fodor, J.A. (1983) *The modularity of mind*. Cambridge, Massachusetts: MIT Press.

Fodor, J.A. & Pylyshyn, Z.W. (1981) How direct is visual perception? Some reflections on Gibson's 'ecological approach'. *Cognition*, *9*, 139–96.

Fodor, J.A. & Pylyshyn, Z.W. (1988) Connectionism and cognitive architecture: A critical analysis. *Cognition*, *28*, 3–71.

Fogelman, K. (1976) *Britain's sixteen-year-olds*. London: National Children's Bureau.

Fonagy, P. (1981) Research on psychoanalytic concepts. In F. Fransella, (Ed.), *Personality – theory, measurement and research*. London: Methuen.

Fonagy, P. (1995) Psychoanalysis. In A.M. Colman (Ed.) *Applications of psychology*. London:Longman.

Fonagy, P. & Higgitt, A. (1984) *Personality, theory and clinical practice*. London: Methuen.

Fontana, D. (1981a) Play. In D. Fontana (Ed.) *Psychology for teachers* London: British Psychologucal Society/ Macmillan Press.

Fontana, D. (1981b) Intelligence. In D. Fontana (Ed.), *Psychology for Teachers*. London: British Psychological Society/Macmillan Press.

Fouts, R.S. (1973) Acquisition and testing of gestural signs in four young chimpanzees. *Science*, *180*, 978–80.

Foxx, R. & Azrin, N. (1973) *Toilet training the retarded*. Illinois: Research Press.

Frank, I.D. (1973) *Persuasion and healing* (2nd ed.). Baltimore: John Hopkins University Press.

Frank, I.D. (1989) Non-specific aspects of treatment: the view of a psychotherapist. In M. Shepherd & N. Sartorius (Eds.) *Non-specific aspects of treatment*. Toronto: Hans Huber.

Frankenhaeuser. F. (1975) Experimental approaches to the study of catecholamines and emotion. In L. Levi (Ed.) *Emotions: The parameters and measurement*. New York: Raven Press.

Frankenhaeuser, M. (1983) The sympathetic-adrenal and pituitary-adrenal response to challenge: Comparison between the sexes. In T.M. Dembroski, T.H. Schmidt & G. Blumchen (Eds.) *Behavioural bases of coronary heart disease*. Basel: S. Karger.

Fransella, F. (1970) ...And then there was one. In D. Bannister (Ed.) *Perspectives in personal construct theory*. London: Academic Press.

Fransella, F. (1972) *Personal change and reconstruction: Research on a treatment of stuttering*. London: Academic Press.

Fransella, F. (1975) *Need to change?* London: Methuen.

Fransella, F. (1981) Personal construct psychology and repertory grid technique. In F. Fransella (Ed.), *Personality–theory, measurement and research*. London: Methuen.

Fransella, F. (1984) Personal construct therapy. In W. Dryden (Ed.), *Individual therapy in Britain*. London: Harper & Row.

Freedman, A.M., Kaplan, H.I. & Sadock, B.J. (1975) *Comprehensive textbook of psychiatry*, vol. 2. Baltimore: Williams & Williams Co.

Freedman, J.L. (1963) Attidudinal effects of inadequate justification. *Journal of Personality*, *31*, 371–385.

Freedman, J.L. (1965) Long-term behavioural effects of cognitive dissonance. *Journal of Experimental & Social Psychology*, *1*, 145–55.

Freeman, W. & Watts, J.W. (1942) *Psychosurgery*. Springfield, ILL.: Thomas.

French, J.R.P. & Raven, B.H. (1959) The bases of social power. In D. Cartwright (Ed.) *Studies in social power*. Ann Arboiur, MI: Institute for Social Research, University of Michigan.

Friedman, M. & Rosenman, R.H. (1974) *Type A behaviour and*

your heart. New York: Knopf.

Freud, A. (1936) *The ego and the mechanisms of defence*. London: Chatto & Windus.

Freud, A. & Dann, S. (1951) An experiment in group upbringing. *Psychoanalytic Study of the Child*, *6*, 127–68.

Freud, S. (1926) Inhibitions, symptoms and anxiety. In *Standard edition of the complete psychological works of Sigmund Freud*. London: Hogarth Press.

Freud, S. (1933) *New introductory lectures on psychoanalysis*. London: Hogarth Press.

Freud, S. (1976a) *The interpretation of dreams*. Pelican Freud Library (4) Harmondsworth, Middlesex: Penguin. (Original work published 1900).

Freud, S. (1976b) *The psychopathology of everyday life*. Pelican Freud Library (5) Harmondsworth, Middlesex: Penguin. (Original work published 1901).

Freud, S. (1977a) *Three essays on the theory of sexuality*. Pelican Freud Library (7) Harmondsworth, Middlesex: Penguin. (Original work published 1905).

Freud, S. (1977b) *Analysis of a phobia in a five-year-old boy*. Pelican Freud Library (8) Harmondsworth, Middlesex: Penguin. (Original work published 1909).

Freud, S. (1984) *Beyond the pleasure principle*. Pelican Freud Library (11) Harmondsworth, Middlesex: Penguin. (Original work published 1920).

Freud, S. (1984) *The ego and the id*. Pelican Freud Library (11) Harmondsworth, Middlesex: Penguin. (Original work published 1923.)

Frijda, N.H. (1994) Varieties of Affect: Emotions and Episodes, moods, and sentiments. In P. Ekman & R. J. Davidson (Eds.) *The nature of emotion: Fundamental questions*. New York: Oxford University Press.

Frisby, J.P. (1986) The computational approach to vision. In I. Roth & J.P. Frisby (Eds.), *Perception and representation*. Milton Keynes: Open University Press.

Frith, C. & Cahill, C. (1995) Psychotic disorders: Schizophrenia, affective psychoses and paranoia. In A.A. Lazarus & A.M. Colman (Eds.) *Abnormal psychology*. London: Longman.

Fromant, S. (1988) Helping each other. *Nursing Times*, 84(36), 30–2.

Fromm, E. (1941) *Escape from freedom*. New York: Farrar & Rhinehart.

Fromm, E. (1962) *The art of loving*. London: Unwin Books.

Fromm, E. (1970) *The crisis of psychoanalysis – Essays on Freud, Marx and social psychology*. Harmondsworth, Middlesex: Penguin.

Fromm, E. (1977) *The anatomy of human destructiveness*. Harmondsworth, Middlesex: Penguin.

Frueh, T. & McGhee, P.E. (1975) Traditional sex-role development and amount of time spent watching television. *Developmental Psychology*, *11*, 109.

Furth, H.G. (1966) *Thinking without language*. New York: Free Press.

Gaertner, S.L. & Dovidio, J.F. (1977) The subtlety of white racism, arousal, and helping. *Journal of Personality & Social Psychology*, *35*, 691–707.

Gaertner, S.L. & Dovidio, J.F. (1986) The aversive form of racism. In J.F. Dovidio & S.L. Gaertner (Eds.) *Prejudice, discrimination and racism*. Orlando, FL: Academic Press.

Gagné, R.M. (1970) *The conditions of learning* (2nd ed.). New York: Holt, Rinehart & Winston.

Gagné, R.M. (1974) *Essentials of learning for instruction*. New York: Dryden Press.

Gahagan, J. (1975) *Interpersonal and group behaviour*. London: Methuen.

Gahagan, J. (1984) *Social interaction and its management*. London: Methuen.

Gahagan, J. (1991) Understanding other people; understanding self. In J. Radford & E. Govier (Eds.) *A textbook of psychology* (2nd ed.) London: Routledge.

Gale, A. (1990) *Thinking about psychology?* (2nd ed.) Leicester: British Psychological Society.

Gale, A. (1995) Ethical issues in psychological research. In A.M. Colman (Ed.) *Psychological research methods and statistics*. London: Longman.

Galin, D. (1974) Implication for psychiatry of left and right cerebral specialization. *Archives of General Psychiatry*, *31*, 572–83.

Gallup, G.G. (1977) Self-recognition in primates. *American Psychologist*, *32*, 329–38.

Garber, H.L. (1988) *The Milwaukee Project; preventing mental retardation in children at risk*. Washington, D.C.: American Association on Mental Retardation.

Garcia, J. & Koelling, R.A. (1966) Relation of cue to consequence in avoidance learning. *Psychonomic Science*, *4*, 123–4.

Garcia, J., Ervin, F.R. & Koelling, R. (1966) Learning with prolonged delay of reinforcement. *Psychonomic Science*, *5* (3), 121–2.

Gardner, B.T. & Gardner, R.A. (1971) Two-way communication with an infant chimpanzee. In A. Schrier & F. Stollitz (Eds.), *Behaviour of non-human primates, Vol. 4*. New York: Academic Press.

Gardner, B.T. & Gardner, R.A. (1975) Evidence for sentence constituents in the early utterances of child and chimp. *Journal of Experimental Psychology: General*, *104*, 244–67.

Gardner, B.T. & Gardner, R.A. (1980) Two comparative psychologists look at language acquisition. In K. Nelson (Ed.), *Children's language, Vol. 2*. New York: Gardner Press.

Gardner, H. (1983) *Frames of mind: The theory of multiple intelligence*. New York: Basic Books.

Gardner, H. (1985) *The mind's new science*. New York: Basic Books.

Gardner, H. (1987) Epilogue: Cognitive science after 1984. In Gardner, H. (1985), *The mind's new science*. New York: Basic Books.

Gardner, R.A. & Gardner, B.T. (1969) Teaching sign language to a chimpanzee. *Science*, *165* (3894), 664–72.

Gardner, R.A. & Gardner, B.T. (1978) Comparative psychology and language acquisition. *Psychology: The state of the art. Annals of the New York Academy of Sciences*, *309*, 37–76.

Garfield, S. (1992) Response to Hans Eysenck. In W. Dryden & C. Feltham (Eds.) *Psychotherapy and its discontents*. Buckingham: Open University Press.

Garland, C. & White, S. (1980) *Children and day nurseries*. London: Grant McIntyre.

Garnham, A. (1988) *Artificial intelligence: An introduction*. London: Routledge, Kegan Paul.

Garnham, A. (1991) *The mind in action*. London: Routledge.

Garvey, C. (1977) *Play*. London: Fontana/Open Books.

Gatchel, R.J. (1995) Stress and coping. In B. Parkinson & A.M. Colman (Eds.) *Emotion and motivation*. London: Longman.

Gauker, C. (1990) How to learn a language like a chimpanzee. *Philosophical Psychology*, *3* (1), 31–53.

Gaze, H. (1988) Stressed to the limit. *Nursing Times, 84 (36)*, 16–17.

Gazzaniga, M.S. (1985) *The social brain: Discovering the networks of the mind*. New York: Basic Books.

Geen, R.G. (1990) *Human aggression*. Milton Keynes: Open University Press.

Geen, R.G. (1995) Social motivation. In B. Parkinson & A.M.

Colman (Eds.) *Emotion and motivation*. London: Longman.

Gelder, M., Gath, D. & Mayon, R. (1989) *Oxford textbook of psychiatry* (2nd ed.). Oxford: Oxford University Press.

Gerard, H.B., Wilhelmy, R.A. & Connolly, E.S. (1968) Conformity and group size. *Journal of Personality and Social Psychology, 8*, 79–82.

Gerbner, G. (1972) Violence in television drama: Trends and symbolic functions. In G.A Comstock & E.A. Rubinstein (Eds.), *Television and social behaviour, Vol. 1, Media content and control*. Washington, DC: US Government Printing Office.

Gerbner, G. & Gross, L. (1976) Living with television: The violence profile. *Journal of Communication, 26*, 173–99.

Gergen, K.J. (1973) Social psychology as history. *Journal of Personality & Social Psychology, 26*, 309–20.

Gergen, K.J. & Gergen, M.M. (1981) *Social psychology*. New York: Harcourt Brace Jovanovich.

Gergen, K.J., Gergen, M.M. & Barton, W. (1973) Deviance in the dark. *Psychology Today, 7*, 129–30.

Gershon, E.S. & Rieder, R.O. (1992) Major disorders of mind and brain. *Scientific American, 267 (3)*, 88–95.

Gibson, E.J. & Walk, P.D. (1960) The visual cliff. *Scientific American, 202*, 64–71.

Gibson, J.J. (1950) *The perception of the visual world*. Boston: Houghton Mifflin.

Gibson, J.J. (1966) *The senses considered as perceptual systems*. Boston: Houghton Mifflin.

Gibson, J.J. (1979) *The ecological approach to visual perception*. Boston: Houghton Mifflin.

Gillham, W.E.C. (1975) Intelligence: The persistent myth. *New Behaviour, June 26*, 433–5.

Gillham, W.E.C. (1978) Measurement constructs and psychological structure: Psychometrics. In A. Burton & J. Radford (Eds.), *Thinking in perspective*. London: Methuen.

Gilligan, C. (1977) In a different voice: Womens' conceptions of self and morality. *Harvard Educational Review, 47*, 481–517.

Gilligan, C. (1982) *In a different voice: Psychological theory and womens' development*. Cambridge, Massachusetts: Harvard University Press.

Gilling, D. & Brightwell, R. (1982) *The human brain*. London: Orbis Publishing.

Gilmore, D.D. (1990) *Manhood in the making: Cultural concepts of masculinity*. New Haven: Yale University Press.

Ginsburg, H.P. (1981) Piaget and education: The contributions and limits of genetic epistemology. In K. Richardson & S. Sheldon (Eds.), *Cognitive development to adolescence*. Hove, E. Sussex/Milton Keynes: Lawrence Erlbaum/Open University.

Glanzer, M. & Cunitz, A.R. (1966) Two storage mechanisms in free recall. *Journal of Verbal Learning and Verbal Behaviour, 5*, 351–60.

Glanzer, M. & Meinzer, A. (1967) The effects of intralist activity on free recall. *Journal of Verbal Learning & Verbal Behaviour, 6*, 928–35.

Glassman, W.E. (1995) *Approaches to psychology* (2nd ed.). Buckingham: Open University Press.

Glueck, S. & Glueck, E.T. (1950) *Unravelling juvenile delinquency*. New York: Commonwealth Fund.

Godden, D. & Baddeley, A.D. (1975) Context-dependent memory in two natural environments: On land and under water. *British Journal of Psychology, 66*, 325–31.

Goetsch, V.L. & Fuller, M.G. (1995) Stress and stress management. In D. Wedding (Ed.) *Behaviour and medicine* (2nd ed.). St. Louis, MO: Mosby-Year Book.

Goffman, E. (1968) *Asylums – essays on the social situation of mental patients and other inmates*. Harmondsworth, Middlesex: Penguin.

Goffman, E. (1963) *Stigma – notes on the management of spoiled identity*. Englewood Cliffs, N.J.: Prentice-Hall.

Goffman, E. (1971) *The presentation of self in everyday life*. Harmondsworth, Middlesex: Penguin.

Goldfarb, W. (1943) The effects of early institutional care on adolescent personality. *Journal of Experimental Education, 12*, 106–29.

Goldfarb, W. (1945) Effects of psychological deprivation in infancy and subsequent stimulation. *American Journal of Psychiatry, 102*, 18–33.

Goldin-Meadow, S. & Feldman, H. (1977) The development of a language-like communication without a language model. *Science, 197*, 401–3.

Goldman, R.J. & Goldman, J.D.G. (1981) How children view old people and ageing: a developmental study of children in four countries. *Australian Journal of Psychology, 3*, 405–18.

Goldman-Eisler, F. (1948) Breast-feeding and character formation. *Journal of Personality, 17*, 83–103.

Goldman-Eisler, F. (1951) The problem of 'orality' and its origin in early childhood. *Journal of Mental Science, 97*, 765–82.

Goldwyn, E. (1979) The fight to be male. *Listener, May 24*, 709–12.

Golombok, S., Spencer, A. & Rutter, M. (1983) Children in lesbian and single-parent households: Psychosexual and psychiatric appraisal. *Journal of Child Psychology and Psychiatry, 24*, 551–72.

Gombrich, E.H. (1960) *Art and illusion*. London: Phaidon.

Goodall, J. (1978) Chimp killings: is it the man in them ? *Science News, 113*, 276.

Gordon, I.E. (1989) *Theories of visual perception*. Chichester: John Wiley & Sons.

Gottesman, I.I. & Shields, J. (1976) A critical review of recent adoption, twin and family studies of schizophrenia: Behavioural genetics perspectives. *Schizophrenia Bulletin, 2*, 360–98.

Gottesman, I.I. & Shields, J.(1982) *Schizophrenia: The epigenetic puzzle*. Cambridge: Cambridge University Press.

Gould, R.L. (1978) *Transformations: Growth and change in adult life*. New York: Simon & Schuster.

Gould, R.L. (1980) Transformational tasks in adulthood. In S.I. Greenspan & G.H. Pollock (Eds.), *The course of life: Psychoanalytic contributions toward understanding personality development, Vol. 3: Adulthood and the ageing process*. Washington DC: National Institution for Mental Health.

Gould, S.J. (1981) *The mismeasure of man*. Harmondsworth, Middlesex: Penguin.

Gouldner, A.W. (1960) The norm of reciprocity: a preliminary statement. *American Sociological Review, 25*, 161–78.

Graham, H. (1986) *The human face of psychology*. Milton Keynes: Open University Press.

Grasha, A.F. (1983) *Practical applications of psychology* (2nd ed.). Boston: Little, Brown & Co.

Gray, J. & Wedderburn, A. (1960) Grouping strategies with simultaneous stimuli. *Quarterly Journal of Experimental Psychology, 12*, 180–4.

Gray, J.A. (1971) *The psychology of fear and stress*. London: Weidenfeld & Nicolson.

Gray, J.A. (1975) *Elements of a two-process theory of learning*. London: Academic Press.

Gray, J.A. (1987) The ethics and politics of animal experimentation. In H. Beloff & A.M. Colman (Eds.), *Psychology Survey, No. 6*. Leicester: British Psychological Society.

Gray, J.A. (1991) On the morality of speciesism. *The Psychologist, 4 (5)*, 196–8.

Green, R. (1978) Sexual identity of 37 children raised by homosexual or transsexual parents. *American Journal of Psychiatry, 135*, 692–7.

Green, S. (1980) Physiological studies I and II. In J. Radford & E. Govier (Eds.), *A textbook of psychology*. London: Sheldon Press.

Green, S. (1994) *Principles of biopsychology*. Hove: Lawrence Erlbaum Associates.

Greene, J. (1975) *Thinking and language*. London: Methuen.

Greene, J. (1987) *Memory, thinking and language*. London: Methuen.

Greene, J. (1990) Perception. In I. Roth (Ed.), *Introduction to psychology, Vol. 2*. Milton Keynes/Hove: Open University/Lawrence Erlbaum Associates Ltd.

Greene, J. & Hicks, C. (1984) *Basic cognitive processes*. Milton Keynes: Open University Press.

Greenfield, P.M. & Smith, J.H. (1976) *The structure of communication in early language development*. New York: Academic Press.

Greer, A., Morris, T. & Pettingale, K.W. (1979) Psychological response to breast cancer: Effect on outcome. *Lancet, 13*, 785–7.

Gregor, A.J. & McPherson, D. (1965) A study of susceptibility to geometric illusions among cultural outgroups of Australian aborigines. *Psychologia Africana, 11*, 490–9.

Gregory, R.L. (1966) *Eye and brain*. London: Weidenfeld & Nicolson.

Gregory, R.L. (1970) *The intelligent eye*. London: Weidenfeld & Nicolson.

Gregory, R.L. (1972) Visual illusions. In B.M. Foss (Ed.), *New horizons in psychology, 1*. Harmondsworth, Middlesex: Penguin.

Gregory, R.L. (1980) Perceptions as hypotheses. *Philosophical Transactions of the Royal Society of London, Series B, 290*, 181–97.

Gregory, R.L. (1981) *Mind in science*. Harmondsworth, Middlesex: Penguin.

Gregory, R.L. (1983) Visual illusions. In J. Miller (Ed.), *States of mind*. London: BBC Publications.

Gregory, R.L. (1987) In defence of artificial intelligence –a reply to John Searle. In C. Blakemore & S. Greenfield (Eds.), *Mindwaves*. Oxford: Blackwell.

Gregory, R.L. & Wallace, J. (1963) *Recovery from early blindness*. Cambridge: Heffer.

Griffit, W. & Veitch, R. (1974) Pre-acquaintance attitude similarity and attraction revisited: Ten days in a fallout shelter. *Sociometry, 37*, 163–73.

Gross, A.E. & Crofton, C. (1977) What is good is beautiful. *Sociometry, 40*, 85–90.

Gross, R.D. (1994) *Key studies in psychology*.(2nd ed.) London: Hodder & Stoughton.

Gross, R. (1995) *Themes, issues and debates in psychology*. London: Hodder & Stoughton.

Guilford, J.P. (1959) Three faces of intellect. *American Psychologist, 14*, 469–79.

Guilford, J.P. (1967) *The nature of human intelligence*. New York: McGraw-Hill.

Guilford, J.P. (1982) Cognitive psychology's ambiguities: Some suggested remedies. *Psychological Review, 89*, 48–59.

Guiton, P. (1958) The effect of isolation on the following response of brown leghorn chicks. *Proceeding of the Royal Physical Society, Edinburgh, 27*, 9–14.

Guiton, P. (1966) Early experience and sexual object choice in the brown leghorn. *Animal Behaviour, 14*, 534–8.

Gunter, B. (1986) *Television and sex-role stereotyping*. London: IBA and John Libbey.

Gunter, B. & McAleer, J.L. (1990) *Children and television – the one-eyed monster?* London: Routledge.

Guntrip, H. (1968) *Schizoid phenomena: Object relations and the self*. London: Hogarth.

Guthrie, E.R. (1938) *Psychology of human conflict*. New York: Harper.

Hall, C.S. (1966) *The meaning of dreams*. New York: McGraw-Hill.

Hall, C.S. & Lindzey, G. (1957) *Theories of personality*. New York: Wiley.

Hall, C.S. & Nordby, V.J. (1973) *A primer of Jungian psychology*. New York: Mentor.

Hall, E.T. (1959) *The silent language*. New York: Doubleday.

Hall, E.T. (1966) *The hidden dimension*. Gaeden City, NY: Doubleday & Company.

Hall, G.S. (1904) *Adolescence*. New York: Appleton & Co.

Halloran, J.D. & Croll, P. (1972) Television programmes in Great Britain. In G.A. Comstock & E.A. Rubinstein (Eds.), *Television and social behaviour, Vol. 1., Media content and control*. Washington DC: US Government Printing Office.

Hamilton, D.L. & Gifford, R.K. (1976) Illusory correlation in interpersonal perception: A cognitive basis of stereotypic judgements. *Journal of Experimental Social Psychology, 12*, 392–407.

Hamilton, L. W. & Timmons, C.R. (1995) Psychopharmacology. In D. Kimble & A. M. Colman (Eds.) *Biological Aspects of Behaviour*. London: Longman.

Hamilton, W.D. (1964) The genetical evolution of social behaviour, I and II. *Journal of Theoretical Biology, 7*, 1–16, 17–52.

Hampson, P.J. (1989) Aspects of attention and cognitive science. *Irish Journal of Psychology, 10*, 261–75.

Hampson, S.E. (1995) The construction of personality. In S.E. Hampson & A.M. Colman (Eds.) *Individual differences and personality*. London: Longman.

Harari, H. & McDavid, J.W. (1973) Teachers' expectations and name stereotypes. *Journal of Educational Psychology, 65*, 222–5.

Hardy, G.R. & Legge, D. (1968) Cross-modal induction of changes in sensory thresholds. *Quarterly Journal of Experimental Psychology, 20*, 20–9.

Hargreaves, D., Molloy, C. & Pratt, A. (1982) Social factors in conservation. *British Journal of Psychology, 73*, 231–4.

Hargreaves, D.J. (1986) Psychological theories of sex-role stereotyping. In D.J. Hargreaves & A.M. Colley (Eds.) *The psychology of sex roles*. London: Harper & Row.

Harkins, S.G. & Jackson, J.M. (1985) The role of evaluation in eliminating social loafing. *Personality & Social Psychology Bulletin, 11*, 456–65.

Harlow, H.F. (1949) Formation of learning sets. *Psychological Review, 56*, 51–65.

Harlow, H.F. (1953) Mice, monkeys, men and motives. *Psychological Review, 60*, 23–32.

Harlow, H.F. (1959) Love in infant monkeys. *Scientific American, 200* (6), 68–74.

Harlow, H.F. & Harlow, M.K. (1962) Social deprivation in monkeys. *Scientific American, 207* (5), 136.

Harlow, H.F., Harlow, M.K. & Meyer, D.R. (1950) Learning motivated by a manipulation drive. *Journal of Experimental Psychology, 40*, 228–34.

Harlow, H.F., Harlow, M.K. & Suomi, S.J. (1971) From thought to therapy: Lessons from a primate laboratory. *American Scientist, 59*, 74–83.

Harlow, H.F. & Zimmerman, R.R. (1959) Affectional responses in the infant monkey. *Science, 130*, 421–32.

Harré, R. (1985) The language game of self-ascription: a note. In K.J. Gergen & K.E. Davis (Eds.) *The social construction of the person*. New York: Springer-Verlag.

Harré, R. (1989) Language games and the texts of identity. In J. Shotter & K.J. Gergen (Eds.) *Texts of identity*. London: Sage.

Harré, R., Clarke, D. & De Carlo, N. (1985) *Motives and mechanisms*. London: Methuen.

Harris, M.G. & Humphreys, G.W. (1995) Computational theories of vision. In R.L. Gregory & A.M. Colman (Eds.) *Sensation and perception*. London: Longman.

Harrison, P. (1995) Schizophrenia: A misunderstood disease. *Psychology Review, 2 (2)*, 2–6.

Hartshorne, H. & May, M. (1930) *Studies in the nature of character*. New York: Macmillan.

Hartup, W.W. (1989) Social relationships and their developmental significance. *American Psychologist, 44*, 120–6.

Hass, R.G. & Linder, D.E. (1972) Counterargument availability and the effects of message structure on persuasion. *Journal of Personality and Social Psychology, 23*, 319–33.

Hass, R.G. & Mann, R. (1976) Anticipatory belief change: Persuasion or impression management? *Journal of Personality and Social Psychology, 34*, 105–11.

Hatfield, E., Traupmann, J. & Walster, G.W. (1978) Equity and extramarital sexuality. *Archives of Sexual Behaviour, 7*, 127–42.

Hatfield, E., Walster, G.W. & Traupmann, J. (1978) Equity and premarital sex. *Journal of Personality and Social Psychology, 37*, 82–92.

Havighurst, R.J. (1964) Stages of vocational development. In H. Borow (Ed.) *Man in a world of work*. Boston: Houghton Mifflin.

Havighurst, R.J., Neugarten, B.L. & Tobin, S.S. (1968) Disengagement and patterns of ageing. In B.L. Neugarten (Ed.), *Middle age and ageing*. Chicago: University of Chicago Press.

Hawkins, L.H. & Armstrong-Esther, C.A. (1978) Circadian rhythms and night shift working in nurses. *Nursing Times, May 4*, 49–52.

Haworth, G. (1992) The use of non-human animals in psychological research: the current status of the debate. *Psychology Teaching*, 46–54, New Series, No. 1.

Hayes, K.H. & Hayes, C. (1951) Intellectual development of a house-raised chimpanzee. *Proceedings of the American Philosophical Society, 95*, 105–9.

Hayslip, B. & Panek, P.E. (1989) *Adult development and ageing*. New York: Harper & Row.

Hazan, C. & Shaver, P.R. (1987) Romantic love conceptualized as an attachment process. *Journal of Personality & Social Psychology*, 52 (3) , 511–24.

Heather, N. (1976) *Radical perspectives in psychology*. London: Methuen.

Hebb, D.O. (1949) *The organization of behaviour*. New York: Wiley.

Hediger, H. (1951) *Wild animals in captivity*. London: Butterworth.

Heider, E. (1972) Universals in colour naming and memory. *Journal of Experimental Psychology, 93*, 10–20.

Heider, F. (1958) *The psychology of interpersonal relations*. New York: John Wiley & Sons.

Heider, F. & Simmel, M. (1944) An experimental study of apparent behaviour. *American Journal of Psychology, 57*, 243–59.

Heim, A. (1970) *Intelligence and personality – their assessment and relationship*. Harmondsworth, Middlesex: Penguin.

Heim, A. (1975) *Psychological testing*. London: Oxford University Press.

Held, R. (1965) Plasticity in sensory-motor systems. *Scientific American, 213* (5), 84–94.

Held, R. & Hein, A. (1963) Movement-produced stimulation in the development of visually guided behaviour. *Journal of Comparative and Physiological Psychology, 56*, 607–13.

Hendrick, C. & Constanini, A. (1970) Effects of varying trait inconsistency and response requirements on the primacy effect on impression formation. *Journal of Personality and Social Psychology, 15*, 158–64.

Heron, W. (1957) The pathology of boredom. *Scientific American, 196*, 52–69.

Herrnstein, R. (1971) IQ. *Atlantic Monthly, September, 43–64*.

Hershenson, M., Munsinger, H. & Kessen, W. (1965) Preference for shapes of intermediate variability in the newborn human. *Science, 147*, 630–1.

Hess, E.H. (1956) Space perception in the chick. *Scientific American*, July, 71–80.

Hess, E.H. (1958) Imprinting in animals. *Scientific American*, March, 71–80.

Hess, R.D. & Shipman, V. (1965) Early experience and the socialization of cognitive modes in children. *Child Development, 36*, 860–86.

Heston, L.J. (1966) Psychiatric disorders in foster home reared children of schizophrenic mothers. *British Journal of Psychiatry, 112*, 819–25.

Hetherington, A.W. & Ranson, S.W. (1942) The relation of various hypothalamic lesions to adiposity in the rat. *Journal of Comparative Neurology, 76*, 475–99.

Hetherington, E.M. (1972) Effects of father absence on personality development in adolescent daughters. *Developmental Psychology, 7*, 313–26.

Hetherington, E.M. (1989) Coping with family transitions: Winners, losers and survivors. *Child Development, 60*, 1–14.

Hetherington, E.M. & Baltes, P.B. (1988) Child psychology and life-span development. In E.M. Hetherington, R. Lerner, & M. Perlmutter (Eds.) *Child development in life-span perspective*. Hillsdale, NJ.: Erlbaum.

Hetherington, E.M., Cox, M. & Cox, R. (1978) The aftermath of divorce. In M.H. Stevens & M. Mathews (Eds.), *Mother/child, father/child relationships*. Washington DC: National Association for the Education of Young Children.

Hewstone, M. & Brown, R.J. (1986) Contact is not enough: An intergroup perspective on the contact hypothesis. In M. Hewstone & R. Brown (Eds.), *Contact and conflict in intergroup encounters*. Oxford: Basil Blackwell.

Hilgard, E.R. (1974) Towards a neo-dissociationist theory: Multiple cognitive controls in human functioning. *Perspectives in Biology and Medicine, 17*, 301–16.

Hilgard, E.R. (1975) Hypnosis. *Annual Review of Psychology, 26*, 19–44.

Hilgard, E.R. (1977) Neodissociation theory of multiple cognitive control systems. In G.E. Schwartz & D. Shapiro (Eds.), *Consciousness and self-regulation, Vol. 1*. New York: Plenum Press.

Hilgard, E.R. (1978) Hypnosis and consciousness. *Human Nature*, January, 42–9.

Hilgard, E.R. (1981) Hypnosis gives rise to fantasy and is not a truth serum. *Skeptical enquirer, 5*, 25.

Hilgard, E.R., Atkinson, R.L. & Atkinson, R.C. (1979) *Introduction to psychology* (7th ed.). New York: Harcourt Brace Jovanovich.

Hilgard, J.R. (1970) *Personality and hypnosis*. Chicago: University of Chicago Press.

Hill, C.Y., Rubin, Z. & Peplau, A. (1976) Breakups before marriage: The end of 103 affairs. *Journal of Social Issues, 32*, 147–67.

Hill, J.J.M. (1977) The social and psychological impact of unemployment: a pilot study (Document No. 2T 74). London: Tavistock Institute.

Hill, P. (1993) Recent advances in selected aspects of adolescent development. *Journal of Child Psychology & Psychiatry, 34 (1),* 69–99.

Hinde, R.A. (1959) Unitary drives. *Animal Behaviour, 7,* 130–41.

Hinde, R.A. (1974) *Biological bases of human social behaviour.* New York: McGraw Hill.

Hinde, R.A. (1982) *Ethology.* London: Fontana.

Hinde, R.A. & Spencer-Booth, Y. (1970) Individual differences in the responses of rhesus monkeys to a period of separation from their mothers. *Journal of Child Psychology and Psychiatry, 11,* 159–76.

Hinton, J. (1975) *Dying.* Harmondsworth, Middlesex: Penguin.

Hirsch, H. (1995) *Genocide and the Politics of Memory.* Chapel Hill, NC: The University of North Carolina Press.

Hobson, J.A. (1995) Sleeping and dreaming. In D. Kimble & A.M. Colman (Eds.) *Biological aspects of behaviour.* London: Longman.

Hobson, J.A. & McCarley, R.W. (1977) The brain as a dream state generator: An activation–synthesis hypothesis of the dream process. *American Journal of Psychiatry, 134,* 121.

Hochberg, J. (1978) Art and perception. In E.C. Carterette & H. Friedman (Eds.), *Handbook of perception. Vol. 10.* London: Academic Press.

Hocket, C.D. (1960) The origins of speech. *Scientific American, 203,* 88–96.

Hodges, B. (1974) Effect of volume on relative weighting in 'impression' formation. *Journal of Personality and Social Psychology, 30,* 378–81.

Hodges, J. & Tizard, B. (1989) Social and family relationships of ex-institutional adolescents. *Journal of Child Psychology and Psychiatry, 30* (1), 77–97.

Hodgkinson, P.E. (1980) Treating abnormal grief in the bereaved. *Nursing Times,* January, 126–8.

Hoffman, J.P., Ireland, T.O.& Widom, C.S. (1994) Traditional socialization theories of violence: A critical examination. In J. Archer (Ed.) *Male violence.* London: Routledge.

Hoffman, L.W. (1977) Fear of success in 1965 and 1974: A follow-up study. *Journal of Consulting and Clinical Psychology, 45,* 310–12.

Hoffman, L.W. (1974) Effects of maternal employment on the child: A review of the research. *Developmental Psychology, 10,* 204–28.

Hoffman, M.L. (1970) Conscience, personality and socialization techniques. *Human Development, 13,* 90–126.

Hoffman, M.L. (1975) Altruistic behaviour and the parent child relationship. *Journal of Personality & Social Psychology, 31,* 937–43.

Hoffman, M.L. (1976) Empathy, role taking, guilt and development of altruistic motives. In T. Lickona (Ed.), *Moral development and behaviour.* New York: Holt, Rinehart & Winston.

Hofling, K.C., Brotzman, E., Dalrymple, S., Graves, N. & Pierce, C.M. (1966) An experimental study in the nurse-physician relationship. *Journal of Nervous and Mental Disorders, 143,* 171–80.

Hogg, M.A. & Abrams, D. (1988) *Social identifications: A social psychology of intergroup relations and group processes.* London: Routledge.

Hogg, M.A. & Vaughan, G.M. (1995) *Social psychology: An introduction.* Hemel Hempstead: Prentice Hall/Harvester Wheatsheaf.

Hohmann, G.W. (1966) Some effects of spinal cord lesions on experienced emotional feelings. *Psychophysiology, 3,* 143–56.

Hollander, E.P. (1958) Conformity, status, and idiosyncrasy credit. *Psychological Review,* 65, 117–27.

Hollander, E.P. & Willis, R.H. (1964) Conformity, independence and anticonformity as determiners of perceived influence and attraction. In E.P. Hollander (Ed.), *Leaders, groups and influence.* New York: Oxford University Press.

Holmes, D.S. (1994) *Abnormal psychology* (2nd ed.) New York ; HarperCollins.

Holmes, J. (1992) Response to Jeffrey Masson. In W. Dryden & C. Feltham (Eds.) *Psychotherapy and its discontents.* Buckingham: Open University Press.

Holmes, J. (1993) *John Bowlby and attachment theory.* London: Routledge.

Holmes, T.H. & Masuda, M. (1974) Life change and illness susceptibility. In B.S. Dohrenwend and B.P. Dohrenwend (Eds.), *Stressful life events: Their nature and effects.* New York: Wiley.

Holmes, T.H. & Rahe, R.H. (1967) The social readjustment rating scale. *Journal of Psycho-somatic Research, 11,* 213–18.

Holt, R.R. (1967) Individuality and generalization in the psychology of personality. In R.S. Lazarus & E.M. Opton (Eds.) *Personality.* Harmondsworth: Penguin.

Homans, G.C. (1961) *Social behaviour: Its elementary forms.* New York: Harcourt Brace Jovanovich.

Homans, G.C. (1974) *Social behaviour: Its elementary forms* (2nd ed.). New York: Harcourt Brace Jovanovich.

Honzik, M.P., Macfarlane, H.W. & Allen, L. (1948) The stability of mental test performance between two and eighteen years. *Journal of Experimental Education, 17,* 309–24.

Hopson, B. & Scally, M. (1980) Change and development in adult life: Some implications for helpers. *British Journal of Guidance and Counselling, 8* (2), 175–87.

Horgan, J. (1993) Eugenics revisited. *Scientific American,* June, 92–100.

Horgan, J. (1995) The new social Darwinists. *Scientific American,* October, 150–7.

Horn, J.L. (1982) The ageing of human abilities. In B. Wolman (Ed.) *Handbook of developmental psychology.* Englewood Cliffs, NJ.: Prentice-Hall.

Horn, J.L. & Cattell, R.B. (1967) Age differences in fluid and crystallized intelligence. *Acta Psychologica, 26,* 107–29.

Horn, J.L. & Cattell, R.B. (1982) Whimsy and misunderstanding of Gf–Gc theory: A comment on Guilford. *Psychology Bulletin, 91,* 623–33.

Horn, J.M., Loehlin, J.L. & Willerman, L. (1979) Intellectual resemblance among adoptive and biological relatives: The Texas adoption project. *Behaviour Genetics, 9,* 177–207.

Horne, J. (1988) *Why we sleep: The functions of sleep in humans and other mammals.* Oxford: Oxford University Press.

Horner, M.S. (1970) The motive to avoid success and changing aspirations of college women. In *Women on campus 1970: A symposium.* Ann Arbor, Michigan: Center for Continuing Education of Women.

Horner, M.S. (1972) Toward an understanding of achievement-related conflicts in women. *Journal of Social Issues, 28,* 157–76.

Horney, K. (1924) On the genesis of the castration complex in women. *International Journal of Psychoanalysis, V,* 50–65.

Horowitz, L.M., Rosenberg, S.M. & Bartholomew, K. (1993) Interpersonal problems, attachment styles, and outcome in Brief Dynamic Psychotherapy. *Journal of Consulting & Clinical Psychology, 61 (4),* 549–560.

Hovland, C.I., Campbell, E. & Brock, B.T. (1957) The effects of 'commitment' on opinion change following communication. In C.I. Hovland (Ed.), *The order of presentation in persuasion.*

New Haven, Connecticut: Yale University Press.

Hovland, C.I. & Janis, I.L. (1959) *Personality and persuasibility.* New Haven, Connecticut: Yale University Press.

Hovland, C.I., Janis, I.L. & Kelley, H.H. (1953) *Communication and persuasion: Psychological studies of opinion change.* New Haven, CT: Yale University Press.

Hovland, C.I., Lumsdaine, A.A. & Sheffield, F.D. (1949) *Experiments in mass communication.* Princeton, New Jersey: Princeton University Press.

Hovland, C.I. & Sears, R.R. (1940) Minor studies in aggression , VI: Correlation of lynchings with economic indices. *Journal of Psychology, 2*, 301–10.

Hovland, C.I. & Weiss, W. (1951) The influence of source credibility on communication effectiveness. *Public Opinion Quarterly, 15*, 635–50.

Howard, J.W. & Rothbart, M. (1980) Social categorization and memory for ingroup and outgroup behaviour. *Journal of Personality and Social Psychology, 38*, 301–10.

Howe, M.J.A. (1980) *The psychology of human learning.* London: Harper & Rowe.

Howe, M.J.A. (1989) The strange achievements of idiots savants. In A.M. Colman & J.G. Beaumont (Eds.), *Psychology Survey, No. 7.* Leicester: British Psychological Society.

Howes, D. & Solomon, R.L. (1950) A note on McGinnies' emotionality and perceptual defence. *Psychological Review, 57*, 229–34.

Howie, D. (1952) Perceptual defence. *Psychological Review, 59*, 308–15.

Howlin, P.A. (1981) The effectiveness of operant language training with autistic children. *Journal of Autism and Developmental Disorders, 11*, 89–106.

Hrdy, S.B. (1977) *The Langurs of Abu.* Cambridge, Massachusetts: Harvard University Press.

Hubel, D.H. (1979) The brain. *Scientific American*, September, 38–47.

Hubel, D.H. & Wiesel, T.N. (1959) Receptive fields of single neurons in the cat's striate cortex. *Journal of Physiology, 148*, 579–91.

Hubel, D.H. & Wiesel, T.N. (1962) Receptive fields, binocular interaction and functional architecture in the cat's visual cortex. *Journal of Physiology, 160*, 106–54.

Hubel, D.H. & Wiesel, T.N. (1968) Receptive fields and functional architecture of monkey striate cortex. *Journal of Physiology, 195*, 215–43.

Hubel, D.H. & Wiesel, T.N. (1977) Functional architecture of macaque monkey visual cortex. *Proceedings of the Royal Society of London, Series B, 198*, 1–59.

Hubel, D.H. & Wiesel, T.N. (1979) Brain mechanisms of vision. *Scientific American, 241*, 150–62.

Huczynski, A. & Buchanan, D. (1991) *Organizational behaviour: An introductory text* (2nd ed.). Hemel Hempstead: Prentice-Hall.

Hudson, W. (1960) Pictorial depth perception in sub-cultural groups in Africa. *Journal of Social Psychology, 52*, 183–208.

Hudson, W. (1962) Pictorial perception and educational adaptation in Africa. *Psychologica Africana, 9*, 226–39.

Huesmann, L.R. & Eron, L.D. (1984) Cognitive processes and the persistence of aggressive behaviour. *Aggressive Behaviour, 10*, 243–51.

Hull, C.L. (1943) *Principles of behaviour.* New York: Appleton, Century Crofts.

Humphrey, N. (1986) *The inner eye.* London: Faber & Faber.

Humphrey, N. (1993) Introduction. In N. Humphrey (1986) *The inner eye* London: Vintage.

Humphreys, G.W. & Riddoch, M.J. (1987) *To see but not to see – a case study of visual agnosia.* London: Lawrence Erlbaum

Associates Ltd.

Hunt, J.McV. (1961) *Intelligence and experience.* New York: Ronald Press.

Hunt, J.McV. (1969) Has compensatory education failed? Has it been attempted? *Harvard Educational Review, 39*, 278–300.

Hunter, I. (1964) *Memory* (revised ed.) Harmondsworth, Middlesex: Penguin.

Hutt, C. (1972) *Males and females.* Harmondsworth, Middlesex: Penguin.

Hyde, T.S. & Jenkins, J.J. (1973) Recall for words as a function of semantic, graphic and syntactic orienting tasks. *Journal of Verbal Learning and Behaviour, 12*, 471–80.

Ickes, W.J. & Barnes, R.D. (1977) The role of sex and self-monitoring in unstructured dyadic interactions. *Journal of Personality & Social Psychology, 35*, 315–30.

Illman, J. (1977) ECT: Therapy or trauma? *Nursing Times*, August *11*, 1226–7.

Immelman, K. & Suomi, S.J. (1981) Sensitive phases in development. In K. Immelman, G. Barlow, M. Main & L. Petrinovich (Eds.), *Issues in behavioural development. The Bielefelt Interdisciplinary Conference.* New York: Cambridge University Press.

Imperato-McGinley, J., Guerro, L., Gautier, T. & Peterson, R.E. (1974) Steroid 5-reductase deficiency in man: An inherited form of male pseudohermaphroditism. *Science, 186*, 1213–16.

Inhelder, B. & Piaget, J. (1958) *The growth of logical thinking.* London: Routledge & Kegan Paul.

Insko, C.A., Arkoff, A. & Insko, V.M. (1965) Effects of high and low fear-arousing communications upon opinion change towards smoking. *Journal of Experimental Social Psychology, 1*, 256–66.

Insko, C.A., Drenan, S., Solomon, M.R., Smith, R. & Wade, T.J. (1983) Conformity as a function of the consistency of positive self-evaluation with being liked and being right. *Journal of Experimental Social Psychology, 19*, 341–58.

Israels, H. & Schatzman, M. (1993) The seduction theory. *History of Psychiatry, 4*, 32–59.

Ittleson, W.H. (1952) *The Ames demonstrations in perception.* Princeton, New Jersey: Princeton University Press.

Iversen, L.L. (1979) The chemistry of the brain. *Scientific American, 241*, 134–49.

Izard, C. (1977) *Human emotions.* New York: Plenum Press.

Jackendoff, R. (1993) *Patterns in the mind: Language and human nature.* Hemel Hempstead: Harvester Wheatsheaf.

Jackson, G. (1992) *Women and psychology—what might that mean ?* Paper given at Annual Conference, Association for the Teaching of Psychology, July.

Jacobs, M. (1984) Psychodynamic therapy: The Freudian approach. In W. Dryden (Ed.), *Individual therapy in Britain.* London: Harper & Row.

Jacobs, M. (1992) *Freud.* London: Sage Publications.

Jahoda, G. (1966) Geometric illusions and environment: A study in Ghana. *British Journal of Psychology, 57*, 193–9.

Jahoda, M. (1958) *Current concepts of positive mental health.* New York: Basic Books.

Jahoda, M. (1979) The impact of unemployment in the 1930s and the 1970s. *Bulletin of the British Psychological Society, 32*, 309–14.

James, W. (1884) What is an emotion? *Mind, 9*, 188–205.

James, W. (1890) *Principles of psychology.* New York: Holt.

James, W. (1902) *The varieties of religious experience.* New York: Longmans, Green.

Janis, I. (1971) *Stress and frustration.* New York: Harcourt Brace.

Janis, I.L. (1982) *Groupthink: Psychological studies of policy decisions and fiascoes* (2nd ed.). Boston, MA: Houghton-Mifflin.

Janis, I.L. & Feshbach, S. (1953) Effects of fear-arousing communication. *Journal of Abnormal and Social Psychology, 48*, 78–92.

Janis, I.L. & Field, P.B. (1959) Sex differences and personality factors related to persuasability. In C.I. Hovland & I.L. Janis (Eds.), *Personality and persuasability*. New Haven, Connecticut: Yale University Press.

Janis, I.L., Kaye, D. & Kirschner, P. (1965) Facilitating effects of 'eating-while-reading' on responsiveness to persuasive communications. *Journal of Personality & Social Psychology, 1*, 181–6.

Janis, I.L. & Mann, L. (1965) Effectiveness of emotional role-playing in modifying smoking habits and attitudes. *Journal of Experimental Personality Research, 1*, 84–90.

Janis, I.L. & Terwilllinger, R.T. (1962) An experimental study of psychological resistance to fear-arousing communication. *Journal of Abnormal and Social Psychology, 65*, 403–10.

Jarvis, M. (1994) Attention and the information processing approach. *Psychology Teaching*, New Series (No. 3). December, 12–22.

Jenkins, J.G. & Dallenbach, K.M. (1924) Oblivescence during sleep and waking. *American Journal of Psychology, 35*, 605–12.

Jenness, A. (1932) The role of discussion in changing opinion regarding matter of fact. *Journal of Abnormal and Social Psychology, 27*, 279–96.

Jensen, A.R. (1969) How much can we boost IQ and scholastic achievement? *Harvard Educational Review, 39*, 1–123.

Jensen, A.R. (1980) *Bias in mental testing*. London: Methuen.

Jersild, A.T. (1963) *The psychology of adolescence* (2nd ed.). New York: Macmillan.

Johnson, J.H. & Scileppi, I.D. (1969) Effects of ego involvement conditions on attitude change in high and low credibility communications. *Journal of Personality and Social Psychology, 13*, 31–6.

Johnson-Laird, P.N., Herrman, D.J. & Chaffin, R. (1984) Only connections: A critique of semantic networks. *Psychological Bulletin, 96* (2), 292–315.

Johnston, W.A. & Heinz, S.P. (1978) Flexibility and capacity demands of attention. *Journal of Experimental psychology: General, 107*, 420–35.

Jonas, K., Eagly, A.H. & Stroebe, W. (1995) Attitudes and persuasion. In M. Argyle & A.M. Colman (Eds.) *Social psychology*. London: Longman.

Jones, E.E., Caputo, C., Legant, P. & Marecek, J. (1973) Behaviour as seen by the actor and as seen by the observer. *Journal of Personality and Social Psychology, 27* (2), 154–64.

Jones, E.E. & Davis, K.E. (1965) From acts to dispositions: The attribution process in person perception. In L. Berkowitz (Ed.), *Advances in experimental social psychology, Vol. 2*. New York: Academic Press.

Jones, E.E., Davis, K.E. & Gergen, K. (1961) Role playing variations and their informational value for person perception. *Journal of Abnormal & Social Psychology, 63*, 302–10.

Jones, E.E. & Nisbett, R.E. (1971) *The actor and the observer: Divergent perceptions of the causes of behaviour*. Morristown, New Jersey: General Learning Press.

Jones E.E., Rock, L., Shaver, K.G., Goethals, G.R. & Wand, L.M. (1968) Patterns of performance and ability attribution: An unexpected primacy effect. *Journal of Personality and Social Psychology, 10*, 317–40.

Jones, E.E. & Sigall, H. (1971) The bogus pipeline: a new paradigm for measuring affect and attitude. *Psychological Bulletin, 76*, 349–64.

Jones, J. (1995) New breed of non-parents turn back on family way. *Observer*, April 16.

Jones, M.C. (1924) The elimination of childrens' fears. *Journal of Experimental Psychology, 7*, 382–90.

Jones, M. (1953) *The therapeutic community*. New York: Basic Books.

Jones, M.C. & Bayley, N. (1950) Physical maturity among boys related to behaviour. *Journal of Educational Psychology, 41*, 129–48.

Jost, A. (1970a) Hormonal factors in the development of the male genital system. In E. Rosenberg & C.A. Paulsen (Eds.), *The human testis*. New York: Plenum Press.

Jost, A. (1970b) Hormonal factors in sexual differentiation. *Philosophical Transactions of the Royal Society of London, B259*, 119–30.

Jourard, S.M. (1966) An exploratory study of body accessibility. *British Journal of Social and Clinical Psychology, 5*, 221–31.

Jourard, S.M. (1971) *Self-disclosure: An experimental analysis of the transparent self*. New York: Wiley Interscience.

Jouvet, M. (1967) Mechanisms of the states of sleep: A neuropharmacological approach. *Research Publications of the Association for the Research in Nervous and Mental Diseases, 45*, 86–126.

Joynson, R.B. (1972) The return of mind. *Bulletin of the British Psychological Society, 25*, 1–10.

Joynson, R.B. (1974) *Psychology and common sense*. London: Routledge & Kegan Paul.

Joynson, R.B. (1980) Models of man: 1879–1979. In A.J. Chapman & D.M.Jones (Eds.) *Models of man*. Leicester: British Psychological Society.

Juel-Nielson, N. (1965) Individual and environment: A psychiatric and psychological investigation of monozygous twins raised apart. *Acta Psychiatrica et Neurologica Scandinavia*, (Suppl. 183).

Jung, C.G. (1963) *Memories, dreams, reflections*. London: Collins/Routledge & Kegan Paul.

Jung, C.G. (Ed.). (1964) *Man and his symbols*. London: Aldus-Jupiter Books.

Kadushin, A. (1970) *Adopting older children*. New York: Columbia University Press.

Kagan, J., Kearsley, R.B. & Zelago, P.R. (1980) *Infancy – its place in human development*.(2nd ed.) Cambridge, Massachusetts: Harvard University Press.

Kahneman, D. (1973) *Attention and effort*. Englewood Cliffs, New Jersey: Prentice Hall.

Kahneman, D. & Henik, A. (1979) Perceptual organization and attention. In M. Kubovy & J.R. Pomerants (Eds.), *Perceptual organization*. Hillsdale, New Jersey: Lawrence Erlbaum Associates Inc.

Kalish, R.A. (1975) *Late adulthood: Perspectives on human development*. Monterey, California: Brooks-Cole.

Kalish, R.A. (1979) The new ageism and the failure models: A polemic. *Gerontologist, 19*, 398–402.

Kalish, R.A. (1982) *Late adulthood: Perspectives on human development* (2nd ed.). Monterey, CA: Brooks/Cole.

Kamin, L.J.(1969) Predictability, surprise, attention and conditioning. In B.A.Campbell & R.M. Church (Eds.) *Punishment and aversive behaviour*. New York: Appleton-Century-Crofts.

Kamin, L.J. (1977) *The science and politics of IQ*. Harmondsworth, Middlesex: Penguin.

Kaminer, H. & Lavie, P. (1991) Sleep and dreaming in Holocaust survivors: dramatic decrease in dream recall in well adjusted survivors. *Journal of Nervous and Mental Disease, 179*, 664–9.

Karlins, M., Coffman, T.L. & Walters, G. (1969) On the fading of social stereotypes: Studies in three generations of college students. *Journal of Personality and Social Psychology*, *13*, 1–16.

Karniol, R. (1978) Childrens' use of intention cues in evaluating behaviour. *Psychological Bulletin*, *85*, 76–85.

Kastenbaum, R. (1979) *Growing old—years of fulfilment*. London: Harper & Row.

Katz, D. (1960) The functional approach to the study of attitudes. *Public Opinion Quarterly*, *24*, 163–204.

Katz, D. & Braly, K. (1933) Racial stereotypes of one hundred college students. *Journal of Abnormal and Social Psychology*, *28*, 280–90.

Katz, E. (1957) The two-step flow of conversion. *Public Opinion Quarterly*, *21*, 61–78.

Kazdin, A.E. & Wilcoxin, L.A. (1976) Systematic desensitization and nonspecific treatment effects: A methodological evaluation. *Psychological Bulletin*, *83*, 729–58.

Keasey, C.B. (1978) Children's developing awareness and usage of intentionality and motives. In C.B. Keasey (Ed.), *Nebraska Symposium on Motivation, Vol. 25*. Lincoln: University of Nebraska Press.

Kelley, H.H. (1950) The warm–cold variable in first impressions of people. *Journal of Personality*, *18*, 431–9.

Kelley, H.H. (1967) Attribution theory in social psychology. In D. Levine (Ed.), *Nebraska Symposium on Motivation, Vol. 15*. Lincoln: Nebraska University Press.

Kelley, H.H. (1972) Causal schemata and the attribution process. In E.E. Jones, D.E. Kanouse, H.H.Kelley, R.E. Nisbett, S. Valins & B. Weiner (Eds.) *Attribution: Perceiving the causes of behaviour*. Morristown, N.J.: General Learning Press.

Kelley, H.H. (1973) The processes of causal attribution. *American Psychologist*, *28*, 107–28.

Kelly, G.A. (1955) *A theory of personality – the psychology of personal constructs*. New York: Norton.

Kelly, G.A. (1962) Europe's matrix of decision. In M.R. Jones (Ed.) *Nebraska Symposiom on Motivation*. Lincoln, NA: University of Nebraska Press.

Kellogg, W.N. & Kellogg, L.A. (1933) *The ape and the child*. New York: McGraw Hill.

Kelman, H.C. (1958) Compliance, identification and internalization: Three processes of attitude change. *Journal of Conflict Resolution*, *2*, 51–60.

Kelman, H.C. & Hovland, C.I. (1953) Reinstatement of the communication in delayed measurement of opinion change. *Journal of Abnormal and Social Psychology*, *48*, 327–35.

Kelman, H. & Lawrence, L. (1972) Assignment of responsibility in the case of Lt. Calley: Preliminary report on a national survey. *Journal of Social Issues*, *28(1)*, 177–212.

Kelvin, P. (1981) Work as a source of identity: The implications of unemployment. *British Journal of Guidance and Counselling*, *9* (1), 2–11.

Kelvin, P. & Jarrett, J. (1985) *The social psychological effects of unemployment*. Cambridge: Cambridge University Press.

Kendell, R.E. (1983) The principles of classification in relation to mental disease. In M. Shepherd & O.L. Zangwill (Eds.), *Handbook of psychiatry: 1, general psychopathology*. Cambridge: Cambridge University Press.

Kenrick, D.T. (1994) Evolutionary social psychology: from sexual selection to social cognition. *Advances in Experimental Social Psychology*, *26*, 75–121.

Kerckhoff, A.C. (1974) The social context of interpersonal attraction. In T.L. Huston (Ed.), *Foundations of interpersonal attraction*. New York: Academic Press.

Kerckhoff, A.C. & Davis, K.E. (1962) Value consensus and need complementarity in mate selection. *American Sociological*

Review, *27*, 295–303.

Kerr, N.L. (1983) Motivation losses in small groups: a social dilemma analysis. *Journal of Personality & Social Psychology*, *45*, 819–28.

Kety, S., Rosenthal, D., Wender, P.H., Schulsinger, F. & Jacobson, B. (1975) Mental illness in the biological and adoptive families of adoptive individuals who have become schizophrenic. In R.R. Fieve, D. Rosenthal & H. Bull (Eds.), *Genetic research in psychiatry*. Baltimore: Johns Hopkins University Press.

Kilham, W. & Mann, L. (1974) Level of destructive obedience as a function of transmitter and executant roles in the Milgram obedience paradigm. *Journal of Personality and Social Psychology*, *29*, 696–702.

Kimball, R.K. & Hollander, E.P. (1974) Independence in the presence of an experienced but deviant group member. *Journal of Social Psychology*, *93*, 281–92.

Kimura, D. (1992) Sex differences in the brain. *Scientific American*, 80–7, September (Special Issue).

Kintsch, W. & Buschke, H. (1969) Homophones and synonyms in short-term memory. *Journal of Experimental Psychology*, *80*, 403–7.

Kirby, R. & Radford, J. (1976) *Individual differences*. London: Methuen.

Kitzinger, C. & Coyle, A. (1995) Lesbian and gay couples: speaking of difference. *The Psychologist, 8(2)*, 64–9.

Klaus, H.M. & Kennell, J.H. (1976) *Maternal infant bonding*. St Louis: Mosby.

Klaus, R.A. & Gray, S.W. (1968) The early training project for disadvantaged children: A report after five years. *Monographs of the Society for Research in Child Development 33* (4), (Serial No. 120).

Kleinmuntz, B. (1980) *Essentials of abnormal psychology* (2nd ed.). London: Harper & Row.

Kleitman, N. (1927) Studies on the physiology of sleep; V; Some experiments on puppies. *American Journal of Physiology*, *84*, 386–95.

Kline, P. (1972) *Fact and fantasy in Freudian theory*. London: Methuen.

Kline, P. (1981a) The work of Eysenck and Cattell. In F. Fransella (Ed.), *Personality–theory, measurement and research*. London: Methuen.

Kline. P. (1981b) Personality. In D. Fontana (Ed.) *Psychology for teachers*. British Psychological Society/Macmillan Press.

Kline, P. (1982) Personality and individual assessment. In A.J. Chapman & A. Gale (Eds.) *Psychology and people: A tutorial text*. London: BPS/Macmillan Press.

Kline, P. (1983) *Personality – measurement and theory*. London: Hutchinson.

Kline, P. (1988) *Psychology exposed*. London: Routledge.

Kline, P. (1989) Objective tests of Freud's theories. In A.M. Colman & J.G. Beaumont (Eds.), *Psychology Survey, No. 7*. Leicester: British Psychological Society.

Kline, P. (1993) Comments on 'Personality traits are alive and well'. *The Psychologist*, 6 (7), 304.

Kline, P. (1995) Personality tests. In S.E. Hampson & A.M. Colman (Eds.) *Individual differences and personality*. London: Longman.

Kline, P. & Storey, R. (1977) A factor analytic study of the oral character. *British Journal of Social & Clinical Psychology*, *16*, 317–28.

Kluckhohn, C. & Murray, H.A. (1953) Personality formation: The determinants. In C. Kluckhohn, H.A. Murray & D.M. Schneider (Eds.) *Personality in nature, society and culture* (2nd ed.) New York: Knopf.

Klüver, H. & Bucy, P.C. (1937) 'Psychic blindness' and other symptoms following bilateral temporal lobectomy in rhesus monkeys. *American Journal of Physiology*, *119*, 352–3.

Kobasa, S.C. (1979) Stressful events and health: An enquiry into hardiness. *Journal of Personality & Social Psychology, 37*, 1–11.

Koestler, A. (1970) *The act of creation*. London: Pan Books.

Koffka, K. (1935) *The principles of Gestalt psychology*. New York: Harcourt Brace & World.

Kohlberg, L. (1963) The development of children's orientations toward a moral order: 1. Sequence in the development of moral thought. *Human Development, 6,* 11–33.

Kohlberg, L. (1966) A cognitive–developmental analysis of childrens' sex-role concepts and attitudes. In E.E. Maccoby (Ed.), *The development of sex differences*. Stanford, California: Stanford University Press.

Kohlberg, L. (1969) Stage and sequence: The cognitive developmental approach to socialization. In D.A. Goslin (Ed.), *Handbook of socialization theory and research*. Chicago: Rand McNally.

Kohlberg, L. (1975) The cognitive-developmental approach to moral education. *Phi Delta Kappa*, June, 670–7.

Kohlberg, L. (1976) Moral stages and moralization. In T. Likona (Ed.), *Moral development and behaviour*. New York: Holt, Rinehart & Winston.

Kohlberg, L. (1978) Revisions in the theory and practice of moral development. *Directions for Child Development, 2*, 83–8.

Kohlberg, L. (1981) *Essays on moral development, Vol. 1*. New York: Harper & Row.

Kohler, I. (1962) Experiments with goggles. *Scientific American*, *206*, 67–72.

Kohler, I. (1964) The formation and transformation of the visual world. *Psychological Issues*, *3*, 28–46/116–33.

Köhler, W. (1925) *The mentality of apes*. New York: Harcourt Brace Jovanovich.

Köhler, W. (1947) *Gestalt psychology*. New York: Liveright.

Koffka, K. (1935) *Principles of Gestalt psychology*. New York: Harcourt Brace.

Kolers, P.A. (1972) *Aspects of motion perception*. New York: Pergamon Press.

Koluchova, J. (1972) Severe deprivation in twins: A case study. *Journal of Child Psychology and Psychiatry*, *13*, 107–14.

Koluchova, J. (1976) The further development of twins after severe and prolonged deprivation: A second report. *Journal of Child Psychology and Psychiatry*, *17*, 181–8.

Kotelchuk, M. (1976) The infant's relationship to the father: experimental evidence. In M.E. Lamb (Ed.) *The role of the father in child development*. New York: Wiley.

Kraepelin, E. (1896) *Dementia Praecox* (trans.). In J. Cutting & M. Shepherd (Eds.) (1987) *The clinical routes of the schizophrenia concept*. Cambridge: Cambridge University Press.

Kraepelin, E. (1913) *Psychiatry* (8th ed.). Leipzig: Thieme.

Krahé, B. (1992) *Personality and social psychology: Towards a synthesis*. London: Sage.

Kraus, A.S. & Lilienfeld, A.M. (1959) Some epidemiological aspects of the high mortality rate in the young widowed group. *Journal of Chronic Diseases*, *10*, 207–17.

Krebs, D. & Adinolfi, A. (1975) Physical attractiveness, social relations and personality style. *Journal of Personality and Social Psychology*, *31*, 245–53.

Kretschmer, E. (1936) *Physique and character* (2nd ed.) (W.J.H. Sprott & K. Paul Trench, trans). New York: Trubner.

Kroger, J. (1985) Separation-individuation and ego identity status in New Zealand university students. *Journal of Youth and Adolescence*, *14*, 133–47.

Kruger, A.C. (1992) The effect of peer and adult-child transactive discussions on moral reasoning. In M. Gauvain & M. Cole (Eds.) *Readings on the development of children*. New York: W.H. Freeman & Company.

Kruglanski, A.W. (1977) The place of naive contents in a theory of attribution: Reflections on Calder and Zuckerman's critiques of the endogenous–exogenous partition. *Personality and Social Psychology Bulletin*, *3*, 592–605.

Kruglanski, A.W. (1979) Causal explanation, teleological expansion: On radical particularism in attribution theory. *Journal of Personality and Social Psychology*, *37*, 1447–57.

Krupat, E. & Garonzik, R. (1994) Subjects' expectations and the search for alternatives to deception in social psychology. *British Journal of Social Psychology*, *33*, 211–22.

Kübler-Ross, E. (1969) *On death and dying*. London: Tavistock/Routledge.

Kuhn, D., Nash, S.C. & Brucker, J.A. (1978) Sex role concepts of two- and three-year-olds. *Child Development*, *49*, 445–51.

Kuhn, H.H. (1960) Self attitudes by age, sex and professional training. *Sociology Quarterly*, *1*, 39–55.

Kuhn. H.H. & McPartland, T.S. (1954) An empirical investigation of self attitudes. *American Sociological Review*, *47,* 647–52.

Kuhn, T.S. (1962) *The structure of scientific revolutions*. Chicago: University of Chicago Press.

Kuhn, T.S. (1970) *The structure of scientific revolutions* (2nd ed.) Chicago: Chicago University Press.

Kulick, J.A. & Brown, R. (1979) Frustration, attribution of blame and aggression. *Journal of Experimental and Social Psychology*, *15*, 183–94.

Kulik. J.A. & Mahler, H.I.M. (1989) Stress and affiliation in a hospital setting: Pre-operative roommate preferences. *Personality & Social Psychology Bulletin*, *15*, 183–93.

Kurtines, W. & Greif, E.B. (1974) The development of moral thought: Review and evaluation of Kohlberg's approach. *Psychological Bulletin*, *81* (8), 453–70.

Labouvie-Vief, G. (1979) *Does intelligence decline with age?* Bethesda, Maryland: National Institute of Health.

Labouvie-Vief, G. (1985) Intelligence and cognition. In J.E. Birren & K.W. Schaie (Eds.) *Handbook of the psychology of ageing* (2nd ed.). New York: Van Nostrand Reinhold.

Labov, W. (1970) The logic of non-standard English. In F. Williams (Ed.), *Language and poverty*. Chicago: Markham.

Lahey, B.B. (1983) *Psychology: An introduction*. Dubuque, Iowa: William C. Brown Co.

Laing, R.D. (1959) *The divided self: An existential study of sanity and madness*. London: Tavistock.

Laing, R.D. (1961) *Self and others*. London: Tavistock.

Laing, R.D. (1967) *The politics of experience and the bird of paradise*. Harmondsworth, Middlesex: Penguin.

Laing, R.D. (1971) *Knots*. Harmondsworth, Middlesex: Penguin.

Laing, R.D. & Esterson, A. (1964) *Sanity, madness and the family*. London: Tavistock.

Laird, J.D. (1974) Self-attribution of emotion: The effects of facial expression on the quality of emotional experience. *Journal of Personality and Social Psychology*, *29*, 475–86.

Lamb, M.E. (1977) Father–infant and mother–infant interaction in the first year of life. *Child Development*, *48*, 167–81.

Lamb, M.E. (1979) The changing American family and its implications for infant social development: The sample case of maternal employment. In M. Lewis & L.A. Rosenblum (Eds.) *The Social Network of the Developing Infant*. New York: Wiley.

Lamb, M.E., Thompson, R.A., Gander, W. & Charnov, E.L. (1985) *Infant-mother attachment: the origins and significance of individual differences in strange situation behaviour*.

Hillsdale, NJ: Erlbaum.

Lambert, M.J., Shapiro, D.A. & Bergin, A.E. (1986) The effectiveness of psychotherapy. In S.L. Garfield & A.E. Bergin (Eds.) *Handbook of psychotherapy and behaviour change* (3rd ed). New York: Wiley.

Lambie, J. (1991) The misuse of Kuhn in psychology. *The Psychologist, 4* (1), 6–11.

Land, E.H. (1964) The retinex. *American Scientist, 52,* 247–64.

Land, E.H. (1977) The retinex theory of colour vision. *Scientific American, 237* (6), 108–28.

Landis, C. (1938) Statistical evaluation of psychotherapeutic methods. In S.E. Hinde (Ed.) *Concepts and problems of psychotherapy.* London: Heineman.

La Piere, R.T. (1934) Attitudes versus action. *Social Forces, 13,* 230–7.

Larsen, K.S. (1974) Conformity in the Asch experiment. *Journal of Social Psychology, 94,* 303–4.

Larsen, K.S. (1982) Cultural conditions and conformity: The Asch effect. *Bulletin of the British Psychological Society, 35,* 347.

Larsen, K.S., Triplett, J.S., Brant, W.D. & Langenberg, D. (1979) Collaborator status, subject characteristics and conformity in the Asch paradigm. *Journal of Social Psychology, 108,* 259–63.

Larson, P.C. (1981) Sexual identification and self-concept. *Journal of Homosexuality, 7,* 15–32.

Lashley, K. (1929) *Brain mechanisms and intelligence: A quantitative study of injuries to the brain.* Chicago, Illinois: University of Chicago Press.

Lashley, K. S. (1950) In search of the engram. *Proceedings from Social Experimental Biology,* 4, 454–82. Reprinted in F.A. Beach, D.O. Hebb, C.T.Morgan & H.W.Nissen (Eds.) *The neuropsychology of Lashley.* New York: McGraw-Hill.

Laswell, H.D. (1948) The structures and function of communication in society. In L. Bryson (Ed.), *Communication of ideas.* New York: Harper.

Latané, B. & Darley, J.M. (1968) Group inhibitions of bystander intervention in emergencies. *Journal of Personality and Social Psychology, 10,* 215–21.

Latané, B. & Darley, J.M. (1970) *The unresponsive bystander: Why does he not help?* New York: Appleton-Century-Croft.

Latané, B. & Nida, S. (1980) Social impact theory and group influence: A social engineering perspective. In P. Paulus (Ed.) *The psychology of group influence.* Hillsdale, NJ: Lawrence Erlbaum.

Latané, B., Nida, S. & Williams, D.W. (1981) The effects of group size on helping behaviour. In J.P. Rushton & R.M. Sorrentino (Eds.) *Altruism and Helping Behaviour.* Hillsdale, NJ.: Erlbaum.

Latané, B. & Rodin, J. (1969) A lady in distress: Inhibiting effects of friends and strangers on bystander intervention. *Journal of Experimental Social Psychology, 5,* 189–202.

Latané, B., Williams, K. & Harkins, S.G.(1979) Many hands make light work: The causes and consequences of social loafing. *Journal of Personality & Social Psychology, 37,* 822–32.

Latané, B. & Wolf, S. (1981) The social impact of majorities and minorities. *Psychological Review, 88,* 438–53.

Lazarsfeld, P.F., Berelson, B. & Gaudet, H. (1948) *The peoples' choice: How the voter makes up his mind in a presidential campaign.* New York: Columbia University Press.

Lazarus, A.A. (1976) *Multimodal behaviour therapy.* New York: Springer.

Lazarus, A.A. (1977) *Behaviour therapy and beyond.* New York: McGraw Hill.

Lazarus, R.S. (1966) *Psychological stress and the coping process.* New York: McGraw-Hill.

Lazarus, R.S. (1982) Thoughts on the relations between emotion and cognition. *American Psychologist, 37,* 1019–24.

Lazarus, R.S. & Folkman, S. (1984) *Stress, appraisal and coping.* New York: Springer-Verlag.

Lazarus, R.S. & McCleary, R.A. (1951) Automatic discrimination without awareness: A study of subception. *Psychological Review, 58,* 113–22.

Lea, S.E.G. (1984) *Instinct, environment and behaviour.* London: Methuen.

Le Bon, G. (1895) *The crowd: a study of the popular mind.* London: T. Fisher Unwin.

Leahy, A.M. (1935) Nature–nurture and intelligence. *Genetic Psychology Monograph, 17,* 235–308.

Leavitt, J.J. (1951) Some effects of certain communication patterns on group performance. *Journal of Abnormal and Social Psychology, 46,* 38–50.

LeDoux, J.E. (1994) Emotion-specific physiological activity: Don't forget about CNS physiology. In P. Ekman & R. J. Davidson (Eds.) *The nature of emotion: Fundamental questions.* New York: Oxford University Press.

Lee, D.N. & Lishman, J.R. (1975) Visual proprioceptive control of stance. *Journal of Human Movement Studies, 1,* 87–95.

Lee, L. (1984) Sequences in separation: A framework for investigating endings of the personal (romantic) relationship. *Journal of Social and Personal Relationships, 1,* 49–74.

Leekam, S. (1993) Children's understanding of mind. In M. Bennett (Ed.) *The child as psychologist: An introduction to the development of social cognition.* Hemel Hempstead, Herts.: Harvester Wheatsheaf.

LeFrancois, G.R. (1983) *Psychology.* Belmont, California: Wadsworth Publishing Co.

Legge, D. (1975) *An introduction to psychological science.* London: Methuen.

Lemyre, L. & Smith, P.M. (1985) Intergroup discrimination and self-esteem in the minimal group paradigm. *Journal of Personality and Social Psychology, 62,* 99–105.

Lenneberg, E.H. (1960) Review of speech and brain mechanisms by W. Penfield and L. Roberts. In R.C. Oldfield & J.C. Marshall (Eds.), *Language.* Harmondsworth, Middlesex: Penguin.

Lenneberg, E.H. (1967) *Biological foundations of language.* New York: Wiley.

Lenneberg, E.H. & Roberts, J.M. (1956) *The language of experience, Memoir 13.* Indiana: University of Indiania, Publications in Anthropology & Linguistics.

Lepper, M.R. & Greene, D. (1978) Overjustification research and beyond: Towards a means–end analysis of intrinsic and extrinsic motivation. In M.R. Lepper & D. Greene (Eds.), *The hidden costs of reward.* Hillsdale, New Jersey: Lawrence Erlbaum Associates Inc.

Lepper, M.R., Greene, D. & Nisbett, R.E. (1973) Undermining children's intrinsic interest with extrinsic reward: A test of the the overjustification hypothesis. *Journal of Personality & Social Psychology, 28,* 129–37.

Lerner, M.J. (1965) The effect of responsibility and choice on a partner's attractiveness following failure. *Journal of Personality, 33,* 178–87.

Lerner, M.J. (1980) *The belief in a just world ; A fundamental delusion.* New York: Plenum.

Leslie, A.M. (1987) Pretence and representation: The origins of 'theory of mind'. *Psychological Review, 94,* 412–26.

Leslie, A,M, & Roth, D. (1993) What autism teaches us about metarepresentation. In S. Baron-Cohen, H. Tager-Flusberg & D.J. Cohen (Eds.) *Understanding other minds: Perspectives from autism.* Oxford: Oxford University Press.

Levenson, R.W. (1994) The search for autonomic specificity. In P. Ekman & R.J. Davidson (Eds.) *The nature of emotion: Fundamental questions.* New York: Oxford University Press.

Levenson, R. W., Ekman, P.& Friesen, W.V. (1990) Voluntary facial action generates emotion-specific autonomic nervous system activity. *Psychophysiology, 27,* 363–84.

Levenson, R.W., Ekman. P., Heider, K. & Friesen, W.V. (1992) Emotion and autonomic nervous system activity in the Minangkabau of West Sumatra. *Journal of Personality & Social Psychology, 62,* 972–88.

Levinger, G. (1980) Toward the analysis of close relationships. *Journal of Experimental Social Psychology, 16,* 510–44.

Levinger, G. & Clark, J. (1961) Emotional factors in the forgetting of word associations. *Journal of Abnormal and Social Psychology, 62,* 99–105.

Levinson, D.J., Darrow, D.N., Klein, E.B., Levinson, M.H. & McKee, B. (1978) *The seasons of a man's life.* New York: A.A. Knopf.

Levinson, D. J. (1986) A conception of adult development. *American Psychologist, 41,* 3–13.

Levy-Agresti, J. & Sperry, R.W. (1968) Differential perceptual capacities in major and minor hemispheres. *Proceedings of the National Academy of Sciences, 61,* 1151.

Lewin, K., Lippitt, R. & White, R. (1939) Patterns of aggressive behaviour in experimentally created 'social climates'. *Journal of Social Psychology, 10,* 271–99.

Le Voi, M. (1993) Parallel distributed processing and its application in models of memory. In G. Cohen, G. Kiss & M. Le Voi, *Memory: Current issues* (2nd ed.). Buckingham: Open University Press.

Lewin, R. (1991) Look who's talking now. *New Scientist, 130* (1766), 48–52.

Lewis, M. & Brooks-Gunn, J. (1979) *Social cognition and the acquisition of self.* New York: Plenum.

Leyens, J.P. & Codol, J.P. (1988) Social cognition. In M.Hewstone, W. Stroebe, J.P. Codol & G.M. Stephenson (Eds.) *Introduction to social psychology.* Oxford: Blackwell.

Lieberman, M.A. (1993) Bereavement self-help groups ; A review of conceptual and methodological issues. In M.S. Stroebe, W. Stroebe & R.O. Hansson (Eds.) *Handbook of bereavement: Theory, research and intervention.* New York: Cambridge University Press.

Light, P. (1986) Context, conservation and conversation. In M. Richards & P. Light (Eds.), *Children of social worlds.* Cambridge: Polity Press.

Light, P., Buckingham, N. & Robbins, A.H. (1979) The conserva-tion task as an interactional setting. *British Journal of Educational Psychology, 49,* 304–10.

Light, P. & Gilmour, A. (1983) Conservation or conversation? Contextual facilitation of inappropriate conservation judge-ments. *Journal of Experimental Child Psychology, 36,* 356–63.

Likert, R. (1932) A technique for the measurement of attitudes. *Archives of Psychology, 22,* 140.

Likert, R. (1961) New patterns of management. New York: McGraw-Hill.

Lilienfeld, S.O. (1995) *Seeing both sides: Classic controversies in abnormal psychology.* Pacific Grove, CA.: Brooks/Cole Publishing Company.

Linder, D.E., Cooper, J. & Jones, E.E. (1967) Decision freedom as a determinant of the role of incentive magnitude in attitude change. *Journal of Personality and Social Psychology, 6,* 245–54.

Lindsay, W.R. (1982) The effects of labelling: Blind and non-blind ratings of social skills in schizophrenic and non-schizophrenic

control subjects. *American Journal of Psychiatry, 139,* 216–19.

Linville, P.W., Fischer, G.W. & Salovey, P. (1989) Perceived distri-butions of the characteristics of in-group and out-group members: empirical evidence and a computer simulation. *Journal of Personality & Social Psychology, 57,* 165–88.

Linville, P.W. & Jones, E.E. (1980) Polarized appraisals of out-group members. *Journal of Personality and Social Psychology, 38,* 689–703.

Lipsitt, L.P. (1977) The study of sensory and learning processes of the newborn. *Clinics in Perinatology, 4,* 163–86.

Lippman, W. (1922) *Public opinion.* New York: Harcourt.

Littlewood, R. & Lipsedge, M. (1989) *Aliens and alienists :Ethnic minorities and psychiatry* (2nd ed.) London: Routledge.

Lloyd, P., Mayes, A., Manstead, A.S.R., Mendell, P.R. & Wagner, H.L. (1984) *Introduction to psychology – an integrated approach.* London: Fontana.

Locke, S.E. (1982) Stress, adaptation and immunity: Studies in humans. *General Hospital Psychiatry, 4,* 49–58.

Locksley, A., Ortiz, V. & Hepburn, C. (1980) Social categorization and discriminatory behaviour. Extinguishing the minimal intergroup discrimination effect. *Journal of Personality and Social Psychology, 39,* 773–83.

Loehlin, J.C. (1989) Partitioning environmental and genetic con-tributions to behavioural development. *American Psychologist, 44,* 1285.

Loehlin, J.C., Willerman, L. & Horn, J.M. (1988) Human behaviour genetics. *Annual Review of Psychology, 39,* 101–33.

Loftus, E.F. (1979) Reactions to blatantly contradictory informa-tion. *Memory and Cognition, 7,* 368–74.

Loftus, E.F. (1984) Expert testimony on the eyewitness. In G.L. Wells & E.F. Loftus (Eds.), *Eyewitness testimony: Psychological perspectives.* Cambridge: Cambridge University Press.

Loftus, E.F., Freedman, J.L. & Loftus, G.R. (1970) Retrieval of words from sub-ordinate and superordinate categories in semantic hierarchies. *Psychonomic Science, 21,* 235–6.

Loftus, E.F., Miller, D.G. & Burns, H.J. (1978) Semantic integra-tion of verbal information into a visual memory. *Journal of Experimental Psychology, 4* (1), 19–31.

Loftus, E.F. & Palmer, J.C. (1974) Reconstruction of automobile destruction: An example of the interaction between language and memory. *Journal of Verbal Learning and Verbal Behaviour, 13,* 585–9.

Loftus, E.F. & Zanni, G. (1975) Eyewitness testimony: The influ-ence of the wording of a question. *Bulletin of the Psychonomic Society, 5,* 86–8.

Logan, G.D. (1988) Toward an instance theory of automisation. *Psychological Review, 95,* 492–527.

Lorenz, K.Z. (1935) The companion in the bird's world. *Auk, 54,* 245–73.

Lorenz, K.Z. (1966) *On aggression.* London: Methuen.

Lott, A.J. & Lott, B.E. (1974) The role of reward in the formation of positive interpersonal attitudes. In T.Huston (Ed.) *Foundations of interpersonal attraction.* New York: Academic Press.

Lovaas, O.I., Freitas, L., Nelson, K. & Whalen, C. (1967) The establishment of imitation and its use for the development of complex behaviour in schizophrenic children. *Behaviour Research and Therapy, 5,* 171–81.

Lubinski, D., Tellegen, A. & Butcher, J.N. (1981) The relationship between androgyny and subjective indicators of emotional well-being. *Journal of Personality & Social Psychology, 40,* 722–30.

Lubinski, D., Tellegen, A. & Butcher, J.N. (1983) Masculinity, feminity and androgyny. *Journal of Personality & Social Psychology, 44,* 428–39.

Luborsky, L., Singer, B. & Luborsky, L. (1975) Comparative studies of psychotherapies: is it true that 'everyone has won and all must have prizes'? *Archives of General Psychiatry, 32,* 995–1008.

Luchins, A.S. (1942) Mechanisation in problem solving. The effect of Einstellung. *Psychological Monographs,* 54 (Whole No. 248).

Luchins, A.S. (1957) Primacy–recency in impression formation. In C. Hovland (Ed.), *The order of presentation in persuasion.* New Haven, Connecticut: Yale University Press.

Luchins, A.S. & Luchins, E.H. (1959) *Rigidity of behaviour.* Eugene, Oregon: University of Oregon Press.

Luria, A.R. (1968) *The mind of a mnemonist.* New York: Basic Books.

Luria, A.R. (1975) *The man with a shattered world.* Harmondsworth, Middlesex: Penguin.

Luria, A.R. (1987) Reductionism. In R. Gregory (Ed.), *The Oxford companion to the mind.* Oxford: Oxford University Press.

Luria, A.R. & Yudovich, F.I. (1971) *Speech and the development of mental processes in the child.* Harmondsworth, Middlesex: Penguin.

Lyons, J. (1970) *Chomsky.* London: Fontana.

Lytton, H. (1977) Do parents create, or respond to, differences in twins? *Developmental Psychology, 13,* 456–9.

Maccoby, E.E. (1980) *Social development – psychological growth and the parent child relationship.* New York: Harcourt Brace Jovanovich.

Maccoby, E.E. & Jacklin, C.N. (1974) *The psychology of sex differences.* Stanford, California: Stanford University Press.

Mackay, D. (1975) *Clinical psychology – theory and therapy.* London: Methuen.

Mackay, D. (1984) Behavioural psychotherapy. In W. Dryden (Ed.), *Individual therapy in Britain.* London: Harper & Row.

Mackinnon, D. (1938) Violations of prohibitions. In H.A. Murray (Ed.), *Explorations in personality.* New York: Oxford University Press.

Mackintosh, N.J. (1978) Cognitive or associative theories of conditioning: implications of an analysis of blocking. In S.H. Hulse, M. Fowler & W.K. Honig (Eds.) *Cognitive processes in animal behaviour.* Hillsdale, NJ.: Lawrence Erlbaum.

Mackintosh, N. (1984) In search of a new theory of conditioning. In G. Ferry (Ed.), *The understanding of animals.* Oxford: Blackwell and New Scientist.

MacNamara, J. (1982) *Names for things.* Cambridge, Massachusetts: Bradford MIT Press.

Maddison, D. & Viola, A. (1968) The health of widows in the year following bereavement. *Journal of Psychosomatic Research, 12,* 297.

Maddox, G.L. (1964) Disengagement theory: A critical evaluation. *The Gerontologist, 4,* 80–3.

Maher, B.A. (1966) *Principles of psychopathology: An experimental approach.* New York: McGraw-Hill.

Mahoney, M.J. (1974) *Cognition and behaviour modification.* Cambridge, Massachusetts: Ballinger.

Maier, N.R.F. (1931) Reasoning in humans II: The solution of a problem and its appearance in consciousness. *Journal of Comparative Psychology, 12,* 181–94.

Maier, S.F. & Seligman, M.E.P. (1976) Learned helplessness: Theory and evidence. *Journal of Experimental Psychology: General, 105,* 3–46.

Mair, K. (1992) The myth of therapist expertise. In W. Dryden & C. Feltham (Eds.) *Psychotherapy and its Discontents.,* Buckingham: Open University Press.

Malan, D. (1976) *Toward the validation of dynamic psychotherapy.* New York: Plenum.

Main, M. (1991) Metacognitive knowledge, metacognitive monitoring, and singular (coherent) vs. multiple (incoherent) model of attachment: Findings and directions for future research. In C.M.Murray Parkes, J.M. Stevenson-Hinde & P. Marris (Eds.) *Attachment across the life cycle.* London: Routledge.

Main, M., Kaplan, N. & Cassidy, J. (1985) Security in infancy, childhood and adulthood: A move to the level of representation. In I. Bretherton & E. Waters (Eds.) *Growing points of attachment theory and research* (Monographs of the Society for Research in Child Development, Vol. 50, Serial No. 209). Chicago: University of Chicago Press.

Main, M. & Weston, D.R. (1981) The quality of the toddler's relationship to mother and to father: Related to conflict behaviour and the readiness to establish new relationships. *Child Development, 52,* 932–40.

Major, B. (1980) Information acquisition and attribution processes. *Journal of Personality & Social Psychology, 39,* 1010–23.

Malinowski, B. (1929) *The sexual life of savages.* New York: Harcourt, Brace and World.

Mandler, G. (1967) Organization and memory. In K.W. Spence & J.T. Spence (Eds.) *The psychology of learning and motivation* (vol. 1). New York: Academic Press.

Mandler, G. (1984) Representation and recall in infancy. In M. Moscovitch (Ed.) *Infant Memory.* New York: Plenum Press.

Mandler, J.M. & Johnson, N.S. (1977) Remembrance of things parsed: Story structure and recall. *Cognitive Psychology, 9,* 111–51.

Mann, L. (1969) *Social psychology.* New York: Wiley.

Mapstone, E. (1991) Special issue on animal experimentation. *The Psychologist, 4* (5), 195.

Marañon, G. (1924) Contribution a l'etude de l'action emotive de l'adrenaline. *Revue Française Endocrinol., 2,* 301–25.

Marcia, J.E. (1966) Development and validation of ego identity status. *Journal of Personality and Social Psychology, 3,* 551–8.

Marcia, J.E. (1967) Ego identity status: Relationship to change in self-esteem, general maladjustment and authoritarianism. *Journal of Personality, 35,* 118–33.

Marcia, J.E. (1968) The case history of a construct: Ego identity status. In E. Vinacke (Ed.), *Readings in general psychology.* New York: Van Nostrand–Reinhold.

Marcia, J.E. (1980) Identity in adolescence. In J. Adelson (Ed.) *Handbook of adolescent psychology.* New York: Wiley.

Marcus, D.E. & Overton, W.F. (1978) The development of cognitive gender constancy and sex role preferences. *Child Development, 49,* 434–44.

Marks, I.M. (1973) The reduction of fear: Towards a unifying theory. *Journal of the Canadian Psychiatric Association, 18,* 9–12.

Marks, I.M. (1978) Exposure treatments: conceptual issues. In W.S. Agras (Ed.) *Behaviour Modification.* Boston: Little Brown.

Marks, I.M. (1981) Space phobia: pseudo-agoraphobic syndrome. *Journal of Neurology, Neurosurgery & Psychiatry, 44,* 387–91.

Marks, I.M., Gelder, M. & Bancroft, J. (1970) Sexual deviants two years after electric aversion. *British Journal of Psychiatry, 117,* 173–85.

Markus, H. & Nurius, P. (1986) Possible selves. *American Psychologist, 41,* 954–69.

Marr, D. (1976) Early processing of visual information.

Philosophical Transactions of the Royal Society of London, B275, 483–524.

Marr, D. (1982) *Vision: A computational investigation into the human representation and processing of visual information.* San Francisco: W.H. Freeman.

Marr, D. & Hildreth, E. (1980) Theory of edge detection. *Proceedings of the Royal Society of London,* B, 207, 187–217.

Marr, D. & Nishihara, K.H. (1978) Representation and recognition of the spatial organization of three-dimensional shapes. *Proceedings of the Royal Society of London,* B, 200, 269–94.

Marris, P. (1958) *Widows and their families.* London, Routledge & Kegan Paul.

Marshall, G.D. & Zimbardo, P.G. (1979) Affective consequences of inadequately explained physiological arousal. *Journal of Personality and Social Psychology,* 37, 970–88.

Marsland, D. (1987) *Education and youth.* London: Falmer.

Martin, G. & Pear, J. (1992) *Behaviour modification: What it is and how to do it* (4th ed). Englewood Cliffs, NJ: Prentice-Hall.

Maslach, C. (1979) Negative emotional biasing of unexplained arousal. *Journal of Personality and Social Psychology,* 37, 953–69.

Maslach, C. Stapp, J. & Santee, R.T. (1985) Individuation: Conceptual analysis and assessment. *Journal of Personality & Social Psychology,* 49, 729–38.

Maslach, C., Santee, R.T. & Wade, C. (1987) Individuation, gender role and dissent: Personality mediators of situational forces. *Journal of Personality and Social Psychology,* 53, 1088–93.

Maslach, C, Stapp, J. & Santee, R.T. (1985) Individuation: Conceptual analysis and assessment. *Journal of Personality & Social Psychology,* 49, 729–38.

Maslow, A. (1954) *Motivation and personality.* New York: Harper & Row.

Maslow, A. (1968) *Towards a psychology of being* (2nd ed.). New York: Van Nostrand–Reinhold.

Maslow, A. (1970) *Motivation and personality* (2nd ed.). New York: Harper & Row.

Maslow, C., Yoselson, K. & London, M. (1971) Persuasiveness of confidence expressed via language and body language. *British Journal of Social and Clinical Psychology,* 10, 234–40.

Mason, M.K. (1942) Learning to speak after six and one half years of silence. *Journal of Speech and Hearing Disorders,* 7, 295–304.

Masson, J. (1984) *The assault on truth: Freud's suppression of the seduction theory.* London: Faber & Faber.

Masson, J. (1988) *Against therapy: Emotional tyranny and the myth of psychological healing.* New York: Atheneum.

Masson, J. (1992) The tyranny of psychotherapy. In W. Dryden & C. Feltham (Eds.) *Psychotherapy and its discontents.* Buckingham: Open University Press.

Matson, J.L., Ollendick, T.H. & Adkins, J. (1980) A comprehensive dining program for mentally retarded adults. *Behaviour Research & Therapy,* 18, 107–12.

Maunsell, J.H.R. & Newsome, W.T. (1987) Visual processing in monkey extrastriate cortex. *Annual Review of Neuroscience,* 10, 363–401.

Mayall, B. & Petrie, P. (1977) *Minder, mother and child.* London: University of London Institute of Education.

Mayer, J. (1955) Regulation of energy intake and the body weight: The glucostatic theory and the lipostatic hypothesis. *Annals of the New York Academy of Sciences,* 63, 15–43.

Maykovich, M.K. (1975) Correlates of racial prejudice. *Journal of Personality and Social Psychology,* 32, 1014–20.

McArthur, L.A. (1972) The how and why of why: Some determinants and consequences of causal attribution. *Journal of*

Personality and Social Psychology, 22, 171–93.

McCall, R.B. (1975) *Intelligence and heredity.* Homewood, Illinois: Learning Systems Co.

McCall, R.B., Applebaum, M.I. & Hogarty, P.S. (1973) Developmental changes in mental test performance. *Monographs of the Society for Research in Child Development* 38, (3, Whole No. 150).

McCann, J.J. (1987) Retinex theory and colour constancy. In R. Gregory (Ed.), *Oxford companion to the mind.* Oxford: Oxford University Press.

McCarley, R.M. (1983) REM dreams, REM sleep and their isomorphism. In M.H. Chase & E.D. Weitzman (Eds.), *Sleep disorders: Basic and clinical research, Vol. 8* (published as book). New York: Spectrum.

McClelland, D.C., Atkinson, J., Clark, R. & Lowell, E. (1953) *The achievement motive.* New York: Appleton-Century-Croft.

McCrae, R.R. & Costa, P.T. (1989) More reasons to adopt the five-factor model. *American Psychologist,* 44, 451–2.

McDougall, W. (1908) *An introduction to social psychology.* London: Methuen.

McGarrigle, J. & Donaldson, M. (1974) Conservation accidents. *Cognition,* 3, 341–50.

McGeoch, J.A. (1936) Studies in retroactive inhibition. VIII: Retroactive inhibition as a function of the length and frequency of the interpolated task. *Journal of Experimental Psychology,* 19, 674–93.

McGeoch, J.A. (1942) *The psychology of learning.* New York: Spectrum.

McGinn, C. (1987) Could a machine be conscious? In C. Blakemore & S. Greenfield (Eds.), *Mindwaves.* Oxford: Blackwell.

McGinnies, E. (1949) Emotionality and perceptual defence. *Psychological Review,* 56, 244–51.

McGlynn, F.D., Mealiea, W.L. & Landau, D.L. (1981) The current status of systematic desensitization. *Clinical Psychology Review,* 1, 149–79.

McGuire, W.J. (1957) Order of presentation as a factor in "conditioning" persuasiveness. In C.I. Hovland (Ed.), *The order of presentation in persuasion.* New Haven: Yale University Press.

McGuire, W.J. (1968) Personality and susceptibility to social influence. In E.F. Borgatta & W.W. Lambert (Eds.) *Handbook of personality: Theory and research.* Chicago, IL: Rand-McNally.

McGuire, W.J. (1969) The nature of attitudes and attitude change. In G. Lindzey & E. Aronson (Eds.) *Handbook of social psychology* (2nd ed., vol. 3). Reading, MA: Addison-Wesley.

McGuire, W.J. & Papegeorgis, D. (1961) Effectiveness of forewarning in developing resistance to persuasion. *Public Opinion Quarterly,* 26, 24–34.

McGurk, H. (1975) *Growing and changing.* London: Methuen.

McNally, R.J. & Reiss, S. (1982) The preparedness theory of phobias and human safety-signal conditioning. *Behaviour Research and Therapy,* 20, 153–9.

McNeill, D. (1966) The creation of language. In R.C. Oldfield & J.C. Marshall (Eds.), *Language.* Harmondsworth, Middlesex: Penguin.

McNeill, D. (1970) *The acquisition of language.* New York: Harper & Row.

Mead, G.H. (1925) The genesis of the self and social control. *International Journal of Ethics,* 35, 251–73.

Mead, G.H. (1934) *Mind, self and society.* Chicago: University of Chicago Press.

Mead, M. (1928) *Coming of age in Samoa.* Harmondsworth, Middlesex: Penguin.

Mead, M. (1930) *Growing up in New Guinea.* Harmondsworth,

Middlesex: Penguin.

Mead, M. (1935) *Sex and temperament in three primitive societies*. New York: Dell.

Mead, M. (1949) *Male and female: A study of the sexes in a changing world*. New York: Dell.

Meadows, S (1986) *Understanding child development*. London: Hutchinson.

Meadows, S. (1988) Piaget's contribution to understanding cognitive development: An assessment for the late 1980's. In K. Richardson & S. Sheldon (Eds.), *Cognitive development to adolescence*. Milton Keynes/Hove: Open University/Lawrence Erlbaum Associates Ltd.

Meadows, S. (1993) *The child as thinker: The acquisition and development of cognition in childhood*. London: Routledge.

Meadows, S. (1995) Cognitive development. In P.E. Bryant & A.M. Colman (Eds.) *Developmental psychology*. London: Longman.

Medawar, P.B. (1963) *The art of the soluble*. Harmondsworth, Middlesex: Penguin.

Meddis, R. (1975) On the function of sleep. *Animal Behaviour, 23*, 676–91.

Meddis, R. (1977) *The sleep instinct*. London: Routledge & Kegan Paul.

Medvedev, Z.A. (1975) Aging and longevity: New approaches and new perspectives. *The Gerontologist, 15*, 196–201.

Megargee, E.I. (1966) Uncontrolled and overcontrolled personality types in extreme antisocial aggression. *Psychological Monographs: General and Applied* (Whole No. 611).

Mehrabian, A. (1972) Nonverbal communication. In J. Cole (Ed.) *Nebraska Symposium on Motivation* (vol. 19). Lincoln, NE: University of Nebraska Press.

Meichenbaum, D. (1977) *Cognitive behaviour modification: An integrative approach*. New York: Plenum.

Meichenbaum, D.H. & Goodman, J. (1971) Training impulsive children to talk to themselves: A means of developing self-control. *Journal of Abnormal Psychology, 77*, 115–26.

Melhuish, E.C. (1982) Visual attention to mothers' and strangers' faces and facial contrast in 1 month olds. *Developmental Psychology, 18*, 299–331.

Melton, A.W. & Irwin, J.M. (1940) The influence of degree of interpolated learning on retroactive inhibition and the overt transfer of specific responses. *American Journal of Psychology, 53*, 173–203.

Melville, J. (1980) Anorexia – fear eats the soul. *New Society*, September, 612–13.

Merei, F. (1949) Group leadership and institutionalization. *Human Relations, 2*, 18–30.

Meyer, V. & Chesser, E.S. (1970) *Behaviour therapy in clinical psychiatry*. Harmondsworth: Penguin.

Miell, D. (1990) Issues in social psychology. In I. Roth (Ed.) *Introduction to psychology, vol.2*. Hove: Lawrence Erlbaum/Open University.

Milavsky, J.R., Kessler, R.C., Stipp, H. & Rubens, W.S. (1982) *Television and aggression: A panel study*. New York: Academic Press.

Miles. T.R. (1967) On defining intelligence. In S. Wiseman (Ed.) *Intelligence and ability*. Harmondsworth: Penguin.

Milgram, S. (1963) Behavioural study of obedience. *Journal of Abnormal and Social Psychology, 67*, 391–8.

Milgram, S. (1965) Liberating effects of group pressure. *Journal of Personality and Social Psychology, 1(2), 127–34.*

Milgram, S. (1969) The lost-letter technique. *Psychology Today, 3(3)*, June, 30–3.

Milgram, S. (1974) *Obedience to authority*. New York: Harper & Row.

Milgram, S. (1992) *The individual in a social world* (2nd ed.).

New York: McGraw-Hill.

Millar, S. (1968) *The psychology of play*. Harmondsworth, Middlesex: Penguin.

Miller, D.T. & Ross, M. (1977) Self-serving biases in the attribution of causality: Fact or fiction? *Psychological Bulletin, 82*, 213–25.

Miller, E. & Morley, S. (1986) *Investigating abnormal behaviour*. London: Lawrence Erlbaum Associates Ltd.

Miller, G.A. (1956) The magical number seven, plus or minus two: Some limits on our capacity for processing information. *Psychological Review, 63*, 81–97.

Miller, G.A. (1962) *Psychology – the science of mental life*. Harmondsworth, Middlesex: Penguin.

Miller, G.A. (1968) *The psychology of communication – seven essays*. Harmondsworth, Middlesex: Penguin.

Miller, G.A. (1969) Psychology as a means of promoting human welfare. *American Psychologist, 24*, 1063–75.

Miller, G.A. & McNeill, D. (1969) Psycholinguistics. In G. Lindzey & E. Aronson (Eds.), *The handbook of social psychology, Vol. 3*. Reading, Massachusetts: Adison-Wesley.

Miller, G.A. & Selfridge, J.A. (1950) Verbal context and the recall of meaningful material. *American Journal of Psychology, 63*, 176–85.

Miller, I. & Norman, W. (1979) Learned helplessness in humans: A review and attribution theory model. *Psychological Bulletin, 86*, 93–118.

Miller, N. & Campbell, D. (1959) Recency and primacy in persuasion as a function of the timing of speeches and measurements. *Journal of Abnormal and Social Psychology, 59*, 1–9.

Miller, N.E. (1941) The frustration–aggression hypothesis. *Psychology Review, 48*, 337–42.

Miller, N.E. (1948) Theory and experiment relating psychoanalytic displacement to stimulus-response generalization. *Journal of Abnormal & Social Psychology,43*, 155–78.

Miller, N.E. (1978) Biofeedback and visceral learning. *Annual Review of Psychology, 29*, 373–404.

Miller, N.E. & Dicara, L.V. (1967) Instrumental learning of heart-rate changes in curarised rats: Shaping and specificity to discriminative stimulus. *Journal of Comparative and Physiological Psychology, 63*, 12–19.

Milner, B. (1971) Interhemispheric differences in the localization of psychological processes in man. *British Medical Bulletin, 27*, 272–7.

Milner, B., Corkin, S. & Teuber, H.L. (1968) Further analysis of the hippocampal amnesic syndrome: 14-year follow-up study of H.M. *Neuropsychologia, 6*, 215–34.

Minard, R.D. (1952) Race relations in the Pocohontas coalfield. *Journal of Social Issues, 8*, 29–44.

Minsky, M. (1975) A framework for representing knowledge. In P.H. Winston (Ed.), *The psychology of computer vision*. New York: McGraw Hill.

Mischel, W. (1968) *Personality and assessment*. New York: Wiley.

Mischel, W. (1969) Continuities and change in personality. *American Psychologist, 24*, 1012–18.

Mischel, W. (1973) Toward a cognitive social learning reconceptualization of personality. *Psychological Review, 80*, 252–83.

Mischel, W. & Mischel, H.N. (1976) A cognitive social learning approach to morality and self-regulation. In T. Lickona (Ed.), *Moral development and behaviour: Theory, research and social issues*. New York: Holt, Rinehart & Winston.

Mistry, J. & Rogoff, B. (1994) Remembering in cultural context. In W.J. Lonner & R.S. Malpass (Eds.) *Psychology and culture*. Boston: Allyn & Bacon.

Mitchell, J. (1974) *Psychoanalysis and feminism*.

Harmondsworth, Middlesex: Penguin.

Mitchel, R. (1982) *Phobias*. Harmondsworth, Middlesex: Penguin.

Moghaddam, F.M., Taylor, D.M. & Wright, S.C. (1993) *Social psychology in cross-cultural perspective*. New York: W H Freeman & Co.

Moltz, H. & Stettner, L.J. (1961) The influences of patterned-light deprivation on the critical period for imprinting. *Journal of Comparative and Physiological Psychology*, *54*, 279–83.

Monahan, F. (1941) *Women in crime*. New York: Ives Washburn.

Money, J. (1971) Sexually dimorphous behaviour, normal and abnormal. In N. Kretchner & D.N. Walcher (Eds.), *Environmental influences on genetic expression*. Washington DC: US Government Printing Office.

Money, J. (1974) Prenatal hormones and postnatal socialization in gender identity differentiation. In J.K. Cole & R. Dienstbier (Eds.), *Nebraska Symposium on Motivation*. Lincoln: University of Nebraska Press.

Money, J. & Ehrhardt, A.A. (1972) *Man and woman, boy and girl*. Baltimore: Johns Hopkins University Press.

Money, J., Hampson, J.G. & Hampson, J.L. (1957) Imprinting and the establishment of gender role. *Archives of Neurology & Psychiatry, 77*, 333–6.

Moore, C. & Frye, D. (1986) The effect of the experimenter's intention on the child's understanding of conservation. *Cognition*, *22*, 283–98.

Moray, N. (1959) Attention in dichotic listening: Affective cues and the influence of instructions. *Quarterly Journal of Experimental Psychology*, *11*, 56–60.

Moreno, J.L. (1953) *Who shall survive?* (2nd ed.). New York: Beacon.

Morgan, M. (1982) Television and adolescents' sex role stereotypes: A longitudinal study. *Journal of Personality and Social Psychology*, *43*, 947–55.

Morris, C.D., Bransford, J.D. & Franks, J.J. (1977) Levels of processing versus transfer appropriate processing. *Journal of Verbal Learning and Verbal Behaviour*, *16*, 519–33.

Morris, D. (1967) *The naked ape*. London: Jonathan Cape.

Morris, D. (1969) *The human zoo*. London: Jonathan Cape.

Morris, P.E. (1978) Models of long-term memory. In M.M. Gruneberg & P.E. Morris (Eds.), *Aspects of memory*. London: Methuen.

Morton, J. (1970) A functional model for memory. In D.A. Norman (Ed.) *Models of Human Memory*. New York: Academic Press.

Moruzzi, G. & Magoun, H.W. (1949) Brain stem reticular formation and activation of the EEG. *Electroencephalography and Clinical Neurophysiology*, *1*, 455–73.

Moscovici, S. (1961) *La psychoanlyse: son image et son public*. Paris ; Presses Universitaires de France.

Moscovici, S. (1976) *Social influence and social change*. London: Academic Press.

Moscovici, S. (1980) Towards a theory of conversion behaviour. In L. Berkowitz (Ed.) *Advances in experimental social psychology 13*, 209–39.

Moscovici, S. (1981) On social representation. In J.P. Forgas (Ed.) *Social cognition: Perspectives in everyday understanding*. London: Academic Press.

Moscovici, S. (1982) The coming era of representations. In J-P Codol & J.P.Leyens (Eds.) *Cognitive analysis of social behaviour*. The Hague: Martinus Nijhoff.

Moscovici, S. (1985) Social influence and conformity. In G. Lindzey & E. Aronson (Eds.) *Handbook of social psychology* (3rd ed.). New York: Random House.

Moscovici, S. & Faucheux, C. (1972) Social influence, conforming bias and the study of active minorities. In L. Berkowitz (Ed.) *Advances in experimental social psychology* (vol. 6). New York: Academic Press.

Moscovici, S. & Hewstone, M. (1983) Social representations and social explanations: from the 'naive' to the 'amateur' scientist. In M. Hewstone (Ed.) *Attribution Theory: Social and functional extensions*. Oxford: Blackwell.

Moscovici, S. & Zavalonni, M. (1969) The group as a polarizer of attitudes. *Journal of Personality & Social Psychology*, *12*, 125–35.

Moser, K.A., Fox, A.J. & Jones, D.R. (1984) Unemployment and mortality in the OPCS longitudinal study. *Lancet*, *2*, 1324–9.

Moskovitz, S. (1983) *Love despite hate – child survivors of the Holocaust and their adult lives*. New York: Schocken.

Mowrer, O.H. (1950) *Learning theory and personality dynamics*. New York: Ronald Press.

Mowrer, O.H. (1960) *Learning theory and behaviour*. New York: John Wiley.

Moyer, K.E. (1976) *The psychobiology of aggression*. New York: Harper & Row.

Mundy-Castle, A.C. & Nelson, G.K. (1962) A neuropsychological study of the Kuysma forest workers. *Psychologia Africana*, *9*, 240–72.

Murdock, B.B. (1962) The serial position effect of free recall. *Journal of Experimental Psychology*, *64*, 482–8.

Murphy, G. (1947) *Personality: A bio-social approach to origins and structure*. New York: Harper & Row.

Murray, E.J. & Foote, F. (1979) The origins of fear of snakes. *Behaviour Research and Therapy*, *17*, 489–93.

Murray, H.A. (Ed.) (1938) *Explorations in personality*. New York: Oxford University Press.

Murstein, B.I. (1972) Physical attractiveness and marital choice. *Journal of Personality and Social Psychology*, *22* (1), 8–12.

Murstein, B.I. (1976) The stimulus-value-role theory of marital choice. In H. Grunebaum & J. Christ (Eds.) *Contemporary marriage: Structures, dynamics and therapy*. Boston: Little, Brown.

Murstein, B.I. (1978) *Exploring intimate lifestyles*. New York: Springer.

Murstein, B.I. (1986) *Paths to marriage*. Beverly Hills, CA: Sage.

Murstein, B.I. (1987) A clarification and extension of the SVR theory of dyadic pairing. *Journal of Marriage and the Family*, *49*, 929–33.

Murstein, B.I. & MacDonald, M.G. (1983) The relation of 'exchange orientation' and 'commitment' scales to marriage adjustment. *International Journal of Psychology*, *18*, 297–311.

Murstein, B.I., MacDonald, M.G. & Cerreto, M. (1977) A theory of the effect of exchange-orientation on marriage and friendship. *Journal of Marriage and the Family*, *39*, 543–8.

Mussen, P.H. & Jones, M. (1957) Self-conceptions, motivations and interpersonal attitudes of late and early maturing boys. *Child Development*, *28*, 243–56.

Myers. D. (1994) *Exploring social psychology*. New York: McGraw-Hill.

Myers, D. G. & Lamm, H. (1975) The group polarization phenomenon. *Psychological Bulletin*, *83*, 602–27.

Navon, D. (1977) Forest before trees: The precedence of global features in visual perception. *Cognitive Psychology*, *9*, 353–83.

Neisser, U. (1964) Visual search. *Scientific American*, *210*, 94–102.

Neisser, U. (1967) *Cognitive psychology*. New York: Appleton-Century-Crofts.

Neisser, U. (1976) *Cognition and reality*. San Francisco: W.H. Freeman.

Neisser, U. (1979) The concept of intelligence. In R.J. Sternberg

& D.K. Detterman (Eds.), *Human intelligence: Perspectives on its theory and measurement*. New Jersey: Norwood.

Neisser, U. (1982) *Memory observed*. San Francisco, CA: Freeman.

Nelson, K. (1973) Structure and strategy in learning to talk. *Monographs of the Society for Research in Child Development, 38,* 149.

Nelson, S.A. (1980) Factors influencing young children's use of motives and outcomes as moral criteria. *Child Development, 51,* 823–9.

Nelson, T.O. & Vining, S.K. (1978) Effect of semantic versus structural processing on long-term retention. *Journal of Experimental Psychology: Human learning and memory, 4,* 198–209.

Nesselroade, J.R., Schaie, K.W. & Batter, P.B. (1972) Ontogenetic and generational components of structural and quantitative change in adult behaviour. *Journal of Gerontology, 27,* 222–8.

Neugarten, B.L. (1965) Personality and patterns of ageing. *Gawein, 13,* 249–56.

Neugarten, B.L. (1975) The future of the young-old. *The Gerontologist, 15,* 4–9.

Neugarten, B.L. & Havighurst, R.J. (1969) Disengagement reconsidered in a cross national context. In R.J. Havighurst (Ed.), *Adjustment to retirement*. Assess, Netherlands: Van Gorcum.

Neugarten, B.L., Moore, J.W. & Lowe, J.C. (1965) Age norms, age constraints and adult socialization. *American Journal of Sociology, 70,* 710–17.

Newcomb, T.M. (1943) *Personality and social change*. New York: Holt, Rinehart & Winston.

Newcomb, T.M. (1947) Autistic hostility and social reality. *Human Relations, 1,* 69–86.

Newcomb, T.M. (1961) *The aquaintanceship process*. New York: Holt, Rinehart & Winston.

Newell, A. (1973) Production systems: Models of control structures. In W.G. Chase (Ed.), *Visual information processing*. New York: Academic Press.

Newell, A., Shaw, J.C. & Simon, H.A. (1958) Elements of a theory of human problem solving. *Psychological Review, 65,* 151–66.

Newell, A. & Simon, H.A. (1972) *Human problem solving*. Englewood Cliffs, New Jersey: Prentice-Hall.

Newman, H.H., Freeman, F.N. & Holzinger, K.J. (1937) *Twins: A study of heredity and environment*. Chicago, Illinois: University of Chicago Press.

Newson, E. (1994) Video violence: And the protection of children. *Psychology Review, 1* (2), 2–5.

Newstead, S. (1995) Language and thought: The Whorfian hypothesis. *Psychology Review, 1* (3), 5–7.

Nicholson, J. (1977) *Habits*. London: Macmillan.

Nicholson, J. (1993) *Men and women: How different are they ?* (2nd ed.) Oxford: Oxford University Press.

Nisbett, R.E. & Borgida, E. (1975) Attribution and the psychology of prediction. *Journal of Personality and Social Psychology, 32,* 923–43.

Nisbett, R.E., Caputo, C., Legant, P. & Maracek, J. (1973) Behaviour as seen by the actor and as seen by the observer. *Journal of Personality and Social Psychology, 27,* 154–65.

Nisbett, R.E. & Ross, L. (1980) *Human inference: Strategies and shortcomings of social judgement*. Englewood Cliffs, New Jersey: Prentice-Hall.

Nisbett, R.E. & Wilson, T. (1977) Telling more than we can know: Verbal reports on mental processes. *Psychology Review, 84,* 231–59.

Norman, D.A. (1969) Memory while shadowing. *Quarterly Journal of Experimental Psychology, 21,* 85–93.

Norman, D.A. (1976) *Memory and attention* (2nd ed.).

Chichester: Wiley.

Norman, D.A. & Bobrow, D.G. (1975) On data-limited and resource-limited processing. *Cognitive Psychology, 7,* 44–64.

Norman, D.A. & Shallice, T. (1980) *Attention to action: Willed and automatic control of behaviour (CHIP Report 99)*. San Diego, California: University of California.

Oakes, P.J., Haslam, S.A. & Turner, J.C. (1994) *Stereotyping and social reality*. Oxford: Blackwell.

Oakes, P.J. & Turner, J.C. (1980) Social categorization and intergroup behaviour: Does minimal intergroup discrimination make social identity more positive? *European Journal of Psychology, 10,* 295–301.

Oakley, D.A. (1983) The varieties of memory: A phylogenetic approach. In A.R. Mayes (Ed.) *Memory in humans and animals*. Wokingham: Van Nostrand.

Oatley, K. (1981) The self with others: The person and the interpersonal context in the approaches of C.R. Rogers and R.D. Laing. In Fransella, F. (Ed.), *Personality – theory, measurement and research*. London: Methuen.

Oatley, K. (1984) *Selves in relation: An introduction to psychotherapy and groups*. London: Methuen.

O'Connor, N. & Hermelin, B. (1988) Low intelligence and special abilities. *Journal of child psychology and psychiatry, 29* (4), 391–6.

Offer, D. (1969) *The psychological world of the teenager*. New York: Basic Books.

Offer, D. & Offer, J.B. (1975) *From teenage to young manhood: A psychological study*. New York: Basic Books.

Offer, D., Ostrov, E., Howard, K.I. & Atkinson, R.(1988) *The teenage world: Adolescents' self-image in ten countries*. New York: Plenum Press.

Offer, D., Rostov, E. & Howard, K.I. (1981) *The adolescent: A psychological self-portrait*. New York: Basic Books.

O'Grady, M. (1977) Effects of subliminal pictorial stimulation on skin resistance. *Perceptual and Motor Skills, 44,* 1051–6.

Öhman, A., Erikkson, A. & Olofsson, C. (1975 a) One-trial learning and superior resistance to extinction of autonomic responses conditioned to potentially phobic stimuli. *Journal of Comparative & Physiological Psychology, 88,* 619–27.

Öhman, A., Erixson, G. & Lofberg, L. (1975 b) Phobias and preparedness: phobic and neutral pictures as conditioned stimuli for human autonomic responses. *Journal of Abnormal Psychology, 84,* 41–5.

Olds, J. (1956) Pleasure centres in the brain. *Scientific American, October,* 105–6.

Olds, J. (1958) Self-stimulation of the brain. *Science, 127,* 315–23.

Olds, J. (1962) Hypothalmic substrates of reward. *Physiological Review, 42,* 554–604.

Olds, J. & Milner, P. (1954) Positive reinforcement produced by electrical stimulation of septal area and other regions of the rat brain. *Journal of Comparative and Physiological Psychology, 47,* 419–27.

Olson, J.M. & Ross, M. (1988) False feedback about placebo effectiveness: Consequences for the misattribution of speech activity. *Journal of Experimental Social Psychology, 24,* 275–91.

Olson, R.K. & Attneave, F. (1970) What variables produce similarity grouping? *American Journal of Psychology, 83,* 1–21.

Ora, J.P. (1965) *Characteristics of the volunteer for psychological investigation*. Office of Naval Research, Contract 2149 (03), Technical Report 27.

Orne, M.T. (1959) The nature of hypnosis: Artifact and essence. *Journal of Abnormal & Social Psychology, 58,* 277–99.

Orne, M.T. (1962) On the social psychology of the psychological experiment – with particular reference to demand characteristics and their implications. *American Psychologist, 17* (11), 776–83.

Orne, M.T. (1966) Hypnosis, motivation and compliance. *American Journal of Psychiatry, 122,* 721–6.

Orne, M.T. (1979) On the simulating subject as quasi-control group in hypnosis research: what, why and how ? In E. Fromm & R.E.Shor (Eds.) *Hypnosis: Research developments and perspectives.* New York: Aldine.

Ornstein, R. (1975) *The psychology of consciousness.* Harmondsworth: Penguin.

Ornstein, R. (1986) *The psychology of consciousness* (2nd ed. revised). Harmondsworth: Penguin.

Orvis, B.R. Cunningham, J.D. & Kelley, H.H. (1975) A closer examination of causal inference: The roles of consensus, distinctiveness and consistency information. *Journal of Personality and Social Psychology, 32,* 605–16.

Osgood, C.E. (1966) Dimensionality of the semantic space for communication via facial expression. *Scandinavian Journal of Psychology, 7,* 1–30.

Osgood, C.E., Suci, G.J. & Tannenbaum, P.H. (1957) *The measurement of meaning.* Urbana, Illinois: University of Illinois Press.

Osgood, C.E. & Tannenbaum, P.H. (1955) The principle of congruity in the prediction of attitude change. *Psychological Review, 62,* 42–55.

Oswald, I. (1966) *Sleep.* Harmondsworth, Middlesex: Penguin.

Oswald, I. (1969) Human brain protein, drugs and dreams. *Nature, 223,* 893–7.

Oswald, I. (1974) *Sleep* (2nd ed.). Harmondsworth, Middlesex: Penguin.

Oswald, I. (1980) Sleep as a restorative process: Human clues. *Process in Brain Research, 53,* 279–88.

Owen, L. & Stoneman, C. (1972) Education and the nature of intelligence. In D. Rubinstein & C. Stoneman (Eds.) *Education for democracy* (2nd ed.) Harmondsworth: Penguin.

Owen, W. (1990) After Hillsborough. *Nursing Times, 86 (25),* 16–17.

Packer, C. (1977) Reciprocal altruism in *Papio anubis. Nature, 265,* 441–2.

Packer, O., Hartmann, E.E. & Teller, D.Y. (1985) Infant colour vision: The effect of test field size on Rayleigh discriminations. *Vision Research, 24,* 1247–60.

Paivio, A. (1969) Mental imagery in associative learning and memory. *Psychological Review, 76,* 241–63.

Paivio, A. (1971) *Imagery and verbal processes.* New York: Holt, Rinehart & Winston.

Paivio, A. (1986) *Mental representations: A dual coding approach.* Oxford: Oxford University Press.

Palermo, D.S. (1971) Is a scientific revolution taking place in psychology? *Psychological Review, 76,* 241–63.

Palmer, S.E. (1975) The effects of contextual scenes on the identification of objects. *Memory & cognition,* 3, 519–26.

Palmore, E. (1977) Facts on aging. *The Gerontologist, 17,* 315–20.

Panskepp, J. (1994) The basics of basic emotion. In P. Ekman & R.J. Davidson (Eds.) *The Nature of emotion: Fundamental questions.* New York: Oxford University Press.

Papez, J.W. (1937) A proposed mechanism of emotion. *Archives of Neurology and Psychiatry, 38,* 725–43.

Parke, R.D. (1969) Effectiveness of punishment as an interaction of intensity, timing agent nurturance and cognitive structuring. *Child Development, 40,* 213–36.

Parke, R.D. (1972) Some effects of punishment on childrens' behaviour. In W.W. Harting (Ed.), *The young child, Vol. 2.* Washington DC: National Association for the Education of Young Children.

Parke, R.D. (1974) Rules, roles and resistance to deviation: Recent advances in punishment, discipline and self control. In A.D. Pick (Ed.), *Minnesota Symposium on Child Psychology,* Vol. 8. Minneapolis, Minnesota: University of Minnesota Press.

Parke, R.D. (1977) Some effects of punishment on childrens' behaviour – revisited. In E.M. Hetherington & R.D. Parke (Eds.), *Contemporary readings in child psychology.* New York: McGraw Hill.

Parke, R.D. (1978) Perspectives on father–infant interaction. In J.D. Osofsky (Ed.), *Handbook of infancy.* New York: John Wiley & Sons.

Parke, R.D. (1981) *Fathering.* London: Fontana.

Parke, R.D., Berkowitz, L., Leyens, J.P., West, S.G. & Sebastian, R.J. (1977) Some effects of violent and non-violent movies on the behaviour of juvenile delinquents. In L. Berkowitz (Ed.), *Advances in experimental psychology, Vol. 10.* New York: Academic Press.

Parkes, C.M. (1962) *Reactions to bereavement.* Unpublished Masters Thesis, London University.

Parkes, C.M. (1964) Recent bereavement as a cause of mental illness. *British Journal of Psychiatry, 110,* 198–204.

Parkes, C.M. (1965) Bereavement and mental illness. *British Journal of Medical Psychology, 38,* 1.

Parkes, C.M. (1970) The first year of bereavement: A longitudinal study of the reaction of London widows to the death of their husbands. *Psychiatry, 33,* 444–67.

Parkes, C.M. (1975) *Bereavement – studies of grief in adult life.* Harmondsworth, Middlesex: Penguin.

Parkes, C.M. (1993) Bereavement as a psychosocial transition: Processes of adaptation to change. In M.S. Stroebe, W. Stroebe & R.O. Hansson (Eds.) *Handbook of bereavement: Theory, research and intervention.* New York: Cambridge University Press.

Parkes, C.M., Benjamin, B. & Fitzgerald, R.G. (1969) Broken heart: A statistical study of increased mortality among widowers. *British Medical Journal, 1,* 740–3.

Parkes, C.M. & Weiss, R.S. (1983) *Recovery from bereavement.* New York: Basic Books.

Parkin, A.J. (1987) *Memory and amnesia: An introduction.* Oxford: Blackwell.

Parkin, A.J. (1993) *Memory: phenomena, experiment and theory.* Oxford: Blackwell.

Parkin, A.J., Lewinson, J. & Folkard, S. (1982) The influence of emotion on immediate and delayed retention: Levinger and Clark reconsidered. *British Journal of Psychology, 73,* 389–93.

Parkinson, B. (1987) Emotion – cognitive approaches. In H. Beloff and A.M. Colman (Eds.), *Psychology survey, No. 6.* Leicester: British Psychological Society.

Patel, K. (1994) Memory of Freud may be forgotten in court. *Times Higher Education Supplement,* May 20.

Patterson, F.G. (1978) The gestures of a gorilla: Language acquisition in another pongid. *Brain and Language, 5,* 72–97.

Patterson, F.G. (1980) Innovative uses of language by a gorilla: A case study. In K. Nelson (Ed.), *Childrens' language, Vol. 2.* New York: Gardner Press.

Patterson, F.G. & Linden, E. (1981) *The education of Koko.* New York: Holt, Rinehart & Winston.

Paul, G.L. (1966) *Insight versus desensitization in psychotherapy: An experiment in anxiety reduction.* Stanford, CA.: Stanford University Press.

Paul, G.L. & Lentz, R.J. (1977) *Psychosocial treatment of chronic mental patients: Milieu versus social learning programs.* Cambridge, MA.: Harvard University Press.

Paul, G.L. & Menditto, A.A. (1992) Effectiveness of inpatient treatment programs for mentally ill adults in public psychiatric facilities. *Applied and Preventative Psychology: Current Scientific Perspectives, 1,* 41–63.

Pavlov, I.P. (1927) *Conditioned reflexes.* London: Oxford University Press.

Peck, D. & Whitlow, D. (1975) *Approaches to personality theory.* London: Methuen.

Peck, R.C. (1968) Psychological developments in the second half of life. In B.L. Neugarten (Ed.) *Middle age and ageing.* Chicago, ILL;: University of Chicago Press.

Penfield, W. (1958) The role of the temporal cortex in recall of past experiences and interpretation of the present. In W. Penfield (Ed.), *Neurological bases of behaviour.* Boston: Little Brown.

Penrose, R. (1987) Minds, machines and mathematics. In C. Blakemore & S. Greenfield (Eds.) *Mindwaves.* Oxford: Blackwell.

Penrose, R. (1990) *The Emperor's new mind.* Oxford: Oxford University Press.

Peplau, L.A. (1991) Lesbian and gay relationships. In J.C. Gonsorek & J.D. Weinrich (Eds.) *Homosexuality: Research implications for public policy.* Newbury Park, CA.: Sage.

Perrin, S. & Spencer, C. (1981) Independence or conformity in the Asch experiment as a reflection of cultural and situational factors. *British Journal of Social Psychology, 20,* 205–9.

Perry, D.G. & Bussey, K. (1979) The social learning theory of sex differences: Imitation is alive and well. *Journal of Personality and Social Psychology, 37* (10), 1699–712.

Perry, D.G. & Parke, R.D. (1975) Punishment and alternative response training as determinants of response inhibition in children. *Genetic Psychology Monographs, 91,* 257–79.

Pervin, L.A. & Lewis, M. (1978) *Perspective in interactional psychology.* New York: Plenum Press.

Peters, R.S. (1974) Moral development: A plea for pluralism. In R.S. Peters (Ed.), *Psychology and ethical development.* London: Allen & Unwin.

Peterson, L.R. & Peterson, M.J. (1959) Short term retention of individual items. *Journal of Experimental Psychology, 58,* 193–8.

Petkova, B. (1995) New views on the self: Evil women – witchcraft or PMS? *Psychology Review, 2* (1), 16–19.

Pettito, L.A. & Seidenberg, M.S. (1979) On the evidence from linguistic abilities in signing apes. *Brain and Language, 8,* 162–83.

Pettigrew, T.F. (1959) Regional difference in anti-negro prejudice. *Journal of Abnormal and Social Psychology, 59,* 28–56.

Pettigrew, T.F. (1971) *Racially separate or together?* New York: McGraw Hill.

Petty, R.E. & Cacioppo, J.T. (1981) *Attitudes and persuasion: Classic and contemporary approaches.* Dubuque, Iowa: Brown.

Phillips, J.L. (1969) *The origins of intellect: Piaget's theory.* San Francisco: W.H. Freeman.

Piaget, J. (1932) *The moral judgement of the child.* London: Routledge & Kegan Paul.

Piaget, J. (1950) *The psychology of intelligence.* London: Routledge & Kegan Paul.

Piaget, J. (1951) *Play, dreams and imitation in children.* London: Routledge & Kegan Paul.

Piaget, J. (1952) *The child's conception of numbers.* London: Routledge & Kegan Paul.

Piaget, J. (1963) *The origins of intelligence in children.* New York: Norton.

Piaget, J. (1970) Piaget's theory. In P.H. Mussen (Ed.), *Manual of child psychology.* London: Wiley.

Piaget, J. (1972) Intellectual evolution from adolescence to adulthood. *Human Development, 15,* 1–21.

Piaget, J. (1973) *The child's conception of the world.* London: Paladin.

Piaget, J. & Inhelder, B. (1956) *The child's conception of space.* London: Routledge & Kegan Paul.

Piaget, J. & Inhelder, B. (1969) *The psychology of the child.* London: Routledge & Kegan Paul.

Piaget, J. & Szeminska, A. (1952) *The child's conception of number.* London: Routledge & Kegan Paul.

Piliavin, I.M., Piliavin, J.A. & Rodin, S. (1975) Costs, diffusion and the stigmatised victim. *Journal of Personality and Social Psychology, 32,* 429–38.

Piliavin, I.M., Rodin, J. & Piliavin, J.A. (1969) Good samaritanism: An underground phenomenon? *Journal of Personality and Social Psychology, 13,* 289–99.

Piliavin, J.A., Dovidio, J.F., Gaertner, S.L. & Clark, R.D. (1981) *Emergency intervention.* New York: Academic Press.

Piliavin, J.A. & Piliavin, I.M. (1972) Effects of blood on reactions to a victim. *Journal of Personality and Social Psychology, 23,* 353–62.

Piliavin, J.A., Piliavin, I.M., Loewenton, E.P., McCauley, C. & Hammond, P. (1969) On observers' reproductions of dissonance effects: The right answers for the wrong reasons? *Journal of Personality and Social Psychology, 13,* 98–106.

Pinel, J.P.J. (1993) *Biopsychology* (2nd ed.). Boston: Allyn & Bacon.

Place, U.T. (1956) Is consciousness a brain process ? *British Journal of Psychology, 47,* 44–51.

Plomin, R. & Loehlin, J.C.(1989) Direct and indirect IQ heritability estimates: a puzzle. *Behavioural Genetics, 19,* 331–42.

Plunkett, K. (1981) Psycholinguistics. In B. Gilliam (Ed.), *Psychology for today* (2nd ed.). Sevenoaks: Hodder & Stoughton.

Plutchik, R. (1980) *Emotion: A psychobioevolutionary synthesis.* New York: Harper & Row.

Plutchik, R. (1986) *Emotion: A psychoevolutionary synthesis.* New York: Harper & Row.

Plutchik, R. & Ax, A.F. (1967) A critique of determinants of emotional state by Schachter and Singer (1962). *Psychophysiology, 4,* 79–82.

Pokorny, M. (1994) Appendix A: Structure of the United Kingdom Council for Psychotherapy and list of its member organizations. In P.Clarkson & M.Pokorny (Eds.) *The Handbook of psychotherapy.* London: Routledge.

Polanyi, M. (1958) *Personal knowledge.* London: Routledge & Kegan Paul.

Pollak, J.M. (1979) Obsessive-compulsive personality: a review. *Psychological Bulletin, 86,* 225–41.

Pomerantz, J. & Garner, W.R. (1973) Stimulus configuration in selective attention tasks. *Perception and Psychophysics, 14,* 565–9.

Pomerantz, J. & Schwaitzberg. S.D. (1975) Grouping by proximity: Selective attention measures. *Perception and Psychophysics, 18,* 355–61.

Popper, K. (1945) *The open society and its enemies.* London: Routledge & Kegan Paul.

Popper, K. (1950) Indeterminism in quantum physics and in classical physics. *British Journal of Philosophy and Science, 1,* 117–33/173–95.

Popper, K. (1959) *The logic of scientific discovery.* London: Hutchinson.

Popper, K. (1968) *Conjecture and refutations: The growth of scientific knowledge.* New York: Harper & Row.

Popper, K. (1972) *Objective knowledge: An evolutionary approach*. Oxford: Oxford University Press.

Porteous, M.A. (1985) Developmental aspects of adolescent problem disclosure in England and Ireland. *Journal of Child Psychology and Psychiatry*, *26*, 465–78.

Poskocil, A. (1977) Encounters between blacks and white liberals: The collision of stereotypes. *Social Forces*, *55*, 715–27.

Postman, L., Bruner, J.S. & McGinnies, E. (1948) Personal values as selective factors in perception. *Journal of Abnormal and Social Psychology*, *43*, 142–54.

Postman, L., Bronson, W.C. & Gropper, G.L. (1953) Is there a mechanism of perceptual defence? *Journal of Abnormal and Social Psychology*, *48*, 215.

Potter, J. & Wetherell, M.S. (1987) *Discourse and social psychology: Beyond attitudes and behaviour*. London: Sage.

Powell, R.A. & Boer, D.P. (1994) Did Freud mislead patients to confabulate memories of abuse? *Psychological reports*, 74, 1283–98.

Premack, D. (1971) Language in chimpanzee? *Science*, *172*, 808–22.

Premack, D. (1976) *Intelligence in ape and man*. Hillsdale, New Jersey: Lawrence Erlbaum Associates Inc.

Premack, D. & Woodruff, G. (1978) Does the chimpanzee have a 'theory of mind'? *Behavioural & Brain Sciences*, *4*, 515–26.

Price, R.A. & Vandenberg, S.G. (1979) Matching for physical attractiveness in married couples. *Personality and Social Psychology Bulletin*, *5*, 398–400.

Price-Williams, D. (1966) Cross-cultural studies. In B.M. Foss (Ed.), *New horizons in psychology, 1*. Harmondsworth, Middlesex: Penguin.

Pringle, M.L. Kellmer, (1986) *The needs of children* (3rd ed) London: Hutchinson.

Prioleau, L., Murdock, M. & Brody, N. (1983) An analysis of psychotherapy versus placebo studies. *The Behavioural & Brain Sciences*, *6*, 275–310.

Putnam, H. (1975) The meaning of meaning. In H. Putnam (Ed.) *Mind, language and reality: Philosophical papers of Hilary Putnam, vol.2*. Cambridge: Cambridge University Press.

Quattrone, G.A. (1982) Overattribution and unit formation: When behaviour engulfs the person. *Journal of Personality and Social Psychology*, *42*, 593–607.

Quattrone, G.A. (1986) On the perception of a group's variability. In S. Worchel & W. Austin (Eds.) *The psychology of intergroup relations*. Vol. 2. New York: Nelson-Hall.

Rabbitt, P.M.A. (1967) Ignoring irrelevant information . *American Journal of Psychology*, *80*, 1–13.

Rachman, S. (1977) The conditioning theory of fear-acquisition: A critical examination. *Behaviour Research and Therapy*, *15*, 375–87.

Rachman, S. (1978) *Fear and courage*. San Francisco: W.H. Freeman.

Rachman, S. (1984) Agoraphobia – a safety-signal perspective. *Behaviour Research and Therapy*, *22*, 59–70.

Rachman, S. & Wilson, G. (1980) *The effects of psychological therapy*. Oxford: Pergamon.

Ramsay, R. & de Groot, W. (1977) A further look at bereavement. Paper presented at EATI conference, Uppsala (cited in P.E. Hodgkinson (1980), Treating abnormal grief in the bereaved. *Nursing Times*, 17 January, 126–8.

Raphael, B. (1984) *The anatomy of bereavement*. London: Hutchinson.

Rassool, G.H. & Winnington, J. (1993) Using psychoactive drugs. *Nursing Times*, *89(47)*, 38–40.

Rawlins, R. (1979) Forty years of rhesus research. *New Scientist*, *82* (1150), 105–10.

Reason, P. & Rowan, J. (Eds.,1981) *Human inquiry: A sourcebook of new paradigm research*. Chichester: Wiley.

Rebok, G.W. (1987) *Life-span cognitive development*. New York: Holt, Rinehart & Winston.

Rechtschaffen, A., Bergmann, B.M., Everson, C.A., Kushida, C.A. & Gilliland, M.A. (1989a) Sleep deprivation in the rat: 1. Conceptual issues. *Sleep*, 12, 1–4.

Rechtschaffen, A. Bergmann, B.M., Everson, C.A., Kushida, C.A. & Gilliland, M.A. (1989 b) Sleep deprivation in the rat: X. Integration and discussion of the findings. *Sleep*, 12, 68–87.

Rees, W.D. & Lutkins, S.G. (1967) Mortality of bereavement. *British Medical Journal*, *4*, 13.

Reich, B. & Adcock, C. (1976) *Values, attitudes and behaviour change*. London: Methuen.

Reichard, S., Livson, F. & Peterson, P.G. (1982) *Ageing and personality*. New York: Wiley.

Rescorla, R.A. (1967) Pavlovian conditioning and its proper control procedures. *Psychological Review*, *74*, 71–80.

Rescorla, R.A. (1968) Probability of shock in the presence and absence of CS in fear conditioning. *Journal of Comparative and Physiological Psychology*, *66*, 1–5.

Rest, J.R. (1983) Morality. In J.H. Flavell & E.M. Markman (Eds.), *Handbook of child psychology, Vol. 3*. New York: Wiley.

Rest, J., Turiel, E. & Kohlberg, L. (1969) Level of moral development as a determinant of preference and comprehension of moral judgement made by others. *Journal of Personality*, *37*, 225–52.

Restle, F. (1957) Discrimination of cues in mazes: A resolution of the 'place versus response' question. *Psychological Review*, *64*, 217–28.

Restle, F. (1974) Critique of pure memory. In R. Solso (Ed.), *Theories in cognitive psychology: The Loyola symposium*. New York: Wiley.

Rheingold, H.L. (1961) The effect of environmental stimulation upon social and exploratory behaviour in the human infant. In B.M. Foss (Ed.), *Determinants of infant behaviour, Vol. 1*. London: Methuen.

Rheingold, H.L. (1969) The effect of a strange environment on the behaviour of infants. In B.M. Foss (Ed.), *Determinants of infant behaviour, Vol. 4*. London: Methuen.

Rheingold, H.L. & Eckerman, C.O. (1973) Fear of a stranger – a critical examination. In H.W. Reese (Ed.), *Advances in child development and behaviour, Vol. 8*. New York: Academic Press.

Rice, R.W. (1978) Construct validity of the esteem for least preferred coworker (LPC) scale. *Psychological Bulletin*, *85*, 1199–1237.

Rice, R.W., Bender, L.R. & Vitters, A.G. (1980) Leader sex, follower attitudes toward women and leadership effectiveness: A laboratory experiment. *Organizational Behaviour and Human Performance*, *25*, 46–78.

Richards, M. (1987) Parents and kids: The new thinking. *New Society*, *March 27*, 12–15.

Richardson, J.T.E. (1974) Imagery and free recall. *Journal of Verbal Learning & Verbal Behaviour*, *13*, 709–13.

Richardson, K. (1991) *Understanding intelligence*. Milton Keynes: Open University Press.

Riegel, K.F. (1973) Dialetic operations: The final period of cognitive development. *Human Development*, *16*, 346–70.

Riesen, A.H. (1947) The development of visual perception in man and chimpanzee. *Science*, *106*, 107–8.

Riesen, A.H. (1965) Effects of early deprivation of photic stimulation. In S. Oster & R. Cook (Eds.), *The biosocial basis of mental retardation*. Baltimore: Johns Hopkins University Press.

Riley, V. (1981) Neuroendocrine influences on immunity and neoplasia. *Science, 211*, 1100–9.

Rips, L.J., Shoben, E.H. & Smith, E.E. (1973) Semantic distance and the verification of semantic relations. *Journal of Verbal Learning and Verbal Behaviour, 12*, 1–20.

Rivers, W.H.R. (1901) Vision. In A.C. Haddon (Ed.), *Reports of the Cambridge Anthropological Expedition to the Torres Straits, Vol. 2, part 1.* Cambridge: Cambridge University Press.

Roberts, R. & Newton, P.M. (1987) Levinsonian studies of women's adult development. *Psychology & Ageing, 39*, 165–74.

Robertson, J. & Robertson, J. (1971) Young children in brief separation: a fresh look. *Psychoanalytic Study of the Child, 26*, 264–315.

Robinson, J.O. (1972) *The psychology of visual illusions.* London: Hutchinson.

Rogers, C.R. (1942) *Counselling and psychotherapy: Newer concepts in practice.* Boston: Houghton Mifflin.

Rogers. C.R. (1951) *Client-centred therapy – its current practices, implications and theory.* Boston: Houghton Mifflin.

Rogers, C.R. (1959) A theory of therapy, personality and interpersonal relationships, as developed in the client-centred framework. In S. Koch (Ed.), *Psychology: A study of a science, Vol. 3.* New York: McGraw Hill.

Rogers, C.R. (1961) *On becoming a person.* Boston: Houghton Mifflin.

Rogers, C.R. (1969) *Freedom to learn: A view of what education might become.* Columbus, OH: Charles E. Merrill.

Rogers, C.R. (1970) *Encounter groups.* New York: Harper & Row.

Rogoff, B. & Morelli, G. (1989) Perspectives on children's development from cultural psychology. *American Psychologist, 44*, 343–8.

Rokeach, M. (1960) *The open and closed mind.* New York: Basic Books.

Rokeach, M. (1968) *Beliefs, attitudes and values.* San Francisco: Jossey-Bass.

Rolls, E.T. & Rolls, B.J. (1982) Brain mechanisms involved in feeding. In L.M. Barker (Ed.) *The psychobiology of human food selection.* Westport, CT: AVI Publishing Company.

Rosch, E. (1973) Natural categories. *Cognitive Psychology, 4*, 328–50.

Rose, P. & Platzer, H. (1993) Confronting prejudice. *Nursing Times,* 89(31), 52–4.

Rose, S. (1976) *The conscious brain.* Harmondsworth, Middlesex: Penguin.

Rose, S. (1992) *The making of memory: From molecules to mind.* London: Bantam Books.

Rose, S., Lewontin, R.C. & Kamin, L.J. (1984) *Not in our genes.* Harmondsworth, Middlesex: Penguin.

Rose, S.A. & Blank, M. (1974) The potency of context in childrens' cognition: An illustration through conservation. *Child Development, 45*, 499–502.

Rosenberg, M. (1965) *Society and the adolescent self-image.* Princeton, New Jersey: Princeton University Press.

Rosenberg, M.J. & Hovland, C.I. (1960) Cognitive, affective, and behavioural components of attitude. In M.J. Rosenberg, C.I. Hovland, W.J. McGuire, R.P. Abelson & J.W. Brehm (Eds.) *Attitude organization and change: An analysis of consistency among attitude components.* New Haven, CT: Yale University Press.

Rosenblatt, F. (1959) Two theorems of statistical separability in the perceptron. In *Mechanisation of thought processes: Proceedings of a symposium held at the National Physical Laboratory, November 1958, Vol. 1.* London: HMSO.

Rosenblum, L.A. & Harlow, H.F. (1963) Approach-avoidance conflict in the mother surrogate situation. *Psychological Reports, 12*, 83–5.

Rosenhan, D.L. (1973) On being sane in insane places. *Science, 179*, 250–8.

Rosenman, R.H., Friedman, M., Straus, R., Wurm, M., Kositichek, R., Hahn, W. & Werthessen, N.T. (1964) A predicitve study of coronary heart disease. *Journal of the American Medical Association, 189*, 103–10.

Rosenman, R.H., Brand, R.J., Jenkins, C.D., Friedman, M., Strauss, R. & Wurm, M. (1975) Coronary heart disease in the Western Collaborative Group Study. *Journal of the American Medical Association, 233*, 872–7.

Rosenthal, D., Wender, P.H., Kety, S.S. & Welner, J. (1971) The adopted-away offspring of schizophrenics. *American Journal of Psychiatry, 128*, 307–11.

Rosenthal, N.E., Sack, D.A., Gillin, J.C., Lewy, A.J., Goodwin, F.K., Davenport, Y., Mudler, P.S., Newsome, D.A. & Weher, T.A. (1984) Seasonal affective disorder. *Archives of General Psychiatry, 41*, 72–80.

Rosenthal, R. (1966) *Experimenter effects in behavioural research.* New York: Appleton-Century-Crofts.

Rosenthal, R. & Jacobson, L. (1968) *Pygmalion in the classroom.* New York: Holt, Rinehart & Winston.

Rosenthal, R. & Rosnow, R.L. (1966) Volunteer subjects and the results of opinion change studies. *Psychological Reports, 19*, 1183.

Ross, L. (1977) The intuitive psychologist and his shortcomings. In L. Berkowitz (Ed.) *Advances in experimental social psychology.* Vol. 10. New Yory: Academic Press.

Ross, L. & Nisbett, R.E. (1991) *The person and the situation: Perspectives of social psychology.* New York: McGraw-Hill.

Roth, I. (1986) An introduction to object perception. In I. Roth and J.P. Frisby (Eds.), *Perception and representation.* Milton Keynes: Open University Press.

Roth I. (1995) Object recognition. In I.Roth & V. Bruce, *Perception and representation: Current issues* (2nd ed.) . Buckingham: Open University Press.

Rothbart, M., Evans, M. & Fulero, S. (1979) Recall for confirming events: Memory processes and the maintenance of social stereotyping. *Journal of Experimental Social Psychology, 15*, 343–55.

Rotter, J.B. (1966) Generalized expectancies for internal versus external control of reinforcement. *Psychological Monographs, 30* (1), 1–26.

Rotter, J.P., Seerman, M. & Liverant, S. (1962) Internal versus external locus of control of reinforcement: A major variable in behaviour theory. In N.F. Washburne (Ed.), *Decisions, values and groups.* New York: Pergamon Press.

Rubin, J.Z., Proveyzano, F.J. & Luria, Z. (1974) The eye of the beholder: Parents' views on sex of newborns. *American Journal of Orthopsychiatry, 44*, 512–19.

Rubin, K.H. (1973) Decentration skills in institutionalized and non-institutionalized elderly. *Proceedings of the 81st Annual Convention of American Psychology Association, 8*, 759–60.

Rubin, Z. (1973) *Liking and loving.* New York: Holt Rinehart & Winston.

Rubin, Z. & McNeil, E.B. (1983) *The psychology of being human* (3rd ed.). London: Harper & Row.

Rubinstein, J.L. & Howes, C. (1979) Caregiving and infant behaviour in day care and in homes. *Developmental Psychology, 15*, 1–24.

Ruble, D.N., Balaban, T. & Cooper, J. (1981) Gender constancy and the effects of sex-typed televised toy commercials. *Child Development, 52*, 667–73.

Rubovits, P.C. & Maehr, M.L. (1973) Pygmalion in black and

white. *Journal of Personality and Social Psychology, 25,* 210–18.

Ruch, J.C. (1984) *Psychology – the personal science.* Belmont, California: Wadsworth Publishing Company.

Rumbaugh, D.M., Gill, T.V. & Glaserfeld, E.C. (1973) Reading and sentence completion by a chimpanzee. *Science, 182,* 731–3.

Rumbaugh, D.M., Warner, H. & Von Glaserfeld, E. (1977) The Lana project: Origin and tactics. In D.M. Rumbaugh (Ed.) *Language Learning by a Chimpanzee: The LANA Project.* New York: Academic Press.

Rumelhart, D.E. (1975) Notes on a schema for stories. In D.G. Bobrow & A. Collins (Eds.), *Representation and understanding: Studies in cognitive science.* New York: Academic Press.

Rumelhart, D.E., Hinton, G.E. & McClelland, J.L. (1986) A general framework for parallel distributed processing. In D. Rumelhart, J.L. McClelland & the PDP Research Group (Eds.), *Parallel distributed processing: Vol. 1. Foundations.* Cambridge, Massachusetts: MIT Press.

Rumelhart, D.E. & Norman, D.A. (1983) Representation in memory. In R.C. Atkinson, R.J. Herrstein, B. Lindzey & R.D. Luce (Eds.), *Handbook of experimental psychology.* Chichester: Wiley.

Rumelhart, D.E. & Norman, D.A. (1985) Representation of knowledge. In M.M. Aitkenhead & J.M. Slack (Eds.), *Issues in cognitive modelling.* London: Lawrence Erlbaum Associates Ltd.

Runciman, W.G. (1966) *Relative deprivation and social justice.* London: Routledge & Kegan Paul.

Rushton, J.P. (1980) *Altruism, socialization and society.* Englewood Cliffs, New Jersey: Prentice Hall.

Rushton, W.A.H. (1987) Colour vision: Eye mechanism. In R. Gregory (Ed.), *The Oxford companion to the mind.* Oxford: Oxford University Press.

Russell, J. (1984) *Explaining mental life: Some philosophical issus in psychology.* London: Macmillan Press.

Rutter, M. (1976) Sex differences in childrens' responses to family stress. In E.J. Anthony and C.M. Konpernick (Eds.), *The child in his family.* New York: Wiley.

Rutter, M. (1979a) Maternal deprivation, 1972–1978: New findings, new concepts, new approaches. *Child Development, 50,* 283–305.

Rutter, M. (1979b) Separation experiences: A new look at an old topic. *Journal of Paediatrics, 95,* 147–54.

Rutter, M. (1981) *Maternal deprivation reassessed* (2nd ed.). Harmondsworth, Middlesex: Penguin.

Rutter, M. (1989) Pathways from childhood to adult life. *Journal of Child Psychology and Psychiatry, 30,* (1), 23–51.

Rutter, M., Graham, P., Chadwick, D.F.D. & Yule, W. (1976) Adolescent turmoil: Fact or fiction. *Journal of Child Psychology and Psychiatry, 17,* 35–56.

Rutter, M. & Rutter, M. (1992) *Developing minds: Challenge and continuity across the life span.* Harmondsworth: Penguin.

Ryan, J. (1972) IQ – the illusion of objectivity. In K. Richardson & D. Spears (Eds.), *Race, culture and intelligence.* Harmondsworth, Middlesex: Penguin.

Ryan, R.M. & Lynch, J.H. (1989) Emotional autonomy versus detachment: revisiting the vicissitudes of adolescence and young adulthood. *Child Development, 60,* 340–56.

Ryder, R. (1990) Open reply to Jeffrey Gray. *The Psychologist* 3, 403.

Ryder, R. (1991) Sentientism: A comment on Gray and Singer. *The Psychologist,* May, 201.

Ryle, A. (1975) Psychotherapy research: The role of the repertory grid. *New Behaviour, August 28,* 326–8.

Ryle, G. (1949) *The concept of mind.* London: Hutchinson.

Sachs, J. & Truswell, L. (1976) Comprehension of two-word instructions by children in the one-word stage. *Journal of Child Language, 5,* 17–24.

Sackeim, H.A. (1989) The efficacy of electroconvulsive therapy in the treatment of major depressive disorder. In S. Fisher & R.P. Greenberg (Eds.) *The limits of biological treatments for psychological distress: Comparisons with therapy and placebo.* Hillsdale, NJ.: Lawrence Erlbaum.

Saegert, S.C., Swap, W. & Zajonc, R.B. (1973) Exposure context and interpersonal attraction. *Journal of Personality and Social Psychology, 25,* 234–42.

Salamé, P. & Baddeley, A.D. (1982) Disruption of short-term memory by unattended speech: Implications for the structure of working memory. *Journal of Verbal Learning and Verbal Behaviour, 21,* 150–64.

Salapatek, P. (1975) Pattern perception in early infancy. In L.B. Cohen and P. Salapatek (Eds.), *Infant perception: From sensation to cognition, Vol. 1. Basic visual processes.* London: Academic Press.

Samuel, J. & Bryant, P. (1984) Asking only one question in the conservation experiment. *Journal of Child Psychology and Psychiatry, 25* (2), 315–18.

Sapir, E. (1929) The status of linguistics as a science. *Language, 5,* 207–14.

Sarbin, T.R. & Mancuso, J.C. (1980) *Schizophrenia: Medical diagnosis or moral verdict?* New York: Pergamon.

Sartorius, N., Kaeber, C., & Cooper, L. (1993) Progress toward achieving a common language in psychiatry. *Archives of General Psychiatry,* 50, 115–24.

Savage-Rumbaugh, E.S. (1990) Language as a cause–effect communication system. *Philosophical Psychology, 3* (1), 55–76.

Savage-Rumbaugh, E.S., Rumbaugh, D.M. & Boysen, S.L. (1978) Symbolic communication between two chimpanzees (*Pan troglodytes*). *Science, 201,* 641–4.

Savage-Rumbaugh, E.S., Rumbaugh, D.M. & Boysen, S.L. (1980) Do apes use language? *American Scientist, 68,* 49–61.

Savickas, M.L. (1995) Work and adjustment. In D. Wedding (Ed.) *Behaviour and medicine* (2nd ed.). St. Louis, MO: Mosby-Year Book.

Savin, H.B. (1973) Professors and psychological researchers: Conflicting values in conflicting roles. *Cognition, 2* (1), 147–9.

Scarr, S. & Weinberg, R.A. (1977) Intellectual similarities within families of both adopted and biological children. *Intelligence, 1,* 170–91.

Scarr, S. & Weinberg, R.A. (1983) The Minnesota adoption studies – genetic difference and malleability. *Child Development, 54,* 260–7.

Scarr-Salapatek, S. (1971) Social class and IQ. *Science, 174,* 28–36.

Scarr-Salapatek, S. (1976) An evolutionary perspective on infant intelligence – species patterns and individual variations. In M. Lewis (Ed.), *Origins of intelligence.* New York: Plenum.

Schachter, S. (1959) *The psychology of affiliatio.: Experimental studies of the sources of gregariousness.* Stanford, CA: Stanford University Press.

Schachter, S. (1964) The interaction of cognitive and physiological determinants of emotional state. In L. Berkowitz (Ed.), *Advances in experimental social psychology, Vol. 1.* New York: Academic Press.

Schachter, S. (1971) *Emotion, obesity and crime.* New York: Academic Press.

Schachter, S. & Singer, J.E. (1962) Cognitive, social and physiological determinants of emotional state. *Psychological Review, 69,* 379–99.

Schachter, S. & Wheeler, L. (1962) Epinephrine, chlorpromazine and amusement. *Journal of Abnormal and Social Psychology*, *65*, 121–8.

Schaffer, H.R. (1966) The onset of fear of strangers and the incongruity hypothesis. *Journal of Child Psychology & Psychiatry*, *7*, 95–106.

Schaffer, H.R. (1971) *The growth of sociability*. Harmondsworth, Penguin.

Schaffer, R. (1977) *Mothering*. London: Fontana/Open Books.

Schaffer, R. (1989) In A. Slater & G. Bremner (Eds.) *Infant development*. Hove & London: Lawrence Erlbaum.

Schaffer, H.R. & Emerson, P.E. (1964) The development of social attachments in infancy. *Monographs of the Society for Research in Child Development*, *29* (Whole No. 3).

Schaie, K.W. & Hertzog, C. (1983) Fourteen year cohort-sequential analysis of adult intellectual development. *Developmental Psychology*, *19*, 531–43.

Schaie, K.W. & Labouvie-Vief, G. (1974) Generational versus autogenetic components of change in adult cognitive behaviour: A fourteen year cross-sequential study. *Developmental Psychology*, *101*, 305–20.

Schaie, K.W. & Strother, C.R. (1968) The effect of time and cohort differences upon age changes in cognitive behaviour. *Multivariate Behaviour Research*, *3*, 259–94.

Schank, R.C. (1975) *Conceptual information processing*. Amsterdam: North-Holland.

Schank, R.C. (1982) *Dynamic memory*. New York: Cambridge University Press.

Schank, R.C. & Abelson, R.P. (1977) *Scripts, plans, goals and understanding*. Hillsdale, New Jersey: Lawrence Erlbaum Associates Inc.

Scheerer, M. (1963) Problem solving. *Scientific American*, *208* (4), 118–28.

Scheff, T.J. (1966) *Being mentally ill: A sociological theory*. Chicago: Aldine Press.

Scherer, K.R. (1994) Toward a concept of 'Modal Emotions'. In P. Ekman & R. J. Davidson (Eds.) *The nature of emotion: Fundamental questions*. New York: Oxford University Press.

Schiff, M., Duyne, M., Dumaret, A., Stewart, J., Tomkiewicz, S. & Fenigold, J. (1978) Intellectual status of working-class children adopted early into upper-middle class families. *Science*, *200*, 1503–4.

Schiffman, R. & Wicklund, R.A. (1992) The minimal group paradigm and its minimal psychology. *Theory & Psychology*, *2*(1), 29–50.

Schlosberg, H.S. (1941) A scale for the judgement of facial expression. *Journal of experimental psychology*, *29*, 497–510.

Schlossberg, N.K., Troll, L.E. & Leibowitz, Z. (1978) *Perspectives on counselling adults: Issues and skills*. Monterey, CA.; Brooks/Cole.

Schneider, K. (1959) Primary and secondary symptoms in schizophrenia. In S.R. Hirsch & M. Shepherd (Eds.), (1974) *Themes and variations in European psychiatry*. New York: John Wright.

Schneirla, T.C. (1965) Aspects of stimulation and organization in approach/withdrawal processes underlying vertebrate behaviour development. In D.S. Lehrman, R.A. Hinde & E. Shaw (Eds.), *Advances in the study of behaviour. Vol. 1*. New York: Academic Press.

Schreiber, F.R. (1973) *Sybil*. Harmondsworth, Middlesex: Penguin.

Schroeder, D.A., Penner, L.A., Dovidio, J.F. & Piliavin, J.A. (1995) *The psychology of helping and altruism: Problems and puzzles*. New York: McGraw-Hill.

Schulman, A. (1974) Memory for words recently classified. *Memory and Cognition*, *2*, 47–52.

Schlenker, B.R. (1982) Translating action into attitudes: an identity-analytic approach to the explanation of social conduct. In L. Berkowitz (Ed.) *Advances in Experimental Social Psychology*, vol. 15. New York: Academic Press.

Schuster, R.H. (1978) Ethological theories of aggression. In I.L. Kutash, S.B. Kutash & L.B. Schlesinger (Eds.), *Violence: Perspectives on murder and aggression*. San Francisco: Jossey-Bass.

Schwartz, S. & Johnson, J.H. (1981) *Psychopathology of childhood*. New York: Pergamon Press.

Science as Ideology Group of the British Society for Social Responsibility in Science (1976) The new synthesis is an old story. *New Scientist, May 13*.

Scodel, A. (1957) Heterosexual somatic preference and fantasy dependence. *Journal of Consulting Psychology*, *21*, 371–4.

Scollon, R. (1976) *Conversations with a one year old*. Honolulu: University of Hawaii Press.

Searle, J.R. (1980) Minds, brains and programs. *The Behaviour and Brain Sciences*, *3*, 417–57.

Searle, J.R. (1987) Minds and brains without programs. In C. Blakemore and S. Greenfield (Eds.), *Mindwaves*. Oxford: Blackwell.

Sears, R.R., Maccoby, E. & Levin, H. (1957) *Patterns of child rearing*. Evanston, Illinois: Row, Petersen and Co.

Sears, R.R., Rau, L. & Alpert, R. (1965) *Identification in child rearing*. Stanford, California: Stanford University Press.

Secord, P.F. & Backman, C.W. (1964) *Social psychology*. New York: McGraw Hill.

Segall, M.H. (1994) A cross-cultural research contribution to unravelling the nativist–empiricist controversy. In W.J. Lonner & R.S. Malpass (Eds.) *Psychology and culture*. Boston: Allyn & Bacon.

Segall, M.H., Campbell, D.T. & Herskovits, M.J. (1963) Cultural differences in the perception of geometrical illusions. *Science*, *139*, 769–71.

Segall, M.H., Campbell, D.T. & Herskovits, M.J. (1966) *The influence of culture on visual perception*. Indianapolis: Bobbs-Merrill.

Segall, M.H., Dasen, P.R., Berry, J.W. & Poortinga, Y.H. (1990) *Human behaviour in global perspective: An introduction to cross-cultural psychology*. New York: Pergamon.

Seidenberg, M.S. & McClelland, J.L. (1989) A distributed, developmental model of word recognition and naming. *Psychological Review, 96*, 523–68.

Seidenberg, M.S. & Petitto, L.A. (1987) Communication, symbolic communications and language: Comment on Savage-Rumbaugh, McDonald, Sevcik, Hopkins and Rupert (1986). *Journal of Experimental Psychology: General*, *116*, 279–87.

Selfridge, O.G. (1959) Pandemonium: A paradigm for learning. In *The mechanisation of thought processes*. London: HMSO.

Selfridge, O.G. & Neisser, U. (1960) Pattern recognition by machine. *Scientific American*, *203*, 60–8.

Seligman, M.E.P. (1970) On the generality of the laws of learning. *Psychological Review, 77*, 406–18.

Seligman, M.E.P. (1971) Phobias and preparedness. *Behaviour Therapy*, *2*, 307–20.

Seligman, M.E.P. (1972) *Biological boundaries of learning*. New York: Appleton-Century-Crofts.

Seligman, M.E.P. (1974) Depression and learned helplessness. In R.J. Friedman & M.M. Katz (Eds.) *The psychology of depression: Contemporary theory and research*. Washington, D.C.: Winston-Wiley.

Seligman, M.E.P. (1975) *Helplessness: On depression, develop-*

ment and death. San Francisco: W.H. Freeman.

Seligman, M.E.P., Maier, S.F. & Solomon, R,L. (1971) Unpredictable and uncontrollable aversive events. In F.R. Brush (Ed.), *Aversive conditioning and learning*. New York: Academic Press.

Selye, H. (1956) *The stress of life*. New York: McGraw-Hill.

Senatore, V., Matson, J.L & Kazdin, A.E. (1982) A comparison of behavioural methods to teach social skills to mentally retarded adults. *Behaviour Therapy, 13*, 313–24.

Serpell, R.S. (1976) *Culture's influence on behaviour*. London: Methuen.

Serpell, R. S. (1979) How specific are perceptual skills ? A cross-cultural study of pattern reproduction. *British Journal of Psychology, 70*, 365–80.

Serpell, R. S. (1994) The cultural construction of intelligence. In W.J.Lonner & R.S. Malpass (Eds.) *Psychology and culture*. Boston: Allyn & Bacon.

Seymour, J. (1995) Counting the cost. *Nursing Times*, 91(22), 24–7.

Shackleton, V.J. & Fletcher, C.A. (1984) *Individual differences – theories and applications*. London: Methuen.

Schaffer, D.R. (1985) *Developmental psychology – theory, research and applications*. Monterey, California: Brooks Cole Publishers.

Schaffer, L.H. (1975) Multiple attention in continuous verbal tasks. In P.M.A. Rabbit and S. Dormi (Eds.), *Attention and performance, Vol. 5*. London: Academic Press.

Schlenker, B.R. (1980) *Impression management*. Monterey, CA: Brooks/Cole.

Schneider, D.J. (1995) Attribution and social cognition. In M. Argyle & A.M.Colman (Eds.) *Social psychology*. London: Longman.

Shaffer, L.H. (1975) Multiple attention in continuous verbal tasks. In P.M.A.Rabbit & S. Dornic (Eds.) *Attention and performance* (vol.V). London: Academic Press.

Shallice, T. (1982) Specific impairments of planning. *Philosophical Transactions of the Royal Society of London*, *13298*, 199–209.

Shapiro, D.A. & Shapiro, D. (1982) Meta-analysis of comparative therapy outcome studies: A replication and refinement. *Psychological Bulletin, 92*, 581–604.

Shatz, M. (1994) *A toddler's life: Becoming a person*. New York: Oxford University Press.

Shatz, M. & Gelman, R. (1973) The development of communication skills: Modification in the speech of young children as a function of the listener. *Monographs of the Society for Research in Child Development, 38*, No. 152.

Shaver, J.P. & Strong, W. (1976) *Facing value decisions: Rationale-building for teachers*. Belmont, California: Wadsworth.

Shavitt, S. (1990) The role of attitude objects in attitude functions. *Journal of Experimental Social Psychology, 26*, 124–8.

Sheehy, G. (1976) *Passages – predictable crises of adult life*. New York: Bantam Books.

Sherif, M. (1935) A study of social factors in perception. *Archives of Psychology, 27* (Whole No. 187).

Sherif, M. (1936) *The psychology of social norms*. New York: Harper & Row.

Sherif, M. (1966) *Group conflict and co-operation: Their social psychology*. London: Routledge & Kegan Paul.

Sherif, M., Harvey, O.J., White, B.J., Hood, W.R. & Sherif, C.W. (1961) *Intergroup conflict and co-operation: The Robber's Cave experiment*. Norman, Oklahoma: University of Oklahoma Press.

Sherif, M. & Hovland, C.I. (1961) *Social judgement: Assimilation and contrast in communication and attitude change*. New Haven, Connecticut: Yale University Press.

Sherif, M. & Sherif, C. (1969) *Social psychology*. New York: Harper & Row.

Sherrington, C.S. (1900) Experiments on the value of vascular and visceral factors for the genesis of emotion. *Proceedings of the Royal Society, 66*, 390–403.

Shields, J. (1962) *Monozygotic twins brought up apart and brought up together*. London: Oxford University Press.

Shields, J. (1976) Heredity and environment. In H.J. Eysenck & G.D. Wilson (Eds.), *Textbook of human psychology*. Lancaster: MTP.

Shields, J. (1978) Genetics. In J.K. Wing (Ed.), *Schizophrenia – towards a new synthesis*. London: Academic Press.

Shiffrin, R.M. & Schneider, W. (1977) Controlled and automatic human information processing: 11 – perceptual learning, automatic attending and a general theory. *Psychological Review, 84*, 127–90.

Shotland, R.L. & Straw, M.K. (1976) Bystander response to an assault: When a man attacks a woman. *Journal of Personality and Social Psychology, 34*, 990–9.

Shotter, J. (1975) *Images of man in psychological research*. London: Methuen.

Shuey, A. (1966) *The testing of negro intelligence*. New York: Social Science Press.

Shweder, R.A. (1991) *Thinking through cultures: Expeditions in cultural psychology*. Cambridge, Mass.: Harvard University Press.

Siann, G. (1985) *Accounting for aggression – perspectives on aggression and violence*. London: Allen & Unwin.

Siddique, C.M. & D'Arcy, C. (1984) Adolescence, stress and psychological well-being. *Journal of Youth and Adolescence*, 13, 459–74.

Sigall, H. (1970) The effects of competence and consensual validation of a communicator's liking for the audience. *Journal of Personality and Social Psychology, 16*, 251–8.

Sigall, H. & Landy, D. (1973) Radiating beauty: Effects of having a physically attractive partner on person perception. *Journal of Personality and Social Psychology, 28*, 218–24.

Sigall, H. & Ostrove, N. (1975) Beautiful but dangerous: Effects of offender attractiveness and nature of crime on juridic judgement. *Journal of Personality and Social Psychology, 31*, 410–14.

Simmons, R.& Blyth, D.A. (1987) *Moving into adolescence*. New York: Aldine de Gruyter.

Simmons, R. & Rosenberg, S. (1975) Sex, sex roles and self-image. *Journal of Youth and Adolescence*, 4, 229–56.

Simon, B. (1971) *Intelligence, psychology and education: A Marxist critique*. London: Lawrence & Wishart.

Simon, H.A. (1979) Information-processing theory of human problem solving. In W. Estes (Ed.), *Handbook of learning and cognitive processes, Vol. 5*. Hillsdale, New Jersey: Lawrence Erlbaum Associates Inc.

Sinclair-de-Zwart, H. (1969) Developmental psycholinguistics. In D. Elkind and J. Flavell (Eds.), *Studies in cognitive development*. New York: Oxford University Press.

Sistruuk, F. & McDavid, J.W. (1971) Sex variable in conforming behaviour. *Journal of Personality and Social Psychology, 2*, 200–7.

Skeels, H.M. (1966) Adult status of children with contrasting early life experiences. *Monographs of the Society for Research in Child Development, 31* (Whole No. 3).

Skeels, H.M. & Dye, H.B. (1939) A study of the effects of differential stimulation on mentally retarded children. *Proceedings of the American Association of Mental Deficiency, 44*, 114–36.

Skinner, B.F. (1938) *The behaviour of organisms.* New York: Appleton-Century-Crofts.

Skinner, B.F. (1948) *Walden two.* New York: Macmillan.

Skinner, B.F. (1950) Are theories of learning necessary? *Psychological Review, 57,* 193–216.

Skinner, B.F. (1953) *Science and human behaviour.* New York: Macmillan.

Skinner, B.F. (1957) *Verbal behaviour.* New York: Appleton-Century-Crofts.

Skinner, B.F. (1958) Teaching machines. *Science, 128,* 969–77.

Skinner, B.F. (1971) *Beyond freedom and dignity.* New York: Knopf.

Skodak, M. & Skeels, H. (1949) A final follow-up study of 100 adopted children. *Journal of Genetic Psychology, 75,* 85–125.

Skuse, D. (1984a) Extreme deprivation in early childhood – I. Diverse outcome for three siblings from an extraordinary family. *Journal of Child Psychology and Psychiatry, 25* (4), 523–41.

Skuse, D. (1984b) Extreme deprivation in early childhood – II. Theoretical issues and a comparative review. *Journal of Child Psychology and Psychiatry, 25* (4), 543–72.

Slaby, R.G. & Frey, K.S. (1975) Development of gender constancy and selective attention to same-sex models. *Child Development, 46,* 849–56.

Slater, A. (1989) Visual memory and perception in early infancy. In A. Slater and G. Bremner (Eds.), *Infant development.* Hove, East Sussex: Lawrence Erlbaum Associates Ltd.

Slater, A., Slater, E. & Roth, M. (1969) *Clinical psychiatry* (3rd ed.). London, Ballière Tindall and Cassell.

Sluckin, W. (1965) *Imprinting and early experiences.* London: Methuen.

Slobin, D.I. (1975) On the nature of talk to children. In E.H. Lenneberg and E. Lenneberg (Eds.), *Foundation of language development, Vol. 1.* New York: Academic Press.

Smail, D. (1987) Psychotherapy and 'change': Some ethical considerations. In S. Fairbairn and G. Fairbairn (Eds.), *Psychology, ethics and change.* London: Routledge & Kegan Paul.

Smart, J.J.C. (1959) Sensations and brain processes. *The Philosophical Review, 68,* 141–56.

Smith, C.U.M. (1994) You are a group of neurons. *The Times Higher Educational Supplement,* 27 May, 20–1.

Smith, E.M., Brown, H.O., Toman, J.E.P., & Goodman, L.S. (1947) The lack of cerebral effects of D-tubo-curarine. *Anaesthesiology, 8,* 1–14.

Smith, H.B., Bruner, J.S. & White, R.W. (1956) *Opinions and personality.* New York: John Wiley.

Smith, M.L. & Glass, G.V. (1977) Meta-analysis of psychotherapeutic outcome studies. *American Psychologist, 32,* 752–60.

Smith, M.L., Glass, G.V. & Miller, B.L. (1980) *The benefits of psychotherapy.* Baltimore, Maryland: Johns Hopkins University Press.

Smith, P.B. (1995) Social influence processes. In M. Argyle & A.M. Colman (Eds.) *Social psychology.* London: Longman.

Smith, P.B. & Bond, M.H. (1993) *Social psychology across cultures: Analysis and perspectives.* Hemel Hempstead, Herts: Harvester Wheatsheaf.

Smith, P.B. & Peterson, M.F. (1988) *Leadership, organizations and culture.* London: Sage.

Smith, P.K. (1990) Ethology, sociobiology and developmental psychology: In memory of Niko Tinbergen and Konrad Lorenz. *British Journal of Developmental Psychology, 8* (2), 187–96.

Smith, P.K. (1995) Social development. In P. E. Bryant & A.M.Colman (Eds.) *Developmental psychology.* London: Longman.

Smith, P.K. & Cowie, H. (1991) *Understanding children's development.*(2nd ed.) Oxford: Basil Blackwell.

Smith, R.E., Sarason, I.G. & Sarason, B.R. (1986) *Psychology – the frontiers of behaviour* (3rd ed.). New York: Harper & Row.

Smith, V.L. & Ellsworth, P.C. (1987) The social psychology of eyewitness accuracy: Misleading questions and communicator expertise. *Journal of Applied Psychology, 72,* 294–300.

Snow, C.E. (1977) Mother's speech research: From input to interaction. In C.E. Snow & C.A. Ferguson (Eds.), *Talking to children: Language input and acquisition.* New York: Cambridge University Press.

Snyder, F.W. & Pronko, N.H. (1952) *Vision with spatial inversion.* Wichita, Kansas: University of Wichita Press.

Snyder, M. (1979) Self-monitoring processes. In L. Berkowitz (Ed.) *Advances in experimental social psychology.* Vol. 18. New York: Academic Press.

Snyder, M. (1987) *Public appearance/private realities. The psychology of self-monitoring.* New York: W H Freeman.

Snyder, M. (1995) Self-monitoring: Public appearances versus private realities. In G.G.Brannigan & M.R. Merrens (Eds.) *The social psychologists: Research adventures.* New York: McGraw-Hill.

Sobesky, W. (1983) The effects of situational factors on moral judgements. *Child Development, 54,* 575–84.

Solomon, R.L. & Howes, D.W. (1951) Word frequency, personal values and visual duration thresholds. *Psychological Review, 58,* 256.

Solomon, R.L., Turner, L.H. & Lessac, M.S. (1968) Some effects of delay of punishment on resistance to temptation in dogs. *Journal of Personality & Social Psychology, 8,* 233–8.

Solomon, R.L. & Wynne, L.C. (1953) Traumatic avoidance learning: Acquisition in normal dogs. *Psychological Monographs, 67,* (4, Whole No. 354).

Solso, R.L. (1979) *Cognitive psychology.* New York: Harcourt Brace Jovanovich.

Solso, R.L. (1995) *Cognitive Psychology* (4th ed.) Boston: Allyn & Bacon.

Sommer, R. (1969) *Personal space: The behavioural basis of design.* Englewood Cliffs, NJ.: Prentice-Hall.

Sorrentino, R.M. & Boutillier, R.G. (1975) The effect of quantity and quality of verbal interaction on ratings of leadership ability. *Journal of Experimental and Social Psychology, 11,* 403–11.

Sorrentino, R.M. & Field, N. (1986) Emergent leadership over time: The functional value of positive motivation. *Journal of Personality and Social Psychology, 50,* 1091–9.

Spanos, N.P. (1989) Experimental research on hypnotic analgesia. In N.P. Spanos & J.F. Chaves (Eds.) *Hypnosis: the cognitive-behavioural perspective.* Buffalo, N.Y.: Prometheus.

Spanos, N.P. (1991) A sociocognitive approach to hypnosis. In S.J. Lynn & J.W. Rhue (Eds.) *Theories of hypnosis: Current models and perspectives.* New York: Guilford.

Spearman, C. (1904) General intelligence, objectively determined and measured. *American Journal of Psychology, 15,* 201–93.

Spearman, C. (1967) The doctrine of two factors. In S. Wiseman (Ed.), *Intelligence and ability.* Harmondsworth, Middlesex: Penguin. (Original work published 1927.)

Speisman, J.C., Lazarus, R.S., Mordkoff, A.M. & Davidson, L.A. (1964) The experimental reduction of stress based on ego defence theory. *Journal of Abnormal and Social Psychology, 68,* 397–8.

Spelke, E., Zelazo, P., Kagan, J. & Kotelchuck, M. (1973) Father interaction and separation protest. *Developmental Psychology, 9,* 83–90.

Spelke, E.S., Hirst, W.C. & Neisser, U. (1976) Skills of divided attention. *Cognition*, *4*, 215–30.

Spence, J.T. & Helmreich, R.L. (1978) *Masculinity and femininity: Their psychological dimensions, correlates and antecedents*. Austin, Texas: University of Texas Press.

Spence, J.T., Helmreich, R.L. & Stapp, J. (1975) Ratings of self and peers on sex role attributes and their relation to self-esteem and concepts of masculinity and femininity. *Journal of Personality and Social Psychology*, *32*, 29–39.

Sperling, G. (1960) The information available in brief visual presentation. *Psychological Monographs*, *74* (Whole No. 498).

Sperling, G. (1963) A mode for visual memory tasks. *Human Factors*, *5*, 19–31.

Sperling, G. & Speelman, R.G. (1970) Acoustic similarity and auditory short-term memory: Experiments and a model. In D.A. Norman (Ed.), *Models of human memory*. New York: Academic Press.

Sperry, R.W. (1943) The effect of 180 degree rotation in the retinal field of visuo-motor co-ordination. *Journal of Experimental Zoology*, *92*, 263–79.

Sperry, R.W. (1964) The great cerebral commissure. *Scientific American*, *210* (1), 42–52.

Sperry, R.W. (1968) Hemisphere deconnection and unity in conscious awareness. *American Psychologist*, *23*, 723–33.

Sperry, R.W. & Gazzaniga, M.S. (1967) Language following surgical disconnection of the hemispheres. In F. Darley (Ed.), *Brain mechanisms underlying speech and language*. New York: Grune and Stratton.

Spitz, R.A. (1945) Hospitalism: An inquiry into the genesis of psychiatric conditions in early childhood. *Psychoanalytic Study of the Child*, *1*, 53–74.

Spitz, R.A. (1946) Hospitalism: A follow-up report on investigation described in Vol. 1, 1945. *Psychoanalytic Study of the Child*, *2*, 113–17.

Spitz, R.A. & Wolf, K.M. (1946) Anaclitic depression. *Psychoanalytic Study of the Child*, *2*, 313–42.

Spitzer, R.L. (1976) More on pseudoscience in science and the case for psychiatric diagnosis. *Archives of General Psychiatry*, *33*, 459–70.

Spitzer, R.L., Endicott, J. & Robins, E. (1978) Research diagnostic criteria: Rationale and reliability. *Archives of General Psychiatry*, *35*, 773–82.

Sroufe, L.A. & Waters, E. (1977) Attachment as an organizational construct. *Child Development*, *48*, 1184–99.

Staats, A.W. & Staats, C.K. (1963) *Complex human behaviour*. New York: Holt Rinehart & Winston.

Stacey, M., Dearden, R., Pill, R. & Robinson, D. (1970) *Hospitals, children and their families: The report of a pilot study*. London: Routledge & Kegan Paul.

Stafford, E.M., Jackson, P.R. & Banks, M.H. (1980) Employment, work involvement and mental health in less qualified young people. *Journal of Occupational Psychology*, *53*, 291–304.

Stahlberg, D. & Frey, D. (1988) Attitudes 1: Structure, measurement and functions. In M. Hewstone, W. Stroebe, J.P. Codol & G.M. Stephenson (Eds.) *Introduction to social psychology*. Oxford: Blackwell.

Stainton Rogers, R., Stenner, P., Gleeson, K. & Stainton Rogers, W. (1995) *Social psychology: A critical agenda*. Cambridge: Polity Press.

Stampfl, T. & Levis, D. (1967) Essentials of implosive therapy. *Journal of Abnormal Psychology*, *72*, 496–503.

Stayton, D.J. & Ainsworth, M.D.S. (1973) Individual differences in infant response to brief, everyday separations as related to other infant and maternal behaviours. *Developmental Psychology*, *9*, 226–35.

Stayton, D.J., Ainsworth, M.D.S. & Main, M.B. (1973) Development of separation behaviour in the first year of life: Protest, following and greeting. *Developmental Psychology*, *9*, 213–25.

Stein, B.S., Morris, C.D. & Bransford, J.D. (1978) Constraints on effective elaboration. *Journal of Verbal Learning and Verbal Behaviour*, *17*, 707–14.

Steinberg, L. & Silverberg, S.B. (1986) The vicissitudes of autonomy in early adolescence. *Child Development*, *57*, 841–51.

Steiner, J.E. (1977) Facial expressions of the neonate infant indicating the hedonics of food-related chemical stimuli. In J.M. Weiffenbach (Ed.), *Taste and Development*. Bethesda, Maryland: DHEW.

Steiner, J.E. (1979) Human facial expressions in response to taste and smell stimulation. In H. Reese & L. Lipsitt (Eds.), *Advances in Child Development and Behaviour, Vol. 13.* New York: Academic Press.

Stephan, W.G. (1978) School desegregation: An evaluation of predictions made in Brown vs. the Board of Education. *Psychological Bulletin, 85*, 217–38.

Stephenson, G.M. (1988) Applied social psychology. In M. Hewstone, W Stroebe, J.P. Codol & G.M. Stephenson (Eds.), *Introduction to social psychology*. Oxford: Basil Blackwell.

Sternberg, R.J. (1979) The nature of mental abilities. *American Psychologist, 34*, 214–30.

Sternberg, R.J. (1985) *Beyond IQ: A triarchic theory of human intelligence*. Cambridge: Cambridge University Press.

Sternberg, R.J. (1987) Intelligence. In R. Gregory (Ed.), *The Oxford companion to the mind*. Oxford: Oxford University Press.

Sternberg, R.J. (1988a) *The triarchic mind: A new theory of human intelligence*. New York: Viking.

Sternberg, R.J. (1988b) Triangulating love. In R.J. Sternberg & M.L. Barnes (Eds.) *The psychology of love*. New Haven, CT; Yale University Press.

Sternberg, R.J. (1990) *Metaphors of mind*. Cambridge: Cambridge University Press.

Sternberg, R.J. (1995) Intelligence and cognitive styles. In S.E. Hampson & A.M. Colman (Eds.) *Individual differences and personality*. London: Longman.

Sternglanz, S.H. & Serbin, L.A. (1974) Sex role stereotyping in childrens' television programs. *Developmental Psychology, 10*, 710–15.

Stevens, R. (1995) Freudian theories of personality. In S.E. Hampson & A.M. Colman (Eds.) *Individual differences and personality*. London: Longman.

Stewart, V.M. (1973) Tests of the 'carpentered world' hypothesis by race and environment in America and Zambia. *International Journal of Psychology, 8*, 83–94.

Stogdill, R.M. (1974) *Handbook of leadership*. New York: Free Press.

Stone, A.A. & Neale, J.M. (1982) Development of a methodology for assessing daily experiences. In A. Baum & J. Singer (Eds.) *Environment and health*. Hillsdale, NJ.: Erlbaum.

Stone, A.A., Reed, B.R., & Neale, J.M. (1987) Changes in daily event frequency precede episodes of physical symptoms. *Journal of Human Stress, 13*, 70–4.

Stoner, J. A. F. (1961) *A comparison of individual and group decisions involving risk*. Unpublished master's thesis, Massachusetts Institute of Technology.

Stones, E. (1971) *Educational psychology*. London: Methuen.

Storms, M.D. (1973) Videotape and the attribution process: reversing actors' and observers' points of view. *Journal of Personality & Social Psychology, 27* (2), 165–75.

Storr, A. (1966) The concept of cure. In C. Rycroft (Ed.), *Psychoanalysis observed*. London: Constable.

Storr, A. (1966) *Human aggression.* Harmondsworth, Middlesex: Penguin.

Storr, A. (1987) Why psychoanalysis is not a science. In C. Blakemore and S. Greenfield (Eds.), *Mindwaves*. Oxford: Blackwell.

Stouffer, S.A., Suchman, E.A., DeVinney, L.C., Starr, S.A. & Williams, R.M. (1949) *The American soldier: Adjustment during army life, Vol. 1.* Princeton, New Jersey: Princeton University Press.

Stratton, G.M. (1896) Some preliminary experiments on vision. *Psychological Review, 3,* 611–17.

Stroebe, M.S., Stroebe, W. & Hansson, R.O. (1993) Contemporary themes and controversies in bereavement research. In M.S. Stroebe, W. Stroebe & R.O. Hansson (Eds.) *Handbook of bereavement: Theory, research and intervention.* New York: Cambridge University Press.

Stroebe, W., Insko, C.A., Thompson, V.D. & Layton, B.D. (1971) Effects of physical attractiveness, attitude similarity, and sex on various aspects of interpersonal attraction. *Journal of Personality and Social Psychology, 18,* 79–91.

Stroop, J.R. (1935) Interference in serial verbal reactions. *Journal of Experimental Psychology, 18,* 643–61.

Sugarman, L. (1986) *Life span development.* London: Methuen.

Suomi, S.J. (1982) Biological foundations and developmental psychobiology. In C.B. Kopp and J.B. Krakow (Eds.), *Child development in a social context.* Reading, Massachusetts: Addison-Wesley.

Suomi, S.J. & Harlow, H.F. (1972) Depressive behaviour in young monkeys subjected to vertical chamber confinement. *Journal of Comparative and Physiological Psychology. 80,* 11–18.

Sutherland, S.N. (1976) *Breakdown.* London: Weidenfeld & Nicolson.

Szasz, T. (1960) The myth of mental illness. *American Psychologist, 15,* 113–18.

Szasz, T. (1972) *The myth of mental illness.* London: Paladin.

Szasz, T. (1973) *The manufacture of madness.* London: Paladin.

Szasz, T. (1974) *Ideology and insanity.* Harmondsworth, Middlesex: Penguin.

Szymanski, K. & Harkins, S.G. (1987) Social loafing and self-evaluation with a social standard. *Journal of Personality & Social Psychology, 53,* 891–7.

Tagiuri, R. (1969) Person perception. In G. Lindzey and E. Aronson, (Eds.), *Handbook of psychology, Vol. 2.* Reading, Massachusetts: Addison-Wesley.

Tajfel, H. (1969) Social and cultural factors in perception. In G. Lindzey & E. Aronson (Eds.) *Handbook of social psychology* (Vol. 3). Reading, MA: Addison-Wesley.

Tajfel, H. (Ed.) (1978) *Differentiation between social groups. Studies in the social psychology of intergroup relations.* London: Academic Press.

Tajfel, H. (1981) *Human group and social categories.* Cambridge: Cambridge University Press.

Tajfel, H., Billig, M.G. & Bundy, R.P. (1971) Social categorization and intergroup behaviour. *European Journal of Social Psychology, 1* (2), 149–78.

Tajfel, H. & Turner, J. (1979) An integrative theory of intergroup conflict. In G.W. Austin and S. Worchel, (Eds.), *The social psychology of intergroup relations.* Monterey, California: Brooks Cole.

Tajfel, H. & Turner, J.C. (1986) The social identity theory of intergroup behaviour. In S. Worchel & W. Austin (Eds.) *Psychology of intergroup relations.* Chicago: Nelson-Hall.

Tavris, C. (1993) The mismeasure of woman. *Feminism & Psychology, 3* (2), 149–68.

Taylor, D.M. & Porter, L.E. (1994) A multicultural view of stereotyping. In W.J. Lonner & R.S. Malpass (Eds.) *Psychology and culture.* Boston: Allyn & Bacon.

Taylor, J. (1992) A questionable treatment. *Nursing Times, 88* (40), 41–3.

Taylor, S.E. (1981) A categorization approach to stereotyping. In D.L. Hamilton (Ed.) *Cognitive processes in stereotyping and intergroup behaviour.* Hillsdale, NJ: Erlbaum.

Taylor, S.E., Peplau, L.A. & Sears, D.O. (1994) *Social psychology* (8th ed) . Englewood Cliffs, NJ: Prentice Hall`cx.

Tedeschi, J.T. & Rosenfield, P. (1981) Impression management theory and the forced compliance situation. In J.T. Tedeschi (Ed.), *Impression management theory and social psychological research.* New York: Academic Press.

Tedeschi, J.T., Schlenker, B.R. & Bonoma, T.V. (1971) Cognitive dissonance: Private ratiocination or public spectacle? *American Psychologist, 26,* 685–95.

Teichman, J. (1988) *Philosophy and the mind.* Oxford: Blackwell.

Teitelbaum, P. (1967) Motivation and control of food intake. In C.F. Code (Ed.), *Handbook of physiology: Alimentary canal, Vol. 1.* Washington, DC: American Physiological Society.

Teitelbaum, P. (1971) The encephalization of hunger. In E. Stellar and J.M. Sprague (Eds.), *Progress in physiological psychology, Vol. 4.* London: Academic Press.

Teitelbaum, P. & Stellar, E. (1954) Recovery from the failure to eat produced by hypothalamic lesions. *Science, 120,* 894–5.

Terman, L.M. (1921) In symposium: Intelligence and its measurement. *Journal of Educational Psychology, 12,* 127–33.

Terman, L.M. (1954) The discovery and encouragement of exceptional talent. *American Psychologist, 9,* 221–38.

Terman, L.M. & Merrill, M.A. (1937) *Measuring intelligence.* London: Harrap.

Terrace, H.S. (1979) *Nim.* New York: Knopf.

Terrace, H.S. (1987) Thoughts without words. In C. Blakemore & S. Greenfield (Eds.), *Mindwaves.* Oxford: Basil Blackwell.

Thibaut, J.W. & Kelley, H.H. (1959) *The social psychology of groups.* New York: Wiley.

Thigpen, C.H. & Cleckley, H. (1954) A case of multiple personality. *Journal of Abnormal and Social Psychology, 49,* 135–51.

Thigpen, C.H. & Cleckley, H. (1957) *The three faces of Eve.* New York: McGraw Hill.

Thomas, K. (1990) Psychodynamics: The Freudian approach. In I. Roth (Ed.), *Introduction to psychology, Vol. 1.* Hove, E. Sussex/Milton Keynes: Open University/Lawrence Erlbaum Associates Ltd.

Thomas, R.M. (1985) *Comparing theories of child development* (2nd ed.). Belmont, California: Wadsworth Publishing Company.

Thorndike, E.L. (1898) Animal intelligence: An experimental study of the associative processes in animals. *Psychological Review, Monograph Supplement, 2* (Whole No. 8).

Thorne, B. (1984) Person-centred therapy. In W. Dryden (Ed.), *Individual therapy in Britain.* London: Harper & Row.

Thorpe, W.H. (1963) *Learning and instinct in animals* (2nd ed.). London: Methuen.

Thurstone, L.L. (1928) Attitudes can be measured. *American Journal of Sociology, 33,* 529–54.

Thurstone, L.L. (1938) Primary mental abilities. *Psychometric Monographs, No. 1.*

Tillman, W.S. & Carver, C.S. (1980) Actors' and observers' attributions for success and failure: A comparative test of predictions from Kelley's cube, self-serving bias and positivity bias formulations. *Journal of Experimental Social Psychology, 16,* 18–32.

Tinbergen, N. (1951) *The study of instinct.* Oxford: Clarendon

Press.

Tinbergen, N. & Perdeck, A.C. (1950) On the stimulus situation releasing the begging response in the newly-hatched herring-gull chick. *Behaviour*, *3*, 1–39.

Tizard, B. (1977) *Adoption: A second chance*. London: Open Books.

Tizard, B. (1986) *The care of young children*. London: Institute of Education.

Tizard, B. & Hodges, J. (1978) The effect of early institutional rearing on the development of eight-year old children. *Journal of Child Psychology and Psychiatry*, *19*, 99–118.

Tizard, B., Joseph, A., Cooperman, O. & Tizard, J. (1972) Environmental effects on language development: A study of young children in long-stay residential nurseries. *Child Development*, *43*, 337–58.

Tizard, B. & Rees, J. (1974) A comparison of the effects of adoption, restoration to the natural mother and continued institutionalization on the cognitive development of four-year old children. *Child Development*, *45*, 92–9.

Tizard, J. & Tizard, B. (1971) Social development of 2-year-old children in residential nurseries. In H.R. Schaffer (Ed.), *The origins of human social relations*. London: Academic Press.

Tolman, E.C. (1948) Cognitive maps in rats and men. *Psychological Review*, *55*, 189–208.

Tolman, E.C. & Honzik, C.H. (1930) Introduction and removal of reward and maze learning in rats. *University of California Publications in Psychology*, *4*, 257–75.

Tolman, E.C., Ritchie, B.F. & Kalish, D. (1946) Studies in spatial learning. 1: Orientation and the short-cut. *Journal of Experimental Psychology*, 36, 13–25.

Torrance, S. (1986) Breaking out of the Chinese room. In M. Yazdani, (Ed.), *Artificial intelligence: Principles and applications*. London: Chapman & Hall.

Traupmann, J., Hatfield, E. & Wexer, P. (1983) Equity and sexual satisfaction in dating couples. *British Journal of Social Psychology*, *22*, 33–40.

Treisman, A.M. (1960) Contextual cues in selective listening. *Quarterly Journal of Experimental Psychology*, *12*, 242–8.

Treisman, A.M. (1964) Verbal cues, language and meaning in selective attention. *American Journal of Psychology*, *77*, 206–19.

Treisman, A.M. & Geffen, G. (1967) Selective attention: Perception or response? *Quarterly Journal of Experimental Psychology*, *19*, 1–18.

Treisman, A.M. & Gelade, G. (1980) A feature integration theory of selection. *Cognitive Psychology*, *12*, 97–136.

Treisman, A.M. & Riley, J.G.A. (1969) Is selective attention selective perception or selective response: A further test. *Journal of Experimental Psychology*, *79*, 27–34.

Triandis, H.C. (1990) Theoretical concepts that are applicable to the analysis of ethnocentrism. In R.W.Brislin (Ed.) *Applied Cross-Cultural Psychology*. Newbury Park, CA.: Sage.

Triplett, N. (1898) The dynamogenic factors in pacemaking and competition. *American Journal of Psychology*, *9*, 507–33.

Triseliotis, J. (1980) Growing up in foster care and after. In J. Triseliotis (Ed.), *New developments in foster care and adoption*. London: Routledge & Kegan Paul.

Trivers, R.L. (1971) The evolution of reciprocal altruism. *Quarterly Review of Biology*, *46*, 35–57.

Trivers, R.L. (1972) Parental investment and sexual selection. In B. Campbell (Ed.) *Sexual selection and the descent of man 1871–1971*. Chicago, ILL: Aldine.

Trivers, R. (1985) *Social Evolution*. Menlo Park, CA.: Benjamin/Cummings.

Trivers, R.L. & Hare, H. (1976) Haplodiploidy and the evolution of

social insects. *Science*, *191*, 249–63.

Troscianko, T. (1987) Colour vision: Brain mechanisms. In R. Gregory (Ed.), *The Oxford companion to the mind*. Oxford: Oxford University Press.

Trower, P. (1987) On the ethical bases of 'scientific' behaviour therapy. In S. Fairbairn & G. Fairbairn (Eds.), *Psychology, ethics and change*. London: Routledge & Kegan Paul.

Truax, C. & Mitchell, K. (1971) Research on certain therapist interpersonal skills in relation to process and outcome. In A.E. Bergin & S.L. Garfield (Eds.), *Handbook of psychotherapy and behaviour change: An empirical analysis*. New York: Wiley.

Tulving, E. (1962) Subjective organization in free recall of unrelated words. *Psychological Review*, *69*, 344–54.

Tulving, E. (1972) Episodic and semantic memory. In E. Tulving & W. Donaldson (Eds.), *Organization of memory*. London: Academic Press.

Tulving, E. (1974) Cue-dependent forgetting. *American Scientist*, 62, 74–82.

Tulving, E. (1983) *Elements of episodic memory*. London: ClarendonPress/Oxford University Press.

Tulving, E. (1985) How many memory systems are there? *American Psychologist*, *40*, 385–98.

Tulving, E. (1979) Relation between encoding specificity and levels of processing. In L.S. Cermak & F.I.M. Craik (Eds.), *Levels of processing in human memory*. Hillsdale, New Jersey: Lawrence Erlbaum Associates Inc.

Tulving, E. & Pearlstone, Z. (1966) Availability versus accessibility of information in memory for words. *Journal of Verbal Learning and Verbal Behaviour*, *5*, 381–91.

Tulving, E. & Psotka, J. (1971) Retroactive inhibition in free recall: Inaccessibility of information available in the memory store. *Journal of Experimental Psychology*, *87*, 1–8.

Turiel, E. (1966) An experimental test of the sequentiality of developmental stages in the child's moral judgements. *Journal of Personality and Social Psychology*, *3*, 611–18.

Turiel, E. (1978) Distinct conceptual and developmental domains: Social convention and morality. In C.B. Keasey (Ed.), *Nebraska Symposium on Motivation, Vol. 25*. Lincoln, Nebraska: Nebraska University Press.

Turing, A.M. (1950) Computing machinery and intelligence. *Mind*, *59*, 433–60.

Turnbull, C.M. (1961) *The forest people*. New York: Simon & Schuster.

Turnbull, S.K. (1995) The middle years. In D. Wedding (Ed.) *Behaviour and medicine* (2nd ed.). St. Louis, MO: Mosby-Year Book.

Turner, E.A. & Wright, J. (1965) Effects of severity of threat and perceived availability on the attractiveness of objects. *Journal of Personality and Social Psychology*, *2*, 128–32.

Turner, J.C. (1982) Towards a cognitive redefinition of the social group. In H. Tajfel (Ed.), *Social identity and intergroup relations*. Cambridge: Cambridge University Press.

Turner, J.C. (1985) Social categorizations and the self-concept: A social cognitive theory of group behaviour. In E.J. Lawler (Ed.), *Advances in group processes: Theory and research, Vol. 2*. Greenwich, Connecticut: JAI Press.

Turner, J.C. (1991) *Social influence*. Milton Keynes: Open University Press.

Turner, J.C., Hogg, M.A., Oakes, P.J., Reicher, S.D. & Wetherell, M.S. (1987) *Rediscovering the social group: A self-categorization theory*. Oxford: Blackwell.

Turner, J.S. & Helms, D.B. (1989) *Contemporary adulthood* (4th ed.). Fort Worth, Florida: Holt, Rinehart & Winston.

Tversky, A. & Kahneman, D. (1974) Judgement under uncertainty: Heuristics and biases. *Science*, 185, 1124–31.

Twombly, R. (1994) Shock therapy returns. *New Scientist, 5 March*, 21–3. Warrington, E.K. & Weiskrantz, L. (1968) New method of testing long-term retention with special reference to amnesic patients. *Nature, 217*, 972–4.

Tyerman, A. & Spencer, C. (1983) A critical test of the Sheriffs' Robbers' Cave experiment: Intergroup competition and co-operation between groups of well-acquainted individuals. *Small Group Behaviour, 14* (4), 515–31.

Ullmann, L.P. & Krasner, L.A. (1975) *A psychological approach to abnormal behaviour*. Englewood Cliffs, New Jersey: Prentice Hall.

Underwood, B.J. (1948) Retroactive and proactive inhibition after 5 and 48 hours. *Journal of Experimental Psychology, 38*, 29–38.

Underwood, B.J. (1957) Interference and forgetting. *Psychological Review, 64*, 49–60.

Underwood, G. (1974) Moray vs. the rest: The effects of extended shadowing practice. *Quarterly Journal of Experimental Psychology, 26*, 368–72.

Unger, R.K. (1979) *Female and male*. London: Harper & Row.

Valentine, E.R. (1992) *Conceptual issues in psychology*.(2nd ed.) London: Routledge.

Valins, S. (1966) Cognitive effects of false heart-rate feedback. *Journal of Personality and Social Psychology, 4*, 400–8.

Van Avermaet, E. (1988) Social influence in small groups. In M. Hewstone, W. Stroebe, J.P. Codol & G.M. Stephenson (Eds.), *Introduction to social psychology*. Oxford: Basil Blackwell.

van Essen, D.C. (1985) Functional organization of primate visual cortex. In A. Peters & E.G. Jones (Eds.), *Cerebral cortex. Vol. 2 – Visual cortex*. New York: Plenum Press.

Vanneman, R.D. & Pettigrew, T.F. (1972) Race and relative deprivation in the urban United States. *Race*, 13, 461–86.

Vaughn, B.E., Gove, F.L. & Egeland, B.R. (1980) The relationship between out-of-home care and the quality of infant–mother attachment in an economically disadvantaged population. *Child Development, 51*, 1203–14.

Vernon, M.D.(1955) The functions of schemata in perceiving. *Psychological Review, 62*, 180–92.

Vernon, P.E. (1950) The hierarchy of ability. In S. Wiseman (Ed.), *Intelligence and ability*. Harmondsworth, Middlesex: Penguin.

Vernon, P.E. (1969) *Intelligence and cultural environment*. London: Methuen.

Vernon, P.E. (1979) *Intelligence: Heredity and environment*. San Francisco: W.H. Freeman.

von Bekesy, G. (1960) *Experiments in hearing*. New York: McGraw-Hill.

Vivian, J. & Brown, R. (1995) Prejudice and intergroup conflict. In M. Argyle & A.M. Colman (Eds.) *Social psychology*. London: Longman.

Von Senden, M. (1960) *Space and sight: The perception of space and shape in the congenitally blind before and after operations* (P. Heath, trans.). London: Methuen. (Original work published 1932.)

Von Wright, J.M., Anderson, K. & Stenman, U. (1975) Generalization of conditioned GSRs in dichotic listening. In P.M.A. Rabbit & S. Dornic (Eds.), *Attention and performance, Vol. 1*. London: Academic Press.

Vygotsky, L.S. (1962) *Thought and language*. Cambridge, Massachusetts: MIT Press. (Original work published 1934.)

Vygotsky, L.S. (1978) *Mind in society*. Cambridge, Massachusetts: Harvard University Press.

Vygotsky, L.S. (1981) The genesis of higher mental functions. In J.V. Wertsch (Ed.) *The concept of activity in Soviet psychol-*

ogy. Armonk, NY.: Sharpe.

Wachtel, P.L. (1977) *Psychoanalysis and behaviour therapy: Toward an integration*. New York: Basic Books.

Wachtel, P.L. (1989) Preface to the paperback edition. In *Psychoanalysis and behaviour therapy*. New York: Basic Books.

Wade, C. & Tavris, C. (1994) The longest war: Gender and culture. In W.J. Lonner & R.S. Malpass (Eds.) *Psychology and Culture*. Boston: Allyn & Bacon.

Wagstaff, G.F. (1981) *Hypnosis, compliance and belief*. Brighton: Harvester.

Wagstaff, G.F. (1989) Forensic aspects of hypnosis. In N.P. Spanos & J.F. Chaves (Eds.) *Hypnosis: The cognitive-behavioural perspective*. Buffalo, N.Y.: Prometheus.

Wagstaff, G.F. (1995) Hypnosis. In A.M. Colman (Ed.) *Controversies in psychology*. London: Longman.

Walker, S. (1984) *Learning theory and behaviour modification*. London: Methuen.

Walster, E. (1966) The assignment of responsibility for an accident. *Journal of Personality and Social Psychology, 5*, 508–16.

Walster, E. (1970) The effect of self-esteem on liking for dates of various social desirabilities. *Journal of Experimental and Social Psychology, 6*, 248–53.

Walster, E., Aronson, E. & Abrahams, D. (1966) On increasing the persuasiveness of a low prestige communicator. *Journal of Experimental and Social Psychology, 2*, 325–42.

Walster, E., Aronson, E., Abrahams, D. & Rottman, L. (1966) Importance of physical attractiveness in dating behaviour. *Journal of Personality and Social Psychology, 4*, 508–16.

Walster, E.H., Walster, G.W. & Berscheid, E. (1978) *Equity theory and research*. Boston, Massachusetts: Allyn and Bacon.

Walster, E. & Festinger, L. (1962) The effectiveness of 'overheard' persuasive communication. *Journal of Abnormal and Social Psychology, 65*, 395–402.

Warr, P.B. (1984) Work and unemployment. In P.J.D. Drenth (Ed.), *Handbook of work and organisational psychology*. Chichester: Wiley.

Warr, P.B. (1987) *Work, unemployment and mental health*. Oxford: Clarendon Press.

Warren, S. & Jahoda, M. (Eds.). (1973) *Attitudes* (2nd ed.). Harmondsworth, Middlesex: Penguin.

Warrington, E.K. & Saanders, H.I. (1971) The fate of old memories. *Quarterly Journal of Experimental Psychology, 23*, 432–42.

Warrington, E.K. & Weiskrantz, L. (1968) New methods of testing long-term retention with special reference to amnesic patients. *Nature, 217* 972–4

Warrington, E.K. & Weiskrantz, L. (1970) Amnesic syndrome: Consolidation or retrieval ? *Nature, 228* 628–30

Waters, E. (1978) The reliability and stability of individual differences in infant–mother attachments. *Child Development, 49*, 483–94.

Waters, E., Wippman, J & Sroufe, L.A. (1979) Attachment, positive affect and competence in the peer group: Two studies in construct validation. *Child Development, 50*, 821–9.

Watson, J.B. (1913) Psychology as the behaviourist views it. *Psychological Review, 20*, 158–77.

Watson, J.B. (1919) *Psychology from the standpoint of a behaviourist*. Philadelphia: J.B. Lippincott.

Watson, J.B. (1924) *Behaviourism*. New York: J.B. Lippincott.

Watson, J.B. & Rayner, R. (1920) Conditioned emotional reactions. *Journal of Experimental Psychology, 3*, 1–14.

Watson, O.N. & Graves, T.D. (1966) Quantitative research in proxemic behaviour. *American Anthropologist, 68*, 971–85.

Waugh, N.C. & Norman, D. (1965) Primary memory. *Psychological*

Review, 72, 89–104.

Weatherley, D. (1961) Anti-semitism and expression of fantasy aggression. *Journal of Abnormal and Social Psychology, 62*, 454–7.

Weatherley, D. (1964) Self-perceived rate of physical maturation and personality in late adolescence. *Child Development, 35*, 1197–210.

Weinman, J. (1995) Health psychology. In A.M. Colman (Ed.) *Controversies in psychology*. London: Longman.

Wechsler, D. (1944) *The measurement of adult intelligence* (3rd ed.). Baltimore: Williams & Wilkins.

Wechsler, D. (1958) *The measurement and appraisal of adult intelligence* (4th ed.). Baltimore: Williams & Wilkins.

Wechsler, D. (1974) *Wechsler Intelligence Scale for Children*. New York: Psychological Corporation.

Weiner, B. (1986) *An attributional theory of motivation and emotion*. New York: Springer-Verlag.

Weiner, B. (1992) *Human motivation: Metaphors, theories and research*. Newbury Park, CA.: Sage.

Weisfeld, G. (1994) Aggression and dominance in the social world of boys. In J. Archer (Ed.) *Male Violence*. London: Routledge.

Weiskrantz, L. (1956) Behavioural changes associated with ablation of the amygdaloid complex in monkeys. *Journal of Comparative and Physiological Psychology, 49*, 381–91.

Weiskrantz, L. (1982) Comparative aspects of of studies of amnesia. *Philosophical Transactions of the Royal Society*. London B, *298*, 97–109.

Weiss, J.M. (1972) Influence of psychological variables on stress-induced pathology. In J. Knight & R. Porter (Eds.) *Physiology, emotion and psychosomatic illness*. Amsterdam: Elsevier.

Weiss, R.S. (1993) Loss and recovery. In M.S. Stroebe, W. Stroebe & R.O. Hansson (Eds.) *Handbook of bereavement: Theory, research and intervention*. New York: Cambridge University Press.

Weisstein, N. (1993) Psychology constructs the female; or, The fantasy life of the male psychologist (with some attention to the fantasies of his friend, the male biologist and the male anthropologist). *Feminism & Psychology, 3* (2), 195–210.

Weitzenhoffer, A.M. & Hilgard, E.R. (1959) *Stanford hypnotic susceptibility scale, forms A and B*. Palo Alto, California: Consulting Psychologists' Press.

Wellman, H.M. (1990) *The child's theory of mind.* Cambridge, MA: MIT Press.

Wells, G.L. & Harvey, J.H. (1977) Do people use consensus information in making causal attributions? *Journal of Personality and Social Psychology, 35*, 279–93.

Werner, E.E. (1987) Children of the Garden Island. *Scientific American*, April, 106–111.

Wessler, R.L. (1986) Conceptualizing cognitions in the cognitive–behavioural therapies. In W. Dryden & W. Golden (Eds.), *Cognitive–behavioural approaches to psychotherapy*. London: Harper & Row.

Westley, W.A. & Elkin, F. (1957) The protective environment and adolescent socialization. *Social Forces, 35*, 243–9.

Weston, D. & Turiel, E. (1980) Act-rule relations: children's concepts of social rules. *Developmental Psychology, 16*, 417–24.

Wetherell, M. (1982) Cross-cultural studies of minimal groups: Implications for the social identity theory of intergroup relations. In H. Tajfel (Ed.), *Social identity and intergroup relations*. London: Cambridge University Press.

Wetherell, M.S. (1987) Social identity and group polarization. In J.C. Turner, M.A. Hogg, P.J. Oakes, S.D.,Reicher & M.S. Wetherell, *Rediscovering the social group: A self-categorization theory*. Oxford: Blackwell.

Whitbourne, S.K. & Weinstock, C.S. (1979) *Adult development: The differentiation of experience*. New York: Holt, Rinehart & Winston.

White, D. (1975) The growth of conscience. *New Society*, December 4th, 538–40.

White, R.W. (1959) Motivation reconsidered: The concept of competence. *Psychological Review, 66*, 297–333.

Whorf, B.L. (1956) In J.B. Carroll (Ed.) *Language, thought and reality*. Cambridge, Mass.: MIT Press.

Wickelgren, W.A. (1965) Acoustic similarity and retroactive interference in short term memory. *Journal of Verbal Learning and Verbal Behaviour, 4*, 53–61.

Wickelgren, W.A. (1973) The long and the short of memory. *Psychological Bulletin, 80*, 425–38.

Wickelgren, W.A. (1974) Single trace fragility theory of memory dynamics. *Memory and Cognition, 2*, 775–80.

Wickens, C.D. (1984) Processing resources in attention. In R. Parasuraman & D.R. Davies, (Eds.), *Varieties of attention*. London: Academic Press.

Wickens, D.D. (1972) Characteristics of word encoding. In A. Melton & E. Martin (Eds.), *Coding processes in human memory*. Washington, DC: Winston.

Wicker, A.W. (1969) Attitude versus actions: The relationship of verbal and overt behavioural responses to attitude objects. *Journal of Social Issues, 25* (4), 41–78.

Wiemann, J.M. & Giles, H. (1988) Interpersonal communication. In M. Hewstone, W. Stroebe, J-P Codol, & G.M. Stephenson (Eds.) *Introduction to social psychology*. Oxford: Blackwell.

Wilder, D.A. (1977) Perceptions of groups, size of opposition and influence. *Journal of Experimental Social Psychology, 13*, 253–68.

Wilding, J.M. (1982) *Perception – from sense to object*. London: Hutchinson.

Wilkinson, S. (1989) The impact of feminist research: Issues of legitimacy . *Philosophical Psychology, 2* (3), 261–9.

Williams, K, Harkins, S.G. & Latané, B. (1981) Identifiability as a deterrant to social loafing: Two cheering experiments. *Journal of Personality & Social Psychology, 40*, 303–11.

Williams, J.B.W. & Spitzer, R.L. (1982) Idiopathic pain disorder: A critique of pain-prone disorder and a proposal for a revision of the DSM III Category psychogenic pain disorder. *Journal of Nervous and Mental Disorders, 170*, 415–19.

Williams, J.E. & Best, D.L. (1994) Cross-cultural views of women and men. In W.J. Lonner & R.S. Malplass (Eds.) *Psychology and culture*. Boston: Allyn & Bacon.

Williams, J. M. G. & Hargreaves, I.R. (1995) Neuroses: Depressive and anxiety disorders. in A.A. Lazarus & A.M. Colman (Eds.) *Abnormal Psychology*. London: Longman.

Williams, T.M. (Ed.). (1986) *The impact of television: A national experiment in three communities*. New York: Academic Press.

Willis, R.H. (1963) Two dimensions of conformity–nonconformity. *Sociometry, 26*, 499–513.

Wilson, E.O. (1975) *Sociobiology – the new synthesis*. Cambridge, Massachusetts: Harvard University Press.

Wilson, E.O. (1976) Sociobiology – a new basis for human nature. *New Scientist, May 13*.

Wilson, E.O. (1978) *On human nature*. Cambridge, Massachusetts: Harvard University Press.

Wilson, G.D. (1976) Personality. In H.J. Eysenck & G.D. Wilson (Eds.) *A textbook of human psychology*. Lancaster: MTP.

Wilson, J.E. & Barkham, M. (1994) A practitioner-scientist approach to psychotherapy process and outcome research. In P. Clarkson & M. Pokorny (Eds.) *The handbook of psychotherapy*. London: Routledge.

Winch, R.F. (1955) The theory of complementary needs in mate selection: A test of one kind of complementariness. *American Sociological Review, 20*, 52–6.

Winch, R.F. (1958) *Mate selections: A study of complementary needs.* New York: Harper.

Wing, J.K., Cooper, J.E. & Sartorious, N. (1974) *Measurement and classification of psychiatric symptoms.* Cambridge: Cambridge University Press.

Wingfield, A. & Byrnes, D. (1972) Decay of information in short-term memory. *Science, 176*, 690–2.

Winnicott, D.W. (1958) *Through paediatrics to psycho-analysis.* London: Hogarth Press.

Wishner, J. (1960) Reanalysis of 'Impressions of personality'. *Psychological Review, 67*, 96–112.

Wittgenstein, L. (1953) *Philosophical investigations.* Oxford: Blackwell.

Wober, J.M., Reardon, G. & Fazal, S. (1987) *Personality, character aspirations and patterns of viewing among children.* London: IBA Research Papers.

Wohlwill, J.F. (1965) Texture of the stimulus field and age as variables in the perception of relative distance. *Journal of Experimental Child Psychology, 2*, 163–77.

Wolf, T.M. (1973) Effects of live-modeled sex-inappropriate play behaviour in a naturalistic setting. *Developmental Psychology, 9*, 120–3.

Wolfe, J.B. (1936) Effectiveness of token-rewards for chimpanzees. *Comparative Psychology, 12*, No. 60.

Wollen, K.A., Weber, A. & Lowry, D.H. (1972) Bizareness versus interaction of mental images as determinants of learning. *Cognitive Psychology*, 3, 518–23.

Wollheim, R. (1971) *Freud.* London: Fontana.

Wolpe, J. (1958) *Psychotherapy by reciprocal inhibition.* Stanford, California: Stanford University Press.

Wolpe, J. (1978) Cognition and causation in human behaviour and its therapy. *American Psychologist, 33*, 437–46.

Wolpe, J. & Rachman, S. (1960) Psychoanalytic evidence: A critique based on Freud's case of little Hans. *Journal of Nervous and Mental Disease, 131*, 135–45.

Wood, D.J., Bruner, J.S. & Ross, G. (1976) The role of tutoring in problem solving. *Journal of Child Psychology & Psychiatry, 17*, 89–100.

Woodworth, R.S. (1938) *Experimental Psychology.* New York: Holt.

Word, C.O., Zanna, M.P. & Cooper, J. (1974) The non-verbal mediation of self-fulfilling prophecies in interracial interaction. *Journal of Experimental Social Psychology, 10*, 109–20.

World Health Organization (1973) *Report of the International Pilot Study of Schizophrenia, Vol. 1.* Geneva: WHO.

World Health Organization (1992) *The ICD-10 Classification of Mental and Behavioural Disorders: Clinical descriptions and diagnostic guidelines.* Geneva: WHO.

World Health Organization (1993) *The ICD-10 Classification of Mental and Behavioural Disorders: Diagnostic criteria for research.* Geneva: WHO.

Worthington, A.G. (1964) Differential rates of dark adaptation to 'taboo' and 'neutral' stimuli. *Canadian Journal of Psychology, 18*, 257–68.

Worthington, A.G. (1969) Paired comparison scaling of brightness judgements: A method for the measurement of perceptual defence. *British Journal of Psychology, 60* (3), 363–8.

Wright, D. (1971) *The psychology of moral behaviour.* Harmondsworth, Middlesex: Penguin.

Yarbus, A.L. (1967) *Eye movements and vision* (B. Haigh, trans.) New York: Plenum.

Yarrow, L.J. (1961) Maternal deprivation: Towards an empirical

and conceptual re-evaluation. *Psychological Bulletin, 58*, 459–90.

Yates, A.J. (1970) *Behaviour therapy.* New York: Wiley.

Young, S. (1994) Brain cells hit the big time. *New Scientist*, February, 23–7.

Zaidel, E. (1978) Auditory language comprehension in the right hemisphere following cerebral commissurotomy and hemispherectomy. In A. Caramassa & E. Zuriff (Eds.), *Acquisition and language breakdown: Parallels and divergences.* Baltimore, Maryland: Johns Hopkins University Press.

Zajonc, R.B. (1965) Social facilitation. *Science*, 1429, 269–74.

Zajonc, R.B. (1968) Attitudinal effects of mere exposure. *Journal of Personality and Social Psychology*, Monograph Supplement 9, Part 2, 1–27.

Zajonc R.B. (1980) Feeling and thinking: Preferences need no inferences. *American Psychologist, 35*, 151–75.

Zajonc, R.B. (1984) On the primacy of affect. *American Psychologist, 39*, 117–23.

Zajonc, R.B. (1989) Styles of explanation in social psychology. *European Journal of Social Psychology, 19*, 345–68.

Zajonc, R.B., Marcus, H.M. & Wilson, W.R. (1974) Exposure effects and associative learning. *Journal of Experimental Social Psychology, 10*, 248–63.

Zajonc, R.B., Shaver, P., Tarvis, C. & Van Kreveld, D. (1972) Exposure, satiation and stimulus discriminability. *Journal of Personality and Social Psychology, 21*, 270–80.

Zajonc. R.B., Swap, W.C., Harrison, A. & Roberts, P. (1971) Limiting conditions of the exposure effect: Satiation and relativity. *Journal of Personality and Social Psychology, 18*, 384–91.

Zanna, M.P. & Cooper, J. (1974) Dissonance and the pill: An attribution approach to studying the arousal propensities of dissonance. *Journal of Personality and Social Psychology, 29*, 703–9.

Zborowski, M. (1952) Cultural components in response to pain. *Journal of Social Issues, 8*, 16–30

Zebrowitz, L.A. (1990) *Social perception.* Milton Keynes: Open University Press.

Zeki, S.M. (1978) Uniformity and diversity of structure and function in rhesus monkey prestriate visual cortex. *Journal of Physiology, 277*, 273–90.

Zillman, D. (1978) Attribution and misattribution of excitatory reactions. In J.H. Harvey, W. Ickes & R.F. Kidd (Eds.), *New directions in attribution research, Vol. 2.* New York: Lawrence Erlbaum Associates Inc.

Zimbardo, P.G. (1969) The human choice: Individuation, reason and order versus deindividuation, impulse and chaos. In W.J. Arnold and D. Levine (Eds.), *Nebraska Symposium on Motivation.* Lincoln: University of Nebraska Press.

Zimbardo, P.G. (1973) On the ethics of intervention in human psychological research with special reference to the "Stanford Prison Experiment". *Cognition, 2* (2), 243–55.

Zimbardo, P.G. (1992) *Psychology and life* (13th ed.) New York: HarperCollins.

Zimbardo, P.G., Banks, W.C., Craig H, & Jaffe, D. (1973) A Pirandellian prison: The mind is a formidable jailor. *New York Times Magazine*, April 8th, 38–60.

Zimbardo, P.G. & Leippe, M. (1991) *The psychology of attitude change and social influence.* New York: McGraw-Hill.

Zimbardo, P.G.& Ruch, F.L. (1973) *Psychology and life.* New York: Scott Foreman.

Zubin, J. & Spring, B. (1977) Vulnerability – a new view of schizophrenia. *Journal of Abnormal Psychology, 86*, 103–26.

Zuckerman, M. (1978) Actions and occurrences in Kelley's cube. *Journal of Personality and Social Psychology, 36*, 647–56.

ACKNOWLEDGEMENTS

Many people have contributed to the production of this book, in a variety of ways, directly and indirectly, both solicited and unsolicited. Thanks to Hugh Coolican, Roger Lindsay and Rob McIlveen for detailed comments on the second edition. Thanks to Roz Brody, Rob McIlveen and Mike Stanley for making extremely helpful and constructive criticism of a sample chapter for the current edition: all three have contributed to some of the changes in both content and design, not just in that particular chapter but throughout the book. Thanks also to Allen Esterson for sending me unsolicited material relating to Freud's seduction theory, which I have incorporated into this edition, albeit in a very abbreviated form. Special thanks go to David Mackin, Daniel Tero and Denise Stewart at GreenGate Publishing Services for all their technical assistance on the production side and in picture research.

Last, but not least, thanks to Julie Hill and Tim Gregson-Williams at Hodder; the latter has remained the stable thread running through a sometimes rather unstable publishing world and just being on the other end of the telephone was sometimes enough.

The publishers would like to thank the following for permission to reproduce photos and illustrations:

Page 34, William Vandivert, Dennis, MA, USA/ Scientific American; p.72, Alan Hobson/Science Photo Library; p.87, David Parker/Science Photo Library; p.110, University of Wisconsin Primate Laboratory; p.119, Oscar Burriel/Science Photo Library; p.121, 'Unmasking the Face' by P. Ekman and W. V. Friesen, Consulting Psychologists Press, 1984; p.129, Robert Estall Photo Library; p.135, Will & Deni Mcintyre/Science Photo Library; p.157, Science Photo Library; p.161, The Hulton Picture Company/ Bettmann Archive, Inc.; p.172, Albert Bandura, Stanford University; p.182 and p.188, John Raffo/Science Photo Library; p.201, Cordon Art; p.216, Weidenfeld and Nicholson Ltd; p.235, BSIP, LECA/Science Photo Library; p.236 Barnaby's Picture Library; p.263, Nick Hedges/Barnaby's Picture Library; p.264, Professor Harold Edgerton/Science Photo Library; p.271, Paul Thompson/ACE Photo Agency; p.276, Bill Angove/Barnaby's Picture Library; p.285, Eve Lucas; p.315, Hubertus Kanus/Barnaby's Picture Library; p.317, Robert Estall Photo Library; p.330, US Department of Energy/Science Photo Library; p.354, Barnaby's Picture Library; p.359, Andrew Warrington; p.389, Michael Melia/Ace Photo Agency; p.401 (left) Geoff Tompkinson/Science Photo Library; p.401 (right) Conor Cafrey/Science Photo Library; p.412, Gerald Cubitt/Barnaby's Picture Library; p.438, Popperfoto/Reuter; p.443, Karen Hoddle/Barnaby's Picture Library; p.445, Health Education Authority; p.457, Barnaby's Picture Library; p.477, David Simson/Barnaby's Picture Library; p.484, William Vandivert, Dennis, MA, USA/Scientific American; p.489, Barnaby's Picture Library; p.496, Stanley Milgram, 1965. From the film 'Obedience', distributed by the Pennsylvania State University, Audio Visual Services; p.507, National Library of Medicine/Science Photo Library; p.516, UPI/Bettmann Archive, Inc.; p.529, Olive Pierce/Black Star; p.548, A. Bruce/Barnaby's Picture Library; p.554, Harlow Primate Laboratory, University of Wisconsin; p.556, Dmitri Kasterine/Radio Times Picture Library; p.574, John Raffo/Science Photo Library; pp.577/8, by permission of the Johns Hopkins Press, Maryland, Baltimore; p.597 Popperfoto; pp.603/4, Popperfoto; p.627, Yves de Braine/Black Star; p.644, by permission of Harvard University Press; p.653, by permission of Georgia State University/Enrico Ferrorelli/Colorific!; p.690, Albert Bandura, Stanford University; p.692, Walter Mischel, Columbia University; p.708 (left) Sara Ellis/Barnaby's Picture Library; p.708 (right) Barnaby's Picture Library p.746, UPI/Bettmann Archive, Inc.; p.748 Thompson/Popperfoto; p.824, Freud Museum Publications Ltd.

The publishers would also like to thank the following for permission to reproduce diagrams.

Figure 5.4. Anorexia Nervosa A.H. Crisp. *Let me be.* Florida: Academic Press Inc.; Figure 9.24. Yabus A.L. (1977) *Eye movements and vision* (B Haigh trans.) New York: Plenum Publishing Corporation; Figures 16.2, 16.6, 16.7 based on Brehm S.S. (1992) *Intimate Relationships* (2nd ed.) New York, McGraw Hill; Figure 18.1, Hovland and Rosenburg (eds) *Attitude, Organisation and Change.* 1960 Yale University Press; Figure 19.2. Hogg M.A. and Vaughan (1995) *Social Psychology: An Introduction.* Hemel Hempstead: Prentice-Hall/Harvester Wheatsheaf; Figure 19.3. J. Kuhl from *Experiments in Integroup Discrimination.* Copyright © 1990 by Scientific American, Inc. All rights reserved; Figure 20.7. Based on Fiedler F.E. (1965) A contingency model of leadership effectiveness. In L. Berkowitz (ed) *Advances in Experimental Social Psychology, volume 1.* Florida: Academic Press Inc.; Figure 21.6. Coleman J.C. and Hendry L (1990) *The nature of adolescence* 2nd ed. London: Routledge; Figure 22.3 Horowitz L.M., Rosenber S.M. and Bartholomew K. (1993) Interpersonal Problems, Attachment Styles and Outcome in Brief Dynamic Psychotherapy. *Journal of Consulting and Clinical Psychology* 61 (4) 549–60. Copyright © 1993 by the American Psychological Association. Adapted with permission.

Every effort has been made to obtain necessary permission with reference to copyright material. The publishers apologise if inadvertently any sources remain unacknowledged and will be glad to make the necessary arrangements at the earliest opportunity.

Index compiled by Frank Merrett, Cheltenham, Gloucester.

INDEX

Italicised headings indicate publications. Italicised page numbers indicate a table, diagram or picture by way of illustration.